STATUTORY INSTRUMENTS 1970

PART II
(in two Sections)

SECTION 1

Published by Authority

LONDON
HER MAJESTY'S STATIONERY OFFICE
1970

PRINTED AND PUBLISHED BY HER MAJESTY'S STATIONERY OFFICE

To be purchased from

49 High Holborn, LONDON, WC1V 6HB

13a Castle Street, EDINBURGH, EH2 3AR
109 St. Mary Street, CARDIFF, CF1 1JW
Brazennose Street, MANCHESTER, M60 8AS
50 Fairfax Street, BRISTOL, BS1 3DE
258 Broad Street, BIRMINGHAM, 1
7 Linenhall Street, BELFAST, BT2 8AY

or through any Bookseller

1970

Price for the two Sections: £10 15*s.* 0*d.* [£10·75] net

PRINTED IN ENGLAND

SBN 11 840065 7*

Contents of the Volume

PART I, Section 1

PART I, Section 2

PART II, Section 1

PART II, Section 2

PART III

Preface

Scope and arrangement of the Volume

1. This volume gives the full text of the statutory instruments registered in the year 1970 which were classified as general, and gives particulars of those which were classified as local(**a**). Other instruments are contained in the Appendix (as to which see para. 3 below).

2. The general instruments are arranged according to their S.I. numbers(**b**), that is to say, in the order of their registration as statutory instruments. The volume is published in three Parts, containing the instruments registered between 1st January and 30th April, 1st May and 31st August, and 1st September and 31st December respectively.

Contents of the Volume

3. **Parts I and II.** At the beginning of each of these Parts is a list of the instruments whose text is contained in that Part, showing their S.I. numbers and titles. The list is followed by the text of the statutory instruments registered in the relevant period and an **Appendix of Instruments not registered as Statutory Instruments** issued in that period. This Appendix includes Orders in Council issued under the royal prerogative or otherwise outside the definition of a statutory instrument, Royal Proclamations which are of a legislative nature, and Letters Patent and Royal Instructions which relate to the constitutions, etc. of overseas territories.

At the end of each Part is a Table showing the modifications to legislation and an Index. Each Table is confined to the instruments in its own Part and gives particulars of those Acts and instruments which have been amended, extended, excluded, repealed or revoked by instruments in the Part. The Index to Part II will be cumulative to both Parts.

4. **Part III.** At the beginning is a list of the instruments in Part III similar to the lists in Parts I and II. It is followed by the text of the instruments comprising Part III, as in Parts I and II.

At the end of Part III are the features which are required by reg. 10 of the Statutory Instruments Regulations 1947 to be included in the Annual Volume of Statutory Instruments. They cover the instruments in all three Parts. In the order in which they occur in the Volume, they are as follows:—

The **Classified List of Local Instruments** gives particulars, including the dates of making, and the S.I. numbers, of all local statutory instruments registered in the S.I. series of the year to which the Annual Volume relates. They are grouped in classes according to their subject-matter.

(**a**) *See* Statutory Instruments Regulations 1947 (S.I. 1948/1 (Rev. XXI, p. 498: 1948 I. p. 4002)), reg. 4 of which provides that S.I. which are in the nature of public general Acts of Parliament shall be classified as general and those which are in the nature of local and personal or private Acts shall be classified as local.

(**b**) Reg. 3 of the Statutory Instruments Regulations 1947 provides for instruments to be numbered in a separate series for each calendar year. Certain instruments bear a subsidiary number—

C. Commencement Orders (bringing an Act or part of an Act into operation).
L. Instruments relating to fees or procedure in courts in England or Wales.
S. Instruments made by a Scottish rule-making authority and applying to Scotland only.

The **Tables.** " Table A " gives particulars of the Acts of Parliament, and " Table B " particulars of statutory and other instruments, the operation of which was affected by the instruments appearing in the Volume. They include the information as to amendments, repeals, revocations, etc., already given in tables of " Modifications to Legislation " in Parts I and II and corresponding information with respect to the instruments in Part III, and also give particulars of Acts or instruments modified or restricted by general instruments throughout the Volume. In addition, Table B gives particulars of general instruments whose operation was affected expressly by Public General Acts of the year in question, or which ceased to operate through becoming spent during that year as a result of legislation of the year.

The **Numerical and Issue List** gives particulars of all statutory instruments which were printed and put on sale by the Queen's Printer of Acts of Parliament under the provisions of the Statutory Instruments Act 1946(**a**), during the year, with, in each case, the date of making and the date of first issue by Her Majesty's Stationery Office.

The **Index** will be cumulative to Parts I and II.

Definition of a statutory instrument

5. To determine whether or not any instrument is required to be a statutory instrument, reference must be made to s. 1 of the Statutory Instruments Act 1946, reg. 2 of the Statutory Instruments Regulations 1947, and arts. 1 and 2 of the Statutory Instruments (Confirmatory Powers) Order 1947(**b**).

The definition of what constitutes a statutory instrument, as respects instruments made under Acts passed before the commencement (1 Jan. 1948) of the 1946 Act, is governed by definitions contained in the Rules Publications Act 1893(**c**) (which was repealed and replaced by the 1946 Act); for those made under Acts passed after the commencement of the 1946 Act, the document is a statutory instrument if it is an Order in Council or if it is made by a Minister of the Crown and the Act provides that the power is to be exercisable by statutory instrument.

Citation

6. For the purposes of citation, statutory instruments are given a title. In addition, all statutory instruments may be identified by the year and number. The first instrument in Part I of this Volume would, by this method, be cited as " S.I. 1970/8 ". When a statutory instrument is referred to in another statutory instrument, a lettered footnote is provided in the latter, giving the identification of the first instrument as above, and also its Part and page reference in the Annual Volume The footnote reference for the same instrument would therefore be " S.I. 1970/8 (1970 I, p. 1) ".

If the text of the instrument is set out in the current edition of *S.R. & O. and S.I. Revised* (Third Edition, as at 31st Dec., 1948) the footnote references give the volume reference in that edition as well as the page reference in the Annual Volume (see, for example, footnote (**b**) below). If a footnote contains the references of a number of instruments, they may in certain circumstances be run together, so as to give all the instrument numbers together and all the volume references together, e.g. " S.R. & O. 1946/157; S.I. 1948/1073, 1961/1942 (1946 II, p. 26; 1948 II, p. 13; 1961 III, p. 2650) ".

(**a**) 1946 c. 36.
(**b**) S.I. 1948/2 (Rev. XXI, p. 504: 1948 I, p. 4008).
(**c**) 1893 c. 66.

Production in Court

7. Under section 2 of the Documentary Evidence Act 1868(**a**), read with section 2 of the Documentary Evidence Act 1882(**b**), *prima facie* evidence of any proclamation, order or regulation made by certain rule-making authorities may be given in courts of justice by production of a copy purporting to be printed by the Government Printer or under the superintendence or authority of Her Majesty's Stationery Office. The Act of 1868 has since been extended by numerous Acts(**c**) to rules, etc., made thereunder by other rule-making authorities. The copies of proclamations, orders, regulations, etc., made by the authorities referred to above as printed in these volumes may therefore be produced as *prima facie* evidence.

Up to date information on statutory instruments

8. The *Index to Government Orders* contains, under subject headings, summaries of all powers to make subordinate legislation conferred by statute on H.M. in Council, the Privy Council, government departments and certain other public bodies. Below each summary appear particulars of any general instruments made in exercise of it which were in force at the date of publication of the *Index*. Details are also given of certain instruments made under prerogative powers. The work contains also a Table of Statutes showing the subject headings under which references to particular sections of enabling Acts appear. (The *Index* is published every two years by H.M.S.O.).

9. Information as to whether any instrument is still in operation, or whether anything has happened to it since it was made, can be obtained from the *Table of Government Orders*. This Table lists general statutory rules and orders and statutory instruments in numerical order, and gives the history of those which have been affected (i.e. revoked, amended, etc.) by subsequent legislation, whether statute or subordinate legislation, identifying the Act or instrument in question. Where any instrument has been amended, the Table gives particulars of the article, section, rule, etc., affected. A user who is interested in one particular provision only of the earlier instrument can thus ascertain whether or not he need consult the text of the amending enactment at all. The *Table of Government Orders* is published annually by H.M.S.O. and is cumulative. A Noter-Up is issued twice yearly.

Authority for Publication

10. The Annual Volumes of Statutory Instruments are published in pursuance of reg. 10 of the Statutory Instruments Regulations 1947 and are prepared under the direction of the Statute Law Committee. Any suggestion or communication relating to their contents should be addressed to the Editor, Statutory Publications Office, Queen Anne's Chambers, 41, Tothill Street, S.W.1.

(**a**) 1868 c. 37. (**b**) 1882 c. 9.

(**c**) *See* the entries relating to extensions of the 1868 Act in the *Chronological Table of the Statutes*.

Abbreviations

Addnl. Instructions ...	Additional Instructions.
A.S.	Act of Sederunt.
am., amdg., amdt. ...	amended, amending, amendment.
appx.	appendix.
art(s).	article(s).
bd(s).	board(s).
c.	chapter(s).
cl(s).	clause(s).
Cmd., Cmnd.	Command Paper.
cont.	continued.
ct(s).	court(s).
E.	England.
exc.	except, excepted.
excl.	excluded.
expl.	explained.
ext.	extended.
G.B.	Great Britain.
gen.	generally.
govt.	government.
H.C.	House of Commons Paper.
H.M.	Her Majesty, Her Majesty's.
incl.	included, including.
instrt.	instrument.
L.P.	Letters Patent.
Min(s).	Minister(s).
mod., mod(s).	modified, modification(s).
N.I.	Northern Ireland.
No.	number.
O.	Order(s).
O. in C., O. of C. ...	Order(s) in Council, Order(s) of Council.
p., pp.	page(s).
para(s).	paragraph(s).
prerog.	prerogative.
prosp.	prospectively.
prov.	provisional, proviso.
pt.	part.
r.	revoked.
R.C.	Rules of the Court of Session.
R. Instructions	Royal Instructions.
R. Warrant	Royal Warrant.
reg(s).	regulation(s).
rep.	repealed.
restr.	restricted.
retrosp.	retrospectively.
Rev.	Statutory Rules and Orders and Statutory Instruments Revised (Third Edition, 1948).
Rev. 1903	Statutory Rules and Orders Revised (Second Edition, 1903).
revn.	revocation.
S.	Scotland.
s., ss.	section(s).
S.I.	Statutory Instrument(s).
S.R. & O.	Statutory Rule(s) and Order(s).

ABBREVIATIONS

sch(s).	schedule(s).
Secy.	Secretary.
susp.	suspended.
temp.	temporarily.
transfd.	transferred.
Treas.	Treasury.
U.K.	United Kingdom of Great Britain and Northern Ireland.
vol.	volume.
W.	Wales.

Statutory Instruments in Part II

OTHER INSTRUMENTS IN PART II

1970 No. 647

SUGAR

The Sugar (Rates of Surcharge and Surcharge Repayments) (No. 6) Order 1970

Made - - - -	30*th April* 1970
Laid before Parliament	4*th May* 1970
Coming into Operation	5*th May* 1970

The Minister of Agriculture, Fisheries and Food, in exercise of the powers conferred on him by sections 7(4), 8(6) and 33(4) of the Sugar Act 1956(**a**) having effect subject to the provisions of section 3 of, and Part II of Schedule 5 to, the Finance Act 1962(**b**), and section 58 of the Finance Act 1968(**c**) and of all other powers enabling him in that behalf, with the concurrence of the Treasury, on the advice of the Sugar Board, hereby makes the following order:—

1.—(1) This order may be cited as the Sugar (Rates of Surcharge and Surcharge Repayments) (No. 6) Order 1970; and shall come into operation on 5th May 1970.

(2) The Interpretation Act 1889(**d**) shall apply for the interpretation of this order as it applies for the interpretation of an Act of Parliament.

2. Notwithstanding the provisions of Article 2 of the Sugar (Rates of Surcharge and Surcharge Repayments) (No. 5) Order 1970(**e**), the rates of surcharge payable under and in accordance with the provisions of section 7 of the Sugar Act 1956, having effect as aforesaid, in respect of sugar and invert sugar imported or home produced or used in the manufacture of imported composite sugar products shall on and after 5th May 1970 be those rates specified in Schedule 1 to this order.

3. For the purpose of section 8(3)(*b*) of the Sugar Act 1956, having effect as aforesaid, the rates of surcharge repayments in respect of invert sugar produced in the United Kingdom from materials on which on or after 5th May 1970 sugar duty has been paid or, by virtue of paragraph 1 of Part II of Schedule 5 to the Finance Act 1962, is treated as having been paid shall, notwithstanding the provisions of Article 3 of the Sugar (Rates of Surcharge and Surcharge Repayments) (No. 5) Order 1970 be those specified in Schedule 2 to this order.

(**a**) 1956 c. 48. (**b**) 1962 c. 44.
(**c**) 1968 c. 44. (**d**) 1889 c. 63.
(**e**) S.I. 1970/552 (1970 I, p. 1772).

In Witness whereof the Official Seal of the Minister of Agriculture, Fisheries and Food is hereunto affixed on 29th April 1970.

(L.S.)

R. P. Fraser,
Authorised by the Minister.

We concur.

30th April 1970.

Joseph Harper,
Ernest Armstrong,
Two of the Lords Commissioners of Her Majesty's Treasury.

SCHEDULE 1

PART I

SURCHARGE RATES FOR SUGAR

Polarisation	Rate of Surcharge per cwt. s.	d.
Exceeding—		
99°	9	4·0
98° but not exceeding 99°	8	9·6
97° „ „ „ 98°	8	7·0
96° „ „ „ 97°	8	4·3
95° „ „ „ 96°	8	1·6
94° „ „ „ 95°	7	10·9
93° „ „ „ 94°	7	8·2
92° „ „ „ 93°	7	5·6
91° „ „ „ 92°	7	2·9
90° „ „ „ 91°	7	0·2
89° „ „ „ 90°	6	9·5
88° „ „ „ 89°	6	6·8
87° „ „ „ 88°	6	4·6
86° „ „ „ 87°	6	2·3
85° „ „ „ 86°	6	0·3
84° „ „ „ 85°	5	10·3
83° „ „ „ 84°	5	8·3
82° „ „ „ 83°	5	6·3
81° „ „ „ 82°	5	4·5
80° „ „ „ 81°	5	2·7
79° „ „ „ 80°	5	0·9
78° „ „ „ 79°	4	11·1
77° „ „ „ 78°	4	9·3
76° „ „ „ 77°	4	7·5
Not exceeding 76°	4	6·0

PART II

SURCHARGE RATES FOR INVERT SUGAR

Sweetening matter content by weight	Rate of Surcharge per cwt.
	s. d.
70 per cent. or more	5 11
Less than 70 per cent. and more than 50 per cent.	4 3
Not more than 50 per cent.	2 1

SCHEDULE 2

SURCHARGE REPAYMENT RATES FOR INVERT SUGAR

Sweetening matter content by weight	Rate of Surcharge Repayment per cwt.
	s. d.
More than 80 per cent.	7 0
More than 70 per cent. but not more than 80 per cent.	5 11
More than 60 per cent. but not more than 70 per cent.	4 3
More than 50 per cent. but not more than 60 per cent.	3 4
Not more than 50 per cent. and the invert sugar not being less in weight than 14 lb. per gallon	2 1

EXPLANATORY NOTE

(*This Note is not part of the Order.*)

This order prescribes—

(*a*) reductions equivalent to 2s. 4d. per cwt. of refined sugar in the rates of surcharge payable on sugar and invert sugar which become chargeable with surcharge on or after 5th May 1970;

(*b*) correspondingly reduced rates of surcharge repayment in respect of invert sugar produced in the United Kingdom from materials on which surcharge has been paid.

1970 No. 648

SUGAR

The Composite Sugar Products (Surcharge and Surcharge Repayments—Average Rates) (No. 7) Order 1970

Made - - - -	30*th April* 1970
Laid before Parliament	4*th May* 1970
Coming into Operation	5*th May* 1970

Whereas the Minister of Agriculture, Fisheries and Food (hereinafter called " the Minister ") has on the recommendation of the Commissioners of Customs and Excise (hereinafter called " the Commissioners ") made an order(**a**) pursuant to the powers conferred upon him by sections 9(1) and 9(4) of the Sugar Act 1956(**b**), having effect subject to the provisions of section 3 of, and Part II of Schedule 5 to, the Finance Act 1962(**c**), to the provisions of section 52(2) of the Finance Act 1966(**d**), and to the provisions of section 58 of the Finance Act 1968(**e**), providing that in the case of certain descriptions of composite sugar products surcharge shall be calculated on the basis of an average quantity of sugar or invert sugar taken to have been used in the manufacture of the products, and that certain other descriptions of composite sugar products shall be treated as not containing any sugar or invert sugar, and that in the case of certain descriptions of goods in the manufacture of which sugar or invert sugar is used, surcharge repayments shall be calculated on the basis of an average quantity of sugar or invert sugar taken to have been so used:

Now, therefore, the Minister, on the recommendation of the Commissioners and in exercise of the powers conferred upon him by sections 9(1), 9(4) and 33(4) of the Sugar Act 1956, having effect as aforesaid, and of all other powers enabling him in that behalf, hereby makes the following order:—

1.—(1) This order may be cited as the Composite Sugar Products (Surcharge and Surcharge Repayments—Average Rates) (No. 7) Order 1970, and shall come into operation on 5th May 1970.

(2) The Interpretation Act 1889(**f**) shall apply for the interpretation of this order as it applies for the interpretation of an Act of Parliament.

2. Surcharge payable on or after 5th May 1970 under and in accordance with the Sugar Act 1956, having effect as aforesaid, in respect of sugar and invert sugar used in the manufacture of the descriptions of imported composite sugar products specified in column 2 of Schedule 1 to this order shall, notwithstanding the provisions of the Sugar (Rates of Surcharge and Surcharge Repayments) (No. 6) Order 1970(**g**) and the Composite Sugar Products (Surcharge and Surcharge Repayments—Average Rates) (No. 6) Order 1970(**a**), be calculated by reference to the weight of the products at the rates specified in relation thereto in column 3 of the said Schedule.

(**a**) S.I. 1970/553 (1970 I, p. 1775). (**b**) 1956 c. 48. (**c**) 1962 c. 44.
(**d**) 1966 c. 18. (**e**) 1968 c. 44. (**f**) 1889 c. 63.
(**g**) S.I. 1970/647 (1970 II, p. 2089).

3. Imported composite sugar products other than those of a description specified in Schedules 1 and 2 to this order shall be treated as not containing any sugar or invert sugar for the purposes of surcharge payable on or after 5th May 1970.

4. Surcharge repayments payable on and after 5th May 1970 under and in accordance with the provisions of section 8 of the Sugar Act 1956, having effect as aforesaid, in respect of sugar and invert sugar used in the manufacture of the descriptions of goods specified in column 1 of Schedule 3 to this order shall, notwithstanding the provisions of the Sugar (Rates of Surcharge and Surcharge Repayments) (No. 6) Order 1970(**a**) and the Composite Sugar Products (Surcharge and Surcharge Repayments—Average Rates) (No. 6) Order 1970(**b**), be calculated by reference to the quantity of the goods at the rates specified in relation thereto in column 2 of the said Schedule.

In Witness whereof the Official Seal of the Minister of Agriculture, Fisheries and Food is hereunto affixed on 30th April 1970.

(L.S.)

R. P. Fraser,
Authorised by the Minister.

SCHEDULE 1

In this Schedule:—

" Tariff heading " means a heading or, where the context so requires, a subheading of the Customs Tariff 1959 (see paragraph (1) of Article 2 of the Import Duties (General) (No. 3) Order 1969(**c**)).

Tariff heading	Description of Imported Composite Sugar Products	Rate of Surcharge
		Per cwt. s. d.
04.02	Milk and cream, preserved, concentrated or sweetened, containing more than 10 per cent. by weight of added sugar	4 2
17.02 (B) (2) and 17.05 (B)	Syrups containing sucrose sugar, whether or not flavoured or coloured, but not including fruit juices containing added sugar in any proportion:—	
	containing 70 per cent. or more by weight of sweetening matter	5 11
	containing less than 70 per cent., and more than 50 per cent., by weight of sweetening matter . .	4 3
	containing not more than 50 per cent. by weight of sweetening matter	2 1

(**a**) S.I. 1970/647 (1970 II, p. 2089). (**b**) S.I. 1970/553 (1970 I, p. 1775).
(**c**) S.I. 1969/1413 (1969 III, p. 4150).

Tariff heading	Description of Imported Composite Sugar Products	Rate of Surcharge
		Per cwt.
		s. d.
17.02 (F) ..	Caramel:—	
	Solid	9 4
	Liquid	6 6
17.04	Sugar confectionery, not containing cocoa ..	7 7
18.06	Chocolate and other food preparations containing cocoa and added sugar:—	
	Chocolate couverture not prepared for retail sale; chocolate milk crumb, liquid ..	4 2
	Chocolate milk crumb, solid	5 1
	Solid chocolate bars or blocks, milk or plain, with or without fruit or nuts; other chocolate confectionery consisting wholly of chocolate or of chocolate and other ingredients not containing added sugar, but not including such goods when packed together in retail packages with goods liable to surcharge at a higher rate	4 2
	Other	5 5
19.08	Pastry, biscuits, cakes and other fine bakers' wares containing added sugar:—	
	Biscuits, wafers and rusks containing more than 12½ per cent. by weight of added sugar, and other biscuits, wafers and rusks included in retail packages with such goods.. ..	2 4
	Cakes with covering or filling containing added sugar; meringues	3 1
	Other	1 2
20.01	Vegetables and fruit, prepared or preserved by vinegar or acetic acid, containing added sugar:—	
	Containing 10 per cent. or more by weight of added sugar	3 3
	Other	8
20.03	Fruit preserved by freezing, containing added sugar	1 2
20.04	Fruit, fruit-peel and parts of plants, preserved by sugar (drained, glacé or crystallised)	6 2
20.05	Jams, fruit jellies, marmalades, fruit purée and fruit pastes, being cooked preparations, containing added sugar	5 10
20.06	Fruit otherwise prepared or preserved, containing added sugar:—	
	Ginger	4 8
	Other	1 2

SCHEDULE 2

Tariff heading	Description of Imported Composite Sugar Products
17.05 (A) and (B)	Sugar and invert sugar, flavoured or coloured.

SCHEDULE 3

Description of goods	Rate of surcharge repayment per bulk barrel of 36 gallons
Lager	4·6d.
All beer other than lager	4·1d.

EXPLANATORY NOTE

(*This Note is not part of the Order.*)

This order provides for reductions on and after 5th May 1970 in the average rates of surcharge payable on imported composite sugar products of the descriptions specified in Schedule 1 and in the average rates of surcharge repayment in respect of exported goods of the descriptions specified in Schedule 3. These correspond to the reductions in surcharge rates effected by the Sugar (Rates of Surcharge and Surcharge Repayments) (No. 6) Order 1970 (S.I.1970/647). Provision is also made for certain imported composite sugar products to be treated as not containing any sugar or invert sugar.

1970 No. 649

ROAD TRAFFIC

The Drivers' Hours (Passenger Vehicles) (Exemptions) (Amendment) Regulations 1970

Made - - -	30*th April* 1970
Laid before Parliament	11*th May* 1970
Coming into Operation	12*th May* 1970

The Minister of Transport, in exercise of his powers under section 96(10) of the Transport Act 1968(**a**) and of all other enabling powers, and after consultation with representative organisations in accordance with section 101(6) of the said Act of 1968, hereby makes the following Regulations:—

1. These Regulations shall come into operation on the 12th May 1970, and may be cited as the Drivers' Hours (Passenger Vehicles) (Exemptions) (Amendment) Regulations 1970.

2. The Drivers' Hours (Passenger Vehicles) (Exemptions) Regulations 1970(**b**) shall have effect as though, after Regulation 4, there were added the following Regulation:—

"**5.** Any driver of a passenger vehicle who spends time on duty during a working day to meet a special need, that is to say work done in connection with the carriage of persons suffering from physical or mental disability to or from any place at which social or recreational facilities for them are specially provided, is hereby exempted from the requirements of section 96(3) in relation to that day, subject to the conditions that—

(*a*) he is able to obtain rest and refreshment during that day for a period which is, or for periods which taken together are, not less than the time by which the working day exceeds 10 hours,

(*b*) that day does not exceed 14 hours, and

(*c*) he has not taken advantage of this exemption from the requirements of section 96(3) on more than one previous working day which forms part of the working week of which that day forms part.".

Given under the Official Seal of the Minister of Transport the 30th April 1970.

(L.S.)

Fred Mulley,
Minister of Transport.

(**a**) 1968 c. 73. (**b**) S.I. 1970/145 (1970 I, p. 635).

EXPLANATORY NOTE

(This Note is not part of the Regulations.)

The Drivers' Hours (Passenger Vehicles) (Exemptions) Regulations 1970 provide (inter alia) an exemption from the requirements of section 96(3) of the Transport Act 1968 (which specifies the length of a working day for drivers of passenger vehicles) to enable such drivers to meet a special need. These Regulations amend the 1970 Regulations to provide a similar exemption where the special need is for the carriage of handicapped persons for certain social and recreational purposes.

1970 No. 655

INDUSTRIAL TRAINING

The Industrial Training Levy (Paper and Paper Products) Order 1970

Made - - -	1*st May* 1970
Laid before Parliament	12*th May* 1970
Coming into Operation	20*th May* 1970

The Secretary of State after approving proposals submitted by the Paper and Paper Products Industry Training Board for the imposition of a further levy on employers in the paper and paper products industry and in exercise of her powers under section 4 of the Industrial Training Act 1964(**a**) and of all other powers enabling her in that behalf hereby makes the following Order :—

Title and commencement

1. This Order may be cited as the Industrial Training Levy (Paper and Paper Products) Order 1970 and shall come into operation on 20th May 1970.

Interpretation

2.—(1) In this Order unless the context otherwise requires :—

(*a*) "agriculture" has the same meaning as in section 109(3) of the Agriculture Act 1947(**b**) or, in relation to Scotland, as in section 86(3) of the Agriculture (Scotland) Act 1948(**c**) ;

(*b*) "an appeal tribunal" means an industrial tribunal established under section 12 of the Industrial Training Act 1964 ;

(*c*) "assessment" means an assessment of an employer to the levy ;

(*d*) "the Board" means the Paper and Paper Products Industry Training Board ;

(*e*) "business" means any activities of industry or commerce ;

(*f*) "charity" has the same meaning as in section 360 of the Income and Corporation Taxes Act 1970(**d**) ;

(*g*) "emoluments" means all emoluments assessable to income tax under Schedule E (other than pensions), being emoluments from which tax under that Schedule is deductible, whether or not tax in fact falls to be deducted from any particular payment thereof ;

(*h*) "employer" means a person who is an employer in the paper and paper products industry at any time in the second levy period ;

(*i*) "the industrial training order" means the Industrial Training (Paper and Paper Products Board) Order 1968(**e**) ;

(**a**) 1964 c. 16.
(**b**) 1947 c. 48.
(**c**) 1948 c. 45.
(**d**) 1970 c. 10.
(**e**) S.I. 1968/787 (1968 II, p. 2194).

(*j*) "the levy" means the levy imposed by the Board in respect of the second levy period ;

(*k*) "notice" means a notice in writing ;

(*l*) "paper and paper products establishment" means an establishment in Great Britain engaged in the second base period wholly or mainly in the paper and paper products industry for a total of twenty-seven or more weeks or, being an establishment that commenced to carry on business in the second base period, for a total number of weeks exceeding one half of the number of weeks in the part of the said period commencing with the day on which business was commenced and ending on the last day thereof ;

(*m*) "the paper and paper products industry" means any one or more of the activities which, subject to the provisions of paragraph 2 of Schedule 1 to the industrial training order, are specified in paragraph 1 of that Schedule as the activities of the paper and paper products industry ;

(*n*) "the second base period" means the period of twelve months that commenced on 6th April 1969 ;

(*o*) "the second levy period" means the period commencing with the day upon which this Order comes into operation and ending on 5th April 1971 ;

(*p*) other expressions have the same meanings as in the industrial training order.

(2) In the case where a paper and paper products establishment is taken over (whether directly or indirectly) by an employer in succession to, or jointly with, another person, a person employed at any time in the second base period at or from the establishment shall be deemed, for the purposes of this Order, to have been so employed by the employer carrying on the said establishment on the day upon which this Order comes into operation, and any reference in this Order to persons employed by an employer at or from a paper and paper products establishment in the second base period shall be construed accordingly.

(3) Any reference in this Order to an establishment that commences to carry on business or that ceases to carry on business shall not be taken to apply where the location of the establishment is changed but its business is continued wholly or mainly at or from the new location, or where the suspension of activities is of a temporary or seasonal nature.

(4) For the purposes of this Order no regard shall be had to the emoluments of a person wholly engaged in the supply of food or drink for immediate consumption or in agriculture.

(5) The Interpretation Act 1889(**a**) shall apply to the interpretation of this Order as it applies to the interpretation of an Act of Parliament.

Imposition of the Levy

3.—(1) The levy to be imposed by the Board on employers in respect of the second levy period shall be assessed in accordance with the provisions of this Article.

(2) The levy shall be assessed by the Board separately in respect of each paper and paper products establishment of an employer, not being an employer to whom paragraph (5) of this Article applies or an employer who is exempt

(**a**) 1889 c. 63.

from the levy by virtue of paragraph (6), but in agreement with the employer one assessment may be made in respect of any number of such establishments, in which case those establishments shall be deemed for the purposes of that assessment to constitute one establishment.

(3) Subject to the provisions of the next following paragraph, the levy assessed in respect of a paper and paper products establishment of an employer shall be an amount equal to 1·0 per cent. of the sum of the emoluments of all the persons employed by the employer at or from that establishment in the second base period.

(4) The amount of the levy imposed in respect of a paper and paper products establishment that ceases to carry on business in the second levy period shall be in the same proportion to the amount that would otherwise be due under the foregoing provisions of this Article as the number of days between the commencement of the said levy period and the date of cessation of business (both dates inclusive) bears to the number of days in the said levy period.

(5) The levy shall be assessed by the Board in respect of each employer (not being an employer who is exempt from the levy by virtue of paragraph (6) of this Article) in whose case the sum of the emoluments of all the persons employed by him in the second base period at or from the paper and paper products establishment or establishments of the employer (including any persons employed in that period at or from a paper and paper products establishment by an associated company of the employer) is not less than £15,000 but is less than £20,000 and, subject to the provisions of paragraph (7), the amount of the levy shall be 1·0 per cent. of the amount obtained by deducting from the sum of the emoluments of all the persons employed by the employer in the second base period at or from the paper and paper products establishment or establishments of the employer—

(*a*) £12,000, in the case where the sum of the emoluments of all the persons so employed by the employer or by an associated company of the employer is less than £17,500 ; or

(*b*) £6,000, in the case where the said sum of the emoluments is not less than £17,500 but is less than £20,000.

(6) There shall be exempt from the levy—

(*a*) an employer in whose case the sum of the emoluments of all the persons employed by him in the second base period at or from the paper and paper products establishment or establishments of the employer (including any persons employed in that period at or from a paper and paper products establishment by an associated company of the employer) is less than £15,000 ;

(*b*) a charity.

(7) Where any persons whose emoluments are taken into account for the purposes of paragraph (5) or (6)(*a*) of this Article were employed in an establishment that ceases to carry on business in the second levy period the sum of the emoluments of those persons shall, for the purposes of this Article, be reduced in the same proportion as the number of days between the commencement of the said levy period and the date of cessation of business (both dates inclusive) bears to the number of days in the said levy period.

Assessment Notices

4.—(1) The Board shall serve an assessment notice on every employer assessed to the levy, but one notice may comprise two or more assessments.

(2) The amount of any assessment payable under an assessment notice shall be rounded down to the nearest £1.

(3) An assessment notice shall state the Board's address for the service of a notice of appeal or of an application for an extension of time for appealing.

(4) An assessment notice may be served on the person assessed to the levy either by delivering it to him personally or by leaving it, or sending it to him by post, at his last known address or place of business in the United Kingdom or, if that person is a corporation, by leaving it, or sending it by post to the corporation, at such address or place of business or at its registered or principal office.

Payment of the Levy

5.—(1) Subject to the provisions of this Article and of Articles 6 and 7, the amount of each assessment appearing in an assessment notice served by the Board shall be due and payable to the Board one month after the date of a further notice requiring payment of that amount, which notice shall be served by the Board on the person assessed to the levy in the same manner as an assessment notice.

(2) The amount of an assessment shall not be recoverable by the Board until there has expired the time allowed for appealing against the assessment by Article 7(1) of this Order and any further period or periods of time that the Board or an appeal tribunal may have allowed for appealing under paragraph (2) or (3) of that Article or, where an appeal is brought, until the appeal is decided or withdrawn.

Withdrawal of Assessment

6.—(1) The Board may, by a notice served on the person assessed to the levy in the same manner as an assessment notice, withdraw an assessment if that person has appealed against that assessment under the provisions of Article 7 of this Order and the appeal has not been entered in the Register of Appeals kept under the appropriate Regulations specified in paragraph (5) of that Article.

(2) The withdrawal of an assessment shall be without prejudice to the power of the Board to serve a further assessment notice in respect of any establishment or, as the case may be, persons to which that assessment related.

Appeals

7.—(1) A person assessed to the levy may appeal to an appeal tribunal against the assessment within one month from the date of the service of the assessment notice or within any further period or periods of time that may be allowed by the Board or an appeal tribunal under the following provisions of this Article.

(2) The Board by notice may for good cause allow a person assessed to the levy to appeal to an appeal tribunal against the assessment at any time within the period of four months from the date of the service of the assessment notice or within such further period or periods as the Board may allow before such time as may then be limited for appealing has expired.

(3) If the Board shall not allow an application for extension of time for appealing, an appeal tribunal shall upon application made to the tribunal by the person assessed to the levy have the like powers as the Board under the last foregoing paragraph.

(4) In the case of an assessment that has reference to an establishment that ceases to carry on business in the second levy period on any day after the date of the service of the relevant assessment notice, the foregoing provisions of this Article shall have effect as if for the period of four months from the date of the service of the assessment notice mentioned in paragraph (2) of this Article there were substituted the period of six months from the date of the cessation of business.

(5) An appeal or an application to an appeal tribunal under this Article shall be made in accordance with the Industrial Tribunals (England and Wales) Regulations 1965(**a**) as amended by the Industrial Tribunals (England and Wales) (Amendment) Regulations 1967(**b**) except where the relevant assessment relates to an establishment that is wholly in Scotland or, as the case may be, to persons employed at or from any such establishment or establishments and to no other persons, in which case the appeal or application shall be made in accordance with the Industrial Tribunals (Scotland) Regulations 1965(**c**) as amended by the Industrial Tribunals (Scotland) (Amendment) Regulations 1967(**d**).

(6) The powers of an appeal tribunal under paragraph (3) of this Article may be exercised by the President of the Industrial Tribunals (England and Wales) or by the President of the Industrial Tribunals (Scotland) as the case may be.

Evidence

8.—(1) Upon the discharge by a person assessed to the levy of his liability under an assessment the Board shall if so requested issue to him a certificate to that effect.

(2) The production in any proceedings of a document purporting to be certified by the Secretary of the Board to be a true copy of an assessment or other notice issued by the Board or purporting to be a certificate such as is mentioned in the foregoing paragraph of this Article shall, unless the contrary is proved, be sufficient evidence of the document and of the facts stated therein.

1st May 1970.

Barbara Castle,
First Secretary of State and Secretary of State
for Employment and Productivity.

EXPLANATORY NOTE

(*This Note is not part of the Order.*)

This Order gives effect to proposals submitted by the Paper and Paper Products Industry Training Board to the Secretary of State for Employment and Productivity for the imposition of a further levy upon employers in the paper and paper products industry for the purpose of raising money towards the expenses of the Board.

The levy is to be imposed in respect of the second levy period commencing on the day upon which this Order comes into operation and ending on 5th April 1971. The levy will be assessed by the Board and there will be a right of appeal against an assessment to an industrial tribunal.

(**a**) S.I. 1965/1101 (1965 II, p. 2805).
(**b**) S.I. 1967/301 (1967 I, p. 1040).
(**c**) S.I. 1965/1157 (1965 II, p. 3266).
(**d**) S.I. 1967/302 (1967 I, p. 1050).

STATUTORY INSTRUMENTS

1970 No. 656

WAGES COUNCILS

The Wages Regulation (Brush and Broom) Order 1970

Made - - -	1*st May* 1970
Coming into Operation	8*th June* 1970

Whereas the Secretary of State has received from the Brush and Broom Wages Council (Great Britain) the wages regulation proposals set out in the Schedule hereto;

Now, therefore, the Secretary of State in exercise of her powers under section 11 of the Wages Councils Act 1959(**a**), and of all other powers enabling her in that behalf, hereby makes the following Order:—

1. This Order may be cited as the Wages Regulation (Brush and Broom) Order 1970.

2.—(1) In this Order the expression "the specified date" means the 8th June 1970, provided that where, as respects any worker who is paid wages at intervals not exceeding seven days, that date does not correspond with the beginning of the period for which the wages are paid, the expression "the specified date" means, as respects that worker, the beginning of the next such period following that date.

(2) The Interpretation Act 1889(**b**) shall apply to the interpretation of this Order as it applies to the interpretation of an Act of Parliament and as if this Order and the Orders hereby revoked were Acts of Parliament.

3. The wages regulation proposals set out in the Schedule hereto shall have effect as from the specified date and as from that date the Wages Regulation (Brush and Broom) Order 1967(**c**) and the Wages Regulation (Brush and Broom) (Amendment) (No. 2) Order 1969(**d**) shall cease to have effect.

Signed by order of the Secretary of State.
1st May 1970.

A. A. Jarratt,
Deputy Under Secretary of State,
Department of Employment and Productivity.

(**a**) 1959 c. 69.
(**b**) 1889 c. 63.
(**c**) S.I. 1967/1759 (1967 III, p. 4669).
(**d**) S.I. 1969/909 (1969 II, p. 2718).

ARRANGEMENT OF SCHEDULE

Article 3

SCHEDULE

The following minimum remuneration shall be substituted for the statutory minimum remuneration fixed by the Wages Regulation (Brush and Broom) Order 1967 (Order M. (105)) as amended by the Wages Regulation (Brush and Broom) (Amendment) (No. 2) Order 1969 (Order M. (111)).

STATUTORY MINIMUM REMUNERATION

PART I

APPLICATION

1. Subject to the provisions of this Schedule, the minimum remuneration payable to a worker to whom this Schedule applies for all work except work to which a minimum overtime rate applies under Part V is:—

(1) in the case of a time worker, other than a worker referred to in (3) of this paragraph, the general minimum time rate payable to the worker under Part II or Part III of this Schedule;

(2) in the case of a worker employed on piece work, other than a worker referred to in (3) of this paragraph;

(*a*) where a minimum piece rate is specified in Part VII or Part VIII of this Schedule, that rate, increased in accordance with Part VI of this Schedule;

(*b*) where no such minimum piece rate applies, piece rates each of which would yield, in the circumstances of the case, to an ordinary worker at least the same amount of money as the piece work basis time rate applicable to the worker under Part II or Part III of this Schedule, or, where no piece work basis time rate is applicable, at least the same amount of money as the general minimum time rate which would be applicable if the worker were a time worker;

(3) in the case of a female apprentice to pan setting or of a male apprentice to whom the provisions of Part IV of this Schedule apply respectively, the general minimum time rate or the piece rates specified in that Part of this Schedule: Provided that where a guaranteed time rate is applicable to a male apprentice who is employed on piece work, and the worker's minimum remuneration calculated on a time work basis at that guaranteed time rate exceeds the minimum remuneration calculated at the said piece rates, the worker shall be paid not less than that guaranteed time rate.

2. In this Schedule "a female pan hand" means a female worker (of any age) who is employed in pan setting, that is to say, the making or setting by hand of a pan knot or both such making and setting with or without the operations of boring and trimming or either of them.

3. This Schedule does not apply to workers employed as carmen, engineers, powermen, enginemen or stokers, but, save as aforesaid, applies to workers in relation to whom the Brush and Broom Wages Council (Great Britain) operates, that is to say, workers employed in Great Britain in the trade specified in the Regulations made by the Minister and dated 10th July 1919**(a)**, with respect to the constitution and proceedings of the Brush and Broom Trade Board (Great Britain), that is to say:—

the manufacture of brushes (other than feather brushes) or brooms, including the following operations, where all or any of them are carried on in association with or in conjunction with the manufacture of such brushes of brooms:—

(*a*) the drafting, dressing or mixing of bass, whisk or similar fibres or animal bristles or hair and the working of wood, bone, ivory or celluloid;

(*b*) all finishing, warehousing, packing or other operations incidental to or appertaining to the manufacture of such brushes or brooms;

but excluding the following operations:—

The sawing and turning of wood as a preliminary operation to the manufacture of such brushes or brooms; the making of metal parts and the mounting of brushes with metal or tortoise-shell backs.

PART II

GENERAL MINIMUM TIME RATES AND PIECE WORK BASIS TIME RATE FOR MALE WORKERS

GENERAL MINIMUM TIME RATES

4.—(1) The general minimum time rates payable to male workers other than the apprentices to whom Part IV of this Schedule applies are as follows:—

	Per hour s. d.
(*a*) Workers (of any age) who have completed an apprenticeship of not less than three years in one or more of the operations or branches of work specified in (*a*) of sub-paragraph (2) of this paragraph ...	6 9
(*b*) Workers (other than those specified at (*a*) of this sub-paragraph) who are employed in any of the operations or branches of work specified in (*a*) or (*b*) of sub-paragraph (2) of this paragraph and have had not less than *one year's* experience in one or more of them, being aged:—	
(i) 19 years or over	6 9
(ii) 18 years and under 19 years	5 9

(a) S.R. & O. 1919/969 (1919 II, p. 539).

(*c*) Workers who are wholly or mainly employed in any of the operations specified in (*c*) of sub-paragraph (2) of this paragraph and have had not less than *one year's* experience in one or more of them, being aged:—

	Per hour s. d.
21 years or over	*6 9*

(*d*) All other workers, being aged:—

	s. d.
21 years or over	*6 3*
20 „ and under 21 years	*6 0*
19 „ „ „ 20 „	*5 3*
18 „ „ „ 19 „	*4 9*
17½ „ „ „ 18 „	*4 4*
17 „ „ „ 17½ „	*4 0*
16½ „ „ „ 17 „	*3 8*
16 „ „ „ 16½ „	*3 4*
15½ „ „ „ 16 „	*3 0*
under 15½ years	*2 9*

(2) The operations or branches of work referred to in the last foregoing sub-paragraph are as follows:—

(*a*) "Pan" (hair and bass), "Hairs", "Finishing" (that is, the work of all wood-workers employed in finishing or part-finishing brushes or brooms by hand or machine), "Boring or Drilling" (hand and machine), "Drawing", "Bone brush cutting", "Bone brush fashioning", "Bone brush drilling", "Bone brush profiling", the manufacture of artists', medical, painting, whitewash and tar brushes, and brushes not otherwise specified; and (i) the drafting, dressing (including cutting), or mixing of animal hair, bass, whisk or other fibre where the operative performs the aforesaid operations singly or in combination by hand or partly by hand and partly by machine; (ii) the working of ivory or celluloid; (iii) the turning of bone; where all or any of the operations specified in (i), (ii) or (iii) are carried on in association with or in conjunction with the manufacture of brushes (other than feather brushes) or brooms.

(*b*) The dressing of bass or fibre by hand or by machine; the cutting and preparation of material for toilet or tooth-brush manufacture; the shaping (including the setting-up of knives and other incidental work) of wooden or plastic boards or handles by spindle moulding or automatic shaping machine or by both such machines; boring; hand finishing; hand drawing; machine fllling; the flirting, brushing, trimming, examining of brushes; polishing or hand polishing, dipping and cellulose spraying; sand-papering and buffing, the making of twisted wire brushes; the making of artists' brushes.

(*c*) The receiving, keeping and storing of stock including raw materials; the packing and despatching of the finished products.

PIECE WORK BASIS TIME RATE

5. The piece work basis time rate applicable to workers specified in (*a*) or (*b*) of sub-paragraph (1) of paragraph 4 is *7s. 6d. per hour*.

PART III

GENERAL MINIMUM TIME RATES AND PIECE WORK BASIS TIME RATES FOR FEMALE WORKERS

6.—(1) The following rates apply to female workers other than the apprentices to pan setting to whom paragraph 7 applies:—

	General minimum time rates Per hour	Piecework basis time rates Per hour
(*a*) Pan Hands of any age employed on:—	s. d.	s. d.
(i) Coco or any other fibre brooms or banisters of any length (except bass and bassine heads on stocks over 12 in. in length and more than 30 knots round, and whisk brooms and banisters). Bass heads up to 12 in. stock, 30 knots round	*5 3*	*5 5*
(ii) Broom heads up to 11½ in. stock, or banisters up to 8¼ in. blade, middles being made of all fibre or fibre and drafts mixed up to 3½ in., and outsides of any material up to and including 3½ in. Banisters (whisk) up to 7½ in. blade made with common Venetian tops (imported as tops); sweeps' hand brushes up to and including 5 in. blade, or toy hearth brushes up to and including 3½ in., both made with fibre, fibre and drafts, drafts only or china below 3 in. But excluding any brushes provided for in (*a*) (i) of this sub-paragraph.	*5 9*	*5 11*
(iii) Work other than that provided for in (*a*) (i) and (ii) of this sub-paragraph	*6 9*	*7 1*
(*b*) Drawing Hands employed on drawing wire brushes (with or without the operation of trimming) of:—		
(i) 38 gauge wire or finer	*5 3*	*5 5*
(ii) thicker than 38 gauge wire	*5 7*	*5 9*
(*c*) Workers employed on any of the operations specified in sub-paragraph (2) of this paragraph who have had not less than *one year's* experience in one or more of such operations *being aged 18 years or over* ...	*5 0*	*5 4*
(*d*) All other workers being aged:—		
18 years or over	*4 9*	*5 4*
17½ years and under 18 years	*4 4*	
17 " " " 17½ "	*4 0*	
16½ " " " 17 "	*3 8*	
16 " " " 16½ "	*3 4*	
15½ " " " 16 "	*3 0*	
under 15½ years	*2 9*	

(2) The operations referred to in (*c*) and (*d*) of the last foregoing sub-paragraphs are as follows:—

The dressing of bass or fibre by hand or by machine; the cutting and preparation of material for toilet or tooth-brush manufacture; the shaping (including the setting-up of knives and other incidental work) of wooden or plastic boards or handles by spindle moulding or automatic shaping machine or by both such machines; boring; hand finishing; hand drawing (other than the hand drawing of wire brushes); machine filling; the flirting, brushing, trimming, examining of brushes; polishing or hand polishing, dipping and cellulose spraying; sand-papering and buffing, the making of twisted wire brushes; the making of artists' brushes; making painting brushes by sectional methods; finishing painting brushes by sectional methods; making shaving brushes by sectional methods; finishing shaving brushes by sectional methods.

PART IV

MINIMUM RATES FOR APPRENTICES

FEMALE APPRENTICES TO PAN SETTING

7.—(1) The general minimum time rate specified in Column (2) of the next following Table is payable during the first six months of apprenticeship to female apprentices to pan setting employed in accordance with the conditions specified in this paragraph, and the piece rates specified in Column (3) are payable to such workers during the remainder of their apprenticeship:

Provided that the said rates shall not be payable to a worker in respect of more than one such apprenticeship.

Column (1) Period of Apprenticeship	Column (2) General Minimum Time Rate	Column (3) Piece Rates
First six months ...	The general minimum time rate applicable to a female worker of 15½ and under 16 years as set out in (*d*) of sub-paragraph (1) of Paragraph 6.	—
Second six months ...	—	Two-thirds of the rates specified in sub-paragraph (2).
Third six months ...	—	Three-quarters of the rates specified in sub-paragraph (2).
Fourth six months ...	—	Five-sixths of the rates specified in sub-paragraph (2).

(2) The piece rates referred to in Column (3) of the said Table are the general minimum piece rates which would be payable under Part VI of this Schedule if the worker were a female pan hand, or, where no such piece rate is payable, piece rates each of which would yield, in the circumstances of the case, to an ordinary worker at least the same amount of money as the appropriate piece work basis time rate applicable under sub-paragraph (1)(*a*) or (1)(*d*) of paragraph 6 to a female pan hand.

(3) Subject to the provisions of this Schedule, the minimum rates of wages specified in this paragraph apply only where the following conditions are fufilled:—

(*a*) the apprentice shall be employed during the whole of her time for a period of two years under a written contract of apprenticeship which has been duly executed and which contains the following provisions, which the Wages Council considers necessary for the effective instruction of the apprentice, or provisions substantially to the same effect and no provisions contrary thereto, that is to say,

(i) that whereas the apprentice is desirous of being trained in the branch of the brush and broom trade known as the operation of "pan setting" and the employer, being engaged in the said trade, is willing to give her such training, the employer shall receive and retain the said worker in his service as an apprentice for a period of two years, subject to the condition that if the apprentice wilfully disobeys any lawful order of the employer or otherwise wilfully misconducts herself towards the employer or those in his employment, it shall be lawful for the employer to discharge the apprentice from his service and absolutely determine the contract of apprenticeship;

(ii) that during the said term of service, the employer shall cause the apprentice to be well and sufficiently instructed in the said operation;

(iii) that, subject to the provisions of the agreement, the working hours shall be those applying for the time being to the female pan hands at the factory of the employer.

(*b*) The number of female apprentices to pan setting employed at any time shall be one female apprentice where not more than three journeywomen are employed with one additional female apprentice for every three journeywomen in excess of three in the service of the employer in the branch of the trade to which the apprentice is bound:

Provided that the temporary absence of a journeywoman or a casual vacancy for a short period in the number of journeywomen employed, shall not affect compliance with this condition.

(*c*) The apprentice shall be the holder of a certificate of registration of apprenticeship issued by, or on behalf of, the Wages Council or shall have made application for such a certificate which has been duly acknowledged and is still under consideration:

Provided that the Wages Council may refuse certification if it is not satisfied that facilities exist which will enable the conditions laid down by the Wages Council for female apprentices to pan setting to be complied with.

(4) In the event of any non-compliance with the conditions specified in the last foregoing sub-paragraph, the minimum rate payable to the apprentice shall be the appropriate minimum rate for a female pan hand other than an apprentice to pan setting.

(5) In this paragraph "journeywoman" means a female worker who has had not less than two years' experience in the pan setting branch of the trade.

MALE APPRENTICES

8.—(1) This paragraph applies to male apprentices to any one of the following branches of the trade: (i) pan work (hair and bass); (ii) hairs; (iii) the making throughout of whitewash brushes and tar brushes; (iv) the making throughout of painting brushes, where the conditions following are fulfilled:—

(*a*) The apprentice shall be employed during the whole of his time for a period of three years under a written contract of apprenticeship which has been duly executed and which contains the following provisions, which the Wages

Council considers necessary for the effective instruction of the apprentice, or provisions substantially to the same effect and no provisions contrary thereto, namely:—

(i) the employer shall keep the apprentice as his apprentice during the said term and to the best of his power, skill and knowledge instruct the apprentice or cause him to be instructed in the branch of the trade specified in the contract;

(ii) the employer shall keep the apprentice under his own supervision or place him under one or more fully qualified journeymen;

(iii) where on account of slackness of trade or other cause beyond the control of the employer the majority of the journeymen employed by the employer in the aforesaid branch of the trade are not working full time, notwithstanding anything contained in provisions (i) and (ii), the employer shall be bound to provide instruction or employment for the apprentice for at least as many hours as are being worked by such majority of journeymen, and, in respect of any hours in which the apprentice is not under instruction or employed, the employer shall not be bound to pay wages to the apprentice and the apprentice shall not be bound to serve the employer:

Provided that, if the employer in each of four successive weeks provides the apprentice neither with instruction nor with employment for at least one-half of the number of working hours constituting full time, the said contract may be determined by seven days' notice in writing given to the employer by the guardian and apprentice jointly.

(*b*) The number of apprentices employed at any time shall be one male apprentice where not more than three journeymen are employed with one additional male apprentice for every three journeymen in excess of three in the service of the employer in the branch or branches of the trade to which the apprentice is bound:

Provided that—

(i) the temporary absence of a journeyman or a casual vacancy for a short period in the number of journeymen employed, shall not affect compliance with this condition;

(ii) where an employer is himself performing the work of a journeyman he shall be treated as a journeyman for the purpose of this condition.

(*c*) The apprentice shall be the holder of a certificate of registration of apprenticeship issued by, or on behalf of, the Wages Council, or shall have made application for such certificate which has been duly acknowledged and is still under consideration:

Provided that—

the Wages Council may refuse certification if it is not satisfied that facilities exist which will enable the conditions laid down by the Wages Council for apprentices to be complied with.

(*d*) (i) A journeyman instructor shall have responsibility for the work of the apprentice during the first 12 months and supervision of the apprentice during the remainder of the apprenticeship in the journeyman's own section of the trade; and

(ii) during the first 18 months of the apprentice's employment in the painting brush making branch of the trade and during the first nine months of the apprentice's employment in any other of the specified branches of the trade a journeyman shall be paid by the employer in each week in respect of the instruction of, and the responsibility for, the apprentice a sum equal to the difference between the actual piece work earnings of the apprentice in that week at the minimum rate applicable to him, and the sum which would be payable under this Schedule to a journeyman if employed on the same work as the apprentice.

(2) The minimum piece rates payable to the apprentices to whom this paragraph applies during the period of apprenticeship specified in Column 1 of the next following Table are the rates specified in Column 2.

Column 1 Period of Apprenticeship	Column 2 Minimum Piece Rates
1st six months	One-half of the piece rates specified in paragraph 10
2nd six months	Two-thirds of the piece rates specified in paragraph 10
3rd six months	Three-quarters of the piece rates specified in paragraph 10
4th six months	Five-sixths of the piece rates specified in paragraph 10
3rd year	Eleven-twelfths of the piece rates specified in paragraph 10

GUARANTEED TIME RATES

9. The following guaranteed time rates are applicable to apprentices to whom paragraph 8 applies—

(1) during the first 12 months of apprenticeship a rate equal to the general minimum time rate payable to a worker aged under 15½ years, under sub-paragraph (1)(*d*) of paragraph 4 other than the proviso thereto;

(2) during the first six months of employment in a section of the trade other than that in which he began his apprenticeship, a rate equal to the general minimum time rate payable to a worker of his age, under the said sub-paragraph (1)(*d*) other than the proviso thereto.

10.—(1) The piece rates referred to in Column 2 of the Table to paragraph 8(2) are—

(*a*) the general minimum piece rates which would be payable under Part VI of this Schedule if the apprentice were a journeyman; or

(*b*) where no such rate applies, piece rates each of which would yield, in the circumstances of the case, to an ordinary worker, at least the same amount of money as the piece work basis time rate specified in paragraph 5.

(2) For the purposes of paragraphs 8 and 9 a "journeyman" is a male worker who has had not less than five years' experience in the branch or branches of the trade to which the apprentice is bound.

(3) Where the employment of a male apprentice does not comply with the provisions of paragraph 8, the minimum rate payable shall be that payable to a male worker of the same age, who is not an apprentice.

PROSPECTIVE APPRENTICES

11. Notwithstanding the foregoing provisions of this Schedule, where an employer employs a worker as a prospective apprentice for a probationary period not exceeding four months and such of the foregoing provisions as to apprentices (other than those with regard to employment under a written contract of apprenticeship and certification by the Wages Council) as are appropriate to the case of that worker are fulfilled, the minimum remuneration applicable to that worker during the said period shall be that applicable to an apprentice employed in accordance with the appropriate provisions specified in paragraph 7, 8 or 9, and, in the event of the worker being continued thereafter at his employment as an apprentice, the said probationary period shall, for the purposes of this Schedule, be treated as part of the period of apprenticeship.

PART V
WAITING TIME AND OVERTIME
WAITING TIME

12.—(1) A worker is entitled to payment of the minimum remuneration specified in this Schedule for all the time during which he is present on the premises of the employer, unless he is present thereon in any of the following circumstances, that is to say:—

(*a*) without the employer's consent, express or implied;

(*b*) for some purpose unconnected with his work and other than that of waiting for work to be given to him to perform;

(*c*) by reason only of the fact that he is resident thereon; or

(*d*) during normal meal times in a room or place in which no work is being done, and he is not waiting for work to be given to him to perform.

(2) The minimum remuneration payable under sub-paragraph (1) of this paragraph to a piece worker when not engaged on piece work is that which would be payable if he were a time worker.

MINIMUM OVERTIME RATES

13.—(1) Minimum overtime rates are payable to any worker as follows:—

(*a*) on any day other than a Saturday, Sunday or customary holiday—

(i) for the first 2 hours worked in excess of 8½ hours ... time-and-a-quarter

(ii) thereafter ... ... time-and-a-half

Provided that where the employer normally requires the worker's attendance on 6 days in the week, the said minimum overtime rates of time-and-a-quarter and time-and-a-half shall be payable after 8 and 10 hours' work respectively;

(*b*) on a Saturday, not being a customary holiday—

(i) where the employer normally requires the worker's attendance on 6 days in the week—
for all time worked in excess of 4 hours ... double time

(ii) where the employer normally requires the worker's attendance on 5 days only in the week— ...
for the first 2 hours worked ... ... time-and-a-quarter
for the next 2 hours ... ... time-and-a-half
thereafter ... ... double time

(*c*) on a Sunday or a customary holiday—
for all time worked ... ... double time

(*d*) in any week, exclusive of any time in respect of which any minimum overtime rate is payable under the foregoing provisions of this sub-paragraph—
for all time worked in excess of 40 hours ... time-and-a-quarter

(2) The minimum overtime rates set out in sub-paragraph (1)(*a*), (*b*) or (*c*) of this paragraph are payable in any week whether or not the minimum overtime rate set out in sub-paragraph (1)(*d*) is also payable.

14. In this Schedule—

(1) The expression "customary holiday" means

(*a*) (i) In England and Wales—

Christmas Day (or, if Christmas Day falls on a Sunday, such weekday as may be appointed by national proclamation, or, if none is so appointed, the next following Tuesday), Boxing Day, Good Friday, Easter Monday, Whit Monday (or where another day is substituted therefor by national proclamation, that day) and August Bank holiday;

(ii) In Scotland—

New Year's Day (or, if New Year's Day falls on a Sunday, the following Monday);

the local Spring holiday;

the local Autumn holiday; and

three other days (being days on which the worker normally works) in the course of a calendar year, to be fixed by agreement between the employer and the worker;

or (*b*) in the case of each of the said days (other than a day in Scotland fixed by agreement between the employer and the worker) a day substituted therefor by agreement between the employer and the worker, being a day recognised by local custom as a day of holiday in substitution for the said day.

(2) The expressions "time-and-a-quarter", "time-and-a-half" and "double time" mean respectively—

(*a*) In the case of a time worker, one and a quarter times, one and a half times and twice the general minimum time rate otherwise payable to the worker;

(*b*) In the case of a worker employed on piece work, other than a male apprentice to whom the rates specified in paragraph 8 or 9 apply—

(i) a time rate equal respectively to one-quarter, one-half and the whole of the piece work basis time rate otherwise applicable to the worker, or where none is applicable, of the general minimum time rate which would be payable if the worker were a time worker and a minimum overtime rate did not apply, and, in addition thereto,

(ii) the general minimum piece rate otherwise payable under Part VI of this Schedule, or where no such piece rate applies, piece rates each of which would yield, in the circumstances of the case, to an ordinary worker at least the same amount of money as the said piece work basis time rate, or, where none is applicable to the worker, at least the same amount of money as the general minimum time rate which would be payable if the worker were a time worker and a minimum overtime rate did not apply;

(*c*) In the case of a male apprentice to whom the rates specified in paragraph 8 or 9 apply and who is employed on piece work;

(i) a time rate equal respectively to one-quarter, one-half and the whole of the general minimum time rate which would be payable to a worker of the same age (other than an apprentice) if he were a time worker and a minimum overtime rate did not apply, and in addition thereto,

(ii) the minimum piece rate otherwise payable under Part IV of this Schedule.

PART VI

GENERAL MINIMUM PIECE RATES FOR MALE OR FEMALE WORKERS

15. The general minimum piece rates payable to the workers to whom this Schedule applies, other than the female apprentices to pan setting and the male apprentices to whom the minimum rates specified in Part IV respectively apply, are the piece rates specified in Part VII or Part VIII of the Schedule increased by *190 per cent.*

PART VII

MINIMUM PIECE RATES FOR MALE WORKERS

PAN WORK—BORING, SETTING AND TRIMMING UNLESS OTHERWISE STATED

16.—(1) Subject to the provisions of this paragraph, the minimum piece rates for pan work (boring, setting and trimming unless otherwise stated) are as follows:—

Description	Filling material		
	Materials other than bass and bassine, whisk and badger hair	Bass and bassine	Whisk
	Column 2	Column 3	Column 4
Column 1	Knots per penny	Knots per penny	Knots per penny
BANISTERS			
1. Other than those specified in items 2 to 14 below	6	5½	5½
2. Comber or Fly (bodies)	5½	—	—
3. Comber or Fly (wings)	4¾	—	—
4. Carpet	6	5½	5½
5. Double: one side soft, the other a material other than whisk or bass (both sides)	5½	—	—
6. Double: one side soft, the other whisk or bass (both sides)	5	—	—
7. Double: toy or toilet, soft side	5½	—	—
8. Double: toy or toilet, hard side, whisk	—	—	4¾
9. Double: toy or toilet, hard side, Kitool	3¾	—	—
10. Mill or moulders	5½	—	—
11. Rubber	5	—	—
12. Toilet or toy	5½	—	4¾
13. Toilet or turnover	4¾	—	—
14. Winged (bodies and wings)	5¾	—	—

BROOMS			
Other than those specified in items 20 to 30 below:—			
15. Stock not exceeding 14 in.	6	—	5½
16. Stock over 14 in. and not exceeding 20 in.	5¾	—	5½
17. Stock exceeding 20 in. and not exceeding 24 in.	5½	—	—
17a. Stock exceeding 24 in.	5¼	—	—
18. Stock not exceeding 16 in.	—	5½	—
19. Stock exceeding 16 in.	—	5	—
20. Carpet	6	5½	5½
21. Golf course stock under 24 in.	—	5½	—
22. Golf course stock 24 in.	—	5¼	—
23. Golf course stock over 24 in. and not exceeding 30 in.	—	4¾	—
24. Golf course stock over 30 in. and not exceeding 36 in.	—	4¼	—
25. Hair outside bass middles	6	5½	—
26. Rubber	3¼	—	—
27. Scrubs	5¾	—	—
28. Wall on broom stocks, ends filled only	5	—	—
29. Wall on Turk's Head pattern	4¾	—	—
30. Winged (bodies and wings)	5¾	—	—
OTHER BRUSHES			
31. Bee-hive boot wipers, stock under 12½ in.	4¼	4	—
32. Bee-hive boot wipers, stock 12½ in.	3¼	3	—
33. Bee-hive boot wipers, stock over 12½ in.	2¼	2	—
34. Bed pan	4¼	—	—
35. Blocks: Ashworth's	4¼	—	—
36. Card top, long handle	5	—	—
37. Carpet sweeping machine (circular brush)	4¾	—	—
38. Celery	6	—	—
39. Chimney sweep block heads	—	5	—
40. Closet	4¾	4¾	4¾
41. Cloth: flat face	5	—	—
42. Cloth: roached face	4½	—	—
43. Compo	—	5½	—
44. Corporation rollers including Karrier rollers: new (boring and setting only)	—	5¼	—
45. Refilling (setting only)	—	6	—
46. Lewin or similar types with holes bored at contrasting angles: new (boring and setting only)	—	4¾	—

Description	Filling material		
	Materials other than bass and bassine, whisk and badger hair	Bass and bassine	Whisk
	Column 2	Column 3	Column 4
Column 1	Knots per penny	Knots per penny	Knots per penny
OTHER BRUSHES—continued			
Corporation rollers, including Karrier rollers—continued			
47. Lewin or similar types with holes bored at contrasting angles: refilling (setting only)	—	5¾	—
48. Laffley: refilling (setting only), material 11 in. or over	—	4¼	—
49. Laffley: refilling (setting only), material 10 in.	—	4¾	—
50. Laffley: refilling (setting only), material under 10 in.	—	5¼	—
51. Currant cleaners: grooved machine	5¼	—	—
52. Curtain or bed (fitting up 6d. per doz. extra)	4¼	—	—
53. Dust or sweeps: porcupine	5¾	5¼	—
54. Dust or sweeps: porcupine union fibre	5½	—	—
55. Dust or sweeps: other than porcupine	6	—	—
56. Dusters: bell, picture, cornice, Venetian	5	—	—
57. Dusters: glaziers, jamb, painters (round or flat)	5½	—	—
58. Dusters: potters, flat	6	5½	6
59. Dusters: potters, round	5¾	5¼	5¾
60. Fire	5¼	—	—
61. Flower pot	4¾	—	—
62. Furniture	4¾	—	4¼
63. Gun: stock up to and including 9 in.	4¾	—	—
64. Gun: stock over 9 in.	4¼	—	—
65. Hearth: gilt or fancy	5¼	—	—
66. Hearth: cased or metal sliding hearth, stock 3½ in. or under	4¾	—	—
67. Hearth: cased or metal sliding hearth, stock over 3½ in.	5¼	—	—
68. Hearth: Scotch	6	—	—
69. Hearth: telescope	4¾	—	—
70. Hearth: slipper or shoe	5¼	—	—

71. Hearth: toy, 4 in. and under	5¼	—	—
72. Hearth: other than those specified in items 65 to 71	5¾	4½	—
73. Jug	3¾	—	—
74. Lamp	4¼	—	—
75. Lamp Colliers	5¼	—	—
76. Mattress	—	—	5¾
77. Orderly	—	5¾	—
78. Paper hangers, flatteners, stainers	5¼	—	—
79. Painters' pegs or ring pegs	5¾	—	—
80. Pointsman	—	5½	—
81. Potato cleaners	—	5½	—
82. Pope's head and pulley cleaning brushes	5¼	—	—
83. Press lags	5¼	—	—
84. Ring	5	—	—
85. Satin stainers	2¼	—	—
86. Scrubs: deck or boat, flat face	5¾	—	—
87. Scrubs: deck or boat, round face	5¼	—	—
88. Scrubs: porcupine	5¼	5	—
89. Seed	4¾	—	—
90. Sieve: round	4¾	—	—
91. Stipplers	3¾	—	—
92. Spoke	4¾	—	—
93. Tiering	5¼	—	—
94. Travis: Toy	—	5½	—
95. Turk's Head	4¾	—	—
96. Wardrobe	4¾	—	4¼
97. Whitewash: round or flat	4¾	—	—
98. Window cleaners	5¼	—	—
99. Window cleaners toy	4¾	—	—

(2) A Toilet or Toy banister has a blade which does not exceed 7 inches in length, and in the case of straight ended handles does not exceed 1 inch in diameter at the heel and 1½ inches at the nose, or in the case of spoon nose shapes does not exceed 1¾ inches at the widest point

All work set with Badger hair shall be charged 4 Knots per penny.

(3) EXTRAS TO COLUMN 2 ARE AS FOLLOWS:—

	Knots less per penny
Banisters and dust (sweeps) with handles (excluding blade), 20 inches long or over	½
Setting with Gumati	½
Setting with Kitool	¼
Setting all work with a mixture of another material with Kitool, Gumati, bone or bassine	½
Setting all work with used hair	1
Setting all work with riflings, drafts, rough undressed hair or shake-up	1
Setting all work except stipplers with China 3 in. and up to and including 3¼ in.	½
Setting all work, except stipplers, with China under 3 in.	1
Setting all work, except stipplers, with any material (dressed or undressed) under 3 in., other than China	½
Cutting off toilet banisters	1
Setting with glue	1
Cement prepared by operator	½
Cutting off carpet banisters and brooms	½
Cutting coco 2d. per doz. brushes.	
Boring and setting banisters of over ⅝-in. and not exceeding ⅞-in. diam. ...	½
Boring and setting banisters ⅝ in. diam. and under	1
Setting brushes containing only 5 knots	½
Setting brushes containing only 4 knots	½
Setting brushes containing only 3 knots	1
Setting brushes containing only 2 knots	1½
Setting brushes containing only 1 knot	2
Work with synthetic monofilaments up to and including ·008-in. gauge ...	1
Work with synthetic monofilaments gauges ·009 to ·019-in. inclusive ...	¾
Work with synthetic monofilaments gauges ·020-in. and over	1
Work with mixtures containing more than one-third synthetic monofilaments and materials other than Kitool, Gumati, bone or bassine	¾

Provided that not more than three of these extras on one job shall be counted being three giving the maximum yield to the worker.

(4) EXTRAS TO COLUMN 3 ARE AS FOLLOWS:—

	Knots less per penny
Setting banisters with seconds or riflings	½
Setting banisters with used bass	1
Setting banisters with whalebone...	¼
Setting brooms with seconds or riflings	½
Setting brooms with used bass	1
Setting brooms with monkey bass	¼
Setting brooms with cane	1¼
Setting brooms with whalebone	½
Setting brooms with Union (mixture of bass with cane and/or whalebone)...	½
Setting brooms and road sweeping machine rollers with monofilament with forged, barbed end	1¼
Setting bass and bassine above 3 ins. to 3½ ins.	¼
Setting bass and bassine 3 ins. and under	½
If a ⅝-in. or larger bit is used in item 18 or items 44 to 50	½
Cutting off banisters	¾

Putting wire in bass or cane—each wire 4d. in 1s. extra.

Putting wire in bass or cane if wire bent by pan hand each wire 5d. in 1s. extra.

(5) EXTRAS TO COLUMN 4 ARE AS FOLLOWS:—

	Knots less per penny
Setting undressed whisk	½
If whisk is cut by pan hand	1

(6) OTHER EXTRAS TO COLUMNS 2, 3 AND 4 ARE AS FOLLOWS:—

	Knots less per penny
If pan hand is required to bore on a foot lathe	¼

All odd knots to be paid for at proportionate rates.

When fewer than half-dozen brushes of one pattern are given out at a time—1d. per brush extra.

For putting up and sharpening bits—bass pan work 6d. in the £1.

For putting up and sharpening bits—other pan work 5d. in the £1.

PAN WORK—SETTING ONLY

17. For SETTING ONLY the minimum piece rates are the minimum piece rates for male workers on pan work (boring, setting and trimming) in paragraph 16, subject to a deduction of 20 per cent.

PAN WORK—SETTING AND TRIMMING ONLY

18. For SETTING AND TRIMMING ONLY the minimum piece rates are the minimum piece rates for male workers on pan work (boring, setting and trimming) in paragraph 16, subject to a deduction of 12½ per cent.

PAN WORK—BORING AND SETTING ONLY

19. For BORING AND SETTING ONLY the minimum piece rates are the minimum piece rates for male workers on pan work (boring, setting and trimming) in paragraph 16, subject to a deduction of 7½ per cent.

MACHINE PAN WORK

20.—(1) Subject to the provisions of this paragraph, the minimum piece rates for machine pan work are as follows:—

Description	Filling material				
	All materials other than those specified in Columns 3, 4, 5 and 6	Monkey bass bassine Gumati Kitool or mixtures of same	Bass or bass mixtures	Whisk	Badger or badger and drafts
	Column 2	Column 3	Column 4	Column 5	Column 6
Column 1	Knots per penny	Knots per penny	Knots per penny	Knots per penny	Knots per penny
Card, flock, cloth, weavers and burlers (hand brushes)	5	4¾	—	—	—
Hollows for French worsted	5	—	—	—	—
Hollows crossing brushes (velvet)	5½	5	—	—	—
Hollow or flat cord 29 in. and under	5	4½	—	—	—
Hollow or flat cord over 29 in.	4½	4	—	—	—
Lags, slips and other machine brushes not specified below	5½	4¾	4½	4	3¾
Lags, slips—not exceeding 10 knots long	5	4½	4	—	—
Lags, slips—Jig	4½	—	—	—	3¾
Lags, slips—Press	4½	—	—	—	3¾
Sieve (round)	4½	—	—	—	3¾
Rollers: other than those specified below	5	4¾	4½	4	3¾
Rollers: spiral	4½	4¼	4	3¾	3½
Rollers: sieve or threshing machine	—	4½	—	—	—
Rollers: sprinklers, dampers or stainers	5	4¾	—	—	3¾
Wheel or Polishing	5½	4¾	4½	—	3¾

(2) The rates in the above Table are subject to the following reductions where the cutting off is not performed by the pan hand:—

(*a*) as respects (i) hair or (ii) hair and fibre mixture (other than in the case of spiral rollers)—a reduction of 7½ per cent.

(*b*) as respects all materials other than hair or hair and fibre mixture and in the case of all spiral rollers—a reduction of 10 per cent.

(3) EXTRAS OR ALLOWANCES ARE AS FOLLOWS:—

	Knots less per penny
Work with synthetic monofilaments up to and including ·008 in. gauge ...	¼
Work with synthetic monofilaments of gauges ·009 in. to ·019 in. inclusive	½
Work with synthetic monofilaments of gauges ·020 in. and over	¾
Work with mixtures containing more than one-third synthetic monofilaments	¾
Work cut off under ⅜ in.	½
Where shaft will not allow hold being at least ⅜ in. deep	1¼
If whisk cut by pan hand	½
Pegged work	1¼
Setting with glue	1
Setting with cement prepared by pan hand	½
Setting with shake-up	¾
Setting with all materials under 3 in. except hairs previously used, riflings or shake-up	½
Setting with hairs or bristles previously used or with riflings or drafts ...	1
Setting with mixture containing whalebone or over one-third Kitool ...	½
Metal tube dampers	½
Old rollers, boring out or pulling to pieces	½
All rollers, cut slanting	½
Rollers over 9 ft. in length	¼
Where the pitch of the holes both along and across, but not diagonally is $\frac{5}{16}$ in. centre to centre or less	¼

Cutting off tops and re-using in same job ½d. in 1s. extra.

Nailing 4d. in 1s. extra.

If hollows for French worsted machines set only, 4d. in the 1s. less:

Provided that not more than three of these extras on one job shall be counted being three giving the maximum yield to the worker.

MINIMUM PIECE RATES FOR MALE WORKERS EMPLOYED ON HAIRS

21.—(1) For the purposes of this Part of this Schedule:—

"Dressed bristles" are bristles which have been mixed, dragged, or are from shoe hairs engined in Great Britain or Ireland.

All other materials are classified as follows:—

CLASS 1

Indian, 5 in. and above.
Chinas, 5 in. and above.
China dressed Siberian, 4½ in. and above.
Waste or Engined Refuse.

CLASS 2

German bleached, all lengths.
Indian, 4 in. to 4¾ in.
Chinas, 4 in. to 4¾ in.
Dressed horsehair, except as provided in class 4.
German boiled (Gekochte).
Caucasian, 4¼ in. and above.
China dressed Siberian, 4¼ in. and below.
Synthetic monofilaments.

Above materials, if washed, to be reckoned in class 1.

CLASS 3

Fine bone, Finner hair, Kitool, Bass, Bassine.

CLASS 4

Chinas, 3¾ in. and below.
Tops.
Dressed riflings.
Madagascar fibre.
Indian, 3¾ in. and below.
Dressed horsehair cut from up to 9 in., other than best English, American and Australian.
Mixture horsehair and fibre.

Above materials, if washed, to be reckoned in class 2.

(2) The following materials shall be paid for as extras as provided in paragraph 24:—

Coco. Manila. Flagged fibre. Mexican fibre. Gumati fibre.

MIXING

22.—(1) In Tables 1 to 5 of this paragraph the rate per dozen lbs. for the whole job (on weight returned) is governed by:—

(*a*) the lowest classed material in the job,

(*b*) the addition of "extras" as provided in paragraph 24,

(*c*) the length of the material which forms the greater part of the job judged by the weight.

(2) Subject to the provisions of paragraph 24, the minimum piece rates for mixing are as follows:—

—	Table 1 Dressed bristles	Table 2 Class 1 materials	Table 3 Class 2 materials	Table 4 Class 3 materials	Table 5 Class 4 materials
	Per dozen lbs.				
	s. d.	s. d.	s. d.	s. d.	s. d.
2¾ in.	8 6	10 0	10 6	11 0	11 6
3 in.	7 6	8 6	9 0	9 6	10 0
3¼ in.	6 6	7 6	8 0	8 6	9 0
3½ in., 3¾ in. ...	5 6	6 6	7 0	7 6	8 0
4 in., 4¼ in.	5 0	6 0	6 6	7 0	7 6
4½ in., 4¾ in. ...	4 6	5 6	6 0	6 6	7 0
5 in., 5¼ in.	4 0	5 0	5 6	6 0	6 6
Above 5¼ in. ...	3 6	4 6	5 0	5 6	6 0

DRAGGING, AND MIXING SIZES

23. Dragging:

(1) In Tables 6 to 8 in this paragraph the rate per dozen lbs. for the whole job (on weight returned) including the sizes, is governed by:

(*a*) the lowest classed material in the job,

(*b*) the addition of "extras" as provided below and in paragraph 24,

(*c*) the lowest length to which the material is dragged.

(2) Mixing Sizes. The rates per dozen lbs. in Table 9 of this paragraph are additional to the rates for dragging and are payable (on weight returned) according to the length of each size.

(3) Subject to the provisions of paragraph 24, the minimum piece rates for dragging and mixing sizes are as follows:—

—	For Dragging only			For mixing sizes and/or bottoms when part of a dragging job
	Table 6 Class 1 materials	Table 7 Class 2 materials	Table 8 Class 4 materials	Table 9
	Per dozen lbs.			
	s. d.	s. d.	s. d.	s. d.
2¼ in.	12 6	14 0	15 0	5 0
2¾ in.	11 0	12 6	13 6	4 6
3 in.	9 6	11 0	12 0	4 0
3¼ in.	8 6	10 0	11 0	3 6
3½ in., 3¾ in.... ...	7 6	9 0	10 0	3 0
4 in., 4¼ in.	7 0	8 6	9 6	2 6
4½ in., 4¾ in.... ...	6 6	8 0	9 0	2 3
5 in., 5¼ in.	6 0	7 6	8 6	2 0
Above 5¼ in.	5 6	7 0	8 0	2 0

(4) The extra is as follows:—

Dragging the following material: Indian (all lengths), 2s. per dozen lbs. extra on the amount put into the job.

24. The EXTRAS ON PIECE RATES SPECIFIED IN PARAGRAPHS 22 AND 23 are:—

	Per doz. lbs. for whole job on weight returned
	s. d.
Manila, flagged fibre and coco	2 0
Dressed Mexican and/or Gumati fibre	1 0
Mixing white or yellow into a grey job	1 0
Mixing white Mexican into a grey job	1 6
Tying up bristles in 1 lb. bundles by weight (including weighing) ...	1 6
Working riflings into job (if unturned)	0 6
Working riflings into job (if turned)	1 0
If bleached bristle mixed in with unbleached	2 0

	Per doz. lbs. of bristles cut back
	s. d.
Cutting back bristles, 2¾ in.	6 3
Cutting back bristles, 3 in., 3½ in.	4 2
Cutting back bristles, 3¾ in., 4¼ in.	2 1
Cutting back bristles, above 4¾ in.	1 0

	Per doz. lbs. cut down
	s. d.
Cutting down above 4¾ in.	1 0

	Per oz. lbs. opened
	s. d.
Indians, opening knots, 4 in. and above	0 6
Indians, opening knots, 3¾ in. and below	1 0
Taking out turned hairs from dressing by engine:	
(*a*) Per doz. lbs. on weight returned, below 4½ in.	1 0
(*b*) Per doz. lbs. on weight returned, 4½ in. and above	0 6
Taking out turned hairs from dressing by sieve:	
(*a*) Per doz. lbs. on weight returned, below 4½ in.	5 0
(*b*) Per doz. lbs. on weight returned, 4½ in. and above	3 0

Samples of any job to be paid for at the proportionate rates.

25. Minimum piece rates are as follows:—

(1) WASHING AND BLEACHING AND TYING UP

	Per doz. lbs.
	s. d.
Shoe hairs	6 0
Other dressed bristles, 4½ in. and above	6 6
Other dressed bristles, 4¼ in. and 4 in.	7 0
Other dressed bristles, 3½ in. and 3¾ in.	7 6
Other dressed bristles, 3 in. and 3¼ in.	10 6
Other dressed bristles, 2¾ in.	13 6

Lecks and extras, 4¾ in. and above, 8d. per dozen lbs. extra.

Other undressed bristles, below 4¾ in., 2s. per dozen lbs. extra.

(2) POINTING AND STRAIGHTENING

	s. d.
Pointing and straightening washed bristles up to 4 in.	3 6
Pointing and straightening washed bristles 4 in. and longer ...	2 6
Pointing and straightening other than washed bristles above 4 in.	2 6
Pointing and straightening other than washed bristles 4 in. and below	3 6

Note.—These rates are not applicable when cones are used.

26. The minimum piece rates for ENGINING SHOE HAIRS are as follows:—

—	Below 4½ in.	4½ in., 4¾ in.	5 in., 5¼ in., 5½ in.	Above 5½ in.
	Per dozen lbs.			
	s. d.	s. d.	s. d.	s. d.
1 or 2 engines	6 0	5 6	4 3	3 9
3 engines	6 9	6 0	4 9	4 6
4 engines	7 6	6 6	5 6	5 0
5 engines	8 0	7 0	6 0	5 6
6 engines	8 9	8 0	6 6	6 3

	Per doz. lbs. s. d.
Re-engining (cleansing)	6 0
Re-engining (cleansing) if four engines...	6 6

Each pull to be calculated as one engine.

All hairs that require roughing for engining, 1s. 6d. per doz. lbs. extra.

27. MISCELLANEOUS MINIMUM PIECE RATES

Per doz. lbs.
s. d.

Jumping to be the same price as dragging (see paragraph 23).

	Per doz. lbs. s. d.
Shake-up, any materials:	
3 in.	14 0
3½ in.	12 0
Riflings, getting up:	
3½ in.	13 0
4 in.	12 0
4½ in. and above	10 0
Shoe hairs, mixing and knotting:	
1 oz.	10 6
½ oz.	14 6
¼ oz.	20 6

MINIMUM PIECE RATES FOR MALE WORKERS EMPLOYED ON HAND FINISHING

28. DEFINITIONS

For the purpose of this Part of this Schedule:—

(1) Hand finishing means the finishing of a brush throughout by one single man, without the assistance of machinery (except so far as the list provides for an allowance to be made in respect of brushes which are partly shaped or finished by machinery).

(2) HARD WOODS are

Satinwood. Ebony. Sabacu. Beech.
Rosewood. Sycamore. Oak. Walnut.

(3) SOFT WOODS are

Cherry. Spanish Chestnut. Lime. Kauri Pine.
Elm. Alder. Ordinary Chestnut. Mahogany.

29. Subject to the provisions of paragraph 31, the minimum piece rates for hand finishing are as follows:—

	Per doz. pairs of brushes s.	d.
APHIS BRUSHES	2	1
APHIS BRUSHES including fitting up	3	2

	Per doz. brushes s.	d.
BILLIARD BRUSHES:		
Flat boards:		
If ¼ in. back, bevelled	5	3
If ¼ in. back, cushioned or domed	5	9
Roached boards:		
Veneers scraped	5	3
¼ in. backs, cushioned	6	10
½ in. backs, roached	7	4
BREECHES OR BOOT TOP BRUSHES:		
Solid:		
⅜ in. backs, roached	3	6
½ in. backs, roached	3	10
BREWERS' OR BARREL BRUSHES:		
Cover or veneer:		
Straight sides, pinned	2	1
Grooved...	2	10
Solid backs:		
⅜ in. nailed up to and including 14 nails, glued	3	2
⅜ in. screwed up to and including 10 screws	4	2
Handled, bent, cover or thick veneer, pinned, handle already sawn out, finished rounded handle	3	2
Handled, bent, pinned, handle already sawn out, finished flat handle	2	1
Handled, bent, solid backs, glued, handle already sawn out, finished rounded handle...	4	2
Handled, bent, glued, handle already sawn out, finished flat handle	3	2
(Cover or thick veneer, glued, 2d. per doz. extra.)		
Solid, hollow sides:		
Four screws grooved and glued	4	9
Bent screws grooved and glued	5	3
Flat hollow sides, pinned and grooved	3	2
Cover (thick veneer), dumb-bell or egg-shape:		
Pinned only	3	2
Glued and pinned	3	8
Solid, dumb-bell or egg-shaped, screwed	5	3
CLOTH AND HAT BRUSHES:		
Flat, veneer scraped, grooved sides	3	2
Roached, all sizes	3	2
Solid, $\frac{3}{16}$ in. or ¼ in. backs, cushioned, straight sides, and grooved:		
Oak, mahogany or walnut	4	2
Rosewood or satinwood	5	3
Ebony	6	4
Ebony sides, rounded	5	3
Ebony, ⅜ in. back, roached, sides grooved	7	4
Ebony, ½ in. back, roached, sides grooved	8	5
Small (or pocket) size, ½ in. or ⅝ in. back, mahogany, cushioned	5	3

	Per doz. brushes s. d.
CLOTH AND HAT BRUSHES (contd.)	
Extra: Round ends grooved	1 1
Concave backs, straight sides, grooved, not hollowed:	
Mahogany, walnut, oak	7 4
Satinwood, rosewood	10 6
Ebony	12 7
Dumb-bell shape, rosewood	12 7
Dumb-bell shape, ebony	14 8
Leather or flexible, oblong, ⅛ in., rosewood or satin backs 9 in. long and upward and rounded	6 4
Leather or flexible, oblong, $\frac{1}{16}$ in. flat veneer up to 9 in. long ...	4 2
Handled:	
Veneered mahogany board	6 4
Veneered cherry board	5 3
With solid back of oak, mahogany or walnut	7 4
With solid back of rosewood or satinwood	8 5
Extra: Splash	1 1
Handled, extra large, or Stock Exchange	10 6
CRUMB BRUSHES:	
Board sawn to shape and size.	
Plain finished without neck, ¼ in. cherry or soft board not exceeding ⅛ in. back	5 3
Mahogany veneer	6 4
Rosewood or satinwood veneer	7 4
Solid backs of mahogany up to ½ in.	10 6
Extra: Rosewood or satinwood backs	2 1
DANDY AND DOG BRUSHES:	
Flat:	
Pinned	1 7
Pinned and glued	1 11
Pinned and glued and grooved	2 5
Solid:	
⅜ in. backs, 4 screws and pins at end, roached	3 8
½ in. backs, 4 screws and pins at end, roached	4 2
⅝ in. backs, 4 screws and pins at end, roached	4 9
Extra:	
Backs, roached and rounded	0 4
Ends, rounded, flat or solid	0 4
Additional screws (each screw)	0 2
Solid oval:	
⅜ in. backs, cushioned, up to 6 pins	4 2
½ in. backs, straight sides, grooved and pinned, up to 6 pins ...	3 2
DISH BRUSHES:	
Planed or sliced veneer	2 8
Veneer scraped	3 2
Solid, up to ¼ in. backs	3 2
FLESH BRUSHES:	
Round or oval or unhandled:	
Veneer planed	3 2
Veneer scraped	3 8
Solid, bevelled	4 2

	Per doz. brushes s. d.
FLESH BRUSHES (contd.)	
Handled:	
Straight	7 4
With shape or neck	9 5
Extras:	
Bent	1 1
Backs cushioned	0 6
Sides grooved	0 8
If boards are already sawn out, 1s. 4d. per dozen less than above prices.	
FURNITURE BRUSHES:	
Crevice or sash, handled	4 9
Double-ended, hollow waist:	
Veneered	4 9
Solid	5 3
Double, straight or slightly hollow sides grooved	4 9
Cater corner:	
⅜ in. backs, cushioned, grooved	3 10
½ in. backs, cushioned, grooved	4 2
Flat, cater, soft veneer	2 1
Triangle or table, veneered	3 8
Triangle or table, solid	4 2
Round or table, backs turned	2 1
Handle, wing, or chair seat, veneered	6 4
Handle, wing, or chair seat, ¼ in. solid backs	7 4
HAIR BRUSHES (HANDLED):	
Scurf boards, and rose or satin veneers scraped	3 8
Cherry or birch boards and backs	4 9
Cherry or birch boards, satin backs	5 9
Satinwood boards and backs	6 4
Rosewood boards and backs	6 4
Ebony—1s. per doz. above satinwood rates.	
Concave, ½ in. solid backs	14 8
Inlaid veneer board, recessed	6 4
Inlaid solid (panel ready made)	8 5
Small size, or Infant's, soft wood boards, satin veneer backs	2 10
Small size, or Infant's, soft wood boards, solid backs	3 8
Small size, or Infant's, hard wood boards, solid backs	4 2
HAIR BRUSHES (MILITARY):	
Army pattern	2 1
Navy pattern	2 8
Birch or cherry boards and backs	4 9
Birch or cherry boards, satin backs, ⅜ in.	5 9
Satinwood boards and backs, ⅜ in.	6 4
Satinwood boards and backs, ½ in.	7 4
Satinwood boards and backs, above ⅝ in.	8 5
Ebony—1s. per doz. above satinwood rates.	
Concave, ½ in. solid backs	11 7
Concave, ⅝ in solid backs	14 8
HAT BRUSHES:	
Straight, veneers scraped, not grooved	2 8
Solid: same prices as corresponding style in cloth.	

	Per doz. brushes s. d.
HAT BRUSHES (contd.)	
Handled or brim and serpentine:	
Veneered sycamore, mahogany or walnut boards and backs ...	3 2
Veneered rosewood or satinwood boards and backs	3 6
Solid sycamore, mahogany, walnut, or oak boards and backs ...	4 2
Solid rosewood or satinwood boards and backs	4 9
Solid ebony	5 9
HORSE BRUSHES:	
Flat, sliced or planed veneer	2 10
Flat, sawn veneer scraped	3 6
Solid:	
¼ in. backs, upright	3 8
¼ in. backs, bevelled	4 2
⅜ in. backs, bevelled	4 9
½ in. backs, bevelled	5 3
Extras:	
Rosewood backs or other hard wood	1 1
Backs rounded and roached extra on bevelled prices	0 6
Backs cushioned or domed	0 8
Webbing	1 1
JEWELLERS' AND TYPEWRITER BRUSHES:	
Flat, straight sides	2 5
Flat, with neck	3 2
Bent, 4d. per doz. above rates of flat.	
Double bent, 8d. per doz. above rates of flat.	
LAUNDRY BRUSHES:	
Without backs	1 1
Flat, cover or thick veneer, pinned	1 7
Flat, cover or thick veneer, pinned and glued	1 11
Solid:	
¼ in. backs, bevelled	2 5
½ in. backs, bevelled	2 8
Extra: backs, cushioned	0 4
MOTOR BRUSHES:	
Body, cover (thick veneer) pinned on, cleaned	3 2
Spoke, triangle, filled in, covers pinned only	3 8
Spoke, triangle, not filled in	3 2
Spoke, semi-circular, filled in, covers pinned only	3 8
Spoke, semi-circular, not filled in	3 2
Mudguard, handles already sawn out, solid back, pinned	7 4
NAIL BRUSHES:	
Flat, straight sides	1 5
Flat, straight grooved	1 9
Solid back, straight sides, roached back	2 3
Solid back, straight sides, grooved	2 8
Solid back, oval roached	2 8
Extras:	
Backs cushioned	0 4
Satinwood, or other hard wood	1 1
Solid backs, concaved	2 1
PLATE AND CREST BRUSHES:	
Straight, up to and including 4 rows	2 10
Every additional row extra	0 2
Bent, 4d. per doz. above prices of straight.	

	Per doz. brushes s. d.
SCRUBBING BRUSHES:	
Flat, "cover" or thick veneer, pinned	1 7
Flat, "cover" or thick veneer, pinned and glued	2 1
Bent	2 5
Solid:	
¼ in. back, bevelled or roached up to and including 8 pins	2 10
⅜ in. back, bevelled or roached up to and including 8 pins	3 2
½ in. back, bevelled or roached up to and including 8 pins	3 6
Bent ¼ in. back, bevelled or roached up to and including 8 pins	3 2
Bent ⅜ in. back, bevelled or roached up to and including 8 pins	3 6
Solid S-shaped	3 10
Extras:	
Backs cushioned	0 4
Dummy screws up to and including 2	0 2
Dummy screws over 2	0 4
Sides grooved	0 8
Toy:	
¼ in. backs	2 10
⅜ in. backs	3 2
Deck or boat, nailed	2 5
Deck or boat, screwed	2 10
Extra: Blocks cleaned	0 8
Butchers:	
Pinned only	1 9
Pinned and glued	2 5
Block, handles already sawn out finished round handles	4 2
Block, handles already sawn out finished flat handles	3 2
SHOE BRUSHES:	
Flat	1 7
Flat grooved	1 11
Flat veneer to be scraped	2 3
Roached boards, sliced or planed veneer	2 3
Roached boards, sawn veneer to be scraped	2 8
Dumb-bell or hollow sides	3 0
Solid, up to ⅜ in. backs, roached	3 6
Solid, up to ½ in. backs, roached	3 10
Extras:	
Dumb-bell or hollow sides	0 4
Oak backs	0 4
Pocket or camp size, up to and including 6 in., 4d. per doz. less.	
Extras:	
Backs, rounded and roached	0 6
Burnishing	1 1
SPOKE BRUSHES:	
Flat:	
Pinned, plain and handled	2 10
Pinned, and glued handle	3 4
Solid:	
Straight, including screws from face	5 3
Bent or straight, turned handle	5 9
Taper, or bicycle, up to 9 in.	3 8
Taper, or bicycle, above 9 in. to 12 in.	4 2
Taper, or bicycle, above 12 in.	5 3
Taper, and turned end	6 10

	Per doz. brushes s. d.
SPOKE BRUSHES (contd.)	
Scotch, or semi-circular rolled, solid back	4 2
Scotch, or semi-circular rolled, flat back, filled in	3 8
Scotch, or semi-circular rolled, flat back, not filled in	3 2
STOVE BRUSHES:	
Flat	1 9
Bent	2 1
Convex	2 8
Solid:	
¼ in. backs	3 2
⅜ in. backs	3 6
Extra: Grooved all round	1 1
Porcupine, veneer	2 1
Porcupine, filled in and veneer	2 5
Extra: Finished dumb-bell	0 8
Porcupine, solid ¼ in. backs, bevelled	3 2
Porcupine, ⅜ in. backs, bevelled	3 6
Extras:	
Filled in	0 4
Backs, cushioned	0 4
Handles, screwed from front	0 6
Veneers scraped	0 4
Veneers of Rosewood	0 6
WATER BRUSHES:	
Flat, glued, pinned	3 2
Solid:	
⅜ in. backs, roached, 6 screws, or 4 screws and 4 pins	4 2
½ in. backs, roached, 6 screws, or 4 screws and 4 pins	4 11
⅝ in. backs, roached, 6 screws, or 4 screws and 4 pins	5 7
Extras:	
Backs, rounded and roached	0 6
Additional screws. Up to and including 10 in all	0 4
Screwing from front in addition	0 8
WEAVERS' CLOTH BRUSHES:	
Set:	
Round edge	2 1
Grooved	3 2
Cleaning up after setting	1 7
Fancy card	4 2
MISCELLANEOUS BRUSHES:	
Banister (ordinary), (drawn), backs pinned on	2 5
Banister (ordinary), (drawn), backs pinned and glued	2 10
Banisters and brooms (drawn), whisk or bass, veneered (veneer scraped), stock already shaped at end	2 8
Banisters and brooms (drawn), whisk or bass, veneered (veneer scraped), stock to be shaped at end	3 2
Bass brooms, cover pinned, shaved edges, length of stock up to 12 in.	1 1
Bass brooms, cover pinned, shaved edges, length of stock over 12 in.	1 5
Bit brushes, round edge	0 8
Boiler, shaped handle	1 9
Carriage washers, blocks made to shape, screwed	4 9
Carriage washers, blocks rough sawn, screwed	6 4

	Per doz. brushes s. d.
MISCELLANEOUS BRUSHES (contd.)	
Celery, resembling plate	3 2
Celery, solid back	6 4
Celery, made on "spoke board", veneered	4 9
Churn, boards already sawn out, veneer glued and pinned	4 2
Churn, boards not sawn out, veneer glued and pinned	6 4
Extra: Bent boards	9 5
Clamp nailed	3 2
Clamp screwed	4 2
Clamp heavy, undressed	5 3
Cog wheel	1 5
Curriers'	5 3
Dressing:	
⅝ in. backs, round ends	5 3
1 in. backs, round ends	6 4
Grooving sides extra	0 8
Flat back, length of stock under 40 in.	8 5
Flat back, length of stock under 50 in.	10 6
Flat back, length of stock under 60 in.	12 7
Extra: Machine driving on above	2 1
Dabbing:	
5 in. and under across the broad end	6 4
(For every ½ in. above 5 in. 1s. per doz. extra.)	
Warp dressing, length of stock 30 to 36 in.	8 5
Circular dabbing	8 5
Roach or gill dabbing	12 7
Dabbing board facing	0 6
Davy lamp, filling up	0 8
Double rubbers	2 5
Drawn whisk or bass, camel back	5 3
Dubbin or handled shoe, veneered	3 6
Dyers' rolled back	5 3
Fettlers:	
Roach back	1 1
Roach back grooved at each end	1 5
Bass, no cover, cleaned up	0 4
Fish or can and dairy, flat or veneer, straight, pinned	1 3
Fish or can and dairy, flat or veneer, straight, pinned and glued	1 7
Fish or can and dairy, flat or veneer, bent, pinned	1 7
Fish or can and dairy, flat or veneer, bent, pinned and glued	2 1
Floor polishers	4 2

	Each brush s. d.
Extra:	
Loaded with one block	1 1
Loaded with sheet lead (per layer of lead)	0 5
Fitted with swivel, including cutting slot for pin	1 1
Fitted with swivel, if slot already cut	0 8

	Per doz. brushes s. d.
Grease:	
Straight, veneered	3 2
Bent	3 8
Moulders:	
Cover, or thick veneer, glued and pinned	2 1
Solid	3 2
Paint cleaner, handle already sawn	3 2
Pan:	
Double or dumb-bell, cover pinned	2 1
Handled, dumb-bell, cover pinned	3 2

	Per doz. brushes s. d.
MISCELLANEOUS BRUSHES (contd.)	
Paperhangers:	
Drawn, ½ in. board, ⅞ in. back	4 2
Set, plain backs	2 1
Set, turned stocks, dromedary backs	3 2
Set, unturned stocks, dromedary backs	7 4
Set, unturned stocks, special round backs, hard wood	6 4
Set, London handle	8 5
Hamilton's new London pattern	3 2
Manchester handle	4 2
Pot or saucepan (drawn)	2 8
Printers' beater's, handle already sawn	12 7
Extra: Screwing up to and including 8 screws	1 1
Printers' lye	5 3
Extra: Grooved sides	0 8
Printers':	
Pick, flat, pinned only	1 9
Pick, flat, glued	1 9
Pick, flat, solid	2 10
Ring roller	2 1
Ring throstle	1 9
Separators:	
Pointed, cover pinned	1 7
Handled, cover pinned, turned	3 2
Sink oblong, solid, roached	3 2
Starch-making and boxing:	
10 in. and under	3 2
10 in. to 12 in.	4 9
12½ in. and over	5 3
Steel, hand brushes, pinned, cleaned, bound (2 bands) and webbed	3 6
Steel, firebrooms, screwed from front (4 screws) and cleaned	3 6
Steel, brooms, screwed from back	1 5
Steel, brooms, screwed from front	1 9
Street orderly:	
Pinned only	2 1
Pinned and glued	2 5
Stipplers:	
3 in. by 4 in. bridge or neck handle, 8 screws	16 10
4 in. by 6 in. to 6 in. by 8 in. bridge or neck handle, 8 screws	25 2
Making handles	8 5
Sweeps:	
(Drawn), backs pinned on	1 9
(Drawn), backs pinned and glued	2 1
Travis, handled	3 2
Warehouse or bundle	3 2
Warehouse or bundle handled	5 3
Washers	3 2
W.C., 2 screws, or 1 screw and pins	1 7
Window sash, handles already turned	1 7
Window sash, handles not turned	4 2
Window washers:	
Porcupine, blocks already made, screwed	3 8
Flat boards, blocks already made, screwed	4 2
GENERAL EXTRAS:	
Screwing: All screws to be turned in.	
Up to and including 2 screws	0 4
Up to and including 6 screws	0 8
Up to and including 10 screws	1 7

	Per doz. brushes s. d.
GENERAL EXTRAS (contd.)	
Pinning:	
Up to and including 6 pins	0 4
Up to and including 10 pins	0 6

Veneers: Intermediate veneers, 2d. per dozen.

GENERAL

30. In case of straight-sided brushes, boards and backs are to be within ½ in. of extreme width and length of finished article. If larger are used, extra payment to be made.

Any particular brush or article not specified herein to be paid for at the price of specified brush it most nearly resembles. Allowance in the price to be made for differences.

All glue, pins, screws, sand-paper, etc., to be provided by employer.

31. THE ALLOWANCES TO BE MADE FROM THE MINIMUM PIECE RATES SET OUT IN PARAGRAPH 29 FOR BOARDS AND/OR BACKS SHAPED BY MACHINERY ARE AS FOLLOWS:—

	If bandsawn per doz. brushes d.	If spindled per doz. brushes d.
HAIR BRUSHES (HANDLED):		
Cherry boards and back	4	6
Hardwood	6	9
HAIR BRUSHES (MILITARY):		
Soft wood	4	6
Hard wood	6	9
CLOTH AND HAT BRUSHES:		
Flat (solid) not handled:		
Soft	4	6
Hard	6	9
Handled:		
Soft	4	6
Hard	6	9
Dandy, dog and shoe	3	4
Scrubbing, up to ½ in.	3	4
Scrubbing, over ½ in. board at edge or end	4	6
FLESH AND HORSE BRUSHES:		
Soft wood	4	6
Hard wood	6	9
CREVICE OR SASH BRUSHES: ...		
Over ½ in.	6	—
½ in. or under	4	—
PLATE AND CREST BRUSHES: ...		
Boards and handles, including bevelling handles ...	—	8
STOVE BRUSHES:		
Flat	—	2
Bent	—	4
WATER BRUSHES (same as Dandy).		
BANDSAWING BOARDS and Backs AFTER GLUED:		
Scrubbing brushes (not including bandsawing round wings):		
Single wing	—	4½
Double wing	—	2
Shoe brushes	—	4½

32. MINIMUM PIECE RATES FOR MALE WORKERS EMPLOYED ON PAINTING BRUSH MAKING GROUND BRUSHES

(1) Rates include grinding and pointing, or damping and pointing, but not finishing. If unground for dusters, etc., minimum piece rates include finishing, washing handles, trimming flat, and one coat of varnish or paint.

Size	10/0	8/0	6/0	4/0	3/0	2/0	1/0	1	2	3	4	5	6
Weight (ozs.)	6½	6	5½	5	4½	4	3½	3	2½	2	1½	1¼	1
	s. d.	s. d.	s. d.	s. d.	s. d.	s. d.	s. d.	s. d.	s. d.	s. d.	s. d.	s. d.	s. d.
(A) Paper socket, S.B., per doz.	5 9	5 5	5 5	4 11	4 11	4 9	4 7	4 2	4 2	3 8	3 8	—	—
(B) Zinc socket, S.B., per doz.	4 9	4 5	4 5	3 10	3 10	3 8	3 6	3 2	3 2	2 8	2 8	—	—
(C) Metal ferrule socket, per doz.	4 0	3 8	3 8	3 4	3 4	3 2	3 0	2 10	2 10	2 1	2 1	—	—
(D) Copper cup, per doz. ...	—	3 10	3 10	3 4	3 4	3 2	3 0	2 10	2 10	2 5	2 5	—	—
(E) Copper oval, solid centre, per doz.	4 7	4 2	4 2	3 10	3 10	3 8	3 8	3 6	3 6	2 10	2 10	—	—
(F) Oval metal, hair through, varnish or flat paint set with varnish, per doz. ...	—	5 5	5 1	4 9	4 9	4 5	4 2	3 10	3 10	3 6	3 6	3 2	3 2
(G) Metal ferrule socket, mixture, per doz.	3 10	3 4	3 4	3 2	3 2	2 10	2 5	2 3	2 3	1 11	1 11	—	—
(H) Zinc socket, mixture, S.B., per doz.	4 7	4 2	4 2	3 8	3 8	3 4	3 0	2 8	2 8	2 3	2 3	—	—

(I) Old pattern, S.B.— Size ...	10/0	8/0	6/0	4/0	3/0	2/0	1/0	1	2	3	4	5	6	7
Weight (ozs.)	8	7¼	6½	6	5½	5	4½	4	3½	3	2½	1¾	1¼	1
	s. d.	s. d.	s. d.	s. d.	s. d.	s. d.	s. d.	s. d.	s. d.	s. d.	s. d.	s. d.	s. d.	s. d.
Per doz. ...	4 7	4 5	4 2	4 0	3 10	3 8	3 4	3 2	3 0	2 10	2 8	2 5	2 3	2 1

GROUND BRUSHES (contd.)

O.K. OVAL GROUND

Size ...	14½	13½	12½	11½	10½	9½	8½	7½	6½
Weight (ozs.) ...	5½	5	4¼	3¾	3¼	2½	2	1¾	1½
Price (per doz.) ...	s. d. 4 5	s. d. 4 5	s. d. 4 0	s. d. 4 0	s. d. 3 9	s. d. 3 6	s. d. 3 6	s. d. 2 10	s. d. 2 10

All intermediate weights to be charged to the size above.

(2) EXTRAS ARE AS FOLLOWS:—

Casing brushes with bristle, 6d. per doz. knots.

Lily and yellow work, sizes 10/0—1/0 inclusive, 8d. per doz.; below size 1/0, 4d. per doz.

Setting with other than the ordinary resin cement, (F) excepted, 6d. per doz.

Bevelling 6½ oz.—3½ oz. inclusive, 2s. 1d. per doz.; 3 oz. and 2½ oz., 1s. 7d. per doz.; below 2½ oz., 1s. 1d. per doz.

If bevelled on the flag in a mould, an additional 6d. per doz. on above bevelling prices.

Shaping handles for socket work, 8d. per doz. Shaping woods, 1s. 5d. per doz. Plain bridling, 2s. 1d. per doz.

Varnishing ferrules, 2d. per doz.

(A), (B), (H), (I).—Binding with copper wire, 1s. 5d. per doz.; binding with iron wire, 2s. 1d. per doz.

(A), (B), (C), (G), (H), (I).—If ovalled, 4d. per doz.

(G), (H).—Made only of fibre and drafts middles. Damping and pointing. Washing hair for cappings, extra.

(I).—Prices include hair through metal ring. Chaining above three rounds, 1s. 1d. per doz. brushes.

For pointing with thrumbs. One knot and ground brushes—below size 1/0, 1s. 5d. per gross; size 1/0 and above, 2s. 1d. per gross.

33. DISTEMPER BRUSHES, ONE, TWO AND THREE KNOT, AND METAL BAND DISTEMPER BRUSHES

(1) Rates include grinding and pointing, or damping and pointing, but not finishing

Weight (ozs.) ...	12	11	10	9	8	7	6½	6	5½	5	4½	4	3½	3	2½	2	1½	1
	s. d.	s. d.	s. d.	s. d.	s. d.	s. d.	s. d.	s. d.	s. d.	s. d.	s. d.	s. d.	s. d.	s. d.	s. d.	s. d.	s. d.	s. d.
(A) One knot, S.B. or C.B., per doz.	—	—	—	—	4 10	4 10	4 8	See (F) below as respects weights 6-3½ ozs.						3 8	3 6	3 4	3 1	3 1
(B) Two knot, S.B. or C.B., per doz.	8 0	7 8	7 3	7 1	6 11	6 8	—	6 6	—	6 3	—	—	—	—	—	—	—	—
(C) Three knot, S.B. or C.B., per doz.	8 5	8 1	7 8	7 6	7 4	7 2	—	7 0	—	6 10	—	—	—	—	—	—	—	—
(D) Hair through C.B., per doz.	9 9	9 9	9 2	9 2	8 10	8 10	—	8 5	—	8 5	—	—	—	—	—	—	—	—
(E) Metal band on tongued handle, per doz. ...	10 4	9 11	9 6	9 2	8 10	8 10	—	—	—	—	—	—	—	—	—	—	—	—

All intermediate weights to be charged to the size above.

Weight (ozs.)	6	5½	5	4½	4	3½
Width of handle	2¾ in. to 3⅛ in.	2⅝ in. to 2¾ in.	2½ in. to 2⅝ in.	2⅜ in. to 2½ in.	2¼ in. to 2⅜ in.	2⅛ in. to 2¼ in.
	s. d.	s. d.	s. d.	s. d.	s. d.	s. d.
(F) One knot, S.B. or C.B., per doz. ...	4 6	4 6	4 2	4 2	4 0	3 10

Any of the above weights made on a smaller handle to be charged by weight only.
Any of the above weights made on a larger handle to be charged by width of handle only.

(2) EXTRAS ARE AS FOLLOWS:—

Casing brushes with bristle, 6d. per dozen knots.
Tying with iron wire, 1s. per doz. for one knot; 6d. per doz. for each additional knot. Plain bridling, 2s. 1d. per doz.
Setting with other than ordinary resin cement 6d. per doz.
Lily and yellow work down to and including 3½ oz., 8d. per doz.; below 3½ oz., 4d. per doz.
Preparing shouldered handles for hood cornering, 2d. per doz.
Soldering C.B. ferrules. 4d. per doz. strips.
(A), (B), (C).—Looping, including tacking, 6d. per doz. Corner clipping, including tacking, 10d. per doz.
Side clipping, 6d. per doz. knots. Chaining, 4d. per doz. knots. Varnishing wires, 2d. per doz. knots.
(B).—Lily and yellow work, 1s. per doz. Preparing handles for hood cornering, 6d. per doz.
(D), (E).—Including varnishing of bands before bleaching.
Cornering on all of above, 4d. per doz.; soldering, 4d. per doz.
Bevelling 1 knot down to and including 3½ oz., 2s. 1d. per doz.; 3 oz. and 2½ oz., 1s. 7d. per doz.; 2 oz. and 1½ oz., 1s. per doz.; 1 oz., 8d. per doz.
If bevelled on the flag in a mould 6d. per doz. in addition to above bevelling prices.

34. SASH TOOLS AND MARBLE TOOLS

(1) Rates include grinding and pointing, but not finishing.

	Size	24	22	20	18	16	14	12	10	9
		s. d.	s. d.	s. d.	s. d.	s. d.	s. d.	s. d.	s. d.	s. d.
(A)	S.B. forked, per doz.	7 10	7 2	6 8	6 1	5 1	4 8	4 1	3 9	3 4
(C)	S.B. socket, per doz....	—	—	—	5 6	4 6	4 1	3 9	3 4	2 11
(D)	S.B. scene painters, per doz.	8 7	8 0	7 5	6 10	6 3	5 8	4 10	4 6	4 1
(E)	Metal ferrule, per doz.	—	—	—	5 3	4 3	3 11	3 6	3 1	2 9
(B)	S.B. forked marble, per doz.	—	—	—	—	—	—	4 8	4 3	3 11
	Size	8	7	6	5	4	3	2	1	0
		s. d.	s. d.	s. d.	s. d.	s. d.	s. d.	s. d.	s. d.	s. d.
(A)	S.B. forked, per doz.	2 11	2 9	2 6	2 4	2 2	2 2	1 11	1 11	1 11
(C)	S.B. socket, per doz....	2 6	2 6	2 4	2 2	1 11	1 11	1 9	1 9	1 9
(D)	S.B. scene painters, per doz.	3 9	3 6	3 1	2 11	2 9	2 6	2 2	2 2	2 2
(E)	Metal ferrule, per doz.	2 4	2 2	1 11	1 9	1 7	1 7	1 5	1 5	1 5
(B)	S.B. forked marble, per doz.	3 6	3 4	2 11	2 9	2 6	2 4	1 11	1 11	1 11

Rates include trimming and one coat of glue or varnish (A), (C), (D), (E). Unground, 2d. per doz. less.

(2) EXTRAS ARE AS FOLLOWS:—

Setting with other than ordinary resin cement, 4d. per doz.

Bevelling, 18-14, 2s. 1d. per doz.; 12-9, 1s. 7d. per doz.; 8-6, 1s. per doz.; 5-1, 8d. per doz.

Bridling, 24-10, 2s. 1d. per doz.; 9-7, 1s. 5d. per doz.; 6-0, 1s. per doz., including one coat of glue or varnish.

For pointing with thrumbs—Sash tools: up to size 4, 8d. per gross; sizes 5-8, 1s. per gross; size 9 and above, 1s. 5d. per gross.

(A), (B), (C), (D).—Binding with copper wire, 24-20, 3s. 4d. per doz.; 18-14, 2s. 3d. per doz.; 12-10, 1s. 11d. per doz.; 9-7, 1s. 7d. per doz.; 6-4, 1s. 5d. per doz.; 4-0, 1s. per doz.; Soldering, 4d. per doz. strips.

(A), (B), (C), (D).—Binding with iron wire, 4d. per doz. above copper wire.

(B).—Trimming and pointing, 8d. per doz.

(E).—Making with peg -top handle, 2d. per doz. Tied on peg-top handles, 4d. per doz.

35. UNGROUND DISTEMPER, WASH DOWNS AND STOCK BRUSHES

(1) Rates include finishing i.e., trimming flat, washing handles, and one coat of varnish.

Weight (ozs.)	12	11	10	9	8	7	6	5	4	3	2	1
S.B. and C.B.	s. d.	s. d.	s. d.	s. d.	s. d.	s. d.	s. d.	s. d.	s. d.	s. d.	s. d.	s. d.
(A) Two knot, per doz.	7 3	6 11	6 7	6 5	6 3	6 1	5 11	5 9	5 7	5 4	—	—
(B) Three knot, per doz.	8 0	8 0	7 8	7 8	7 3	6 11	6 3	6 1	5 9	5 2	5 0	4 7
(C) Four knot, per doz.	8 10	8 10	8 5	8 5	8 0	7 8	7 5	6 11	6 6	5 11	5 9	5 4
(D) Copper band, hair through, per doz.	8 10	8 10	8 4	8 4	8 0	8 0	7 8	7 8	—	—	—	—
(E) Metal band, tongued handle, per doz.	9 4	9 0	8 8	8 4	8 0	8 0	—	—	—	—	—	—

All intermediate sizes to be charged to the size above.

(2) EXTRAS ARE AS FOLLOWS:—

Casing brushes with bristle, 6d. per dozen knots.

(A), (B), (C).—Tying with iron wire, 1s. 7d. per doz. for 2 knot; 6d. per doz. for each additional knot.

(A), (B), (C).—Looping, including tacking, 6d. per doz. brushes. Corner clipping, including tacking, 10d. per doz. brushes. Side clipping, 6d. per doz. knots. Chaining, 4d. per doz. knots. Preparing handles for hood cornering, 6d. per doz.

Cornering, 4d. per doz. Soldering, 4d. per doz.

36. TIERING OR CALICO BRUSHES

Three knot. Rates include finishing, i.e., trimming flat, washing handles, and one coat of varnish.

	s. d.		s. d.
Worsted bound (per doz.)	8 0	Copper bound (per doz.)	6 0

37. FIBRE WORK

(1) Rates include finishing, i.e., washing handles, flat trimming, and one coat of varnish.

Weight (ozs.)	12	11	10	9	8	7	6½	6	5½	5	4½	4	3½	3	2½	2	1½	1
(A) S.B. or C.B.	s. d.	s. d.	s. d.	s. d.	s. d.	s. d.	s. d.	s. d.	s. d.	s. d.	s. d.	s. d.	s. d.	s. d.	s. d.	s. d.	s. d.	s. d.
One knot, per doz. ...	—	—	—	—	4 2	4 2	3 10	3 10	3 10	3 6	3 6	3 4	3 4	3 2	3 2	3 0	2 10	2 10
Two knot, per doz. ...	4 11	4 11	4 7	4 7	4 2	4 2	—	3 10	—	3 10	—	—	—	—	—	—	—	—
Three knot, per doz. ...	7 6	6 11	6 7	6 0	6 0	5 5	—	5 0	—	5 0	—	—	—	—	—	—	—	—
Four knot, per doz. ...	8 3	7 8	7 4	6 9	6 9	6 1	—	5 9	—	5 9	—	—	—	—	—	—	—	—
Bath brushes, S.B., per doz.	—	—	5 1	4 11	4 9	4 7	—	4 5	—	4 2	—	—	—	—	—	—	—	—
(B) Zinc socket, S.B., per doz.	—	—	—	—	—	—	—	—	3 6	3 0	3 0	2 10	2 8	2 3	2 3	2 3	2 3	—

All intermediate weights to be charged to the size above.

(2) EXTRAS ARE AS FOLLOWS:—

(A).—Tying with iron wire, 1s. per doz. for one knot; 6d. per doz. for each additional knot.
Above four knot, 8d. per doz. knots for making.
Damping and pointing, 6d. per doz.
Cornering, 4d. per doz. Soldering, 4d. per doz.

(B).—Binding with copper wire, 1s. 4d. per doz. Iron wire, 2s. per doz.

38. COMMONWEALTH FIBRE STOCK

Made on a handle bored in a similar manner to a string stock brush, using 12-in. Fibre, 1½ oz. to each knot passed through each hole and tied with four round of copper wire.

	s. d.		s. d.		s. d.
Five knot, per doz....	5 7	Four knot, per doz.	4 9	Three knot, per doz....	3 10

Rates include trimming.

FLAT TIN FIBRE.—1 oz. made in stencil tin, compressed at top, 1s. 11d. per doz. including 2 pins and trimming.

39. FLAT LIMERS AND NAIL STOCK

(1) Excluding all fibre brushes:—

Width of handle, inches	11	10½	10	9½	9	8½	8	7½	7	6½	6	5½	5	4½
Weight (ozs.)	14	13	12	11	10	9	8	7	6	5	4	3	2	1
	s. d.	s. d.	s. d.	s. d.	s. d.	s. d.	s. d.	s. d.	s. d.	s. d.	s. d.	s. d.	s. d.	s. d.
Uncapped (per doz.)	9 8	9 2	8 9	8 4	7 11	7 5	7 0	6 7	6 2	5 8	5 3	4 10	4 5	3 11
Capped (per doz.)	10 7	10 2	9 8	9 2	8 8	8 3	7 8	7 3	6 9	6 4	5 9	5 4	4 10	4 5

Rates include finishing, trimming flat, washing handles, and one coat of varnish.

Any of the above weights made on a smaller handle to be charged by weight; made on a larger handle to be charged by width of handle.

(2) For fibre brushes:—

Size (measurement by width of handle), inches	10	9½	9	8½	8	7½	7	6½	6	5½	5	4½
	s. d.	s. d.	s. d.	s. d.	s. d.	s. d.	s. d.	s. d.	s. d.	s. d.	s. d.	s. d.
Per doz.	8 0	7 3	7 0	6 7	5 9	5 6	5 4	4 10	4 6	4 5	3 11	3 7

Rates include finishing, trimming flat, and one coat of varnish.

(3) EXTRAS ARE AS FOLLOWS:—

Perforated metal bands with ordinary brush flats, 1s. 5d. per doz.

Small-headed nails, 8d. per doz. brushes extra up to 7 in.; above 7 in., 1s. 1d. per doz.

Making with shellac, 7 in. and above, 8d. per doz.; below 7 in., 4d. per doz.

Capped with white material, 6d. per doz.

40. ROUND LIMERS

(1) Excluding all fibre brushes:—

Uncapped—weight (ozs.)	12	11	10	9	8	7	6	5	4	3	2	1
Handle (diameter in inches)	4½	4¼	4	3¾	3½	3¼	3	2¾	2½	2¼	2	1½
	s. d.	s. d.	s. d.	s. d.	s. d.	s. d.	s. d.	s. d.	s. d.	s. d.	s. d.	s. d.
(Per doz.)	7 8	7 4	7 0	6 8	6 4	5 11	5 7	5 1	4 7	4 2	3 8	3 4

Prices include finishing same as flat limers.

(2) For fibre brushes:—

Size (diameter of handle), inches	3¼	3
	s. d.	s. d.
Per doz.	4 8	4 5

Rates include finishing, trimming flat, and one coat of varnish.

Any of the above weights made on a smaller handle to be charged by weight; made on a larger handle to be charged by width of handle.

(3) EXTRAS ARE AS FOLLOWS:—

Perforated metal bands with ordinary brush flats, 1s. 5d. per doz.
Small-headed nails, 8d, per doz. extra up to 7 oz.; above 7 oz., 1s. 1d. per doz.
Making with shellac, 7 oz. and above, 8d. per doz. extra; below 7 oz., 4d. per doz.
Capped with other than white material, 6d. per doz.
Capped with white material, 1s. 1d. per doz.

41.

WEATHER BOARDS

(1)

Weight (ozs.)	9	8½	8	7½	7	6½	6	5½	5	4½	4	3½	3
Width of handle (inches) ...	8½	8	7½	7	6½	6	5½	5	4½	4	3½	3	2½
	s. d.	s. d.	s. d.	s. d.	s. d.	s. d.	s. d.	s. d.	s. d.	s. d.	s. d.	s. d.	s. d.
(Per doz.)	12 6	11 11	11 4	10 9	10 2	9 8	9 1	8 6	7 11	7 4	6 11	6 9	6 2

Rates exclude washing hair and finishing.

(2) EXTRAS ARE AS FOLLOWS:—

One-third extra if made with two rows of nails.
Perforated metal bands, 1s. per doz.

42.

KALSOMINE, PADDLE AND WALL BRUSHES

(1) Rates exclude washing hair and finishing. All intermediate sizes to be charged to the size above.

(Inches)	8	7½	7	6½	6	5½	5	4½	4	3½	3
	s. d.	s. d.	s. d.	s. d.	s. d.	s. d.	s. d.	s. d.	s. d.	s. d.	s. d.
(A) Kalsomine (per doz.)	23 0	—	18 6	—	16 6	14 6	12 6	10 6	10 6	—	—
(B) Paddle or Wall (per doz.)	15 6	14 6	13 6	12 6	11 6	10 6	9 6	8 6	8 6	7 6	6 0
(C) Common Kalsomine or common Wall:—											
(i) Made of fibre and drafts, uncapped. To be made in perforated bands nailed all round, with holes not less than ½ in. apart. To be made with wedge, and not on tongued handle.											
Per doz.	9 6	9 0	8 6	8 0	7 6	7 0	6 0	5 6	5 0	4 6	4 0
If capped, 1s. per doz. extra.											

(ii) With tin band made from yellow, grey or china bristles, dressed or straightened, ½ in. thick wedge, the shorter width across the band not exceeding 1 in.; holes not less than ½ in. apart; nailed all round; made with wedge and not with tongued handle.

	s. d.
Longer width across band not exceeding 4 in., weight not exceeding 1¾ oz., length of bristle not exceeding 3¼ in.	5 0 per dozen.
Longer width across band exceeding 4 in., but not exceeding 5 in., weight not exceeding 2 oz., length of bristle not exceeding 3½ in.	6 0 per dozen.
Longer width across band exceeding 5 in., but not exceeding 6 in., weight not exceeding 2⅝ oz., length of bristle not exceeding 3½ in.	7 6 per dozen.

(2) THE FOLLOWING IS EXTRA:—

(B).—Beating bands over for Army pattern 2s. 1d. per doz. extra.

43. (*a*) UNGROUND PASTE BRUSHES, SPRINKLERS, AND IRON BOUND GLUE BRUSHES
(*b*) TAR BRUSHES exceeding 4½ oz.

Weight (ozs.)	14	13	12	11½	11	10½	10	9½	9	8½	8	7½	7
Per doz.	s. d. 18 3	s. d. 18 3	s. d. 13 9	s. d. 13 9	s. d. 11 5	s. d. 11 5	s. d. 10 4	s. d. 10 4	s. d. 9 2	s. d. 9 2	s. d. 6 11	s. d. 6 11	s. d. 5 9
Weight (ozs.)	6½	6	5½	5	4½	4	3½	3	2½	2	1½	1	½
Per doz.	s. d. 5 2	s. d. 4 7	s. d. 4 7	s. d. 4 0	s. d. 4 0	s. d. 3 6	s. d. 3 6	s. d. 2 10	s. d. 2 6	s. d. 2 3	s. d. 2 1	s. d. 1 11	s. d. 1 6

All intermediate weights to be charged to the size above.
Above 14 oz., 2s. 3d. per doz. extra, for each oz.
Narrow ring glue brushes, 6d. per doz. extra, including trimming and washing handles.

44. SAUCEPAN BRUSHES

	s. d.
Tin band, dipped and drawn through, per doz. ... ... (If pegged, 2d. extra; if tied at base, 2d. extra.)	1 0
String bound, per doz.	1 0
Copper wire bound, per doz.	2 5

45. STENCIL BRUSHES

(1) Size	12	11	10	9	8	7	6	5	4	3	2	1
	s. d.	s. d.	s. d.	s. d.	s. d.	s. d.	s. d.	s. d.	s. d.	s. d.	s. d.	s. d.
(A) Socket S.B., per doz.	4 6	—	4 1	3 9	3 4	2 11	2 9	2 9	2 6	2 6	2 4	2 4
(B) Tin band, per doz.	2 11	2 9	2 6	2 4	2 2	1 11	1 9	1 9	1 7	1 7	1 5	1 5

Including trimming.

(2) EXTRAS ARE AS FOLLOWS:—

Making with other than the ordinary resin cement, 4d. per doz.

(A)—Prices include trimming and glueing bindings. If bound with wire same price as sash tools.

46. FLAT VARNISH BRUSHES, GRAINERS, etc., IN TIN

Rates include trimming.

Size, in.	6	5½	5	4½	4	3½	3	2½	2	1½	1
	s. d.	s. d.	s. d.	s. d.	s. d.	s. d.	s. d.	s. d.	s. d.	s. d.	s. d.
Hog unbevelled (per doz.)	—	—	—	—	7 3	6 9	6 3	5 2	4 2	3 6	2 9
Flat oval nickelled steel or copper compressed (finishing extra) (per doz.)	—	—	—	—	—	—	6 9	5 9	4 8	3 8	3 1
Thin hair grainers (per doz.)	—	—	—	—	5 2	5 2	4 2	4 2	3 1	3 1	2 1
French mottlers (per doz.)	—	—	—	—	5 2	5 2	4 2	4 2	3 1	3 1	2 1
Oak grainers (per doz.)	—	—	—	—	12 6	10 11	9 4	7 3	6 3	4 8	—
Flat badger (per doz.)	—	—	—	18 9	16 8	14 7	12 6	10 5	8 4	7 3	4 2
Hair grainers (per doz.)	7 3	7 3	6 3	6 3	5 2	5 2	4 2	4 2	3 1	3 1	—

COMMON VARNISH BRUSHES OR "CARD WORK"

Bevelled varnish in tin made dry, one row of nails if possible. To include two rows of nails, and up to and including ⅞ in. thickness:—

Size, in.	4	3½	3	2½	2	1½	1
Per doz.	s. d. 12 6	s. d. 11 5	s. d. 10 5	s. d. 8 10	s. d. 6 11	s. d. 5 7	s. d. 4 2

Small bevelled varnish metal band or one knot, put on wheel, pegged or not, but not finished. Made with glue or cement:—

Weight, oz.	3	2½	2	1½	1¼	1	¾	½
Per doz.	s. d. 5 9	s. d. 5 4	s. d. 5 0	s. d. 3 8	s. d. 3 1	s. d. 2 11	s. d. 2 11	s. d. 2 11

Including trimming.

IRON BAND MAN HELPS

47.

Including grinding and pointing, cutting off handles and singeing.

Made in 1¼-in. glue ring (per doz.), 2s. 9d.

If made in narrow ring, 6d. per doz. extra.

(1) TAR BRUSHES SHORT

48.

(Not exceeding 4½ oz.)

Including trimming and washing handles.

Mixture not containing bristle turned out, 1s. 6d. per doz., turned in, 4½d. per doz. extra.

Mixture containing bristle or pure bristle; turned out, 2s. 3d. per doz., turned in, 5d. per doz. extra.

(2) TURK'S HEAD TAR BRUSHES

(Not exceeding 4½ oz.)

Uncapped (per doz.), 4s. 8d. Capped (per doz.), 5s. 2d.

Setting knots, 2d. per doz. knots extra, including trimming and washing handles.

(3) TAR HEADS

(Not exceeding 4½ oz.)

Mixture not containing bristle; turned out, 1s. 9d. per doz.; turned in, 4½d. per doz. extra.

Mixture containing bristle, or pure bristle; turned out, 2s. 5d. per doz.; turned in, 5d. per doz. extra.

Nailing on long handles, 1s. 1d. per doz. extra on short tar brush prices. Nailing limer stocks, 1s. 1d. per doz. heads extra.

Screwing with 1 or 2 screws, 1s. 5d. per doz. heads extra. Bolting, 1s. 1d. per doz. heads extra.

Long tar handling, above 50 in. in length, 4d. per doz. extra on above prices.

Navy tar, narrow ring, 3s. 6d. per doz., including pinning, trimming and washing handles.

Extra long driving handles, 4d. per doz. extra for all tar brushes.

Making with a plug driven on a metal dummy driving handle, 5d. per doz. extra.

(Note.—For tar brushes over 4½ ozs. in weight, see paragraph 43.)

IMPROVED OR TINNED GLUE

49.

Size	6	5	4	3	2	1
Weight (ozs.)	2½	2	1½	1	¾	½
	s. d.	s. d.	s. d.	s. d.	s. d.	s. d.
Per doz.	2 5	2 3	2 1	1 11	1 9	1 7

Rates include trimming. All intermediate weights to be charged to the size above.

GENERAL

50.

All work given out in quantities of less than ½ doz. to be charged 1½d. per brush extra.

All work requiring pinning, 1½d. per doz. pins extra.

Finishing ground work: anything after pointing to be paid extra.

Unground driven work includes trimming.

Dry tied work includes trimming, singeing, washing handles, and one coat of varnish on wires and across the handle.

Dry work, with the exception of tar and glue brushes, includes finishing, trimming, washing handles, and one coat of varnish or paint, not stamping.

All work, unless specially excluded, to be charged extra if made with cement other than the ordinary resin mixture.

Cornering and soldering to be charged extra, and to be reckoned as part of the making.

Tar brushes, Turk's head and iron band glue brushes made with hand or power press less 5 per cent.

All rates per doz., etc., refer to per doz. brushes except where otherwise stated.

MINIMUM PIECE RATES FOR MALE DRAWING HANDS ON MACHINE BRUSHES

51.—(1) The minimum piece rates are in respect of boring, drawing and trimming unless otherwise specified.

(2) In this Part of this Schedule:—

LAG—means a detached segment, made of wood, aluminium or other metal, to be attached to a centre core or bearer with screws or bolts. A set of lags fitted together forms a roller or part of a roller.

SLIP—means a flat or roached faced stock, bored through pattern, up to and including 1 in. thick at thickest part; if over 1 in. thick whether bored through pattern or not, or more than 72 in. long irrespective of the thickness, to be regarded as a lag.

52.—(1) The minimum piece rates for male drawing hands on machine brushes are:—

Types of Brushes	Filling Material						Wire (inclusive)		
	All materials other than wire and those specified in Columns 3-7	Badger hair drawn root in hole	Bass, African or Bahia (other than fine drawing Bahia)	Monkey bass or bassine other than H.V. bassine	H.V. bassine or fine drawing Bahia	Bone	Fine wire over 40 gauge	35 to 40 gauge	27 to 34 gauge
Column 1	Column 2	Column 3	Column 4	Column 5	Column 6	Column 7	Column 8	Column 9	Column 10
	Knots per penny	Knots per penny	Knots per penny	Knots per penny	Knots per penny	Knots per penny	Knots per penny	Knots per penny	Knots per penny
Lags	9	8	6	8	8	7	7	6	4
Lags drawn specially tight	8	—	—	—	—	—	—	—	—
Wheel or pulley (tentering or polishing) ...	9	—	6	8	8	7	7	6	4
Slips	9	8	6	8	8	7	7	—	—
Metal work ready bored	9	7	—	—	—	—	7	—	—
Silk weavers, dressers and thread polishers. Lags	9	—	—	—	—	—	—	—	—
Silk weavers, dressers and thread polishers. Slips	10	—	—	—	—	—	—	—	—
Roller brushes in two halves (comber)	9	—	6	9	8	7	8	—	—
Card brushes	9	—	—	—	—	8	—	—	—

Dabbing other than metal or composition including boring	9	—	—	—	—	—	—	—	—
Dabbing metal or composition ready bored ...	10	—	—	—	—	—	—	—	—
Dabbing and circular disc, refilled or repaired...	8½	—	—	—	—	—	—	—	—
Hollow or cord	8	—	—	—	—	—	—	—	—
Grain cleaner, flat or roached stocks, under 7 in. wide or 24 in. long	10	—	—	—	—	—	—	—	—
Grain cleaner, flat or roached stocks, 7 in. wide or over, or over 24 in. long up to and including 30 in. long	9	—	—	—	—	—	—	—	—
Grain cleaner, flat or roached stocks, 7 in. wide or over, or over 30 in. long	8	—	—	—	—	—	—	—	—
Grain cleaner, flat or roached stocks, circular, concave or convex	7	—	—	—	—	—	—	—	—
Leather straps or brush belts, eyeletted ...	9*	—	—	—	—	—	—	—	—
Leather straps or brush belts, not eyeletted ...	9	—	—	—	—	—	8	6	—
Leather straps or brush belts, in Kitool (or in hair drawn double over 3½ in. out overall) ...	8	—	—	7	—	—	—	—	—

*This price does not include fitting the eyelets.

(2) EXTRAS TO COLUMN 2 ARE AS FOLLOWS:—

	Knots less per penny
Work with synthetic monofilaments gauges ·005 to ·013 in. inclusive	½
Work with synthetic monofilaments gauges ·014 to ·020 in. inclusive	1
Work with synthetic monofilaments gauges ·021 in. and over	2
Work with mixtures containing more than one-third synthetic monofilaments, gauges ·005 to ·013 in. inclusive	½
Work with mixtures containing more than one-third synthetic monofilaments, gauges ·014 to ·020 in. inclusive	1
Work with mixtures containing more than one-third synthetic monofilaments, gauges ·021 in. and over	1½

(3) OTHER EXTRAS AND ALLOWANCES ARE AS FOLLOWS:—

All work drawn through side—1 knot per 1d. less.

All work drawn root in hole (other than badger hair work)—1 knot per 1d. less.

All work drawn penetrating—1 knot per 1d. less.

Cutting off or trimming, when done by worker other than drawing hand, 7½ per cent. less.

Time spent on marking out spiral rollers—the appropriate piece work basis time rate per hour extra net.

MINIMUM PIECE RATES FOR MALE WORKERS EMPLOYED ON BONE BRUSH MAKING

53.

	Per score s. d.
(1) For cutting	0 9

	Per gross s. d.
(2) For profiling:	
Children's	1 3
If cutters sharpened for profiler	1 2
Others	1 7
If cutters sharpened for profiler	1 6

(3) For fashioning:

	Child's	3 Row and Ladies'	4 Row	5 Row
	per gross s. d.	per gross s. d.	per gross s. d.	per gross s. d.
Common	—	16 6	18 0	—
Regulars	14 6	18 6	19 0	24 6
Corners	17 0	20 6	23 0	27 6
Pierrepont	19 0	22 6	25 0	32 0
Tom Thumb	13 6	—	—	—

PART VIII

MINIMUM PIECE RATES FOR FEMALE WORKERS

MINIMUM PIECE RATES FOR FEMALE PAN HANDS (OTHER THAN FEMALE APPRENTICES TO PAN SETTING TO WHOM THE MINIMUM RATES SPECIFIED IN PARAGRAPH 7 APPLY)

54. Workers employed on work other than:—

(1) Coco and any other fibre brooms and banisters of any length (except bass and bassine heads on stocks over 12 in. in length and more than 30 knots round, and whisk brooms and banisters).
Bass heads up to 12 in. stock, 30 knots round
and other than

(2) Broom heads up to 11½ in. stock and banisters up to 8½ in. blade, middles made of all fibre or fibre and drafts mixed up to 3½ in., and outsides of any material up to and including 3¼ in.
Banisters (whisk) up to 7½ in. blade made with common Venetian tops (imported as tops).
Sweeps' hand brushes up to and including 5 in. blade and toy hearth brushes up to and including 3½ in. both made with fibre, fibre and drafts, drafts only or China below 3 in.

(*a*) Pan hands who set but neither bore nor trim work other than that specified in (1) and (2) above.	The piece rates for male workers employed on pan work set out in paragraph 16.—Less 25 per cent.
(*b*) Pan hands who set and trim but do not bore work other than that specified in (1) and (2) above.	The piece rates for male workers employed on pan work set out in paragraph 16.—Less 15 per cent.
(*c*) Pan hands who set and bore but do not trim work other than that specified in (1) and (2) above.	The piece rates for male workers employed on pan work set out in paragraph 16.—Less 10 per cent.
(*d*) Pan hands who set, bore and trim work other than that specified in (1) and (2) above.	The piece rates for male workers employed on pan work set out in paragraph 16.

MINIMUM PIECE RATES FOR FEMALE DRAWING HANDS

55.—(1) Subject to the provisions of paragraph 58, the minimum piece rates for hand drawing TOILET BRUSHES are as follows:—

	Per 100 knots d.
Cloth	4¾
Flesh	4¾
Flesh long handled	5
Hair	4¾
Hair bristle mixed with horn or bone	5
Hair ball cut or cushion	5¼
Hair whalebone, flat cut	5½
Hair whalebone, ball cut	5¾
Hat	4½
Nail	4½
Trepanned brushes:	
Cloth	6½
Hair	6½
Hat	6
Nail	6

Ivory brushes:

1s. 6d. per dozen extra on rates for hair, hat and cloth brushes.

1s. 0d. per dozen extra on rates for nail and other small brushes.

(2) In the case of hair brushes the minimum piece rates specified in this paragraph include trimming but are payable without deduction where the drawing hand is not required to do the trimming.

In the case of all brushes other than hair brushes, the minimum piece rates specified in this paragraph include trimming. The deduction to be made where the brushes are trimmed by a worker other than the drawing hand is set out in paragraph 58(1).

Work with synthetic monofilaments and mixtures containing more than one-third of same, 15 per cent. extra.

56. Subject to the provisions of paragraph 58, the minimum piece rates for hand drawing HOUSEHOLD BRUSHES are as follows:—

	Per 100 knots d.
Billiard	5
Boot top:	
Shear cut	4½
Hard, shear cut	4¾
Can:	
Fibre or bass, shear cut	4½
Pure Bahia, shear cut	5
Carriage washing:	
Drawn doubled	5½
Root in hole	7
Churn, long handled, shear cut	5
Churn bass, shear cut	5¾
Crevice or sash, single end, bristle	5½
Crumb	4¾
Dandy:	
Whisk, shear cut	5½
Bassine, shear cut	5
Bass, shear cut	5¾
Bone, shear cut	5½
Quill, shear cut	6
Davy lamp	6

HOUSEHOLD BRUSHES (contd.)

	Per 100 knots d.
Dish:	
Shear cut	4½
Hard, shear cut	4¾
Floor polishing:	
Up to 10 in. by 5 in.	5
Over 10 in. by 5 in.	6
Furniture	4¾
Furniture porcupine	7
Horse:	
Fibre or mixed, shear cut	5
Bristle, shear cut	5½
Moulders' pattern brushes	5
Paperhanging, drawn, root in hole	7
Pick and Lye	4¾
Plate:	
Shear cut	4½
Hard, shear cut	4¾
Round oil, shear cut	4½
Saucepan, drawn-handled, shear cut	5
Scrubs, deck	5¾
Scrubs, household:	
Bristle and mixed, shear cut	4¾
Fibre, bass (other than Bahia) and union, shear cut	4½
Pure Bahia, shear cut	5
Shoe:	
Blacking and polishing, shear cut	4½
Hard, shear cut	4¾
Sink, bristle, oblong pattern, shear cut	4¾
Spoke:	
Fibre or mixed, shear cut	5
Bristle, shear cut	5½
Porcupine, shear cut	6
Stove:	
Shear cut	4½
Hard, shear cut	4¾
Porcupine, shear cut	5
Water:	
Fibre or mixed, shear cut	5
Bristle, shear cut	5½
W.C., porcupine, shear cut	6

Work with synthetic monofilaments and mixtures containing more than one-third of same, 15 per cent. extra.

57. Subject to the provisions of paragraph 58, the minimum piece rates for hand drawing BROOMS, SWEEPS, etc., are as follows:—

	Per 100 knots d.
Brooms:	
Coco	5¾
Whisk	6
Drawn bass—single wire	6½
Drawn bass—double wire	7½
Window	5
Bassine, monkey bass, Madagascar fibre, Kitool and union fibre	5¾
Brooms and banisters, double drawn	5½

BROOMS, SWEEPS (contd.)

Banisters:	d.
Coco	5¾
Whisk	6
Bassine, monkey bass, Madagascar fibre, Kitool and union fibre	5¾
Bass	6½
Hair work, root in hole	6½

58. The extras and allowances on the minimum piece rates specified in paragraphs 55-57 are as follows:—

(1) As respects all brushes other than hair brushes:

5 per cent. deduction to be made where the brushes are trimmed by a worker other than the drawing hand.

(2) As respects shoe and stove brushes made with C. Hong Kong, ½d. per 100 knots extra.

(3) As respects brushes referred to in paragraphs 56 and 57, for each wing snout or tuft, 2d. extra per dozen brushes.

59. The minimum piece rates for hand drawing TOOTH BRUSHES are as follows:—

	Per gross s.	d.
9 or 10 holes, total holes 38-42	18	6
10 or 11 holes, total holes 42-46	19	6
12 or 13 holes, total holes 50-54	21	0
14 or 15 holes, total holes 58-62	22	0
3 rows (40 holes and upwards)	18	6
Tom Thumb (28 holes and upwards)	16	0
Child's (34 holes and upwards)	17	6
5 rows	29	6

Work with synthetic monofilaments and mixtures containing more than one-third of same, 15 per cent. extra.

60. The minimum piece rates for hand drawing (including trimming) POTTERY BRUSHES are as follows:—

		Per 100 knots d.
BISCUIT STUMPER	New	6¾
BISCUIT STUMPER	Refills	7¼
GLOST STUMPER (hair, bristle or a mixture of hair and bristle)	New	7¾
GLOST STUMPER (hair, bristle or a mixture of hair and bristle)	Refills	8¼
JUG	New	8½
JUG	Refills	9½
MACHINE DISC BRUSHES—		
Face of brush not exceeding 6 in. diameter	New	8
Face of brush exceeding 6 in. diameter	New	9
Face of brush not exceeding 6 in. diameter	Refills	8½
Face of brush exceeding 6 in. diameter	Refills	9½

The diameter means the diameter of the stock occupied by the holes, not the diameter of the whole stock.

The rates for refills set out above are applicable only when the old brush is pulled to pieces by the drawing hand.

Work with synthetic monofilaments and mixtures containing more than one-third of same, 15 per cent. extra.

MINIMUM PIECE RATES FOR FEMALE DRAWING HANDS ON MACHINE BRUSHES

61.—(1) The minimum piece rates are in respect of drawing only.

(2) In this Part of this Schedule:—

LAG—means a detached segment, made of wood, aluminium or other metal, to be attached to a centre core or bearer with screws or bolts. A set of lags fitted together forms a roller or part of a roller.

SLIP—means a flat or roached faced stock, bored through pattern, up to and including 1 in. at thickest part; if over 1 in. thick whether bored through pattern or not, or more than 72 in. long irrespective of the thickness, to be regarded as a lag.

62.—(1) The minimum piece rate for female drawing hands on machine brushes are:—

Types of brushes	Filling material						
	All materials other than those specified in Columns 3 to 8	Gumati, Kitool or finner, synthetic monofilaments from ·005 in. to ·013 in. and mixtures containing same	Synthetic monofilaments from ·014 in. to ·018 in. and mixtures containing same	Badger hair drawn root in hole	Bass, African or Bahia (other than fine drawing Bahia)	Monkey bass or bassine other than H.V. bassine	H.V. bassine or fine drawing Bahia, synthetic monofilaments from ·019 in. upwards and mixture containing same
Column 1	Column 2	Column 3	Column 4	Column 5	Column 6	Column 7	Column 8
	Per 100 knots	Per 100 knots	Per 100 knots	Per 100 knots	Per 100 knots	Per 100 knots	Per 100 knots
	d.	d.	d.	d.	d.	d.	d.
Lags	6	6½	7	9¼	10¼	6½	8¼
Wheel or pulley tentering or polishing	6¾	7¼	7¾	9¾	10¾	7¼	8¾
Slips including heald varnish	5¾	6¼	6¾	9	10	6¼	8
Roller brushes in two halves	6	6½	7	9¼	10¼	6½	8¼
Card brushes	5½	6	6½	—	—	—	—
Dabbing, drawn in wood	5½	—	—	—	—	—	—
Dabbing, drawn in metal or composition	6	—	—	—	—	—	—
Dabbing and circular disc refilled or repaired	6	—	—	—	—	—	—
Bar, cog wheel, roller and ring	5½	6	—	—	—	—	—
Collier's lamp	6½	—	—	—	—	—	—

Asa Lees bobbins	8	—	—	—	—	—	—
Asa Lees circular	6	—	—	—	—	—	—
Platts bobbins	9	—	—	—	—	—	—
Hollow or cord, 4 in. radius and under	$7\frac{3}{4}$	$8\frac{1}{4}$	—	—	—	—	—
Hollow or cord, over 4 in. radius	$6\frac{1}{2}$	7	—	—	—	—	—
Grain cleaner, flat or roached stocks under 7 in. wide or 24 in. long	$6\frac{1}{2}$	—	—	—	—	—	—
Grain cleaner, 7 in. wide or over 24 in. long	7	—	—	—	—	—	—
Grain cleaner, circular, concave or convex	$8\frac{1}{4}$	—	—	—	—	—	—
Leather straps or brush belts, eyeletted	$6\frac{1}{2}$	7	—	—	—	—	—
Leather straps or brush belts, not eyeletted	$6\frac{1}{2}$	7	—	—	—	—	—

EXTRAS ARE AS FOLLOWS:—

(2)

Lags when over 100 in. long—$\frac{1}{2}$d. per 100 knots extra.
All work drawn through side—$\frac{1}{2}$d. per 100 knots extra.
All work drawn root in hole (other than badger)—1d. per 100 knots extra.
All work drawn penetrating—1d. per 100 knots extra.
All work, other than with synthetic monofilaments, cut off or trimmed by drawing hand, except metal work—1d. in 1s. extra.
All metal work cut-off and trimmed by drawing hand—2d. in 1s. extra.
All work drawn for materials $2\frac{1}{4}$ in. and under—$\frac{1}{2}$d. per 100 knots extra.
All work drawn in holes $\frac{6}{64}$ in. diameter and under $\frac{7}{64}$ in. diameter—$\frac{1}{2}$d. per 100 knots extra.
All work drawn in holes $\frac{4}{64}$ in. diameter and $\frac{5}{64}$ in. diameter—1d. per 100 knots extra.
All work drawn in holes $\frac{2}{64}$ in. diameter and $\frac{3}{64}$ in. diameter—$1\frac{1}{2}$d. per 100 knots extra.
All work drawn with double wire—$1\frac{1}{2}$d. per 100 knots extra.
All work drawn with string or nylon (instead of wire)—1d. per 100 knots extra.
Spiral lags when wire is fastened off in sections—1d. per 100 knots extra.
Columns 2 to 4 inclusive—Lags and wheel or pulley drawn especially tight—$\frac{1}{2}$d. per 100 knots extra.
Columns 2 to 8 inclusive—Wheel or pulley below 3 in. diameter stock—$\frac{1}{4}$d. per 100 knots extra.
Columns 2 to 8 inclusive—Roller Brushes in two halves below 3 in. internal diameter—$\frac{1}{2}$d. per 100 knots extra.
Columns 2 to 4 inclusive—Lags, wheel or pulley, slips and roller brushes in two halves in metal work—$1\frac{1}{4}$d. per 100 knots extra.
Work with synthetic monofilaments and mixtures containing more than one-third of same, cut off or trimmed by the drawing hand, except metal work, $1\frac{1}{2}$d. in the 1s. extra.

EXPLANATORY NOTE

(This Note is not part of the Order.)

This Order, which has effect from 8th June 1970, sets out the statutory minimum remuneration payable in substitution for that fixed by the Wages Regulation (Brush and Broom) Order 1967 (Order M. (105)), as amended by the Wages Regulation (Brush and Broom) (Amendment) (No. 2) Order 1969 (Order M. (111)), which Orders are revoked.

New provisions are printed in italics.

STATUTORY INSTRUMENTS

1970 No. 657

WAGES COUNCILS

The Wages Regulation (Brush and Broom) (Holidays) Order 1970

Made - - -	1*st May* 1970
Coming into Operation	8*th June* 1970

Whereas the Secretary of State has received from the Brush and Broom Wages Council (Great Britain) the wages regulation proposals set out in the Schedule hereto ;

Now, therefore, the Secretary of State in exercise of her powers under section 11 of the Wages Councils Act 1959(**a**), and of all other powers enabling her in that behalf, hereby makes the following Order :—

1. This Order may be cited as the Wages Regulation (Brush and Broom) (Holidays) Order 1970.

2.—(1) In this Order the expression "the specified date" means the 8th June 1970, provided that where, as respects any worker who is paid wages at intervals not exceeding seven days, that date does not correspond with the beginning of the period for which the wages are paid, the expression "the specified date" means, as respects that worker, the beginning of the next such period following that date.

(2) The Interpretation Act 1889(**b**) shall apply to the interpretation of this Order as it applies to the interpretation of an Act of Parliament and as if this Order and the Order hereby revoked were Acts of Parliament.

3. The wages regulation proposals set out in the Schedule hereto shall have effect as from the specified date and as from that date the Wages Regulation (Brush and Broom) (Holidays) Order 1969(**c**) shall cease to have effect.

Signed by order of the Secretary of State.

1st May 1970.

A. A. Jarratt,
Deputy Under Secretary of State,
Department of Employment and Productivity.

(**a**) 1959 c. 69.
(**b**) 1889 c. 63.
(**c**) S.I. 1969/209 (1969 I, p. 532).

Article 3

SCHEDULE

The following provisions as to holidays and holiday remuneration shall be substituted for the provisions as to holidays and holiday remuneration set out in the Wages Regulation (Brush and Broom) (Holidays) Order 1969 (hereinafter referred to as "Order M. (109)").

PART I
APPLICATION

1. This Schedule applies to every worker (other than an outworker) for whom statutory minimum remuneration has been fixed.

PART II
CUSTOMARY HOLIDAYS

2.—(1) An employer shall allow to every worker in his employment to whom this Schedule applies a holiday (hereinafter referred to as a "customary holiday") in each year on the days specified in the following sub-paragraph, provided that the worker was in his employment for a period of not less than eight weeks immediately preceding the customary holiday and worked for the employer during the whole or part of that period and (unless excused by the employer or absent by reason of the proved illness of the worker) throughout the last working day on which work was available to him immediately preceding the customary holiday.

(2) The said customary holidays are:—

(*a*) (i) In England and Wales—

Christmas Day (or, if Christmas Day falls on a Sunday, such weekday as may be appointed by national proclamation, or, if none is so appointed, the next following Tuesday), Boxing Day, Good Friday, Easter Monday, Whit Monday (or where another day is substituted therefor by national proclamation, that day) and August Bank Holiday;

(ii) In Scotland—

New Year's Day (or, if New Year's Day falls on a Sunday, the following Monday);

the local Spring holiday;

the local Autumn holiday; and

three other days (being days on which the worker normally works) in the course of a calendar year, to be fixed by agreement between the employer and the worker; or

(*b*) in the case of each of the said days (other than a day in Scotland fixed by agreement between the employer and the worker), a day substituted therefor by agreement between the employer and the worker, being a day recognised by local custom as a day of holiday in substitution for the said day.

(3) Where in England and Wales, Christmas Day or Boxing Day, or in Scotland New Year's Day (or any day substituted for any one of these days under the provisions of (*b*) of sub-paragraph (2) of this paragraph), falls on a Saturday, the employer shall allow:—

(*a*) to a worker who normally works for the employer on five days a week but does not normally work for him on a Saturday, instead of the customary holiday, a holiday on a day on which the worker normally works for the employer during the eight weeks immediately following the customary holiday;

(*b*) to a worker who normally works for the employer on six days a week (including Saturday) but normally works on a Saturday for not more than five hours, in addition to the customary holiday, a holiday on a Saturday during the eight weeks immediately following the customary holiday:

Provided that a worker shall not be entitled to a holiday in pursuance of this sub-paragraph:—

(i) if he is not qualified under sub-paragraph (1) of this paragraph to be allowed the customary holiday and would not be so qualified if he normally worked for the employer on a Saturday ; or

(ii) if, in the case of a worker to whom (*a*) of this sub-paragraph applies, he has been allowed a day of holiday (not being a customary holiday or a day of annual holiday or additional annual holiday) on a day on which he would normally work for the employer in the four weeks immediately preceding the customary holiday and has been paid for that holiday not less than the amount to which he would have been entitled had the day been a customary holiday allowed to him under sub-paragraph (1) of this paragraph ; or

(iii) if, in the case of a worker to whom (*b*) of this sub-paragraph applies, he has been allowed not less than 4 hours off from work during his normal working hours on a day on which the worker would normally have worked for the employer (not being a customary holiday or a day of annual holiday or additional annual holiday) during the ten days immediately preceding the customary holiday and has been paid in respect of the hours off so allowed to him not less than the statutory minimum remuneration to which he would have been entitled as a time worker if he had worked throughout those hours on his usual work.

(4) Notwithstanding the preceding provisions of this paragraph, an employer may (except where in the case of a woman or young person such a requirement would be unlawful) require a worker who is otherwise entitled to any customary holiday under the foregoing provisions of this Schedule to work thereon, and, in lieu of any holiday on which he so works, the employer shall allow to the worker a day's holiday (hereinafter referred to as a "holiday in lieu of a customary holiday") on a weekday on which he would normally work for the employer within the period of two months next ensuing.

(5) A worker who is so required to work on a customary holiday shall be paid:—

(*a*) for all time worked thereon at the minimum rate then appropriate to the worker for work on a customary holiday ; and

(*b*) in respect of the holiday in lieu of the customary holiday, holiday remuneration in accordance with paragraph 8.

PART III

ANNUAL HOLIDAY AND ADDITIONAL ANNUAL HOLIDAY

ANNUAL HOLIDAY

3.—(1) Subject to the provisions of paragraph 4, in addition to the holidays specified in Part II of this Schedule an employer shall, between the date on which the provisions of this Schedule become effective and 30th September 1970, and in each succeeding year between 1st June and the 30th September, allow a holiday (hereinafter referred to as an "annual holiday") to every worker in his employment to whom this Schedule applies who has been employed by him during the 12 months ended on the 5th April immediately preceding the commencement of the holiday season for any of the periods of employment (calculated in accordance with the provisions of paragraph 13) set out in the table below, and the duration of the annual holiday shall, in the case of each such worker, be related to his period of employment during that 12 months as follows:—

Period of employment	Duration of annual holiday for workers with a normal working week of:—			
	6 days	5 days	4 days	3 days
At least 48 weeks	12 days	10 days	8 days	6 days
" " 44 "	11 "	9 "	7 "	5 "
" " 40 "	10 "	8 "	6 "	5 "
" " 36 "	9 "	7 "	6 "	4 "
" " 32 "	8 "	6 "	5 "	4 "
" " 28 "	7 "	5 "	4 "	3 "
" " 24 "	6 "	5 "	4 "	3 "
" " 20 "	5 "	4 "	3 "	2 "
" " 16 "	4 "	3 "	2 "	2 "
" " 12 "	3 "	2 "	2 "	1 day
" " 8 "	2 "	1 day	1 day	1 "

(2) In this Schedule the expression "holiday season" means in relation to an annual holiday in the year 1970 the period commencing on 1st June 1970 and ending on 30th September 1970, and in each succeeding year the period commencing on 1st June and ending on 30th September of the same year and in relation to an additional annual holiday means a period of one year commencing on 1st June.

(3) The duration of the worker's annual holiday during the holiday season ending on the 30th September 1970, shall be reduced by any days of annual holiday and additional annual holiday duly allowed to him by the employer under the provisions of Order M.(109) between 1st June 1970 and the date on which the provisions of this Schedule became effective.

4.—(1) Subject to the provisions of this paragraph, an annual holiday shall be allowed on consecutive working days, being days on which the worker is normally called upon to work for the employer.

(2) Where the number of days of annual holiday for which a worker has qualified exceeds the number of days constituting his normal working week, the holiday may, by agreement in writing made between the employer and the worker, be allowed in two periods of consecutive working days ; so however that when a holiday is so allowed, one of the periods shall consist of a number of such days not less than the number of days constituting the normal worker's working week.

(3) For the purposes of this paragraph, days of annual holiday shall be treated as consecutive notwithstanding that a day of holiday allowed to a worker under Part II of this Schedule or a day upon which he does not normally work for the employer intervenes.

(4) Subject to the provisions of sub-paragraph (5) of this paragraph, where a day of holiday allowed to a worker under Part II of this Schedule immediately precedes a period of annual holiday or occurs during such a period and the total number of days of annual holiday required to be allowed in the period under the foregoing provisions of this paragraph, together with any such day of holiday allowed under Part II of this Schedule, exceeds the number of days constituting the worker's normal working week then, notwithstanding the foregoing provisions of this paragraph, the duration of that period of annual holiday may be reduced by one day and in such a case one day of annual holiday shall be allowed on any working day in the holiday season, or with the consent of the worker on any working day prior to the commencement of the next holiday season.

(5) Any day of annual holiday or additional annual holiday under this Schedule may be allowed on a day on which the worker is entitled to a day of holiday or to a half-holiday under any enactment other than the Wages Councils Act 1959, except that a day of annual holiday allowed under sub-paragraph (4) of this paragraph shall not be allowed on the worker's weekly short day.

ADDITIONAL ANNUAL HOLIDAY

5. Subject to the provisions of this paragraph, in addition to the holidays specified in paragraphs 2 and 3 an employer shall in each year commencing on 1st June allow a holiday (hereinafter referred to as an "additional annual holiday") to every worker in his employment to whom this Schedule applies who has been employed by him at the preceding 5th April for a continuous period of *one year* or more (calculated in accordance with paragraph 13) and the duration of the additional annual holiday shall be *three days*.

6. Where a worker becomes entitled to any days of additional annual holiday in accordance with the provisions of paragraph 5 those days of additional annual holiday shall be allowed by the employer, by agreement with the worker, on a day or days on which the worker is normally called upon to work for the employer, at any time (or times) during the period of 12 months commencing on 1st June immediately following 5th April upon which the worker becomes entitled as aforesaid.

GENERAL

7. An employer shall give to a worker notice of the commencing date or dates and duration of the period or periods of his annual holiday and the date or dates of his additional holiday. Such notice shall be given at least 28 days before:—

(*a*) the first day of the annual holiday or, where under the provisions of paragraph 4 an annual holiday is allowed in more than one period, before each separate period;
and

(*b*) the said date or dates of the additional annual holiday.

Notice may be given individually to the worker or by the posting of a notice in the place where the worker is employed.

PART IV—HOLIDAY REMUNERATION

A.—CUSTOMARY HOLIDAYS AND HOLIDAYS IN LIEU OF CUSTOMARY HOLIDAYS

8.—(1) Subject to the provisions of this paragraph, for each day of holiday which a worker is allowed under Part II of this Schedule he shall be paid by the employer as holiday remuneration whichever of the following sums is the greater, that is to say either:—

(*a*) (i) In the case of a worker whose normal working week exceeds five days, two-elevenths
(ii) In the case of a worker whose normal working week is five days, one-fifth
(iii) In the case of a worker whose normal working week is four days, one-quarter
(iv) In the case of a worker whose normal working week is three days, one-third

of the average weekly earnings of the worker during the 12 months ended on the 5th April immediately preceding the holiday such average weekly earnings to be determined by dividing, by the number of weeks of employment with the employer during the said period, the total remuneration (as defined in paragraph 14) paid to him by the employer during that period; or

(*b*) a sum equal to the appropriate statutory minimum remuneration to which he would have been entitled if the day had not been a day of holiday and he had been employed on work entitling him to statutory minimum remuneration for the time normally worked by him on that day of the week.

Provided that payment of the said holiday remuneration is subject to the condition that the worker (unless excused by the employer or absent by reason of proved illness of the worker) works throughout his normal working hours on the first working day following the holiday.

(2) Holiday remuneration in respect of any holiday allowed under Part II of this Schedule shall be paid to the worker not later than on the pay day on which the wages are paid for the first working day following the holiday: Provided that where a worker ceases to be employed before being allowed a holiday in lieu of a customary holiday or a holiday under sub-paragraph (3) of paragraph 2, he shall be paid the holiday remuneration for that day immediately upon the termination of his employment and in such a case the condition contained in the proviso to sub-paragraph (1) of this paragraph shall not apply.

B.—ANNUAL HOLIDAY

9.—(1) Subject to the provisions of paragraph 11, a worker qualified to be allowed an annual holiday under this Schedule shall be paid as holiday remuneration by his employer in respect thereof, not later than the last pay day preceding such annual holiday, whichever of the following sums is the greater, that is to say either:—

(*a*) a sum equal to two fifty-seconds of the total remuneration (as defined in paragraph 14) paid by the employer to the worker during the 12 months ended on the 5th April immediately preceding the holiday ; or,

(*b*) one day's holiday pay in respect of each day thereof.

(2) Where under the provisions of paragraph 4 an annual holiday is allowed in more than one period the holiday remuneration shall be apportioned accordingly.

C.—ADDITIONAL ANNUAL HOLIDAY

10.—(1) A worker entitled to be allowed an additional annual holiday under this Schedule shall be paid by his employer in respect thereof on the last pay day preceding such additional annual holiday as follows:—

Where the worker's normal working week is 6 days	...	*three-elevenths*
" " " " " " " 5 days	...	*three-tenths*
" " " " " " " 4 days	...	*three-eighths*
" " " " " " " 3 days	...	*one-half*

of the amount he would be entitled to receive at the date of the holiday for an annual holiday of two normal working weeks determined in accordance with paragraph 9.

(2) Where an employer allows the days of additional annual holiday otherwise than on consecutive days the remuneration shall be apportioned accordingly.

11. Where any accrued holiday remuneration has been paid by the employer to the worker (in accordance with the provisions of paragraph 12 of this Schedule or under Order M. (109)) in respect of employment during any of the periods referred to in that paragraph or that Order respectively, the amount of holiday remuneration payable by the employer in respect of any annual holiday for which the worker has qualified by reason of employment during the said period shall be reduced by the amount of the said accrued holiday remuneration unless that remuneration has been deducted from a previous payment of holiday remuneration made under the provisions of this Schedule.

ACCRUED HOLIDAY REMUNERATION PAYABLE ON TERMINATION OF EMPLOYMENT

12.—(1) Subject to the provisions of this paragraph, where a worker ceases to be employed by an employer after the provisions of this Schedule become effective, the employer shall, immediately on the termination of the employment, pay to the worker as accrued holiday remuneration:—

(*a*) in respect of employment in the 12 months up to and including the immediately preceding 5th April a sum equal to the holiday remuneration for any days of annual holiday for which he has qualified ;

(*b*) in respect of employment up to and including the immediately preceding 5th April a sum equal to the holiday remuneration for any days of additional annual holiday for which he has qualified ; and

(*c*) in respect of any employment since the said 5th April for a period of at least 8 weeks duration (calculated in accordance with paragraph 13) whichever of the following sums is the greater, that is to say either:—

(i) a sum equal to two fifty-seconds of the total remuneration (as defined in paragraph 14) paid by the employer to the worker since that date; or,

(ii) a sum equal to the holiday remuneration for any days of annual holiday which would have been payable to him if he could have been allowed an annual holiday in respect of that employment at the time of leaving it and if paid at the rate of one day's holiday pay in respect of each day thereof.

(2) Accrued holiday remuneration is not payable in respect of any days of annual holiday which the worker has been allowed or become entitled to be allowed under this Schedule or under Order M. (109).

(3) Subject to the provisions of sub-paragraph (4) hereof, where a worker has been allowed in a holiday season part only of the annual holiday for which he has qualified under this Schedule or under Order M. (109) and his employment is terminated before he becomes entitled to the rest of that holiday the accrued holiday remuneration payable shall be the appropriate amount under the foregoing provisions less the amount received by the worker in respect of that part of the holiday which has been allowed.

(4) Any accrued holiday remuneration payable under the provisions of this paragraph shall be reduced by the amount of any accrued holiday remuneration already paid by the employer to the worker in pursuance of this Schedule or Order M. (109) in respect of the same period of employment or part thereof.

PART V—GENERAL

13. For the purposes of calculating any period of employment qualifying a worker for an annual holiday, additional annual holiday or for any accrued holiday remuneration under this Schedule, the worker shall be treated—

(1) as if he were employed for a week in respect of any week in which—

(*a*) he has worked for the employer on not less than three days and has performed some work for which statutory minimum remuneration is payable;

(*b*) he has been absent throughout the week or he has worked for the employer on less than 3 days, by reason, in either case, of the proved illness of, or accident to, the worker: Provided that the number of weeks which may be treated as weeks of employment for such reasons shall not exceed four in the aggregate in the period of 12 months ended on the 5th April immediately preceding the commencement of the holiday season; and

(2) as if he were employed on any day of holiday allowed under the provisions of this Schedule or of Order M. (109) and for the purpose of the provisions of sub-paragraph (1) of this paragraph, a worker who is absent on such a holiday shall be treated as having worked thereon for the employer on work for which statutory minimum remuneration is payable.

14. In this Schedule, unless the context otherwise requires, the following expressions have the meanings hereby respectively assigned to them, that is to say:—

"APPROPRIATE RATE OF STATUTORY MINIMUM REMUNERATION" means, where the worker is usually employed as:—

(1) a time worker	the general minimum time rate applicable to the worker.
(2) a piece worker and is a female worker under 21 years of age ...	the general minimum time rate which would apply if the worker were employed as a time worker.
(3) a piece worker and is not a worker specified in (2) of this definition	a time rate equal to the basis rate.

For the purpose of this definition—

(*a*) the expression "basis rate" means the piece work basis time rate applicable to the worker or which is applicable when no general minimum piece rate applies or where no such piece work basis time rate is applicable the general minimum time rate which would apply if the worker were a time worker;

(*b*) where a worker is employed on work to which more than one minimum rate applies, the rate shall be ascertained by reference to the work on which he has been mainly employed in the 12 months prior to the holiday in the case of a customary holiday or holiday in lieu of a customary holiday, the commencement of the holiday season in the case of an annual holiday or additional annual holiday or the date of the termination of the employment where accrued holiday remuneration is payable;

(*c*) where a worker is usually employed partly on time work and partly on piece work, he shall be treated as having been employed on piece work for the whole of his time;

(*d*) where a female worker aged under 21 years is employed on pan work the general minimum time rate applicable shall be the rate for all "other workers" which would apply to the worker if no other general work minimum time rate applied.

"NORMAL WORKING WEEK" means the number of days on which it has been usual for the worker to work in a week in the employment of the employer in the 12 months ended on 5th April immediately preceding the commencement of the holiday season or, where under paragraph 12 accrued holiday remuneration is payable on the termination of the employment, in the 12 months immediately preceding the date of the termination of the employment:

Provided that—

(1) part of a day shall count as a day;

(2) no account shall be taken of any week in which the worker did not perform any work for which statutory minimum remuneration has been fixed.

"ONE DAY'S HOLIDAY PAY" means the appropriate proportion of the remuneration which the worker would be entitled to receive from his employer at the date of the annual holiday (or, where the holiday is taken in more than one period, at the date of the first period) or date or dates of the additional annual holiday, or at the termination date, as the case may be, for one week's work if working his normal working week and the number of daily hours normally worked by him (exclusive of overtime), and if paid at the appropriate rate of statutory minimum remuneration for work for which statutory minimum remuneration is payable and at the same rate for any work for the same employer for which such remuneration is not payable, and in this definition "appropriate proportion" means—

where the worker's normal working week is six days—two-elevenths

where the worker's normal working week is five days—one-fifth

where the worker's normal working week is four days—one-quarter

where the worker's normal working week is three days—one-third.

"OUTWORKER" means a worker who works in his own home or in any other place not under the control or management of the employer.

"STATUTORY MINIMUM REMUNERATION" means statutory minimum remuneration (other than holiday remuneration) fixed by a wages regulation order made by the Secretary of State to give effect to proposals submitted to her by the Brush and Broom Wages Council (Great Britain).

"TOTAL REMUNERATION" means any payments paid or payable to the worker under his contract of employment, for time (other than hours of overtime) worked or piece work done by him (other than during hours of overtime), holiday remuneration, any productivity or long service bonus payable to the worker on a weekly, fortnightly or monthly basis and merit payments so payable but does not include any other payments.

"WEEK" means "pay week".

15. The provisions of this Schedule are without prejudice to any agreement for the allowance of any further holidays with pay or for the payment of additional holiday remuneration.

EXPLANATORY NOTE

(*This Note is not part of the Order.*)

This Order, which has effect from 8th June 1970, sets out the holidays which an employer is required to allow to workers and the remuneration payable for those holidays, in substitution for the holidays and holiday remuneration fixed by the Wages Regulation (Brush and Broom) (Holidays) Order 1969 (Order M. (109)), which Order is revoked.

New provisions are printed in italics.

1970 No. 666

INCOME TAX

The Income Tax (Employments) (No. 5) Regulations 1970

Made - - -	*4th May* 1970
Laid before the House of Commons	*8th May* 1970
Coming into Operation	*6th July* 1970

The Commissioners of Inland Revenue, in exercise of the powers conferred upon them by section 204 of the Income and Corporation Taxes Act 1970(**a**), hereby make the following Regulations:—

1.—(1) These Regulations may be cited as the Income Tax (Employments) (No. 5) Regulations 1970, and shall come into operation on the 6th day of July 1970.

(2) The Interpretation Act 1889(**b**) shall apply for the interpretation of these Regulations as it applies for the interpretation of an Act of Parliament.

(3) In these Regulations the expression "the Principal Regulations" means the Income Tax (Employments) Regulations 1965(**c**) as amended by the Income Tax (Employments) (No. 2) Regulations 1966(**d**), the Income Tax (Employments) (No. 3) Regulations 1969(**e**) and the Income Tax (Employments) (No. 4) Regulations 1969(**f**).

2. Regulations 19 and 29 of the Principal Regulations shall have effect, as regards payments of emoluments made on or after the 6th day of July 1970, as if for any reference to a rate of £6 5s. 0d. or more a week there were substituted a reference to a rate of £8 or more a week, and as if for any reference to a rate of £27 or more a month there were substituted a reference to a rate of £34 10s. 0d. or more a month.

By Order of the Commissioners of Inland Revenue.

J. Webb,
Secretary.

4th May 1970.

(**a**) 1970 c. 10. (**b**) 52 & 53 Vict. c. 63. (**c**) S.I. 1965/516 (1965 I, p. 1321).
(**d**) S.I. 1966/1373 (1966 III, p. 3691). (**e**) S.I. 1969/170 (1969 I, p. 440).
(**f**) S.I. 1969/688 (1969 II, p. 1859).

EXPLANATORY NOTE

(*This Note is not part of the Regulations.*)

These Regulations provide for raising the limit of weekly or monthly pay above which an employer has to operate the Pay as You Earn scheme for every employee, to take into account the increased Income Tax allowances proposed in the Finance Bill 1970.

1970 No. 670

SEA FISHERIES

WHITE FISH INDUSTRY

The White Fish Authority (Quality and Handling) (Northern Ireland) Regulations Confirmatory Order 1970

Made - - -	30*th April* 1970
Laid before Parliament	11*th May* 1970
Coming into Operation	1*st June* 1970

Whereas the White Fish Authority (hereinafter referred to as "the Authority") have made the White Fish Authority (Quality and Handling) (Northern Ireland) Regulations 1969 :

And Whereas the Authority have transmitted to the Minister of Agriculture, Fisheries and Food, the Secretary of State for Scotland, being the Secretary of State concerned with the sea fishing industry in Scotland, and the Secretary of State for the Home Department, being the Secretary of State concerned with the sea fishing industry in Northern Ireland, (hereinafter referred to as "the Ministers") an objection to the Regulations which has been duly made to the Authority and has not been withdrawn and the Ministers have considered the objection :

And Whereas the Ministers, after consultation with the Authority, have considered it desirable to make such modifications in the Regulations as hereinafter appear and have caused notice thereof to be published in such manner as they thought best adapted for informing persons affected :

Now, therefore, the Ministers, in exercise of the powers conferred on them by section 5(6) of the Sea Fish Industry Act 1951(**a**), as having effect in Northern Ireland by virtue of the Northern Ireland (Sea Fish Industry) Order 1951(**b**) and of section 20(2) of that Act, hereby make the following Order :—

1. This Order may be cited as the White Fish Authority (Quality and Handling) (Northern Ireland) Regulations Confirmatory Order 1970 and shall come into operation on 1st June 1970.

2. The White Fish Authority (Quality and Handling) (Northern Ireland) Regulations 1969, having been modified by the Ministers in the three respects specified in Article 3 of this Order so as to read as set out in the Schedule to this Order, are hereby confirmed.

3. The said modifications were—

(*a*) the substitution in Regulation 2 of the words "the Interpretation Act (Northern Ireland) 1954(**c**)" for the words "the Interpretation Act 1889 as applied by the Interpretation Act 1921" ;

(*b*) the substitution in Regulation 8(*b*) of the words "place of purchase" for the words "place of sale" ;

(**a**) 1951 c. 30. (**b**) S.I. 1951/1797 (1951 I, p. 738).
(**c**) 1954 c. 33 (N.I.).

(*c*) the deletion of the following Regulation entitled "Administration"—

"10. These Regulations shall be administered by the Committee constituted for Scotland and Northern Ireland under Section 2(1) of the Sea Fish Industry Act 1951, extended as aforesaid, in accordance with the functions delegated to them by the Authority.".

In witness whereof the Official Seal of the Minister of Agriculture, Fisheries and Food is hereunto affixed on 28th April 1970.

(L.S.)

Cledwyn Hughes,
Minister of Agriculture, Fisheries and Food.

Given under the Seal of the Secretary of State for Scotland on 30th April 1970.

(L.S.)

William Ross,
Secretary of State for Scotland.

Given under the hand of the Secretary of State for the Home Department on 27th April 1970.

James Callaghan,
Secretary of State for the Home Department.

SCHEDULE Article 2

THE WHITE FISH AUTHORITY (QUALITY AND HANDLING) (NORTHERN IRELAND) REGULATIONS 1969

Whereas it appears to the Authority that it is desirable to bring into force regulations for the purpose of improving the condition in which white fish are offered for sale in Northern Ireland:

And Whereas the Authority have consulted with such bodies as appear to them to be representative of the interests concerned:

Now, therefore, the Authority, in exercise of the powers conferred upon them by Section 5 of the Sea Fish Industry Act 1951, as extended to Northern Ireland by the Northern Ireland (Sea Fish Industry) Order 1951, hereby make the following Regulations:—

Citation and Interpretation

1. These Regulations may be cited as the White Fish Authority (Quality and Handling) (Northern Ireland) Regulations 1969 and shall apply only to Northern Ireland.

2. The Interpretation Act (Northern Ireland) 1954 shall apply to the interpretation of these Regulations as it applies to the interpretation of an Act of Parliament.

3. In these Regulations, unless the context otherwise requires—

"the Authority" means—

the White Fish Authority;

"box" means—

a container of any kind;

"firsthand" means—

in relation to a sale or purchase of white fish the first sale or purchase thereof after it has been landed from a fishing vessel in Northern Ireland;

"registered length" in relation to a fishing vessel means—

its length as measured for the purposes of the Merchant Shipping Act 1894(a) or any amendment thereof;

"fishing vessel" means—

(*a*) any vessel, registered as a fishing vessel under the Merchant Shipping Act 1894 or any amendment thereof and owned or chartered by a person residing or having a place of business in Northern Ireland, from which white fish is landed for sale at the ports of Portavogie, Kilkeel and Ardglass in the County of Down, Northern Ireland, and

(*b*) any such vessel of a registered length of or exceeding forty feet from which white fish is landed for sale in Northern Ireland, elsewhere than at those ports previously specified;

"processing" means—

preserving or preparing white fish or manufacturing products from white fish, by any method for human consumption;

"white fish" has the same meaning as in the Sea Fish Industry Act 1951, except that it does not include sprats, sand-eels, Norway Pout, blue whiting, mackerel or shellfish (other than Nephrops Norvegicus).

Cleanliness, etc. of boxes, fish rooms and fish pounds

4. Any person engaged in the catching and landing for firsthand sale of white fish shall ensure that boxes, fish rooms and fish pounds for stowing or handling white fish on board a fishing vessel shall

(*a*) be kept clean, and

(*b*) be so constructed, be of such materials and be kept in such good order, repair and condition as to

(i) enable them to be effectively cleaned, and

(ii) prevent, so far as is reasonably practicable, any risk of contamination of the fish.

Handling of white fish

5. No person shall land white fish from a fishing vessel unless it has, whilst at sea, been—

(*a*) (except in the case of Nephrops Norvegicus) both gutted and washed free from guts, blood and dirt;

(*b*) sorted so as to separate skate, ray, dogfish and saithe from other species of fish;

(*c*) both packed in boxes and chilled by the use of ice in such a manner that its temperature at the time of landing does not exceed 2°C. (36°F.); and

(*d*) protected from direct exposure to sun or wind.

(a) 1894 c. 60.

6. Any person offering white fish for firsthand sale for human consumption shall ensure that while so offered it is—

(*a*) kept sorted and chilled as laid down in Regulation 5(*b*) and (*c*) respectively;

(*b*) kept in boxes; and

(*c*) so placed as to avoid, so far as reasonably practicable, any risk of contamination.

7. Any person required under these Regulations to pack or keep white fish in ice in a box shall ensure that it is packed or kept in such a manner that the depth of ice and fish in the box does not exceed the depth of the box.

8. Any person who has purchased white fish at firsthand for the purpose of carrying on a business of selling white fish for human consumption shall ensure that it is

(*a*) packed in boxes and maintained by the use of ice or by mechanical refrigeration at a temperature not exceeding 2°C. (36°F.) until it has been removed from the place of purchase; and

(*b*) removed without delay from the place of purchase to the premises where he carries on that business.

9. Any person who has purchased white fish at firsthand sale for the purpose of carrying on a business of selling white fish for human consumption by wholesale shall ensure that—

(*a*) so long as it remains in his premises, the white fish (with the exception of dry salted fish) is not directly exposed to sun or wind and (with the exception of smoked or wet salted or dry salted fish) is maintained by the use of ice or mechanical refrigeration at a temperature not exceeding 2°C. (36°F.), and

(*b*) all offal is removed from processing benches and stored clear of all other white fish intended for human consumption.

EXPLANATORY NOTE

(*This Note is not part of the Order.*)

This Order confirms, with minor modifications, Regulations made by the White Fish Authority to regulate the handling of white fish for the purpose of improving the condition in which they are offered for sale in Northern Ireland.

STATUTORY INSTRUMENTS

1970 No. 671 (L.14)

SUPREME COURT OF JUDICATURE, ENGLAND

PROCEDURE

The Rules of the Supreme Court (Amendment) 1970

Made - - - - -	30*th April* 1970
Laid before Parliament	11*th May* 1970
Coming into Operation	26*th May* 1970

We, the Rule Committee of the Supreme Court, being the authority having for the time being power under section 99(4) of the Supreme Court of Judicature (Consolidation) Act 1925(**a**) to make, amend or revoke rules regulating the practice and procedure of the Supreme Court of Judicature, hereby exercise those powers and all other powers enabling us in that behalf as follows:—

1.—(1) These rules may be cited as the Rules of the Supreme Court (Amendment) 1970 and shall come into operation on 26th May 1970.

(2) In these rules an Order referred to by number means the Order so numbered in the Rules of the Supreme Court 1965(**b**), as amended(**c**), and a Form referred to by number means the Form so numbered in Appendix A to those Rules.

(3) The Interpretation Act 1889(**d**) shall apply to the interpretation of these rules as it applies to the interpretation of an Act of Parliament.

2. In Order 47, rule 4, for the words "£40" there shall be substituted the words "£100".

3. The following Appendix shall be substituted for Appendix 3 to Order 62:—

"APPENDIX 3

FIXED COSTS

(*In this Appendix decimal equivalents are shown in italics and brackets*)

PART I

Costs on recovery of a liquidated sum without trial

1. The scale of costs following paragraph 2 of this Part of this Appendix shall apply in relation to the following cases if the writ of summons therein was issued on or after 26th May 1970 and was indorsed in accordance with Order 6, rule 2(1)(*b*), with a claim for a debt or liquidated demand only of £100 or upwards, that is to say—

(**a**) 1925 c. 49.
(**b**) S.I. 1965/1776 (1965 III, p. 4995).
(**c**) The relevant amending instrument is S.I. 1968/1244 (1968 II, p. 3360).
(**d**) 1889 c. 63.

(*a*) cases in which the defendant pays the amount claimed or a sum of not less than £100 within the time and in the manner required by the indorsement of the writ;

(*b*) cases in which the plaintiff obtains judgment in default of appearance under Order 13, rule 1, or under that rule by virtue of Order 83, rule 4, or Order 84, rule 3, or judgment in default of defence under Order 19, rule 2, or under that rule by virtue of Order 83, rule 4, or Order 84, rule 3, being in any case judgment for a sum of £100 or upwards;

(*c*) cases in which the plaintiff obtains judgment under Order 14, for a sum of £100 or upwards, either unconditionally or unless that sum is paid into court or to the plaintiff's solicitors.

2. In every case to which the said scale applies there shall be added to the basic costs set out in the said scale the fee paid on the issue of the writ.

SCALE OF COSTS

A. Basic costs

	Amount to be allowed in cases under the following sub-paragraphs of paragraph 1 of this Appendix		
	(*a*)	(*b*)	(*c*)
	£. s. (£. *p*)	£. s. (£. *p*)	£. s. (£. *p*)
If the amount recovered is:—			
not less than £100 but less than £500	7 0 (*7·00*)	8 10 (*8·50*)	11 0 (*11·00*)
not less than £500	10 5 (*10·25*)	16 0 (*16·00*)	21 0 (*21·00*)

B. Additional costs

		Amount to be allowed where the amount recovered is—	
		(i) *not less than £100 but less than £500*	(ii) *not less than £500*
		£. s. (£. *p*)	£. s. (£. *p*)
(1)	Where there is more than one defendant, in respect of each additional defendant served	1 0 (*1·00*)	1 10 (*1·50*)
(2)	Where substituted service is ordered and effected, in respect of each defendant served	2 0 (*2·00*)	6 5 (*6·25*)
(3)	Where the plaintiff's solicitor has no place of business within 5 miles of the Royal Courts of Justice or his nearest District Registry, or where he has a place of business within that area but any defendant is served outside that area	10 (*0·50*)	1 10 (*1·50*)
(4)	Where service out of the jurisdiction is ordered and effected, in the case of service—		
	(*a*) in Scotland, Northern Ireland, the Isle of Man or the Channel Islands ...	6 0 (*6·00*)	8 10 (*8·50*)
	(*b*) in any other place out of the jurisdiction	9 0 (*9·00*)	13 0 (*13·00*)
(5)	In the case of judgment in default of defence or judgment under Order 14, where notice of appearance is not given on the day		

	Amount to be allowed where the amount recovered is— (i) not less than £100 but less than £500 £. s. (£. p)	(ii) not less than £500 £. s. (£. p)
on which the appearance is entered, and the plaintiff makes an affidavit of service for the purpose of a judgment in default of appearance (the allowance to include the search fee)	1 5 (*1·25*)	2 10 (*2·50*)
(6) In the case of judgment under Order 14 where an affidavit of service of the summons is required	1 5 (*1·25*)	2 10 (*2·50*)
(7) In the case of judgment under Order 14, for each adjournment of the summons ...	1 0 (*1·00*)	1 10 (*1·50*)
(8) In the case of judgment in default of appearance or defence on an application by summons under Order 83, rule 4—		
(*a*) where judgment is given for interest at a rate exceeding 48 per cent. per annum on production of an affidavit justifying that rate	2 10 (*2·50*)	4 0 (*4·00*)
(*b*) in any other case	1 10 (*1·50*)	3 0 (*3·00*)
(*c*) where there is more than one defendant, in respect of each additional defendant	10 (*0·50*)	1 10 (*1·50*)
(9) In the case of judgment in default of appearance or defence on an application by summons under Order 84, rule 3 ...	2 10 (*2·50*)	3 10 (*3·50*)
and, where there is more than one defendant in respect of each additional defendant ...	10 (*0·50*)	1 0 (*1·00*)

	Costs to be allowed £ s. (£. p)
(10) Where the amount recovered is not less than £500 and there is no available solicitor carrying on business within 2 miles of the place where the defendant is served, a mileage allowance in respect of each mile after the first two miles between that place and the nearest place of business of an available solicitor	2 (*0·10*)

PART II

Costs on judgment without trial for possession of land

1.—(1) Where the writ of summons is indorsed with a claim for the possession of land and the plaintiff obtains judgment—

(*a*) under Order 13, rule 4 or 5, in default of appearance, or

(*b*) under Order 19, rule 5 or 6, in default of defence, or

(*c*) under Order 14,

for possession of the land and costs, then, subject to sub-paragraph (2), there shall be allowed the costs prescribed by paragraph 2 of this Part of this Appendix.

(2) Where the plaintiff is also entitled under the judgment to damages to be assessed, or where the plaintiff claims any relief of the nature specified in Order 88, rule 1, this Part of this Appendix shall not apply.

2. The costs to be allowed under this Part of this Appendix shall be the costs which would be allowed under Part I (together with the fee paid on the writ) if judgment had been obtained in the same circumstances, that is to say, in default of appearance or defence or under Order 14, but the writ has been indorsed with a claim for a debt or liquidated demand only of £100 or upwards and judgment for not less than £100 but less than £500 had been obtained.

PART III

Miscellaneous

1. Where a plaintiff or defendant signs judgment for costs under rule 10, there shall be allowed—

Costs of the judgment ... ... £1. 12s. (£*1·60*)

2. Where a certificate of a judgment or decree is registered in the High Court in the Register for Irish Judgments or the Register for Scottish Judgments under the Judgments Extension Act 1868 (a), within 12 months of the date of the judgment and without an order, there shall be allowed—

Costs of registration ... ... £7. 0s. (£*7·00*)

3. Where the Court orders a judgment or order of an inferior court to be removed into the High Court for enforcement, there shall be allowed in the case of a judgemnt or order—

(*a*) of the Mayor's and City of London Court ... ... £2. 10s. (£*2·50*)

(*b*) of the Salford Hundred Court, the Liverpool Court of Passage or any other court ... ... £5. 5s. (£*5·25*)

4. Where, upon the application of any person who has obtained a judgment or order against a debtor for the recovery or payment of money, a garnishee order, is made under Order 49, rule 1, against a garnishee attaching debts due or accruing due from him to the debtor, the following costs shall be allowed—

(*a*) to the garnishee, to be deducted by him from any debt due by him as aforesaid before payment to the applicant—

	If no affidavit used £. s.	(£. *p*)	*If affidavit used* £. s.	(£. *p*)
(i) where the garnishee resides within 5 miles of the court office from which the garnishee order was obtained ...	1 10	(*1·50*)	3 5	(*3·25*)
(ii) where the garnishee does not so reside	2 10	(*2·50*)	4 10	(*4·50*)

(*b*) to the applicant, to be retained, unless the Court otherwise orders, out of the money recovered by him under the garnishee order and in priority to the amount of the debt owing to him under the judgment or order—

(a) 1868 c. 54.

Basic costs	£. s. (£. *p*)
If the amount recovered by the applicant from the garnishee is—	
less than £5	Nil
not less than £5 but not more than £10	2 5 (*2·25*)
more than £10	7 0 (*7·00*)
Additional costs	
Where the garnishee fails to attend the hearing of the application and an affidavit of service is required	2 10 (*2·50*)

5. Where a charging order is made—

(*a*) in respect of any securities, under Order 50, rule 2; or

(*b*) in respect of any partnership property or profits, under section 23 of the Partnership Act 1890**(a)**; or

(*c*) in respect of land, under section 35 of the Administration of Justice Act 1956**(b)**;

there shall be allowed—

	£. s. (£. *p*)
Basic costs	9 0 (*9·00*)
Additional costs where an affidavit of service is required	2 10 (*2·50*)

6. Where leave is given under Order 45, rule 3, to enforce a judgment or order for the giving of possession of land by writ of possession, if costs are allowed on the judgment or order there shall be allowed the following costs, which shall be added to the judgment or order—

	£. s. (£. *p*)
Basic costs	2 10 (*2·50*)
Where notice of the proceedings has been given to more than one person, in respect of each additional person	8 (*0·40*)

7. Where a writ of execution within the meaning of Order 46, rule 1, is issued against any party, there shall be allowed—

	£. s. (£. *p*)
Costs of issuing execution	3 10 (*3·50*)"

4. In Form 53 for the words "the sums of £ and £ for costs of execution" there shall be substituted the words "the sum[s] of £ ‡[and £ for costs of execution]" and in the note for the words "£40" there shall be substituted the words "£100".

Dated 30th April 1970.

Gardiner, C.
Parker of Waddington, C.J.
Denning, M.R.
J. E. S. Simon, P.
Cyril Salmon, L.J
Denys B. Buckley, J.
John R. Willis, J.
Nigel Bridge, J.
E. S. Fay.
Oliver Lodge.
W. O. Carter.
Arthur J. Driver.

(a) 1890 c. 39. (b) 1956 c. 46.

EXPLANATORY NOTE

(This Note is not part of the Rules.)

These Rules are mainly consequential on the amendments made by section 4 of the Administration of Justice Act 1969 (C.58) in the provisions of section 47 of the County Courts Act 1959 relating to the costs of actions brought in the High Court which could have been brought in a county court. Rule 2 prevents a plaintiff recovering any costs of execution where he issues a writ of *fieri facias* to enforce a judgment without costs for less than £100, instead of £40 as at present. Rule 3 substitutes new items of fixed costs for those set out in Appendix 3 to Order 62. Rule 4 makes minor drafting and consequential amendments in the form of writ of *fieri facias*.

1970 No. 672 (C.14)

SUPREME COURT OF JUDICATURE, ENGLAND COUNTY COURTS

The Administration of Justice Act 1969 (Commencement No. 2) Order 1970

Made - - - - *30th April* 1970

The Lord Chancellor, in exercise of the powers conferred on him by section 36(5) and (6) of the Administration of Justice Act 1969**(a)**, hereby makes the following Order:—

1.—(1) This Order may be cited as the Administration of Justice Act 1969 (Commencement No. 2) Order 1970.

(2) In this Order—

"the 1959 Act" means the County Courts Act 1959**(b)** as amended**(c)**;

"the 1969 Act" means the Administration of Justice Act 1969; and

"the appointed day" means 26th May 1970.

(3) The Interpretation Act 1889**(d)** shall apply to the interpretation of this Order as it applies to the interpretation of an Act of Parliament.

2. The provisions of the 1969 Act which were not brought into operation by the Administration of Justice Act 1969 (Commencement No. 1) Order 1969**(e)** shall come into operation on the appointed day.

3. This Order shall have effect subject to the transitional provisions set out in the Schedule.

Dated 30th April 1970.

Gardiner, C.

SCHEDULE

TRANSITIONAL PROVISIONS

Transfer of proceedings from county court

1. The amendments made by the 1969 Act in section 44 of the 1959 Act shall apply to proceedings begun before, as well as on or after, the appointed day, and in relation to proceedings begun before that day a county court judge may, if he sees fit, refuse to make an order under section 66 of the 1959 Act, if the proceedings are within the jurisdiction of the court as extended by the 1969 Act; but nothing in this Order shall be taken to affect any order made before the appointed day.

(a) 1969 c. 58.
(b) 1959 c. 22.
(c) The relevant amending instrument is S.I. 1965/2141 (1965 III, p. 6290).
(d) 1889 c. 63.
(e) S.I. 1969/1607 (1969 III, p. 5089).

Transfer of proceedings to county court

2. The amendments made by the 1969 Act in sections 45, 68 and 146 of the 1959 Act shall apply to proceedings begun before, as well as on or after, the appointed day, and in relation to proceedings begun before the appointed day the High Court or a judge thereof shall have the same powers under section 54 as he would have if the proceedings had been begun after that day.

Costs of proceedings in High Court

3. The amendments made by the 1969 Act in sections 47 and 60 of the 1959 Act shall not apply to proceedings begun before the appointed day.

Miscellaneous

4. In relation to proceedings begun before the appointed day nothing in the provisions of the 1969 Act brought into force by this Order shall affect the operation of section 19 of the City of London (Courts) Act 1964**(a)**.

EXPLANATORY NOTE

(*This Note is not part of the Order.*)

This Order brings into operation on 26th May 1970 sections 1 to 5, 9(1) and 10 of the Administration of Justice Act 1969, together with the relevant consequential amendments and repeals. These are the only provisions of the Act not already in force and they increase the jurisdiction of the county court; amend section 47 of the County Courts Act 1959 (which relates to the costs of actions brought in the High Court which could have been brought in a county court); and enable increased jurisdiction to be conferred on county court registrars. The Order also makes the necessary transitional provisions.

(a) 1964 c. iv.

1970 No. 673 (L.15)

COUNTY COURTS

PROCEDURE

The County Court (Amendment No. 3) Rules 1970

Made - - -	30*th April* 1970
Coming into Operation	26*th May* 1970

1.—(1) These Rules may be cited as the County Court (Amendment No. 3) Rules 1970.

(2) In these Rules an Order and Rule referred to by number means the Order and Rule so numbered in the County Court Rules 1936(**a**), as amended (**b**); Appendices B and D mean respectively Appendices B and D to those Rules, and a form referred to by number means the form so numbered in Appendix A to those Rules.

(3) The Interpretation Act 1889(**c**) shall apply for the interpretation of these Rules as it applies for the interpretation of an Act of Parliament.

2. In each of the following Rules, for the words "£500" wherever they appear there shall be substituted the words "£750":—

Order 7, Rules 1(2) and 2;

Order 15, Rule 8;

Order 27, Rules 2 and 3; and

Order 28, Rule 16(3)(*d*).

3. Order 13 shall be amended as follows:—

(1) For paragraph (1) of Rule 4A, there shall be substituted the following paragraph:—

"(1) Where the same judge is the judge for two or more districts and proceedings which are to be heard and determined by him are pending in the court for one of those districts, the judge or, by leave of the judge, the registrar of that court may at any time, upon application or of his own motion, direct that the

(**a**) S.R. & O. 1936/626 (1936 I, p. 282).
(**b**) The relevant amending instruments are S.R. & O. 1937/239, 1938/18, 731, 1475, 1939/815, 1942/1070, S.I. 1950/1231, 1993, 1951/1354, 1952/2198, 1953/1728, 1955/1799, 1956/1851, 1957/174, 1136, 1958/2226, 1959/1251, 1960/1275, 1961/1526, 1965/2147, 1969/585, 1970/204 (1937 I, p. 532; 1938 I, pp. 977, 986, 990; 1939 I, p. 469; 1942 I, p. 91; 1950 I, pp. 400, 440; 1951 I, p. 357; 1952 I, p. 635; 1953 I, p. 404; 1955 I, p. 530; 1956 I, p. 545; 1957 I, pp. 512, 517; 1958 I, p. 372; 1959 I, p. 795; 1960 I, p. 809; 1961 II, p. 3177; 1965 III, p. 6292; 1969 I, p. 1551; 1970 I, p. 911). (**c**) 1889 c.63.

hearing in those proceedings shall take place in the court for another of those districts".

(2) For Rule 8, there shall be substituted the following Rule :—

Application for injunction

"8.—(1) An application for the grant of an injunction may be made to the judge by any party to an action or matter before or after the trial or hearing, whether or not a claim for the injunction was included in that party's particulars of claim, originating application, petition, counterclaim or third party notice, as the case may be.

(2) Where the applicant is the plaintiff and the case is one of urgency, the application may be made *ex parte* on affidavit but, except as aforesaid, the application must be made on notice.

(3) The plaintiff may not make an application before the issue of the summons, originating application or petition by which the action or matter is to be commenced except where the case is one of urgency and in that case—

(*a*) the affidavit on which the application is made shall show that the action or matter is one which the court to which the application is made has jurisdiction to hear and determine, and

(*b*) the injunction applied for shall, if granted, be on terms providing for the issue of the summons, originating application or petition in the court granting the application and on such other terms, if any, as the judge thinks fit."

4. In Order 22, Rules 3 and 6, for the words "£30" wherever they appear there shall be substituted the words "£75".

5. Order 23 shall be amended as follows :—

(1) In Rules 1, 4 and 5, for the words "£30" wherever they appear there shall be substituted the words "£75";

(2) Rule 13 shall be revoked.

6. In Order 25, Rule 24(2), for the words "£10" there shall be substituted the words "£20".

7. At the end of Order 31, Rule 12, there shall be added the words "or, except as provided by Order 47, Rule 42(6), to a review of taxation where the judge exercises his power to appoint assessors without any application being made by any party to the proceedings."

8. Order 47 shall be amended as follows :—

(1) In Rule 5(1) for the words "three Higher Scales, namely Scale 1, Scale 2 and Scale 3" there shall be substituted the words "four Higher Scales, namely Scale 1, Scale 2, Scale 3 and Scale 4".

(2) For the table set out in Rule 5(3) there shall be substituted the following table :—

" Sum of Money	Scale applicable
Exceeding £5 and not exceeding £20	Lower Scale
Exceeding £20 and not exceeding £50	Scale 1
Exceeding £50 and not exceeding £200	Scale 2
Exceeding £200 and not exceeding £500	Scale 3
Exceeding £500	Scale 4 "

(3) For the words "Scale 2 or 3" in paragraph (1) of Rule 21 there shall be substituted the words "Scale 2, 3 or 4" and for the words "Scale 3" in paragraph (5) of that Rule there shall be substituted the words "Scale 3 or 4".

(4) In Rule 29(2) for the words "Scale 3" there shall be substituted the words "Scale 3 or 4".

(5) For paragraph (4) of Rule 42 there shall be substituted the following paragraph :—

"(4) Any party who is dissatisfied with the registrar's decision to allow or disallow any item in whole or in part, or with the amount allowed by the registrar, on his reconsideration of a taxation may apply for a review of the taxation by the judge."

(6) After paragraph (5) of Rule 42 there shall be inserted the following paragraph :—

"(6) If the judge sees fit to exercise in relation to the application his power to appoint assessors under section 91 of the Act without any application being made by any party to the proceedings, he shall appoint not less than two assessors, of whom one shall be a registrar, and Order 31, Rules 7 and 9, shall apply as if the assessors had been summoned on the application of a party."

(7) The existing paragraph (6) of Rule 42 shall stand as paragraph (7).

(8) The following Rule shall be added after Rule 49 :—

Personal liability of solicitor for costs

"50.—(1) Subject to the following provisions of this Rule, where in any proceedings costs are incurred improperly or without reasonable cause or are wasted by undue delay or by any other misconduct or default, the judge may make against any solicitor whom he considers to be responsible (whether personally or through a servant or agent) an order—

(*a*) disallowing the costs as between the solicitor and his client, and

(*b*) directing the solicitor to repay to his client costs which the client has been ordered to pay to other parties to the proceedings ; or

(*c*) directing the solicitor personally to indemnify such other parties against costs payable by them.

(2) No order under this Rule shall be made against a solicitor unless he has been given a reasonable opportunity to appear before the judge and show cause why the order should not be made, except where any proceeding in court or in chambers cannot conveniently proceed, and fails or is adjourned without useful progress being made,—

(*a*) because of the failure of the solicitor to attend in person or by a proper representative ; or

(*b*) because of the failure of the solicitor to deliver any document for the use of the court which ought to have been delivered or to be prepared with any proper evidence or account or otherwise to proceed.

(3) Before making an order under this Rule the judge may, if he thinks fit, refer the matter (save in the cases excepted from paragraph (2)) to the registrar for inquiry and report and direct the solicitor in the first place to show cause before the registrar.

(4) The judge may direct that notice of any proceedings or order against a solicitor under this Rule shall be given to his client in such manner as may be specified in the direction."

9. In Form 87 after the words "the Judge" there shall be inserted the words "[*or* Registrar]".

10. In the recital in Form 98, for the words "£500" there shall be substituted the words "£5,000".

11. In Forms 113, 114 and 273, for the words "£10" wherever they appear there shall be substituted the words "£50".

12. In Form 124 and Form 125, for the words "£5" wherever they appear there shall be substituted the words "£20".

13. In Form 205 and Form 222, for the words "£500" wherever they appear there shall be substituted the words "£750".

14. In Forms 231 and 381, for the words "£100" wherever they appear there shall be substituted the words "£400".

15. Form 266 shall be amended—

(*a*) by substituting for the words "twenty pounds" the words "£50 [*or in the case of rescuing goods* £20]"; and

(*b*) by deleting the word "(and)" appearing before the words "for rescuing".

16. Appendix B shall be amended as follows:—

(1) In items 29(*a*) and (*b*), for the figures "10 0" in Scale 2 there shall be substituted the figures "13 0".

(2) For items 35, 36 and 37, there shall be substituted the following item:—

	Scale 1	*Scale* 2	*Scale* 3
	£ s.	£ s.	£ s.
"35. Where the solicitor does not carry on business within two miles of the place of trial of an action or matter, the place of hearing of an application to which item 8 relates, the place of inspection of documents or the place where a taxation is carried out—			
(*a*) the travelling and out of pocket expenses reasonably incurred by him in attending that place; or ...	—	—	—
(*b*) if an agent is employed, for correspondence with the agent ...	1 0	2 0	3 0

Note. Where in the opinion of the registrar, it would have been reasonable to employ a solicitor carrying on business nearer to the relevant place, he shall not allow under paragraph (*a*) more than he would have allowed to such a solicitor."

(3) There shall be inserted on the right-hand side of the column headed "*Scale* 3" an additional column headed "*Scale* 4" and the following amounts shall be inserted in that column opposite the items to which they relate:—

Item No.	*Amount to be inserted*
1	£2 to £8
2(*a*)	£1.10 to £4
(*b*)	10s.
and for every folio or part thereof beyond 5	2s.
3(*a*)	—
(*b*)	1s.
(*c*)	1s.
4	5s.
and per folio beyond 5	1s.
5	Such sum as is fair and reasonable in all the circumstances *not exceeding* £125
6(*a*)	£5 to £35
(*b*)	£3 to £12
7(*a*)	£5 to £15
(*b*)	£1.10 to £8
8(*a*)	£3 to £15
(*b*)	£3 to £7
9	£2.10
10(*a*)	£3 to £5
(*b*)	£3
11	£2 to £4
12(*a*)	£1.10
(*b*)	£1.10
(*c*)	£1
(*d*)	£2
13(*a*)	£3 to £10
(*b*)	£2 to £5
14(*a*)	£3
(*b*)	£2
15	15s.
16	15s.
17	15s.
18	£1 to £2
19(*a*) (*b*)	5s.
20(*a*)	£3.10 to £5
(*b*)	£1.10
21	—
22	10s.
23	15s.
24	5s.
25(*a*)	£3 to £12
(*b*)	£2 to £5

Item No.	*Amount to be inserted*
26	£9 to £45
27	£4
28	£2.10
and for leading counsel if case certified fit for more counsel than one	£3.10
29(*a*) (*b*)	£3 to £23
(*c*)	£3 to £14
30(*a*)	£4 to £6
(*b*)	£4 to £6
31	—
32(*a*)	
(*b*)	
(*c*)	—
33	—
34(*a*)	£5
(*b*)	—
35(*a*)	—
(*b*)	£4.

(4) After the number of each of the following items there shall be inserted an asterisk:—

items 1, 2, 5, 6, 7, 8, 18, 26, 29 and 30;

and at the end of the Appendix there shall be inserted the following note:—

"*These items are subject to increase under Order 47, Rule 21(3)."

17. Appendix D shall be amended as follows:—

(1) In paragraph 4 of Part I for the words "3*s*." there shall be substituted the words "5*s*.".

(2) The following new Part shall be added at the end:—

"PART III

JUDGMENT SUMMONSES AND APPLICATIONS ON LOWER SCALE

The following Table shows the amount to be allowed where costs awarded on the Lower Scale fall to be fixed and allowed without taxation under Order 25, Rule 66(2)(*b*), or Order 47, Rule 37(4).

	Amount to be allowed
1. For each attendance on the hearing of a judgment summons	£1
2. For making or opposing an application in the course of or relating to the proceedings.	£1
3. For making or opposing an application for a new trial or to set aside a judgment	£1. 10s"

We, the undersigned members of the Rule Committee appointed by the Lord Chancellor under section 102 of the County Courts Act 1959(**a**), having by virtue of the powers vested in us in this behalf made the foregoing Rules, do hereby certify the same under our hand and submit them to the Lord Chancellor accordingly.

D. O. McKee.
Connolly H. Gage.
Hugh Mais.
H. S. Ruttle.
David Pennant.
W. Ralph Davies.
E. A. Everett.
Arthur Figgis.
A. F. Stapleton Cotton.
D. A. Marshall.

I allow these Rules, which shall come into operation on 26th May 1970.

Dated 30th April 1970.

Gardiner, C.

EXPLANATORY NOTE

(*This Note is not part of the Rules.*)

Most of the provisions of these Rules are occasioned by the coming into force of those sections of the Administration of Justice Act 1969 which specially affect county courts and, in particular, increase their jurisdiction. A new Higher Scale 4 is prescribed for costs on claims exceeding £500, and appropriate changes are made in the relevant rules and forms (Rules 2, 8, 10, 13 and 16). The limit of the registrar's jurisdiction is raised from £30 to £75 (Rules 4 and 5). Fresh provision is made with respect to applications for injunctions, including applications made before the commencement of proceedings (Rules 3(2) and 5(2)). The judge is enabled to review a taxation of costs on a question of quantum, and provision is made for the summoning of assessors on a review (Rule 8(5) and (6)). The registrar is given power, by leave of the judge, to direct proceedings to be heard at another court of the same judge (Rule 3(1)). A solicitor may be made personally responsible for costs incurred through his misconduct or default (Rule 8(8)). Various forms are amended to reflect increases in some of the fines which may be imposed under the County Courts Act 1959 (Rules 11, 12 and 15). Among the remaining miscellaneous amendments the most important are those relating to the costs of judgment summonses and other proceedings on the Lower Scale (Rules 6 and 17(2)).

(**a**) 1959 c. 22.

STATUTORY INSTRUMENTS

1970 No. 675

RIGHTS OF WAY

The National Parks and Access to the Countryside (Amendment) Regulations 1970

Made - - -	1*st May* 1970
Laid before Parliament	11*th May* 1970
Coming into Operation	26*th May* 1970

The Minister of Housing and Local Government, in exercise of his powers under sections 38(1) and 110 of the National Parks and Access to the Countryside Act 1949(**a**) and of all other powers enabling him in that behalf, hereby makes the following regulations :—

1.—(1) These regulations may be cited as the National Parks and Access to the Countryside (Amendment) Regulations 1970 and shall come into operation on 26th May 1970.

(2) The Interpretation Act 1889(**b**) shall apply to the interpretation of these regulations as it applies to the interpretation of an Act of Parliament.

2. Regulation 2 of the National Parks and Access to the Countryside (Amendment) Regulations 1963(**c**) is hereby revoked.

3. The following regulation shall be substituted for regulation 5 of the National Parks and Access to the Countryside Regulations 1950(**d**) :—

"5. Rights of way or alleged rights of way shall be shown on a rights of way map in any of the following manners :—

Footpath, by a continuous purple line, or by a continuous line with short bars at intervals, as thus :—

or by a broken black line with short intervals, as thus :—

Bridleway, by a continuous green line, or by a continuous line with cross bars, at intervals, as thus :—

(**a**) 1949 c. 97.
(**b**) 1889 c. 63.
(**c**) S.I. 1963/968 (1963 II, p. 1609).
(**d**) S.I. 1950/1066 (1950 II, p. 186).

or by a broken line with cross bars in the intervals, as thus :—

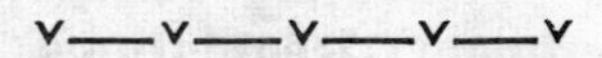

Road used as a public path or byway open to all traffic by a broken green line, or by a broken line and small arrowheads, as thus :—

v—v—v—v—v

Given under the official seal of the Minister of Housing and Local Government on 1st May 1970.

(L.S.)

Anthony Greenwood,
Minister of Housing and Local Government.

EXPLANATORY NOTE

(This Note is not part of the Regulations.)

These regulations, made by the Minister of Housing and Local Government after consultation with the Secretary of State for Wales, replace regulation 5 of the National Parks and Access to the Countryside Regulations 1950, as amended by regulation 2 of the National Parks and Access to the Countryside Regulations 1963.

The regulations make provision for alternative notations for rights of way maps under Part IV of the National Parks and Access to the Countryside Act 1949, as amended by the Countryside Act 1968 (1968 c. 41), in order to facilitate the reproduction of those maps in monochrome. The regulations repeat the provisions of the said regulation 2, with an addition to provide notations for byways open to all traffic. The addition takes account of the provisions of Part III of Schedule 3 to the Countryside Act 1968.

STATUTORY INSTRUMENTS

1970 No. 677

PROBATION AND AFTER-CARE

The Probation (Conditions of Service) (Amendment) Rules 1970

Made - - -	1*st May* 1970
Coming into Operation	1*st May* 1970

In pursuance of the powers conferred on me by Schedule 5 to the Criminal Justice Act 1948(**a**) and section 1 of the Police, Fire and Probation Officers Remuneration Act 1956(**b**), I hereby make the following Rules :—

1.—(1) These Rules may be cited as the Probation (Conditions of Service) (Amendment) Rules 1970.

(2) These Rules shall come into operation forthwith and shall take effect from 1st April 1970.

2. For Schedule 1 to the Probation (Conditions of Service) Rules 1965(**c**), as substituted by Rule 2 of the Probation (Conditions of Service) (Amendment) Rules 1968(**d**), there shall be substituted the following Schedule :—

"SCHEDULE 1 Rule 2

TABLE

SCALE OF ANNUAL SALARY FOR SENIOR PROBATION OFFICERS

Column 1 Length of Service	Column 2 Rate of Annual Salary
	£
Up to 1 year's service	2,046
Over 1 and up to 2 years' service	2,115
Over 2 and up to 3 years' service	2,187
Over 3 and up to 4 years' service	2,259
Over 4 years' service	2,331 "

(**a**) 1948 c. 58.
(**b**) 1956 c. 1 (5 & 6 Eliz. 2).
(**c**) S.I. 1965/722 (1965 I, p. 2230).
(**d**) S.I. 1968/386 (1968 I, p. 1043).

3. For Schedule 2 to the said Rules of 1965, as substituted by Rule 3 of the said Rules of 1968, there shall be substituted the following Schedule :—

"SCHEDULE 2 Rule 3(1)

TABLE

SCALE OF ANNUAL SALARY FOR PROBATION OFFICERS

Column 1 Length of Service	Column 2 Rate of Annual Salary
	£
Up to 1 year's service	975
Over 1 and up to 2 years' service	1,035
Over 2 and up to 3 years' service	1,095
Over 3 and up to 4 years' service	1,155
Over 4 and up to 5 years' service	1,215
Over 5 and up to 6 years' service	1,275
Over 6 and up to 7 years' service	1,341
Over 7 and up to 8 years' service	1,404
Over 8 and up to 9 years' service	1,476
Over 9 and up to 10 years' service	1,551
Over 10 and up to 11 years' service	1,626
Over 11 and up to 12 years' service	1,701
Over 12 and up to 13 years' service	1,776
Over 13 years' service	1,851 "

4. At the end of Rule 2(2) of the said Rules of 1965 (which specifies the reckonable service of senior probation officers) there shall be added the following sub-paragraph :—

"(*c*) such other period of employment (not being employment as a probation officer) before the commencement of his current period of continuous service as the Secretary of State at the request of the probation and after-care committee employing him approves.".

James Callaghan,
One of Her Majesty's Principal Secretaries of State.

Home Office,
Whitehall.
1st May 1970.

EXPLANATORY NOTE

(*This Note is not part of the Rules.*)

These Rules amend the Probation (Conditions of Service) Rules 1965 by introducing higher scales of annual salary for senior probation officers and probation officers, and by enabling the Secretary of State to approve, in the case of the former rank, the counting of outside service for calculating the starting point on the salary scale. The Rules, in pursuance of the powers conferred by section 1 of the Police, Fire and Probation Officers Remuneration Act 1956, take effect from 1st April 1970.

1970 No. 678

WILD BIRDS

The Wild Birds (Various Species) Order 1970

Made - - -	30*th April* 1970
Coming into Operation	18*th May* 1970

In exercise of the power conferred on me by sections 9(1) and 13(1) of the Protection of Birds Act 1954(**a**), and after consulting the Advisory Committee on the Protection of Birds for England and Wales, I hereby make the following Order :—

1.—(1) This Order may be cited as the Wild Birds (Various Species) Order 1970 and shall come into operation on 18th May 1970.

(2) In this Order "the Act" means the Protection of Birds Act 1954.

2. The wild birds specified in Schedule 1 to this Order shall, with respect to England and Wales, be added to Part I of Schedule 1 to the Act (which confers protection by special penalties at all times).

3. The wild birds specified in Schedule 2 to this Order shall, with respect to England and Wales, be removed from Part I of Schedule 1 to the Act.

4. The two following wild birds shall, with respect to England and Wales, be removed from Part II of Schedule 1 to the Act (which confers protection by special penalties during the close season) and shall be added to Part I of that Schedule, namely brambling and black-tailed godwit.

5. Wild geese of the species grey lag goose shall, with respect to England and Wales, be removed from Part II of Schedule 1 to the Act and shall be added to Schedule 3 to the Act (which specifies wild birds which may be killed or taken outside the close season).

6. The Wild Birds (Bramblings and Black-Tailed Godwits) Order 1957(**b**) is hereby revoked.

7. In accordance with the provisions of this Order and of the other subsisting Orders (**c**) by which birds have been added to, or removed from, Schedule 1, 2 or 3 to the Act, those Schedules have effect, with respect to England and Wales, as set out in the Appendix to this Order.

James Callaghan,
One of Her Majesty's Principal
Secretaries of State.

Home Office,
Whitehall.
30th April 1970.

(**a**) 1954 c. 30.
(**b**) S.I. 1957/318 (1957 II, p. 3061).
(**c**) S.I. 1955/354; 1956/25, 500; 1961/482; 1962/2592; 1963/1244; 1966/1575 (1962 III, p. 3483; 1966 III, p. 4856).

Article 2

SCHEDULE 1

WILD BIRDS TO BE ADDED TO PART I OF SCHEDULE 1

Bluethroat
Crake, spotted
Crossbill
Diver, all species
Fieldfare
Firecrest
Harrier, all species
Kingfisher
Owl, snowy
Quail, European
Redwing
Sandpiper, wood
Serin
Tern, little
Warbler, Savi's
Woodlark

Article 3

SCHEDULE 2

WILD BIRDS TO BE REMOVED FROM PART I OF SCHEDULE 1

Bustard
Crossbill, common
Diver, black-throated
Diver, great northern
Diver, red-throated
Hen-harrier
Marsh-harrier
Montagu's harrier
Quail, common
Roller
Swan, Bewick's
Wren, St. Kilda

Article 7

APPENDIX

Sections 1, 4, 6, 9.

SCHEDULE 1

WILD BIRDS AND THEIR EGGS PROTECTED BY SPECIAL PENALTIES

PART I

AT ALL TIMES

Avocet
Bee-eater, all species
Bittern, all species
Bluethroat
Brambling
Bunting, snow
Buzzard, honey
Chough
Corncrake (landrail)
Crake, spotted
Crossbill
Diver, all species
Dotterel
Eagle, all species
Fieldfare
Firecrest
Godwit, black-tailed
Goshawk
Grebe, black-necked
Grebe, Slavonian
Greenshank
Harrier, all species
Hobby
Hoopoe
Kingfisher
Kite
Merlin
Oriole, golden
Osprey
Owl, barn
Owl, snowy
Peregrine
Phalarope, red-necked
Plover, Kentish
Plover, little ringed
Quail, European
Redstart, black
Redwing
Ruff and reeve
Sandpiper, wood
Serin
Shrike, red-backed
Sparrow-hawk
Spoonbill
Stilt, black-winged
Stint, Temminck's
Stone curlew
Swan, whooper
Tern, black
Tern, little
Tern, roseate
Tit, bearded
Tit, crested
Warbler, Dartford
Warbler, marsh
Warbler, Savi's
Woodlark
Wryneck

PART II

DURING THE CLOSE SEASON

Whimbrel
Wild duck of the following species—
 Common scoter
 Garganey teal
 Goldeneye
 Long-tailed duck
 Scaup-duck
 Velvet scoter

SCHEDULE 2

Sections 2, 3, 5, 9, 10.

WILD BIRDS WHICH MAY BE KILLED OR TAKEN AT ANY TIME BY AUTHORISED PERSONS

Bullfinch (only in certain areas (a))
Cormorant
Crow, carrion
Crow, hooded
Domestic pigeon gone feral
Gull, greater black-backed
Gull, lesser black-backed
Gull, herring
Jackdaw
Jay
Magpie
Oyster-catcher (only in certain areas(b))
Rook
Shag
Sparrow, house
Starling
Stock-dove
Wood-pigeon

SCHEDULE 3

Sections 2, 6, 7, 9.

WILD BIRDS WHICH MAY BE KILLED OR TAKEN OUTSIDE THE CLOSE SEASON

Any wild bird included in Part II of Schedule 1 to this Act.

Capercaillie
Coot
Curlew (other than stone curlew)
Godwit, bar-tailed
Moorhen
Plover, golden
Plover, grey
Redshank, common
Snipe, common
Snipe, jack

Wild duck of the following species—
 Common pochard
 Gadwall
 Mallard
 Pintail
 Shoveler
 Teal
 Tufted duck
 Wigeon

Wild geese of the following species—
 Bean-goose
 Canada goose
 Grey lag goose
 Pink-footed goose
 White-fronted goose
Woodcock

(a) *See* S.I. 1955/354; 1961/482. (b) *See* S.I. 1956/25, 500; 1963/1244.

EXPLANATORY NOTE

(*This Note is not part of the Order.*)

Any person who at any time commits an offence under the Protection of Birds Act 1954 in respect of a bird included in Part I of Schedule 1 to the Act or in respect of the nest or egg of such a bird is liable to special penalties. This Order, which has effect in England and Wales, adds the birds listed in Schedule 1 to, and in Article 4 of, the Order to Part I of Schedule 1 to the Act and removes those listed in Schedule 2 to the Order from that Part so that the latter enjoy only the general protection under the Act afforded to the majority of wildbird species. The grey lag goose is removed from Part II of Schedule 1 to the Act and added to Schedule 3, so that it will no longer be protected by special penalties during the close season and may be killed or taken outside that season. Schedules 1, 2 and 3 to the Act will now have effect, in England and Wales, as set out in the Appendix to the Order. The present changes are shown in bold type in the Schedules to the Order and the Appendix except where they relate to nomenclature only.

STATUTORY INSTRUMENTS

1970 No. 679

CUSTOMS AND EXCISE

The Anti-Dumping (Provisional Charge to Duty) (No. 3) Order 1970

Made - - - - -	*4th May* 1970
Laid before the House of Commons - -	*8th May* 1970
Coming into Operation -	*9th May* 1970

The Board of Trade in pursuance of the powers conferred upon them by sections 1, 2, 8 and 9(3) of the Customs Duties (Dumping and Subsidies) Act 1969(**a**), hereby make the following Order:—

1. This Order may be cited as the Anti-Dumping (Provisional Charge to Duty) (No. 3) Order 1970 and shall come into operation on 9th May 1970.

2. Goods of the description set out in the Schedule hereto (being goods classified in the Customs Tariff 1959(**b**) under the heading mentioned in the first column of that Schedule) shall be subject to a provisional charge to duty in respect of a duty of customs at the rate set out in the third column of that Schedule.

3. Section 2 of the Customs Duties (Dumping and Subsidies) Act 1969 (which allows relief to be given where goods are shown not to have been dumped or where the margin of dumping is less than the provisional charge) shall apply to the provisional charge imposed by this Order.

Gwyneth Dunwoody,
Parliamentary Secretary
to the Board of Trade.

4th May 1970.

SCHEDULE

Relevant Tariff Heading	Description of Goods	Relevant Rate
ex 28.28 (P)	Zirconium dioxide originating in the Union of Soviet Socialist Republics	£275 per ton

(**a**) 1969 c. 16. (**b**) *see* S.I. 1969/1413 (1969 III, p. 4150).

EXPLANATORY NOTE

(*This Note is not part of the Order.*)

This Order makes imports of zirconium dioxide originating in the Union of Soviet Socialist Republics subject to a provisional charge in respect of an anti-dumping duty.

The making of the Order enables the Commissioners of Customs and Excise to require security for the payment of any anti-dumping duty which may be imposed retrospectively on such imports under section 8(1) of the Customs Duties (Dumping and Subsidies) Act 1969. If any duty is imposed retrospectively, it may only be so imposed on goods imported while the Order is in force, and its rate may not exceed the rate mentioned in the Schedule to the Order.

The Order expires automatically after three months unless previously revoked or extended (for not more than three months) by a further Order.

The Order applies section 2 of the 1969 Act to the charge, which enables relief to be granted where particular goods have not been dumped or the margin of dumping is less than the amount of the provisional charge.

STATUTORY INSTRUMENTS

1970 No. 682 (S. 48)

COURT OF SESSION, SCOTLAND

Act of Sederunt (Rules of Court Amendment No. 3) 1970

Made - - -	1*st May* 1970
Coming into Operation	1*st June* 1970

The Lords of Council and Session, under and by virtue of the powers conferred upon them by section 2 of the Courts of Law Fees (Scotland) Act 1895**(a)** and section 16 of the Administration of Justice (Scotland) Act 1933**(b)** and of all other powers competent to them in that behalf, with the approval of the Treasury for the exercise of the said powers under section 2 of the Courts of Law Fees (Scotland) Act 1895**(a)**, do hereby enact and declare as follows:—

1. Section I of Rule 346 of the Rules of Court**(c)**, as applied by paragraph 2 of the Act of Sederunt (Rules of Court Amendment No. 3) 1969**(d)**, shall cease to have effect.

2. Rule 346 of the Rules of Court**(c)**, as substituted by paragraph 1(2) of the Act of Sederunt (Rules of Court Amendment No. 2) 1969**(e)**, shall be amended by the addition after Section H of a Section I as set forth in the Schedule annexed hereto.

3. This Act of Sederunt may be cited as the Act of Sederunt (Rules of Court Amendment No. 3) 1970, and shall come into operation on 1st June 1970.

And the Lords appoint this Act of Sederunt to be inserted in the Books of Sederunt.

J. L. CLYDE

I.P.D.

Edinburgh,
1st May 1970.

SCHEDULE

I.—*ACCOUNTANT OF COURT'S DEPARTMENT*

I.—*In Factories and Curatories*

	£	s.	d.
1. For registering case and receiving and delivering up Bond of Caution:			
In Court of Session appointments	2	0	0
In Sheriff Court appointments	1	10	0
2. For examining factor's Inventory where estate:			
(*a*) does not exceed £500	1	0	0
(*b*) exceeds £500—for first £500	1	0	0
plus an additional fee of £1 for each further £1,000 or part thereof, but fee not to exceed £20			
3. For each search of the records		4	0
plus 6s. correspondence fee if applicable			

(a) 1895 c. 14. (b) 1933 c. 41. (c) S.I. 1965/321 (1965 I,p. 803).
(d) S.I. 1969/1702 (1969 III, p. 5359).
(e) S.I. 1969/475 (1969 I, p. 1362).

	£.	s.	d.
4. For auditing each Account:			
(*a*) where factor's commissions is £4 or less, or where no commission is allowable	1	0	0
(*b*) where factor's commission is above £4, the fee shall be ...	1	0	0
plus 15 per cent on the factor's commission as fixed (or what would have been the factor's full commission if chargeable or fully allowed)			
5. For reporting *re* Discharge, Special Powers or on other special matters	1 to 12	0 to 0	0 to 0
6. For report on scheme of division	2	0	0
plus £1 extra for each £1,000, or part thereof, to be divided amongst the preferable and ordinary creditors; but fee not to exceed £25			
7. For certificate under Seal		10	0

II.—*In Bankruptcies*

	£.	s.	d.
8. For registering case, and related work	1	0	0
9. For supervising proceedings in sequestration 1½ per cent on amount to be divided amongst preferable and ordinary creditors			
10. For report on bankrupt's petition for discharge	2	0	0
11. For concurrences in private sale of heritage, if £1,000 or under ...	2	0	0
plus £1 extra for each additional £1,000 or part thereof, but not to exceed £12			
12. For special report	2	0	0
13. For report on appeal against trustee's commission	1	0	0
plus 2 per cent on the trustee's commission as fixed, but not to exceed £20			
14. For each inspection of sederunt book or search of the records... ...		4	0
plus 6s. correspondence fee if applicable			
15. For auditing the accounts and fixing the commission of trustee under voluntary trust deed, 12½ per cent on commission allowed to trustee			
16. For examining and issuing acknowledgment for sederunt book ...	3	0	0

III.—*In Consignations*

	£.	s.	d.
17. For lodging Consignation		4	0
18. For producing or delivering up		4	0
plus 2s. for every £100 or part thereof uplifted, but not to exceed £3			
19. For examining Register		4	0
plus 6s. correspondence fee if applicable			

IV.—*Copying Fees*

	£.	s.	d.
20. For photostats or other copies, each foolscap page		2	0

V.—*Liquidations*

	£.	s.	d.
21. For receiving and uplifting Bond of Caution		10	0

EXPLANATORY NOTE

(*This Note is not part of the Act of Sederunt.*)

This Act of Sederunt prescribes a new table of Fee-fund Dues in the Department of the Accountant of Court.

1970 No. 684 (S. 50)

NATIONAL HEALTH SERVICE (SCOTLAND)

The National Health Service (Constitution of Standing Advisory Committees) (Scotland) Amendment Order 1970

Made - - - 30*th April* 1970

The Secretary of State in exercise of the powers conferred on him by section 2(3) of the National Health Service (Scotland) Act 1947(**a**) and after consulting the Scottish Health Services Council, hereby makes the following order:—

1. This order may be cited as the National Health Service (Constitution of Standing Advisory Committees) (Scotland) Amendment Order 1970.

2. This order, the National Health Service (Constitution of Standing Advisory Committees) (Scotland) Order 1948(**b**) (hereinafter referred to as "the principal order") the National Health Service (Constitution of Standing Advisory Committees) (Scotland) Amendment Order 1959(**c**) and the National Health Service (Constitution of Standing Advisory Committees) (Scotland) Amendment Order 1960(**d**) shall be read as one and may be cited as the National Health Service (Constitution of Standing Advisory Committees) (Scotland) Orders 1948 to 1970.

3. The Interpretation Act 1889(**e**) shall apply for the interpretation of this order as it applies for the interpretation of an Act of Parliament.

4. At the end of the schedule to the principal order as amended there shall be added in the columns indicated the words and numbers specified in the Schedule to this order.

Given under the seal of the Secretary of State for Scotland.

(L.S.)

R. E. C. Johnson,
Secretary.

Scottish Home and Health Department,
St. Andrew's House,
Edinburgh.
30th April 1970.

(**a**) 1947 c. 27.
(**b**) S.I. 1948/1875 (Rev. XV, p. 818: 1948 I, p. 2453).
(**c**) S.I. 1959/400 (1959 I, p. 1825).
(**d**) S.I. 1960/2438 (1960 II, p. 2111).
(**e**) 1889 c. 63.

SCHEDULE

(Column 1)	(Column 2)	(Column 3)	(Column 4)
Standing Advisory Committee on Ophthalmic Services	All Ophthalmic Services to which Parts II and IV of the Act apply	2	6

EXPLANATORY NOTE

(*This Note is not part of the Order.*)

This Order constitutes the Standing Advisory Committee on Ophthalmic Services to advise the Secretary of State and the Scottish Health Services Council on the administration and development of ophthalmic services in Scotland and fixes the maximum numbers of members to be appointed to this Committee by the Council itself and by the Secretary of State.

1970 No. 686

NATIONAL HEALTH SERVICE, ENGLAND AND WALES

The National Health Service (The University Hospital of Wales (Cardiff) Designation) Order 1970

Made - - -	5*th May* 1970
Laid before Parliament	13*th May* 1970
Coming into Operation	1*st October* 1970

The Secretary of State for Wales, being satisfied that the group of hospitals specified in Schedule 1 to this order and vested in him is to provide for the University of Wales facilities for undergraduate and post-graduate clinical teaching and after consultation with that University, in exercise of his powers under section 5 of the Health Services and Public Health Act 1968(**a**) and of all other powers enabling him in that behalf, hereby makes the following order:—

1.—(1) This order may be cited as the National Health Service (The University Hospital of Wales (Cardiff) Designation) Order 1970 and shall come into operation on 1st October 1970.

(2) The Interpretation Act 1889(**b**) applies to the interpretation of this order as it applies to the interpretation of an Act of Parliament.

2. The group of hospitals specified in Schedule 1 to this order (hereinafter in this order referred to as "the group") is hereby designated as a university hospital.

3. Part II of Schedule 3 to the National Health Service Act 1946(**c**) (Constitution of Hospital Management Committees) shall have effect in relation to the Committee appointed to exercise functions with respect to the management and control of the group, as modified and set out in Schedule 2 to this order.

(**a**) 1968 c. 46. (**b**) 1889 c. 63. (**c**) 1946 c. 81.

SCHEDULE 1

List of Hospitals

1. Cardiff Royal Infirmary (including William Nicholls Convalescent Home).
2. Maternity Hospital, Cardiff.
3. Llandough Hospital, Penarth.
4. Lord Pontypridd Hospital, Dulwich House, Cardiff.
5. St. David's Hospital, Cardiff.
6. Prince of Wales Orthopaedic Hospital (including the Out-Patient Clinic, The Walk, Cardiff).
7. Royal Hamadryad General and Seamen's Hospital, Cardiff.
8. Lansdowne Hospital, Cardiff.
9. Caerau Hospital.
10. Children's E.N.T. Hospital, Cardiff.
11. Barry Accident and Surgical Hospital.
12. Barry Neale-Kent Hospital.
13. Sully Hospital.
14. Glan Ely Hospital.
15. St. Mary's Hospital, Penarth.
16. Rookwood Hospital, Cardiff.
17. Barry Maternity Hospital.
18. Whitchurch Hospital.
19. Ely Hospital.
20. Velindre Hospital.
21. Caerphilly District Miners' Hospital (including Van Annexe).
22. Energlyn Hospital.
23. Gelligaer Hospital.
24. Ystrad Mynach Hospital.
25. University Hospital of Wales, Heath, Cardiff.
26. V.D. Clinic, Barry.
27. Chest Clinic, Cardiff.
28. Chest Clinic, Caerphilly.
29. Amy Evans Memorial Clinic, Barry.

SCHEDULE 2

Constitution of the University Hospital of Wales (Cardiff) Hospital Management Committee

The provisions of Part II of Schedule 3 to the National Health Service Act 1946 shall have effect as modified and set out below:—

(1) the Hospital Management Committee shall consist of a Chairman, appointed by the Welsh Hospital Board after consultation with the University of Wales, and 25 other members appointed by the Board;

(2) of the 25 other members 10 shall be nominated by the University of Wales, and of these 10 members 5 shall be nominated by the medical and dental teaching staff of the group;

(3) other members shall include persons appointed after consultation with the senior medical and dental staff of the group, and with such local health authorities, Executive Councils and other organisations as appear to the Board to be concerned;

(4) not more than 10 members shall be medical practitioners or dental practitioners of whom not more than 8 shall be persons nominated by the University under paragraph (2) of this Schedule;

(5) before making appointments to fill vacancies, the Board shall consult the Committee.

George Thomas,

Secretary of State for Wales.

5th May 1970.

EXPLANATORY NOTE

(*This Note is not part of the Order.*)

This order designates the group of hospitals set out in Schedule 1 as a university hospital, associated with the University of Wales, and provides for a modified form of Hospital Management Committee (as set out in Schedule 2) to manage and control it.

STATUTORY INSTRUMENTS

1970 No. 690 (L.15)

LEGAL AID AND ADVICE, ENGLAND

The Legal Aid (General) (Amendment) Regulations 1970

Made - - -	*4th May* 1970
Laid before Parliament	*12th May* 1970
Coming into Operation	*1st June* 1970

The Lord Chancellor in exercise of the powers conferred on him by sections 1, 2, 3, 4, 5, 6 and 12 of, and the Third Schedule to, the Legal Aid and Advice Act 1949(**a**) as amended by the Legal Aid Act 1960(**b**) hereby makes the following Regulations :—

1.—(1) These Regulations may be cited as the Legal Aid (General) (Amendment) Regulations 1970 and shall come into operation on 1st June 1970.

(2) The Interpretation Act 1889(**c**) shall apply to the interpretation of these Regulations as it applies to the interpretation of an Act of Parliament.

(3) In these Regulations a Regulation referred to by number means the Regulation so numbered in the Legal Aid (General) Regulations 1962(**d**) as amended (**e**).

2. In the Arrangements of Regulations at the beginning of the Legal Aid (General) Regulations 1962 after "24. Remuneration of Counsel and Solicitors in Magistrates' Courts, etc." there shall be inserted "24(A). The Lands Tribunal."

3. In Regulation 5(11) (which makes provision for applications for legal aid by persons concerned in proceedings only in a representative, fiduciary or official capacity) after the words "for the purpose of determining" there shall be inserted the words "whether legal aid is available or the amount of".

4. The following Regulation shall be inserted after Regulation 24 :—

"*The Lands Tribunal*

24(A).—(1) In this Regulation the expression "the Tribunal" means the Lands Tribunal as established by section 1(1)(*b*) of the Lands Tribunal Act 1949(**f**) and the expression "the Registrar" means the Registrar of the Tribunal.

(2) Except in so far as otherwise provided by this Regulation these Regulations shall apply to applications for legal aid for proceedings in the Tribunal and to the conduct of all proceedings in it for which a Civil Aid Certificate is granted in like manner as they apply to applications for legal aid for, and the conduct of, proceedings in any Court.

(**a**) 1949 c. 51. (**b**) 1960 c. 28. (**c**) 1889 c. 63.
(**d**) S.I. 1962/148 (1962 I, p. 117). (**e**) The relevant amending instruments are S.I. 1962/1714, 1965/865 (1962 II, p. 2122; 1965 I, p. 2340). (**f**) 1949 c. 42.

(3) Where any power to do any act or exercise any jurisdiction or discretion is conferred by these Regulations on a Court it shall be exercised by the Tribunal and may, unless it is exercisable only during the hearing of the proceedings, be exercised by the Registrar.

(4) The provisions of the Third Schedule to the Act (which relates to the remuneration to be paid to Counsel and Solicitors giving legal aid under Part 1 of the Act) shall apply to proceedings in the Tribunal as they apply to proceedings in a County Court.

(5) Notwithstanding anything in Regulation 19, the following provisions shall have effect in relation to proceedings in the Tribunal to which an assisted person is a party :—

(*a*) Where a final decision is given in writing by the Tribunal, it shall, in addition to any direction as to costs, contain a direction that the costs of any assisted person shall be taxed in accordance with the provisions of the Third Schedule to the Act and the costs shall be so taxed by the Registrar.

(*b*) Where the proceedings are brought to an end without a direction having been given under the foregoing sub-paragraph of this Regulation the costs of any assisted person shall be taxed by the Registrar in accordance with the Third Schedule to the Act.

(*c*) In taxing the costs of any assisted person the Registrar shall have power to determine the appropriate scale for the taxation, being a scale of costs prescribed by the Rules of the Supreme Court or by the County Court Rules."

Dated 4th May 1970.

Gardiner, C.

EXPLANATORY NOTE

(*This Note is not part of the Regulations.*)

These Regulations amend the Legal Aid (General) Regulations, as amended, so as to provide that the personal resources of an applicant concerned in proceedings only in a representative, fiduciary or official capacity shall not be taken into account in considering eligibility for legal aid, so as to apply the Regulations to legally aided proceedings in the Lands Tribunal and to make provision for the taxation of costs in those proceedings.

1970 No. 691

EXCHANGE CONTROL

The Exchange Control (Authorised Dealers and Depositaries) Order 1970

Made - - -	*6th May* 1970
Coming into Operation	*20th May* 1970

The Treasury, in exercise of the powers conferred upon them by sections 36(5) and 42(1) of the Exchange Control Act 1947(**a**), hereby make the following Order :—

1.—(1) This Order may be cited as the Exchange Control (Authorised Dealers and Depositaries) Order 1970, and shall come into operation on 20th May 1970.

(2) The Interpretation Act 1889(**b**) shall apply for the interpretation of this Order as it applies for the interpretation of an Act of Parliament.

2. Offices in the United Kingdom or the Channel Islands of the persons specified in Schedules 1 and 2 to this Order are authorised to act for the purposes of the said Act as authorised dealers in relation to gold.

3. Offices in the United Kingdom or the Channel Islands of the persons specified in Schedule 2 to this Order are authorised to act for the purposes of the said Act as authorised dealers in relation to all foreign currencies.

4. The following are authorised to act as authorised depositaries for the purposes of Part III of the said Act :—

(*a*) the Bank of England, and the Quotations Department of the Stock Exchange, London ;

(*b*) offices in the United Kingdom or the Channel Islands of the persons specified in Schedule 2 to this Order ;

(*c*) the persons specified in Schedule 3 to this Order.

5. The Orders specified in Schedule 4 to this Order are hereby revoked.

6. This Order shall extend to the Channel Islands, and any reference in this Order to the Exchange Control Act 1947 includes a reference to that Act as extended by the Exchange Control (Channel Islands) Order 1947(**c**).

Neil McBride,
Walter Harrison,
Two of the Lords Commissioners of Her Majesty's Treasury.

6th May 1970.

(**a**) 1947 c. 14.
(**b**) 1889 c. 63.
(**c**) S.R. & O. 1947/2034 (Rev. VI, p. 1001: 1947 I, p. 660).

SCHEDULE 1

Authorised Dealers in Gold

The Bank of England.
Mocatta & Goldsmid Ltd.
Sharps, Pixley & Co. Ltd.

SCHEDULE 2

Authorised Dealers in Gold and in all Foreign Currencies and Authorised Depositaries

Afghan National Bank Ltd.
African Continental Bank Ltd.
Algemene Bank Nederland N.V.
Allied Bank International.
American Express International Banking Corporation.
American National Bank and Trust Company of Chicago.
Anglo-Israel Bank Ltd.
Anglo-Portuguese Bank Ltd.
Ansbacher & Co. Ltd., Henry.
Arbuthnot Latham & Co., Ltd.
Atlantic International Bank Ltd.
Australia and New Zealand Bank Ltd.
Baer International Ltd., Julius.
Banco de Bilbao.
Banco Español en Londres, S.A.
Bangkok Bank Ltd.
Bank Melli Iran.
Bank of Adelaide.
Bank of America National Trust & Savings Association.
Bank of Baroda.
Bank of Ceylon.
Bank of China.
Bank of Cyprus (London) Ltd.
Bank of India.
Bank of Ireland.
Bank of Kobe, Ltd., The.
Bank of London & South America Ltd.
Bank of Montreal.
Bank of New South Wales.
Bank of New York, The.
Bank of New Zealand.
Bank of Nova Scotia.
Bank of Scotland.
Bank of Tokyo Ltd., The.
Bankers Trust Company.
Bankers Trust International Ltd.
Banque Belge Ltd.
Banque Belgo-Congolaise S.A.
Banque de l'Indochine.
Banque de Paris et des Pays-Bas.
Barclays Bank D.C.O.
Barclays Bank Ltd.
Barclays Bank (London and International) Ltd.
Baring Brothers & Co., Ltd.
Belfast Banking Company, Ltd.
Brandt's Sons & Co., Ltd., Wm.
British and Continental Banking Company Ltd.
British and French Bank Ltd.

British Bank of the Middle East, The.
British Linen Bank.
Brown, Shipley & Co. Ltd.
Burston & Texas Commerce Bank Ltd.
Canadian Imperial Bank of Commerce.
Central Bank of India.
Chartered Bank, The.
Charterhouse Japhet & Thomasson Ltd.
Chase and Bank of Ireland (International) Ltd.
Chase Manhattan Bank N.A., The.
Chemical Bank.
City National Bank of Detroit.
Clydesdale Bank Ltd.
Commercial Bank of Australia, Ltd.
Commercial Bank of the Near East Ltd.
Commercial Banking Company of Sydney, Ltd.
Commonwealth Trading Bank of Australia.
Continental Illinois National Bank and Trust Company of Chicago.
Co-operative Wholesale Society Ltd.
County Bank Ltd.
Coutts & Co.
Crédit Industriel et Commercial.
Crédit Lyonnais.
Crocker-Citizens National Bank.
Dai-Ichi Bank, Ltd., The.
Daiwa Bank Ltd., The.
Detroit Bank & Trust Company, The.
Discount Bank (Overseas) Ltd.
District Bank Ltd.
Eastern Bank, Ltd., The.
English, Scottish and Australian Bank, Ltd.
First National Bank of Boston, The.
First National Bank of Chicago, The.
First National City Bank.
First Pennsylvania Banking and Trust Company, The.
First Wisconsin National Bank of Milwaukee.
Fleming, Suez, Brown Brothers Ltd.
French Bank of Southern Africa Ltd.
Fuji Bank Ltd., The.
Ghana Commercial Bank.
Gibbs & Sons, Ltd., Antony.
Girard Trust Bank.
Glyn, Mills & Co.
Guinness Mahon & Co. Ltd.
Habib Bank (Overseas) Ltd.
Hambros Bank Ltd.
Hambros (Guernsey) Ltd.
Hambros (Jersey) Ltd.
Hibernian Bank Ltd.
Hill Samuel & Co. (Guernsey) Ltd.
Hill Samuel & Co. (Jersey) Ltd.
Hill Samuel & Co. Ltd.
Hoare & Co., C.
Hongkong & Shanghai Banking Corporation, The.
International Commercial Bank Ltd.
Ionian Bank Ltd.
Irving Trust Company.
Isle of Man Bank Ltd.
Israel-British Bank (London) Ltd.
Johnson Matthey (Bankers) Ltd.
Joseph & Sons, Ltd., Leopold.

Keyser Ullmann Ltd.
Kleinwort, Benson (Channel Islands) Ltd.
Kleinwort, Benson (Guernsey) Ltd.
Kleinwort, Benson Ltd.
Korea Exchange Bank.
Lazard Brothers & Co., Ltd.
Lloyds Bank Europe Ltd.
Lloyds Bank Ltd.
Manufacturers Hanover Trust Company.
Marine Midland Grace Trust Company of New York.
Mellon National Bank and Trust Company.
Mercantile Bank Ltd.
Midland and International Banks Ltd.
Midland Bank Ltd.
Mitsubishi Bank, Ltd., The.
Mitsui Bank, Ltd., The.
Montagu & Co., Ltd., Samuel.
Morgan Grenfell & Co. Ltd.
Morgan Guaranty Trust Company of New York.
Moscow Narodny Bank, Ltd.
Munster and Leinster Bank Ltd.
National and Grindlays Bank Ltd.
National Bank Ltd.
National Bank of Australasia, Ltd.
National Bank of Commerce of Seattle, The.
National Bank of Detroit.
National Bank of Greece.
National Bank of Ireland Ltd., The.
National Bank of New Zealand, Ltd., The.
National Bank of Nigeria Ltd.
National Bank of Pakistan.
National Commercial & Glyns Ltd.
National Provincial Bank Ltd.
National Westminster Bank Ltd.
Netherlands Bank of South Africa Ltd.
Nippon Kangyo Bank Ltd., The.
Northern Bank Ltd.
Northern Trust Company, The.
Overseas Union Bank Ltd.
Provincial Bank of Ireland Ltd.
Rafidain Bank.
Rea Brothers Ltd.
Reserve Bank of Australia.
Rothschild & Sons, N.M.
Rothschild & Sons (C.I.) Ltd., N.M.
Rothschild Intercontinental Bank Ltd.
Royal Bank of Canada, The.
Royal Bank of Scotland Ltd., The.
Sanwa Bank Ltd., The.
Sassoon Banking Co., Ltd., E.D.
Scandinavian Bank Ltd.
Schroder, Wagg & Co. Ltd., J. Henry.
Scottish Co-operative Wholesale Society Ltd.
Security Pacific National Bank.
Singer & Friedlander Ltd.
Slater, Walker Ltd.
Société Centrale de Banque.
Société Générale pour favoriser le développement du Commerce et de l'Industrie en France.
Standard Bank C.I. Ltd.
Standard Bank Ltd., The.

Standard Bank of West Africa Ltd.
State Bank of India.
Sumitomo Bank, Ltd., The.
Swiss Bank Corporation.
Swiss-Israel Trade Bank.
Tokai Bank, Ltd., The.
Toronto-Dominion Bank, The.
Trade Development Bank.
Ulster Bank Ltd.
Union Bank of Switzerland.
United Bank Ltd.
United Bank of Kuwait Ltd., The.
United California Bank.
United Commercial Bank.
Warburg & Co., Ltd., S.G.
Western American Bank (Europe) Ltd.
Westminster Bank Ltd.
Westminster Foreign Bank Ltd.
Williams Deacon's Bank Ltd.
Yorkshire Bank Ltd.
Zivnostenska Banka National Corporation.

SCHEDULE 3

AUTHORISED DEPOSITARIES

1. Members in the United Kingdom or the Channel Islands of:—
   - The Stock Exchange, London.
   - The Scottish Stock Exchange.
   - The Midlands & Western Stock Exchange.
   - The Northern Stock Exchange.
   - The Belfast Stock Exchange.
   - The Provincial Brokers' Stock Exchange.
   - The Association of Stock and Share Dealers.
   - The London Discount Market Association.
   - The Association of Canadian Investment Dealers and Members of the Toronto and Montreal Stock Exchanges in Great Britain.
   - The Association of New York Stock Exchange Member Firms having Representation in the United Kingdom.
   - The Issuing Houses Association.
   - The Association of Investment Trust Companies.
   - The British Insurance Association.

2. Solicitors practising in the United Kingdom or the Channel Islands, advocates practising in the Isle of Man, and advocates and écrivains of the Royal Courts of Jersey and Guernsey practising in the Channel Islands.

3. The Public Trustee and the Accountant General of the Supreme Court.

4. Persons in the United Kingdom not included in paragraphs 1, 2 or 3 of this Schedule who are holders of a principal's licence or are exempted (whether by definition, class or name) for the purposes of the Prevention of Fraud (Investments) Act 1958(**a**) or the Prevention of Fraud (Investments) Act (Northern Ireland) 1940(**b**), and the offices in the Channel Islands of such persons.

(**a**) 1958 c. 45. (**b**) 1940 c. 9. (N.I.).

SCHEDULE 4

ORDERS REVOKED

The Exchange Control (Authorised Dealers and Depositaries) Order 1969.	S.I. 1969/517 (1969 I, p. 1432).
The Exchange Control (Authorised Dealers and Depositaries) (Amendment) (No. 3) Order 1969.	S.I. 1969/1414 (1969 III, p. 4475).
The Exchange Control (Authorised Dealers and Depositaries) (Amendment) (No. 4) Order 1969.	S.I. 1969/1624 (1969 III, p. 5119).
The Exchange Control (Authorised Dealers and Depositaries) (Amendment) Order 1970.	S.I. 1970/25 (1970 I, p. 220).
The Exchange Control (Authorised Dealers and Depositaries) (Amendment) (No. 2) Order 1970.	S.I. 1970/561 (1970 I, p. 1803).

EXPLANATORY NOTE

(*This Note is not part of the Order.*)

This Order, which consolidates the 1969 Order, as amended, lists :—

(*a*) the banks and other persons authorised under the Exchange Control Act 1947 to deal in gold and foreign currencies ; and

(*b*) those who are entitled to act as authorised depositaries for the purpose of the deposit of securities as required by that Act.

It also amends paragraph 2 of Schedule 3 and authorises solicitors practising in the Channel Islands to act as authorised depositaries even if they are not advocates or écrivains of the Royal Courts of Jersey and Guernsey.

1970 No. 694

CUSTOMS AND EXCISE

The Import Duties (Temporary Exemptions) (No. 5) Order 1970

Made - - - - -	*7th May* 1970
Laid before the House of Commons	*8th May* 1970
Coming into Operation	*9th May* 1970

The Lords Commissioners of Her Majesty's Treasury, by virtue of the powers conferred on them by sections 3(6) and 13 of the Import Duties Act 1958(**a**), and of all other powers enabling them in that behalf on the recommendation of the Board of Trade hereby make the following Order:—

1.—(1) This Order may be cited as the Import Duties (Temporary Exemptions) (No. 5) Order 1970.

(2) The Interpretation Act 1889(**b**) shall apply for the interpretation of this Order as it applies for the interpretation of an Act of Parliament.

(3) This Order shall come into operation on 9th May 1970.

2.—(1) Until the beginning of 1st January 1971 or, in the case of goods in relation to which an earlier day is specified in Schedule 1 to this Order, until the beginning of that day, any import duty which is for the time being chargeable on goods of a heading of the Customs Tariff 1959 specified in that Schedule shall not be chargeable in respect of goods of any description there specified in relation to that heading.

(2) Any entry in column 2 in the Schedule to this Order is to be taken to comprise all goods which would be classified under an entry in the same terms constituting a subheading (other than the final subheading) in the relevant heading in the Customs Tariff 1959.

(3) For the purposes of classification under the Customs Tariff 1959, in so far as that depends on the rate of duty, any goods to which paragraph (1) above applies shall be treated as chargeable with the same duty as if this Order had not been made.

Neil McBride,
Ernest Armstrong,
Two of the Lords Commissioners
of Her Majesty's Treasury

7th May 1970

(**a**) 1958 c. 6. (**b**) 1889 c. 63.

SCHEDULE

Goods Temporarily Exempt from Import Duty

Tariff heading	*Description*
12.05	Dried chicory root (until 2nd July 1970)
28.17	Sodium peroxide (until 2nd July 1970)
28.43	Cuprous potassium cyanide (until 2nd July 1970)
29.35	3-(4-Amino-2-methyl-5-pyrimidyl)methyl-5-(2-hydroxyethyl)-4-methylthiazoline-2-thione
73.40	Circular can ends of tinplate, of a thickness of not less than 0·2 millimetre nor more than 0·24 millimetre, of an overall diameter of not less than 81 millimetres nor more than 83 millimetres, lacquered on both sides and having a curled edge (until 2nd July 1970)

EXPLANATORY NOTE

(*This Note is not part of the Order.*)

This Order provides for the temporary exemption from import duty, for specified periods, of dried chicory root, certain tinplate ends for cans, and three chemicals, all as specified in the Schedule to the Order.

1970 No. 700

CUSTOMS AND EXCISE

The Anti-Dumping (Provisional Charge to Duty) (No. 4) Order 1970

Made - - - - - -	8*th May* 1970
Laid before the House of Commons - -	8*th May* 1970
Coming into Operation -	11*th May* 1970

The Board of Trade in pursuance of the powers conferred upon them by sections 1, 2, 8 and 9(3) of the Customs Duties (Dumping and Subsidies) Act 1969(**a**), hereby make the following Order:—

1. This Order may be cited as the Anti-Dumping (Provisional Charge to Duty) (No. 4) Order 1970 and shall come into operation on 11th May 1970.

2. Goods of the description set out in the Schedule hereto (being goods classified in the Customs Tariff 1959(**b**) under the heading mentioned in the first column of that Schedule) shall be subject to a provisional charge to duty in respect of a duty of customs at the rate set out in the third column of that Schedule.

3. Section 2 of the Customs Duties (Dumping and Subsidies) Act 1969 (which allows relief to be given where goods are shown not to have been dumped or where the margin of dumping is less than the provisional charge) shall apply to the provisional charge imposed by this Order.

Gwyneth Dunwoody,

Parliamentary Secretary
to the Board of Trade.

8th May 1970.

SCHEDULE

Relevant Tariff Heading	Description of Goods	Relevant Rate
07.01 (D)	Cucumbers originating in Rumania	£2 per cwt.

(**a**) 1969 c. 16. (**b**) *see* S.I. 1969/1413 (1969 III, p. 4150).

EXPLANATORY NOTE

(*This Note is not part of the Order.*)

This Order makes imports of cucumbers originating in Rumania subject to a provisional charge in respect of an anti-dumping duty.

The making of the Order enables the Commissioners of Customs and Excise to require security for the payment of any anti-dumping duty which may be imposed retrospectively on such imports under section 8(1) of the Customs Duties (Dumping and Subsidies) Act 1969. If any duty is imposed retrospectively, it may only be so imposed on goods imported while the Order is in force, and its rate may not exceed the rate mentioned in the Schedule to the Order.

The Order expires automatically after three months unless previously revoked or extended (for not more than three months) by a further Order.

The Order applies section 2 of the 1969 Act to the charge, which enables relief to be granted where particular goods have not been dumped or the margin of dumping is less than the amount of the provisional charge.

STATUTORY INSTRUMENTS

1970 No. 701

PENSIONS

The Pensions Increase (Federated Superannuation Scheme for Nurses and Hospital Officers) (Metropolitan Civil Staffs) Regulations 1970

Made - - -	*7th May* 1970
Laid before Parliament	*15th May* 1970
Coming into Operation	*20th May* 1970

In pursuance of subsections (2)(*a*)(iv) and (4) of section 3 of the Pensions (Increase) Act 1965(**a**) (as amended by section 2(5) of the Pensions (Increase) Act 1969(**b**), and extended by section 1(4) of, and paragraph 10 of Schedule 2 to, that Act), I hereby, with the consent of the Minister for the Civil Service, make the following Regulations :—

Citation and commencement

1. These Regulations may be cited as the Pensions Increase (Federated Superannuation Scheme for Nurses and Hospital Officers) (Metropolitan Civil Staffs) Regulations 1970, and shall come into operation on 20th May 1970.

Interpretation

2.—(1) In these Regulations, unless the context otherwise requires, the expression—

"the Act of 1969" means the Pensions (Increase) Act 1969 ;

"average remuneration", in relation to any person, means the average annual amount of the salary and emoluments of his office during the last three years of his reckonable service ;

"an F.S.S.N. scheme" means a superannuation scheme operated under the Federated Superannuation Scheme for Nurses and Hospital Officers ;

"member of the metropolitan civil staffs" has the meaning assigned to it by section 15(1) of the Superannuation (Miscellaneous Provisions) Act 1967(**c**) ;

"the 1969 pension increase" means the benefits conferred by section 1 of the Act of 1969 on persons whose superannuation benefits are regulated under the Superannuation Act 1965(**d**) ;

"notional pension", in relation to any person, means the notional pension referred to in Regulation 5 of these Regulations ;

"reckonable service", in relation to any person, means any period of employment as a member of the metropolitan civil staffs during which the

(**a**) 1965 c. 78.
(**b**) 1969 c. 7.
(**c**) 1967 c. 28.
(**d**) 1965 c. 74.

person was subject to an F.S.S.N. scheme and in respect of which the contribution authorised or required to be paid under the scheme by the employer were duly paid.

(2) The Interpretation Act 1889(a) shall apply for the interpretation of these Regulations as it applies for the interpretation of an Act of Parliament.

Effect of the Regulations

3. These Regulations shall apply for the payment to persons described in Regulation 4 of these Regulations of the allowances described in Regulation 6 of these Regulations, being allowances which appear to the Secretary of State to be appropriate having regard to the 1969 pension increase.

Persons to whom the Regulations apply

4. These Regulations shall apply to any person who—

(*a*) has retired from employment as a member of the metropolitan civil staffs after attaining the age of sixty years ; and

(*b*) at the date of his retirement was subject to an F.S.S.N. scheme and had completed 10 years' reckonable service ; and

(*c*) has received or become entitled to receive payment of any retirement benefit under that scheme.

Notional pension

5.—(1) There shall be ascribed to each person to whom these Regulations apply a notional pension calculated by multiplying one eightieth of his average remuneration by the number of completed years of his reckonable service.

(2) In calculating a notional pension any fraction of a pound shall be treated as a whole pound.

Payments of benefits equivalent to statutory pension increases

6. The Secretary of State may, in respect of any period beginning on or after 1st April 1969, direct payment out of the Metropolitan Police Fund to any person to whom these Regulations apply of an allowance equal to the 1969 pension increase which would have been payable to him if he had been eligible under the Superannuation Act 1965 for a pension, beginning on the day after the last day of his reckonable service, of the same amount as his notional pension.

James Callaghan,
One of Her Majesty's Principal
Secretaries of State.

5th May 1970.

Consent of the Minister for the Civil Service given under his Official Seal on 7th May 1970.

(L.S.)

J. E. Herbecq,
Authorised by the
Minister for the Civil Service.

(a) 1889 c. 63.

EXPLANATORY NOTE

(*This Note is not part of the Regulations.*)

Where a person on retirement from employment as a member of the civil staff of the Metropolitan Police was entitled to superannuation benefits under a scheme operated under the Federated Superannuation Scheme for Nurses and Hospital Officers (F.S.S.N.), those benefits will not have been increased by the Pensions (Increase) Act 1969, since they are provided by means of insurance policies.

These Regulations enable benefits to be paid to such a person out of the Metropolitan Police Fund corresponding to the benefits conferred by that Act on retired civil servants who are in receipt of pensions under the Superannuation Act 1965.

The benefit of the Regulations is made retrospective to 1st April 1969 under powers conferred by paragraph 10 of Schedule 2 to the 1969 Act read with section 3(4) of the Pensions (Increase) Act 1965.

1970 No. 702

WAGES COUNCILS

The Wages Regulation (Keg and Drum) Order 1970

Made - - -	*7th May* 1970
Coming into Operation	*4th June* 1970

Whereas the Secretary of State has received from the Keg and Drum Wages Council (Great Britain) the wages regulation proposals set out in the Schedule hereto ;

Now, therefore, the Secretary of State in exercise of her powers under section 11 of the Wages Councils Act 1959(**a**), and of all other powers enabling her in that behalf, hereby makes the following Order :—

1. This Order may be cited as the Wages Regulation (Keg and Drum) Order 1970.

2.—(1) In this Order the expression "the specified date" means the 4th June 1970, provided that where, as respects any worker who is paid wages at intervals not exceeding seven days, that date does not correspond with the beginning of the period for which the wages are paid, the expression "the specified date" means, as respects that worker, the beginning of the next such period following that date.

(2) The Interpretation Act 1889(**b**) shall apply to the interpretation of this Order as it applies to the interpretation of an Act of Parliament and as if this Order and the Orders hereby revoked were Acts of Parliament.

3. The wages regulation proposals set out in the Schedule hereto shall have effect as from the specified date and as from that date the Wages Regulation (Keg and Drum) Order 1966(**c**) and the Wages Regulation (Keg and Drum) (Amendment) Order 1968(**d**) shall cease to have effect.

Signed by order of the Secretary of State.
7th May 1970.

A. A. Jarratt,
Deputy Under Secretary of State,
Department of Employment and Productivity.

Article 3

SCHEDULE

The following minimum remuneration shall be substituted for the statutory minimum remuneration fixed by the Wages Regulation (Keg and Drum) Order 1966 (Order K.D. (80)) as amended by the Wages Regulation (Keg and Drum) (Amendment) Order 1968 (Order K.D. (82)).

(**a**) 1959 c. 69.
(**b**) 1889 c. 63.
(**c**) S.I. 1966/266 (1966 I, p. 712).
(**d**) S.I. 1968/1429 (1968 III, p. 4163).

STATUTORY MINIMUM REMUNERATION

Part I

GENERAL

1. The minimum remuneration payable to a worker, to whom this Schedule applies, is as follows:—

(1) where the worker is employed on time work,

(*a*) for all work except work to which a minimum overtime rate applies under Part III of this Schedule,

(i) the general minimum time rate payable to the worker under Part II of this Schedule, and in addition thereto,

(ii) in the case of a regular night worker, the supplemental time rate payable under paragraph 4;

(*b*) for all work to which a minimum overtime rate applies under Part III of this Schedule, that rate;

(2) where the worker is employed on piece work,

(*a*) piece rates, each of which would yield, in the circumstances of the case, to an ordinary worker, at least the same amount of money as the piece work basis time rate applicable to the worker under Part II of this Schedule and, in addition thereto,

(*b*) in the case of a regular night worker, in respect of all time worked (except time to which a minimum overtime rate would apply under Part III of this Schedule if the worker were employed on time work) the supplemental time rate payable under paragraph 4.

DEFINITION OF REGULAR NIGHT WORKER

2. For the purposes of this Schedule, a regular night worker is a worker whose normal hours of work fall between the hours of 5 p.m. on one day and 7.30 a.m. on the next day.

Part II

GENERAL MINIMUM TIME RATES AND PIECE WORK BASIS TIME RATES

3. The general minimum time rates payable to male or female workers employed on time work and the piece work basis time rates applicable to such workers when employed on piece work are as follows:—

	General minimum time rates per hour	Piece work basis time rates per hour
(1) MALE WORKERS aged—	s. d.	s. d.
21 years or over	*6 0*	*6 7¼*
20 and under 21 years	*5 2½*	*5 8¾*
19 „ „ 20 „	*4 7*	*5 0½*
18 „ „ 19 „	*3 11¾*	*4 4¾*
17 „ „ 18 „	*3 5*	*3 9¼*
16 „ „ 17 „	*2 9*	*3 0½*
under 16 years	*2 2¼*	*2 5*

	General minimum time rates per hour s. d.	Piece work basis time rates per hour s. d.
(2) FEMALE WORKERS aged—		
21 years or over	4 8¼	5 2
20 and under 21 years	4 4	4 9¼
19 „ „ 20 „	4 0¾	4 5¾
18 „ „ 19 „	3 11¾	4 4¾
17 „ „ 18 „	3 1	3 4¾
16 „ „ 17 „	2 8¼	2 11½
under 16 years	2 2¼	2 5

SUPPLEMENTAL TIME RATE FOR REGULAR NIGHT WORKERS

4. The supplemental time rate payable to a regular night worker is an amount equal to one-third of the following rate:—

(1) in the case of a worker employed on time work, the general minimum time rate payable to the worker,

(2) in the case of a worker employed on piece work, the general minimum time rate which would be payable if the worker were employed on time work.

Part III

OVERTIME AND WAITING TIME

MINIMUM OVERTIME RATES FOR TIME WORKERS

5.—(1) Subject to the provisions of this paragraph, minimum overtime rates are payable to a worker employed on time work as follows:—

(*a*) On any day other than a Saturday, Sunday or customary holiday:—

(i) For the first 2 hours worked in excess of 8 hours .. .. time-and-a-third

(ii) Thereafter .. .. time-and-a-half

Provided that where the worker normally attends on five days only in the week, the said minimum overtime rates of time-and-a-third and time-and-a-half shall be payable after 8½ and 10½ hours' work respectively.

(*b*) On a Saturday, not being a customary holiday:—

(i) For the first 2 hours worked in excess of 4 hours .. .. time-and-a-third

(ii) Thereafter .. .. time-and-a-half

Provided that where the worker normally attends on five days only in the week, the following minimum overtime rates shall apply:—

(i) For the first 2 hours worked .. .. .. time-and-a-third

(ii) Thereafter .. .. time-and-a-half

(*c*) On a Sunday or a customary holiday:—

For all time worked .. .. double time

(*d*) In any week for all time worked in excess of 40 hours (exclusive of any time in respect of which any minimum overtime rate is payable under the foregoing provisions of this sub-paragraph):—

(i) for the first 2 hours so worked .. .. .. time-and-a-third

(ii) thereafter .. .. time-and-a-half

(2) In ascertaining whether any minimum overtime rate is payable, regard shall be had to the whole of the worker's turn of duty, which shall be treated as worked on the day upon which it commences, except that where the full turn of duty of a regular night worker ordinarily extends from one day to the next each such turn of duty in the week shall be treated as worked wholly on the day after it commences.

6. In this Part of this Schedule—

(1) the expression "customary holiday" means—

(*a*) (i) In England and Wales—

Christmas Day (or, if Christmas Day falls on a Sunday, such week day as may be appointed by national proclamation, or, if none is so appointed, the next following Tuesday), Boxing Day, Good Friday, Easter Monday, Whit Monday (*or where another day is substituted therefor by national proclamation, that day*) and August Bank Holiday ;

(ii) In Scotland—

New Year's Day (or, if New Year's Day falls on a Sunday, the following Monday) ;
the local Spring holiday ;
the local Autumn holiday ; and
three other days (being days on which the worker normally works for the employer) in the course of a calendar year to be fixed by the employer and notified to the worker not less than three weeks before the holiday ;

or (*b*) in the case of each of the said days (other than a day fixed by the employer in Scotland and notified to the worker as aforesaid) a day substituted by the employer therefor, being a day recognised by local custom as a day of holiday in substitution for the said day.

(2) the expressions "time-and-a-third", "time-and-a-half" and "double time" mean, respectively, one and a third times, one and a half times, and twice the general minimum time rate otherwise payable to the worker under paragraph 3.

WAITING TIME

7.—(1) A worker is entitled to payment of the minimum remuneration specified in this Schedule for all time during which he is present on the premises of his employer unless he is present thereon in any of the following circumstances:—

(*a*) without the employer's consent, express or implied ;

(*b*) for some purpose unconnected with his work and other than that of waiting for work to be given to him to perform ;

(*c*) by reason only of the fact that he is resident thereon ;

(*d*) during normal meal times in a room or place in which no work is being done, and he is not waiting for work to be given to him to perform.

(2) The minimum remuneration payable under sub-paragraph (1) of this paragraph to a piece worker when not engaged on piece work, is that which would be payable if he were a time worker.

PART IV

APPLICABILITY OF STATUTORY MINIMUM REMUNERATION

8. This Schedule applies to workers in relation to whom the Keg and Drum Wages Council (Great Britain) operates, that is to say, workers employed in Great Britain in the Keg and Drum Branch of the Hollow-ware Making Trade as specified in the Schedule to the Trade Boards (Keg and Drum Trade, Great Britain) (Constitution and Proceedings) Regulations 1928(**a**), which reads as follows:—

(**a**) S.R. & O. 1928/844 (1928, p. 1276).

"1. Subject to the provisions of this Schedule the Keg and Drum Branch of the Hollow-ware Making Trade consists of the following operations:—

(*a*) All work in connection with—

(i) the manufacture of kegs, drums, tapers, taper-necked cans and painters' pots, or parts thereof:—

from sheet iron or sheet steel (hereinafter called black plate) of an average thickness of less than ·125 of an inch (10 Birmingham Gauge); or

from black plate coated with any metal and of an average thickness exceeding ·01745 of an inch (27 Birmingham Gauge) but less than ·125 of an inch (10 Birmingham Gauge);

and the repair thereof;

(ii) the manufacture of boxes, canisters and bottles, or parts thereof from black plate whether coated or not with metal when carried on in a department mainly engaged in the manufacture or repair specified in paragraph 1 (*a*) (i) hereof;

(iii) the manufacture of kegs, drums, tapers, taper-necked cans and painters' pots, or parts thereof from black plate coated with any metal and of an average thickness not exceeding ·01745 of an inch (27 Birmingham Gauge) when carried on in a department mainly engaged in the manufacture or repair specified in paragraph 1 (*a*) (i) hereof;

and the repair thereof;

(iv) the manufacture from any iron or steel of forged, stamped or pressed mountings or fittings, or parts thereof, for the articles to the manufacture or repair of which paragraph 1 (*a*) (i) hereof applies when done by workers wholly or mainly so engaged or in association or conjunction with the said manufacture or repair.

(*b*) all work in connection with—

(i) the manufacture from black plate of articles of hollow-ware or parts thereof;

(ii) the manufacture of baths and dustbins from black plate or from black plate coated with any metal, of an average thickness not exceeding ·0392 of an inch (20 Birmingham Gauge);

(iii) the manufacture from any iron or steel of forged, stamped or pressed mountings or fittings or parts thereof for the articles specified in paragraph 1(*b*) (i) and (ii) hereof

when done in a department mainly engaged in the work specified in paragraph 1 (*a*) hereof.

2. Work in connection with the manufacture specified in paragraph 1 hereof includes—

(*a*) finishing;

(*b*) the work of persons employed in the factory or workshop in counting or weighing materials handed to workers and articles or parts thereof received from workers;

(*c*) packing, warehousing, despatching, the work of inside messengers, yard-workers and stokers and work of a similar nature.

3. Notwithstanding anything in this Schedule the following operations are not operations in the Keg and Drum Branch of the Hollow-ware Making Trade:—

(*a*) work specified in paragraph 1 hereof when performed in an establishment, branch or department mainly engaged in other work and in which the jointing and finishing of the articles or parts of articles specified in paragraph 1 hereof are done by workers mainly employed in jointing and finishing other articles;

(*b*) finishing when performed in a department mainly engaged in the finishing of articles other than articles specified in paragraph 1 hereof and in which no manufacture specified in paragraph 1 hereof is carried on ;

(*c*) packing, warehousing, despatching, the work of inside messengers, yard-workers and stokers, and work of a similar nature when performed in an establishment not otherwise engaged in operations in the Keg and Drum Branch of the Hollow-ware Making Trade ;

(*d*) the manufacture of component parts of motor vehicles, motor plants, aircraft, cycles or motor-cycles ;

(*e*) the manufacture of any article or part of any article when made in an establishment mainly engaged in the manufacture of motor vehicles, motor plants, aircraft, cycles or motor-cycles or of component parts thereof ;

(*f*) all clerical work other than work specified in paragraph 2 (*b*) hereof ;

(*g*) the manufacture of tin rollers, tin roller drums, card cases, coiler cans and other articles for use with textile or other machinery ;

(*h*) all processes of lithographic printing and processes of varnishing or lacquering done in connection therewith ;

(*i*) all work in connection with the maintenance or upkeep of premises, machinery or plant ;

(*j*) all work included under the Trade Boards (Hollow-ware Trade, Great Britain) (Constitution and Proceedings) Regulations 1928(**a**) ;

(*k*) all work included under the Trade Boards (Tin Box Trade, Great Britain) (Constitution and Proceedings) Regulations 1928(**b**).

4. The expression 'finishing' includes operations of coating, polishing and cleaning articles."

EXPLANATORY NOTE

(*This Note is not part of the Order.*)

This Order, which has effect from 4th June 1970, sets out the statutory minimum remuneration payable in substitution for that fixed by the Wages Regulation (Keg and Drum) Order 1966 (Order K.D. (80)), as amended by the Wages Regulation (Keg and Drum) (Amendment) Order 1968 (Order K.D. (82)), which Orders are revoked.

New provisions are printed in italics.

(**a**) S.R. & O. 1928/843 (1928, p. 1272). (**b**) S.R. & O. 1928/847 (1928, p. 1289).

1970 No. 703

WAGES COUNCILS

The Wages Regulation (Keg and Drum) (Holidays) Order 1970

Made - - -	*7th May* 1970
Coming into Operation	*4th June* 1970

Whereas the Secretary of State has received from the Keg and Drum Wages Council (Great Britain) the wages regulation proposals set out in the Schedule hereto ;

Now, therefore, the Secretary of State in exercise of her powers under section 11 of the Wages Councils Act 1959(**a**), and of all other powers enabling her in that behalf, hereby makes the following Order :—

1. This Order may be cited as the Wages Regulation (Keg and Drum) (Holidays) Order 1970.

2.—(1) In this Order the expression "the specified date" means the 4th June 1970, provided that where, as respects any worker who is paid wages at intervals not exceeding seven days, that date does not correspond with the beginning of the period for which the wages are paid, the expression "the specified date" means, as respects that worker, the beginning of the next such period following that date.

(2) The Interpretation Act 1889(**b**) shall apply to the interpretation of this Order as it applies to the interpretation of an Act of Parliament and as if this Order and the Order hereby revoked were Acts of Parliament.

3. The wages regulation proposals set out in the Schedule hereto shall have effect as from the specified date and as from that date the Wages Regulation (Keg and Drum) (Holidays) Order 1965(**c**), as amended by Schedule 2 to the Wages Regulation (Keg and Drum) Order 1966(**d**), shall cease to have effect.

Signed by order of the Secretary of State.
7th May 1970.

A. A. Jarratt,
Deputy Under Secretary of State,
Department of Employment and Productivity.

SCHEDULE

Article 3

The following provisions as to holidays and holiday remuneration shall be substituted for the provisions as to holidays and holiday remuneration set out in the Wages Regulation (Keg and Drum) (Holidays) Order 1965 (hereinafter referred to as "Order K.D. (78)"), as amended by Schedule 2 to the Wages Regulation (Keg and Drum) Order 1966 (Order K.D. (80)).

(**a**) 1959 c. 69.
(**b**) 1889 c. 63.
(**c**) S.I. 1965/551 (1965 I, p. 1702).
(**d**) S.I. 1966/266 (1966 I, p. 712).

Part I

APPLICATION

1. This Schedule applies to every worker for whom statutory minimum remuneration has been fixed.

Part II

CUSTOMARY HOLIDAYS

2.—(1) An employer shall allow to every worker in his employment to whom this Schedule applies a holiday (hereinafter referred to as a "customary holiday") in each year on the days specified in the following sub-paragraph provided that the worker was in his employment on the day immediately preceding the customary holiday and (unless excused by the employer or absent by reason of the proved illness of the worker) has worked for the employer throughout the last working day on which work was available to him immediately preceding the customary holiday.

(2) The said customary holidays are—

(*a*) (i) In England and Wales—

Christmas Day (or, if Christmas Day falls on a Sunday, such week day as may be appointed by national proclamation, or, if none is so appointed, the next following Tuesday), Boxing Day, Good Friday, Easter Monday, Whit Monday (*or where another day is substituted therefor by national proclamation, that day*) and August Bank Holiday;

(ii) In Scotland—

New Year's Day (or, if New Year's Day falls on a Sunday, the following Monday);
the local Spring holiday;
the local Autumn holiday; and
three other days (being days on which the worker normally works for the employer) in the course of a calendar year to be fixed by the employer and notified to the worker not less than three weeks before the holiday;

or (*b*) in the case of each of the said days (other than a day fixed by the employer in Scotland and notified to the worker as aforesaid) a day substituted by the employer therefor, being a day recognised by local custom as a day of holiday in substitution for the said day.

(3) Where in England and Wales, Christmas Day or Boxing Day, or in Scotland, New Year's Day (or any day substituted for any one of these days under the provisions of (*b*) of sub-paragraph (2) of this paragraph) falls on a Saturday, the employer shall allow—

(*a*) to a worker who normally works for the employer on five days a week but does not normally work for him on a Saturday, instead of the customary holiday, a holiday on a day on which the worker normally works for the employer during the week immediately following the customary holiday;

(*b*) to a worker who normally works for the employer on six days a week (including Saturday) but normally works on a Saturday for not more than 4½ hours exclusive of overtime, in addition to the customary holiday a holiday on a Saturday during the two weeks immediately following the customary holiday:

Provided that a worker shall not be entitled to a holiday in pursuance of this sub-paragraph—

(i) if he is not qualified under sub-paragraph (1) of this paragraph to be allowed the customary holiday and would not be so qualified if he normally worked for the employer on a Saturday;

or (ii) if, in the case of a worker to whom (*a*) of this sub-paragraph applies, he has been allowed a day of holiday (not being a customary holiday or a day of annual holiday) on a day on which he would normally work for the employer in the week immediately preceding the customary holiday and has been paid for that holiday not less than the amount to which he would have been entitled had the day been a customary holiday allowed to him under sub-paragraph (1) of this paragraph ;

or (iii) if, in the case of a worker to whom (*b*) of this sub-paragraph applies, he has been allowed not less than 4½ hours off from work during his normal working hours on a day on which he would normally work for the employer (not being a customary holiday or a day of annual holiday) in the week immediately preceding or in the week immediately following the customary holiday and has been paid in respect of the hours off so allowed to him not less than the appropriate rate of statutory minimum remuneration to which he would have been entitled if he had worked throughout those hours on his usual work.

(4) Notwithstanding the provisions of sub-paragraph (1) of this paragraph, an employer may (unless it is not lawful for him to do so) require a worker who is otherwise qualified to be allowed a customary holiday to work thereon and where he does so the employer shall allow the worker a day's holiday (hereinafter referred to as a "holiday in lieu of a customary holiday") on a day on which he normally works for the employer within the three weeks immediately following the customary holiday.

PART III

ANNUAL HOLIDAY

3.—(1) In addition to the holidays specified in Part II of this Schedule and subject to the provisions of paragraph 4, an employer shall between the date on which the provisions of this Schedule become effective and 31st October 1970, and in each succeeding year between 1st April and 31st October, allow a holiday (hereinafter referred to as an "annual holiday") to every worker in his employment to whom this Schedule applies who has been employed by him during the 12 months immediately preceding the commencement of the holiday season for any of the periods of employment (*calculated in accordance with the provisions of paragraph* 10) specified below, and the duration of the annual holiday shall in the case of each such worker be related to that period as follows:—

Period of employment	Duration of annual holiday for workers with a normal working week of—		
	Six days	Five days	Four days or less
Column 1	Column 2	Column 3	Column 4
At least 48 weeks	*18 days*	*15 days*	*12 days*
„ „ 44 „	*16* „	*13* „	*11* „
„ „ 40 „	*15* „	*12* „	*10* „
„ „ 36 „	*13* „	*11* „	*9* „
„ „ 32 „	*12* „	*10* „	*8* „
„ „ 28 „	*10* „	*8* „	*7* „
„ „ 24 „	*9* „	*7* „	*6* „
„ „ 20 „	*7* „	*6* „	*5* „
„ „ 16 „	*6* „	*5* „	*4* „
„ „ 12 „	*4* „	*3* „	*3* „
„ „ 8 „	*3* „	*2* „	*2* „
„ „ 4 „	*1 day*	*1 day*	*1 day*

(2) Notwithstanding the provisions of the last foregoing sub-paragraph:—

(*a*) the number of days of annual holiday which an employer is required to allow to a worker in any holiday season shall not exceed in the aggregate *three times* the number of days constituting the worker's normal working week.

(*b*) the duration of the worker's annual holiday in the holiday season ending on 31st October 1970 shall be reduced by any days of annual holiday duly allowed to him by the employer under the provisions of Order K.D. (78) as amended by Schedule 2 to Order K.D. (80) between 1st April 1970 and the date on which the provisions of this Schedule become effective.

(3) In this Schedule the expression "holiday season" means, in any year, the period commencing on 1st April and ending on 31st October in that year.

4.—(1) An annual holiday shall be allowed on consecutive working days, being days on which the worker is normally called upon to work for the employer, and days of annual holiday shall be treated as consecutive notwithstanding that a Sunday, or a day of holiday allowed under Part II of this Schedule, intervenes:

Provided that where the duration of an annual holiday which an employer is required to allow to a worker exceeds the number of days constituting the worker's normal working week the said holiday may be allowed in three separate periods of such consecutive working days, and in that event, notwithstanding the foregoing provisions of this Schedule, the annual holiday shall be allowed as follows:—

(*a*) as to one period, not being less than the period constituting the worker's normal working week, during the holiday season;

(*b*) as to a second period, during the holiday season or within the period ending on 31st March immediately following the holiday season; and

(*c*) as to *any days exceeding twice the number of days constituting the worker's normal working week,* on days to be fixed by the employer, either during the holiday season or within the period ending on 31st March immediately following the holiday season.

(2) Subject to the provisions of sub-paragraph (1) of this paragraph, any day of annual holiday under this Schedule may be allowed on a day on which the worker is entitled to a day of holiday or to a half-holiday under any enactment other than the Wages Councils Act 1959.

5. An employer shall give to a worker reasonable notice of the commencing date or dates and duration of the period or periods of his annual holiday either individually to the worker or by the posting of a notice in the place where the worker is employed.

PART IV

HOLIDAY REMUNERATION

A—CUSTOMARY HOLIDAYS AND HOLIDAYS IN LIEU OF CUSTOMARY HOLIDAYS

6.—(1) Subject to the provisions of this paragraph, for each day of holiday which the worker is allowed under Part II of this Schedule he shall be paid by the employer holiday remuneration equal to the amount to which he would have been entitled, calculated at the general minimum time rate applicable to the worker (or which would be applicable if he were a time worker) increased by ten per cent., if the day had not been a day of holiday and he had been employed on work entitling him to statutory minimum remuneration for the time normally worked by him on that day of the week:

Provided that payment of the said holiday remuneration is subject to the condition that the worker (unless excused by the employer or absent by reason of the proved illness of the worker) presents himself for employment at the usual commencing hour on the first working day following the holiday and works his normal hours of work on that day.

(2) Holiday remuneration in respect of any holiday allowed under Part II of this Schedule shall be paid to the worker not later than the pay day on which the wages are paid for the first working day following the holiday:

Provided that where a worker ceases to be employed before being allowed a holiday in lieu of a customary holiday or a holiday under sub-paragraph (3) of paragraph 2, he shall be paid the holiday remuneration for that day immediately upon the termination of his employment and in such a case the condition contained in the proviso to sub-paragraph (1) of this paragraph shall not apply.

B—ANNUAL HOLIDAY

7.—(1) Subject to the provisions of paragraph 8, a worker qualified to be allowed an annual holiday under this Schedule shall be paid by his employer in respect thereof, on the last pay day preceding such annual holiday, one day's holiday pay (as defined in paragraph 11) in respect of each day thereof.

(2) Where under the provisions of paragraph 4 an annual holiday is allowed in more than one period, the holiday remuneration shall be apportioned accordingly.

8. Where any accrued holiday remuneration has been paid by the employer to the worker in accordance with paragraph 9 of this Schedule or with Order K.D. (78) as amended in respect of employment during any of the periods referred to in that paragraph or that Order, the amount of holiday remuneration payable by the employer in respect of any annual holiday for which the worker has qualified by reason of employment during the said period shall be reduced by the amount of the said accrued holiday remuneration unless that remuneration had been deducted from a previous payment of holiday remuneration made under the provisions of this Schedule or of Order K.D. (78) as amended.

ACCRUED HOLIDAY REMUNERATION PAYABLE ON TERMINATION OF EMPLOYMENT

9. Where a worker ceases to be employed by an employer after the provisions of this Schedule become effective the employer shall, immediately on the termination of the employment (hereinafter referred to as "the termination date") pay to the worker as accrued holiday remuneration:—

(1) in respect of employment in the 12 months ended on the 31st day of the preceding March, a sum equal to the holiday remuneration for any days of annual holiday for which he has qualified, except days of annual holiday which he has been allowed or has become entitled to be allowed before leaving the employment; and

(2) in respect of any employment after the said 31st March, a sum equal to the holiday remuneration which would have been payable to him if he could have been allowed an annual holiday in respect of that employment at the time of leaving it.

PART V

GENERAL

10. For the purposes of calculating any period of employment qualifying a worker for an annual holiday or for any accrued holiday remuneration under this Schedule, the worker shall be treated:—

(1) as if he were employed for a week in respect of any week in which—

(*a*) he has worked for the employer for not less than 24 hours and has performed some work for which statutory minimum remuneration is payable ; or (*b*) he has been absent throughout the week, or he has worked for the employer for less than 24 hours, solely by reason of the proved illness of or accident to the worker, provided that the number of weeks which may be treated as weeks of employment for such reason shall not exceed six in the aggregate in the period of 12 months immediately preceding the commencement of the holiday season ; or

(*c*) he is absent from work owing to suspension due to shortage of work, provided that the number of weeks which may be treated as weeks of employment for such reason shall not exceed four in the aggregate in the period of 12 months last mentioned, and

(2) as if he were employed on any day of holiday allowed under the provisions of this Schedule, and for the purposes of the provisions of sub-paragraph (1) of this paragraph, a worker who is absent on such a holiday shall be treated as having worked thereon for the employer for the number of hours ordinarily worked by him on that day of the week on work for which statutory minimum remuneration is payable.

11. In this Schedule, unless the context otherwise requires, the following expressions have the meanings hereby respectively assigned to them, that is to say:—

"NORMAL WORKING WEEK" means the number of days on which it has been usual for the worker to work in a week in the employment of the employer during the 12 months immediately preceding the commencement of the holiday season or, where under paragraph 9 accrued holiday remuneration is payable on the termination of the employment, during the 12 months immediately preceding the termination date:

Provided that—

(1) part of a day shall count as a day ;

(2) no account shall be taken of any week in which the worker did not perform any work for which statutory minimum remuneration has been fixed.

"ONE DAY'S HOLIDAY PAY" means the appropriate proportion of the remuneration which the worker would be entitled to receive from his employer at the date of the annual holiday (or where the holiday is allowed in more than one period at the date of the first period) or at the termination date, as the case may require, for one week's work if working his normal working week and the number of daily hours normally worked by him (exclusive of overtime) and if paid at the general minimum time rate applicable to the worker (or which would be applicable if he were a time worker) increased by ten per cent., for work for which statutory minimum remuneration is payable and at the same rate (increased as aforesaid) for any work for which such remuneration is not payable, and in this definition "appropriate proportion" means—

where the worker's normal working week is six days ..	one-sixth
where the worker's normal working week is five days ..	one-fifth
where the worker's normal working week is four days or less	one-quarter

"STATUTORY MINIMUM REMUNERATION" means minimum remuneration (other than holiday remuneration) fixed by a wages regulation order made by the Secretary of State to give effect to proposals submitted to her by the Keg and Drum Wages Council (Great Britain).

"WEEK" in paragraphs 3 and 10 means "pay week".

12. The provisions of this Schedule are without prejudice to any agreement for the allowance of any further holidays with pay or for the payment of additional holiday remuneration.

EXPLANATORY NOTE

(*This Note is not part of the Order.*)

This Order, which has effect from 4th June 1970, sets out the holidays which an employer is required to allow to workers and the remuneration payable for those holidays in substitution for the holidays and holiday remuneration fixed by the Wages Regulation (Keg and Drum) (Holidays) Order 1965 (Order K.D. (78)), as amended by Schedule 2 to the Wages Regulation (Keg and Drum) Order 1966 (Order K.D. (80)). Order K.D. (78) is revoked.

New provisions are printed in italics.

STATUTORY INSTRUMENTS

1970 No. 704

INDUSTRIAL TRAINING

The Industrial Training Levy (Food, Drink and Tobacco) Order 1970

Made - - -	*7th May* 1970
Laid before Parliament	*18th May* 1970
Coming into Operation	*20th May* 1970

The Secretary of State after approving proposals submitted by the Food, Drink and Tobacco Industry Training Board for the imposition of a further levy on employers in the food, drink and tobacco industry and in exercise of her powers under section 4 of the Industrial Training Act 1964(**a**) and of all other powers enabling her in that behalf hereby makes the following Order:—

Title and commencement

1. This Order may be cited as the Industrial Training Levy (Food, Drink and Tobacco) Order 1970 and shall come into operation on 20th May 1970.

Interpretation

2.—(1) In this Order unless the context otherwise requires:—

(a) "agriculture" has the same meaning as in section 109(3) of the Agriculture Act 1947(**b**) or, in relation to Scotland, as in section 86(3) of the Agriculture (Scotland) Act 1948(**c**);

(b) "an appeal tribunal" means an industrial tribunal established under section 12 of the Industrial Training Act 1964;

(c) "assessment" means an assessment of an employer to the levy;

(d) "the Board" means the Food, Drink and Tobacco Industry Training Board;

(e) "business" means any activities of industry or commerce;

(f) "charity" has the same meaning as in section 360 of the Income and Corporation Taxes Act 1970(**d**);

(g) "emoluments" means all emoluments assessable to income tax under Schedule E (other than pensions), being emoluments from which tax under that Schedule is deductible, whether or not tax in fact falls to be deducted from any particular payment thereof;

(h) "employer" means a person who is an employer in the food, drink and tobacco industry at any time in the second levy period;

(i) "food, drink and tobacco establishment" means an establishment in Great Britain engaged in the second base period wholly or mainly in

(**a**) 1964 c. 16. (**b**) 1947 c. 48. (**c**) 1948 c. 45. (**d**) 1970 c. 10.

the food, drink and tobacco industry for a total of twenty-seven or more weeks or, being an establishment that commenced to carry on business in the second base period, for a total number of weeks exceeding one half of the number of weeks in the part of the said period commencing with the day on which business was commenced and ending on the last day thereof;

(j) "the food, drink and tobacco industry" means any one or more of the activities which, subject to the provisions of paragraph 2 of Schedule 1 to the industrial training order, are specified in paragraph 1 of that Schedule as the activities of the food, drink, and tobacco industry;

(k) "the industrial training order" means the Industrial Training (Food, Drink and Tobacco Board) Order 1968**(a)**;

(l) "the levy" means the levy imposed by the Board in respect of the second levy period;

(m) "notice" means a notice in writing;

(n) "the second base period" means the period of twelve months that commenced on 6th April 1969;

(o) "the second levy period" means the period commencing with the day upon which this Order comes into operation and ending on 5th April 1971;

(p) other expressions have the same meanings as in the industrial training order.

(2) In reckoning the amount of emoluments for the purposes of this Order no regard shall be had to the emoluments of any person employed as follows:—

(a) by a local authority;

(b) by a milk marketing board in the provision of—
(i) services of artificial insemination for livestock at a centre providing such services; or
(ii) any services in respect of milk recording;

(c) wholly in agriculture;

(d) as a member of the crew of an aircraft, as the master or a member of the crew of a ship or, in the case of a person employed as a seaman, in or about a ship in port by the owner or charterer thereof on work of a kind ordinarily done by a seaman on a ship while it is in port;

(e) wholly as a registered dock worker in dock work; or

(f) wholly in the supply (including any preparation thereof by the person engaged in such supply) of food or drink to persons, being a supply—
(i) for immediate consumption;
(ii) of hot fried fish or hot chipped potatoes; or
(iii) by means of an automatic vending machine at or in connection with an hotel, restaurant, café, snack bar, canteen, mess room or similar place of refreshment.

(a) S.I. 1968/1033 (1968 II, p. 2721).

(3) Any reference in this Order to persons employed at or from a food, drink and tobacco establishment shall in any case where the employer is a company be construed as including a reference to any director of the company (or any person occupying the position of director by whatever name he was called) who was, at the material time, in receipt of a salary from the company.

(4) In the case where a food, drink and tobacco establishment is taken over (whether directly or indirectly) by an employer in succession to, or jointly with, another person, a person employed at any time in the second base period at or from the establishment shall be deemed, for the purposes of this Order, to have been so employed by the employer carrying on the said establishment on the day upon which this Order comes into operation, and any reference in this Order to persons employed by an employer at or from a food, drink and tobacco establishment in the second base period shall be construed accordingly.

(5) Any reference in this Order to an establishment that commences to carry on business or that ceases to carry on business shall not be taken to apply where the location of the establishment is changed but its business is continued wholly or mainly at or from the new location, or where the suspension of activities is of a temporary or seasonal nature.

(6) The Interpretation Act 1889**(a)** shall apply to the interpretation of this Order as it applies to the interpretation of an Act of Parliament.

Imposition of the levy

3.—(1) The levy to be imposed by the Board on employers in respect of the second levy period shall be assessed in accordance with the provisions of this Article.

(2) The levy shall be assessed by the Board separately in respect of each food, drink and tobacco establishment of an employer (not being an employer who is exempt from the levy by virtue of paragraph (5) of this Article), but in agreement with the employer one assessment may be made in respect of any number of such establishments, in which case those establishments shall be deemed for the purposes of that assessment to constitute one establishment.

(3) Subject to the provisions of this Order, the levy assessed in respect of a food, drink and tobacco establishment of an employer shall be an amount equal to 0.9 per cent. of the sum of the emoluments of all the persons employed by the employer at or from that establishment in the second base period.

(4) The amount of the levy imposed in respect of a food, drink and tobacco establishment that ceases to carry on business in the second levy period shall be in the same proportion to the amount that would otherwise be due under paragraph (3) of this Article as the number of days between the commencement of the said levy period and the date of cessation of business (both dates inclusive) bears to the number of days in the said levy period.

(5) There shall be exempt from the levy—

(a) an employer in whose case the sum of the emoluments of all the persons employed by him in the second base period at or from the food, drink and tobacco establishment or establishments of the employer (including any persons employed in that period at or from a food, drink and tobacco establishment by an associated company of the employer) is less than £15,000;

(b) a charity.

(a) 1889 c. 63.

Assessment Notices

4.—(1) The Board shall serve an assessment notice on every employer assessed to the levy, but one notice may comprise two or more assessments.

(2) The amount of any assessment payable under an assessment notice shall be rounded down to the nearest £1.

(3) An assessment notice shall state the Board's address for the service of a notice of appeal or of an application for an extension of time for appealing.

(4) An assessment notice may be served on the person assessed to the levy either by delivering it to him personally or by leaving it, or sending it to him by post, at his last known address or place of business in the United Kingdom or, if that person is a corporation, by leaving it, or sending it by post to the corporation, at such address or place of business or at its registered or principal office.

Payment of the Levy

5.—(1) Subject to the provisions of this Article and of Articles 6 and 7, the amount of each assessment appearing in an assessment notice served by the Board shall be due and payable to the Board one month after the date of a further notice requiring payment of that amount, which notice shall be served by the Board on the person assessed to the levy in the same manner as an assessment notice.

(2) The amount of an assessment shall not be recoverable by the Board until there has expired the time allowed for appealing against the assessment by Article 7(1) of this Order and any further period or periods of time that the Board or an appeal tribunal may have allowed for appealing under paragraph (2) or (3) of that Article or, where an appeal is brought, until the appeal is decided or withdrawn.

Withdrawal of Assessment

6.—(1) The Board may, by a notice served on the person assessed to the levy in the same manner as an assessment notice, withdraw an assessment if that person has appealed against that assessment under the provisions of Article 7 of this Order and the appeal has not been entered in the Register of Appeals kept under the appropriate Regulations specified in paragraph (5) of that Article.

(2) The withdrawal of an assessment shall be without prejudice to the power of the Board to serve a further assessment notice in respect of any establishment to which that assessment related.

Appeals

7.—(1) A person assessed to the levy may appeal to an appeal tribunal against the assessment within one month from the date of the service of the assessment notice or within any further period or periods of time that may be allowed by the Board or an appeal tribunal under the following provisions of this Article.

(2) The Board by notice may for good cause allow a person assessed to the levy to appeal to an appeal tribunal against the assessment at any time within the period of four months from the date of the service of the assessment notice or within such further period or periods as the Board may allow before such time as may then be limited for appealing has expired.

(3) If the Board shall not allow an application for extension of time for appealing, an appeal tribunal shall upon application made to the tribunal by the person assessed to the levy have the like powers as the Board under the last foregoing paragraph.

(4) In the case of an establishment that ceases to carry on business in the second levy period on any day after the date of the service of the relevant assessment notice the foregoing provisions of this Article shall have effect as if for the period of four months from the date of the service of the assessment notice mentioned in paragraph (2) of this Article there were substituted the period of six months from the date of the cessation of business.

(5) An appeal or an application to an appeal tribunal under this Article shall be made in accordance with the Industrial Tribunals (England and Wales) Regulations 1965(**a**) as amended by the Industrial Tribunals (England and Wales) (Amendment) Regulations 1967(**b**) except where the establishment to which the relevant assessment relates is wholly in Scotland in which case the appeal or application shall be made in accordance with the Industrial Tribunals (Scotland) Regulations 1965(**c**) as amended by the Industrial Tribunals (Scotland) (Amendment) Regulations 1967(**d**).

(6) The powers of an appeal tribunal under paragraph (3) of this Article may be exercised by the President of the Industrial Tribunals (England and Wales) or by the President of the Industrial Tribunals (Scotland) as the case may be.

Evidence

8.—(1) Upon the discharge by a person assessed to the levy of his liability under an assessment the Board shall if so requested issue to him a certificate to that effect.

(2) The production in any proceedings of a document purporting to be certified by the Secretary of the Board to be a true copy of an assessment or other notice issued by the Board or purporting to be a certificate such as is mentioned in the foregoing paragraph of this Article shall, unless the contrary is proved, be sufficient evidence of the document and of the facts stated therein.

7th May 1970.

Barbara Castle,
First Secretary of State and Secretary of State for Employment and Productivity.

EXPLANATORY NOTE

(*This Note is not part of the Order.*)

This Order gives effect to proposals submitted by the Food, Drink and Tobacco Industry Training Board to the Secretary of State for Employment and Productivity for the imposition of a further levy on employers in the food, drink and tobacco industry for the purpose of raising money towards the expenses of the Board.

The levy is to be imposed in respect of the second levy period commencing with the date upon which this Order comes into operation and ending on 5th April, 1971. The levy will be assessed by the Board and there will be a right of appeal against an assessment to an industrial tribunal.

(**a**) S.I. 1965/1101 (1965 II, p. 2805).
(**b**) S.I. 1967/301 (1967 I, p. 1040).
(**c**) S.I. 1965/1157 (1965 II, p. 3266).
(**d**) S.I. 1967/302 (1967 I, p. 1050).

STATUTORY INSTRUMENTS

1970 No. 705 (S.51)

LOCAL GOVERNMENT, SCOTLAND

The Rate Support Grant (Scotland) Amendment Regulations 1970

Made - - -	*5th May* 1970
Laid before Parliament	*14th May* 1970
Coming into Operation	*16th May* 1970

In exercise of the powers conferred on me by section 6(1) of and paragraph 5 of Part I of Schedule 1 to the Local Government (Scotland) Act 1966(**a**), and of all other powers enabling me in that behalf, and after consultation with such associations of local authorities as appear to me to be concerned, I hereby make the following regulations :—

1. These regulations may be cited as the Rate Support Grant (Scotland) Amendment Regulations 1970 and shall come into operation on 16th May 1970.

2.—(1) In these regulations any reference to "the principal regulations" is a reference to the Rate Support Grant (Scotland) Regulations 1967(**b**) as amended (**c**).

(2) The Interpretation Act 1889(**d**) shall apply for the interpretation of these regulations as it applies for the interpretation of an Act of Parliament.

3. In regulation 2(2) of the principal regulations—

(*a*) for the words "special educational treatment" there shall be substituted the words "special education" ;

(*b*) the definition of "voluntary home" shall be omitted ; and

(*c*) there shall be added at the end the following words :—

" "voluntary residential establishment" means an establishment managed by a voluntary organisation, or any other person not being a local authority, which provides residential accommodation for the purposes of the Social Work (Scotland) Act 1968(**e**), whether for reward or not."

4. In regulation 4 of the principal regulations—

(1) in paragraph (4)—

(*a*) the words "and approved" shall be omitted ;

(*b*) there shall be added after "1962" the words "as amended by paragraph 9 of Schedule 2 to the Education (Scotland) Act 1969"(**f**) ;

(2) for paragraph (5) there shall be substituted the following paragraph:—

"(5) the provision of education for pupils attending public schools and residing in voluntary residential establishments, other than—

(**a**) 1966 c. 51.
(**b**) S.I. 1967/715 (1967 II, p. 2162).
(**c**) The amending regulations are not relevant to the subject matter of these regulations.
(**d**) 1889 c. 63.
(**e**) 1968 c. 49.
(**f**) 1969 c. 49.

(*a*) children within the meaning of section 15 of the Social Work (Scotland) Act 1968 in the care of a local authority under that section ;

(*b*) children within the meaning of Part III of the Social Work (Scotland) Act 1968 subject to a supervision requirement under section 44(1) of that Act ; and

(*c*) pupils sent by an education authority to a voluntary residential establishment for the purpose of enabling them to attend a school where they will receive special education ;".

Provided that until section 44(1) of the said Act of 1968 comes into operation, the said paragraph (5) (as set out in this paragraph), shall have effect as if for sub-paragraph (*b*) thereof there were substituted the following sub-paragraph :—

"(*b*) children or young persons within the meaning of the Children and Young Persons (Scotland) Act 1937(**a**) committed to the care of a local authority as a fit person under that Act and remaining in their care ;".

(3) for paragraph (9) there shall be substituted the following paragraph :—

"(9) the exercise of any of the functions specified in subsection (1) of section 86 of the Social Work (Scotland) Act 1968 in respect of a person determined by the Secretary of State under subsection (2) of that section to have no ordinary residence."

William Ross,
One of Her Majesty's Principal
Secretaries of State.

St. Andrew's House,
Edinburgh.
5th May 1970.

EXPLANATORY NOTE

(*This Note is not part of the Regulations.*)

These Regulations amend existing Regulations dealing with the pooling of expenditure, incurred by certain local authorities, among all authorities by means of adjustments to rate support grants. Pooling arrangements will now extend to the provision of accommodation and certain other social work services for persons of all ages instead of to the provision only of certain services for children. Certain minor amendments are made in consequence of recent legislation.

(**a**) 1937 c. 37.

1970 No. 706 (S.52)

EDUCATION, SCOTLAND

The Teaching Council (Scotland) Election Scheme 1970 Approval Order 1970

Made - - - -	6*th May* 1970
Laid before Parliament	15*th May* 1970
Coming into Operation	16*th May* 1970

Whereas the General Teaching Council for Scotland have, in exercise of their powers under paragraph 1(6) of Part I of Schedule 1 to the Teaching Council (Scotland) Act 1965**(a)**, as amended by the Teaching Council (Scotland) Act 1965 (Amendment of Constitution of the Council) Order 1970**(b)**, made the Teaching Council (Scotland) Election Scheme 1970 which makes provision for the election of certain categories of members of the said Council and have submitted the said scheme to me for approval;

Now, therefore, in exercise of the powers conferred on me by paragraph 1(8) of Part I of the said Schedule, and of all other powers enabling me in that behalf, I hereby make the following order:—

1. This order may be cited as the Teaching Council (Scotland) Election Scheme 1970 Approval Order 1970, and shall come into operation on 16th May 1970.

2. The Teaching Council (Scotland) Election Scheme 1970, which is set out in the Schedule to this order, is hereby approved.

William Ross,
One of Her Majesty's
Principal Secretaries of State.

St. Andrew's House,
Edinburgh.

6th May 1970.

(a) 1965 c. 19. **(b)** S.I. 1970/523 (1970 I, p. 1724).

SCHEDULE

THE TEACHING COUNCIL (SCOTLAND) ELECTION SCHEME 1970

Scheme for the Election of Registered Teachers to the General Teaching Council for Scotland made under Schedule 1, Part I of the Teaching Council (Scotland) Act 1965 (as amended)

Interpretation

1.—(1) The Interpretation Act 1889**(a)** shall apply for the interpretation of this Scheme as it applies for the interpretation of an Act of Parliament.

(2) In this Scheme, unless the context otherwise requires, any reference to any enactment shall be construed as a reference to the said enactment as amended by any subsequent enactment or to any enactment substituted for that enactment.

Definitions

2.—(1) In this Scheme unless the context otherwise requires:—

"the Act" means the Teaching Council (Scotland) Act 1965;

"arbiter" means the person appointed on or before the 31st day of October in each election year by the Sheriff of the Lothians and Peebles at Edinburgh on the application of the Council;

"the Council" means the General Teaching Council for Scotland constituted under section 1 of the Act;

"election year" means the year 1970 and every fourth year thereafter;

"register" means the register established by the Council under section 6 of the Act and "registered" shall be construed accordingly;

"Registrar" means the registrar employed by the Council under paragraph 14(1) of Part II of Schedule 1 to the Act;

"Returning Officer" means a person appointed as returning officer under paragraph 4 of this Scheme and includes a Deputy Returning Officer so appointed;

"teacher" means a registered person whether in employment as a teacher or not and includes a conditionally registered person employed as a teacher in a further education centre but does not include any other conditionally registered person;

(2) Unless the context otherwise requires, any reference to a "category of employment" shall be construed as a reference to a category of educational establishment mentioned in paragraph 1(2) of Part I of Schedule 1 to the Act and any reference, in relation to a person, to his category of employment shall be construed as a reference to that one of the said categories of educational

(a) 1889 c. 63.

establishment in which he is employed, or which he has chosen as his category for purposes of the election, as provided for in Article 3(3)(*b*) below.

Notification of election

3.—(1) The Registrar shall notify every teacher twice within an election year, the first occasion being not later than 30th April and the second not later than 15th June, that an election of twenty-six teachers to be members of the Council will take place later that year.

(2) The first notification may be given by bulletin, circular or otherwise and the second notification shall be in writing in the form as nearly as may be of Form A in the Appendix to this Scheme.

(3) The Registrar shall secure so far as reasonably practicable that every teacher—

(*a*) is informed of his category of employment; and

(*b*) is given the opportunity to verify this category or to request that an amendment be made thereto stating the grounds for amendment;

and the Registrar shall, if he is satisfied with the grounds for amendment, change the category in accordance with the request.

Returning officer

4.—(1) The Council shall, at least six months before the date on which an election is to take place in an election year, appoint a person, not being a member of the Council or a teacher, to be the Returning Officer for the ensuing election.

(2) The Council shall at the same time also appoint a Deputy Returning Officer, not being a member of the Council or a teacher, to act for the Returning Officer in the event of his absence or inability to act.

(3) The Returning Officer shall have power, subject to the approval of the Council, to employ staff necessary for the conduct of the election and pay them out of the monies provided to him by the Council.

(4) Subject to the provisions of this Scheme the Returning Officer shall be responsible for the conduct of the election.

Voting categories

5. For the purposes of an election under this Scheme—

(*a*) there shall be four voting categories each of which bears the number specified in relation thereto in column (1) of the following Table and corresponds to that one of the categories of educational establishment mentioned in paragraph 1(2) of Schedule 1 to the Act which is specified in relation thereto in column (2) of the said Table;

(*b*) the teachers eligible to stand for election in a voting category, who shall not include conditionally registered teachers, are those specified in relation to that category in column (3) of the said Table; and

(*c*) the number of Council members to be elected in a voting category are those specified in relation thereto in column (4) of the said Table:—

TABLE

(1) No. of Voting Category	(2) Category of employment	(3) Teachers eligible to stand for election	(4) No. of Council Members to be elected in voting category
I	Colleges of Education	Teachers other than Principals employed in colleges of education	1
II	Further education centres	All teachers employed in further education centres	3
III	Secondary schools and departments	All teachers employed in secondary schools and departments	11
IV	Primary schools and departments	All teachers employed in primary schools departments	11
		Total	26

Qualifications of Candidates and Electors

6.—(1) *Candidates*

(*a*) Only teachers employed on a whole-time basis on 1st September of an election year in post in a category of employment shall be eligible to be nominated for election for that category;

(*b*) for the purposes of any election under this Scheme, a candidate for election shall be taken to belong to the category of employment appearing against his name on the register on 1st September in each election year;

(*c*) a teacher who shall have attained the age of 70 years on 1st February of the year succeeding an election shall not be eligible to be nominated for election.

(2) *Electors*

An elector must be a teacher whose name is on the register on 15th October in an election year.

Publication of notice of election

7.—(1) The Council shall fix 30th September in an election year and, if this falls on a Saturday or Sunday, the preceding Friday as the last day on which nomination papers are to be accepted and at least twenty-eight clear days before the day so fixed shall cause a notice of the election to be published specifying the number of members to be elected, the place to which nomination papers are to be sent and the latest time by which they are to be accepted.

(2) The said notice shall be in the form as nearly as may be of Form A in the Appendix to this Scheme and shall be published once in a daily newspaper circulated in each of the following places, namely, Aberdeen, Dundee, Edinburgh,

Glasgow, and such other places as the Council may determine, and in such periodical journals as the Council may determine.

Nomination

8.—(1) Each candidate for election shall be nominated on a separate nomination paper signed by a proposer and seconder being teachers in his category of employment and supported by twenty others in the same category at the date of signature.

(2)(*a*) Each nomination paper shall be in the form as nearly as may be of Form B in the Appendix to this Scheme and shall state only the name and private address of the nominated candidate, the educational establishment in which he is employed and his category of employment, and also the names and registered numbers of the proposer, seconder and the twenty other supporters.

(*b*) The nomination paper shall also be signed by the nominee to signify his willingness to be nominated and to confirm that he is employed both in the educational establishment and in the category of employment specified in the nomination paper and that the other particulars so specified are correct.

(3) Any person having the requisite qualifications for nominating or supporting a candidate may nominate or support any number of candidates not exceeding the number to be elected.

(4)(*a*) Every nomination paper shall, by twelve noon on the last day fixed under article 7 above for the receipt of nomination papers, be delivered whether by post or otherwise to the Returning Officer, the General Teaching Council for Scotland, 140 Princes Street, Edinburgh EH2 4BS, or such other address as may be fixed by the Council.

(*b*) Every nomination paper in respect of which any requirement of this Scheme has not been complied with, or which is not received by the Returning Officer by twelve noon of the last day fixed for the receipt of nomination papers shall be null and void:

provided that no misnomer or inaccurate or incomplete description of any person or place named in any nomination paper shall invalidate that paper if, in the opinion of the Returning Officer, the description of the person or place is such as to be commonly understood.

(5) The Returning Officer shall, within three days after the last day fixed under Article 7 above for the receipt of nomination papers, send a list of the nominated candidates in each category to the candidates in that category and any candidate may within seven days of the dispatch of such list intimate to the Returning Officer in writing that he does not wish to stand for the election and that his nomination is to be withdrawn and any such intimation to the Returning Officer shall be final.

(6) If a candidate validly nominated changes his category of employment or dies at or before the last time fixed for the sending in of nomination papers or after that time but before the poll his nomination shall be treated as having been withdrawn.

Roll of electors

9.—(1) The roll of electors in an election year shall consist of the teachers on the register on 15th October of that year.

(2)(*a*) Subject to sub-paragraphs (*e*) and (*f*) below the voting in Voting Category I of the election shall be confined to teachers who are employed in colleges of education on 15th October in an election year.

(*b*) Subject to sub-paragraphs (*e*) and (*f*) below the voting in Voting Category II shall be confined to teachers who are employed in further education centres on 15th October in an election year.

(*c*) Subject to sub-paragraphs (*e*) and (*f*) below the voting in Voting Category III shall be confined to teachers who are employed in secondary schools or departments on 15th October in an election year.

(*d*) Subject to sub-paragraphs (*e*) and (*f*) below the voting in Voting Category IV shall be confined to teachers who are employed in primary schools or departments on 15th October in an election year.

(*e*) A teacher employed on 15th October in an election year in two or more categories of employment may vote in one only of the corresponding voting categories, namely the category appearing against his name on the register.

(*f*) A teacher who on 15th October in an election year is not employed in any of the categories of employment mentioned in sub-paragraphs (*a*) to (*d*) above may, notwithstanding, vote in respect of one of those categories if he has been employed at any time in that category or if he holds a qualification which would enable him to be employed as a teacher in that category.

Conduct of the election

10. The election of the persons to represent teachers shall be conducted in the following manner:—

(1) If the number of duly and properly nominated candidates in a category does not exceed the number of persons to be elected in that category the Returning Officer shall forthwith declare the said candidates to be elected.

(2) If the number of duly and properly nominated candidates in a category exceeds the number of persons to be elected in that category the Returning Officer shall cause ballot papers and identification envelopes to be prepared.

(3) The ballot paper for a category shall be in the form as nearly as may be of Form C in the Appendix to this Scheme and shall contain only the names, addresses and places of employment of all the persons duly and properly nominated as candidates for that category, shall state the last day and time by which the ballot paper may be received and the place to which it is to be returned.

(4) The identification envelopes shall be in the form as nearly as may be of Form D in the Appendix to this Scheme.

(5) The Returning Officer shall, at least twenty-one days prior to the last time fixed for the receipt of ballot papers, such time being not later than twelve noon on 30th November, cause to be forwarded by post to each person qualified to take part in the election at his registered address a ballot paper appropriate to the category of the person together with an identification envelope and each teacher shall be entitled to receive one ballot paper appropriate to his category or where he has two or more categories, the category chosen under Article 9(2)(*e*) above, and one identification envelope, and it shall not be lawful to vote otherwise than by using the ballot paper provided by the Returning Officer.

(6)(*a*) Each elector shall

(i) vote by marking the ballot paper delivered to him with an 'X' against the name or names of the person or persons (not exceeding the number of persons to be elected) for whom he votes and should place his ballot paper folded face inwards in the appropriate identification envelope and should seal this securely; and

(ii) sign the declaration printed on the said envelope, place the said envelope inside a covering envelope which should then be sealed and sent by post or otherwise to the Returning Officer.

(*b*) Every ballot paper in respect of which any requirement of this Scheme has not been complied with or on which the elector has placed any mark whereby he may be afterwards identified or which is not received by the Returning Officer by twelve noon on the last day fixed for the receipt of ballot papers shall be null and void.

(7)(*a*) The Returning Officer immediately after the last time fixed for the receipt of ballot papers shall cause the validity of the votes to be ascertained by an examination of the identification envelopes and by such other evidence if any as he may think necessary and shall cause such of the identification envelopes as are found to be valid to be opened and the ballot papers withdrawn, kept folded face inwards, and placed in a separate ballot box dependent upon the category in which the said vote is appropriate.

(*b*) When all the ballot papers have been transferred to the ballot boxes, they shall be examined and counted and the number of valid votes given for each candidate shall be ascertained.

(*c*) Any candidate or any agent appointed by him may be present during the examination of the identification envelopes and the counting of the ballot papers.

(8) The appropriate number of candidates in each category having the greatest number of votes shall be declared elected by the Returning Officer. In this paragraph "appropriate number" in relation to a category means the number specified in column (4) of the Table in Article 5 above in relation to that category. If the same number of votes has been cast in favour of two or more candidates and the addition of a vote would entitle any of such candidates to be elected, the Returning Officer shall determine by lot which of the candidates whose votes are equal shall be declared elected.

(9) At the time of the declaration of the result of the election the Returning Officer shall intimate the name and address of the arbiter to whom any appeal under Article 11(2) below may be made.

Powers of returning officer

11.—(1) Any question arising with regard to the validity of a nomination or a ballot paper or otherwise in connection with any election shall be determined by the Returning Officer.

(2) No election shall be invalidated by reason of misdescription or non-compliance with the provisions of this Scheme, or by reason of any miscount or of the non-delivery, loss or miscarriage in the course of post of any document required under this Scheme to be dispatched by post, if the Returning Officer

certifies in writing that the election was conducted substantially in accordance with the provisions of this Scheme and if the result of such misdescription, non-compliance, miscount, non-delivery, loss or miscarriage did not affect the result of the election provided that any unsuccessful candidate or his agent may within fourteen days after the declaration by the Returning Officer of the result of the election appeal to the arbiter against a certificate given by the Returning Officer under this sub-paragraph and the decision of the arbiter shall be final.

(3) The identification envelopes and ballot papers shall be destroyed by the Returning Officer on the expiry of one calendar month from the date of the declaration of the election unless there shall have been an appeal as provided for under sub-paragraph (2) above, in which event the arbiter shall order the destruction of the said envelopes and ballot papers as soon as may be after the appeal is disposed of.

Notice and publication of results of election

12. The Returning Officer shall—

(*a*) forthwith give to every person elected notice in writing of his election and shall furnish the Registrar with a list of the persons certified by him to be duly elected showing the number of votes cast for each of the said persons; and

(*b*) publish the names and addresses of the elected candidates in the same newspapers and other periodicals as those in which the election notice was published under Article 7 of this Scheme.

Secrecy of ballot

13. The Returning Officer, and every Officer, Clerk or servant employed in connection with the election, shall maintain and aid in maintaining the secrecy of the ballot and shall not communicate to any persons any information as to the manner in which any elector has recorded his vote.

DAVID LEES

.... Chairman.

GEORGE D GRAY

.... Registrar.

140 Princes Street,
EDINBURGH.
10th April 1970.

APPENDIX

Form A

NOTICE OF ELECTION

Teaching Council (Scotland) Act 1965

The General Teaching Council for Scotland

Notice is hereby given that pursuant to the Teaching Council (Scotland) Act 1965 as amended an election of twenty-six members of the General Teaching Council for Scotland to represent the teachers who are on the Register of that Council is about to be held.

Each teacher to be elected shall be:—

(*a*) a registered or provisionally registered teacher but not a conditionally registered teacher,

(*b*) in post in one or other of the categories (set out in the table below) on a whole-time basis on 1st September of the election year, and

(*c*) under 70 years of age on 1st February of

The following table shows for each voting category the numbers, and categories of employment of the teachers to be elected, and the qualifications of the persons entitled to nominate each candidate and to vote in the election:—

TABLE

(1) *No. of Voting* Category	(2) *No. of Council Members to be elected*	(3) *Categories of Employment*	(4) *Qualifications of persons entitled to nominate candidates and vote in the election*
I	One	I Colleges of Education	Registered teachers employed in colleges of education
II	Three	II Further Education Centres	Registered teachers employed in further education centres
III	Eleven	III Secondary Schools and Departments	Registered teachers employed in secondary schools and departments other than conditionally registered teachers
IV	Eleven	IV Primary Schools and Departments	Registered teachers employed in primary schools and departments other than conditionally registered teachers

N.B. Registered teachers (*a*) employed in more than one category of employment, or (*b*) not serving as teachers will vote in the Voting Category for which they have intimated an option and which corresponds to an appropriate entry in the Register.

Each candidate for election shall be nominated on a separate nomination paper. Each nomination paper shall state only the name, address and place of employment and the category of employment of the nominated candidate. It shall be signed by two teachers in his category of employment and supported by twenty others in the same category. The twenty-two signatories shall give their registration numbers.

Any person having the requisite qualifications for nominating a candidate in a category may nominate any number of candidates not exceeding the number to be elected in that category.

The nomination papers shall be signed by the nominee signifying his willingness to be nominated and that his particulars are correct, and must be delivered by post or otherwise not later than twelve noon on the day of 19 to the Returning Officer, General Teaching Council for Scotland, 140 Princes Street, Edinburgh EH2 4BS.

Every nomination paper in respect of which any requirement has not been complied with or which is not received at the address given above by twelve noon on the said day of 19 shall be null and void.

Nomination papers may be obtained on application to the Returning Officer at the above address.

(Date)......................................(Signed)..............................Returning Officer

FORM B

FORM OF NOMINATION PAPER

N.B. A teacher shall be nominated only by teachers in his own category

WE, THE UNDERSIGNED, being teachers registered or provisionally registered or, in the case of teachers employed in further education centres, conditionally registered with the General Teaching Council for Scotland as

Teachers employed in a College of Education (Category I)	*Delete so as to leave your category only.*
Teachers employed in a Further Education Centre (Category II)	
Teachers employed in a Secondary School or Department (Category III)	
Teachers employed in a Primary School or Department (Category IV)	

HEREBY NOMINATE

(BLOCK CAPITALS)

Mr./Mrs./Miss ....

Private Address ....

....

Educational establishment in which employed and category of employment ....

....

....

Registration No...

(*Insert full name of candidate, private address, educational establishment in which employed with full postal address, and registration number.*)

WHO IS REGISTERED IN CATEGORY.......................
as a proper person to be elected to the General Teaching Council as representing Category.....................................

Proposer	*Seceonder*
Name	Name ....
Registration Number	Registration Number ....
Signature	Signature ....

Supporters

Signature	*Reg. No.*	*Signature*	*Reg. No.*
1.	....	11.	....
2.	....	12.	....
3.	....	13.	....
4.	....	14.	....
5.	....	15.	....
6.	....	16.	....
7.	....	17.	....
8.	....	18.	....
9.	....	19.	....
10.	....	20.	....

I consent to be nominated as a candidate for election as a representative of the teachers registered in Category...... to serve on the General Teaching Council. I declare that the statements in this nomination paper with regard to my candidature are correct.

(Signed)..............................

(Date)..............................

FORM C

BALLOT PAPER

Election to the General Teaching Council for Scotland by teachers registered in Category.........

Elector's Mark		*Name of Candidate*	*Address of Candidate*	*Educational Establishment in which employed*
	1			
	2			
	3			
	4			
	5			
	6			
	7			
	8			
	9			
	10			
	11			

The electors must put a mark thus 'X' against the name(s) of the candidate(s) for whom he votes.

The elector must not vote for more than ( ) candidates. If he does so his ballot paper will be null and void. (The elector may vote for fewer candidates than are to be elected.)

If the elector places any mark on this ballot paper by which such elector may be afterwards identified, the ballot paper will be null and void.

This paper should be folded face inwards and placed in the identification envelope which must be signed by the elector in the place marked for that purpose, securely fastened, and placed in a covering envelope which must then be sent by post or otherwise to the Returning Officer, General Teaching Council for Scotland, 140 Princes Street, Edinburgh EH2 4BS and must be received there by twelve noon on the day of 19 .

FORM D

FORM OF IDENTIFICATION ENVELOPE

GENERAL TEACHING COUNCIL FOR SCOTLAND
ELECTION

(Identification Envelope)

I, the undersigned, hereby declare that I am the person to whom the enclosed ballot paper is addressed, that I am a teacher in Category............and that I have not marked any other ballot paper in this election.

Registration
Number........... Signature.......................................

EXPLANATORY NOTE

(*This Note is not part of the Order.*)

This Order approves the scheme of election for teacher-members (other than principals of colleges of education) of the General Teaching Council for Scotland who are required to be elected by virtue of Schedule 1 to the Teaching Council (Scotland) Act 1965 as amended.

1970 No. 708

BORROWING AND SECURITIES

The Control of Borrowing (Amendment) Order 1970

Made - -	8*th May* 1970
Laid before Parliament	14*th May* 1970
Coming into Operation	15*th May* 1970

The Treasury, in exercise of the powers conferred upon them by sections 1 and 3(4) of the Borrowing (Control and Guarantees) Act 1946(**a**) and of all other powers enabling them in that behalf, hereby make the following Order :—

1. This Order may be cited as the Control of Borrowing (Amendment) Order 1970, and shall come into operation on 15th May 1970.

2. The Interpretation Act 1889(**b**) shall apply for the interpretation of this Order as it applies for the interpretation of an Act of Parliament.

3. The Control of Borrowing Order 1958(**c**), as amended by the Control of Borrowing (Amendment) Order 1967(**d**), shall be further amended by the substitution, for article 8A thereof, of the following article :—

"8A.—(1) Subject to the provisions of this article, nothing in Part I of this Order applies to any transaction unless—

(*a*) the transaction is effected by or on behalf of a person resident outside the United Kingdom, and is not a transaction consisting of or including the issue of non-sterling securities, or

(*b*) the transaction is effected by or on behalf of an investment trust company which is resident in the scheduled territories but outside the United Kingdom, or

(*c*) the transaction is effected by a local authority.

(2) The exemption contained in the foregoing paragraph shall not apply to—

(*a*) the issue of any of the securities mentioned in paragraphs 1 to 5 of Part II of Schedule 1 to the Trustee Investments Act 1961(**e**), unless the terms on which the securities are to be issued have, before the making of the issue, been approved by the Bank of England on behalf of the Treasury ;

(*b*) the issue of any sterling securities where the amount of the money to be raised by the issue is not less than £1 million, unless the time at which the securities are to be issued has, before the making of the issue, been approved by the Bank of England on behalf of the Treasury.

(**a**) 1946 c. 58. (**b**) 1889 c. 63.
(**c**) S.I. 1958/1208 (1958 I, p. 203). (**d**) S.I. 1967/69 (1967 I, p. 150).
(**e**) 1961 c. 62.

(3) In this article—

"investment trust company" means a body corporate whose functions consist wholly or mainly in the holding of investments or other property ;

"non-sterling securities" means securities on which capital moneys, dividends and interest are payable solely in a currency other than sterling, and "sterling securities" means any securities other than non-sterling securities.

(4) For the purposes of this article, a person being a body corporate shall be deemed to be resident where the central management and control of its trade or business is exercised."

4. The Control of Borrowing (Amendment) Order 1967 is hereby revoked.

Roy Jenkins,
E. G. Perry,
Two of the Lords Commissioners
of Her Majesty's Treasury.

8th May 1970.

EXPLANATORY NOTE

(This Note is not part of the Order.)

This Order further amends the Control of Borrowing Order 1958. The only change is that this Order removes the exemption from control of the borrowing or raising of money in Great Britain by the issue of non-sterling securities by or on behalf of investment trust companies resident in the scheduled territories but outside the United Kingdom.

1970 No. 709

DECIMAL CURRENCY

The Decimal Currency (Amendment of Enactments) Order 1970

Made - - -	*7th May* 1970
Laid before Parliament	*15th May* 1970
Coming into Operation	*15th February* 1971

The Treasury, in exercise of the powers conferred on them by section 11(1)(*c*) of the Decimal Currency Act 1969(**a**), hereby make the following Order :—

1. This Order may be cited as the Decimal Currency (Amendment of Enactments) Order 1970, and shall come into operation on 15th February 1971.

2. The Interpretation Act 1889(**b**) shall apply for the interpretation of this Order as it applies for the interpretation of an Act of Parliament.

3. The Church Funds Investment Measure 1958(**c**) shall be amended by substituting, in paragraph 9(3) of the Schedule thereto, for the words "one-tenth of one penny", the figures "0·05p".

Ernest Armstrong,
Neil McBride,
Two of the Lords Commissioners
of Her Majesty's Treasury.

7th May 1970.

EXPLANATORY NOTE

(*This Note is not part of the Order.*)

This Order amends, in connection with the introduction of decimal currency, paragraph 9(3) of the Schedule to the Church Funds Investment Measure 1958, which provides that, in calculating the basic value of a share in an Investment Fund, the figure found shall be rounded off to the nearest one-tenth of one penny. The effect of the Order is that the rounding off will be to the nearest 0·05p.

(**a**) 1969 c. 19. (**b**) 1889 c. 63. (**c**) 1958 No. 1.

STATUTORY INSTRUMENTS

1970 No. 716 (S.53)

WILD BIRDS

The Wild Birds (Various Species) (Scotland) Order 1970

Made - - -	8*th May* 1970
Coming into Operation	18*th May* 1970

In exercise of the power conferred on me by sections 9(1) and 13(1) of the Protection of Birds Act 1954(**a**), and after consulting the Advisory Committee on the Protection of Birds for Scotland and giving an opportunity to submit objections or representations, I hereby make the following order :—

1.—(1) This order, which shall apply to Scotland, may be cited as the Wild Birds (Various Species) (Scotland) Order 1970 and shall come into operation on 18th May 1970.

(2) In this order "the Act" means the Protection of Birds Act 1954.

(3) The Interpretation Act 1889(**b**) shall apply for the interpretation of this order as it applies for the interpretation of an Act of Parliament.

2. The wild birds specified in Schedule 1 to this order shall, with respect to Scotland, be added to Part I of Schedule 1 to the Act (which confers protection by special penalties at all times).

3. The wild birds specified in Schedule 2 to this order shall, with respect to Scotland, be removed from Part I of Schedule 1 to the Act.

4. The two following wild birds shall, with respect to Scotland, be removed from Part II of Schedule 1 to the Act (which confers protection by special penalties during the close season) and shall be added to Part I of that Schedule, namely Brambling and Black-tailed Godwit.

5. The Wild Birds (Bramblings and Black-Tailed Godwits) (Scotland) Order 1957(**c**) is hereby revoked.

6. In accordance with the provisions of this order and of the other subsisting orders (**d**) by which birds have been added to, or removed from, Schedule 1, 2

(**a**) 1954 c. 30. (**b**) 1889 c. 63.
(**c**) S.I. 1957/326 (1957 II, p. 3062).
(**d**) S.I. 1955/496; 1955/1751; 1956/332; 1962/2591; 1965/2181; 1967/1181; 1967/1724; 1967/1887 (1962 III, p. 3482; 1967 II, p. 3466; 1967 III, pp. 4649, 5130).

or 3 to the Act, those Schedules have effect, with respect to Scotland, as set out in the Appendix to this order.

William Ross,
One of Her Majesty's Principal
Secretaries of State.

St. Andrew's House,
Edinburgh.
8th May 1970.

Article 2

SCHEDULE 1

WILD BIRDS TO BE ADDED TO PART I OF SCHEDULE 1

Bluethroat
Crake, spotted
Crossbill
Diver, all species
Fieldfare
Firecrest
Harrier, all species
Kingfisher
Owl, barn
Quail, European
Redwing
Sandpiper, wood
Serin
Shrike, red-backed
Sparrow-hawk
Tern, little
Warbler, Savi's
Woodlark

Article 3

SCHEDULE 2

WILD BIRDS TO BE REMOVED FROM PART I OF SCHEDULE 1

Bustard
Diver, black-throated
Diver, great northern
Diver, red-throated
Hen-harrier
Marsh-harrier
Montagu's harrier
Quail, common
Roller
Swan, Bewick's
Wren, St. Kilda

APPENDIX

Article 6 — SCHEDULE 1 — Sections 1, 4, 6, 9

WILD BIRDS AND THEIR EGGS PROTECTED BY SPECIAL PENALTIES

PART I

AT ALL TIMES

Avocet
Bee-eater (all species)
Bittern (all species)
Owl, barn
Owl, snowy
Peregrine

Bluethroat
Brambling
Bunting, snow
Buzzard, honey
Chough
Corncrake (landrail)
Crake, spotted
Crossbill
Diver (all species)
Dotterel
Eagle (all species)
Fieldfare
Firecrest
Godwit, black-tailed
Goshawk
Grebe, black-necked
Grebe, Slavonian
Greenshank
Harrier (all species)
Hobby
Hoopoe
Kingfisher
Kite
Merlin
Oriole, golden
Osprey
Phalarope, red-necked
Plover, Kentish
Plover, little ringed
Quail, European
Redstart, black
Redwing
Ruff and reeve
Sandpiper, wood
Serin
Shrike, red-backed
Sparrow-hawk
Spoonbill
Stilt, black-winged
Stint, Temminck's
Stone curlew
Swan, whooper
Tern, black
Tern, little
Tern, roseate
Tit, bearded
Tit, crested
Warbler, Dartford
Warbler, marsh
Warbler, Savi's
Woodlark
Wryneck

PART II

DURING THE CLOSE SEASON

Whimbrel
Wild duck of the following species—
Common scoter
Garganey teal
Goldeneye
Long-tailed duck
Scaup-duck
Velvet scoter

SCHEDULE 2 Sections 2, 3, 5, 9, 10

WILD BIRDS WHICH MAY BE KILLED OR TAKEN AT ANY TIME BY AUTHORISED PERSONS

Cormorant
Crow, carrion
Crow, hooded
Domestic pigeon gone feral
Magpie
Raven (in Argyll and Skye)
Red-breasted merganser (in Scotland only)

Dove, collared (in Scotland only)
Goosander (in Scotland only)
Gull, greater black-backed
Gull, lesser black-backed
Gull, herring
Jackdaw
Jay
Rock-dove (in Scotland only)
Rook
Shag
Sparrow, house
Starling
Stock-dove
Wood-pigeon

Sections 2, 6, 7, 9

SCHEDULE 3

WILD BIRDS WHICH MAY BE KILLED OR TAKEN OUTSIDE THE CLOSE SEASON

Any wild bird included in Part II of Schedule 1 to this Act.

Capercaillie
Coot
Curlew (other than stone curlew)
Gannet (on the island of Sula Sgeir in Ross and Cromarty)
Godwit, bar-tailed
Moorhen
Plover, golden
Plover, grey
Redshank, common
Snipe, common
Snipe, jack
Wild duck of the following species—
- Common pochard
- Gadwall
- Mallard
- Pintail
- Shoveler
- Teal
- Tufted duck
- Wigeon

Wild geese of the following species—
- Barnacle goose (in the Western Isles)
- Bean-goose
- Canada goose
- Grey lag goose
- Pink-footed goose
- White-fronted goose

Woodcock

EXPLANATORY NOTE

(*This Note is not part of the Order.*)

Any person who at any time commits an offence under the Protection of Birds Act 1954 in respect of a bird included in Part I of Schedule 1 to the Act or in respect of the nest or egg of such a bird is liable to special penalties. This Order, which has effect in Scotland, adds the birds listed in Schedule 1 to, and in Article 4 of, the Order, to Part I of Schedule 1 to the Act and removes those listed in Schedule 2 to the Order from that Part so that the latter enjoy only the general protection under the Act afforded to the majority of wild bird species. Schedules 1, 2 and 3 to the Act will now have effect, in Scotland, as set out in the Appendix to the Order. The present changes are shown in bold type in the Schedules to the Order and the Appendix, except where they relate to nomenclature only.

1970 No. 717 (S. 54)

LAND COMMISSION

The Betterment Levy (Tenancies and Reversions) (Scotland) (Amendment) Regulations 1970

Made - - - - - -	*6th May* 1970
Laid before the House of Commons	*20th May* 1970
Coming into Operation - - -	*25th May* 1970

In exercise of the powers conferred on me by section 98 of, and paragraph 12 of Schedule 6 and paragraph 8 of Schedule 7 to, the Land Commission Act 1967**(a)**, section 47(3) of the Finance Act 1969**(b)**, and of all other powers enabling me in that behalf, I being for the purposes of these regulations the appropriate Minister in relation to Scotland, hereby make the following regulations:—

Citation, extent, commencement and interpretation

1.—(1) These regulations, which may be cited as the Betterment Levy (Tenancies and Reversions) (Scotland) (Amendment) Regulations 1970, apply to Scotland and shall come into operation on 25th May 1970.

(2) The Interpretation Act 1889**(c)** applies for the interpretation of these regulations as it applies for the interpretation of an Act of Parliament.

Amendment of the Betterment Levy (Tenancies and Reversions) (Scotland) Regulations 1967

2. The Betterment Levy (Tenancies and Reversions) (Scotland) Regulations 1967**(d)** as amended**(e)** shall be deemed always to have had effect as if further amended and are hereby further amended.

(*a*) by the addition after regulation 7(2)(*a*) of the following sub-paragraph: "(*aa*) was a disposition made on or after 23rd September 1965 and before the first appointed day to which paragraph 10A or paragraph 10B of Schedule 5 applies, or";

(*b*) in regulation 7(3) by the substitution for the words "paragraphs (5) and (6)" of the words "paragraphs (5), (6) and (7)";

(*c*) in regulation 7(5)(*a*) by the substitution for the words "falling within the antecedent period" of the words "to which paragraph 2(*a*) or (2)(*aa*) refers";

(*d*) in regulation 7(6) by the addition at the end of the words "subject to paragraph (7) of this regulation"; and

(a) 1967 c. 1. **(b)** 1969 c. 32. **(c)** 1889 c. 63. **(d)** S.I. 1967/324 (1967 I, p. 1102).
(e) The amending regulations are not relevant to the subject matter of these regulations.

(*e*) by the addition after regulation 7(6) of the following paragraph:
"(7) Where the grant was a disposition to which paragraph 10B of Schedule 5 applies, the amount of the consideration given for the grant shall be taken to be the amount determined under paragraph (6) of this regulation but subject to any adjustment made under sub-paragraphs (1), (2) or (3) of the said paragraph 10B which shall be construed as if the references therein to the amount of the consideration given for the disposition were references to the amount determined under paragraph (6) of this regulation."

3. The Betterment Levy (Tenancies and Reversions) (Scotland) Regulations 1967 as amended shall from the date on which these regulations come into operation be further amended by the addition at the end of regulation 15(1)(*a*) of the following words "and not being a mining lease the subject of a disposition to which Part II of the Betterment Levy (Minerals) (Scotland) (Amendment) Regulations 1969(**a**) applies and in respect of which an operative assessment of effective rate occurs or has occurred under that Part of those regulations".

William Ross,
One of Her Majesty's Principal
Secretaries of State.

St. Andrew's House,
Edinburgh.

6th May 1970.

EXPLANATORY NOTE

(*This Note is not part of the Regulations.*)

These Regulations contain amendments to the Betterment Levy (Tenancies and Reversions) (Scotland) Regulations 1967 consequential upon the Finance Act 1969 and the Betterment Levy (Minerals) (Scotland) (Amendment) Regulations 1969.

Firstly, Regulation 2 amends Regulation 7 of the 1967 Regulations, which concerns the base value of tenancies derived from the consideration given for the grant of a tenancy, to take account of the modifications to Schedule 5 of the Land Commission Act 1967 introduced by section 47 of the Finance Act 1969. Under the power conferred by section 47(3) of that Act this amendment is made retrospective to 6th April 1967, the first appointed day under the Land Commission Act 1967.

Grants of tenancies during the interim period (23rd September 1965 to 5th April 1967) were excluded from Regulation 7 because a disposition during that period is not a relevant disposition under paragraph 3 of Schedule 5 to the Act of 1967. It is now, however, provided by section 47 of the Act of 1969 which introduces into that Schedule a new paragraph 10A (plots for single houses) and a new paragraph 10B (certain other dispositions), that, if it is to the levypayer's advantage, a disposition during that period, and falling within either of those paragraphs, may be treated as a relevant disposition. Regulation 2 makes corresponding amendments to paragraph 7 of the 1967 Regulations, which are to be read as if always so amended.

(**a**) S.I. 1970/457 (1970 I, p. 1535).

Secondly, Regulation 3 disapplies Regulation 15 of the 1967 Regulations in certain circumstances to which the Betterment Levy (Minerals) (Scotland) (Amendment) Regulations 1969 apply.

Levy is normally assessed in Case B on the grant of a tenancy as a single principal amount which takes into account, amongst other things, the capital value of the right to receive rent payable in respect of the tenancy on the assumption that the tenancy will run its course and that the landlord will receive all the consideration in respect of which he is assessed to levy. Regulation 15 of the 1967 regulations deals with the situation which arises upon the tenancy being prematurely determined, e.g. by abandonment. If this happens the assumption referred to is falsified. Regulation 15 accordingly makes provision for adding to the landlord's base value on an assessment on a future chargeable act or event an amount which will reflect the capitalised value of the rent he failed to obtain during the tenancy which has been determined but which he would have received, had the tenancy run its course. This provision requires modification in the case of a mining lease which has been granted, renewed, extended or varied by a disposition assessed to levy under Part II of the 1969 Regulations. That Part of those Regulations provides that levy shall be charged from time to time on the actual amount of rents, royalties, etc. As levy is payable only in respect of rent etc., actually received or receivable, no levy is charged on rents etc., which would have been received or receivable but for the premature determination of the mining lease. Regulation 3 accordingly provides that Regulation 15 of the 1967 Regulation shall not apply to dispositions assessed to levy on this basis.

STATUTORY INSTRUMENTS

1970 No. 718

TERMS AND CONDITIONS OF EMPLOYMENT

The Baking Industry Exemption Order 1970

Made - - - -	8*th May* 1970
Coming into Operation	1*st July* 1970

The Secretary of State being satisfied that there is in force the agreement mentioned in Article 2 hereof, the parties to which are an organisation representing employers in the baking industry and a trade union representing the bakery workers, and that, having regard to the terms of that agreement the Baking Industry (Hours of Work) Act 1954**(a)** should not apply in relation to bakery workers to whom that agreement relates, and in exercise of her powers under section 9(1) of the said Act, and of all other powers enabling her in that behalf, hereby makes the following Order:—

Citation, commencement, revocation and interpretation

1.—(1) This Order, which may be cited as the Baking Industry Exemption Order 1970, shall come into operation on 1st July 1970.

(2) The Baking Industry Exemption Order, 1959**(b)**, is hereby revoked.

(3) The Interpretation Act 1889**(c)** shall apply to the interpretation of this Order as it applies to the interpretation of an Act of Parliament and as if this Order and the Order hereby revoked were Acts of Parliament.

Exemption from statutory restrictions on night work

2. The provisions of sections one to eight of the Baking Industry (Hours of Work) Act 1954 shall not apply in relation to bakery workers to whom the following agreement relates employed by any employer to whom the agreement applies, that is to say, the agreement made on 27th January 1970 between the National Association of Master Bakers, Confectioners and Caterers, the Participating Employers referred to in the said agreement and the Bakers' Union.

Signed by order of the Secretary of State.
8th May 1970.

A. A. Jarratt,
Deputy Under Secretary of State,
Department of Employment and Productivity.

(a) 1954 c. 57. **(b)** S.I. 1959/1398 (1959 I, p. 277). **(c)** 1889 c. 63.

EXPLANATORY NOTE

(This Note is not part of the Order.)

This Order, which has effect from 1st July 1970, provides that the restrictions on night work in the baking industry imposed by the Baking Industry (Hours of Work) Act 1954 shall not apply in relation to bakery workers covered by the agreement referred to in Article 2 of this Order, and is in substitution of the Baking Industry Exemption Order 1959, which Order is revoked.

STATUTORY INSTRUMENTS

1970 No. 719

CRIMINAL PROCEDURE, ENGLAND AND WALES

The Fixed Penalty (Procedure) (Amendment) (No. 2) Regulations 1970

Made - - -	*8th May* 1970
Laid before Parliament	*18th May* 1970
Coming into Operation	*1st June* 1970

In pursuance of the powers conferred upon me by section 80(11) of the Road Traffic Regulation Act 1967(**a**), I hereby make the following Regulations :—

1.—(1) These Regulations may be cited as the Fixed Penalty (Procedure) (Amendment) (No. 2) Regulations 1970.

(2) The Interpretation Act 1889(**b**) shall apply to the interpretation of these Regulations as it applies to the interpretation of an Act of Parliament.

(3) These Regulations shall not extend to Scotland.

(4) These Regulations shall come into operation on 1st June 1970.

2.—(1) In Regulation 4(1)(*a*) of the Fixed Penalty (Procedure) Regulations 1970(**c**), as amended by the Fixed Penalty (Procedure) (Amendment) Regulations 1970(**d**), after the words "the Middlesex area" there shall be inserted the words "or the south-east London area".

(2) Regulation 4(1)(*c*) of the first-mentioned Regulations shall be omitted.

James Callaghan,
One of Her Majesty's Principal
Secretaries of State.

Home Office,
Whitehall.
8th May 1970

(**a**) 1967 c. 76.
(**b**) 1889 c. 63.
(**c**) S.I. 1970/198 (1970 I, p. 869).
(**d**) S.I. 1970/449 (1970 I, p. 1522).

EXPLANATORY NOTE

(This Note is not part of the Regulations.)

These Regulations provide that payment of a fixed penalty for an offence committed in the south-east London area shall be made to the chief clerk at the Marylebone magistrates' court instead of to the clerk to the justices for the Croydon petty sessional division.

STATUTORY INSTRUMENTS

1970 No. 720 (S.55)

COURT OF SESSION SCOTLAND

SHERIFF COURT, SCOTLAND

Act of Sederunt (Variation and Recall of Orders in Consistorial Causes) 1970

Made - - -	*8th May* 1970
Coming into Operation	*4th July* 1970

The Lords of Council and Session, by virtue of the powers conferred upon them by sections 16 and 34 of the Administration of Justice (Scotland) Act 1933(**a**) and section 8(4) of the Law Reform (Miscellaneous Provisions) (Scotland) Act 1966(**b**), do hereby enact and declare as follows :—

1. All applications to the Sheriff for variation or recall of any order to which the provisions of section 8(1) and (6) of the Law Reform (Miscellaneous Provisions (Scotland) Act 1966(**b**) apply, shall be commenced by an initial writ under the Sheriff Courts (Scotland) Acts 1907(**c**) and 1913(**d**) and the proceedings therein shall be subject to the same rights of appeal to the Court of Session as any ordinary action in the Sheriff Court.

2. Subject to the provisions of this Act of Sederunt, every such application shall proceed as an ordinary action, and it shall not be competent for the Sheriff to direct that it be tried as a summary cause nor to shorten the *induciae*.

3. Within three days after the date of lodging the initial writ in the Sheriff court, there shall be lodged in the process of the Court of Session action in which the original order was made, a copy of the initial writ certified by the solicitor lodging the same ; provided that on cause shown the Court of Session, on a motion enrolled for that purpose, may allow such copy to be lodged late on such terms and conditions as shall appear to be just.

4. Any of the parties referred to in section 8(3) of the Law Reform (Miscellaneous Provisions) (Scotland) Act 1966(**b**) who is entitled under said subsection to request that the application in the Sheriff Court shall be remitted to the Court of Session, may do so by a note lodged in the Sheriff Court and signed by the party desiring such a remit or by his solicitor.

5. Where such a note is lodged the Sheriff shall, at tabling of the cause, order that the application be remitted forthwith to the Court of Session and the Sheriff Clerk shall as soon as possible thereafter transmit the whole process to the Court of Session.

(**a**) 1933 c. 41.
(**b**) 1966 c. 19.
(**c**) 1907 c. 51.
(**d**) 1913 c. 28, (2 & 3 Geo. 5).

6. An application remitted to the Court of Session as aforesaid shall form part of the process of the Court of Session action in which the original order was made. The initial writ and each step of process lodged in the Sheriff Court shall be allocated a separate number of process therein. The initial writ shall be deemed to be a minute craving variation of the order, and the defender in the initial writ shall lodge answers thereto in the Court of Session within fourteen days after the date of transmission.

7. In a defended application in which no request is made for a remit to the Court of Session, the pursuer in the Sheriff Court process shall, at tabling of the cause, lodge with the process a note certifying that a certified copy of the initial writ has been lodged in the Court of Session.

8. If, in any application to which paragraph 7 hereof applies, the pursuer shall fail to lodge the note referred to in that paragraph, the cause shall be deemed not to have been tabled and it shall drop from the roll ; provided that within three months the Sheriff may direct it to be again enrolled for tabling under such conditions as to notice, or re-service, or expenses, or otherwise as he shall think fit.

9. In a defended application in which no request is made for a remit to the Court of Session, the pursuer shall, at the tabling of the cause or within six days thereafter, lodge in process in the Sheriff Court each step in the Court of Session process which may be borrowed and a copy, certified by the solicitor lodging the same, of each step in the Court of Session process which may not be borrowed.

10. In the defences lodged to an application in which no request is made for a remit to the Court of Session, the defender shall be entitled to apply for variation or recall of any order to which the provisions of section 8 of the Law Reform (Miscellaneous Provisions) (Scotland) Act 1966 apply made in the action to which the application relates, and he may insist upon such application notwithstanding the abandonment of the pursuer's claim.

11. As soon as possible after any application in which no request is made for a remit to the Court of Session shall have been disposed of by the Sheriff the Sheriff Clerk shall transmit the whole Sheriff Court process to the Court of Session.

12. A process transmitted to the Court of Session as aforesaid shall form part of the Court of Session action in which the original order was made, and each step of the Sheriff Court process shall be allocated a separate number of process therein. The principal initial writ, the principal interlocutor sheets, and the borrowing inventory of process shall not thereafter be borrowed from the Court of Session process.

13. This Act of Sederunt may be cited as the Act of Sederunt (Variation and Recall of Orders in Consistorial Causes) 1970 and shall come into operation on 4th July 1970.

And the Lords appoint this Act of Sederunt to be inserted in the Books of Sederunt.

J. L. Clyde,
I.P.D.

Edinburgh,
8th May 1970.

EXPLANATORY NOTE

(This Note is not part of the Act of Sederunt.)

This Act of Sederunt prescribes certain procedure in applications for variation or recall by the sheriff of those orders in consistorial causes to which section 8 of the Law Reform (Miscellaneous Provisions) (Scotland) Act 1966 applies.

1970 No. 721

COAL INDUSTRY

The Opencast Coal (Rate of Interest on Compensation) (No. 2) Order 1970

Made - - -	11*th May* 1970
Laid before Parliament	19*th May* 1970
Coming into Operation	20*th May* 1970

The Treasury, in exercise of the powers conferred upon them by sections 35(8) and 49(4) of the Opencast Coal Act 1958**(a)** and of all other powers enabling them in that behalf, hereby make the following Order:—

1. This Order may be cited as the Opencast Coal (Rate of Interest on Compensation) (No. 2) Order 1970, and shall come into operation on 20th May 1970.

2. The Interpretation Act 1889**(b)** shall apply for the interpretation of this Order as it applies for the interpretation of an Act of Parliament.

3. The rate of interest for the purposes of section 35 of the Opencast Coal Act 1958 shall be 8 per cent. per annum.

4. The Opencast Coal (Rate of Interest on Compensation) Order 1970**(c)** is hereby revoked.

Neil McBride,
Ernest Armstrong,
Two of the Lords Commissioners
of Her Majesty's Treasury.

11th May 1970.

EXPLANATORY NOTE

(*This Note is not part of the Order.*)

Section 35 of the Opencast Coal Act 1958 provides that interest shall be payable in addition to compensation in certain circumstances. This Order reduces the rate of interest from $8\frac{1}{2}$ per cent. to 8 per cent. per annum and revokes the Opencast Coal (Rate of Interest on Compensation) Order 1970.

(a) 1958 c. 69. **(b)** 1889 c. 63. **(c)** S.I. 1970/542 (1970 I, p. 1749).

1970 No. 722

WAGES COUNCILS

The Wages Regulation (Boot and Shoe Repairing) Order 1970

Made - - -	11*th May* 1970
Coming into Operation	18*th June* 1970

Whereas the Secretary of State has received from the Boot and Shoe Repairing Wages Council (Great Britain) the wages regulation proposals set out in the Schedule hereto ;

Now, therefore, the Secretary of State in exercise of her powers under section 11 of the Wages Councils Act 1959(**a**), and of all other powers enabling her in that behalf, hereby makes the following Order :—

1. This Order may be cited as the Wages Regulation (Boot and Shoe Repairing) Order 1970.

2.—(1) In this Order the expression "the specified date" means the 18th June 1970, provided that where, as respects any worker who is paid wages at intervals not exceeding seven days, that date does not correspond with the beginning of the period for which the wages are paid, the expression "the specified date" means, as respects that worker, the beginning of the next such period following that date.

(2) The Interpretation Act 1889(**b**) shall apply to the interpretation of this Order as it applies to the interpretation of an Act of Parliament and as if this Order and the Order hereby revoked were Acts of Parliament.

3. The wages regulation proposals set out in the Schedule hereto shall have effect as from the specified date and as from that date the Wages Regulation (Boot and Shoe Repairing) Order 1969(**c**) shall cease to have effect.

Signed by order of the Secretary of State.

11th May 1970.

A. A. Jarratt,
Deputy Under Secretary of State,
Department of Employment and Productivity.

(**a**) 1959 c. 69. (**b**) 1889 c. 63.
(**c**) S.I. 1969/428 (1969 I, p. 1221).

ARRANGEMENT OF SCHEDULE

Article 3

SCHEDULE 1

The following minimum remuneration shall be substituted for the statutory minimum remuneration fixed by the Wages Regulation (Boot and Shoe Repairing) Order 1969 (Order D. (149)).

STATUTORY MINIMUM REMUNERATION

PART I

APPLICATION

1.—(1) Subject to the provisions of this Schedule, the minimum remuneration payable to a worker to whom this Schedule applies for all work except work to which a minimum overtime rate applies under Part VI of this Schedule is:—

(*a*) in the case of a time worker, the hourly general minimum time rate applicable to the worker under the provisions of this Schedule;

(*b*) in the case of a worker employed on piece work,

(i) where a general minimum piece rate applies under Part VIII of this Schedule, that piece rate;

(ii) where no general minimum piece rate applies, piece rates each of which would yield, in the circumstances of the case, to an ordinary worker at least the same amount of money as the hourly general minimum time rate which would be applicable if the worker were a time worker:

Provided that where a guaranteed time rate is applicable to the worker under paragraph 3 or 5 and the worker's minimum remuneration calculated on a time work basis at the hourly guaranteed time rate exceeds the minimum remuneration calculated under the provisions of (*b*) of this sub-paragraph, the worker shall be paid at not less than the hourly guaranteed time rate.

(2) In this Schedule, the expressions "hourly general minimum time rate" and "hourly guaranteed time rate" mean respectively the general minimum time rate and the guaranteed time rate applicable to the worker under Part II, Part III or Part IV of this Schedule divided by 41.

2.—(1) Subject to the provisions of sub-paragraph (2) of this paragraph, this Schedule applies to workers in relation to whom the Boot and Shoe Repairing Wages Council (Great Britain) operates, that it to say, workers employed in Great Britain in the circumstances specified in the Schedule to the Boot and Shoe Repairing Wages Council (Great Britain) (Variation) Order 1948(a), namely:—

(i) all workers employed in Great Britain in a boot and shoe repairing undertaking as defined in sub-paragraph (3) of this paragraph on any of the following work:—

(*a*) the repairing, altering or dyeing of boots, shoes, slippers and all other similar kinds of footwear;

(*b*) the making of bespoke footwear;

(*c*) work incidental or ancillary to any of the above-mentioned operations;

(*d*) shop duties in connection with the above operations, including attending to customers and sale by retail of boot and shoe laces and materials and articles used in connection with the cleaning or repair of boots or shoes;

(*e*) collection or despatch in connection with the operations in (*a*) and (*b*) above, and work ancillary thereto;

(*f*) canvassing for boot or shoe repairs and the collection of accounts in connection with the undertaking;

(*g*) clerical or other office work in connection with the undertaking, including costing and the work of a cashier;

(ii) all outworkers employed by way of trade in Great Britain on any of the operations specified in (*a*), (*b*) or (*c*) of (i) above.

(2) Notwithstanding the provisions of sub-paragraph (1) of this paragraph, this Schedule does not apply:—

(i) to workers employed in any shop or in any department in a shop, being a shop or department which is wholly or mainly engaged in the sale by retail of footwear (including operations in connection with such sale), in respect of their employment:—

(*a*) on retail sales at such shop and operations incidental thereto; or

(*b*) on transport or clerical work relating to such sales; or

(ii) to workers employed in or in connection with a factory which is wholly or mainly engaged on the manufacture of leather footwear on a large scale, in respect of their employment:—

(*a*) on the making of bespoke footwear and work incidental or ancillary thereto; or

(*b*) on transport or clerical work relating to bespoke footwear; or

(iii) to workers who are persons registered as handicapped by disablement in pursuance of the Disabled Persons (Employment) Acts 1944 and 1958(b), in respect of their employment by Remploy Limited.

(3) For the purpose of this Schedule a "boot and shoe repairing undertaking" means any undertaking or any part of an undertaking which is wholly or mainly engaged by way of trade on any of the following operations, including operations incidental or ancillary thereto, that is to say—

(i) the repairing of leather footwear;

(ii) the making of bespoke footwear:

Provided that as regards trainees who, under the Government Vocational Training Scheme for resettlement training, have been placed by the Department of Employment and Productivity with, and are being trained by, an employer for a period of approved training, this Schedule shall not (subject to the condition that the requirements of the Training Scheme are complied with) apply during the period in respect of which the trainees are in receipt of allowances as provided under the Scheme.

(a) S.I. 1948/706 (Rev. XXIII, p. 453: 1948 I, p. 4398).
(b) 1944 c. 10 and 1958 c. 33.

PART II

MALE OR FEMALE WORKERS AGED 21 YEARS OR OVER

GENERAL MINIMUM TIME RATE AND GUARANTEED TIME RATE FOR FOREMEN OR MANAGERS

	Per week of 41 hours s. d.
3.—(1) The general minimum time rate applicable to all male or female workers aged 21 years or over and employed as foremen or managers is ...	*276 0*
(2) The guaranteed time rate applicable to the workers specified in sub-paragraph (1) when employed on piece work is	*276 0*

(3) For the purposes of this paragraph,

(*a*) a foreman or manager is a male or female worker who either—

(i) exercises sole supervisory authority over all journeyworkers who must exceed three in number (excluding himself) working in the same shop or department, or

(ii) (whether working alone or with any other worker) under the terms of his employment and, in addition to any work which may be required of him as a journeyworker, fits up or supervises the fitting up, of the work and has control of the repairing or making and the technical direction thereof;

(*b*) a journeyworker is a male or female worker to whom there applies under this Schedule either a general minimum piece rate or a general minimum time rate of not less than *243s. 0*d. per week of 41 hours or to whom such a general minimum time rate would be applicable if he were a time worker.

GENERAL MINIMUM TIME RATES

4. The general minimum time rates applicable to all male or female workers aged 21 years or over, except (i) the foremen or managers specified in paragraph 3 and (ii) learners to whom the minimum rates specified in Part IV of this Schedule apply, are as follows:—

	Per week of 41 hours s. d.
(*a*) sewing or stitching machine operators employed in operating—	
(i) power sole stitchers or both power sole stitchers and Blake or other sole sewing machines on the Blake principle ...	*266 0*
(ii) Blake or other sole sewing machines on the Blake principle or edge trimming machines	*257 0*
Provided that where the worker, for the purpose of training thereon, is employed on such machines for one probationary period not exceeding four months, the general minimum time rate applicable during the said period shall be	*247 0*
(*b*) (i) press cutters responsible for cutting and costing	*265 0*
(ii) press cutters other than those responsible for cutting and costing	*247 0*
(*c*) workers employed—	
(i) as makers of bespoke (which term includes surgical) footwear	*280 0*
(ii) as repairers engaged in sewing down caps, re-welting, welt repairs, linking or any other hand stitching operation ...	*253 0*
(iii) in clicking	*253 0*
(iv) in clicking and closing	*253 0*

	Male workers	Female workers
	Per week of 41 hours	
	s. d.	s. d.
(v) as closers (that is, in fitting and machining) in the making of uppers for bespoke (which term includes surgical) footwear and not employed in clicking	*253 0*	*188 0*

	All workers Per week of 41 hours
	s. d.
(*d*) workers employed in altering footwear or on benching or finishing operations (whether performed by hand or machine) in repairing leather footwear	*246 0*

	Male workers	Female workers
	Per week of 41 hours	
	s. d.	s. d.
(*e*) all other workers to whom this paragraph applies ...	*243 0*	*182 0*

PART III

MALE OR FEMALE WORKERS AGED UNDER 21 YEARS

GENERAL MINIMUM TIME RATES AND GUARANTEED TIME RATE

5.—(1) The general minimum time rates applicable to all male or female workers aged under 21 years, being—

(*a*) foremen or managers as defined in paragraph 3(3),

(*b*) press cutters responsible for cutting and costing, or

(*c*) workers who have worked at least five years in the trade under a contract of apprenticeship,

are the general minimum time rates which would be applicable to those workers under paragraph 3 or 4 if they were aged 21 years or over.

	Per week of 41 hours
	s. d.
(2) The guaranteed time rate applicable to the workers specified in sub-paragraph (1)(*a*) of this paragraph when employed on piece work is	*276 0*

GENERAL MINIMUM TIME RATES

6.—(1) The general minimum time rates applicable to all male or female workers aged under 21 years except (i) the workers specified in paragraph 5 and (ii) learners or apprentices to whom the minimum rates specified in Part IV of this Schedule apply are those specified in the following Table.

	Column 1	Column 2	Column 3
	The workers specified in sub-para. (2) of this paragraph	Other male workers	Other female workers
	Per week of 41 hours		
	s. d.	s. d.	s. d.
Aged 20 and under 21 years	*198 0*	*198 0*	*161 0*
" 19 " " 20 "	*178 0*	*178 0*	*145 0*
" 18 " " 19 "	*164 0*	*164 0*	*134 0*
" 17 " " 18 "	*137 0*	*137 0*	*114 0*
" 16 " " 17 "	*128 0*	*128 0*	*106 0*
Under 16 years	*121 0*	*121 0*	*99 0*

(2) The workers referred to in Column 1 of the foregoing Table are male or female workers who are—

(*a*) operators of sole stitching, sole sewing or edge trimming machines,

(*b*) press cutters not responsible for cutting and costing,

(*c*) employed as makers of bespoke (which term includes surgical) footwear,

(*d*) repairers engaged in sewing down caps, re-welting, welt repairs, linking or any other hand stitching operation,

(*e*) employed in clicking,

(*f*) employed in clicking and closing,

(*g*) employed in altering footwear or on benching operations (whether performed by hand or machine) in repairing leather footwear, or

(*h*) employed in finishing operations (whether performed by hand or machine) in repairing leather footwear.

PART IV

GENERAL MINIMUM TIME RATES FOR LEARNERS AND APPRENTICES

LEARNERS

7.—(1) The following general minimum time rates are applicable to male or female learners employed in accordance with the conditions set out in paragraph 9.

	Learners to bespoke hand sewn making	All others learners
	Per week of 41 hours	
	s. d.	s. d.
Aged 20 and under 21 years	*192 0*	*191 0*
„ 19 „ „ 20 „	*172 0*	*171 0*
„ 18 „ „ 19 „	*158 0*	*157 0*
„ 17 „ „ 18 „	*131 0*	*130 0*
„ 16 „ „ 17 „	*121 0*	*120 0*
„ under 16 years	*115 0*	*114 0*

(2) The general minimum time rate applicable to a learner to bespoke hand sewn making who is aged 21 years or over and who has not completed a period of five years in such learnership shall, until he attains the age of 22 years or until he completes the said period of learnership (whichever period is the less), be the rate applicable to a learner aged 20 and under 21 years, increased by 5s. 0d. weekly.

APPRENTICES

8. The following general minimum time rates are applicable to male or female apprentices—

(*a*) who are employed under contracts of apprenticeship in writing to be taught one or more of the following sections of the trade—

(i) bespoke hand sewn making including hand finishing,

(ii) boot and shoe repairing in all its operations as performed in the establishment, including benching by hand and by such benching machines as are used in the establishment, hand sewing, re-stitching, re-welting, finishing by hand, by any finishing machine used in the establishment, by hand and such machine, patching by hand, by machine and by solution, and all other upper repairing,

(iii) clicking (including pattern cutting) and closing (including fitting and machining) of uppers for bespoke work or either of such operations, and

(*b*) in whose case the conditions specified in paragraph 10 are fulfilled.

	Per week of 41 hours
	s. d.
Aged 20 and under 21 years	*189 0*
„ 19 „ „ 20 „	*169 0*
„ 18 „ „ 19 „	*155 0*
„ 17 „ „ 18 „	*129 0*
„ 16 „ „ 17 „	*119 0*
„ under 16 years	*114 0*

Part V

CONDITIONS AS TO LEARNERS AND APPRENTICES

LEARNERS

9.—(1) The general minimum time rates specified in paragraph 7 apply only to a male or female learner in whose case the conditions following are fulfilled—

(*a*) if he is a learner to bespoke hand sewn making, he shall be employed for not less than two-thirds of his time in learning the bespoke hand sewn making branch of the trade and shall, during the whole or a substantial part of such time, receive adequate instruction in either (i) bespoke hand sewn making, (ii) clicking, or (iii) clicking and closing of uppers for bespoke work;

(*b*) if he is a learner employed in a factory in which machinery driven by mechanical power is used for benching or finishing operations, he shall be employed, during the whole or a substantial part of his time, as a learner in the trade and shall receive, during such time, adequate instruction in a progressive manner in either—

(i) benching by hand and all operations of benching by machine which are carried out in the factory, or

(ii) benching by hand or machine and finishing by hand or machine, not less than one-third of the learner's time being spent in benching:

Provided that where the learner has been so employed for not less than three years he may be employed thereafter, in conjunction with a journeyworker finisher, as a learner to finishing by machine, and in such case the learner shall be employed for at least one-third of his time in learning the operations of edge trimming, edge setting and heel scouring;

(*c*) any other learner shall be employed during the whole or a substantial part of his time, as a learner in the trade and shall receive during such time adequate instruction in a progressive manner in either—

(i) benching by hand, throughout the whole period of his employment, or

(ii) benching by hand and finishing by hand or machine, not less than one-third of the learner's time being spent in benching;

(*d*) in the establishment in which the learner is employed the proportion of learners to journeyworkers shall not exceed that of one learner to two journeyworkers:

Provided that one learner of each of the classes specified at (*a*), (*b*) or (*c*) of this sub-paragraph may be employed in an establishment in which only one journeyworker is employed on the operation or group of operations in which the learner is receiving instruction.

(2) For the purposes of sub-paragraph (1) of this paragraph,

(*a*) the "bespoke hand sewn making branch of the trade" shall mean that branch in which workers are employed for not less than two-thirds of their time on bespoke hand sewn making, clicking or closing of uppers or on one or more of such operations for bespoke work;

(*b*) the expression "journeyworker" shall, save as is hereinafter provided in this sub-paragraph, have the same meaning as in paragraph 3(3);

(*c*) a worker aged under 21 years to whom a general minimum time rate specified in paragraph 6 applies shall not be reckoned as a learner, apprentice or journeyworker;

(*d*) where an employer is wholly or mainly performing the work of a journeyworker he shall be reckoned as a journeyworker.

(3) For the purposes of determining the proportion of learners to journeyworkers in accordance with condition (*d*) of sub-paragraph (1) of this paragraph,

(*a*) a casual absence of a journeyworker or a casual vacancy for a short period in the number of journeyworkers employed shall not be treated as a failure to comply with the said condition;

(*b*) an apprentice shall be reckoned as a learner notwithstanding that the general minimum rates set out in paragraph 7 do not apply to him.

APPRENTICES

10.—(1) The general minimum time rates specified in paragraph 8 apply only to a male or female apprentice employed under a contract of apprenticeship in writing in whose case the conditions following are fufilled:—

(*a*) The apprentice shall be employed under a written contract of apprenticeship which has been duly executed and which contains the following provisions (which the Wages Council considers necessary for the effective instruction of the apprentice) or provisions substantially to the like effect and no provisions contrary thereto;

(i) A description of the section or sections of work in the trade to which the worker is apprenticed;

(ii) The date of the commencement of the apprenticeship and a provision for its continuance until the date on which the apprentice shall have completed five years' apprenticeship or reached his 21st birthday whichever is the earlier;

(iii) A term that during the period of apprenticeship the employer will pay to the apprentice not less than the appropriate statutory minimum remuneration from time to time;

(iv) A covenant or agreement by the employer that, throughout the period of apprenticeship, he will keep the apprentice under his supervision and instruct the apprentice himself, or place him in the hands of one or more competent journeyworkers for instruction, so that in either case the apprentice shall receive throughout the period of apprenticeship and in a progressive manner effective instruction in the section or sections of work in the trade to which he is apprenticed;

(v) A covenant or agreement by the apprentice whereby, throughout the period of apprenticeship, he binds himself to the employer to learn the section or sections of work in the trade to which he is apprenticed;

(vi) A term, in the case of an apprentice who is apprenticed to the boot and shoe repairing section of work in the trade, that the employment of the apprentice on benching shall alternate regularly with his employment on finishing, so that not more than one-third of his time is spent on finishing operations;

(vii) A provision that, during the apprenticeship, the apprentice shall not be put on piece work and shall not be employed on any work to which any minimum overtime rate applies under Part VI of this Schedule.

(*b*) In the establishment in which the apprentice is employed the proportion of apprentices to journeyworkers in either branch of the trade shall not at any time exceed that of one apprentice to two journeyworkers:

Provided that—

(i) one apprentice may be employed in each branch of the trade if only one journeyworker is employed in the same branch;

(ii) where an employer who works personally at the trade and does not employ a journeyworker has one apprentice who has completed at least four years' apprenticeship, he may employ a second apprentice during the last year of the apprenticeship of the first apprentice, and for the purpose of calculating the proportion of apprentices to journeyworkers the first apprentice shall not be taken into account.

(*c*) The apprentice shall be the holder of a certificate of registration as an apprentice issued by, or on behalf of, the Wages Council or shall have made application for such a certificate which has been duly acknowledged and is still under consideration:

Provided that the certification of an apprentice may be cancelled by the Wages Council if the other conditions of apprenticeship are not complied with.

(2) For the purpose of determining the proportion of apprentices to journeyworkers in accordance with condition (*b*) of the last preceding sub-paragraph,

(*a*) one of the said branches of the trade shall be that branch in which workers are employed for not less than two-thirds of their time on one or more of the operations of (i) bespoke hand sewn making, (ii) hand sewn repairing, (iii) clicking (cutting), and (iv) the closing of uppers for bespoke work, and the other branch shall be any other section of the trade;

(*b*) a casual absence of a journeyworker or a casual vacancy for a short period in the number of journeyworkers employed shall not be treated as a failure to comply with the said condition;

(*c*) where an employer is wholly or mainly performing the work of a journeyworker he shall be reckoned as a journeyworker;

(*d*) a learner shall be reckoned as an apprentice notwithstanding that the general minimum time rates set out in paragraph 8 do not apply to him;

(*e*) a worker aged under 21 years to whom a general minimum time rate specified in paragraph 6 applies shall not be reckoned as a learner, apprentice or journeyworker;

(*f*) save as aforesaid, the expression "journeyworker" shall have the same meaning as in paragraph 3(3).

(3) Notwithstanding the foregoing provisions of this Schedule, where an employer employs a worker as a prospective apprentice for a probationary period not exceeding three months and the conditions of apprenticeship set out in sub-paragraph (1) of this paragraph, other than employment under a written contract of apprenticeship and certification by the Wages Council are fulfilled, the minimum remuneration payable to that worker during the said period shall be that applicable to an apprentice employed in accordance with the condition specified in sub-paragraph (1) of this paragraph, and, in the event of the worker being continued thereafter at his employment as an apprentice, the said probationary period shall, for the purposes of this Schedule, be treated as part of the period of apprenticeship, whether or not it is included therein:

Provided that where the employer does not, on or before the last day of the said probationary period, enter into with the worker such a contract of apprenticeship as is mentioned in sub-paragraph (1) of this paragraph, the employer shall pay to the worker a sum equal to the difference between the minimum remuneration payable to him as a prospective apprentice and the amount that would have been payable to him had the provisions of this sub-paragraph not applied.

PART VI

OVERTIME AND WAITING TIME

MINIMUM OVERTIME RATES

11. Minimum overtime rates are payable to a worker to whom this Schedule applies as follows:—

(1) on any day other than a Sunday or customary holiday or a day on which a rest period occurs,

(*a*) for the first 2 hours worked in excess of 10 hours ... time-and-a-quarter

(*b*) thereafter ... ... time-and-a-half

(2) in any week for all time worked during rest periods,

(*a*) for the first 2 hours worked ... ... time-and-a-quarter

(*b*) thereafter ... ... time-and-a-half

(3) on a Sunday or customary holiday, for all time worked ... double time

(4) in any week, for all time worked in excess of 41 hours, exclusive of any time for which a minimum rate is payable under the foregoing provisions of this paragraph,

(*a*) for the first 3 hours so worked ... ... time-and-a-quarter

(*b*) thereafter ... ... time-and-a-half

12. In this Schedule

(1) the expressions "time-and-a-quarter", "time-and-a-half" and "double time" mean respectively—

(*a*) in the case of a time worker, one and a quarter times, one and a half times and twice the hourly general minimum time rate otherwise applicable to the worker,

(*b*) in the case of a worker employed on piece work

(i) a time rate equal respectively to one quarter, one half and the whole of the hourly general minimum time rate which would be applicable to the worker if he were a time worker and a minimum overtime rate did not apply, and in addition thereto,

(ii) the minimum remuneration otherwise applicable to the worker under paragraph 1(1)(*b*).

(2) the expression "customary holiday" means—

(*a*) in England and Wales

(i) Christmas Day, Boxing Day, Good Friday, Easter Monday, Whit Monday (or where another day is substituted therefor by national proclamation, that day), August Bank Holiday and any day proclaimed as a public holiday or additional bank holiday, or

(ii) in the case of each of the named holidays, such other day (not being a day on which a rest period occurs) as may be substituted therefor by the employer by a notice posted in the factory throughout the three weeks immediately preceding the holiday for which it is substituted;

(*b*) in Scotland

(i) New Year's Day, Good Friday, the local Spring holiday, the day observed as Victoria Day or Queen's Birthday, the local Autumn holiday, Christmas Day and any day proclaimed as a public holiday or additional bank holiday, or

(ii) in the case of each of the named holidays, such other day (not being a day on which a rest period occurs) as may be substituted therefor by the employer by a notice posted in the factory throughout the three weeks immediately preceding the holiday for which it is substituted:

Provided that notification of days of holiday made by the employer for the purpose of Section 94 of the Factories Act 1961**(a)**, shall be treated for the purposes of this sub-paragraph as effective notice of substitution.

(3) the expression "rest period" means—

(*a*) a day (other than a Sunday or customary holiday) in each week of employment (or where one or more customary holidays fall in any such week either in that week or at the employer's option in the next succeeding week), appointed by the employer by giving at least three weeks' notice to the worker as the day upon which the worker will not normally be required to work, or

(*b*) each of the periods during which a worker will not normally be required to work on two days (other than Sundays or customary holidays) in each week of employment (or where one or more customary holidays fall in any such week either in that week or at the employer's option in the next succeeding week) similarly appointed by the employer as days upon which the worker will not normally be required to work for more than 5 hours, or

(*c*) in default of any such appointment by the employer as is mentioned in the preceding sub-paragraphs (*a*) and (*b*) hereof, Saturday or if Saturday is a customary holiday the last working day preceding it.

WAITING TIME

13.—(1) A worker is entitled to payment of the minimum remuneration specified in this Schedule for all time during which he is present on the premises of his employer, unless he is present thereon in any of the following circumstances:—

(*a*) without the employer's consent, express or implied,

(*b*) for some purpose unconnected with his work and other than that of waiting for work to be given to him to perform,

(*c*) by reason only of the fact that he is resident thereon,

(*d*) during normal meal times in a room or place in which no work is being done and he is not waiting for work to be given to him to perform.

(2) The minimum remuneration payable under sub-paragraph (1) of this paragraph to a piece worker when not engaged on piece work is that which would be applicable if he were a time worker.

PART VII

GUARANTEED REMUNERATION

GUARANTEED WEEKLY REMUNERATION

14.—(1) This paragraph applies to a worker (other than a casual worker) who ordinarily works for the employer for at least 36 hours weekly on work to which this Schedule applies.

(2) Notwithstanding anything contained in this Schedule, where in any week:—

(*a*) no remuneration is payable to the worker under the foregoing provisions of this Schedule or by way of holiday remuneration under any wages regulation order made by the Secretary of State to give effect to the proposals of the Wages Council, or

(*b*) the total amount of any such remuneration is less than the guaranteed weekly remuneration provided for by this paragraph,

the minimum remuneration payable to that worker for that week in lieu of any amount aforesaid shall, subject to the provisions of this paragraph, be the guaranteed weekly remuneration.

(a) 1961 c. 34.

(3) Subject to the provisions of the next following sub-paragraph the amount of the guaranteed weekly remuneration is as follows:—

(*a*) in the case of a worker who ordinarily works for the employer on work to which this Schedule applies for at least 41 hours weekly, 32 hours' pay calculated at the general minimum time rate ordinarily applicable to the worker, or

(*b*) in the case of a worker who ordinarily works for the employer for less than 41 but not less than 36 hours weekly on such work, 32/41sts of the amount payable at the said rate for the hours ordinarily worked by the worker in a week for the employer on such work.

(4) Payment of the guaranteed weekly remuneration in any week is subject to the condition that the worker throughout the period of his ordinary employment in that week, excluding any day allowed to him as a holiday, is (*a*) capable of and available for work and (*b*) willing to perform such duties outside his normal occupation as the employer may reasonably require if his normal work is not available to him in the establishment in which he is employed:

Provided that guaranteed weekly remuneration shall not cease to be payable to a worker in respect of any week by reason only of the fact that he is absent during any part of that week by reason of proved illness or with the consent of the employer but, in the case of any such absence (other than absence on a holiday with pay allowed under the provisions of a wages regulation order) the amount of the guaranteed weekly remuneration shall be reduced by the amount to which he would have been entitled under this Schedule as a time worker had he worked the number of hours ordinarily worked by him during the period of such absence in that week.

(5) If the employer is unable to provide the worker with work by reason of a strike, failure of supplies or any cause (other than shortage of work) outside the control of the employer, guaranteed weekly remuneration shall not be payable in respect of any week during which, or part of which, the employer is unable to provide work as aforesaid.

(6) The amount of the guaranteed weekly remuneration applicable to a piece worker shall be the sum to which he would be entitled if he were a time worker.

(7) In this paragraph the expression "week" means "pay week".

GUARANTEED DAILY REMUNERATION FOR CASUAL WORKERS

15.—(1) Notwithstanding anything contained in this Schedule, where the time worked by a casual worker on work to which this Schedule applies is less than 5 hours on a weekly short day (not being a customary holiday) or 8 hours on any other day, he shall be treated for the purposes of this Schedule (except Part VI) as if he had worked on such work 5 and 8 hours respectively.

(2) A casual worker who, in accordance with his employer's instructions, reports on any day for work to which this Schedule applies, but does not perform any such work, shall be treated as if the provisions of sub-paragraph (1) of this paragraph applied in respect of that day.

(3) For the purposes of this paragraph:—

(*a*) A casual worker is a worker who undertakes short engagements on an hourly or a day to day basis.

(*b*) A piece worker shall be treated as though he were a time worker.

PART VIII

GENERAL MINIMUM PIECE RATES FOR MALE OR FEMALE WORKERS

16.—(1) The general minimum piece rates applicable to male or female workers employed on repairing are the piece rates set out in Part IX of this Schedule increased by *106* per cent.

(2) The general minimum piece rates applicable to male or female workers employed on bespoke making are the piece rates set out in Part X of this Schedule increased by *106* per cent.

PART IX

PIECE RATES FOR MALE OR FEMALE WORKERS EMPLOYED ON REPAIRING

A.—SOLES—COMPLETED WORK

17.—(1) Subject to the provisions of paragraph 19 and the provisions as to extras and reductions specified in paragraphs 20 to 29 inclusive, the piece rates for male or female workers employed on repairing soles (completed work) are set out in the following Table.

(2) "Benching throughout" means the performance by a single worker of all the separate operations of benching, the appropriate rates for which, in paragraph 42, amount to the appropriate rate for benching throughout, and includes in the case of riveted work the operations of riveting round soles by machine when the riveting machine is operated by the benchman but does not include the sewing or stitching of the new soles where the work is sewn or stitched.

(3) The piece rates for "benching throughout" shall be increased by 2d. per pair where nails have to be removed from full nailed or bradded work.

(4) The piece rates for "hand stitching (with square awl)" shall be increased by one-third when old stitches are taken out from welts before restitching.

	RIVETED WORK								SEWN OR STITCHED WORK							
	Men's	Ladies'	Youths'	Boys'		Girls' and infants'			Men's	Ladies'	Youths'	Boys'		Girls' and infants'		
Size	6–11	2–8	2–5½	11–1½	7–10½	11–1½	7–10½	Under 7	6–11	2–8	2–5½	11–1½	7–10½	11–1½	7–10½	Under 7
Column	1	2	3	4	5	6	7	8	9	10	11	12	13	14	15	16
	Per pair s. d.	Per pair s. d.	Per pair s. d.	Per pair s. d.	Per pair s. d.	Per pair s. d.	Per pair s. d.	Per pair s. d.	Per pair s. d.	Per pair s. d.	Per pair s. d.	Per pair s. d.	Per pair s. d.	Per pair s. d.	Per pair s. d.	Per pair s. d.
(*a*) (i) HALF SOLE (other than pumps and slippers):—																
Benching throughout	7½	6½	7	6½	5½	5½	5½	4¾	8¼	7¼	7¾	7¼	6¼	6¼	6¼	5½
Hand sewing	—	—	—	—	—	—	—	—	1 0¾	10¼	11¼	10¼	9¼	9¼	8	8
Hand stitching (with square awl) ...	—	—	—	—	—	—	—	—	1 5½	1 2¼	1 3¾	1 2½	1 0½	1 0½	10	9
Hand finishing	7	6	6½	5	4	4	3½	3	7	6	6½	5	4	4	3½	3

	RIVETED WORK								SEWN OR STITCHED WORK							
	Men's	Ladies'	Youths'	Boys'		Girls' and infants'			Men's	Ladies'	Youths'	Boys'		Girls' and infants'		
Size	6–11	2–8	2–5½	11–1½	7–10½	11–1½	7–10½	Under 7	6–11	2–8	2–5½	11–1½	7–10½	11–1½	7–10½	Under 7
Column	1	2	3	4	5	6	7	8	9	10	11	12	13	14	15	16
	Per pair s. d.	Per pair s. d.	Per pair s. d.	Per pair s. d.	Per pair s. d.	Per pair s. d.	Per pair s. d.	Per pair s. d.	Per pair s. d.	Per pair s. d.	Per pair s. d.	Per pair s. d.	Per pair s. d.	Per pair s. d.	Per pair s. d.	Per pair s. d.
(ii) SOLE UNDER HEEL (other than pumps and slippers):—																
Benching throughout	1 2	1 1	1 1½	1 1	10½	10½	10	9	1 3	1 2	1 2½	1 2	11½	11½	11	9¾
Hand sewing	—	—	—	—	—	—	—	—	1 5	1 1	1 2½	1 1	11	11	9	8½
Hand stitching (with square awl) ...	—	—	—	—	—	—	—	—	1 11	1 5½	1 7½	1 5½	1 2	1 2	1 0	11
Hand finishing (whether heeled or not)	1 1	10½	1 0	10½	9	9	8	8	1 1	10½	1 0	10½	9	9	8	8
(b) HALF SOLE, SLIPPERS (other than pumps):—																
Benching	6½	5½	6	5½	4½	4½	4	3	7¼	6¼	6¾	6¼	5¼	5¼	4¾	3¾
Hand sewing	—	—	—	—	—	—	—	—	10¾	8¾	9½	8½	7¼	7¼	6¼	6
Hand finishing	6	5	5½	4	3	3	2½	2	6	5	5½	4	3	3	2½	2

	PUMPS TURNED								PUMPS TURNED AND GRAFTED							
	Men's	Ladies'	Youths'	Boys'		Girls' and infants'			Men's	Ladies'	Youths'	Boys'		Girls' and infants'		
Size	6–11	2–8	2–5½	11–1½	7–10½	11–1½	7–10½	Under 7	6–11	2–8	2–5½	11–1½	7–10½	11–1½	7–10½	Under 7
Column	1	2	3	4	5	6	7	8	9	10	11	12	13	14	15	16
	Per pair s. d.	Per pair s. d.	Per pair s. d.	Per pair s. d.	Per pair s. d.	Per pair s. d.	Per pair s. d.	Per pair s. d.	Per pair s. d.	Per pair s. d.	Per pair s. d.	Per pair s. d.	Per pair s. d.	Per pair s. d.	Per pair s. d.	Per pair s. d.
(*c*) HALF SOLE, PUMPS (other than slippers):—																
Benching and hand sewing of soles complete	2 1	1 9	1 10	1 9	1 7	1 7	1 6	1 5	2 5	2 1	2 2	2 1	1 10	1 10	1 9	1 8
Hand finishing	7	6	6½	5	4	4	3½	3	7	6	6½	5	4	4	3½	3
Pumps which are slippers—																
Benching and hand sewing of soles complete	1 10½	1 6¼	1 7½	1 6¼	1 4¼	1 4¼	1 3¼	1 2¼	2 2½	1 10¼	1 11¼	1 10¼	1 7¼	1 7¼	1 6¼	1 5½
Hand finishing	7	6	6½	5	4	4	3½	3	7	6	6½	5	4	4	3½	3

(*d*) FITTING LADIES' BREASTED SOLES

(i) Where splitting and butting is completed by benchman by hand and cemented to heel breasts ... ... 1s. 0d. per pair

(ii) Where splitting and butting is completed by benchman by machine and cemented to heel breasts ... ... 6d. per pair

18. LEATHER SOLES CEMENTED ON

	MEN'S		LADIES'	
	By Hand	Machine only	By Hand	Machine only
	Per pair d.	Per pair d.	Per pair d.	Per pair d.
(a) Stripping and levelling, including filling	2¾	2¾	2¼	2¼
(b) Skiving and securing old soles at waist	1½	1¼	1	1
(c) Rolling and moulding soles	¼	¼	¼	¼
(d) Skiving new soles	¼	¼	¼	¼
(e) Roughing upper or welt	1¼	1¼	1¼	1¼
(f) Roughing new soles	1¼	1¼	1¼	¾
(g) Applying cement to upper or welt	¾	¾	¾	¾
(h) Applying cement to soles	¾	¾	¾	¾
(i) Attaching new soles and hammering down by hand	1¼	—	1¼	—
(j) Fixing new soles in press (including use of activator)	—	¾	—	½
(k) Securing with rivets at waist and toe as necessary	½	¼	½	¼
(l) Rounding	1	½	1	½
	11½	10	10½	8½

19.—The piece rates for benching set out in paragraphs 17 and 18 do not include payment for:—

(a) Pegging the waists,

(b) Repairing insoles of welted work,

(c) In the case of sole under heel, the sewing or repairing of hand sewn or welted seats.

Where the benchman performs any of these operations, he shall be paid in respect of such work the piece rates specified in paragraph 1 (1) (b)(ii).

20. SOLEING MATERIAL NOT CUT TO SHAPE

The piece rates for benching throughout set out in paragraphs 17 and 18 in respect of soles apply where the soleing material is cut into separate soles shaped rights and lefts. If the soleing material is not given out in this form, 1d. per pair extra is payable.

21. OUTSIZES

For men's work over size 11 the piece rates provided in paragraph 17 for soleing men's work sizes 6-11 and in paragraph 18 for men's work and for ladies' work over size 8 the piece rates provided in paragraph 17 for soleing ladies' work sizes 2-8 and in paragraph 18 for ladies' work shall be respectively payable, with the following additions:—

	Per pair
(*a*) Hand sewn or hand stitched work where the benching and the sewing (or stitching) are done by the same worker	1½d.
(*b*) Benching of riveted work, machine sewn work or machine stitched work	½d.
(*c*) Hand sewing or hand stitching only	1d.
(*d*) Hand finishing	½d.

22. LONG WORK

(*a*) Repairing men's or youths' Napoleon, jockey or riding boots, long Wellingtons, short Wellingtons, field boots or sea boots which reach to the knee or above—

(i) Sole only, men's (all sizes) and youths' (sizes 2-5½): 1½d. per pair extra to the rates for benching;

(ii) Soleing and heeling (or half heeling) when done together, men's (all sizes) and youths' (sizes 2-5½): 2½d. per pair extra to the rates for benching;

(*b*) Repairing ladies' long work—

(i) Sole only, or

(ii) Soleing and heeling (or half heeling) when done together: ¾d. per pair extra to the rates for benching.

23. RIVETING SOLES ON WELTED BOOTS OR SHOES

Riveting soles by hand on welted boots or shoes, 1d. per pair extra to the rates for benching riveted work. This extra does not apply when the new sole is riveted on the top of the old sole or middle sole.

24. SEWING THROUGH (SOLES OR CLUMPS)

Soles or clumps, sewn through by hand on Blake principle, 5d. per pair extra to the rates for hand sewing.

25. SOLEING WITH LEATHER SUBSTITUTES

Soleing with leather substitutes, but excluding the work for which rates are provided in paragraphs 67 and 68:—

(*a*) Where the worker has to prepare or roughen or prepare and roughen both the new sole and the bottom and to apply an adhesive for the purpose of fixing the new sole before sewing or riveting	4d. per pair extra.
(*b*) Where the worker has no preparatory work to perform to the new sole but prepares or roughens or prepares and roughens the bottom and applies an adhesive for the purpose of fixing the new sole before sewing or riveting	2d. per pair extra.

26. SOLEING WITH WATERPROOF LEATHERS OTHER THAN CHROME

Benching throughout ... ... ¾d. per pair extra.

Hand finishing ... ... 1¼d. per pair extra.

27. WOOD PEGGING BY HAND

Soleing, 5¼d. per pair extra to the rates for benching riveted work.

28. FINISHING (PART ONLY), EXCLUDING LEATHER SUBSTITUTES

Finishing edges only, bottoms not touched, 25 per cent. less.

Finishing edges and finishing waist from heel to joint, foreparts of bottoms not touched, 12½ per cent. less.

29. FINISHING (PART ONLY), LEATHER SUBSTITUTES

Finishing edges only by hand, 12½ per cent. less.

Finishing edges and surface of the waist by hand, 7½ per cent. less.

B.—HEELING OR HALF HEELING, TOE BITS, SIDE BITS, UNDERLAYS AND CROSS PIECES

30.—Subject to the provisions of paragraph 31 and to the provisions as to addition and subtraction set out in paragraphs 32 to 41, the piece rates specified in the following Table apply to male or female workers employed on repairing.

	Men's	Ladies'	Youths'	Boys'		Girls' and infants'		
Size	6–11	2–8	2–5½	11–1½	7–10½	11–1½	7–10½	Under 7
Column...	1	2	3	4	5	6	7	8
	Per pair d.	Per pair d.	Per pair d.	Per pair d.	Per pair d.	Per pair d.	Per pair d.	Per pair d.
(*a*) HEELING OR HALF HEELING WITH LEATHER OR LEATHER SUBSTITUTES								
(1) WORK OTHER THAN SLIPPERS								
BENCHING—								
(*a*) Stripping top piece, removing old grindery, levelling and securing under lifts	2	1¼	1¾	1¾	1¾	1¼	1¼	1¼
(*b*) Tacking on top pieces	¼	¼	¼	¼	¼	¼	¼	¼
(*c*) Rounding by hand	¼	¼	¼	¼	¼	¼	¼	¼
(*d*) Nailing round by hand	¾	½	½	½	½	½	½	½
(*e*) Hammering down and filing nails	¼	¼	¼	¼	¼	¼	¼	¼
HAND FINISHING...	3½	2	2½	2	1½	2	1	1
(2) SLIPPERS								
Benching, including nailing by machine when the nailing or slugging machine is operated by the benchman	3	2	2½	2½	2	2½	2	1½
Hand finishing...	2½	2	2	2	1½	1½	1	1
Benching for nailing round or slugging by machine when the nailing or slugging machine is not operated by the benchman	The rates for benching set out above, subject to the following reductions:— (i) Boys' (size 11 and over), youths' (sizes 2 to 5½) and men's work ... ... ¾d. per pair (ii) All other sizes ... ... ½d. per pair When the work is returned to the same benchman for hammering down and filing the heels after nailing round or slugging by machine the rates for benching shall be subject in respect of all sizes to a reduction of ¼d. per pair only.							

	HAND SEWN								RIVETED							
	Men's	Ladies'	Youths'	Boys'		Girls' and infants'			Men's	Ladies'	Youths'	Boys'		Girls' and infants'		
Size ...	6–11	2–8	2–5½	11–1½	7–10½	11–1½	7–10½	Under 7	6–11	2–8	2–5½	11–1½	7–10½	11–1½	7–10½	Under 7
Column ...	1	2	3	4	5	6	7	8	9	10	11	12	13	14	15	16
	Per pair d.	Per pair d.	Per pair d.	Per pair d.	Per pair d.	Per pair d.	Per pair d.	Per pair d.	Per pair d.	Per pair d.	Per pair d.	Per pair d.	Per pair d.	Per pair d.	Per pair d.	Per pair d.
(*b*) TOE BITS, SIDE BITS OR UNDERLAYS																
Benching, exclusive of hand sewing	3½	2½	3	3	2½	2½	2	1½	3½	2½	3	3	2½	2½	2	1½
Hand sewing	4½	4	4	4	3½	3½	3	3	—	—	—	—	—	—	—	—
Hand finishing	3½	2	2½	2	1½	2	1	1	3½	2	2½	2	1½	2	1	1

(*c*) FIXING MOULDED RUBBER HEELS WHERE NO PARING REQUIRED ... ... MEN'S, 3d. per pair. All other sizes, 2d. per pair.

	HAND SEWN								RIVETED							
	Men's	Ladies'	Youths'	Boys'		Girls' and infants'			Men's	Ladies'	Youths'	Boys'		Girls' and infants'		
Size ...	6–11	2–8	2–5½	11–1½	7–10½	11–1½	7–10½	Under 7	6–11	2–8	2–5½	11–1½	7–10½	11–1½	7–10½	Under 7
Column ...	1	2	3	4	5	6	7	8	9	10	11	12	13	14	15	16
	Per pair d.	Per pair d.	Per pair d.	Per pair d.	Per pair d.	Per pair d.	Per pair d.	Per pair d.	Per pair d.	Per pair d.	Per pair d.	Per pair d.	Per pair d.	Per pair d.	Per pair d.	Per pair d.
(*d*) CROSS PIECES																
Benching, exclusive of hand sewing	5½	4	5	3½	3	3½	3	2½	5½	4	5	3½	3	3½	3	2½
Benching, cemented work ...	7½	6	7	5½	5	5½	5	4½	7½	6	7	5½	5	5½	5	4½
Hand sewing	7	6	6½	5½	5	5	4	4	—	—	—	—	—	—	—	—
Hand finishing	3½	2½	3	2	1½	2	1	1	3½	2½	3	2	1½	2	1	1

31.—As respects the work specified in paragraph 30:—

(i) If benching (other than hand sewing) is not completed by one worker, the piece rates specified in paragraph 1 (1) (*b*)(ii) apply.

(ii) The piece rates for benching are payable to the benchman whether his work includes or does not include the filing of heels, toe plates and metal tips.

(iii) The piece rates for benching heels do not apply to the removing of old heels and the fixing (including knifing up) of new ready made heels of pulp or leather. If the benchman performs these operations he shall be paid the piece rates specified in paragraph 1(1)(*b*)(ii).

32. TOP PIECES CUT TO SHAPE AND SIZE

The piece rates for benching heels set out in paragraph 30 shall be reduced by ¼d. per pair where no knifing up is required before the top pieces are nailed or riveted round.

33. OUTSIZES, HEEL OR HALF HEEL

For men's work over size 11, the piece rate provided in paragraph 30 for men's work sizes 6-11, and for ladies' work over size 8, the piece rate provided in paragraph 30 for ladies' work sizes 2-8 shall be payable respectively with the following additions:—

For benching (whether complete or in preparation for the riveting or slugging machine)	¼d. per pair.
For hand finishing	¼d. per pair.

34. NEW LIFTS AND PART LIFTS

(1) (*a*) New lifts—for each quarter of an inch or part thereof, 1d. per pair extra;

(*b*) Part lifts—where parts of heels have to be cut out to the depth of ½ inch or more for the purpose of levelling the heels, although complete new lifts may not be inserted, 1d. per pair extra.

(2) Where heels are stripped down to the seat piece, the piece rates for re-building heels and heeling (benching) set out in paragraph 64 shall apply.

35. QUARTER OR HALF-TIPS

(1) (*a*) Inserted iron quarter or half-tips	1d. per pair extra.
(*b*) Inserted rubber tips:	
(i) When solutioned	2d. per pair extra.
(ii) When not solutioned	1d. per pair extra.
(*c*) Where the top piece has a quarter rubber tip already attached when the top piece is given out:	
(i) For solutioning on the quarter rubber tip in the process of fixing the top piece to the heel ...	1d. per pair extra.
(ii) For attaching any additional leather to the top piece to make up the difference between the thickness of the quarter rubber tip and the top piece	½d. per pair extra.

(2) No extra is payable for affixing the top piece which has a quarter rubber tip already attached.

36. ELONGATED HEELS

Repairing elongated heels (where waists already filled in):

Men's (all sizes) and youths' (sizes 2 to 5½).	1¾d. per pair extra to the rates for benching.
All other sizes	¾d. per pair extra to the rates for benching.

37. LONG WORK—HEELING

(*a*) Repairing men's and youths' Napoleon, jockey, or riding boots, long Wellingtons, short Wellingtons, field boots or sea boots which reach to the knee or above—

(i) Heeling or half heeling:
1d. per pair extra to the rates for benching;

(ii) Toe bits, side bits, underlays, and cross pieces or any of them:
1d. per pair extra to the rates for benching.

(*b*) Repairing ladies' long work—

(i) Heeling or half heeling:
½d. per pair extra to the rates for benching;

(ii) Heeling or half heeling when done together with toe bits, side bits, underlays, and cross pieces or any of them:
¾d. per pair extra to the rates for benching;

(iii) Toe bits, side bits, underlays, and cross pieces or any of them:
½d. per pair extra to the rates for benching.

38. TOE PIECES (SHAPED)

Shaped toe pieces:

Hand sewn and benched, 3½d. per pair extra;
Riveted, 1d. per pair extra.

39. WOOD PEGGING BY HAND

Heeling, 1¾d. per pair extra to the rates for benching riveted work.

40. FINISHING (PART ONLY), EXCLUDING LEATHER SUBSTITUTES

Finishing edges only, bottoms not touched, 25 per cent. less.

41. FINISHING (PART ONLY), LEATHER SUBSTITUTES

Finishing edges only by hand 12½ per cent. less.

C.—PIECE RATES FOR SEPARATE OPERATIONS OF BENCHING SOLES

42.—(1) Subject to the provisions of paragraphs 43 and 44 and to the provisions as to extras set out in paragraphs 47 to 50, the piece rates for separate operations of benching soles set out in the following Table apply to male or female workers employed on repairing.

(2) If benching throughout is not performed by a single worker, the piece rates for any of the separate operations of benching specified in the said Table are the rates for the individual operations or, where more than one of these operations is performed by a single worker, the sum of the appropriate rates for the individual operations involved.

	RIVETED WORK								SEWN OR STITCHED WORK							
	Men's	Ladies'	Youths'	Boys'		Girls' and infants'			Men's	Ladies'	Youths'	Boys'		Girls' and infants'		
Size ...	6–11	2–8	2–5½	11–1½	7–10½	11–1½	7–10½	Under 7	6–11	2–8	2–5½	11–1½	7–10½	11–1½	7–10½	Under 7
Column ...	1	2	3	4	5	6	7	8	9	10	11	12	13	14	15	16
	Per pair d.	Per pair d.	Per pair d.	Per pair d.	Per pair d.	Per pair d.	Per pair d.	Per pair d.	Per pair d.	Per pair d.	Per pair d.	Per pair d.	Per pair d.	Per pair d.	Per pair d.	Per par d.
(*a*) HALF SOLE (other than pumps and slippers):—																
1. Stripping and levelling, including filling	2¾	2¼	2½	2¼	1¾	1¾	1¾	1¾	2½	2	2¼	2¼	1¾	1¾	1¾	1¾
2. Skiving old soles at waist ...	1	½	¾	½	½	½	½	½	1	½	¾	½	½	½	½	½
3. Tacking on new soles	½	½	½	½	½	½	½	½	½	½	½	½	½	½	½	½
4. Rolling or moulding	¼	¼	¼	¼	¼	¼	¼	¼	¼	¼	¼	¼	¼	¼	¼	¼
5. Skiving new soles by hand or machine	¼	¼	¼	¼	¼	¼	¼	¼	¼	¼	¼	¼	¼	¼	¼	¼
6. Riveting across waist by hand	¼	¼	¼	¼	¼	¼	¼	¼	½	½	½	¼	¼	¼	¼	¼
7. Rounding by hand	¾	¾	¾	¾	½	½	½	¼	1	1	1	1	¾	¾	¾	½
8. Riveting round soles by hand	1¼	1¼	1¼	1¼	1	1	1	¾	—	—	—	—	—	—	—	—
9. Hammering down rivets ...	½	½	½	½	½	½	½	¼	—	—	—	—	—	—	—	—
10. Cutting channels by hand ...	—	—	—	—	—	—	—	—	½	½	½	½	½	½	½	½
11. Opening channels by hand ...	—	—	—	—	—	—	—	—	½	½	½	½	½	½	½	½
12. Laying channels by hand ...	—	—	—	—	—	—	—	—	¾	¾	¾	¾	½	½	½	¼
13. Hammering down bottoms ...	—	—	—	—	—	—	—	—	½	½	½	½	½	½	½	¼

	RIVETED WORK							
	Men's	Ladies'	Youths'	Boys'		Girls' and infants'		
Size ...	6–11	2–8	2–5½	11–1½	7–10½	11–1½	7–10½	Under 7
Column ...	1	2	3	4	5	6	7	8
	Per pair d.	Per pair d.	Per pair d.	Per pair d.	Per pair d.	Per pair d.	Per pair d.	Per pair d.
(*b*) SOLE UNDER HEEL (other than pumps and slippers):—								
1. Stripping and levelling, including filling	4½	3½	4	3½	3	3	2½	2¼
2. Tacking on	1¼	1¼	1¼	1¼	1¼	1¼	1¼	1¼
3. Removing old heels	1¾	1¾	1¾	1¾	1¼	1¼	1¼	1¼
4. Rolling or moulding	¼	¼	¼	¼	¼	¼	¼	¼
5. Fitting new sole to seat ...	¼	¼	¼	¼	¼	¼	¼	¼
6. Securing seat by hand riveting	¼	¼	¼	¼	¼	¼	¼	¼
7. Rounding by hand	1½	1½	1½	1½	1	1	1	¾
8. Riveting round soles by hand	1¾	1¾	1¾	1¾	1¼	1¼	1¼	1
9. Hammering down rivets ...	¾	¾	¾	¾	¾	¾	¾	½
10. Replacing old heels by hand...	1¾	1¾	1¾	1¾	1¼	1¼	1¼	1¼
11. Cutting channels by hand ...	—	—	—	—	—	—	—	—
12. Opening channels by hand ...	—	—	—	—	—	—	—	—
13. Laying channels by hand ...	—	—	—	—	—	—	—	—
14. Hammering down bottoms ...	—	—	—	—	—	—	—	—

	SEWN OR STITCHED WORK							
	Men's	Ladies'	Youths'	Boys'		Girls' and infants'		
Size ...	6–11	2–8	2–5½	11–1½	7–10½	11–1½	7–10½	Under 7
Column ...	9	10	11	12	13	14	15	16
	Per pair d.	Per pair d.	Per pair d.	Per pair d.	Per pair d.	Per pair d.	Per pair d.	Per pair d.
(*b*) SOLE UNDER HEEL (other than pumps and slippers):—								
1. Stripping and levelling, including filling	4½	3½	4	3½	3	3	2½	2¼
2. Tacking on	1¼	1¼	1¼	1¼	1¼	1¼	1¼	1¼
3. Removing old heels	1¾	1¾	1¾	1¾	1¼	1¼	1¼	1¼
4. Rolling or moulding	¼	¼	¼	¼	¼	¼	¼	¼
5. Fitting new sole to seat ...	¼	¼	¼	¼	¼	¼	¼	¼
6. Securing seat by hand riveting	¼	¼	¼	¼	¼	¼	¼	¼
7. Rounding by hand	1¾	1¾	1¾	1¾	1¼	1¼	1¼	¾
8. Riveting round soles by hand	—	—	—	—	—	—	—	—
9. Hammering down rivets ...	—	—	—	—	—	—	—	—
10. Replacing old heels by hand...	1¾	1¾	1¾	1¾	1¼	1¼	1¼	1¼
11. Cutting channels by hand ...	¾	¾	¾	¾	½	½	½	½
12. Opening channels by hand ...	¾	¾	¾	¾	½	½	½	½
13. Laying channels by hand ...	1	1	1	1	1	1	1	¾
14. Hammering down bottoms ...	¾	¾	¾	¾	¾	¾	¾	½

43.—(1) The piece rates for stripping and levelling including filling set out at (*a*) and (*b*) of the last foregoing Table shall be increased by 1d. per pair where nails have to be removed from full nailed or bradded work.

(2) Where new lifts are required, the piece rate for replacing old heels by hand set out at (*b*) of the said Table shall be increased as if paragraph 34 applied.

(3) Where piece rates for riveting round soles by hand, hammering down rivets, laying channels by hand and hammering down bottoms set out at (*a*) and (*b*) of the said Table are payable and:—

(*a*) the operations of riveting round soles is performed by hand, the worker shall also be paid the appropriate rate for hammering down rivets;

(*b*) the channels have not been laid by machine and hammering down bottoms is performed, the worker shall also be paid the appropriate rate for laying channels by hand.

44. The piece rates for benching set out in paragraphs 42 and 43 do not include payment for:—

(*a*) Pegging the waists,
(b) Repairing insoles of welted work,
(*c*) In the case of sole under heel, the sewing or repairing of hand sewn or welted seats,

Where the benchman performs any of these operations, he shall be paid in respect of such work the piece rates specified in paragraph 1 (1)(*b*)(ii).

(*d*) Fitting ladies' breasted through soles—see paragraph 45.

45. FITTING LADIES' BREASTED THROUGH SOLES

(*a*) Where splitting and butting is completed by benchman by hand and cemented to heel breasts ... ... 1s. per pair.

(*b*) Where splitting and butting is completed by benchman by machine and cemented to heel breasts ... ... 6d. per pair.

46. LADIES' PLATFORM THROUGH SOLES

	By Hand		Machine only	
	Per pair			
	s.	d.	s.	d.
1. Stripping and levelling, including securing and filling ...		4¾		4¾
2. Roughing uppers		2¼		1¼
3. Roughing new soles		2		1¼
4. Cementing uppers		1½		1
5. Cementing soles...		1½		1
6. Attaching bottoms (including use of activator)		2½		2
7. Rounding		1½		¾
	1	4	1	0

47. SOLEING MATERIAL NOT CUT TO SHAPE

The piece rates for stripping and levelling including filling set out in paragraph 42 apply where soleing material is cut into separate soles shaped rights and lefts. If the soleing material is not given out in this form, an addition of 1d. per pair is payable.

48. OUTSIZES

For men's work over size 11, the piece rates provided in paragraph 42 for soleing men's work size 6-11 and for ladies' work over size 8 the piece rates provided in paragraph 42 for soleing ladies' work size 2-8 shall be payable respectively, with the following addition:—

Riveted work, machine sewn work or machine stitched work:

For stripping, levelling and tacking-on ... ... ½d. per pair.

49. RIVETING SOLES ON WELTED BOOTS OR SHOES

Riveting soles by hand on welted boots or shoes—

1d. per pair extra to the appropriate rate for riveting round soles.

This extra does not apply when the new sole is riveted on the top of the old sole or middle sole.

50. SOLEING WITH LEATHER SUBSTITUTES

Soleing with leather substitutes, but excluding the work for which rates are provided in paragraphs 67 and 68:—

(*a*) Where the worker has to prepare or roughen or prepare and roughen both the new sole and the bottom and to apply an adhesive for the purpose of fixing the new sole before sewing or riveting,

4d. per pair extra.

(*b*) Where the worker has no preparatory work to perform to the new sole but prepares or roughens or prepares and roughens the bottom and applies an adhesive for the purpose of fixing the new sole before sewing or riveting,

2d. per pair extra.

D.—PIECE RATES FOR OTHER REPAIRS TO SOLES

51.—(1) INSOLES OR HALF INSOLES—SHAPING AND SLIPPING IN

(excluding welted insoles).

Men's (all sizes) and youths' (sizes 2 to 5½)	4d. per pair.
Ladies'	3d. per pair.
Boys' and girls' (up to size 1½)	2d. per pair.

(2) Where either the whole or half of the present insole has to be removed and a new insole (either whole or half) is fitted and the upper is lasted in, the above piece rates do not apply, and a piece worker doing such work shall be paid the piece rates specified in paragraph 1(1)(*b*)(ii).

52. MIDDLES, (TOE TO JOINT) SECURELY ATTACHED BY EITHER GRINDERY OR SOLUTION, AND ROUNDING BY HAND

Men's (all sizes) and youths' (sizes 2 to 5½)	4d. per pair.
Ladies'	3d. per pair.
Boys' and girls' (up to size 1½)...	2d. per pair.
Fitting of press cut slip middles, being a reinforcement and not separately attached or rounded, by hand	1d. per pair.

53. HALF MIDDLES (slotted and fitted)

Where half middles are slotted and fitted into the old middles:—

Men's (all sizes) and youths' (sizes 2 to 5½)	2d. per pair.
Ladies'	1½d. per pair.
Boys' and girls' (up to size 1½)	1d. per pair.

54. TOE PLATES OR TOE TIPS (separate job)

Nailed on...	1d. per pair.
Nailed on and sunk or inserted	3½d. per pair.
Screwed on	2d. per pair.
Screwed on and sunk or inserted	4½d. per pair.

Provided that these rates shall not apply to toe plates or toe tips when combined with nailing to which the rates in paragraph 55 apply.

55. NAILS OR BRADS

(1)(*a*) Nailing or bradding foreparts (with or without toe plates or toe tips nailed on): the piece rates specified in the following Table:—

Column 1	Column 2	Column 3	Column 4	Column 5
—	Men's	Youths' (sizes 2 to 5½)	Ladies'	Children's (i.e., all under size 2)
	Per pair d.	Per pair d.	Per pair d.	Per pair d.
NAILS:				
Full rows round, each row	1¾	1½	1¼	1
Rows up middle, each row ...	¾	½	½	¼
Toe and joint:—One row... ...	1¼	1	1	—
Two rows	2	1¾	1¾	—
RADS				
Full rows round, each row ...	2	1¾	1½	1¼
Rows up middle, each row ...	1	1	¾	¾
Toe and joint:—One row ...	1½	1¼	1	—
Two rows ...	2½	2¼	2	—

If toe plates or toe tips screwed on, 1d. per pair extra.
If toe plates or toe tips sunk or inserted, 2½d. per pair extra.

(*b*) Nailing waists:—1¾d. per pair.

(2) The rates for nailing or bradding foreparts and for nailing waists set out in this paragraph do not include payments for fitters, clinkers, ice, climbing, cricket or golf nails, the removing of old nails or the filling up of old holes with wood pegs. If the benchman performs any of these operations, he shall be paid in respect thereof the piece rates specified in paragraph 1(1)(*b*)(ii).

56. RE-SEWING

(*a*) Re-sewing old soles or waists:—
Up to 4 inches, 3d.; ¾d. per inch thereafter.

(*b*) Re-sewing old pumps:—
Joint to joint:—
Men's (all sizes) and youths' (sizes 2 to 5½), 1s. 6d. per pair.
Ladies' and other sizes, 1s. 2d. per pair.
Turning and re-turning, 6d. per pair extra.
Heel to heel:—
8d. per pair additional to the rates for re-sewing from joint to joint set out above.
Part re-sewing only:—
Sewing, 2d. per inch with a minimum of 2d.
Turning and re-turning, 6d. per pair extra.

57. LINK STITCHING OR LOOPING

1½d. per inch with a minimum of 3d.

58. STIFFENERS (NEW)

New stiffeners (Blake or riveted work) lasted in:
Men's (all sizes) and youths' (sizes 2 to 5½), 1s. 6d. per pair.
Ladies' and boys' and girls' (sizes 11 to 1½), 1s. 3d. per pair.
Boys' and girls' (sizes 7 to 10½ and 4 to 6), 10d. per pair.
If welted:
With tingled or braced seats, 6d. per pair extra.
With sewn seats, 1s. 0d. per pair extra.

59. WELTS

(*a*) Re-welting (including taking out old welts):—

Heel to heel—

Men's (all sizes)	3s. 0d. per pair.
Youths' (sizes 2 to 5½)	2s. 6d. per pair.
Ladies' and other sizes	2s. 0d. per pair.

Joint to joint—

Men's (all sizes)	2s. 0d. per pair.
Youths' (sizes 2 to 5½)	1s. 9d. per pair.
Ladies' and other sizes	1s. 8d. per pair.
New pieces of welt on a job (that is on one boot or shoe or on a pair of boots or shoes)	Up to one inch 3¼d., with 1¼d. per inch thereafter.

(*b*) Re-sewing of old welts:—

Joint to joint—

Men's (all sizes)	1s. 8d. per pair.
Youths' (sizes 2 to 5½)	1s. 4d. per pair.
Ladies' and other sizes	1s. 2d. per pair.
Re-sewing old welts whether of one boot or shoe or of a pair of boots or shoes	Up to 2 inches 2d., with 1d. per inch thereafter.

E.—PIECE RATES FOR OTHER REPAIRS TO HEELS

60. HAND FINISHING NEW HEELS

Ladies' French	5½d. per pair.
Ladies' Cuban	4d. per pair.
Ladies' Square	3d. per pair.
Men's	3½d. per pair.

61. HEEL SUPPORTS

Metal or other ready made heel breast supports, 2d. per pair.

62. HEELING WITH LEATHER SUBSTITUTES

The piece rates appropriate under paragraph 67 and 68.

63. NAILING HEELS

(1) Nailing heels when boots are not heeled or when performed as a job additional to complete heeling:

Less than two rows, 1d. per pair.

Two or more rows, 2d. per pair.

(2) The rates for nailing heels set out in this paragraph do not include payment for fitters, clinkers, ice, climbing, cricket or golf nails, the removing of old nails or the filling up of old holes with wood pegs. If the benchman performs any of these operations, he shall be paid in respect thereof the piece rates specified in paragraph 1(1)(*b*)(ii).

64.—(1) REBUILDING HEELS AND HEELING (BENCHING)

(i) Ladies' French	1s. 2d. per pair up to 2 inches.
Ladies' Cuban	10½d. per pair up to 1½ inches.
Ladies' Square	7d. per pair up to 1¼ inches.
Men's	9d. per pair up to 1¼ inches.

The measurement of the height of the heel is to be taken from the upper at the breast of the heel.

(ii) For every quarter inch or part thereof higher, 1d. per pair extra.

(iii) When sole seat piece is required, 2d. per pair extra.

(2) The above rates do not apply to sewn seats.

65. REFASTENING HEELS

Refastening heels with pieced insoles and nailing through seat by hand, 3d. each.

66. WOOD HEELS

Turning back covers and lowering heels, 1d. per pair.
Replacing covers, 1d. per pair.

F.—PIECE RATES FOR FIXING COMPLETE RUBBER SETS, RUBBER FOREPARTS AND RUBBER OR LEATHER SUBSTITUTE HEELS

67.—(1) The piece rates for fixing complete rubber sets, rubber foreparts, and rubber or leather substitute heels are set out in the following Table:—

Column 1	Column 2	Column 3	Column 4
—	Men's (all sizes)	Ladies' (all sizes) and youths' (sizes 2 to 5½)	Children's (i.e., all sizes under 2)
	Per pair d.	Per pair d.	Per pair d.
(*a*) REMOVING RUBBER SETS Removing old rubber sets and plugging holes: ...			
(i) Foreparts	2	1½	1½
(ii) Heels	1	1	1
(*b*) FIXING COMPLETE RUBBER SETS			
(i) Solutioning complete rubber sets (when nails or screws also used) additional to the rates in (ii) below	2	2	2
(ii) Fixing complete rubber sets (that is, heels and two or more parts or sections on each sole) by screwing or nailing	6	4	4
(*c*) FIXING RUBBER FOREPARTS			
(i) Solutioning rubber foreparts (when nails or screws also used) additional to the rates in (ii) and (iii) below	1	1	1
(ii) Fixing rubber foreparts (one piece) by screwing or nailing	3	2	1½
(iii) Fixing rubber foreparts (two or more parts or sections on each sole) by screwing or nailing...	4	3	3
(*d*) FIXING RUBBER FOREPARTS BY SOLUTION (with or without screws or nails) where the new or old soles are roughened by the worker in preparation for fixing by any adhesive process	8	6	4
(*e*) RUBBER OR LEATHER SUBSTITUTE HEELS			
(i) Where rubber shaped to the heels or leather substitute is used in conjunction with heeling and no lift is placed underneath, the piece rates for heeling shall apply	(see paragraph 30)		
(ii) Fixing rubbers or leather substitute already shaped to the heel when there is no removal of lift or top piece and no building up ...	2	1½	1½
(iii) Solutioning rubber or leather substitute heels (when nails or screws also used), additional to the rates for the work specified in (i) and (ii) above	1	1	1
(iv) Attaching revolving rubber heels without removing lifts or top piece	1	1	1
(v) Finishing heels when fixing of rubbers or leather substitute is not combined with heeling	1	1	1

(2) The rates set out in this paragraph do not apply to (*a*) other rubber soles for which the worker shall be paid the piece rates specified in paragraph 1 (1)(*b*)(ii), or (*b*) rubber tips, the rates for which are set out in paragraph 35.

G.—PIECE RATES FOR CREPE WORK

68. The piece rates for crepe work are set out in the following Table:—

	Men's	Ladies'	Youths' 2-5½	Boys' and Girls' 11-1½	Boys' and Girls' 7-10½
Column ...	1	2	3	4	5
	Per pair s. d.	Per pair s. d.	Per pair s. d.	Per pair s. d.	Per pair s. d.
(1) THROUGH SOLE					
(a) Stripping, levelling and filling ...	5½	4½	4½	3¼	3
(b) Preparing and solutioning bottoms	2½	2½	2½	2	1¾
(c) Solutioning new middle soles ...	1¾	1¼	1¼	1	1
(d) Fixing and hammering down middles	2¾	1¾	1¾	1¼	1
(e) Solutioning outsoles and middles ...	2½	2¼	2¼	1½	1¼
(f) Fixing and hammering down outsoles	2½	2¼	2¼	2	1½
(g) Rounding both middles and outsoles	4	3½	3½	2½	2
	1 9½	1 6	1 6	1 1½	11½
(2) HALF-SOLE					
(a) Stripping, levelling, filling and skiving	4½	3½	3½	2¾	2¼
(b) Preparing and solutioning bottoms	1¾	1¼	1¼	1	1
(c) Solutioning crepe middle soles ...	1	1	1	¾	¾
(d) Fixing and hammering down middles	1¾	1¼	1¼	1¼	1
(e) Solutioning outsoles and middles ...	2¼	1¾	1¾	1¼	1
(f) Fixing and hammering down outsoles	1¾	1¾	1¾	1¼	1
(g) Rounding outsoles and middles ...	3	3	3	2½	2
	1 4	1 1½	1 1½	10¾	9
(3) HEEL					
(a) Scouring and levelling old heel ...	2½	2	2	1¼	1
(b) Solutioning old heel...	¾	½	½	½	¼
(c) Solutioning new top pieces... ...	¾	½	½	½	¼
(d) Fixing and hammering down top pieces...	½	½	½	½	½
(e) Rounding by hand	¾	¾	¾	¾	¾
	5¼	4¼	4¼	3½	2¾
(4) TOE PIECES OR SIDE PIECES					
(a) Stripping, levelling and skiving old soles	2¾	2¼	2¼	2	1½
(b) Fitting piece of new middle sole ...	1¼	1	1	1	¾
(c) Attaching toe or side piece... ...	1½	1½	1½	1½	1¼
(d) Rounding by hand	¾	¾	¾	½	½
(e) Hammering down by hand ...	¾	¾	¾	½	½
	7	6¼	6¼	5½	4½

(5) EXTRAS ON CREPE WORK	Per pair d.
(a) Rands, joint to joint, solutioned, fixed and pared to sole	7
(b) Rands, joint to joint, frictioned, fixed and pared to sole	4
(c) Rands, full, solutioned, fixed and pared to sole	10½
(d) Rands, full, frictioned, fixed and pared to sole	7
(e) All round welts, solutioned, turned down and pared to sole	10½
(f) Building heels by single press cut lifts	2
(g) Wedge shape lifts	2
(h) Attaching ready-built heels (solutioned)	2

H.—REPAIRS TO UPPERS

69. BACK STRAPS

(*a*) Completed work machined:

(i) When not put under seat:

Up to 4 inches, 2½d. each.

Over 4 inches, 1d. each per inch or part thereof extra.

(ii) When put under seat:

Up to 4 inches, 4d. each.

Over 4 inches, 1d. each per inch or part thereof extra.

(iii) When stabbed to seat:

Up to 4 inches, 5d. each.

Over 4 inches, 1d. each per inch or part thereof extra.

(*b*) Completed work solutioned:

2d. each additional to the rates for machined work set out in (*a*) of this paragraph.

70. The piece rates for PATCHES (other than seat patches) are set out in the following Table:—

	Each
	d.
(*a*) Patches machined (when not soled):	
(i) If neither sewn to sole nor put under	4
(ii) If put under sole	6
(iii) If sewn down to sole or welt...	7
(*b*) Patches machined (when to be soled):	
(i) If neither sewn to sole nor put under	4
(ii) If put under sole	4½
(iii) If sewn down to sole or welt...	7
(*c*) Patches solutioned: to be paid at the rates for machined work in (*a*) and (*b*) of this Table with the addition of	2
(*d*) Lasted in or put under (when to be soled)	1
(*e*) Put under (when not soled)	2
(*f*) Sewn down to sole or welt only	3

(*g*) Hand stabbed on, 2½d. each extra to the rates for machined work set out in this Table.

(*h*) Saddle or cross patches to be paid for as two patches.

71. The piece rates for SEAT PATCHES are set out in the following Table:—

Column 1	Column 2	Column 3
—	Men's (all sizes) and youths' (sizes 2 to 5½)	Ladies' and other sizes
	Each s. d.	Each s. d.
Completed work:		
(*a*) Machined and lasted in:		
(i) Half way round heel or less	7	6
(ii) Over half way round heel	1 1	11
(*b*) Machined and sewn down to seat:		
(i) Half way round heel or less	9	7
(ii) Over half way round heel	1 4	1 1
(*c*) Solutioned on and lasted in:		
(i) Half way round heel or less	9	8
(ii) Over half way round heel	1 5	1 3
(*d*) Solutioned on and sewn down to seat:		
(i) Half way round heel or less	11	9
(ii) Over half way round heel	1 8	1 5
Separate operations:		
(*e*) Shaping, fitting and machining:		
(i) Half way round heel or less	3½	3½
(ii) Over half way round heel	6	6
(*f*) Shaping, fitting and solutioning:		
(i) Half way round heel or less	6	6
(ii) Over half way round heel	10	10
(*g*) Lasting-in:		
(i) Half way round heel or less	4	4
(ii) Over half way round heel	8	7
(*h*) Sewing down to seat:		
(i) Half way round heel or less	6	4
(ii) Over half way round heel	1 3	1 0

Hand stabbed on, 5d. each extra to the rates for machined work set out in this Table.

72. The piece rates for TOE CAPS are set out in the following Table:—

Column 1	Column 2	Column 3
—	Men's (all sizes) and youths' (sizes 2 to 5½)	Ladies' and other sizes
	Per pair s. d.	Per pair s. d.
(*a*) Toe caps machined and lasted in:		
(i) When boots are soled	10	8
(ii) When boots are not soled	1 3	1 0
(iii) When boots are made longer (including piecing the insoles)	1 10	1 6
(*b*) Toe caps, solutioned: to be paid at the rates for machined work in (*a*) of this Table with the addition of	2	2
(*c*) Lasted in only:		
(i) When boots are soled	6	4½
(ii) When boots are not soled	1 2	9
(iii) When boots are made longer (including piecing the insoles)	1 6	1 0
(*d*) When sewn down to sole or welt, machined	1 0	10
(*e*) When sewn down to sole or welt, solutioned	1 5	1 2
(*f*) Sewn down only	9	6

(*g*) When caps are sewn in under welt, the appropriate rates specified in paragraph 59 are to be paid in addition to the rates in (*a*), (*b*) and (*c*) of this Table.

(*h*) Toe caps fitted and machined only, 3½d. per pair; if solutioned only, 5½d. per pair.

(*i*) All work when uppers are pulled up to joint for re-capping is to be paid for as lasting vamps with caps as set out in paragraph 74.

(*j*) Toe caps of waxed kips, waxed splits and heavy chrome leathers, 2d. each extra.

73. TOE PUFFS

(*a*) Toe puffs when not re-capped to be paid for as toe caps.

(*b*) When toe puffs are put in and the material is not prepared for the worker, an extra of 2d. per pair shall apply in addition to the rates for toe caps.

74. The piece rates for VAMPS (re-vamping) are set out in the following Table:—

Column 1	Column 2	Column 3	Column 4
—	Men's (all sizes) and youths' (sizes 2 to 5½)	Ladies'	Other sizes
	Per pair s. d.	Per pair s. d.	Per pair s. d.
(*a*) Vamps machined and fitted	11	9	7
If solutioned, extra	6	6	5
(*b*) Lasting	11	10	8
(*c*) Sewing down to sole or welt	1 4	1 2	1 0

(*d*) When vamps are sewn in under welt, the appropriate rates specified in paragraph 59 are to be paid in addition to the rates in (*a*), (*b*) and (*c*) of this Table.

(*e*) Toe capped vamps:

Machined and fitted, 1d. per pair ... ...
Lasted in, 1d. per pair ... ...
Sewn down through welt, 2½d. per pair
} extra to the rates in (*a*), (*b*) and (*c*) of this Table.

(*f*) Lasting vamps of single soled boots, when being soled, 2½d. per pair less.

I.—SURGICAL REPAIRING AND EXTRAS

75. The piece rates for repairing set out in this Part of this Schedule apply to surgical repairing. The additional extras provided in paragraphs 77 and 78 for bespoke hand sewn surgical making apply also to bespoke hand sewn surgical repairing.

PART X

PIECE RATES FOR MALE OR FEMALE WORKERS EMPLOYED ON BESPOKE MAKING BESPOKE HAND SEWN WORK (INCLUDING BESPOKE HAND SEWN SURGICAL WORK)

76.—(1) Subject to the provisions of this Part of this Schedule, the piece rates applicable to male or female workers employed on the bespoke making of bespoke hand sewn work (including bespoke hand sewn surgical work) are set out in the following Table.

(2) Where surgical work is not hand stitched by the maker, the rates for completed work shall be reduced by an amount equal to the appropriate rate for "hand stitching" specified in Column 7 of the said Table.

(3) Where surgical work is not finished by the maker, the rates for completed work shall be reduced by an amount equal to the appropriate rate for "finishing by hand alone" specified in Column 8 of the said Table.

(4) In this Part of this Schedule, the expression "groundwork" includes the making of all boots and shoes of black leathers (other than patent) whether made with or without toe caps, puffs, or box, block or stiffened toes.

GROUND WORK

		Work on sectional system					
	Completed work	Lasting-up (tacking on, rounding and holeing insoles, including preparing stiffeners and toe puffs and trimming uppers out for sewer)	Hand sewing (including preparing and setting up of welts)	Rounding (fill up bottom, round sole, channel)	Heeling, closing channels, building heel, getting ready for finishing	Hand stitching	Finishing by hand alone
Column 1	Column 2	Column 3	Column 4	Column 5	Column 6	Column 7	Column 8
	Per pair s. d.	Per pair s. d.	Per pair s. d.	Per pair s. d.	Per pair s. d.	Per pair s. d.	Per pair s. d.
(*a*) MEN'S, LADIES' AND YOUTHS' LONG WORK: Napoleon, jockey or riding boots, long Wellingtons, short Wellingtons, field boots	40 2	6 2	5 8	4 3½	3 9½	8 1	7 6

	Completed work	Work on sectional system					
		Lasting-up (tacking on, rounding and holeing insoles, including preparing stiffeners and toe puffs and trimming uppers out for sewer)	Hand sewing (including preparing and setting up of welts)	Rounding (fill up bottom, round sole, channel)	Heeling, closing channels, building heel, getting ready for finishing	Hand stitching	Finishing by hand alone
Column 1	Column 2	Column 3	Column 4	Column 5	Column 6	Column 7	Column 8
	Per pair s. d.	Per pair s. d.	Per pair s. d.	Per pair s. d.	Per pair s. d.	Per pair s. d.	Per pair s. d.
(*b*) MEN'S, LADIES' AND YOUTHS' SHORT WORK:							
Boots and Shoes	33 4	4 10	4 10	3 0	3 3	6 6	7 6
(*c*) BOYS' AND GIRLS':							
Boots and Shoes	23 1	3 5½	3 3½	2 1	2 5	4 0½	5 1
(*d*) INFANTS':							
Boots and Shoes under size 9	20 1½	2 10	2 10	1 7	2 3	3 7	4 10
(*e*) Chrome leather soles in hand stitched work, extra...	2 0	—	—	6½	—	1 0	5½
(*f*) Outsizes (i.e. men's size 11 and over, ladies' size 8 and over), extra	1 8	3	3	3	3	3	3

EXTRAS TO GROUND WORK

77. The extras set out in the following Table apply to the piece rates specified in paragraph 76:—

	Completed work	Work on sectional system					
		Lasting	Hand sewing	Rounding	Heeling	Hand stitching	Finishing by hand
Column 1	Column 2	Column 3	Column 4	Column 5	Column 6	Column 7	Column 8
	Per pair s. d.	Per pair s. d.	Per pair s. d.	Per pair s. d.	Per pair s. d.	Per pair s. d.	Per pair s. d.
(*a*) MEN'S LONG WORK:							
(1) Ham or thigh boots	2 3½	8	5½	3½	3½	3½	3½
(2) Patent uppers or fronts:							
When patent calf used	3 6	2 1½	9	—	—	—	7½
When patent leathers other than patent calf used	3 1½	1 11	9	—	—	—	5½
(3) Spur boxes	4 11½	—	—	—	3 10½	—	1 1
(4) Stabbing seats	2 4	—	—	—	—	—	—
(5) Middles to field boots	1 8½	—	—	5½	—	1 1	2
(6) Stiff leg	1 11½	—	—	—	—	—	—
(7) White, coloured or velvet finished leathers, whether covers are used or not (employer to find material for covers)...	3 5½	8	4½	4½	4½	10	10
(8) Other extras as set out in paragraphs 78 and 81...							
(*b*) MEN'S SHORT WORK:							
(1) Patent uppers:							
When patent calf used	2 11½	10	5½	2½	2½	7½	7½
When patent leathers other than patent calf used	2 6½	9	5½	2	2	6½	5½
(2) Crupp uppers	1 0	2½	2	1	1	3½	2
(3) Patent golosh:							
When patent calf used	2 5½	10	3½	2½	2½	5½	5½
When patent leathers other than patent calf used	1 11	7½	3½	2½	2½	3½	3½

Column 1	Completed work	Work on sectional system					
		Lasting	Hand sewing	Rounding	Heeling	Hand stitching	Finishing by hand
	Column 2	Column 3	Column 4	Column 5	Column 6	Column 7	Column 8
	Per pair s. d.	Per pair s. d.	Per pair s. d.	Per pair s. d.	Per pair s. d.	Per pair s. d.	Per pair s. d.
(4) Patent vamp:							
When patent calf used	1 4	9	3½	—	—	3½	—
When patent leathers other than patent calf used	1 2½	7½	3½	—	—	3½	—
(5) Patent toe cap:							
When patent calf used	11½	6½	2½	—	—	2½	—
When patent leathers other than patent calf used	8½	4½	2	—	—	2	—
(6) Patent back golosh:							
When patent calf used	1 0½	6½	2	—	—	2	2
When patent leathers other than patent calf used	8½	2½	2	—	—	2	2
(7) Cloth leg	1 0½	2½	2	2	2	2	2
(8) Wing toe cap	11½	8	3½	—	—	—	—
(9) Middle soles, through	2 4	—	—	9	—	1 1½	5½
(10) Middle soles to joint	1 4½	—	—	5½	—	9	2
(11) Welts from ¼ inch to ⅜ inch in width	1 0	—	4½	2	—	2	3½
(12) Welts over ⅜ inch in width	1 11½	—	9	3½	—	3½	7½
(13) Bevel clumps	2 11½	—	—	1 11½	—	—	1 0
(14) Square clumps	2 4	—	—	1 6	—	—	10
(15) Heels, for each ¼ inch over and above 1¼ inches per pair	6½	—	—	—	4½	—	2
(16) Seats welted or sewn	2 8	—	1 0	5½	—	9	5½
(17) Seats braced...	6	—	6	—	—	—	—
(18) Heels seats sewn down	6	—	—	—	6	—	—
(19) Seats randed...	2 8	—	1 0	5½	—	9	5½
(20) German seats	2 6	—	1 0	—	9	5½	3½
(21) Spur boxes	4 11½	—	—	—	3 10½	—	1 1
(22) Sock linings sewn in	2 4½	1 3½	1 1	—	—	—	—
(23) Arched insoles	2 0	2 0	—	—	—	—	—
(24) Inserted rubberettes or iron tips	6½	—	—	—	4½	—	2
(25) Stitching aloft and bunked	1 3	—	—	—	—	7½	7½
(26) French corks	6 11	6 0	11	—	—	—	—

Column 1	Completed work	Work on sectional system					
		Lasting	Hand sewing	Rounding	Heeling	Hand stitching	Finishing by hand
	Column 2	Column 3	Column 4	Column 5	Column 6	Column 7	Column 8
	Per pair s. d.	Per pair s. d.	Per pair s. d.	Per pair s. d.	Per pair s. d.	Per pair s. d.	Per pair s. d.
(27) Mock corks	5 11	5 0	11	—	—	—	—
(28) Inside corks, not surgical	2 6	2 6	—	—	—	—	—
(29) White, coloured or velvet finished leathers whether covers are used or not (employer to find material for covers)	2 0	5½	2	2	3½	5½	5½
(30) Full bradding or nailing	1 2½	—	—	—	—	—	—
(31) Bradding or nailing toe and joint...	7½	—	—	—	—	—	—
(32) Clinkered round	1 2½	—	—	—	—	—	—
(33) Clinkered round toes	7½	—	—	—	—	—	—
(34) Other extras as set out in paragraphs 78 and 81.							
(*c*) LADIES' LONG WORK:							
(1) Patent uppers or fronts:							
When patent calf used	2 8	1 11	4½	—	—	—	4½
When patent leathers other than patent calf used	2 4	1 7	4½	—	—	—	4½
(2) Other extras the same as for "Men's long work" as set out in this paragraph and in paragraphs 78 and 81.							
(*d*) LADIES' SHORT WORK:							
(1) Cloth leg up to 7 inches	1 0½	2½	2	2	2	2	2
(2) Cloth leg over 7 inches	1 6½	3½	4½	2	2	2	4½
(3) Middle soles...	1 0	—	—	3½	—	6½	2
(4) Welts above ½ inch in width	1 0	—	4½	2	—	2	3½
(5) Heels above 1⅜ inches in height, for each ¼ inch or part of ¼ inch	6½	—	—	—	4½	—	2
(6) French corks...	5 11	5 0	11	—	—	—	—
(7) Mock corks	4 8	4 0½	7½	—	—	—	—
(8) Inside corks, not surgical	1 11½	1 11½	—	—	—	—	—
(9) White, coloured or velvet finished leathers whether covers are used or not (employer to find material for covers)	1 4½	3½	2	2	2	3½	3½

78.—(1) Additional extras to ground work for bespoke hand sewn surgical work (including repairing) are set out in the following Table.

(2) For the purposes of (*a*) to (*f*) all measurements of the heights of corks are to be taken from the centre of the heel base or under the joint, whichever is the greater.

	Completed work	Work on sectional system				
		Preparing work ready for lasting (excluding covering)	Covering	Lasting	Sewing	Finishing by hand
Column 1	Column 2	Column 3	Column 4	Column 5	Column 6	Column 7
	Each s. d.	Each s. d.	Each s. d.	Each s. d.	Each s. d.	Each s. d.
(*a*) Outside through cork (box randed):						
(1) Rising to 1 inch	18 8	6 10	—	4 6½	7 3½	—
(2) For every additional half-inch or part thereof	1 8	1 1	—	3½	3½	—
(3) Bridge or arched waists, add	1 2½	—	—	—	11	3½
(4) Steel bridge plate, fixing	5½	—	—	—	—	—
(*b*) Outside through cork (randed other than box randed):						
(1) Rising to 1 inch	14 7	4 10½	—	2 11	6 9½	—
(2) For every additional half-inch or part thereof	1 8	1 1	—	3½	3½	—
(3) Bridge or arched waists, add	1 2½	—	—	—	11	3½
(4) Steel bridge plate, fixing	5½	—	—	—	—	—
(*c*) Outside cork forepart:						
(1) Rising from joint to 1 inch	10 6	3 2½	—	2 1½	5 2	—
(2) For every additional half-inch or part thereof	1 0	8	—	2	2	—
(*d*) Outside heel cork, cased:						
(1) Rising to 1 inch	3 6	1 8	—	9	1 1	—
(2) For every additional half-inch or part thereof	8½	4½	—	2	2	—
(*e*) Through inside corks, covered:						
(1) Rising to 1 inch:						
(i) Loose	8 8	5 5½	11	1 10	5½	—
(ii) Sewn in	9 4½	3 10½	11	2 9	1 10	—
(2) For every additional half-inch or part thereof	2 3½	1 1	2	9	3½	—

Column 1	Completed work	Work on sectional system: Preparing work ready for lasting (excluding covering)	Covering	Lasting	Sewing	Finishing by hand
	Column 2	Column 3	Column 4	Column 5	Column 6	Column 7
	Each s. d.	Each s. d.	Each d.	Each s. d.	Each s. d.	Each d.
(*f*) Inside heel cork, covered:						
(1) Rising to 1 inch:						
(i) Loose	5 11	3 2½	9	1 8	3½	—
(ii) Sewn in	6 10½	3 3	9	1 11½	11	—
(2) For every additional half-inch or part thereof	1 0	4½	2	3½	2	—
(*g*) Extra heel, loose cork fitted inside up to joint	3 6	—	—	—	—	—
(*h*) Cork fillers for Chopart's boots or false toe parts:						
(1) 2 inches long and over	3 0	2 3	9	—	—	—
(2) Under 2 inches long	1 5	9	8	—	—	—
(*i*) Fitting in brace or tack	2 6	—	—	1 6	1 0	—

	Each s. d.
(*j*) Fitting heel round fixed iron heel stop (exclusive of riveting)	1 0
(*k*) Stiffeners:	
(1) High stiffeners carried above ankle	1 2½
(2) Double high stiffeners to cover each side of ankle	1 9
(3) Long stiffeners	5½
(*l*) Completely filled in waist from heel to joint, completed job (if not finished by maker, 7d. each less)	3 6
(*m*) (1) Meta bars (outside)	10
(2) Meta bars (concealed)	1 2½
(*n*) (1) Wedges or layers (either forepart or heel), sewn in	5½
(2) Wedges or layers riveted on or sewn in made-up boot, on forepart, when not soled	10
(3) Wedges or layers in made-up boot, on heel, when not heeled	7½
(4) Through wedges or layers from forepart to heel (including making up waist on stock boots)	2 8
(5) Where the wedge or layer sewn in is over ⅓ inch thick at the thickest point, 2½d. additional to above rates.	

		Each s. d.
(o)	(1) "T" straps ...	5½
	(2) "T" straps if stabbed on to finished boot...	10
(p)	"D" straps ...	5½
(q)	Buckles ...	4½
(r)	Sponge rubber insoles, cut, cemented to sock, inserted and, if required, cemented to leather insole ...	1 6
(s)	Valgus or Meta rubber pads with socks, fixing ...	10
(t)	Mechanical appliances:	
	(1) Concealed ankle support springs (exclusive of riveting, see item (8) below) ...	1 9
	(2) Inserted metal arch supports (exclusive of riveting, see item (8) below) ...	1 9
	(3) Single or double sockets and fixed shoe pieces (exclusive of riveting, see item (8) below) ...	1 9
	(4) Sole or foot springs (exclusive of riveting, see item (8) below) ...	10
	(5) Fixing to heel and building round undetachable leg appliance...	3 6
	(6) Riveting in socket, single or double ...	9
	(7) Taking down heel, fixing in socket by riveting, rebuilding heel and working over socket ...	2 6
	(8) For the work of riveting referred to in items (1) to (4) above, the worker must be paid the piece rates specified in paragraph 1 (1) (*b*) (ii).	
(u)	Shaped oblique or elongated heels:	
	(1) For an elongation up to and including ¼ inch ...	(No extra)

		Benching Each s. d.	Finishing Each d.
	(2) For an elongation exceeding ¼ inch but not exceeding 1 inch ...	4½	2
	(3) For an elongation exceeding 1 inch but not extending more than half-way from the position of the ordinary heel to the joint...	1 1	3½
	(4) For an elongation extending more than half-way from the position of the ordinary heel to the joint ...	2 1½	7½
(v)	For any extra work involved in the building or re-building of a heel from the seat which is necessitated by the floating out of the heel above ¼ inch from the ordinary contour of the heel...	4½	2
(w)	Converting stock boot into surgical boot to be paid for on the basis of new work.		

		Each Side d.
(x)	Sewing waist by hand where foreparts are stitched by machine ...	2

BESPOKE PEGGED WORK

79. The piece rates for all completed bespoke pegged work are 2s. 0d. per pair less than the rates for completed bespoke hand sewn work as set out in paragraph 76. The piece rates for extras to bespoke pegged work are the same as those set out in paragraphs 77 and 78 for the extras to hand sewn work.

BESPOKE RIVETED WORK

80. The piece rates for bespoke riveted work are set out in the following Table:—

	Men's	Ladies' and youths'	Boys' and girls', sizes 11 to 1½	Boys' and girls', sizes 7 to 10½
Column 1	Column 2	Column 3	Column 4	Column 5
	Per pair s. d.	Per pair s. d.	Per pair s. d.	Per pair s. d.
(*a*) Benched (stuff cut by machinery)	2 4	2 1	1 9	1 6
(*b*) Finished by hand throughout	1 4	10	7	6
(*c*) Finished by hand (edges and heels only)	10	7	5	4½
(*d*) Extras:—				
(i) Nailing or bradding soles by hand ...	7	7	5	5
(ii) Stuff not press cut	4½	4½	3½	3½

(*e*) Light Bluchers (no cap):—
- (i) Putting-up ... ... 1s. 9d. per pair.
- (ii) Nailing or bradding ... ... 5d. per pair.
- (iii) Finishing by hand (edges and heels only) ... 9½d. per pair.

Part XI

GENERAL

81.—(1) For each try on, or re-try on, outworkers shall be paid 1s. 4d. extra for one boot or shoe or pair of boots or shoes, and indoor workers, 8d. extra for one boot or shoe or pair of boots or shoes. These rates do not include bracing. Alterations (other than operations to which general minimum piece rates are applicable) are to be paid at the piece rates specified in paragraph 1 (1)(*b*)(ii).

(2) Scafe or similar soles, 2s. 6d. per pair extra to the rates for completed work set out in paragraphs 76, 77 and 78.

(3) The minimum rates of wages specified in this Schedule do not include the cost of grindery.

82. Rates per pair—where a piece rate is specified in this Schedule as a rate per pair one-half of such rate shall be payable where only one boot or shoe is involved

DEFINITIONS

83. (*a*) "German seat" is a piece of butt leather sewn round the heel.

(*b*) "Inside corks" are extra insoles of cork which are made with the boot.

(*c*) "Shaped toe piece" is a toe piece that is larger than the ordinary toe bit and extends along the side up to the joint.

(*d*) "Underlays" are inserted and slotted toe bits or side bits.

(*e*) "Grindery" is all material apart from tools used by the worker in the making or repairing of leather footwear.

(*f*) "Box randed"—a box rand is a rand which is made from a piece of bend, butt, fore-end, shoulder or belly leather.

EXPLANATORY NOTE

(*This Note is not part of the Order.*)

This Order, which has effect from 18th June 1970, sets out the statutory minimum remuneration payable in substitution for that fixed by the Wages Regulation (Boot and Shoe Repairing) Order 1969 (Order D. (149)) which Order is revoked.

New provisions are printed in italics.

STATUTORY INSTRUMENTS

1970 No. 723

WAGES COUNCILS

The Wages Regulation (Boot and Shoe Repairing) (Holidays) Order 1970

Made - - - *11th May* 1970

Coming into Operation *18th June* 1970

Whereas the Secretary of State has received from the Boot and Shoe Repairing Wages Council (Great Britain) the wages regulation proposals set out in the Schedule hereto;

Now, therefore, the Secretary of State in exercise of her powers under section 11 of the Wages Councils Act 1959(**a**), and of all other powers enabling her in that behalf, hereby makes the following Order:—

1. This Order may be cited as the Wages Regulation (Boot and Shoe Repairing) (Holidays) Order 1970.

2.—(1) In this Order the expression "the specified date" means the 18th June 1970, provided that where, as respects any worker who is paid wages at intervals not exceeding seven days, that date does not correspond with the beginning of the period for which the wages are paid, the expression "the specified date" means, as respects that worker, the beginning of the next such period following that date.

(2) The Interpretation Act 1889(**b**) shall apply to the interpretation of this Order as it applies to the interpretation of an Act of Parliament and as if this Order and the Order hereby revoked were Acts of Parliament.

3. The wages regulation proposals set out in the Schedule hereto shall have effect as from the specified date and as from that date the Wages Regulation (Boot and Shoe Repairing) (Holidays) Order 1967(**c**), as amended by Schedule 2 to the Wages Regulation (Boot and Shoe Repairing) Order 1969(**d**), shall cease to have effect.

Signed by order of the Secretary of State.
11th May 1970.

A. A. Jarratt,
Deputy Under Secretary of State,
Department of Employment and Productivity.

(**a**) 1959 c. 69.
(**b**) 1889 c. 63.
(**c**) S.I. 1967/641 (1967 I, p. 1967).
(**d**) S.I. 1969/428 (1969 I, p. 1221).

Article 3

SCHEDULE

The following provisions as to holidays and holiday remuneration shall be substituted for the provisions as to holidays and holiday remuneration set out in the Wages Regulation (Boot and Shoe Repairing) (Holidays) Order 1967 (Order D. (145)) as amended by Schedule 2 to the Wages Regulation (Boot and Shoe Repairing) Order 1969 (Order D. (149)).

PART I

APPLICATION

1. This Schedule applies to every worker (other than an outworker) for whom statutory minimum remuneration has been fixed.

PART II

CUSTOMARY HOLIDAYS

2.—(1) Subject to the following provisions of this paragraph, an employer shall allow to every worker in his employment to whom this Schedule applies a holiday (hereinafter referred to as a "customary holiday") in each year on the days specified in the following sub-paragraph provided that the worker (unless excused by the employer or absent by reason of the proved illness of or accident to the worker) has worked for the employer throughout the last working day on which work was available to him immediately preceding the customary holiday.

(2) The said customary holidays are:—

(*a*) in England and Wales—

(i) Christmas Day, Boxing Day, Good Friday, Easter Monday, Whit Monday (or where another day is substituted therefor by national proclamation, that day), August Bank Holiday and any day proclaimed as a public holiday or additional bank holiday, or

(ii) in the case of each of the named holidays, such other day (not being a day on which a rest period occurs) as may be substituted therefor by the employer by a notice posted in the factory throughout the three weeks immediately preceding the holiday for which it is substituted;

(*b*) in Scotland—

(i) New Year's Day, Good Friday, the local Spring holiday, the day observed as Victoria Day or Queen's Birthday, the local Autumn holiday, Christmas Day and any day proclaimed as a public holiday or additional bank holiday, or

(ii) in the case of each of the named holidays, such other day (not being a day on which a rest period occurs) as may be substituted therefor by the employer by a notice posted in the factory throughout the three weeks immediately preceding the holiday for which it is substituted:

Provided that notification of days of holiday made by the employer for the purposes of Section 94 of the Factories Act 1961(**a**), shall be treated for the purposes of this sub-paragraph as effective notice of substitution.

(3) Notwithstanding the preceding provisions of this paragraph, an employer may (except where in the case of a woman or young person, such a requirement would be unlawful) require a worker who is otherwise entitled to any customary holiday under the foregoing provisions of this Schedule to work thereon and,

(**a**) 1961 c. 34.

in lieu of any customary holiday on which he so works, the worker shall be entitled to be allowed a day's holiday (hereinafter referred to as a "holiday in lieu of a customary holiday") on a week-day other than a day on which a rest period occurs, being a day upon which he would normally work, within the period of four weeks next ensuing.

(4) A worker who is required to work on a customary holiday shall be paid:—

(*a*) for all time worked thereon at the minimum rate then appropriate to the worker for work on a customary holiday; and

(*b*) in respect of the holiday in lieu of the customary holiday, holiday remuneration in accordance with paragraph 7.

PART III

ANNUAL HOLIDAY

3.—(1) In addition to the holidays specified in Part II of this Schedule and subject to the provisions of sub-paragraph (2) of this paragraph and of paragraph 4, an employer shall between the date on which this Schedule becomes effective and 30th November 1970, and in each succeeding year between 1st April and 30th November, allow a holiday (hereinafter referred to as an "annual holiday") to every worker in his employment to whom this Schedule applies who has been employed by him during the 12 months immediately preceding the commencement of the holiday season for any one of the periods of employment (calculated in accordance with the provisions of paragraph 11) set out in the table below and the duration of the annual holiday shall in the case of each such worker be related to that period as follows:—

Period of employment	Duration of annual holiday			
	Where the worker's normal working week is:—			
	Six days	Five days	Four days	Three days or less
At least 48 weeks	*15 days*	*13 days*	*11 days*	*9 days*
" " 44 "	11 days	9 days	7 days	5 days
" " 40 "	10 "	8 "	6 "	5 "
" " 36 "	9 "	7 "	6 "	4 "
" " 32 "	8 "	6 "	5 "	4 "
" " 28 "	7 "	5 "	4 "	3 "
" " 24 "	6 "	5 "	4 "	3 "
" " 20 "	5 "	4 "	3 "	2 "
" " 16 "	4 "	3 "	2 "	2 "
" " 12 "	3 "	2 "	2 "	1 day
" " 8 "	2 "	2 "	1 day	1 "
" " 4 "	1 day	1 day	1 "	—

(2) Notwithstanding the provisions of the last foregoing sub-paragraph, the number of days of annual holiday which an employer is required to allow to a worker in any holiday season shall not exceed in the aggregate twice the number of days constituting the worker's normal working week.

(3) The duration of the worker's annual holiday in the holiday season ending on 30th November 1970, shall be reduced by any days of annual holiday duly allowed to him by the employer under the provisions of Order D. (145) between 1st April 1970, and the date on which the provisions of this Schedule become effective.

(4) In this Schedule the expression "holiday season" means, in relation to an annual holiday during the year 1970, the period commencing on 1st April and ending on 30th November 1970, and, in relation to each subsequent year, the period commencing on 1st April and ending on 30th November in that year.

4.—(1) Subject to the provisions of this paragraph, an annual holiday under this Schedule shall be allowed on consecutive working days being days on which the worker is normally called upon to work for the employer and days of holiday shall be treated as consecutive notwithstanding that a Sunday or some other holiday intervenes.

(2) (*a*) Where the number of days of annual holiday for which a worker has qualified exceeds the number of days constituting the worker's normal working week but does not exceed twice that number, the said holiday may, by agreement between the employer and the worker or his representative, be allowed in two or three separate periods of such consecutive working days, provided that one of the periods is of not less duration than the number of days constituting the worker's normal working week and that the remaining days of holiday are allowed on whole days upon which the worker is normally employed by the employer.

(*b*) Where the number of days of annual holiday for which a worker has qualified exceeds twice the number of days constituting his normal working week the holiday may be allowed as follows:—

(i) as to the period comprising twice the number of days constituting the worker's normal working week, in accordance with sub-paragraph (*a*) of this paragraph ; and

(ii) as to any additional days, on working days which need not be consecutive, to be fixed by agreement between the employer and the worker or his representative, during the period 1st December and 31st March immediately following the holiday season.

5. Subject to the provisions of paragraph 4, any day of annual holiday under this Schedule:—

(1) may be allowed on a day on which the worker is entitled to a half-holiday under any enactment other than the Wages Councils Act 1959 ;

(2) shall not be allowed on any whole day of holiday to which the worker is so entitled.

6. An employer shall give a worker notice of the commencing date and duration of his annual holiday. Such notice shall be given at least 28 days before the first day of the holiday or, where, under the provisions of paragraph 4, an annual holiday is allowed in more than one period, before each separate period, and may be given individually to a worker or by the posting of a notice in the place where the worker is employed.

PART IV

HOLIDAY REMUNERATION

CUSTOMARY HOLIDAYS

7.—(1) For each day of holiday to which a worker is entitled under Part II of this Schedule he shall be paid by the employer as holiday remuneration whichever of the following amounts is the greater—

(*a*) one-fifth of the appropriate statutory minimum remuneration to which he would have been entitled as a time worker for a week's work if he had worked the number of hours normally worked by him (exclusive of overtime) during the week ; or (*b*) the appropriate statutory minimum remuneration (exclusive of overtime) to which he would have been entitled as a time worker if the day had not been a day of holiday and he had been employed on work for which statutory minimum remuneration is payable for the time usually worked by him on that day of the week:

Provided that payment of the said holiday remuneration is subject to the condition that the worker (unless excused by the employer or absent by reason of the proved illness of or accident to the worker) works throughout the first day on which work is available to him immediately following the holiday.

(2) Holiday remuneration in respect of any customary holiday shall be paid by the employer to the worker on the day on which wages are paid for the first working day following the said holiday.

(3) Holiday remuneration in respect of any holiday in lieu of a customary holiday shall be paid on the day on which wages are paid for the first working day following the holiday in lieu of the customary holiday:

Provided that the said payment shall be made immediately upon the termination of the worker's employment in the case where he ceases to be employed before being allowed a holiday in lieu of a customary holiday to which he is entitled and in that case the condition specified in sub-paragraph (1) of this paragraph shall not apply.

ANNUAL HOLIDAY

8.—(1) Subject to the provisions of paragraph 9, a worker qualified to be allowed an annual holiday under this Schedule shall be paid by his employer, on the last pay day preceding such holiday, one day's holiday pay (as defined in paragraph 12) in respect of each day thereof.

(2) Where under the provisions of paragraph 4 an annual holiday is allowed in more than one period the holiday remuneration shall be apportioned accordingly.

9. Where any accrued holiday remuneration has been paid by the employer to the worker (in accordance with paragraph 10 of this Schedule or under the provisions of Order D. (145)) in respect of employment during any of the periods referred to in paragraph 10, the amount of holiday remuneration payable by the employer in respect of any annual holiday for which the worker has qualified by reason of employment during the said period shall be reduced by the amount of the said accrued holiday remuneration unless that remuneration has been deducted from a previous payment of holiday remuneration made under the provisions of this Schedule or of Order D. (145).

ACCRUED HOLIDAY REMUNERATION PAYABLE ON TERMINATION OF EMPLOYMENT

10.—(1) Where a worker ceases to be employed by an employer after the provisions of this Schedule become effective, the employer shall, subject to the provisions of sub-paragraph (2) of this paragraph, immediately on the termination of the employment (hereinafter referred to as "the termination date") pay to the worker accrued holiday remuneration, that is to say:—

(*a*) in respect of any period of employment occurring before 1st April immediately preceding the termination date, an amount equal to the holiday remuneration to which the worker would have been entitled under the provisions of paragraph 8, if he had been allowed an annual holiday in respect of that period of employment at the termination date, LESS any holiday remuneration already paid for any day or days of annual holiday allowed subsequently to 1st April aforesaid in respect of that period of employment, and (*b*) in respect of any period of employment since 31st March immediately preceding the termination date, an amount equal to one day's holiday pay (as defined in paragraph 12) multiplied by the number of days of annual holiday to which the worker would have been entitled under the provisions of paragraph 3 if by virtue of such period of employment he could have been allowed an annual holiday at the termination date, LESS any accrued holiday remuneration already paid by the employer to the worker in accordance with this paragraph or in accordance with the provisions of Order D. (145) in respect of that period:

Provided that—

(*a*) no worker shall be entitled to the payment by his employer of accrued holiday remuneration if he is dismissed on the grounds of dishonesty and is so informed by the employer at the time of dismissal;

(*b*) where a worker is employed under a contract of service under which not less than one week's notice on either side is required to terminate the employment and the worker, without the consent of his employer, terminates his employment without having given not less than one week's notice or before one week has expired from the beginning of such notice, the amount of accrued holiday remuneration payable to the worker shall be the amount payable under the foregoing provisions of this paragraph less an amount equal to one day's holiday pay multiplied by the number of days constituting the worker's normal working week.

(2) Accrued holiday remuneration is not payable in respect of any period of employment for which the worker has been allowed or become entitled to be allowed an annual holiday under this Schedule.

PART V

GENERAL

11. For the purposes of calculating any period of employment qualifying a worker for an annual holiday or for any accrued holiday remuneration under this Schedule, the worker shall be treated—

(1) as if he were employed for a week in respect of any week in which—

(*a*) he has worked for the employer for not less than 24 hours and has performed some work for which statutory minimum remuneration is payable; or

(*b*) he has worked for the employer for less than 24 hours, or has performed no work, solely by reason of the proved illness of or accident to the worker, provided that the number of weeks which may be treated as weeks of employment for such reason shall not exceed four in any such period as aforesaid; or

(*c*) he has worked for the employer for less than 24 hours, or has performed no work, solely by reason of a stoppage of work due to a trade dispute (except a stoppage due to a strike which is unauthorised at its inception by the worker's Trade Union); and

(2) as if he were employed on any day of holiday allowed under the provisions of this Schedule and for the purpose of the provisions of (*a*) of this paragraph, a worker who is absent on such a holiday shall be treated as having worked thereon for the employer for the number of hours ordinarily worked by him on that day of the week on work to which statutory minimum remuneration applies.

12. In this Schedule, unless the context otherwise requires, the following expressions have the meanings hereby respectively assigned to them, that is to say:—

"NORMAL WORKING WEEK" means the number of days on which it has been usual for the worker to work in a week in the employment of the employer during the 12 months immediately preceding the commencement of the holiday season, or where, under paragraph 10, accrued holiday remuneration is payable on the termination of the employment, in the 12 months immediately preceding the termination date:

Provided that:—

(i) part of a day shall count as a day; and

(ii) no account shall be taken of any week in which the worker did not perform any work for which statutory minimum remuneration has been fixed.

"ONE DAY'S HOLIDAY PAY" means the appropriate proportion of the remuneration which the worker would be entitled to receive from his employer at the date of the annual holiday (or where the holiday is taken in more than one period at the date of the first period) or at the termination date, as the case may be, for one week's work if working his normal working week and the number of daily hours normally worked by him (exclusive of overtime) and if he were paid:—

(1) where the worker is employed as a time worker, the amount which the worker would be entitled to receive from the employer under the arrangement current immediately prior to the holiday;

(2) where the worker is employed as a piece worker, a time rate equal to the hourly general minimum time rate applicable to the worker (or which would be applicable if he were a time worker) increased by ten per cent., for work to which statutory minimum remuneration applies and at the same rate (increased as aforesaid) for any work for the same employer to which such remuneration does not apply;

and in this definition "appropriate proportion" means—

where the worker's normal working week is 6 days — one-sixth
" " " " " " " 5 " — one-fifth
" " " " " " " 4 " — one-quarter
" " " " " " " 3 " — one-third
" " " " " " " 2 " — one-half
" " " " " " " 1 day — the whole.

"REST PERIOD" means—

(1) a day (other than a Sunday or customary holiday) in each week of employment (or where one or more customary holidays fall in any such week either in that week or at the employer's option in the next succeeding week), appointed by the employer by giving at least three weeks' notice to the worker as the day upon which the worker will not normally be required to work, or

(2) each of the periods during which a worker will not normally be required to work on two days (other than Sundays or customary holidays) in each week of employment (or where one or more customary holidays fall in any such week either in that week or at the employer's option in the next succeeding week) similarly appointed by the employer as days upon which the worker will not normally be required to work for more than 5 hours, or

(3) in default of any such appointment by the employer as is mentioned in the preceding sub-paragraphs (1) and (2) hereof, Saturday or if Saturday is a customary holiday the last working day preceding it.

"STATUTORY MINIMUM REMUNERATION" means minimum remuneration (other than holiday remuneration) fixed by a wages regulation order made by the Secretary of State to give effect to proposals submitted to her by the Boot and Shoe Repairing Wages Council (Great Britain).

"WEEK" means pay week.

13. The provisions of this Schedule are without prejudice to any agreement for the allowance of any further holidays with pay or for the payment of additional holiday remuneration.

EXPLANATORY NOTE

(This Note is not part of the Order.)

This Order, which has effect from 18th June 1970, sets out the holidays which an employer is required to allow to workers and the remuneration payable for those holidays, in substitution for the holidays and holiday remuneration fixed by the Wages Regulation (Boot and Shoe Repairing) (Holidays) Order 1967 (Order D. (145)), as amended by Schedule 2 to the Wages Regulation (Boot and Shoe Repairing) Order 1969 (Order D. (149)). Order D. (145) is revoked.

New provisions are printed in italics.

STATUTORY INSTRUMENTS

1970 No. 739

EDUCATION, ENGLAND AND WALES

The Remuneration of Teachers (Primary and Secondary Schools) (Amendment No. 3) Order 1970

Made - - -	11*th May* 1970
Coming into Operation	12*th May* 1970

Whereas:—

(1) in pursuance of section 2(2) of the Remuneration of Teachers Act 1965**(a)** (hereinafter referred to as "the Act") the Committee constituted under section 1 of the Act for the purpose of considering the remuneration payable to teachers in primary and secondary schools maintained by local education authorities (hereinafter referred to as "the Committee") have transmitted to the Secretary of State for Education and Science (hereinafter referred to as "the Secretary of State") recommendations agreed on by them with respect to the remuneration of such teachers;

(2) there are in force orders made under section 2 of the Act with respect to the remuneration of such teachers, namely, the Remuneration of Teachers (Primary and Secondary Schools) Order 1969**(b)**, the Remuneration of Teachers (Primary and Secondary Schools) (Amendment) Order 1970**(c)** and the Remuneration of Teachers (Primary and Secondary Schools) (Amendment No. 2) Order 1970**(d)**;

(3) it appears to the Secretary of State that effect can more conveniently be given to the recommendations of the Committee by further amending the scales and other provisions set out in the document referred to in the said Orders, namely, the document published by Her Majesty's Stationery Office on 28th April 1969 under the title "SCALES OF SALARIES FOR TEACHERS IN PRIMARY AND SECONDARY SCHOOLS, ENGLAND AND WALES, 1969" (hereinafter referred to as "the Document");

(4) in pursuance of section 2(5) of the Act the Secretary of State has prepared a draft Order setting out the further amendments of the scales and other provisions contained in the said document which, in his opinion, are requisite for giving effect to the recommendations of the Committee; and

(5) the Secretary of State, as required by section 2(6) of the Act, has consulted the Committee with respect to the draft Order and the Committee have made no representations with respect thereto.

(a) 1965 c. 3.
(b) S.I. 1969/618 (1969 I, p. 1725).
(c) S.I. 1970/28 (1970 I, p. 222).
(d) S.I. 1970/251 (1970 I, p. 981).

Now therefore the Secretary of State, in pursuance of section 2(6) of the Act. hereby orders as follows:—

Citation and Commencement

1. This Order may be cited as the Remuneration of Teachers (Primary and Secondary Schools) (Amendment No. 3) Order 1970 and shall come into operation on 12th May 1970.

Interpretation

2. The Interpretation Act 1889**(a)** shall apply for the interpretation of this Order as it applies for the interpretation of an Act of Parliament.

Amendment of Order

3. The scales and other provisions set out in the Document are hereby further amended so as to give effect to the provisions of this Order.

Increase of Remuneration

4.—(1) Subject as in paragraph (2) below provided, the remuneration payable to every full-time teacher in a primary or secondary school maintained by a local education authority, as determined in accordance with the scales and other provisions set out in the Document, shall, with effect from 1st April 1970, be increased by £120 a year.

(2) The said increase of remuneration and any like increase payable to any teacher in a college of education or by virtue of an order made under the Act shall be disregarded for the purpose of determining at what incremental point a teacher shall enter any scale set out in the Document.

Given under the Official Seal of the Secretary of State for Education and Science on 11th May 1970.

(L.S.)

Alice Bacon,
Minister of State for Education and Science.

EXPLANATORY NOTE

(*This Note is not part of the Order.*)

This Order increases by £120 a year the salaries of teachers in primary and secondary schools maintained by local education authorities in accordance with the agreement reached in the Committee for the consideration of the remuneration of such teachers.

The Order has retrospective effect by virtue of section 7(3) of the Remuneration of Teachers Act 1965.

(a) 1889 c. 63.

STATUTORY INSTRUMENTS

1970 No. 740

EDUCATION, ENGLAND AND WALES

The Remuneration of Teachers (Farm Institutes) (Amendment) Order 1970

Made - - -	11*th May* 1970
Coming into Operation	12*th May* 1970

Whereas:—

(1) in pursuance of section 2(2) of the Remuneration of Teachers Act 1965**(a)** (hereinafter referred to as "the Act") the Committee constituted under section 1 of the Act for the purpose of considering the remuneration payable to teachers in farm institutes and teachers of agricultural subjects on the staff of local education authorities (hereinafter referred to as "the Committee") have transmitted to the Secretary of State for Education and Science (hereinafter referred to as "the Secretary of State") recommendations agreed on by them with respect to the remuneration of such teachers;

(2) there is in force an order made under section 2 of the Act with respect to the remuneration of such teachers, namely, the Remuneration of Teachers (Farm Institutes) Order 1969**(b)**;

(3) it appears to the Secretary of State that effect can more conveniently be given to the recommendations of the Committee by amending the scales and other provisions set out in the document referred to in the said Order, namely, the document published by Her Majesty's Stationery Office on 11th December 1969 under the title "SCALES OF SALARIES FOR THE TEACHING STAFF OF FARM INSTITUTES AND FOR TEACHERS OF AGRICULTURAL (INCLUDING HORTICULTURAL) SUBJECTS, ENGLAND AND WALES, 1969" (hereinafter referred to as "the Document");

(4) in pursuance of section 2(5) of the Act the Secretary of State has prepared a draft Order setting out the amendments of the scales and other provisions contained in the Document which, in his opinion, are requisite for giving effect to the recommendations of the Committee; and

(5) the Secretary of State, as required by section 2(6) of the Act, has consulted the Committee with respect to the draft Order and the Committee have made no representations with respect thereto.

Now therefore the Secretary of State, in pursuance of section 2(6) of the Act, hereby orders as follows:—

Citation and Commencement

1. This Order may be cited as the Remuneration of Teachers (Farm Institutes) (Amendment) Order 1970 and shall come into operation on 12th May 1970.

(a) 1965 c. 3. **(b)** S.I. 1969/1780 (1969 III, p. 5575).

Interpretation

2. The Interpretation Act 1889(**a**) shall apply for the interpretation of this Order as it applies for the interpretation of an Act of Parliament.

Amendment of Document

3. The scales and other provisions set out in the Document are hereby amended so as to give effect to the provisions of this Order.

Increase of Remuneration

4.—(1) Subject as in paragraph (2) below provided, the remuneration payable to every full-time teacher employed as a member of the teaching staff of a farm institute maintained by a local education authority or as a teacher of agricultural subjects (including horticultural and related subjects) on the staff of a local education authority, as determined in accordance with the scales and other provisions set out in the Document, shall, with effect from 1st April 1970, be increased by £120 a year.

(2) The said increase of remuneration and any like increase payable to any teacher in a college of education or by virtue of an order made under the Act shall be disregarded for the purpose of determining at what incremental point a teacher shall enter any scale set out in the Document.

Given under the Official Seal of the Secretary of State for Education and Science on 11th May 1970.

(L.S.)

Alice Bacon,
Minister of State for Education and Science.

EXPLANATORY NOTE

(*This Note is not part of the Order.*)

This Order increases by £120 a year the salaries of full-time teachers in farm institutes and teachers of agricultural subjects on the staff of local education authorities in accordance with the agreement reached in the Committee for the consideration of the remuneration of such teachers.

The Order has retrospective effect by virtue of section 7(3) of the Remuneration of Teachers Act 1965.

(a) 1889 c. 63.

STATUTORY INSTRUMENTS

1970 No. 741

EDUCATION, ENGLAND AND WALES

The Remuneration of Teachers (Further Education) (Amendment) Order 1970

Made - - -	11*th May* 1970
Coming into Operation	12*th May* 1970

Whereas:—

(1) in pursuance of section 2(2) of the Remuneration of Teachers Act 1965**(a)** (hereinafter referred to as "the Act") the Committee constituted under section 1 of the Act for the purpose of considering the remuneration payable to teachers in establishments for further education (other than farm institutes) maintained by local education authorities (hereinafter referred to as "the Committee") have transmitted to the Secretary of State for Education and Science (hereinafter referred to as "the Secretary of State") recommendations agreed on by them with respect to the remuneration of such teachers;

(2) there is in force an order made under section 2 of the Act with respect to the remuneration of such teachers, namely, the Remuneration of Teachers (Further Education) Order 1969**(b)**;

(3) it appears to the Secretary of State that effect can more conveniently be given to the recommendations of the Committee by amending the scales and other provisions set out in the document referred to in the said Order, namely, the document published by Her Majesty's Stationery Office on 28th November 1969 under the title "SCALES OF SALARIES FOR TEACHERS IN ESTABLISHMENTS FOR FURTHER EDUCATION, ENGLAND AND WALES, 1969" (hereinafter referred to as "the Document");

(4) in pursuance of section 2(5) of the Act the Secretary of State has prepared a draft Order setting out the amendments of the scales and other provisions contained in the Document which, in his opinion, are requisite for giving effect to the recommendations of the Committee; and

(5) the Secretary of State, as required by section 2(6) of the Act, has consulted the Committee with respect to the draft Order and the Committee have made no representations with respect thereto.

Now therefore the Secretary of State, in pursuance of section 2(6) of the Act, hereby orders as follows—

Citation and Commencement

1. This Order may be cited as the Remuneration of Teachers (Further Education) (Amendment) Order 1970 and shall come into operation on 12th May 1970.

(a) 1965 c. 3. **(b)** S.I. 1969/1713 (1969 III, p. 5387).

Interpretation

2. The Interpretation Act 1889**(a)** shall apply for the interpretation of this Order as it applies for the interpretation of an Act of Parliament.

Amendment of Document

3. The scales and other provisions set out in the Document are hereby amended so as to give effect to the provisions of this Order.

Increase of Remuneration

4.—(1) Subject as in paragraph (2) below provided, the remuneration payable to every full-time teacher in an establishment for further education (other than farm institutes) maintained by a local education authority, as determined in accordance with the scales and other provisions set out in the Document, shall, with effect from 1st April 1970, be increased by £120 a year.

(2) The said increase of remuneration and any like increase payable to any teacher in a college of education or by virtue of an order made under the Act shall be disregarded for the purpose of determining at what incremental point a teacher shall enter any scale set out in the Document.

Given under the Official Seal of the Secretary of State for Education and Science on 11th May 1970.

(L.S.)

Alice Bacon,
Minister of State for Education and Science.

EXPLANATORY NOTE

(*This Note is not part of the Order.*)

This Order increases by £120 a year the salaries of full-time teachers in establishments for further education (other than farm institutes) maintained by local education authorities in accordance with the agreement reached in the Committee for the consideration of the remuneration of such teachers.

The Order has retrospective effect by virtue of section 7(3) of the Remuneration of Teachers Act 1965.

(a) 1889 c. 63.

STATUTORY INSTRUMENTS

1970 No. 743

WAGES COUNCILS

The Wages Regulation (Retail Newsagency, Tobacco and Confectionery) (Scotland) (Amendment) Order 1970

Made - - -	12*th May* 1970
Coming into Operation	15*th June* 1970

Whereas the Secretary of State has received from the Retail Newsagency, Tobacco and Confectionery Trades Wages Council (Scotland) the wages regulation proposals set out in the Schedule hereto ;

Now, therefore, the Secretary of State in exercise of her powers under section 11 of the Wages Councils Act 1959(**a**), and of all other powers enabling her in that behalf, hereby makes the following Order :—

1. This Order may be cited as the Wages Regulation (Retail Newsagency, Tobacco and Confectionery) (Scotland) (Amendment) Order 1970.

2.—(1) In this Order the expression "the specified date" means the 15th June 1970, provided that where, as respects any worker who is paid wages at intervals not exceeding seven days, that date does not correspond with the beginning of the period for which the wages are paid, the expression "the specified date" means, as respects that worker, the beginning of the next such period following that date.

(2) The Interpretation Act 1889(**b**) shall apply to the interpretation of this Order as it applies to the interpretation of an Act of Parliament.

3. The wages regulation proposals set out in the Schedule hereto shall have effect as from the specified date.

Signed by order of the Secretary of State.
12th May 1970.

A. A. Jarratt,
Deputy Under Secretary of State,
Department of Employment and Productivity.

(**a**) 1959 c. 69. (**b**) 1889 c. 63.

Article 3

SCHEDULE

STATUTORY MINIMUM REMUNERATION

The Wages Regulation (Retail Newsagency, Tobacco and Confectionery) (Scotland) Order 1967(a) (Order R.N.T.S. (34)) shall have effect as if in the Schedule thereto:—

1. For paragraph 3 there were substituted the following paragraph:—

"WORKERS OTHER THAN MANAGERS AND MANAGERESSES

3. Subject to the provision of paragraph 1, the minimum remuneration payable to male or female workers (other than managers or manageresses) employed in Area 1 or Area 2, as the case may be, shall be the appropriate amount set out in the following tables:—

	Male Workers		Female Workers	
	Area 1 per week	Area 2 per week	Area 1 per week	Area 2 per week
	s. d.	s. d.	s. d.	s. d.
(A) Clerks Grade I aged 23 years or over ...	*225 6*	*218 6*	*178 6*	*172 6*
(B) Clerks Grade I under 23 years of age, Clerks Grade II, Shop Assistants, Central Warehouse workers, and all other workers (except the workers referred to in (C) below) aged:—				
22 years or over	*219 6*	*212 6*	*175 0*	*169 0*
21 and under 22 years	*201 6*	*194 6*	*157 6*	*153 6*
20 " " 21 "	*167 0*	*161 0*	*138 6*	*134 6*
19 " " 20 "	*156 0*	*151 0*	*134 6*	*129 6*
18 " " 19 "	*146 0*	*141 0*	*131 0*	*125 0*
17 " " 18 "	*120 0*	*115 0*	*114 6*	*109 6*
16 " " 17 "	*113 0*	*108 0*	*106 6*	*101 6*
15 " " 16 "	*105 6*	*101 6*	*103 0*	*98 0*

(C) Transport Workers

Age of transport worker	Type of Vehicle		Area 1	Area 2
	Mechanically propelled vehicle with carrying capacity of	Horse-drawn vehicle	per week	per week
			s. d.	s. d.
21 years or over	1 ton or less	One-horse	*222 6*	*213 6*
20 and under 21 years ...	1 ton or less	One-horse	*183 0*	*177 0*
19 " " 20 "	1 ton or less	One-horse	*171 6*	*165 6*
18 " " 19 "	1 ton or less	One-horse	*161 0*	*155 0*
Under 18 years	1 ton or less	One-horse	*139 0*	*133 0*
All ages...	Over 1 ton and up to 5 tons	Two-horse	*225 6*	*216 6*
	Over 5 tons	—	*229 6*	*220 6*"

(a) S.I. 1967/1626 (1967 III, p. 4467).

2. In paragraph 19 for the definition of 'Customary Holiday' there were substituted the following:—

" 'CUSTOMARY HOLIDAY' means New Year's Day (or, if New Year's Day falls on a Sunday, the following day), the local Spring holiday, the local Autumn holiday and three other days, observed by local custom as holidays, to be fixed by the employer and notified to the worker; *and one other day (being a day on which the worker normally works) in the period commencing on 25th December and ending on the next following 8th January, to be fixed by the employer and notified to the worker not less than seven clear days before 25th December.*"

EXPLANATORY NOTE

(*This Note is not part of the Order.*)

This Order, which has effect from 15th June 1970, amends the Wages Regulation (Retail Newsagency, Tobacco and Confectionery) (Scotland) Order 1967 (Order R.N.T.S. (34)) by increasing the statutory minimum remuneration fixed by that Order and providing for an additional day of customary holiday.

New provisions are printed in italics.

1970 No. 744

PENSIONS

The Superannuation (Transfers between the Civil Service and Public Boards) (Amendment) Rules 1970

Made - - -	13*th May* 1970
Laid before Parliament	21*st May* 1970
Coming into Operation	1*st June* 1970

The Minister for the Civil Service, in exercise of the powers conferred upon him by sections 2 and 15 of the Superannuation (Miscellaneous Provisions) Act 1948(**a**) and article 2(1)(*c*) of the Minister for the Civil Service Order 1968(**b**), and of all other powers enabling him in that behalf, hereby makes the following Rules :—

1. These Rules may be cited as the Superannuation (Transfers between the Civil Service and Public Boards) (Amendment) Rules 1970, and shall come into operation on 1st June 1970.

2. The Interpretation Act 1889(**c**) shall apply for the interpretation of these Rules as it applies for the interpretation of an Act of Parliament.

3. The Superannuation (Transfers between the Civil Service and Public Boards) Rules 1950(**d**) (hereafter in these Rules referred to as "the principal Rules"), as amended (**e**), shall have effect as if the following bodies were added to the Schedule thereto, that is to say :—

The Arts Council of Great Britain.

The British National Export Council.

The Clyde Port Authority.

The Consumer Council.

The Highlands and Islands Development Board.

The Welsh Industrial Estates Corporation.

The Clothing and Allied Products Industry Training Board.

The Hairdressing and Allied Services Industry Training Board.

4. In their application to any person who becomes employed as a civil servant after ceasing to be in the pensionable employment of one of the bodies mentioned in the last preceding Rule the principal Rules shall have effect as if :—

(**a**) 1948 c. 33.
(**b**) S.I. 1968/1656 (1968 III, p. 4485).
(**c**) 1889 c. 63.
(**d**) S.I. 1950/1539 (1950 II, p. 291).
(**e**) The relevant amending instruments are S.I. 1966/454, 1968/471 (1966 I, p. 974; 1968 I, p. 1187).

(*a*) the reference to the date of the making of the principal Rules in Rule 3(1)(*d*) and (*e*) thereof were references to the date of the making of these Rules; and

(*b*) the references to the coming into operation of the principal Rules in Rule 3(2) thereof were references to the coming into operation of these Rules.

5. In their application to any person who enters the pensionable employment of one of the bodies mentioned in Rule 3 of these Rules after ceasing to be employed as a civil servant the principal Rules shall have effect as if :—

(*a*) the reference to the date of the making of the principal Rules in Rule 7(1)(*e*) thereof were a reference to the date of the making of these Rules; and

(*b*) the references to the coming into operation of the principal Rules in Rule 7(2) thereof were references to the coming into operation of these Rules.

Given under the official seal of the Minister for Civil Service on 13th May 1970.

(L.S.)

K. H. McNeill,
Authorised by the Minister
for the Civil Service.

EXPLANATORY NOTE

(*This Note is not part of the Rules.*)

These Rules add certain Industrial Training Boards, the Arts Council of Great Britain, the British National Export Council, the Clyde Port Authority, the Consumer Council, the Highlands and Islands Development Board and the Welsh Industrial Estates to the Schedule to the Superannuation (Transfers between the Civil Service and Public Boards) Rules 1950. The principal Rules provide for the aggregation of service and for a single superannuation award in cases where a person transfers from pensionable service with one of the bodies specified to an established post in the Civil Service or vice versa.

Under the powers of Section 2(5) of the Superannuation (Miscellaneous Provisions) Act 1948, the Rules apply, subject to certain conditions, to persons who have transferred from one employment to the other before the coming into operation of the Rules.

1970 No. 745

CUSTOMS AND EXCISE

The Anti-Dumping (Provisional Charge to Duty) (Revocation) Order 1970

Made - - -	13*th May* 1970
Laid before the House of Commons - -	19*th May* 1970
Coming into Operation	20*th May* 1970

The Board of Trade, in pursuance of the powers conferred upon them by sections 1, 2, 8, 9(3) and 15(4) of the Customs Duties (Dumping and Subsidies) Act 1969**(a)**, hereby make the following Order:—

1.—(1) This Order may be cited as the Anti-Dumping (Provisional Charge to Duty) (Revocation) Order 1970 and shall come into operation on 20th May 1970.

(2) The Interpretation Act 1889**(b)** shall apply to the interpretation of this Order as it applies to the interpretation of an Act of Parliament and as if this Order and the Orders hereby revoked were Acts of Parliament.

2. The Anti-Dumping (Provisional Charge to Duty) Order 1970**(c)** and the Anti-Dumping (Provisional Charge to Duty) (No. 2) Order 1970**(d)** are hereby revoked.

Gwyneth Dunwoody,
Parliamentary Secretary
to the Board of Trade.

13th May 1970.

EXPLANATORY NOTE

(*This Note is not part of the Order.*)

This Order revokes the two Orders made earlier this year making imports of calcium ammonium nitrate originating in Belgium, the Federal Republic of Germany, Austria, Italy, the Netherlands and Sweden subject to a provisional charge to duty in respect of an anti-dumping duty.

(a) 1969 c. 16. **(b)** 1889 c. 63. **(c)** S.I. 1970/213 (1970 I, p. 945).
(d) S.I. 1970/342 (1970 I, p. 1229).

STATUTORY INSTRUMENTS

1970 No. 746

MEDICINES

The Medicines Commission and Committees Regulations 1970

Made - - - -	11*th May* 1970
Laid before Parliament	21*st May* 1970
Coming into Operation	26*th May* 1970

The Secretaries of State respectively concerned with health in England and in Wales, the Secretary of State concerned with health and with agriculture in Scotland, the Minister of Health and Social Services for Northern Ireland, the Minister of Agriculture, Fisheries and Food and the Minister of Agriculture for Northern Ireland, acting jointly, in exercise of their powers under paragraph 1 of Schedule 1 to the Medicines Act 1968(**a**), as having effect subject to the provisions of section 2(2) of and Schedule 1 to, the Transfer of Functions (Wales) Order 1969(**b**), and of all other powers enabling them in that behalf, hereby make the following regulations :—

Citation and commencement

1. These regulations may be cited as the Medicines Commission and Committees Regulations 1970 and shall come into operation on 26th May 1970.

Interpretation

2.—(1) In these regulations, unless the context otherwise requires—

"the Act" means the Medicines Act 1968 ;

"the Commission" means the Medicines Commission established by section 2 of the Act ;

"the Ministers" has the same meaning as in the Act.

(2) The Interpretation Act 1889(**c**) shall apply to the interpretation of these regulations as it applies to the interpretation of an Act of Parliament.

Terms of office of members of the Commission

3.—(1) In this regulation "retirement day" means 31st December 1971 or any 31st day of December occurring at two yearly intervals thereafter.

(2) Except as provided in the following paragraphs of this regulation, a member appointed to the Commission shall hold office until the second retirement day following his appointment and shall then vacate office.

(3) One half of the original members of the Commission, who shall be determined by the Commission, shall hold office until 31st December 1971 and shall then vacate office.

(4) Where two or more members (other than a member appointed as des-

(**a**) 1968 c. 67. (**b**) S.I. 1969/388 (1969 I, p. 1070).
(**c**) 1889 c. 63.

cribed in paragraph (6) of this regulation) are appointed to the Commission at any one time and the total membership of the Commission is thereby increased, a number of the newly-appointed members, being in the circumstances described in column 1 of the Schedule to these regulations the number specified in column 2 thereof, shall vacate office on the first, instead of the second, retirement day following their appointment; and the Commission shall as soon as is practicably convenient following the appointment determine which members shall vacate office on the earlier date.

(5) Where the appointment of a single member to the Commission (other than a member appointed as described in paragraph (6) of this regulation) increases the total membership of the Commission to an even number, that member shall vacate office on the first, instead of the second retirement day following his appointment.

(6) A member appointed to the Commission to take the place of a member who during his term of office ceased to be a member by reason of death, resignation or otherwise shall hold office for the remainder of the term of office of the person whose place he has taken.

(7) A member of the Commission may resign office at any time by notice in writing to the Ministers.

Terms of office of members of Committees established under section 4 *of the Act*

4. A member of a committee established under section 4 of the Act shall hold and vacate office, and the chairman of such a committee shall hold and vacate office as chairman, under the terms of the instrument under which he is appointed, but such a member or chairman shall not be appointed for a period of more than 6 years and may resign office at any time by notice in writing to the Ministers.

Committees of the Commission

5.—(1) The Commission may, with the approval of the Ministers, appoint one or more committees for the purpose of reporting to them on any matter in relation to their functions under the Act except any matter included in the purposes for which a committee has been established under section 4 of the Act.

(2) A committee appointed by the Commission shall include at least one member who is a member of the Commission.

(3) A person appointed to a committee by reason of his membership of the Commission, who during his term of office as a member of the committee ceases to be a member of the Commission, and is not immediately re-appointed thereto, shall also cease to be a member of the committee; but nothing in this paragraph shall prevent him from being re-appointed to that committee.

(4) The Commission shall appoint one of the members of a committee to be chairman of that committee.

Sub-committees of Committees established under section 4 *of the Act*

6.—(1) A committee established under section 4 of the Act, or two or more such committees acting jointly may, with the approval of the Ministers or such of them by whom the committee or committees, as the case may be, were established, appoint one or more sub-committees and shall appoint a member of each such sub-committee to be chairman of the sub-committee.

(2) The members of a sub-committee shall include at least one member of the committee, or of each of the committees, as the case may be, by which they were appointed.

(3) Subject to the provisions of paragraph (5) of this regulation, a member of a sub-committee shall hold office, and the chairman of a sub-committee shall hold office as chairman, for such term, not exceeding 6 years, as the committee or committees, as the case may be, by which he was appointed may determine and shall then vacate office.

(4) A member of a sub-committee may resign office at any time by notice in writing to the committee or committees, as the case may be, by which he was appointed.

(5) A person appointed as a member of a sub-committee by reason of his membership of a committee by which the sub-committee was appointed, who during his term of office as a member of the sub-committee ceases to be a member of such a committee and is not immediately re-appointed thereto, shall also cease to be a member of the sub-committee ; but nothing in this paragraph shall prevent his re-appointment to the sub-committee.

R. H. S. Crossman,
Secretary of State for Social Services.

29th April 1970.

Given under my hand on 30th April 1970.

George Thomas,
Secretary of State for Wales.

Given under the seal of the Secretary of State for Scotland on 5th May 1970.

(L.S.)

William Ross,
Secretary of State for Scotland.

Given under my hand on 11th May 1970.

W. K. Fitzsimmons,
Minister of Health and Social Services
for Northern Ireland.

In Witness whereof the official seal of the Minister of Agriculture, Fisheries and Food is hereunto affixed on 7th May 1970.

(L.S.) *Cledwyn Hughes,*
Minister of Agriculture, Fisheries and Food.

Given under my hand on 11th May 1970.

Phelim R. H. O'Neill,
Minister of Agriculture for Northern Ireland.

Regulation 3(4)

SCHEDULE

Column 1 Circumstances	Column 2 Number of newly-appointed members to retire on first retirement day following their appointment
Where the number of newly-appointed members is an even number.	Half the number of members.
Where the number of newly-appointed members is an odd number and the total membership of the Commission is by their appointment increased to an even number.	The number of members plus one divided by two.
Where the number of newly-appointed members is an odd number and the total membership of the Commission is by their appointment increased to an odd number.	The number of members less one divided by two.

EXPLANATORY NOTE

(*This Note is not part of the Regulations.*)

These Regulations provide for the terms of office of members of the Medicines Commission established by section 2 of the Medicines Act 1968 and Committees established under section 4 of that Act and for the appointment by the former of committees and by the latter of sub-committees.

STATUTORY INSTRUMENTS

1970 No. 748

EXCHANGE CONTROL

The Exchange Control (Scheduled Territories) (Amendment) Order 1970

Made - - -	14*th May* 1970
Laid before Parliament	21*st May* 1970
Coming into Operation	4*th June* 1970

The Treasury, in exercise of the powers conferred upon them by sections 1(3)(*b*) and 36(5) of the Exchange Control Act 1947(**a**), hereby make the following Order:—

1.—(1) This Order may be cited as the Exchange Control (Scheduled Territories) (Amendment) Order 1970, and shall come into operation on 4th June 1970.

(2) The Interpretation Act 1889(**b**) shall apply for the interpretation of this Order as it applies for the interpretation of an Act of Parliament.

2. Schedule 1 to the Exchange Control Act 1947, as amended by the Exchange Control (Scheduled Territories) Order 1967(**c**) and as further amended (**d**), shall be further amended by inserting after paragraph 29 the following paragraph :—

"29A. Tonga."

3. This Order shall extend to the Channel Islands, and any reference in this Order to the Exchange Control Act 1947 includes a reference to that Act as extended by the Exchange Control (Channel Islands) Order 1947(**e**).

Joseph Harper,
Neil McBride,
Two of the Lords Commissioners of Her Majesty's Treasury.

14th May 1970.

(**a**) 1947 c. 14. (**b**) 1889 c. 63.
(**c**) S.I. 1967/1767 (1967 III, p. 4736).
(**d**) S.I. 1968/333, 1399 (1968 I, p. 971: II, p. 4047).
(**e**) S.R. & O. 1947/2034 (Rev. VI, p. 1001: 1947 I, p. 660).

EXPLANATORY NOTE

(This Note is not part of the Order.)

Tonga ceases, on 4th June 1970, to be a protected state and attains full independence. This Order amends the list of Scheduled territories contained in the First Schedule to the Exchange Control Act 1947 by the inclusion by name of Tonga, which was previously included by definition.

STATUTORY INSTRUMENTS

1970 No. 749

TRANSPORT

PENSIONS AND COMPENSATION

The Passenger Transport (Compensation to Officers) Regulations 1970

Made - - -	14*th May* 1970
Laid before Parliament	27*th May* 1970
Coming into Operation	30*th May* 1970

ARRANGEMENT OF REGULATIONS

PART V

RETIREMENT COMPENSATION AND PAYMENTS ON DEATH

PART VI

ADJUSTMENT, REVIEW AND COMPOUNDING OF COMPENSATION

PART VII

PROCEDURE AND MISCELLANEOUS

SCHEDULE

The Minister of Transport, in exercise of the power conferred by section 1 of the Water Officers Compensation Act 1960(**a**) as that section is applied by section 17(3) of the Transport Act 1968(**b**), and of all other enabling powers, hereby makes the following regulations :—

PART I

PRELIMINARY

Citation and commencement

1.—(1) These regulations may be cited as the Passenger Transport (Compensation to Officers) Regulations 1970.

(2) These regulations shall come into operation on the 30th May 1970 and shall have effect from the 2nd September 1969.

Interpretation

2.—(1) In these regulations, unless the context otherwise requires, the following expressions have the meanings hereby respectively assigned to them, that is to say :—

"accrued pension", in relation to a pensionable officer who has suffered loss of employment, means—

(*a*) if his last relevant pension scheme provided benefits in which he had a right to participate, the pension to which he would have become entitled in respect of his pensionable service according to the method of calculation, modified where necessary for the purpose of giving effect to these regulations, prescribed by that scheme if, at the date on which he ceased to be subject to that scheme, he had attained normal retiring age and complied with any requirement of that scheme as to a minimum period of qualifying service or contribution and completed any additional contributory payments or payments in respect of added years which he was in the course of making ; and

(*b*) in any other case, such portion of the pension (if any) of which he had reasonable expectations as the compensating authority consider equitable, having regard to his age, the length of his employment at the date of loss and all the other circumstances of the case ;

"accrued retiring allowance", in relation to a pensionable officer who has suffered loss of employment, means—

(*a*) if his last relevant pension scheme provided benefits in which he had a right to participate, any lump sum payment to which he would have become entitled in respect of his pensionable service according to the method of calculation, modified where necessary for the purpose of giving effect to these regulations, prescribed by that scheme if, at the date on which he ceases to be subject to that scheme, he had attained normal retiring age and complied with any requirement of that scheme as to a minimum period of qualifying service or contribution and completed any additional contributory payments or payments in respect of added years which he was in the course of making ; and

(**a**) 8 & 9 Eliz. 2 c. 15.

(**b**) 1968 c. 73.

(*b*) in any other case, such portion of the lump sum payment (if any) of which he had reasonable expectations as the compensating authority consider equitable, having regard to his age, the length of his employment at the date of loss and all the other circumstances of the case ;

"accrued incapacity pension" and "accrued incapacity retiring allowance" have the same respective meanings as "accrued pension" and "accrued retiring allowance" except that the reference to a person's attaining normal retiring age shall be construed as a reference to his becoming incapable of discharging efficiently the duties of his employment by reason of permanent ill-health or infirmity of mind or body ;

"the Act" means the Transport Act 1968 ;

"added years", in relation to a person who suffers loss of employment, means—

(*a*) in the case of a contributory employee or local Act contributor any additional years of service reckonable by him in his employment immediately prior to the loss in question under regulation 12 of the Local Government Superannuation (Benefits) Regulations 1954(**a**) as amended (**b**), or, in Scotland, under regulation 12 of the Local Government Superannuation (Benefits) (Scotland) Regulations 1954(**c**) as amended (**d**), any corresponding provision of a local Act scheme, or those regulations or any such provision as aforesaid as applied by or under any enactment, and includes any additional years of service which, having been granted under any such provision or under any similar provision contained in any other enactment or scheme, have subsequently become and are so reckonable under or by virtue of rules made under section 2 of the Superannuation (Miscellaneous Provisions) Act 1948(**e**), or any other enactment ; and

(*b*) in the case of any other person, any additional years of service, similar to those mentioned in paragraph (*a*) of this definition, reckonable by him under his last relevant pension scheme ;

"additional contributory payments" means—

(*a*) additional contributory payments of the kind referred to in section 2(3) and (4) of the Local Government Superannuation Act 1953(**f**); or

(*b*) any similar payments made under a local Act scheme or other pension scheme as a condition of reckoning any period of employment as service or as a period of contribution for the purposes of the scheme, or, where the scheme provides for the reckoning of non-contributing service, as contributing service for the purposes of the scheme ; or

(*c*) any payments made for the purpose of increasing the length at which any period of service or of contribution would be reckonable for the purpose of calculating a benefit under a local Act scheme ; or

(*d*) any payments similar to any of those mentioned in the foregoing subparagraphs made in pursuance of rules under section 2 of the Superannuation (Miscellaneous Provisions) Act 1948 ;

"appropriate transfer order", in relation to a person who has suffered loss of employment or loss or diminution of emoluments, means the order under section 17(1) of the Act to which, or, as the case may be, to anything done in pursuance of which, that loss or that diminution is attributable ;

(**a**) S.I. 1954/1048 (1954 II, p. 1595).
(**b**) S.I. 1955/1041 (1955 II, p. 1825).
(**c**) S.I. 1954/1059 (1954 II, p. 1632).
(**d**) S.I. 1955/1226 (1955 II, p. 1831).
(**e**) 11 & 12 Geo. 6 c. 33.
(**f**) 1 & 2 Eliz. 2 c. 25.

"attributable loss" means loss of employment or loss or diminution of emoluments which is attributable to the appropriate transfer order or to anything done in pursuance thereof;

"bus service" has the same meaning as in the Act;

"compensating authority" in relation to any person who has suffered attributable loss, means the Executive in relation to which provision is made by the appropriate transfer order for any transfer such as is mentioned in section 17(1) of the Act;

"compensation question" means a question arising in relation to these regulations—

(*a*) as to a person's entitlement to compensation for loss of office or employment, or for loss or diminution of emoluments, or

(*b*) as to the manner of a person's employment or the comparability of his duties;

"contributory employee", "contributing service", "non-contributing service", "local Act contributor" and "local Act scheme" have the same meanings as in the Local Government Superannuation Act 1937(**a**) or, in Scotland, as in the Local Government Superannuation (Scotland) Act 1937(**b**);

"emoluments" means all salary, wages, fees and other payments paid or made to an officer as such for his own use, and also the money value of any apartments, rations or other allowances in kind appertaining to his employment, but does not include payments for overtime, other than payments which are a usual incident of his employment, or any allowances payable to him to cover the cost of providing office accommodation or clerical or other assistance, or any travelling or subsistence allowance or other moneys to be spent, or to cover expenses incurred, by him for the purposes of his employment; and "net emoluments", in relation to any employment, means the annual rate (modified where necessary in accordance with regulation 42) of the emoluments of that employment less such part of those emoluments as the officer was liable to contribute under a pension scheme, and in relation to any employment which has been lost or the emoluments of which have been diminished, the expression means the annual rate of emoluments as aforesaid immediately before the loss or diminution, as the case may be:

Provided that, where fees or other variable payments were paid to an officer as part of his emoluments during any period immediately preceding the loss or diminution, the amount in respect of fees or other variable payments to be included in the annual rate of emoluments shall be the annual average of the fees or other payments paid to him during the period of 5 years immediately preceding the loss or diminution, or such other period as the compensating authority may think reasonable in the circumstances;

"enactment" means any Act or any instrument made under an Act;

"Executive" means a Passenger Transport Executive for the establishment of which provision has been made by an order under section 9(1) of the Act;

"ferry service" has the same meaning as in the Act;

"local authority" means, in England and Wales, the council of a county, county borough, metropolitan borough, London borough, county district, rural parish or borough included in a rural district, the Greater London Council, the Common Council of the City of London and the council of the Isles of Scilly, any two or more of those authorities acting jointly and any joint committee, combined authority or joint board and a police authority

(**a**) 1 Edw. 8 & 1 Geo. 6 c. 68. (**b**) 1 Edw. 8 & 1 Geo. 6 c. 69.

for a county, a borough or a combined police area ; and means in Scotland, any county council, town council or district council including any joint committee or joint board of such authorities appointed under any enactment, order or scheme ;

"long-term compensation" means compensation payable in accordance with the provisions of Part IV of these regulations for loss of employment or loss or diminution of emoluments ;

"material date", in relation to any person who suffers attributable loss, means—

(*a*) for the purposes of regulation 3 and regulation 5, the date on which the appropriate transfer order is made and

(*b*) for any other purpose of these regulations, the date appointed by the appropriate transfer order for the transfer of persons to the service of the Executive or the date on which that person suffered attributable loss whichever is the earlier ;

"minimum pensionable age" means, in relation to a pensionable officer, the earliest age at which, under his last relevant pension scheme, he could have become entitled to receive payment of a pension, other than a pension payable in consequence of his redundancy, the termination of his employment in the interests of efficiency or his incapacity to discharge efficiently the duties of his employment by reason of permanent ill-health or infirmity of mind or body ;

"Minister" means the Minister of Transport ;

"national service" means service which is relevant service within the meaning of the Reserve and Auxiliary Forces (Protection of Civil Interests) Act 1951(**a**), and includes service immediately following such service as aforesaid, being service in any of Her Majesty's naval, military or air forces pursuant to a voluntary engagement entered into with the consent of the authority or person under whom an officer held his last relevant employment ;

"normal retiring age" means, in the case of a pensionable officer to whom an age of compulsory retirement applied by virtue of any enactment to which he was subject in the employment which he has lost or the emoluments of which have been diminished or by virtue of the conditions of that employment, that age, and, in any other case, the age of 65 years if the officer is a male, or 60 years if the officer is a female ;

"officer" includes the holder of any place, situation or employment (other than membership of a Passenger Transport Authority) whether by virtue of an agreement for the rendering by him of personal services, by appointment, or otherwise, and the expression "office" shall be construed accordingly ;

"Passenger Transport Authority" means a Passenger Transport Authority for the establishment of which provision has been made by an order under section 9(1) of the Act ;

"pensionable officer", in relation to a person who has suffered attributable loss means a person who immediately before suffering such loss was subject to a pension scheme ;

"pension scheme", in relation to a pensionable officer, means any form of arrangement associated with his employment for the payment of superannuation benefits, whether subsisting by virtue of Act of Parliament, trust, contract or otherwise ; and "last relevant pension scheme", in relation to a pensionable officer means a pension scheme to which he was subject immediately before suffering attributable loss ;

(**a**) 14 & 15 Geo. 6 c. 65.

"reckonable service", in relation to a person, means any period of whole-time or part-time employment in any relevant employment and includes any period of war service or national service undertaken on his ceasing to hold any such employment but does not include employment of which account has been taken, or is required to be taken, in calculating the amount of any superannuation benefit to which he has become entitled;

"relevant employment", in relation to a person who suffers attributable loss, means employment—

(*a*) under the Crown or in the service of an Executive, a subsidiary thereof, or a local authority, or

(*b*) as an officer of a Passenger Transport Authority, or

(*c*) by any authority or body for the purposes of the Crown, an Executive, a subsidiary thereof or of local government in Great Britain, or

(*d*) in the service of a person whose business consists of, or includes, the provision of bus services or ferry services, being employment in connection with such provision, or

(*e*) under any officer employed as mentioned in either paragraph (*a*), (*b*) or (*c*) of this definition for the purposes of the functions of the employing authority or body, or

(*f*) preceding any of the foregoing employments, being employment which is reckonable for the purposes of his last relevant pension scheme;

but, except as provided in regulations 7(1)(*c*) and 13(1)(*c*), the expression "relevant employment" does not include service in the armed forces of the Crown;

"resettlement compensation" means compensation payable in accordance with Part III of these regulations for loss of employment;

"retirement compensation" means compensation payable in accordance with the provisions of regulation 20, 21, 22 or 23;

"subsidiary", in relation to an Executive, has the same meaning as in the Transport Act 1962(**a**), and in this connection no account shall be taken of the provisions of section 51(5) of the Act;

"tribunal" means a tribunal established under section 12 of the Industrial Training Act 1964(**b**);

"war service" means war service within the meaning of the Local Government Staffs (War Service) Act 1939(**c**), the Teachers Superannuation (War Service) Act 1939(**d**) (or, in Scotland, the Education (Scotland) (War Service Superannuation) Act 1939(**e**)), the Police and Firemen (War Service) Act 1939(**f**) or employment for war purposes within the meaning of the Superannuation Schemes (War Service) Act 1940(**g**) and includes any period of service in the First World War in the armed forces of the Crown or in the forces of the Allied or Associated Powers if such service immediately followed a period of relevant employment and was undertaken either compulsorily or with the permission of the employer in that employment.

(2) (*a*) Where under any provision of these regulations an annual value is to be assigned to a capital sum or a capital value to an annual amount, the annual or capital value shall be ascertained in accordance with the tables set

(**a**) 10 & 11 Eliz. 2 c. 46.
(**b**) 1964 c. 16.
(**c**) 2 & 3 Geo. 6 c. 94.
(**d**) 2 & 3 Geo. 6 c. 95.
(**e**) 2 & 3 Geo. 6 c. 96.
(**f**) 2 & 3 Geo. 6 c. 103.
(**g**) 3 & 4 Geo. 6 c. 26.

out in the Schedule to these regulations in so far as they provide for the particular case.

(*b*) For the purpose of determining the application of the said tables the headings and the note to each table shall be treated as a part of the table.

(*c*) Where the said tables do not provide for a case in which an annual value is to be assigned to a capital sum or a capital value to an annual amount, the annual or capital value shall be such as may be agreed between the compensating authority and the person to whom the capital sum or annual amount is payable.

(3) Unless the context otherwise requires, references in these regulations to the provisions of any enactment shall be construed as references to those provisions as amended, re-enacted or modified by or under any subsequent enactment.

(4) References in these regulations to a numbered regulation shall, unless the reference is to a regulation of specified regulations, be construed as references to the regulation bearing that number in these regulations.

(5) References in any of these regulations to a numbered paragraph shall, unless the reference is to a paragraph of a specified regulation, be construed as references to the paragraph bearing that number in the first-mentioned regulation.

(6) The Interpretation Act 1889(**a**) shall apply for the interpretation of these regulations as it applies for the interpretation of an Act of Parliament.

PART II

ENTITLEMENT TO COMPENSATION

Persons to whom the regulations apply

3. These regulations shall apply to any person who—

(*a*) was employed immediately before the material date, either for the whole or for a part only of his time, as an officer of a local authority or under such an officer for the purposes of the functions of the local authority, or

(*b*) would have been so employed at that time but for any national service on which he was then engaged.

Grounds of entitlement to compensation

4. Subject to the provisions of these regulations, any person to whom these regulations apply and who suffers loss of employment or loss or diminution of emoluments which is attributable to an order made under section 17(1) of the Act or to anything done in pursuance of such order shall be entitled to have his case considered for the payment of compensation under these regulations, and such compensation shall be determined in accordance with these regulations.

National service

5.—(1) Where any person to whom these regulations apply would have been employed immediately before the material date as an officer of a local authority or under such an officer for the purposes of the functions of the local authority

(**a**) 52 & 53 Vict. c. 63.

but for any national service on which he was then engaged, then if before the expiry of 2 months after ceasing to be so engaged, or, if prevented by sickness or other reasonable cause, as soon as practicable thereafter, he gives notice to the compensating authority that he is available for employment, that person shall be entitled to have his case considered for the payment of compensation on the ground—

(*a*) if he is not given or offered re-employment in his former office or in any reasonably comparable office (whether in the same or in a different service), of loss of employment ; or

(*b*) if he is so re-employed with diminished emoluments as compared with the emoluments which he would have enjoyed had he continued in his former employment, of diminution of emoluments.

(2) The loss of employment which is the cause of a claim for compensation under paragraph (1)(*a*) shall be treated as having occurred on the earlier of the two following dates, that is to say, the date of the refusal of re-employment or a date one month after the date on which the person gave notice that he was available for employment ; and the person shall be deemed to have been entitled to the emoluments which he would have enjoyed at such earlier date had he continued in his former employment.

Part III

Resettlement Compensation

Resettlement compensation for loss of employment

6. The compensating authority shall, subject to the provisions of these regulations, pay resettlement compensation to any person to whom these regulations apply and who satisfies the conditions set out in regulation 7.

Conditions for payment of resettlement compensation

7.—(1) Without prejudice to any other requirement of these regulations, the conditions for the payment of resettlement compensation to any person are that—

(*a*) he has suffered, not later than 10 years after the material date, loss of employment attributable to the appropriate transfer order or to anything done in pursuance of such order ;

(*b*) he has not at the date of the loss attained normal retiring age ;

(*c*) he has, for a period beginning 3 years immediately before the material date and ending on the date of the occurrence of the loss, been continuously engaged (disregarding breaks not exceeding in the aggregate 6 months) for the whole or part of his time in relevant employment ; and for this purpose the expression "relevant employment" includes any period of national service immediately following such employment ;

(*d*) he has made a claim for such compensation in accordance with the provisions of Part VII of these regulations not later than 13 weeks after the loss of employment which is the cause of his claim or 13 weeks after the coming into operation of these regulations, whichever is the later ;

(*e*) the loss of employment which is the cause of his claim has occurred for some reason other than misconduct or incapacity to perform such duties as, immediately before the loss, he was performing or might reasonably have been required to perform ; and (*f*) he has not, subject to paragraph (3), been offered any reasonably comparable employment under the Crown, in the service of a local authority, a Passenger Transport Authority, an Executive or a subsidiary thereof.

(2) In ascertaining for the purposes of this regulation whether a person has been offered employment which is reasonably comparable with the employment which he has lost, no account shall be taken of the fact that the duties of the employment offered are in relation to a different service from that in connection with which his employment was held or are duties which involve a transfer of his employment from one place to another within Great Britain.

(3) No account shall be taken for the purposes of this regulation of an offer of employment where the compensating authority are satisfied—

(*a*) that acceptance would have involved undue hardship to the person, or

(*b*) that he was prevented from accepting the offer by reason of ill-health or other circumstances beyond his control.

Amount of resettlement compensation

8.—(1) The amount of resettlement compensation which may be paid to a person shall, for each week for which such compensation is payable, be a sum ascertained by taking two thirds of the weekly rate of the net emoluments which that person has lost and deducting therefrom, in addition to the items mentioned in regulation 33(3) and (4), such of the following items as may be applicable—

(*a*) unemployment, sickness or injury benefit under any Act relating to National Insurance claimable by him in respect of such week (excluding any amount claimable by him in respect of a dependant) ; and

(*b*) two thirds of the net emoluments received by him in respect of such week from work or employment undertaken as a result of the loss of employment.

(2) For the purposes of this regulation the weekly rate of a person's net emoluments shall be deemed to be seven three hundred and sixty-fifths of those emoluments.

Period for payment of resettlement compensation

9. Subject to the provisions of these regulations, resettlement compensation shall be payable to a person only in respect of the period of 13 weeks next succeeding the week in which he lost the employment in respect of which his claim has been made or, in the case of a person who has attained the age of 45 years, the said 13 weeks and one additional week for every year of his age after attaining the age of 45 years and before the date of the loss of employment, subject to a maximum addition of 13 such weeks.

Additional provisions relating to resettlement compensation

10.—(1) Resettlement compensation shall be payable to a person at intervals equivalent to those at which the emoluments of his employment were previously paid or at such other intervals as may be agreed between the person and the compensating authority.

(2) Resettlement compensation shall be terminated by the compensating authority—

(*a*) if without reasonable cause the recipient fails to comply with any of the provisions of regulation 11, or

(*b*) if on being requested to do so, he fails to satisfy the compensating authority that, so far as he is able, he is seeking suitable employment.

Claimant for resettlement compensation to furnish particulars of employment

11. Every person claiming or in receipt of resettlement compensation shall (after as well as before the compensation begins to be paid)—

(*a*) forthwith supply the compensating authority in writing with particulars of any employment which he obtains or of any change in his earnings from any such employment, and

(*b*) if the compensating authority so require, so long as he is out of employment and is not receiving sickness or injury benefit, register with the Department of Employment and Productivity.

PART IV

LONG-TERM COMPENSATION FOR LOSS OF EMPLOYMENT OR LOSS OR DIMINUTION OF EMOLUMENTS

Long-term compensation

12. The compensating authority shall, subject to the provisions of these regulations, pay long-term compensation to any person to whom these regulations apply and who satisfies the conditions set out in regulation 13.

Conditions for payment of long-term compensation

13.—(1) Without prejudice to any other requirement of these regulations, the conditions for the payment of long-term compensation to any person are that—

(*a*) he has suffered attributable loss not later than 10 years after the material date ;

(*b*) he has not, save as is provided in regulation 29, at the date of such loss attained normal retiring age ;

(*c*) he has, for a period beginning not less than 8 years immediately before the material date and ending on the date of the occurrence of the attributable loss, been continuously engaged (without a break of more than 12 months at any one time) for the whole or part of his time in relevant employment ; and for this purpose the expression "relevant employment" includes any period of national service immediately following such employment ;

(*d*) he has made a claim for such compensation in accordance with the provisions of Part VII of these regulations not later than 2 years after the attributable loss which is the cause of the claim or 2 years after the coming into operation of these regulations, whichever is the later ; and (*e*) if the cause of the claim for compensation is loss of employment—

(i) the loss has occurred for some reason other than misconduct or incapacity to perform such duties as, immediately before the loss, he was performing or might reasonably have been required to perform ; and

(ii) he has not been offered any reasonably comparable employment under the Crown or in the service of a local authority, a Passenger Transport Authority, an Executive or a subsidiary thereof.

(2) Paragraphs (2) and (3) of regulation 7 (which relate to offers of employment) shall apply for the purposes of this regulation as they apply for the purposes of regulation 7.

(3) Claims for long-term compensation for loss of employment shall in all respects be treated as claims for such compensation for the loss of emoluments occasioned thereby and the provisions of these regulations shall apply to all such claims accordingly.

Factors to be considered in determining payment of long-term compensation

14.—(1) For the purpose of determining the amount (subject to the limits set out in these regulations) of long-term compensation (if any) payable under these regulations to any person for loss or diminution of emoluments, the compensating authority shall have regard to such of the following factors as may be relevant, that is to say—

(*a*) the conditions upon which the person held the employment which he has lost, including in particular its security of tenure, whether by law or practice ;

(*b*) the emoluments and other conditions, including security of tenure, whether by law or practice, of any work or employment undertaken by the person as a result of the loss of employment ;

(*c*) the extent to which he has sought suitable employment and the emoluments which he might have acquired by accepting other suitable employment offered to him ;

(*d*) all the other circumstances of his case :

Provided that no account shall be taken of the fact that he entered the employment which he has lost or the emoluments of which have been diminished after the date on which any order under section 9(1) of the Act is made.

(2) In ascertaining for the purposes of paragraph (1)(*c*) whether a person has been offered suitable employment, regulation 7(3) shall apply as it applies for the purpose of ascertaining whether employment is reasonably comparable with employment which has been lost.

Amount of long-term compensation payable for loss of emoluments

15.—(1) Long-term compensation for loss of emoluments shall, subject to the provisions of these regulations, be payable until the normal retiring age or death of a person to whom it is payable, whichever first occurs, and shall not exceed a maximum annual sum calculated in accordance with the provisions of paragraphs (2) to (4).

(2) The said maximum annual sum shall, subject as hereinafter provided, be the aggregate of the following sums, namely—

(*a*) for every year of the person's reckonable service, one sixtieth of the net emoluments which he has lost ; and

(*b*) in the case of a person who has attained the age of 40 years at the date of the loss, a sum calculated in accordance with the provisions of paragraph (3) appropriate to his age at that date ;

but the said maximum annual sum shall in no case exceed two thirds of the net emoluments which the person has lost.

(3) The sum referred to in paragraph (2)(*b*) shall be—

(*a*) in the case of a person who has attained the age of 40 years but has not attained the age of 50 years at the date of the loss, the following fraction of the net emoluments which he has lost—

(i) where his reckonable service is less than 10 years, one sixtieth for each year of such service after attaining the age of 40 years ; or

(ii) where his reckonable service amounts to 10 years but is less than 15 years, one sixtieth for each year of such service after attaining the age of 40 years and one additional sixtieth ; or

(iii) where his reckonable service amounts to 15 years but is less than 20 years, one sixtieth for each year of such service after attaining the age of 40 years and two additional sixtieths ; or

(iv) where his reckonable service amounts to 20 years or more, one sixtieth for each year of such service after attaining the age of 40 years and three additional sixtieths ;

but the sum so calculated shall not in any case exceed one sixth of the said net emoluments ;

(*b*) in the case of a person who has attained the age of 50 years but has not attained the age of 60 years at the date of the loss, one sixtieth of the said net emoluments for each year of his reckonable service after attaining the age of 40 years, up to a maximum of 15 such years ; and

(*c*) in the case of a person who has attained the age of 60 years at the date of the loss, one sixtieth of the said net emoluments for each year of his reckonable service after attaining the age of 45 years.

(4) Where a person has become entitled (whether immediately or prospectively on attaining some greater age) to a superannuation benefit by way of annual amounts under a pension scheme associated with the employment which he has lost, the maximum annual sum referred to in paragraph (1) shall be the maximum sum calculated under paragraphs (2) and (3) as if he had not become so entitled.

(5) Where long-term compensation is payable in respect of any period and resettlement compensation has also been paid in respect of that period, the long-term compensation shall be limited to the amount (if any) by which it exceeds the resettlement compensation paid as aforesaid.

(6) Long-term compensation shall be payable to a person at intervals equivalent to those at which the emoluments of his employment were previously paid or at such other intervals as may be agreed between the person and the compensating authority.

Long-term compensation for diminution of emoluments

16. Long-term compensation for diminution of emoluments in respect of any employment shall, subject to the provisions of these regulations, be awarded and paid in accordance with the following provisions:—

(*a*) the compensation shall consist of an annual sum which shall be payable to a person at intervals equivalent to those at which the emoluments of his employment are or were previously paid or at such other intervals as may be agreed between the person and the compensating authority, and shall, subject to the provisions of these regulations, be payable until normal retiring age or death, whichever first occurs ; and

(*b*) the said annual sum shall not exceed the maximum annual sum which could have been awarded under regulation 15 if the person had suffered loss of employment and the loss of emoluments occasioned thereby had been equivalent to the amount of the diminution :

Provided that no compensation shall be payable if the emoluments have been diminished by less than 2½ per cent.

Date from which long-term compensation is to be payable

17.—(1) Long-term compensation shall be payable with effect from the date of the claim or from any earlier date permitted by the succeeding provisions of this regulation.

(2) Where a claim for long-term compensation is duly made within 13 weeks of the occurrence of the loss or diminution which is the cause of the claim, or within 13 weeks of the coming into operation of these regulations, whichever is the later, the award shall be made retrospective to the date on which the loss or diminution occurred.

(3) Where a claim for long-term compensation is made after the expiry of the period mentioned in paragraph (2), the award may, at the discretion of the compensating authority, be made retrospective to a date not earlier than 13 weeks prior to the date on which the claim was made :

Provided that if the compensating authority are satisfied that the failure to make the claim within the period mentioned in paragraph (2) was due to ill-health or other circumstances beyond the claimant's control, the award may be made retrospective to a date not earlier than that on which the loss or diminution occurred.

PART V

RETIREMENT COMPENSATION AND PAYMENTS ON DEATH

Entitlement to retirement compensation and other payments

18.—(1) The compensating authority shall, subject to the provisions of these regulations, pay retirement compensation to any person to whom this Part of these regulations applies, and shall make the other payments for which provision is made in regulations 26 to 30.

(2) Save as is provided in regulation 29, this Part of these regulations applies to a pensionable officer who satisfies the conditions set out in regulation 13 and for the purposes of such application paragraph (3) of that regulation shall have effect as if for the reference therein to claims for long-term compensation there were substituted a reference to claims for retirement compensation.

(3) Regulation 14 shall apply in relation to retirement compensation as it applies in relation to long-term compensation.

Additional factors governing payment of retirement compensation

19.—(1) Where retirement compensation is payable under any one of regulations 20, 21, 22 and 23, such compensation shall not be payable under any other of those regulations.

(2) If a person has attained the age of 40 years at the date on which he lost his employment or suffered a diminution of his emoluments, the compensating authority, in calculating the amount of the retirement compensation payable to him, shall credit him with additional years of service or an additional period of contribution on the following basis, namely—

(*a*) 2 years, whether or not he has completed any years of service after attaining the age of 40 years, and

(*b*) 2 years for each of the first 4 completed years of his reckonable service between the date when he attained the age of 40 years and the date of the loss or diminution, and

(*c*) one year for each such year of service after the fourth, but the additional years of service or period of contribution so credited shall not exceed the shortest of the following periods, namely—

(i) such number of years as, when added to his pensionable service, would amount to the maximum period of such service which would have been reckonable by him had he continued in his employment until attaining normal retiring age, or

(ii) the number of years of his reckonable service, or

(iii) 15 years;

and in calculating the amount of any retirement compensation payable to him any period so added shall be aggregated with any years of service or period of contribution entailing reduction of the relevant pension or retiring allowance because of a retirement pension payable under section 30 of the National Insurance Act 1965(**a**).

(3) When retirement compensation is awarded, or when an award is reviewed under regulation 35, the additional compensation payable in consequence of any years of service or period of contribution credited to a person under paragraph (2) may be reduced or withheld to such extent as the compensating authority may think reasonable having regard to the pension scheme (if any) associated with any further employment obtained by him.

(4) If under his last relevant pension scheme the amount of any benefit to which a person might have become entitled could have been increased at the discretion of the authority administering the pension scheme or of any other body, the compensating authority may increase, to an extent not exceeding that to which his accrued pension, accrued retiring allowance, accrued incapacity pension or accrued incapacity retiring allowance might have been increased or supplemented, the corresponding component of any retirement compensation payable to him; and in this connection the compensating authority shall have regard to the terms of any relevant resolution of the authority or body with regard to the increase of benefits and to the provisions of any enactment protecting the interests of that person.

(**a**) 1965 c. 51.

(5) If under his last relevant pension scheme a person would have been entitled to surrender a proportion of any pension which might have become payable to him in favour of his spouse or any dependant, then, if he so desires and informs the compensating authority by notice in writing accordingly within one month after becoming entitled to retirement compensation under these regulations, he may surrender a proportion of so much of the said compensation as is payable by way of an annual sum on the like terms and conditions and in consideration of the like payments by the compensating authority as if the said annual sum were a pension to which he had become entitled under the said pension scheme.

(6) In calculating for the purposes of regulation 20, 21 or 22 the amount of the annual sum which is equal to a person's accrued pension, no account shall be taken of any reduction falling to be made in that pension by reason of the provisions of any Act relating to National Insurance until the person reaches the age at which under his last relevant pension scheme the pension would have been so reduced.

(7) In paragraph (2) the expression "reckonable service" includes any period of employment of which account has been taken or is required to be taken in calculating the amount of any superannuation benefit to which a person has become entitled under a pension scheme associated with the employment which he has lost or, as the case may be, the employment in which his emoluments were diminished.

Retirement compensation for loss of emoluments payable to pensionable officer on attainment of normal retiring age

20.—(1) Subject to the provisions of these regulations, when a person to whom this Part of these regulations applies reaches normal retiring age, the retirement compensation payable to him for loss of emoluments shall be—

(*a*) an annual sum equal to the amount of his accrued pension, and

(*b*) a lump sum equal to the amount of his accrued retiring allowance (if any).

(2) Where an annual sum is payable under this regulation in respect of any period and resettlement compensation is also payable in respect of that period, the said annual sum shall be limited to the amount (if any) by which it exceeds the resettlement compensation so payable as aforesaid.

Retirement compensation payable to pensionable officer on his becoming incapacitated or reaching minimum pensionable age

21.—(1) Where a person to whom this Part of these regulations applies and who has suffered loss of employment before attaining what would have been his normal retiring age—

(*a*) becomes incapacitated in circumstances in which, if he had continued in the employment which he has lost, he would have become entitled to a pension under his last relevant pension scheme ; or

(*b*) attains the age which, had he continued to serve in the employment which he has lost, would have been his minimum pensionable age,

he shall be entitled on the happening of either event to claim, in lieu of any compensation to which he would otherwise be entitled under these regulations—

(i) in the case mentioned in sub-paragraph (*a*) of this paragraph, an annual sum equal to the amount of his accrued incapacity pension and a lump sum equal to the amount of his accrued incapacity retiring allowance (if any), and

(ii) in the case mentioned in sub-paragraph (*b*) of this paragraph, an annual sum equal to the amount of his accrued pension and a lump sum equal to the amount of his accrued retiring allowance (if any),

subject however to the conditions specified in paragraph (5).

(2) On receipt of a claim under paragraph (1) the compensating authority shall consider whether the claimant is a person to whom that paragraph applies, and within 13 weeks after the date of the receipt of the claim—

(*a*) if they are satisfied that he is not such a person, they shall notify him in writing accordingly ; or

(*b*) if they are satisfied that he is such a person, they shall assess the amount of compensation payable to him and notify him in writing accordingly ;

and any such notification shall, for the purposes of these regulations, be deemed to be a notification by the authority of a decision on a claim for compensation.

(3) A compensating authority may require any person who makes a claim under paragraph (1)(*a*) to submit himself to a medical examination by a registered medical practitioner selected by that authority and, if they do so, they shall also afford the person an opportunity of submitting a report from his own medical adviser as a result of an examination by him, and the authority shall take that report into consideration together with the report of the medical practitioner selected by them.

(4) If a person wishes to receive compensation under this regulation, he shall so inform the compensating authority in writing within one month from the receipt of a notification under paragraph (2) or, where the claim has been the subject of an appeal, from the decision of the tribunal thereon, and the compensation shall be payable as from the date on which the compensating authority received the claim.

(5) The calculation of compensation under this regulation shall be subject to the following conditions—

(*a*) where the compensating authority, by virtue of regulation 19, have credited the person with additional years of service or an additional period of contribution, no account shall be taken of any additional years or period beyond the number of years which he could have served, had he not lost his employment, before the date on which the claim was received by the compensating authority ; and

(*b*) if, by reason of any provision of the relevant pension scheme for a minimum benefit, the amount of any such pension or retiring allowance is in excess of that attributable to the person's actual service, no account shall be taken of any such additional years or period except to the extent (if any) by which they exceed the number of years represented by the difference between his actual service and the period by reference to which the minimum benefit has been calculated ; and

(*c*) if the number of years by reference to which an accrued incapacity pension or accrued incapacity retiring allowance is to be calculated is less than any minimum number of years of qualifying service prescribed by the relevant pension scheme, the amount of such pension or retiring allowance shall, notwithstanding any minimum benefit prescribed by the pension scheme, not exceed such proportion of such minimum benefit as the number of years of pensionable service bears to the minimum number of years of qualifying service.

Option to take retirement compensation prematurely

22.—(1) If a person to whom this Part of these regulations applies has suffered loss of employment after attaining the age of 50 years and so requests the compensating authority by notice in writing, he shall be entitled, as from the date on which the compensating authority receive such notice, to an annual sum equal to the amount of his accrued pension and a lump sum equal to the amount of his accrued retiring allowance (if any), and in that event he shall not be entitled to receive any further payment of long-term compensation after that date :

Provided that—

(i) in calculating the amount of the compensation payable to a person who has given such notice as aforesaid no account shall be taken of any additional years of service or period of contribution credited to him under regulation 19 ; and

(ii) where the person has claimed long-term compensation the said notice shall be given not later than 2 years after a decision on the claim has been notified or, where the decision has been reviewed under regulation 35(3), not later than 2 years after the review, or if there has been more than one such review, after the latest.

(2) Regulation 21(2) shall apply in relation to a notice given under the last foregoing paragraph as it applies to a claim made under paragraph (1) of that regulation.

(3) Where an annual sum is payable under this regulation in respect of any period and resettlement compensation is also payable in respect of that period, the said annual sum shall be limited to the amount (if any) by which it exceeds the resettlement compensation so payable as aforesaid.

Retirement compensation for diminution of emoluments

23. Regulations 20 and 21 shall apply to a person to whom this Part of these regulations applies and who has suffered a diminution of his emoluments, as if he had suffered loss of employment and as if the loss of emoluments occasioned thereby had been equivalent to the amount of the diminution :

Provided that no compensation shall be payable—

(i) if the emoluments have been diminished by less than $2\frac{1}{2}$ per cent ; or

(ii) if the person has continued to pay superannuation contributions as if his emoluments had not been diminished.

Superannuation contributions

24.—(1) A person entitled to retirement compensation under regulation 20, 21 or 22 shall pay to the compensating authority an amount equal to any sum which was paid to him by way of return of superannuation contributions, including any interest, after ceasing to be employed, and the compensating authority may at his request repay that amount to him at any time before he becomes entitled as aforesaid, but if that amount is not paid to the compensating authority, or is repaid by them to the person, the compensation shall be reduced by an annual amount the capital value of which is equal to the amount of the said superannuation contributions.

(2) For the purposes of this regulation the expression "superannuation contributions" shall include payments made by the person in respect of added years and any additional contributory payments made by him.

(3) Any sums paid to a compensating authority under this regulation in respect of returned contributions shall, except in so far as they are repaid to the officers concerned, be applied for the payment of compensation which the authority is liable to pay under this Part of these regulations.

Retirement compensation of a person who obtains further pensionable employment

25.—(1) Where a person to whom this Part of these regulations applies, after suffering loss of employment or diminution of emoluments, enters employment in which he is subject to a pension scheme and thereafter becomes entitled to reckon for the purposes of that scheme any service or period of contribution which falls to be taken into account for the purpose of assessing the amount of any retirement compensation payable to him, his entitlement to retirement compensation shall be reviewed and no retirement compensation shall be payable in respect of such service or period unless the annual rate of the emoluments to which he was entitled immediately before such loss or diminution exceeds the annual rate on entry of the emoluments of the new employment by more than $2\frac{1}{2}$ per cent. of such first mentioned emoluments, and any retirement compensation so payable to him shall, in so far as it is calculated by reference to remuneration, be calculated by reference to the difference between the said annual rates:

Provided that—

(i) if on entering the new employment a person—

(*a*) becomes a contributory employee or local Act contributor and

(*b*) becomes entitled to reckon as non-contributing service, or as service at half length for purposes of a local Act scheme, any service or period of contribution which immediately before the loss of employment or the diminution of emoluments was reckonable as contributing service or a period of contribution,

one-half of that service or period shall not be subject to the provisions of this paragraph;

(ii) this paragraph shall not operate to increase the amount of any retirement compensation payable in respect of diminution of emoluments beyond the amount which would have been payable if the person had attained normal retiring age immediately before he ceased to hold the employment in which he suffered the diminution of emoluments.

(2) No retirement compensation shall be payable in the circumstances mentioned in paragraph (1) if the person has continued to pay superannuation contributions as if his emoluments had not been diminished.

Compensation payable to widow or dependants of a claimant

26.—(1) Payments in accordance with this regulation and regulations 27 and 28 shall be made to or for the benefit of the widow, child or other dependant or to the personal representatives of a person to whom this Part of these regulations applies or, as the case may be, to trustees empowered by such a person to stand possessed of any benefit under his last relevant pension scheme.

(2) If the widow, child or other dependant of that person might have become entitled but for the loss of his employment to a pension under his last relevant pension scheme, the widow, child or other dependant, as the case may be, shall be entitled to receive—

(*a*) where the pension scheme provides for a prescribed proportion, an annual sum equal to the prescribed proportion of any retirement compensation by way of annual amounts payable to the person under regulation 20, 21 or 22 immediately before his death or, if he dies before becoming entitled to receive compensation under any of those regulations, the prescribed proportion of the compensation by way of annual amounts which he would have received under regulation 21 had he become entitled thereto immediately before his death, and

(*b*) where the pension scheme does not provide for a prescribed proportion, such an annual sum as is provided by paragraph (3):

Provided that—

(i) where any retirement compensation has been surrendered under regulation 19(5) or compounded under regulation 36, any sum payable under sub-paragraph (*a*) shall be calculated as if such surrender or compounding had not taken place, and

(ii) in calculating the sum payable under sub-paragraph (*a*) it shall be assumed that the retirement compensation payable, or which would have been payable, to a person under regulation 20, 21 or 22 had been such sum as would have been payable if the accrued pension or accrued incapacity pension had not been reduced by reason of the provisions of any Act relating to National Insurance.

(3) The sum mentioned in paragraph (2)(*b*) shall be an annual sum equal to the annual amount of the pension (calculated in the manner specified in paragraph (4)) to which the widow, child or other dependant of the person in question would have become entitled if he had died immediately before the date on which he suffered the loss of employment, having then complied with any requirements of the last relevant pension scheme as to a minimum period of qualifying service or contribution and completed any additional contributory payments or payments in respect of added years which he was then in the course of making.

(4) The calculation referred to in paragraph (3) shall be made on the basis of the method prescribed by the last relevant pension scheme of the person in question for the calculation of benefits for a widow, child or other dependant and in so far as the age at which he died is relevant for the purposes of the said calculation, the date on which he died shall be taken to be the actual date of his death, the provisions of paragraph (3) to the contrary notwithstanding.

(5) Any annual sum payable to or for the benefit of a widow, child or other dependant under this regulation shall cease to be payable in any circumstances in which a corresponding pension under the last relevant pension scheme would have ceased to be payable; and where that scheme provides for pay-

ment of the pension to any person on behalf of a child or other dependant, any annual sum payable under this regulation to a child or other dependant shall be paid to that person on behalf of the child or dependant in the like manner and for the like period as is provided in the pension scheme.

(6) Except where the compensation has been reduced under regulation 24, compensation payable under this regulation and regulation 27 shall in the aggregate be reduced by an amount the capital value whereof is equal to the amount of any superannuation contributions as defined in regulation 24(2) returned to the person in respect of whom the compensation is payable and either not paid to the compensating authority or repaid to him by the compensating authority, the compensation under each such regulation being reduced in proportion to the capital value of each amount.

(7) If the person in question suffered a diminution of emoluments, then

(*a*) where his last relevant pension scheme provides for a prescribed proportion, the provisions of paragraph (2)(*a*) shall apply with the substitution of references to diminution of emoluments for references to loss of employment, and the annual sum payable to a widow, child or other dependant of such a person shall be calculated as if he had suffered loss of employment and as if the loss of emoluments occasioned thereby had been equivalent to the amount of the diminution:

Provided that no sum shall be payable under this sub-paragraph—

(i) if the emoluments have been diminished by less than 2½ per cent; or

(ii) if the person has continued to pay superannuation contributions as if his emoluments had not been diminished; and

(*b*) where the said scheme does not provide for a prescribed proportion, the provisions of paragraph (2)(*b*) and of regulation 33(4)(*a*) shall apply with the substitution of references to diminution of emoluments for the references to loss of employment and of a reference to employment in which he has suffered such a diminution for the reference to employment which he has lost:

Provided that no sum shall be payable under this sub-paragraph if the sum calculated thereunder amounts to less than 2½ per cent of such sum as would have been payable had the person in question suffered a loss of employment instead of a diminution of emoluments.

(8) In this regulation "prescribed proportion" means the proportion which, by the provisions contained in the last relevant pension scheme of a person to whom this Part of these regulations applies, the pension payable to his widow, child or other dependant is to bear to that person's pension.

Compensation where death grant would have been payable

27.—(1) If the widow, the personal representatives of a person to whom this Part of these regulations applies or trustees empowered by such a person to stand possessed of any benefit under his last relevant pension scheme, might have become entitled to a death grant under his last relevant pension scheme, she or they, as the case may be, shall be entitled to receive a sum calculated in accordance with the provisions of regulation 26(6) and paragraph (2) of this regulation.

(2) The amount of the sum referred to in paragraph (1) shall be ascertained in accordance with the method of calculation prescribed by the last relevant pension scheme for the ascertainment of death grant as if the person had died immediately before losing his employment, subject to the following modifications—

(*a*) except where the person had been in receipt of retirement compensation under regulation 22, account shall be taken of any additional years of service or period of contribution credited to him under regulation 19(2)—

(i) in the case of a person who had been in receipt of retirement compensation under regulation 21, to the extent of the period between the loss of employment and the date of the claim made under that regulation; and

(ii) in any other case, to the extent of the period between the loss of employment and the person's death;

(*b*) if the number of years of the person's service or period of contribution is less than the minimum number of years of qualifying service or period prescribed by the pension scheme for the receipt of a death grant, the said sum shall not exceed such proportion of the death grant calculated as aforesaid as the number of years of the person's pensionable service or period of contribution bears to the minimum number of years of qualifying service or period prescribed by the pension schemes; and

(*c*) there shall be deducted from such sum the amount of any retirement compensation paid to the person under regulation 20, 21 or 22, or where any part of the compensation has been surrendered under regulation 19(5), the amount which would have been so paid but for any such surrender.

(3) For the purpose of calculating such death grant, an annual sum payable under either paragraph (2)(*a*) or paragraph (7)(*a*) of regulation 26 to or for the benefit of a widow, child or other dependant shall be deemed to be a pension payable to or for the benefit of the widow, child or dependant, as the case may be.

(4) This regulation shall apply in the case of a person who has suffered a diminution of emoluments with the substitution of references to diminution of emoluments for references to loss of employment, and the sum payable to the said widow, personal representatives or trustees of such a person shall be calculated as if he had suffered loss of employment and as if the loss of emoluments occasioned thereby had been equivalent to the amount of the diminution:

Provided that no sum shall be payable under this paragraph—

(i) if the emoluments have been diminished by less than 2½ per cent; or

(ii) if the person has continued to pay superannuation contributions as if his emoluments had not been diminished.

Balance payable to claimant's widow or personal representatives

28.—(1) If no annual sum is payable to the widow, child or other dependant of any person under regulation 26(2)(*a*) or (7)(*a*) and no sum is payable under regulation 27 and the person dies before he has received in the aggregate by way of retirement compensation a sum equivalent to the amount of any contributions repaid by him under regulation 24, together with compound interest thereon calculated at the rate of 3 per cent per annum with half-yearly rests up to the date of his death as from the 1st April or 1st October following the half year in which the amount was paid, there shall be paid to his personal representatives the difference between the aggregate amount received by way of retirement compensation as aforesaid and the said equivalent sum.

(2) If an annual sum becomes payable to a widow under either paragraph (2)(*a*) or paragraph (7)(*a*) of regulation 26 and on her re-marriage or death the sum ceases to be payable, and any sum payable to a child or other dependant under either of those paragraphs has ceased to be payable, and if the aggregate amount of the payments which were made as aforesaid to her husband by way of retirement compensation and to the widow, personal representatives or trustees under regulation 27 is less than a sum equivalent to the amount which would have been payable to the personal representatives under that regulation if no annual sum had been payable under either of the said paragraphs (2)(*a*) or (7)(*a*), there shall be paid to her or her personal representatives the difference between such aggregate amount and the said equivalent sum.

(3) For the purposes of this regulation a person who has surrendered any part of his retirement compensation under regulation 19(5) shall be deemed to have received during any period the amount of compensation for that period which he would have received but for any such surrender.

Compensation payable to non-pensionable officer on reaching retiring age

29.—(1) Where a person who is not a pensionable officer is receiving long-term compensation for loss of employment and attains normal retiring age, the compensating authority may, if satisfied that the person would, but for the loss, have continued in the employment he has lost for a substantial period beyond that age, continue to pay compensation to him for the remainder of his life at half its former rate.

(2) Where a person who is not a pensionable officer suffers loss of employment on or after attaining normal retiring age, the compensating authority may, if satisfied that the person would in the normal course have continued in the employment he has lost for a further substantial period, pay compensation to him for the remainder of his life at half the rate to which he would have been entitled under regulation 15 had he not attained normal retiring age at the date on which he lost his employment.

Persons subject to policy schemes

30.—(1) Regulations 20, 21, 22, 23 and 27 shall not apply to a person (in this regulation referred to as a "policy scheme participant") who has been participating in a scheme associated with his employment for providing superannuation benefits by means of contracts or policies of insurance, and who, after the loss of his employment or the diminution of his emoluments, continued to participate in that scheme, or became entitled to a benefit or prospective benefit thereunder other than a return of contributions.

(2) If a policy scheme participant has lost his employment, the compensating authority may, if the relevant scheme so permits, make such payments to or in respect of him, whether by way of the payment of premiums or otherwise, as are actuarially equivalent to the amounts by which his retirement compensation might have been increased under regulation 19(2) or (4) had he been a person to whom regulation 20, 21 or 22 applied.

(3) If a policy scheme participant has suffered a diminution of his emoluments, the compensating authority may, if the relevant scheme so permits, make such payments to or in respect of him, whether by way of the payment of premiums or otherwise, as will secure to him the like benefits as if his emoluments had not been diminished.

(4) If a policy scheme participant becomes entitled to a benefit under such a scheme as is mentioned in paragraph (1) before reaching normal retiring age, the compensating authority may reduce any long-term compensation payable to him by the amount of such benefit.

Intervals for payment of compensation under Part V

31. Any compensation awarded as an annual sum under this Part of these regulations to or in respect of any person shall be payable at intervals equivalent to those at which the corresponding benefit would have been payable under the person's last relevant pension scheme or at such other intervals as may be agreed between the person entitled to receive the compensation and the compensating authority.

PART VI

ADJUSTMENT, REVIEW AND COMPOUNDING OF COMPENSATION

Adjustment of compensation where superannuation benefit is also payable

32.—(1) Where any period of service of which account was taken in calculating the amount of any compensation payable under Part IV or V of these regulations is subsequently taken into account for the purpose of calculating the amount of any superannuation benefit payable to or in respect of any person in accordance with a pension scheme associated with any employment undertaken subsequent to the loss of employment or diminution of emoluments which was the subject of the claim for compensation, the compensating authority may in accordance with this regulation withhold or reduce the compensation payable in respect of any period for which such superannuation benefit is being received.

(2) If the part of any superannuation benefit by way of annual amounts which is attributable to a period of service mentioned in paragraph (1) equals or exceeds the part of any compensation by way of annual amounts which is attributable to the same period, that part of the compensation may be withheld, or if such part of the superannuation benefit is less than such part of the compensation, the compensation may be reduced by an amount not exceeding such part of the superannuation benefit.

(3) In the case of a death benefit payable in respect of any person, the sum payable under regulation 27 may be reduced by an amount not greater than the proportion of the death benefit which the period of service mentioned in paragraph (1) bears to the total period of service of which account was taken in the calculation of the death benefit.

(4) In addition to any reduction authorised by paragraph (2) or (3), if, in the circumstances mentioned in paragraph (1), compensation by way of annual amounts is attributable in part to any provision of the relevant pension scheme for a minimum benefit, the compensation may be reduced by an amount not exceeding that part.

(5) Where any additional years of service or period of contribution have been credited to a person under regulation 19(2), if the number of such years or such period is equal to or less than the period spent in the subsequent employment mentioned in paragraph (1), the compensation by way of annual amounts may be reduced (in addition to any other reduction authorised by this regulation) by an amount not exceeding that attributable to the additional years or period so

credited or, if the number of such years or such period is greater than the period spent in the subsequent employment, by such proportion of that amount as the period spent in the subsequent employment bears to the number of additional years or the period so credited.

(6) Where compensation has been calculated in accordance with regulation 25, the provisions of this regulation shall only apply—

(*a*) in relation to such part (if any) of the superannuation benefit as is attributable to annual emoluments in excess of those to which the person was entitled on entering the new employment referred to in regulation 25, and

(*b*) in relation to any non-contributing service which becomes reckonable as contributing service pursuant to section 2 of the Local Government Superannuation Act 1953.

(7) Where compensation is payable in respect of diminution of emoluments, the provisions of this regulation shall apply only in relation to such part (if any) of the superannuation benefit as is attributable to annual emoluments in excess of those to which the person was entitled immediately prior to the diminution.

Reduction of compensation in certain cases

33.—(1) If under a person's last relevant pension scheme any benefit for which the scheme provided would have been subject to reduction or suspension on his taking up other specified employment, any retirement compensation to which he is entitled for loss of employment or diminution of emoluments shall, where such employment is taken up, be reduced or suspended in the like manner and to the like extent:

Provided that in calculating the amount of the reduction there shall be aggregated with the emoluments of the employment taken up the amount of any superannuation benefit by way of annual amounts payable to the person under a pension scheme associated with the employment which he has lost or, as the case may be, the employment in which the emoluments were diminished.

(2) There shall be deducted from the retirement compensation payable to any person any additional contributory payments remaining unpaid at the date when he suffered loss of employment; and any such payments not recovered at the date of his death shall be deducted from any compensation payable in respect of that person under regulation 26, 27 or 28(2).

(3) Where a person is entitled to compensation under these regulations and the circumstances are such that he is also entitled to—

(*a*) a redundancy payment under the Redundancy Payments Act 1965(**a**), or

(*b*) any similar payment in consequence of the loss of his employment under any contract or arrangement with the authority by whom he was employed (other than payments by way of a return of contributions under a pension scheme), or

(*c*) any payment under or by virtue of the provisions of any enactment relating to the reinstatement in civil employment of persons who have been in the service of the Crown,

(**a**) 1965 c. 62.

the compensation which would, apart from this paragraph, become due to the person, whether by instalments or lump sum or both, shall in the aggregate be reduced by the amount of the payments referred to in this paragraph.

(4) Where compensation under these regulations is payable to or in respect of any person, and that person or his widow, child or other dependant or his personal representatives or trustees such as are mentioned in regulation 27(1) is or are also entitled (whether immediately or on the person's attaining some greater age) to a superannuation benefit under a pension scheme associated with the employment which he has lost—

(*a*) any instalment of such compensation which is payable in respect of any period shall be reduced by the amount of the instalment of such superannuation benefit which is payable in respect of the same period; and

(*b*) any such compensation which is payable as a lump sum shall be reduced by the amount of any lump sum superannuation benefit.

(5) For the purposes of paragraph (4) no account shall be taken of any sum payable in consequence of the surrender by any person of part of his superannuation benefit under any provision in that behalf in the relevant pension scheme with a view to obtaining or increasing allowances for his widow, child or other dependant; and the person shall be deemed to have received during any period the amount of superannuation benefit which he would have received but for any such surrender.

(6) Where in any week a person is entitled to long-term compensation for loss or diminution of emoluments and is also entitled to unemployment, sickness or injury benefit under any Act relating to National Insurance, other than a benefit claimable by him in respect of a dependant, there shall be deducted from the long-term compensation payable for that week a sum equal to the amount by which the aggregate of such National Insurance benefit claimable in respect of that week and the weekly rate at which the long-term compensation would be payable but for this regulation exceeds two thirds of the weekly rate of the net emoluments of the employment which he has lost or in which the emoluments have been diminished:

Provided that this paragraph shall not apply in relation to any such sickness or injury benefit in so far as—

(*a*) an equivalent sum is deducted from the emoluments of his current employment, and

(*b*) such deduction from those emoluments has not occasioned an increase in his long-term compensation.

(7) In paragraph (6) the expression "weekly rate" means seven three hundred and sixty-fifths of the relevant annual rate.

Notification of change of circumstances

34. Where—

(*a*) a pensionable officer after suffering loss of employment or diminution of emoluments enters any employment referred to in regulation 25 or becomes entitled to any superannuation benefit on ceasing to hold such employment, or (*b*) a person entitled to long-term compensation enters employment the remuneration whereof is payable out of public funds, or ceases to hold such employment, or receives any increase in his remuneration in such employment, or

(*c*) a person entitled to retirement compensation enters employment in which the compensation is subject to reduction or suspension under regulation 33, or ceases to hold such employment, or receives any increase in his remuneration in such employment, or

(*d*) a person entitled to long-term compensation starts to receive any benefit, any increase in benefit or any further benefit under any Act relating to National Insurance,

he shall forthwith inform the compensating authority in writing of that fact.

Review of awards of long-term or retirement compensation

35.—(1) The compensating authority shall, within a period of 2 years after the date on which any decision on a claim for long-term or retirement compensation for loss of employment (other than compensation payable under regulation 22) is notified to a claimant under regulation 37 or within such longer period as is specified in the subsequent provisions of this regulation, and at intervals of not more than 6 months, review their decision or, where the claim has been the subject of an appeal, the decision of the tribunal, and these regulations shall apply in relation to any such review as they apply in relation to the initial determination of the claim; and on such review, in the light of any material change in the circumstances of the case, compensation may be awarded, or compensation previously awarded may be increased, reduced or discontinued, subject to the limits set out in these regulations.

(2) The person to whom the decision relates may require the compensating authority to carry out the review mentioned in paragraph (1) at any time within the period of 2 years mentioned in that paragraph if he considers that there has been a change in the circumstances of his case which is material for the purposes of these regulations.

(3) The compensating authority shall carry out a review in accordance with paragraph (1), notwithstanding the expiration of the period mentioned in that paragraph, if—

(*a*) the emoluments of employment or work undertaken as a result of the loss of employment had been taken into account in determining the amount of any compensation awarded, and

(*b*) such employment or work has been lost or the emoluments thereof reduced, otherwise than by reason of misconduct or incapacity to perform such duties as the person might reasonably have been required to perform, and

(*c*) the compensating authority are satisfied that such loss or reduction is causing him hardship,

and where any decision is so reviewed, the decision shall be subject to further review in accordance with paragraph (1) as if the review carried out under this paragraph had been the initial determination of the claim.

(4) Paragraphs (1) and (2) shall apply in relation to any decision on a claim for long-term or retirement compensation in respect of diminution of emoluments as they apply in relation to any decision mentioned in the said paragraph (1):

Provided that—

(i) where the person to whom the decision relates ceases to hold the employment in which his emoluments were diminished, a review shall be held within 3 months after that date, but no further review shall be held after the expiry of that period, and

(ii) while that person continues to hold that employment, there shall be no limit to the period within which a review may take place.

(5) Notwithstanding anything contained in the foregoing provisions of this regulation, the compensating authority shall review a decision (whether of the authority or the tribunal) on a claim for long-term compensation for loss of employment or diminution of emoluments after the expiration of any period within which a review is required to be made if at any time—

(*a*) the person to whom the decision relates becomes engaged in employment (hereinafter referred to as his "current employment") the remuneration whereof is payable out of public funds and which he has undertaken subsequent to the loss or diminution, and

(*b*) the aggregate of the net emoluments of his current employment, any superannuation benefit by way of annual amounts payable to him in respect of the employment which he has lost or the employment in which his emoluments have been diminished and the long-term compensation payable to him exceeds the net emoluments of the employment which he has lost or, as the case may be, in which the emoluments have been diminished.

(6) The compensating authority shall further review any decision reviewed under paragraph (5) whenever the net emoluments of the person's current employment are increased.

(7) If on any review under paragraph (5) or (6) the compensation is reduced, it shall not be reduced below the amount by which the net emoluments of the person's current employment, together with any superannuation benefit by way of annual amounts payable to him in respect of the employment which he has lost or the employment in which his emoluments have been diminished, falls short of the net emoluments of the employment which he has lost or, as the case may be, in which the emoluments have been diminished.

(8) The compensating authority shall give to a person to whom a decision relates not less than 14 days' notice of any review of that decision to be carried out under this regulation unless the review is carried out at his request.

(9) Nothing in this regulation shall preclude the making of any adjustments of compensation required by regulation 32 or 33.

Compounding of awards

36.—(1) In a case where an annual sum which has been or might be awarded under these regulations does not exceed £26, the compensating authority may, at their discretion, compound their liability in respect thereof by paying a lump sum equivalent to the capital value of the annual sum and, if any lump sum payment has been or might be awarded in addition to such annual sum under regulation 20, 21, 22 or 23, the compensating authority may likewise discharge their liability in respect thereof by an immediate payment.

(2) In any other case, if the person who has been awarded long-term or retirement compensation requests them to do so, the compensating authority may, after having regard to the state of health of that person and the other

circumstances of the case, compound up to one quarter of their liability to make payments under the award (other than payments to a widow, child or other dependant under regulation 26) by the payment of an equivalent amount as a lump sum or, where any compensation has been awarded as a lump sum, by increasing that compensation to such equivalent amount; and in calculating for this purpose the liability of the authority to make such payments, account shall be taken of the annual value of lump sum payments of compensation.

(3) The making of a composition under paragraph (2) in relation to an award of long-term or retirement compensation shall not prevent the subsequent making of a composition under paragraph (1) in relation to that award, but, subject as aforesaid, not more than one composition may be made in relation to any award.

PART VII

PROCEDURE AND MISCELLANEOUS

Procedure on making claims

37.—(1) Every claim for compensation under these regulations and every request for a review of an award of long-term or retirement compensation shall be made in accordance with this regulation.

(2) Every such claim and request shall be made to the compensating authority in writing, shall set out the grounds on which the claim or request is made and shall state whether any other claim for compensation has been made by the claimant under these regulations.

(3) Resettlement compensation shall be claimed separately from any other form of compensation claimable under these regulations.

(4) The compensating authority shall consider any such claim or request in accordance with the relevant provisions of these regulations and shall notify the person making the claim or request in writing of their decision—

(*a*) in the case of a claim for resettlement compensation, not later than one month after the receipt of the claim, and

(*b*) in the case of a claim for, or request for the review of an award of, compensation under Part IV or V of these regulations, not later than 13 weeks after the receipt of the claim or request, and

(*c*) in any other case, as soon as possible after the decision; but the decision of a compensating authority shall not be invalidated by reason of the fact that notice of the decision is given after the expiry of the period mentioned in this paragraph.

(5) Every notification of a decision by the compensating authority (whether granting or refusing compensation or reviewing an award, or otherwise affecting any compensation under these regulations) shall contain a statement—

(*a*) giving reasons for the decision;

(*b*) showing how any compensation has been calculated and, in particular, if the amount is less than the maximum which could have been awarded under these regulations, showing the factors taken into account in awarding that amount; and (*c*) directing the attention of the claimant to his right under regulation 44, if he is aggrieved by the decision, to institute proceedings before a tribunal and giving him the address to which the application instituting such proceedings should be sent.

Claimants to furnish information

38.—(1) Any person claiming or receiving compensation or whose award of compensation is being reviewed shall furnish all such information as the compensating authority may at any time reasonably require; and he shall verify the same in such manner, including the production of books or of original documents in his possession or control, as may be reasonably so required.

(2) Any such person shall, on receipt of reasonable notice, present himself for interview at such place as the compensating authority may reasonably require: and any person who attends for interview may, if he so desires, be represented by his adviser.

Procedure on death of claimant

39.—(1) In the event of the death of a claimant or of a person who, if he had survived, could have been a claimant, a claim for compensation under these regulations may be continued or made, as the case may be, by his personal representatives.

(2) Where any such claim is continued or made as aforesaid by personal representatives, the personal representatives shall, as respects any steps to be taken or thing to be done by them in order to continue or make the claim, be deemed for the purposes of these regulations to be the person entitled to claim, but, save as aforesaid, the person in whose right they continue or make the claim shall be deemed for the purposes of these regulations to be such person, and the relevant provisions of these regulations shall be construed accordingly:

Provided that the compensating authority may in any such case extend the period within which a claim is required to be made by regulation 7 or 13.

Calculation of service

40.—(1) For the purpose of determining the amount of any compensation payable in respect of the loss of an office to which, or of any two or more offices to which in the aggregate, a person devoted substantially the whole of his time, any previous period of part-time employment shall be treated as though it were whole-time employment for a proportionately reduced period.

(2) For the purpose of making any calculations under these regulations in respect of a person's reckonable service, all periods of such service shall be aggregated and, except where reference is made to completed years of service, if the aggregated service includes a fraction of a year, that fraction shall, if it equals or exceeds 6 months, be treated as a year, and shall, in any other case be disregarded.

Emoluments of part-time employments

41. In ascertaining for the purposes of these regulations whether, and how far, the remuneration of alternative employment falls short of emoluments which have been lost where these emoluments were payable in respect of two or more part-time employments, the remuneration of the alternative employment or of the aggregate of two or more such employments shall be apportioned in the proportion which the emoluments of the part-time employments bore to each other.

Temporary variation of emoluments

42. In calculating for the purposes of these regulations the amount of any emoluments lost, or the amount by which any emoluments have been diminished, and in determining the net emoluments, the accrued pension or the accrued retiring allowance of any person who has suffered such a loss or diminution, no account shall be taken of any increase in the amount of the person's emoluments which is attributable to any temporary allowance made in consequence of the appropriate transfer order and otherwise than in the ordinary course of his employment.

Compensation not assignable

43. Subject to any statutory provision in that behalf, any compensation to which a person becomes entitled under these regulations shall be paid by the compensating authority and shall be payable to, or in trust for, the person who is entitled to receive it, and shall not be assignable:

Provided that, without prejudice to any other right of recovery, any compensation paid in error to a person may be recovered by the compensating authority from him by deduction from any compensation payable to him under these regulations.

Right of appeal from decision of compensating authority

44.—(1) Every person who is aggrieved by any decision of the compensating authority with respect to a compensation question or by any failure on the part of the compensating authority to notify him of any such decision within the appropriate time prescribed by these regulations, may within 13 weeks of the notification to him of the decision or the expiry of the prescribed time, as the case may be, institute proceedings for the determination of the question by a tribunal in accordance with the Industrial Tribunals (Employment and Compensation) Regulations 1967(**a**), or in Scotland, the Industrial Tribunals (Employment and Compensation) (Scotland) Regulations 1967(**b**) and these regulations; and the tribunal shall determine the question accordingly.

(2) For the purpose of any such proceedings a person or persons may be appointed to sit with the tribunal as assessor or assessors.

(3) The compensating authority shall give effect to the decision of the tribunal subject to any modifications that may be required in consequence of any appeal from that decision on a point of law.

Given under the Official Seal of the Minister of Transport the 14th May 1970.

(L.S.)

Fred Mulley,
Minister of Transport.

(**a**) S.I. 1967/361 (1967 I, p. 1205). (**b**) S.I. 1967/362 (1967 I, p. 1220).

Regulation 2(2)

SCHEDULE

TABLE I

Table showing the capital value of an annual amount of £1 payable for life

Age	Capital value of £1 per annum payable for life					
	Female			Male		
	£	s.	d.	£	s.	d.
Under 35	15	11	0	15	3	0
35 and under 40	15	2	0	14	12	0
40 and under 45	14	11	0	13	19	0
45 and under 50	13	18	0	13	2	0
50	13	9	0	12	11	0
51	13	5	0	12	7	0
52	13	2	0	12	3	0
53	12	18	0	11	18	0
54	12	14	0	11	14	0
55	12	10	0	11	9	0
56	12	6	0	11	5	0
57	12	2	0	11	0	0
58	11	18	0	10	15	0
59	11	13	0	10	10	0
60	11	8	0	10	5	0
61	11	4	0	10	0	0
62	10	19	0	9	14	0
63	10	14	0	9	9	0
64	10	8	0	9	3	0
65	10	3	0	8	18	0
66	9	18	0	8	12	0
67	9	12	0	8	7	0
68	9	7	0	8	1	0
69	9	1	0	7	16	0
70	8	15	0	7	10	0

NOTE:—This table is for use in connection with regulation 36(1) and (2) for the compounding of annual retirement compensation which a person is currently entitled to receive under regulation 20, 21, 22 or 23. Where the compensation is payable before age 60 (females), 65 (males) but will be reduced on the attainment of that age (in connection with National Insurance pension) the table should be used in conjunction with Table II, i.e. Table II should be used for valuing that part of the compensation which ceases to be payable at age 60 or 65 as the case may be and this table should be used for valuing the remainder.

TABLE II

Table showing the capital value of an amount of £1 per annum ceasing at age 60 (females), 65 (males)

Age	Capital Value					
	Female			Male		
	£	s.	d.	£	s.	d.
Under 35	13	8	0	14	2	0
35 and under 40	12	5	0	13	3	0
40 and under 45	10	14	0	11	19	0
45 and under 50	8	13	0	10	8	0
50	7	3	0	9	6	0
51	6	12	0	8	18	0
52	6	0	0	8	9	0
53	5	7	0	7	19	0
54	4	13	0	7	10	0
55	3	18	0	6	19	0
56	3	3	0	6	8	0
57	2	6	0	5	17	0
58	1	9	0	5	4	0
59		10	0	4	11	0
60	—			3	17	0
61	—			3	2	0
62	—			2	6	0
63	—			1	8	0
64	—				10	0

NOTE:—This table is for use in connection with regulation 36(1) and (2) for the compounding of any part of annual retirement compensation which will cease to be payable on the attainment of age 60 (females), 65 (males). Table I should be used in relation to the remainder of such compensation, i.e. the part which is payable for life—see note on that table.

TABLE III

Table showing the capital value of an annual amount of £1 payable to a widow until death or remarriage

Age of widow at date of widowhood	Capital value of £1 per annum as at date of widowhood	Age of widow at date of widowhood	Capital value of £1 per annum as at date of widowhood
	£ s. d.		£ s. d.
20	6 0 0	45	11 18 0
21	6 0 0	46	12 1 0
22	6 0 0	47	12 3 0
23	6 0 0	48	12 5 0
24	6 0 0	49	12 6 0
25	6 5 0	50	12 6 0
26	6 12 0	51	12 6 0
27	6 19 0	52	12 5 0
28	7 6 0	53	12 4 0
29	7 13 0	54	12 3 0
30	8 0 0	55	12 1 0
31	8 8 0	56	11 19 0
32	8 15 0	57	11 16 0
33	9 2 0	58	11 13 0
34	9 8 0	59	11 10 0
35	9 15 0	60	11 6 0
36	10 1 0	61	11 3 0
37	10 6 0	62	10 19 0
38	10 11 0	63	10 14 0
39	10 16 0	64	10 8 0
40	11 1 0	65	10 3 0
41	11 5 0	66	9 18 0
42	11 9 0	67	9 12 0
43	11 12 0	68	9 7 0
44	11 15 0	69	9 1 0
		70	8 15 0

NOTE:—This table is for use in connection with regulation 36(1) for compounding annual compensation payable to a widow under regulation 26. It should also be used, where a reduction of compensation under regulation 26(6) falls to be apportioned between the compensation payable under that regulation and under regulation 27, for ascertaining the capital value of annual compensation to a widow.

TABLE IV

Table showing the annual amount payable for life equivalent in value to a lump sum of £100

Age	Annual sum, payable for life, equal in value to a lump sum of £100	
	Female	Male
	£ s. d.	£ s. d.
Under 35	6 8 7	6 12 0
35 and under 40	6 12 5	6 17 0
40 and under 45	6 17 5	7 3 4
45 and under 50	7 3 11	7 12 8
50	7 8 8	7 19 4
51	7 10 11	8 1 11
52	7 12 8	8 4 7
53	7 15 0	8 8 1
54	7 17 6	8 10 11
55	8 0 0	8 14 8
56	8 2 7	8 17 9
57	8 5 3	9 1 10
58	8 8 1	9 6 0
59	8 11 8	9 10 6
60	8 15 5	9 15 1
61	8 18 7	10 0 0
62	9 2 8	10 6 2
63	9 6 11	10 11 8
64	9 12 4	10 18 7
65	9 17 0	11 4 9
66	10 2 0	11 12 7
67	10 8 4	11 19 6
68	10 13 11	12 8 5
69	11 1 0	12 16 5
70	11 8 7	13 6 8

NOTE:—This table is for use in connection with regulation 24(1) for ascertaining the annual amount by which retirement compensation under regulation 20, 21 or 22 is to be reduced where a claimant has not paid to the compensating authority an amount equal to any sum paid to him by way of superannuation contributions or that amount has been repaid to him by the compensating authority at his request. It should also be used in connection with regulation 36(2) for calculating for the purposes of that paragraph the annual value of retirement compensation awarded as a lump sum.

TABLE V

Table showing the annual amount payable to a widow until death or remarriage equivalent in value to a lump sum of £100

Age of widow at date of widowhood	Annual amount equal in value to a lump sum of £100	Age of widow at date of widowhood	Annual amount equal in value to a lump sum of £100
	£ s. d.		£ s. d.
20	16 13 4	45	8 8 1
21	16 13 4	46	8 6 0
22	16 13 4	47	8 4 7
23	16 13 4	48	8 3 3
24	16 13 4	49	8 2 7
25	16 0 0	50	8 2 7
26	15 3 0	51	8 2 7
27	14 7 9	52	8 3 3
28	13 14 0	53	8 3 11
29	13 1 5	54	8 4 7
30	12 10 0	55	8 6 0
31	11 18 1	56	8 7 4
32	11 8 7	57	8 9 6
33	10 19 9	58	8 11 8
34	10 12 9	59	8 13 11
35	10 5 2	60	8 17 0
36	9 19 0	61	8 19 5
37	9 14 2	62	9 2 8
38	9 9 7	63	9 6 11
39	9 5 2	64	9 12 4
40	9 1 0	65	9 17 0
41	8 17 9	66	10 2 0
42	8 14 8	67	10 8 4
43	8 12 5	68	10 13 11
44	8 10 3	69	11 1 0
		70	11 8 7

NOTE:—This table is for use in connection with regulation 26(6) for ascertaining the annual amount by which compensation to a widow is to be reduced in the circumstances described in that paragraph. If a reduction is required to be apportioned between compensation payable under regulations 26 and 27, the capital value of annual compensation to a widow should be ascertained by reference to Table III.

TABLE VI

Table showing, according to the outstanding period of long-term compensation, the capital value of each £100 of the total amount of long-term compensation compounded

Outstanding number of complete years of long-term compensation	Capital value of each £100 of the total amount of long-term compensation	
	Female	Male
	£ s. d.	£ s. d.
0	98 8 0	98 4 0
1	95 4 0	94 16 0
2	92 2 0	91 10 0
3	89 4 0	88 6 0
4	86 8 0	85 8 0
5	83 16 0	82 14 0
6	81 6 0	80 2 0
7	78 18 0	77 14 0
8	76 14 0	75 8 0
9	74 12 0	73 4 0
10	72 12 0	71 4 0
11	70 12 0	69 6 0
12	68 16 0	67 10 0
13	67 0 0	65 14 0
14	65 6 0	64 2 0
15	63 14 0	62 10 0
16	62 2 0	61 0 0
17	60 12 0	59 12 0
18	59 4 0	58 4 0
19	57 16 0	56 18 0
20	56 10 0	55 12 0
21	55 4 0	54 8 0
22	54 0 0	53 4 0
23	52 16 0	52 0 0
24	51 12 0	50 18 0
25	50 10 0	49 18 0
26	49 8 0	48 18 0
27	48 8 0	47 18 0
28	47 8 0	46 18 0
29	46 8 0	45 18 0
30	45 10 0	45 0 0

NOTE:—This table is for use in connection with regulation 36(1) and (2) for compounding awards of long-term compensation under Part IV of these regulations. The total amount of the annual long-term compensation which is to be compounded must first be calculated, i.e. the amount which the person would receive on account of that compensation or the part of it which is to be compounded, if it were paid until "normal retiring age" (as defined in these regulations). For each £100 so calculated, the lump sum payment will be the amount shown in the table according to the number of complete years in the period between the date of compounding and "normal retiring age".

EXPLANATORY NOTE

(This Note is not part of the Regulations.)

1. These regulations, made by the Minister of Transport under section 1 of the Water Officers Compensation Act 1960, as applied by section 17(3) of the Transport Act 1968 have, by virtue of paragraph (2) of the said section 1, been framed so as to have effect from 2 September 1969, a date earlier than the making of the regulations. They provide for the payment of compensation to or in respect of local authority officers who suffer loss of employment or loss or diminution of emoluments which is attributable to an order under section 17(1) (transfer of local authority transport undertakings) of the said Act of 1968 or to anything done in pursuance of any such order.

2. Part I of the regulations contains definitions. Part II specifies the persons to whom the regulations apply and the grounds of entitlement to compensation. The regulations apply to persons employed whole-time or part-time by or on behalf of a local authority.

3. The compensation payable is—

(*a*) resettlement compensation for loss of employment (Part III of the regulations);

(*b*) long-term compensation for loss of employment or loss or diminution of emoluments (Part IV);

(*c*) retirement compensation for loss of employment or loss or diminution of emoluments (Part V);

(*d*) compensation to the widow, child or other dependant or to the personal representatives of a claimant who was a pensionable officer (Part V).

4. Resettlement compensation is payable for a period not exceeding 26 weeks to officers with at least 3 years' service in relevant employment before the material date. The qualifying conditions and factors to be considered are set out in regulation 7. The method of calculating the amount of compensation is contained in regulation 8.

5. Long-term and retirement compensation is payable to officers with at least 8 years' service in relevant employment before the material date. The qualifying and other conditions are set out in regulation 13.

6. The method of calculating the maximum amount of long-term compensation is laid down in regulations 15 (loss of employment) and 16 (diminution of emoluments). This amount is a proportion, not exceeding two thirds, of the net emoluments lost or of the amount by which the emoluments have been diminished, as the case may be. This compensation is payable from a date determined under regulation 17 and can be payable up to normal retiring age. In the case of a non-pensionable officer, compensation not exceeding one half of the rate of long-term compensation may be paid beyond normal retiring age (regulation 29).

7. Retirement compensation payable to a pensionable officer is based upon his accrued pension rights (regulations 20 and 23) supplemented in the case of persons aged 40 or over at the date of loss by the addition of notional years of service (regulation 19). Special provision is made for any persons whose pension arrangements are by way of policies of insurance (regulation 30). Retirement compensation is ordinarily payable from normal retiring age but in certain circumstances is payable earlier (regulations 21 and 22).

8. Compensation is payable to the widow, child or other dependant or to the personal representatives or trustees of a claimant who dies where such persons would have benefited under the relevant pension scheme (regulations 26 to 28).

9. Part VI of the regulations provides for long-term and retirement compensation to be reviewed and for awards to be varied in the light of changing circumstances (regulation 35). It also contains provisions for the adjustment, suspension and compounding of compensation in certain circumstances.

10. Part VII contains provisions relating to the procedure for making claims and notifying decisions, and confers upon a claimant who is aggrieved by a decision on a compensation question or a failure of a compensating authority to notify their decision a right to refer the question for determination by a tribunal established under Section 12 of the Industrial Training Act 1964.

1970 No. 752

FOOD AND DRUGS

COMPOSITION AND LABELLING

The Cream Regulations 1970

Made - - -	13*th May* 1970
Laid before Parliament	21*st May* 1970
Coming into Operation	1*st June* 1970

The Minister of Agriculture, Fisheries and Food and the Secretary of State for Social Services, acting jointly, in exercise of the powers conferred upon them by sections 4, 7, 123 and 136(2) of, and paragraph 2(2) of Schedule 12 to, the Food and Drugs Act 1955(**a**), as read with the Secretary of State for Social Services Order 1968(**b**), and of all other powers enabling them in that behalf, hereby make the following regulations after consultation with such organisations as appear to them to be representative of interests substantially affected by the regulations and reference to the Food Hygiene Advisory Council under section 82 of the said Act (insofar as the regulations are made in exercise of the powers conferred by the said section 7) :—

Citation and commencement

1. These regulations may be cited as the Cream Regulations 1970, and shall come into operation on 1st June 1970.

Interpretation

2.—(1) In these regulations, unless the context otherwise requires—

"the Act" means the Food and Drugs Act 1955;

"appropriate designation", in relation to food, means a name or description or a name and description sufficiently specific, in each case, to indicate to an intending purchaser the true nature of the food to which it is applied ;

"clotted cream" means cream which has been produced and separated by the scalding, cooling and skimming of milk or cream ;

"container" includes any form of packaging of food for sale as a single item, whether by way of wholly or partly enclosing the food or by way of attaching the food to some other article and in particular includes a wrapper or confining band ;

"cream" means that part of milk rich in fat which has been separated by skimming or otherwise and which is intended for sale for human consumption ;

(**a**) 4 & 5 Eliz. 2. c. 16. (**b**) S.I. 1968/1699 (1968 III, p. 4585).

"flavouring" includes flavouring essence and flavouring extract and means any product consisting of a flavouring agent and such other substances, if any, the use of which in food is not forbidden and which are reasonably necessary to produce a solid, a solution or an emulsion, but no other ingredient or ingredients;

"flour confectionery" means any solid or semi-solid product complete in itself and suitable for consumption without further preparation or processing other than heating, of which the characteristic ingredient, apart from any filling, is ground cereal, whether or not flavoured, coated with or containing any carbohydrate sweetening matter, chocolate or cocoa; and includes shortbread, sponges, pastry, pastry cases, crumpets, muffins, macaroons, ratafias, meringues and petits fours, but does not include pharmaceutical products, bread, biscuits or any product containing a filling which has as an ingredient any meat or fish;

"food" means food intended for sale for human consumption and includes drink, chewing gum and other products of a like nature and use, and articles and substances used as ingredients in the preparation of food or drink or of such products, but does not include—

(*a*) water, live animals or birds,

(*b*) fodder or feeding stuffs for animals, birds or fish, or

(*c*) articles or substances used only as drugs;

"food and drugs authority" has the meaning assigned to it by section 83 of the Act;

"pasteurised cream" means cream which has been subjected to heat treatment so as to pasteurise it or has been produced from pasteurised milk;

"pre-packed" means made up in advance in or on a container ready for sale by retail;

"sell" includes offer or expose for sale or have in possession for sale and "sale" and "sold" shall be construed accordingly;

"sell by retail" means sell to a person buying otherwise than for the purpose of re-sale, but does not include selling to a caterer for the purposes of his catering business or to a manufacturer for the purposes of his manufacturing business; and "sale by retail" and "sold by retail" shall be construed accordingly;

"sterilised cream" means cream which has been subjected to a process of sterilisation by heat treatment in the container in which it is to be supplied to the consumer;

"sugar" means any soluble carbohydrate sweetening matter;

"ultra heat treated cream" means cream which has been subjected in continuous flow to an appropriate heat treatment and has been packaged aseptically;

"untreated cream" means cream which has not been treated by heat or in any manner likely to affect its nature and qualities and has been derived from milk which has not been so treated;

AND other expressions have the same meaning as in the Act.

(2) The Interpretation Act 1889(**a**) shall apply to the interpretation of these regulations as it applies to the interpretation of an Act of Parliament and as if these regulations and the order hereby revoked were Acts of Parliament.

(**a**) 1889 c. 63.

(3) All percentages mentioned in these regulations are percentages calculated by weight of the cream including added ingredients, if any, permitted by regulation 5, save that as respects the calculation of the milk fat content, specified in regulation 4, of any cream which contains added sugar in accordance with the provisions of these regulations, the percentages specified in regulation 4 are percentages by weight of the cream excluding any such sugar.

(4) Any reference in these regulations to a label borne on a container shall be construed as including a reference to any legible marking on the container however effected.

(5) For the purposes of these regulations, the supply of food, otherwise than by sale, at, in or from any place where food is supplied in the course of a business shall be deemed to be a sale of that food, and a reference to purchasing and purchaser shall be construed accordingly.

(6) Any reference in these regulations to any order or other regulations shall be construed as a reference to such order or regulations as amended by any subsequent order or regulations.

(7) Any reference in these regulations to a numbered regulation shall, unless the reference is to a regulation of specified regulations, be construed as a reference to the regulation bearing that number in these regulations.

Exemptions

3. The following provisions of these regulations shall not apply in relation to any cream—

(*a*) sold, consigned or delivered for exportation to any place outside the United Kingdom ;

(*b*) supplied under Government contracts for consumption by Her Majesty's forces or supplied for consumption by a visiting force within the meaning of any of the provisions of Part I of the Visiting Forces Act 1952(**a**).

Description and composition of cream

4.—(1) Subject to the provisions of this regulation, any cream sold, consigned or delivered shall bear one of the following descriptions and shall comply with such of the following compositional requirements as are specified in relation to that description :—

(*a*) "clotted cream" if the cream is clotted cream and contains not less than 55 per cent. milk fat ;

(*b*) "double cream" if the cream contains not less than 48 per cent. milk fat:

Provided that, for the purposes of any sale, consignment or delivery on or before 29th February 1972, the word "thick" may be substituted for the word "double" ;

(*c*) "whipping cream" if the cream contains not less than 35 per cent. milk fat ;

(*d*) "whipped cream" if the cream contains not less than 35 per cent. milk fat and has been whipped ;

(*e*) "sterilised cream" if the cream is sterilised cream and contains not less than 23 per cent. milk fat:

(**a**) 1952 c. 67.

Provided that, for the purposes of any sale, consignment or delivery on or before 29th February 1972, the word "sterilised" may be omitted ;

(*f*) "cream" or "single cream" if the cream, not being sterilised cream contains not less than 18 per cent. milk fat ;

(*g*) "sterilised half cream" if the cream is sterilised cream and contains not less than 12 per cent. milk fat ;

(*h*) "half cream" if the cream, not being sterilised cream, contains not less than 12 per cent. milk fat:

Provided that the provisions of this paragraph shall not have effect as respects any sale, consignment or delivery before 1st March 1972 of—

(i) any clotted cream which bears the description "clotted cream" and which contains not less than 48 per cent. milk fat ;

(ii) any sterilised cream which contains less than 23 per cent. milk fat but not less than 18 per cent. milk fat.

(2) If any cream, other than cream bearing the description "clotted cream", which is sold, consigned or delivered is pasteurised cream, ultra heat treated cream or untreated cream, the description specified in relation to that cream in paragraph (1) of this regulation shall include the expression or letters "pasteurised", "ultra heat treated" or "U.H.T.", or "untreated" as appropriate :

Provided that the provisions of this paragraph shall not have effect as respects any sale, consignment or delivery before 1st March 1972 of any cream (other than cream in an aerosol container) which contains not less than 18 per cent. milk fat and which bears the description "cream", "single cream", "double cream" or "thick cream".

(3) In the case of cream derived from milk other than cows' milk, each of the descriptions specified in paragraph (1) of this regulation shall include the name of the kind of animal from which the milk has been obtained.

(4) If any cream which complies with any of the requirements as to composition specified in paragraph (1) of this regulation is used as an ingredient of another food, it shall be sufficient compliance with paragraphs (1) and (2) of this regulation if the description "cream" is applied to any such cream containing not less than 18 per cent. milk fat or if the description "half cream" is applied to any such cream containing not less than 12, and not more than 18 per cent. milk fat.

(5) No person shall sell, consign or deliver any cream in contravention of this regulation.

Permitted ingredients in cream

5.—(1) Subject to the provisions of this regulation, any cream sold, consigned or delivered shall contain no flavouring or other added ingredient whether or not that ingredient is a constituent of milk :

Provided that—

(*a*) clotted cream may contain nisin ;

(*b*) cream which may bear the description "whipped cream" in pursuance of regulation 4(1) and cream in an aerosol container may contain—

(i) sodium alginate, or a mixture of sodium bicarbonate, tetrasodium pyrophosphate and alginic acid,

(ii) sodium carboxymethyl cellulose,

(iii) carrageenan,

(iv) gelatine,

so however that the percentage of any or, as the case may be, all of the ingredients specified in this sub-paragraph (*b*) present in the cream shall not exceed 0·3 per cent.;

(*c*) cream which may bear the description "whipped cream" in pursuance of regulation 4(1) and cream in an aerosol container may contain—

(i) not more than 13 per cent. of sugar,

(ii) nitrous oxide ;

(*d*) cream in an aerosol container may contain not more than 0·5 per cent. of glyceryl monostearate ;

(*e*) sterilised cream or ultra heat treated cream may contain—

(i) calcium chloride,

(ii) sodium or potassium salts of—

(*aa*) carbonic acid,

(*ab*) citric acid,

(*ac*) orthophosphoric acid,

so however that the percentage of any or, as the case may be, all of the ingredients specified in this sub-paragraph (*e*) present in the cream shall not exceed 0·2 per cent..

(2) Notwithstanding the provisions of the last preceding paragraph, any cream sold, consigned or delivered to a manufacturer for the purposes of his manufacturing business or to a caterer for the purposes of his catering business may contain any or all of the following ingredients where appropriate to the circumstances or the description of cream specified in relation thereto, namely—

(*a*) cream intended for use in flour confectionery may contain not more than 13 per cent. of sugar ;

(*b*) cream which may bear the description "whipping cream" in pursuance of regulation 4(1) may contain not more than 13 per cent. of sugar ;

(*c*) cream which may bear the description "whipping cream" in pursuance of regulation 4(1) may contain—

(i) sodium alginate, or a mixture of sodium bicarbonate, tetrasodium pyrophosphate and alginic acid,

(ii) sodium carboxymethyl cellulose,

(iii) carrageenan,

(iv) gelatine,

so however that the percentage of any or, as the case may be, all of the ingredients specified in this sub-paragraph (*c*) present in the cream shall not exceed 0·3 per cent..

(3) Notwithstanding the preceding provisions of this regulation, no product derived from milk and substantially similar to and resembling cream shall be deemed not to be cream solely by reason of the presence of any flavouring or other added ingredient or of any ingredient in an amount in excess of the amount permitted by this regulation.

(4) No person shall sell, consign or deliver any cream in contravention of this regulation.

Amendment of the Emulsifiers and Stabilisers in Food Regulations 1962

6. The Emulsifiers and Stabilisers in Food Regulations 1962(**a**) shall be amended as follows :—

(*a*) by adding at the end of regulation 4(1) thereof the following words "save that cream may contain any such substance of a kind and to the extent permitted by regulation 5 of the Cream Regulations 1970." ;

(*b*) by deleting therefrom regulation 7 thereof.

Sales by description

7.—(1) No person shall sell any food under such a description as to lead an intending purchaser to believe that he is purchasing any kind of cream for which compositional requirements are specified in regulation 4 unless the food complies with the appropriate compositional requirements having effect in relation to that kind of cream.

(2) Where a person sells any food to a purchaser in response to a request for any kind of cream for which compositional requirements are specified in regulation 4, he shall be deemed to sell cream of that kind and under such a description as is specified in these regulations in relation to that kind of cream unless he clearly notifies the purchaser at the time of sale that the food is not that kind of cream.

Labelling and advertisement of cream

8. On and after 1st January 1973 no person shall—

(*a*) give with any food sold by him any label, whether attached to or borne on the container or not, or display with any food offered or exposed for sale by him any ticket, or

(*b*) publish, or be a party to the publication of, any advertisement for food, which bears or includes the word "cream" or any derivative thereof or any word substantially similar thereto otherwise than in accordance with provisions of the Act or any regulations made thereunder which, in either case, expressly provide for the use of that word unless—

(i) the food is cream which complies with the appropriate compositional requirements having effect in relation thereto by virtue of these regulations, or

(ii) that word is used in such a context as to indicate explicitly or by clear implication that the substance to which it relates is an ingredient of that food and unless the substance is cream which complies with such appropriate compositional requirements, or

(iii) that word is used in such a context as to indicate explicitly or by clear implication that such food is not, or does not contain, cream :

Provided that nothing in this regulation shall prohibit the use of the word "creamed" in relation to food which is not butter, milk, cream, condensed milk, evaporated milk, dried milk, cheese, skimmed milk or skimmed milk with non-milk fat.

9.—(1) No person shall sell, consign or deliver to a manufacturer for the purposes of his manufacturing business or to a caterer for the purposes of his catering business any cream which contains sugar, unless—

(**a**) S.I. 1962/720 (1962 I, p. 729).

(*a*) there appears clearly and legibly on the label borne on, or securely attached to, the container of such cream and in immediate proximity to, and so prominent in height and visual emphasis as to be conspicuous by comparison with, the description of the cream required by regulation 4 the following statement "contains X per cent. Y", and the statement is completed by inserting at "X" the amount of sugar in the cream expressed as a percentage of the mixture of cream and sugar and at "Y" the common or usual name or appropriate designation of the sugar, or

(*b*) the vendor furnishes to the purchaser not later than the time of delivery of such cream to the purchaser an invoice or other document bearing a statement as aforesaid.

(2) No person shall sell by retail any cream in an aerosol container or any cream which may bear the description "whipped cream" in pursuance of regulation 4(1), being cream which in each case contains sugar, unless there appears clearly and legibly on the label borne on, or securely attached to, the container of such cream and in immediate proximity to, and so prominent in height and visual emphasis as to be conspicuous by comparison with, the description of the cream required by regulation 4 the statement referred to in paragraph (1)(*a*) of this regulation.

10.—(1) Notwithstanding the provisions of article 5(1)(*a*) of, and Table C of Schedule 1 to, the Labelling of Food Order 1953(**a**), as amended (**b**), (whereby the ingredients of certain foods pre-packed for sale as such need not be specified in certain circumstances) and of regulation 6(1) of, and items 1 and 3 in Part I of Schedule 2 to, the Labelling of Food Regulations 1970(**c**) (whereby the use of certain generic, rather than specific, expressions is permitted in relation to certain food when forming an ingredient of some other food) no person shall sell by retail pre-packed any cream containing all or any of the substances specified in regulation 5, unless the appropriate designations of such substances appear on a label borne on the container of that cream in order of the proportion by weight in which they were used in the manufacturing process (the appropriate designation of the substance used in the greatest proportion by weight being listed first):

Provided that the provisions of this paragraph shall not have effect as respects any such sale by retail before 1st March 1972 of—

(*a*) any clotted cream which bears the description "clotted cream" and which contains not less than 48 per cent. milk fat;

(*b*) any sterilised cream which contains not less than 18 per cent. milk fat;

(*c*) any cream (other than cream in an aerosol container) which contains not less than 18 per cent. milk fat and which bears the description "cream", "single cream", "double cream" or "thick cream".

(2) Notwithstanding the provisions of regulation 9(2) of the Labelling of Food Regulations 1970 (whereby the use of certain generic, rather than specific, expressions is permitted in certain circumstances in relation to certain substances contained in food for sale by retail otherwise than pre-packed), no

(**a**) S.I. 1953/536 (1953 I, p. 665).
(**b**) The relevant amending instruments are S.I. 1953/1889, 1959/471, 1965/2199, 1967/861 (1953 I, p. 685; 1959 I, p. 1326; 1965 III, p. 6422; 1967 II, p. 2569).
(**c**) S.I. 1970/400 (1970 I, p. 1383).

person shall sell by retail otherwise than pre-packed any cream which has been dispensed from an aerosol container or any cream which may bear the description "whipped cream" in pursuance of regulation 4(1), being cream which in either case contains all or any of the substances specified in regulation 5, unless the appropriate designations of such substances in order of the proportion by weight in which they were used in the manufacturing process (the appropriate designation of the substance used in the greatest proportion by weight being listed first) appear on a ticket displayed on or in immediate proximity to, such cream so as to be clearly visible to an intending purchaser :

Provided that where any such cream is so sold for immediate consumption at or near the place of sale without having been previously exposed for sale, there shall be deemed to be sufficient compliance with the provisions of this paragraph if the purchaser is clearly notified, at or before the time of delivery of the cream to him, that the cream contains all or some of the substances specified in regulation 5.

Requirements as to marking on labels on containers and on tickets

11. Any description required or permitted by regulation 4 to be borne on any cream shall appear, when the said cream is—

(*a*) sold, consigned or delivered in a container, on a label borne on the container of the said cream ;

(*b*) sold by retail otherwise than in a container, on a ticket displayed on or in immediate proximity to the said cream so as to be clearly visible to an intending purchaser ;

and every letter or word of such description shall be in characters of uniform colour and size, save that the initial letter of any word may be taller than any other letter in that word.

Penalties and enforcement

12.—(1) If any person contravenes or fails to comply with any of the foregoing provisions of these regulations he shall be guilty of an offence and shall be liable to a fine not exceeding one hundred pounds or to imprisonment for a term not exceeding three months, or to both, and, in the case of a continuing offence, to a further fine not exceeding five pounds for each day during which the offence continues after conviction.

(2) Each food and drugs authority shall enforce and execute such provisions in their area.

(3) The requirement of section 109(3) of the Act (which requires notice to be given to the Minister of Agriculture, Fisheries and Food of intention to institute proceedings for an offence against any provisions of these regulations made under section 7 of the Act) shall not apply as respects any proceedings instituted by a Council for an offence against any such provisions of these regulations.

Defences

13.—(1) In any proceedings for an offence against these regulations in relation to the publication of an advertisement, it shall be a defence for the defendant to prove that, being a person whose business it is to publish or arrange for the publication of advertisements, he received the advertisement for publication in the ordinary course of business.

(2) In any proceedings against the manufacturer or importer of any cream for an offence against these regulations in relation to the publication of an advertisement, it shall rest on the defendant to prove that he did not publish, and was not a party to the publication of, the advertisement.

Application of various sections of the Act

14.—(1) Sections 108(3) and (4) (which relate to prosecutions), 110(1), (2) and (3) (which relate to evidence of analysis), 112 (which relates to the power of a court to require analysis by the Government Chemist), 113 (which relates to a contravention due to some person other than the person charged), 115(2) (which relates to the conditions under which a warranty may be pleaded as a defence) and 116 (which relates to offences in relation to warranties and certificates of analysis) of the Act shall apply for the purposes of these regulations as if references therein to proceedings or a prosecution, under or taken or brought under the Act included references to proceedings, or a prosecution as the case may be, taken or brought for an offence under these regulations and as if the reference in the said section 112 to subsection (4) of section 108 included a reference to that subsection as applied by these regulations.

(2) Paragraph (*b*) of the proviso to section 108(1) of the Act shall apply for the purposes of these regulations as if the reference therein to section 116 of the Act included a reference to that section as applied by these regulations.

Revocation

15. The Food Standards (Cream) Order 1951(**a**) is hereby revoked.

In witness whereof the Official Seal of the Minister of Agriculture, Fisheries and Food is hereunto affixed on 11th May 1970.

(L.S.)

Cledwyn Hughes,
Minister of Agriculture, Fisheries and Food.

R. H. S. Crossman,
Secretary of State for Social Services.

13th May 1970.

(a) S.I. 1951/668 (1951 III, p. 13).

EXPLANATORY NOTE

(This Note is not part of the Regulations.)

These regulations, which apply to England and Wales only, supersede the Food Standards (Cream) Order 1951 and come into operation on 1st June 1970.

The principal provisions of these regulations—

(*a*) specify requirements for the description and composition of cream (regulation 4);

(*b*) specify permitted added ingredients for cream, subject to specified limits (regulation 5), and make consequential amendments to the Emulsifiers and Stabilisers in Food Regulations 1962 (regulation 6);

(*c*) specify requirements for the labelling and advertisement of cream (regulations 8 to 11);

(*d*) provide that certain requirements relating to the description and composition of cream (regulation 4(1) and (2)) and relating to labelling (regulation 10(1)) shall have modified effect before 1st March 1972.

The regulations do not apply to any cream intended for export or supplied for consumption by Her Majesty's forces or a visiting force (regulation 3(1)).

1970 No. 753

EDUCATION, ENGLAND AND WALES

The Teachers' Superannuation (Amendment No. 2) Regulations 1970

Made - - -	15*th May* 1970
Laid before Parliament	27*th May* 1970
Coming into Operation	28*th May* 1970

The Secretary of State for Education and Science, with the consent of the Minister for the Civil Service and after consultation with representatives of local education authorities and of teachers appearing to him to be likely to be affected, in exercise of the powers conferred upon him by section 1 of the Teachers' Superannuation Act 1967(**a**) as amended by the Minister for the Civil Service Order 1968(**b**), hereby makes the following Regulations :—

1.—(1) These Regulations shall come into operation on 28th May 1970.

(2) These Regulations may be cited as the Teachers' Superannuation (Amendment No. 2) Regulations 1970 and shall be included among the regulations which may be cited together as the Teachers' Superannuation Regulations 1967 to 1970.

2. In these Regulations "the principal Regulations" means the Teachers' Superannuation Regulations 1967(**c**).

3. Regulation 7 of the principal Regulations (which relates to qualifying service) shall be amended by the addition at the end thereof of the following paragraph :—

"(*d*) any service which under any provisions relating to the superannuation of teachers in force in Scotland or Northern Ireland is treated in like manner as qualifying service.

4. Regulation 70 of the principal Regulations (which relates to organisers) shall be amended as follows :—

(*a*) in sub-paragraph (*a*)(ii) of paragraph (1) after the words "local education authority" (where those words secondly occur) there shall be inserted the words "or under the Physical Training and Recreation Act 1937"(**d**) ; and

(*b*) to the bodies specified in paragraph (2) there shall be added a Regional Advisory Council for Further Education and the British India Steam Navigation Company Limited.

5. Part I of Schedule 1 to the principal Regulations (which specifies the kinds of service as a teacher which are reckonable service) shall be amended as follows :—

(**a**) 1967 c. 12.
(**b**) S.I. 1968/1656 (1968 III, p. 4485).
(**c**) S.I. 1967/489 (1967 I, p. 1562).
(**d**) 1937 c. 46.

(*a*) in sub-paragraph (*b*) of paragraph 9 after the words "local education authority" there shall be inserted the words "or under the Physical Training and Recreation Act 1937"; and

(*b*) after paragraph 18 there shall be inserted the following paragraph:—

"18A. Teacher employed by the Royal National Institute for the Blind for the purposes of its National Mobility Centre if—

(*a*) he was previously employed for not less than three years in reckonable service or class A external service; and

(*b*) within three months of becoming so employed by the said Institute, with the agreement of the Secretary of State and the said Institute, he elects by notice in writing to the Secretary of State that his employment shall be reckonable service."

Given under the Official Seal of the Secretary of State for Education and Science on 11th May 1970.

(L.S.)

Alice Bacon,
Minister of State for Education and Science.

Consent of the Minister for the Civil Service given under his Official Seal on 15th May 1970.

(L.S.)

K. H. McNeill,
Authorised by the Minister for the Civil Service.

EXPLANATORY NOTE

(*This Note is not part of the Regulations.*)

These Regulations make minor changes with respect to categories of service counting as reckonable and qualifying service under the Teachers' Superannuation Regulations 1967 to 1970.

1970 No. 757 (C.15)

ROAD TRAFFIC

The Vehicle and Driving Licences Act 1969 (Commencement No. 6) Order 1970

Made - - -	14*th May* 1970
Laid before Parliament	27*th May* 1970
Coming into Operation	1*st June* 1970

The Minister of Transport hereby makes this Order in exercise of his powers under section 38(2) of the Vehicle and Driving Licences Act 1969(**a**) and of all other enabling powers.

1. This Order may be cited as the Vehicle and Driving Licences Act 1969 (Commencement No. 6) Order 1970.

2. Paragraph 1 of Schedule 1 to the Vehicle and Driving Licences Act 1969 shall come into operation on 1st June 1970.

Given under the Official Seal of the Minister of Transport the 14th May 1970.

(L.S.)

Fred Mulley,
Minister of Transport.

EXPLANATORY NOTE

(*This Note is not part of the Order.*)

This Order brings into operation paragraph 1 of Schedule 1 to the Vehicle and Driving Licences Act 1969 which amends section 115 of the Road Traffic Act 1960 to provide a new definition of licensing authority for the purposes of Part II of that Act.

(**a**) 1969 c. 27.

1970 No. 758

ROAD TRAFFIC

The Motor Vehicles (Driving Licences) (Amendment) Regulations 1970

Made - - -	14*th May* 1970
Laid before Parliament	27*thMay* 1970
Coming into Operation	1*st June* 1970

The Minister of Transport, in exercise of his powers under sections 98 and 101(2) of the Road Traffic Act 1960(**a**) as respectively amended by sections 16 and 14 of the Vehicle and Driving Licences Act 1969(**b**), and under section 113 of the said Act of 1960, and of all other enabling powers, and after consultation with representative organisations in accordance with section 260(2) of that Act, hereby makes the following Regulations:—

1.—These Regulations shall come into operation on 1st June 1970, and may be cited as the Motor Vehicles (Driving Licences) (Amendment) Regulations 1970.

2.—The Motor Vehicles (Driving Licences) Regulations 1970(**c**) shall have effect as though—

(*a*) in paragraph (1)(*d*) of Regulation 6 (conditions attached to provisional licences), for the word "cycle" there were substituted the word "bicycle"; and

(*b*) in paragraph (3) of Regulation 23 (persons who become resident in Great Britain), for sub-paragraph (*a*) there were substituted the following sub-paragraph—

"(*a*) subsections (1) and (2) of section 112 of the Act of 1960 (which relate to the duties of a court when they order a disqualification or an endorsement or allow an appeal against such an order) shall apply as if—

(i) in the case of subsection (1), for the words "shall send notice of the order to the licensing authority" onwards there were substituted the words "shall send notice of the order to the Minister, and, in a case where a person is so disqualified, shall also on the production of the permit retain it and forward it to the Minister who shall keep the permit until the disqualification has expired or been removed or the person entitled to the permit leaves Great Britain and in any case has made a demand in writing for its return to him.", and

(**a**) 1960 c. 16. (**b**) 1969 c. 27. (**c**) S.I. 1970/170 (1970 I, p. 727).

(ii) in the case of subsection (2), for the words "the licensing authority" onwards there were substituted the words "the Minister"."

Given under the Official Seal of the Minister of Transport the 14th May 1970.

(L.S.) *Fred Mulley,*
Minister of Transport.

EXPLANATORY NOTE

(This Note is not part of the Regulations.)

These Regulations amend the Motor Vehicles (Driving Licences) Regulations 1970 as follows:—

(*a*) the condition attached to a provisional licence which prohibits the licence holder when riding a motor cycle from carrying an unqualified driver is amended so as to apply only to the riding of a motor bicycle; and

(*b*) revised provision is made in relation to driving permits held by persons who become resident in Great Britain as regards the duties of a court when ordering a disqualification or an endorsement or when allowing an appeal against such an order.

STATUTORY INSTRUMENTS

1970 No. 759

AGRICULTURE

CEREALS MARKETING

The Home-Grown Cereals Authority (Rate of Supplementary Levy) Order 1970

Made - - -	18*th May* 1970
Laid before Parliament	21*st May* 1970
Coming into Operation	1*st June* 1970

Whereas the Home-Grown Cereals Authority (hereinafter referred to as "the Authority"), established by the Cereals Marketing Act 1965(a) (hereinafter referred to as "the Act"), have prepared and submitted to the Ministers hereinafter named, pursuant to paragraph 1 of Schedule 3 to the Act, a supplementary estimate for the period of twelve months beginning with 1st July 1969 (hereinafter referred to as "the relevant year") for the purposes of the Authority's functions under Part I of the Act:

And whereas pursuant to the said paragraph the Authority duly submitted to the Ministers with such supplementary estimate a proposal that the kind of home-grown cereals in respect of which a supplementary levy should be raised shall be wheat:

And whereas the Ministers have determined that the additional amount to be raised by levy for the relevant year for such purposes shall be £81,000 and have determined that the kind of home-grown cereals in respect of which a supplementary levy is to be raised for that year shall be wheat:

And whereas by virtue of section 14 of the Act the levy in respect of the relevant year is imposed as mentioned in section 15(1) of the Act, as it has effect by virtue of paragraph 3 of Schedule 3 to the Act:

Now, therefore, the Minister of Agriculture, Fisheries and Food, the Secretaries of State respectively concerned with agriculture in Scotland and Northern Ireland and the Secretary of State for Wales, acting jointly in exercise of the powers conferred upon them by section 13(5) of, and paragraph 2 of Schedule 3 to, the Act, as read with the Transfer of Functions (Wales) Order 1969(b), and of all other powers enabling them in that behalf, hereby make the following order:—

Citation and commencement

1. This order may be cited as the Home-Grown Cereals Authority (Rate of Supplementary Levy) Order 1970, and shall come into operation on 1st June 1970.

(a) 1965 c. 14.

(b) S.I. 1969/388 (1969 I, p. 1070).

Interpretation

2.—(1) In this order—

"cereals (guarantee payments) order" means an order under section 1 of the Agriculture Act 1957(**a**) which provides for payments to growers of home-grown cereals ;

"deficiency payment" means a payment made in pursuance of any cereals (guarantee payments) order ;

"home-grown cereals" means cereals grown in the United Kingdom and being either wheat, barley, oats or rye, and "home-grown wheat" shall be construed accordingly ;

"registered grower" means a person for the time being registered as a grower for the purposes of any cereals (guarantee payments) order.

(2) The Interpretation Act 1889(**b**) shall apply to the interpretation of this order as it applies to the interpretation of an Act of Parliament.

Rate of supplementary levy

3. The rate of supplementary levy for the relevant year, which appears to the Ministers to be sufficient (but not more than sufficient) to meet the amount to be raised in respect of home-grown wheat, shall be 0·3d. per cwt. and the rate of levy shall apply in respect of the quantity of home-grown wheat delivered as determined in accordance with the provisions of article 4 of this order.

Home-grown wheat subject to levy

4. The quantity of home-grown wheat on which the levy is to be imposed shall be that quantity (any quantity of less than 1 cwt. to be ignored)—

(*a*) which is delivered by registered growers during the relevant year to, or in accordance with the instructions of, purchasers thereof ; and

(*b*) in respect of which deficiency payments would, apart from section 15 of the Act, be paid to or in respect of the registered growers thereof.

In Witness whereof the Official Seal of the Minister of Agriculture, Fisheries and Food is hereunto affixed on 7th May 1970.

(L.S.)

Cledwyn Hughes,
Minister of Agriculture, Fisheries and Food.

Given under the Seal of the Secretary of State for Scotland on 8th May 1970.

(L.S.)

William Ross,
Secretary of State for Scotland.

(**a**) 1957 c. 57. (**b**) 1889 c. 63.

Given under the hand of the Secretary of State for the Home Department on 15th May 1970.

James Callaghan,
Secretary of State for the Home Department.

Given under my hand on 18th May 1970.

George Thomas,
Secretary of State for Wales.

EXPLANATORY NOTE

(This Note is not part of the Order.)

This order specifies the rate of supplementary levy to be raised in respect of home-grown wheat for the year beginning with 1st July 1969 to meet the additional amount determined by the Ministers to finance the Home-Grown Cereals Authority in the performance of their non-trading functions under Part I of the Cereals Marketing Act 1965. This amount is additional to those for which provision was made in the Home-Grown Cereals Authority (Rates of Levy) Order 1969 (S.I. 1969/752).

The order includes provisions as to the quantity of wheat in respect of which the levy is to be imposed.

The levy will be recovered as mentioned in section 15 of the Act, which provides for recovery by deduction from cereals deficiency payments.

1970 No. 760

AGRICULTURE

CEREALS MARKETING

The Home-Grown Cereals Authority (Rates of Levy) Order 1970

Made - - -	18*th May* 1970
Laid before Parliament	21*st May* 1970
Coming into Operation	1*st July* 1970

Whereas the Home-Grown Cereals Authority (hereinafter referred to as "the Authority"), established by the Cereals Marketing Act 1965(**a**) (hereinafter referred to as "the Act"), have prepared and submitted to the Ministers hereinafter named, pursuant to section 13(1)(*a*) of the Act, an estimate of the amount required to be raised by levy for the period of twelve months beginning with 1st July 1970 (hereinafter referred to as "the relevant year") for the purposes of the Authority's functions under Part I of the Act:

And whereas pursuant to section 13(2) of the Act the Authority duly submitted to the Ministers with such estimate proposals as to the kinds of home-grown cereals in respect of which a levy should be imposed and as to the apportionment of the amount specified in the estimate as between those kinds of home-grown cereals:

And whereas the Ministers have determined that the amount to be raised by levy for the relevant year for such purposes shall be £1,746,000 and have determined that the kinds of home-grown cereals in respect of which the levy is to be imposed for that year shall be wheat and barley:

And whereas the Ministers have apportioned the amount so determined as between those kinds of home-grown cereals:

And whereas by virtue of section 14 of the Act the levy in respect of the relevant year will be imposed as mentioned in section 15(1) of the Act:

Now, therefore, the Minister of Agriculture, Fisheries and Food, the Secretaries of State respectively concerned with agriculture in Scotland and Northern Ireland and the Secretary of State for Wales, acting jointly in exercise of the powers conferred upon them by section 13 of the Act, as read with the Transfer of Functions (Wales) Order 1969(**b**), and of all other powers enabling them in that behalf, hereby make the following order:—

Citation and commencement

1. This order may be cited as the Home-Grown Cereals Authority (Rates of Levy) Order 1970, and shall come into operation on 1st July 1970.

(**a**) 1965 c. 14. (**b**) S.I. 1969/388 (1969 I, p. 1070).

Interpretation

2.—(1) In this order—

"cereals (guarantee payments) order" means an order under section 1 of the Agriculture Act 1957(**a**) which provides for payments to growers of home-grown cereals ;

"cereals (protection of guarantees) order" means an order made under section 5 of the Agriculture Act 1957 for the purpose of supporting any arrangements in force by virtue of a cereals (guarantee payments) order ;

"deficiency payment" means a payment made in pursuance of any cereals (guarantee payments) order ;

"home-grown cereals" means cereals grown in the United Kingdom and being either wheat, barley, oats or rye, and "home-grown wheat" and "home-grown barley" shall be construed accordingly ;

"registered buyer" means a person for the time being registered as a buyer of barley for the purposes of any cereals (protection of guarantees) order ;

"registered grower" means a person for the time being registered as a grower for the purposes of any cereals (guarantee payments) order.

(2) The Interpretation Act 1889(**b**) shall apply to the interpretation of this order as it applies to the interpretation of an Act of Parliament.

Rates of levy

3. The rate of levy for the relevant year, which appears to the Ministers to be sufficient (but not more than sufficient) to meet the amount apportioned to—

(*a*) home-grown wheat, shall be 2·2d. per cwt ;

(*b*) home-grown barley shall be 1·8d. per cwt. and 1s. 0d. per acre ;

and the rate of levy shall apply respectively in respect of the quantity of home-grown wheat delivered and the quantity of home-grown barley delivered and the acreage of land used for the growing of such barley as determined in accordance with the following provisions of this order.

Home-grown wheat subject to levy

4. The quantity of home-grown wheat on which the relevant levy is to be imposed shall be that quantity (any quantity of less than 1 cwt. to be ignored)—

(*a*) which is delivered by or on behalf of registered growers during the relevant year to, or in accordance with the instructions of, purchasers thereof ; and

(*b*) in respect of which deficiency payments would, apart from section 15 of the Act, be paid to or in respect of the registered growers thereof.

Home-grown barley subject to levy

5.—(1) The quantity of home-grown barley on which the relevant part of the levy in respect of that barley is to be imposed shall be that quantity (any quantity of less than 1 cwt. to be ignored)—

(*a*) which is delivered by or on behalf of registered growers during the relevant year to, or in accordance with the instructions of, registered buyers thereof ; and

(**a**) 1957 c. 57. (**b**) 1889 c. 63.

(*b*) in respect of which deductions or additions would be made in accordance with a cereals (guarantee payments) order from or to deficiency payments which would, apart from section 15 of the Act, be paid to or in respect of the registered growers thereof.

(2) The acreage of land on which the relevant part of the levy in respect of home-grown barley is to be imposed shall be the acreage of land (any area of less than one-quarter of an acre to be ignored) used for the growing of home-grown barley for harvesting during the relevant year being land in relation to which deficiency payments would, apart from section 15 of the Act, be paid to or in respect of the registered growers of such barley.

In Witness whereof the Official Seal of the Minister of Agriculture, Fisheries and Food is hereunto affixed on 7th May 1970.

(L.S.) *Cledwyn Hughes,*
Minister of Agriculture, Fisheries and Food.

Given under the Seal of the Secretary of State for Scotland on 8th May 1970.

(L.S.) *William Ross,*
Secretary of State for Scotland.

Given under the hand of the Secretary of State for the Home Department on 15th May 1970.

James Callaghan,
Secretary of State for the Home Department.

Given under my hand on 18th May 1970.

George Thomas,
Secretary of State for Wales.

EXPLANATORY NOTE

(*This Note is not part of the Order.*)

This order specifies, in respect of home-grown wheat and home-grown barley, the rates of levy to be raised in respect of the year beginning with 1st July 1970 to meet the amounts apportioned by the Ministers to these kinds of home-grown cereals to finance the Home-Grown Cereals Authority in the performance of their non-trading functions under Part I of the Cereals Marketing Act 1965. These functions include the implementation of bonus payment schemes for growers of wheat and barley.

The order also includes provisions as to the quantity of wheat or barley, and acreage of land used for growing barley, in respect of which the levy is to be imposed.

The levy will be recovered as mentioned in section 15 of the Act, which provides for recovery by deduction from cereals deficiency payments.

STATUTORY INSTRUMENTS

1970 No. 761 (L.16)

LEGAL AID AND ADVICE, ENGLAND

The Legal Aid (Extension of Proceedings) Regulations 1970

Made - - -	24*th April* 1970
Laid before Parliament	4*th May* 1970
Coming into Operation	1*st June* 1970

The Lord Chancellor, in exercise of the powers conferred on him by sections 1 and 12 of the Legal Aid and Advice Act 1949(**a**), hereby makes the following Regulations:—

1.—(1) These Regulations may be cited as the Legal Aid (Extension of Proceedings) Regulations 1970 and shall come into operation on 1st June 1970.

(2) The Interpretation Act 1889(**b**) shall apply to these Regulations as it applies to the interpretation of an Act of Parliament.

2. The proceedings in which legal aid may be given shall include proceedings in the Lands Tribunal.

Dated 24th April 1970.

Gardiner, C.

EXPLANATORY NOTE

(*This Note is not part of the Regulations.*)

These Regulations make legal aid available for proceedings in the Lands Tribunal.

(**a**) 1949 c. 51. (**b**) 1889 c. 63.

1970 No. 762 (L.17)

MAGISTRATES' COURTS

PROCEDURE

The Maintenance Orders (Facilities for Enforcement) (Amendment) Rules 1970

Made - - -	15*th May* 1970
Laid before Parliament	22*nd May* 1970
Coming into Operation	1*st July* 1970

The Lord Chancellor, in exercise of the power conferred on him by Section 15 of the Justices of the Peace Act 1949(**a**), as extended by section 122 of the Magistrates' Courts Act 1952(**b**), after consultation with the Rule Committee appointed under the said section 15, hereby makes the following Rules :—

1. These Rules may be cited as the Maintenance Orders (Facilities for Enforcement) (Amendment) Rules 1970 and shall come into operation on 1st July 1970.

2. In Rule 6 of the Maintenance Orders (Facilities for Enforcement) Rules 1922(**c**) there shall be inserted, after the words "originally issued" where first occurring, the words "or to such other person or authority as that court or the Secretary of State may from time to time direct".

Dated 15th May 1970.

Gardiner, C.

EXPLANATORY NOTE

(*This Note is not part of the Rules.*)

Rule 6 of the Maintenance Orders (Facilities for Enforcement) Rules 1922 provides that the person collecting money due under a maintenance order registered or confirmed in England under the Maintenance Orders (Facilities for Enforcement) Act 1920 shall send that money to the court from which the order originally issued. These Rules amend Rule 6 to enable the money collected to be sent to such other person or authority as the court which made the order or the Secretary of State may from time to time direct.

(**a**) 1949 c. 101. (**b**) 1952 c. 55.
(**c**) S.R. & O. 1922/1355 (Rev. XIII, p. 128: 1922, p. 526).

STATUTORY INSTRUMENTS

1970 No. 764

AGRICULTURE

The Price Stability of Imported Products (Rates of Levy) (Eggs) (No. 4) Order 1970

Made - - - - 18*th May* 1970

Coming into Operation 19*th May* 1970

The Minister of Agriculture, Fisheries and Food, in exercise of the powers conferred upon him by section 1(2), (4), (5), (6) and (7) of the Agriculture and Horticulture Act 1964(a) and of all other powers enabling him in that behalf, hereby makes the following order:—

1. This order may be cited as the Price Stability of Imported Products (Rates of Levy) (Eggs) (No. 4) Order 1970, and shall come into operation on 19th May 1970.

2.—(1) In this order—

" the Principal Order " means the Price Stability of Imported Products (Levy Arrangements) (Eggs) Order 1970(b) as amended by any subsequent order, and if any such order is replaced by any subsequent order the expression shall be construed as a reference to such subsequent order;

AND other expressions have the same meaning as in the Principal Order.

(2) The Interpretation Act 1889(c) shall apply to the interpretation of this order as it applies to the interpretation of an Act of Parliament and as if this order and the order hereby revoked were Acts of Parliament.

3. In accordance with and subject to the provisions of the Principal Order (which provides for the charging of levies on imports of those eggs and egg products which are specified commodities for the purposes of the Agriculture and Horticulture Act 1964) the rate of general levy for such imports into the United Kingdom of any specified commodity as are described in column 2 of the Schedule to this order in relation to a tariff heading indicated in column 1 of that Schedule shall be the rate set forth in relation thereto in column 3 of that Schedule.

4. The Price Stability of Imported Products (Rates of Levy) (Eggs) (No. 3) Order 1970(d) is hereby revoked.

In Witness whereof the Official Seal of the Minister of Agriculture, Fisheries and Food is hereunto affixed on 18th May 1970.

(L.S.)

J. A. Barrah,
Assistant Secretary.

(a) 1964 c. 28. (b) S.I. 1970/359 (1970 I, p. 1277). (c) 1889 c. 63.
(d) S.I. 1970/631 (1970 I, p. 2035).

SCHEDULE

1. Tariff Heading	2. Description of Imports	3. Rate of General Levy
	Imports of:—	
04.05	*Birds' eggs in shell:—*	(per 120 eggs) s. d.
	1. Not exceeding 11 lb. in weight per 120 ..	2 0
	2. Over 11 lb. but not exceeding 12½ lb. in weight per 120	3 6
	3. Over 12½ lb. but not exceeding 14 lb. in weight per 120	3 6
	4. Over 14 lb. but not exceeding 15½ lb. in weight per 120	4 0
	5. Over 15½ lb. but not exceeding 17 lb. in weight per 120	4 6
	6. Over 17 lb. in weight per 120	4 6

EXPLANATORY NOTE

(*This Note is not part of the Order.*)

This order, which comes into operation on 19th May 1970, supersedes the Price Stability of Imported Products (Rates of Levy) (Eggs) (No. 3) Order 1970. It—

(*a*) increases the rates of general levy on imports of eggs in shell for those eggs in the weight grades which are numbered 2 to 5 in the Schedule to the order ;

(*b*) reimposes unchanged the rates of general levy for the other two weights of eggs which were in force immediately before the commencement of this order.

STATUTORY INSTRUMENTS

1970 No. 765

AGRICULTURE

The Price Stability of Imported Products (Rates of Levy No. 7) Order 1970

Made - - - - 18*th May* 1970

Coming into Operation - 19*th May* 1970

The Minister of Agriculture, Fisheries and Food, in exercise of the powers conferred upon him by section 1(2), (4), (5), (6) and (7) of the Agriculture and Horticulture Act 1964(**a**) and of all other powers enabling him in that behalf, hereby makes the following order:—

1. This order may be cited as the Price Stability of Imported Products (Rates of Levy No. 7) Order 1970, and shall come into operation on 19th May 1970.

2.—(1) In this order—

" the Principal Order " means the Price Stability of Imported Products (Levy Arrangements) Order 1966(**b**) as amended(**c**) and as amended by any subsequent order, and if any such order is replaced by any subsequent order the expression shall be construed as a reference to such subsequent order;

AND other expressions have the same meaning as in the Principal Order.

(2) The Interpretation Act 1889(**d**) shall apply to the interpretation of this order as it applies to the interpretation of an Act of Parliament.

3. In accordance with and subject to the provisions of Part II of the Principal Order (which provides for the charging of levies on imports of certain specified commodities), and notwithstanding the provisions of Article 3(*b*) of the Price Stability of Imported Products (Rates of Levy No. 6) Order 1970(**e**), the rate of country levy for such imports into the United Kingdom of any specified commodity as are described in column 2 of the Schedule to this order in relation to a tariff heading indicated in column 1 of that Schedule shall on and after 19th May 1970 be the rate set forth in relation thereto in column 3 of that Schedule.

In Witness whereof the Official Seal of the Minister of Agriculture, Fisheries and Food is hereunto affixed on 18th May 1970.

(L.S.)

R. J. E. Taylor,
Assistant Secretary.

(**a**) 1964 c. 28. (**b**) S.I. 1966/936 (1966 II, p. 2271).
(**c**) S.I. 1969/758, 1564 (1969 II, p. 2137; III, p. 5018). (**d**) 1889 c. 63.
(**e**) S.I. 1970/641 (1970 I, p. 2066).

SCHEDULE

1. Tariff Heading	2. Description of Imports	3. Rate of Country Levy
		per ton £ s. d.
	Imports of:—	
10.03	Barley which has been grown in and consigned to the United Kingdom from—	
	Canada	1 5 0
	the French Republic	15 0
	the Kingdom of the Netherlands	15 0

EXPLANATORY NOTE

(*This Note is not part of the Order.*)

This Order, which comes into operation on 19th May 1970, reduces on and after that date the rates of country levy on imports of barley grown in and consigned to the United Kingdom from Canada to 25*s*. per ton and from France or the Netherlands to 15*s*. per ton.

STATUTORY INSTRUMENTS

1970 No. 766

SUGAR

The Sugar (Rates of Surcharge and Surcharge Repayments) (No. 7) Order 1970

Made - - - -	18*th May* 1970
Laid before Parliament	20*th May* 1970
Coming into Operation	21*st May* 1970

The Minister of Agriculture, Fisheries and Food, in exercise of the powers conferred on him by sections 7(4), 8(6) and 33(4) of the Sugar Act 1956(**a**) having effect subject to the provisions of section 3 of, and Part II of Schedule 5 to, the Finance Act 1962(**b**), and section 58 of the Finance Act 1968(**c**) and of all other powers enabling him in that behalf, with the concurrence of the Treasury, on the advice of the Sugar Board, hereby makes the following order:—

1.—(1) This order may be cited as the Sugar (Rates of Surcharge and Surcharge Repayments) (No. 7) Order 1970; and shall come into operation on 21st May 1970.

(2) The Interpretation Act 1889(**d**) shall apply for the interpretation of this order as it applies for the interpretation of an Act of Parliament.

2. Notwithstanding the provisions of Article 2 of the Sugar (Rates of Surcharge and Surcharge Repayments) (No. 6) Order 1970(**e**), the rates of surcharge payable under and in accordance with the provisions of section 7 of the Sugar Act 1956, having effect as aforesaid, in respect of sugar and invert sugar imported or home produced or used in the manufacture of imported composite sugar products shall on and after 21st May 1970 be those rates specified in Schedule 1 to this order.

3. For the purpose of section 8(3)(*b*) of the Sugar Act 1956, having effect as aforesaid, the rates of surcharge repayments in respect of invert sugar produced in the United Kingdom from materials on which on or after 21st May 1970 sugar duty has been paid or, by virtue of paragraph 1 of Part II of Schedule 5 to the Finance Act 1962, is treated as having been paid shall, notwithstanding the provisions of Article 3 of the Sugar (Rates of Surcharge and Surcharge Repayments) (No. 6) Order 1970 be those specified in Schedule 2 to this order.

(**a**) 1956 c. 48. (**b**) 1962 c. 44.
(**c**) 1968 c. 44. (**d**) 1889 c. 63.
(**e**) S.I. 1970/647 (1970 II, p. 2089).

In Witness whereof the Official Seal of the Minister of Agriculture, Fisheries and Food is hereunto affixed on 18th May 1970.

(L.S.)

R. G. R. Wall,
Authorised by the Minister.

We concur.

18th May 1970.

Walter Harrison,
E. G. Perry,
Two of the Lords Commissioners of Her Majesty's Treasury.

SCHEDULE 1

PART I

SURCHARGE RATES FOR SUGAR

Polarisation	Rate of Surcharge per cwt. s.	d.
Exceeding—		
99°	11	8·0
98° but not exceeding 99°	11	0·0
97° " " " 98°	10	8·8
96° " " " 97°	10	5·4
95° " " " 96°	10	2·0
94° " " " 95°	9	10·7
93° " " " 94°	9	7·3
92° " " " 93°	9	4·0
91° " " " 92°	9	0·6
90° " " " 91°	8	9·2
89° " " " 90°	8	5·9
88° " " " 89°	8	2·5
87° " " " 88°	7	11·7
86° " " " 87°	7	8·9
85° " " " 86°	7	6·4
84° " " " 85°	7	3·9
83° " " " 84°	7	1·4
82° " " " 83°	6	10·8
81° " " " 82°	6	8·6
80° " " " 81°	6	6·4
79° " " " 80°	6	4·1
78° " " " 79°	6	1·9
77° " " " 78°	5	11·6
76° " " " 77°	5	9·4
Not exceeding 76°	5	7·5

PART II

SURCHARGE RATES FOR INVERT SUGAR

Sweetening matter content by weight	Rate of Surcharge per cwt.
	s. d.
70 per cent. or more	7 5
Less than 70 per cent. and more than 50 per cent.	5 4
Not more than 50 per cent.	2 7

SCHEDULE 2

SURCHARGE REPAYMENT RATES FOR INVERT SUGAR

Sweetening matter content by weight	Rate of Surcharge Repayment per cwt.
	s. d.
More than 80 per cent.	8 9
More than 70 per cent. but not more than 80 per cent.	7 5
More than 60 per cent. but not more than 70 per cent.	5 4
More than 50 per cent. but not more than 60 per cent.	4 3
Not more than 50 per cent. and the invert sugar not being less in weight than 14 lb. per gallon	2 7

EXPLANATORY NOTE

(*This Note is not part of the Order.*)

This order prescribes—

(*a*) increases equivalent to 2s. 4d. per cwt. of refined sugar in the rates of surcharge payable on sugar and invert sugar which become chargeable with surcharge on or after 21st May 1970;

(*b*) correspondingly increased rates of surcharge repayment in respect of invert sugar produced in the United Kingdom from materials on which surcharge has been paid.

1970 No. 767

SUGAR

The Composite Sugar Products (Surcharge and Surcharge Repayments—Average Rates) (No. 8) Order 1970

Made - - - -	18*th* *May* 1970
Laid before Parliament	20*th* *May* 1970
Coming into Operation	21*st* *May* 1970

Whereas the Minister of Agriculture, Fisheries and Food (hereinafter called " the Minister ") has on the recommendation of the Commissioners of Customs and Excise (hereinafter called " the Commissioners ") made an order(**a**) pursuant to the powers conferred upon him by sections 9(1) and 9(4) of the Sugar Act 1956(**b**), having effect subject to the provisions of section 3 of, and Part II of Schedule 5 to, the Finance Act 1962(**c**), to the provisions of section 52(2) of the Finance Act 1966(**d**), and to the provisions of section 58 of the Finance Act 1968(**e**), providing that in the case of certain descriptions of composite sugar products surcharge shall be calculated on the basis of an average quantity of sugar or invert sugar taken to have been used in the manufacture of the products, and that certain other descriptions of composite sugar products shall be treated as not containing any sugar or invert sugar, and that in the case of certain descriptions of goods in the manufacture of which sugar or invert sugar is used, surcharge repayments shall be calculated on the basis of an average quantity of sugar or invert sugar taken to have been so used:

Now, therefore, the Minister, on the recommendation of the Commissioners and in exercise of the powers conferred upon him by sections 9(1), 9(4) and 33(4) of the Sugar Act 1956, having effect as aforesaid, and of all other powers enabling him in that behalf, hereby makes the following order:—

1.—(1) This order may be cited as the Composite Sugar Products (Surcharge and Surcharge Repayments—Average Rates) (No. 8) Order 1970, and shall come into operation on 21st May 1970.

(2) The Interpretation Act 1889(**f**) shall apply for the interpretation of this order as it applies for the interpretation of an Act of Parliament.

2. Surcharge payable on or after 21st May 1970 under and in accordance with the Sugar Act 1956, having effect as aforesaid, in respect of sugar and invert sugar used in the manufacture of the descriptions of imported composite sugar products specified in column 2 of Schedule 1 to this order shall, notwithstanding the provisions of the Sugar (Rates of Surcharge and Surcharge Repayments) (No. 7) Order 1970(**g**) and the Composite Sugar Products (Surcharge and Surcharge Repayments—Average Rates) (No. 7) Order 1970(**a**), be calculated by reference to the weight of the products at the rates specified in relation thereto in column 3 of the said Schedule.

(**a**) S.I. 1970/648 (1970 II, p. 2092). (**b**) 1956 c. 48. (**c**) 1962 c. 44.
(**d**) 1966 c. 18. (**e**) 1968 c. 44. (**f**) 1889 c. 63.
(**g**) S.I. 1970/766 (1970 II, p. 2411).

3. Imported composite sugar products other than those of a description specified in Schedules 1 and 2 to this order shall be treated as not containing any sugar or invert sugar for the purposes of surcharge payable on or after 21st May 1970.

4. Surcharge repayments payable on and after 21st May 1970 under and in accordance with the provisions of section 8 of the Sugar Act 1956, having effect as aforesaid, in respect of sugar and invert sugar used in the manufacture of the descriptions of goods specified in column 1 of Schedule 3 to this order shall, notwithstanding the provisions of the Sugar (Rates of Surcharge and Surcharge Repayments) (No. 7) Order 1970(**a**) and the Composite Sugar Products (Surcharge and Surcharge Repayments—Average Rates) (No. 7) Order 1970(**b**), be calculated by reference to the quantity of the goods at the rates specified in relation thereto in column 2 of the said Schedule.

In Witness whereof the Official Seal of the Minister of Agriculture, Fisheries and Food is hereunto affixed on 18th May 1970.

(L.S.) *R. G. R. Wall*,
Authorised by the Minister.

SCHEDULE 1

In this Schedule:—

" Tariff heading " means a heading or, where the context so requires, a subheading of the Customs Tariff 1959 (see paragraph (1) of Article 2 of the Import Duties (General) (No. 3) Order 1969(**c**)).

Tariff heading	Description of Imported Composite Sugar Products	Rate of Surcharge
		Per cwt. s. d.
04.02	Milk and cream, preserved, concentrated or sweetened, containing more than 10 per cent. by weight of added sugar	5 2
17.02 (B) (2) and 17.05 (B)	Syrups containing sucrose sugar, whether or not flavoured or coloured, but not including fruit juices containing added sugar in any proportion:—	
	containing 70 per cent. or more by weight of sweetening matter	7 5
	containing less than 70 per cent., and more than 50 per cent., by weight of sweetening matter..	5 4
	containing not more than 50 per cent. by weight of sweetening matter	2 7

(**a**) S.I. 1970/766 (1970 II, p. 2411). (**b**) S.I. 1970/648 (1970 II, p. 2092).
(**c**) S.I. 1969/1413 (1969 III, p. 4150).

Tariff heading	Description of Imported Composite Sugar Products	Rate of Surcharge
		Per cwt.
		s. d.
17.02 (F) ..	Caramel:—	
	Solid	11 8
	Liquid	8 2
17.04	Sugar confectionery, not containing cocoa ..	9 6
18.06	Chocolate and other food preparations containing cocoa and added sugar:—	
	Chocolate couverture not prepared for retail sale; chocolate milk crumb, liquid	5 2
	Chocolate milk crumb, solid	6 5
	Solid chocolate bars or blocks, milk or plain, with or without fruit or nuts; other chocolate confectionery consisting wholly of chocolate or of chocolate and other ingredients not containing added sugar, but not including such goods when packed together in retail packages with goods liable to surcharge at a higher rate	5 3
	Other	6 9
19.08	Pastry, biscuits, cakes and other fine bakers' wares containing added sugar:—	
	Biscuits, wafers and rusks containing more than 12½ per cent. by weight of added sugar, and other biscuits, wafers and rusks included in retail packages with such goods.. ..	2 11
	Cakes with covering or filling containing added sugar; meringues	3 11
	Other	1 5
20.01	Vegetables and fruit, prepared or preserved by vinegar or acetic acid, containing added sugar:—	
	Containing 10 per cent. or more by weight of added sugar	4 1
	Other	10
20.03	Fruit preserved by freezing, containing added sugar	1 5
20.04	Fruit, fruit-peel and parts of plants, preserved by sugar (drained, glacé or crystallised)	7 8
20.05	Jams, fruit jellies, marmalades, fruit purée and fruit pastes, being cooked preparations, containing added sugar	7 4
20.06	Fruit otherwise prepared or preserved, containing added sugar:—	
	Ginger	5 10
	Other	1 5

SCHEDULE 2

Tariff heading	Description of Imported Composite Sugar Products
17.05 (A) and (B)	Sugar and invert sugar, flavoured or coloured.

SCHEDULE 3

Description of goods	Rate of surcharge repayment per bulk barrel of 36 gallons
Lager	5·8d.
All beer other than lager	5·2d.

EXPLANATORY NOTE

(*This Note is not part of the Order.*)

This order provides for increases on and after 21st May 1970 in the average rates of surcharge payable on imported composite sugar products of the descriptions specified in Schedule 1 and in the average rates of surcharge repayment in respect of exported goods of the descriptions specified in Schedule 3. These correspond to the increases in surcharge rates effected by the Sugar (Rates of Surcharge and Surcharge Repayments) (No. 7) Order 1970 (S.I.1970/766). Provision is also made for certain imported composite sugar products to be treated as not containing any sugar or invert sugar.

1970 No. 768

CIVIL AVIATION

The Air Corporations (General Staff, Pilots and Officers Pensions) (Amendment) Regulations 1970

Made - - -	18*th May* 1970
Coming into Operation	1*st June* 1970

The Board of Trade, in exercise of their powers under section 24 of the Air Corporations Act 1967(**a**) and of all other powers enabling them in that behalf, after consulting with each of the Corporations and with such organisations representative of the employees to whom the Regulations will relate as appear to the Board to be appropriate, hereby make the following Regulations :—

1.—(1) These Regulations shall come into operation on 1st June 1970 and may be cited as the Air Corporations (General Staff, Pilots and Officers Pensions) (Amendment) Regulations 1970.

(2) These Regulations—

(*a*) shall be construed as one with the Air Corporations (General Staff Pensions) Regulations 1948(**b**) ;

(*b*) may be cited together with the Air Corporations (Pensions) Regulations 1948 to 1969(**c**) as the Air Corporations (Pensions) Regulations 1948 to 1970.

(3) The Interpretation Act 1889(**d**) shall apply for the purpose of the interpretation of these Regulations as it applies for the purpose of the interpretation of an Act of Parliament.

2.—(1) The Joint Pension Scheme established and maintained by virtue of the Air Corporations (Pensions) Regulations 1948 to 1969 shall be in accordance with the provisions of the Trust Deed and Amending Deeds, copies of which are set out in the Schedules to those Regulations as further amended by a Deed dated 10th March 1970 a copy of which is set out in the Schedule to these Regulations.

(2) The said Deed dated 10th March 1970 is accordingly confirmed and shall come into operation on 1st June 1970.

3. BEA Airtours Limited (being a subsidiary of the British European Airways Corporation) whose employees are admitted to the Scheme by virtue of the said Deed dated 10th March 1970, and each of their employees who is a member of the Scheme shall, for the purpose of providing funds from which benefits under the said Scheme may be paid, pay contributions in accordance with the provisions of the said Trust Deeds.

(**a**) 1967 c. 33.
(**b**) S.I. 1948/2361 (Rev. I, p. 1275; 1948 I, p. 437).
(**c**) See S.I. 1948/2361 (Rev. I, p. 1275; 1948 I, p. 437) and amending instruments down to S.I. 1969/834 (1969 II, p. 2338).
(**d**) 1889 c. 63.

4. Contributions and benefits shall be paid in respect of the service of such an employee with BEA Airtours Limited before the coming into force of these Regulations in accordance with the provisions of the said Trust Deeds.

Geoffrey Parker,
An Under Secretary of the
Board of Trade.

18th May 1970.

SCHEDULE

THIS DEED is made the tenth day of March One thousand nine hundred and seventy BETWEEN BRITISH OVERSEAS AIRWAYS CORPORATION whose principal office is situate at Speedbird House, Heathrow Airport (London) Hounslow in the County of Middlesex and BRITISH EUROPEAN AIRWAYS CORPORATION whose principal office is situate at Bealine House Ruislip in the County of Middlesex BOAC RESTAURANTS LIMITED and BEA HELICOPTERS LIMITED (hereinafter called "the Employers") of the first part BEA AIRTOURS LIMITED (hereinafter called "Airtours") of the second part Rankin Lorimer Weir Derek Harding Glover Angus John Dore Betts Robert Gilchrist Cunningham Ralph Arthur Fuller Charles Victor Green Cyril Alfred Herring Oliver James Hinch Reginald Banwell Johnson Charles George Klimcke Thomas Nisbet and John Charles William Springbett the Management Trustees for the time being of The Airways Corporations Joint Pension Scheme (hereinafter called "the Management Trustees") of the third part and AIRWAYS CORPORATIONS JOINT PENSION FUND TRUSTEES LIMITED (hereinafter called "the Custodian Trustees" which expression shall include the Custodian Trustees for the time being) of the fourth part AND IS supplemental to the various Deeds set out in the Air Corporations Pensions Regulations 1948 to 1969.

WHEREAS

(1) Airtours is a subsidiary of British European Airways Corporation for the purposes of Section 24 of the Air Corporations Act 1967.

(2) The parties hereto are desirous of extending the Airways Corporations Joint Pension Scheme so as to enable employees of Airtours to be admitted to membership of the Scheme.

(3) At a meeting of the Management Trustees held on the tenth day of September One thousand nine hundred and sixty nine the said Rankin Lorimer Weir and the said Robert Gilchrist Cunningham were appointed to execute this Deed in accordance with the provisions of Clause 18 of the Trust Deed.

NOW IT IS HEREBY AGREED AND DECLARED BY AND BETWEEN THE PARTIES HERETO AS FOLLOWS:—

1. Airtours shall be deemed to be a party to the various Deeds set out in the Air Corporations Pensions Regulations 1948 to 1969.

2. Airtours shall enjoy all the rights and shall assume all the obligations of an Employer arising under the Trust Deed and Rules of the Scheme.

3. The Trust Deed shall be amended as follows:—

(*a*) In Clause 1 of the Trust Deed for the definition of "Employer" there shall be substituted the following definition:—

"Employer" means whichever of the following persons or bodies is the Employer of a Member for the time being:—

(*a*) British Overseas Airways Corporation

(*b*) British European Airways Corporation

(*c*) BOAC Restaurants Limited

(*d*) BEA Helicopters Limited

(*e*) BEA Airtours Limited

(*b*) In Clauses 19A and 19A(*a*) the words "BRL or Helicopters" shall be deleted and replaced by the words "BRL, Helicopters or Airtours".

4. Save as expressly altered amended or varied hereby the Trust Deed and the Schedules thereto as heretofore amended shall continue and remain in force and shall have effect as if the alterations amendments or variations herein set out were where applicable inserted therein.

5. This Deed is conditional on its being confirmed by Regulations made by the Board of Trade under Section 24 of the Air Corporations Act 1967 and if so confirmed shall come into force on such date as may be specified in that behalf in such Regulations.

IN WITNESS WHEREOF the parties of the first and second and fourth parts have caused their respective Common Seals to be hereunto affixed and the Management Trustees have hereunto set their hands and seals the day and year first before written.

THE COMMON SEAL OF BRITISH OVERSEAS AIRWAYS CORPORATION was hereunto affixed in the presence of:

(L.S.)

D. H. GLOVER
Member

R. M. FORREST
Secretary

THE COMMON SEAL OF BRITISH EUROPEAN AIRWAYS CORPORATION was hereunto affixed in the presence of:

(L.S.)

M. J. LESTER
Secretary

THE COMMON SEAL OF BOAC RESTAURANTS LIMITED was hereunto affixed in the presence of:

(L.S.)

D. H. GLOVER
Director

D. G. DODSON
Secretary

THE COMMON SEAL OF BEA HELICOPTERS LIMITED was hereunto affixed in the presence of:

(L.S.)

J. A. CAMERON
Director

R. D. KEEFE
Secretary

THE COMMON SEAL OF BEA AIRTOURS LIMITED was hereunto affixed in the presence of:

(L.S.)

W. BAILLIE
Director

R. L. NORTHRIDGE
Secretary

SIGNED SEALED AND DELIVERED by the said RANKIN LORIMER WEIR in the presence of:

R. L. WEIR

CHRISTINE LOOSEN (Secretary)
21, Windsor Road,
Bray, Berks.

SIGNED SEALED AND DELIVERED by the said ROBERT GILCHRIST CUNNINGHAM in the presence of:

R. G. CUNNINGHAM

M. C. SLATER (Secretary)
1, Burlington Road,
Isleworth, Middlesex.

THE COMMON SEAL OF AIRWAYS CORPORATIONS JOINT PENSION FUND TRUSTEES LIMITED was hereunto affixed in the presence of:

(L.S.)

R. L. WEIR
Director

H. BROMAGE
Secretary

EXPLANATORY NOTE

(*This Note is not part of the Regulations.*)

These Regulations amend the Airways Corporations Joint Pension Scheme so as to make provision whereby employees of BEA Airtours Limited, a subsidiary of BEA, can be admitted to the Scheme. Provision is also made for the subsidiary to have the rights and obligations of an employer under the Trust Deed and Rules of the Scheme and for payment of contributions by the subsidiary and its employees.

1970 No. 771

CUSTOMS AND EXCISE

The Import Duty Drawbacks (No. 4) Order 1970

Made - - - -	19*th May* 1970
Laid before the House of Commons	28*th May* 1970
Coming into Operation	4*th June* 1970

The Lords Commissioners of Her Majesty's Treasury, by virtue of the powers conferred on them by sections 9 and 13 of, and Schedule 5 to, the Import Duties Act 1958(**a**) and section 2(5) of the Finance Act 1965(**b**), and of all other powers enabling them in that behalf, on the recommendation of the Board of Trade hereby make the following Order:—

1.—(1) This Order may be cited as the Import Duty Drawbacks (No. 4) Order 1970.

(2) The Interpretation Act 1889(**c**) shall apply for the interpretation of this Order as it applies for the interpretation of an Act of Parliament.

(3) In this Order " the No. 10 Order of 1968 " means the Import Duty Drawbacks (No. 10) Order 1968(**d**).

(4) This Order shall come into operation on 4th June 1970.

2. In Schedule 1 to the No. 10 Order of 1968 (which relates to the drawbacks to be allowed on the exportation of imported articles or goods incorporating them), in each of the following entries, in column 2, for the words " on or after 1st July 1970 " there shall be substituted the words " on or after 1st January 1971"—

(*a*) the entry relating to headings 69.11, 69.12 and 69.13 of the Customs Tariff 1959 (tableware and other articles of a kind commonly used for domestic or toilet purposes, of porcelain, china or other pottery; certain ornaments and furniture of ceramic);

(*b*) the entry relating to heading 70.13 (glassware of a kind commonly used for table, kitchen, toilet or office purposes, for indoor decoration or similar uses); and

(*c*) the entry relating to heading 70.14 (illuminating glassware, signalling glassware and optical elements of glass).

3.—(1) In Schedule 2 to the No. 10 Order of 1968 (which relates to the drawbacks to be allowed on the exportation of goods produced or manufactured from imported articles), in the entry relating to linseed oil and goods

(**a**) 1958 c. 6. (**b**) 1965 c. 25. (**c**) 1889 c. 63.
(**d**) S.I. 1968/1881 (1968 III, p. 4969)

made therewith (as amended by the Import Duty Drawbacks (No. 2) Order 1970(e)) the following paragraphs shall be omitted—

paragraph 3 (certain mixtures consisting of cobalt linoleate, linseed oil and linseed oil fatty acids),

paragraph 5 (printed linoleum and floorcloth),

paragraph 8 (linoleum not printed, manufactured on a base of resin coated paper felt), and

paragraph 11 (oil baize and leathercloth);

and paragraphs 4, 6, 7, 9, 10, 12, 13 and 14 shall respectively become paragraphs 3, 4, 5, 6, 7, 8, 9 and 10.

(2) In Schedule 3 to the No. 10 Order of 1968 (goods excluded from operation of the Import Duties Act 1958, Schedule 5, paragraph 3(2)(*a*)), for " Linseed oil (paragraphs 3 to 12 only) " there shall be substituted " Linseed oil (paragraphs 3 to 8 only) ".

Ernest Armstrong,
Walter Harrison,
Two of the Lords Commissioners of Her Majesty's Treasury

19th May 1970

EXPLANATORY NOTE

(*This Note is not part of the Order.*)

This Order—

(1) extends the period for which drawback of import duty is allowed on the exportation of certain imported ceramic products and glassware; and

(2) revokes the provisions for drawback of import duty on certain goods manufactured from imported linseed oil.

(e) S.I. 1970/270 (1970 I, p. 1021).

1970 No. 772

CUSTOMS AND EXCISE

The Import Duties (General) (No. 3) Order 1970

Made - - - -	19*th May* 1970
Laid before the House of Commons	28*th May* 1970
Coming into Operation	4*th June* 1970

The Lords Commissioners of Her Majesty's Treasury, by virtue of the powers conferred on them by sections 1, 2 and 13 of the Import Duties Act 1958(**a**) and of all other powers enabling them in that behalf, on the recommendation of the Board of Trade hereby make the following Order:—

1.—(1) This Order may be cited as the Import Duties (General) (No. 3) Order 1970.

(2) The Interpretation Act 1889(**b**) shall apply for the interpretation of this Order as it applies for the interpretation of an Act of Parliament.

(3) This Order shall come into operation on 4th June 1970.

2. Esparto wax shall cease to be included among the goods chargeable with import duty under heading 15.16 of the Customs Tariff 1959 (vegetable waxes, whether or not coloured); and accordingly Schedule 1 to the Import Duties (General) (No. 3) Order 1969(**c**) (which by reference to the Tariff sets out the import duties chargeable under the Import Duties Act 1958) shall be amended by substituting for sub-headings (A) and (B) of heading 15.16 the following—

" (A) Carnauba wax; candelilla wax; esparto wax; ouricury wax	—	—
(B) Other	6%	—"

Neil McBride,
Ernest Armstrong,
Two of the Lords Commissioners of Her Majesty's Treasury

19*th May*, 1970.

EXPLANATORY NOTE

(*This Note is not part of the Order.*)

This Order removes the import duty on esparto wax.

(**a**) 1958 c. 6. (**b**) 1889 c. 63. (**c**) S.I. 1969/1413 (1969 III, p. 4150).

STATUTORY INSTRUMENTS

1970 No. 773

AGRICULTURE

AGRICULTURAL GRANTS, GOODS AND SERVICES

The Ploughing Grants Scheme 1970

Laid before Parliament in draft

Made - - - *18th May* 1970

The Minister of Agriculture, Fisheries and Food and the Secretary of State, acting jointly, in pursuance of sections 1, 2, 3 and 5 of the Agriculture (Ploughing Grants) Act 1952(**a**), as read with the Transfer of Functions (Wales) Order 1969(**b**), and all their other enabling powers, with the approval of the Treasury, hereby make the following scheme, a draft of which has been laid before Parliament and has been approved by resolution of each House of Parliament :—

1. This scheme, which may be cited as the Ploughing Grants Scheme 1970, shall apply to England and Wales and Northern Ireland.

2.—(1) In this scheme, unless the context otherwise requires, the following expressions have the meanings hereby respectively assigned to them :—

"the Act" means the Agriculture (Ploughing Grants) Act 1952 ;

"grass" includes clover, lucerne or sainfoin or mixtures of clover, lucerne or sainfoin with grass ;

"land under grass" includes any grazing land ;

"the appropriate Minister", in relation to land in England or Northern Ireland, means the Minister and, in relation to land in Wales, means the Minister and the Secretary of State, acting jointly ;

"the Minister" means the Minister of Agriculture, Fisheries and Food ;

"occupier" in Northern Ireland includes the person who, by virtue of an agreement, whether written or otherwise, has the right to the use of the land at the time of the completion of the operations referred to in this scheme.

(2) For the purposes of this scheme grass shall be regarded as a crop.

(3) The Interpretation Act 1889(**c**) applies to the interpretation of this scheme as it applies to the interpretation of an Act of Parliament.

(**a**) 1952 c. 35. (**b**) S.I. 1969/388 (1969 I, p. 1070). (**c**) 1889 c. 63.

3.—(1) Subject to the provisions of this scheme a grant may be made by the Minister in respect of the following operations—

(*a*) the ploughing up of land under grass ;

(*b*) after ploughing, the carrying out of such further operations on the land as may be required by the appropriate Minister and as are necessary, or form part of the operations necessary, to bring the land into a state of cleanliness, fertility, and fitness for cropping ; and

(*c*) the sowing on that land of a crop, unless the appropriate Minister otherwise determines.

(2) A grant shall not be made under this scheme in respect of any land unless before the commencement of any operations in respect of which such a grant may be made the appropriate Minister has approved those operations in relation to that land and is satisfied that the carrying out thereof on that land, together with any necessary preliminary operations, is likely to involve expenditure which is substantially heavier than normal for operations such as are specified in sub-paragraph (1) of this paragraph.

(3) Where operations in relation to any land have been approved for the purposes of the Ploughing Grants Scheme 1968(**a**) or the Ploughing Grants Scheme 1969(**b**), not being operations deemed to have been so approved by virtue of paragraph 3(3) of the said Ploughing Grants Scheme 1968, and any part of the said land has not been ploughed up from grass before 1st June 1970, such operations shall be deemed to have been approved for the purposes of this scheme also.

(4) The person to whom such a grant may be made shall be the occupier of the land on completion of the operations in respect of which the grant is payable.

(5) A grant shall not be made under this scheme in respect of any land which has been the subject of a grant under Part II of any previous scheme made under the Act.

4. The rate of grant to be made in accordance with this scheme shall be £12 per acre :

Provided that in calculating the amount of a grant fractions of an acre less than one quarter of an acre shall be disregarded.

5. A grant under this scheme may only be made where the land ploughed up—

(*a*) is not less than one acre in area ;

(*b*) was ploughed up from grass within the period beginning with 1st June 1970 and ending with 31st May 1971 ; and

(*c*) at the time when such ploughing up was begun was under grass that had been sown not later than 1st June 1958, or had been continuously under grass since before that date.

6. The appropriate Minister may require an applicant for a grant under this scheme to give to any person authorised by the Minister in that behalf, or, in

(**a**) S.I. 1968/852 (1968 II, p. 2280). (**b**) S.I. 1969/769 (1969 II, p. 2180).

relation to land in Wales, by the Minister and the Secretary of State or either of them, adequate facilities for the inspection of any land to which the application relates.

7. Where in the opinion of the appropriate Minister—

(*a*) the ploughing or any other operation in respect of which a grant under this scheme may be made has been inefficiently carried out, or

(*b*) any preliminary operations the expenditure or likely expenditure on which has been taken into account by the appropriate Minister for the purpose of satisfying himself that a grant may be made under this scheme have not been carried out or have been inefficiently carried out, or

(*c*) adequate facilities for the inspection of the land in respect of which any such grant as aforesaid may be made have not been given ;

payment of the grant may be withheld or the amount of the grant may be reduced to such amount as the appropriate Minister considers reasonable.

8. If in respect of any of the operations in respect of which a grant is payable under this scheme payments of moneys provided by Parliament under any enactment other than the Act are available, the Minister in determining the amount of grant payable under this scheme may take into consideration such payments, and may withhold or reduce the amount payable under this scheme accordingly.

9. A grant shall not be made under this scheme in respect of any land which has been the subject of a grassland renovation grant made by virtue of a scheme under section 11 of the Agriculture (Miscellaneous Provisions) Act 1963(**a**).

In Witness whereof the Official Seal of the Minister of Agriculture, Fisheries and Food is hereunto affixed on 13th May 1970.

(L.S.)

Cledwyn Hughes,
Minister of Agriculture,
Fisheries and Food.

Given under my hand on 14th May 1970.

George Thomas,
Secretary of State for Wales.

Approved on 18th May 1970.

Walter Harrison,
E. G. Perry,
Two of the Lords Commissioners
of Her Majesty's Treasury.

(**a**) 1963 c. 11.

EXPLANATORY NOTE

(This Note is not part of the Scheme.)

This scheme, which is made under the Agriculture (Ploughing Grants) Act 1952, provides for the making of grants by the Minister of Agriculture, Fisheries and Food at the rate of £12 per acre in respect of land ploughed up from grass, where after ploughing the operations described in the scheme are carried out. The land must have been under grass since 1st June 1958 and the ploughing must be carried out within the period from 1st June 1970 to 31st May 1971.

Prior approval must be obtained from the appropriate Minister, and this will only be given where he is satisfied that the carrying out of the operations (together with any necessary preliminary operations) is likely to involve expenditure which is substantially heavier than normal for operations of the kind.

Where operations have been expressly approved for the purposes of the 1968 scheme or the 1969 scheme, but any of the ploughing is carried out during the period to which this scheme applies, the approval is to be treated as though it were given for the purposes of this scheme also.

In other respects, except for the advancement of the dates by one year, the scheme is materially the same as the 1969 scheme.

STATUTORY INSTRUMENTS

1970 No. 774 (S.57)

CENSUS

The Census (Scotland) Regulations 1970

Made - - -	19*th May* 1970
Laid before Parliament	28*th May* 1970
Coming into Operation	15*th June* 1970

In exercise of the powers conferred on me by section 3(1) of the Census Act 1920(**a**), and of all other powers enabling me in that behalf, I hereby make the following regulations:—

Citation and commencement

1. These regulations may be cited as the Census (Scotland) Regulations 1970, and shall come into operation on 15th June 1970.

Interpretation

2.—(1) In these regulations, unless the context otherwise requires—

"the Act" means the Census Act 1920;

"assistant census officer" means an officer appointed under regulation 4(1)(*b*);

"the census" means the census directed to be taken by the Census Order 1970(**b**) (hereinafter referred to as "the Census Order");

"census day" means 25th April 1971;

"census district" means a district so referred to in regulation 3;

"census night" means the night of 25th to 26th April 1971;

"census officer" means an officer appointed under regulation 4(1)(*a*);

"enumeration district" means a district so referred to in regulation 3;

"enumerator" means an officer appointed under regulation 4(1)(*c*);

"prescribed person" means a person required by the Census Order to make a return;

"Registrar General" means the Registrar General of Births, Deaths and Marriages for Scotland.

(2) Any reference in these regulations to a numbered regulation or schedule shall, unless the context otherwise requires, be construed as a reference to the regulation or schedule bearing that number in these regulations.

(3) The Interpretation Act 1889(**c**) shall apply for the interpretation of these regulations as it applies for the interpretation of an Act of Parliament.

(**a**) 1920 c. 41.
(**b**) S.I. 1970/481 (1970 I, p. 1599).
(**c**) 1889 c. 63.

Census districts and enumeration districts

3. For the purpose of the census the Registrar General shall divide Scotland into census districts, and shall divide each census district into enumeration districts.

Appointment of officers

4.—(1) For the purpose of the census the Registrar General may—

(*a*) appoint a census officer for each census district;

(*b*) appoint, or authorise a census officer to appoint, such number of assistant census officers for each census district as the Registrar General may determine;

(*c*) appoint, or authorise a census officer or assistant census officer to appoint, an enumerator for each enumeration district.

(2) The officers appointed under this regulation shall perform the duties assigned to them under the Act and these regulations.

Instructions by the Registrar General

5. The Registrar General may give to officers appointed under regulation 4, or may authorise a census officer or assistant census officer to give, such instructions as the Registrar General may consider necessary for the performance of the duties assigned to them under the Act and these regulations, and any such instructions shall be complied with by any officer to whom they are given.

Undertakings

6. Every census officer, assistant census officer and enumerator, and every person assisting any such officer in the performance of his duties shall, before performing any duties, grant an undertaking in the form set out in Schedule 1 faithfully to perform his duties under the Act and these regulations.

Forms of return

7. The form of return to be made by a prescribed person mentioned in column (1) of Schedule 2 shall be the form set out in Schedule 3 which bears the identification particulars appropriate to his case shown in column (2) of Schedule 2, and a prescribed person shall comply with the instructions contained in such form.

Provision of forms and other documents for enumerators

8. Every census officer shall enter in the enumeration books provided by the Registrar General such particulars as the Registrar General may require, and shall, before census day, provide every enumerator appointed to act for an enumeration district within his census district with an enumeration book, a sufficient number of forms of return and such other forms or documents as may be necessary for the purpose of the census.

Delivery of forms of return

9.—(1) The enumerator shall, within such period as may be specified by the Registrar General, deliver—

(*a*) to the head, or person for the time being acting as the head, of every private household occupying a dwelling or part of a dwelling mentioned in Group I in Schedule 1 to the Census Order, form H in Schedule 3 ;

(*b*) to the manager, chief resident officer or other person for the time being in charge of any premises mentioned in Groups II or III in Schedule 1 to the Census Order and to the person appointed for the purposes of article 5(3) of the Census Order in any premises mentioned in Group IV in that Schedule, the number of forms L and P in Schedule 3 as the enumerator shall estimate to be required.

(2) The enumerator shall, on delivering each form, enter thereon such particulars as the Registrar General may require and shall, if so requested by any prescribed person or by any person acting on his behalf, give such explanations as are reasonably necessary to enable the prescribed person to make a proper return.

(3) An enumerator shall be deemed to have fulfilled the obligation placed upon him to deliver a form of return under this regulation if he hands it to the person mentioned in paragraph (1) of this regulation or to some responsible person acting on behalf of that person or if he leaves the form at the dwelling or premises where persons are to be enumerated.

(4) The Registrar General shall make such arrangements as he thinks fit for the delivery—

(*a*) of forms S, F and P in Schedule 3, as may be appropriate to the case in accordance with Schedule 2, to the captain, master or other person in charge of a vessel mentioned in Group V in Schedule 1 to the Census Order and to the person appointed for the purposes of article 5(3) of the Census Order in any vessel mentioned in Group IV in that Schedule;

(*b*) of a form P in Schedule 3 to every person mentioned in Group VI in Schedule 1 to the Census Order.

(5) The person to whom forms are delivered under paragraph (1)(*b*) or paragraph (4)(*a*) of this regulation shall deliver a form P to every prescribed person on the premises or vessel who is capable of completing the form, after having caused to be entered on each such form the address of the premises or the name of the vessel, as the case may be, as required by article 5(3) of the Census Order :

Provided that a manager or other person in charge of premises mentioned in Group II in Schedule 1 to the Census Order, who has arranged for the form of return with respect to a person incapable of completing it himself to be completed by a relative or other person accompanying him, shall deliver for that purpose a form P to the said relative or other person.

Personal returns

10.—(1) Any member of a private household or other person mentioned in Group I in Schedule 1 to the Census Order being a person aged 16 years or over on census day, who is capable of completing a form of return and is not himself the head or the person for the time being acting as the head of that household, may make a personal return if he complies with the procedure prescribed in the following paragraphs of this regulation.

(2) Subject to the foregoing paragraph a person claiming to make a personal return (hereinafter called "the applicant"), or a person acting on his behalf, shall apply to the enumerator for a separate form of return ; or if the applicant

cannot for any reason obtain a form of return from the enumerator he, or a person acting on his behalf, may apply to the census officer for such a form.

(3) The enumerator or census officer, as the case may be, shall issue to the applicant, or the person acting on his behalf, form P in Schedule 3 and shall, if so requested, give such explanations as are reasonably necessary to enable the applicant to make a proper return.

(4) The prescribed person who would otherwise have to make a return in respect of the applicant on form H shall enter on that form no particulars relating to the applicant other than his name and the relationship in which he stands to the prescribed person.

Collection of returns

11.—(1) Where under regulation 9(5) forms P have been delivered to persons mentioned in article 5(2) of the Census Order, the person responsible for delivering the forms shall collect the completed forms on the day after census day or as soon thereafter as is reasonably practicable.

(2) The enumerator shall on the day after census day, or as soon thereafter as is reasonably practicable, collect all forms of return delivered by him and all separate forms of return issued in accordance with regulation 10 to persons within his enumeration district, and shall examine each return and satisfy himself that the entries thereon are properly and sufficiently made, and shall make all such inquiries as are reasonably necessary for that purpose.

(3) The Registrar General shall make such arrangements as he thinks fit for the collection of completed forms of return made by persons in vessels mentioned in Groups IV and V in Schedule 1 to the Census Order and by persons in places mentioned in Group VI in that Schedule.

Particulars to be obtained by enumerators

12.—(1) For the purpose of obtaining the particulars required to be stated in item 17 in Schedule 2 to the Census Order the enumerator shall, when delivering or collecting form H make such enquiries as are reasonably necessary to enable him to complete the panel headed "To be completed by enumerator" on the form.

(2) When delivering forms of return under regulation 9(1)(*b*) the enumerator shall make such enquiries as are reasonably necessary to ascertain the nature of the premises, and in the case of premises in Group II in Schedule 1 to the Census Order the number of rooms in the premises, and shall enter the information on form L.

Further duties of enumerators

13.—(1) The enumerator shall within such period as may be specified by the Registrar General—

(*a*) enter in the enumeration book and in any forms of return collected by him such particulars as the Registrar General may require ; and

(*b*) deliver to the census officer the enumeration book and all returns collected by him.

(2) If required to do so by the census officer or assistant census officer, the enumerator shall make such enquiries as may be reasonably necessary to secure the completion of any incomplete return.

Further duties of census officers

14.—(1) The census officer or, if so directed by him, the assistant census officer shall examine the enumeration books delivered to him under the foregoing regulation, and where it appears to him that any book is incomplete he shall require the enumerator to take such steps as may be reasonably necessary to complete the book and to send it duly completed to the census officer within a time to be specified by the census officer.

(2) When so directed by the Registrar General, the census officer shall send all completed enumeration books relating to enumeration districts within his census district, together with the returns delivered to him by enumerators or assistant census officers, to the Registrar General.

Replacement of census officer, assistant census officer or enumerator

15.—(1) Where in the opinion of the Registrar General any census officer is unable to perform his duties in connection with the census, the Registrar General may appoint some fit and proper person in his place to perform such duties.

(2) Where in the opinion of the census officer any assistant census officer or enumerator is unable to perform his duties in connection with the census, the census officer may appoint some fit and proper person in his place to perform such duties.

Giving of information

16.—(1) Every prescribed person shall give to the enumerator such information as he may reasonably require for the performance of his duties under these regulations, and every other person in respect of whom it is the duty of a prescribed person to make a return shall give to that prescribed person such information as he may reasonably require for that purpose.

(2) Otherwise than in accordance with these regulations no person shall use, publish or communicate to any other person any information given under the Census Order and these regulations.

Safe custody of forms and documents

17. A person having custody, whether on his own behalf or on behalf of any other person, of any forms of return, enumeration books or other documents containing confidential information relating to the census shall keep such forms, books and other documents in such manner as to prevent any unauthorised person having access thereto.

Revocation

18. The Census (Scotland) Regulations 1965(**a**) are hereby revoked.

St. Andrew's House,
Edinburgh.
19th May 1970.

William Ross,
One of Her Majesty's Principal
Secretaries of State.

(**a**) S.I. 1965/1262 (1965 II, p. 3560).

Regulation 6

SCHEDULE 1

FORM OF UNDERTAKING TO BE MADE BY CERTAIN PERSONS

I, ... being a person appointed in accordance with the Census (Scotland) Regulations 1970 to act as *census officer/*assistant census officer/*enumerator/*a person assisting .... for the purposes of the census, hereby undertake and promise faithfully to perform the duties imposed by the Census Act 1920, and the Census (Scotland) Regulations 1970, so far as applicable to me, and to fulfil all the obligations required of me by the Act and Regulations, and I hereby state that I have read and understand the provisions hereunto annexed of section 8 of the Act as amended by Schedule 3 to the Criminal Justice Act 1967(**a**), and regulation 17 of the Regulations.

Signed ....

In the presence of ....

*Strike out words which do not apply.

Section 8 *of the Census Act* 1920 *as amended, is as follows*:—

"**8**.—(1) If any person—

(*a*) refuses or neglects to comply with or acts in contravention of any of the provisions of this Act or any Order in Council or regulations made under this Act ; or

(*b*) being a person required under this Act to make a statutory declaration with respect to the performance of his duties, makes a false declaration ; or

(*c*) being a person required by any Order in Council or regulations made under this Act to make, sign, or deliver any document, makes, signs, or delivers, or causes to be made, signed, or delivered a false document ; or

(*d*) being a person required in pursuance of any such Order in Council or regulations to answer any question, refuses to answer or gives a false answer to that question ;

he shall for each offence be liable on summary conviction to a fine not exceeding fifty pounds.

(2) If any person—

(*a*) being a person employed in taking a census, without lawful authority publishes or communicates to any person otherwise than in the ordinary course of such employment any information acquired by him in the course of his employment ; or

(*b*) having possession of any information which to his knowledge has been disclosed in contravention of this Act, publishes or communicates that information to any other person ;

he shall be guilty of a misdemeanour, and shall on conviction be liable to imprisonment with or without hard labour, for a term not exceeding two years or to a fine, or to both such imprisonment and fine."

Regulation 17 *of the Census* (*Scotland*) *Regulations* 1970 *is as follows*:—

"**17**. A person having custody, whether on his own behalf or on behalf of any other person, of any forms of return, enumeration books or other documents containing confidential information relating to the census shall keep such forms, books and other documents in such manner as to prevent any unauthorised person having access thereto."

(**a**) 1967 c. 80.

Regulation 7

SCHEDULE 2

(1) Prescribed Persons	(2) Identification Particulars of Form
(*a*) The head or person for the time being acting as the head of every private household.	The form entitled "H Form For Private Households".
(*b*) The manager, chief resident officer or other person in charge of any premises mentioned in Groups II or III in Schedule 1 to the Census Order and the person appointed for the purposes of article 5(3) of the Census Order in any premises mentioned in Group IV in that Schedule.	The form entitled "L Form for Hotels, Boarding Houses, Hospitals, Schools and Institutions etc."
(*c*) The person appointed for the purposes of article 5(3) of the Census Order in any vessel mentioned in Group IV in Schedule 1 to the Census Order.	The form entitled "F Form for H.M. Ships".
(*d*) The captain, master or other person in charge of any vessel mentioned in Group V in Schedule 1 to the Census Order.	The form entitled "S Form for Vessels (other than H.M. Ships)".
(*e*) Any person mentioned in column 2 in Groups II, III, IV, V or VI in Schedule 1 to the Census Order.	The form entitled "P Form For Making A Personal Return".
(*f*) Any person making a personal return under Regulation 10.	The form entitled "P Form For Making A Personal Return".

Regulation 7

SCHEDULE 3

Forms of Return for 1971 Census

Form H
(private households)

B14
Has the person obtained **any** of the following qualifications since reaching the age of 18?

a H.N.C. or H.N.D.
b Nursing qualifications
c Teaching qualifications
d Degrees, diplomas or other educational qualifications
e Graduate or corporate membership of professional institutions
f Any other professional or vocational qualifications

If so, give full details of **all** such qualifications in the order in which they were obtained, even if not relevant to the present job or if the person is not working.

Please check these details by asking each person about his qualifications.
If **none,** write 'NONE'.
This question need not be answered for persons under 18 or retired persons over 70.

To be answered for persons who can speak, read or write Scottish Gaelic.

G

a If the person can **speak** Scottish Gaelic, tick the appropriate box.

b If the person can **read** or **write** Scottish Gaelic, tick the appropriate box(es).

Qualification	Major Subject or Subjects	Awarding Institution	G
			a ☐ speaks Gaelic and English ☐ speaks Gaelic but not English *b* ☐ reads Gaelic ☐ writes Gaelic
			a ☐ speaks Gaelic and English ☐ speaks Gaelic but not English *b* ☐ reads Gaelic ☐ writes Gaelic
			a ☐ speaks Gaelic and English ☐ speaks Gaelic but not English *b* ☐ reads Gaelic ☐ writes Gaelic
			a ☐ speaks Gaelic and English ☐ speaks Gaelic but not English *b* ☐ reads Gaelic ☐ writes Gaelic
			a ☐ speaks Gaelic and English ☐ speaks Gaelic but not English *b* ☐ reads Gaelic ☐ writes Gaelic
			a ☐ speaks Gaelic and English ☐ speaks Gaelic but not English *b* ☐ reads Gaelic ☐ writes Gaelic

PLEASE TURN OVER TO THE NEXT PAGE →

The remaining questions in Part B do not apply to children under 15 years of age.

Answer questions B15—B17 in respect of the main employment last week, or of the most recent job if retired or out of work.

For persons who have never had a job and for a housewife who did not have a job last week write 'NONE' at B15.

For

	B15	B16	B17	B18
	What was the **name and business** of the person's employer (if self-employed, the name and nature of the person's business)? (see note B15) *Give the trading name if one was used.*	*a* What was the person's **occupation**? Give full details. (see note B16) *b* Describe the **actual work** done in that occupation.	Was the person an employee, or self-employed employing others (see note B17), or self-employed without employees?	If the person is an **apprenti** **or trainee,** write 'Apprentice', 'Articled clerk', 'Articled pupil', 'Student apprentice', 'Graduate apprentice', 'Management trainee', 'Trainee technician', or 'Trainee craftsman' as appropriate. (see note B
1st person	*a* Name of business *b* Nature of business	*a* Occupation *b* Description of work	1 ☐ An employee 2 ☐ Self-employed employing others (see note B17) 3 ☐ Self-employed without employees	
2nd person	*a* Name of business *b* Nature of business	*a* Occupation *b* Description of work	1 ☐ An employee 2 ☐ Self-employed employing others (see note B17) 3 ☐ Self-employed without employees	
3rd person	*a* Name of business *b* Nature of business	*a* Occupation *b* Description of work	1 ☐ An employee 2 ☐ Self-employed employing others (see note B17) 3 ☐ Self-employed without employees	
4th person	*a* Name of business *b* Nature of business	*a* Occupation *b* Description of work	1 ☐ An employee 2 ☐ Self-employed employing others (see note B17) 3 ☐ Self-employed without employees	
5th person	*a* Name of business *b* Nature of business	*a* Occupation *b* Description of work	1 ☐ An employee 2 ☐ Self-employed employing others (see note B17) 3 ☐ Self-employed without employees	
6th person	*a* Name of business *b* Nature of business	*a* Occupation *b* Description of work	1 ☐ An employee 2 ☐ Self-employed employing others (see note B17) 3 ☐ Self-employed without employees	

Form L
(hotels, boarding houses, hospitals, schools, institutions, etc.)

Form F
(H.M. ships)

Form S
(vessels other than H.M. ships)

Form P
(personal return)

EXPLANATORY NOTE

(*This Note is not part of the Regulations.*)

The Regulations provide for the appointment of officers and for the detailed arrangements necessary for the conduct of the census directed to be taken by the Census Order 1970. The forms of return to be completed by householders, by managers and other persons in charge of premises or vessels and by individual persons in certain premises, vessels and other places, are prescribed by the Regulations and set out in Schedule 3.

1970 No. 775

CIVIL AVIATION

The Air Navigation (Fees) (Fifth Amendment) Regulations 1970

Made - - - 15*th May* 1970

Coming into Operation 1*st June* 1970

The Board of Trade with the consent of the Treasury and in exercise of their powers under Article 77 of the Air Navigation Order 1966(**a**), as amended (**b**), and of all other powers enabling them in that behalf hereby make the following Regulations.

1. These Regulations shall come into operation on 1st June 1970 and may be cited as the Air Navigation (Fees) (Fifth Amendment) Regulations 1970.

2. The Interpretation Act 1889(**c**), shall apply for the purpose of the interpretation of these Regulations as it applies for the purpose of the interpretation of an Act of Parliament.

3. The Schedule to the Air Navigation (Fees) Regulations 1966(**d**), as amended in particular by the Air Navigation (Fees) (Second Amendment) Regulations 1967(**e**), shall be further amended as follows:

In paragraph 7 for "£50 0s. 0d." there shall be substituted "£80 0s. 0d.".

Robert Burns,
A Second Secretary of
the Board of Trade.

15th May 1970.

We consent to the making of these Regulations.

E. G. Perry,
Neil McBride,
Lords Commissioners of
Her Majesty's Treasury.

15th May 1970.

EXPLANATORY NOTE

(*This Note is not part of the Regulations.*)

These Regulations amend the Air Navigation (Fees) Regulations 1966, as amended, by providing for an increased fee for the approval of persons who may make reports in connection with the issue, validation and renewal of certificates of airworthiness and who issue certificates of compliance.

(**a**) S.I. 1966/1184 (1966 III, p. 3073).
(**b**) There is no amendment expressly relating to the subject matter of these Regulations.
(**c**) 1889 c. 63. (**d**) S.I. 1966/1255 (1966 III, p. 3404). (**e**) S.I. 1967/915 (1967 II, p. 2733).

STATUTORY INSTRUMENTS

1970 No. 776

CENSUS

The Census Regulations 1970

Made - - - -	15*th May* 1970
Laid before Parliament	28*th May* 1970
Coming into Operation	15*th June* 1970

The Secretary of State for Social Services in exercise of his powers under section 3(1) of the Census Act 1920**(a)**, and of all other powers enabling him in that behalf, hereby makes the following regulations:—

Citation and commencement

1. These regulations may be cited as the Census Regulations 1970, and shall come into operation on 15th June 1970.

Interpretation

2.—(1) In these regulations, unless the context otherwise requires—

"the Act" means the Census Act 1920;

"assistant census officer" means an officer appointed under regulation 5(1)(*b*);

"the census" means the census directed to be taken by the Census Order 1970**(b)**; (hereinafter referred to as "the Census Order");

"census day" means 25th April 1971;

"census district" means a district so referred to in regulation 3;

"census night" means the night of 25th to 26th April 1971;

"census officer" means an officer appointed under regulation 5(1)(*a*);

"census supervisor" means an officer appointed under regulation 4;

"enumeration district" means a district so referred to in regulation 3;

"enumerator" means an officer appointed under regulation 5(1)(*c*);

"prescribed person" means a person required by the Census Order to make a return;

(2) Any reference in these regulations to a numbered regulation or schedule shall, unless the context otherwise requires, be construed as a reference to the regulation or schedule bearing that number in these regulations.

(a) 1920 c. 41. **(b)** S.I. 1970/481 (1970 I, p. 1599).

(3) The Interpretation Act 1889(a) shall apply to the interpretation of these regulations as it applies to the interpretation of an Act of Parliament.

Census districts and enumeration districts

3. For the purpose of the census the Registrar General shall divide England and Wales into census districts, and shall divide each census district into enumeration districts.

Appointment of census supervisors

4. For the purpose of the census the Registrar General may appoint census supervisors who shall perform the duties assigned to them under the Act and these regulations.

Appointment of other officers

5.—(1) For the purpose of the census the Registrar General may—

(*a*) appoint, or authorise a census supervisor to appoint, a census officer for each census district;

(*b*) appoint, or authorise a census officer to appoint, such number of assistant census officers for each census district as the Registrar General may determine;

(*c*) appoint, or authorise a census officer or assistant census officer to appoint, an enumerator for each enumeration district.

(2) The officers appointed under this regulation shall perform the duties assigned to them under the Act and these regulations.

Instructions by the Registrar General

6. The Registrar General may give to officers appointed under regulations 4 and 5 or may authorise a census supervisor, census officer or assistant census officer to give, such instructions as the Registrar General may consider necessary for the performance of the duties assigned to them under the Act and these regulations and any such instructions shall be complied with by any officer to whom they are given.

Undertakings

7. Every census supervisor, census officer, assistant census officer and enumerator and every person assisting any such officer in the performance of his duties shall, before performing any duties, give an undertaking in the form set out in Schedule 1 faithfully to perform his duties under the Act and these regulations.

Forms of return

8.—(1) The form of return to be made by a prescribed person mentioned in column (1) of Schedule 2 shall be the form set out in Schedule 3 which bears the identification particulars appropriate to his case shown in column (2) of Schedule 2, and a prescribed person shall comply with the instructions contained in such form.

(2) The Registrar General may cause any such form to be translated into Welsh and such translation may be used for the purposes of the census.

(a) 1889 c. 63.

Provision of forms and other documents for enumerators

9. Every census officer shall enter in the enumeration books provided by the Registrar General such particulars as the Registrar General may require, and shall, before census day, provide every enumerator appointed to act for an enumeration district within his census district with an enumeration book, a sufficient number of forms of return and such other forms or documents as may be necessary for the purpose of the census.

Delivery of forms of return

10.—(1) The enumerator shall, within such period as may be specified by the Registrar General, deliver—

(*a*) to the head, or person for the time being acting as the head, of every private household occupying a dwelling or part of a dwelling mentioned in Group I in Schedule 1 to the Census Order, form H or form W in Schedule 3;

(*b*) to the manager, chief resident officer or other person for the time being in charge of any premises mentioned in Groups II or III in Schedule 1 to the Census Order and to the person appointed for the purposes of article 5(3) of the Census Order in any premises mentioned in Group IV in that Schedule, the number of forms L and P or of forms L and Pw in Schedule 3 as the enumerator shall estimate to be required.

(2) The enumerator shall, on delivering each form, enter thereon such particulars as the Registrar General may require and shall, if so requested by any prescribed person or by any person acting on his behalf, give such explanations as are reasonably necessary to enable the prescribed person to make a proper return.

(3) An enumerator shall be deemed to have fulfilled the obligation placed upon him to deliver a form of return under this regulation if he hands it to the person mentioned in paragraph (1) of this regulation or to some responsible person acting on behalf of that person or if he leaves the form at the dwelling or premises where persons are to be enumerated.

(4) The Registrar General shall make such arrangements as he thinks fit for the delivery—

(*a*) of forms S, F and P or Pw in Schedule 3, as may be appropriate to the case in accordance with Schedule 2, to the captain, master or other person in charge of a vessel mentioned in Group V in Schedule 1 to the Census Order and to the person appointed for the purposes of article 5(3) of the Census Order in any vessel mentioned in Group IV in that Schedule;

(*b*) of a form P in Schedule 3 to every person mentioned in Group VI in Schedule 1 to the Census Order.

(5) The person to whom forms are delivered under paragraph (1)(*b*) or paragraph (4)(*a*) of this regulation shall deliver a form P or Pw, as the case may be, to every prescribed person on the premises or vessel who is capable of completing the form, after having caused to be entered on each such form the address of the premises or the name of the vessel, as the case may be, as required by article 5(3) of the Census Order:

Provided that a manager or other person in charge of premises mentioned in Group II in Schedule 1 to the Census Order, who has arranged for the form of return with respect to a person incapable of completing it himself to be completed by a relative or other person accompanying him, shall deliver for that purpose a form P or Pw, as the case may be, to the said relative or other person.

Personal returns

11.—(1) Any member of a private household or other person mentioned in Group I in Schedule 1 to the Census Order being a person aged 16 years or over on census day, who is capable of completing a form of return and is not himself the head or the person for the time being acting as the head of that household, may make a personal return if he complies with the procedure prescribed in the following paragraphs of this regulation.

(2) Subject to the foregoing paragraph a person claiming to make a personal return (hereinafter called "the applicant"), or a person acting on his behalf, shall apply to the enumerator for a separate form of return; or if the applicant cannot for any reason obtain a form of return from the enumerator he, or a person acting on his behalf, may apply to the census officer for such a form.

(3) The enumerator or census officer, as the case may be, shall issue to the applicant, or the person acting on his behalf, form P or Pw in Schedule 3 and shall if so requested, give such explanations as are reasonably necessary to enable the applicant to make a proper return.

(4) The prescribed person who would otherwise have to make a return in respect of the applicant on form H or W, as the case may be, shall enter on that form no particulars relating to the applicant other than his name and the relationship in which he stands to the prescribed person.

Collection of returns

12.—(1) Where under regulation 10(5) forms P or Pw have been delivered to persons mentioned in article 5(2) of the Census Order, the person responsible for delivering the forms shall collect the completed forms on the day after census day or as soon thereafter as is reasonably practicable.

(2) The enumerator shall on the day after census day, or as soon thereafter as is reasonably practicable, collect all forms of return delivered by him and all separate forms of return issued in accordance with regulation 11 to persons within his enumeration district, and shall examine each return and satisfy himself that the entries thereon are properly and sufficiently made, and shall make all such inquiries as are reasonably necessary for that purpose.

(3) The Registrar General shall make such arrangements as he thinks fit for the collection of completed forms of return made by persons in vessels mentioned in Groups IV and V in Schedule 1 to the Census Order and by persons in places mentioned in Group VI in that Schedule.

Particulars to be obtained by enumerators

13.—(1) For the purpose of obtaining the particulars required to be stated in item 17 in Schedule 2 to the Census Order the enumerator shall, when delivering or collecting form H or W, make such inquiries as are reasonably necessary to enable him to complete the panel headed "To be completed by enumerator" on the form.

(2) When delivering forms of return under regulation 10(1)(*b*) the enumerator shall make such inquiries as are reasonably necessary to ascertain the nature of

the premises, and in the case of premises in Group II in Schedule 1 to the Census Order the number of rooms in the premises, and shall enter the information on form L.

Further duties of enumerators

14.—(1) The enumerator shall within such period as may be specified by the Registrar General—

(*a*) enter in the enumeration book and in any forms of return collected by him such particulars as the Registrar General may require; and

(*b*) deliver to the census officer the enumeration book and all returns collected by him.

(2) If required to do so by the census officer or assistant census officer, the enumerator shall make such inquiries as may be reasonably necessary to secure the completion of any incomplete return.

Further duties of census officers

15.—(1) The census officer or, if so directed by him, the assistant census officer shall examine the enumeration books delivered to him under the foregoing regulation, and where it appears to him that any book is incomplete he shall require the enumerator to take such steps as may be reasonably necessary to complete the book and to send it duly completed to the census officer within a time to be specified by the census officer.

(2) When so directed by the Registrar General, the census officer shall send all completed enumeration books relating to enumeration districts within his census district, together with the returns delivered to him by enumerators or assistant census officers, to the Registrar General.

Replacement of census supervisor, census officer, assistant census officer or enumerator

16.—(1) Where in the opinion of the Registrar General any census supervisor or census officer is unable to perform his duties in connection with the census, the Registrar General may appoint some fit and proper person in his place to perform such duties.

(2) Where in the opinion of the census officer any assistant census officer or enumerator is unable to perform his duties in connection with the census, the census officer may appoint some fit and proper person in his place to perform such duties.

Giving of information

17.—(1) Every prescribed person shall give to the enumerator such information as he may reasonably require for the performance of his duties under these regulations, and every other person in respect of whom it is the duty of a prescribed person to make a return shall give to that prescribed person such information as he may reasonably require for that purpose.

(2) Otherwise than in accordance with these regulations no person shall use, publish or communicate to any other person any information given under the Census Order and these regulations.

Safe custody of forms and documents

18. A person having custody, whether on his own behalf or on behalf of any other person, of any forms of return, enumeration books or other documents containing confidential information relating to the census shall keep such forms, books and other documents in such manner as to prevent any unauthorised person having access thereto.

Revocation

19. The Census Regulations 1965(**a**) are hereby revoked.

Regulation 7

SCHEDULE 1

Form of Undertaking to be made by Certain Persons

I, ... being
*a person appointed in accordance with the Census Regulations 1970 to act as *census supervisor/*census officer/*assistant census officer/*enumerator
*a person assisting..for the purposes of the census, hereby undertake and promise faithfully to perform the duties imposed by the Census Act 1920, and the Census Regulations 1970 so far as applicable to me, and to fulfil all the obligations required of me by the Act and Regulations, and I hereby state that I have read and understand the provisions hereunto annexed of section 8 of the Act as amended by Schedule 3 to the Criminal Justice Act 1967(**b**), and regulation 18 of the Regulations.

Signed...

In the presence of ....

Section 8 of the Census Act 1920 as amended, is as follows:—

"8.—(1) If any person—

(*a*) refuses or neglects to comply with or acts in contravention of any of the provisions of this Act or any Order in Council or regulations made under this Act; or

(*b*) being a person required under this Act to make a statutory declaration with respect to the performance of his duties, makes a false declaration ; or

(*c*) being a person required by any Order in Council or regulations made under this Act to make, sign, or deliver any document, makes, signs, or delivers, or causes to be made, signed, or delivered a false document; or

(*d*) being a person required in pursuance of any such Order in Council or regulations to answer any question, refuses to answer or gives a false answer to that question;

he shall for each offence be liable on summary conviction to a fine not exceeding fifty pounds.

*Strike out words which do not apply.

(**a**) S.I. 1965/1267 (1965 II, p. 3601). (**b**) 1967 c. 80.

(2) If any person—

(*a*) being a person employed in taking a census, without lawful authority publishes or communicates to any person otherwise than in the ordinary course of such employment any information acquired by him in the course of his employment; or

(*b*) having possession of any information which to his knowledge has been disclosed in contravention of this Act, publishes or communicates that information to any other person;

he shall be guilty of a misdemeanour, and shall on conviction be liable to imprisonment with or without hard labour, for a term not exceeding two years or to a fine, or to both such imprisonment and fine."

Regulation 18 of the Census Regulations 1970 is as follows:—

"18. A person having custody, whether on his own behalf or on behalf of any other person, of any forms of return, enumeration books or other documents containing confidential information relating to the census shall keep such forms, books and other documents in such manner as to prevent any unauthorised person having access thereto."

Regulation 8

SCHEDULE 2

(1) *Prescribed Persons*	(2) *Identification Particulars of Form*
(*a*) The head or person for the time being acting as the head of every private household in England.	The form entitled "H Form For Private Households".
(*b*) The head or person for the time being acting as the head of every private household in Wales (including Monmouthshire).	The form entitled "W Form For Private Households".
(*c*) The manager, chief resident officer or other person in charge of any premises mentioned in Groups II or III in Schedule 1 to the Census Order and the person appointed for the purposes of article 5(3) of the Census Order in any premises mentioned in Group IV in that Schedule.	The form entitled "L Form For Hotels, Boarding Houses, Hospitals, Schools and Institutions etc.".
(*d*) The person appointed for the purposes of article 5(3) of the Census Order in any vessel mentioned in Group IV in Schedule 1 to the Census Order.	The form entitled "F Form For H.M. Ships".
(*e*) The captain, master or other person in charge of any vessel mentioned in Group V in Schedule 1 to the Census Order.	The form entitled "S Form For Vessels (other than H.M. Ships)".
(*f*) Any person in England mentioned in column 2 in Groups II, III, IV, V or VI in Schedule I to the Census Order.	The form entitled "P Form For Making A Personal Return".
(*g*) Any person in Wales (including Monmouthshire) mentioned in column 2 in Groups II, III, IV, V or VI in Schedule 1 to the Census Order.	The form entitled "Pw Form For Making A Personal Return".
(*h*) Any person in England making a personal return under Regulation 11.	The form entitled "P Form For Making A Personal Return".
(*i*) Any person in Wales (including Monmouthshire) making a personal return under Regulation 11.	The form entitled "Pw Form For Making A Personal Return".

(1) Prescribed Persons	(2) Identification Particulars of Form
(a) The head or person for the time being acting as the head of every private household in England.	The form entitled "H Form For Private Households".
(b) The head or person for the time being acting as the head of every private household in Wales (including Monmouthshire).	The form entitled "W Form For Private Households".
(c) The manager, chief resident officer or other person in charge of any premises mentioned in Groups II or III in Schedule 1 to the Census Order and the person appointed for the purposes of article 5(3) of the Census Order in any premises mentioned in Group IV in that Schedule.	The form entitled "L Form For Hotels, Boarding Houses, Hospitals, Schools and Institutions etc.".
(d) The person appointed for the purposes of article 5(3) of the Census Order in any vessel mentioned in Group IV in Schedule 1 to the Census Order.	The form entitled "R Form For H.M. Ships".
(e) The captain, master or other person in charge of any vessel mentioned in Group V in Schedule 1 to the Census Order.	The form entitled "S Form For Vessels (other than H.M. Ships)".
(f) Any person in England mentioned in column 2 in Groups II, III, IV, V or VI in Schedule 1 to the Census Order.	The form entitled "P Form For Making A Personal Return".
(g) Any person in Wales (including Monmouthshire) mentioned in column 2 in Groups II, III, IV, V or VI in Schedule 1 to the Census Order.	The form entitled "Pw Form For Making A Personal Return".
(h) Any person in England making a personal return under Regulation 11.	The form entitled "P Form For Making A Personal Return".
(i) Any person in Wales (including Monmouthshire) making a personal return under Regulation 11.	The form entitled "Pw Form For Making A Personal Return".

SCHEDULE 3

Regulation 8

Forms of Return for 1971 Census

Form H
(private households in England)

B8 Will the person be a **student** attending **full-time** at an educational establishment during the term starting April/May 1971? (see note B8) *This question need not be answered for children under 15 years of age.*	**B9** *a* If the person was born in England or Wales or Scotland or Northern Ireland tick the appropriate box. or *b* If the person was born in another country, write the name of the country (using the name by which it is known today) and the year in which the person first entered the United Kingdom (that is England, Wales, Scotland and Northern Ireland).	**B10** Write the country of birth of: *a* the person's **father** *b* the person's **mother** *This question should be answered even if the person's father or mother is no longer alive. (If country not known, write 'NOT KNOWN'.)* *Give the name by which the country is known today.*
☐ YES ☐ NO	*a* Born in ☐ England 01 ☐ Scotland 02 ☐ Wales (incl. Monmouthshire) 03 ☐ Northern Ireland or *b* Born in .... (country) and entered U.K. in .... (year)	*a* Father born in (country) *b* Mother born in (country)
☐ YES ☐ NO	*a* Born in ☐ England 01 ☐ Scotland 02 ☐ Wales (incl. Monmouthshire) 03 ☐ Northern Ireland or *b* Born in .... (country) and entered U.K. in .... (year)	*a* Father born in (country) *b* Mother born in (country)
☐ YES ☐ NO	*a* Born in ☐ England 01 ☐ Scotland 02 ☐ Wales (incl. Monmouthshire) 03 ☐ Northern Ireland or *b* Born in .... (country) and entered U.K. in .... (year)	*a* Father born in (country) *b* Mother born in (country)
☐ YES ☐ NO	*a* Born in ☐ England 01 ☐ Scotland 02 ☐ Wales (incl. Monmouthshire) 03 ☐ Northern Ireland or *b* Born in .... (country) and entered U.K. in .... (year)	*a* Father born in (country) *b* Mother born in (country)
☐ YES ☐ NO	*a* Born in ☐ England 01 ☐ Scotland 02 ☐ Wales (incl. Monmouthshire) 03 ☐ Northern Ireland or *b* Born in .... (country) and entered U.K. in .... (year)	*a* Father born in (country) *b* Mother born in (country)
☐ YES ☐ NO	*a* Born in ☐ England 01 ☐ Scotland 02 ☐ Wales (incl. Monmouthshire) 03 ☐ Northern Ireland or *b* Born in .... (country) and entered U.K. in .... (year)	*a* Father born in (country) *b* Mother born in (country)

PLEASE TURN OVER TO THE NEXT PAGE →

Answers should be written on the line on which the person's name appears in column B1

B11 Was the person's **usual address one year ago (on 25th April 1970)** the same as that shown by the answer to **question B4?** Write 'YES' or 'NO'. If no, write also the usual address on 25th April 1970. *For a child now under one year of age, write* 'UNDER ONE'. BLOCK CAPITALS PLEASE	**B12** Was the person's **usual address five years ago (on 25th April 1966)** the same as that shown by the answer to **question B11?** Write 'YES' or 'NO'. If no, write also the usual address on 25th April 1966. *For a child now under five years of age, write* 'UNDER FIVE'. BLOCK CAPITALS PLEASE	**B13** Has the person obtained any of the following? G.C.E. **'A' level** Higher School Certificate (HSC) **Higher** grade of Scottish Certificate of Education (SCE) **Higher** grade of Scottish Leaving Certificate (SLC) Ordinary National Certificate (ONC) Ordinary National Diploma (OND) *This question need not be answered for children under 15 or retired persons over 70.*
1st person		1 ☐ GCE 'A' level or HSC 2 ☐ SCE higher or SLC higher 3 ☐ ONC or OND 4 ☐ None of these
2nd person		1 ☐ GCE 'A' level or HSC 2 ☐ SCE higher or SLC higher 3 ☐ ONC or OND 4 ☐ None of these
3rd person		1 ☐ GCE 'A' level or HSC 2 ☐ SCE higher or SLC higher 3 ☐ ONC or OND 4 ☐ None of these
4th person		1 ☐ GCE 'A' level or HSC 2 ☐ SCE higher or SLC higher 3 ☐ ONC or OND 4 ☐ None of these
5th person		1 ☐ GCE 'A' level or HSC 2 ☐ SCE higher or SLC higher 3 ☐ ONC or OND 4 ☐ None of these
6th person		1 ☐ GCE 'A' level or HSC 2 ☐ SCE higher or SLC higher 3 ☐ ONC or OND 4 ☐ None of these

1971 CENSUS FORM

NOTES

These notes are to help you answer some of the questions in Part B (for persons present). In cases where they also apply to Part C (absent persons) this is shown in Part C.

If you have any further difficulty with these, or any other questions please ask the enumerator about them when he calls to collect your form.

B7 Job last week

A job means any work for payment or profit. In particular it includes:

(a) work on a person's own account

(b) part-time work, even if only for a few hours, such as jobbing gardening or paid domestic work

(c) casual or temporary work of any kind (for example seasonal work, week-end work and vacation work by students)

(d) unpaid work in a family business, for example a shop or farm.

Unpaid work, other than in a family business, does not count as a job.

B8 Students

Do not count as full-time students people who are:

(a) on day release from work to attend school or college

(b) attending night school only

(c) attending an educational establishment provided by employers, such as an apprenticeship school.

B15 Employer's name and business

Describe the business fully and try to avoid abbreviations or initials. General terms such as 'manufacturer', 'merchant', 'agent', 'broker', 'factor', 'dealer', 'engineering', are not enough by themselves and further details should be given about the articles manufactured or dealt in.

For civil servants, local government officers and other public officials give the name of the Government department, local authority or public body and the branch in which they are employed.

For people employed solely in private domestic service write 'PRIVATE' in answer to this question.

For members of Armed Forces see special note overleaf.

B16 Occupation

Full and precise details of occupation are required.

If a person's job is known in the trade or industry by a special name use that name.

Terms such as 'scientist', 'technician', 'engineer' 'machinist', 'fitter', 'foreman', 'checker' should not be used by themselves. Greater detail is required as for example:—

woodworking machinist, civil engineer, toolroom foreman.

For civil servants, local government officers and other public officials give their rank or grade.

B17 Self-employed

'Self-employed, employing others' means having one or more employees other than 'family workers A family worker' is one who lives in the same household as the employer and is related to him. Although 'family workers' are not counted for the purpose of deciding whether an employer has employees, they should themselves be recorded as employees.

B18 Apprentices, etc.

Answer this question only for a person who is undergoing training for a period fixed in advance and leading to recognition as a skilled worker or technician or to a recognised technical, commercial or professional qualification or managerial post.

Do not answer this question for a young person undergoing probationary training who has not yet entered into formal apprenticeship.

B20 Place of work

For people who do not work regularly at one place or who travel during the course of their work (for example, sales representatives, seamen and some building and transport workers):

(a) if they report daily to a depot or other fixed address give that address

(b) if they do not report daily to a fixed address write 'NO FIXED PLACE'

For people such as building workers employed on a site for a long period give the address of the site.

For dock workers give the name and address of the dock or wharf at which they are usually employed.

B21 Means of transport

If the person uses different means of transport on different days give the means used most often.

Do not use terms such as 'public transport' or 'private transport' but give the actual means used, for example, 'train', 'bus', 'car', 'bicycle'.

SPECIAL NOTE FOR MEMBERS OF ARMED FORCES

At B15 (or, if appropriate, C5) give arm and branch of service.

At B16 (or C6) give rank or rating only.

Questions B17 (or C7), B18, B19 and B22 need not be answered.

Form W
(private households in Wales)

B8	B9	B10
Will the person be a **student** attending **full-time** at an educational establishment during the term starting April/May 1971 ? (see note B8) *This question need not be answered for children under 15 years of age.*	*a* If the person was born in England or Wales or Scotland or Northern Ireland tick the appropriate box. or *b* If the person was born in another country, write the name of the country (using the name by which it is known today) and the year in which the person first entered the United Kingdom (that is England, Wales, Scotland and Northern Ireland).	Write the country of birth of: *a* the person's **father** *b* the person's **mother** *This question should be answered even if the person's father or mother is no longer alive. (If country not known, write 'NOT KNOWN'.)* *Give the name by which the country is known today.*
☐ YES ☐ NO	*a* Born in ☐ England 01 ☐ Scotland 02 ☐ Wales (incl. Monmouthshire) 03 ☐ Northern Ireland or *b* Born in .... (country) and entered U.K. in .... (year)	*a* Father born in (country) *b* Mother born in (country)
☐ YES ☐ NO	*a* Born in ☐ England 01 ☐ Scotland 02 ☐ Wales (incl. Monmouthshire) 03 ☐ Northern Ireland or *b* Born in .... (country) and entered U.K. in .... (year)	*a* Father born in (country) *b* Mother born in (country)
☐ YES ☐ NO	*a* Born in ☐ England 01 ☐ Scotland 02 ☐ Wales (incl. Monmouthshire) 03 ☐ Northern Ireland or *b* Born in .... (country) and entered U.K. in .... (year)	*a* Father born in (country) *b* Mother born in (country)
☐ YES ☐ NO	*a* Born in ☐ England 01 ☐ Scotland 02 ☐ Wales (incl. Monmouthshire) 03 ☐ Northern Ireland or *b* Born in .... (country) and entered U.K. in .... (year)	*a* Father born in (country) *b* Mother born in (country)
☐ YES ☐ NO	*a* Born in ☐ England 01 ☐ Scotland 02 ☐ Wales (incl. Monmouthshire) 03 ☐ Northern Ireland or *b* Born in .... (country) and entered U.K. in .... (year)	*a* Father born in (country) *b* Mother born in (country)
☐ YES ☐ NO	*a* Born in ☐ England 01 ☐ Scotland 02 ☐ Wales (incl. Monmouthshire) 03 ☐ Northern Ireland or *b* Born in .... (country) and entered U.K. in .... (year)	*a* Father born in (country) *b* Mother born in (country)

PLEASE TURN OVER TO THE NEXT PAGE →

Answers should be written on the line on which the person's name appears in column B1

	B11	B12	B13
	B11 Was the person's **usual address one year ago (on 25th April 1970)** the same as that shown by the answer to **question B4**? Write 'YES' or 'NO'. If no, write also the usual address on 25th April 1970. *For a child now under one year of age, write* 'UNDER ONE'. BLOCK CAPITALS PLEASE	**B12** Was the person's **usual address five years ago (on 25th April 1966)** the same as that shown by the answer to **question B11**? Write 'YES' or 'NO'. If no, write also the usual address on 25th April 1966. *For a child now under five years of age, write* 'UNDER FIVE'. BLOCK CAPITALS PLEASE	**B13** Has the person obtained any of the following? G.C.E. **'A' level** Higher School Certificate (HSC) **Higher** grade of Scottish Certificate of Education (SCE) **Higher** grade of Scottish Leaving Certificate (SLC) Ordinary National Certificate (ONC) Ordinary National Diploma (OND) *This question need not be answered for children under 15 or retired persons over 70.*
1st person			1 ☐ GCE 'A' level or HSC 2 ☐ SCE higher or SLC higher 3 ☐ ONC or OND 4 ☐ None of these
2nd person			1 ☐ GCE 'A' level or HSC 2 ☐ SCE higher or SLC higher 3 ☐ ONC or OND 4 ☐ None of these
3rd person			1 ☐ GCE 'A' level or HSC 2 ☐ SCE higher or SLC higher 3 ☐ ONC or OND 4 ☐ None of these
4th person			1 ☐ GCE 'A' level or HSC 2 ☐ SCE higher or SLC higher 3 ☐ ONC or OND 4 ☐ None of these
5th person			1 ☐ GCE 'A' level or HSC 2 ☐ SCE higher or SLC higher 3 ☐ ONC or OND 4 ☐ None of these
6th person			1 ☐ GCE 'A' level or HSC 2 ☐ SCE higher or SLC higher 3 ☐ ONC or OND 4 ☐ None of these

1971 CENSUS FORM

NOTES

These notes are to help you answer some of the questions in Part B (for persons present). In cases where they also apply to Part C (absent persons) this is shown in Part C.

If you have any further difficulty with these, or any other questions please ask the enumerator about them when he calls to collect your form.

B7 Job last week

A job means any work for payment or profit. In particular it includes:

(a) work on a person's own account

(b) part-time work, even if only for a few hours, such as jobbing gardening or paid domestic work

(c) casual or temporary work of any kind (for example seasonal work, week-end work and vacation work by students)

(d) unpaid work in a family business, for example a shop or farm.

Unpaid work, other than in a family business, does not count as a job.

B8 Students

Do not count as full-time students people who are:

(a) on day release from work to attend school or college

(b) attending night school only

(c) attending an educational establishment provided by employers, such as an apprenticeship school.

B15 Employer's name and business

Describe the business fully and try to avoid abbreviations or initials. General terms such as 'manufacturer', 'merchant', 'agent', 'broker', 'factor', 'dealer', 'engineering', are not enough by themselves and further details should be given about the articles manufactured or dealt in.

For civil servants, local government officers and other public officials give the name of the Government department, local authority or public body and the branch in which they are employed.

For people employed solely in private domestic service write 'PRIVATE' in answer to this question.

For members of Armed Forces see special note overleaf.

B16 Occupation

Full and precise details of occupation are required.

If a person's job is known in the trade or industry by a special name use that name.

Terms such as 'scientist', 'technician', 'engineer' 'machinist', 'fitter', 'foreman', 'checker' should not be used by themselves. Greater detail is required as for example:—

woodworking machinist, civil engineer, toolroom foreman.

For civil servants, local government officers and other public officials give their rank or grade.

B17 Self-employed

'Self-employed, employing others' means having one or more employees other than 'family workers A family worker is one who lives in the same household as the employer and is related to him. Although 'family workers' are not counted for the purpose of deciding whether an employer has employees, they should themselves be recorded as employees.

B18 Apprentices, etc.

Answer this question only for a person who is undergoing training for a period fixed in advance and leading to recognition as a skilled worker or technician or to a recognised technical, commercial or professional qualification or managerial post.

Do not answer this question for a young person undergoing probationary training who has not yet entered into formal apprenticeship.

B20 Place of work

For people who do not work regularly at one place or who travel during the course of their work (for example, sales representatives, seamen and some building and transport workers):

(a) if they report daily to a depot or other fixed address give that address

(b) if they do not report daily to a fixed address write 'NO FIXED PLACE

For people such as building workers employed on a site for a long period give the address of the site.

For dock workers give the name and address of the dock or wharf at which they are usually employed.

B21 Means of transport

If the person uses different means of transport on different days give the means used most often.

Do not use terms such as 'public transport' or 'private transport' but give the actual means used, for example, 'train', 'bus', 'car', 'bicycle'.

SPECIAL NOTE FOR MEMBERS OF ARMED FORCES

At B15 (or, if appropriate, C5) give arm and branch of service.

At B16 (or C6) give rank or rating only.

Questions B17 (or C7), B18, B19 and B22 need not be answered.

Form L

(hotels, boarding houses, hospitals, schools, institutions, etc.)

Form F
(H.M. ships)

Form S
(vessels other than H.M. ships)

Form P
(personal return in England)

Form Pw
(personal return in Wales)

R. H. S. Crossman,
Secretary of State for Social Services.

15th May 1970.

EXPLANATORY NOTE

(*This Note is not part of the Regulations.*)

The Regulations provide for the appointment of officers and for the detailed arrangements necessary for the conduct of the census directed to be taken by the Census Order 1970. The forms of return to be completed by householders, by managers and other persons in charge of premises or vessels and by individual persons in certain premises, vessels and other places are prescribed by the regulations and set out in Schedule 3.

STATUTORY INSTRUMENTS

1970 No. 777

ROAD TRAFFIC

The Motor Vehicles (Construction and Use) (Amendment) (No. 2) Regulations 1970

Made - - -	18*th May* 1970
Laid before Parliament	29*th May* 1970
Coming into Operation	15*th June* 1970

The Minister of Transport, in exercise of his powers under section 64(1) of the Road Traffic Act 1960(**a**) as amended by section 51 of and Schedule 4 to the Road Traffic Act 1962(**b**), section 72(5) of the said Act of 1960, and of all other enabling powers, and after consultation with representative organisations in accordance with the provisions of section 260(2) of the said Act of 1960, hereby makes the following Regulations:—

1.—(1) These Regulations shall come into operation on the 15th June 1970 and may be cited as the Motor Vehicles (Construction and Use) (Amendment) (No. 2) Regulations 1970.

(2) The Interpretation Act 1889(**c**) shall apply for the interpretation of these Regulations as it applies for the interpretation of an Act of Parliament.

2. The Motor Vehicles (Construction and Use) Regulations 1969(**d**), as amended (**e**), shall have effect as though—

(1) for Regulation 97 there were substituted the following Regulation—

"97. No person shall cause or permit to be on a road any motor vehicle which is not attended by a person duly licensed to drive it unless the engine is stopped and the parking brake required by Regulation 11 is effectively set:

Provided that the requirements of this Regulation as to the stopping of the engine shall not apply in the case of—

(*a*) a fire brigade vehicle the engine of which is being used for any fire brigade purpose;

(*b*) a vehicle which is propelled by gas produced in plant carried on the vehicle or on a trailer drawn by the vehicle;

(*c*) a vehicle when it is being used for police or ambulance purposes; or

(*d*) a vehicle engaged in operations which require its engine to be used—

(i) to drive special machinery or apparatus forming part of the vehicle or mounted thereon, such machinery or apparatus being that used for purposes other than in connection with the driving of the vehicle; or

---

(**a**) 1960 c. 16.
(**b**) 1962 c. 59.
(**c**) 1889 c. 63.
(**d**) S.I. 1969/321 (1969 I. p, 829).
(**e**) There is no relevant amending instrument.

(ii) to maintain the electrical power in the batteries of the vehicle at a level required for the driving of such machinery or apparatus,

so, however, that paragraph (*d*) of this proviso shall not have effect in the case of a vehicle which is stationary on a road in such a position or in such condition or in such circumstances (including the gradient of the road) as to be likely to cause danger to any person or property.";

(2) in Regulation 115—

(*a*) in paragraph (1), for sub-paragraph (*n*) there were substituted the following sub-paragraph:—

"(*n*) where a motor vehicle is drawing a trailer or trailers and every such trailer is fitted with power assisted or power operated brakes which can be operated by the driver of the drawing vehicle and are not rendered ineffective by the non-rotation of the engine of the drawing vehicle—

(i) where one such trailer is drawn; or

(ii) where two or more such trailers are drawn, if one attendant is carried either on the drawing vehicle or a trailer for the purpose of attending to the trailers.;";

(*b*) after paragraph (1), there were inserted the following paragraph—

"(1A) The requirements of the said section 72 with regard to the employment of persons to drive or attend a locomotive whilst being driven on a highway shall not apply in the case of a locomotive propelled by the combustion of liquid fuel or by electrical power, whether or not the locomotive is drawing a trailer or trailers.".

Given under the Official Seal of the Minister of Transport the 18th May 1970.

(L.S.)

Fred Mulley,
Minister of Transport.

EXPLANATORY NOTE

(*This Note is not part of the Regulations.*)

These Regulations further amend the Motor Vehicles (Construction and Use) Regulations 1969. The principal changes are:—

1. Regulation 97 is amended to allow motor vehicles, the engines of which are used to drive special machinery, to be left on roads in certain circumstances unattended and with the engine running.

2. Regulation 115 is amended so as to vary the requirements with regard to employment of attendants on motor vehicles and trailers.

1970 No. 781 (S.58)

BETTING AND GAMING

The Gaming Clubs (Hours and Charges) (Scotland) Regulations 1970

Made - - -	*18th May* 1970
Laid before Parliament	*29th May* 1970
Coming into Operation	*1st July* 1970

In exercise of the powers conferred on me by sections 14(2) and (3), 22(4) and 51 of the Gaming Act 1968(**a**), and of all other powers enabling me in that behalf, and after consultation with the Gaming Board for Great Britain, I hereby make the following regulations:—

Citation and commencement

1. These regulations may be cited as the Gaming Clubs (Hours and Charges) (Scotland) Regulations 1970 and shall come into operation on 1st July 1970.

Interpretation

2.—(1) In these regulations, the expression—

"the Act" means the Gaming Act 1968;

"bingo club premises" has the meaning assigned to it by section 20(1) of the Act;

"charging period" has the meaning assigned to it by regulation 5(2) of these regulations; and

"gaming" does not include gaming by means of any machine to which Part III of the Act applies.

(2) A reference in these regulations to a charge in respect of gaming does not include an amount paid for a chance of winning a prize in gaming to which section 21 of the Act applies.

(3) Nothing in these regulations precludes the making of different charges thereunder in respect of different facilities (whether provided in different parts of the same premises or by way of different games or of the same game played at different tables or otherwise) or in respect of gaming facilities provided on the premises during different sessions of play.

(4) The Interpretation Act 1889(**b**) applies for the interpretation of these regulations as it applies for the interpretation of an Act of Parliament.

Bingo hours

3.—(1) No gaming shall take place on bingo club premises except—

(*a*) between the hours of two in the afternoon and midnight of a Saturday or New Year's Eve;

(**a**) 1968 c. 65. (**b**) 1889 c. 63.

(*b*) between the hours of two in the afternoon and eleven in the evening of any other day.

(2) This regulation does not apply to gaming which is prohibited by section 18(2) of the Act (which relates to gaming in Scotland between certain hours on Sundays).

General gaming hours

4. No gaming shall take place on any premises (not being bingo club premises) in respect of which a licence under the Act is for the time being in force on any weekday between the hours of four in the morning and two in the afternoon.

Bingo charges

5.—(1) Any charge which, apart from this regulation, would be prohibited by section 3 as applied by section 14(1) of the Act may be made in respect of gaming on bingo club premises if the charge satisfies the following requirements, that is to say—

(*a*) the charge shall be in respect of one person and be for admission to or otherwise in respect of gaming which takes place within a charging period ;

(*b*) the charge shall be of a fixed amount of money not exceeding ten shillings ;

(*c*) where in relation to one charging period more than one charge can be incurred, or the same charge can be incurred more than once, by one person (without leaving the premises and being readmitted), every charge shall be in accordance with a scheme of charging so devised that the aggregate amount of the charges which can be incurred by any one person (without leaving the premises and being readmitted) in relation to that charging period does not exceed ten shillings ; and

(*d*) where charges are made for permission to take part in games of bingo of the kind whose rules permit a player to withdraw any part of his initial stake after the game has begun, the number of times that one person can incur such a charge (whether by incurring different charges of that kind, or by incurring the same charge more than once or by incurring charges partly in one way and partly in another) shall not exceed three in relation to one charging period.

(2) There may be specified for the purposes of this regulation, in a notice displayed on the premises at or near the principal entrance, one or more periods of time (not being wholly or partly concurrent) identified by reference to the clock and not being shorter in duration than two hours each, and in any such case a reference in this regulation to a charging period is a reference to a period so specified. In any other case, that reference is a reference to a period of twenty-four hours beginning with midnight.

General gaming charges

6.—(1) Any charge which, apart from this regulation would be prohibited by section 3 as applied by section 14(1) of the Act may be made in respect of gaming on any premises (not being bingo club premises) in respect of which a licence under the Act is for the time being in force, if the charge satisfies the following requirements, that is to say,—

(*a*) the charge shall be of a fixed amount of money and shall be in respect of one or more facilities accorded to one person ; and (*b*) subject to paragraph (2) below, where the charge is of such a nature that it can be incurred more than once by one person (otherwise than by leaving and being readmitted to the premises, or any particular part of the premises or any particular table), the charge shall not be capable of being incurred again by the same person within one hour of the time when it was last incurred by him.

(2) A charge may be made for permission to take part in a series of games of *chemin de fer* (including a series which has already begun), notwithstanding that the charge may recur within one hour, if—

(*a*) the games comprised in the series consist of all the games which can be played with a shoe of not fewer than six packs of playing cards of fifty-two cards each ; and

(*b*) neither the holder of the licence nor any person acting on his behalf holds the bank, or has a share or interest in it, in any of the games in the series.

William Ross,
One of Her Majesty's Principal
Secretaries of State.

St. Andrew's House,
Edinburgh.
18th May 1970.

EXPLANATORY NOTE

(*This Note is not part of the Regulations.*)

These Regulations relate to premises licensed for gaming in Scotland. Regulations 3 and 4 restrict the hours during which gaming is to be permitted in bingo clubs and other licensed clubs respectively. Regulations 5 and 6 authorise the making of charges in respect of gaming in bingo and other licensed clubs respectively. The charges permitted are in addition to any stakes hazarded in the gaming.

STATUTORY INSTRUMENTS

1970 No. 782

INDUSTRIAL TRAINING

The Industrial Training Levy (Air Transport and Travel) Order 1970

Made - - -	20*th May* 1970
Laid before Parliament	28*th May* 1970
Coming into Operation	3*rd June* 1970

The Secretary of State after approving proposals submitted by the Air Transport and Travel Industry Training Board for the imposition of a further levy on employers in the air transport and travel industry and in exercise of her powers under section 4 of the Industrial Training Act 1964(**a**) and of all other powers enabling her in that behalf hereby makes the following Order:—

Title and commencement

1. This Order may be cited as the Industrial Training Levy (Air Transport and Travel) Order 1970 and shall come into operation on 3rd June 1970.

Interpretation

2.—(1) In this Order unless the context otherwise requires :—

(*a*) "agriculture" has the same meaning as in section 109(3) of the Agriculture Act 1947(**b**) or, in relation to Scotland, as in section 86(3) of the Agriculture (Scotland) Act 1948(**c**) ;

(*b*) "Air Corporation" means the British Overseas Airways Corporation or the British European Airways Corporation, and includes B.O.A.C. Associated Companies Limited, British Engine Overhaul Limited and BEA Helicopters Limited ;

(*c*) "air transport and travel establishment" means an establishment in Great Britain that was engaged in the relevant base period wholly or mainly in the air transport and travel industry for a total of twenty-seven or more weeks or, being an establishment that commenced to carry on business in that period, for a total number of weeks exceeding one-half of the number of weeks in the part of the said period commencing with the day on which business was commenced and ending on the last day thereof ;

(*d*) "the air transport and travel industry" means any one or more of the activities which, subject to the provisions of paragraph 2 of the Schedule to the industrial training order, are specified in paragraph 1 of that Schedule as the activities of the air transport and travel industry ;

(*e*) "an appeal tribunal" means an industrial tribunal established under section 12 of the Industrial Training Act 1964 ;

(*f*) "assessment" means an assessment of an employer to the levy ;

(**a**) 1964 c. 16. (**b**) 1947 c. 48. (**c**) 1948 c. 45.

(*g*) "the Board" means the Air Transport and Travel Industry Training Board;

(*h*) "British air carrier" means any company that undertakes or offers to undertake for hire or reward the carriage by air of passengers (including their baggage) or of freight, being a company which, or an associated company of which, has its sole or principal place of business in Great Britain and is engaged in activities specified in paragraph 1(*b*) of the Schedule to the industrial training order;

(*i*) "business" means any activities of industry or commerce;

(*j*) "emoluments" means all emoluments assessable to income tax under Schedule E (other than pensions), being emoluments from which tax under that Schedule is deductible, whether or not tax in fact falls to be deducted from any particular payment thereof;

(*k*) "employer" means a person who is an employer in the air transport and travel industry at any time in the relevant levy period;

(*l*) "the industrial training order" means the Industrial Training (Air Transport and Travel Industry Board) Order 1970(**a**);

(*m*) "the levy" means the levy imposed by the Board in respect of the relevant levy period;

(*n*) "notice" means a notice in writing;

(*o*) "relevant levy period" means. as the case may require, the third levy period or the fourth levy period, and the expression "relevant base period" means, in relation to the levy to be imposed in respect of the third levy period, the third base period or, in relation to the levy to be imposed in respect of the fourth levy period, the fourth base period;

(*p*) "the third base period" and "the fourth base period" mean respectively the periods of twelve months that commenced on 6th April 1969 and on 6th April 1970;

(*q*) "the third levy period" means the period commencing with the day on which this Order comes into operation and ending on 31st March 1971, and the "fourth levy period" means the period commencing on 1st April 1971 and ending on 31st March 1972;

(*r*) "travel agency establishment" means an air transport and travel establishment engaged, wholly or mainly, in the business of a travel agent or of providing packaged tours (being activities to which sub-paragraph (*g*) of paragraph 1 of the Schedule to the industrial training order applies) or in any related or other activities to which sub-paragraph (*h*) of that paragraph applies in the case of an employer or of an associated company engaged in the first mentioned activities;

(*s*) other expressions have the same meanings as in the industrial training order.

(2) In the case where an air transport and travel establishment is taken over (whether directly or indirectly) by an employer in succession to, or jointly with, another person, a person who was employed at any time in a relevant base period at or from the establishment shall be deemed, for the purposes of this Order, to have been so employed by the employer carrying on the establishment on the first day of the relevant levy period, and any reference in this Order to persons employed by the employer in the relevant base period at or from an establishment shall be construed accordingly.

(3) Any reference in this Order to an establishment that commences to carry on business or that ceases to carry on business shall not be taken to apply

(**a**) S.I. 1970/252 (1970 I, p. 983).

where the location of the establishment is changed but its business is continued wholly or mainly at or from the new location, or where the suspension of activities is of a temporary or seasonal nature.

(4) The Interpretation Act 1889(**a**) shall apply to the interpretation of this Order as it applies to the interpretation of an Act of Parliament.

Imposition of the Levy

3.—(1) The levy to be imposed by the Board on employers in respect of the third levy period and of the fourth levy period respectively shall be assessed in accordance with the provisions of this Article.

(2) The levy shall be assessed by the Board separately in respect of each air transport and travel establishment of an employer, not being an Air Corporation, the British Airports Authority or an employer who is exempted from the levy by virtue of paragraph (7) of this Article, but in agreement with the employer one assessment may be made in respect of any number of such establishments in which case those establishments shall be deemed for the purposes of that assessment to constitute one establishment.

(3) The levy assessed in respect of an air transport and travel establishment of an employer shall, subject to the provisions of this Article, be an amount equal to 2·0 per cent. (or in the case of an establishment of a British air carrier 3·8 per cent.) of the sum of the emoluments of all the persons employed by the employer at or from that establishment in the relevant base period.

(4) In the case of an air transport and travel establishment that ceases to carry on business in a relevant levy period the said sum of emoluments mentioned in the last foregoing paragraph shall be reduced in the same proportion as the number of days between the commencement of that levy period and the date of cessation of business (both dates inclusive) bears to the number of days in the said period.

(5) The levy shall be assessed by the Board in respect of each Air Corporation and of the British Airports Authority and shall, subject to the provisions of this Article, be an amount equal to 3·8 per cent. in the case of an Air Corporation and 2·0 per cent. in the case of the said Authority of the sum of the emoluments of all the persons employed by the Corporation or Authority, as the case may be, at or from its establishment or establishments in the relevant base period.

(6) For the purposes of this Article, no regard shall be had to any person employed as follows:—

(*a*) by a local authority in—

(i) any activities to which paragraph 1(*h*) or 1(*i*) of the Schedule to the industrial training order applies, not being activities mentioned in head (ii) or head (iv) of paragraph 3(*q*) thereof; or

(ii) any operations (being certain building work or civil engineering work) specified in paragraph 2(*c*)(i) of that Schedule;

(*b*) as a member of the crew of an aircraft that is operated by an employer having his sole or principal place of business outside Great Britain;

(*c*) wholly in agriculture;

(*d*) wholly in the supply of food or drink for immediate consumption, except where such person is a member of the crew of an aircraft; or

(**a**) 1889 c. 63.

(*e*) wholly at or from a travel agency establishment in the third base period.

(7) There shall be exempted from the levy to be imposed in respect of the third levy period an employer in whose case the principal activities of the air transport and travel industry in the third base period were limited to the business of a travel agent or of providing packaged tours.

Assessment Notices

4.—(1) The Board shall serve an assessment notice on every employer assessed to the levy, but one notice may comprise two or more assessments.

(2) An assessment notice shall state the amount (rounded down, where necessary, to the nearest £1) of the levy payable by the person assessed thereto, and where the notice comprises two or more assessments the said amount shall, before any such rounding down, be equal to the total amount of the levy assessed by the Board under Article 3 of this Order in respect of each establishment included in the notice.

(3) An assessment notice shall state the Board's address for the service of a notice of appeal or of an application for an extension of time for appealing.

(4) An assessment notice may be served on the person assessed to the levy either by delivering it to him personally or by leaving it, or sending it to him by post, at his last known address or place of business in the United Kingdom or, if that person is a corporation, by leaving it, or sending it by post to the corporation, at such address or place of business or at its registered or principal office.

Payment of the Levy

5.—(1) Subject to the provisions of this Article and of Articles 6 and 7, the amount of the levy payable under an assessment notice served by the Board shall be payable to the Board in two instalments determined in accordance with the provisions of the next following paragraph, and the first instalment shall be due one month after the date of the assessment notice and the second instalment one month after the date (not being earlier than five months after the date of the assessment notice) of a notice requiring payment of that instalment, which notice shall be served by the Board on the person assessed to the levy in the same manner as an assessment notice.

(2) The first of the said instalments shall be equal to 0·3 per cent. of the sum of emoluments by reference to which the amount of the said levy has been assessed in accordance with the provisions of Article 3 of this Order, and the second instalment shall be equal to the balance of the amount payable under the assessment notice.

(3) The amount of an instalment mentioned in the last foregoing paragraph, may be rounded up or down by the Board to a convenient figure, but so that the aggregate amount of both instalments shall be equal to the amount of the levy stated in the assessment notice in accordance with Article 4(2) of this Order.

(4) An instalment of an assessment shall not be recoverable by the Board until there has expired the time allowed for appealing against the assessment by Article 7(1) of this Order and any further period or periods of time that the Board or an appeal tribunal may have allowed for appealing under paragraph (2) or (3) of that Article or, where an appeal is brought, until the appeal is decided or withdrawn.

Withdrawal of Assessment

6.—(1) The Board may, by a notice served on the person assessed to the levy in the same manner as an assessment notice, withdraw an assessment if that person has appealed against that assessment under the provisions of Article 7 of this Order and the appeal has not been entered in the Register of Appeals kept under the appropriate Regulations specified in paragraph (5) of that Article.

(2) The withdrawal of an assessment shall be without prejudice—

(*a*) to the power of the Board to serve a further assessment notice in respect of any establishment or, as the case may be, persons to which that assessment related and, where the withdrawal is made by reason of the fact that an establishment has ceased to carry on business in the relevant levy period, the said notice may provide that the whole amount payable thereunder in respect of the establishment shall be due one month after the date of the notice ; or

(*b*) to any other assessment included in the original assessment notice, and such notice shall thereupon have effect as if any assessment withdrawn by the Board had not been included therein.

Appeals

7.—(1) A person assessed to the levy may appeal to an appeal tribunal against the assessment within one month from the date of the service of the assessment notice or within any further period or periods of time that may be allowed by the Board or an appeal tribunal under the following provisions of this Article.

(2) The Board by notice may for good cause allow a person assessed to the levy to appeal to an appeal tribunal against the assessment at any time within the period of four months from the date of the service of the assessment notice or within such further period or periods as the Board may allow before such time as may then be limited for appealing has expired.

(3) If the Board shall not allow an application for extension of time for appealing, an appeal tribunal shall upon application made to the tribunal by the person assessed to the levy have the like powers as the Board under the last foregoing paragraph.

(4) In the case of an establishment that ceases to carry on business in a relevant levy period on any day after the date of the service of an assessment notice that applies in respect of that period, the foregoing provisions of this Article shall have effect as if for the period of four months from the date of the service of the assessment notice mentioned in paragraph (2) of this Article there were substituted the period of six months from the date of the cessation of business.

(5) An appeal or an application to an appeal tribunal under this Article shall be made in accordance with the Industrial Tribunals (England and Wales) Regulations 1965(**a**) as amended by the Industrial Tribunals (England and Wales) (Amendment) Regulations 1967(**b**) except where the assessment relates to an establishment that is wholly in Scotland in which case the appeal or application shall be made in accordance with the Industrial Tribunals (Scotland) Regulations 1965(**c**) as amended by the Industrial Tribunals (Scotland) (Amendment) Regulations 1967(**d**).

(a) S.I. 1965/1101 (1965 II, p. 2805).
(b) S.I. 1967/301 (1967 I, p. 1040).
(c) S.I. 1965/1157 (1965 II, p. 3266).
(d) S.I. 1967/302 (1967 I, p. 1050).

(6) The powers of an appeal tribunal under paragraph (3) of this Article may be exercised by the President of the Industrial Tribunals (England and Wales) or by the President of the Industrial Tribunals (Scotland) as the case may be.

Evidence

8.—(1) Upon the discharge by a person assessed to the levy of his liability under an assessment the Board shall if so requested issue to him a certificate to that effect.

(2) The production in any proceedings of a document purporting to be certified by the Secretary of the Board to be a true copy of an assessment or other notice issued by the Board or purporting to be a certificate such as is mentioned in the foregoing paragraph of this Article shall, unless the contrary is proved, be sufficient evidence of the document and of the facts stated therein.

20th May 1970.

Barbara Castle
First Secretary of State and Secretary of State for Employment and Productivity.

EXPLANATORY NOTE

(*This Note is not part of the Order.*)

This Order gives effect to proposals submitted by the Air Transport and Travel Industry Training Board (formerly known as the Civil Air Transport Industry Training Board) to the Secretary of State for Employment and Productivity for the imposition of two further levies upon employers in the air transport and travel industry (formerly the civil air transport industry) for the purpose of raising money towards the expenses of the Board.

A levy is to be imposed in respect of the third and of the fourth levy periods. The third levy period will commence on the day upon which this Order comes into operation and end on 31st March 1971 and the fourth levy period will commence on 1st April 1971 and end on 31st March 1972. Each levy will be assessed by the Board and there will be a right of appeal against the assessment to an industrial tribunal.

STATUTORY INSTRUMENTS

1970 No. 783

WAGES COUNCILS

The Wages Regulation (Retail Bespoke Tailoring) (England and Wales) Order 1970

Made - - -	20*th May* 1970
Coming into Operation	24*th June* 1970

Whereas the Secretary of State has received from the Retail Bespoke Tailoring Wages Council (England and Wales) (hereafter in this Order referred to as "the Wages Council") the wages regulation proposals set out in the Schedule hereto;

Now, therefore, the Secretary of State, in exercise of her powers under section 11 of the Wages Councils Act 1959(**a**), and of all other powers enabling her in that behalf, hereby makes the following Order:—

1. This Order may be cited as the Wages Regulation (Retail Bespoke Tailoring) (England and Wales) Order 1970.

2.—(1) In this Order the expression "the specified date" means the 24th June 1970, provided that where, as respects any worker who is paid wages at intervals not exceeding seven days, that date does not correspond with the beginning of the period for which the wages are paid, the expression "the specified date" means, as respects that worker, the beginning of the next such period following that date.

(2) The Interpretation Act 1889(**b**) shall apply to the interpretation of this Order as it applies to the interpretation of an Act of Parliament and as if this Order and the Orders hereby revoked were Acts of Parliament.

3. The wages regulation proposals set out in the Schedule hereto shall have effect as from the specified date and as from that date the Wages Regulation (Retail Bespoke Tailoring) (England and Wales) Order 1966(**c**) and the Wages Regulation (Retail Bespoke Tailoring) (England and Wales) (Amendment) Order 1968(**d**) shall cease to have effect and the Wages Regulation (Retail Bespoke Tailoring) (England and Wales) (Holidays) Order 1967(**e**) shall have effect as if Schedule 2 were omitted.

Signed by order of the Secretary of State.

20th May 1970.

A. A. Jarratt,
Deputy Under Secretary of State,
Department of Employment and Productivity.

(**a**) 1959 c. 69.
(**b**) 1889 c. 63.
(**c**) S.I. 1966/1505 (1966 III, p. 4176).
(**d**) S.I. 1968/1795 (1968 III, p. 4807).
(**e**) S.I. 1967/1631 (1967 III, p. 4483).

ARRANGEMENT OF SCHEDULE

Article 3

SCHEDULE

The following minimum remuneration shall be substituted for the statutory minimum remuneration fixed by the Wages Regulation (Retail Bespoke Tailoring) (England and Wales) Order 1966 (Order R.B. (66)), as amended by the Wages Regulation (Retail Bespoke Tailoring) (England and Wales) (Amendment) Order 1968 (Order R.B. (71)) and Schedule 2 to the Wages Regulation (Retail Bespoke Tailoring) (England and Wales) (Holidays) Order 1967 (Order R.B. (69)).

STATUTORY MINIMUM REMUNERATION

PART I

GENERAL

1.—(1) The minimum remuneration payable to a worker to whom this Schedule applies for all work except work to which a minimum overtime rate applies under Part V is:—

(*a*) in the case of a time worker, the hourly general minimum time rate applicable to the worker under the provisions of this Schedule;

(*b*) in the case of a worker employed on piece work, piece rates each of which would yield, in the circumstances of the case, to an ordinary worker (that is to say, a worker of ordinary skill and efficiency of the class in question) at least the same amount of money as the piece work basis time rate applicable to the worker or, where no piece work basis time rate is applicable, at least the same amount of money as the hourly general minimum time rate which would be applicable to the worker if he were a time worker.

(2) In this Schedule, in relation to a worker to whom a weekly general minimum time rate applies, the expression hourly general minimum time rate means the weekly general minimum time rate applicable to the worker divided by 40.

APPLICABILITY OF STATUTORY MINIMUM REMUNERATION

2.—(1) Subject to the provisions of sub-paragraph (2) of this paragraph, this Schedule applies to workers in relation to whom the Retail Bespoke Tailoring Wages Council (England and Wales) operates, that is to say, workers employed in England and Wales in any of the branches of work in the retail bespoke tailoring trade as specified in the Schedule to the Trade Boards (Retail Bespoke Tailoring Trade, England and Wales) (Constitution and Proceedings) Regulations 1924(**a**), which are set out below, that is to say:—

Those branches of men's, women's, boys' and girls' bespoke tailoring in which the tailor supplies the garment direct to the individual wearer and employs the worker direct.

(**a**) S.R. & O. 1924/835 (1924, p. 1769).

A worker shall be deemed to be employed by the tailor direct, if employed by another worker in the employ of the tailor, to whom a minimum rate of wages fixed under the Wages Councils Act 1959 is applicable; or if employed by a sub-contractor engaged in cutting, making or finishing garments exclusively for the tailor in the tailor's shop or in a building of which the shop forms part or to which the shop is attached;

including:—

(*a*) (i) The altering, repairing, renovating, or re-making of men's, women's, boys' or girls' tailored garments where carried out for the individual wearer by a tailor who employs the worker direct as defined above;

(ii) The cleaning of such garments where carried on in association with or in conjunction with the repairing, renovating or re-making of the garments;

(*b*) The lining with fur of the above-mentioned garments where carried out in association with or in conjunction with the making of such garments;

(*c*) All processes of embroidery or decorative needlework where carried out in association with or in conjunction with the above-mentioned branches of tailoring;

(*d*) The packing and all other operations incidental to or appertaining to any of the above-mentioned branches of tailoring;

but excluding:—

(*a*) All or any of the above-mentioned operations where carried on in a factory where garments are made up for three or more retail establishments;

(*b*) The making of head-gear.

(2) Notwithstanding the provisions of sub-paragraph (1) of this paragraph, this Schedule does not apply to workers employed as cutters, trimmers or packers.

PART II

MALE WORKERS

GENERAL MINIMUM TIME RATES

3. Subject to the provisions of this Schedule, the general minimum time rates applicable to male workers employed in Areas A and B respectively are as follows:—

	Area A per hour		Area B per hour	
	s.	d.	s.	d.
(1) JOURNEYMAN TAILOR (as defined in paragraph 17(3))	*7*	*2*	*7*	*0½*
(2) ASSISTANT JOURNEYMAN TAILOR (as defined in paragraph 17(4))	*6*	*9*	*6*	*7¼*
(3) MALE WORKERS (other than the workers specified in sub-paragraphs (1) and (2) of this paragraph) after five years' employment in the trade	*6*	*2¾*	*6*	*1¼*
(4) MALE WORKERS (other than apprentices and learners) who have not completed five years' employment in the trade:—	s.	d.	s.	d.
During the 1st year	*2*	*9½*	*2*	*8¼*
During the 2nd year	*3*	*5*	*3*	*4*
During the 3rd year	*4*	*1*	*3*	*11¾*
During the 4th year	*4*	*8½*	*4*	*6¾*
During the 5th year	*5*	*4¼*	*5*	*3½*

	Area A	Area B
(5) INDENTURED APPRENTICES whose employment complies with the conditions specified in paragraph 15 during the following periods of apprenticeship—	per week s. d.	per week s. d.
The 1st year of apprenticeship	90 6¾	88 5½
The 2nd year of apprenticeship	114 8½	112 7¼
The 3rd year of apprenticeship	144 10¾	142 9½
	per hour s. d.	per hour s. d.
The 4th year of apprenticeship	4 6¼	4 5¼
The 5th year of apprenticeship	5 9	5 7¾
(6) LEARNERS whose employment complies with the conditions specified in paragraph 17(5) during the following periods of learnership—	per week s. d.	per week s. d.
The 1st year of learnership	90 6¾	88 5½
The 2nd year of learnership	114 8½	112 7¼
The 3rd year of learnership	144 10¾	142 9½
	per hour s. d.	per hour s. d.
The 4th year of learnership	4 6¼	4 5¼
The 5th year of learnership	5 6¾	5 5½

PIECE WORK BASIS TIME RATES

4. The piece work basis time rate applicable to a male worker, irrespective of his experience in the trade, who is employed on piece work in Area A or Area B shall be a rate equal to the general minimum time rate which would be payable if the worker were a time worker who has completed five years' employment in the trade, increased by *twelve* per cent, provided that, where the worker is of a class specified in sub-paragraph (1) or (2) of paragraph 3 the piece work basis time rate for that worker shall be a rate equal to the appropriate general minimum time rate applicable to that class of worker, increased by *twelve* per cent.

WORKERS ON SPECIAL CLASSES OF WORK

5. Notwithstanding the provisions of paragraphs 3 and 4, where a male worker who has completed five years' employment in the trade is employed in the making of (i) military dress uniforms (other than khaki), (ii) naval frock and dress uniforms, (iii) hunt coats and hunt riding breeches, (iv) frock and dress coats and (v) court and diplomatic garments, or any of those garments, the general minimum time rate or the piece work basis time rate applicable to the worker shall be increased by 2½d. an hour.

PART III

FEMALE WORKERS
GENERAL MINIMUM TIME RATES

6. Subject to the provisions of this Schedule, the general minimum time rates applicable to female workers employed in Areas A and B respectively are as follows:—

	Area A per hour s. d.	Area B per hour s. d.
(1) JOURNEYMAN TAILORESS (as defined in paragraph 17(3))	5 8¼	5 7½
(2) ASSISTANT JOURNEYMAN TAILORESS (as defined in paragraph 17(4))	5 4	5 3½
(3) FEMALE WORKERS (other than the workers specified in sub-paragraphs (1) and (2) of this paragraph) after five years' employment in the trade	4 11¼	4 10¾

(4) FEMALE WORKERS (other than apprentices and learners) who have not completed five years' employment in the trade—

	s. d.	s. d.
During the 1st year	*2 11*	*2 10½*
During the 2nd year	*3 3¼*	*3 2¾*
During the 3rd year	*3 8*	*3 7½*
During the 4th year	*4 0½*	*3 11¾*
During the 5th year	*4 5*	*4 4¼*

(5) INDENTURED APPRENTICES whose employment complies with the conditions specified in paragraph 15 during the following periods of apprenticeship—

	Area A per week s. d.	Area B per week s. d.
The 1st year of apprenticeship	*90 6¾*	*88 5½*
The 2nd year of apprenticeship	*114 8½*	*112 7¼*
The 3rd year of apprenticeship	*144 10¾*	*142 9½*
	per hour s. d.	per hour s. d.
The 4th year of apprenticeship	*4 4*	*4 3¼*
The 5th year of apprenticeship...	*4 11½*	*4 11*

(6) LEARNERS whose employment complies with the conditions specified in paragraph 17(5) during the following periods of learnership—

	per week s. d.	per week s. d.
The 1st year of learnership	*90 6¾*	*88 5½*
The 2nd year of learnership	*114 8½*	*112 7¼*
The 3rd year of learnership	*144 10¾*	*142 9½*
	per hour s. d.	per hour s. d.
The 4th year of learnership	*4 4*	*4 3¼*
The 5th year of learnership	*4 9¼*	*4 8¾*

PIECE WORK BASIS TIME RATES

7. The piece work basis time rate applicable to a female worker, irrespective of her experience in the trade, who is employed on piece work in Area A or Area B shall be a rate equal to the general minimum time rate which would be payable if the worker were a time worker who has completed five years' employment in the trade, increased by *twelve* per cent, provided that, where the worker is of a class specified in sub-paragraphs (1) or (2) of paragraph 6 the piece work basis time rate for that worker shall be a rate equal to the appropriate general minimum time rate applicable to that class of worker, increased by *twelve* per cent.

PART IV

RECKONING OF EXPERIENCE

Previous Instruction in an Approved Technical Class

8. Where any worker has, after attaining the age of 15 years and prior to his employment on work to which this Schedule applies, received instruction in tailoring processes and related studies in a technical class at any school or other institution and such instruction has been approved by the Wages Council, for the purpose of reckoning the period of his apprenticeship, learnership or other employment in

the trade each complete one hundred hours of such instruction shall be treated as four weeks of apprenticeship, learnership or other employment in the trade: Provided that the period to be so treated as employment in the trade shall not exceed the total number of weeks during which the worker attended the technical class.

Previous Experience in the Tailoring Trade

9. Where any worker has at any time been employed as a worker in relation to whom there operated one or more of the following Wages Councils, that is to say, the Retail Bespoke Tailoring Wages Council (England and Wales), the Retail Bespoke Tailoring Wages Council (Scotland), the Ready-made and Wholesale Bespoke Tailoring Wages Council (Great Britain) and the Wholesale Mantle and Costume Wages Council (Great Britain), each such period of employment shall, for the purpose of reckoning the period of the worker's learnership or other employment (not being apprenticeship) in the trade, be treated as though it were an equal period of learnership or other employment in the trade.

Experience under the Government Vocational Training Scheme

10. Where any worker has completed the full period of training in retail bespoke tailoring in respect of which training allowances are payable under the Government Vocational Training Scheme, such period of training shall, for the purpose of reckoning the period of the worker's employment in the trade, be treated as though it were a period of five years' employment therein.

PART V

OVERTIME AND WAITING TIME

NORMAL NUMBER OF HOURS

11. Minimum overtime rates set out in paragraph 12 are payable to any worker as follows:—

(1) in any week,
for all time worked in excess of ... ... 40 hours

(2) on any day other than a Saturday, Sunday or a customary holiday,
for all time worked in excess of ... ... 7¼ hours

Provided that where the worker normally attends on five days only in the week, minimum overtime rates shall apply to all time worked in excess of the hours following:—
where the normal working hours exceed 8½ ... ... 9 hours
or
where the normal working hours are more than 8 but not more than 8½ ... ... 8½ hours
or
where the normal working hours are not more than 8 ... 8 hours

(3) on a Saturday, not being a customary holiday—
(*a*) where the worker normally attends on six days in the week, for all time worked in excess of ... 4 hours
(*b*) where the worker normally attends on five days only in the week... ... ... for all time worked

(4) on a Sunday or a customary holiday ... ... for all time worked

MINIMUM OVERTIME RATES

12.—(1) Minimum overtime rates are payable to any worker as follows:—

(*a*) on any day other than a Saturday, Sunday or customary holiday—

(i) for the first 2 hours of overtime worked ... ... time-and-a-quarter

(ii) for the next 2 hours ... ... time-and-a-half

(iii) thereafter ... ... double time

(*b*) on a Saturday, not being a customary holiday—

(i) where the worker normally attends on six days in the week—

for all time worked in excess of 4 hours ... double time

(ii) where the worker normally attends on five days only in the week—

for the first 2 hours worked ... ... time-and-a-quarter

for the next 2 hours ... ... time-and-a-half

thereafter ... ... double time

(*c*) on a Sunday or a customary holiday—

for all time worked... ... ... double time

(*d*) in any week, exclusive of any time in respect of which a minimum overtime rate is payable under the foregoing provisions of this sub-paragraph—

for all time worked in excess of 40 hours ... ... time-and-a-quarter

(2) Where it is the practice in a Jewish undertaking for the employer to require attendance of the worker on Sunday and not on Saturday (except where such attendance on Sunday is unlawful) Saturday shall be treated as a Sunday, and, subject to the provisions of sub-paragraph (3) of this paragraph, Sunday as a Saturday.

(3) Where the worker normally attends on six days in the week and an ordinary week-day is substituted for Saturday, or in a case where the provisions of sub-paragraph (2) of this paragraph apply, for Sunday, as the worker's weekly short day, for the purposes of this Part of this Schedule (except where such substitution is unlawful) that ordinary week-day shall be treated as a Saturday, and Saturday or Sunday, as the case may be, as an ordinary week-day.

(4) Where the worker normally attends on five days only in the week and Saturday is one of his normal working days, the ordinary week-day on which he does not normally attend shall for the purposes of this Part of this Schedule be treated as a Saturday and Saturday as an ordinary week-day.

13. In this Part of this Schedule—

(1) the expression "CUSTOMARY HOLIDAY" means—

(*a*) Christmas Day (or, if Christmas Day falls on a Sunday, such weekday as may be appointed by national proclamation, or, if none is so appointed, the next following Tuesday), Boxing Day, Good Friday, Easter Monday, Whit Monday (or where another day is substituted therefor by national proclamation, that day) and August Bank Holiday ; or

(*b*) in the case of each of the said days, a day substituted by the employer therefor, being a day recognised by local custom as a day of holiday in substitution for the said day ;

(2) the expressions "time-and-a-quarter", "time-and-a-half" and "double time" mean, respectively,

(*a*) in the case of a time worker, one and a quarter times, one and a half times and twice the hourly general minimum time rate otherwise applicable to the worker;

(*b*) in the case of a worker employed on piece work,

(i) a time rate equal respectively to one quarter, one half, and the whole of the piece work basis time rate otherwise applicable to the worker or, where no piece work basis time rate is otherwise applicable, of the hourly general minimum time rate which would be applicable to the worker if he were a time worker and a minimum overtime rate did not apply, and in addition thereto,

(ii) the piece rates otherwise applicable to the worker under paragraph 1(1).

WAITING TIME

14.—(1) A worker is entitled to payment of the minimum remuneration specified in this Schedule for all time during which he is present on the premises of his employer unless he is present thereon in any of the following circumstances:—

(*a*) without the employer's consent, express or implied;

(*b*) for some purpose unconnected with his work and other than that of waiting for work to be given to him to perform;

(*c*) by reason only of the fact that he is resident thereon;

(*d*) during normal meal times in a room or place in which no work is being done and he is not waiting for work to be given to him to perform.

(2) The minimum remuneration payable under sub-paragraph (1) of this paragraph to a piece worker when not engaged on piece work is that which would be applicable if he were a time worker.

PART VI

APPRENTICES

CONDITIONS AS TO RATES FOR APPRENTICES

15. The general minimum time rates specified in (5) of paragraphs 3 and 6 respectively apply only to an apprentice in whose case the conditions following are fulfilled:—

(1) the apprentice shall be employed for a period of five years under, and in accordance with, a written contract of apprenticeship which has been duly executed and which contains the following provisions, which the Wages Council considers necessary for the effective instruction of the apprentice, or provisions substantially to the same effect, and no provisions contrary thereto, namely,—

(*a*) the apprentice, of his own free will and with the consent of his guardian, binds himself to serve the employer as his apprentice in his trade of retail bespoke tailoring for a term of five years;

(*b*) the employer shall keep the apprentice as his apprentice during the said term and to the best of his power, skill and knowledge shall instruct the apprentice, or cause him to be instructed by a fully qualified tailor or tailoress, in the making throughout of such one or more of the following garments, namely, coats, skirts, trousers, breeches, waistcoats or cassocks as shall be specified in the said contract of apprenticeship and in everything relative to the work of making and completing the same;

(*c*) during the first three years of apprenticeship the employer shall not require the apprentice to work during any period for which a minimum overtime rate is payable under the provisions of Part V; and (*d*) during the said term of apprenticeship the employer shall not put the apprentice on piece work ;

(2) the apprentice shall be the holder of a certificate of registration of apprenticeship issued by or on behalf of the Wages Council, or shall have made application for such a certificate which has been duly acknowledged and is still under consideration:

Provided that the certification of the apprentice may be cancelled by the Wages Council if the other conditions of apprenticeship are not complied with.

PROSPECTIVE APPRENTICES

16.—(1) Notwithstanding the foregoing provisions of this Schedule an employer may employ a worker as a prospective apprentice where all the foregoing conditions of apprenticeship other than those with regard to employment under a written contract of apprenticeship and certification by the Wages Council are fulfilled, for a probationary period:—

(*a*) not exceeding 12 months where the employer has given to the worker a written undertaking that he will permit the worker to attend a full-time course of instruction in tailoring processes approved by the Wages Council ;

(*b*) not exceeding six months in any other case.

(2) The minimum remuneration applicable to such a prospective apprentice during the probationary period shall be that applicable to an indentured apprentice employed in accordance with the conditions specified in the preceding paragraph.

(3) Where before the expiration of the probationary period a Wages Council has received from the employer written notification of the intention of the employer and worker to enter into a written contract of apprenticeship and has acknowledged the same in writing the probationary period may be extended as the Wages Council considers necessary for the drawing up and execution of the written contract.

(4) If the employer and worker enter into a written contract of apprenticeship at the end of any probationary period then for the purposes of this Schedule such probationary period shall be included in reckoning the period of five years referred to in paragraph 15(1) hereof.

PART VII

DEFINITIONS AND INTERPRETATION

17.—(1) In this Schedule—

Area A—comprises the whole of England and Wales except Area B.

Area B—comprises each area in England and Wales which at the date of the 1961 census was administered by

(*a*) a Rural District Council or

(*b*) a Municipal Borough Council or an Urban District Council having according to the said census a population of less than 10,000, but does not include any areas within the Metropolitan Police District.

(2) For the purposes of the Schedule:—

(*a*) an outworker shall be deemed to be employed in the area in which the employer's establishment from which work is given out to that worker is situated ;

(*b*) "outworker" means a worker who works in his own home or in some other place not under the control or management of the employer.

(3) The expression:—

"Journeyman Tailor" or "Journeyman Tailoress" means a worker who

(*a*) has completed

(i) an apprenticeship complying with the conditions specified in paragraph 15, or

(ii) five years' employment on work to which this Schedule applies (of which at least two years shall have been completed after he attained the age of 18 years), including employment in the trade reckoned in accordance with the provisions of paragraphs 8, 9 and 10; and

(*b*) is capable of making throughout, without supervision, one or more of the following garments, namely, coats, skirts, trousers, breeches, waistcoats or cassocks.

(4) The expression:—

"Assistant Journeyman Tailor" or "Assistant Journeyman Tailoress" means a worker other than a Journeyman Tailor or Journeyman Tailoress who

(*a*) has completed

(i) five years' employment as a learner, as defined in sub-paragraph (5) of this paragraph, or

(ii) five years' employment on work to which this Schedule applies (of which at least two years shall have been completed after he attained the age of 18 years), including employment in the trade reckoned in accordance with the provisions of paragraphs 8, 9 and 10; and

(*b*) is either:—

(i) skilled in the general trade of under pressing and pressing off, or

(ii) is capable of carrying out, in the making of coats (including overcoats and ladies' coats) or vests or trousers or breeches or cassocks or skirts, without supervision, three or more of the operations specified below:—

COATS

Marking and fitting up
Baisting for try on
Piecing up by hand or machine
Putting in pockets by hand or machine
Making sleeves by hand or machine
Making linings and putting in same by hand or machine
Canvassing
Baisting under
Baisting out
Padding collars and lapels by hand
Making collars
Putting on collars by hand or machine
Working button holes
Stitching edges by hand or machine
Under pressing
Pressing off

VESTS

Marking and fitting up
Baisting for try on
Putting in pockets

VESTS (*cont.*)

Canvassing
Making up edges
Making back and putting in linings
Working button holes
Under pressing and pressing off
Stitching edges by hand or machine

TROUSERS, BREECHES OR SKIRTS

Marking and fitting up
Baisting for try on
Piecing up and seaming seams by hand or machine
Making up fly or placket by hand or machine
Making up tops by hand or machine
Putting in pockets by hand or machine
Making up bottoms by hand or machine
Under pressing and pressing off

CASSOCKS

Marking and fitting up
Baisting for try on
Piecing up by hand or machine
Putting in pockets by hand or machine
Making collars
Putting on collars by hand or machine
Working button holes by hand or machine
Under pressing and pressing off

(5) The expression "learner" means any worker, male or female, who,

(*a*) not being—

(i) an apprentice employed in accordance with the conditions specified in paragraph 15 ;

(ii) a worker who has completed the full period of training in retail bespoke tailoring in respect of which training allowances are payable under the Government Vocational Training Scheme ;

(iii) a worker who has been employed for more than five years in the retail bespoke section of the tailoring trade, the ready-made and wholesale bespoke tailoring trade, and the wholesale mantle and costume trade, or in one or more of such trades ; or

(iv) a worker who works in a room used for dwelling purposes unless he is in the employment of his parent or guardian ;

(*b*) is employed by an employer who provides him with reasonable facilities for learning—

(i) the general trade of under pressing and pressing off, or

(ii) three or more of the operations specified in sub-paragraph (4)(*b*)(ii) of this paragraph in the making of coats (including overcoats and ladies' coats) or vests or trousers or breeches or cassocks or skirts, and who, until at least three operations on any one garment have been taught, is not employed by the same employer for more than six months on any one operation, and (*c*) has received a certificate of registration of learnership from the Wages Council, or has made an application for such certificate which has been duly acknowledged and is still under consideration:

Provided that the certificate may be cancelled by the Wages Council if the other conditions of learnership are not complied with.

EXPLANATORY NOTE

(*This Note is not part of the Order.*)

This Order, which has effect from 24th June 1970, sets out the statutory minimum remuneration payable in substitution for that fixed by the Wages Regulation (Retail Bespoke Tailoring) (England and Wales) Order 1966 (Order R.B. (66)) as amended by Schedule 2 to the Wages Regulation (Retail Bespoke Tailoring) (England and Wales) (Holidays) Order 1967 (Order R.B. (69)) and the Wages Regulation (Retail Bespoke Tailoring) (England and Wales) (Amendment) Order 1968 (Order R.B. (71)). Orders R.B. (66) and R.B. (71) are revoked.

New provisions are printed in italics.

STATUTORY INSTRUMENTS

1970 No. 785

LEGAL AID AND ADVICE, ENGLAND

The Legal Advice (Amendment) Regulations 1970

Made - - -	19*th May* 1970
Laid before Parliament	29*th May* 1970
Coming into Operation	1*st August* 1970

The Lord Chancellor, in exercise of the powers conferred on him by sections 7 and 12 of the Legal Aid and Advice Act 1949(**a**) as amended by the Legal Aid Act 1960(**b**), hereby makes the following Regulations :—

1.—(1) These Regulations may be cited as the Legal Advice (Amendment) Regulations 1970 and shall come into operation on 1st August 1970.

(2) The Interpretation Act 1889(**c**) shall apply to the interpretation of these Regulations as it applies to the interpretation of an Act of Parliament.

(3) In these Regulations a Regulation referred to by number means a Regulation so numbered in the Legal Advice Regulations 1959(**d**) as amended by the Legal Advice (Amendment) Regulations 1960(**e**).

2. Regulation 3 (which relates to the financial conditions for legal advice) shall be amended as follows :—

(1) In paragraph (1) there shall be substituted for the expression "£7 10s. 0d." the expression "£9 10s. 0d.";

(2) In paragraph (4) there shall be substituted for the expression "£2 5s. 0d." (wherever it occurs) the expression "£3 1s. 0d.";

(3) There shall be substituted for sub-paragraph (*b*) the following sub-paragraph :—

"(*b*) In respect of any child wholly or substantially maintained by him, or by any spouse of his where the capital and income of the spouse are treated as his resources—

Where the child is under 5 years of age ...	£1 8 0
Where the child is 5 or more years of age but under 11 years of age	£1 13 0
Where the child is 11 or more years of age but under 13 years of age	£2 1 0
Where the child is 13 or more years of age but under 16 years of age	£2 4 0"

(**a**) 1949 c. 51. (**b**) 1960 c. 28. (**c**) 1889 c. 63.
(**d**) S.I. 1959/47 (1959 I, p. 1550). (**e**) S.I. 1960/729 (1960 II, p. 1804).

3. In paragraph (2) of Regulation 6 (which relates to payment of solicitors) there shall be substituted for the expression "£1" (wherever it occurs) the expression "£2".

Dated 19th May 1970.

Gardiner, C.

EXPLANATORY NOTE

(*This Note is not part of the Regulations.*)

The Regulations relax the financial conditions on which legal advice is available under section 7 of the Legal Aid and Advice Act 1949. In future it will be available to those having an income (after certain deductions) of not more than £9 10s. 0d. in the week preceding the application for legal advice (instead of £7 10s. 0d.). The Regulations also increase the fee paid to solicitors giving legal advice from £1 per half hour to £2 per half hour.

STATUTORY INSTRUMENTS

1970 No. 787

LEGAL AID AND ADVICE, ENGLAND

The Legal Aid (General) (Amendment No. 2) Regulations 1970

Made - - -	21*st May* 1970
Laid before Parliament	29*th May* 1970
Coming into Operation	1*st August* 1970

The Lord Chancellor, in exercise of the powers conferred on him by sections 4, 5 and 12 of the Legal Aid and Advice Act 1949(**a**) as amended by the Legal Aid Act 1960(**b**) and with the concurrence of the Treasury, hereby makes the following Regulations :—

1.—(1) These Regulations may be cited as the Legal Aid (General) (Amendment No. 2) Regulations 1970 and shall come into operation on 1st August 1970.

(2) The Interpretation Act 1889(**c**) shall apply to the interpretation of these Regulations as it applies to the interpretation of an Act of Parliament.

(3) In these Regulations a paragraph referred to by number means a paragraph so numbered in the First Schedule to the Legal Aid (General) Regulations 1962(**d**) as amended (**e**).

2. Paragraph 9(*b*) (which relates to computing income) shall be amended as follows :—

(1) There shall be substituted for the expression "£117" (wherever it occurs) the expression "£159" and for the expression "£65" there shall be substituted the expression "£182" ;

(2) There shall be substituted for sub-paragraph (ii) the following sub-paragraph :—

"(ii) In respect of any child wholly or substantially maintained by him or any spouse of his where the capital and income of the spouse are treated as his resources—

Where the child is under 5 years of age ...	£73
Where the child is 5 or more years of age but under 11 years of age	£86

(**a**) 1949 c. 51.
(**b**) 1960 c. 28.
(**c**) 1889 c. 63.
(**d**) S.I. 1962/148 (1962 I, p. 117).
(**e**) There are no relevant amendments.

Where the child is 11 or more years of age but under 13 years of age	£107
Where the child is 13 or more years of age but under 16 years of age	£114 ;"

Dated 19th May 1970.

Gardiner, C.

We concur.

Dated 21st May 1970.

Neil McBride,
E. G. Perry,
Two of the Lords Commissioners of Her Majesty's Treasury.

EXPLANATORY NOTE

(*This Note is not part of the Regulations.*)

The Regulations increase the allowances which may be made in computing the income of an applicant for a Certificate for a Claim.

1970 No. 789

EXCHANGE CONTROL

The Exchange Control (Purchase of Foreign Currency) Order 1970

Made - - -	25*th May* 1970
Laid before Parliament	29*th May* 1970
Coming into Operation	1*st June* 1970

The Treasury, in exercise of the powers conferred upon them by sections 31 and 36(5) of the Exchange Control Act 1947**(a),** hereby make the following Order:—

1.—(1) This Order may be cited as the Exchange Control (Purchase of Foreign Currency) Order 1970, and shall come into operation on 1st June 1970.

(2) In this Order the following expressions have the meanings hereby respectively assigned to them, that is to say:—

"cheque card" means a card issued by any of the banks specified in the Schedule to this Order to a customer guaranteeing, subject to the conditions and limitations stated thereon or otherwise communicated to holders of such cheque cards, that cheques drawn by that customer will, when presented for payment, be honoured; and

"travel expenditure" means expenditure of foreign currency incurred outside the United Kingdom and the Channel Islands on and in connection with travel outside the United Kingdom and the Channel Islands and does not include the use of foreign currency for any form of capital expenditure or investment outside the scheduled territories, and in particular does not include the use of foreign currency for the purchase of any freehold or leasehold land or building outside the scheduled territories or for the development, repair or maintenance thereof or for the payment of any deposit thereon or the use of foreign currency for the purchase of any securities or business outside the scheduled territories or for the purchase of any life or endowment assurance policy or the payment of any premium thereon or the purchase of any annuity.

(3) The Interpretation Act 1889**(b)** shall apply for the interpretation of this Order as it applies for the interpretation of an Act of Parliament and as if this Order and the Orders hereby revoked were Acts of Parliament.

2. There shall be exempted from the provisions of section 1(1) of the Exchange Control Act 1947 the purchase outside the United Kingdom and the Channel Islands of foreign currency with notes which—

(*a*) are or have at any time been legal tender in any territory which is part of the scheduled territories; and

(*b*) have been exported from the United Kingdom or the Channel Islands under the exemption granted by article 5(1)(i) of the Exchange Control (Import and Export) Order 1966**(c)** as amended **(d).**

(a) 1947 c. 14. **(b)** 1889 c. 63. **(c)** S.I. 1966/1351 (1966 III, p. 3681).
(d) S.I. 1969/1883 (1969 III, p. 5825).

3. There shall be exempted from the provisions of the said section 1(1) the purchase outside the United Kingdom and the Channel Islands of foreign currency by any person who is the holder of a current cheque card issued to him by any bank specified in the Schedule to this Order if the purchase is effected by means of a cheque expressed in sterling drawn by him, being a cheque drawn in accordance with the conditions relating to, and within the limitations applying to, the drawing of cheques stated on the drawer's cheque card or otherwise communicated to holders of such cheque cards by the issuing bank.

4. The exemptions from the said section 1(1) granted by this Order are granted subject to the following conditions, namely that—

(*a*) the purchaser uses any foreign currency purchased under the said exemptions for travel expenditure only; and

(*b*) any foreign currency so purchased which, when the purchaser next returns to the United Kingdom or the Channel Islands, has not been used as aforesaid shall not be retained by the purchaser for more than one month after his said return.

5. There shall be exempted from the provisions of sections 5, 6 and 7 of the said Act any payment made by any bank specified in the Schedule to this Order in the course of honouring any cheque used to purchase foreign currency under the exemption granted by article 3 of this Order.

6. The Exchange Control (Purchase of Foreign Currency) Order 1965(**a**) and the Exchange Control (Purchase of Foreign Currency) (Amendment) Order 1966(**b**) are hereby revoked.

7. This Order shall extend to the Channel Islands, and any reference in this Order to the Exchange Control Act 1947 includes a reference to that Act as extended by the Exchange Control (Channel Islands) Order 1947(**c**).

E. G. Perry,
Neil McBride,
Two of the Lords Commissioners
of Her Majesty's Treasury.

25th May 1970.

(**a**) S.I. 1965/757 (1965 I, p. 2259). (**b**) S.I. 1966/1352 (1966 III, p. 3685).
(**c**) S.R. & O. 1947/2034 (Rev. VI, p. 1001: 1947 I, p. 660).

SCHEDULE

The banks specified for the purposes of articles 3 and 5 of this Order are the offices in the United Kingdom or the Channel Islands of the following banks, namely:—

Bank of Ireland.
Bank of Scotland.
Barclays Bank D.C.O.
Barclays Bank Ltd.
Belfast Banking Company, Ltd.
British Linen Bank.
Clydesdale Bank Ltd.
Coutts & Co.
Glyn, Mills & Co.
Hibernian Bank Ltd.
Isle of Man Bank Ltd.
Lewis's Bank Ltd.
Lloyds Bank Ltd.
Midland Bank Ltd.
Munster and Leinster Bank Ltd.
National Bank Ltd.
National Bank of Ireland Ltd., The.
National Westminster Bank Ltd.
Northern Bank Ltd.
Provincial Bank of Ireland Ltd.
Royal Bank of Ireland, Ltd.
Royal Bank of Scotland Ltd., The.
Ulster Bank Ltd.
Williams Deacon's Bank Ltd.
Williams & Glyn's Bank Ltd.
Yorkshire Bank Ltd.

EXPLANATORY NOTE

(*This Note is not part of the Order.*)

This Order exempts from section 1(1) of the Exchange Control Act 1947 the purchase outside the United Kingdom and the Channel Islands by travellers resident here of foreign currency—

(*a*) with sterling or scheduled territories currency notes which they may export on their persons or in their baggage (this Order revokes and article 2 replaces the Exchange Control (Purchase of Foreign Currency) Order 1965 as amended); and

(*b*) by the encashment of sterling cheques if the traveller holds a cheque card issued by a bank specified in the Schedule and the cheque is drawn within the limits imposed on the use of the cheque card.

Both exemptions are subject to conditions limiting the use to which such foreign currency may be put to travel expenditure (as defined) and limiting the period for which it may be retained to one month after the traveller's return.

1970 No. 791 (C.16)

COMMONWEALTH IMMIGRANTS

The Immigration Appeals Act 1969 (Commencement No. 2) Order 1970

Made - - - *21st May* 1970

In exercise of the power conferred on me by section 24(5) of the Immigration Appeals Act 1969(**a**), I hereby make the following Order:—

1. This Order may be cited as the Immigration Appeals Act 1969 (Commencement No. 2) Order 1970.

2. The following provisions of the Immigration Appeals Act 1969 shall come into operation on 1st July 1970, that is to say:—

(*a*) section 1, together with Schedule 1 (the adjudicators and the Tribunal);

(*b*) subsections (1) and (2) of section 2, in so far as they relate to an appeal to an adjudicator under subsection (1)(*c*) against a refusal of an application for the grant of an entry certificate;

(*c*) subsections (1), (3) and (4) of section 3, in so far as they relate to an appeal to an adjudicator under subsection (1)(*b*) against the variation of a condition of admission or under subsection (1)(*c*) against a refusal to revoke or vary such a condition;

(*d*) section 4 (appeal against deportation orders);

(*e*) section 6 (notice of matters in respect of which there are rights of appeal);

(*f*) section 7 (review by Tribunal of determination of adjudicator);

(*g*) section 8 (determination of appeals);

(*h*) section 9 (special procedure in cases involving national security or forgery of documents);

(*i*) section 10 (reference of cases for further consideration);

(*j*) section 11 (rules of procedure);

(*k*) section 12 (release of appellants pending hearing) together with Schedule 3;

(*l*) section 15 (financial support for organisations providing advice and assistance for persons with rights of appeal);

(*m*) Part II (deportation of Commonwealth citizens for breach of conditions of admission);

(**a**) 1969 c. 21.

(*n*) Part III (miscellaneous and supplementary provisions), except sections 20 and 21 (which came into operation on the passing of the Act).

James Callaghan,
One of Her Majesty's Principal
Secretaries of State.

Home Office,
Whitehall.
21st May 1970.

EXPLANATORY NOTE

(*This Note is not part of the Order.*)

This Order brings into operation on 1st July 1970 the provisions of the Immigration Appeals Act 1969 mentioned in the Order. These include the provisions for appeals to the adjudicators or Tribunal against decisions other than the refusal of admission to the United Kingdom, directions for removal or the imposition of a condition of admission.

1970 No. 792 (C.17)

ALIENS

The Aliens (Appeals) (Commencement No. 1) Order 1970

Made - - - *21st May* 1970

In exercise of the power conferred on me by Article 1(3) of the Aliens (Appeals) Order 1970(**a**), I hereby make the following Order:—

1. This Order may be cited as the Aliens (Appeals) (Commencement No. 1) Order 1970.

2. The following provisions of the Aliens (Appeals) Order 1970 shall come into operation on 1st July 1970, that is to say:—

(*a*) paragraphs (1) and (2) of Article 2, in so far as they relate to an appeal to an adjudicator under paragraph (1)(*c*) against a refusal of an application for the grant of a visa;

(*b*) Article 3, in so far as it relates to an appeal to an adjudicator—

(i) under paragraph (1)(*b*) against the variation of a landing condition,

(ii) under paragraph (1)(*c*) against a refusal to revoke or vary a landing condition,

(iii) under paragraph (1)(*d*) against the imposition of a special restriction or a refusal to revoke or vary any such restriction, or

(iv) under paragraph (1)(*e*) against a refusal of permission under paragraph 2 or 3 of Schedule 1 to the Aliens Order 1953(**b**), as amended (**c**), or a refusal of such permission in the terms applied for, or the imposition of a condition as a term of such permission;

(*c*) Article 4 (appeal against deportation orders);

(*d*) Article 6(1) (further appeal from adjudicator to Tribunal);

(*e*) Article 7 (determination of appeals);

(*f*) Article 8 (special procedure in cases involving national security, etc., or forgery of documents);

(*g*) Article 9 (reference of cases for further consideration);

(*h*) Article 10 (release of appellants pending hearing);

(*i*) Article 12(2) and (3) (supplementary provisions);

(**a**) S.I. 1970/151 (1970 I, p. 663). (**b**) S.I. 1953/1671 (1953 I, p. 94).

(**c**) The amending Orders are not relevant to the subject matter of this Order.

(*j*) Article 13 (interpretation of Part II);

(*k*) Part III (amendments of Aliens Order 1953).

James Callaghan,

One of Her Majesty's Principal Secretaries of State.

Home Office,
Whitehall.
21st May 1970.

EXPLANATORY NOTE

(*This Note is not part of the Order.*)

This Order brings into operation on 1st July 1970 the provisions of the Aliens (Appeals) Order 1970 mentioned in the Order. These include the provisions for appeals to the adjudicators or Tribunal against decisions other than the refusal of leave to land in the United Kingdom, directions for removal or the imposition of a landing condition.

1970 No. 793

COMMONWEALTH IMMIGRANTS

ALIENS

The Immigration Appeals (Notices) Regulations 1970

Made - - -	21*st May* 1970
Laid before Parliament	28*th May* 1970
Coming into Operation	1*st July* 1970

In exercise of the powers conferred upon me by section 6 of the Immigration Appeals Act 1969**(a)**, both as enacted and as applied and modified by Article 12(1) of the Aliens (Appeals) Order 1970**(b)**, I hereby make the following Regulations:—

Citation

1. These Regulations may be cited as the Immigration Appeals (Notices) Regulations 1970 and shall come into operation on 1st July 1970.

Interpretation

2.—(1) In these Regulations—

"the Appeals Act" means the Immigration Appeals Act 1969;

"the Appeals Order" means the Aliens (Appeals) Order 1970;

"appeal" means an appeal under Part I of the Appeals Act or Part II of the Appeals Order;

"entry certificate officer" means a person having authority to grant an entry certificate on behalf of the Government of the United Kingdom;

"visa officer" means a person having authority to grant a visa on behalf of the Government of the United Kingdom.

(2) Any reference in these Regulations to a Regulation is a reference to a Regulation contained in these Regulations.

(3) The Interpretation Act 1889**(c)** shall apply to the interpretation of these Regulations as it applies to the interpretation of an Act of Parliament.

Notice of decisions and actions

3.—(1) Subject to the provisions of paragraph (3) below, when any decision or action against which an appeal can be brought is taken, notice in writing thereof shall as soon as practicable be given in accordance with the provisions of these Regulations to the person by whom such an appeal can be brought.

(2) Any such notice shall be given—

(*a*) in the case of a decision or action taken by an immigration officer in the exercise of powers conferred on him as such, by the immigration officer;

(a) 1969 c. 21. **(b)** S.I. 1970/151 (1970 I, p. 663). **(c)** 1889 c. 63.

(*b*) in the case of a refusal of an application for the grant of an entry certificate or visa, by the entry certificate officer or visa officer who refused the application;

(*c*) where the officer required by sub-paragraph (*a*) or (*b*) above to give the notice is for any reason unable to do so, by such immigration officer, entry certificate officer or visa officer as may be designated for the purpose by the Secretary of State;

(*d*) in the case of a decision or action other than one mentioned in sub-paragraph (*a*) or (*b*) above, by the Secretary of State.

(3) It shall not be necessary to give notice in compliance with the requirements of paragraph (1) above if the officer or authority required by paragraph (2) above to give it has no knowledge of the whereabouts or place of abode of the person to whom it is to be given.

Contents of notice

4.—(1) Subject to the provisions of paragraph (2) below, any notice given under Regulation 3 shall—

(*a*) include a statement of the reasons for the decision or action to which it relates;

(*b*) if it relates to the giving of directions for the removal of any person from the United Kingdom, include a statement of the country or territory to which he is to be removed; and

(*c*) be accompanied by a statement informing the person to whom the notice is given of—

(i) his right of appeal and the relevant provision of the Appeals Act or the Appeals Order, as the case may be;

(ii) the manner in which the appeal should be brought and the address to which a notice of appeal should be sent;

(iii) the time within which the appeal should be brought; and

(iv) the facilities available for advice and assistance in connection therewith.

(2) In the case of a notice which relates to any such decision as is mentioned in section 3(1) (*b*) of the Appeals Act or Article 3(1) (*b*) of the Appeals Order (variation of conditions of entry), it shall not be necessary to comply with the requirements of paragraph (1) above if the decision was taken at the request of the person to whom the notice is given and was not less favourable to him than that which was requested.

Notices under Commonwealth Immigrants Act 1962 *and Aliens Order* 1953

5.—(1) Subject to the provisions of paragraph (2) below, where notice in writing of any decision is given under paragraph 2 of Schedule 1 to the Commonwealth Immigrants Act 1962(**a**) or Article 5 of the Aliens Order 1953(**b**) (refusal of entry and conditions of entry) the provisions of these Regulations shall, if the statements required by Regulation 4 are included in or accompany the notice, be deemed to have been complied with in relation to the decision.

(2) Paragraph (1) above shall not apply in the case of a notice given to a person in charge of a party in pursuance of sub-paragraph (2) of the said paragraph 2 or paragraph (2) of the said Article 5.

(**a**) 1962 c. 21. (**b**) S.I. 1953/1671 (1953 I, p. 94).

Service of notice

6. Any notice required by Regulation 3 to be given to any person may be sent by post in a registered letter or by the recorded delivery service or delivered to his last known or usual place of abode.

James Callaghan,
One of Her Majesty's Principal
Secretaries of State.

Home Office,
Whitehall.
21st May 1970.

EXPLANATORY NOTE

(*This Note is not part of the Regulations.*)

These Regulations provide for the giving of notices of decisions and actions against which appeals lie under the Immigration Appeals Act 1969 and the Aliens (Appeals) Order 1970.

1970 No. 794

COMMONWEALTH IMMIGRANTS

ALIENS

The Immigration Appeals (Procedure) Rules 1970

Made - - - -	21*st May* 1970
Laid before Parliament	28*th May* 1970
Coming into Operation	1*st July* 1970

ARRANGEMENT OF RULES

In exercise of the powers conferred upon me by section 11 of the Immigration Appeals Act 1969**(a)**, both as enacted and as applied and modified by Article 12(1) of the Aliens (Appeals) Order 1970**(b)**, and by section 7(2) of the said Act and Article 6(2) of the said Order, I hereby, make the following Rules:—

PART I
INTRODUCTION

Citation and commencement

1. These Rules may be cited as the Immigration Appeals (Procedure) Rules 1970 and shall come into operation on 1st July 1970.

Interpretation

2.—(1) In these Rules, unless the context otherwise requires—

"the Act of 1962" means the Commonwealth Immigrants Act 1962**(c)**;

"adjudicator" means an adjudicator appointed for the purposes of Part I of the Appeals Act;

"the Aliens Order" means the Aliens Order 1953**(d)** as amended **(e)**;

"the Appeals Act" means the Immigration Appeals Act 1969 and, in relation to an appeal under Part II of the Appeals Order, means that Act as applied and modified by that Order;

"the Appeals Order" means the Aliens (Appeals) Order 1970;

"appeal" means an appeal under Part I of the Appeals Act or Part II of the Appeals Order, and "appellant" shall be construed accordingly;

"appellate authority" means an adjudicator or the Tribunal;

"chairman" means any member of the Tribunal appointed under paragraph 13 of Schedule 1 to the Appeals Act to act on behalf of the president;

"entry certificate officer" means a person having authority to grant an entry certificate on behalf of the Government of the United Kingdom;

"the president" means the president of the Tribunal;

"the Tribunal" means the Tribunal appointed for the purposes of Part I of the Appeals Act;

"visa officer" means a person having authority to grant a visa on behalf of the Government of the United Kingdom.

(2) In Part IV of these Rules any reference to an appellant in relation to an appeal to the Tribunal from the determination of an adjudicator under section 7 of the Appeals Act or Article 6 of the Appeals Order shall be construed as a reference to the person against whom the decision or action in question was taken, whether he is the appellant or the respondent in that appeal.

(3) Any reference in these Rules to a Rule is a reference to a Rule contained in these Rules.

(4) Any reference in these Rules to a form is a reference to a form set out in the Schedule to these Rules.

(5) Any reference in these Rules to any enactment is a reference thereto as amended, and includes a reference thereto as extended or applied by or under any other enactment.

(6) The Interpretation Act 1889**(f)** shall apply to the interpretation of these Rules as it applies to the interpretation of an Act of Parliament.

(a) 1969 c. 21. **(b)** S.I. 1970/151 (1970 I, p.663). **(c)** 1962 c. 21. **(d)** S.I. 1953/1671 (1953 I, p. 94). **(e)** S.I. 1953/1671, 1957/597, 1960/2214, 1964/2034, 1967/1282, 1968/1649, 1970/151 (1953 I, p. 94; 1957 I, p. 142; 1960 I, p. 291; 1964 III, p. 5116; 1967 II, p. 3712; 1968 III, p. 4471; 1970 I, p. 663). **(f)** 1889 c. 63.

PART II

APPEAL TO ADJUDICATOR OR TRIBUNAL AT FIRST INSTANCE

Application of Part II

3. This Part applies to appeals to an adjudicator and, under Article 4(1)(*b*) of the Appeals Order, to the Tribunal, and references in this Part to an appeal, an appellant or proceedings shall be construed accordingly.

Time limit for appealing

4.—(1) Notice of appeal—

(*a*) under section 2(1)(*a*) of the Appeals Act against a refusal to admit a person into the United Kingdom; or

(*b*) under Article 2(1)(*a*) of the Appeals Order against a refusal to grant a person leave to land in the United Kingdom,

may be given at any time before the ship or aircraft in which he is to be removed from the United Kingdom departs.

(2) Notice of appeal under section 2(1)(*b*) of the Appeals Act or Article 2(1)(*b*) of the Appeals Order against a prohibition on landing from a ship at a port may be given at any time before the ship departs.

(3) Notice of appeal—

(*a*) under section 2(1)(*c*) of the Appeals Act against a refusal of an application for the grant of an entry certificate; or

(*b*) under Article 2(1)(*c*) of the Appeals Order against a refusal of an application for the grant of a visa,

may be given not later than 3 months after the refusal.

(4) Notice of appeal under Article 2(1)(*d*) of the Appeals Order against a refusal by the Secretary of State to revoke an instruction which names a person who is to be refused leave to land may be given not later than 28 days after the refusal.

(5) Notice of appeal under section 3 of the Appeals Act or Article 3 of the Appeals Order (conditions of entry) against any decision may be given—

(*a*) in the case of an appeal under subsection (1)(*a*) of that section or paragraph (1)(*a*) of that Article (imposition of time conditions), not later than 24 hours after the taking of the decision;

(*b*) in any other case, not later than 14 days after the taking of the decision.

(6) Notice of appeal under section 4 of the Appeals Act or Article 4 of the Appeals Order (deportation) against any decision may be given—

(*a*) in the case of an appeal under subsection (1)(*b*) of that section or paragraph (1)(*a*)(ii) of that Article (refusal by the Secretary of State to revoke a deportation order), not later than 28 days after the taking of the decision;

(*b*) in any other case, not later than 14 days after the taking of the decision.

(7) Notice of appeal under section 5 of the Appeals Act or Article 5 of the Appeals Order against the giving of directions for the removal of a person from the United Kingdom may be given—

(*a*) in the case of an appeal under subsection (3) of that section or paragraph (3) of that Article in respect of directions given in consequence of a refusal of admission under section 2(1) of the Act of 1962 or a refusal of leave to land under Article 1 of the Aliens Order, as the case may be, at any time before the ship or aircraft in which he is to be removed from the United Kingdom departs;

(*b*) in any other case, not later than 14 days after the giving of the directions.

(8) Where notice in writing of any decision or action is required by the Immigration Appeals (Notices) Regulations 1970**(a)** to be given and it is sent by post, the day on which it was so sent shall, for the purposes of this Rule, be deemed to be the day on which the decision or action was taken.

Notice of appeal

5.—(1) Notice of appeal shall be given by completing Part I of Form 1 and so much of Part II thereof as relates to the notice and serving it on the appropriate authority specified in paragraph (2) below:

Provided that notice of appeal under—

(*a*) section 2(1)(*a*) or (*b*) of the Appeals Act or Article 2(1)(*a*) or (*b*) of the Appeals Order (refusal of entry or prohibition on seaman landing); or

(*b*) section 5(3) of the Appeals Act or Article 5(3) of the Appeals Order against the giving of directions for removal in consequence of a refusal of admission under section 2(1) of the Act of 1962 or a refusal of leave to land under Article 1 of the Aliens Order,

may, if the appellant is in the United Kingdom, be given orally to any immigration officer (whether or not responsible for the decision or action in question) by him or by a person duly authorised by him in that behalf or, in the case of an appellant who is a minor or who is for any reason incapable of acting, by any person acting on his behalf.

(2) For the purposes of paragraph (1) above the appropriate authority is—

(*a*) in the case of an appeal under—

(i) section 2(1)(*a*) or (*b*) or 3(1)(*a*) of the Appeals Act (refusal of entry, prohibition on seaman landing or imposition of conditions of entry); or

(ii) Article 2(1)(*a*) or (*b*) or 3(1)(*a*) of the Appeals Order (refusal of entry, prohibition on seaman landing or imposition of conditions of entry); or

(iii) section 5(3) of the Appeals Act or Article 5(3) of the Appeals Order against the giving of directions for removal from the United Kingdom in consequence of a refusal of admission under section 2(1) of the Act of 1962 or a refusal of leave to land under Article 1 of the Aliens Order, as the case may be,

the immigration officer responsible for the decision or action in question;

(*b*) in the case of an appeal under section 2(1)(*c*) of the Appeals Act (refusal of entry certificate), the entry certificate officer responsible for the decision in question;

(*c*) in the case of an appeal under Article 2(1)(*c*) of the Appeals Order (refusal of visa), the visa officer responsible for the decision in question;

(*d*) in any other case, the Secretary of State.

(3) The grounds of an appeal set out in Form 1 may be varied or amplified at any time during the course of the appeal.

(a) S.I. 1970/793 (1970 II, p.2506).

(4) Form 1 shall be signed by the appellant or by a person duly authorised by him in that behalf or, in the case of an appellant who is a minor or who is for any reason incapable of acting, by any person acting on his behalf.

(5)(*a*) An authority to whom notice of appeal has been given in accordance with these Rules shall, unless the appellant subsequently gives notice of the abandonment of his appeal, take such steps as are necessary to ensure that the notice of appeal is referred to an adjudicator or the Tribunal, as appropriate, together with such particulars relating to the nature and grounds of the appeal as have been given by the appellant.

(*b*) The steps required by sub-paragraph (*a*) above shall be taken, in the case of an immigration officer, as soon as practicable after the giving of the notice of appeal or, in any other case, as soon as practicable after the written statement of facts required by Rule 7 has been prepared.

(6) Where a written notice of appeal addressed to any immigration officer, entry certificate officer or visa officer has been sent or delivered in accordance with Rule 40 but that officer is for any reason unable to receive it, the notice shall be deemed to have been served on that officer; and in any such case the Secretary of State shall cause the steps required by paragraph (5) above to be taken by another officer in accordance with that paragraph.

Parties

6.—(1) In the case of an appeal against a decision or action taken by an immigration officer in the exercise of powers conferred on him as such, the appellant and the immigration officer shall be the parties to the appeal.

(2) In the case of an appeal—

(*a*) under section 2(1)(*c*) of the Appeals Act against a refusal of an application for the grant of an entry certificate; or

(*b*) under Article 2(1)(*c*) of the Appeals Order against a refusal of an application for the grant of a visa,

the appellant and the entry certificate officer or visa officer who refused the application shall be the parties to the appeal.

(3) In the case of an appeal against any decision or action other than one mentioned in paragraph (1) or (2) above, the appellant and the Secretary of State shall be the parties to the appeal.

(4) The Secretary of State shall be treated as a party to any appeal, where he would not otherwise be a party to it by virtue of this Rule, upon giving written notice to the appellate authority at any time during the course of the appeal stating that he desires to be so treated.

(5) If any party to an appeal is or claims to be a refugee within the competence of the United Nations High Commissioner for Refugees, the United Kingdom Representative of the High Commissioner shall be treated as a party to the appeal upon giving written notice to the appellate authority at any time during the course of the appeal stating that he desires to be so treated.

(6) If an officer is for any reason unable to take part in the proceedings in any appeal to which he would otherwise be a party by virtue of paragraph (1) or (2) above, the Secretary of State shall be treated as a party to the appeal in place of the officer; and thereupon any notice or other document sent or given by or to the officer for the purposes of the appeal shall be deemed to have been sent or given by or to the Secretary of State.

Explanatory statement by respondent

7.—(1) Subject to the provisions of paragraph (2) below, the respondent in an appeal shall, as soon as practicable after notice of the appeal is given, prepare a written statement of the facts relating to the decision or action in question and the reasons therefor and take such steps as are necessary to ensure that the statement is referred to an adjudicator or the Tribunal, as appropriate, and that a copy thereof is given to the appellant.

(2) It shall not be necessary for an immigration officer who is the respondent in an appeal to comply with the requirements of paragraph (1) above if he is of the opinion that it is not practicable to do so, having regard to the time available before the hearing of the appeal; but he shall then, as soon as practicable after notice of the appeal is given, give written notice to the appellate authority and the appellant that he is of that opinion and that a statement of the facts relating to the decision or action in question and the reasons therefor will be given orally at the hearing of the appeal.

(3) At the commencement of any hearing before an appellate authority, the authority shall give to the respondent an opportunity to amplify orally the written statement given in accordance with paragraph (1) above or, if no such written statement has been given, shall obtain from the respondent an oral statement of the facts relating to the decision or action in question and the reasons therefor.

(4) In this Rule "respondent" in relation to an appeal means the person, other than the appellant, who is a party to the appeal by virtue of Rule 6(1), (2), (3) or (6).

Appeal against directions for removal on grounds of destination

8. In the case of an appeal under section 5(3) of the Appeals Act or Article 5(3) of the Appeals Order (objection to removal to a particular country), the appellant shall submit with the notice of appeal a statement in writing of the matters put forward in support of the appeal.

Supply of documents

9. Subject to the provisions of section 9 of the Appeals Act and Article 8 of the Appeals Order (cases involving national security, etc. or forgery of documents), the appellate authority shall cause copies of all notices and other documents required for an appeal to be supplied to every party to the appeal.

Determination of appeal without hearing

10. An appellate authority may dispose of an appeal without a hearing if—

(*a*) no party to the appeal has requested a hearing; or

(*b*) the appellate authority has decided, after giving every other party to the appeal an opportunity of replying to any representations submitted in writing by or on behalf of the appellant, to allow the appeal; or

(*c*) the appellate authority is satisfied that the appellant is outside the United Kingdom and that no person is authorised to represent him at a hearing; or

(*d*) in the case of an appeal under section 5(3) of the Appeals Act or Article 5(3) of the Appeals Order (objection to removal to a particular country), the appellate authority is of opinion that the matters put forward in support of the appeal in pursuance of Rule 8 do not warrant a hearing.

PART III

APPEAL TO TRIBUNAL FROM ADJUDICATOR

Application of Part III

11. This Part applies to appeals to the Tribunal from the determination of an adjudicator under section 7 of the Appeals Act or Article 6 of the Appeals Order, and references in this Part to an appeal, an appellant or proceedings shall be construed accordingly.

Leave to appeal

12.—(1) An appeal shall lie only with the leave of the adjudicator or the Tribunal in every case except—

(*a*) where the determination relates to an appeal under section 3(1)(*b*) of the Appeals Act or Article 3(1)(*b*) of the Appeals Order against the variation of a condition of admission or landing condition imposed on a person otherwise than in consequence of an application made by him for such a variation; and

(*b*) in the circumstances mentioned in section 7(2)(*a*) of the Appeals Act and Article 6(2)(*a*) of the Appeals Order (certificate by Secretary of State as to public interest that case should be decided by Tribunal).

(2) In addition to the circumstances in which leave to appeal must, by virtue of section 7(2)(*b*) of the Appeals Act and Article 6(2)(*b*) of the Appeals Order (existence of entry certificate or visa), be granted, an appellate authority to whom application for leave to appeal as aforesaid is duly made shall grant it—

(*a*) if the authority is satisfied that the determination of the appeal turns upon an arguable point of law; or

(*b*) where an adjudicator has dismissed an appeal by a person who is in the United Kingdom, if the authority is satisfied that the country or territory to which he is to be removed is one to which he is unwilling to go owing to fear of being persecuted there for reasons of race, religion, nationality, membership of a particular social group or political opinion.

(3) In this Rule "landing condition" has the same meaning as in Article 3(1)(*b*) of the Appeals Order.

Time limit for appealing

13.—(1) Application to an adjudicator for leave to appeal shall be made forthwith after the making of the determination in question.

(2) Application to the Tribunal for leave to appeal or notice of appeal may be made or given not later than 7 days after the making of the determination in question.

(3) Where the applicant or the appellant, as the case may be, is the person against whom the decision or action in question was taken and he is not in the United Kingdom, the Isle of Man, the Channel Islands or the Republic of Ireland, paragraph (2) above shall have effect as if for the words "7 days" there were substituted the words "28 days".

Notice of appeal and application for leave to appeal

14.—(1) Subject to the provisions of paragraph (2) below, notice of appeal or an application for leave to appeal shall be given or made by completing Part I of Form 2 and so much of Part II thereof as relates to the notice and serving it on an adjudicator or the Tribunal, as appropriate.

(2) Notwithstanding the provisions of paragraph (1) above, an application to an adjudicator for leave to appeal may be made orally by the applicant or by a person duly authorised by him in that behalf or, in the case of an applicant who is a minor or who is for any reason incapable of acting, by any person acting on his behalf; but in that event the requirements of paragraph (1) above shall be complied with as soon as practicable thereafter.

(3) The grounds of an appeal or application set out in Form 2 may be varied or amplified at any time during the course of the appeal or application.

(4) Form 2 shall be signed by the appellant or applicant, as the case may be, or by a person duly authorised by him in that behalf or, in the case of an appellant or applicant who is a minor or who is for any reason incapable of acting, by any person acting on his behalf.

(5) Where leave to appeal is not required or is given, a notice of application for leave to appeal shall be treated as a notice of appeal; and where such an appeal lies with the leave of an adjudicator or the Tribunal or with the leave of the Tribunal only and notice of appeal is served on the Tribunal, the notice of appeal shall be treated also as an application for leave to appeal.

Parties

15.—(1) On any appeal against the determination of an adjudicator, the persons who were the parties to the appeal before the adjudicator shall be the parties to the appeal before the Tribunal.

(2) The Secretary of State shall be treated as a party to any appeal, where he would not otherwise be a party to it by virtue of paragraph (1) above, upon giving written notice to the Tribunal at any time during the course of the appeal stating that he desires to be so treated.

(3) If any party to an appeal is or claims to be a refugee within the competence of the United Nations High Commissioner for Refugees, the United Kingdom Representative of the High Commissioner shall be treated as a party to the appeal, where he would not otherwise be a party to it by virtue of paragraph (1) above, upon giving written notice to the Tribunal at any time during the course of the appeal stating that he desires to be so treated.

(4) If an officer is for any reason unable to take part in the proceedings in any appeal to which he would otherwise be a party by virtue of paragraph (1) above, the Secretary of State shall be treated as a party to the appeal in place of the officer; and thereupon any notice or other document sent or given by or to the officer for the purpose of the appeal shall be deemed to have been sent or given by or to the Secretary of State.

Evidence

16.—(1) If any party to an appeal wishes to adduce evidence before the Tribunal further to that which was adduced before the adjudicator in the course of the proceedings to which the appeal relates, he shall give notice in writing to that effect to the Tribunal indicating the nature of the evidence; and any such notice shall—

(*a*) in the case of the appellant, be given with the notice of appeal or as soon as practicable after notice of appeal is given;

(*b*) in the case of any other party, as soon as practicable after a copy of the notice of appeal has been received by him.

(2) In any proceedings on an appeal—

(*a*) the Tribunal may, in its discretion, receive or decline to receive further evidence of which notice has been given in accordance with paragraph (1) above, and if any such further evidence is received as aforesaid it shall, if the Tribunal so directs, be given in writing in such manner and at such time as the Tribunal may require;

(*b*) if it appears to the Tribunal that further evidence of which notice has been given as aforesaid should be received or that the evidence before it is insufficient to enable it to arrive at a proper determination of the appeal, it may remit the appeal to the same or another adjudicator for such further evidence as the Tribunal may require to be obtained; and

(*c*) the summary or record taken or kept in accordance with Rule 36 of any evidence received by the adjudicator in the course of the proceedings to which the appeal relates or by an adjudicator to whom the appeal is remitted as aforesaid shall be received as evidence by the Tribunal.

Supply of documents

17. Subject to the provisions of section 9 of the Appeals Act and Article 8 of the Appeals Order (cases involving national security, etc. or forgery of documents), the Tribunal shall cause copies of all notices and other documents required for an appeal, other than those already supplied in accordance with Rule 9, to be supplied to every party to the appeal.

Determination of appeal without hearing

18. The Tribunal may dispose of an appeal without a hearing if—

(*a*) no party to the appeal has requested a hearing; or

(*b*) where the appellant is the person against whom the decision or action in question was taken, the Tribunal is satisfied that he is not in the United Kingdom and that no other person is authorised to represent him at a hearing.

PART IV

GENERAL PROCEDURE

Application for bail

19. An application by an appellant to be released on bail shall—

(*a*) if to an immigration officer or police officer, be made orally; or

(*b*) if to an appellate authority, be made either orally or in Form 3.

Bail

20.—(1) The recognizance of an appellant shall be in Form 4 and that of a surety in Form 5.

(2) Where an appellate authority directs the release of an appellant on bail and the taking of the recognizance is postponed under paragraph 6 of Schedule 3 to the Appeals Act, the authority shall issue a certificate in Form 6 showing the conditions to be endorsed on the recognizance with a view to the recognizance being taken subsequently and the amounts in which the appellant and any sureties are to be bound.

(3) The person having custody of an appellant shall—

(*a*) on receipt of a certificate in Form 7 signed by the secretary of the Tribunal or by the adjudicator stating that the recognizances of any sureties required have been taken, or on being otherwise satisfied that all such recognizances have been taken; and

(*b*) on being satisfied that the appellant has entered into his recognizance, release the appellant.

(4) Paragraphs (1) and (2) above shall not apply to Scotland, and in their application to Scotland paragraph (3) above and Form 7 shall have effect as if for the references to recognizances of sureties having been taken there were substituted references to bail having been taken and for the references to a recognizance there were substituted references to a bail bond.

Notice of time and place of hearing

21.—(1) Subject to the provisions of paragraph (2) below, as soon as practicable after notice of appeal has been given the appellate authority shall, if there is to be a hearing, give notice in writing to every party to the appeal stating the time and place of the hearing.

(2) Where an appellant is detained under paragraph 4 of Schedule 1 to the Act of 1962 or Article 8 of the Aliens Order (detention pending further examination or removal), the appellate authority may, instead of giving notice in writing as aforesaid, cause any immigration officer to be notified orally as to the time and place of the hearing; and thereupon that officer shall take such steps as are necessary to ensure that every party to the appeal is notified accordingly and that the appellant is produced at the hearing.

Power to require particulars

22. An appellate authority may at any time request any party to the appeal to furnish any particulars which appear to be requisite for the determination of the appeal, and thereupon that party shall send the particulars to the appellate authority.

Representation

23.—(1) In any proceedings on an appeal, a party to the appeal may act in person or be represented—

(*a*) in the case of the appellant, by counsel or a solicitor, a consular officer or a person performing functions corresponding to those of a consular officer, a person appointed in that behalf by any voluntary organisation for the time being in receipt of a grant under section 15 of the Appeals Act or, with the leave of the appellate authority, by any other person appearing to the authority to be acting on behalf of the appellant;

(*b*) in the case of the Secretary of State or any officer, by counsel or a solicitor or any officer of the Home Department;

(*c*) in the case of the United Kingdom Representative of the United Nations High Commissioner for Refugees, by a person appointed by him in that behalf.

(2) A person representing a party to an appeal in accordance with paragraph (1) above may take all such steps and do all such things relating to the proceedings as the person whom he represents is by these Rules required or authorised to take or do.

Summoning of witnesses

24.—(1) An appellate authority may, for the purpose of any appeal, by summons require any person in the United Kingdom to attend as a witness at a hearing of the appeal at such time and place as may be specified in the summons and, subject to the provisions of Rule 26(2), at the hearing to answer any questions or produce any documents in his custody or under his control which relate to any matter in question in the appeal:

Provided that no person shall be required, in obedience to such a summons, to go more than 10 miles from his place of residence unless the necessary expenses of his attendance are paid or tendered to him.

(2) Any such summons shall be in Form 8.

Conduct of proceedings at hearings

25. Subject to the provisions of Rules 16 and 31, at any hearing by an appellate authority—

(*a*) the appellate authority shall give each party to the appeal an opportunity to address the authority, to give evidence and to call witnesses, and any party to the appeal may put questions to any person giving evidence before the authority;

(*b*) after any evidence has been taken the appellate authority shall give each party to the appeal an opportunity of making representations on the evidence and on the subject matter of the appeal generally,

but, save as aforesaid and after complying where appropriate with the provisions of Rule 7(3), the appellate authority shall conduct the proceedings in such manner as it considers appropriate in the circumstances for ascertaining the matters in dispute and determining the appeal.

Evidence

26.—(1) An appellate authority may receive oral, documentary or other evidence of any fact which appears to the authority to be relevant to the appeal, notwithstanding that such evidence would be inadmissible in a court of law.

(2) In any proceedings before an appellate authority, no person shall be compelled to give any evidence or produce any document which he could not be compelled to give or produce on the trial of an action in that part of the United Kingdom in which the proceedings are conducted.

(3) An appellate authority may require any witness to give evidence on oath or affirmation, and for that purpose an oath or affirmation in due form may be administered.

Inspection of documentary evidence

27. Subject to the provisions of section 9 of the Appeals Act and Article 8 of the Appeals Order (cases involving national security, etc. or forgery of documents), when an appellate authority takes into consideration documentary evidence the authority shall give every party to the appeal an opportunity of inspecting that evidence and taking copies thereof.

Burden of proof

28.—(1) If in any proceedings before an appellate authority a party thereto asserts that a decision or action taken against him under any provisions of the Act of 1962, Part II of the Appeals Act or the Aliens Order ought not to have been taken on the grounds that he is not a person to whom those provisions apply, it shall lie on him to prove that he is not such a person.

(2) If in any proceedings before an appellate authority a party thereto asserts any fact of such a kind that, if the assertion were made to the Secretary of State or any officer for the purposes of any of the provisions of the Act of 1962 or any immigration rules, it would by virtue of those provisions or rules be for him to satisfy the Secretary of State or officer of the truth thereof, it shall lie on that party to prove that the assertion is true.

(3) In paragraph (2) above "immigration rules" means immigration rules as defined in section 24(2) of the Appeals Act or immigration rules as defined in Article 13(1) of the Appeals Order.

Exclusion of public

29.—(1) Subject to the provisions of paragraph (2) below, an appellate authority may—

(*a*) at the request of a party, exclude any member of the public or members of the public generally from any hearing by the authority; or

(*b*) whether or not at the request of a party, exclude any member of the public who, in the opinion of the authority, is behaving in a manner likely to interfere with the proper conduct of the proceedings,

but save as aforesaid any hearing of an appeal shall take place in public.

(2) Nothing in this Rule shall prevent a member of the Council on Tribunals or of its Scottish Committee from attending a hearing in his capacity as such, except where the Secretary of State has given a certificate under the provisions of section 9(3)(*a*) of the Appeals Act or Article 8(3)(*a*) of the Appeals Order (cases involving national security) and the hearing takes place in the absence of a party to the appeal and his representatives accordingly.

Transfer of proceedings

30.—(1) Where any proceedings before an adjudicator have not been disposed of by the adjudicator and the chief adjudicator, or any person for the time being carrying out the functions of the chief adjudicator, is of the opinion that it is not practicable without undue delay for the proceedings to be completed by that adjudicator, he shall make arrangements for them to be dealt with by another adjudicator; and any adjudicator to whom any proceedings are transferred as aforesaid shall have power to deal with them as if they had been commenced before him.

(2) In the case of an appeal to an adjudicator under section 2(1)(*a*) of the Appeals Act or Article 2(1)(*a*) of the Appeals Order (refusal of entry), if the adjudicator considers that it is expedient for the appeal to be dealt with by another adjudicator—

(*a*) at a place elsewhere by reason of the existence there of facilities for the medical examination or further medical examination of the appellant; or

(*b*) by reason of the first-mentioned adjudicator's personal connection with or interest in the circumstances of the appeal,

the first-mentioned adjudicator may make arrangements for it to be dealt with by that other adjudicator; and any adjudicator to whom an appeal is transferred as aforesaid shall have power to deal with it as if it had been commenced before him.

(3) Where any proceedings are transferred to an adjudicator in accordance with paragraph (1) or (2) above or referred to the Tribunal in accordance with directions given under section 9(1) of the Appeals Act or Article 8(1)(*a*) of the Appeals Order (cases involving national security, etc.), any notice or other document sent or given by or to the adjudicator from whom the proceedings were transferred or referred shall be deemed to have been sent or given by or to the first-mentioned adjudicator or the Tribunal, as the case may be.

Hearing of appeal in absence of appellant

31. An appellate authority may hear an appeal in the absence of the appellant if satisfied that he is not in the United Kingdom.

Summary determination of appeals

32.—(1) Subject to the provisions of paragraph (2) below, where it appears to an appellate authority that the issues raised on an appeal have been determined—

(*a*) in the case of an appeal before an adjudicator, by the same or another adjudicator or by the Tribunal, or

(*b*) in the case of an appeal before the Tribunal, by the Tribunal,

in previous proceedings under Part I of the Appeals Act or Part II of the Appeals Order to which the appellant was a party on the basis of facts which did not materially differ from those to which the appeal relates, the authority may forthwith determine the appeal without a hearing.

(2) Before an appellate authority determines an appeal without a hearing in accordance with paragraph (1) above, the authority shall give the parties an opportunity of making representations to the effect that the appeal ought not to be so determined.

(3) Where an appeal is determined without a hearing in accordance with paragraph (1) above, the appellate authority shall give written notice to the parties that the appeal has been so determined, and any such notice shall contain a statement of the issues raised on the appeal and specify the previous proceedings in which those issues were determined.

Miscellaneous powers

33. An appellate authority may—

(*a*) postpone the time fixed for the hearing of an appeal;

(*b*) give directions on any matter arising in connection with an appeal to any party who requests them;

(*c*) if notice of the abandonment of an appeal is given, dismiss the appeal;

(*d*) if the parties to an appeal agree in writing upon the terms of a determination to be made by the appellate authority, determine the appeal accordingly;

(*e*) adjourn the hearing of any evidence or representations or the consideration of an appeal to such date as the authority may determine; and

(*f*) subject to the provisions of the Appeals Act, the Appeals Order and these Rules, regulate its own procedure.

Irregularities

34. Any irregularity resulting from failure to comply with these Rules before an appellate authority has reached its decision shall not of itself render the proceedings void, but the appellate authority may, and shall if it considers that any person may have been prejudiced, take such steps as it thinks fit before reaching its decision to cure the irregularity, whether by amendment of any document, the giving of any notice or otherwise.

Recording of determinations and reasons therefor

35.—(1) The determination on any appeal shall be recorded by the appellate authority in a document signed by the adjudicator or, as the case may be, the president or presiding chairman and the reasons for the determination shall be set out therein.

(2) The appellate authority shall, as soon as practicable, cause a copy of the document referred to in paragraph (1) above to be sent to every party to the appeal.

Record of proceedings

36. The appellate authority shall cause a summary of the proceedings before it to be taken, except insofar as a record of them is kept by means of shorthand notes or by mechanical means.

Part V

Miscellaneous

References by the Secretary of State

37. An appellate authority shall consider any matter referred to it by the Secretary of State for further consideration under section 10 of the Appeals Act or Article 9 of the Appeals Order in whatever manner it thinks appropriate.

Performance of functions of Tribunal

38. Any function conferred on the Tribunal by Schedule 3 to the Appeals Act or Rule 24 and any function of the Tribunal in relation to applications for leave to appeal may be performed by the president or a chairman acting alone.

Time

39.—(1) Where the time provided by these Rules for doing any act expires on a Sunday or public holiday and by reason thereof the act cannot be done on that day, the act shall be in time if done on the next working day.

(2) Where, under these Rules, an act is to be done not later than a specified period after any event, the period shall be calculated from the expiry of the day on which the event occurred.

Notices etc.

40.—(1) Any notice or other document required or authorised by these Rules to be sent or given to any person or authority may be sent by post in a registered letter or by the recorded delivery service or delivered—

(*a*) in the case of a document directed to the Tribunal, to the secretary of the Tribunal;

(*b*) in the case of a document directed to an adjudicator, to any person employed as his clerk;

(*c*) in the case of a document directed to the Secretary of State, to the Under Secretary of State, Home Office, Immigration and Nationality Department (Appeals Section), Princeton House, 271-277 High Holborn, London, W.C.1;

(*d*) in the case of a document directed to an immigration officer, entry certificate officer or visa officer, to the address specified in the statement issued in relation to the decision or action in question under Regulation 4(1)(*c*) of the Immigration Appeals (Notices) Regulations 1970 or, if no such statement has been issued, to the address specified in sub-paragraph (*c*) above;

(*e*) in the case of a document directed to any other person, to his address for service specified in any notice given under these Rules, or to his last known or usual place of abode,

and, if sent or given to a person representing a party to an appeal in accordance with Rule 23(1), shall be deemed to have been sent or given to that party.

(2) A party to an appeal may at any time by notice to the appellate authority change his address for service under these Rules.

Variation of forms

41. The forms set out in the Schedule to these Rules or forms substantially to the like effect may be used with such variations as the circumstances may require.

James Callaghan,
One of Her Majesty's Principal
Secretaries of State.

Home Office,
Whitehall.
21st May 1970.

Rules 2(4) and 41

SCHEDULE

FORMS

Rule 5

Form 1

IMMIGRATION APPEALS ACT 1969

Notice of appeal to adjudicator or Tribunal at first instance

To the *Adjudicator/*Tribunal

PART I

Particulars of appellant:

	Forenames	Surname	Date of birth
Full name: (Block letters)			

Nationality:

Address:
(If detained
give address
where detained)

Particulars of decision or action appealed against:—

The grounds of appeal are as follows:—

A hearing of the appeal *is/*is not requested

PART II

*The appellant is applying for bail (*see* Note (*a*) below)

*The appellant objects to removal to the country/territory to which he is to be removed, namely...

on the grounds set out in the attached statement (*see* Note (*b*) below)

A copy of the notice of the decision or action appealed against is annexed hereto.

Signed...
(Appellant or authorised representative)

Date...

---

*Delete words which are inapplicable.

Notes (a) An application for bail should normally be supported by the appropriate form, but may be made orally. Such an application may be made subsequently.

(b) An objection to removal to a particular country or territory must be accompanied by a written statement as to the grounds for the objection.

Form 2 Rule 14

IMMIGRATION APPEALS ACT 1969

Notice of appeal or application for leave to appeal from adjudicator

To the *Adjudicator/*Tribunal

PART I

Particulars of appellant:

	Forenames	Surname	Date of birth
Full name: (Block letters)			

Nationality:

Address:
(if detained
give address
where detained)

Particulars of determination of the adjudicator appealed against:—

The grounds of appeal are as follows:—

A hearing of the appeal *is/*is not requested

PART II

The appellant is applying for

*Leave to appeal to the Tribunal

*Bail (*see* Note (*a*) below)

*The appellant objects to removal to the country/territory to which he is to be removed, namely..
on the grounds set out in the attached statement (*see* Note (*b*) below)

*The appellant wishes to adduce further evidence before the Tribunal as follows:—

A copy of the notice of the determination of the adjudicator appealed against is annexed hereto.

Signed......................................
(Appellant or authorised representative)

Date...

---

*Delete words which are inapplicable.

Notes (a) An application for bail should normally be supported by the appropriate form, but may be made orally. Such an application may be made subsequently.

(b) An objection to removal to a particular country or territory must be accompanied by a written statement as to the grounds for the objection.

Rule 19 Form 3

IMMIGRATION APPEALS ACT 1969

Application to appellate authority for bail

To the *Adjudicator/*Tribunal

Particulars of appellant:

	Forenames	Surname
Full name: (Block letters)		

Address where detained:

Give the appellant's address if bail were granted, and the amount of the recognizance in which he would agree to be bound.
Address if granted bail
Amount of recognizance offered £..

Give the names, addresses and occupations of two persons who might act as sureties if bail were granted and the amounts of the recognizances in which they might agree to be bound.

1st Surety:
Name, address, occupation
Amount of recognizance offered £..

2nd Surety:
Name, address,occupation
Amount of recognizance offered £..

---

*If bail has been granted by an adjudicator in the course of the appeal state:—
Amount of recognizances:

Appellant	Sureties	
£..	£....................	£..............

Were the sureties the persons named above?

What, if any, special conditions were imposed?

The appellant applies for bail on the following grounds:—

Signed..
(Appellant or authorised representative)

Date...

*Delete words which are inapplicable.

Form 4 Rule 20(1)

IMMIGRATION APPEALS ACT 1969

Recognizance of appellant

I, ...(hereinafter called the appellant) acknowledge that I owe to Her Majesty The Queen the sum of £.............., payment thereof to be enforced against me by due process of law if I fail to comply with the condition[s] endorsed hereon.

Signed..

Address at which appellant proposes to reside pending appeal ....
....
....
....

Taken before me the............................day of........................, 19......, at..

Signed..

Office..

(*Endorsement*)

Condition[*s*]

The condition[s] of this recognizance is [are] that if the appellant appears before ....(appellate authority) at............................ (time and place) unless the appellate authority otherwise orders, then this recognizance shall be void, but otherwise shall remain in full force(1).

(1) Conditions appearing to the appellate authority to be likely to result in the appellant's appearance at the time and place required may be added.

Form 5 Rule 20(1)

IMMIGRATION APPEALS ACT 1969

Recognizance of appellant's surety

I,..acknowledge that I owe to Her Majesty the Queen the sum of.., payment thereof to be enforced against me by due process of law if.......................... detained in..fails to comply with the condition endorsed hereon.

Signed ....

Address ....
....
....
....

Taken before me the..............................day of ...., 19......, at...

Signed.....................................

Office.......................................

(*Endorsement*)

Condition

The condition of the recognizance is that if the said.. appears before...(appellate authority) at.............. ....(time and place) unless the appellate authority otherwise orders, then this recognizance shall be void, but otherwise shall remain in full force.

Rule 20(2) Form 6

IMMIGRATION APPEALS ACT 1969

Certificate of conditions of bail

I hereby certify that...(appellate authority) has granted bail and has fixed the amount of the recognizance to be entered into by..
....
detained in..at the sum of...and.....................surety in......... [each] conditioned for the appearance of the said........... .... before ....(appellate authority) at...(time and place) unless the appellate authority otherwise orders.*

Signed...

Date ....

*Add, in the case of the appellant, any other conditions specified by the appellate authority.

Rule 20(3) and (4) Form 7

IMMIGRATION APPEALS ACT 1969

Certificate that all recognizances taken

I hereby certify that the recognizances of the sureties of.. ....detained in ....have been taken.

Signed...

(Secretary of the Tribunal/Adjudicator)

Date ....

Form 8 Rule 24

IMMIGRATION APPEALS ACT 1969

Summons to witness

To .... (name)

of ....(address)

An appeal has been lodged by..

against the* {decision / action / determination}* of ....

to the effect that:—

.... { State shortly the particulars of the decision, action or determination appealed against

....

....

And I, the undersigned, am satisfied that you are likely to be able to [give material evidence] [and] [produce the undermentioned document[s] likely to be material evidence] therein.

You are therefore summoned to attend as a witness at the hearing of the appeal at .... (time and place) and at the hearing to [answer any questions] [and] [produce the following document[s]]:—

Signed..

(President/Chairman of the Tribunal/Adjudicator)

Date..

*Delete words which are inapplicable.

Note Failure to comply with this summons without reasonable excuse is an offence carrying a maximum fine of £100 (s. 11(3), Immigration Appeals Act 1969).

EXPLANATORY NOTE

(This Note is not part of the Rules.)

These Rules (which have been prepared in consultation with the Council on Tribunals) set out the procedure to be followed in bringing appeals under Part I of the Immigration Appeals Act 1969 and the Aliens (Appeals) Order 1970 and in proceedings before the Tribunal and adjudicators established for that purpose.

Part II of the Rules relates to appeals to the adjudicators and the Tribunal at first instance, Part III to appeals to the Tribunal from determinations of the adjudicators and Part IV to the general procedure applicable in either case. Provisions are included for limiting the time within which appeals at first instance (Rule 4) and from the determinations of the adjudicators (Rule 13) are to be brought; for the release of appellants on bail (Rules 19 and 20); and for the summoning of witnesses before the Tribunal and adjudicators (Rule 24).

1970 No. 795

ALIENS

The Aliens (Approved Ports) (Amendment) Order 1970

Made - - - -	21*st May* 1970
Coming into Operation	1*st July* 1970

In pursuance of the power conferred upon me by Articles 1(3) and 29 of the Aliens Order 1953(**a**), I hereby make the following Order:—

1. This Order may be cited as the Aliens (Approved Ports) (Amendment) Order 1970 and shall come into operation on 1st July 1970.

2. In the list of seaports set out in the Schedule to the Aliens (Approved Ports) Order 1969(**b**) for the entry " Bristol " there shall be substituted the entry " Bristol and Avonmouth " and after the entry " Falmouth " there shall be inserted the entry " Felixstowe ".

James Callaghan,
One of Her Majesty's Principal
Secretaries of State.

Home Office,
Whitehall.
21st May 1970.

EXPLANATORY NOTE

(*This Note is not part of the Order.*)

This Order revises the list of seaports approved for the purposes of the Aliens Order 1953 by including Avonmouth with Bristol and adding Felixstowe to the list.

(**a**) S.I. 1953/1671 (1953 I, p. 94). (**b**) S.I. 1969/840 (1969 II, p. 2347).

1970 No. 796

CUSTOMS AND EXCISE

The Export of Goods (Control) (Amendment No. 3) Order 1970

Made - - - 26*th May* 1970

Coming into Operation 1*st June* 1970

The Board of Trade, in exercise of the powers conferred on them by section 1 of the Import, Export and Customs Powers (Defence) Act 1939(**a**), hereby order as follows:—

1.—(1) This Order may be cited as the Export of Goods (Control) (Amendment No. 3) Order 1970 and shall come into operation on 1st June 1970.

(2) The Interpretation Act 1889(**b**) shall apply to the interpretation of this Order as it applies to the interpretation of an Act of Parliament and as if this Order and the Order hereby revoked were Acts of Parliament.

2. The Export of Goods (Control) Order 1967(**c**), as amended (**d**), shall have effect as if the entry relating to potatoes in Schedule 1, Part I, Group 8 were omitted.

3. The Export of Goods (Control) (Amendment No. 3) Order 1969(**e**) is hereby revoked.

R. L. Davies,
An Assistant Secretary of
the Board of Trade.

26th May 1970.

EXPLANATORY NOTE

(*This Note is not part of the Order.*)

This Order further amends the Export of Goods (Control) Order 1967 by removing potatoes from the goods of which the export is controlled.

(**a**) 1939 c. 69. (**b**) 1889 c. 63. (**c**) S.I. 1967/675 (1967 I, p. 2080).

(**d**) The relevant amending orders are S.I. 1968/132, 1969/1887 (1968 I, p. 353; 1969 III, p. 5827).

(**e**) S.I. 1969/1887 (1969 III, p. 5827).

1970 No. 797

POISONS

The Poisons List Order 1970

Made - - - -	21*st May* 1970
Laid before Parliament	28*th May* 1970
Coming into Operation	8*th July* 1970

Whereas the Poisons Board has recommended to me that the list of substances which are to be treated as poisons for the purposes of the Pharmacy and Poisons Act 1933(**a**) should be amended so that certain substances should be omitted from, and certain additional substances should be included in, the said list, either from or in Part I thereof (which Part specifies those poisons which, subject to the provisions of the said Act, are not to be sold except by a person who is an authorised seller of poisons) or from or in Part II thereof (which Part specifies those poisons which, subject to the provisions of the said Act, are not to be sold except by a person who is an authorised seller of poisons or whose name is entered on a local authority's list):

Now, therefore, in pursuance of section 17(5) of the said Act, I hereby order as follows:—

1. This Order may be cited as the Poisons List Order 1970 and shall come into operation on 8th July 1970.

2. The Poisons List(**b**) shall be amended and varied as follows, that is to say:—

(*a*) Part I shall be amended and varied in the manner specified in paragraph 1 of Schedule 1 to this Order;

(*b*) Part II shall be amended and varied in the manner specified in paragraph 2 of that Schedule;

and accordingly the list of substances which are to be treated as poisons for the purposes of the Pharmacy and Poisons Act 1933 shall be as set out in Schedule 2 to this Order.

James Callaghan,
One of Her Majesty's Principal
Secretaries of State.

Home Office,
Whitehall.
21st May 1970.

(**a**) 1933 c. 25. (**b**) See Schedule 2 to the Poisons List (No. 2) Order 1968, S.I. 1968/1682 (1968 III, p. 4514).

SCHEDULE 1

Amendments and Variations in the Poisons List

1. In Part I of the Poisons List—

(*a*) there shall be inserted, at the appropriate points in the list therein set out in alphabetical order, the following items, that is to say:—

" Bezitramide; its salts "

" Dihydrocodeinone *O*-carboxymethyloxime; its salts; its esters; their salts "

" 3-(3,4-Dihydroxyphenyl)alanine; its salts "

" Dothiepin; its salts "

" Quinine; its salts "

" Salbutamol; its salts ";

(*b*) in the item beginning with the word " Antimony " the words " oxides of antimony; sulphides of antimony; " shall be omitted;

(*c*) in the item beginning with the word " α-Methylphenethylamine " for the words " ephedrine and its optical isomers," there shall be substituted the words " ephedrine, its optical isomers and ".

2. In Part II of the Poisons List—

(*a*) the item " Calcium arsenates ", under the heading " Arsenical substances ", shall be omitted;

(*b*) in the item beginning with the words " Hydrofluoric acid ", after those words there shall be inserted the words " alkali metal bifluorides; ammonium bifluoride ".

SCHEDULE 2

The Poisons List

Part I

Acetanilide; alkyl acetanilides
Acetohexamide
Acetorphine; its salts; its esters and ethers; their salts
Acetylcarbromal
Acetyldihydrocodeine; its salts
Alcuronium chloride
Alkali fluorides other than those specified in Part II of this List
Alkaloids, the following; their quaternary compounds; any salt, simple or complex, of any substance falling within the following:—

Aconite, alkaloids of
Atropine
Belladonna, alkaloids of
Brucine
Calabar bean, alkaloids of
Coca, alkaloids of
Cocaine
Codeine; its esters and ethers
Colchicum, alkaloids of
Coniine
Cotarnine
Curare, alkaloids of; curare bases
Ecgonine; its esters and ethers
Emetine
Ephedra, alkaloids of
Ergot, alkaloids of, whether hydrogenated or not; their homologues
Gelsemium, alkaloids of
Homatropine
Hyoscine
Hyoscyamine
Jaborandi, alkaloids of

Lobelia, alkaloids of
Morphine; its esters and ethers
Papaverine
Pomegranate, alkaloids of
Quebracho, alkaloids of, other than the alkaloids of red quebracho
Rauwolfia, alkaloids of; their derivatives
Sabadilla, alkaloids of
Solanaceous alkaloids not otherwise included in this List
Stavesacre, alkaloids of
Strychnine
Thebaine
Veratrum, alkaloids of
Yohimba, alkaloids of

Allylisopropylacetylurea
Allylprodine; its salts
Alphameprodine; its salts
Alphaprodine; its salts
Amidopyrine; its salts; amidopyrine sulphonates; their salts
Amino-alcohols esterified with benzoic acid, phenylacetic acid, phenylpropionic acid, cinnamic acid or the derivatives of these acids; their salts
p-Aminobenzenesulphonamide; its salts; derivatives of *p*-aminobenzenesulphonamide having any of the hydrogen atoms of the *p*-amino group or of the sulphonamide group substituted by another radical; their salts
p-Aminobenzoic acid, esters of; their salts
Aminorex; its salts
Amitriptyline; its salts
Amyl nitrite
Androgenic, oestrogenic and progestational substances, the following:—

Benzoestrol
Derivatives of stilbene, dibenzyl or naphthalene with oestrogenic activity; their esters
Steroid compounds with androgenic or oestrogenic or progestational activity; their esters

Anileridine; its salts
Anti-histamine substances, the following; their salts; their molecular compounds:-

Antazoline
Bromodiphenhydramine
Buclizine
Carbinoxamine
Chlorcyclizine
Chlorpheniramine
Cinnarizine
Clemizole
Cyclizine
Cyproheptadine
3-Di-*n*-butylaminomethyl-4,5,6-trihydroxyphthalide
Diphenhydramine
Diphenylpyraline
Doxylamine
Isothipendyl
Mebhydrolin
Meclozine
Phenindamine
Pheniramine
Phenyltoloxamine
Promethazine
Pyrrobutamine
Thenalidine
Tolpropamine
Triprolidine
Substances being tetra-*N*-substituted derivatives of ethylenediamine or propylenediamine

Antimony, chlorides of; antimonates; antimonites; organic compounds of antimony
Apomorphine; its salts
Arsenical substances, the following, except those specified in Part II of this List; halides of arsenic; oxides of arsenic; arsenates; arsenites; organic compounds of arsenic
Azacyclonol; its salts

Barbituric acid; its salts; derivatives of barbituric acid; their salts; compounds of barbituric acid, its salts, its derivatives, their salts, with any other substance
Barium, salts of, other than barium sulphate and the salts of barium specified in Part II of this List
Benactyzine; its salts
Benzethidine; its salts
Benzhexol; its salts
Benzoylmorphine; its salts
Benztropine and its homologues; their salts
Benzylmorphine; its salts
Betameprodine; its salts
Betaprodine; its salts
Bezitramide; its salts
Bromvaletone
Busulphan; its salts
Butylchloral hydrate

Cannabis (the dried flowering or fruiting tops of *Cannabis sativa* Linn.); the resin of cannabis; extracts of cannabis; tinctures of cannabis; cannabin tannate
Cantharidin; cantharidates
Captodiame; its salts
Caramiphen; its salts
Carbachol
Carbromal
Carisoprodol
Carperidine; its salts
Chloral; its addition and its condensation products; their molecular compounds
Chlordiazepoxide; its salts
Chlormethiazole; its salts
Chloroform
Chlorothiazide and other derivatives of benzo-1,2,4-thiadiazine-7-sulphonamide 1, 1-dioxide, whether hydrogenated or not
Chlorphenoxamine; its salts
Chlorphentermine; its salts
Chlorpropamide; its salts
Chlorprothixene and other derivatives of 9-methylenethiaxanthen; their salts
Chlorthalidone and other derivatives of *o*-chlorobenzene sulphonamide
Clonitazene; its salts
Clorexolone
Clorprenaline; its salts
Corticotrophins, natural and synthetic
Creosote obtained from wood
Croton, oil of
4-Cyano-2-dimethylamino-4,4-diphenylbutane; its salts
4-Cyano-1-methyl-4-phenylpiperidine; its salts
Cyclarbamate
Cycrimine; its salts

Dehydroemetine; its salts
Demecarium bromide
Desipramine; its salts
Desomorphine; its salts; its esters and ethers; their salts
Dextromethorphan; its salts

Dextromoramide; its salts
Dextrorphan; its salts
Diacetylmorphine; its salts
Diacetylnalorphine; its salts
Diampromide; its salts
Diazepam and other compounds containing the chemical structure of dihydro-1, 4-benzodiazepine substituted to any degree; their salts
Digitalis, glycosides of; other active principles of digitalis
Dihydrocodeine; its salts; its esters and ethers; their salts
Dihydrocodeinone; its salts
Dihydrocodeinone *O*-carboxymethyloxime; its salts; its esters; their salts
Dihydromorphine; its salts; its esters; their salts; its ethers; their salts
3-(3,4-Dihydroxyphenyl)alanine; its salts
Dimenoxadole; its salts
Dimepheptanol; its salts; its esters and ethers; their salts
Dinitronaphthols; dinitrophenols; dinitrothymols
Dioxaphetyl butyrate; its salts
Diperodon; its salts
Diphenoxylate; its salts
Dipipanone; its salts
Disulfiram
Dithienylallylamines; dithienylalkylallylamines; their salts
Dothiepin; its salts
Dyflos

Ecothiopate iodine
Ectylurea
Elaterin
Embutramide
Emylcamate
Erythrityl tetranitrate
Ethacrynic acid; its salts
Ethchlorvynol
Ethinamate
Ethionamide
Ethoheptazine; its salts
Ethylmorphine; its salts; its esters and ethers; their salts
Ethylnoradrenaline; its salts
Etonitazene; its salts
Etorphine; its salts; its esters and ethers; their salts
Etoxeridine; its salts

Fenfluramine; its salts
Fentanyl; its salts
Fluanisone
Flufenamic acid; its salts; its esters; their salts
Fluoroacetamide
Fluoroacetanilide
Furethidine; its salts

Gallamine; its salts; its quaternary compounds
Glutethimide; its salts
Glyceryl trinitrate
Glymidine
Guanidines, the following:—
polymethylene diguanidines; di-*p*-anisyl-*p*-phenetylguanidine

Haloperidol and other 4-substituted derivatives of *N*-(3-*p*-fluorobenzoylpropyl) piperidine
Hexapropymate
Hydrazines, benzyl, phenethyl and phenoxyethyl; their α-methyl derivatives; acyl derivatives of any of the foregoing substances comprised in this item; salts of any compounds comprised in this item

Hydrocyanic acid; cyanides, other than ferrocyanides and ferricyanides
Hydromorphinol; its salts; its esters and ethers; their salts
Hydromorphone; its salts; its esters; their salts; its ethers; their salts
Hydroxycinchoninic acids; derivatives of; their salts; their esters
Hydroxy-*N*,*N*-dimethyltryptamines; their esters or ethers; any salt of any substance falling within this item
Hydroxypethidine; its salts; its esters and ethers; their salts
Hydroxyurea
Hydroxyzine; its salts

Imipramine; its salts
Indomethacin; its salts
Insulin
Iprindole; its salts
Isoaminile; its salts
Isoetharine; its salts
Isomethadone (isoamidone); its salts
Isoprenaline; its salts

Ketobemidone; its salts; its esters and ethers; their salts

Laudexium; its salts
Lead acetates; compounds of lead with acids from fixed oils
Levomethorphan; its salts
Levomoramide; its salts
Levophenacylmorphan; its salts; its esters and ethers; their salts
Levorphanol; its salts; its esters and ethers; their salts
Lysergide; its salts, simple or complex; its quaternary compounds

Mannityl hexanitrate
Mannomustine; its salts
Mebezonium iodide
Mebutamate
Meclofenoxate; its salts
Mefenamic acid; its salts; its esters; their salts
Mephenesin; its esters
Meprobamate
Mercaptopurine; its salts; derivatives of mercaptopurine; their salts
Mercury, oxides of; nitrates of mercury; mercuric ammonium chlorides; potassio-mercuric iodides; organic compounds of mercury which contain a methyl (CH_3) group directly linked to the mercury atom; mercuric oxycyanides; mercuric thiocyanate
Mescaline and other derivatives of phenethylamine formed by substitution in the aromatic ring; their salts
Metaxalone
Metazocine; its salts; its esters and ethers; their salts
Metformin; its salts
Methadone (amidone); its salts
Methadyl acetate; its salts
Methaqualone; its salts
Methixene; its salts
Methocarbamol
Methoxsalen
Methoxyphenamine; its salts
Methylaminoheptane; its salts
Methyldesorphine; its salts; its esters and ethers; their salts
Methyldihydromorphine; its salts; its esters and ethers; their salts
2-Methyl-3-morpholino-1,1-diphenylpropanecarboxylic acid; its salts; its esters; their salts
Methylpentynol; its esters and other derivatives

α-Methylphenethylamine, β-methylphenethylamine and α-ethylphenethylamine; any synthetic compound structurally derived from any of those substances by substitution in the aliphatic part or by ring closure therein (or by both such substitution and such closure) or by substitution in the aromatic ring (with or without substitution at the nitrogen atom), except **ephedrine, its optical isomers and** *N*-substituted derivatives, fenfluramine, hydroxyamphetamine, methoxyphenamine, phenylpropanolamine, pholedrine and prenylamine; any salt of any substance falling within this item
1-Methyl-4-phenylpiperidine-4-carboxylic acid; esters of; their salts
Methyprylone
Metoclopramide; its salts
Metopon; its salts; its esters and ethers; their salts
Mitopodozide; its salts
Monofluoroacetic acid; its salts
Morpheridine; its salts
Mustine and any other *N*-substituted derivatives of di-(2-chloroethyl)amine; their salts
Myrophine; its salts

Nalorphine; its salts
Nicocodine; its salts
m-Nitrophenol; *o*-nitrophenol; *p*-nitrophenol
Noracymethadol; its salts
Norcodeine; its salts; its esters and ethers; their salts
Norlevorphanol; its salts; its esters and ethers; their salts
Normethadone; its salts
Normorphine; its salts; its esters and ethers; their salts
Norpipanone
Nortryptyline; its salts
Nux Vomica

Opium
Orciprenaline; its salts
Orphenadrine; its salts
Orthocaine; its salts
Ouabain
Oxalic acid
Oxethazaine
Oxycodone; its salts; its esters; their salts; its ethers; their salts
Oxymorphone; its salts; its esters and ethers; their salts
Oxyphenbutazone
Oxytocins, natural and synthetic

Paraldehyde
Paramethadione
Pargyline; its salts
Pemoline; its salts
Pentazocine; its salts
Phenacemide
Phenadoxone; its salts
Phenaglycodol
Phenampromide; its salts
Phenazocine; its salts; its esters and ethers; their salts
Phenbutrazate
Phencyclidine; its salts
Phenetidylphenacetin
Phenformin; its salts
Phenols (any member of the series of phenols of which the first member is phenol and of which the molecular composition varies from member to member by one atom of carbon and two atoms of hydrogen) except in substances containing less than sixty per cent., weight in weight, of phenols; compounds of phenol with a metal, except in substances containing less than the equivalent of sixty per cent., weight in weight, of phenols

Phenomorphan; its salts; its esters and ethers; their salts
Phenoperidine; its salts; its esters and ethers; their salts
Phenothiazine, derivatives of; their salts; except dimethoxanate, its salts and promethazine, its salts and its molecular compounds
Phenylbutazone; its salts
2-Phenylcinchoninic acid; 2-salicylcinchoninic acid; their salts; their esters
5-Phenylhydantoin; its alkyl and aryl derivatives; their salts
4-Phenylpiperidine-4-carboxylic acid ethyl ester; its salts
Pholcodine; its salts; its esters and ethers; their salts
Phosphorus, yellow
Picric acid
Picrotoxin
Piminodine; its salts
Piritramide; its salts
Pituitary gland, the active principles of
Podophyllum resin
Polymethylenebistrimethylammonium salts
Procainamide; its salts
Procarbazine; its salts
Procyclidine; its salts
Proheptazine; its salts
Promoxolan
Propoxyphene; its salts
Propylhexedrine; its salts
Prothionamide
Prothipendyl; its salts

Quinethazone
Quinine; its salts

Racemethorphan; its salts
Racemoramide; its salts
Racemorphan; its salts; its esters and ethers; their salts

Salbutamol; its salts
Savin, oil of
Strophanthus; glycosides of strophanthus
Styramate
Sulphinpyrazone
Sulphonal; alkyl sulphonals
Suprarenal gland medulla, the active principles of; their salts
Syrosingopine

Tetrabenazine; its salts
Thalidomide; its salts
Thallium, salts of
Thebacon; its salts
Thiocarlide; its salts
Thyroid gland, the active principles of; their salts
Tolbutamide
Tretamine; its salts
Triaziquone
Tribromethyl alcohol
2,2,2-Trichloroethyl alcohol, esters of; their salts
Trimeperidine; its salts
Trimipramine; its salts
Troxidone
Tybamate

Vasopressins, natural and synthetic
Verapamil; its salts

Zoxazolamine; its salts

PART II

Ammonia

Arsenical substances, the following:—

Arsenic sulphides
Arsenious oxide
Calcium arsenites
Copper acetoarsenite
Copper arsenates
Copper arsenites
Lead arsenates
Potassium arsenites
Sodium arsenates
Sodium arsenites
Sodium thioarsenates

Barium, salts of, the following:—

Barium carbonate
Barium silicofluoride

Diamines, the following; their salts:—

phenylene diamines; tolylene diamines; other alkylated-benzene diamines

Dinitrocresols (DNOC); their compounds with a metal or a base
Dinosam; its compounds with a metal or a base
Dinoseb; its compounds with a metal or a base

Endosulfan
Endothal; its salts
Endrin

Formaldehyde
Formic acid

Hydrochloric acid
Hydrofluoric acid; **alkali metal bifluorides; ammonium bifluoride;** potassium fluoride; sodium fluoride; sodium silicofluoride

Mercuric chloride; mercuric iodide; organic compounds of mercury except compounds which contain a methyl (CH_3) group directly linked to the mercury atom
Metallic oxylates

Nicotine; its salts
Nitric acid
Nitrobenzene

Organo-tin compounds, the following:—

Compounds of fentin

Paraquat; salts of
Phenols as defined in Part I of this List in substances containing less than sixty per cent., weight in weight, of phenols; compounds of phenol with a metal in substances containing less than the equivalent of sixty per cent., weight in weight, of phenols
Phosphoric acid
Phosphorus compounds, the following:—

Amiton, azinphos-ethyl, azinphos-methyl, chlorfenvinphos, demeton-O, demeton-S, demeton-O-methyl, demeton-S-methyl, dichlorvos, diethyl 4-methyl-7-coumarinyl phosphorothionate, diethyl *p*-nitrophenyl phosphate, dimefox, disulfoton, ethion, ethyl *p*-nitrophenyl phenylphosphonothionate, mazidox, mecarbam, mevinphos, mipafox, oxydemeton-methyl, parathion, phenkapton, phorate, phosphamidon, schradan, sulfotep, TEPP (HETP), thionazin, triphosphoric pentadimethylamide, vamidothion

Potassium hydroxide

Sodium hydroxide
Sodium nitrite
Sulphuric acid

Zinc phosphide

EXPLANATORY NOTE

(*This Note is not part of the Order.*)

This Order provides for the omission of certain substances from Parts I and II of the Poisons List, the substances omitted being set out, respectively, in paragraph 1(*b*) and in paragraph 2(*a*) of Schedule 1.

It also makes other changes in the list, including the insertion therein of certain additional substances.

The Poisons List, as amended by this Order, is set out in Schedule 2; the changes referred to in the preceding paragraph being indicated by the use of **heavy type.**

1970 No. 798

POISONS

The Poisons Rules 1970

Made - - -	21*st May* 1970
Laid before Parliament	28*th May* 1970
Coming into Operation	8*th July* 1970

ARRANGEMENT OF RULES

Storage and Transport

Special Provisions with respect to the supply and storage of medicines, etc.

Miscellaneous

SCHEDULES

SCHEDULE 13: Restriction of sale and supply of strychnine and certain other substances.

SCHEDULE 14. Substances in which poison is exempted by Rule 7 from section 18(2) of the Act.

SCHEDULE 15: Poisons required to be coloured in certain cases.

In pursuance of section 23 of the Pharmacy and Poisons Act 1933(**a**), on the recommendation of the Poisons Board I hereby make the following Rules :—

Citation, commencement and revocation

1.—(1) These Rules may be cited as the Poisons Rules 1970.

(2) These Rules shall come into operation on 8th July 1970.

(3) The Poisons (No. 2) Rules 1968(**b**) are hereby revoked.

(4) Notwithstanding anything in paragraph (3)—

(*a*) any authority or certificate issued for the purposes of Rule 18 of the said Rules of 1968 before the coming into operation of these Rules and still in force shall continue in force for the same time as if these Rules had not been made and shall be deemed to have been issued for the purposes of the corresponding provision of Rule 18 of these Rules and Schedule 13 thereto ;

(*b*) any record required to be kept under Rule 29(3) or 38(2)(*b*) of the said Rules of 1968 and any book required under Rule 37 or 38(2)(*b*) of those Rules to be preserved in accordance therewith shall be kept or preserved in the same manner and for the same period as if these Rules had not been made.

Interpretation

2.—(1) In these Rules, unless the context otherwise requires—

"the Act" means the Pharmacy and Poisons Act 1933 ;

"animal" includes poultry ;

"antimonial poisons" means chlorides of antimony, antimonates, antimonites and organic compounds of antimony ;

"arsenical poisons" means halides of arsenic, oxides of arsenic, sulphides of arsenic, arsenates, arsenites, copper acetoarsenite, sodium thioarsenates and organic compounds of arsenic ;

"food" includes a beverage ;

"listed seller of Part II poisons" means a person entitled, subject to the provisions of the Act and of these Rules, to sell poisons included in Part II of the Poisons List(**c**) by virtue of the entry of his name in a local authority's list kept in pursuance of section 21 of the Act ;

"medicine for the internal treatment of human ailments" includes any medicine to be administered by hypodermic injection, but does not include any mouth wash, eye drops, eye lotion, ear drops, douche or similar articles ;

"sale exempted by section 20 of the Act" means a sale made in such circumstances as to be entitled, except as provided by these Rules, to exemption under section 20 of the Act from the foregoing provisions of Part II of the Act ;

(**a**) 1933 c. 25. (**b**) S.I. 1968/1683 (1968 III, p. 4525).

(**c**) See Schedule 2 to the Poison List Order 1970 S.I. 1970/797, (1970 II, p.2532).

"transaction exempted by section 19 of the Act" means the supply of a medicine in such circumstances as to be entitled to exemption under section 19 of the Act from the provisions of section 18 of the Act.

(2) In these Rules any reference to a Rule or Schedule shall be construed as a reference to a Rule contained in these Rules or, as the case may be, to a Schedule thereto ; and any reference in a Rule to a paragraph shall be construed as a reference to a paragraph of that Rule.

(3) Any reference in these Rules to the British Pharmacopoeia (except in a context which specifies a particular edition thereof), the British Pharmaceutical Codex, the British National Formulary, the British Veterinary Codex or the name published by the General Medical Council as the approved name of a poison shall be construed as a reference to the edition or publication having effect on the date on which these Rules were made, together with any amendments made thereto before that date.

(4) Any reference in the Schedules to the percentage of a poison contained in any substance or preparation shall, unless otherwise expressly provided, be construed in the following manner, that is to say, a reference to a substance or preparation containing one per cent. of any poison means—

(*a*) in the case of a solid, that one gramme of the poison is contained in every hundred grammes of the substance or preparation ;

(*b*) in the case of a liquid, that one millilitre of the poison, or, if the poison itself is a solid, one gramme of the poison, is contained in every hundred millilitres of the substance or preparation ;

and so in proportion for any greater or lesser percentage.

(5) References in these Rules to the provisions of any enactment shall be construed as references to those provisions as amended, re-enacted or modified by any subsequent enactment.

(6) The Interpretation Act 1889(**a**) shall apply to the interpretation of these Rules as it applies to the interpretation of an Act of Parliament, and as if these Rules and the Rules revoked by these Rules were Acts of Parliament.

Metric system and imperial system

3.—(1) For the purposes of these Rules a poison shall not be regarded as sold, issued or supplied otherwise than in accordance with a prescription or other order by reason only that the prescription or order specifies a quantity of the poison in terms of the imperial system and the quantity sold, issued or supplied is the equivalent of that amount in the metric system, or by reason only that the prescription or order specifies a quantity of the poison in terms of the metric system and the quantity sold, issued or supplied is the equivalent of that amount in the imperial system.

(2) In the case of a poison which is a drug within the meaning of the Weights and Measures (Equivalents for dealings with drugs) Regulations 1969(**b**) the quantity of the poison in the metric system which is the equivalent of a particular quantity in the imperial system shall, for the purposes of these Rules, be deemed to be the appropriate equivalent quantity ascertained in accordance with the provisions of those Regulations.

APPLICATION AND RELAXATION OF PART II OF THE ACT

Restriction of sales by shopkeepers

4. It shall not be lawful for any shopkeeper to sell poisons on any premises used for or in connection with his retail business, notwithstanding that the

(**a**) 1889 c. 63. (**b**) S.I. 1969/101 (1969 I, p. 328).

sale is exempted by section 20 of the Act, unless he complies with the provisions of paragraph (*a*) or paragraph (*b*), as the case may be, of section 18(1) of the Act.

Exemption of animal medicines

5. The provisions of section 18(1)(*a*) and (*b*) of the Act shall not apply with respect to any medicine for the treatment of animals sold by a person carrying on a business which comprises the manufacture of medicines for the treatment of animals, if the following requirements are complied with :—

(*a*) a statement in writing signed by the owner of the business, or, in the case of a corporate body, on behalf of that body, stating the name of the business, the principal place where it is carried on, the name of the person in charge of the sale of the medicines, and the premises on which the medicines are to be sold must be furnished prior to the sale to the registrar of the Pharmaceutical Society ; and

(*b*) the sale must be effected on the premises specified in the statement ; and

(*c*) an inspector appointed under section 25 of the Act must be permitted at all reasonable times to enter the premises and be given all reasonable facilities to make such examination and enquiry and to do such other things (including the taking, on payment therefor, of samples) as may be necessary for ascertaining whether the provisions of the Act and of these Rules are being complied with.

Extension of labelling provisions and relaxation with respect to poisons in Schedule 2 *and in Part B of Schedule* 4 *and consignments to Northern Ireland*

6.—(1) Subject as hereinafter provided, the provisions of section 18(1)(*c*) of the Act and of Rules 19 to 24 (which provisions relate to the labelling of poisons) shall apply to sales exempted by section 20 of the Act, other than sales of poisons to be exported to purchasers outside the United Kingdom ; and shall also apply to the supply of poisons (otherwise than on sale) in like manner as if references in the said provisions to the sale and the seller of poisons included references to the supply and the supplier of poisons respectively.

(2) The said provisions, except the provisions of Rule 23 and of section 18(1)(*c*)(iv) of the Act as modified by Rule 24, shall not apply to the sale or supply of any of the poisons included in Schedule 2 to a person who—

(*a*) carries on a business in the course of which poisons are regularly sold by way of wholesale dealing or are regularly used in the manufacture of other articles, and

(*b*) requires the poison for the purpose of that business,

if the outside of the package in which the poison is sold or supplied is labelled conspicuously with words indicating the dangerous properties of the poison.

(3) The provisions of section 18(1)(*c*)(iii) of the Act and of Rule 22 shall not apply to sales exempted by section 20 of the Act of any of the poisons included in Part B of Schedule 4.

(4) The said provisions shall not apply to the sale or supply of poisons to be consigned to purchasers in Northern Ireland if the poisons are labelled in accordance with the corresponding provisions of the law in force in Northern Ireland relating to the labelling of poisons.

Substances to which section 18(2) *of the Act applies*

7. The provisions of section 18(2) of the Act (which makes provision as to persons to whom poisons may be sold and to the keeping of records of sales) shall apply with respect to all substances included in Schedule 1, whether or not the poison sold is a poison included in Part I of the Poisons List, and shall not apply with respect to any other substance:

Provided that—

(i) paragraph (*a*) of the said section 18(2) shall, in its application to sales by listed sellers of Part II poisons, be deemed to be satisfied if the person to whom the poison is sold is known by the person in charge of the premises on which the poison is sold or of the department of the business in which the sale is effected to be a person to whom the poison may properly be sold, and

(ii) the provisions of the said section 18(2) shall not apply, so far as the poison specified in the first column of Schedule 14 is concerned, to sales of substances specified in the second column of that Schedule.

Extension of section 18(2) *to sales wholesale, etc., and relaxation of the said subsection*

8.—(1) The provisions of section 18(2) of the Act as modified by Rule 7 shall apply to sales exempted by section 20 of the Act, except sales of poisons to be exported to purchasers outside the United Kingdom; and shall also apply to the supply in the form of commercial sample, otherwise than on sale, of any substance included in Schedule 1 in like manner as if references in the said provisions to the sale and seller of poisons respectively included references to the supply and the supplier of poisons in the form of commercial samples:

Provided that the said provisions shall not apply to the sale or supply of any article by the manufacturer thereof or by a person carrying on a business in the course of which poisons are regularly sold by way of wholesale dealing, if—

(*a*) the article is sold or supplied to a person carrying on a business in the course of which poisons are regularly sold or are regularly used in the manufacture of other articles, and

(*b*) the seller or supplier is reasonably satisfied that the purchaser requires the article for the purpose of that business.

(2) Paragraph (*a*) of the said section 18(2) shall, in its application to sales exempted by section 20 of the Act and to the supply in the form of commercial samples of substances included in Schedule 1, be deemed to be satisfied if the person to whom the poison or sample is sold or supplied is known by the person in charge of the department of the business through which the sale or supply is effected to be a person to whom the poison or sample may properly be sold or supplied.

(3) So much of paragraph (*b*) of the said section 18(2) as requires an entry in a book to be signed by the purchaser of a poison shall not, as respects the sale of a poison to a person for the purposes of his trade, business or profession, apply if the following requirements are satisfied:—

(*a*) the seller must obtain before the completion of the sale an order in writing signed by the purchaser stating his name and address, trade, business or profession, and the following particulars in regard to the article to be purchased, that is to say, the purpose for which it is required and the total quantity to be purchased, or, in the case of an article packed in ampoules, either the said total quantity or the total quantity intended to be administered or injected ;

(*b*) the seller must be reasonably satisfied that the signature is that of the person purporting to have signed the order, and that that person carries on the trade, business or profession stated in the order, being one in which the poison to be purchased is used ;

(*c*) the seller must insert in the entry prescribed by Rule 36 the words "signed order" and a reference number by which the order can be identified :

Provided that where a person represents that he urgently requires a poison for the purpose of his trade, business or profession, the seller may, if he is reasonably satisfied that the person so requires the poison and is, by reason of some emergency, unable before delivery either to furnish to the seller an order in writing duly signed or to attend and sign the entry in the book, deliver the poison to the purchaser on an undertaking by the purchaser to furnish such an order within the twenty-four hours next following.

If any purchaser by whom any such undertaking has been given fails to deliver to the seller a signed order in accordance with the undertaking, or if any person for the purpose of obtaining delivery of any poison under the foregoing proviso makes a statement which is to his knowledge false, he shall be deemed to have contravened the provisions of this Rule.

(4) Where the seller of a poison is reasonably satisfied that the poison is required for the purpose of medical, dental or veterinary treatment, there shall not apply—

(*a*) in the case of a sale to a hospital, infirmary, health centre, dispensary or clinic, such of the provisions of this Rule as require the purchaser to state his trade, business or profession and the seller to be satisfied with respect thereto ;

(*b*) in the case of a sale of the poison not being a poison to which any Part of the Dangerous Drugs Act 1965(**a**) applies to a duly qualified medical practitioner, registered dentist, registered veterinary surgeon or registered veterinary practitioner or to a hospital, infirmary, health centre, dispensary or clinic, such of the provisions of this Rule as require the purchaser to state the purpose for which the poison is required.

Relaxation of section 19(3) *in the case of certain medicines*

9. The requirements mentioned in section 19(3) of the Act (which requires particulars of medicines supplied or dispensed under that section to be entered in a book) need not be satisfied in the case of—

(*a*) any medicine, not being a substance included in Schedule 1, which is supplied by—

(i) a duly qualified medical practitioner for the purposes of medical treatment, or

(ii) an authorised seller of poisons on and in accordance with a prescription given by a duly qualified medical practitioner or a registered dentist ; or

(*b*) any medicine, notwithstanding that it is a substance included in Schedule 1, which is supplied on and in accordance with a prescription given by a duly qualified medical practitioner or a registered dentist

(**a**) 1965 c. 15.

upon a form issued by a local authority (whether a local authority as defined in the Act or not) for use in connection with a health service of that authority, provided that the following requirements are complied with :—

(i) the prescription or a true copy thereof must be kept upon the premises upon which the medicine was dispensed for a period of at least two years in such a manner as to be readily available for inspection, and

(ii) the prescription or copy must bear on it particulars of the date of dispensing, the ingredients and quantity of the medicine supplied, and the name of the person by whom, the name and address of the person to whom, and the date on which the prescription was given ; or

(*c*) any medicine, notwithstanding that it is a substance included in Schedule 1, which is supplied on and in accordance with a prescription given by a registered dentist under and in accordance with the National Health Service Act 1946(**a**) or the National Health Service (Scotland) Act 1947(**b**).

General exemption of section 19 *transactions*

10. Nothing in these Rules shall apply, except as is expressly provided therein, to transactions exempted by section 19 of the Act.

Exemption from the provisions applying solely to Schedule 1

11. Such of the provisions of these Rules and of Part II of the Act as modified by these Rules, as apply solely with respect to the substances included in Schedule 1, shall not apply with respect to—

(*a*) machine-spread plasters ; or

(*b*) surgical dressings ; or

(*c*) articles containing barium carbonate or zinc phosphide and prepared for the destruction of rats or mice ; or

(*d*) corn paints in which the only poison is a poison included in the Poisons List under the heading of "Cannabis".

Complete exemption for articles and substances in Schedule 3

12. Nothing in Part II of the Act or in these Rules shall apply—

(*a*) with respect to any article included in Group I of Schedule 3 ; or

(*b*) so far as any poison specified in the first column of Group II of that Schedule is concerned, with respect to any of the articles or substances specified in the second column opposite the description of the poison.

ADDITIONAL RESTRICTIONS ON THE SALE OF POISONS

Additional restriction of sale of poisons in Schedule 4

13.—(1) It shall not be lawful to sell any poison included in Schedule 4, except on and in accordance with a prescription complying with the requirements of paragraph (3) given by a duly qualified medical practitioner, registered dentist, registered veterinary surgeon or registered veterinary practitioner :

(**a**) 1946 c. 81. (**b**) 1947 c. 27.

Provided that where an authorised seller of poisons is reasonably satisfied that a person ordering any such poison is a duly qualified medical practitioner who is by reason of some emergency unable to furnish such a prescription immediately, he may, notwithstanding that no such prescription has been given, if the said person undertakes to furnish him within the twenty-four hours next following with such a prescription, deliver the poison ordered in accordance with the directions of the said person, so, however, that, notwithstanding anything in any such directions, the supply shall not be repeated unless such a prescription has been given.

If any person by whom any such undertaking has been given fails to deliver to the seller a prescription in accordance with the undertaking, or if any person for the purpose of obtaining delivery of any poison under the foregoing proviso makes a statement which is to his knowledge false, he shall be deemed to have contravened the provisions of this Rule.

(2) This Rule shall apply to the sale of any such poison, notwithstanding that it is a transaction exempted by section 19 of the Act, but shall not apply to any sale exempted by section 20 of the Act.

(3) For the purposes of this Rule a prescription shall, in the case of any poison included in Schedule 4, be in writing and be signed by the person giving it with his usual signature and be dated by him and, in the case of any poison included in Part A of Schedule 4—

(*a*) except in the case of a health prescription, specify the address of the person giving it ;

(*b*) specify the name and address of the person for whose treatment it is given or, if the prescription is given by a veterinary surgeon or practitioner, of the person to whom the medicine is to be delivered ;

(*c*) have written thereon, if given by a dentist, the words "For dental treatment only" or, if given by a veterinary surgeon or practitioner, the words "For animal treatment only" ;

(*d*) when the medicine is packed otherwise than in ampoules, indicate—

(i) except in the case of a preparation contained in the British National Formulary, the total amount to be supplied, and

(ii) except in the case of a preparation which is to be used for external treatment only, the dose to be taken ;

(*e*) when the medicine is packed in ampoules, indicate—

(i) except in the case of a preparation contained in the British National Formulary, either the total amount to be supplied or the total amount intended to be administered or injected, and

(ii) in any case, the amount intended to be administered or injected in each dose.

(4) The person dispensing the prescription shall comply with the following requirements :—

(*a*) the prescription must not be dispensed more than once unless the prescriber has directed thereon either that it may be dispensed a stated number of times or that it may be dispensed at stated intervals ;

(*b*) if the prescription contains a direction that it may be dispensed a stated number of times or at stated intervals it must not be dispensed otherwise than in accordance with the direction ;

(*c*) a prescription which contains a direction that it may be dispensed a stated number of times but no direction as to the intervals at which it may be dispensed shall not be dispensed more often than once in three days, and a prescription which contains a direction that it is to be dispensed at stated intervals but no direction as to the number of times that it may be dispensed shall not be dispensed more often than three times ;

(*d*) at the time of dispensing or, where a poison has been delivered under the proviso to paragraph (1), on the subsequent receipt of the prescription there must be noted on the prescription above the signature of the prescriber the name and address of the seller and the date on which the prescription is dispensed or, as the case may be, the poison was delivered ;

(*e*) except in the case of a health prescription or a prescription which may be dispensed again, the prescription must, for a period of two years, be retained and kept on the premises on which it was dispensed in such manner as to be readily available for inspection.

(5) In this Rule "health prescription" means a prescription given by a duly qualified medical practitioner or registered dentist under and in accordance with the National Health Service Act 1946, or the National Health Service (Scotland) Act 1947, or given by a duly qualified medical practitioner or registered dentist upon a form issued by a local authority (whether a local authority as defined in the Act or not) for use in connection with a health service of that authority.

Additional restriction of sales by authorised sellers of poisons

14. It shall not be lawful for any authorised seller of poisons to sell any substance included in Schedule 1, notwithstanding that the substance is a poison included in Part II of the Poisons List, unless the sale is effected by, or under the supervision of, a registered pharmacist.

Restriction of sales by listed sellers of Part II poisons

15.—(1) No shopkeeper shall be entitled by virtue of being a listed seller of Part II poisons to sell—

(*a*) any poison other than ammonia, hydrochloric acid, nitric acid, potassium quadroxalate and sulphuric acid, except in a closed container as closed by the manufacturer or other person from whom the poison was obtained ;

(*b*) any substance included in Schedule 1 unless the sale is effected by himself or by a responsible deputy.

In this paragraph the expression "responsible deputy" means a person nominated as a deputy on the seller's form of application, as hereinafter prescribed, for entry as a listed seller of Part II poisons, or any person substituted, by notice in writing to the local authority, for a person so nominated, and not more than two deputies shall be nominated at the same time in respect of one set of premises.

(2) No person shall be entitled by virtue of being a listed seller of Part II poisons to sell—

(*a*) any poison included in the first column of Part A of Schedule 5 unless the article or substance sold is one of the articles or substances specified against the description of the poison in the second column of that Part, and the container of the substance is, in addition to any other direction of the Act or of these Rules with respect to labelling, labelled clearly with a notice of the special purpose for which the article or substance is intended, and a warning that it is only to be used for that purpose ;

(*b*) any poison included in Part B of Schedule 5, unless the purchaser thereof is engaged in the trade or business of agriculture or horticulture and requires the poison for the purpose of that trade or business.

Requirement as to colouring in certain cases

16. It shall not be lawful to sell any poison included in Schedule 15 which is intended for use as a weed killer or in the prevention or treatment of infestation by animals, plants or other living organisms unless there has been added to the poison a dye or other substance which, in the case of a poison included in that Schedule as a poison in solution, renders it of a distinctive colour or, in the case of any other poison, renders it of a distinctive colour whether dry or wet or in solution :

Provided that this Rule shall not apply in the case of—

(*a*) poisons which are themselves of a distinctive colour,

(*b*) sheep dips which are already of a distinctive colour, or

(*c*) articles to be exported to purchasers outside the United Kingdom.

Restriction of sales of Part I poisons to shopkeepers

17. It shall not be lawful to sell by way of wholesale dealing any poison included in Part I of the Poisons List to a person carrying on a business of shopkeeping unless the seller—

(*a*) has reasonable grounds for believing that the purchaser is an authorised seller of poisons ; or

(*b*) has received a statement signed by the purchaser or by a person authorised by him on his behalf to the effect that the purchaser does not intend to sell the poison on any premises used for or in connection with his retail business.

Restriction of sale and supply of strychnine and certain other substances

18.—(1) Except in the cases mentioned in paragraphs 1, 2, 3 and 4 of Part I of Schedule 13, it shall not be lawful to sell or supply strychnine.

(2) Except in the cases mentioned in paragraphs 1, 2 and 5 of the said Part I, it shall not be lawful to sell or supply monofluoroacetic acid, any salt thereof, fluoroacetamide or fluoroacetanilide.

(3) Except in the cases mentioned in paragraphs 1, 2, 3 and 6 of the said Part I, it shall not be lawful to sell or supply sodium arsenites or potassium arsenites.

(4) Except in the cases mentioned in paragraphs 1 and 7 of the said Part I, it shall not be lawful to sell or supply lysergide or its salts, mescaline or its salts, other derivatives of phenethylamine formed by substitution in the aromatic ring or their salts, or psilocybin.

(5) Except in the cases mentioned in paragraphs 1, 2 and 8 of the said Part I, it shall not be lawful to sell or supply embutramide or mebezonium iodide.

(6) Except in the cases mentioned in paragraphs 1, 2 and 9 of the said Part I, it shall not be lawful to sell or supply fluanisone.

(7) Except in the cases mentioned in paragraphs 1, 2 and 10 of the said Part I, it shall not be lawful to sell or supply zinc phosphide.

(8) Any authority or certificate issued for the purposes of paragraph 4 or 5 of the said Part I shall be retained by the seller of the poison to which the authority or certificate relates.

SUPPLEMENTARY PROVISIONS WITH RESPECT TO LABELLING AND CONTAINERS

Manner of labelling containers

19.—(1) Subject to the provisions of these Rules, the particulars with which the container of a poison is required to be labelled under section 18(1)(*c*) of the Act and under these Rules, must appear in a conspicuous position on the container in which the poison is sold and on every box or other covering of whatever nature enclosing the container, and the particulars must be clearly and distinctly set out and not in any way obscured or obliterated.

(2) Where the poison is contained in an ampoule, cachet or similar article it shall not be necessary to label the article itself, if every box or other covering in which the article is enclosed is duly labelled.

(3) Nothing in section 18(1)(*c*) of the Act or in Rules 19 to 24 shall require the labelling of any transparent cover or any wrapper, hamper, packing case, crate or other covering used solely for the purposes of transport or delivery.

Labelling of name of poison

20.—(1) Subject as hereinafter provided, for the purposes of section 18(1)(*c*)(i) of the Act and of Rule 29(3)(*a*) the name of a poison shall be—

(*a*) where the term under which a poison is included in the Poisons List describes the poison specifically—

(i) the said term ; or

(ii) the name published by the General Medical Council as the approved name of the poison ; or

(iii) if the poison is the subject of a monograph in the British Pharmacopoeia, the British Pharmaceutical Codex or the British Veterinary Codex, one of the names or synonyms or abbreviated names set out at the head of the monograph ;

(*b*) where the said term describes a group of poisons and not the poison specifically—

(i) if the poison is the subject of a monograph in the British Pharmacopoeia, the British Pharmaceutical Codex or the British Veterinary Codex, one of the names or synonyms or abbreviated names set out at the head of the monograph ; and

(ii) in any other case, the accepted scientific name, the name descriptive of the true nature and origin of the poison or the name published by the General Medical Council as the approved name of the poison.

(2) For the purposes aforesaid it shall, in the case of—

(*a*) a substance which is the subject of a monograph in the British Pharmacopoeia, the British Pharmaceutical Codex or the British Veterinary Codex, or any dilution, concentration or admixture of such a substance; or

(*b*) a preparation contained in the British Pharmacopoeia, the British Pharmaceutical Codex, the British National Formulary or the British Veterinary Codex, or any dilution, concentration or admixture of such a preparation ; or (*c*) a surgical dressing for which a standard is prescribed in the British Pharmaceutical Codex,

by sufficient, notwithstanding anything in paragraph (2), to state the name, synonym or abbreviated name used to describe the substance, preparation or surgical dressing in the British Pharmacopoeia, the British Pharmaceutical Codex, the British National Formulary or the British Veterinary Codex with the addition of the letters "B.P.", or "B.P.C.", "B.N.F." or "B.Vet.C.", as the case may be.

(3) For the purposes aforesaid it shall, in the case of a preparation containing a poison specified in the first column of Schedule 6, be sufficient, notwithstanding anything in paragraph (1), to state the name of the poison or substance mentioned in the second column of that Schedule in respect of which the proportion of the poison to the total ingredients of the preparation is in accordance with the provisions of Rule 21(2) expressed.

(4) For the purposes aforesaid it shall, in the case of a preparation derived from nux vomica or from opium and containing one or more alkaloids of nux vomica or of opium named in the Poisons List, be sufficient, notwithstanding anything in paragraph (1), to state the name of strychnine or morphine, as the case may be, or one of the names or abbreviated names of strychnine or morphine, as the case may be, set out at the head of the monographs in the British Pharmacopoeia, the British Pharmaceutical Codex or the British Veterinary Codex.

Labelling of particulars as to proportion of the poison

21.—(1) For the purposes of section 18(1)(*c*)(ii) of the Act (which requires preparations containing poisons to be labelled with the prescribed particulars as to the proportion of poison therein) the label of the container of any preparation containing a poison as one of its ingredients shall, subject as hereinafter provided, include a statement of the proportion which the poison bears to the total ingredients of the preparation.

(2) In the case of a preparation containing a poison specified in the first column of Schedule 6, it shall be sufficient to state on the label the particulars specified in the second column of that Schedule against the description of the poison.

(3) In the case of a preparation derived from nux vomica or from opium and containing one or more alkaloids of nux vomica or of opium named in the Poisons List, it shall be sufficient, so far as those alkaloids are concerned, to state on the label the proportion of strychnine or of morphine, as the case may be, contained in the preparation.

(4) In the case of a substance, preparation or surgical dressing which is named in accordance with paragraph (2) of Rule 20, it shall not be necessary to state on the label the proportion of the poison contained in the substance, preparation or surgical dressing and, in the case of any dilution, concentration or admixture of such a substance or preparation, it shall be sufficient to state the proportion which the substance or preparation bears to the total ingredients of the dilution, concentration or admixture.

(5) Where the poison is in tablets, pills, cachets, capsules, lozenges or similar articles, or in ampoules, it shall be sufficient to state on the label of the box or other covering in which the articles are enclosed the number of the articles and the amount of the poison, or in the case of such a preparation as is mentioned in the last foregoing paragraph the amount of the preparation, contained in each article.

(6) Where any proportion is stated as a percentage, the statement shall indicate whether the percentage is calculated on the basis of weight in weight, weight in volume, or volume in volume.

Indication of character of the poison

22.—(1) In pursuance of section 18(1)(*c*)(iii) of the Act (which requires the containers of poisons to be labelled with the word "Poison" or other prescribed indication of character), the container of any article specified in Schedule 7 shall, instead of being labelled with the word "Poison", be labelled with the words specified in that Schedule as applicable to that article.

(2) The said words specified as aforesaid or the word "Poison", as the case may be, must not be modified in meaning by the addition of any other words or marks, and—

(*a*) in the case of a substance included in Schedule 1, must either be in red lettering or be set against a red background ; and

(*b*) in all cases must either be on a separate label or be surrounded by a line within which there must be no other words except words with which the container of the poison is required to be labelled under the Act or these Rules.

Special precautions in the case of certain articles

23.—(1) It shall not be lawful to sell or supply any poison—

(*a*) in the case of a liquid other than a medicine, contained in a bottle of a capacity of not more than one hundred and twenty fluid ounces, unless the bottle is labelled with the words "Not to be taken" ;

(*b*) in the case of an embrocation, liniment, lotion, liquid antiseptic or other liquid medicine for external application, unless the container is labelled with the name of the article and the words "For external use only".

(2) It shall not be lawful to sell or supply any compressed hydrocyanic acid unless the container is labelled with the words "Warning. This container holds poisonous gas and should only be opened and used by persons having expert knowledge of the precautions to be taken in its use".

(3) This Rule shall be in addition to the other requirements of the Act and of these Rules with respect to labelling and shall apply to transactions exempted by section 19 of the Act, but shall not apply to the sale or supply of poisons to be exported to purchasers outside the United Kingdom.

Name of seller and address of premises

24.—(1) The provisions of section 18(1)(*c*)(iv) of the Act (which requires the container of a poison to be labelled with the name of the seller and the address of the premises on which it was sold) shall not apply in the case of an article sold for the purpose of being sold again in the same container.

(2) The requirements of section 18(1)(*c*)(iv) of the Act shall be deemed to be satisfied, in the case of a poison supplied from a warehouse or depot, if the container of the poison is labelled with the address of the supplier's principal place of business or, in the case of a limited company, of the registered office of the company.

(3) Where any poison is sold in a container and outer covering, being the container and covering in which it was obtained by the seller, it shall be sufficient if the name of the seller and the address of the premises on which it was sold appear only on the outer covering.

(4) Where the names of more than one person or more than one address appear on any label, there must also be words on the label indicating clearly which person is the seller and at which of the addresses the poison was sold.

Form of containers

25.—(1) It shall not be lawful to sell, whether wholesale or retail, or supply any poison unless—

(*a*) it is contained in a container impervious to the poison and sufficiently stout to prevent leakage arising from the ordinary risks of handling and transport ; and

(*b*) in the case of a liquid contained in a bottle of a capacity of not more than one hundred and twenty fluid ounces, not being—

(i) a medicine made up ready for the internal treatment of human or animal ailments, or

(ii) a local anaesthetic for injection in the treatment of human or animal ailments, or

(iii) a sterile ophthalmic solution in a single dose sterile bottle enclosed in a sealed container,

the outer surface of the bottle is fluted vertically with ribs or grooves recognisable by touch.

(2) Sub-paragraph (*a*) of paragraph (1) shall apply to transactions exempted by section 19 of the Act, and sub-paragraph (*b*) shall not apply to the sale or supply of poisons to be exported to purchasers outside the United Kingdom or the sale or supply of poisons to a person or institution concerned with scientific education or research or chemical analysis, for the purposes of that education or research or analysis.

STORAGE AND TRANSPORT

Storage of poisons

26.—(1) It shall not be lawful to store any poison except in a container impervious to the poison and sufficiently stout to prevent leakage from the container arising from the ordinary risks of handling.

(2) It shall not be lawful to store any substance included in Schedule 1 in any retail shop or premises used in connection therewith unless the substance is stored—

(*a*) in a cupboard or drawer reserved solely for the storage of poisons ; or

(*b*) in a part of the premises which is partitioned off or otherwise separated from the remainder of the premises and to which customers are not permitted to have access ; or

(*c*) on a shelf reserved solely for the storage of poisons and—

(i) no food is kept directly under the shelf, and

(ii) the container of the substance is distinguishable by touch from the containers of articles and substances other than poisons stored upon the same premises :

Provided that, in the case of any such substance to be used in agriculture or horticulture, it shall not be lawful to store the substance on any shelf, or in any such part of the premises as aforesaid if food is kept in that part, or in any cupboard or drawer unless the cupboard or drawer is reserved solely for the storage of poisons to be used as aforesaid.

Transport of poisons

27. It shall not be lawful to consign any poison for transport unless it is sufficiently stoutly packed to avoid leakage arising from the ordinary risks of handling and transport.

Special provisions with respect to the transport of poisons specified in Schedule 8

28.—(1) It shall not be lawful to consign for transport by carrier any poison included in Schedule 8 unless the outside of the package containing the article is labelled conspicuously with the name or description of the poison as set forth in that Schedule and a notice indicating that it is to be kept separate from food and from empty containers in which food has been contained.

(2) It shall not be lawful for any person knowingly to transport any such poison as aforesaid, either on his own behalf or for another person, in any vehicle in which food is being transported, unless the food is carried in a part of the vehicle effectively separated from that containing the poison, or is otherwise adequately protected from the risk of contamination.

(3) This Rule shall not apply with respect to medicines.

SPECIAL PROVISIONS WITH RESPECT TO THE SUPPLY AND STORAGE OF MEDICINES, ETC.

Supply of medicines to out-patients from certain hospitals, etc.

29.—(1) The provisions of Part II of the Act and of these Rules, except the provisions of Rule 23, shall not apply with respect to—

(*a*) any medicine for the treatment of human ailments dispensed from a hospital, infirmary, health centre or dispensary maintained by any public authority, or out of public funds, or by a charity ;

(*b*) any medicine for the treatment of animals supplied from a veterinary hospital which is under the superintendence of a registered veterinary surgeon or registered veterinary practitioner,

if the requirements contained in the following provisions of this Rule are satisfied in relation thereto.

(2) The medicine must not be supplied except by, or on and in accordance with a prescription of, a duly qualified medical practitioner for the purposes of medical treatment, or a registered dentist for the purposes of dental treatment, or a registered veterinary surgeon or registered veterinary practitioner for the purposes of animal treatment.

(3) In a case where a substance included in Schedule 1 is supplied, a record must be kept on the premises in such a way that there can readily be traced at any time during a period of two years after the date on which the substance was supplied the following particulars :—

(*a*) the name and quantity of the poison supplied ; and

(*b*) the date on which the poison was supplied ; and

(*c*) the name and address of the person to whom the poison was supplied ; and

(*d*) the name of the person who supplied the poison or who gave the prescription upon which it was supplied :

Provided that this paragraph shall not apply to a medicine supplied on and in accordance with a prescription given by a duly qualified medical practitioner or registered dentist under and in accordance with the National Health Service Act 1946 or the National Health Service (Scotland) Act 1947.

(4) The container of the medicine must be labelled—

(*a*) with a designation and address sufficient to identify the hospital, infirmary, health centre or dispensary from which it was supplied ;

(*b*) except in the case of a medicine made up ready for treatment, with the word "Poison" ;

(*c*) in the case of a poison supplied from a veterinary hospital, with the words "For animal treatment only",

and in the case of a medicine to which Rule 23 applies the requirements of that Rule shall be satisfied in addition to the requirements aforesaid.

Supply of medicines for use in institutions

30.—(1) In any institution in which medicines are dispensed in a dispensing or pharmaceutical department in charge of a person appointed for that purpose, no medicine containing a poison shall be issued from that department for use in the wards, operating theatres or other sections of the institution, except in accordance with the requirements contained in the following provisions of this Rule.

(2) The medicines must not be issued except upon a written order signed by a duly qualified medical practitioner, registered dentist, or by a sister or nurse in charge of a ward, theatre or other section of the institution :

Provided that in a case of emergency a medicine containing a poison may be issued, notwithstanding that no such written order is produced, on an undertaking by the person ordering the medicine to furnish such a written order within the twenty-four hours next following.

(3) The container of the medicine must be labelled—

(*a*) with words describing its contents ; and

(*b*) in the case of substances included in Schedule 1 to these Rules, with a distinguishing mark or other indication indicating that the poison is to be stored in a cupboard reserved solely for the storage of poisons and other dangerous substances.

(4) In this Rule "institution" means any hospital, infirmary, health centre, dispensary, clinic, nursing home or other institution at which human ailments are treated.

Supply of oral contraceptives

31.—(1) The provisions of Part II of the Act and of these Rules shall not apply with respect to any oral contraceptive supplied—

(*a*) from a family planning clinic, if the requirements contained in paragraphs (2) and (3) are satisfied in relation thereto ; or

(*b*) by a duly qualified medical practitioner otherwise than from a family planning clinic.

(2) An oral contraceptive must not be supplied from a family planning clinic except on and in accordance with a prescription given by a duly qualified medical practitioner.

(3) The container of an oral contraceptive supplied from a family planning clinic must be labelled with words describing its contents and with a designation and address sufficient to identify the family planning clinic from which it was supplied.

(4) In this Rule :—

"family planning clinic" means a health centre, dispensary or clinic which is maintained by any public authority or by a charity or by an institution approved for the purposes of paragraph (4) of section 20 of the Act by an order made thereunder and at which contraceptive substances are supplied.

Storage of poisons in institutions

32.—(1) In any institution in which medicines are dispensed in a dispensing or pharmaceutical department in the charge of a person appointed for that purpose, all poisons other than those issued for use shall be stored in that department.

(2) In any institution to which paragraph (1) does not apply, all poisons other than those issued for use shall be stored—

(*a*) in the charge of a person appointed for the purpose by the governing body or person in control of the institution ;

(*b*) otherwise than on an open shelf, unless the container of the poison is distinguishable by touch from containers of substances other than poisons kept on the same premises ; and

(*c*) in the case of substances included in Schedule 1, either in a cupboard or drawer or on a shelf reserved solely for the storage of poisons.

(3) Every substance included in Schedule 1 kept in a ward in any institution, shall be stored in a cupboard reserved solely for the storage of poisons and other dangerous substances.

(4) All places in which poisons are kept in an institution shall be inspected at intervals of not more than three months by a pharmacist or other person appointed for the purpose by the governing body or person in control of the institution.

(5) In this Rule "institution" means any hospital, infirmary, health centre, dispensary, clinic, nursing home or other institution at which human ailments are treated or any family planning clinic as defined in Rule 31(4).

MISCELLANEOUS

Manufacture of pharmaceutical preparations

33. In all establishments in which pharmaceutical preparations containing any poison are manufactured for the purpose of the internal treatment of human ailments, the preparation must be manufactured by, or under the supervision of, a registered pharmacist or a person having one of the following qualifications in chemistry :—

(*a*) the Fellowship of the Royal Institute of Chemistry,

(*b*) the Associateship of the Royal Institute of Chemistry :

Provided that this Rule shall not apply to—

(i) the manufacture by, or under the supervision of, a duly qualified medical practitioner of preparations containing insulin, the active principles or pituitary, suprarenal or thyroid glands or the salts of the active principles of thyroid gland ;

(ii) the manufacture of any preparation by, or under the supervision of, a person who, for a period of at least three years before 1st May 1936, was continuously engaged in the manufacture of pharmaceutical preparations containing poisons and prepared for the internal treatment of human ailments, and has furnished to the registrar of the Pharmaceutical Society a statement in writing, verified by a statutory declaration, to that effect.

Form of application to a local authority, fees to be paid by listed sellers of Part II poisons and form of local authority's list

34.—(1) Every application made to a local authority for the entry of a name on the list kept by the authority in pursuance of section 21(1) of the Act, being a list of persons entitled, subject to the provisions of the Act and of these Rules, to sell poisons included in Part II of the Poisons List, shall be made in the form set out in Schedule 9 and there shall be attached to the form of application a statement of the poisons included in Part II of the Poisons List, a summary of the requirements of section 18 of the Act and of these Rules so far as they relate to the storage, sale and consignment for transport of poisons by or on behalf of persons entitled as aforesaid and a statement of the fees payable under this Rule.

(2) The following fees shall be paid to a local authority by every person whose name is entered in the list kept by that authority—

(*a*) in respect of the entry of his name in the list, a fee of twenty-five shillings ;

(*b*) in respect of the making of any alteration in the list in relation to the premises on which he is entitled to sell, a fee of five shillings ;

(*c*) in respect of the retention of his name on the list in any year subsequent to the year in which his name is first entered therein, a fee of fifteen shillings :

Provided that, in the case of a person whose name is entered in or retained on the list as a person entitled to sell on more than one set of premises, the fees payable shall be increased—

(i) in the case of the entry of his name, by the sum of twenty-five shillings for each additional set of premises on which he is entitled to sell ;

(ii) in the case of the retention of his name, by the sum of fifteen shillings for each additional set of premises.

(3) The said list shall be kept in the form set out in Schedule 10.

Certificates of persons to whom poisons may be sold

35.—(1) A certificate given for the purposes of section 18(2)(*a*) of the Act, being a certificate certifying a person to be a person to whom a poison may properly be sold, shall be in the form, and shall contain the particulars, set out in Schedule 11.

(2) All householders are hereby authorised to give such certificates as aforesaid :

Provided that a certificate given by a householder who is not known to the seller of the poison to be a responsible person of good character shall not be a sufficient certificate for the said purposes unless it is endorsed in the manner specified in Schedule 11 by a police officer in charge of a police station.

(3) On any sale of a poison upon such a certificate as aforesaid, the certificate shall be retained by the seller.

Form of record of sales

36. The particulars of sales of poisons which are required by section 18(2)(*b*) of the Act to be entered in a book shall be entered in the form set out in Schedule 12.

Preservation of records

37. All books kept for the purposes of Part II of the Act shall be preserved on the premises on which the sales recorded therein were made for a period of two years from the date on which the last entry was made therein.

James Callaghan,
One of Her Majesty's Principal
Secretaries of State.

Home Office,
Whitehall.
21st May 1970.

SCHEDULE 1

Rules 7, 8, 9, 11, 14, 15(1), 22(2), 26(2), 29(3), 30(3) and 32

Substances included in the Poisons List to which special restrictions apply unless exempted by Rule 11

Acetorphine; its salts; its esters and ethers; their salts

Acetyldihydrocodeine; its salts

Alcuronium chloride

Alkaloids, the following; their quaternary compounds; any salt, simple or complex, of any substance falling within the following:—

Aconite, alkaloids of, except substances containing less than 0·02 per cent. of the alkaloids of aconite

Atropine except substances containing less than 0·15 per cent. of atropine or not more than one per cent. of atropine methonitrate

Belladonna, alkaloids of, except substances containing less than 0·15 per cent. of the alkaloids of belladonna calculated as hyoscyamine

Brucine except substances containing less than 0·2 per cent. of brucine

Calabar bean, alkaloids of

Coca, alkaloids of, except substances containing less than 0·1 per cent. of the alkaloids of coca

Cocaine except substances containing less than 0·1 per cent. of cocaine

Codeine; its esters and ethers; except substances containing less than 1·5 per cent. of codeine

Coniine except substances containing less than 0·1 per cent. of coniine

Cotarnine except substances containing less than 0·2 per cent. of cotarnine

Curare, alkaloids of; curare bases

Ecgonine; its esters and ethers; except substances containing less than the equivalent of 0·1 per cent. of ecgonine

Emetine except substances containing less than one per cent. of emetine

Ephedrine; its optical isomers; except when contained in liquid preparations or preparations not intended for the internal treatment of human ailments and except solid preparations containing less than ten per cent. of ephedrine or its optical isomers otherwise than in an inert diluent.

Gelsemium, alkaloids of, except substances containing less than 0·1 per cent. of the alkaloids of gelsemium

Homatropine except substances containing less than 0·15 per cent. of homatropine

Hyoscine except substances containing less than 0·15 per cent. of hyoscine

Hyoscyamine except substances containing less than 0·15 per cent. of hyoscyamine

Jaborandi, alkaloids of, except substances containing less than 0·5 per cent. of the alkaloids of jaborandi

Lobelia, alkaloids of, except substances containing less than 0·5 per cent. of the alkaloids of lobelia

Morphine; its esters and ethers; except substances containing less than 0·2 per cent. of morphine calculated as anhydrous morphine

Nicotine

Papaverine except substances containing less than one per cent. of papaverine

Pomegranate, alkaloids of, except substances containing less than 0·5 per cent. of the alkaloids of pomegranate

Quebracho, alkaloids of

Sabadilla, alkaloids of, except substances containing less than one per cent. of the alkaloids of sabadilla

Solanaceous alkaloids, not otherwise included in this Schedule, except substances containing less than 0·15 per cent. of solanaceous alkaloids calculated as hyoscyamine

Stavesacre, alkaloids of, except substances containing less than 0·2 per cent. of the alkaloids of stavesacre

Strychnine except substances containing less than 0·2 per cent. of strychnine

Thebaine except substances containing less than one per cent. of thebaine

Veratrum, alkaloids of, except substances containing less than one per cent. of the alkaloids of veratrum

Yohimba, alkaloids of

Allylisopropylacetylurea

Allylprodine; its salts

Alphameprodine; its salts

Alphaprodine; its salts

Amino-alcohols esterified with benzoic acid, phenylacetic acid, phenylpropionic acid, cinnamic acid or the derivatives of these acids, except substances containing less than ten per cent. of esterified amino-alcohols and except procaine when in a preparation containing any substance to which Part II of the Thereapeutic Substances Act 1956(a) for the time being applies; their salts

---

(a) 1956 c. 25.

Anileridine; its salts

Antimonial poisons except substances containing less than the equivalent of one per cent. of antimony trioxide

Apomorphine; its salts; except substances containing less than 0·2 per cent. of apomorphine

Arsenical poisons except substances containing less than the equivalent of 0·01 per cent. of arsenic trioxide and except dentrifices containing less than 0·5 per cent. of acetarsol

Barbituric acid; its salts; derivatives of barbituric acid; their salts; compounds of barbituric acid, its salts, its derivatives, their salts, with any other substance

Barium, salts of

Benzethidine; its salts

Benzoylmorphine; its salts

Benzylmorphine; its salts

Betameprodine; its salts

Betaprodine; its salts

Bezitramide; its salts

Busulphan; its salts

Cannabis; the resin of cannabis; extracts of cannabis; tinctures of cannabis; cannabin tannate

Cantharidin except substances containing less than 0·01 per cent. of cantharidin

Cantharidates except substances containing less than the equivalent of 0·01 per cent. of cantharidin

Carbachol

Carperidine; its salts

Chloroform, except substances containing not more than 5 per cent. of chloroform or when in preparations not intended for the internal treatment of human ailments

Clonitazene; its salts

4-Cyano-2-dimethylamino-4,4-diphenylbutane; its salts

4-Cyano-1-methyl-4-phenylpiperidine; its salts

Dehydroemetine; its salts

Demecarium bromide

Desomorphine; its salts; its esters and ethers; their salts

Dextromethorphan; its salts; except substances containing less than 1·5 per cent. of dextromethorphan

Dextromoramide; its salts

Dextrorphan; its salts

Diacetylmorphine; its salts

Diacetylnalorphine; its salts

Diampromide; its salts

Digitalis, glycosides and other active principles of, except substances containing less than one unit of activity (as defined in the British Pharmacopoeia) in two grammes of the substance

Dihydrocodeine; its salts; its esters and ethers; their salts

Dihydrocodeinone; its salts

Dihydrocodeinone *O*-carboxymethyloxime; its salts; its esters; their salts

Dihydromorphine; its salts; its esters and ethers; their salts

Dimenoxadole; its salts

Dimepheptanol; its salts; its esters and ethers; their salts

Dinitrocresols (DNOC); their compounds with a metal or a base; except winter washes containing not more than the equivalent of five per cent. of dinitrocresols

Dinitronaphthols; dinitrophenols; dinitrothymols

Dinosam; its compounds with a metal or a base

Dinoseb; its compounds with a metal or a base

Dioxaphetyl butyrate; its salts

Diphenoxylate; its salts; except (*a*) pharmaceutical preparations in solid or liquid form containing not more than 2·5 milligrammes of diphenoxylate calculated as base and not less than 25 microgrammes of atropine calculated as atropine sulphate per dosage unit and containing no other substance to which any Part of the Dangerous Drugs Act 1965(**a**) applies and (*b*) liquid preparations containing 0·5 milligrammes diphenoxylate hydrochloride, 0·005 milligrammes atropine sulphate, 0·16 millilitres ethyl alcohol, 0·002 millilitres imitation cherry flavour, 0·45 millilitres glycerine, 0·4 millilitres sorbital solution (70 per cent.), 0·01 milligrammes red dye colour index No. 14700 (F.D. 4C. Red No. 4), 0·0008 millilitres water

Dipipanone; its salts

Disulfiram

Dithienylallylamines; dithienylalkylallylamines; their salts

Dyflos

Ecothiopate iodine

Embutramide

Endosulfan

Endothal; its salts

Endrin

Ethylmorphine; its salts; its esters and ethers; their salts; except substances containing less than 0·2 per cent. of ethylmorphine

Etonitazene; its salts

Etorphine; its salts; its esters and ethers; their salts

Etoxeridine; its salts

Fentanyl; its salts

Fluanisone

Fluoroacetamide; fluoroacetanilide

Furethidine; its salts

Gallamine; its salts; its quaternary compounds

Guanidines, the following:—

polymethylene diguanidines; di-*p*-anisyl-*p*-phenetylguanidine

Hydrocyanic acid except substances containing less than 0·15 per cent., weight in weight, of hydrocyanic acid (HCN); cyanides, other than ferrocyanides and ferricyanides, except substances containing less than the equivalent of 0·1 per cent., weight in weight, of hydrocyanic acid (HCN)

Hydromorphinol; its salts; its esters and ethers; their salts

Hydromorphone; its salts; its esters and ethers; their salts

Hydroxycinchoninic acids; derivatives of; their salts; their esters; except substances containing less than three per cent. of a hydroxycinchoninic acid or a derivative thereof

Hydroxypethidine; its salts; its esters and ethers; their salts

Hydroxyurea

Isomethadone (isoamidone); its salts

Ketobemidone; its salts; its esters and ethers; their salts

Laudexium; its salts

(**a**) 1965 c. 15.

Lead, compounds of, with acids from fixed oils

Levomethorphan; its salts

Levomoramide; its salts

Levophenacylmorphan; its salts; its esters and ethers; their salts

Levorphanol; its salts; its esters and ethers; their salts

Mannomustine; its salts

Mebezonium iodide

Mercaptopurine; its salts; derivatives of mercaptopurine; their salts

Mercuric chloride except substances containing less than one per cent. of mercuric chloride; mercuric iodide except substances containing less than two per cent. of mercuric iodide; nitrates of mercury except substances containing less than the equivalent of three per cent., weight in weight, of mercury (Hg); potassiomercuric iodides except substances containing less than the equivalent of one per cent. of mercuric iodide; organic compounds of mercury except substances, not being aerosols, containing less than the equivalent of 0·2 per cent., weight in weight, of mercury (Hg)

Mescaline, and other derivatives of phenethylamine formed by substitution in the aromatic ring; their salts

Metazocine; its salts; its esters and ethers; their salts

Methadone (amidone); its salts

Methadyl acetate; its salts

Methyldesorphine; its salts; its esters and ethers; their salts

Methyldihydromorphine; its salts; its esters and ethers; their salts

2-Methyl-3-morpholino-1,1-diphenylpropanecarboxylic acid; its salts; its esters; their salts

1-Methyl-4-phenylpiperidine-4-carboxylic acid; esters of; their salts

Metopon; its salts; its esters and ethers; their salts

Monofluoroacetic acid; its salts

Morpheridine; its salts

Mustine and any other *N*-substituted derivative of di-(2-chloroethyl)amine; their salts

Myrophine; its salts

Nalorphine; its salts

Nicocodine; its salts

m-Nitrophenol; *o*-nitrophenol; *p*-nitrophenol

Noracymethadol; its salts

Norcodeine; its salts; its esters and ethers; their salts

Norlevorphanol; its salts; its esters and ethers; their salts

Normethadone; its salts

Normorphine; its salts; its esters and ethers; their salts

Norpipanone

Nux Vomica except substances containing less than 0·2 per cent. of strychnine

Opium except substances containing less than 0·2 per cent. of morphine calculated as anhydrous morphine

Organo-tin compounds, the following:—
 Compounds of fentin

Ouabain

Oxycodone; its salts; its esters and ethers; their salts

Oxymorphone; its salts; its esters and ethers; their salts

Phenacemide

Phenadoxone; its salts

Phenampromide; its salts

Phenazocine; its salts; its esters and ethers; their salts

Phencyclidine; its salts

Phenomorphan; its salts; its esters and ethers; their salts

Phenoperidine; its salts; its esters and ethers; their salts

2-Phenylcinchoninic acid; 2-salicylcinchoninic acid; their salts; their esters

4-Phenylpiperidine-4-carboxylic acid ethyl ester; its salts

Pholcodine; its salts; its esters and ethers; their salts; except substances containing less than 1·5 per cent. of pholcodine

Phosphorus compounds, the following:—

- Amiton
- Azinphos-ethyl
- Azinphos-methyl
- Chlorfenvinphos except sheep dips containing not more than ten per cent., weight in weight, of chlorfenvinphos
- Demeton-O
- Demeton-S
- Demeton-O-methyl
- Demeton-S-methyl
- Dichlorvos
- Diethyl 4-methyl-7-coumarinyl phosphorothionate
- Diethyl *p*-nitrophenyl phosphate
- Dimefox
- Disulfoton
- Ethion
- Ethyl-*p*-nitrophenyl phenylphosphonothionate
- Mazidox
- Mecarbam
- Mevinphos
- Mipafox
- Oxydemeton-methyl
- Parathion
- Phenkapton
- Phorate
- Phosphamidon
- Schradan
- Sulfotep
- TEPP (HETP)
- Thionazin
- Triphosphoric pentadimethylamide
- Vamidothion

Picrotoxin

Piminodine; its salts

Piritramide; its salts

Polymethylenebistrimethylammonium salts

Proheptazine; its salts

Propoxyphene; its salts
Racemethorphan; its salts
Racemoramide; its salts
Racemorphan; its salts; its esters and ethers; their salts
Savin, oil of
Strophanthus, glycosides of
Thallium, salts of
Thebacon; its salts
Tretamine; its salts
Triaziquone
Trimeperidine; its salts
Zinc phosphide

SCHEDULE 2

Rule 6(2)

Poisons exempted from labelling provisions when sold or supplied in certain circumstances

Alkali fluorides; alkali metal bifluorides; ammonium bifluoride
Ammonia
Antimony, chlorides of; antimonates; antimonites
Chloroform
Dinitrocresols (DNOC)
Dinitronaphthols; dinitrophenols
Formaldehyde
Formic acid
Glyceryl trinitrate
Hydrochloric acid
Hydrofluoric acid; sodium silicofluoride
Lead acetates; compounds of lead with acids from fixed oils
Mercuric chloride; mercuric iodide; organic compounds of mercury
Mercury, oxides of; nitrates of mercury
Nitric acid
Nitrobenzene
m-Nitrophenol; *o*-nitrophenol; *p*-nitrophenol
Oxalic acid; metallic oxalates
Phenols; compounds of phenol with a metal
Phosphorus, yellow
Picric acid
Potassium hydroxide
Sodium hydroxide
Sulphuric acid

Rule 12

SCHEDULE 3

Articles exempted from the provisions of the Act and of these Rules

GROUP I

GENERAL EXEMPTIONS

Adhesives; anti-fouling compositions; builders' materials; ceramics; distempers; electrical valves; enamels; explosives; fillers; fireworks; fluorescent lamps; glazes; glue; inks; lacquer solvents; loading materials; matches; motor fuels and lubricants; paints other than pharmaceutical paints; photographic paper; pigments; plastics; propellants; rubber; varnishes; vascular plants and their seeds.

GROUP II

SPECIAL EXEMPTIONS

Poison	*Substance or article in which exempted*
Acetanilide; alkyl acetanilides	Substances not being preparations for the treatment of human ailments
Alkaloids, the following:—	
Brucine	Surgical spirit containing not more than 0·015 per cent. of brucine
Emetine	Ipecacuanha; extracts and tinctures of ipecacuanha; substances containing less than 0·05 per cent. of emetine
Ephedra, alkaloids of	Substances containing less than one per cent. of the alkaloids of ephedra
Jaborandi, alkaloids of	Substances containing less than 0·025 per cent. of the alkaloids of jaborandi
Lobelia, alkaloids of	Preparations for the relief of asthma in the form of cigarettes, smoking mixtures or fumigants; substances containing less than 0·1 per cent. of the alkaloids of lobelia
Nicotine	Tobacco; preparations in aerosol dispensers containing not more than 0·2 per cent. of nicotine, weight in weight; other liquid preparations, and solid preparations with a soap base, containing not more than 7·5 per cent. of nicotine, weight in weight
Pomegranate, alkaloids of	Pomegranate bark
Solanaceous alkaloids	Stramonium contained in preparations for the relief of asthma in the form of cigarettes, smoking mixtures or fumigants
Stavesacre, alkaloids of	Soaps; ointments; lotions for external use
p-Aminobenzenesulphonamide; its salts; derivatives of *p*-aminobenzenesulphonamide having any of the hydrogen atoms of the *p*-amino group or of the sulphonamide group substituted by another radical; their salts	Feeding stuffs containing not more than 0·5 per cent. of total sulphonamides; sulphaquinoxaline when contained, to a concentration not exceeding 0·5 per cent., in preparations for the destruction of rats and mice

Poison	*Substance or article in which exempted*
Ammonia	Substances not being solutions of ammonia or preparations containing solutions of ammonia; substances containing less than five per cent., weight in weight, of ammonia (NH_3); refrigerators; smelling bottles
Androgenic, oestrogenic and progestational substances, the following:— Benzoestrol; Derivatives of stilbene, dibenzyl or naphthalene with oestrogenic activity; their esters; Steroid compounds with androgenic or oestrogenic or progestational activity; their esters	Preparations intended for external application only, except preparations containing more than four milligrammes of oestrogenic substance per hundred grammes of inert substance; feeding stuffs containing hexoestrol or stilboestrol or both and not containing any other androgenic, oestrogenic or progestational substance
Anti-histamine substances, the following; their salts; their molecular compounds:— Antazoline; Bromodiphenhydramine; Buclizine; Carbinoxamine; Chlorcyclizine; Chlorpheniramine; Cinnarizine; Clemizole; Cyclizine; 3-Di-*n*-butylaminomethyl-4,5,6-trihydroxyphthalide; Diphenhydramine; Diphenylpyraline; Doxylamine; Isothipendyl; Mebhydrolin; Meclozine; Phenindamine; Pheniramine; Phenyltoloxamine; Promethazine; Pyrrobutamine; Thenalidine; Tolpropamine; Triprolidine; Substances being tetra-*N*-substituted derivatives of ethylenediamine or propylenediamine	Preparations intended for external application only and preparations containing not more than one per cent. of anti-histamine substances for application in the nose or eye
Antimony, chlorides of	Polishes
Arsenical poisons	Pyrites ores or sulphuric acid containing arsenical poisons as natural impurities; poultry or pig feeding stuffs containing not more than 0·005 per cent. of 4-hydroxy-3-nitrophenylarsonic acid

Poison	*Substance or article in which exempted*
	and not containing any other arsenical poison; animal feeding stuffs containing not more than 0·01 per cent. of arsanilic acid and not containing any other arsenical poison
Barbituric acid; its salts; derivatives of barbituric acid; their salts; compounds of barbituric acid, its salts, its derivatives, their salts, with any other substance	Self heating preparations, in aerosol dispensers, intended for external application only, containing 1,5-diethyl-2-thio-4,6-pyrimidinedione and not containing any other substance mentioned opposite hereto in the first column
Barium, salts of	Witherite other than finely ground witherite; barium carbonate bonded to charcoal for case hardening; fire extinguishers containing barium chloride
Carbarsone	Poultry feeding stuffs containing not more than 0·0375 per cent. of carbarsone
Chloroform	Substances containing less than one per cent. of chloroform; solid preparations; toothpaste
Creosote obtained from wood	Substances containing less than fifty per cent. of creosote obtained from wood
Diamines, the following; their salts:—phenylene diamines; tolylene diamines; other alkylated-benzene diamines	Substances other than preparations for the dyeing of hair
Dinitrocresols (DNOC); their compounds with a metal or a base	Substances being neither preparations for the treatment of human ailments nor preparations for use in agriculture or horticulture
Dinitrophenols	Substances not being preparations for the treatment of human ailments
Dinosam; its compounds with a metal or a base	Substances not being preparations for use in agriculture or horticulture
Dinoseb; its compounds with a metal or a base	Substances not being preparations for use in agriculture or horticulture
Diperodon; its salts	Preparations intended for external application only, containing not more than one per cent. of diperodon, calculated as anhydrous base
Disulfiram	Substances not being preparations for the treatment of human ailments
Formaldehyde	Substances containing less than five per cent., weight in weight, of formaldehyde (H.CHO); photographic glazing or hardening solutions
Formic acid	Substances containing less than five per cent., weight in weight, of formic acid (H.COOH)

Poison	*Substance or article in which exempted*
Hydrochloric acid	Substances containing less than nine per cent., weight in weight, of hydrochloric acid (HCl)
Hydrocyanic acid	Preparations of wild cherry; in reagent kits supplied for medical or veterinary purposes, substances containing less than the equivalent of 0·1 per cent., weight in weight, of hydrocyanic acid (HCN)
Lead acetate	Substances containing less than four per cent. of lead acetate
Lead, compounds of	Machine-spread plasters
Mercuric chloride	Batteries
Mercuric chloride; mercuric iodide; organic compounds of mercury	Dressings on seeds or bulbs
Mercury, nitrates of	Ointments containing less than the equivalent of three per cent., weight in weight, of mercury (Hg)
Mercury, oxides of	Canker and wound paints (for trees) containing not more than three per cent., weight in weight, of yellow mercuric oxide
Mescaline; its salts	Living plants
Nitric acid	Substances containing less than nine per cent., weight in weight, of nitric acid (HNO_3)
Nitrobenzene	Substances containing less than 0·1 per cent. of nitrobenzene; soaps containing less than one per cent. of nitrobenzene; polishes
p-Nitrobenzyl cyanide	Photographic solutions containing less than the equivalent of 0·1 per cent., weight in weight, of hydrocyanic acid (HCN)
p-Nitrophenol	Preparations for use in agriculture or horticulture containing not more than 0·5 per cent. of *p*-nitrophenol as preservative
Organo-tin compounds, the following:—	
Compounds of fentin	Substances other than preparations for use in agriculture or horticulture
Oxalic acid; metalic oxalates	Laundry blue; polishes; cleaning powders or scouring products, containing the equivalent of not more than ten per cent. of oxalic acid dihydrate
Paraquat	Preparations in pellet form containing not more than five cent. of salts of paraquat calculated as paraquat ion
Phenols	Butylated hydroxytoluene; carvacrol; creosote obtained from coal tar; essential oils in which phenols occur naturally;

Poison	*Substance or article in which exempted*
	medicines containing less than one per cent. of phenols; nasal sprays, mouth washes, pastilles, lozenges, capsules, pessaries, ointments or suppositories containing less than 2·5 per cent. of phenols; in reagent kits supplied for medical or veterinary purposes; smelling bottles; soaps for washing; solid substances, other than pastilles, lozenges, capsules, pessaries, ointments and suppositories, containing less than sixty per cent. of phenols; tar (coal or wood), crude or refined; *p-tertiary*-amylphenol; *tertiary*-butylcresol; *p-tertiary*-butylphenol; *p*-(1,1,3,3-tertramethylbutyl) phenol; thymol
Phenyl mercuric salts	Toilet, cosmetic and therapeutic preparations containing not more than 0·01 per cent. of phenyl mercuric salts as a preservative; antiseptic dressings on toothbrushes; in textiles containing not more than 0·01 per cent. of phenyl mercuric salts as a bacteriostat and fungicide
Phosphoric acid	Substances containing phosphoric acid, not being descaling preparations containing more than fifty per cent., weight in weight, of ortho-phosphoric acid
Phosphorus compounds, the following:—	
Amiton Azinphos-ethyl Azinphos-methyl	Substances other than preparations for use in agriculture or horticulture
Chlorfenvinphos	Substances other than preparations, not being granular preparations, for use in agriculture or horticulture
Demeton-O Demeton-S	Substances other than preparations for use in agriculture or horticulture
Dichlorvos	Substances other than preparations for use in agriculture or horticulture, not being preparations in— (*a*) impregnated materials containing not more than twenty per cent., weight in weight, of dichlorvos in a resinous or plastic base, or (*b*) aerosols containing not more than one per cent., weight in weight, of dichlorvos, or (*c*) thermal vaporisers containing not more than thirty per cent., weight in weight, of dichlorvos in an impregnated, fixed, rigid and porous base

Poison	*Substance or article in which exempted*
Diethyl 4-methyl-7-coumarinyl phosphorothionate Diethyl *p*-nitrophenyl phosphate Dimefox	Substances other than preparations for use in agriculture or horticulture
Disulfoton	Substances other than preparations, not being granular preparations, for use in agriculture or horticulture
Ethion Ethyl *p*-nitrophenyl phenylphosphonothionate Mazidox Mecarbam Mevinphos Mipafox	Substances other than preparations for use in agriculture or horticulture
Oxydemeton-methyl	Substances other than preparations for use in agriculture or, except in aerosol canisters containing not more than 0·25 per cent., weight in weight, of oxydemeton-methyl, for use in horticulture
Parathion	Substances other than preparations, not being granular preparations, for use in agriculture or horticulture
Phenkapton	Substances other than preparations for use in agriculture or horticulture
Phorate	Substances other than preparations, not being granular preparations, for use in agriculture or horticulture
Phosphamidon Schradan Sulfotep TEPP (HETP)	Substances other than preparations for use in agriculture or horticulture
Thionazin	Substances other than preparations, not being granular preparations, for use in agriculture or horticulture
Triphosphoric penta-dimethylamide Vamidothion	Substances other than preparations for use in agriculture or horticulture
Picric acid	Substances containing less than five per cent. of picric acid
Podophyllum resin	Preparations containing not more than 1·5 per cent., weight in weight, of podophyllum resin
Potassium hydroxide	Substances containing the equivalent of less than seventeen per cent. of total caustic alkalinity expressed as potassium hydroxide; accumulators; batteries
Procaine	Feeding stuffs containing any substance to which Part II of the Therapeutic Substances Act 1956 for the time being applies

Poison	*Substance or article in which exempted*
Quinine; its salts	Preparations containing not more than one per cent. of quinine or its salts; soft drinks, wines or tonic wines; preparations containing not more than fifteen per cent. of quinine or its salts for use in the manufacture of soft drinks, wines, tonic wines or confectionery
Sodium ethyl mercurithiosalicylate	Therapeutic substances containing less than 0·1 per cent. of sodium ethyl mercurithiosalicylate as a preservative
Sodium fluoride	Substances containing less than three per cent. of sodium fluoride as a preservative; dentifrices containing not more than 0·3 per cent. of sodium fluoride; mouth wash tablets containing not more than 0·2 per cent. of sodium fluoride and liquid mouth washes containing not more than 0·05 per cent. thereof
Sodium hydroxide	Substances containing the equivalent of less than twelve per cent. of total caustic alkalinity expressed as sodium hydroxide
Sodium nitrite	Substances other than preparations containing more than 0·1 per cent. of sodium nitrite for the destruction of rats or mice
Sodium silicofluoride	Substances containing less than three per cent. of sodium silicofluoride as a preservative
Sulphuric acid	Substances containing less than nine per cent., weight in weight, of sulphuric acid (H_2SO_4); accumulators; batteries and sealed containers in which sulphuric acid is packed together with car batteries for use in those batteries; fire extinguishers

In Group II in this Schedule the expression "granular preparation" in relation to a poison means a preparation—

(*a*) which consists of absorbent mineral or synthetic solid particles impregnated with the poison, the size of the particles being such that not more than four per cent., weight in weight, of the preparation is capable of passing a sieve with a mesh of 250 microns, and not more than one per cent. a sieve with a mesh of 150 microns;

(*b*) which has an apparent density of not less than 0·4 grammes per millilitre if compacted without pressure; and

(*c*) not more than 12 per cent. of which, weight in weight, consists of the poison.

Rules 6(3) and 13

SCHEDULE 4

Substances required to be sold by retail only upon a prescription given by a duly qualified medical practitioner, registered dentist, registered veterinary surgeon or registered veterinary practitioner.

Part A

Alcuronium chloride
Allylisopropylacetylurea

Barbituric acid; its salts; derivatives of barbituric acid; their salts; compounds of barbituric acid, its salts, its derivatives, their salts, with any other substance

Busulphan; its salts

Demecarium bromide

Dinitrocresols (DNOC); their compounds with a metal or a base, except preparations for use in agriculture or horticulture

Dinitronaphthols; dinitrophenols; dinitrothymols

Disulfiram

Dithienylallylamines; dithienylalkylallylamines; their salts; except diethylthiambutene, dimethylthiambutene and ethylmethylthiambutene

Gallamine; its salts; its quaternary compounds

Hydroxyurea

Mannomustine; its salts

Mercaptopurine; its salts; derivatives of mercaptopurine; their salts

Mustine and any other *N*-substituted derivatives of di-(2-chloroethyl)amine; their salts

Phenacemide

Phencyclidine; its salts

2-Phenylcinchoninic acid; 2-salicylcinchoninic acid; their salts; their esters

Polymethylenebistrimethylammonium salts

Tretamine; its salts

Triaziquone

PART B

Acetanilide; alkyl acetanilides

Acetohexamide

Acetylcarbromal

Amidopyrine; its salts; amidopyrine sulphonates; their salts

p-Aminobenzenesulphonamide; its salts; derivatives of *p*-aminobenzenesulphonamide having any of the hydrogen atoms of the *p*-amino group or of the sulphonamide group substituted by another radical; their salts; except when contained in ointments or surgical dressings or in preparations for the prevention and treatment of diseases in poultry

Aminorex; its salts

Amitriptyline; its salts

Androgenic, oestrogenic and progestational substances, the following:—

Benzoestrol

Derivatives of stilbene, dibenzyl or naphthalene with oestrogenic activity; their esters

Steroid compounds with androgenic or oestrogenic or progestational activity; their esters

Azacyclonol; its salts

Benactyzine; its salts

Benzhexol; its salts

Benztropine and its homologues; their salts

Bromvaletone

Captodiame; its salts

Caramiphen; its salts; except tablets containing not more than the equivalent of 7·5 milligrammes of caramiphen base, and liquid preparations containing not more than the equivalent of 0·1 per cent. of caramiphen base

Carbromal

Carisoprodol

Chloral; its addition and its condensation products; their molecular compounds; except when contained, in the form of chloral hydrate, in preparations intended for external application only and except when contained, in the form of alpha-chloralose, in preparations intended for indoor use in the destruction of rats or mice containing not more than four per cent., weight in weight, of alpha-chloralose

Chlordiazepoxide; its salts

Chlormethiazole; its salts

Chlorothiazide and other derivatives of benzo-1,2,4-thiadiazine-7-sulphonamide 1, 1-dioxide, whether hydrogenated or not

Chlorphenoxamine; its salts

Chlorphentermine; its salts

Chlorpropamide; its salts

Chlorprothixene and other derivatives of 9-methylenethiaxanthen; their salts

Chlorthalidone and other derivatives of *o*-chlorobenzene sulphonamide

Clorexolone

Clorprenaline; its salts; when contained in aerosol dispensers

Colchicum, alkaloids of; their salts

Corticotrophins, natural and synthetic

Cyclarbamate

Cycrimine; its salts

Desipramine; its salts

Diazepam and other compounds containing the chemical structure of dihydro-1, 4-benzodiazepine substituted to any degree; their salts

3-(3,4-Dihydroxyphenyl)alanine; its salts

Diphenoxylate and its salts contained in (*a*) pharmaceutical preparations in solid or liquid form containing not more than 2·5 milligrammes of diphenoxylate calculated as base and not less than 25 microgrammes of atropine calculated as atropine sulphate per dosage unit and containing no other substance to which any Part of the Dangerous Drugs Act 1965 applies or (*b*) liquid preparations containing 0·5 milligrammes diphenoxylate hydrochloride, 0·005 milligrammes atropine sulphate, 0·16 millilitres ethyl alcohol, 0·002 millilitres imitation cherry flavour 0·45 millilitres glycerine, 0·4 millilitres sorbital solution (70 per cent.), 0·01 milligrammes red dye colour index No. 14700 (F.D. 4C. Red No. 4), 0·0008 millilitres water

Dothiepin; its salts

Ectylurea

Emylcamate

Ephedrine; its optical isomers; their salts; when contained in aerosol dispensers

Ergot, alkaloids of, whether hydrogenated or not; their homologues; any salt of any substance falling within this item

Ethacrynic acid; its salts

Ethchlorvynol

Ethinamate

Ethionamide

Ethoheptazine; its salts

Ethylnoradrenaline; its salts; when contained in aerosol dispensers

Fenfluramine; its salts

Flufenamic acid; its salts; its esters; their salts

Glutethimide; its salts

Glymidine

Haloperidol and other 4-substituted derivatives of *N*-(3-*p*-fluoro-benzoylpropyl) piperidine

Hexapropymate

Hydrazines, benzyl phenethyl or phenoxyethyl; their α-methyl derivatives; acyl derivatives of any of the foregoing substances comprised in this item; salts of any compounds comprised in this item

Hydroxy-*N*,*N*-dimethyltryptamines; their esters or ethers; any salt of any substance falling within this item

Hydroxyzine; its salts

Imipramine; its salts

Indomethacin; its salts

Iprindole; its salts

Isoaminile; its salts

Isoetharine; its salts; when contained in aerosol dispensers

Isoprenaline; its salts; when contained in aerosol dispensers

Mebutamate

Meclofenoxate; its salts

Mefenamic acid; its salts; its esters; their salts

Mephenesin; its esters

Meprobamate

Metaxalone

Metformin; its salts

Methaqualone; its salts

Methixene; its salts

Methocarbamol

Methoxsalen

Methoxyphenamine; its salts; when contained in aerosol dispensers

Methylaminoheptane; its salts; when contained in aerosol dispensers

Methylpentynol; its esters and other derivatives

α-Methylphenethylamine, β-methylphenethylamine and α-ethylphenethylamine; any synthetic compound structurally derived from any of those substances by substitution in the aliphatic part or by ring closure therein (or by both such substitution and such closure) or by substitution in the aromatic ring (with or without substitution at the nitrogen atom), except ephedrine, its optical isomers and *N*-substituted derivatives, fenfluramine, hydroxyamphetamine, methoxyphenamine, phenylpropanolamine, pholedrine and prenylamine; any salt of any substance falling within this item

Methyprylone

Metoclopramide; its salts

Mitopodozide; its salts

Nortryptyline; its salts

Orciprenaline; its salts; when contained in aerosol dispensers

Orphenadrine; its salts

Oxethazaine

Oxyphenbutazone

Oxytocins, natural and synthetic

Paraldehyde

Paramethadione

Poison	*Form to which sale is restricted*
Nitrobenzene	Agricultural and horticultural insecticides; substances for the treatment of bee disease; ointments for the treatment of animals
Organo-tin compounds, the following:—	
Compounds of fentin	Preparations for use in agriculture or horticulture
Phosphorus compounds, the following:—	
Amiton Azinphos-ethyl Azinphos-methyl Chlorfenvinphos Demeton-O Demeton-S Dichlorvos Diethyl 4-methyl-7-coumarinyl phosphorothionate Diethyl *p*-nitrophenyl phosphate Dimefox Disulfoton Ethion Ethyl *p*-nitrophenyl phenylphosphonothionate Mazidox Mecarbam Mevinphos Mipafox Oxydemeton-methyl Parathion Phenkapton Phorate Phosphamidon Schradan Sulfotep TEPP (HETP) Thionazin Triphosphoric pentadimethylamide Vamidothion	Preparations for use in agriculture or horticulture
Zinc phosphide	Preparations for the destruction of rats or mice

PART B

Poisons which may be sold by listed sellers of Part II poisons only to persons engaged in the trade or business of agriculture or horticulture and for the purpose of that trade or business

Arsenical poisons other than lead arsenates and copper acetoarsenite

Dinitrocresols (DNOC); their compounds with a metal or a base; except winter washes containing not more than the equivalent of five per cent. of dinitrocresols

Dinosam; its compounds with a metal or a base

Dinoseb; its compounds with a metal or a base

Mercuric chlorides; mercuric iodides; organic compounds of mercury; except solutions containing not more than five per cent., weight in volume, of phenyl mercuric acetate for use in swimming baths

Organo-tin compounds, the following:—
Compounds of fentin
Phosphorus compounds, the following:—
Amiton
Azinphos-ethyl
Azinphos-methyl
Chlorfenvinphos
Demeton-O
Demeton-S
Dichlorvos
Diethyl 4-methyl-7-coumarinyl phosphorothionate
Diethyl *p*-nitrophenyl phosphate
Dimefox
Disulfoton
Ethion
Ethyl *p*-nitrophenyl phenylphosphonothionate
Mazidox
Mecarbam
Mevinphos
Mipafox, except in the form of a cap on a stick or wire
Oxydemeton-methyl
Parathion
Phenkapton
Phorate
Phosphamidon
Schradan
Sulfotep
Thionazin
Triphosphoric pentadimethylamide
Vamidothion

Rules 20(3) and 21(2)

SCHEDULE 6

Statement of particulars permitted in certain cases as to proportion of poison

Name of Poison	*Particulars*
Alkaloids Aconite, alkaloids of	The proportion of any one alkaloid of aconite that the preparation would be calculated to contain on the assumption that all the alkaloids of aconite in the preparation were that alkaloid.
Belladonna, alkaloids of Calabar bean, alkaloids of Coca, alkaloids of Colchicum, alkaloids of Ephedra, alkaloids of Ergot, alkaloids of Gelsemium, alkaloids of Jaborandi, alkaloids of Lobelia, alkaloids of Pomegranate, alkaloids of Quebracho, alkaloids of, other than the alkaloids of red quebracho Sabadilla, alkaloids of Solanaceous alkaloids not otherwise included in the Poisons List Stavesacre, alkaloids of Veratrum, alkaloids of Yohimba, alkaloids of	The same as above, with the substitution for the reference to aconite of a reference to belladonna, calabar bean or such other of the said poisons as the case may require.

Name of Poison	*Particulars*
Antimonial poisons	The proportion of antimony trioxide (Sb_2O_3) or antimony pentoxide (Sb_2O_5) that the preparation would be calculated to contain on the assumption that the antimony (Sb) in the poison had been wholly converted into antimony trioxide or antimony pentoxide as the case may be.
Arsenical poisons	The proportion of arsenic trioxide (As_2O_3) or arsenic pentoxide (As_2O_5) that the preparation would be calculated to contain on the assumption that the arsenic (As) in the poison had been wholly converted into arsenic trioxide or arsenic pentoxide as the case may be.
Barium, salts of	The proportion of one particular barium salt which the preparation would be calculated to contain on the assumption that the barium (Ba) in the poison had been wholly converted into that salt.
Digitalis, glycosides of; other active principles of digitalis	The number of units of activity as defined in the British Pharmacopoeia contained in a specified quantity of the preparation.
Hydrocyanic acid; cyanides, other than ferrocyanides and ferricyanides	The proportion of hydrocyanic acid (HCN) that the preparation would be calculated to contain on the assumption that the cyanides in the poison had been wholly converted into hydrocyanic acid.
Insulin	The number of units of activity as defined in the British Pharmacopoeia contained in a specified quantity of the preparation.
Lead, compounds of, with acids from fixed oils	The proportion of lead oxide (PbO) that the preparation would be calculated to contain on the assumption that the lead in the poison had been wholly converted into lead oxide.
Mercury, organic compounds of	The proportion of organically-combined mercury (Hg) contained in the preparation.
Nux Vomica	The proportion of strychnine contained in the preparation.
Opium	The proportion of morphine contained in the preparation.
Phenols	The proportion of phenols (added together) contained in the preparation.
Compounds of a phenol with a metal	The proportion of phenols (added together) that the preparation would be calculated to contain on the assumption that the compounds of

Name of Poison	*Particulars*
	phenols with a metal had been wholly converted into the corresponding phenols.
Pituitary gland, the active principles of	Either— (*a*) the number of units of activity as defined in the British Pharmacopoeia contained in a specified quantity of the preparation; or (*b*) the proportion of pituitary gland, or of anterior or of posterior lobe of the gland, as the case may be, contained in the preparation; or (*c*) the amount of pituitary gland, or of anterior or of posterior lobe of the gland, as the case may be, from which a specified quantity of the preparation was obtained together with an indication whether the amount relates to fresh or to dried gland substance.
Potassium hydroxide	The proportion of potassium monoxide (K_2O) which the preparation would be calculated to contain on the assumption that the potassium hydroxide in the preparation had been wholly converted into potassium monoxide.
Sodium hydroxide	The proportion of sodium monoxide (Na_2O) which the preparation would be calculated to contain on the assumption that the sodium hydroxide in the preparation had been wholly converted into sodium monoxide.
Strophanthus, glycosides of	The amount of Standard Tincture of Strophanthus as defined in the British Pharmacopoeia 1948 which possesses the same activity as a specified quantity of the preparation when assayed by the method described in the said Pharmacopoeia.
Suprarenal gland medulla, the active principles of; their salts	Either— (*a*) the proportion of suprarenal gland or of the medulla of the gland, as the case may be, contained in the preparation; or (*b*) the amount of suprarenal gland or of the medulla of the gland, as the case may be, from which a specified quantity of the preparation was obtained, together with an indication whether the amount relates to fresh or to dried gland substance.

Name of Poison	*Particulars*
Thyroid gland, the active principles of; their salts	Either— (*a*) the proportion of thyroid gland contained in the preparation; or (*b*) the amount of thyroid gland from which a specified quantity of the preparation was obtained, together with an indication whether the amount relates to fresh or to dried gland.

Rule 22(1)

SCHEDULE 7

Indication of character of article prescribed for the purposes of section 18(1)(*c*)(iii) *of the Act*

1. To be labelled with the words "*Caution. It is dangerous to take this preparation except under medical supervision.*":—

Medicines made up ready for the internal treatment of human ailments and containing insulin.

2. To be labelled with the words "*Caution. It is dangerous to exceed the stated dose.*":—

Medicines (other than medicines containing insulin and medicines mentioned in paragraph 9 of this Schedule) made up ready for the internal treatment of human ailments except in the case of a substance included in Schedule 1.

3. To be labelled with the words "*Poison. For animal treatment only.*":—

Medicines made up ready for the treatment of animals.

4. To be labelled with the words "*Caution. This preparation may cause serious inflammation of the skin in certain persons and should be used only in accordance with expert advice.*":—

Preparations for the dyeing of hair containing phenylene diamines, tolylene diamines or other alkylated-benzene diamines or their salts.

5. To be labelled with the words "*Caution. This substance is caustic.*":—

Potassium hydroxide, sodium hydroxide, and articles containing either of those substances.

6. To be labelled with the words "*Caution. This substance is poisonous. The inhalation of its vapour, mist, spray or dust may have harmful consequences. It may also be dangerous to let it come into contact with the skin or clothing.*":—

Dinitrocresols (DNOC); their compounds with a metal or a base; except preparations for the treatment of human ailments and except winter washes containing not more than the equivalent of five per cent. of dinitrocresols.

Dinosam, its compounds with a metal or a base
Dinoseb, its compounds with a metal or a base
Endosulfan
Endothal; its salts
Endrin
Fluoroacetamide; fluoroacetanilide
Organic compounds of mercury in aerosols
Organo-tin compounds, the following:—
  Compounds of fentin
Phosphorous compounds, the following:—
  Amiton
  Azinphos-cthyl
  Azinphos-methyl

Chlorfenvinphos
Demeton-O
Demeton-S
Dichlorvos
Diethyl 4-methyl-7-coumarinyl phosphorothionate
Diethyl *p*-nitrophenyl phosphate
Dimefox
Disulfoton
Ethion
Ethyl *p*-nitrophenyl phenylphosphonothionate
Mazidox
Mecarbam
Mevinphos
Mipafox
Oxydemeton-methyl
Parathion
Phenkapton
Phorate
Phosphamidon
Schradan
Sulfotep
TEPP (HETP)
Thionazin
Triphosphoric pentadimethylamide
Vamidothion

7. To be labelled with the words "*Caution. This preparation should be administered only under medical supervision. The vapour is dangerous.*":—

Medicines made up ready for the internal or external treatment of human ailments and containing dyfloes.

8. To be labelled with the words "*Caution. This substance is poisonous. Inhalation of the powder is dangerous. It is also dangerous to let the substance come into contact with the skin or clothing.*":—

Monofluoroacetic acid; its salts.

9. To be labelled with the words "*Caution. This may cause drowsiness. If affected, do not drive or operate machinery.*":—

Medicines made up ready for the internal treatment of human ailments if the poison is one of the following:—

Anti-histamine substances, the following: their salts; their molecular compounds:—

Antazoline
Bromodiphenhydramine
Buclizine
Carbinoxamine
Chlorcyclizine
Chlorpheniramine
Cinnarizine
Clemizole
Cyclizine
Cyproheptadine
3-Di-*n*-butylaminomethyl-4,5,6-trihydroxyphthalide
Diphenhydramine
Diphenylpyraline
Doxylamine
Isothipendyl
Mebhydrolin
Meclozine
Phenindamine

Pheniramine
Phenyltoloxamine
Promethazine
Pyrrobutamine
Thenalidine
Tolpropamine
Triprolidine
Substances being tetra-*N*-substituted derivatives of ethylenediamine or propylenediamine.

Rule 28

SCHEDULE 8

Poisons required to be specially labelled for transport

Arsenical poisons

Barium, salts of

Dinitrocresols (DNOC), their compounds with a metal or a base, when contained in preparations for use in agriculture or horticulture, except winter washes containing not more than the equivalent of five per cent. of dinitrocresols

Dinosam, its compounds with a metal or a base, when contained in preparations for use in agriculture or horticulture.

Dinoseb, its compounds with a metal or a base, when contained in preparations for use in agriculture or horticulture

Endosulfan

Endothal; its salts

Endrin

Fluoroacetamide; fluoroacetanilide

Hydrocyanic acid; cyanides, other than ferrocyanides and ferricyanides, except preparations containing less than the equivalent of 0·1 per cent., weight in weight, of hydrocyanic acid (HCN)

Monofluoroacetic acid; its salts

Nicotine, except in solid preparations containing less than four per cent. of nicotine

Organo-tin compounds, the following:—
Compounds of fentin

Phosphorus compounds, the following:—
Amiton
Azinphos-ethyl
Azinphos-methyl
Chlorfenvinphos
Demeton-O
Demeton-S
Demeton-O-methyl
Demeton-S-methyl
Dichlorvos
Diethyl 4-methyl-7-coumarinyl phosphorothionate
Diethyl *p*-nitrophenyl phosphate
Dimefox
Disulfoton
Ethion
Ethyl *p*-nitrophenyl phenylphosphonothionate
Mazidox
Mecarbam
Mevinphos
Mipafox
Oxydemeton-methyl

Parathion
Phenkapton
Phorate
Phosphamidon
Schradan
Sulfotep
TEPP (HETP)
Thionazin
Triphosphoric pentadimethylamide
Vamidothion

Strychnine

Thallium, salts of

SCHEDULE 9

Rule 34(1)

Form of application for entry in the list kept by a local authority under section 21 of the Act

PHARMACY AND POISONS ACT 1933
(1933 c. 25)

Form of application by a person to have his name entered in a local authority's list of persons entitled to sell poisons included in Part II of the Poisons List

To the {Town Clerk / Clerk of the County Council} of ....

I, ...

being engaged in the business of ....
hereby apply to have my name entered in the list kept in pursuance of section 21 of the above Act in respect of the following premises, namely, ...

....

....

....

....

as a person entitled to sell from those premises poisons included in Part II of the Poisons List.

I hereby nominate ....

....

to act as my deputy (deputies) for the sale of poisons in accordance with Rule 15(1) of the Poisons Rules 1970.

Signature of applicant ....

Date ....

This space is for the use of the local authority.

....

....

....

....

....

Rule 34(3)

SCHEDULE 10

Form of the list to be kept by a local authority in pursuance of section 21(1) *of the Act*

PHARMACY AND POISONS ACT 1933
(1933 c. 25)

List of persons entitled to sell poisons in Part II of the Poisons List

Full Name	Address of premises	Description of business carried on at the premises	Name of deputy (or deputies) permitted to sell

Rule 35

SCHEDULE 11

Certificate for the purchase of a poison

For the purposes of section 18(2)(*a*)(i) of the Pharmacy and Poisons Act 1933, I, the undersigned, a householder occupying (*a*)........................ hereby certify from my knowledge of (*b*)........................of (*a*)........................ that he is a person to whom (*c*)........................may properly be supplied.

I further certify that (*d*)........................is the signature of the said (*b*)........................

....
Signature of householder giving certificate.

Date........................

(*a*) Insert full postal address.
(*b*) Insert full name of intending purchaser.
(*c*) Insert name of poison.
(*d*) Intending purchaser to sign his name here.

Endorsement required by Rule 35 *of the Poisons Rules* 1970 *to be made by a police officer in charge of a police station when, but only when, the householder giving the certificate is not known to the seller of the poison to be a responsible person of good character.*

I hereby certify that in so far as is known to the police of the district in which *........................resides he is a responsible person of good character.

Signature of Police Officer........................
Rank........................
In charge of Police Station at........................
Date........................

Office Stamp of
Police Station.

*Insert full name of householder giving the certificate.

Rule 36

SCHEDULE 12

Form of entry to be made in the book to be kept by sellers of poisons in accordance with section 18(2)(*b*) *of the Act*

Date of Sale	Name and quantity of poison supplied	Purchaser's			Purpose for which stated to be required	Date of certificate (if any)	Name and address of person giving certificate (if any)	Signature of purchaser or, where a signed order is permitted by the Poisons Rules 1970, the date of the signed order
		Name	Address	Business, trade or occupation				

Rule 18

SCHEDULE 13

Restriction of sale and supply of strychnine and certain other substances

PART I

Cases of sale or supply to which provisions of Rule 18 *do not apply*

1. The provisions of Rule 18 shall not apply in the case of the sale of a substance—

(*a*) to be exported to purchasers outside the United Kingdom, or

(*b*) to a person or institution concerned with scientific education or research or chemical analysis, for the purposes of that education or research or analysis.

2. The provisions of Rule 18, other than those of paragraph (4) (lysergide, mescaline etc.), shall not apply in the case of the sale of a substance by way of wholesale dealing.

3. The following provisions of Rule 18, namely, paragraph (1) (strychnine) and paragraph (3) (sodium and potassium arsenites), shall not apply in the case of—

(*a*) the sale or supply of a substance as an ingredient in a medicine, or

(*b*) the sale of a substance for the purpose of being compounded in medicines prescribed or administered by a duly qualified medical practitioner, registered veterinary surgeon or registered veterinary practitioner.

4. The following provision of Rule 18, namely, paragraph (1) (strychnine), shall not apply in the case of the sale of strychnine—

(*a*) to a person producing a written authority in form "A" of the forms set out in Part II of this Schedule issued, in England or Wales, by a person duly authorised by the Minister of Agriculture, Fisheries and Food, or, in Scotland, by the chairman or secretary of an Agricultural Executive Committee or by a person duly authorised by the Secretary of State, authorising the purchase of strychnine for the purpose of killing moles, or

(*b*) to a person producing a written authority in form "B" of the said forms issued by a person duly authorised by the Secretary of State authorising the purchase of strychnine for the purpose of killing seals at the place or places mentioned in the authority;

so, however, that the authority in question has been issued within the preceding three months and the quantity sold does not exceed the quantity, not being more than four ounces, specified therein.

5.—(1) The following provision of Rule 18, namely, paragraph (2) (monofluoroacetic acid etc.), shall not apply in the case of the sale of a substance—

(*a*) to a person producing a certificate in form "A" of the forms set out in Part III of this Schedule issued by the medical officer of health of a local authority or port health authority certifying that the substance is required for use as a rodenticide by employees of that local authority or port health authority being such use—

(i) in ships or sewers in such places as are identified in the certificate; or

(ii) in such drains as are identified in the certificate, being drains which are situated in restricted areas and wholly enclosed and to which all means of access are, when not in actual use, kept closed; or

(iii) in such warehouses as are identified in the certificate, being warehouses which are situated in restricted dock areas and to which all means of access are, when not in actual use, kept securely locked or barred, or

(*b*) to a person producing a certificate in form "B" of the said forms issued by the medical officer of health of a local authority or port health authority certifying that the substance is required for use as a rodenticide by such person or by the employees of such body of persons, carrying on a business of pest control, as is named in the certificate, being such use as is mentioned in sub-paragraph (1)(*a*)(i) or (ii) of this paragraph, or (*c*) to a person producing a certificate in form "B" of the said forms issued, in England or Wales, by a person duly authorised by the Minister of Agriculture, Fisheries and Food or, in Scotland, by an officer of the Department of Agriculture and Fisheries for Scotland, not below the rank (according to the post in which he serves) of Senior Executive Officer or Senior Experimental Officer certifying that the substance is required for use as rodenticide by officers of the Ministry of Agriculture, Fisheries and Food or of the Department of Agriculture and Fisheries for Scotland, being such use as is mentioned in sub-paragraph (1)(*a*)(i) or (ii) of this paragraph;

so, however, that the certificate in question has been issued within the preceding three months and the quantity sold does not exceed the quantity specified therein.

(2) In this paragraph the following expressions have the meanings hereby respectively assigned to them, that is to say:—

"dock area" means an area in the vicinity of a dock as defined in section 57(1) of the Harbours Act 1964**(a)**;

"drain" and "sewer" have the meanings respectively assigned to them by section 343(1) of the Public Health Act 1936**(b)**;

"local authority" in Greater London means the Common Council of the City of London or the council of a London borough, elsewhere in England or Wales means the council of a county, a county borough or a county district and, in Scotland, has the same meaning as in the Public Health (Scotland) Act 1945**(c)**;

"port health authority" means, in England or Wales, the port health authority of the Port of London or a port health authority for the purposes of the Public Health Act 1936 and, in Scotland, a port health authority as constituted in terms of section 172 of the Public Health (Scotland) Act 1897**(d)**;

"restricted", in relation to any area, means controlled in such manner that access to the area by unauthorised persons is in normal circumstances prevented.

6. The following provision of Rule 18, namely, paragraph (3) (sodium and potassium arsenites), shall not apply in the case of the sale or supply of a substance as an ingredient in a sheep dip or sheep wash in a container clearly labelled with a notice of the special purpose for which the substance is intended and a warning that it is only to be used for that purpose, such labelling being additional to any labelling required by the Act or any other provision of these Rules.

7. The following provision of Rule 18, namely, paragraph (4) (lysergide, mescaline etc.), shall not apply in the case of the sale of a substance to a duly qualified medical practitioner for the purpose of his profession as such.

8. The following provision of Rule 18, namely, paragraph (5) (embutramide and mebezonium iodide), shall not apply in the case of the sale of a substance to a registered veterinary surgeon or registered veterinary practitioner for the purpose of killing animals or birds in the course of his profession as such.

9. The following provision of Rule 18, namely, paragraph (6) (fluanisone), shall not apply in the case of the sale of a substance to a registered veterinary surgeon or registered veterinary practitioner for the purposes of his profession as such.

10.—(1) The following provision of Rule 18, namely, paragraph (7) (zinc phosphide), shall not apply in the case of the sale of a substance—

(*a*) to a local authority for the purposes of the exercise of its statutory powers, or

(*b*) to a government department or an officer of the Crown, for the purposes of the public service, or

(*c*) to a person, or body of persons, carrying on a trade or business, for the purposes of that trade or business.

(2) In this paragraph the expression "local authority" has the meaning assigned to it by paragraph 5(2) of this Part of this Schedule.

(a) 1964 c. 40.
(b) 1936 c. 49.
(c) 1945 c. 15 (9 & 10 Geo. 6).
(d) 1897 c. 38.

PART II

Forms of authority for purchasing strychnine for killing moles and seals

FORM A

Authority for the purchase of strychnine for killing moles

For the purposes of Rule 18(1) of the Poisons Rules 1970 and of paragraph 4 of Part I of Schedule 13 thereto I hereby authorise..

....to purchase within three months from the date hereof

....of strychnine for the purpose of killing moles.

....

[A person authorised by the Minister of Agriculture, Fisheries and Food/Secretary of State for Scotland.
Chairman/Secretary of the...............
.... Agricultural Executive Committee]

Date..

FORM B

Authority for the purchase of strychnine for killing seals

Authority No...

For the purposes of Rule 18(1) of the Poisons Rules 1970 and of paragraph 4 of Part I of Schedule 13 thereto I, being a person duly authorised by the Secretary of State, hereby authorise..to purchase within three months of the date hereof..of strychnine for the purpose of killing seals at..

....

A person authorised by the Secretary of State

Department..

Date..

Part III

Forms of certificate authorising the purchase of monofluoroacetic acid, a salt thereof, fluoroacetamide or fluoroacetanilide as a rodenticide

Form A

Certificate authorising the purchase of monofluoroacetic acid, a salt thereof, fluoroacetamide or fluoroacetanilide as a rodenticide for use by employees of a local authority or a port health authority (in Scotland, a port local authority)

For the purposes of Rule 18(2) of the Poisons Rules 1970 and paragraph 5 of Part I of Schedule 13 thereto, I hereby certify that..........
of..........is required for use by employees of
..........as a rodenticide in [ships] [sewers]
situated at..........
[the following warehouses] viz..........
situated in the restricted dock area at..........
being warehouses to which all means of access are, when not in actual use, kept securely locked or barred
[the following drains] viz..........
situated in the restricted area at..........
being drains which are wholly enclosed and to which all means of access are, when not in actual use, kept closed.

....
Medical Officer of Health of

Date.......... ....

Form B

Certificate authorising the purchase of monofluoroacetic acid, a salt thereof, fluoroacetamide or fluoroacetanilide as a rodenticide for use by a person, or the employees of a body of persons, carrying on a business of pest control or for use by officers of the Ministry of Agriculture, Fisheries and Food or of the Department of Agriculture and Fisheries for Scotland

For the purposes of Rule 18(2) of the Poisons Rules 1970 and paragraph 5 of Part I of Schedule 13 thereto, I hereby certify that..........
of..........is required for use by [..........
..........] [employees of..........]
[officers of the Ministry of Agriculture, Fisheries and Food/Department of Agrculture and Fisheries for Scotland] as a rodenticide in—

[ships] [sewers] situated at..........
[the following drains] viz..........
situated in the restricted areas at..........
being drains which are wholly enclosed and to which all means of access are, when not in actual use, kept closed.

....
[Medical Officer of Health of
....
A person duly authorised by the Minister of Agriculture, Fisheries and Food]
An officer of the Department of Agriculture and Fisheries for Scotland holding the rank of..........

Date.......... ....]

Rule 7

SCHEDULE 14

Substances in which poison is exempted by Rule 7 from section 18(2) *of the Act*

Poison	*Substances in which exempted*
Nicotine	Agricultural and horticultural insecticides consisting of nicotine dusts containing not more than four per cent., weight in weight, of nicotine.

SCHEDULE 15

Rule 16

Poisons required to be coloured in certain cases

Arsenical poisons
Fluoroacetamide; fluoroacetanilide
Monofluoroacetic acid; its salts
Organo-tin compounds, the following:—
  Compounds of fentin
Phosphorus compounds, the following:—
  Azinphos-ethyl
  Azinphos-methyl
  Chlorfenvinphos
  Dichlorvos
  Disulfoton in solution
  Ethion
  Mecarbam
  Mevinphos
  Oxydemeton-methyl
  Phenkapton
  Phorate in solution
  Phosphamidon
  Thionazin
  Vamidothion

EXPLANATORY NOTE

(This Note is not part of the Rules.)

These Rules revoke and reproduce with amendments the Poisons (No. 2) Rules 1968. The principal changes are described below.

The Poisons List Order 1970 (S.I. 1970/797) adds various substances to, and makes certain other alterations in, the Poisons List; related changes are made in Rule 2(1) and in Schedules 1 to 5.

Rule 3(2) provides that equivalent quantities in the metric and imperial systems are to be determined in accordance with the Weights and Measures (Equivalents for dealings with drugs) Regulations 1969 (S.I. 1969/101) instead of in accordance with the Tables of Equivalents in the British Pharmacopoeia, the British Pharmaceutical Codex and the British Veterinary Codex.

Rule 12(*b*) provides that nothing in Part II of the Pharmacy and Poisons Act 1933 or in the Rules shall apply to poisons specified in Group II of Schedule 3 when contained in articles or substances so specified. The specified poisons include alkaloids (in particular, nicotine), arsenical poisons, hydrocyanic acid, phenols, phosphorus compounds (in particular, thionazin), potassium hydroxide and sodium hydroxide. Changes are made in the list of articles and substances containing these poisons which are exempted from the provisions referred to above; these changes are additional to those referred to in the second paragraph of this Note.

Rule 18 and Schedule 13 contain provisions restricting the sale and supply of strychnine and certain other substances. Changes are made in these provisions so far as they relate to the sale of monofluoroacetic acid etc. for use as a rodenticide and they are extended to an additional substance, namely, zinc phosphide.

1970 No. 799

BETTING AND GAMING

The Gaming Clubs (Hours and Charges) Regulations 1970

Made - - -	21*st May* 1970
Laid before Parliament	29*th May* 1970
Coming into Operation	1*st July* 1970

In pursuance of sections 14(2) and (3), 22(4) and 51 of the Gaming Act 1968(**a**), and after consultation with the Gaming Board for Great Britain, I hereby make the following Regulations :—

Citation, commencement and extent

1.—(1) These Regulations may be cited as the Gaming Clubs (Hours and Charges) Regulations 1970 and shall come into operation on 1st July 1970.

(2) These Regulations shall not extend to Scotland.

Interpretation

2.—(1) In these Regulations, the expression—

"the Act" means the Gaming Act 1968 ;

"bingo club premises" has the meaning assigned to it by section 20(1) of the Act ;

"charging period" has the meaning assigned to it by Regulation 5(2) of these Regulations ; and

"gaming" does not include gaming by means of any machine to which Part III of the Act applies.

(2) A reference in these Regulations to a charge in respect of gaming does not include an amount paid for a chance of winning a prize in gaming to which section 21 of the Act applies.

(3) Nothing in these Regulations precludes the making of different charges thereunder in respect of different facilities (whether provided in different parts of the same premises or by way of different games or of the same game played at different tables or otherwise) or in respect of gaming facilities provided on the premises during different sessions of play.

(4) The Interpretation Act 1889(**b**) applies for the interpretation of these Regulations as it applies for the interpretation of an Act of Parliament.

Bingo hours

3.—(1) No gaming shall take place on bingo club premises except—

(*a*) between the hours of two in the afternoon and midnight of a Saturday or New Year's Eve ;

(**a**) 1968 c. 65. (**b**) 1889 c. 63.

(*b*) between the hours of two in the afternoon and eleven in the evening of any other day.

(2) This Regulation does not apply to gaming which is prohibited by section 18 of the Act (which relates to gaming between certain hours on Sundays).

General gaming hours

4. No gaming shall take place on any premises (not being bingo club premises) in respect of which a licence under the Act is for the time being in force on any weekday between the hours of four in the morning and two in the afternoon.

Bingo charges

5.—(1) Any charge which, apart from this Regulation, would be prohibited by section 3 as applied by section 14(1) of the Act may be made in respect of gaming on bingo club premises if the charge satisfies the following requirements, that is to say,—

(*a*) the charge shall be in respect of one person and be for admission to or otherwise in respect of gaming which takes place within a charging period ;

(*b*) the charge shall be of a fixed amount of money not exceeding ten shillings ;

(*c*) where in relation to one charging period more than one charge can be incurred, or the same charge can be incurred more than once, by one person (without leaving the premises and being readmitted), every charge shall be in accordance with a scheme of charging so devised that the aggregate amount of the charges which can be incurred by any one person (without leaving the premises and being readmitted) in relation to that charging period does not exceed ten shillings ; and

(*d*) where charges are made for permission to take part in games of bingo of the kind whose rules permit a player to withdraw any part of his initial stake after the game has begun, the number of times that one person can incur such a charge (whether by incurring different charges of that kind, or by incurring the same charge more than once or by incurring charges partly in one way and partly in another) shall not exceed three in relation to one charging period.

(2) There may be specified for the purposes of this Regulation, in a notice displayed on the premises at or near the principal entrance, one or more periods of time (not being wholly or partly concurrent) identified by reference to the clock and not being shorter in duration than two hours each, and in any such case a reference in this Regulation to a charging period is a reference to a period so specified. In any other case, that reference is a reference to a period of twenty-four hours beginning with midnight.

General gaming charges

6.—(1) Any charge which, apart from this Regulation would be prohibited by section 3 as applied by section 14(1) of the Act may be made in respect of gaming on any premises (not being bingo club premises) in respect of which a licence under the Act is for the time being in force, if the charge satisfies the following requirements, that is to say,—

(*a*) the charge shall be of a fixed amount of money and shall be in respect of one or more facilities accorded to one person ; and (*b*) subject to paragraph (2) below, where the charge is of such a nature that it can be incurred more than once by one person (otherwise than by leaving and being readmitted to the premises, or any particular part of the premises or any particular table), the charge shall not be capable of being incurred again by the same person within one hour of the time when it was last incurred by him.

(2) A charge may be made for permission to take part in a series of games of *chemin de fer* (including a series which has already begun), notwithstanding that the charge may recur within one hour, if—

(*a*) the games comprised in the series consist of all the games which can be played with a shoe of not fewer than six packs of playing cards of fifty-two cards each ; and

(*b*) neither the holder of the licence nor any person acting on his behalf holds the bank, or has a share or interest in it, in any of the games in the series.

James Callaghan,
One of Her Majesty's Principal
Secretaries of State.

Home Office,
Whitehall.
21st May 1970.

EXPLANATORY NOTE

(*This Note is not part of the Regulations.*)

These Regulations relate to premises licensed for gaming in England and Wales. Regulations 3 and 4 restrict the hours during which gaming is to be permitted in bingo clubs and other licensed clubs respectively. Regulations 5 and 6 authorise the making of charges in respect of gaming in bingo and other licensed clubs respectively. The charges permitted are in addition to any stakes hazarded in the gaming.

STATUTORY INSTRUMENTS

1970 No. 801

CUSTOMS AND EXCISE

The Import Duties (Temporary Exemptions) (No. 6) Order 1970

Made - - - -	26*th May* 1970
Laid before the House of Commons -	28*th May* 1970
Coming into Operation	1*st June* 1970

The Lords Commissioners of Her Majesty's Treasury, by virtue of the powers conferred on them by sections 3(6) and 13 of the Import Duties Act 1958(**a**) and of all other powers enabling them in that behalf, on the recommendation of the Board of Trade hereby make the following Order:—

1.—(1) This Order may be cited as the Import Duties (Temporary Exemptions) (No. 6) Order 1970.

(2) The Interpretation Act 1889(**b**) shall apply for the interpretation of this Order as it applies for the interpretation of an Act of Parliament.

(3) This Order shall come into operation on 1st June 1970.

2.—(1) Until the beginning of 1st August 1970, any import duty which is for the time being chargeable on goods of heading 03.03 (B) of the Customs Tariff 1959 (oysters) shall not be chargeable in respect of oysters in shell, not exceeding 60 millimetres in diameter, other than of the kind *Ostrea virginica*.

(2) For the purposes of classification under the Customs Tariff 1959, in so far as that depends on the rate of duty, any goods to which paragraph (1) of this Article applies shall be treated as chargeable with the same duty as if this Order had not been made.

E. G. Perry,

Ernest Armstrong,

Two of the Lords Commissioners of Her Majesty's Treasury.

26th May 1970

EXPLANATORY NOTE

(*This Note is not part of the Order.*)

This Order provides for the temporary exemption from import duty, until 1st August 1970, of certain seed oysters.

(**a**) 1958 c. 6. (**b**) 1889 c. 63.

1970 No. 802

LANDLORD AND TENANT

The Irish Land (Finance) (Amendment) Rules 1970

Made - - -	26*th May* 1970
Laid before Parliament	29*th May* 1970
Coming into Operation	2*nd July* 1970

The Treasury, in exercise of the powers conferred upon them by sections 41, 45 and 46 of the Irish Land Act 1903**(a)** and section 14 of the Irish Land Act 1909**(b)** and of all other powers enabling them in that behalf, hereby make the following Rules:—

1. These Rules may be cited as the Irish Land (Finance) (Amendment) Rules 1970, and shall come into operation on 2nd July 1970.

2. The Interpretation Act 1889**(c)** shall apply for the interpretation of these Rules as it applies for the interpretation of an Act of Parliament.

3. The Irish Land (Finance) Rules 1912**(d)**, as amended **(e)**, shall be further amended, in Rule 16(2)(*b*) thereof, by substituting for the words "fifty-six per cent." the words "fifty-nine per cent.", and by substituting for the words "seventy per cent." the words "seventy-three per cent.".

E. G. Perry,
Ernest Armstrong,
Two of the Lords Commissioners
of Her Majesty's Treasury.

26th May 1970.

EXPLANATORY NOTE

(*This Note is not part of the Rules.*)

These Rules further amend the Irish Land (Finance) Rules 1912, relating to the ascertainment of the amount repaid in respect of advances under the Irish Land Acts of 1903 and 1909.

(a) 1903 c. 37.
(b) 1909 c. 42.
(c) 1889 c. 63.
(d) S.R. & O. 1912/69 (1912, p. 405).
(e) See S.R. & O. 1913, p. 349; S.I. 1961/1012, 1969/851 (1961 II, p. 1958; 1969 II, p. 2386).

STATUTORY INSTRUMENTS

1970 No. 803

BETTING AND GAMING

The Gaming Clubs (Bankers' Games) Regulations 1970

Made - - -	26*th May* 1970
Laid before Parliament	29*th May* 1970
Coming into Operation	1*st July* 1970

In pursuance of sections 13(2) and 51 of the Gaming Act 1968(**a**), and after consultation with the Gaming Board for Great Britain, I hereby make the following Regulations :—

Citation, commencement and extent

1.—(1) These Regulations may be cited as the Gaming Clubs (Bankers' Games) Regulations 1970 and shall come into operation on 1st July 1970.

(2) These Regulations shall not extend to Scotland.

Interpretation

2.—(1) In these Regulations "the Act" means the Gaming Act 1968.

(2) Nothing in these Regulations shall be construed as requiring any wager to be accepted, or as precluding the cancellation of any wager by mutual consent of the parties to it.

(3) The Interpretation Act 1889(**b**) applies for the interpretation of these Regulations as it applies for the interpretation of an Act of Parliament.

Roulette

3.—(1) Section 13(1) of the Act (which prohibits bankers' games) shall not have effect in relation to a game of roulette which is played on premises in respect of which a licence under the Act is for the time being in force, if the game is so played as to comply with the following provisions of this Regulation.

(2) Any wager in relation to the game shall be made with the banker and the bank shall be held by the holder of the licence, or by a person acting on his behalf in pursuance of a contract of service between the holder of the licence and that person.

(3) No person other than the holder of the licence shall have any share or interest in the bank.

(4) The game shall be played with a single ball and with a roulette wheel having thirty-seven equal compartments, and no more, which shall be numbered (in any order) from 0 to 36.

(**a**) 1968 c. 65. (**b**) 1889 c. 63.

(5) Any wager in relation to the game shall be payable, if won, at the appropriate odds indicated below, and shall be a wager that the score in the game will be :—

(*a*) one specific number (35 to 1);

(*b*) one of two specific numbers (17 to 1);

(*c*) one of three specific numbers (11 to 1);

(*d*) one of four specific numbers (8 to 1);

(*e*) one of six specific numbers (5 to 1);

(*f*) one of twelve specific numbers (2 to 1);

(*g*) one of eighteen specific numbers not including 0 (1 to 1); or

(*h*) one of twenty-four specific numbers (1 to 2).

(6) Any wager that the score in the game will be one of eighteen specific numbers not including 0 shall be subject to the limitation that, if the score should be 0, the stake will be divided equally between the bank and the person wagering.

Dice

4.—(1) Section 13(1) of the Act shall not have effect in relation to a game of dice which is played on premises in respect of which a licence under the Act is for the time being in force, if the game is so played as to comply with the following provisions of this Regulation.

(2) Any wager in relation to the game shall be made with the banker and the bank shall be held by the holder of the licence, or by a person acting on his behalf in pursuance of a contract of service made between the holder of the licence and that person.

(3) No person other than the holder of the licence shall have any share or interest in the bank.

(4) Two dice, and no more, shall be thrown at every throw made in the course of the game, and the sides of each of the dice shall be marked with values from 1 to 6, so arranged that the sum of the values of any pair of opposite sides is 7.

(5) Any wager in relation to the game shall be of a kind specified in the Schedule to these Regulations, and shall be payable, if won, at the appropriate odds there specified.

Baccarat

5.—(1) In this Regulation, "baccarat" means any version of that card-game (whether it is *baccarat banque, chemin de fer, punto banco* or some other version) in which one hand of cards (the banker's hand) is played against one opposing hand or against each of two opposing hands, and no more.

(2) Section 13(1) of the Act shall not have effect in relation to a game of baccarat which is played on premises in respect of which a licence under the Act is for the time being in force, if the game is so played as to comply with the following provisions of this Regulation.

(3) Any wager in relation to the game shall be made with the banker and, subject to paragraph (7) below, shall be payable, if the wager is won, at odds of 1 to 1.

(4) Any wager in relation to the game shall, subject to paragraph (7) below, be a wager that the opposing hand (or, in the case of a game against two opposing hands, a specific one or both of them) will win the game ; but the wager shall be subject to the limitation that it will be treated as void if the game should result,—

(*a*) in the case of a wager that one hand will win, in a draw between the banker's hand and that hand ; or

(*b*) in the case of a wager that two hands will win, in a draw between the banker's hand and one or both of those hands or in the banker's hand winning against one of those hands and losing against the other.

(5) Except in the case of *chemin de fer* played under rules which require the banker to give up being banker immediately an opposing hand wins a game,—

(*a*) the bank shall be held by the holder of the licence, or by a person acting on his behalf in pursuance of a contract of service made between the holder of the licence and that person ; and

(*b*) no person other than the holder of the licence shall have any share or interest in the bank.

(6) In the case of *chemin de fer* played under rules which require the banker to give up being banker immediately an opposing hand wins a game, neither the holder of the licence nor any person acting on his behalf shall hold the bank or have a share or interest in it.

(7) Where in any game—

(*a*) the bank is held as mentioned in paragraph (5)(*a*) above ;

(*b*) there is only one opposing hand in the game ; and

(*c*) the rules of the game are such that no person has an option in any circumstances as to whether or not a third card should be added to either hand in the game,

the banker may, notwithstanding paragraphs (3) and (4) above, accept a wager (payable, if won, at odds of 19 to 20) that the banker's hand will win the game ; but the wager shall be subject to the limitation that, if the game should result in a draw, the wager will be treated as void.

Blackjack

6.—(1) In this Regulation, "blackjack" means that version of the card-game of pontoon or *vingt-et-un* in which—

(*a*) one player (the banker) plays against each of two or more other players (the opposing players), cards being dealt to each of the players ;

(*b*) the cards are dealt from a shoe containing a shuffled stack of cards consisting, at the commencement of any series of games, of four standard packs of playing cards of fifty-two cards each and no more ;

(*c*) the cards are dealt face upwards so as to be disclosed immediately to all the players ;

(*d*) one card only is dealt to the banker initially in any game and it is dealt before any opposing player is required to decide, after considering the first two cards dealt to him, whether himself to take a third or any subsequent card ;

(*e*) an opposing player is not required to take a third or any subsequent card in any circumstances other than those mentioned in paragraph (8) below ;

(*f*) the banker is required to take further cards, one by one, until he has a score of more than 16 and is not permitted to take a further card once he has such a score ; and

(*g*) for the purpose of scoring, the cards have the values mentioned in paragraph (10) below.

(2) Section 13(1) of the Act shall not have effect in relation to a game of blackjack which is played on premises in respect of which a licence under the Act is for the time being in force, if the game is so played as to comply with the following provisions of this Regulation.

(3) Any wager in relation to the game shall be made with the banker and the bank shall be held by the holder of the licence, or by a person acting on his behalf in pursuance of a contract of service made between the holder of the licence and that person.

(4) No person other than the holder of the licence shall have any share or interest in the bank.

(5) Subject to the following provisions of this Regulation, any wager in relation to the game shall be made with the banker by an opposing player ; shall be made before any cards are dealt in the game ; and shall be a wager (hereafter in this Regulation referred to as an "initial wager") that the person wagering will get a score not exceeding 21, and either—

(*a*) the banker's score will exceed 21 ; or

(*b*) the person wagering will get a higher score than the banker ; or

(*c*) if the person wagering and the banker should both get a score of 21, the person wagering will get it with a hand of two cards only and the banker will not :

but the wager shall be subject to the limitation that it will be treated as void (instead of being lost) if the person wagering and the banker both get the same score of less than 21, or both get a score of 21 with a hand of two cards only, or both get a score of 21 with more than two cards.

(6) The odds payable, if the initial wager is won, shall—

(*a*) where the person wagering gets a score of 21 with a hand of two cards only, be 3 to 2 ; and

(*b*) in any other case, be 1 to 1.

(7) Where the first card dealt to the banker is an Ace and the first two cards dealt to an opposing player give a score of 21, nothing in paragraph (5) above shall prevent that player from wagering with the banker a stake equivalent to not more than half the amount staked on his initial wager that the banker's second card will have a value of 10 ; and a wager under this paragraph, if won, shall be payable at odds of 2 to 1.

(8) Where two cards only have been dealt to an opposing player and they give a score of 9, 10 or 11, nothing in paragraph (5) above shall prevent that player from doubling the amount of his initial stake, on the condition that he is to receive for his hand a third card and no more.

(9) Where two cards only have been dealt to an opposing player and they are cards of equal value (other than a value of 4, 5 or 10 each), nothing in paragraph (5) above shall prevent that player from separating those two cards into two separate hands (to each of which, in the case of Aces being separated, only one card may be added) and, for the purposes of the separation, making

a further initial wager of the same amount as that already staked ; and where this is done—

(*a*) those wagers shall have effect in relation to the two hands respectively, but as if any score of 21 made by either of them with two cards only had been made with more than two cards ;

(*b*) paragraph (7) above shall not apply ;

(*c*) paragraph (8) above shall not apply where the cards separated were Aces but, in any other case, it shall apply as if the two hands had been separate from the outset ; and

(*d*) this paragraph shall not apply so as to allow either of the two hands itself to be separated.

(10) The values of the cards referred to in paragraph (1) above are as follows :—

(*a*) the first Ace dealt to any one player in any game has the value of 11 unless that would give the player a score of more than 21 at the end of the game and, subject to that, any Ace has the value of 1 ;

(*b*) any card from 2 to 10 has its face value ; and

(*c*) any Jack, Queen or King has a value of 10.

(11) For the purposes of this Regulation, one person (not being the banker) may act as two or more opposing players and any reference in this Regulation to a player or to a person wagering shall be construed accordingly.

James Callaghan,
One of Her Majesty's Principal
Secretaries of State.

Home Office,
Whitehall.
26th May 1970.

SCHEDULE Regulation 4(5)

DICE

Permitted Wagers

"Win"
"Come"
"Behind" wagers

1.—(1) A wager that the score on the next throw of the dice will not be 2, 3 or 12, but that either it will be 7 or 11 or, if it should be 4, 5, 6, 8, 9 or 10, then that same score of 4, 5, 6, 8, 9 or 10, as the case may be, will occur again before a score of 7 occurs.

The odds payable if the wager is won shall be 1 to 1.

(2) Where a person has made a wager under sub-paragraph (1) above and, on the first throw of the dice following the making of that wager, a score of 4, 5, 6, 8, 9 or 10 has occurred, that person may under this sub-paragraph wager a stake equiv-

alent to not more than the amount staked on his wager under sub-paragraph (1) above that that same score of 4, 5, 6, 8, 9 or 10, as the case may be, will occur before a score of 7 occurs.

The odds payable if a wager under this sub-paragraph is won shall, where the score wagered on is—

(*a*) 4 or 10, be 2 to 1;

(*b*) 5 or 9, be 3 to 2;

(*c*) 6 or 8, be 6 to 5.

"Don't win bar 2"
"Don't come bar 2"
"Behind" wagers

2.—(1) A wager that the score on the next throw of the dice (disregarding any throw giving a score of 2) will not be 7 or 11, but that either it will be 3 or 12 or, if it should be 4, 5, 6, 8, 9 or 10, then a score of 7 will occur before that same score of 4, 5, 6, 8, 9 or 10, as the case may be, occurs again.

The odds payable if the wager is won shall be 1 to 1.

(2) Where a person has made a wager under sub-paragraph (1) above and, on the first throw of the dice following the making of that wager (disregarding any throw giving a score of 2), a score of 4, 5, 6, 8, 9 or 10 has occurred, that person may under this sub-paragraph wager a stake sufficient to win not more than the amount staked on his wager under sub-paragraph (1) above that a score of 7 will occur before that same score of 4, 5, 6, 8, 9 or 10, as the case may be, occurs again.

The odds payable if a wager under this sub-paragraph is won, shall, where the score wagered against is—

(*a*) 4 or 10, be 1 to 2;

(*b*) 5 or 9, be 2 to 3;

(*c*) 6 or 8, be 5 to 6.

"Place Bets (Box Numbers) to Win"

3. A wager (not being a wager under paragraph 1(2) above) that a specific score, being one of the following, that is to say, 4, 5, 6, 8, 9 or 10, will occur before a score of 7 occurs.

The odds payable if the wager is won shall, where the score wagered on is—

(*a*) 4 or 10, be 9½ to 5;

(*b*) 5 or 9, be 7 to 5;

(*c*) 6 or 8, be 7 to 6.

"Place Bets (Box Numbers) to Lose"

4. A wager (not being a wager under paragraph 2(2) above) that a score of 7 will occur before a specific score, being one of the following, that is to say, 4, 5, 6, 8, 9 or 10, occurs.

The odds payable if the wager is won shall, where the score wagered against is—

(*a*) 4 or 10, be 5 to 11;

(*b*) 5 or 9, be 5 to 8;

(*c*) 6 or 8, be 4 to 5.

"Hard Ways"

5. A wager that a specific score, being one of the following, that is to say, 4, 6, 8 or 10, will occur made up of two of the same number, before it occurs made up of different numbers and before a score of 7 occurs.

The odds payable if the wager is won shall, where the score wagered on is—

(*a*) 4 or 10, be 7½ to 1;

(*b*) 6 or 8, be 9½ to 1.

"Craps"

6. A wager that on the next throw of the dice the score will be one or another of the following, that is to say, 2, 3 and 12.

The odds payable if the wager is won shall be 7½ to 1.

"Field"

7. A wager that on the next throw of the dice the score will be one or another of the following, that is to say, 2, 3, 4, 9, 10, 11 and 12.

The odds payable if the wager is won shall, where the score which occurs is—

(*a*) 12, be 3 to 1;

(*b*) 2, be 2 to 1;

(*c*) 3, 4, 9, 10 or 11, be 1 to 1.

"Single Number" Wagers

8. A wager that on the next throw of the dice a specific score being one of the following, that is to say, 2, 3, 11 or 12, will occur.

The odds payable if the wager is won shall, where the score wagered on is—

(*a*) 2 or 12, be 33 to 1;

(*b*) 3 or 11, be 16 to 1.

EXPLANATORY NOTE

(*This Note is not part of the Regulations.*)

Section 13(1) of the Gaming Act 1968 prohibits the playing of bankers' games and games of unequal chance on premises licensed under that Act. Section 13(2), however, authorises the making of regulations to provide that this prohibition shall not have effect in relation to games specified in the regulations, if so played as to comply with the regulations.

These Regulations specify for this purpose the game of roulette, the dice game sometimes known as craps, the various versions of baccarat (including *chemin de fer* and *punto banco*), and blackjack, and the manner in which they are to be played. The effect of the Regulations is slightly to modify the games of dice and blackjack as commonly played in casinos abroad.

The Regulations do not affect any restriction contained in a licence under the Act as to the games which may be played on the premises.

1970 No. 804 (S.59)

BETTING AND GAMING

The Gaming Clubs (Bankers' Games) (Scotland) Regulations 1970

Made - - -	21*st May* 1970
Laid before Parliament	29*th May* 1970
Coming into Operation	1*st July* 1970

In exercise of the powers conferred on me by sections 13(2) and 51 of the Gaming Act 1968(**a**), and of all other powers enabling me in that behalf, and after consultation with the Gaming Board for Great Britain, I hereby make the following regulations :—

Citation and commencement

1. These regulations may be cited as the Gaming Clubs (Bankers' Games) (Scotland) Regulations 1970 and shall come into operation on 1st July 1970.

Interpretation

2.—(1) In these regulations "the Act" means the Gaming Act 1968.

(2) Nothing in these regulations shall be construed as requiring any wager to be accepted, or as precluding the cancellation of any wager by mutual consent of the parties to it.

(3) The Interpretation Act 1889(**b**) applies for the interpretation of these regulations as it applies for the interpretation of an Act of Parliament.

Roulette

3.—(1) Section 13(1) of the Act (which prohibits bankers' games) shall not have effect in relation to a game of roulette which is played on premises in respect of which a licence under the Act is for the time being in force, if the game is so played as to comply with the following provisions of this regulation.

(2) Any wager in relation to the game shall be made with the banker and the bank shall be held by the holder of the licence, or by a person acting on his behalf in pursuance of a contract of service between the holder of the licence and that person.

(3) No person other than the holder of the licence shall have any share or interest in the bank.

(4) The game shall be played with a single ball and with a roulette wheel having thirty-seven equal compartments, and no more, which shall be numbered (in any order) from 0 to 36.

(**a**) 1968 c. 65. (**b**) 1889 c. 63.

(5) Any wager in relation to the game shall be payable, if won, at the appropriate odds indicated below, and shall be a wager that the score in the game will be :—

(*a*) one specific number (35 to 1);

(*b*) one of two specific numbers (17 to 1);

(*c*) one of three specific numbers (11 to 1);

(*d*) one of four specific numbers (8 to 1);

(*e*) one of six specific numbers (5 to 1);

(*f*) one of twelve specific numbers (2 to 1);

(*g*) one of eighteen specific numbers not including 0 (1 to 1); or

(*h*) one of twenty-four specific numbers (1 to 2).

(6) Any wager that the score in the game will be one of eighteen specific numbers not including 0 shall be subject to the limitation that, if the score should be 0, the stake will be divided equally between the bank and the person wagering.

Dice

4.—(1) Section 13(1) of the Act shall not have effect in relation to a game of dice which is played on premises in respect of which a licence under the Act is for the time being in force, if the game is so played as to comply with the following provisions of this regulation.

(2) Any wager in relation to the game shall be made with the banker and the bank shall be held by the holder of the licence, or by a person acting on his behalf in pursuance of a contract of service made between the holder of the licence and that person.

(3) No person other than the holder of the licence shall have any share or interest in the bank.

(4) Two dice, and no more, shall be thrown at every throw made in the course of the game, and the sides of each of the dice shall be marked with values from 1 to 6, so arranged that the sum of the values of any pair of opposite sides is 7.

(5) Any wager in relation to the game shall be of a kind specified in the schedule to these regulations, and shall be payable, if won, at the appropriate odds there specified.

Baccarat

5.—(1) In this regulation, "baccarat" means any version of that card-game (whether it is baccarat banque, chemin de fer, punto banco or some other version) in which one hand of cards (the banker's hand) is played against one opposing hand or against each of two opposing hands, and no more.

(2) Section 13(1) of the Act shall not have effect in relation to a game of baccarat which is played on premises in respect of which a licence under the Act is for the time being in force, if the game is so played as to comply with the following provisions of this regulation.

(3) Any wager in relation to the game shall be made with the banker and, subject to paragraph (7) below, shall be payable, if the wager is won, at odds of 1 to 1.

(4) Any wager in relation to the game shall, subject to paragraph 7 below, be a wager that the opposing hand (or, in the case of a game against two opposing hands, a specific one or both of them) will win the game ; but the wager shall be subject to the limitation that it will be treated as void if the game should result,—

(*a*) in the case of a wager that one hand will win, in a draw between the banker's hand and that hand ; or

(*b*) in the case of a wager that two hands will win, in a draw between the banker's hand and one or both of those hands, or in the banker's hand winning against one of those hands and losing against the other.

(5) Except in the case of chemin de fer played under rules which require the banker to give up being banker immediately an opposing hand wins a game,—

(*a*) the bank shall be held by the holder of the licence, or by a person acting on his behalf in pursuance of a contract of service made between the holder of the licence and that person ; and

(*b*) no person other than the holder of the licence shall have any share or interest in the bank.

(6) In the case of chemin de fer played under rules which require the banker to give up being banker immediately an opposing hand wins a game, neither the holder of the licence nor any person acting on his behalf shall hold the bank or have a share or interest in it.

(7) Where in any game—

(*a*) the bank is held as mentioned in paragraph (5)(*a*) above ;

(*b*) there is only one opposing hand in the game ; and

(*c*) the rules of the game are such that no person has an option in any circumstances as to whether or not a third card should be added to either hand in the game,

the banker may, notwithstanding paragraphs (3) and (4) above, accept a wager (payable, if won, at odds of 19 to 20) that the banker's hand will win the game ; but the wager shall be subject to the limitation that, if the game should result in a draw, the wager will be treated as void.

Blackjack

6.—(1) In this regulation, "blackjack" means that version of the card-game of pontoon or vingt-et-un in which—

(*a*) one player (the banker) plays against each of two or more other players (the opposing players), cards being dealt to each of the players ;

(*b*) the cards are dealt from a shoe containing a shuffled stack of cards consisting, at the commencement of any series of games, of four standard packs of playing cards of fifty-two cards each and no more ;

(*c*) the cards are dealt face upwards so as to be disclosed immediately to all the players ;

(*d*) one card only is dealt to the banker initially in any game and it is dealt before any opposing player is required to decide, after considering the first two cards dealt to him, whether himself to take a third or any subsequent card ;

(*e*) an opposing player is not required to take a third or any subsequent card in any circumstances other than those mentioned in paragraph (8) below ;

(*f*) the banker is required to take further cards, one by one, until he has a score of more than 16 and is not permitted to take a further card once he has such a score ; and

(*g*) for the purpose of scoring, the cards have the values mentioned in paragraph (10) below.

(2) Section 13(1) of the Act shall not have effect in relation to a game of blackjack which is played on premises in respect of which a licence under the Act is for the time being in force, if the game is so played as to comply with the following provisions of this regulation.

(3) Any wager in relation to the game shall be made with the banker and the bank shall be held by the holder of the licence, or by a person acting on his behalf in pursuance of a contract of service made between the holder of the licence and that person.

(4) No person other than the holder of the licence shall have any share or interest in the bank.

(5) Subject to the following provisions of this regulation, any wager in relation to the game shall be made with the banker by an opposing player ; shall be made before any cards are dealt in the game ; and shall be a wager (hereafter in this regulation referred to as an "initial wager") that the person wagering will get a score not exceeding 21, and either—

(*a*) the banker's score will exceed 21 ; or

(*b*) the person wagering will get a higher score than the banker ; or

(*c*) if the person wagering and the banker should both get a score of 21, the person wagering will get it with a hand of two cards only and the banker will not :

but the wager shall be subject to the limitation that it will be treated as void (instead of being lost) if the person wagering and the banker both get the same score of less than 21, or both get a score of 21 with a hand of two cards only, or both get a score of 21 with more than two cards.

(6) The odds payable, if the initial wager is won, shall—

(*a*) where the person wagering gets a score of 21 with a hand of two cards only, be 3 to 2 ; and

(*b*) in any other case, be 1 to 1.

(7) Where the first card dealt to the banker is an Ace and the first two cards dealt to an opposing player give a score of 21, nothing in paragraph (5) above shall prevent that player from wagering with the banker a stake equivalent to not more than half the amount staked on his initial wager that the banker's second card will have a value of 10 ; and a wager under this paragraph, if won, shall be payable at odds of 2 to 1.

(8) Where two cards only have been dealt to an opposing player and they give a score of 9, 10 or 11, nothing in paragraph (5) above shall prevent that player from doubling the amount of his initial stake, on the condition that he is to receive for his hand a third card and no more.

(9) Where two cards only have been dealt to an opposing player and they are cards of equal value (other than a value of 4, 5 or 10 each), nothing in paragraph (5) above shall prevent that player from separating those two cards

into two separate hands (to each of which, in the case of Aces being separated, only one card may be added) and, for the purposes of the separation, making a further initial wager of the same amount as that already staked ; and where this is done—

(*a*) those wagers shall have effect in relation to the two hands respectively, but as if any score of 21 made by either of them with two cards only had been made with more than two cards ;

(*b*) paragraph (7) above shall not apply ;

(*c*) paragraph (8) above shall not apply where the cards separated were Aces but, in any other case, it shall apply as if the two hands had been separate from the outset ; and

(*d*) this paragraph shall not apply so as to allow either of the two hands itself to be separated.

(10) The values of the cards referred to in paragraph (1) above are as follows :—

(*a*) the first Ace dealt to any one player in any game has the value of 11 unless that would give the player a score of more than 21 at the end of the game and, subject to that, any Ace has the value of 1 ;

(*b*) any card from 2 to 10 has its face value ; and

(*c*) any Jack, Queen or King has a value of 10.

(11) For the purposes of this regulation, one person (not being the banker) may act as two or more opposing players and any reference in this regulation to a player or to a person wagering shall be construed accordingly.

William Ross,
One of Her Majesty's Principal
Secretaries of State.

St. Andrew's House,
Edinburgh.
21st May 1970.

Regulation 4(5)

SCHEDULE

Dice

Permitted Wagers

"Win"
"Come"
"Behind" wagers

1.—(1) A wager that the score on the next throw of the dice will not be 2, 3 or 12, but that either it will be 7 or 11 or, if it should be 4, 5, 6, 8, 9 or 10, then that same score of 4, 5, 6, 8, 9 or 10, as the case may be, will occur again before a score of 7 occurs.

The odds payable if the wager is won shall be 1 to 1.

(2) Where a person has made a wager under sub-paragraph (1) above and, on the first throw of the dice following the making of that wager, a score of 4, 5, 6, 8, 9 or 10 has occurred, that person may under this sub-paragraph wager a stake equivalent to not more than the amount staked on his wager under sub-paragraph (1) above that that same score of 4, 5, 6, 8, 9 or 10, as the case may be, will occur before a score of 7 occurs.

The odds payable if a wager under this sub-paragraph is won shall, where the score wagered on is—

(*a*) 4 or 10, be 2 to 1;

(*b*) 5 or 9, be 3 to 2;

(*c*) 6 or 8, be 6 to 5.

"Don't win bar 2"
"Don't come bar 2"
"Behind" wagers

2.—(1) A wager that the score on the next throw of the dice (disregarding any throw giving a score of 2) will not be 7 or 11, but that either it will be 3 or 12 or, if it should be 4, 5, 6, 8, 9 or 10, then a score of 7 will occur before that same score of 4, 5, 6, 8, 9 or 10, as the case may, occurs again.

The odds payable if the wager is won shall be 1 to 1.

(2) Where a person has made a wager under sub-paragraph (1) above and, on the first throw of the dice following the making of that wager (disregarding any throw giving a score of 2), a score of 4, 5, 6, 8, 9 or 10 has occurred, that person may under this sub-paragraph wager a stake sufficient to win not more than the amount staked on his wager under sub-paragraph (1) above that a score of 7 will occur before that same score of 4, 5, 6, 8, 9 or 10, as the case may be, occurs again.

The odds payable if a wager under this sub-paragraph is won, shall, where the score wagered against is—

(*a*) 4 or 10, be 1 to 2;

(*b*) 5 or 9, be 2 to 3;

(*c*) 6 or 8, be 5 to 6.

"Place Bets (Box Numbers) to Win"

3. A wager (not being a wager under paragraph 1(2) above) that a specific score, being one of the following, that is to say, 4, 5, 6, 8, 9 or 10, will occur before a score of 7 occurs.

The odds payable if the wager is won shall, where the score wagered on is—

(*a*) 4 or 10, be 9½ to 5;

(*b*) 5 or 9, be 7 to 5;

(*c*) 6 or 8, be 7 to 6.

"Place Bets (Box Numbers) to Lose"

4. A wager (not being a wager under paragraph 2(2) above) that a score of 7 will occur before a specific score, being one of the following, that is to say, 4, 5, 6, 8, 9 or 10, occurs.

The odds payable if the wager is won shall, where the score wagered against is—

(*a*) 4 or 10, be 5 to 11;

(*b*) 5 or 9, be 5 to 8;

(*c*) 6 or 8, be 4 to 5.

"Hard Ways"

5. A wager that a specific score, being one of the following, that is to say, 4, 6, 8 or 10, will occur made up of two of the same number, before it occurs made up of different numbers and before a score of 7 occurs.

The odds payable if the wager is won shall, where the score wagered on is—

(*a*) 4 or 10, be 7½ to 1;

(*b*) 6 or 8, be 9½ to 1.

"Craps"

6. A wager that on the next throw of the dice the score will be one or another of the following, that is to say, 2, 3 and 12.

The odds payable if the wager is won shall be 7½ to 1.

"Field"

7. A wager that on the next throw of the dice the score will be one or another of the following, that is to say, 2, 3, 4, 9, 10, 11 and 12.

The odds payable if the wager is won shall, where the score which occurs is—

(*a*) 12, be 3 to 1;

(*b*) 2, be 2 to 1;

(*c*) 3, 4, 9, 10 or 11, be 1 to 1.

"Single Number" Wagers

8. A wager that on the next throw of the dice a specific score being one of the following, that is to say, 2, 3, 11 or 12, will occur.

The odds payable if the wager is won shall, where the score wagered on is—

(*a*) 2 or 12, be 33 to 1;

(*b*) 3 or 11, be 16 to 1.

EXPLANATORY NOTE

(*This Note is not part of the Regulations.*)

Section 13(1) of the Gaming Act 1968 prohibits the playing of bankers' games and games of unequal chance on premises licensed under that Act. Section 13(2), however, authorises the making of regulations to provide that this prohibition shall not have effect in relation to games specified in the regulations, if so played as to comply with the regulations.

These Regulations specify for this purpose the game of roulette, the dice game sometimes known as craps, the various versions of baccarat (including chemin de fer and punto banco), and blackjack, and the manner in which they are to be played. The effect of the Regulations is slightly to modify the games of dice and blackjack as commonly played in casinos abroad.

The Regulations do not affect any restriction contained in a licence under the Act as to the games which may be played on the premises.

STATUTORY INSTRUMENTS

1970 No. 806 (S.61)

LEGAL AID AND ADVICE, SCOTLAND

The Legal Advice (Scotland) Amendment Regulations 1970

Made - - -	25*th May* 1970
Laid before Parliament	29*th May* 1970
Coming into Operation	1*st August* 1970

In exercise of the powers conferred on me by sections 7 and 15 of the Legal Aid (Scotland) Act 1967(**a**), and of all other powers enabling me in that behalf, I hereby make the following regulations:—

1.—(1) These regulations may be cited as the Legal Advice (Scotland) Amendment Regulations 1970 and shall come into operation on 1st August 1970.

(2) The Interpretation Act 1889(**b**) shall apply for the interpretation of these regulations as it applies for the interpretation of an Act of Parliament.

2. Regulation 3 of the Legal Advice (Scotland) Regulations, 1959(**c**), as amended by the Legal Advice (Scotland) Amendment Regulations, 1960(**d**) (which regulation relates to the financial conditions of legal advice) shall be amended as follows:—

(1) In paragraph (1), for the expression "£7 10s.", there shall be substituted the expression "£9 10s.".

(2) In paragraph (4), for the expression "£2 5s.", wherever it occurs, there shall be substituted the expression "£3 1s.".

(3) For paragraph (4)(*b*) there shall be substituted the following sub-paragraph:—

"(*b*) In respect of any child wholly or substantially maintained by him, or by any spouse of his where the capital and income of the spouse are treated as his resources—

Where the child is under five years of age ...	£1 8 0
Where the child is five or more years of age but under eleven years of age	£1 13 0
Where the child is eleven or more years of age but under thirteen years of age	£2 1 0
Where the child is eleven or more years of age but under sixteen years of age ...	£2 4 0"

(**a**) 1967 c. 43.
(**b**) 1889 c. 63.
(**c**) S.I. 1959/174 (1959 I, p. 1563).
(**d**) S.I. 1960/757 (1960 II, p. 1839).

William Ross,
One of Her Majesty's Principal
Secretaries of State.

St. Andrew's House,
Edinburgh.
25th May 1970.

EXPLANATORY NOTE

(*This Note is not part of the Regulations.*)

The Regulations relax the financial conditions upon which oral legal advice is available under section 7 of the Legal Aid (Scotland) Act 1967. Legal advice will in future be available to persons having an income (after certain deductions) of not more than £9 10s. (instead of £7 10s.) in the week preceding the application for legal advice.

STATUTORY INSTRUMENTS

1970 No. 807

CLEAN AIR

The Smoke Control Areas (Authorised Fuels) Regulations 1970

Made - - -	27*th May* 1970
Laid before Parliament	28*th May* 1970
Coming into Operation	1*st June* 1970

The Minister of Housing and Local Government, in exercise of the powers conferred on him by section 34(1) of the Clean Air Act 1956(**a**), and of all other powers enabling him in that behalf, hereby makes the following regulations. :—

Title and commencement

1. These regulations may be cited as the Smoke Control Areas (Authorised Fuels) Regulations 1970 and shall come into operation on 1st June 1970.

Interpretation

2. The Interpretation Act 1889(**b**) shall apply for the interpretation of these regulations as it applies for the interpretation of an Act of Parliament.

Authorised fuels for the purposes of the Clean Air Act 1956

3. The following fuel is hereby declared to be an authorised fuel for the purposes of the Clean Air Act 1956, that is to say—

"Fireglo" manufactured by La Societé Rouennaise de Defumage, Les Combustibles de Normandie, Comptoir Breton de Manutention et de Combustibles and Les Combustibles de l'Ouest from a feed stock of anthracite from South Wales to which about 7% of pitch is added. The briquettes from the mixture are subjected to mild heat treatment.

Given under the official seal of the Minister of Housing and Local Government on 27th May 1970.

(L.S.)

Anthony Greenwood,
Minister of Housing and Local Government.

(**a**) 1956 c. 52. (**b**) 1889 c. 63.

EXPLANATORY NOTE

(This Note is not part of the Regulations.)

Section 11 of the Clean Air Act 1956 makes it an offence to emit smoke from a chimney of a building within a smoke control area unless it can be shown that the emission of smoke was not caused by the use of any fuel other than an authorised fuel. The Regulations declare "Fireglo" as described in Regulation 3 to be an authorised fuel for the purposes of the Act.

STATUTORY INSTRUMENTS

1970 No. 808 (C.18)

NATIONAL HEALTH SERVICE, ENGLAND AND WALES
NATIONAL HEALTH SERVICE, SCOTLAND.

The National Health Service Contributions Act 1970 (Commencement) Order 1970

Made - - - *27th May* 1970

The Secretary of State for Social Services, in exercise of his powers under section 2(2) of the National Health Service Contributions Act 1970(a) and of all other powers enabling him in that behalf, hereby orders as follows :—

1. This Order may be cited as the National Health Service Contributions Act 1970 (Commencement) Order 1970.

2. The day appointed for the coming into force of the National Health Service Contributions Act 1970 shall be 6th July 1970.

R. H. S. Crossman,
Secretary of State for Social Services.

27th May 1970.

EXPLANATORY NOTE

(*This Note is not part of the Order.*)

This Order brings the National Health Service Contributions Act 1970 into force on 6th July 1970.

(a) 1970 c. 16.

1970 No. 809

WAGES COUNCILS

The Wages Regulation (Fur) Order 1970

Made - - - *27th May* 1970

Coming into Operation *23rd June* 1970

Whereas the Secretary of State has received from the Fur Wages Council (Great Britain) the wages regulation proposals set out in the Schedule hereto;

Now, therefore, the Secretary of State in exercise of her powers under section 11 of the Wages Councils Act 1959(**a**) and of all other powers enabling her in that behalf, hereby makes the following Order:—

1. This Order may be cited as the Wages Regulation (Fur) Order 1970.

2.—(1) In this Order the expression "the specified date" means the 23rd June 1970, provided that where, as respects any worker who is paid wages at intervals not exceeding seven days, that date does not correspond with the beginning of the period for which the wages are paid, the expression "the specified date" means, as respects that worker, the beginning of the next such period following that date.

(2) The Interpretation Act 1889(**b**) shall apply to the interpretation of this Order as it applies to the interpretation of an Act of Parliament and as if this Order and the Orders hereby revoked were Acts of Parliament.

3. The wages regulation proposals set out in the Schedule hereto shall have effect as from the specified date and as from that date the Wages Regulation (Fur) Order 1967(**c**) and the Wages Regulation (Fur) (Amendment) Order 1968(**d**) shall cease to have effect.

Signed by order of the Secretary of State.

27th May 1970.

A. A. Jarratt,
Deputy Under Secretary of State,
Department of Employment and Productivity.

(**a**) 1959 c. 69.
(**b**) 1889 c. 63.
(**c**) S.I. 1967/1308 (1967 III, p. 3919).
(**d**) S.I. 1968/1578 (1968 III, p. 4384).

SCHEDULE

Article 3

The following minimum remuneration shall be substituted for the statutory minimum remuneration fixed by the Wages Regulation (Fur) Order 1967 (Order Z. (85)), as amended by the Wages Regulation (Fur) (Amendment) Order 1968 (Order Z. (87)).

STATUTORY MINIMUM REMUNERATION

Part I

APPLICATION

1.—(1) Subject to the provisions of Part III of this Schedule, the minimum remuneration payable to a worker to whom this Schedule applies for all work except work to which a minimum overtime rate applies under Part IV is—

(*a*) in the case of a time worker, the hourly general minimum time rate payable to the worker under the provisions of this Schedule;

(*b*) in the case of a worker employed on piece work (other than an apprentice in the Dressers' and Dyers' Section of the trade to whom paragraph 10 applies);

(i) where a general minimum piece rate applies under Part VI, that rate;

(ii) where no general minimum piece rate applies, piece rates each of which would yield, in the circumstances of the case, to an ordinary worker at least the same amount of money as the piece work basis time rate applicable to the worker or, where no piece work basis time rate applies, at least the same amount of money as the hourly general minimum time rate which would be payable if the worker were a time worker, or

(*c*) in the case of an apprentice in the Dressers' and Dyers' Section of the trade who is employed on piece work and to whom paragraph 10 applies, the piece rates specified in that paragraph:

Provided that where an hourly guaranteed time rate is applicable to the worker and his minimum remuneration calculated on a time work basis at that rate exceeds the minimum remuneration calculated at the said piece rates the worker shall be paid not less than that guaranteed time rate.

(2) In this Schedule the expressions "hourly general minimum time rate" and "hourly guaranteed time rate" mean respectively the general minimum time rate and the guaranteed time rate applicable to the worker under Part II of this Schedule divided in either case by 40.

2. This Schedule applies to workers in relation to whom the Fur Wages Council (Great Britain) operates, that is to say, workers employed in Great Britain in the trade specified in the Regulations made by the Minister and dated 25th October 1919(**a**), with respect to the Constitution and Proceedings of the Trade Board for the Fur Trade (Great Britain), namely:—

The dressing, dyeing and making up of furs or of skins for furriers' purposes including:—

(1) The dressing or dyeing or general preparation of furs or skins;

(2) The manufacture of furs or skins into garments, rugs, or other articles;

(3) The remaking, repairing or cleaning of articles made from furs or skins where carried on by fur dressers or fur manufacturers;

(4) The lining with fur of coats, cloaks, mantles, capes, gloves or similar articles where carried out by fur manufacturers;

(**a**) S.R. & O. 1919/1634 (Rev. XXIII, p. 474: 1919 II, p. 549).

(5) Bundling, packing, warehousing and other operations carried on by fur skin merchants, fur dressers, fur dyers or fur manufacturers;

but excluding:—

(*a*) The making up of fur toys, purses, boots, shoes or slippers;

(*b*) The making of fur hats when carried on in association with or in conjunction with the making or trimming of men's, women's or children's headgear from other materials;

(*c*) Warehousing, packing and other similar operations carried on in shops wholly, mainly, or substantially engaged in the retail distribution of articles of any description that are not made on the premises.

PART II

GENERAL MINIMUM, GUARANTEED AND PIECE WORK BASIS

TIME RATES

CUTTING AND NAILING BRANCH OF THE FURRIERS' SECTION GENERAL MINIMUM TIME RATES

3. Subject to the provisions of this Schedule, the general minimum time rates per week of 40 hours applicable to workers in the cutting and nailing branch of the Furriers' Section are as follows:—

	Up to and including 14th Feb., 1971	*From 15th Feb., 1971*
	£ *s. d.*	(*£p.*)
(1) CUTTERS who, having worked in the said branch for six years or, in the case of workers who were apprentices, for five years, have subsequently worked as cutters for—		
(*a*) not less than one year	*15 0 0*	(*15·0*)
(*b*) less than one year	*13 10 0*	(*13·50*)
(2) NAILERS who, having worked in the said branch for six years or, in the case of workers who were apprentices, for five years, have subsequently worked as nailers for—		
(*a*) not less than one year	*14 0 0*	(*14·0*)
(*b*) less than one year	*13 0 0*	(*13·0*)

Provided that where a nailer performs also the work of a cutter the rate applicable to him in respect of that work shall be that which would be applicable if he were a cutter.

(3)(*a*) APPRENTICES to cutting and nailing, whose employment complies with the provisions of paragraph 18, during the following years of apprenticeship;

(*b*) LEARNERS to cutting and nailing, whose employment complies with the conditions specified in paragraph 21, during the following years of employment; and (*c*) ALL OTHER WORKERS employed in cutting and nailing or in either of such operations, during the following years of employment—

	Workers aged 18 years or over		All Other Workers	
	Up to and including 14th Feb., 1971 £ *s. d.*	*From 15th Feb., 1971* (£*p.*)	*Up to and including 14th Feb., 1971* £ *s. d.*	*From 15th Feb., 1971* (£*p.*)
The first year	*8 10 0*	*(8·50)*	*5 10 0*	*(5·50)*
The second year	*9 0 0*	*(9·0)*	*6 10 0*	*(6·50)*
The third year	*9 14 0*	*(9·70)*	*7 14 0*	*(7·70)*
The fourth year	*10 14 0*	*(10·70)*		
The fifth year	*12 0 0*	*(12·0)*		

	Up to and including 14th Feb., 1971 £ *s. d.*	*From 15th Feb., 1971* (£*p.*)
(4) MALE WORKERS aged 21 years or over and engaged in CLEANING by any method, fur skins or articles manufactured from fur	*12 10 0*	*(12·50)*

PIECE WORK BASIS TIME RATES—CUTTERS OR NAILERS

4. The piece work basis time rate applicable to a cutter or nailer specified in sub-paragraph (1) or sub-paragraph (2) of paragraph 3 when employed on piece work is a rate equal to one-and-one-third times the hourly general minimum time rate which would be applicable if the worker were employed on time work.

MACHINING, LINING, FINISHING AND HAND FUR SEWING BRANCH OF THE FURRIERS' SECTION

GENERAL MINIMUM TIME RATES

5. Subject to the provisions of this Schedule, the general minimum time rates per week of 40 hours applicable to female workers in the machining, lining, finishing and hand fur sewing branch of the Furriers' Section are as follows:—

	Up to and including 14th Feb., 1971 £ *s. d.*	*From 15th Feb., 1971* (£*p.*)
(1) FUR MACHINISTS who have worked for five years in the said branch	*10 12 0*	*(10·60)*
(2) LINERS, FINISHERS, HAND FUR SEWERS OR MACHINISTS (other than fur machinists) who have worked for five years in the said branch	*10 2 0*	*(10·10)*

(3)(*a*) LEARNERS to machining, lining, finishing or hand fur sewing, or to two or more of such operations, whose employment complies with the conditions specified in paragraph 22, during the following years of employment; and

(*b*) ALL OTHER WORKERS employed in the said branch, during the following periods of employment—

	Workers aged 18 years or over		All Other Workers	
	Up to and including 14th Feb., 1971	*From 15th Feb., 1971*	*Up to and including 14th Feb., 1971*	*From 15th Feb., 1971*
	£ s. d.	*(£p.)*	*£ s. d.*	*(£p.)*
The first year	*7 0 0*	*(7·0)*	*5 10 0*	*(5·50)*
The second year	*7 14 0*	*(7·70)*	*6 10 0*	*(6·50)*
The third year	*8 10 0*	*(8·50)*	*6 14 0*	*(6·70)*
The fourth year	*8 14 0*	*(8·70)*		
The fifth year	*9 10 0*	*(9·50)*		

PIECE WORK BASIS TIME RATES

6. The piece work basis time rate applicable to a female worker specified in sub-paragraph (1) or sub-paragraph (2) of paragraph 5 when employed on piece work is a rate equal to one-and-one-third times the hourly general minimum time rate which would be applicable if she were employed on time work.

RECKONING OF EMPLOYMENT IN THE FURRIERS' SECTION

7.—(1) A worker (not being an apprentice) who enters, or has entered, the Furriers' Section at or over the age of 18 years shall be treated for the purpose of this Part of this Schedule as though he had, at the date of his entry, completed the following period of learnership or other employment, as the case may be, in the branch in which he is employed—

(*a*) in the case of a worker in the cutting and nailing branch aged at the date of his entry in the said section—

(i) 18 and under 19 years ... ... 1 year

(ii) 19 and under 20 years ... ... 2 years

(iii) 20 years or over ... ... 3 years

(*b*) in the case of a worker in the machining, lining, finishing and hand fur sewing branch ... ... 1 year

(2) For the purpose of calculating any period of employment in the Furriers' Section, any employment in the machining, lining, finishing and hand fur sewing branch shall count as employment in the cutting and nailing branch and any employment in the cutting and nailing branch shall count as employment in the machining, lining, finishing and hand fur sewing branch.

FUR SORTERS' SECTION

GENERAL MINIMUM TIME RATES

8. The general minimum time rates per week of 40 hours applicable to workers employed in the Fur Sorters' Section in merchants' or brokers' warehouses are as follows:—

	Up to and including 14th Feb., 1971 £ s. d.	From 15th Feb., 1971 (£p.)
(1) MALE FUR SORTERS aged 21 years or over ...	14 0 0	(14·0)
(2) MALE WORKERS aged 21 years or over and employed in a FUR SORTING department under the supervision of a male fur sorter or as COUNTERS, STRIPERS or SIZERS	13 0 0	(13·0)
(3) ALL OTHER MALE WORKERS employed in the Fur Sorters' Section (except male skin packers), being aged—		
18 years or over, after *six* months	13 0 0	(13·0)
18 " " ", during first *six* months	10 10 0	(10·50)
16 and under 18 years	8 0 0	(8·0)
Under 16 years	6 0 0	(6·0)
(4) FEMALE WORKERS employed as FUR SORTERS, ASSISTANTS TO FUR SORTERS, COUNTERS, STRIPERS or SIZERS, being aged—		
18 years or over	9 10 0	(9·50)
16 and under 18 years	7 10 0	(7·50)
Under 16 years	6 10 0	(6·50)

DRESSERS' AND DYERS' SECTION

GENERAL MINIMUM TIME RATES FOR WORKERS OTHER THAN APPRENTICES

9. The general minimum time rates per week of 40 hours applicable to workers (other than the apprentices to whom paragraph 10 applies) in the Dressers' and Dyers' Section are as follows:—

	Up to and including 14th Feb., 1971 £ s. d.	From 15th Feb., 1971 (£p.)
(1) MALE TUBBERS	12 14 0	(12·70)
(2) WORKERS EMPLOYED AS ROLLER FLESHING MACHINE OPERATORS (other than shaving machine operators)—		
(*a*) Male workers	12 14 0	(12·70)
(*b*) Female workers	8 10 0	(8·50)
(3) WORKERS EMPLOYED AS HAND FLESHERS OR ROTARY FLESHING MACHINE OPERATORS—		
(*a*) Male workers	16 10 0	(16·50)
(*b*) Female workers	11 4 0	(11·20)
(4) ALL OTHER MALE WORKERS employed in the Dressers' and Dyers' Section (except the apprentices to whom paragraph 10 applies), being aged—		
19 years or over	10 18 0	(10·90)
17 and under 19 years	8 10 0	(8·50)
Under 17 years	5 14 0	(5·70)

(5) ALL OTHER FEMALE WORKERS employed in the Dressers' and Dyers' Section (except the apprentices to whom paragraph 10 applies), being aged—

18 years or over	7	14	0	(7·70)
Under 18 years	5	16	0	(5·80)

MINIMUM RATES FOR APPRENTICES

10.—(1) The general minimum time rates specified in Column 2 of the next following table are applicable during the first six months of apprenticeship to apprentices employed, in accordance with the conditions specified in paragraph 19, on time work in the Dressers' and Dyers' Section, and the piece rates and guaranteed time rates specified in Columns 3 and 4 respectively are applicable to such workers when employed in accordance with the said conditions on piece work during the remainder of their apprenticeship.

Column 1	Column 2	Column 3	Column 4
Period of Apprenticeship	General Minimum Time Rates	Piece Rates	Guaranteed Time Rates
The first six months	A rate equal to the general minimum time rate applicable to a worker of the same age and sex under sub-paragraph (4) or sub-paragraph (5) of paragraph 9.	—	—
The second six months	—	One-quarter of the piece rates specified in sub-paragraph (2) of this paragraph.	A rate equal to the general minimum time rate applicable to a worker of the same age and sex under sub-paragraph (4) or sub-paragraph (5) of paragraph 9.
The second year	—	One-half of the piece rates specified in sub-paragraph (2) of this paragraph.	
The third year	—	Three-quarters of the piece rates specified in sub-paragraph (2) of this paragraph.	
The fourth year	—	The piece rates specified in sub-paragraph (2) of this paragraph.	—

(2) The piece rates referred to in Column 3 of the said table are the general minimum piece rates specified in Part VI of this Schedule or, where no piece rate is so specified, piece rates each of which would yield, in the circumstances of the case, to an ordinary worker of the same sex at least the same amount of money as the general minimum time rate applicable under sub-paragraph (3) of paragraph 9 to a worker employed as a hand flesher or rotary fleshing machine operator.

PIECE WORK BASIS TIME RATES

ROLLER FLESHING MACHINE OPERATORS

11. The piece work basis time rates per week of 40 hours applicable to male or female workers employed in the Dressers' and Dyers' Section as roller fleshing machine operators (other than shaving machine operators) are as follows:—

	Up to and including 14th Feb., 1971	*From 15th Feb., 1971*
	£ s. d.	*(£p.)*
(1) Male workers	*14 8 0*	*(14·40)*
(2) Female workers	*10 4 0*	*(10·20)*

ALL SECTIONS OF THE TRADE

GENERAL MINIMUM TIME RATES

12. The general minimum time rates per week of 40 hours applicable to all workers to whom the foregoing provisions of this Part of this Schedule do not apply, are as follows:—

	Up to and including 14th Feb., 1971	*From 15th Feb., 1971*
(1) MALE SKIN PACKERS being aged—		
	£ s. d.	*(£p.)*
18 years or over, after *six* months	*12 10 0*	*(12·50)*
18 „ „ „, during first *six* months	*10 10 0*	*(10·50)*
(2) ALL OTHER MALE WORKERS, being aged—		
19 years or over	*11 0 0*	*(11·0)*
17 and under 19 years	*8 14 0*	*(8·70)*
Under 17 years	*5 16 0*	*(5·80)*
(3) ALL FEMALE WORKERS, being aged—		
18 years or over	*8 0 0*	*(8·0)*
Under 18 years	*6 4 0*	*(6·20)*

DEFINITIONS

13. For the purposes of this Part of this Schedule—

"CUTTER" means a person engaged, wholly or mainly, in cutting furs or skins in connection with manufacture, remodelling, alterations or repairing, including any preparation of furs or skins actually performed by such person for such cutting but not including nailing by a worker engaged, wholly or mainly, in nailing;

"FUR SORTER" means a worker who assumes sole responsibility for the proper grading of skins;

"NAILER" means a person engaged, wholly or mainly, in nailing;

"SKIN PACKER" means a worker engaged in and responsible for baling or packing skins for transport;

"TUBBER" means a worker in the Dressers' and Dyers' Section who has at least five years' experience therein and is capable of handling in an expert manner most varieties of fur skins from the raw stage through the various processes (except fleshing) to the finished article.

PART III

NIGHT WORKERS IN ALL SECTIONS OF THE TRADE

14.—(1) Notwithstanding anything contained in this Schedule, a night worker shall be paid for any work between the hours of 7 p.m. on any day and 7 a.m. on the next succeeding day one-and-one-third times the appropriate minimum rate: Provided that this provision shall not apply to a time worker in respect of any overtime.

(2) For the purposes of this paragraph—

"APPROPRIATE MINIMUM RATE" means, in the case of a time worker, the hourly general minimum time rate otherwise applicable to the worker or, in the case of a worker employed on piece work, the minimum rate which would be applicable if he were not a night worker;

"NIGHT WORKER" means a worker whose usual hours of work (exclusive of overtime) include at least 4 hours a night between 7 p.m. and 7 a.m.: Provided that a worker who is usually so employed during part only of the week shall be treated as a night worker in respect of that part of the week;

"OVERTIME" means, in the case of a time worker, any time in respect of which a minimum overtime rate applies or, in the case of a worker employed on piece work, any time in respect of which such a rate would apply if he were a time worker.

PART IV

OVERTIME AND WAITING TIME

MINIMUM OVERTIME RATES

15.—(1) Subject to the provisions of this paragraph, minimum overtime rates are payable to ANY TIME WORKER as follows:—

(*a*) On any day other than a Saturday, Sunday or a customary holiday, for all time worked in excess of 8 hours—Time-and-a-half:

Provided that where the employer normally requires the worker's attendance only from Monday to Friday (inclusive) the said rate shall be payable after 8¼ hours on two of those days and after 8½ hours on the remaining three days;

(*b*) On a Saturday, not being a customary holiday, for all time worked in excess of 4 hours—Time-and-a-half:

Provided that where the employer normally requires the worker's attendance only from Monday to Friday (inclusive) the said rate shall be payable for all time worked on a Saturday;

(*c*) On a Sunday or a customary holiday, for all time worked—Double time.

(*d*) In any week exclusive of any time in respect of which a minimum overtime rate is payable under the provisions of (*a*), (*b*) or (*c*) above—

For all time worked in excess of 40 hours—Time-and-a-half.

(2) For the purpose of calculating the number of hours worked by a worker on any day, regard shall be had to the whole of the worker's turn of duty and, where that turn extends beyond midnight, it shall be regarded as having been worked wholly on the day upon which it commences:

Provided that

(*a*) this provision shall not apply in respect of any time worked between midnight on Saturday and midnight on Sunday and for that time double time shall be payable as provided in sub-paragraph (1)(*c*) of this paragraph;

(*b*) all time worked on a Monday morning as part of a turn of duty normally commencing on Sunday shall be treated as though it were worked on the previous Saturday and included in a turn of duty which commenced on that day.

(3) Where the worker is normally employed on Sunday instead of Saturday and, in the case of a woman or young person, such substitution is not unlawful—

(*a*) for the purposes of sub-paragraph (1) of this paragraph, Saturday shall be treated as a Sunday and Sunday as a Saturday;

(*b*) for the purposes of sub-paragraph (2) of this paragraph, Saturday shall be treated as a Friday, Sunday as a Saturday and Monday as a Sunday.

16. In this Part of this Schedule—

(1) "TIME-AND-A-HALF" and "DOUBLE TIME" mean respectively,

(*a*) in the case of a worker other than a night worker, one-and-a-half times and twice the hourly general minimum time rate otherwise payable to the worker;

(*b*) in the case of a night worker, one-and-a-half times and twice the hourly general minimum time rate which would be payable if the worker were not a night worker and a minimum overtime rate did not apply.

(2) "CUSTOMARY HOLIDAY" means—

(*a*) In England and Wales—

Christmas Day (or, if Christmas Day falls on a Sunday, such weekday as may be appointed by national proclamation, or, if none is so appointed, the next following Tuesday), Boxing Day, Good Friday, Easter Monday, Whit Monday (or, where another day is substituted therefor by national proclamation, that day) and August Bank Holiday;

(*b*) In Scotland—

New Year's Day (or, if New Year's Day falls on a Sunday, the following Monday);

the local Spring holiday;

the local Autumn holiday; and

three other days (being days on which the worker normally works) in the course of a calendar year, to be fixed by the employer and notified to the worker not less than four weeks before the holiday; or

(*c*) in the case of each of the said days (other than a day fixed by the employer in Scotland and notified to the worker as aforesaid) a day substituted therefor, being either a day recognised by local custom as a day of holiday in substitution for the said day or a day fixed by agreement between the employer and the worker or his representative.

(3) "NIGHT WORKER" has the same meaning as in paragraph 14.

WAITING TIME

17.—(1) A worker is entitled to payment of the minimum remuneration specified in this Schedule for all time during which he is present on the premises of his employer unless he is present thereon in any of the following circumstances:—

(*a*) without the employer's consent, express or implied;

(*b*) for some purpose unconnected with his work and other than that of waiting for work to be given to him to perform;

(*c*) by reason only of the fact that he is resident thereon;

(*d*) during normal meal times in a room or place in which no work is being done, and he is not waiting for work to be given to him to perform.

(2) The minimum remuneration payable under sub-paragraph (1) of this paragraph to a piece worker when not engaged on piece work is that which would be payable if he were a time worker.

PART V

CONDITIONS AS TO APPRENTICES AND LEARNERS

APPRENTICES TO CUTTING AND NAILING

18.—(1) Subject to the provisions of this Schedule, the general minimum time rates specified in paragraph 3(3) apply only to an apprentice to cutting and nailing in whose case the conditions following are fulfilled—

(*a*) the apprentice shall be employed during the whole of his time for a period of five years as an apprentice to cutting and nailing under a written contract of apprenticeship which has been duly executed and which includes the following provisions, which the Wages Council considers necessary for securing the effective instruction of the apprentice, or provisions substantially to the same effect and no provisions contrary thereto:—

(i) the apprentice of his own free will and with the consent of the guardian binds himself to serve the employer as his apprentice in his trade of furrier for a term of five years;

(ii) the employer shall keep the worker as his apprentice during the said term, and to the best of his power, skill and knowledge instruct the apprentice or cause him to be instructed in cutting and nailing in the Furriers' Section of the fur trade;

(iii) the employer shall keep the apprentice under his own supervision or place him under one or more fully qualified journeymen;

(iv) during the first three years of apprenticeship the employer shall not require the apprentice to work any time in respect of which any minimum overtime rates would apply under Part IV of this Schedule to a worker employed on time work;

(v) during the first two years of apprenticeship the employer shall not require the apprentice to do any piece work;

(*b*) in the establishment in which the apprentice is employed the number of apprentices to cutting and nailing shall be limited in proportion to the number of journeymen employed in the cutting and nailing branch at the time of the engagement of the apprentice as follows—

Number of Journeymen	Number of Apprentices
5 or under	1
From 6 to 10	2
From 11 to 15	3
From 16 to 20	4
From 21 to 25	5

and thereafter in the proportion of one additional apprentice to each five additional journeymen, any number of journeymen in excess of an exact multiple of five being treated as five;

(*c*) the apprentice shall be the holder of a certificate of registration of apprenticeship issued by the Wages Council or shall have made an application for such a certificate which has been acknowledged and is still under consideration:

Provided that the certification of an apprentice may be cancelled by the Wages Council if the other conditions of apprenticeship are not complied with.

(2) For the purpose of determining the proportion of apprentices to journeymen in accordance with the last preceding sub-paragraph, "journeyman" means a male or female worker other than an apprentice or a learner, and an employer who employs no journeymen but personally instructs an apprentice shall be treated as a journeyman.

APPRENTICES IN THE DRESSERS' AND DYERS' SECTION

19.—(1) Subject to the provisions of this Schedule, the minimum remuneration specified in paragraph 10 applies only to an apprentice to dressing and dyeing in whose case the conditions following are fulfilled:—

(*a*) the apprentice shall be employed during the whole of his time for a period of four years as an apprentice to dressing and dyeing under a written contract of apprenticeship, entered into on or after his sixteenth birthday, which is duly executed and which includes the following provisions which the Wages Council considers necessary for securing the effective instruction of the apprentice or provisions substantially to the same effect and no provisions contrary thereto:—

(i) the apprentice of his own free will and with the consent of the guardian binds himself to serve the employer as his apprentice in his trade of fur dressing and dyeing for a term of four years;

(ii) the apprentice shall during the period of service attend at his own expense or that of his guardian such classes outside the factory as his employer may from time to time recommend;

(iii) the employer shall keep the worker as his apprentice during the said term and to the best of his power, skill and knowledge instruct the apprentice or cause him to be instructed in hand fleshing or rotary machine fleshing or shaving or unhairing, and during the first six months of service shall give the apprentice opportunity for spending a proportion of his time on work in all sections in the dressing and dyeing shop as carried on by the employer;

(iv) the employer shall keep the apprentice under his own supervision or place him under a fully qualified journeyman;

(v) during the first six months of service the employer shall not put the apprentice on piece work;

(*b*) in the establishment in which the apprentice is employed the number of apprentices to dressing and dyeing shall be limited in proportion to the number of journeymen in the service of the employer in the Dressers' and Dyers' Section at the time of the engagement of the apprentice as follows:—

Number of Journeymen	Number of Apprentices
5 or under	1
From 6 to 10	2
From 11 to 15	3
From 16 to 20	4
From 21 to 25	5

and thereafter in the proportion of one additional apprentice to each additional five journeymen, any number of journeymen in excess of an exact multiple of five being treated as five;

(*c*) the apprentice shall be the holder of a certificate of registration of apprenticeship issued by the Wages Council or shall have made application jointly with the employer to the Wages Council for such a certificate which has been acknowledged and is still under consideration:

Provided that the certification of an apprentice may be cancelled by the Wages Council if the other conditions of apprenticeship are not complied with.

(2) For the purpose of determining the proportion of apprentices to journeymen in accordance with the provisions of the last preceding sub-paragraph, "journeyman" means a worker employed as a hand flesher, rotary machine flesher, shaver or unhairer to whom there apply the general minimum piece rates for fleshers, shavers or unhairers specified in Part VI of this Schedule or the general minimum time rates for such workers specified in paragraph 9, and an employer who employs no journeymen but personally instructs the apprentice shall be treated as a journeyman.

PROSPECTIVE APPRENTICES

20. Notwithstanding the foregoing provisions of this Schedule, where an employer employs a worker as a prospective apprentice for a probationary period not exceeding four weeks and all the appropriate conditions as to apprenticeship other than those with regard to employment under a written contract of apprenticeship and certification by the Wages Council are fulfilled, the minimum remuneration applicable to that worker during the said period shall be that applicable to an apprentice employed in accordance with the conditions specified in paragraph 18 or paragraph 19 as the case may be and, in the event of the worker being continued thereafter at his employment as an apprentice, the said probationary period shall for the purpose of this Schedule be treated as part of the period of apprenticeship, whether or not it is included therein.

LEARNERS TO CUTTING AND NAILING

21. The general minimum time rates specified in sub-paragraph (4) of paragraph 3 apply to a learner to cutting and nailing who (not being an apprentice to whom the minimum rates in sub-paragraph (3) of that paragraph apply) is employed during the whole or a substantial part of his time for a period not exceeding *five* years in learning cutting and nailing by an employer who provides him with reasonable facilities for such learning.

LEARNERS TO MACHINING, LINING, FINISHING OR HAND FUR SEWING

22. The minimum rates specified in sub-paragraph (3) of paragraph 5 apply to a learner to machining, lining, finishing or hand fur sewing, or to two or more of such operations, who is employed during the whole or a substantial part of her time for a period not exceeding five years in learning machining, lining, finishing or hand fur sewing, or two or more of such operations, by an employer who provides her with reasonable facilities for such learning.

PART VI

GENERAL MINIMUM PIECE RATES

HAND OR MACHINE FLESHING

23.—(1) The general minimum piece rates applicable to workers employed on piece work (other than apprentices to whom paragraph 10 applies, during the first three years of their apprenticeship) on any of the operations specified in Columns 2, 3 and 4 of table I or Columns 2 and 3 of table II in sub-paragraph (2) of this paragraph are the appropriate piece rates set out in the said tables increased—

(*a*) in respect of Mink (blubbering); Mink, Farm; Musquash, Russian; and Weasel, Chinese, by 12½ per cent.; and

(*b*) in respect of all other skins, by 25 per cent.

(2) The following are the tables of piece rates referred to in sub-paragraph (1) of this paragraph:—

TABLE I

Skin (of any size except where otherwise stated)	Hand Fleshing (per skin except where otherwise stated)		Hand or Machine: Paring out all over from Pickle or Leather (per skin except where otherwise stated)		Hand or Machine: Paring out Heads and Necks from Pickle or Leather (per skin except where otherwise stated)	
Column 1	Column 2		Column 3		Column 4	
	s.	d.	s.	d.	s.	d.
Anteater	4	7	2	4		—
Antelope Furriers (hand or machine) ...		3½		3½		—
„ Cow or large Furriers (hand or machine)		5¼		5¼		—
Badger		11		4		2
Baranduki		1¾		—		—
Bears, Black	5	9	1	11		—
„ „ Cub	2	11	1	0		—
„ Brown	6	9	2	3		—
„ „ Cub	3	4	1	1		—
„ Grizzly	9	8	3	3		—
„ „ Cub	4	9	1	7		—
„ Green	19	4	5	0		—
„ „ Cub	9	8	2	5		—
„ Indian	9	8	2	5		—
„ „ Cub	4	10	1	7		—
„ Polar	14	6	3	9		—
„ „ Cub	7	2	2	5		—
Beaver	2	3½	2	3½		—
„ Cub	1	5¼		8½		—
Buffalo	17	3	8	6		—
Bullock	17	3	8	6		—
Cat, Biscution		8		2¾		1¼
„ Bush	1	0		4		1¾
„ Civet		2½		—		—
„ Dutch		5		1¾		—
„ House		5		1¾		1
„ Leopard (hand or machine) ...		11½	1	1½		—
„ Luke	1	3½		5		2½
„ Lynx	1	8½		6		2½
„ Ocelot (hand or machine)		7		8		—
„ Serval		11½		4		1¾
Cheetah	3	10	1	11		—
Chinchilla, Real		8		—		—
„ Bastard		2½		—		—
„ Rat		2½		—		—
Chinchillona		4		—		—
Cow	17	3	8	6		—
Calf (English)	9	8	4	10		—
„ (English stillborn)	2	7		10		—
„ Other types	1	11		8		—
Coyote	1	2		5		—
Deer, Antelope	6	6	3	3		—
„ Dik Dik		9½		4¾		—
„ Duiker	1	0		6		—
„ Elk	5	9	2	10½		—

TABLE I—*continued*

Skin (of any size expect where otherwise stated)	Hand Fleshing (per skin except where otherwise stated)		Hand or Machine: Paring out all over from Pickle or Leather (per skin except where otherwise stated)		Hand or Machine: Paring out Heads and Necks from Pickle or Leather (per skin except where otherwise stated)	
Column 1	Column 2		Column 3		Column 4	
	s.	d.	s.	d.	s.	d.
Deer, Fawn	1	2½		7¼		—
„ Gazelle	1	9		11½		—
„ Hartbeest	4	9	2	4½		—
„ Park	2	11	1	5½		—
„ Reindeer	2	11	1	5½		—
„ Springbok	1	10		11		—
„ Waterbuck	5	9	2	10½		—
Dogs, Furriers	1	7		6½		—
„ Odd Skins	3	3	1	7½		—
Donkey	17	3	8	6		—
Ermine (including Solongoi)		2		—		—
Fischer	1	9		10½		—
Fitch, Open		3		1½		¾
„ (extra if opened by flesher) ...		½		—		—
„ Cased		3½		1½		¾
Flying Fox } Flying Squirrel }		7		2¼		—
Fox, Australian	1	0		4		1¾
„ Balkan, Caucasian and Persian ...	1	0		4		1¾
„ Black	2	6		—		—
„ Blue	2	6		—		—
„ Cross	2	6		—		—
„ Grey		10½		3½		1½
„ Jap		10½		3½		1½
„ Kit		8½		3		1¼
Fox, South American (other than Kit) ...		11		4		1½
„ Silver	2	6		—		—
„ White	1	9		—		—
„ Russian (Reds and Mongolian) ...	1	3		5		1¾
„ Canadian	1	3		4¾		2
„ American	1	3		4¾		2
„ Platina	2	6		—		—
„ Kamchatka	2	0		8		3½
„ Cape		10½		3½		1½
„ Swedish	1	3		5		2
„ Indian		8½		2¾		1¼
„ King		8½		2¾		1¼
„ All unspecified types (other than Kit)	1	0		4		1¾
„ For boning and/or fleshing tails ...		4		—		—
„ Boning paws (per paw)		2		—		—
Gazelle, Furriers		3		1¼		—
Goats	1	9		7		—
„ Kid		7		2¼		—
Hamster		1¾		—		—
Hare		3¾		—		—
Horse	18	3	9	1		—
„ Pony (British)	18	3	9	1		—
„ Foals for furrier purposes ...	1	9		10½		—
Hyena	3	6	1	9		—
Hyrax		4		1¼		—
Jackal (All types)		10½		3½		1¾
„ Boning paws (per paw)		2		—		—
Jaguar	4	7	2	4		—

TABLE I—*continued*

Skin (of any size except where otherwise stated)	Hand Fleshing (per skin except where otherwise stated)	Hand or Machine: Paring out all over from Pickle or Leather (per skin except where otherwise stated)	Hand or Machine: Paring out Heads and Necks from Pickle or Leather (per skin except where otherwise stated)
Column 1	Column 2	Column 3	Column 4
	s. d.	s. d.	s. d.
Jap Mink	3	3	—
Kangaroo, Large	1 6	9	—
„ Medium	1 2	7	—
„ Small	9½	4½	—
Kolinsky	3	—	—
„ (extra if opened by flesher)	½	—	
Lambs, Indian	7	2¼	—
„ Persian	11	3¾	2
Leopard	4 3	2 4½	—
„ Snow	4 6	2 6	—
Lion	9 0	4 6	—
Lioness	6 0	3 0	—
Llama	3 6	1 2	—
Lynx	2 9	1 6	5
Marmot	3½	1¼	¾
„ Kansu	5	1¾	—
„ Kotel	2½	1	½
„ Mindel	2 4 (per doz.)	—	—
Marten (All species, including Canadian Sable) (hand or machine)	5	5	—
Mink (blubbering)	8	—	—
„ Wild	5	5	—
„ Farm (hand or machine)	5	5	—
Mole	1	¼	—
„ South African	1¾	½	—
Monkey	10½	5¼	—
Musquash, Natural Black	3	1 6 (per doz.)	7 (per doz.)
„ Western	16 9 (per 100)	1 0 (per doz.)	7 (per doz.)
„ Southern	16 9 (per 100)	1 0 (per doz.)	7 (per doz.)
„ French, Finnish and Czech	16 9 (per 100)	1 0 (per doz.)	7 (per doz.)
„ Russian (clean scraped only)	15 6 (per 100)	1 0 (per doz.)	—
„ Chinese	18 0 (per 100)	1 0 (per doz.)	—
„ (Kit and Mice)	1¾	—	—
Nutria	7	2¼	—
Ocelot (proper) (hand or machine)	9	1 2	—
Opossum, American	3	1½	¾
„ Australian	3½	1½	¾
„ Ringtail	3	1½	¾
„ Tasmanian	5	2¼	1
„ Victorian	5	2¼	1
„ New Zealand	5	2¼	1
Otter, Open	1 9	7	—
„ Cased	2 3½	1 2	—
„ Sea	5 9	2 10½	—
„ Cub	2 10½	1 5	—

TABLE I—*continued*

Skin (of any size except where otherwise stated) Column 1	Hand Fleshing (per skin except where otherwise stated) Column 2		Hand or Machine: Paring out all over from Pickle or Leather (per skin except where otherwise stated) Column 3		Hand or Machine: Paring out Heads and Necks from Pickle or Leather (per skin except where otherwise stated) Column 4	
	s.	d.	s.	d.	s.	d.
Pahmi		$2\frac{1}{2}$		$1\frac{1}{4}$	—	
Panther	3	6	1	9	—	
Peschaniki	16	6 (per 100)	5	6 (per 100)	—	
Platypus		7		$2\frac{1}{4}$	—	
Puma	3	6	1	9	—	
Rabbit, Wild		$1\frac{3}{4}$		.67	—	
„ „ (extra if opened by flesher)		$\frac{1}{4}$	—		—	
Rabbit, English and French Tames (Price to include cutting open by the Flesher) ...						
Rabbits Entredeux		3	—		—	
„ Clapier		4		$1\frac{1}{2}$	—	
„ Fortes		$4\frac{1}{2}$		$1\frac{1}{2}$	—	
Racoon	1	0		4		$1\frac{3}{4}$
„ Russian	1	3	1	3	—	
Sable, Russian (hand or machine) ...		8		8	—	
Seal (Fur) ... ... Unhairing s. d.						
„ Wig ... ... 20 8 per skin	—		—		—	
„ Middling ... 14 8 „	—		—		—	
„ Small ... ... 11 2 „	—		—		—	
„ Large Pup ... 8 0 „	—		—		—	
„ Middling Pup ... 6 10 „	—		—		—	
Sheep (odd skins)	2	11	1	0	—	
„ Furriers	1	6	—		—	
Skunk		4		2 (Including heads and necks)	—	
Squirrel, Canadian		$1\frac{1}{2}$	—		—	
„ All other types		2	—		—	
Susliki		$1\frac{3}{4}$	—		—	
Tiger	5	9	2	11	—	
„ Cub	2	$10\frac{1}{2}$	2	0	—	
Vicuna / Guanaco }	2	4	1	2	—	
Viscasha		$5\frac{3}{4}$		$2\frac{1}{2}$	—	
Wallaby, Large		$10\frac{1}{2}$		4	—	
„ Medium		7		3	—	
„ Small		$5\frac{1}{2}$		2	—	
Weasel and Stoat		$1\frac{3}{4}$	—		—	
Weasel, Chinese		$3\frac{1}{2}$		$3\frac{1}{2}$	—	
Wolf, Russian and Large Timber ...	3	6	1	1	—	
„ Other types	1	9		7	—	
Wolverine	1	9		7	—	
Wombat		$10\frac{1}{2}$		$3\frac{1}{2}$		$1\frac{3}{4}$
Zebra	46	0	12	0	—	

TABLE II

HAND BEAM WORK ONLY

Skin Column 1	Cutting down (per skin) Column 2	Shaving (per skin) Column 3
	s. d.	s. d.
Bears, Black	5 9	1 11
„ „ Cub	2 11	1 0
„ Brown	6 6	3 0
„ „ Cub	3 6	1 6
„ Grizzly	10 0	5 0
„ „ Cub	5 0	2 6
„ Green	19 4	5 0
„ „ Cub	9 8	2 5
„ Indian	10 0	5 0
„ „ Cub	5 0	2 6
„ Polar	12 6	7 6
„ „ Cub	7 2	2 10
Bullock	20 0	10 0
Cheetah	5 0	2 6
Cow	20 0	10 0
Donkey	20 0	10 0
Horse	30 0	10 0
Jaguar	5 0	3 0
Leopard	5 0	2 6
„ Snow	5 0	2 6
Lion	10 0	7 6
Lioness	7 6	5 0
Puma	5 0	2 6
Tiger	7 6	5 0
Zebra	46 0	12 0

(3) Subject to the provisions of sub-paragraph (1) of this paragraph the piece rate applicable to workers employed on machine fleshing (except where it is indicated in Column 1 of table I in sub-paragraph (2) of this paragraph that the rate applies to both hand and machine fleshing), is the appropriate rate shown in Column 2 of the said table, LESS 25 per cent.

24.—(1) The general minimum piece rate for paring out all over from pickle or leather, where no piece rate is specified in Column 3 of table I in sub-paragraph (2) of paragraph 23, shall be an amount equal to one-third of the appropriate general minimum piece rate for hand fleshing or machine fleshing applicable to the worker under the provisions of paragraph 23.

(2) The general minimum piece rate for tubbing shall be an amount equal to the appropriate general minimum piece rate for hand fleshing (excluding extras) applicable to the worker under the provisions of paragraph 23.

25.—(1) The general minimum piece rates applicable to workers (other than apprentices to whom paragraph 10 applies, during the first three years of their apprenticeship) employed on fleshing pony or lamb skins where roller or rotary machines are used are the piece rates specified in the next sub-paragraph increased by 25 per cent.

(2) The piece rates referred to in the foregoing sub-paragraph are:—

(*a*) Pony skins, when taken off the roller fleshing machines:—

8¾d. per skin for one operation, with an addition of 5¼d. per skin if paring out is required to be done;

(*b*) Lamb skins:—

(i) rotary machine fleshing 5¼d. per skin,

(ii) when taken off the roller machine for further paring out operation by hand or rotary machine—3½d. per skin,

(iii) cutting down of necks by fleshing (rotary) machine—1d. per skin.

26. In this Part of this Schedule,

(1) "BEAM WORK" means—

(*a*) such damping as may be required on all skins (except beaver, hair or fur seals) after liquoring by tubber has been completed; and

(*b*) cutting down and shaving, or either of these operations;

(2) "HAND FLESHING" means—

(*a*) fleshing throughout after all liquoring and damping has been completed for the fleshers;

(*b*) cleaning off afterwards where imperfect fleshing has been done in the initial stages; and

(*c*) cutting open and pulling over or either of such operations in the raw state before or after fleshing or damping;

(3) "FLESHING THROUGHOUT" does not include boning of fleshing tails, shaving, paring out, thinning edges, boning paws or burring ears (that is to say, taking shells completely out) where separate piece rates are specified for those operations in this Part of this Schedule, but includes, in the case of hand fleshing, any damping of completed skins performed by the flesher at his own option;

(4) "MACHINE FLESHING" means—

(*a*) fleshing throughout on the machine; and

(*b*) cleaning off afterwards on the machine where imperfect fleshing has been done in the inital stages; and

(*c*) cutting open and pulling over or either of such operations in the raw state before or after fleshing or damping;

(5) "PARING OUT" means shaving, paring out, thinning edges;

(6) "PULLING" means removing upper portion of hair;

(7) "TUBBING" means—

(*a*) preparing skins for the flesher and after fleshing leathering them in a tub and completing the dressing, or

(*b*) preparing skins for the flesher and after fleshing preparing them and putting them through the machine for leathering and completing the dressing;

(8) "UNHAIRING" means preparing skins by soaking and heating and removing hair.

EXPLANATORY NOTE

(*This Note is not part of the Order.*)

This Order, which has effect from 23rd June 1970, sets out the statutory minimum remuneration payable in substitution for that fixed by the Wages Regulation (Fur) Order 1967 (Order Z. (85)) as amended by the Wages Regulation (Fur) (Amendment) Order 1968 (Order Z. (87)), which Orders are revoked.

New provisions are printed in italics.

1970 No. 810

WAGES COUNCILS

The Wages Regulation (Fur) (Holidays) Order 1970

Made - - -	27*th May* 1970
Coming into Operation	23*rd June* 1970

Whereas the Secretary of State has received from the Fur Wages Council (Great Britain) the wages regulation proposals set out in the Schedule hereto ;

Now, therefore, the Secretary of State in exercise of her powers under section 11 of the Wages Councils Act 1959(**a**) and of all other powers enabling her in that behalf, hereby makes the following Order :—

1. This Order may be cited as the Wages Regulation (Fur) (Holidays) Order 1970.

2.—(1) In this Order the expression "the specified date" means the 23rd June 1970, provided that where, as respects any worker who is paid wages at intervals not exceeding seven days, that date does not correspond with the beginning of the period for which the wages are paid, the expression "the specified date" means, as respects that worker, the beginning of the next such period following that date.

(2) The Interpretation Act 1889(**b**) shall apply to the interpretation of this Order as it applies to the interpretation of an Act of Parliament and as if this Order and the Order hereby revoked were Acts of Parliament.

3. The wages regulation proposals set out in the Schedule hereto shall have effect as from the specified date and as from that date the Wages Regulation (Fur) (Holidays) Order 1967(**c**), shall cease to have effect.

Signed by order of the Secretary of State.
27th May 1970.

A. A. Jarratt,
Deputy Under Secretary of State,
Department of Employment and Productivity.

(**a**) 1959 c. 69. (**b**) 1889 c. 63. (**c**) S.I. 1967/1166 (1967 II, p. 3411).

SCHEDULE

Article 3

The following provisions as to holidays and holiday remuneration shall be substituted for the provisions as to holidays and holiday remuneration set out in the Wages Regulation (Fur) (Holidays) Order 1967 (Order Z. (84)).

PART I

APPLICATION

1. This Schedule applies to every worker for whom statutory minimum remuneration has been fixed.

PART II

CUSTOMARY HOLIDAYS

2.—(1) An employer shall allow to every worker in his employment to whom this Schedule applies a holiday (hereinafter referred to as a "customary holiday") in each year on the days specified in the following sub-paragraph, provided that the worker was in his employment for a period of not less than four weeks immediately preceding the customary holiday, and has worked for the employer during the whole or part of that period, and (unless excused by the employer or absent by reason of the proved illness of, or accident to, the worker) worked for the employer throughout the last working day on which work was available to him immediately prior to the customary holiday.

(2) The said customary holidays are:—

(*a*) (i) in England and Wales—
Christmas Day (or, if Christmas Day falls on a Sunday, such weekday as may be appointed by national proclamation, or, if none is so appointed, the next following Tuesday), Boxing Day, Good Friday, Easter Monday, Whit Monday (or where another day is substituted therefor by national proclamation, that day) and August Bank Holiday;

(ii) in Scotland—
New Year's Day (or, if New Year's Day falls on a Sunday, the following Monday);
the local Spring holiday;
the local Autumn holiday; and
three other days (being days on which the worker normally works) in the course of a calendar year, to be fixed by the employer and notified to the worker not less than four weeks before the holiday; or

(*b*) in the case of each of the said days (other than a day fixed by the employer in Scotland and notified to the worker as aforesaid), a day substituted therefor, being either a day recognised by local custom as a day of holiday in substitution for the said day, or a day agreed between the employer and the worker or his representative.

(3) Notwithstanding the preceding provisions of this paragraph, an employer may (except where in the case of a woman or young person such a requirement would be unlawful) require a worker who is otherwise entitled to any customary holiday under the foregoing provisions of this Schedule to work thereon, and, in lieu of any customary holiday on which he so works, the worker shall be entitled to be allowed a day's holiday (hereinafter referred to as a "holiday in lieu of a customary holiday") on a weekday on which he would normally work within the period of three weeks next ensuing.

PART III

ANNUAL HOLIDAY

3.—(1) In addition to the holidays specified in Part II of this Schedule, and subject to the following provisions of this paragraph and to paragraph 4, an employer shall, between the date on which the provisions of this Schedule become effective and 31st

October 1970 and in each succeeding year between 1st April and 31st October, allow a holiday (hereinafter referred to as an "annual holiday") to every worker in his employment to whom this Schedule applies who was employed by him during the 12 months immediately preceding the commencement of the holiday season for any of the periods of employment (calculated in accordance with the provisions of paragraph 10) set out in the appropriate column of the table below, and the duration of the annual holiday shall, in the case of each such worker, be related to that period as follows:—

Period of employment	Where the worker's normal working week is six days	Where the worker's normal working week is five days or less
	Duration of annual holiday in 12 months commencing 1st April	Duration of annual holiday in 12 months commencing 1st April
	Days	Days
At least 48 weeks	*18*	15
" " 46 "	*17*	14
" " 45 "	*16*	14
" " 44 "	*16*	13
" " 42 "	*15*	13
" " 40 "	*14*	12
" " 39 "	*13*	12
" " 38 "	*13*	11
" " 36 "	*12*	11
" " 33 "	*11*	10
" " 30 "	*10*	9
" " 27 "	*9*	8
" " 24 "	*8*	7
" " 21 "	*7*	6
" " 18 "	*6*	5
" " 15 "	*5*	4
" " 12 "	*4*	3
" " 9 "	*3*	2
" " 8 "	*2*	2
" " 6 "	*2*	1
" " 4 "	*1*	1
" " 3 "	*1*	—

(2) Notwithstanding the provisions of the last foregoing sub-paragraph:—

(*a*) the number of days of annual holiday which an employer is required to allow to a worker in respect of a period of employment during the 12 months immediately preceding 1st April 1970 and that period in each succeeding year, shall not exceed in the aggregate three times the number of days constituting the worker's normal working week.

(*b*) the duration of the worker's annual holiday during the holiday season ending on 31st October 1970 shall be reduced by any days of annual holiday duly allowed to him by the employer under the provisions of Order Z.(84) during the period from and including 1st April 1970 to the date on which the provisions of this Schedule become effective.

(3) In this Schedule the expression "holiday season" means in relation to an annual holiday during the year 1970 the period commencing on 1st April 1970 and ending on 31st October 1970, and in relation to each subsequent year, the period commencing on 1st April and ending on 31st October in that year.

4.—(1) Subject to the provisions of this paragraph, an annual holiday shall be allowed on consecutive working days and days of holiday shall be treated as consecutive notwithstanding that a day of holiday allowed to a worker under Part II of this Schedule or a day upon which he does not normally work for the employer intervenes.

(2)(*a*) Where the number of days of annual holiday for which a worker has qualified exceeds the number of days constituting his normal working week, but does not exceed twice that number, the holiday may be allowed in two periods of consecutive working days; so, however, that when a holiday is so allowed, one of the periods shall consist of a number of such days not less than the number of days constituting the worker's normal working week.

(*b*) Where the number of days of annual holiday for which a worker has qualified exceeds twice the number of days constituting his normal working week the holiday may be allowed as follows:—

(i) as to two periods of consecutive working days, each such period not being less than the period constituting the worker's normal working week, during the holiday season; and

(ii) as to any additional days, on working days which need not be consecutive, to be fixed by the employer either during the holiday season or on any working day before the beginning of the next following holiday season.

(3) Where a customary holiday immediately precedes a period of annual holiday or occurs during such a period and the total number of days of annual holiday required to be allowed in the period under the foregoing provisions of this paragraph, together with any such customary holiday, exceeds the number of days constituting the worker's normal working week then, notwithstanding the foregoing provisions of this paragraph, the duration of that period of annual holiday may be reduced by one day and in such a case one day of annual holiday may be allowed on any working day (not being the worker's weekly short day) in the holiday season.

(4) A day of annual holiday under this Schedule shall not be allowed on any day on which the worker is entitled to a day of holiday or to a half-holiday under any enactment other than the Wages Councils Act 1959.

5. An employer shall give to a worker notice of the commencing date or dates and duration of the period or periods of his annual holiday. Such notice shall be given at least 28 days before the first day of the annual holiday, or where under the provisions of sub-paragraph (2) of paragraph 4 an annual holiday is allowed in more than one period, before each period, and may be given individually to the worker or by the posting of a notice in the place where the worker is employed.

PART IV

HOLIDAY REMUNERATION

A—CUSTOMARY HOLIDAYS AND HOLIDAYS IN LIEU OF CUSTOMARY HOLIDAYS

6.—(1) Subject to the provisions of this paragraph, for each day of holiday to which a worker is entitled under Part II of this Schedule he shall be paid by the employer holiday remuneration equal to the amount which would be payable in accordance with the provisions of paragraph 7 if the day had been a day of annual holiday except that, for this purpose, the expression "normal working week" in that paragraph shall have the meaning assigned to it in paragraph 11, in relation to a customary holiday or a holiday in lieu of a customary holiday:

Provided, however, that payment of the said holiday remuneration is subject to the condition that the worker (unless excused by the employer or absent by reason of the proved illness of, or accident to, the worker) presents himself for employment at the usual starting hour on the first working day following the holiday.

(2) The holiday remuneration in respect of any customary holiday shall be paid by the employer to the worker not later than the pay day on which the wages are paid for the first working day following the customary holiday.

(3) The holiday remuneration in respect of any holiday in lieu of a customary holiday shall be paid not later than the pay day on which the wages are paid for the first working day following the holiday in lieu of a customary holiday:

Provided that the said payment shall be made immediately upon the termination of the worker's employment in the case where he ceased to be employed before being allowed a holiday in lieu of a customary holiday to which he is entitled, and in that case the proviso contained in sub-paragraph (1) of this paragraph shall not apply.

B—ANNUAL HOLIDAY

7.—(1) Subject to the provisions of paragraph 8, a worker qualified to be allowed an annual holiday under this Schedule shall be paid by his employer in respect thereof, on the last pay day preceding such annual holiday, one day's holiday pay (as defined in paragraph 11) in respect of each day of annual holiday.

(2) Where under the provisions of paragraph 4 an annual holiday is allowed in more than one period, the holiday remuneration shall be apportioned accordingly.

8. Where any accrued holiday remuneration has been paid by the employer to the worker (in accordance with paragraph 9 of this Schedule or in accordance with the provisions of Order Z.(84)) in respect of employment during any period referred to in that paragraph or that Order, the amount of holiday remuneration payable by the employer in respect of any annual holiday for which the worker has qualified by reason of employment during the said period shall be reduced by the amount of the said accrued holiday remuneration unless that remuneration has been deducted from a previous payment of holiday remuneration made under the provisions of this Schedule or of Order Z.(84).

ACCRUED HOLIDAY REMUNERATION PAYABLE ON TERMINATION OF EMPLOYMENT

9. Where a worker ceases to be employed by an employer after the provisions of this Schedule become effective, the employer shall, immediately on the termination of the employment, pay to the worker as accrued holiday remuneration:—

(1) in respect of employment in the 12 months up to the preceding 31st March, a sum equal to the holiday remuneration which would be payable for any days of annual holiday for which he has qualified (except days of annual holiday which he has been allowed or has become entitled to be allowed before leaving the employment) if they were allowed at the time of leaving the employment; and

(2) in respect of any employment since the said 31st March, a sum equal to the holiday remuneration which would have been payable to him if he could have been allowed an annual holiday in respect of that employment at the time of leaving it.

PART V

GENERAL

10. For the purposes of calculating any period of employment qualifying a worker for an annual holiday or for any accrued holiday remuneration under this Schedule, the worker shall be treated:—

(1) as if he were employed for a week in respect of any week in which—

(*a*) he has worked for the employer for not less than 12 hours and has performed some work for which statutory minimum remuneration is payable;

(*b*) he has been absent throughout the week solely by reason of the proved illness of, or accident to, the worker: provided that the number of weeks which may be treated as weeks of employment for such reason shall not exceed eight in the aggregate in the period of 12 months immediately preceding the commencement of the holiday season;

(*c*) he is absent from work throughout the week due to suspension because of shortage of work: provided that the number of weeks which may be treated as weeks of employment for such reason shall not exceed two at any one time;

(*d*) he has been absent throughout the week due to a stoppage of work because of a trade dispute: provided that the number of weeks which may be treated as weeks of employment for such reason shall not exceed three in the aggregate in the period of 12 months last mentioned;

(2) as if he were employed on any day of holiday allowed under the provisions of this Schedule, or of the Schedule to Order Z.(84), and for the purpose of the provisions of sub-paragraph (1) of this paragraph, a worker who is absent on such a holiday shall be treated as having worked thereon for the employer for the number of hours ordinarily worked by him on that day of the week on work for which statutory minimum remuneration is payable.

11. In this Schedule, unless the context otherwise requires, the following expressions have the meanings hereby respectively assigned to them, that is to say:—

"normal working week" means, in relation to—

(1) an annual holiday, or one day's holiday pay, the number of days on which it has been usual for the worker to work in a week in the employment of the employer in the 12 months immediately preceding the commencement of the holiday season, or, where under paragraph 9 accrued holiday remuneration is payable on the termination of the employment, in the 12 months immediately preceding the date of the termination of the employment;

(2) a customary holiday or a holiday in lieu of a customary holiday, the number of days on which it has been usual for the worker to work in a week in the employment of the employer in the four weeks immediately preceding the customary holiday:

Provided that—

(*a*) part of a day shall count as a day;

(*b*) no account shall be taken of any week in which the worker did not perform any work for which statutory minimum remuneration has been fixed.

"one day's holiday pay" means—

(1) the appropriate proportion of the remuneration which the worker would be entitled to receive from his employer at the date of the annual holiday, or at the termination of the employment, as the case may require, for one week's work if working his normal working week and the number of daily hours normally worked by him (exclusive of overtime)—

(*a*) in the case of a time worker, under the arrangement current immediately prior to the holiday;

(*b*) in the case of a piece worker other than a flesher, shaver and unhairer, if he were employed as a time worker at a time rate equal to the piece work basis time rate of statutory minimum remuneration then applicable to him as a piece worker or where no piece work basis time rate is applicable, at the appropriate hourly general minimum time rate of statutory minimum remuneration;

(2) in the case of piece workers employed as fleshers, shavers and unhairers

Males	Females
£2 10s. 6d.	£1 18s. 6d.

In this definition "appropriate proportion" means—

where the worker's normal working week is six days	...	one-sixth
" " " " " " " five days	...	one-fifth
" " " " " " " four days	...	one-quarter
" " " " " " " three days	...	one-third
" " " " " " " two days	...	one-half

"statutory minimum remuneration" means minimum remuneration (other than holiday remuneration) fixed by a wages regulation order.

"week" in paragraphs 3 and 10 means "pay week".

12. The provisions of this Schedule are without prejudice to any agreement for the allowance of any further holidays with pay or for the payment of additional holiday remuneration.

EXPLANATORY NOTE

(*This Note is not part of the Order.*)

This Order, which has effect from 23rd June 1970, sets out the holidays which an employer is required to allow to workers and the remuneration payable for those holidays, in substitution for the holidays and holiday remuneration fixed by the Wages Regulation (Fur) (Holidays) Order 1967 (Order Z. (84)), which Order is revoked.

New provisions are printed in italics.

STATUTORY INSTRUMENTS

1970 No. 811

CONSUMER PROTECTION

The Electrical Appliances (Colour Code) (Amendment) Regulations 1970

Made - - -	27*th May* 1970
Laid before Parliament	29*th May* 1970
Coming into Operation	1*st July* 1970

In pursuance of sections 1 and 2 of the Consumer Protection Act 1961(**a**), and after consulting with such persons and bodies of persons as appear to me to be requisite, I hereby make the following Regulations :—

1. These Regulations may be cited as the Electrical Appliances (Colour Code) (Amendment) Regulations 1970 and shall come into operation on 1st July 1970.

2. Regulation 6 of the Electrical Appliances (Colour Code) Regulations 1969(**b**) shall be amended—

(*a*) by substituting for the words "1st July 1970" the words "the relevant date" ; and

(*b*) by adding at the end the following words—

"For the purposes of this Regulation the relevant date shall,—

(i) in the case of goods and component parts sold, or in the possession of a person for the purpose of being sold, by way of wholesale dealing (that is to say, to a person who buys for the purpose of selling again or of letting on hire), be 1st November 1970 ; and

(ii) in any other case, be 1st April 1971".

James Callaghan,
One of Her Majesty's Principal
Secretaries of State.

Home Office,
Whitehall.

27th May 1970.

(**a**) 1961 c. 40.

(**b**) S.I. 1969/310 (1969 I, p. 816).

EXPLANATORY NOTE

(This Note is not part of the Regulations.)

Regulation 6 of the Electrical Appliances (Colour Code) Regulations 1969 permits the colours red, black and green to be used for marking the wires in the mains lead of a domestic electrical appliance to which those Regulations apply, as an alternative to the new colours brown, blue and green and yellow, until 1st July 1970.

These Regulations substitute 1st April 1971 for 1st July 1970 except that, in the case of goods sold or held for sale by way of wholesale dealing, the new date is 1st November 1970.

1970 No. 812 (S.62)

LEGAL AID AND ADVICE, SCOTLAND

The Legal Aid (Scotland) (Section 5) Amendment Regulations 1970

Made - - -	27*th May* 1970
Laid before Parliament	29*th May* 1970
Coming into Operation	1*st August* 1970

In exercise of the powers conferred on me by sections 4, 5 and 15 of the Legal Aid (Scotland) Act 1967(**a**), and of all other powers enabling me in that behalf, and with the concurrence of the Treasury, I hereby make the following regulations :

1.—(1) These regulations may be cited as the Legal Aid (Scotland) (Section 5) Amendment Regulations 1970 and shall come into operation on 1st August 1970.

(2) The Interpretation Act 1889(**b**) shall apply for the interpretation of these regulations as it applies for the interpretation of an Act of Parliament.

2. The Schedule to the Legal Aid (Scotland) (Section 5) Regulations 1960(**c**) as amended (**d**) (which relates to the assessment of resources of an applicant for a legal aid certificate), shall be amended as follows :—

(1) In paragraph 9 there shall be substituted for the expression "£117" (wherever it occurs) the expression "£159" and for the expression "£65" there shall be substituted the expression "£182" ;

(2) There shall be substituted for sub-paragraph (*b*) of paragraph 9 the following sub-paragraph :—

"(*b*) In respect of any child wholly or substantially maintained by him or where the capital and income of any spouse of his are treated as his resources, by the spouse—

Where the child is under five years of age	£73
Where the child is five or more years of age but under eleven years of age	£86
Where the child is eleven or more years of age but under thirteen years of age	£107
Where the child is thirteen or more years of age but under sixteen years of age	£114"

(**a**) 1967 c. 43. (**b**) 1889 c. 63.
(**c**) S.I. 1960/497 (1960 II, p. 1827).
(**d**) S.I. 1960/756; 1960/1559 (1960 II, pp. 1835; 1837).

William Ross,
One of Her Majesty's Principal Secretaries of State.

St. Andrew's House,
Edinburgh.
25th May 1970.

We concur.

Ernest Armstrong,
Joseph Harper,
Two of the Lord's Commissioners of Her Majesty's Treasury.

27th May 1970.

EXPLANATORY NOTE

(*This Note is not part of the Regulations.*)

The Regulations increase the allowances which may be made in computing the income of an applicant for legal aid under section 5 of the Legal Aid (Scotland) Act 1967.

STATUTORY INSTRUMENTS

1970 No. 815

CUSTOMS AND EXCISE

The European Free Trade Association (Origin of Goods) (Amendment) Regulations 1970

Made - - -	28*th May* 1970
Laid before the House of Commons	29*th May* 1970
Coming into Operation	1*st June* 1970

The Board of Trade, in pursuance of the powers conferred upon them by section 1(1) of the European Free Trade Association Act 1960(**a**), hereby make the following Regulations :—

1.—(1) These Regulations may be cited as the European Free Trade Association (Origin of Goods) (Amendment) Regulations 1970 and shall come into operation on 1st June 1970.

(2) The Interpretation Act 1889(**b**) shall apply to the interpretation of these Regulations as it applies to the interpretation of an Act of Parliament and as if these Regulations and the Regulations hereby revoked were Acts of Parliament.

(3) All the Regulations amending the European Free Trade Association (Origin of Goods) Regulations 1964(**c**) (hereinafter called "the principal Regulations") and in force immediately before the commencement of these Regulations (being those Regulations specified in Schedule 2 hereto) are hereby revoked.

2. The principal Regulations shall—

(*a*) have effect subject to the further amendment relating to polyvinyl acetate mentioned in Part II of Schedule 1 hereto, and

(*b*) continue to have effect subject to the other amendments mentioned in Schedule 1 hereto (being all the subsisting amendments made to the principal Regulations before the commencement of these Regulations).

Brown,
Minister of State.
Board of Trade.

28th May 1970.

(**a**) 1960 c. 19. (**b**) 1889 c. 63.
(**c**) S.I. 1964/1966 (1964 III, p. 4296).

SCHEDULE 1

Part I

Amendments to the body of the principal Regulations

For Regulation 6 there shall be substituted the following:—

"*Consignment*

6.—(1) Goods shall be treated as consigned from a place in the area if it is shown to the satisfaction of the Commissioners—

(*a*) that those goods have been consigned to the United Kingdom from such a place; or

(*b*) that they

(i) have been consigned from such a place to an exhibition outside the area and have been exhibited there, and

(ii) are in the same state as they were in when consigned to the exhibition and have not been used otherwise than for the purpose of exhibiting or demonstrating them at the exhibition since they were so consigned, and

(iii) have been sold or otherwise disposed of by the consignee to a person in the United Kingdom and have been consigned from the exhibition to the United Kingdom during or immediately after the exhibition; or

(*c*) that they

(i) have been consigned from such a place to a Customs warehouse outside the area, and

(ii) have remained continuously in that warehouse and no substitution or addition of other goods has taken place, and

(iii) have been consigned to the United Kingdom from that warehouse, and

(iv) are in the same state as they were in when consigned to that warehouse, and

(v) are entered on importation into the United Kingdom within twelve months from the date of their exportation from a place in the area.

(2) In this regulation:—

"exhibition" means a trade, industrial, agricultural or crafts exhibition, fair or similar show or display, but does not include any such exhibition, fair, show or display organised for private purposes in shops or business premises with a view to the sale of goods foreign to the country where the exhibition is held;

"Customs warehouse" means a place where goods may be stored under the control of Customs authorities without payment of import duties and taxes; the term does not include free ports or free zones, but does include places of the kind described above which are situated inside free ports or free zones.".

Part II

Amendments to Schedule 1 to the principal Regulations

In Schedule 1,—

Chapter 20

(*a*) after Chapter 19, there shall be inserted the following further Chapter:—

"CHAPTER 20

PREPARATIONS OF VEGETABLES, FRUIT OR OTHER PARTS OF PLANTS

1 *Tariff heading and Description*	2 *Qualifying process*
20·02 Potato crisps	Manufacture from materials not falling in 20·02." ;

Chapter 21

(*b*) there shall be added to the exceptions from the description of goods in relation to tariff heading 21·07 the following:—

"yoghourt, with added flavouring or fruit" ;

Chapter 29

(*c*) after the existing entry referring to tariff heading 29·35 (heterocyclic acids etc.), a further entry shall be included as follows:—

in Column 1 *Tariff heading and Description*	in Column 2 *Qualifying process*
"29·35 Furfuryl alcohol." ;	"Manufacture from furfuraldehyde." ;

Chapter 39

(*d*) after the third entry referring to tariff heading 39·02 (polymerisation products made from one monomer (homopolymers), in the forms mentioned in Notes 3(*a*) and 3(*b*) to Chapter 39) a further entry shall be included as follows:—

in Column 1 *Tariff heading and Description*	in Column 2 *Qualifying process*
"39·02 Polyvinyl acetate, in the forms mentioned in Notes 3(*a*) and 3(*b*) to Chapter 39." ;	"Manufacture from monomer vinyl acetate or from any material not being, and not containing, material which has been produced by polymerisation of the monomer." ;

Chapter 65

(*e*) for the description of goods related to tariff heading 65·02 there shall be substituted:—

"Hat-shapes, plaited or made from plaited or other strips of any material (other than materials of the kinds falling in Chapters 39, 50 to 56 and 58 to 62), bleached or dyed, neither blocked to shape nor made with brims." ;

Chapter 84

(*f*) for the description of goods related to tariff heading 84·59 there shall be substituted:—

"Machines and mechanical appliances, having individual functions, not falling within any other heading of this Chapter." ;

Chapter 85

(*g*) for the description of goods related to tariff heading 85·22 there shall be substituted:—

"Electrical appliances and apparatus, having individual functions, not falling within any other heading of this Chapter.";

Chapter 86

(*h*) for the description of goods related to tariff heading 86·08 there shall be substituted:—

"Containers specially designed and equipped for carriage by one or more modes of transport.";

Chapter 90

(*i*) for the description of goods related to tariff heading 90·07, there shall be substituted:—

"Photographic cameras; photographic flashlight apparatus; photocopying apparatus (not contact type).";

Chapter 98

(*j*) for the description of goods related to tariff heading 98·07 there shall be substituted:—

"Date, sealing or numbering stamps and the like (including devices for printing or embossing labels), designed for operating in the hand; hand-operated composing sticks and hand printing sets incorporating such composing sticks.".

PART III

Amendments to Schedule 2 *to the principal Regulations.*

In Schedule 2,—

Introductory Notes

(*a*) for Note 4 of the Introductory Notes there shall be substituted the following:—

"Nothing in the terms of the qualifying processes shall preclude the use of—

(i) materials listed in Schedule 3 to these Regulations, provided that they undergo in the area a process of production or manufacture not being a process listed in Regulation 2(2); or

(ii) materials which are of area origin.";

(*b*) in Note 6, for the list of items to be regarded as single textile materials there shall be substituted the following:—

"(*a*) silk and waste silk

(*b*) man-made fibres (continuous) produced by a process mentioned in Note 1(*a*) to Chapter 51

(*c*) man-made fibres (continuous) produced by a process mentioned in Note 1(*b*) to Chapter 51

(*d*) man-made fibres (discontinuous) produced by a process mentioned in Note 1(*a*) to Chapter 51 (*e*) man-made fibres (discontinuous) produced by a process mentioned in Note 1(*b*) to Chapter 51

(*f*) metallised textiles

(*g*) wool

(*h*) other animal hair

(*i*) flax and ramie

(*j*) cotton

(*k*) other vegetable fibres." ;

Chapter 58

(*c*) for the description of goods related to tariff heading 58·07 there shall be substituted: —

"Chenille yarn (including flock chenille yarn), gimped yarn (other than metallised yarn of heading 52·01 and gimped horsehair yarn)." ;

Chapter 59

(*d*) after the existing entry referring to tariff heading 59·02 there shall be included a further entry, as follows: —

in Column 1	in Column 2
Tariff heading and Description	*Qualifying process*
"59·02 Needled felt, whether or not impregnated or coated." ;	"Manufacture from natural fibres not spun or thrown, and in the case of fibres falling in Chapter 53 or 55 not carded or combed ; or from fibres of polypropylene provided that the value of any such fibres imported from outside the Area or of undetermined origin does not exceed 40 per cent of the export price of the finished product ; or from waste of man-made fibres falling in 56·03 or waste of natural fibres ; or from materials not falling in Chapters 50 to 62." ;

(*e*) for the description of goods related to tariff heading 59·03 there shall be substituted: —

"Bonded fibre fabrics, similar bonded yarn fabrics, and articles of such fabrics, whether or not impregnated or coated." ;

(*f*) for the description of goods related to tariff heading 59·07 there shall be substituted: —

"Textile fabrics coated with gum or amylaceous substances, of a kind used for the outer covers of books and the like ; tracing cloth ; prepared painting canvas ; buckram and similar fabrics for hat foundations and similar uses." ;

(*g*) after the second entry referring to tariff heading 59·17 (bolting cloth) there shall be included a further entry as follows: —

in Column 1	in Column 2
Tariff heading and Description	*Qualifying process*
"*59·17 Fabrics (other than woven textile felts) of a kind commonly used in machinery for making or finishing cellulosic pulp, paper or paperboard, including such fabrics in tubular or endless form." ;	"Manufacture from monofil of polyester (ex 51·02) ; or from materials not falling in Chapters 50 to 62." ;

Chapter 61

(*h*) the qualifying process in the case of goods of the first description mentioned in relation to tariff heading 61·02 shall be the following:—

"Manufacture from fibres or yarns (ex Chapters 50 to 59); or from woven fabric of wild silk (such as honan, pongee, tussore and shantung) which is wholly of tussore yarn produced from the uncultivated silkworm, provided that the fabric has been dyed or printed within the Area (ex 50·09); or from materials not falling in Chapters 50 to 62.".

SCHEDULE 2

(*Regulations revoked.*)

The European Free Trade Association (Origin of Goods) (Amendment), (Amendment No. 2) and (Amendment No. 3) Regulations 1965(**a**).

The European Free Trade Association (Origin of Goods) (Amendment), (Amendment No. 2) and (Amendment No. 3) Regulations 1966(**b**).

The European Free Trade Association (Origin of Goods) (Amendment), (Amendment No. 2) and (Amendment No. 3) Regulations 1967(**c**).

The European Free Trade Association (Origin of Goods) (Amendment) Regulations 1968(**d**).

The European Free Trade Association (Origin of Goods) (Amendment) Regulations 1969(**e**).

EXPLANATORY NOTE

(*This Note is not part of the Regulations.*)

These Regulations amend the European Free Trade Association (Origin of Goods) Regulations 1964 (S.I. 1964/1966).

They—

(i) add a new entry in Schedule 1 of the 1964 Regulations which enables certain polyvinyl acetate (ex tariff heading 39·02) to qualify for EFTA tariff treatment when made in the Area from non-EFTA monomer vinyl acetate; and

(ii) consolidate all previous amendments to the 1964 Regulations.

(**a**) S.I. 1965/1603, 1731, 2148 (1965 II, p. 4620; III, pp.4857, 6299).
(**b**) S.I. 1966/221, 601, 1587 (1966 I, p. 427; II, p. 1372; III, p. 4993).
(**c**) S.I. 1967/443, 932, 1584 (1967 I, p. 1377; II, p. 2809; III, p. 4397).
(**d**) S.I. 1968/653 (1968 I, p. 1485). (**e**) S.I. 1969/1347 (1969 III, p. 4019).

STATUTORY INSTRUMENTS

1970 No. 816

SOCIAL SECURITY

The Supplementary Benefit (Determination of Requirements) Regulations 1970

Laid before Parliament in draft

Made - - - *28th May* 1970

Coming into Operation *2nd November* 1970

Whereas a draft of the following regulations was laid before Parliament and approved by resolution of each House of Parliament:

Now, therefore, the Secretary of State for Social Services, with the consent of the Treasury, in exercise of the powers conferred by section 5 of the Ministry of Social Security Act 1966(**a**), and of all other powers enabling him in that behalf, hereby makes the following regulations:—

Citation, commencement and interpretation

1.—(1) These regulations may be cited as the Supplementary Benefit (Determination of Requirements) Regulations 1970 and shall come into operation on 2nd November 1970.

(2) In these regulations, unless the context otherwise requires, "the Act" means the Ministry of Social Security Act 1966(**a**) and other expressions have the same meaning as in the Act.

(3) The rules for the construction of Acts of Parliament contained in the Interpretation Act, 1889(**b**) shall apply for the purpose of the interpretation of these regulations as they apply for the purpose of the interpretation of an Act of Parliament.

Amendment of provisions for calculating requirements

2.—(1) Part II (calculation of requirements) of Schedule 2 to the Act (provisions for determining the right to and amount of benefit) shall be varied in accordance with the following provisions of this regulation.

(2) For paragraph 9 (normal requirements) and paragraph 10 (blind persons' requirements) of the said Schedule 2, as varied (**c**), there shall be substituted the following paragraphs:—

"*Normal requirements*

9. Requirements of persons other than blind persons—

	£	s.	d.
(*a*) husband and wife or other persons falling within paragraph 3(1) of this Schedule	8	10	0
(*b*) person living alone or householder not falling within sub-paragraph (*a*) of this paragraph who is directly responsible for household necessities and rent (if any)	5	4	0

(**a**) 1966 c. 20. (**b**) 1889 c. 63. (**c**) S.I. 1969/1036 (1969 II, p. 3065).

(*c*) any other person aged—

	£	s.	d.
(i) not less than 21 years	4	3	0
(ii) less than 21 but not less than 18 years ...	3	10	0
(iii) less than 18 but not less than 16 years ...	3	1	0
(iv) less than 16 but not less than 13 years ...	2	8	0
(v) less than 13 but not less than 11 years ...	2	4	0
(vi) less than 11 but not less than 5 years ...	1	16	0
(vii) less than 5 years	1	10	0

Blind persons

10. Requirements of persons who are or include blind persons—

(*a*) husband and wife or other persons falling within paragraph 3(1) of this Schedule—

	£	s.	d.
(i) if one of them is blind	9	15	0
(ii) if both of them are blind	10	11	0

(*b*) any other blind person aged—

	£	s.	d.
(i) not less than 21 years	6	9	0
(ii) less than 21 but not less than 18 years ...	4	10	0
(iii) less than 18 but not less than 16 years ...	3	17	0
(iv) less than 16 but not less than 13 years ...	2	8	0
(v) less than 13 but not less than 11 years ...	2	4	0
(vi) less than 11 but not less than 5 years ...	1	16	0
(vii) less than 5 years	1	10	0"

(3) In paragraph 13(1)(*b*) of the said Schedule 2, as varied (a), (increase on account of rent of the amount specified for requirements where the beneficiary is a non-householder aged 18 or over), for "11 shillings" there shall be substituted "12 shillings".

Signed by authority of the Secretary of State for Social Services.

David Ennals,
Minister of State,
Department of Health and Social Security.

28th May 1970.

We consent,

Walter Harrison,
Neil McBride,
Two of the Lords Commissioners
of Her Majesty's Treasury.

28th May 1970.

EXPLANATORY NOTE

(*This Note is not part of the Regulations.*)

These regulations provide for increases in weekly amounts allowed in respect of requirements for the purpose of determining entitlement to and the amount of supplementary pension or allowance under the Ministry of Social Security Act 1966.

(a) S.I. 1968/1118 (1968 II, p. 3076).

1970 No. 818

FUGITIVE CRIMINAL

The Extradition (Sovereign Base Areas of Akrotiri and Dhekelia) Order in Council 1970

Made - - - - *29th May* 1970

At the Court at Buckingham Palace, the 29th day of May 1970

Present,

The Queen's Most Excellent Majesty in Council

Whereas by section 18 of the Extradition Act 1870(**a**) it is among other things enacted that if, by any law or ordinance made after the passing of the said Act by the legislature of any British possession, provision is made for carrying into effect within such possession the surrender of fugitive criminals who are in, or suspected of being in, such British possession, Her Majesty may, by the Order in Council applying the said Act in the case of any foreign state, or by any subsequent Order, direct that such law or ordinance or any part thereof shall have effect in such British possession with or without modifications and alterations as if it were part of the said Act:

And Whereas by an Ordinance enacted by the Administrator of the Sovereign Base Areas of Akrotiri and Dhekelia, the short title of which is the Extradition Ordinance, 1970, the Extradition Acts 1870 to 1932 are modified in their application to the Sovereign Base Areas to provide that the appropriate courts of those Areas may exercise the functions under those Acts in relation to the surrender and discharge of fugitive criminals in the said Areas:

And Whereas it is further provided by the said Ordinance that it shall be of no effect until Her Majesty shall by Order in Council direct that the said Ordinance shall have effect within the Sovereign Base Areas but that the said Ordinance shall thereafter come into operation on the day on which such Order in Council is published in the Gazette of the Sovereign Base Areas:

Now, therefore, Her Majesty, in pursuance of section 18 of the Extradition Act 1870, is pleased, by and with the advice of Her Privy Council, to direct, and by this Order directs, as follows :—

1. The said Ordinance of 1970 shall have effect in the Sovereign Base Areas of Akrotiri and Dhekelia, without modification or alteration, as if it were part of the Extradition Act 1870.

2. This Order may be cited as the Extradition (Sovereign Base Areas of Akrotiri and Dhekelia) Order in Council 1970.

W. G. Agnew.

(**a**) 1870 Vict. c. 52.

EXPLANATORY NOTE

(*This Note is not part of the Order.*)

This Order gives effect in the Sovereign Base Areas of Akrotiri and Dhekelia to the Extradition Ordinance 1970 of the Areas as if it were part of the Extradition Act 1870.

1970 No. 819

EVIDENCE

The Evidence (Federal Republic of Germany) Order 1970

Made - - - - *29th May* 1970

At the Court at Buckingham Palace, the 29th day of May 1970

Present,

The Queen's Most Excellent Majesty in Council

Whereas Her Majesty in Council is satisfied that there exist in the Federal Republic of Germany and Land Berlin (West Berlin) public registers kept under the authority of the laws of the Federal Republic of Germany and Land Berlin (West Berlin) and recognised by the courts thereof as authentic records, and that those registers are regularly and properly kept:

Now, therefore, Her Majesty, by virtue and in exercise of the powers conferred on Her by section 5(1) of the Oaths and Evidence (Overseas Authorities and Countries) Act 1963(**a**) and all other powers in that behalf in Her vested, is pleased, by and with the advice of Her Privy Council, to order, and it is hereby ordered, as follows:—

1. This Order may be cited as the Evidence (Federal Republic of Germany) Order 1970.

2. This Order extends to all parts of the United Kingdom.

3. The registers of the Federal Republic of Germany and Land Berlin (West Berlin) specified in the first column of the Schedule to this Order shall be deemed to be public registers kept under the authority of the laws of the Federal Republic of Germany and Land Berlin (West Berlin) and recognised by the courts thereof as authentic records and to be documents of such a public nature as to be admissible as evidence of the matters regularly recorded therein.

4. For the purposes of the preceding Article all matters recorded in the registers shall be deemed, until the contrary is proved, to be regularly recorded therein.

5. Subject to any requirements of rules of court, a document which purports to be issued in the Federal Republic of Germany or Land Berlin (West Berlin) as an official copy of an entry in a register specified in the first column of the Schedule to this Order and which purports to be authenticated as such in the manner specified in that Schedule, shall, without evidence as to the custody of the register or of inability to produce it and without any further or other proof, be received as evidence that the register contains such an entry.

6. Nothing in this Order shall be taken to prohibit or restrict the admission in evidence of any copy, extract, summary, certificate or other document whatsoever which, apart from the provisions of this Order, would be admissible as evidence of any particular matter, or to affect any power which, otherwise than by virtue of this Order, is exercisable by any court with respect to the admission of documents in evidence.

W. G. Agnew.

(**a**) 1963 c.27.

SCHEDULE

Register	Certifying Officer	Mode of Authentication
Register of Births ...	The Registrar (Der Standesbeamte).	The signature and seal or stamp of the certifying officer.
Register of Marriages	The Registrar (Der Standesbeamte).	The signature and seal or stamp of the certifying officer.
Register of Deaths ...	The Registrar (Der Standesbeamte).	The signature and seal or stamp of the certifying officer.

EXPLANATORY NOTE

(*This Note is not part of the Order*.)

This Order makes entries contained in specified public registers of the Federal Republic of Germany and Land Berlin (West Berlin) admissible in evidence in the United Kingdom and provides for their proof by official certificates.

STATUTORY INSTRUMENTS

1970 No. 820

SAVINGS BANKS

The Trustee Savings Banks (Isle of Man) Order 1970

Made - - -	*29th May* 1970
Coming into Operation	*8th June* 1970

At the Court at Buckingham Palace, the 29th day of May 1970

Present,

The Queen's Most Excellent Majesty in Council

Her Majesty, in pursuance of the power conferred on Her by section 99 of the Trustee Savings Banks Act 1969**(a)**, is pleased, by and with the advice of Her Privy Council, to order, and it is hereby ordered, as follows:—

1. This Order may be cited as the Trustee Savings Banks (Isle of Man) Order 1970 and shall come into operation on 8th June 1970.

2. The Trustee Savings Banks Act 1969 in its extension to the Isle of Man shall have effect subject to the adaptations and modifications specified in the Schedule to this Order.

W. G. Agnew.

SCHEDULE

ADAPTATIONS AND MODIFICATIONS IN THE EXTENSION OF THE TRUSTEE SAVINGS BANKS ACT 1969 TO THE ISLE OF MAN

1. Section 20(4) shall be omitted.

2. In section 56(7) for the words from "and in any newspapers" to "established" there shall be substituted the words "and, where the bank is established in the Isle of Man, in a newspaper published in the Isle of Man".

3. In section 59(1) for the words from "any judge" where those words first occur to "standing in Scotland" there shall be substituted the words "a Deemster, who, if satisfied that such examination is desirable, may thereupon appoint the High Bailiff or an advocate of not less than seven years standing in the Isle of Man".

4. In section 59(4) for the words from "a master or taxing officer" to "Scotland" there shall be substituted the words "the Taxing Master".

5. For section 64(1)(*b*) there shall be substituted the following paragraph:—

"(*b*) the bank is ordered to be wound up in pursuance of section 307 of the Companies Act 1931 (an Act of Tynwald).".

6. In section 68(2) for the word "indictment" there shall be substituted the word "information" and the words from "by a court" to "Northern Ireland" shall be omitted.

(a) 1969 c. 50.

7. Section 72(2) shall be omitted.

8. In section 92(2) for the word "indictment" there shall be substituted the word "information" and the words from "by a court" to "Northern Ireland" shall be omitted.

EXPLANATORY NOTE

(*This Note is not part of the Order.*)

This Order specifies the adaptations and modifications subject to which the Trustee Savings Banks Act 1969 has effect in the Isle of Man.

STATUTORY INSTRUMENTS

1970 No. 821

CLERK OF THE CROWN IN CHANCERY

The Crown Office (Writs for Dissolving and Summoning Convocations) Rules 1970

Made - - -	29*th May* 1970
Laid before Parliament	29*th May* 1970
Coming into Operation	30*th May* 1970

At the Court at Buckingham Palace, the 29th day of May 1970

Present,

The Queen's Most Excellent Majesty in Council

Whereas by the Crown Office Act 1877(**a**), it is (among other things) enacted that Her Majesty may, by Order in Council, make rules prescribing the form in which documents to which the said Act applies, or any of them, may be worded:

And Whereas the said Act applies to, among other documents, writs directed to the Archbishops of Canterbury and York to dissolve and summon the Convocations of their respective Provinces:

And Whereas it is expedient that the form of such writs currently in use should be changed:

Now, therefore, Her Majesty, in pursuance of section 3 of the said Act, is pleased, by and with the advice of Her Privy Council, to order, and it is hereby ordered, as follows:—

1. These Rules may be cited as the Crown Office (Writs for Dissolving and Summoning Convocations) Rules 1970 and shall come into operation on 30th May 1970.

2. The forms set out in the Schedule to these Rules shall be used for writs dissolving and summoning the Convocations of Canterbury and York.

W. G. Agnew.

SCHEDULE

WRIT FOR DISSOLVING THE CONVOCATION OF CANTERBURY OR YORK

ELIZABETH THE SECOND by the Grace of God of the United Kingdom of Great Britain and Northern Ireland and of Our other Realms and Territories Queen, Head of the Commonwealth, Defender of the Faith:

To the Most Reverend Father in God Our right trusty and well beloved Counsellor [*here insert the name of the Archbishop of Canterbury or York*], by the same Grace Archbishop of [*here insert "Canterbury, Primate of all England" or "York, Primate of England"*] and Metropolitan Greeting;

(**a**) 1877 c. 41.

Whereas the present Convocation of your Province of [*here insert "Canterbury" or "York"*] was by Our Writ called together on the day of and is still continued:

And Whereas We have this day ordered, by and with the advice of Our Privy Council, that the said Convocation be dissolved on the day of :

Therefore We Command you to dissolve the said Convocation on the said day and to signify such dissolution to all Bishops, Deans, Archdeacons and other Clergy whom it does concern.

WITNESS Ourself at Westminster the day of in the year of Our Reign.

WRIT FOR SUMMONING A NEW CONVOCATION OF CANTERBURY OR YORK

ELIZABETH THE SECOND by the Grace of God of the United Kingdom of Great Britain and Northern Ireland and of Our other Realms and Territories Queen, Head of the Commonwealth, Defender of the Faith:

To the Most Reverend Father in God Our right trusty and well beloved Counsellor [*here insert the name of the Archbishop of Canterbury or York*], by the same Grace Archbishop of [*here insert "Canterbury, Primate of All England" or "York, Primate of England"*] and Metropolitan Greeting:

Whereas We have ordered, by and with the advice of Our Privy Council, that writs be issued for dissolving the Convocations of the Provinces of Canterbury and York and for calling together new Convocations of the said Provinces and for electing new members of the Lower Houses of those Convocations:

Therefore We Command you on such dissolution to call together a new Convocation of your Province comprising the Bishops of all the dioceses of your Province, and such of the Deans, Archdeacons and Clergy of your Province as may be elected or otherwise become members of the Lower House of that Convocation in accordance with the Canon for the Representation of the Clergy in the Lower House of the Convocation of [*here insert "Canterbury" or "York"*], to appear before you in [*here insert the place where the Convocation is to meet*] or elsewhere as it shall seem most expedient on the day of :

And this as you love Us, the state of Our Kingdom and the honour and good of the Church of England, by no means omit.

WITNESS Ourself at Westminster the day of in the year of Our Reign.

EXPLANATORY NOTE

(*This Note is not part of the Rules.*)

The Rules prescribe new forms to be used for writs directed to the Archbishops of Canterbury and York for dissolving and summoning the Convocations of their respective Provinces.

STATUTORY INSTRUMENTS

1970 No. 822

JUDGES

The Judges' Remuneration Order 1970

Laid before Parliament in draft

Made - - - - - - *29th May* 1970

At the Court at Buckingham Palace, the 29th day of May 1970

Present,

The Queen's Most Excellent Majesty in Council

Whereas subsection (2) of section 1 of the Judges' Remuneration Act 1965(**a**) enables Her Majesty by Order in Council to direct that any of the salaries specified in schedule 1 to that Act shall be increased to such amount as may be specified in the Order:

And Whereas subsection (3) of the said section 1 provides that no recommendation shall be made to Her Majesty in Council to make an Order under that section unless a draft of the Order has been laid before Parliament and approved by resolution of each House of Parliament:

And Whereas a draft of the following Order was laid before Parliament and approved by resolution of each House:

Now, therefore, in exercise of the powers conferred on Her by the said section 1(2) and all other powers enabling Her in that behalf Her Majesty, by and with the advice of Her Privy Council, is pleased to order, and it is hereby ordered, as follows:—

1. This Order may be cited as the Judges' Remuneration Order 1970.

2. There shall be paid to the holder of any judicial office listed in the schedule to this Order a salary at the annual rate specified in relation to that office in the second column of that schedule instead of the salary specified in the second column of schedule 1 to the Judges' Remuneration Act 1965.

W. G. Agnew.

(**a**) 1965 c. 61.

SCHEDULE

Judicial Office	*Salary*
	£
Lord of Appeal in Ordinary	13,000
Lord Chief Justice	14,250
Master of the Rolls	13,000
President of the Probate, Divorce and Admiralty Division	13,000
Lord Justice of Appeal	11,500
Puisne Judge of the High Court of Justice	11,500
Lord President of the Court of Session	11,500
Lord Justice Clerk	11,250
Ordinary Judge of the Court of Session	9,500
Lord Chief Justice of Northern Ireland	10,750
Lord Justice of Appeal in Northern Ireland	9,300
Puisne Judge of the High Court of Justice in Northern Ireland	9,300

EXPLANATORY NOTE

(*This Note is not part of the Order.*)

This Order increases the salaries of the holders of certain high judicial offices in England and Wales, Scotland and Northern Ireland to the amounts specified in the schedule.

STATUTORY INSTRUMENTS

1970 No. 823

CIVIL AVIATION

The Air Navigation (Noise Certification) Order 1970

Laid before Parliament in draft

Made - - - - - - - -	29*th May* 1970
Coming into Operation - - - - -	
(*a*) *for the purpose of making regulations* -	28*th June* 1970
(*b*) *for purposes of Articles* 3, 5, 9 *and* 16 -	27*th August* 1970
(*c*) *for all other purposes* - - - -	1*st January* 1971

At the Court at Buckingham Palace, the 29th day of May 1970

Present,

The Queen's Most Excellent Majesty in Council

Her Majesty, in exercise of the powers conferred upon Her by sections 8, 57, 58, 59 and 61 of the Civil Aviation Act 1949**(a)** and section 19 of the Civil Aviation Act 1968**(b)**, and of all other powers enabling Her in that behalf, is pleased, by and with the advice of Her Privy Council, to order, and it is hereby ordered, as follows:—

Citation and Operation

1. This Order may be cited as the Air Navigation (Noise Certification) Order 1970 and shall come into operation—

(*a*) thirty days after the date hereof, for the purpose of enabling the Board to make regulations thereunder;

(*b*) ninety days after the date hereof for the purposes of Articles 3, 5, 9 and 16; and

(*c*) on 1st January 1971 for all other purposes.

Interpretation

2.—(1) In this Order—

"An International Standard Atmosphere at sea level" has the meaning specified in Schedule 2 to this Order ;

"By-pass ratio" means the ratio of the air mass flow through the by-pass ducts of a gas turbine engine to the air mass flow through the combustion chambers calculated at maximum thrust when the engine is stationary in an International Standard Atmosphere at sea level;

(a) 1949 c. 67. **(b)** 1968 c. 61.

"EPNdB" means the unit for expressing effective perceived noise level determined in accordance with Board of Trade Civil Aviation Publication CAP 335 dated 13th March 1970 with any modifications which may be prescribed ;

"The Convention" means the Convention on International Civil Aviation signed on behalf of the United Kingdom at Chicago on 7th December 1944;

"Noise certificate" means a certificate issued by the competent authority of a State to the effect that the aeroplane to which the certificate relates complies with the applicable noise certification requirements in force in that State ;

"Prescribed" means prescribed by regulations made by the Board under this Order.

(2) Expressions used in this Order shall, unless the context otherwise requires, have the same respective meanings as in the Air Navigation Order 1966**(a)** as amended **(b)**.

(3) The Interpretation Act 1889**(c)** applies for the purpose of the interpretation of this Order as it applies for the purpose of the interpretation of an Act of Parliament.

(4) A power to make regulations under this Order shall include the power to make different provisions with respect to different classes of aeroplanes and with respect to different circumstances and to make such incidental and supplementary provisions as are necessary or expedient for carrying out the purposes of the Order.

Application of Order

3.—(1) This Order shall apply to every aeroplane having turbojet or turbofan engines which—

(*a*) has a maximum total weight authorised of more than 5,700 kg; and

(*b*) in accordance with its certificate of airworthiness requires for take-off at maximum total weight authorised a runway at least 450 metres long; and

(*c*) is incapable of sustaining level flight at a speed in excess of Flight Mach 1; and

(*d*) (i) is powered by engines having a by-pass ratio of 2 or more, or

(ii) is an aeroplane otherwise powered, unless it is of a description exempted by the Board from the application of this Order as being a description of aeroplane which in their opinion is of the same type as an aeroplane in respect of which the authorities of the State of manufacture received an application for a certificate of airworthiness before 1st January 1969 and did not reject that application.

(2) Nothing in this Article shall prejudice Article 16.

Requirement of noise certificate

4. An aeroplane to which this Order applies shall not land or take off in the United Kingdom unless—

(*a*) there is in force in respect of that aeroplane a noise certificate—

(i) issued by the Board under Article 5 of this Order ; or

(a) S.I. 1966/1184 (1966 III, p. 3073).
(b) The relevant amending instrument is S.I. 1969/1082 (1969 II, p. 3153).
(c) 1889 c. 63.

(ii) issued by the competent authority of the country in which the aeroplane is registered, being a country prescribed as one which applies standards which in the opinion of the Board of Trade are substantially equivalent to those required for the issue of a noise certificate by the Board ; or

(iii) issued in pursuance of the Convention by the competent authority of the State in which the aeroplane is registered, and

(*b*) any conditions subject to which the certificate was issued are complied with:

Provided that the foregoing prohibition shall not apply to:—

(*a*) an aeroplane flying in accordance with the "A Conditions" or the "B Conditions" set forth in Schedule 2 to the Air Navigation Order 1966 as amended;

(*b*) an aeroplane flying in accordance with the conditions of a permit to fly issued under the said Order by the Board in respect of that aeroplane;

(*c*) an aeroplane landing or taking off at a prescribed place.

Issue of noise certificate by the Board of Trade and validity of noise certificate

5.—(1) The Board may issue a noise certificate in respect of any aeroplane to which this Order applies if they are satisfied that the aeroplane complies with the standards specified in Schedule 1 to this Order in relation to the noise made by the aeroplane, and for that purpose the applicant for a certificate shall furnish such evidence and submit the aeroplane to such flying trials and other tests as the Board may require.

(2) The Board shall issue every noise certificate subject to a condition as to the maximum total weights at which the aeroplane may take off and land and may issue such a certificate subject to such other conditions relating to standards as to noise as they think fit.

(3) Subject to the provisions of this Article and of Article 8 of this Order, a noise certificate issued under this Article shall remain in force without limit of time.

(4) A noise certificate issued under this Article in respect of an aeroplane registered in the United Kingdom shall cease to be sufficient for the purposes of Article 4 of this Order—

(*a*) if the aeroplane or any part of it is modified, in any way which affects the ability of the aeroplane to comply with the noise standards required by this Order, otherwise than in a manner and with material of a type approved by the Board either generally or in relation to a class of aeroplane or to the particular aeroplane;

(*b*) until the completion of any inspection or test of the aeroplane required by the Board to be made for the purpose of ascertaining whether the aeroplane continues to comply with the noise standards required by this Order.

(5) The Board may, for the purposes of this Article, accept reports furnished to them by a person whom they may approve, either absolutely or subject to such conditions as they think fit, as qualified to furnish such reports.

Noise certificate to be carried

6.—(1) An aeroplane shall not land or take off in the United Kingdom unless it carries any noise certificate which it is required to carry under the law of the country in which it is registered.

(2) An aeroplane registered in the United Kingdom shall, when in flight, whether within United Kingdom or elsewhere, carry any noise certificate which is required by this Order to be in force in respect of that aeroplane:

Provided that if the flight is intended to begin and end at the same aerodrome, the certificate may be kept at that aerodrome instead of being carried in the aeroplane.

Production of noise certificate

7. The commander of an aeroplane shall, within a reasonable time after being requested to do so by an authorised person, cause to be produced to that person the noise certificate in force in respect of that aeroplane.

Revocation, suspension and variation of noise certificates

8.—(1) The Board may, if they think fit, provisionally suspend any noise certificate, approval, exemption or other document issued under this Order pending investigation of the case. The Board may, after sufficient ground being shown to their satisfaction after due inquiry, revoke, suspend or vary any such certificate.

(2) The holder or any person having the possession or custody of any noise certificate, approval, exemption or other document which has been revoked, suspended or varied under this Order shall surrender it to the Board within a reasonable time after being required to do so by them.

(3) The breach of any condition subject to which any noise certificate, approval, exemption or other document has been issued under this Order shall render the certificate invalid during the continuance of the breach.

Offences in relation to noise certificates

9.—(1) A person shall not with intent to deceive—

(*a*) use any noise certificate issued or required under this Order which has been forged, altered, revoked or suspended, or to which he is not entitled; or

(*b*) lend any such certificate to, or allow it to be used by, any other person; or

(*c*) make any false representation for the purpose of procuring for himself or any other person the issue, renewal or variation of any such certificate.

(2) A person shall not purport to issue any noise certificate under this Order unless he has been authorised to do so.

Power to prevent aeroplanes flying

10.—(1) If it appears to the Board or an authorised person that any aeroplane is intended or likely to be flown in such circumstances that Article 4 of this Order would be contravened in relation to the flight, the Board or that authorised person may direct the operator or the commander of the aeroplane that he is not to permit the aeroplane to make the flight or any other flight of such designation as may be specified in the direction, until the direction has been revoked by the Board or by an authorised person, and the Board or that authorised person may take such steps as are necessary to detain the aeroplane.

(2) For the purposes of paragraph (1) of this Article, the Board or any authorised person may enter upon and inspect any aeroplane.

Right of access to aerodromes and other places

11. The Board and any authorised person shall have for the purpose of ascertaining whether the provisions of this Order are being complied with, the right of access at all reasonable times—

(*a*) to any aerodrome for the purpose of inspecting any aeroplane on the aerodrome or any document which they have, or he has, power to demand under this Order, and for the purpose of detaining any aeroplane under this Order; and

(*b*) to any place where an aeroplane has landed, for the purpose of inspecting the aeroplane or any document which they have, or he has, power to demand under this Order and for the purpose of detaining the aeroplane under this Order:

Provided that access to a Government aerodrome shall only be obtained with the permission of the person in charge of the aerodrome.

Obstruction of persons

12. A person shall not wilfully obstruct or impede any person acting in the exercise of his powers or the performance of his duties under this Order.

Enforcement of directions

13. Any person who fails to comply with any direction given to him by the Board or by any authorised person under any provision of this Order shall be deemed for the purposes of this Order to have contravened that provision.

Penalties

14.—(1) If any provision of this Order is contravened in relation to an aeroplane, the operator of that aeroplane and the commander thereof, if the operator or, as the case may be, the commander is not the person who contravened that provision shall (without prejudice to the liability of any other person under this Order for that contravention) be deemed for the purposes of the following provisions of this Article to have contravened that provision unless he proves that the contravention occurred without his consent or connivance and that he exercised all due diligence to prevent the contravention.

(2) If it is proved that an act or omission of any person which would otherwise have been a contravention by that person of a provision of this Order was due to any cause not avoidable by the exercise of reasonable care by that person, the act or omission shall be deemed not to be a contravention by that person of that provision.

(3) If any person contravenes any provisions of this Order, not being a provision referred to in paragraphs (4) or (5) of this Article, he shall be liable on summary conviction to a fine not exceeding ten pounds; or in the case of a second or subsequent conviction for the like offence to a fine not exceeding twenty pounds.

(4) If any person contravenes Article 12 of this Order he shall be liable on summary conviction to a fine of fifty pounds; or in the case of a second or subsequent conviction for the like offence to a fine of one hundred pounds, or to imprisonment for a term not exceeding three months or to both such fine and imprisonment.

(5) If any person contravenes Article 4, 9 or 13 of this Order he shall be liable on summary conviction or indictment to a fine not exceeding two hundred pounds or to imprisonment for a term of six months or to both such fine and imprisonment.

Application of Order to the Crown and visiting forces etc.

15.—(1) Subject to the following provisions of this Article, the provisions of this Order shall apply to, or in relation to, aeroplanes belonging to or exclusively employed in the service of Her Majesty, as they apply to or in relation to other aeroplanes and for the purposes of such application the Department or other authority for the time being responsible on behalf of Her Majesty for the management of the aeroplane shall be deemed to be the operator of the aeroplane:

Provided that nothing in this Article shall render liable to any penalty any Department or other authority responsible on behalf of Her Majesty for the management of any aeroplane.

(2) The naval, military and air force authorities and members of any visiting force and any international headquarters and the members thereof and property held or used for the purpose of such a force or headquarters shall be exempt from the provisions of this Order to the same extent as if that force or headquarters formed part of the forces of Her Majesty raised in the United Kingdom and for the time being serving there.

(3) Nothing in this Order shall apply to or in relation to any military aircraft.

Exemption

16. The Board may exempt from any of the provisions of this Order or any regulations made thereunder any aeroplane or persons or classes of aeroplanes or persons, either absolutely or subject to such conditions as they think fit.

Extra territorial effect of the Order

17.—(1) Except where the context otherwise requires, the provisions of this Order,

(*a*) in so far as they apply (whether by express reference or otherwise) to aeroplanes registered in the United Kingdom, shall apply to such aeroplanes wherever they may be ;

(*b*) in so far as they apply as aforesaid to other aeroplanes shall apply to such aeroplanes when they are within the United Kingdom ;

(*c*) in so far as they prohibit, require or regulate (whether by express reference or otherwise) the doing of anything by the commander of any aeroplane registered in the United Kingdom, shall apply to him wherever he may be ; and

(*d*) in so far as they prohibit, require or regulate as aforesaid the doing of anything in relation to any aeroplane registered in the United Kingdom by other persons shall, where such persons are British subjects or citizens of the Republic of Ireland, apply to them wherever they may be.

(2) Nothing in this Article shall be construed as extending to make any person guilty of an offence in any case in which it is provided by section 3(1) of the British Nationality Act 1948(**a**) (which limits the criminal liability of certain persons who are not citizens of the United Kingdom and colonies) that that person shall not be guilty of an offence.

W. G. Agnew.

(**a**) 1948 c. 56.

SCHEDULE 1 Article 5(1)

Noise standards required for issue of a noise certificate

1. In this Schedule—

"the noise certification reference conditions" means conditions in which—

(i) atmospheric pressure at sea level is 1013.25 millibars;

(ii) ambient air temperature is 25°C;

(iii) relative humidity is 70%;

(iv) there is zero wind; and

(v) the maximum take-off and landing weights of the aeroplane are those at which noise certification is requested by the applicant for the certificate.

2. The noise levels required by paragraph 3 of this Schedule shall be measured at the following points:

(*a*) on take-off, at a point on a line parallel to and 650 metres from the extended centre-line of the runway where it appears to the Board that the noise after take-off is greatest;

(*b*) on take-off, at a point on the extended centre-line of the runway, 6500 metres from the start of the take-off run; and

(*c*) on the approach to landing, at a point on the extended centre-line of the runway, 120 metres vertically below the 3° descent path.

3.—(1) Subject to the provisions of paragraph 4 of this Schedule, an aeroplane having the maximum total weight authorised specified in the first column of the following Table shall not, at the points referred to at (*a*), (*b*) and (*c*) of paragraph 2 of this Schedule, exceed, in the noise certification reference conditions, the noise levels specified in relation to those points in the second, third and fourth columns of that Table, as shown by flying trials (whether or not conducted at the maximum total weight authorised).

TABLE

Maximum total weight authorised of aeroplane	*Noise level in EPNdB*		
	At point (*a*)	*At point* (*b*)	*At point* (*c*)
272,000 kg or more	108	108	108
34,000 kg or less	102	93	102

(2) Where the maximum total weight authorised of the aeroplane is between the weights specified in the above Table, the noise levels which are not to be exceeded shall vary linearly according to the logarithm of the maximum total weight authorised of the aeroplane.

(3) The necessary corrections shall be made where the flying trials are carried out in conditions other than the noise certification reference conditions.

4. The noise levels specified in paragraph 3 of this Schedule may be exceeded at one or two of the measuring points specified in paragraph 2 if—

(*a*) the sum of the excess does not exceed 4 EPNdB;

(*b*) at no measuring point is the excess greater than 3 EPNdB; and

(*c*) the excesses are completely offset by reductions at the other measuring points.

Article 2

SCHEDULE 2

"An International Standard Atmosphere at sea level" means an atmosphere having the following characteristics:—

(*a*) the air is a perfect dry gas;

(*b*) the physical constants are:

(i) sea level mean molecular weight:
$M_0 = 28.9644 \times 10^{-3}$ kg. mol^{-1}

(ii) sea level atmospheric pressure:
$P_0 = 1013.250$ millibars
$= 1.013250 \times 10^5$ newtons. m^{-2}

(iii) sea level temperature:
$t_0 = 15°C$
$T_0 = 288.15°K$

(iv) sea level atmospheric density:
$\rho_0 = 1.2250$ kg. m^{-3}

(v) temperature of the ice point:
$T_i = 273.15°K$

(vi) universal gas constant:
$R^* = 8.31432$ joules $(°K)^{-1}$. mol^{-1}

EXPLANATORY NOTE

(*This Note is not part of the Order.*)

This Order applies to turbojet and turbofan aeroplanes having a maximum total weight authorised of more than 5700 kilogrammes and incapable of level supersonic flight or of using a runway of 450 metres or less, and which either have engines with a by-pass ratio of 2 or more, or are otherwise powered and are not exempted as being of types developed before 1st January 1969 (Article 3(1)(*d*)(ii)) or otherwise exempted under Article 16 of the Order.

The Order prohibits an aircraft to which it applies, wherever registered, from landing or taking off in the United Kingdom except in accordance with a noise certificate issued by the Board of Trade, or by the competent authority of such countries as may be prescribed by regulations made by the Board, or issued in pursuance of the Chicago Convention of 1944. It makes provision for the issue of noise certificates by the Board of Trade, specifies standards with which an aeroplane must comply in order to obtain such a certificate, and contains ancillary provisions including power to detain aircraft to prevent a contravention of the Order.

The publication CAP 335, referred to in Article 2, can be purchased from H.M. Stationery Office.

1970 No. 824

MERCHANT SHIPPING

The Oil in Navigable Waters (Convention Countries) (Monaco) Order 1970

Made - - -	29*th May* 1970
Laid before Parliament	29*th May* 1970
Coming into Operation	25*th June* 1970

At the Court at Buckingham Palace, the 29th day of May 1970

Present,

The Queen's Most Excellent Majesty in Council

Whereas by section 18(3) of the Oil in Navigable Waters Act 1955**(a)** it is enacted that for the purposes of that section Her Majesty may, if satisfied that the government of any country has accepted the International Convention for the Prevention of Pollution of the Sea by Oil 1954, by Order in Council make a declaration to that effect:

And whereas Her Majesty is satisfied that the Government of the Principality of Monaco has accepted the said Convention:

Now, therefore, Her Majesty, in pursuance of the powers conferred upon Her by the said section 18(3) and of all other powers enabling Her in that behalf, is pleased, by and with the advice of Her Privy Council, to order, and it is hereby ordered, as follows:—

1. This Order may be cited as the Oil in Navigable Waters (Convention Countries) (Monaco) Order 1970 and shall come into operation on 25th June 1970.

2. For the purposes of section 18 of the Oil in Navigable Waters Act 1955 it is hereby declared that the Government of the Principality of Monaco has accepted the International Convention for the Prevention of Pollution of the Sea by Oil 1954.

W. G. Agnew.

(a) 1955 c. 25.

1970 No. 825

CIVIL AVIATION

The Tokyo Convention (Certification of Countries) Order 1970

Made - - - *29th May* 1970

At the Court at Buckingham Palace, the 29th day of May 1970

Present,

The Queen's Most Excellent Majesty in Council

Her Majesty, in exercise of the powers conferred upon Her by section 7(1) of the Tokyo Convention Act 1967(**a**) (which provides that Her Majesty may by Order in Council certify which countries are Convention countries, that is to say countries in which the Convention on Offences and certain other Acts Committed on board Aircraft signed in Tokyo on 14th September 1963 is for the time being in force) and of all other powers enabling Her in that behalf is pleased, by and with the advice of Her Privy Council, to order, and it is hereby ordered, as follows:

1. This Order may be cited as the Tokyo Convention (Certification of Countries) Order 1970.

2. The Tokyo Convention (Certification of Countries) Order 1969(**b**) is hereby revoked and section 38(2) of the Interpretation Act 1889(**c**) (which relates to the effect of repeals) shall apply to this Order as if this Order were an Act of Parliament and as if the Order revoked by this Article were an Act of Parliament thereby repealed.

3. It is hereby certified that the countries listed in the Schedule hereto are Convention countries.

W. G. Agnew.

SCHEDULE

The United Kingdom of Great Britain and Northern Ireland
- The Channel Islands
- The Isle of Man
- Bahamas
- Bermuda
- British Antarctic Territory
- British Honduras
- British Indian Ocean Territory
- British Solomon Islands Protectorate
- British Virgin Islands
- Cayman Islands
- Central and Southern Line Islands
- The Sovereign Base Areas of Akrotiri and Dhekelia in the island of Cyprus

(**a**) 1967 c. 52. (**b**) S.I. 1969/1835 (1969 III, p. 5715).
(**c**) 1889 c. 63.

SCHEDULE (*continued*)

Falkland Islands and Dependencies
Fiji
Gibraltar
Gilbert and Ellice Islands Colony
Hong Kong
Montserrat
Pitcairn
St. Helena and Dependencies
St. Vincent
Seychelles
Turks and Caicos Islands

Brazil

Canada

Denmark and the Faroe Islands

Ecuador

Gabon

The Federal Republic of Germany

Israel

Italy

Malagasy Republic

Mexico

The Netherlands and all territories subject to the sovereignty or authority of the Kingdom of the Netherlands except Surinam and the Netherlands Antilles

Niger

Norway and all territories subject to the sovereignty or authority of Norway

The Philippines

Portugal and all territories subject to the sovereignty or authority of Portugal

Saudi Arabia

Spain and all territories subject to the sovereignty or authority of Spain

Sweden

The United States of America and all territories subject to the sovereignty or authority of the United States of America

Upper Volta

EXPLANATORY NOTE

(*This Note is not part of the Order.*)

This Order revokes and replaces the Tokyo Convention (Certification of Countries) Order 1969. It certifies in which countries the Convention on Offences and certain other Acts Committed on board Aircraft, signed in Tokyo on 14th September 1963, is for the time being in force. Under section 7(1) of the Tokyo Convention Act 1967 this Order is conclusive evidence of the matters certified.

1970 No. 828 (S.63)

AGRICULTURE

AGRICULTURAL GRANTS, GOODS AND SERVICES

The Ploughing Grants (Scotland) Scheme 1970

Laid before Parliament in draft

Made - - - *26th May* 1970

In exercise of the powers conferred upon me by sections 1, 2, 3 and 5 of the Agriculture (Ploughing Grants) Act 1952(**a**), and of all other powers enabling me in that behalf, and with the approval of the Treasury, I hereby make the following scheme, a draft of which has been laid before Parliament and has been approved by resolution of each House of Parliament :—

1. This scheme may be cited as the Ploughing Grants (Scotland) Scheme 1970.

2.—(1) In this scheme, unless the context otherwise requires, the following expressions have the meanings hereby respectively assigned to them—

"the Act" means the Agriculture (Ploughing Grants) Act 1952 ;

"eligible occupier" means a person who is for the time being an eligible occupier within the meaning of the Crofting Counties Agricultural Grants (Scotland) Scheme 1961(**b**), the Crofting Counties Agricultural Grants (Scotland) Scheme 1963(**c**) or the Crofting Counties Agricultural Grants (Scotland) Scheme 1965(**d**) and, except in the case of a person who is a sub-tenant as is mentioned in section 14(1)(*c*) of the Crofters (Scotland) Act 1961(**e**), who has been offered a grant under any of the said schemes ;

"grass" includes rye grass and other rotational grasses, clover and permanent grass ;

"land under grass" includes any grazing land ;

"occupier" in relation to any land means the person who has the right to carry out on that land the operations referred to in this scheme.

(2) For the purposes of this scheme grass shall be regarded as a crop.

(3) Any reference in this scheme to any other scheme shall be construed as a reference to that scheme as amended by any subsequent scheme, and if any scheme referred to in this scheme is replaced by a subsequent scheme the reference shall be construed as a reference to that subsequent scheme.

(4) The Interpretation Act 1889(**f**) shall apply for the interpretation of this scheme as it applies for the interpretation of an Act of Parliament.

(**a**) 1952 c. 35.
(**b**) S.I. 1961/2266 (1961 III, p. 3973).
(**c**) S.I. 1963/1294 (1963 II, p. 2240).
(**d**) S.I. 1965/1519 (1965 II, p. 4399).
(**e**) 1961 c. 58.
(**f**) 1889 c. 63.

3.—(1) Subject to the provisions of this scheme a grant may be made by the Secretary of State in respect of the following operations—

(*a*) the ploughing up of land under grass ;

(*b*) after ploughing, the carrying out of such further operations on the land as may be required by the Secretary of State and as are necessary, or form part of the operations necessary, to bring the land into a state of cleanliness, fertility, and fitness for cropping ; and

(*c*) the sowing on that land of a crop, unless the Secretary of State otherwise determines.

(2) A grant shall not be made under this scheme in respect of any land unless before the commencement of any operations in respect of which such a grant may be made the Secretary of State has approved those operations in relation to that land and is satisfied that the carrying out thereof on that land, together with any necessary preliminary operations, is likely to involve expenditure which is substantially heavier than normal for operations such as are specified in sub-paragraph (1) of this paragraph.

(3) Where the Secretary of State has approved operations in relation to any land for the purposes of the Ploughing Grants (Scotland) Scheme 1968(**a**) or the Ploughing Grants (Scotland) Scheme 1969(**b**), not being operations deemed to have been approved for the purposes of the said scheme of 1968 by virtue of paragraph 3(3) thereof, and any part of the said land has not been ploughed up from grass before 1st June 1970, such operations shall be deemed to have been approved for the purposes of this scheme also.

(4) A grant shall not be made under this scheme in respect of any land which has been the subject of a grant under Part II of any previous scheme made under the Act.

4. The rate of grant to be made in accordance with this scheme shall be £12 per acre :

Provided that in calculating the amount of a grant fractions of an acre less than one-quarter of an acre shall be disregarded.

5. Subject to the provisions of paragraph 7 of this scheme a grant under this scheme may only be made where the land ploughed up—

(*a*) is not less than one acre in area ;

(*b*) was ploughed up from grass within the period beginning with 1st June 1970 and ending with 31st May 1971 ; and

(*c*) at the time when such ploughing up was begun was under grass that had been sown not later than 1st June 1958, or had been continuously under grass since before that date.

6. The person to whom a grant may be made under this scheme in pursuance of an application made in that behalf shall be the occupier of the land ploughed up as at the date of the completion, on that land, of the operations in respect of which the grant is payable :

(**a**) S.I. 1968/860 (1968 II, p. 2283). (**b**) S.I. 1969/778 (1969 II, p. 2191).

Provided that where the occupier is a landholder within the meaning of the Small Landholders (Scotland) Acts 1886 to 1931(**a**) or a crofter within the meaning of the Crofters (Scotland) Acts 1955 and 1961(**b**) or an eligible occupier to whom a grant may be made by virtue of the provisions of the next succeeding paragraph and an application for the grant is made on his behalf as provided by and in the manner specified in head (*c*) of that paragraph, the grant shall be made to the person making the application.

7. Where land is ploughed up by a landholder within the meaning of the Small Landholders (Scotland) Acts 1886 to 1931 or a crofter within the meaning of the Crofters (Scotland) Acts 1955 and 1961 or an eligible occupier then notwithstanding that the area of that land is less than one acre a grant may be made in respect thereof if—

(*a*) the area so ploughed up and any areas of land ploughed up by neighbouring landholders or neighbouring crofters or neighbouring eligible occupiers, as the case may be, together in the aggregate amount to or exceed one acre ;

(*b*) the provisions of this scheme are complied with in relation to all the areas so ploughed up, or in relation to such number of them as, in the aggregate, amount to or exceed one acre ; and

(*c*) an application for grant in respect of all those areas is made on behalf of those landholders or crofters or eligible occupiers, as the case may be, by the Clerk of the Committee appointed for the management of the common grazings or common pasture in which the landholders or crofters or eligible occupiers, as the case may be, all have shares, or, where there is no such Clerk, or, where they do not all have such shares, by a person who has been duly authorised by the landholders or crofters or eligible occupiers, in a manner satisfactory to the Secretary of State, to make the application.

8. The Secretary of State may require an applicant for a grant under this scheme to give to any person authorised by the Secretary of State in that behalf adequate facilities for the inspection of any land to which the application relates.

9. Where in the opinion of the Secretary of State—

(*a*) the ploughing or any other operation in respect of which a grant under this scheme may be made has been inefficiently carried out ; or

(*b*) any preliminary operations the expenditure or likely expenditure on which has been taken into account by the Secretary of State for the purpose of satisfying himself that a grant may be made under this scheme have not been carried out or have been inefficiently carried out ; or

(*c*) adequate facilities for the inspection of the land in respect of which any such grant as aforesaid may be made have not been given ;

payment of the grant may be withheld or the amount of the grant may be reduced to such amount as the Secretary of State considers reasonable.

10. If in respect of any of the operations in respect of which a grant is payable under this scheme payments of moneys provided by Parliament under any enactment other than the Act are available, the Secretary of State in deter-

(**a**) 1886 c. 29; 1887 c. 24; 1891 c. 41; 1908 c. 50; 1911 c. 49; 1919 c. 97; 1931 c. 44.
(**b**) 1955 c. 21; 1961 c. 58.

mining the amount of grant payable under this scheme may take into consideration such payments, and may withhold or reduce the amount payable under this scheme accordingly.

11. A grant shall not be made under this scheme in respect of any land which has been the subject of a grassland renovation grant made by virtue of a scheme under section 11 of the Agriculture (Miscellaneous Provisions) Act 1963(**a**).

William Ross,
One of Her Majesty's Principal
Secretaries of State.

St. Andrew's House,
Edinburgh.
18th May 1970.

We approve.

E. G. Perry,
Neil McBride,
Two of the Lords Commissioners
of Her Majesty's Treasury.

26th May 1970.

EXPLANATORY NOTE

(*This Note is not part of the Scheme.*)

This Scheme, which is made under the Agriculture (Ploughing Grants) Act 1952, provides for the making of grants by the Secretary of State at the rate of £12 per acre in respect of land ploughed up from grass, where after ploughing the operations described in the Scheme are carried out. The land must have been under grass since 1st June 1958 and the ploughing must be carried out within the period from 1st June 1970 to 31st May 1971.

Prior approval must be obtained from the Secretary of State, and this will only be given where he is satisfied that the carrying out of the operations (together with any necessary preliminary operations) is likely to involve expenditure which is substantially heavier than normal for operations of the kind.

Where operations have been expressly approved for the purposes of the 1968 Scheme or the 1969 Scheme, but any of the ploughing is carried out during the period to which this Scheme applies, the approval is to be treated as though it were given for the purposes of this Scheme also. In other respects, except for the advancement of the dates by one year, the Scheme is materially the same as the 1969 Scheme.

(**a**) 1963 c. 11.

1970 No. 830

INDUSTRIAL ORGANISATION AND DEVELOPMENT

The Apple and Pear Development Council (Amendment) Order 1970

Laid before Parliament in draft

Made - - -	29*th May* 1970
Coming into Operation	5*th June* 1970

The Minister of Agriculture, Fisheries and Food in exercise of the powers conferred on him by section 8(1) of the Industrial Organisation and Development Act 1947(**a**) and of all other powers enabling him in that behalf, after consultation with the Apple and Pear Development Council (established under the said Act by the Apple and Pear Development Council Order 1966(**b**)), with the organisations appearing to him to be representative of substantial numbers of persons carrying on business in the industry and with the organisations representative of persons employed in the industry appearing to the Minister to be appropriate, hereby makes the following order a draft whereof has been laid before Parliament and approved by a resolution of each House of Parliament :—

Citation, commencement and interpretation

1.—(1) This order may be cited as the Apple and Pear Development Council (Amendment) Order 1970, and shall come into operation at the expiration of seven days beginning with the day on which it is made.

(2) The Interpretation Act 1889(**c**) shall apply to the interpretation of this order as it applies to the interpretation of an Act of Parliament.

Amendment of principal order

2. The Apple and Pear Development Council Order 1966 shall be amended by substituting in article 10(1) thereof for the words "thirty shillings" the words "sixty shillings".

(a) 1947 c.40. (b) S.I. 1966/1579 (1966 III, p. 4883).
(c) 1889 c.63.

In Witness whereof the Official Seal of the Minister of Agriculture, Fisheries and Food is hereunto affixed on 29th May 1970.

(L.S.)

Cledwyn Hughes,
Minister of Agriculture, Fisheries and Food.

EXPLANATORY NOTE

(*This Note is not part of the Order.*)

This order amends the Apple and Pear Development Council Order 1966 by raising from thirty shillings to sixty shillings per acre the maximum rate of the annual charge which may be imposed by the Apple and Pear Development Council on registered growers.

1970 No. 831 (C.19) (S.64)

NATIONAL HEALTH SERVICE, SCOTLAND

The Health Services and Public Health Act 1968 (Commencement No. 4) (Scotland) Order 1970

Made - - - *25th May* 1970

In exercise of the powers conferred on me by section 79(2) of the Health Services and Public Health Act 1968(a) and of all other powers enabling me in that behalf, I hereby make the following order:—

1. This order, which shall extend to Scotland only, may be cited as the Health Services and Public Health Act 1968 (Commencement No. 4) (Scotland) Order 1970.

2. Section 15 of the Health Services and Public Health Act 1968 shall come into operation on 1st September 1970.

William Ross,
One of Her Majesty's Principal Secretaries of State.

St. Andrew's House,
Edinburgh.

25th May 1970.

EXPLANATORY NOTE

(*This Note is not part of the Order.*)

This Order brings into force on 1st September 1970 Section 15 of the Health Services and Public Health Act 1968, which relates to the provision in Scotland of advice, etc. for purposes of family planning.

(a) 1968 c. 46.

STATUTORY INSTRUMENTS

1970 No. 834

REPRESENTATION OF THE PEOPLE

The Elections (Welsh Forms) (No. 5) Regulations 1970

Made - - -	1*st May* 1970
Laid before Parliament	7*th May* 1970
Coming into Operation	11*th June* 1970

In exercise of the powers conferred on me by sections 42 and 171(5) of the Representation of the People Act 1949(**a**) and by section 2(2) of the Welsh Language Act 1967(**b**), and of all other powers enabling me in that behalf, I hereby make the following Regulations :—

1. These Regulations may be cited as the Elections (Welsh Forms) (No. 5) Regulations 1970 and shall come into operation fourteen days after they have been approved by both Houses of Parliament.

2. The Interpretation Act 1889(**c**) shall apply to the interpretation of these Regulations as it applies to the interpretation of an Act of Parliament.

3. The form set out in Part I of the Schedule to these Regulations is hereby prescribed as the version partly in Welsh and partly in English which shall be used in place of Form A in Schedule 1 to the Representation of the People Regulations 1969(**d**) (return by occupier as to residents) in connection with the preparation of registers of electors in Wales or Monmouthshire.

4. The form set out in Part II of the Schedule to these Regulations is hereby prescribed as the version partly in Welsh and partly in English which shall be used by an electoral registration officer for a constituency in Wales or Monmouthshire in place of Form D in Schedule 1 to the Representation of the People Regulations 1969 (proxy paper).

5. The forms set out in Part III of the Schedule to these Regulations are hereby prescribed as the versions partly in Welsh and partly in English which shall be used at a parliamentary election in Wales or Monmouthshire in place of Forms E and F in Schedule 1 to the Representation of the People Regulations 1969 (official poll cards).

(**a**) 1949 c. 68.
(**b**) 1967 c. 66.
(**c**) 1889 c. 63.
(**d**) S.I. 1969/904 (1969 II, p. 2602).

6. The forms set out in the Schedule to these Regulations may be used with such variations as the circumstances may require.

James Callaghan,
One of Her Majesty's Principal Secretaries of State.

Home Office,
Whitehall.
1st May 1970.

Regulation 3

SCHEDULE

PART I

FORM A: RETURN BY OCCUPIER AS TO RESIDENTS

REPRESENTATION OF THE PEOPLE ACTS

REGISTER OF ELECTORS 19

Qualifying date: 10th October 19 . Register in force for twelve months from 16th February 19

I have to compile and publish an up-to-date Register of Electors for 19 . To do so, I need information which you, as Occupier, are obliged by law to supply. Please complete this form accurately and return it to me now—there is no need to wait until the qualifying date before doing so. You should also complete the form even though you intend to move house some time after the qualifying date.

Registers of Electors are needed so that everyone who is entitled to vote at parliamentary or local elections may do so. A person whose name does not appear in the Register cannot vote.

The notes within tell you how to fill up the form, but if you need any further help, I shall be glad to give it.

The Electoral Registration Officer.

FFURFLEN A: ATEB GAN DDEILIAD YNGLŶN Â PHRESWYLWYR

DEDDFAU CYNRYCHIOLAETH Y BOBL

COFRESTR ETHOLWYR 19

Dyddiad cymhwyster: Hydref 10fed 19 . Cofrestr mewn grym am deuddeng mis o Chwefror 16eg 19

Gofynnir i mi ddarparu a chyhoeddi Cofrestr Etholwyr gyflawn ar gyfer 19 . I wneud hynny y mae arnaf eisiau gwybodaeth y mae'n rhaid i chi, fel Deiliad, ei rhoi i mi yn unol â'r gyfraith. Llenwch y ffurflen hon yn gywir ac anfonwch hi'n ôl i mi yn awr os gwelwch yn dda—nid oes eisiau i chi aros tan y dyddiad cymhwyster cyn gwneud hynny. Dylech lenwi'r ffurflen hefyd hyd yn oed os ydych yn bwriadu symud i dŷ arall rywbryd wedi'r dyddiad cymhwyster.

Y mae'r Cofrestrau Etholwyr yn angenrheidiol oherwydd ni all unrhyw berson bleidleisio mewn etholiad seneddol nac mewn etholiad llywodraeth leol oni fydd ei enw ar y Gofrestr.

Y mae'r nodiadau ar yr ochr fewn yn dweud wrthych sut i lenwi'r ffurflen, ond os bydd arnoch eisiau unrhyw help ychwanegol, byddaf yn falch o'i roi.

Swyddog Cofrestru Etholiadol.

Please complete parts 1, 2 and 3 and sign the declaration (part 4). Byddwch cystal â llenwi rhannau 1, 2 a 3 a llofnodwch y datganiad (rhan 4)

Part 1. Address Rhan 1. Cyfeiriad

No. of flat, room or floor (where applicable)	No. of house (or name if it is not numbered)	Name of street or road	Parish or town: postal district or postcode (if any)
Rhif y fflat, yr ystafell neu'r llawr (lle mae'n gymwys)	Rhif y tŷ (neu enw oni bo rhif)	Enw'r heol neu'r ffordd	Plwyf neu dref: dosbarth post neu god post (os oes un)

Part 2. Residents eligible to be included (*see* Notes 1 and 2)
If there are none, please write "None"

Rhan 2. Preswylwyr sy'n gymwys i'w cynnwys (*gweler* Nodiadau 1 a 2). Os nad oes un, byddwch cystal ag ysgrifennu "Dim Un"

Surname and title (Mr., Mrs., etc.) (BLOCK LETTERS) Cyfenw a theitl (Mr., Mrs., etc.) (LLYTHRENNAU BREISION) Occupier's name first Enw'r deiliad yn gyntaf	Full Christian names or forenames (BLOCK LETTERS) Enwau bedydd neu enwau blaen eraill yn llawn (LLYTHRENNAU BREISION)	If aged 18 on or before 16th February 19 enter a ✓ in this column Os yn 18 oed ar neu cyn Chwefror 16, 19 rhowch ✓ yn y golofn hon	If 18th birthday is after 16th February 19 and on or before the following 15th February give date of birth (See note 1) Os yn 18 oed ar ôl Chwefror 16, 19 ac ar neu cyn y 15ed o'r Chwefror dilynol, rhowch y dyddiad geni (Gweler nodyn 1)	If a merchant seaman enter "M." (See note 1(*e*)) Os morwr (heb fod yn y Llynges) rhowch "M." (Gweler nodyn 1(*e*))

Part 3. Other residents

Is any part of your house/flat separately occupied by persons not entered above?

Answer Yes or No

Part 4. Declaration

I declare that to the best of my knowledge and belief—

(*a*) the particulars given above are true and accurate;

(*b*) all those whose names are entered above are British subjects or citizens of the Irish Republic and are over 18 or will attain their 18th birthday on or before 15th February 19 .

Signature ....

Llofnod ....

Rhan 3. Preswylwyr eraill

A oes unrhyw ran o'ch tŷ/fflat yn cael ei dal ar wahân gan bersonau nad yw eu henwau uchod?

Atebwch OES neu NAC OES

Rhan 4. Datganiad

Yr wyf yn datgan, hyd eithaf fy ngwybodaeth a'm cred fod—

(*a*) y manylion a roddir uchod yn wir ac yn gywir;

(*b*) y cwbl o'r personau a enwir uchod yn DDEILIAID PRYDEINIG neu'n ddinasyddion o Weriniaeth Iwerddon a'u bod dros 18 oed neu'n cael eu pen-blwydd yn 18 ar neu cyn Chwefror 15, 19 .

Date ....

Dyddiad ....

Notes

1. You should enter every British subject (Commonwealth citizens are British subjects) or citizen of the Irish Republic who will be resident at your address on 10th October 19 and who is 18 years of age or over on 16th February next or whose 18th birthday is after 16th February next and on or before the following 15th February (people in this age-group can vote at elections held on or after the date of their 18th birthday).

You should include—

(*a*) Those who normally live at your address but are temporarily away, e.g. on holiday, as a student or in hospital (including informal patients in psychiatric hospitals);

(*b*) Resident guests, other than short-stay visitors;

(*c*) Lodgers and resident domestics;

(*d*) Any person who is away working, unless his absence will be for more than six months;

(*e*) Merchant seamen. Enter "M" against the name of a merchant seaman He will then be invited to appoint a proxy to vote for him, or to vote by post. A merchant seaman may be included if he would have been resident at an address (including a hostel or club for merchant seamen) but for the nature of his occupation;

(*f*) Reservists called up for service or training.

2. Do not enter—

(*a*) Members of H.M. Forces

(*b*) Crown servants employed outside the United Kingdom

(*c*) Persons employed by the British Council in posts outside the United Kingdom

(*d*) Wives or husbands of members of H.M. Forces, of Crown servants or of British Council Staff employed outside the United Kingdom if they are living abroad to be with their husbands or wives, as the case may be

} Their names will be included in the Register if they have made the necessary service declaration; to do this they should apply to their Service or Department or the British Council

(*e*) Aliens.

Nodiadau

1. Dylech gynnwys pob deiliad Prydeinig (y mae dinasyddion y Gymanwlad yn ddeiliaid Prydeinig) neu ddinesydd o Weriniaeth Iwerddon a fydd yn preswylio yn eich cyfeiriad ar Hydref 10, 19 ac sydd yn 18 oed neu drosodd ar yr 16eg o Chwefror nesaf, neu a fydd yn cael ei ben-blwydd yn 18 ar ôl yr 16eg o Chwefror nesaf, ac ar neu cyn y 15ed o'r Chwefror dilynol (gall pobl yn y grŵp oedran hwn bleidleisio mewn etholiadau a gynhelir ar neu ar ôl eu pen-blwydd yn 18 oed).

Dylech gynnwys—

(*a*) Y rhai hynny sy'n byw fel arfer yn eich cyfeiriad chi ond sydd i ffwrdd dros dro, e.e. ar wyliau, fel myfyriwr, neu mewn ysbyty (gan gynnwys cleifion anffurfiol mewn ysbytai seiciatrig);

(*b*) Ymwelwyr preswyl, ond nid ymwelwyr dros amser byr;

(*c*) Lletywyr a gweision a morynion preswyl;

(*d*) Unrhyw berson sy'n gweithio oddi catref oni fyddo'n absennol am fwy na chwe mis;

(*e*) Morwyr (ar wahân i forwyr yn y Llynges). Rhowch "M" wrth enw morwr. Yna fe'i gwahoddir i benodi dirprwy i bleidleisio yn ei le, neu i anfon ei bleidlais drwy'r post. Gellir cynnwys morwr a fyddai, onibai am ei waith, yn preswylio mewn cyfeiriad (gan gynnwys hostel neu glwb i forwyr, ar wahân i forwyr yn y Llynges);

(*f*) Aelodau o'r Lluoedd Cadw (Reservists) a alwyd i fyny am hyfforddiant neu wasanaeth.

2. Peidiwch â chynnwys—

(*a*) Aelodau o Luoedd Ei Mawrhydi

(*b*) Gweision y Goron sy'n gwasanaethu y tu allan i'r Deyrnas Gyfunol

(*c*) Aelodau o staff y Cyngor Prydeinig sy'n gwasanaethu y tu allan i'r Deyrnas Gyfunol

(*d*) Gwŷr neu wragedd y rhain os ydynt yn byw y tu allan i'r Deyrnas Gyfunol er mwyn bod gyda'u gwŷr neu'u gwragedd, fel y bo'r achos

} Rhoddir eu henwau ar y Gofrestr wedi iddynt wneud y datganiad gwasanaeth angenrheidiol; i wneud hyn dylent anfon cais at y Gwasanaeth neu'r Adran, neu at y Cyngor Prydeinig

(*e*) Tramorwyr.

Regulation 4

PART II

FORM D: PROXY PAPER

REPRESENTATION OF THE PEOPLE ACTS

Constituency..

Polling District..

Local government electoral area(s)..

....

(Name of proxy)..

(Address) ....

....

....

is hereby appointed as proxy for
(Name of elector)..

who is qualified as a *service voter / resident to be registered for

(Qualifying address)..

....

to vote for *him/her at *the parliamentary election for the above constituency on .... / *any election for the above parliamentary constituency or local government electoral area(s) (*see* Note 1)

*Delete whichever is inapplicable

This proxy appointment is not valid until..

Signature ....
Electoral Registration Officer

Address ....

....

....

Date..................................

NOTES

1. If your appointment as proxy is for a particular parliamentary election, it will be valid for that election only. In other cases your appointment will continue in force until the electoral registration officer informs you to the contrary (e.g. because the elector cancels it).

If the elector is shown on this form as a resident, your appointment will be valid for all parliamentary and local government elections for the constituency and local government electoral area(s) named above, but not for rural borough or parish council elections.

If the elector is shown on this form as a service voter, your appointment will be valid for all parliamentary and local government elections for the constituency and local government electoral area(s) named above (including rural borough and parish council elections) unless the elector applies to vote by post at a particular parliamentary election. If he does this, your appointment will be suspended for that election only and you will be so informed.

If a ballot paper is issued to the elector at the polling station before you apply for a ballot paper on his behalf, you will not be entitled to vote as proxy.

2. To vote as proxy at an election you must go in person to the polling station for the elector's qualifying address, except that you may apply to vote by post as proxy if either—

(*a*) you are entitled to vote by post in respect of your own vote at the election, or

(*b*) in the case of a parliamentary election only, your address is not in the same borough and constituency as the address for which the elector is registered, or is not within the same urban district, rural borough or parish as that address.

Any application to vote by post as proxy should be made on Form V which may be obtained from the electoral registration officer.

3. It is an offence to vote, whether in person or by post, as proxy for some other person if you know that that person is subject to a legal incapacity to vote, e.g. if that person has been convicted and is detained in a penal institution in pursuance of his sentence.

FFURFLEN D: PAPUR DIRPRWY

DEDDFAU CYNRYCHIOLAETH Y BOBL

Etholaeth ....

Dosbarth Pleidleisio ....

Rhanbarth(au) etholiadol llywodraeth leol..

(Enw'r dirprwy)..

(Cyfeiriad)..

....

....

Penodir y sawl a enwyd uchod drwy hyn yn ddirprwy ar ran

(Enw'r etholwr)..

sy'n gymwys fel *pleidleisiwr lluyddol / preswylydd i gael ei gofrestru oblegid

(Cyfeiriad y cofrestrwyd ef o'i blegid)..

er mwyn iddo bleidleisio *drosto/drosti *yn yr etholiad seneddol ar gyfer yr etholaeth uchod ar........................... / *mewn unrhyw etholiad ar gyfer yr etholaeth seneddol neu ranbarth(au) etholiadol llywodraeth leol uchod (*gweler* Nodyn 1)

*Dileer y rhai nad ydynt yn gymwys

Ni ddaw'r penodiad hwn i fod yn ddirprwy i rym tan..................................

Llofnod ....

Swyddog Cofrestru Etholiadol

Cyfeiriad..

....

....

Dyddiad....................................

NODIADAU

1. Os ar gyfer etholiad seneddol arbennig y penodwyd chwi'n ddirprwy, bydd mewn grym ar gyfer yr etholiad hwnnw'n unig. Mewn achosion eraill, bydd eich penodiad mewn grym nes i'r swyddog cofrestru etholiadol eich hysbysu'n wahanol (e.e. am fod yr etholwr wedi ei ddiddymu).

Os yw'n ymddangos ar y ffurflen hon fod yr etholwr yn breswylydd, bydd eich penodiad yn parhau mewn grym ar gyfer pob etholiad seneddol a llywodraeth leol yn yr etholaeth a'r rhanbarth(au) etholiadol llywodraeth leol a enwyd uchod, ond nid ar gyfer etholiadau cyngor bwrdeistref wledig neu gyngor plwyf.

Os yw'n ymddangos ar y ffurflen mai pleidleisiwr lluyddol yw'r etholwr, bydd eich penodiad mewn grym ar gyfer pob etholiad seneddol a llywodraeth leol yn yr etholaeth a'r rhanbarth(au) etholiadol llywodraeth leol a enwyd uchod (gan gynnwys etholiadau cyngor bwrdeistref wledig a chyngor plwyf), oni fydd yr etholwr yn gwneud cais am bleidleisio drwy'r post mewn etholiad seneddol arbennig. Os gwna hyn, dirymir eich penodiad ar gyfer yr etholiad hwnnw'n unig, ac fe'ch hysbysir am hynny.

2. I bleidleisio fel dirprwy, rhaid i chwi fynd yn bersonol i'r orsaf bleidleisio ar gyfer y cyfeiriad y cofrestrwyd yr etholwr o'i blegid, ond gellwch wneud cais am bleidleisio drwy'r post fel dirprwy—

(*a*) os oes gennych hawl i bleidleisio drwy'r post oherwydd eich pleidlais eich hun yn yr etholiad, neu

(*b*) yn achos etholiad seneddol yn unig, os nad yw eich cyfeiriad yn yr un fwrdeistref ac etholaeth â'r cyfeiriad y cofrestrwyd yr etholwr o'i blegid, neu os nad yw o fewn yr un dosbarth trefol, bwrdeistref wledig, neu blwyf â'r cyfeiriad hwnnw.

Dylid gwneud cais ar Ffurflen V am bleidleisio drwy'r post fel dirprwy, a gellir ei chael oddi wrth y swyddog cofrestru etholiadol.

3. Y mae'n drosedd pleidleisio, naill ai'n bersonol neu drwy'r post, fel dirprwy ar ran rhyw berson arall os gwyddoch nad oes gan y person hwnnw hawl cyfreithiol i bleidleisio, e.e. os dyfarnwyd y person hwnnw'n euog a'i gadw mewn sefydliad cosbi yn unol â'i ddedfryd.

PART III Regulation 5

FORM E: ELECTORS' OFFICIAL POLL CARD
FFURFLEN E: CERDYN PLEIDLEISIO SWYDDOGOL YR ETHOLWR

REPRESENTATION OF THE PEOPLE ACTS
DEDDFAU CYNRYCHIOLAETH Y BOBL

Front of card

OFFICIAL POLL CARD
CERDYN PLEIDLEISIO SWYDDOGOL

Constituency Etholaeth	
Polling Day.................................... Dyddiad Pleidleisio	Number on Register.................. Rhif ar y Gofrestr Name .... Enw
Your polling station will be Yr orsaf bleidleisio i chwi fydd	Address .... Cyfeiriad ....

Back of card

PARLIAMENTARY ELECTION

The poll will be open from 7 a.m. to 10 p.m.

The address of your polling station is shown on the front of this card.

When you go to the polling station tell the clerk your name and address, as shown on the front of this card. The presiding officer will give you a ballot paper; see that he stamps the official mark on it before he gives it to you.

Mark your vote on the ballot paper secretly in one of the voting compartments. Put one X in the space to the right opposite the name of the candidate for whom you wish to vote. You may vote for only one candidate. If you put any other mark on the ballot paper, your vote may not be counted.

Then fold the ballot paper so as to conceal your vote, show the official mark on the back to the presiding officer and put the paper into the ballot box.

If you spoil the ballot paper by mistake do not destroy it; give it back to the presiding officer and ask for another.

ISSUED BY THE RETURNING OFFICER

ETHOLIAD SENEDDOL

Bydd yr orsaf bleidleisio ar agor o 7 a.m. hyd 10 p.m. Gwelir cyfeiriad eich gorsaf bleidleisio ar wyneb y cerdyn hwn.

Wedi i chwi gyrraedd yr orsaf bleidleisio, rhowch eich enw a'ch cyfeiriad i'r clerc, fel y maent ar wyneb y cerdyn hwn. Cewch bapur pleidleisio gan y swyddog llywyddu; mynnwch weld ei fod yn rhoi 'r nod swyddogol arno cyn ei estyn i chwi.

Rhowch arwydd eich pleidlais ar y papur pleidleisio yn ddirgel yn un o'r cabanau pleidleisio. Rhowch un X yn y lle gwag ar y dde gyferbyn ag enw'r ymgeisydd yr ydych am bleidleisio drosto. Dros un ymgeisydd yn unig y cewch bleidleisio. Os rhowch unrhyw farc arall ar y papur pleidleisio, efallai na chaiff eich pleidlais ei chyfrif.

Yna plygwch y papur er mwyn cuddio'ch pleidlais, dangoswch y nod swyddogol ar gefn y papuri 'r swyddog llywyddu, a rhowch y papur yn y blwch pleidleisiau.

Os digwydd i chwi gam-nodi'ch papur pleidleisio drwy gamgymeriad, peidiwch â'i ddinistrio; rhowch ef yn ôl i'r swyddog llywyddu a gofynnwch iddo am un arall.

CYHOEDDWYD GAN Y SWYDDOG CANLYNIADAU

FORM F: PROXY'S OFFICIAL POLL CARD

FFURFLEN F: CERDYN PLEIDLEISIO SWYDDOGOL Y DIRPRWY

REPRESENTATION OF THE PEOPLE ACTS

DEDDFAU CYNRYCHIOLAETH Y BOBL

Front of card

PROXY'S OFFICIAL POLL CARD

CERDYN PLEIDLEISIO SWYDDOGOL Y DIRPRWY

Proxy's name...
Enw'r dirprwy

Proxy's address..
Cyfeiriad y dirprwy

....

Back of card

PARLIAMENTARY ELECTION

....CONSTITUENCY

Polling day..

The poll will be open from 7 a.m. to 10 p.m.

The elector named below whose proxy you are is entitled to vote at the polling station—

....

....

To vote as proxy you must go to that polling station. Tell the clerk that you wish to vote as proxy; give the name and qualifying address of the elector, as follows:—

Number on Register..

Name...

Address ....

....

The presiding officer will give you the elector's ballot paper. The method of voting as proxy is the same as for casting your own vote.

It is an offence to vote as proxy for some other person if you know that that person is subject to a legal incapacity to vote, e.g. if that person has been convicted and is detained in a penal institution in pursuance of his sentence.

ISSUED BY THE RETURNING OFFICER

ETHOLIAD SENEDDOL

ETHOLAETH...

Dyddiad pleidleisio...
Bydd yr orsaf bleidleisio ar agor o 7 a.m. hyd 10 p.m.

Mae gan yr etholwr a enwir isod, yr ydych yn ddirprwy drosto, hawl i bleidleisio yn yr orsaf bleidleisio yma—

....
....

I bleidleisio fel dirprwy, rhaid i chwi fynd i'r orsaf bleidleisio honno. Dywedwch wrth y clerc eich bod am bleidleisio fel dirprwy; rhowch enw'r etholwr, a'r cyfeiriad y cofrestrwyd ef o'i blegid, fel hyn:—

Rhif ar y Gofrestr...
Enw ....
Cyfeiriad ....
....

Fe rydd y swyddog llywyddu bapur pleidleisio'r etholwr i chwi. Y mae'r dull o bleidleisio fel dirprwy yr un fath â'r dull o roi eich pleidlais eich hun.

Y mae'n drosedd i bleidleisio fel dirprwy ar ran rhyw berson arall os gwyddoch nad oes gan y person hwnnw hawl gyfreithiol i bleidleisio, e.e. os dyfarnwyd y person hwnnw'n euog a'i gadw mewn sefydliad cosbi yn unol â'i ddedfryd.

CYHOEDDWYD GAN Y SWYDDOG CANLYNIADAU

EXPLANATORY NOTE

(*This Note is not part of the Regulations.*)

These Regulations prescribe in Welsh and English certain forms to be used in connection with elections in Wales and Monmouthshire.

STATUTORY INSTRUMENTS

1970 No. 835

PARTNERSHIP

The Partnerships (Unrestricted Size) No. 2 Regulations 1970

Made - - - *28th May* 1970

The Board of Trade in pursuance of the powers conferred upon them by section 120(2) of the Companies Act 1967(**a**) hereby make the following Regulations :—

1. These Regulations may be cited as the Partnerships (Unrestricted Size) No. 2 Regulations 1970.

2. Section 434 of the Companies Act 1948(**b**) shall not apply to the formation for the purpose of carrying on practice as actuaries of a partnership consisting of persons each of whom is either a Fellow of the Institute of Actuaries or a Fellow of the Faculty of Actuaries.

C. W. Jardine,
An Under-Secretary
of the Board of Trade.

28th May 1970.

EXPLANATORY NOTE

(*This Note is not part of the Regulations.*)

Section 434 of the Companies Act 1948 prohibits the formation of partnerships consisting of more than 20 members. These Regulations exempt from that prohibition partnerships of the description, and formed for the purpose, specified in the Regulations.

(a) 1967 c. 81. **(b)** 1948 c. 38.

1970 No. 846 (C. 20) (S. 65)

SOCIAL WORK, SCOTLAND

The Social Work (Scotland) Act 1968 (Commencement No. 4) Order 1970

Made - - - *25th May* 1970

In exercise of the powers conferred on me by section 98 of the Social Work (Scotland) Act 1968(a), I hereby make the following order:—

1. This order may be cited as the Social Work (Scotland) Act 1968 (Commencement No. 4) Order 1970.

2. Subsection (3) (accommodation for children's hearings) of section 34 and subsections (1) to (7) of section 36 (the reporter and deputies) of the Social Work (Scotland) Act 1968 shall come into operation on 1st July 1970.

William Ross,
One of Her Majesty's Principal
Secretaries of State.

St. Andrew's House,
Edinburgh 1.
25th May 1970.

EXPLANATORY NOTE

(*This Note is not part of the Order.*)

This Order brings into operation on 1st July 1970 section 34(3) and, insofar as it is not already in operation, section 36 of the Social Work (Scotland) Act 1968.

(a) 1968 c. 49.

STATUTORY INSTRUMENTS

1970 No. 847

RATING AND VALUATION

The Rate Rebates (Limits of Income) Order 1970

Laid before Parliament in draft

Made - - - *2nd June* 1970

Coming into Operation 1*st August* 1970

The Minister of Housing and Local Government, in exercise of his powers under paragraph 14 of Schedule 9 to the General Rate Act 1967(**a**) and of all other powers enabling him in that behalf, with the approval of the Treasury, hereby makes the following order in the terms of a draft which has been laid before Parliament and has been approved by a resolution of each House of Parliament :—

Title, commencement and interpretation

1.—(1) This order may be cited as the Rate Rebates (Limits of Income) Order 1970 and shall come into operation on 1st August 1970.

(2) The Interpretation Act 1889(**b**) shall apply to the interpretation of this order as it applies to the interpretation of an Act of Parliament.

Limits of income

2. The limit of income for the purposes of section 49(1)(*b*) of the General Rate Act 1967 shall, in relation to any rebate application in respect of the period beginning on 1st October 1970 and subsequent rebate periods, be the following amount of income, in place of the amount specified in paragraph 12 of Schedule 9 to that Act as varied by the Rate Rebates (Limits of Income) Order 1968(**c**), namely—

(*a*) if at the date of making of the application the applicant is married and living with his spouse, £318 10s.;

(*b*) in any other case, £260.

(**a**) 1967 c. 9. (**b**) 1889 c. 63.
(**c**) S.I. 1968/1066 (1968 II, p. 2870).

Given under the official seal of the Minister of Housing and Local Government on 29th May 1970.

(L.S.)

Anthony Greenwood,
Minister of Housing and
Local Government.

We approve this order.

E. G. Perry,
Walter Harrison,
Two of the Lords Commissioners of
Her Majesty's Treasury.

2nd June 1970.

EXPLANATORY NOTE

(This Note is not part of the Order.)

The Order raises the income limits governing entitlement to rate rebates in England and Wales. Under section 49 of the General Rate Act 1967 domestic occupiers are entitled to a rebate equal to two-thirds of the amount by which their reckonable rates for a six months rebate period exceed £3 15s. 0d. provided their incomes are within the specified limits. The present limits of income within the relevant six months period, and the limits as raised by this Order, are set out below, with the weekly equivalents given in brackets.

	Present limits		*New limits*	
Married couple	£286	(£11)	£318 10s.	(£12 5s.)
Single person	£234	(£ 9)	£260	(£10)
Addition for each child	£ 52	(£ 2)	(unchanged)	

STATUTORY INSTRUMENTS

1970 No. 848

HOUSING, ENGLAND AND WALES

The Isles of Scilly (Housing) Order 1970

Made - - - *2nd June* 1970

Coming into Operation *10th June* 1970

The Minister of Housing and Local Government, in exercise of his powers under section 87 of the Housing Act 1969(a) (hereinafter called "the Act") and of all other powers enabling him in that behalf, hereby makes the following order:—

1.—(1) This order may be cited as the Isles of Scilly (Housing) Order 1970 and shall come into operation on 10th June 1970.

(2) The Interpretation Act 1889(b) shall apply for the interpretation of this order as it applies for the interpretation of an Act of Parliament.

2. The provisions of the Act (other than Part III thereof) shall have effect, in their application to the Isles of Scilly, subject to the exceptions, adaptations and modifications hereunder—

(i) In section 26 (local authorities for the purposes of Part I of the Act), the word "and" where second occurring shall be omitted and at the end there shall be added the words "and the Council of the Isles of Scilly.";

(ii) In section 27 (interpretation), in the definition of "housing authority", the word "or" where second occurring shall be omitted and at the end there shall be added the words "or the Council of the Isles of Scilly.";

(iii) In Part II (general improvement areas)—

(a) for any reference to a local authority there shall be substituted a reference to the Council of the Isles of Scilly;

(b) in section 33 (conversion of highway into footpath or bridle-way)—

(1) in subsection (1), the words from "whether" onwards shall be omitted;

(2) in subsection (2), the words "who are not the local planning authority" and, in paragraph (a), the words "instead of by the local planning authority" shall be omitted and, in paragraph (b), for the words from "by" onwards there shall be substituted the words "under section 93 of that Act by a competent authority.";

(c) section 39 (local authorities for the purposes of Part II of the Act) shall not apply to the Isles of Scilly;

(a) 1969 c. 33. (b) 1889 c. 63.

(iv) In section 70 (review of housing conditions by local authorities), for the words "every local authority (within the meaning of the enactments mentioned in this section)" there shall be substituted the words "the Council of the Isles of Scilly" and after the words "this Act" there shall be inserted the words "in so far as those enactments for the time being extend to the Isles of Scilly and apply to the Council of the Isles of Scilly";

(v) In section 74 (power of local authorities to make advances repayable on maturity), in subsection (7), the word "and" where second occurring shall be omitted and at the end there shall be added the words "and the Council of the Isles of Scilly.";

(vi) In section 77 (extension of powers under section 14 of the Housing Subsidies Act 1967(a) to contributions in respect of conversion or improvement of dwellings), in subsections (2) and (3), for the words "a local authority" there shall be substituted the words "the Council of the Isles of Scilly".

Given under the official seal of the Minister of Housing and Local Government on 2nd June 1970.

(L.S.)

F. J. Ward,
Under Secretary,
Ministry of Housing and Local Government.

EXPLANATORY NOTE

(*This Note is not part of the Order.*)

Section 87 of the Housing Act 1969 provides that the provisions of that Act (other than Part III) shall have effect, in their application to the Isles of Scilly, subject to such exceptions, adaptations and modifications as the Minister of Housing and Local Government may by order direct. This order makes certain adaptations and modifications (with a consequential exception) to enable the Council of the Isles of Scilly to exercise certain powers conferred by the Act on, and to receive certain contributions payable to, the local authorities therein mentioned.

(a) 1967 c. 29.

STATUTORY INSTRUMENTS

1970 No. 850

REPRESENTATION OF THE PEOPLE

The Returning Officers' Expenses (England and Wales) (Amendment) Regulations 1970

Made - - -	28*th May* 1970
Coming into Operation	29*th May* 1970

The Treasury, in exercise of the powers conferred on them by section 20(2) of the Representation of the People Act 1949(**a**), hereby make the following Regulations:—

1. These Regulations may be cited as the Returning Officers' Expenses (England and Wales) (Amendment) Regulations 1970, and shall come into operation on 29th May 1970.

2. The Interpretation Act 1889(**b**) shall apply for the interpretation of these Regulations as it applies for the interpretation of an Act of Parliament.

3. The Returning Officers' Expenses (England and Wales) Regulations 1970(**c**) shall be amended, in head I of Part B of the Schedule thereto, as follows:

(*a*) in paragraph 5, by substituting for the figures "£4 15s." the figures "£5 10s.";

(*b*) in paragraph 6, by substituting for the figures "£3 10s." the figures "£4", and for the figures "£3" the figures "£3 10s.";

(*c*) in paragraph 7, by substituting for the figures "£3" the figures "£3 10s.".

Neil McBride,
E. G. Perry,
Two of the Lords Commissioners of Her Majesty's Treasury.

28th May 1970.

EXPLANATORY NOTE

(*This Note is not part of the Regulations.*)

These Regulations amend the Returning Officers' Expenses (England and Wales) Regulations 1970. The only change is an increase in the maximum charges to which a returning officer at a parliamentary election in England or Wales is entitled in respect of certain travelling and overnight subsistence allowances of himself and other officers.

(**a**) 1949 c. 68. (**b**) 1889 c. 63. (**c**) S.I. 1970/298 (1970 I, p. 1107).

STATUTORY INSTRUMENTS

1970 No. 851

REPRESENTATION OF THE PEOPLE

The Returning Officers' Expenses (Scotland) (Amendment) Regulations 1970

Made - - - *28th May* 1970
Coming into Operation *29th May* 1970

The Treasury, in exercise of the powers conferred on them by section 20(2) of the Representation of the People Act, 1949(**a**), hereby make the following Regulations:—

1. These Regulations may be cited as the Returning Officers' Expenses (Scotland) (Amendment) Regulations 1970, and shall come into operation on 29th May 1970.

2. The Interpretation Act 1889(**b**) shall apply for the interpretation of these Regulations as it applies for the interpretation of an Act of Parliament.

3. The Returning Officers' Expenses (Scotland) Regulations 1970(**c**) shall be amended, in head I of Part B of the Schedule thereto, as follows:—

(*a*) in paragraph 5, by substituting for the figures "£4 15s." the figures "£5 10s.";

(*b*) in paragraph 6, by substituting for the figures "£3 10s." the figures "£4", and for the figures "£3" the figures "£3 10s.";

(*c*) in paragraph 7, by substituting for the figures "£3" the figures "£3 10s.".

Neil McBride,
E. G. Perry,
Two of the Lords Commissioners of Her Majesty's Treasury.

28th May 1970.

EXPLANATORY NOTE

(*This Note is not part of the Regulations.*)

These Regulations amend the Returning Officers' Expenses (Scotland) Regulations 1970. The only change is an increase in the maximum charges to which a returning officer at a parliamentary election in Scotland is entitled in respect of certain travelling and overnight subsistence allowances of himself and other officers.

(**a**) 1949 c. 68. (**b**) 1889 c. 63. (**c**) S.I. 1970/300 (1970 I, p. 1119).

1970 No. 852

REPRESENTATION OF THE PEOPLE

The Returning Officers' Expenses (Northern Ireland) (Amendment) Regulations 1970

Made - - -	28*th May* 1970
Coming into Operation	29*th May* 1970

The Treasury, in exercise of the powers conferred on them by section 20(2) of the Representation of the People Act 1949(**a**), hereby make the following Regulations:—

1. These Regulations may be cited as the Returning Officers' Expenses (Northern Ireland) (Amendment) Regulations 1970, and shall come into operation on 29th May 1970.

2. The Interpretation Act 1889(**b**) shall apply for the interpretation of these Regulations as it applies for the interpretation of an Act of Parliament.

3. The Returning Officers' Expenses (Northern Ireland) Regulations 1970(**c**) shall be amended, in head I of Part B of the Schedule thereto, as follows:—

(*a*) in paragraph 5, by substituting for the figures "£4 15s." the figures "£5 10s.";

(*b*) in paragraph 6, by substituting for the figures "£3 10s." the figures "£4", and for the figures "£3" the figures "£3 10s.";

(*c*) in paragraph 7, by substituting for the figures "£3" the figures "£3 10s.".

Neil McBride,
E. G. Perry,
Two of the Lords Commissioners of Her Majesty's Treasury.

28th May 1970.

EXPLANATORY NOTE

(*This Note is not part of the Regulations.*)

These Regulations amend the Returning Officers' Expenses (Northern Ireland) Regulations 1970. The only change is an increase in the maximum charges to which a returning officer at a parliamentary election in Northern Ireland is entitled in respect of certain travelling and overnight subsistence allowances of himself and other officers.

(**a**) 1949 c. 68. (**b**) 1889 c. 63. (**c**) S.I. 1970/299 (1970 I, p. 1113).

1970 No. 855

WAGES COUNCILS

The Wages Regulation (Hair, Bass and Fibre) Order 1970

Made - - -	*3rd June* 1970
Coming into Operation	*2nd July* 1970

Whereas the Secretary of State has received from the Hair, Bass and Fibre Wages Council (Great Britain) the wages regulation proposals set out in the Schedule hereto;

Now, therefore, the Secretary of State in exercise of her powers under section 11 of the Wages Councils Act 1959(**a**), and of all other powers enabling her in that behalf, hereby makes the following Order:—

1. This Order may be cited as the Wages Regulation (Hair, Bass and Fibre) Order 1970.

2.—(1) In this Order the expression "the specified date" means the 2nd July 1970, provided that where, as respects any worker who is paid wages at intervals not exceeding seven days, that date does not correspond with the beginning of the period for which the wages are paid, the expression "the specified date" means, as respects that worker, the beginning of the next such period following that date.

(2) The Interpretation Act 1889(**b**) shall apply to the interpretation of this Order as it applies to the interpretation of an Act of Parliament and as if this Order and the Order hereby revoked were Acts of Parliament.

3. The wages regulation proposals set out in the Schedule hereto shall have effect as from the specified date and as from that date the Wages Regulation (Hair, Bass and Fibre) Order 1969(**c**) shall cease to have effect.

Signed by order of the Secretary of State.

3rd June 1970.

A. A. Jarratt,
Deputy Under Secretary of State,
Department of Employment and Productivity.

Article 3

SCHEDULE

The following minimum remuneration shall be substituted for the statutory minimum remuneration fixed by the Wages Regulation (Hair, Bass and Fibre) Order 1969 (Order H.B. (72)).

(**a**) 1959 c. 69. (**b**) 1889 c. 63.
(**c**) S.I. 1969/640 (1969 II, p. 1775).

STATUTORY MINIMUM REMUNERATION

PART I

GENERAL

1. The minimum remuneration payable to a worker to whom this Schedule applies for all work except work to which a minimum overtime rate applies under Part IV is:—

(1) in the case of a time worker, the general minimum time rate payable to the worker under Part II or Part III of this Schedule ;

(2) in the case of a worker employed on piece work, piece rates each of which would yield, in the circumstances of the case, to an ordinary worker at least the same amount of money as the piece work basis time rate applicable to the worker under Part II or Part III of this Schedule, or, where none is applicable, at least the same amount of money as the general minimum time rate which would be payable to the worker if he were a time worker.

PART II

MALE WORKERS

GENERAL MINIMUM TIME RATES

2.—(1) The general minimum time rates payable to male workers are as follows:—

(*a*) where the worker is employed in any of the occupations specified in sub-paragraph (2) of this paragraph and his experience in any one or more of them totals not less than 1 *year*:—

and the worker is aged—	Per hour s. d.
21 years or over	*6 9*
20 and under 21 years	*6 0*
19 „ „ 20 „	*5 3*
18 „ „ 19 „	*4 9*

(*b*) where the worker, not being a worker to whom sub-paragraph (1)(*a*) of this paragraph applies, is aged—

	Per hour s. d.
21 years or over	*6 3*
20 and under 21 years	*6 0*
19 „ „ 20 „	*5 3*
18 „ „ 19 „	*4 9*
17½ „ „ 18 „	*4 4*
17 „ „ 17½ „	*4 0*
16½ „ „ 17 „	*3 8*
16 „ „ 16½ „	*3 4*
15½ „ „ 16 „	*3 0*
Under 15½ years	*2 9*

Provided that the general minimum time rate payable during his first 12 months' employment in the trade to a worker specified in this sub-paragraph who enters or has entered the trade for the first time at or over the age of 17 years shall be that applicable to a worker in the age group immediately junior to his age group.

(2) The occupations referred to in (*a*) of sub-paragraph (1) of this paragraph and in sub-paragraph (1) of paragraph 4 are as follows:—

HAIR DRESSING—Dresser, Opener, Washer, Dyer, Bleacher, Sorter, Hackler or Comber, Drawer or Drafter, Firster, Seconder, Knocker-up, Buncher, Finisher;

HAIR WEAVING (Power loom weaving, damask seating hand loom weaving or carpet weaving)—Weaver, Dyer, Starcher, Hair Carpet Picker;

BASS DRESSING—Sorter, Dyer, Cutter, Rougher, Hackler or Comber, Shaker-up, Roller-up, Mixer or Blender, Jumper, Drawer or Drafter, Bundler, Buncher or Tyer-up, Tightener;

FIBRE DRESSING—Dyer, Bleacher, Hackler or Comber, Shaker-up, Mixer or Blender, Drawer or Drafter, Polisher, Bundler, Buncher or Tyer-up, Hand Trimmer.

PIECE WORK BASIS TIME RATE

	Per hour s. d.
3. The piece work basis time rate applicable to a male worker specified in (*a*) of sub-paragraph (1) of paragraph 2 is	*7 6*

PART III

FEMALE WORKERS

GENERAL MINIMUM TIME RATES

4. The general minimum time rates payable to female workers are as follows:—

	Per hour s. d.
(1) where the worker is employed in any of the occupations specified in sub-paragraph (2) of paragraph 2 and her experience in any one or more of them totals not less than *1 year*	*5 0*
(2) where the worker, not being a worker to whom (1) of this paragraph applies, is aged—	
18 years or over	*4 9*
17½ and under 18 years	*4 4*
17 „ „ 17½ „	*4 0*
16½ „ „ 17 „	*3 8*
16 „ „ 16½ „	*3 4*
15½ „ „ 16 „	*3 0*
Under 15½ years	*2 9*

Provided that the general minimum time rate payable during her first 12 months' employment in the trade to a worker who enters or has entered the trade for the first time at or over the age of 16 years shall be that applicable to a worker in the age group immediately junior to her age group.

PIECE WORK BASIS TIME RATE

	Per hour s. d.
5. The piece work basis time rate applicable to a female worker specified in sub-paragraph (1) of paragraph 4 is	*5 4*

PART IV

OVERTIME AND WAITING TIME—ALL WORKERS MINIMUM OVERTIME RATES

6. Subject to the provisions of this paragraph, minimum overtime rates are payable to any worker as follows:—

(1) In any week, exclusive of any time for which double time is payable under the provisions of (2) or (3) of this paragraph, for time worked in excess of 40 hours—

(*a*) for the first 3 hours so worked .. .. .. time-and-a-quarter

(*b*) thereafter .. .. time-and-a-half

Provided that where in any week a worker is allowed a holiday on any day of customary holiday the said period of 40 hours shall be reduced by 8 hours in respect of each such holiday which is allowed on a day normally worked by the worker.

(2) On a Sunday or a customary holiday—
for all time worked .. .. double time

(3) On a Saturday—
for all time worked after noon .. .. .. double time

7. In this Part of this Schedule—

(1) The expressions "time-and-a-quarter", "time-and-a-half" and "double time" mean respectively:—

(*a*) in the case of a time worker, one and a quarter times, one and a half times and twice the general minimum time rate otherwise payable to the worker;

(*b*) in the case of a piece worker to whom a piece work basis time rate otherwise applies under paragraph 3 or 5,

(i) a time rate equal respectively to one quarter, one half and the whole of the said piece work basis time rate and, in addition thereto,

(ii) piece rates each of which would yield, in the circumstances of the case, to an ordinary worker, at least the same amount of money as the said piece work basis time rate;

(*c*) in the case of any other worker employed on piece work,

(i) a time rate equal respectively to one quarter, one half and the whole of the general minimum time rate which would be payable under Part II or Part III of this Schedule if the worker were a time worker and a minimum overtime rate did not apply and, in addition thereto,

(ii) piece rates each of which would yield, in the circumstances of the case, to an ordinary worker, at least the same amount of money as the said general minimum time rate.

(2) The expression "customary holiday" means—

(*a*) (i) In England and Wales—

Christmas Day (or, if Christmas Day falls on a Sunday, such week-day as may be appointed by national proclamation, or, if none is so appointed, the next following Tuesday), Boxing Day, Good Friday, Easter Monday, Whit Monday and August Bank Holiday.

(ii) In Scotland—

New Year's Day (or, if New Year's Day falls on a Sunday, the following Monday);

the local Spring holiday;

the local Autumn holiday; and

three other days (being days on which the worker normally works) in the course of a calendar year, to be fixed by the employer and notified to the worker not less than three weeks before the holiday ; or

(*b*) in the case of each of the said days (other than a day fixed by the employer in Scotland and notified to the worker as aforesaid) a day substituted therefor by the employer, being a day recognised by local custom as a day of holiday in substitution for the said day.

WAITING TIME

8.—(1) A worker is entitled to payment of the minimum remuneration specified in this Schedule for all time during which he is present on the premises of his employer unless he is present thereon in any of the following circumstances:—

(*a*) without the employer's consent, express or implied,

(*b*) for some purpose unconnected with his work and other than that of waiting for work to be given to him to perform,

(*c*) by reason only of the fact that he is resident thereon,

(*d*) during normal meal times in a room or place in which no work is being done, and he is not waiting for work to be given to him to perform.

(2) The minimum remuneration payable under sub-paragraph (1) of this paragraph to a piece worker when not engaged on piece work is that which would be payable if he were a time worker.

PART V

APPLICABILITY OF STATUTORY MINIMUM REMUNERATION

9. This Schedule does not apply to workers employed in the weaving of hair machine belting or in any preparatory, finishing, warehousing or packing operation incidental to or appertaining to such weaving, but save as aforesaid applies to workers in relation to whom the Hair, Bass and Fibre Wages Council (Great Britain) operates, that is to say, workers to whom the Schedule to the Hair, Bass and Fibre Wages Council (Great Britain) (Variation) Order 1964(**a**) applies, namely:—

Workers employed in Great Britain in any of the following occupations:—

The drafting, dressing or mixing of bass, whisk or similar fibres or horse hair or other hairs and the weaving of hair or fibre or of mixed hair and fibre, and all preparatory, finishing, warehousing or packing operations incidental to or appertaining to all or any of the above processes, but excluding:—

(*a*) any of the above operations or processes where they are carried on in association with or in conjunction with the manufacture of brushes or brooms ;

(*b*) the drafting, dressing or mixing of hair or fibre preparatory to the curling of hair or fibre or of mixed hair and fibre and all preparatory, finishing, warehousing or packing operations incidental to or appertaining to all or any of the last above-mentioned processes, and

(*c*) the dressing of animal skins.

(**a**) S.I. 1964/585 (1964 I, p. 1085).

EXPLANATORY NOTE

(*This Note is not part of the Order.*)

This Order, which has effect from 2nd July 1970, sets out the statutory minimum remuneration payable in substitution for that fixed by the Wages Regulation (Hair, Bass and Fibre) Order 1969 (Order H.B. (72)), which Order is revoked.

New provisions are printed in italics.

STATUTORY INSTRUMENTS

1970 No. 856

WAGES COUNCILS

The Wages Regulation (Hair, Bass and Fibre) (Holidays) Order 1970

Made - - -	*3rd June* 1970
Coming into Operation	*2nd July* 1970

Whereas the Secretary of State has received from the Hair, Bass and Fibre Wages Council (Great Britain) the wages regulation proposals set out in the Schedule hereto;

Now, therefore, the Secretary of State in exercise of her powers under section 11 of the Wages Councils Act 1959(**a**), and of all other powers enabling her in that behalf, hereby makes the following Order:—

1. This Order may be cited as the Wages Regulation (Hair, Bass and Fibre) (Holidays) Order 1970.

2.—(1) In this Order the expression "the specified date" means the 2nd July 1970, provided that where, as respects any worker who is paid wages at intervals not exceeding seven days, that date does not correspond with the beginning of the period for which the wages are paid, the expression "the specified date" means, as respects that worker, the beginning of the next such period following that date.

(2) The Interpretation Act 1889(**b**) shall apply to the interpretation of this Order as it applies to the interpretation of an Act of Parliament and as if this Order and the Order hereby revoked were Acts of Parliament.

3. The wages regulation proposals set out in the Schedule hereto shall have effect as from the specified date and as from that date the Wages Regulation (Hair, Bass and Fibre) (Holidays) Order 1969(**c**) shall cease to have effect.

Signed by order of the Secretary of State.

3rd June 1970.

A. A. Jarratt,
Deputy Under Secretary of State,
Department of Employment and Productivity.

(**a**) 1959 c. 69. (**b**) 1889 c. 63.
(**c**) S.I. 1969/641 (1962 II, p. 1781).

SCHEDULE

Article 3

The following provisions as to holidays and holiday remuneration shall be substituted for the provisions as to holidays and holiday remuneration set out in the Wages Regulation (Hair, Bass and Fibre) (Holidays) Order 1969 (hereinafter referred to as "Order H.B. (73)").

PART I
APPLICATION

1. This Schedule applies to every worker (other than an outworker) for whom statutory minimum remuneration has been fixed.

PART II
CUSTOMARY HOLIDAYS

2.—(1) An employer shall allow to every worker in his employment to whom this Schedule applies a holiday (hereinafter referred to as a "customary holiday") in each year on the days specified in the following sub-paragraph, provided that the worker has been in his employment for a period of not less than eight weeks immediately preceding the customary holiday and has worked for the employer during the whole or part of that period and (unless excused by the employer or absent by reason of the proved illness of the worker) has worked for the employer throughout the last working day on which work was available to him immediately preceding the customary holiday.

(2) The said customary holidays are:—

(*a*) (i) In England and Wales—

Christmas Day (or, if Christmas Day falls on a Sunday, such week-day as may be appointed by national proclamation, or, if none is so appointed, the next following Tuesday), Boxing Day, Good Friday, Easter Monday, Whit Monday and August Bank holiday.

(ii) In Scotland—

New Year's Day (or, if New Year's Day falls on a Sunday, the following Monday);

the local Spring holiday;

the local Autumn holiday; and

three other days (being days on which the worker normally works) in the course of a calendar year to be fixed by the employer and notified to the worker not less than three weeks before the holiday; or

(*b*) In the case of each of the said days (other than a day fixed by the employer in Scotland and notified to the worker as aforesaid) a day substituted therefor by the employer, being a day recognised by local custom as a day of holiday in substitution for the said day.

(3) Notwithstanding the preceding provisions of this paragraph, an employer may (except where in the case of a woman or young person such requirement would be unlawful) require a worker who is otherwise entitled to any customary holiday under the foregoing provisions of this Schedule to work thereon and, in lieu of any holiday on which he so works, the employer shall allow to the worker a day's holiday (hereinafter referred to as a "holiday in lieu of a customary holiday") on a week-day within the period of two months next ensuing.

(4) A worker who is so required to work on a customary holiday shall be paid:—

(*a*) for all time worked thereon, the statutory minimum remuneration then appropriate to the worker for work on a customary holiday; and

(*b*) in respect of the holiday in lieu of the customary holiday, holiday remuneration in accordance with paragraph 8.

PART III

ANNUAL HOLIDAY AND ADDITIONAL ANNUAL HOLIDAY

ANNUAL HOLIDAY

3. Subject to the provisions of paragraph 4, in addition to the holidays specified in Part II of this Schedule, an employer shall, between the date on which the provisions of this Schedule become effective and 30th September 1970 and in each succeeding year between 6th April and 30th September allow a holiday (hereinafter referred to as an "annual holiday") to every worker in his employment to whom this Schedule applies who has been employed by him during the twelve months immediately preceding the commencement of the holiday season for any of the periods of employment (calculated in accordance with the provisions of paragraph 13) set out in the Table below, and the duration of the annual holiday shall, in the case of each such worker, be related to his period of employment during that twelve months as follows:—

Period of employment	Duration of annual holiday where the worker's normal working week is:—		
	5 days	4 days	3 days
At least 48 weeks	10 days	8 days	6 days
" " 44 "	9 "	7 "	5 "
" " 40 "	8 "	6 "	5 "
" " 36 "	7 "	6 "	4 "
" " 32 "	6 "	5 "	4 "
" " 28 "	5 "	4 "	3 "
" " 24 "	4 "	4 "	3 "
" " 20 "	3 "	3 "	2 "
" " 16 "	2 "	2 "	2 "
" " 12 "	2 "	2 "	1 day
" " 8 "	1 day	1 day	1 "

4.—(1) An annual holiday under this Schedule shall be allowed on consecutive working days, being days on which the worker is normally called upon to work for the employer, and days of holiday shall be treated as consecutive notwithstanding that a Sunday, a customary holiday on which the worker is not required to work or a holiday in lieu of a customary holiday intervenes:

Provided that—

(*a*) where the duration of an annual holiday which the employer is required to allow to a worker exceeds the period constituting the worker's normal working week the said holiday may by agreement in writing made between the employer and the worker be allowed in two separate periods of such consecutive working days, if one of such periods is not less than the period constituting the worker's normal working week;

(*b*) one day of an annual holiday may be allowed on a non-consecutive working day falling within the holiday season or with the consent of the worker on any working day prior to the commencement of the next holiday season where the said annual holiday or such separate period, as the case may be, is allowed immediately after a customary holiday on which the worker is not required to work or so that such a customary holiday intervenes;

(*c*) the duration of the worker's annual holiday in the holiday season ending on 30th September 1970 shall be reduced by any days of annual holiday duly allowed to him by the employer under the provisions of Order H.B. (73) between 6th April 1970 and the date on which the provisions of this Schedule become effective.

(2) Subject to the provisions of sub-paragraph (1) of this paragraph, any day of annual holiday or additional annual holiday under this Schedule may be allowed

on a day on which the worker is entitled to a day of holiday or to a half-holiday under any enactment other than the Wages Councils Act 1959.

(3) In this Schedule the expression "holiday season" means, in relation to an annual holiday during the year 1970, the period commencing on 6th April 1970 and ending on 30th September 1970 and, in relation to each subsequent year, the period commencing on 6th April and ending on 30th September in that year and in relation to an additional annual holiday means a period of one year commencing on 6th April.

ADDITIONAL ANNUAL HOLIDAY

5. Subject to the provisions of this paragraph, in addition to the holidays specified in paragraphs 2 and 3 an employer shall in each year commencing on 6th April allow a holiday (hereinafter referred to as an "additional annual holiday") to every worker in his employment to whom this Schedule applies who has been employed by him at the preceding 5th April for a continuous period of *one year* or more (calculated in accordance with paragraph 13) and the duration of the additional annual holiday shall be *three days*.

6. Where a worker becomes entitled to any days of additional annual holiday in accordance with the provisions of paragraph 5 those days of additional annual holiday shall be allowed by the employer, by agreement with the worker, on a day or days on which the worker is normally called upon to work for the employer, at any time (or times) during the period of 12 months immediately following 5th April upon which the worker becomes entitled as aforesaid.

GENERAL

7. An employer shall give to a worker notice of the commencing date or dates and duration of the period or periods of his annual holiday and the date or dates of his additional holiday. Such notice shall be given at least 28 days before—

(*a*) the first day of the annual holiday or, where under the provisions of paragraph 4 an annual holiday is allowed in more than one period, before each separate period ; and

(*b*) the said date or dates of the additional annual holiday.

Notice may be given individually to the worker or by the posting of a notice in the place where the worker is employed.

PART IV
HOLIDAY REMUNERATION
A—CUSTOMARY HOLIDAYS AND HOLIDAYS IN LIEU OF CUSTOMARY HOLIDAYS

8.—(1) Subject to the provisions of this paragraph, for each day of holiday which a worker is allowed under Part II of this Schedule he shall be paid by the employer as holiday remuneration whichever of the following sums is the greater, that is to say either:—

(*a*) (i) in the case of a worker whose normal working week is five days, one-fifth

(ii) in the case of a worker whose normal working week is four days, one-quarter

(iii) in the case of a worker whose normal working week is three days, one-third

of the average weekly earnings (exclusive of overtime but including holiday remuneration) of the worker during the twelve months ended on 5th April immediately preceding the holiday, such average weekly earnings to be determined by dividing, by the number of weeks of employment with the employer during the said period, the total remuneration (as defined in paragraph 14) paid to him by the employer during that period:

Provided that when Good Friday or Easter Monday in England and Wales or the local Spring holiday in Scotland (or days substituted therefor under the provisions of sub-paragraph (2)(*b*) of paragraph 2 or holidays in lieu of such customary holidays) fall after 5th April in any year, the holiday remuneration for any such holiday under this sub-paragraph shall be one-fifth, one-quarter or one-third, as the case may require, of the average weekly earnings (exclusive of overtime but including holiday remuneration) of the worker (calculated as aforesaid) during the twelve months ended on 5th April in the preceding year ; or

(*b*) a sum equal to the appropriate statutory minimum remuneration to which he would have been entitled if the day had not been a day of holiday and he had been employed on work entitling him to statutory minimum remuneration for the time normally worked by him on that day of the week:

Provided that payment of the said holiday remuneration is subject to the condition that the worker (unless excused by the employer or absent by reason of the proved illness of the worker) presents himself for employment at the usual starting hour on the first working day following the holiday.

(2) The holiday remuneration in respect of any customary holiday shall be paid by the employer to the worker on the pay day on which the wages for the pay week including the customary holiday are paid.

(3) The holiday remuneration in respect of any holiday in lieu of a customary holiday shall be paid on the pay day on which the wages for the week including that holiday in lieu of a customary holiday are paid: Provided that the said payment shall be made immediately upon the termination of the worker's employment if he ceases to be employed before being allowed such holiday in lieu of a customary holiday and in that case the condition specified in sub-paragraph (1) of this paragraph shall not apply.

B—ANNUAL HOLIDAY

9.—(1) Subject to the provisions of paragraph 11, a worker qualified to be allowed an annual holiday under this Schedule shall be paid as holiday remuneration by his employer in respect thereof not later than the last pay day preceding such annual holiday—

(*a*) in the case of a worker who has been in the employment of the employer during the whole of the twelve months up to and including the 5th April immediately preceding the commencement of the holiday season whichever of the following sums is the greater, that is to say either:—

(i) a sum equal to two fifty-seconds of the total remuneration (as defined in paragraph 14) paid to him by the employer during the said twelve months ; or

(ii) one day's holiday pay in respect of each day of annual holiday ;

(*b*) in the case of any other worker:—
one day's holiday pay in respect of each day of annual holiday.

(2) Where under the provisions of paragraph 4 an annual holiday is allowed in more than one period the holiday remuneration shall be apportioned accordingly.

C—ADDITIONAL ANNUAL HOLIDAY

10.—(1) A worker entitled to be allowed an additional annual holiday under this Schedule shall be paid by his employer in respect thereof on the last pay day preceding such additional annual holiday as follows:—

Where the worker's normal working week is 5 days ... ... three-tenths
" " " " " " " 4 days ... ... three-eighths
" " " " " " " 3 days ... ... one-half

of the amount he would be entitled to receive at the date of the holiday for an annual holiday of two normal working weeks determined in accordance with paragraph 9.

(2) Where an employer allows the days of additional annual holiday otherwise than on consecutive days the remuneration shall be apportioned accordingly.

11. Where any accrued holiday remuneration has been paid by the employer to the worker (in accordance with paragraph 12 of this Schedule or Order H.B. (73)) in respect of employment during any of the periods referred to in paragraph 12 of this Schedule, the amount of holiday remuneration payable by the employer in respect of any annual holiday for which the worker has qualified by reason of employment during the said period shall be reduced by the amount of the said accrued holiday remuneration unless that remuneration has been deducted from a previous payment of holiday remuneration made under the provisions of this Schedule or of Order H.B. (73).

ACCRUED HOLIDAY REMUNERATION PAYABLE ON TERMINATION OF EMPLOYMENT

12. Where a worker ceases to be employed by an employer after the provisions of this Schedule become effective, the employer shall, immediately on the termination of the employment, pay to the worker as accrued holiday remuneration:—

(1) (*a*) in respect of employment in the twelve months up to and including the immediately preceding 5th April a sum equal to the holiday remuneration for any days of annual holiday for which he has qualified except days of annual holiday which he has been allowed or has become entitled to be allowed before leaving his employment ; and

(*b*) in respect of employment up to and including the immediately preceding 5th April a sum equal to the holiday remuneration for any days of additional annual holiday for which he has qualified except any day or days of additional annual holiday which he has been allowed or has become entitled to be allowed before leaving his employment ;

(2) in respect of any employment since the said 5th April a sum equal to the holiday remuneration which would have been payable to him if he could have been allowed an annual holiday in respect of that employment at the time of leaving it, and if paid at the rate of one day's holiday pay in respect of each day thereof.

PART V

GENERAL

13. For the purposes of calculating any period of employment qualifying a worker for an annual holiday or additional annual holiday or for any accrued holiday remuneration under this Schedule, the worker shall be treated—

(*a*) as if he were employed for a week in respect of any week in which—

(i) he has worked for the employer on not less than three days and has performed some work for which statutory minimum remuneration is payable ; or

(ii) he has been absent throughout the week by reason of the proved illness of or accident to, the worker, but not exceeding four weeks in the aggregate in the period of twelve months immediately preceding the commencement of the holiday season ; and

(*b*) as if he were employed on any day of holiday allowed under the provisions of this Schedule, and for the purposes of the provisions of sub-paragraph (*a*) of this paragraph, a worker who is absent on such a holiday shall be treated as having worked thereon for the employer on work to which statutory minimum remuneration applies.

14. In this Schedule, unless the context otherwise requires, the following expressions have the meanings hereby respectively assigned to them, that is to say:—

"APPROPRIATE RATE OF STATUTORY MINIMUM REMUNERATION" means—

(a) in the case of a worker who is usually wholly employed as a time worker, the general minimum time rate ordinarily applicable to the worker;

(b) in the case of a worker who is usually employed on piece work,

(i) where the worker is aged over 18 years and a piece work basis time rate is applicable, a time rate equal to the piece work basis time rate ordinarily applicable to the worker;

(ii) in any other case the general minimum time rate which would be ordinarily applicable to the worker if he were employed as a time worker:

Provided that for the purposes of this definition—

(i) a rate ordinarily applicable to a worker shall be ascertained by reference to the work on which he has been mainly employed in the twelve months immediately prior to the holiday in the case of a customary holiday, the commencement of the holiday season in the case of an annual holiday or additional annual holiday or the termination date where accrued holiday remuneration is payable;

(ii) where a worker is usually employed partly on time work and partly on piece work, he shall be treated as having been usually employed wholly on piece work.

"NORMAL WORKING WEEK" means the number of days on which it has been usual for the worker to work in a week in the employment of the employer during the twelve months immediately preceding the commencement of the holiday season, or, where under paragraphs 11 and 12, accrued holiday remuneration is payable on the termination of the employment, in the twelve months immediately preceding the termination date:

Provided that:—

(i) part of a day shall count as a day; and

(ii) no account shall be taken of any week in which the worker did not perform any work for which statutory minimum remuneration has been fixed.

"ONE DAY'S HOLIDAY PAY" means the appropriate proportion of the remuneration which the worker would be entitled to receive from his employer at the date of the annual holiday (or, where the holiday is taken in more than one period, at the date of the first period), or date or dates of additional annual holiday or at the termination date, as the case may be, for one week's work if working his normal working week and the number of daily hours normally worked by him (exclusive of overtime), and if paid at the appropriate rate of statutory minimum remuneration for work to which statutory minimum remuneration applies and at the same rate for any work for the same employer to which such remuneration does not apply, and in this definition "appropriate proportion" means—

where the worker's normal working week is five days—one-fifth
" " " " " " " four " —one-quarter
" " " " " " " three " —one-third

"STATUTORY MINIMUM REMUNERATION" means statutory minimum remuneration (other than holiday remuneration) which has been fixed by a wages regulation order.

"TOTAL REMUNERATION" means any payments paid or payable to the worker under his contract of employment, for time (other than hours of overtime) worked or piece work done by him, holiday remuneration, any productivity or long service bonus payable to the worker on a weekly, fortnightly or monthly basis and merit payments so payable but does not include any other payments.

"WAGES REGULATION ORDER" means a wages regulation order made by the Secretary of State to give effect to proposals submitted to her by the Hair, Bass and Fibre Wages Council (Great Britain).

"WEEK" means pay week.

15. The provisions of this Schedule are without prejudice to any agreement for the allowance of any further holidays with pay or for the payment of additional holiday remuneration.

EXPLANATORY NOTE

(*This Note is not part of the Order.*)

This Order, which has effect from 2nd July 1970, sets out the holidays which an employer is required to allow to workers and the remuneration payable for those holidays in substitution for the holidays and holiday remuneration set out in the Wages Regulation (Hair, Bass and Fibre) (Holidays) Order 1969 (Order H.B. (73)), which Order is revoked.

New provisions are printed in italics.

1970 No. 858

LANDS TRIBUNAL

The Lands Tribunal (Amendment) Rules 1970

Made - - - -	1*st June* 1970
Coming into Operation	1*st July* 1970

The Lord Chancellor, in exercise of the powers conferred on him by section 3 of the Lands Tribunal Act 1949**(a)** and section 28(6) of the Law of Property Act 1969**(b)**, after consultation with the Council on Tribunals in accordance with section 8 of the Tribunals and Inquiries Act 1958**(c)**, and with the approval of the Treasury in regard to fees, hereby makes the following Rules:—

1. These Rules may be cited as the Lands Tribunal (Amendment) Rules 1970 and shall come into operation on 1st July 1970.

2.—(1) The Interpretation Act 1889**(d)** shall apply to the interpretation of these Rules as it applies to the interpretation of an Act of Parliament.

(2) In these Rules, unless the context otherwise requires, a Rule, Schedule or Form referred to by number means the Rule, Schedule or Form so numbered in the Lands Tribunal Rules 1963**(e)** as amended by the Lands Tribunal (Amendment) Rules 1968**(f)**.

3. In Rule 19 after the words "Landlord and Tenant Act 1954" there shall be inserted "and section 28 of the Law of Property Act 1969".

4. After Rule 22 there shall be inserted the following Rule:—

"22A. At any time after an objection to the application has been received by the Registrar, the Tribunal may, of its own motion, and shall, on the application of the applicant or of any person having given notice of objection, suspend the proceedings for such time as it may consider appropriate to enable an application to be made to the High Court for the determination of a question arising under subsection (2) of the section."

5. Schedule 1 shall be amended as follows:—

(i) In Forms 1 to 6, 6X and 9, for "W.1." (which appears in the address of the Registrar) there shall be substituted "WIR OER".

(a) 1949 c. 42.
(b) 1969 c. 59.
(c) 1958 c. 66.
(d) 1889 c. 63.
(e) S.I. 1963/483 (1963 I, p. 532).
(f) S.I. 1968/1700 (1968 III, p. 4592).

(ii) In Form 6 after "Estate or interest in respect of which compensation is claimed. . . " there shall be inserted:-

"Where compensation is claimed for compulsory purchase, whether the acquiring authority has entered upon the land or possession has been given to such authority....................

If so, on what date..".

(iii) The following form shall be substituted for Form 7:—

"FORM 7

Application for Discharge or Modification of Restrictive Covenant under section 84 *of the Law of Property Act* 1925 *as amended by section* 28 *of the Law of Property Act* 1969

Rule 20(1)

To:— The Registrar,
Lands Tribunal,
3 Hanover Square,
LONDON,
W1R OER.

1. I/We ....
of...
being entitled to (*here state nature of interest*)...
in (*here describe land in which applicant is entitled to an interest*)..............
..........................which land is subject to a restriction of which particulars are set out in paragraph 2 below, hereby apply for an order that the restriction may be discharged wholly [*or* to the extent of (*here state extent of discharge applied for*)..]

[*or* may be modified by (*here state nature of modification applied for*) ....]

Here state usual address. If there is more than one applicant, these particulars should be completed for each applicant.

Strike out words not applicable.

[If the above-mentioned restriction is discharged [*or* modified] I/we agree that a further restriction may be imposed on the subject land in the following terms..
....]

2. PARTICULARS OF RESTRICTION

Nature of restriction..
....

Land affected by the restriction...
....

Whether freehold land, or leasehold held for a term of more than 40 years whereof 25 years have expired...

Manner and date of imposition of restriction.......................................
....

Nature and amount (if any) of consideration paid for the restriction at the time when it was imposed..
....

Persons entitled to the benefit of the restriction (*here state names and addresses of such persons and the nature of their interests*)....................
....

3. The grounds of this application are that the application falls within paragraph(s)..............................(*here specify* (*a*), (*aa*), (*b*) *or* (*c*) *as appropriate*) of subsection (1) of section 84.

4. PARTICULARS OF APPLICATION

Strike out inapplicable entries.

[*Application within paragraph* (1)(*a*). The following are brief particulars of the changes in the character of the property or the neighbourhood or other circumstances relied on..
....
....]

[*Application within paragraph* (1)(*aa*).

(i) The reasonable user(s) of the land which would be impeded by the continued existence of the covenant is (are)....................
....

[(ii) The restriction in impeding reasonable user(s) does not secure to persons entitled to the benefit of it any practical benefits of substantial value or advantage to them]

[(iii) The restriction is contrary to the public interest because.........
....]]

[*Application within paragraph* (1)(*b*). Brief particulars of the facts relied on to prove the express or implied agreement are...............................
....]

[*Application within paragraph* (1)(*c*). The discharge or modification of the restriction will not injure any person entitled to the benefit of it, because
....]

5. PLANNING FACTORS

Strike out inapplicable entries.

[(i) The following planning permissions have been granted or refused in relation to the property during the last 5 years......
....]

[(ii) The following provisions in the relevant development plan directly affect the property..
....]

[(iii) The following are brief particulars of a declared or ascertainable pattern for the grant or refusal of planning permission in the relevant area...]

All communications regarding this application should be addressed to me/us at the address shown above [*or* to my/our solicitor/agent

Mr... of..............................]

Signed ....

Dated............................... "

(iv) The following form shall be substituted for Form 8:—

"FORM 8

Objection to Application for Discharge or Modification of Restrictive Covenant under section 84 *of the Law of Property Act* 1925 *as amended by section* 28 *of the Law of Property Act* 1969

Rule 22

To:— The Registrar,
Lands Tribunal,
3 Hanover Square,
London,
W1R OER.

In the matter of an application made by.. under section 84 of the Law of Property Act 1925 as amended by section 28 of the Law of Property Act 1969.

Here insert name(s) of applicant(s).

I/We ....
of...
hereby object to the said application.

Here state usual address.

I/We claim to be entitled to the benefit of the restriction to which the application relates by virtue of (*here state nature of interest*)...............
....

Particulars of the grounds of objection are:—(*here state briefly the grounds of objection*)...

[I/We accept the following facts stated in the application:—(*here set out any statements in paragraph* 4 *of the application which are admitted*)........
....]

Strike out words not applicable.

[I/We accept the particulars of the relevant planning position given in paragraph 5 of the application]

[*or* The particulars given in paragraph 5 of the application are inaccurate or insufficient in the following respects:—(*here give corrected or further particulars*)...]

In the event of the said restriction being discharged or modified, I/we claim the sum of £........................to make up for any loss or disadvantage suffered by me/us in consequence of the discharge or modification [*or* (*state other grounds*)...
....]

The sum claimed is arrived at as follows:—
(*here give particulars of loss or disadvantage suffered and of quantification of compensation claimed*)...
....

All communications regarding this objection should be addressed to me/us at the address shown above [*or* to my/our solicitor/agent Mr..................
.... of ....].

Signed ....

Dated ....

Note:— Claims for compensation can be considered only where the Tribunal is satisfied that the objector is entitled to the benefit of the restriction."

6. The following schedule shall be substituted for Schedule 2:—

"SCHEDULE 2

(*In this Schedule decimal equivalents are shown in brackets and italics*)

Rule 62 FEES

Item	Fee
	£ s. d.
Notices of appeal and reference, and applications	
1. On a notice of appeal under Part I or Part III of these Rules (not being an appeal against a determination by the Commissioners of Inland Revenue under the Finance (1909-10) Act 1910) and on a notice of reference under Part IV of these Rules (not being a reference under section 44(6) of the Finance Act 1965)	2 0 0
2. On a notice of appeal under Part II of these Rules	10 0
3. Under Part V of these Rules	
(*a*) on an application	10 0 0
(*b*) on notification to the registrar in accordance with Rule 21(3)	5 0 0
4. On an application under Part VI of these Rules	
(*a*) for a definitive certificate	10 0 0
(*b*) for a temporary and definitive certificate	15 0 0
5. On any application to the President, Tribunal or registrar, or for making a consent order ...	10 0
Hearing fees	
6.—(*a*) On an appeal against the decision of a local valuation court and on an appeal by way of a reference by consent—	
(i) where net annual value does not exceed £250	1 0 0
(ii) where net annual value exceeds £250 but does not exceed £500	2 0 0
(iii) where net annual value exceeds £500 but does not exceed £1,000	5 0 0
(iv) where net annual value exceeds £1,000 but does not exceed £5,000 ...	10 0 0
(v) where net annual value exceeds £5,000	25 0 0

Item	Fee
	£ s. d.
(*b*) On an appeal against a determination under Part I (not being a determination by the Commissioners of Inland Revenue under the Finance (1909-10) Act 1910) or on a reference under Part IV of these Rules (not being a reference on a dispute as to water rates or under section 44(6) of the Finance Act 1965) or on an application for a certificate of value—	
where the amount awarded or determined by the Tribunal or agreed by the parties following a hearing	
(i) does not exceed £250	5 0 0
(ii) exceeds £250 but does not exceed £500	5 0 0 with an addition of £1 in respect of every £50 or part of £50 by which the amount awarded exceeds £250
(iii) exceeds £500 but does not exceed £5,000	10 0 0 with an addition of £1 in respect of every £100 or part of £100 by which the amount awarded exceeds £500
(iv) exceeds £5,000	55 0 0 with an addition of £1 in respect of every £200 or part of £200 by which the amount awarded exceeds £5,000, but not exceeding in any case £250
(*c*) On an appeal or reference where the award is in terms of rent or other annual payment, the following scale of fees shall be substituted for those payable under paragraph (*b*)—	
where the amount awarded	
(i) does not exceed £10 per annum ...	5 0 0
(ii) exceeds £10 per annum but does not exceed £25 per annum	5 0 0 with an addition of £1 in respect of every £2 10s. [£2·50*p*.] or part of £2 10s. [£2·50*p*.] by which the rent etc., awarded exceeds £10 per annum

Item	Fee
	£ s. d.
(iii) exceeds £25 per annum but does not exceed £250 per annum	11 0 0 with an addition of £1 in respect of every £5 or part of £5 by which the rent etc., awarded exceeds £25 per annum
(iv) exceeds £250 per annum	56 0 0 with an addition of £1 in respect of every £10 or part of £10 by which the rent etc., awarded exceeds £250, but not in any case exceeding £250
(*d*) On the hearing of an application or the making of an order under Part V of these Rules ...	15 0 0
(*e*) On the hearing of any other appeal or reference (not being an appeal against a determination by the Commissioners of Inland Revenue under the Finance (1909-10) Act 1910 or a reference under section 44(6) of the Finance Act 1965) in which no fee is payable by reference to an amount awarded	5 0 0
Copies of documents	
7. On supplying and certifying a copy of an order or an award of the Tribunal	10 0 [*50p.*]
8. For a copy of all or part of any document (other than a copy on which Fee No. 7 is payable)—	
(*a*) not over foolscap or I.S.O. A4 size—	
(i) for each sheet of the first copy ...	2 0 [*10p.*]
(ii) for each additional sheet	1 0 [*5p.*]
(*b*) over foolscap or I.S.O. A4 size—	
(i) for each sheet of the first copy ...	4 0 [*20p.*]
(ii) for each additional sheet	2 0 [*10p.*]
9. On a case for the decision of the Court of Appeal—	
(*a*) drawing case, if not drawn by the parties	10 0 [*50p.*]
(*b*) attending the President or the Tribunal settling case	2 0 0
10. On taxation of a bill of costs, for every £2 or fraction thereof allowed	1 0 [*5p.*]

Directions for payment

11. A document transmitted by post for stamping shall be accompanied by a cheque, money order or postal order drawn to the order of the Inland Revenue, for the amount of fee payable."

Dated 28th May 1970.

Gardiner, C.

We approve the amendments made by these Rules to the fees prescribed in Schedule 2 to the Lands Tribunal Rules 1963 as amended by Rule 10 of the Lands Tribunal (Amendment) Rules 1968.

Dated 1st June 1970.

Walter Harrison,
E. G. Perry,
Two of the Lords Commissioners of Her Majesty's Treasury.

EXPLANATORY NOTE

(*This Note is not part of the Rules.*)

These Rules amend the Lands Tribunal Rules 1963. Following the amendment of section 84 of the Law of Property Act 1925 (C.5) by section 28 of the Law of Property Act 1969, changes are made in the procedure on applications for the discharge or modification of restrictive covenants, and revised forms for such applications and for objections to them are prescribed. Among other minor amendments a new schedule of fees contains revised fees for copies of documents and provides for the forthcoming decimalisation of the coinage.

1970 No. 860

WAGES COUNCILS

The Wages Regulation (Retail Food) (Scotland) (Amendment) Order 1970

Made - - -	*4th June* 1970
Coming into Operation	*13th July* 1970

Whereas the Secretary of State has received from the Retail Food Trades Wages Council (Scotland) the wages regulation proposals set out in the Schedule hereto;

Now, therefore, the Secretary of State in exercise of her powers under section 11 of the Wages Councils Act 1959(**a**), and of all other powers enabling her in that behalf, hereby makes the following Order:—

1. This Order may be cited as the Wages Regulation (Retail Food) (Scotland) (Amendment) Order 1970.

2.—(1) In this Order the expression "the specified date" means the 13th July 1970, provided that where, as respects any worker who is paid wages at intervals not exceeding seven days, that date does not correspond with the beginning of the period for which the wages are paid, the expression "the specified date" means, as respects that worker, the beginning of the next such period following that date.

(2) The Interpretation Act 1889(**b**) shall apply to the interpretation of this Order as it applies to the interpretation of an Act of Parliament.

3. The wages regulation proposals set out in the Schedule hereto shall have effect as from the specified date.

Signed by order of the Secretary of State.

4th June 1970.

A. A. Jarratt,
Deputy Under Secretary of State,
Department of Employment and Productivity.

(**a**) 1959 c. 69. (**b**) 1889 c. 63.

Article 3

SCHEDULE

The Wages Regulation (Retail Food) (Scotland) Order 1970(**a**) (Order R.F.C.S. (41)) shall have effect as if in the Schedule thereto:—

1. for paragraphs 4 and 5 there were substituted the following paragraphs:—

"WORKERS OTHER THAN SHOP MANAGERS, SHOP MANAGERESSES, TEMPORARY SHOP MANAGERS, TEMPORARY SHOP MANAGERESSES, CENTRAL TRANSPORT WORKERS AND RETAIL TRANSPORT WORKERS

4. Subject to the provisions of paragraph 1, the minimum remuneration payable to male or female workers of the classes specified in Column 1 of the following table employed in Area 1 or Area 2, as the case may be, shall be the appropriate amount set out in Column 2:—

Column 1	Column 2			
	Male Workers		Female Workers	
	Area 1	Area 2	Area 1	Area 2
	per week s. d.	per week s. d.	per week s. d.	per week s. d.
(1) CLERKS GRADE I other than those referred to in (2) of this paragraph, CLERKS GRADE II, SHOP ASSISTANTS, CENTRAL WAREHOUSE WORKERS, TRANSPORT WORKERS (other than those referred to in paragraph 5) and all other workers being workers aged:—				
15 and under 16 years	*120 0*	*115 0*	*105 0*	*100 0*
16 " " 17 "	*130 0*	*125 0*	*110 0*	*105 0*
17 " " 18 "	*140 0*	*135 0*	*115 0*	*110 0*
18 " " 19 "	160 0	*154 0*	*135 0*	*129 0*
19 " " 20 "	*175 0*	*167 0*	*145 0*	*137 0*
20 " " 21 "	*190 0*	*180 0*	*155 0*	*145 0*
21 " " 22 "	*220 0*	*210 0*	*175 0*	*165 0*
22 years or over..	241 6	228 6	188 6	179 0
(2) CLERKS GRADE I aged 23 years or over..	245 6	232 6	191 6	182 0

(a) S.I. 1970/428 (1970 I, p. 1473).

CENTRAL TRANSPORT WORKERS AND RETAIL TRANSPORT WORKERS

5. Subject to the provisions of paragraph 1, the minimum remuneration payable to Central Transport Workers and Retail Transport Workers employed in Area 1 or Area 2, as the case may be, on the types of vehicle described in Column 2 of the following table, shall be the appropriate amount set out in Column 3:—

Column 1	Column 2		Column 3	
	Type of vehicle			
Age of transport worker	Mechanically propelled vehicle with carrying capacity of	Horse drawn vehicle	Area 1	Area 2
(1) CENTRAL TRANSPORT WORKERS			per week s. d.	per week s. d.
21 years or over	1 ton or less	One-horse	241 6	228 6
20 and under 21 years			*205 0*	*195 0*
19 " " 20 "			*190 0*	*182 0*
18 " " 19 "			*175 0*	*169 0*
Under 18 years			*155 0*	*150 0*
All ages	Over 1 ton up to 2 tons	Two-horse	244 6	231 6
	Over 2 tons up to 5 tons	—	244 6	231 6
	Over 5 tons	—	248 6	235 6
(2) RETAIL TRANSPORT WORKERS All ages	Over 1½ tons up to 2 tons	Two-horse	241 6	228 6
	Over 2 tons up to 5 tons	—	241 6	228 6
	Over 5 tons	—	245 6	232 6"

2. in paragraph 21 for the definition of "Customary Holiday" there were substituted the following:—

" 'CUSTOMARY HOLIDAY' means—

1st *and 2nd January* (or, if either of these days fall on a Sunday, 3rd January shall be substituted for such day);

the local Spring holiday;

the local Autumn holiday;

Christmas Day (or, if Christmas Day falls on a Sunday, 26th December shall be substituted); and

two other days, observed by local custom as holidays, to be fixed by the employer and notified to the worker; and any day proclaimed as a public holiday throughout Scotland."

EXPLANATORY NOTE

(*This Note is not part of the Order.*)

This Order, which has effect from 13th July 1970, amends the Wages Regulation (Retail Food) (Scotland) Order 1970 (Order R.F.C.S. (41)) by increasing the statutory minimum remuneration for workers aged 21 years or below fixed by that Order and providing for an additional day of customary holiday.

New provisions are printed in italics.

1970 No. 862

EDUCATION, ENGLAND AND WALES

The Teachers' Superannuation (Family Benefits) Regulations 1970

Made - - - - *3rd June* 1970

* *To be laid before Parliament*

Coming into Operation *3rd July* 1970

ARRANGEMENT OF REGULATIONS

* This instrument was laid before Parliament on 2nd July 1970.

Part IV

Teachers' Widows' and Children's Pension Scheme

Preliminary

21. The Scheme.
22. Elections.

Application

23. Teachers to whom Scheme applies.
24. Commencement of Application.
25. Application to Deceased Teachers.

Contributions

26. Payment of Contributions.
27. Normal Contributions.
28. Additional Contributions.
29. Additional Contributions on Increase of Previous Service.
30. Commencement of Additional Contributions—Methods I and II.
31. Method I.
32. Method II.
33. Method III.
34. Additional Contributions payable by Re-instated Contributors.
35. Additional Contributions payable by Former External Contributors.
36. Additional Contributions after Termination of Service.
37. Contributions during Intervals in Service.
38. Payment of Outstanding Contributions.
39. Contributions in respect of Deceased Teachers.
40. Service Counting for Benefit.

Repayment of Contributions

41. When Contributions repayable.
42. Amount when no Benefit payable.
43. Amount when Children's Pension only payable.
44. Amount in other Cases.
45. Repayment of Repaid Normal Contributions.

Benefits

46. Widow's Pension.
47. Amount of Widow's Pension.
48. Duration of Widow's Pension.
49. Short Service Widow's Pension.
50. Amount of Short Service Widow's Pension.

PART V

TEACHERS' DEPENDANTS' PENSION SCHEME

PRELIMINARY

NOMINATION OF DEPENDANTS

CONTRIBUTIONS

BENEFITS

PART VI

MISCELLANEOUS AND SUPPLEMENTARY

SCHEDULES

The Secretary of State for Education and Science, with the consent of the Minister for the Civil Service and after consultation with representatives of local education authorities and of teachers appearing to him to be likely to be affected, in exercise of the powers conferred upon him by section 7 of the Teachers' Superannuation Act 1967**(a)** as amended by the Minister for the Civil Service Order 1968**(b)**, hereby makes the following Regulations:—

PART I

GENERAL

Citation and Commencement

1. These Regulations may be cited as the Teachers' Superannuation (Family Benefits) Regulations 1970 and shall come into operation on 3rd July 1970.

Revocation

2.—(1) The Teachers' Superannuation (Family Benefits) Regulations 1966**(c)**, the Teachers' Superannuation (Family Benefits) (Amending) Regulations 1967**(d)** and the Teachers' Superannuation (Family Benefits) (Amending) Regulations 1968**(e)** are hereby revoked.

(2) Section 38(2) of the Interpretation Act 1889**(f)** (which relates to the effect of repeals) shall have effect in relation to the Regulations revoked by this regulation as if they were enactments repealed by an Act.

(3) Without prejudice to the operation of section 38(2) of the Interpretation Act 1889 as applied by paragraph (2), any contribution or pension paid, any appointment, requirement, election, acceptance or nomination made, any approval or determination given, any extension of time allowed and any other thing done under any provision of the Regulations hereby revoked shall be deemed to have been paid, made, given, allowed or done, as the case may be, under the corresponding provision of these Regulations and shall have effect under these Regulations accordingly.

(a) 1967 c. 12.
(b) S.I. 1968/1656 (1968 III, p. 4485).
(c) S.I. 1966/357 (1966 I, p. 813).
(d) S.I. 1967/1856 (1967 III, p. 4975).
(e) S.I. 1968/1914 (1968 III, p. 5069).
(f) 1889 c. 63.

Interpretation

3.—(1) The Interpretation Act 1889 shall apply for the interpretation of these Regulations as it applies for the interpretation of an Act of Parliament.

(2) References in these Regulations to the provisions of any enactment, regulations or rules shall, unless the context otherwise requires, be construed as references to those provisions as amended, modified, affected, extended or re-enacted by or under any subsequent enactment, regulations, rules or other instrument.

(3) References in these Regulations to a regulation or to a Part or to a Schedule shall, unless the context otherwise requires, be construed as references to a regulation or to a Part of, or to a Schedule to, these Regulations, as the case may be.

Definitions

4. In these Regulations, unless the context otherwise requires—

"the Act of 1967" means the Teachers' Superannuation Act 1967;

"additional allowance" means an additional superannuation allowance within the meaning of the Teachers' Regulations exclusive of any part thereof attributable to part-time teaching;

"additional contributions" means the contributions required to be paid by regulations 28 and 29;

"annual superannuation allowance" means an annual superannuation allowance within the meaning of the Teachers' Regulations exclusive of any part thereof attributable to part-time teaching service;

"average salary" means, in relation to a contributor or deceased teacher, his average salary as calculated under section 4(3) of the Act of 1967 without taking into account any part-time teaching service;

"the Board" means the Board of Management constituted as in Part II provided;

"child" means—

(*a*) in Part IV a person who—

(i) has not attained the age of sixteen; or

(ii) having attained the age of sixteen, is receiving full-time education or undergoing full-time training for a trade, profession or calling, which training is of a duration of not less than two years; or

(iii) having attained the age of sixteen, is an incapacitated person by reason of an infirmity which arose either before he attained that age or while receiving such education or undergoing such training as aforesaid; and

(*b*) in Part V a person who has not attained the age of sixteen;

"class A external service" and "class B external service" have the same respective meanings as in the Teachers' Regulations;

"contributor" and "re-instated contributor" have the meanings respectively assigned to them by regulation 23(4);

"deceased teacher" has the meaning assigned to it by regulation 25(3);

"dependant" has in Part V the meaning assigned to it by regulation 57;

"eligible child" means a child, not being a married woman, who is—

(*a*) a legitimate child of a contributor, born before the contributor dies or becomes entitled to be paid superannuation allowances or within one year of his death or becoming so entitled;

(*b*) an adopted child of a contributor, adopted before the contributor becomes entitled to be paid superannuation allowances;

(*c*) a legitimate or adopted child of a deceased teacher; or

(*d*) a step-child or illegitimate child of a contributor or deceased teacher or an adopted child of the wife of a contributor or deceased teacher, being a child wholly or mainly dependent on the contributor both before he becomes entitled to be paid superannuation allowances and at the time of his death or on the deceased teacher at the time of his death, as the case may be;

"external scheme" means a scheme legally in force whereby the payment of pensions to or in respect of the widows and children of persons employed in class A external service is secured, being a scheme requiring the payment of contributions and providing benefits similar to the contributions required and the benefits provided by the Teachers' Widows' and Children's Pension Scheme under Part IV;

"financial year" means the year ending on 31st March;

"former external contributor" means a person who has been a contributor under an external scheme;

"the Fund" means the Teachers' Family Benefits Fund maintained under Part III;

"incapacitated person" means a person who, in the opinion of the Secretary of State, is incapable by reason of infirmity of mind or body of earning a livelihood and who is not wholly or mainly supported out of money provided by Parliament or raised by a rate; and "incapacitated" shall be interpreted accordingly;

"interchange rules" means rules made under section 2 of the Superannuation (Miscellaneous Provisions) Act 1948**(a)** (which section relates to persons transferring to or from certain employments) and includes provisions corresponding to the provisions of such rules contained in regulations made under section 67(1) of the National Health Service Act 1946**(b)** or section 66(1) of the National Health Service (Scotland) Act 1947**(c)**;

"life pension" has in Part V the meaning assigned to it by regulation 68;

"Method I", "Method II" and "Method III" mean the methods of paying additional contributions prescribed by regulations 31, 32 and 33 respectively;

"normal contributions" means the contributions required to be paid by regulation 27;

"part-time teaching service" has the same meaning as in the Teachers' Regulations;

"pensionable age" means, in relation to a contributor or deceased teacher, the age of sixty or any lesser age which under the Teachers' Regulations he is or was required to attain to become qualified to be paid superannuation allowances;

"previous service" means, in relation to a contributor or deceased teacher, service or employment before the day on which the Teachers' Widows' and Children's Pensions Scheme becomes or, as the case may be, again becomes applicable to him, being service which—

(a) 1948 c. 33. **(b)** 1946 c. 81. **(c)** 1947 c. 27.

(*a*) is on that day reckonable service or class A external service;

(*b*) becomes reckonable service by virtue of regulations 15 and 32 of the principal Regulations;

(*c*) becomes reckonable service by virtue of interchange rules; or

(*d*) becomes previous service by virtue of an election made under regulation 29;

"reckonable service" means—

(*a*) reckonable service within the meaning of the Act of 1967 exclusive of any such service attributable to part-time teaching service; and

(*b*) service which for the purposes of the Teachers' Regulations is service as an organiser, a teacher in an admitted school, a services civilian teacher or a services education officer;

"the Regulations of 1966" means the Teachers' Superannuation (Family Benefits) Regulations 1966;

"salary", in relation to any period, means the amount of the salary of a teacher by reference to which superannuation contributions payable by him in respect of that period are calculated;

"the Schemes" means the Teachers' Widows' and Children's Pension Scheme and the Teachers' Dependants' Pension Scheme administered in accordance with the provisions of Part IV and Part V respectively;

"the Secretary of State" means the Secretary of State for Education and Science;

"service counting for benefit" has the meaning assigned to it by regulation 40;

"short service gratuity" means a gratuity payable by virtue of regulation 46 of the principal Teachers' Regulations exclusive of any part thereof attributable to part-time teaching service;

"superannuation allowances" means annual superannuation allowances and additional allowances;

"superannuation contributions" means the contributions payable by a teacher under section 3 of the Act of 1967 or the Teachers' Regulations, other than such contributions in respect of part-time teaching service, and includes, where the context so requires, contributions corresponding to superannuation contributions paid in respect of class A external service;

"teacher" means a person employed in reckonable service and, where the context so requires, includes a person who has ceased to be so employed;

"the Teachers' Regulations" means the Teachers' Superannuation Regulations 1967 to 1970(**a**); and the "principal Teachers' Regulations" means the Teachers' Superannuation Regulations 1967;

"temporary pension" has in Part V the meaning assigned to it by regulation 68;

"terminal sum" includes—

(*a*) an additional superannuation allowance;

(*b*) a short service gratuity;

(*c*) a death gratuity and any other sum payable on death by virtue of regulations 47 and 48 of the principal Teachers' Regulations; and

(*d*) any sum payable under the Teachers' Regulations by way of return of superannuation contributions.

(**a**) S.I. 1967/489, 948, 1286, 1968/1353, 1969/80, 1970/10, 1970/753 (1967 I, p. 1562; II, p. 2904; II, p. 3721; 1968 II, p. 3753; 1969 I, p. 241; 1970 I, p. 11).

Part II

Board of Management

Continuance of Board

5. The Board of Management established by the Regulations of 1966 shall continue in being as a body corporate with perpetual succession and a common seal and shall exercise the powers and functions conferred on it by these Regulations.

Constitution of Board

6.—(1) The Board shall consist of nineteen members, to be appointed—

one by the Association of Agricultural Education Staffs of Local Authorities,

one by the Association of Education Committees,

one by the Association of Municipal Corporations,

one by the Association of Principals of Technical Institutions,

one by the Association of Teachers in Colleges and Departments of Education,

one by the Association of Teachers in Technical Institutions,

one by the Association of University Teachers,

one by the County Councils Association,

one jointly by the Incorporated Association of Headmasters and the Incorporated Association of Assistant Masters,

one jointly by the Association of Headmistresses, Incorporated, and the Association of Assistant Mistresses, Incorporated,

one by the Inner London Education Authority,

one by the National Association of Head Teachers,

one by the National Association of Schoolmasters,

one by the National Society for Art Education,

three by the National Union of Teachers,

one by the Welsh Joint Education Committee, and

one (hereinafter referred to as "an additional member"), in place of the Chairman for the time being of the Board, by the body by which the chairman was appointed to be a member.

(2) A member of the Board appointed by a body specified in paragraph (1) need not be a member of that body.

(3) Members of the Board, other than an additional member, shall be appointed each for a term of three years. An additional member shall be appointed for a term of office ending on the date on which the chairman in whose place he was appointed ceases to be chairman.

(4) Any member of the Board who—

(*a*) communicates in writing to the Board a wish to resign;

(*b*) is absent from all meetings of the Board during a period of one year;

(*c*) is adjudicated a bankrupt or makes a composition or arrangement with his creditors;

(*d*) is compulsorily admitted to hospital or received into guardianship under Part IV, or becomes a patient within the meaning of Part VIII, of the Mental Health Act 1959**(a)**; or

(*e*) is convicted of an offence and ordered to be imprisoned for a period of not less than three months without the option of a fine

shall thereupon cease to be a member of the Board.

(5) Every vacancy in the office of member of the Board shall as soon as possible be notified to the proper appointing body. Any competent person may be reappointed to be a member of the Board.

Chairman and Vice-Chairman

7. The Board shall, whenever it sees fit, elect from among its members a chairman and vice-chairman each of whom shall hold office until his resignation, his ceasing to be a member of the Board or the appointment of his successor, whichever shall first occur. Any member of the Board who has previously held office as chairman or vice-chairman shall be eligible for re-election as such.

Proceedings of Board

8.—(1) The Board shall hold ordinary meetings at least twice in each year. A special meeting may at any time be summoned by the chairman or by four members of the Board upon seven clear days' notice being given to the other members of the matters to be discussed.

(2) There shall be a quorum when not less than one-third of the members of the Board are present at a meeting.

(3) The chairman, or in his absence the vice-chairman, shall preside at meetings of the Board but, if both are absent from any meeting or from any part of a meeting, a chairman of that meeting or of that part of a meeting shall be appointed by the members present before any other business is transacted.

(4) Every matter shall be determined by a majority of the members of the Board present at a meeting and voting on the question. In the case of equality of votes on any matter the person presiding as chairman shall have a second or casting vote.

(5) The proceedings of the Board shall not be invalidated by any vacancy in its membership or by any defect in the appointment or qualification of any member.

Committees

9. The Board may appoint such committees as it thinks fit consisting either wholly or partly of members thereof and may delegate the exercise of any of its powers or functions to such a committee.

Assessor

10. The Secretary of State may appoint a person to be assessor for him at the meetings of the Board and of any committee thereof, and such assessor (or in his absence from any meeting such other person as may be nominated by the Secretary of State for the purpose of that meeting) shall be entitled to attend and speak, but not to vote, at the meetings of the Board and of any committee.

(a) 1959 c. 72.

Conduct of Business

11. Within the limits prescribed by the foregoing provisions of this Part the Board shall conduct its proceedings and manage its business in such manner as it may from time to time determine.

Expenses of Board

12.—(1) The Board shall, in such manner and for such period as the Secretary of State may from time to time require, prepare estimates of its administrative expenses and shall submit such estimates to the Secretary of State.

(2) The Board shall not, except with the consent of the Secretary of State, incur administrative expenses in excess of the amount of the estimates approved by him.

(3) Subject to the foregoing provisions of this regulation, the administrative expenses of the Board shall be paid by the Secretary of State.

(4) The Secretary of State shall pay to members of the Board such travelling, subsistence and other allowances as he may, with the consent of the Treasury, determine.

(5) For the purposes of this regulation administrative expenses shall include expenses incurred in connection with the management of investments other than—

(*a*) brokerage, commission and fees in respect of valuations; and

(*b*) stamp duty on any contract, transfer and other assurance.

Review of Schemes

13. It shall be the duty of the Board to keep the Schemes under review and, where it appears to it to be desirable, to make recommendations to the Secretary of State with respect to any matter, including questions of administrative policy, concerning the Schemes or either of them and, in particular, with respect to any matter—

(*a*) which has been referred to the Board by the Secretary of State; or

(*b*) which has been the subject of representations made to the Board by or on behalf of any person or body interested in, or affected by, the Schemes or either of them, or by a body representing local education authorities or teachers.

Power to Borrow

14. The Board may whenever it thinks it necessary or expedient so to do raise or borrow any sum or sums of money and may secure the repayment thereof in such manner and upon such terms and conditions in all respects as it may think fit.

PART III

THE FUND

Continuance of Fund

15. For the purposes of the Schemes the Teachers' Family Benefits Fund established under the Regulations of 1966 shall continue to be managed by the Board and shall be divided into two parts to be called respectively the General Account and the Investment Account.

General Account

16.—(1) There shall be paid into the General Account—

(*a*) all sums payable to the Secretary of State under Parts IV and V; and

(*b*) such sums as the Board may from time to time authorise to be transferred from the Investment Account for the purpose of avoiding a deficiency in the General Account.

(2) There shall be paid out of the General Account—

(*a*) the benefits and other sums payable under Parts IV and V; and

(*b*) such sums as the Board may from time to time authorise to be transferred to the Investment Account, being sums not for the time being needed for the purposes of the General Account.

Investment Account

17.—(1) There shall be paid into the Investment Account—

(*a*) any sums transferred from the General Account under regulation 16(2)(*b*);

(*b*) all dividends, interest and other moneys accruing from the investment of moneys forming part of the Fund;

(*c*) sums realised on the disposal of investments; and

(*d*) any other sums received by the Board and not required to be paid into the General Account.

(2) There shall be paid out of the Investment Account—

(*a*) any sums transferred to the General Account under regulation 16(1)(*b*);

(*b*) sums expended in the acquisition of investments; and

(*c*) any expenses incurred in connection with any investment or proposed investment which are not administrative expenses for the purposes of regulation 12.

Investments

18.—(1) Subject as hereafter in this regulation provided, the Board shall invest any property for the time being held for the purposes of the Investment Account and not needed as a balance for working purposes, whether at the time in a state of investment or not, in accordance with the provisions of this regulation, and may also from time to time vary any investments so made.

(2) The property held for the purposes of the Investment Account shall consist of two parts, that is to say, a narrower-range part and a wider-range part, and the property comprised in each part on the day on which these Regulations come into operation shall, subject as in this regulation provided, continue to be so comprised.

(3) No transfer shall be made from one part of the Investment Account to the other unless either—

(*a*) the transfer is authorised or required by the following provisions of this regulation; or

(*b*) a compensating transfer is made at the same time.

(4) When any property accrues to the Investment Account—

(*a*) if, not being dividends or interest in respect of investments, it accrues in respect of property comprised in either the narrower-range part or the wider-range part, it shall be treated as belonging to that part; and

(*b*) in any other case, by apportionment of the accruing property or the transfer of property from one part to the other, or both, the value of the wider-range part shall be increased by an amount equal to three-quarters of the value of the accruing property and of the narrower-range part by an amount equal to one-quarter of that value.

(5) Property belonging to the narrower-range part of the Investment Account shall be invested only in investments for the time being falling within Part I or Part II of the First Schedule to the Act of 1961 and any property invested in any other manner which is or becomes comprised in the narrower-range part shall either be transferred to the wider-range part, with a compensating transfer, or be re-invested in such investments as aforesaid as soon as may be.

(6) Subject as hereafter in this regulation provided, property belonging to the wider-range part of the Investment Account shall be invested in—

(*a*) investments for the time being falling within Part I, Part II or Part III of the First Schedule to the Act of 1961;

(*b*) the acquisition, development or management (whether in association with any other person or not) of land situated in the United Kingdom or any interest in such land;

(*c*) fixed interest securities issued by the government of any country outside the United Kingdom or by a public, municipal or local authority or a publicly controlled or nationalised industry or undertaking in such a country; or

(*d*) the stocks, shares, debentures or other securities issued in the United Kingdom or elsewhere by a company incorporated outside the United Kingdom.

(7) No investment shall be made in pursuance of sub-paragraph (*c*) or (*d*) of paragraph (6) if it would result in more than one-tenth of the total value at cost of the property held for the purposes of the Investment Account being invested in securities the price of which is not quoted on a recognised stock exchange within the meaning of the Prevention of Fraud (Investments) Act 1958(**a**) or the Belfast stock exchange.

(8) In relation to investments made in pursuance of paragraph (5) and sub-paragraph (*a*) of paragraph (6)—

(*a*) paragraphs 1, 2 and 3 of Part IV of Schedule 1 to the Act of 1961 shall not apply; and

(*b*) paragraphs 4, 5, 6 and 7 of that Part shall apply.

(9) If for the purposes of paragraph (4) the Board obtains, from a person reasonably believed by the Board to be qualified to make it and whether made in the course of his employment as an officer or servant or not, a valuation in writing of any property, the valuation shall be conclusive in determining whether any transfer or apportionment of property made under paragraph (4) has been duly made.

(**a**) 1958 c. 45.

(10) When property falls to be taken out of the Investment Account nothing in this regulation shall restrict the discretion of the Board as to the choice of property to be taken out.

(11) For the purposes of this regulation the Board may make such arrangements as it thinks fit for the management of investments, including the employment of an investment manager, and for obtaining proper advice in relation to investments.

(12) In this regulation—

"the Act of 1961" means the Trustee Investments Act 1961**(a)**;

"compensating transfer", in relation to any property transferred between the narrower-range part and the wider-range part, means a transfer in the opposite direction of property of equal value;

"proper advice" means the advice of a person who is reasonably believed by the Board to be qualified by his ability in, and practical experience of, investment matters notwithstanding that he may give it in the course of his employment as an officer or servant;

"property" includes real and personal property of any description, including money and things in action, but does not include an interest in expectancy.

Accounts and Audit

19.—(1) The Board shall cause to be kept in relation to the General Account and the Investment Account proper records with respect to—

(*a*) all sums payable into and out of the Accounts and the matters in respect of which those sums are payable; and

(*b*) the assets and liabilities of the Accounts

and such records shall give a true and fair view of the Accounts and explain transactions relating thereto.

(2) In respect of each financial year there shall be prepared—

(*a*) an income and expenditure account relating to the General Account;

(*b*) an income and expenditure account relating to the Investment Account; and

(*c*) a balance sheet giving a true and fair view of the state of the Fund at the end of the year.

(3) The accounts and balance sheet prepared under paragraph (2) shall be audited under arrangements to be approved by the Secretary of State.

(4) After the accounts prepared as required by paragraph (2) have been audited they shall be published by the Board, together with any reports of the auditor, the Secretary of State and the Board on matters within their respective competence, and copies thereof shall be made available without charge to any persons paying contributions or entitled to benefits under either Part IV or Part V who apply for them.

Quinquennial Valuations

20.—(1) The Government Actuary or Deputy Government Actuary shall make an actuarial valuation as at 1st April 1971 and as at 1st April in each fifth year thereafter of the assets and liabilities of the Fund and shall report to the

(a) 1961 c. 62.

Secretary of State and the Board thereon and on the sufficiency or otherwise of the contributions being made to the Fund to support the benefits payable therefrom.

(2) The Government Actuary or Deputy Government Actuary shall include in his report recommendations for the making good of any deficiency or for the disposal of any surplus, as the case may be.

(3) After consideration of the report of the Government Actuary or Deputy Government Actuary the Board shall make to the Secretary of State such proposals, if any, as it considers appropriate for the amendment of these Regulations and for the alteration of either the benefits or the contributions payable thereunder or of both such benefits and such contributions.

PART IV

TEACHERS' WIDOWS' AND CHILDREN'S PENSION SCHEME

PRELIMINARY

The Scheme

21. The Scheme established by Part IV of the Regulations of 1966 for securing the payment of pensions to or in respect of the widows and children of teachers who die shall be continued and be administered in accordance with the provisions of this Part under the name of the Teachers' Widows' and Children's Pension Scheme (hereafter in this Part referred to as "the Scheme").

Elections

22. Any election required or authorised to be made under the provisions of this Part shall—

(*a*) be made in writing and sent by post to the Secretary of State; and

(*b*) if accepted by the Secretary of State, be irrevocable.

APPLICATION

Teachers to whom Scheme applies

23.—(1) The Scheme shall apply to men teachers who—

(*a*) not having been previously employed in reckonable service or class A external service become employed in reckonable service;

(*b*) being former external contributors, become employed or again employed in reckonable service and liable to pay superannuation contributions; or

(*c*) having ceased to be contributors and to be employed in reckonable service and not having been employed in class A external service since so ceasing, again become employed in reckonable service and liable to pay superannuation contributions.

(2) Subject as hereinafter provided, the Scheme shall also apply to men teachers, other than those specified in paragraph (1), of any description specified in column (1) of the following Table who elect that it shall apply to them within three months after the date specified in column (2) thereof in relation to that description:—

TABLE

(1) Description of Teachers	(2) Date
Teachers becoming employed in reckonable service who have been previously employed in such service or class A external service, other than teachers who while so employed were able to elect that the Scheme or an external scheme should apply to them and did not so elect.	The date of becoming employed in reckonable service.
Teachers who marry while employed in reckonable service.	The date of marriage.
Teachers who having been employed in reckonable service or class A external service— (*a*) neither were contributors nor are former external contributors; (*b*) marry after a date 3 months before ceasing to be so employed; and (*c*) subsequently become employed or again employed in reckonable service and liable to pay superannuation contributions.	The date of becoming employed or again employed in reckonable service.

(3) Teachers of any description specified in column (1) of the Table contained in paragraph (2) shall not elect that the Scheme shall apply to them if, at the commencement of the period within which they may so elect, they have attained pensionable age and are qualified to be paid superannuation allowances or benefits in respect of class A external service corresponding to superannuation allowances on ceasing to be employed in reckonable service or class A external service.

(4) In this Part a teacher to whom the Scheme applies by virtue of this regulation is referred to as a "contributor"; and a contributor who is such by virtue of paragraph (1)(*c*) is referred to as a "re-instated contributor".

Commencement of Application

24. The date on which the Scheme shall commence to apply to a contributor shall—

(*a*) in a case to which regulation 23(1) applies, be the date on which he becomes employed or again employed, as the case may be, in reckonable service; and

(*b*) in a case to which regulation 23(2) applies, be the date of the commencement of the period during which he may elect that it shall apply to him.

Application to Deceased Teachers

25.—(1) The Scheme shall apply to men teachers who—

(*a*) before the expiry of the period during which they may under regulation 23(2) elect that the Scheme shall apply to them, die without having so elected; or (*b*) within three months of the expiry of the said period, die without having so elected, if the Secretary of State is satisfied that by reason of sickness or unavoidable cause they have been unable so to elect.

(2) Notwithstanding anything contained in paragraph (1) the Scheme shall not by reason of that paragraph apply—

(*a*) to a teacher who before his death elects that it shall not apply to him;

(*b*) to a teacher who had attained pensionable age and was qualified to be paid superannuation allowances on ceasing to be employed in reckonable service; or

(*c*) to a teacher in respect of whom the Secretary of State is satisfied, after consultation with persons interested, that it would not benefit his widow or eligible children.

(3) A teacher to whom the Scheme applies by virtue of this regulation is in this Part referred to as a "deceased teacher".

CONTRIBUTIONS

Payment of Contributions

26. For the purpose of defraying the cost of the benefits under the Scheme there shall be paid to the Secretary of State—

(*a*) by or in respect of every contributor, normal contributions in respect of reckonable service after the Scheme becomes applicable to him and additional contributions in respect of previous service; and

(*b*) in respect of every deceased teacher, such contributions as are prescribed by regulation 39.

Normal Contributions

27.—(1) Subject as hereinafter provided normal contributions shall be an amount equal to two per cent. of the salary of a contributor and shall be paid, in respect of any period during which he is employed in reckonable service, from the date on which the Scheme commences to apply to him until the date on which he ceases to pay superannuation contributions.

(2) Normal contributions shall not be paid by a contributor who, after attaining pensionable age, has become entitled to be paid superannuation allowances unless, after the termination of a subsequent period of employment in reckonable service, he becomes entitled to a subsequent additional allowance and is then married to the same wife as when he first became entitled to be paid superannuation allowances after attaining pensionable age.

(3) Normal contributions payable by a contributor by reason of paragraph (2) shall, together with compound interest thereon calculated at the rate of four per cent. per annum with yearly rests from 1st October in the financial year next after that in which the period to which they relate fall, be paid by the surrender of the whole or a proportion of his subsequent additional allowance.

Additional Contributions

28.—(1) Subject as hereinafter provided in relation to re-instated contributors and former external contributors, a contributor—

(*a*) shall pay additional contributions in respect of the whole of his previous service not exceeding ten years, and

(*b*) may, if he elects so to do, pay additional contributions in respect of part or all of such service in excess of ten years.

(2) Subject as aforesaid, additional contributions payable by a contributor shall be paid and their amount determined by—

Method I, as provided in regulation 31, or

Method II, as provided in regulation 32, or

Method III, as provided in regulation 33,

or partly by either Method I or Method II and partly by Method III.

(3) A contributor shall elect by which one of the methods or combination of methods specified in paragraph (2) the additional contributions payable by him shall be paid and their amount determined.

(4) A contributor shall not elect to pay additional contributions—

(*a*) by Method I, if he has attained the age of fifty-nine; or

(*b*) by Method II, if he has not attained the age of thirty or has attained the age of sixty-four

on the date on which such contributions commence to be payable by him.

(5) An election made under paragraph (3) shall not be such as to result in the total annual amount of the contributions payable by him being in excess of the amount authorised by regulation 73.

(6) If a contributor to whom this regulation applies elects that the additional contributions payable by him shall be paid and their amount determined by a combination of methods, he shall further elect in respect of what amount of previous service such contributions shall be so paid and determined by Method I or Method II, as the case may be.

(7) Where a contributor does not elect under the preceding provisions of this regulation that the amount of additional contributions payable by him in respect of any period of previous service shall be paid and determined by either Method I or Method II, the amount of such contributions in respect of that period shall be paid and determined by Method III.

(8) For the purposes of this regulation such part of the previous service of a contributor as does not amount to a number of complete years shall be expressed as a fraction of a year, of which fraction the denominator shall be twelve and the numerator shall be the number of months of thirty days comprised in the said part, any number of days exceeding fourteen which remains being reckoned as a month.

(9) Any election authorised or required to be made by this regulation shall be made—

(*a*) by a contributor to whom the Scheme applies by virtue of an election, at the same time as he makes that election; and

(*b*) by any other contributor, within three months of the day on which the Scheme commences to apply to him.

Additional Contributions on Increase of Previous Service

29.—(1) This regulation applies to a contributor who—

(*a*) on becoming a contributor either had no previous service or was required or elected to pay additional contributions in respect of the whole of his then previous service; and

(*b*) after becoming a contributor repays superannuation contributions in respect of a period of reckonable service or class A external service which had been repaid to him.

(2) A contributor to whom this regulation applies may elect that the period mentioned in paragraph (1)(*b*) shall be previous service and, if he does so elect, it shall be such service and he—

(*a*) shall pay additional contributions in respect of so much thereof as when added to his other previous service amounts to not more than ten years; and

(*b*) may, if he elects so to do, pay additional contributions in respect of any further part or all thereof.

(3) Any election under this regulation shall be made by a contributor within three months of the date of the coming into operation of these Regulations or of the date on which he repaid the superannuation contributions repaid to him, whichever shall be the later.

(4) Except as in this regulation provided, the provisions of regulation 28 shall apply to additional contributions payable by virtue of this regulation as if such contributions were payable, and formed part of contributions payable, under that regulation.

Commencement of Additional Contributions—Methods I and II

30. Where, by virtue of an election made under regulation 28 or 29 additional contributions become payable by a contributor by either Method I or Method II or such contributions are increased, the contributions or the increase, as the case may be, shall, except as in regulations 34 and 35 otherwise provided, commence to be payable from the first day of the month beginning next after the day on which notification of acceptance of the election is sent to the contributor by post by the Secretary of State.

Method I

31. Additional contributions payable by Method I shall be paid by a contributor, in respect of any period during which he is employed in reckonable service, from the date on which they commence to be payable until he ceases to be so employed, attains the age of sixty or dies, whichever shall first occur, and shall be the amount ascertained by multiplying—

(*a*) the percentage of his salary for that period which, in column (2) of Schedule 1, is specified opposite to his age in column (1) thereof on the date from which additional contributions commence to be payable by him, by

(*b*) the length in years of the period of previous service in respect of which additional contributions are payable by him by Method I.

Method II

32. Additional contributions payable by Method II shall be paid by a contributor, in respect of any period during which he is employed in reckonable service, from the date on which they commence to be payable until he ceases to be so employed, attains the age of sixty-five or dies, whichever shall first occur, and shall in respect of any period be the amount ascertained by multiplying—

(*a*) the percentage of his salary for that period which, in column (3) of Schedule 1, is specified opposite to his age in column (1) thereof on the date from which additional contributions commence to be payable by him, by

(*b*) the length in years of the period of previous service in respect of which additional contributions are payable by him by Method II.

Method III

33.—(1) Additional contributions payable by Method III shall be paid by the surrender of the whole or a proportion of any terminal sum payable to or in respect of a contributor.

(2) The amount of such additional contributions shall be ascertained by multiplying the length in years of the period of previous service in respect of which additional contributions are payable by Method III by the appropriate percentage of his average salary.

(3) For the purposes of paragraph (2) the appropriate percentage shall be—

(*a*) in respect of any period of previous service of a contributor to whom the Scheme commenced to apply on a day before the beginning of April 1967 (other than any period which is previous service by virtue of an election made under regulation 29), that specified in column (2) of Schedule 2 opposite to his age on that day specified in column (1) thereof;

(*b*) in respect of any period of previous service of a contributor to whom the Scheme commenced to apply on a day after the beginning of April 1967 (other than any period which is previous service by virtue of an election made under regulation 29), that specified in column (3) of Schedule 2 opposite to his age on that day specified in column (1) thereof; and

(*c*) in respect of any period of previous service which is such by virtue of an election made by a contributor under regulation 29, that specified in column (3) of Schedule 2 opposite to his age on the day on which he made such election specified in column (1) thereof.

(4) Except as in paragraph (5) provided, no surrender of the whole or a proportion of a terminal sum shall be made by or in respect of a contributor who—

(*a*) is or would be entitled under regulations 41 to 44 to repayment of additional contributions paid by him; or

(*b*) has not been employed in reckonable service after being employed in service in which he was a contributor under an external scheme.

(5) In the case of a contributor to whom paragraph (4)(*b*) applies, any contributions corresponding to additional contributions which were under an external scheme required to be paid by a method corresponding to Method III and which have not been so paid shall be paid in accordance with the provisions of this regulation as if the period in respect of which they were payable were a period of previous service.

(6) Notwithstanding anything in this regulation before contained, where the surrender of the whole or a proportion of a terminal sum has been made under this regulation there shall, except as in regulations 27(3), 34(6) and 38 provided, be no further surrender of the whole or a proportion of any subsequent terminal sum payable to or in respect of the same contributor.

Additional Contributions payable by Re-instated Contributors

34.—(1) A re-instated contributor who—

(*a*) while previously employed in reckonable service paid additional contributions by either Method I or Method II or would have so paid such contributions if he had continued to be employed in reckonable service after the beginning of April 1967;

(*b*) has discontinued the payment of, or, as the case may be, has not paid, such contributions for a period or periods amounting in the aggregate to more than one year, exclusive of any period to be disregarded under paragraph (2); and

(*c*) has not paid the balance of such contributions payable by him in the manner provided for in regulation 36

shall pay additional contributions in accordance with either paragraph (3) or paragraph (5), as shall be appropriate.

(2) For the purpose of paragraph (1)(*b*) any period during which a re-instated contributor has been absent from employment in reckonable service shall be disregarded if on last ceasing to be so employed in such service—

(*a*) he was paid either superannuation allowances or a short service gratuity; or

(*b*) he was absent on sick leave which was treated as reckonable service and neither his superannuation contributions nor any contributions under the Scheme have been repaid to him.

(3) In the case of a re-instated contributor to whom paragraph (1) applies and who, before becoming such a contributor, had not attained the age at which additional contributions ceased to be payable by him by Method I or Method II, as the case may be—

(*a*) the Secretary of State shall notify to him the period which is to be treated as service counting for benefit by reason of—

(i) the additional contributions paid by him by Method I or Method II while previously employed in reckonable service and not repaid to him; and

(ii) any payments purporting to be additional contributions which have been made by him since again becoming employed in reckonable service and which will be made by him if he continues to be so employed until the end of the month in which he is notified as required by this sub-paragraph and to make such payments at the same rate;

(*b*) additional contributions shall be paid and their amount determined by either Method I or Method II, whichever was the method by which when previously employed in reckonable service he paid, or was liable to pay, such contributions;

(*c*) except as in paragraph (4) provided, the period of previous service shall be deemed to be the period in respect of which he was required or elected under regulations 28 and 29 to pay additional contributions by Method I or Method II, reduced by the period to be treated as service counting for benefit as notified under sub-paragraph (*a*) and increased by any period of service since he last ceased to be employed in reckonable service which has become reckonable service by virtue of interchange rules;

(*d*) the day from which additional contributions again commence to be payable by him shall be—

(i) if he has been repaid superannuation contributions in respect of a period of reckonable service or class A external service in respect of which he had elected or had been required under the Scheme to pay additional contributions, the first day of the month commencing next after the repayment by him of those superannuation contributions;

(ii) if sub-paragraph (*d*)(i) does not apply to him and if he continues to be employed in reckonable service after the end of the month in which he is notified as required by sub-paragraph (*a*), the first day of the month commencing next after that notification; or

(iii) if neither sub-paragraph (*d*)(i) nor sub-paragraph (*d*)(ii) applies to him, the day on which he again becomes employed in reckonable service; and

(*e*) his relevant age shall be his age on the day on which additional contributions again commence to be payable by him.

(4) A re-instated contributor to whom paragraph (3) applies may, within three months of being notified as required by paragraph (3)(*a*), elect that a period of previous service exceeding ten years in respect of which additional contributions are payable by him by Method I or Method II shall be reduced to such an extent as will result in his having not less than ten years of service counting for benefit; and, if the Secretary of State accepts any such election, the period of previous service so reduced shall be substituted for the period specified in paragraph (3)(*c*).

(5) In the case of a re-instated contributor to whom paragraph (1) applies and who, after ceasing to be employed in reckonable service and before becoming such a contributor, had attained the age at which additional contributions would have ceased to be payable by him by Method I or Method II, as the case may be, additional contributions shall be paid by the surrender of the whole or a proportion of any terminal sum payable to or in respect of him and shall be of such amount as shall be determined in accordance with Method III in respect of a period of previous service equal to the difference between—

(*a*) the period of previous service in respect of which he was required or elected under regulations 28 and 29 to pay additional contributions by Method I or Method II; and

(*b*) the period of service counting for benefit by reason of the additional contributions paid by him by Method I or Method II while previously employed in reckonable service and not repaid to him.

(6) A re-instated contributor who, while previously employed in reckonable service, elected or was required to pay additional contributions by Method III shall pay such contributions by that method and, for the purpose of determining the amount thereof—

(*a*) the period of previous service shall be deemed to be the period in respect of which he elected or was required under regulations 28 and 29 to pay additional contributions by Method III, increased by any period of service which has since become reckonable service by virtue of interchange rules; and

(*b*) there shall be deducted therefrom any amount previously paid by him by Method III together with compound interest thereon calculated at three and a half per cent. per annum with yearly rests from the date of payment.

Additional Contributions payable by Former External Contributors

35.—(1) A former external contributor who under an external scheme was paying, or was or would have been liable to pay, contributions corresponding to additional contributions by a method corresponding to either Method I or Method II and who, before becoming a contributor, had not attained the age at which such contributions would have ceased to be payable by him shall pay additional contributions by either Method I or Method II—

(*a*) in accordance with paragraph (3), if he becomes a contributor within one year, exclusive of any period to be disregarded under paragraph (2), of ceasing to be so liable; or

(*b*) in accordance with paragraph (4), if he becomes a contributor more than one year, exclusive of any period to be disregarded under paragraph (2), after ceasing to be so liable.

(2) For the purpose of paragraph (1) any period during which a former external contributor was absent from class A external service shall be disregarded if on last ceasing to be employed in such service—

(*a*) he was granted any benefit by reason of having become permanently incapable through infirmity of mind or body of serving efficiently; or

(*b*) he was absent on sick leave which was treated as class A external service and neither his superannuation contributions nor any contributions under the external scheme last applicable to him have been repaid to him.

(3) In the case of a former external contributor to whom paragraph (1)(*a*) applies—

(*a*) additional contributions shall be paid and their amount determined by either Method I or Method II, whichever shall correspond to the method by which under the external scheme last applicable to him he was paying, or was or would have been liable to pay, contributions corresponding to additional contributions;

(*b*) the period of previous service shall be deemed to be the period of service by reference to which under the external scheme last applicable to him the amount of the contributions corresponding to additional contributions payable by him by a method corresponding to either Method I or Method II was determined;

(*c*) the day from which additional contributions commence to be payable by him shall be the day on which he becomes employed in reckonable service; and

(*d*) his relevant age shall be deemed to be the same as for the purpose of determining under the external scheme last applicable to him the amount of the contributions corresponding to additional contributions payable by him by a method corresponding to either Method I or Method II.

(4) In the case of a former external contributor to whom paragraph (1)(*b*) applies—

(*a*) The Secretary of State shall notify to him—

(i) the period or periods counting for benefit under any external scheme previously applicable to him by reason of the payment by him of contributions corresponding to additional contributions by a method corresponding to either Method I or Method II, as ascertained from the appropriate authority in relation to that scheme; and

(ii) the period which is to be treated as service counting for benefit by reason of any payments purporting to be additional contributions which have been made by him since becoming employed in reckonable service and which will be made by him if he continues to be so employed until the end of the month in which he is notified as required by this sub-paragraph and to make such payments at the same rate;

(*b*) additional contributions shall be paid and their amount determined by either Method I or Method II, whichever shall correspond to the method by which he was last liable under an external scheme to pay contributions corresponding to additional contributions;

(*c*) except as in paragraph (5) provided, the period of previous service shall be deemed to be the period by reference to which under the external scheme first applicable to him the amount of the contributions corresponding to additional contributions payable by him by a method corresponding to either Method I or Method II was determined, reduced by the aggregate of the periods specified in sub-paragraph (*a*) and increased by any period of service since he last ceased to be employed in class A external service which has become reckonable service by virtue of interchange rules;

(*d*) the day from which additional contributions commence to be payable by him shall be—

(i) if, after ceasing to be employed in class A external service his superannuation contributions in respect of that service and his contributions corresponding to normal contributions under the external scheme last applicable to him were repaid to him, the first day of the month commencing next after the repayment by him of those superannuation contributions;

(ii) if sub-paragraph (*d*)(i) does not apply to him and if he continues to be employed in reckonable service after the end of the month in which he is notified as required by sub-paragraph (*a*), the first day of the month commencing next after that notification; or

(iii) if neither sub-paragraph (*d*)(i) nor sub-paragraph (*d*)(ii) applies to him, the day on which he becomes employed in reckonable service; and

(*e*) his relevant age shall be his age on the day on which additional contributions commence to be payable by him.

(5) A former external contributor to whom paragraph (1)(*b*) applies may, within three months of being notified as required by paragraph (4)(*a*), elect that the period of service in respect of which additional contributions are by this regulation required to be paid by him by Method I or Method II, if it exceeds ten years, shall be reduced to such an extent as will result in his having not less than ten years of service counting for benefit; and, if the Secretary of State

accepts any such election, the period of service so reduced shall be substituted for the period specified in paragraph (4)(*c*).

(6) A former external contributor who under an external scheme was paying, or was or would have been liable to pay, contributions corresponding to additional contributions by a method corresponding to either Method I or Method II and who, after the external scheme ceased to be applicable to him and before becoming a contributor, had attained the age at which such contributions would have ceased to be payable by him shall pay additional contributions by, and of an amount determined in accordance with, Method III; and for that purpose—

(*a*) the Scheme shall be deemed to have commenced to apply to him on the day on which an external scheme first commenced to apply to him; and

(*b*) the period of previous service in respect of which additional contributions are payable shall be deemed to be a period equal to the difference between—

(i) the period of service in respect of which he was required or elected under the external scheme last applicable to him to pay contributions corresponding to additional contributions by a method corresponding to either Method I or Method II; and

(ii) the period or periods counting for benefit under any external Scheme previously applicable to him by reason of the payment by him of contributions corresponding to additional contributions.

(7) A former external contributor who was liable under an external scheme to pay contributions corresponding to additional contributions by a method corresponding to Method III shall, if he becomes a contributor, pay additional contributions by Method III; and, for the purpose of determining the amount thereof—

(*a*) the period of previous service shall be deemed to be the period by reference to which under the external scheme last applicable to him the amount of the contributions corresponding to additional contributions payable by him by a method corresponding to Method III was ascertainable, increased by any period of service since he last ceased to be employed in class A external service which has become reckonable service by virtue of interchange rules;

(*b*) the Scheme shall be deemed to have first become applicable to him on the day on which the external scheme last applicable to him became, or was deemed to have become, applicable to him for the purpose of ascertaining the amount of the contributions corresponding to additional contributions payable by him thereunder by a method corresponding to Method III; and

(*c*) there shall be deducted therefrom any amount previously paid by him by a method corresponding to Method III together with compound interest thereon calculated at three and a half per cent. per annum with yearly rests from the date of payment.

Additional Contributions after Termination of Service

36.—(1) In the case of a contributor who—

(*a*) was paying additional contributions by either Method I or Method II;

(*b*) ceased to be employed in reckonable service before attaining the age at which such contributions ceased to be payable;

(*c*) on ceasing to be so employed was qualified to be paid superannuation allowances on attaining pensionable age; and

(*d*) has not become a contributor under an external scheme

the balance of the additional contributions payable by him shall be paid by the surrender of the whole or a proportion of any terminal sum payable to or in respect of him.

(2) For the purposes of paragraph (1) the balance of the additional contributions payable by a contributor shall be the sum equal to the difference between the amount of such contributions already paid by him and the amount which would have been paid by him if he had continued to be employed in reckonable service until the end of the period during which such contributions would have been payable by him at—

(*a*) in the case of a contributor ceasing to be so employed before attaining the age of sixty, the rate of salary being paid to him immediately before he ceased to be so employed; and

(*b*) in the case of a contributor paying contributions by Method II and ceasing to be so employed after attaining the age of sixty and before attaining the age of sixty-five, a rate of salary equal to his average salary

together with, in the case of a contributor ceasing to be so employed before attaining the age of sixty, compound interest calculated at three and one half per cent. per annum with yearly rests from the date of his ceasing to be so employed on such part of that sum as bears the same proportion to the whole thereof as the length of the period from that date to the date of payment bears to the length of the period from that date to the date on which additional contributions would have ceased to be payable by him if he had not ceased to be so employed.

(3) In the case of a contributor who—

(*a*) was paying additional contributions by either Method I or Method II;

(*b*) ceased to be employed in reckonable service before attaining pensionable age;

(*c*) on ceasing to be so employed was not qualified to be paid superannuation allowances on attaining that age;

(*d*) had on ceasing to be so employed service counting for benefit amounting to not less than ten years; and

(*e*) subsequently became entitled to be paid superannuation allowances by virtue of employment or service other than reckonable service

the balance of the additional contributions payable by him shall be paid by the surrender of the whole or a proportion of any terminal sum payable to or in respect of him.

(4) For the purposes of paragraph (3) the balance of the additional contributions payable by a contributor shall be such an amount as shall be determined in accordance with Method III in respect of a period of previous service equal to the difference between—

(*a*) the period of previous service in respect of which he was required or elected under regulations 28 and 29 to pay additional contributions by Method I or Method II; and

(*b*) the period of his service counting for benefit by reason of the additional contributions paid by him by Method I or Method II while employed in reckonable service and not repaid to him.

Contributions during Intervals in Service

37. A contributor who pays under regulation 31 of the principal Teachers' Regulations superannuation contributions in respect of a period of absence from reckonable service shall continue to pay contributions under the Scheme and, for the purpose of determining the amount of such contributions, the amount of his salary shall be taken to be the same as for the purpose of the payment of superannuation contributions by him.

Payment of Outstanding Contributions

38.—(1) In this regulation "outstanding contributions" means the aggregate of—

(*a*) any amount due from a contributor in respect of normal contributions and additional contributions payable by Method I or Method II which have not been paid by him in accordance with the preceding provisions of this Part; and

(*b*) compound interest on any such amount calculated at four per cent. per annum with yearly rests from the day on which payment became due to the day on which payment is made.

(2) Subject as in paragraph (3) provided, a contributor who continues to be employed in reckonable service and would not be entitled to be paid superannuation allowances if he were to cease to be so employed may, with the consent of the Secretary of State, elect to pay outstanding contributions of £20 or more by further annual contributions of such amount as shall be actuarially equivalent thereto.

(3) In relation to further annual contributions payable by virtue of an election made under paragraph (2) the following provisions shall have effect—

(*a*) additional contributions payable by a contributor by Method I or Method II shall be increased by the amount of the further annual contributions;

(*b*) further annual contributions payable by a contributor who has not elected under regulation 28 to pay additional contributions by either Method I or Method II shall be payable as if they were additional contributions payable by whichever of those two Methods he shall, consistently with paragraphs (4) and (5) of regulation 28, elect;

(*c*) further annual contributions shall not be treated as additional contributions for the purposes of paragraphs (3) and (5) of regulation 34;

(*d*) a contributor paying additional contributions by Method I or Method II may not make an election under this regulation after attaining the age one year less than that at which such additional contributions cease to be payable by him; and

(*e*) not more than one election to pay further annual contributions may be made by a contributor.

(4) Any sum in respect of outstanding contributions due from a contributor when he ceases to be employed in reckonable service, dies or attains the age at which additional contributions cease to be payable by him shall be paid to the Secretary of State either—

(*a*) in such manner as may be agreed; or

(*b*) by the surrender of the whole or a portion of any terminal sum payable to or in respect of the contributor.

Contributions in respect of Deceased Teachers

39.—(1) In the case of a deceased teacher the contributions payable shall be the aggregate of—

(*a*) an amount equal to two per cent. of his salary from the commencement of the period during which he could elect that the Scheme should apply to him until his death; and

(*b*) an amount determined in accordance with Method III as if he were a contributor to whom the Scheme first became applicable on the date of the commencement of the said period.

(2) For the purposes of this regulation the previous service of a deceased teacher shall be taken to be the whole of his previous service not exceeding ten years.

(3) Contributions payable under this regulation shall be paid by the surrender of the whole or a proportion of any terminal sum payable in respect of a deceased teacher.

(4) If some or all of any terminal sum payable in respect of a deceased teacher has been paid, such proportion thereof as is required in order to make or complete the payment of contributions in accordance with this regulation shall be refunded to the Secretary of State.

Service Counting for Benefit

40.—(1) For the purposes of the Scheme the following shall be service counting for benefit:—

(*a*) in relation to every contributor, any period of reckonable service in respect of which the full amount of normal contributions is held in the Fund;

(*b*) in relation to every contributor other than a re-instated contributor and a former external contributor, any period of previous service in respect of which the full amount of additional contributions is held in the Fund;

(*c*) in relation to a re-instated contributor—

(i) any period to be treated as service counting for benefit as notified by the Secretary of State under regulation 34(3)(*a*); and

(ii) any other period of previous service in respect of which the full amount of additional contributions is held in the Fund;

(*d*) in relation to a former external contributor—

(i) any period counting for benefit for the purposes of an external scheme;

(ii) any period to be treated as service counting for benefit as notified by the Secretary of State under regulation 35(4)(*a*); and

(iii) any other period of previous service in respect of which the full amount of additional contributions is held in the Fund; and

(*e*) in relation to a deceased teacher, any period in respect of which the full amount of the contributions required to be paid by regulation 39 is held in the Fund.

(2) Where additional contributions are payable by a contributor by Method III and the amount of any terminal sum due to him is insufficient to enable payment to be made in full, then, unless payment of the deficiency is made in

some other manner, so much only of the period of previous service in respect of which the contributions were payable as would under regulation 33 have required the surrender of an amount equal to the terminal sum shall be service counting for benefit.

REPAYMENT OF CONTRIBUTIONS

When Contributions repayable

41.—(1) Such sums as are prescribed by the three regulations next following shall be paid to or in respect of a contributor by way of repayment of contributions paid by him—

(*a*) on his being repaid his superannuation contributions after ceasing to be employed in reckonable service;

(*b*) on his transfer to other employment if interchange rules apply to him on such transfer;

(*c*) on his becoming entitled to be paid superannuation allowances or a short service gratuity if he then has no wife;

(*d*) on his death if no pension is payable to his widow under the Scheme;

(*e*) on his becoming employed in class B external service if—

(i) his service counting for benefit is less than ten years; and

(ii) he elects within three months of becoming so employed that his contributions shall be repaid to him;

(*f*) on his becoming employed in class C external service if—

(i) he becomes liable to pay contributions under a scheme whereby the payment of pensions to or in respect of widows and children of persons employed in the same employment is legally secured, being a scheme under which for the purpose of determining the amount of such pension account is taken of reckonable service; and

(ii) he elects within three months of becoming so employed that his contributions shall be repaid to him; and

(*g*) on his becoming a person who fulfils the conditions specified in paragraph (2).

(2) The conditions referred to in paragraph (1)(*g*) are that a person—

(*a*) has ceased to be employed in reckonable service for more than one year;

(*b*) has been granted in respect of class B or class C external service any benefit by reason of having become permanently incapable through infirmity of mind or body of serving efficiently; and

(*c*) has service counting for benefit of less than ten years.

Amount when no Benefit payable

42. In the case of a contributor who—

(*a*) has service counting for benefit of less than three years;

(*b*) has service counting for benefit of less than ten years, no children and either no wife or a wife who has not attained the age of fifty; or

(*c*) has no children and also had no wife at any time while a contributor the sum to be paid under regulation 41 shall be the aggregate of both the normal and the additional contributions paid by him together with compound interest calculated as in regulation 74 provided.

Amount when Children's Pension only payable

43. In the case of a deceased contributor in respect of whom the only benefit payable under the Scheme is a children's pension the sum to be paid under regulation 41 shall be the aggregate of the additional contributions paid by him together with compound interest calculated as in regulation 74 provided.

Amount in other Cases

44. In the case of a contributor to whom neither regulation 42 nor regulation 43 applies the sum to be paid under regulation 41 shall be the aggregate of—

(*a*) half the normal contributions paid by him in respect of any period ending before the date on which he ceased to have a wife to whom in the event of his death a pension would have been payable under the Scheme;

(*b*) the normal contributions paid by him in respect of any other period; and

(*c*) the additional contributions paid by him

together with compound interest calculated as in regulation 74 provided.

Repayment of Repaid Normal Contributions

45.—(1) A re-instated contributor and a contributor under an external scheme who has repaid superannuation contributions repaid to him may, within three months of making such payment, also repay to the Secretary of State any sum paid to him by way of repayment of normal contributions and interest thereon, together with compound interest on that sum calculated at three and a half per cent. per annum with yearly rests from the day of its payment to him.

(2) A re-instated contributor who—

(*a*) has been paid superannuation allowances by reason of infirmity of mind or body or a short service gratuity; or

(*b*) has been paid under regulation 41(*e*) a sum by way of repayment of contributions; or

(*c*) both on ceasing to be employed in reckonable service and on again becoming employed in reckonable service, was subject to interchange rules

may, within three months of again becoming employed in reckonable service, repay to the Secretary of State any sum paid to him by way of repayment of normal contributions and interest thereon, together with compound interest on that sum calculated at three and a half per cent. per annum with yearly rests from the day of its payment to him.

BENEFITS

Widow's Pension

46.—(1) Subject as hereinafter provided, an annual widow's pension shall be paid to the widow of a contributor or a deceased teacher whose service counting for benefit amounts to not less than ten years and who—

(*a*) immediately prior to his death was entitled to be paid superannuation allowances;

(*b*) having ceased to be employed in reckonable service before attaining pensionable age was qualified on so ceasing to be paid superannuation allowances on attaining that age; or (*c*) was within one year before his death employed in reckonable service or class A external service or in service which would have been such service if he had not attained the age of seventy.

(2) A widow's pension shall not be paid to a widow whose marriage with a deceased contributor took place after he became entitled to be paid superannuation allowances by virtue of regulation 41(1)(*b*) of the principal Teachers' Regulations unless he subsequently again became employed in reckonable service.

Amount of Widow's Pension

47.—(1) The annual amount of a widow's pension shall, unless her husband was at any time a contributor under an external scheme, be determined in accordance with the provisions of this regulation.

(2) Except in the cases specified in paragraph (3), the annual amount of a widow's pension shall be not less than—

(*a*) £125 if her husband, on or after 10th December 1968, ceased to be employed in reckonable service or died while so employed; or

(*b*) £115 if sub-paragraph (*a*) does not apply.

(3) The following are the cases referred to in paragraph (2):—

(*a*) a widow whose husband, not having been qualified on last ceasing to be employed in reckonable service to be paid superannuation allowances on attaining pensionable age, subsequently became entitled to be paid such allowances by virtue of employment or service other than reckonable service; and

(*b*) a widow whose husband, after last ceasing to be employed in reckonable service, was granted in respect of class B or class C external service any benefit by reason of having become permanently incapable through infirmity of mind or body of serving efficiently.

(4) In the case of the widow of a contributor or deceased teacher whose service counting for benefit is equal to the whole of his reckonable service the annual amount of the widow's pension shall be:—

(*a*) if at the time of his death an annual superannuation allowance was payable to him, one-third of that allowance; or

(*b*) if at the time of his death he had ceased to be employed in reckonable service and had not attained pensionable age, one-third of the annual superannuation allowance which would have been payable to him on attaining that age; or

(*c*) if at the time of his death he had attained pensionable age and was employed in class B external service, one-third of the annual superannuation allowance which would have been payable to him if on the day of his death he had ceased to be so employed; or

(*d*) if regulation 46(1)(*c*) applies and neither sub-paragraph (*b*) nor sub-paragraph (*c*) of this paragraph applies, one-third of the annual superannuation allowance which would have been payable to him if on the day of his death he had ceased to be employed in reckonable service by reason of having become permanently incapable through infirmity of mind or body of serving efficiently as a teacher in reckonable service.

(5) In the case of the widow of a contributor or deceased teacher whose service counting for benefit is not equal to the whole of his reckonable service the annual amount of the widow's pension shall be the amount which bears to the amount that would be payable under paragraph (4), if that paragraph were applicable, the same proportion as the service counting for benefit bears to the whole of his reckonable service of which account was, or would have been, taken for the purpose of calculating the rate of his annual superannuation allowance.

(6) For the purposes of this regulation the amount of an annual superannuation allowance shall be deemed to be the amount that would be payable by way of such allowance if—

(*a*) any modification of Section 4(3) of the Act of 1967 made by regulation 77 of the principal Teachers' Regulations were disregarded;

(*b*) no addition were made under regulation 83(1) of the principal Teachers' Regulations to the period of service by reference to which it is calculated;

(*c*) any period of employment to which regulation 41(3) of the principal Teachers' Regulations applies were not disregarded for the purpose of determining entitlement to superannuation allowances; and

(*d*) there were disregarded—

(i) any reduction or withholding thereof under regulation 52 or regulation 54 of the principal Teachers' Regulations;

(ii) the surrender of any part thereof in return for the grant of a pension or other like benefit to a widow or dependant; and

(iii) any modification thereof in consequence of the National Insurance Act 1965(**a**).

(7) For the purpose of determining the amount of a widow's pension payable to the widow of a contributor or deceased teacher who was employed in class A external service but not at any time a contributor under an external scheme—

(*a*) his annual superannuation allowance shall be deemed to be increased by the amount of any like allowance payable in respect of his class A external service; and

(*b*) his reckonable service shall be deemed to be increased by his class A external service.

Duration of Widow's Pension

48.—(1) A widow's pension shall begin to accrue on the day following the death of her husband unless she is then co-habiting with a man.

(2) A widow's pension shall cease to be paid on her death, on her commencing to co-habit with a man to whom she is not married and, unless the Secretary of State otherwise decides, on her re-marriage.

(3) Payment of a widow's pension which has not been made, or which has been discontinued, by reason of her re-marriage or her co-habitation with a man may, if the Secretary of State so decides, be made or resumed, as the case may be, on her again becoming a widow or after the termination of the co-habitation.

(**a**) 1965 c. 51.

Short Service Widow's Pension

49.—(1) Subject as hereinafter provided, an annual short service widow's pension shall be paid to the widow of a contributor or deceased teacher—

(*a*) whose service counting for benefit amounts to less than ten years but not less than three years;

(*b*) who was either—

(i) employed in reckonable service or class A external service within one year before his death; or

(ii) was entitled on his last ceasing to be so employed to annual superannuation allowances by virtue of regulation 41(1)(*b*) of the principal Teachers' Regulations or to a short service gratuity; and

(*c*) who is survived by either—

(i) an eligible child or children; or

(ii) a widow who attained the age of fifty on or before the day of his death.

(2) A short service widow's pension shall not be paid to a widow whose marriage with a deceased contributor took place after he became entitled to be paid superannuation allowances by virtue of regulation 41(1)(*b*) of the principal Teachers' Regulations or a short service gratuity unless he subsequently again became employed in reckonable service.

Amount of Short Service Widow's Pension

50. Subject as in regulation 55 provided, the annual amount of a short service widow's pension shall be the amount which, opposite to the number in column (1) of the following Table of the years of service counting for benefit of her husband, is specified—

(*a*) in column (2) thereof, in the case of a widow whose husband, on or after 10th December 1968, ceased to be employed in reckonable service or class A external service or died while so employed; or

(*b*) in column (3) thereof, in any other case:—

TABLE

(1) Years of Service	(2) Annual Amount	(3) Annual Amount
3	£63	£58
4	£71	£66
5	£80	£74
6	£89	£82
7	£98	£90
8	£107	£98
9	£116	£106

Duration of Short Service Widow's Pension

51.—(1) The provisions of regulation 48 shall apply to a short service widow's pension as they apply to a widow's pension.

(2) Subject as in paragraph (1) provided, a short service widow's pension payable to a widow who has not attained the age of fifty shall be discontinued when there ceases to be any incapacitated child or any other eligible child of her husband who has not attained the age of nineteen.

Children's Pension

52. Subject as in regulation 54 provided, an annual children's pension shall be paid to or for the benefit of an eligible child or eligible children of a deceased contributor or deceased teacher to whose widow there is payable or would be payable if he were survived by a widow who neither re-marries nor co-habits with a man, either—

(*a*) a widow's pension under regulation 46; or

(*b*) a short service widow's pension under regulation 49.

Amount of children's Pension

53.—(1) Subject as hereafter in this regulation and in regulation 55 provided, the annual amount of a children's pension shall be the amount which, opposite to the number of eligible children in respect of whom it is for the time being payable specified in column (1) of the following Table, is specified—

(*a*) under letter A in column (2) or column (3) thereof, whichever column shall for the time being be appropriate, where the pension is payable to or for the benefit of a child or children of a contributor or deceased teacher who, on or after 10th December 1968, ceased to be employed in reckonable service or class A external service or died while so employed; or

(*b*) under letter B in column (2) or (3) thereof, whichever column shall for the time being be appropriate, in any other case:—

TABLE

(1) Number of Eligible Children	(2) Annual Amount of Pension where there is a Surviving Widow of the Contributor or Deceased Teacher		(3) Annual Amount of Pension where there is not a Surviving Widow of the Contributor or Deceased Teacher	
	A	B	A	B
1	£65	£60	£95	£85
2	£120	£110	£180	£165
3	£175	£160	£265	£245
4 or more	£230	£210	£355	£325

(2) Where the eligible child or eligible children to or for whose benefit a children's pension is payable is or include an incapacitated child who has attained the age of sixteen the annual amount of the pension shall be the aggregate of the following two amounts:—

(*a*) the amount for the time being payable under paragraph (1) in respect of four or more eligible children ; and (*b*) the amount, if any, for the time being payable under paragraph (1) in respect of any other eligible children not exceeding three in number.

(3) If an eligible child who has attained the age of sixteen and to whom, or for whose benefit, a children's pension is payable is in receipt of remuneration at a yearly rate in excess of £115, or such other amount as may from time to time be substituted for £115 in section 10(5) of the Income and Corporation Taxes Act 1970(**a**), in respect of full-time training for a trade, profession or calling, the annual amount of the pension shall be reduced by the amount of the excess, or, if it would result in a smaller reduction of the pension, the child shall be disregarded for the purpose of calculating the amount of the pension.

Duration of Children's Pension

54.—(1) A children's pension shall begin to accrue on the day following the death of the contributor or deceased teacher to or for the benefit of whose eligible child or children it is payable.

(2) A children's pension shall be discontinued—

(*a*) in a case to which regulation 52(*a*) applies on there ceasing to be an eligible child to or for whose benefit such pension is payable; and

(*b*) in a case to which regulation 52(*b*) applies, on there ceasing to be either any incapacitated child or any other eligible child under the age of nineteen to or for whose benefit such pension is payable.

Benefits in respect of Contributors under External Schemes

55.—(1) In relation to a contributor in respect of whom benefits are payable both under the Scheme and under an external scheme the annual amount of a widow's pension, short service widow's pension and children's pension shall be such an amount as bears the same proportion to the annual amount thereof which would be payable by virtue of his total service counting for benefit as the amount defined in sub-paragraph (*a*) of paragraph (2) bears to the total of the latter amount and the amount defined in sub-paragraph (*b*) of that paragraph.

(2) The amounts referred to in paragraph (1) shall be—

(*a*) the amount held in the Fund or due thereto which represents the normal and additional contributions paid or payable by or in respect of the contributor, together with compound interest thereon calculated at three and one half per cent. per annum with yearly rests from 1st October in the year in which any such contribution was paid to the end of the month immediately preceding the day on which such amount is determined;

(*b*) the amount of the contributions paid or payable by or in respect of the contributor under an external scheme, together with compound interest thereon calculated at three and one half per cent. per annum with yearly rests from 1st October in the year in which any such contribution was paid or became due to the end of the month immediately preceding the day on which such amount is determined.

(3) For the purposes of this regulation any additional contributions payable by Method III in respect of a period of previous service included in the service counting for benefit shall be deemed to have been paid in full.

(**a**) 1970 c. 10.

PART V

TEACHERS' DEPENDANTS' PENSION SCHEME

PRELIMINARY

The Scheme

56. The Scheme established by Part V of the Regulations of 1966 for securing the payment of pensions to or for the benefit of persons wholly or mainly dependant on teachers (not being persons to whom or for whose benefit pensions may be paid under the Teachers' Widows' and Children's Pension Scheme) shall be continued and be administered in accordance with the provisions of this Part under the name of the Teachers' Dependants' Pension Scheme (hereafter in this Part referred to as "the Scheme").

NOMINATION OF DEPENDANTS

Dependants

57.—(1) The persons to whom or for whose benefit pensions may be paid under the Scheme (hereafter in this Part referred to as "dependants") shall be persons nominated to the Secretary of State by a teacher and shall at the time of nomination be wholly or mainly dependant on the teacher.

(2) A dependant shall be a person who is related to the teacher by whom he is nominated in one of the following ways:—

(*a*) husband;

(*b*) son, step-son, daughter or step-daughter who is not an eligible child for the purposes of Part IV;

(*c*) father or step-father;

(*d*) mother or step-mother;

(*e*) brother or sister;

(*f*) grandson or granddaughter, being the son or daughter of a deceased son or daughter of the teacher;

(*g*) nephew or niece, being the son or daughter of a deceased brother or sister of the teacher.

(3) At the time of nomination a female dependant shall be unmarried and a dependant nominated for a temporary pension shall be under the age of sixteen.

Nomination by Teachers

58.—(1) A teacher who is employed in reckonable service may make a nomination in favour of a dependant if he has been so employed for not less than three years and has not attained the age of fifty-five.

(2) Without prejudice to the provisions of paragraph (1) above, a teacher who, while employed in class A external service made a valid nomination of a dependant under a scheme corresponding to the Scheme, may nominate the same dependant if—

(*a*) on ceasing to be so employed he was not entitled to superannuation benefits in respect of his class A external service and has not been repaid the superannuation contributions paid by him in respect of that service; and (*b*) he becomes employed in reckonable service within one year of ceasing to be employed in class A external service.

(3) Subject as in paragraphs (1), (4) and (5) provided, a teacher may make a further nomination either in favour of a dependant already nominated by him or of another dependant if since his last previous nomination, either—

(*a*) his salary has increased by not less than £120 a year; or

(*b*) not less than three years have elapsed.

(4) A nomination or further nomination shall not be made by a teacher if it would result in there being at one time more than the following dependants nominated by him—

(*a*) nominated for life pensions: one adult and one incapacitated child of whom the teacher is the parent; and

(*b*) nominated for temporary pensions: three children:

Provided that a woman teacher may nominate her husband in addition to the dependants specified above.

(5) A nomination or further nomination shall not be made by a teacher if it would result in there being payable to or in respect of dependants nominated by him pensions the total annual value of which would exceed one-sixth of his annual salary at the time of making the nomination:

Provided that—

(*a*) a woman teacher who nominates her husband for a life pension may—

(i) nominate him for a life pension not exceeding one-sixth of her salary at the time of nomination; and

(ii) nominate another adult for a life pension not exceeding one-sixth of her salary at the time of nomination; and

(iii) nominate her incapacitated child for a life pension not exceeding £230 a year; and

(iv) nominate not more than three children each for temporary pensions not exceeding £60 a year;

(*b*) a teacher who is unmarried may—

(i) nominate an adult for a life pension not exceeding one-sixth of his salary at the time of the nomination; and

(ii) nominate his incapacitated child for a life pension not exceeding £350 a year; and

(iii) nominate not more than three children each for temporary pensions not exceeding £80 a year.

Validity of Nominations

59.—(1) A nomination made by a teacher shall not be valid unless the Secretary of State is satisfied—

(*a*) that the requirements of regulations 57 and 58 are satisfied in respect of the dependant nominated; and

(*b*) that the teacher is, at the time of making the nomination, in good health, regard being had to his age.

(2) For the purpose of paragraph 1(*b*) the Secretary of State may require the teacher to be examined by a duly qualified medical practitioner designated by him.

Avoidance of Nominations

60. A nomination of a dependant shall become void—

(*a*) on the receipt by the Secretary of State of a written notice of revocation from the teacher by whom it was made;

(*b*) on the dependant ceasing to be wholly or mainly dependant on the teacher by whom he was nominated;

(*c*) on the death of the dependant;

(*d*) on the marriage of the dependant if female;

(*e*) on the attainment of the age of sixteen by a dependant nominated for a temporary pension;

(*f*) on the dependant becoming a person to whom or for whose benefit a pension is or may become payable under Part IV;

(*g*) on the teacher by whom it was made being repaid his superannuation contributions after ceasing to be employed in reckonable service; and

(*h*) on the teacher by whom it was made ceasing to be employed in reckonable service for a period exceeding one year without entitlement to superannuation allowances or a short service gratuity unless, having become employed in class A external service, he nominates the dependant and pays contributions in respect of him under a scheme corresponding to the Scheme.

CONTRIBUTIONS

Payment of Contributions

61. For the purposes of defraying the cost of the benefits under the Scheme every teacher by whom a nomination has been made shall pay contributions in respect thereof to the Secretary of State.

Amount of Contributions

62.—(1) Except as in paragraph (2) provided, the contributions to be paid by a teacher in respect of every nomination made by him shall be at a rate to be determined by the Government Actuary or Deputy Government Actuary as at the date of nomination and shall be of a fixed annual amount according to the age and sex of the teacher, the amount and type of the pension which will be payable, the age of the nominee, and, in the case of a life pension, the sex of the nominee.

(2) The contributions to be paid by a teacher in respect of a nomination to which regulation 58(2) applies shall be—

(*a*) the amount of the arrears of the contributions which would, if he had continued to be employed in class A external service, have been payable in respect of the dependant from the time of ceasing to be so employed until becoming employed in reckonable service; and

(*b*) further contributions at the rate at which he was previously paying contributions in respect of the dependant.

Duration of Contributions

63.—(1) Contributions in respect of a nomination shall commence to be payable from the first day of the month commencing next after the Secretary of State sends by post to the teacher by whom it was made a notification that it has been accepted.

(2) Contributions in respect of a nomination shall cease to be payable by the teacher by whom it was made on—

(*a*) his attaining the age of sixty; or

(*b*) on his ceasing to be employed in reckonable service; or

(*c*) on the nomination becoming void.

Contributions in respect of Intervals in Service

64. Where a teacher who is not qualified to be granted superannuation allowances and has not been repaid his superannuation contributions again becomes employed in reckonable service after ceasing to be so employed for a period not exceeding one year, he shall pay the contributions in respect of any nomination made by him which would have been payable by him if he had continued to be so employed throughout that period.

Payment of Contributions on Death

65.—(1) Where a teacher dies while employed in reckonable service or within one year of ceasing to be so employed—

(*a*) any sums due from him at the date of his death by way of contributions in respect of any nomination; and

(*b*) any sum necessary to complete the payment by him of contributions for one year in respect of any nomination

shall be paid by the surrender of the whole or a proportion of any terminal sum payable in respect of him or, if such sum is insufficient for the purpose, may be paid in such other manner as may be agreed.

(2) Where a teacher dies before attaining pensionable age, having previously ceased to be employed in reckonable service and being qualified on so ceasing to be paid superannuation allowances on attaining that age, any sums due from him by way of contributions in respect of any nomination, together with compound interest thereon calculated at four per cent. per annum with yearly rests, shall be paid by the surrender of the whole or a proportion of any terminal sum payable in respect of him.

Repayment of Contributions

66. A sum equal to one-half of the contributions paid by a teacher in respect of the nomination of a dependant for a life pension shall, together with compound interest thereon calculated as in regulation 74 provided, be repaid to him—

(*a*) on his being repaid his superannuation contributions after ceasing to be employed in reckonable service; or

(*b*) unless he has become employed in class A external service and has made a valid nomination of the same dependant under the scheme applicable to that employment corresponding to the Scheme, on his ceasing to be employed in reckonable service for a period exceeding one year without entitlement to superannuation allowances or a short service gratuity.

Benefits

Entitlement to Pensions

67. Pensions shall be payable under the Scheme to or in respect of a dependant on the death of the teacher by whom he was nominated if—

(*a*) the nomination has not become void;

(*b*) contributions for not less than one year have been paid in respect of the nomination; and

(*c*) the teacher dies—

(i) while employed in reckonable service; or

(ii) after ceasing to be so employed, having been on so ceasing either entitled to be paid superannuation allowances by virtue of regulation 41(1)(*b*) of the principal Teachers' Regulations or a short service gratuity or qualified to be paid superannuation allowances on attaining pensionable age; or

(iii) within one year of ceasing to be so employed and any contributions outstanding at the date of his death are paid in accordance with regulation 65; or

(iv) while employed in class A external service, having made a valid nomination of the dependant under the scheme applicable to that employment corresponding to the Scheme.

Life and Temporary Pensions

68.—(1) Pensions payable under the Scheme shall be —

(*a*) life pensions, if at the time of nomination the dependant is over the age of sixteen or is incapacitated; or

(*b*) temporary pensions in other cases

and "life pension" and "temporary pension" shall in this Part be construed accordingly.

Amounts of Pensions

69.—(1) Subject to the provisions of regulation 58 and of paragraphs (2) and (3)—

(*a*) the annual amount of a life pension shall be such amount, being a multiple of £10 not less than £30, as the teacher shall determine at the time of making the nomination of the dependant to or in respect of whom it is payable;

(*b*) the annual amount of a temporary pension shall be such of the following sums, that is to say, £30, £40, £50 or £60, as the teacher shall determine at the time of making the nomination of the dependant to or in respect of whom it is payable.

(2) The annual amount of a pension payable under the Scheme to or in respect of a dependant to or in respect of whom a pension is also payable under a scheme applicable to class A external service corresponding to the Scheme shall be such an amount as bears the same proportion to the amount thereof determined under the foregoing provisions of this Part as the amount determined under sub-paragraph (*a*) below bears to the amount determined under sub-paragraph (*b*) b ow—

(*a*) the amount held in the Fund which represents contributions paid in respect of the dependant, together with compound interest on any such contributions calculated at three and a half per cent. per annum with yearly rests from 1st October in the year in which it was paid to the end of the month immediately preceding the day on which such amount is determined;

(*b*) the total of the amount determined under sub-paragraph (*a*) and the amount of the contributions paid in respect of the dependant under any scheme applicable to class A external service corresponding to the Scheme, together with compound interest on any such contributions calculated at three and a half per cent. per annum with yearly rests from 1st October in the year in which it was paid to the end of the month immediately preceding the day on which such amount is determined.

(3) Where the teacher who nominated the dependant to whom a pension is payable ceased to be employed in reckonable service before attaining the age of sixty, being then qualified to be paid superannuation allowances on attaining that age, the annual amount of the pension shall be reduced by such amount as shall be appropriate having regard to the amount by which the contributions actually paid is less than those which would have been paid if the teacher had continued to be employed in reckonable service until attaining the age of sixty.

Duration of Pensions

70.—(1) A life pension and a temporary pension shall begin to accrue on the day following the death of the teacher by whom the dependant to or in respect of whom it is payable was nominated.

(2) A life pension shall cease to be paid on the death of the dependant to or in respect of whom it is payable, or, in the case of a female dependant, on her marriage.

(3) A temporary pension shall cease to be paid on the death of the dependant to or in respect of whom it is payable or on his attaining the age of sixteen, whichever shall first occur.

PART VI

MISCELLANEOUS AND SUPPLEMENTARY

Functions of Secretary of State and Employers

71.—(1) The Secretary of State shall—

(*a*) maintain records of all elections made under Part IV and of all valid nominations made under Part V;

(*b*) receive all contributions payable under Parts IV and V and arrange for the amounts thereof to be credited to the Fund as provided in Part III;

(*c*) make all payments of benefits and other sums under these Regulations and arrange for the amounts thereof to be debited to the Fund as provided in Part III; and

(*d*) maintain records of all such contributions and of all such payments of benefits and other sums.

(2) Local education authorities and other employers of teachers to whom the Teachers' Widows' and Children's Pension Scheme applies or by whom valid nominations have been made for the purposes of the Teachers' Dependants' Pension Scheme shall—

(*a*) maintain records of the contributions collected for the purposes of each of the Schemes from such teachers employed by them; and

(*b*) make to the Secretary of State such reports and returns and give him such information relating to such teachers as he may require for the purposes of his functions under these Regulations.

(3) Expenses incurred by the Secretary of State and by local education authorities and other employers of teachers for the purposes of the Schemes shall not be charged to the Fund but shall be deemed to be contributions thereto by the Secretary of State or the local education authorities or other employers, as the case may be.

Supplementary Provisions as to Contributions

72.—(1) The provisions of the principal Teachers' Regulations specified in paragraph (2) shall apply in relation to contributions payable under these Regulations (other than additional contributions payable by Method III) in like manner as they apply in relation to superannuation contributions.

(2) The following are the provisions referred to in paragraph (1):—

regulation 20, relating to the payment of contributions by deduction from salary;

regulation 21, relating to the payment of contributions direct to the Secretary of State; and

regulation 27, relating to interest on overdue contributions.

(3) Where a payment on account of contributions payable under these Regulations (other than additional contributions payable by Method III) is less than the amount due, then, without prejudice to regulation 38—

(*a*) there shall be deducted therefrom such an amount as is required to meet any liability in respect of interest under regulation 27 of the principal Teachers' Regulations as applied by this regulation; and

(*b*) the remainder thereof shall be appropriated as the payment for such part of the period in respect of which contributions are payable as the Secretary of State may think fit.

Limitation of Amount of Contributions

73.—(1) Notwithstanding any preceding provisions of these Regulations the aggregate amount of the sums payable by a teacher in any year as—

(*a*) superannuation contributions;

(*b*) normal contributions;

(*c*) additional contributions payable by either Method I or Method II;

(*d*) further annual contributions payable under regulation 38; and

(*e*) contributions payable under Part V

shall not exceed fifteen per cent. of his salary for that year.

(2) For the purposes of this regulation—

(*a*) the amount of the superannuation contributions payable by a teacher shall be deemed to be—

(i) the amount thereof before any modification in consequence of the National Insurance Act 1965; and

(ii) not less than six per cent. nor more than thirteen per cent. of his salary for the year; and

(*b*) "year" means a year of assessment for the purposes of income tax.

Interest on Repaid Contributions

74. Where contributions are repaid under Part IV or Part V compound interest shall be added thereto and, for that purpose, shall be calculated at the rate of three per cent. per annum with yearly rests from 1st October in the year in which the contributions were paid to the day specified in column (2) of the following Table opposite to the paragraph of regulation 41 or regulation 66 by virtue of which the repayment is made specified in column (1) thereof:—

TABLE

(1) Paragraph	(2) Day to which compound interest is to be calculated
Paragraph (*a*) of regulation 41 and paragraph (*a*) of regulation 66	The day three months after that on which the person by whom the contributions were paid last ceased to be employed in reckonable service or class A or class B external service or the day on which he attained the age of seventy, whichever shall be the earlier.
Paragraph (*b*) of regulation 41	The day on which interchange rules become applicable to the person by whom the contributions were paid.
Paragraph (*c*) of regulation 41	The day on which the person by whom the contributions were paid becomes entitled to be paid superannuation allowances or a short service gratuity.
Paragraph (*d*) of regulation 41	The day on which the person by whom the contributions were paid dies.
Paragraphs (*e*), (*f*) and (*g*) of regulation 41	The day three months after that on which the person by whom the contributions were paid last ceased to be employed in reckonable service or class A external service.
Paragraph (*b*) of regulation 66	The day one year after that on which the person by whom the contributions were paid ceased to be employed in reckonable service.

Deductions from Repaid Contributions

75. Any contributions repaid under Part IV or Part V and any interest added thereto shall be reduced by a sum equal to the amount of any income tax payable in consequence of such repayment and addition.

Payment of Pensions

76. Every pension and other sum payable under these Regulations shall, unless it consists of a single payment, be paid monthly in arrear with proportionate payment on death or other terminating event.

Payments in respect of Deceased Persons

77. On the death of a person to whom or to whose estate any sum not exceeding £500 is due under these Regulations the Secretary of State may, without probate or other proof of title, pay the said sum to the persons appearing to him to be beneficially entitled to the personal estate of the deceased, or, as he thinks fit, to one or more of those persons or distribute it among all or any of those persons in such proportion as he may determine.

Payments in respect of Minors and Infirm Persons

78. If a person to or in respect of whom a pension or other sum is payable under these Regulations is a minor, or, in the opinion of the Secretary of State, is incapable by reason of infirmity of mind or body of managing his affairs, the Secretary of State may pay the pension or other sum to any person having the care of that person, and, insofar as it is not so paid, may apply it in such manner as he thinks fit for the benefit of that person or his dependants.

Remission of Debts to Fund

79. The Secretary of State may remit the payment of any sum due to him and payable into the Fund—

(*a*) if it is less than £50; and

(*b*) on the recommendation of the Board, if it is £50 or more.

Benefits not Assignable

80.—(1) Subject to the following provisions of this regulation every assignment of or charge on, and every agreement to assign or charge, any pension payable under these Regulations shall be void.

(2) On the bankruptcy of a person entitled to any such pension, it shall not pass to any trustee or other person acting on behalf of the creditors.

(3) Nothing in the preceding provisions of this regulation shall affect the powers of the court under Section 51(2) of the Bankruptcy Act 1914**(a)** (under which the court may order the payment of the whole or part of certain sums to the trustee in bankruptcy).

Provision of Information

81. Every teacher affected by these Regulations or, if he is dead, his personal representatives, and every person by or in respect of whom any benefit or payment is claimed under these Regulations, shall give such information and produce such documents to the Secretary of State as he may require for the purposes of his functions under these Regulations.

(a) 1914 c. 59.

Extension of Time

82. The Secretary of State may extend the time within which anything is required or authorised to be done under the provisions of these Regulations if he considers that there are reasonable grounds for so doing.

Determination of Questions

83. Any question arising under these Regulations as to—

(*a*) any election;

(*b*) any nomination;

(*c*) liability to pay and the amount of any contributions;

(*d*) the period which in relation to a re-instated contributor or a former external contributor is to be treated under regulation 34 or, as the case may be, regulation 35 as service counting for benefit;

(*e*) the amount by which a pension payable to or in respect of a dependant is to be reduced under regulation 69(3); and

(*f*) the entitlement to receive and the amount of any benefit or payment

shall be decided by the Secretary of State and his decision thereon shall be final.

SCHEDULE 1 Regulations 31 and 32

RATES OF ADDITIONAL CONTRIBUTIONS—METHODS I AND II

(1) Age on date from which additional contributions payable		(2) Percentage of Salary (Method I)	(3) Percentage of Salary (Method II)
Years	Completed months		
24 or under	—	·05	—
25	—	·05	—
26	—	·05	—
27	—	·06	—
28	—	·06	—
29	—	·06	—
30	—	·07	·06
31	—	·07	·06
32	—	·08	·07
33	—	·08	·07
34	—	·09	·08
35	—	·09	·08
36	—	·10	·09
37	—	·10	·09
38	—	·11	·10
39	—	·11	·10
40	—	·12	·10
41	—	·13	·11
42	—	·14	·12

SCHEDULE 1—continued

(1) Age on date from which additional contributions payable		(2) Percentage of Salary (Method I)	(3) Percentage of Salary (Method II)
Years	Completed months		
43	—	·15	·12
44	—	·15	·13
45	—	·16	·13
46	—	·18	·14
47	—	·20	·15
48	—	·21	·16
49	—	·23	·17
50	—	·25	·18
51	—	·28	·19
52	—	·31	·20
53	—	·35	·22
54	—	·41	·24
55	—	·46	·26
	1	·46	·26
	2	·47	·26
	3	·48	·26
	4	·49	·26
	5	·50	·27
	6	·51	·27
	7	·52	·27
	8	·53	·27
	9	·54	·28
	10	·55	·28
	11	·56	·28
56	—	·57	·28
	1	·58	·29
	2	·59	·29
	3	·60	·29
	4	·61	·29
	5	·62	·30
	6	·63	·30
	7	·65	·30
	8	·67	·30
	9	·69	·31
	10	·71	·31
	11	·73	·31
57	—	·75	·32
	1	·77	·32
	2	·79	·32
	3	·81	·32
	4	·84	·33
	5	·86	·33
	6	·89	·33

SCHEDULE 1—continued

(1) Age on date from which additional contributions payable		(2) Percentage of Salary (Method 1)	(3) Percentage of Salary (Method II)
Years	Completed months		
	7	·92	·34
	8	·95	·34
	9	·99	·34
	10	1·03	·35
	11	1·07	·35
58	—	1·11	·36
	1	1·16	·36
	2	1·21	·36
	3	1·27	·37
	4	1·33	·37
	5	1·40	·38
	6	1·48	·38
	7	1·57	·38
	8	1·67	·39
	9	1·78	·39
	10	1·90	·40
	11	2·00	·40
59	—	—	·41
	1	—	·41
	2	—	·42
	3	—	·42
	4	—	·43
	5	—	·43
	6	—	·44
	7	—	·44
	8	—	·45
	9	—	·45
	10	—	·46
	11	—	·46
60	—	—	·46
	1	—	·46
	2	—	·47
	3	—	·48
	4	—	·49
	5	—	·50
	6	—	·51
	7	—	·52
	8	—	·53
	9	—	·54
	10	—	·55
	11	—	·56
61	—	—	·57
	1	—	·58

SCHEDULE 1—continued

(1) Age on date from which additional contributions payable		(2) Percentage of Salary (Method I)	(3) Percentage of Salary (Method II)
Years	Completed months		
	2	—	·59
	3	—	·60
	4	—	·61
	5	—	·62
	6	—	·63
	7	—	·65
	8	—	·67
	9	—	·69
	10	—	·71
	11	—	·73
62	—	—	·75
	1	—	·77
	2	—	·79
	3	—	·81
	4	—	·84
	5	—	·86
	6	—	·89
	7	—	·92
	8	—	·95
	9	—	·99
	10	—	1·03
	11	—	1·07
63	—	—	1·11
	1	—	1·16
	2	—	1·21
	3	—	1·27
	4	—	1·33
	5	—	1·40
	6	—	1·48
	7	—	1·57
	8	—	1·67
	9	—	1·78
	10	—	1·90
	11	—	2·00

SCHEDULE 2 Regulation 33

RATES OF ADDITIONAL CONTRIBUTIONS—METHOD III

(1) Age	(2) Percentage of average salary	(3) Percentage of average salary
24 or under	3·1	3·1
25	3·2	3·2
26	3·2	3·2
27	3·2	3·2
28	3·2	3·2
29	3·2	3·2
30	3·3	3·3
31	3·3	3·3
32	3·3	3·3
33	3·3	3·3
34	3·3	3·3
35	3·3	3·3
36	3·2	3·2
37	3·2	3·2
38	3·2	3·2
39	3·2	3·2
40	3·2	3·2
41	3·1	3·1
42	3·1	3·1
43	3·1	3·1
44	3·1	3·1
45	3·0	3·1
46	2·9	3·0
47	2·8	3·0
48	2·7	3·0
49	2·6	2·9
50	2·5	2·9
51	2·5	2·9
52	2·5	2·8
53	2·5	2·8
54	2·5	2·7
55	2·5	2·7
56	2·5	2·6
57	2·5	2·6
58	2·5	2·5
59	2·4	2·4
60	2·3	2·3
61	2·3	2·3
62	2·2	2·2
63	2·2	2·2
64 or over	2·1	2·1

Given under the Official Seal of the Secretary of State for Education and Science on 28th May 1970.

(L.S.)

Edward Short,
Secretary of State for Education and Science.

Consent of the Minister for the Civil Service given under his Official Seal on 3rd June 1970.

(L.S.)

K. H. McNeill,
Authorised by the Minister for the Civil Service.

EXPLANATORY NOTE

(*This Note is not part of the Regulations.*)

These Regulations consolidate with amendments the existing regulations relating to the payment of pensions to the widows or widowers of teachers and their children and other dependants.

The principal amendments are:—

(*a*) All men teachers entering service for the first time are now (and have been since 1st April 1969) required to participate in the Teachers' Widows' and Children's Pension Scheme and the only option whether to do so or not is for men teachers returning to service for the first time since 1st April 1966 (regulation 23).

(*b*) Provision is made to enable a teacher to increase his service counting for benefit by paying additional contributions in respect of teaching service in the United Kingdom, the Isle of Man or the Channel Islands on repayment of personal superannuation contributions in respect of that service previously withdrawn by him (regulation 29).

(*c*) A teacher who left pensionable service prematurely without qualification for any pension but subsequently completed the qualifying period for his own pension by some other employment will be able to pay the appropriate contributions and a pension will be payable to his widow (regulations 36(3) and 46).

(*d*) Sums owing by reason of non-payment of contributions may be settled by periodic payments (regulation 38).

(*e*) Pensions will be paid to or in respect of the widow and children of a teacher who has less than ten years' service counting for benefit and to whom superannuation benefits or a short service gratuity were payable on the ground of ill health (regulation 49).

(*f*) The Secretary of State is authorised to remit debts to the Teachers' Family Benefits Fund (regulation 79).

1970 No. 863

PENSIONS

The Superannuation (Teaching and Northern Ireland Civil Service) Interchange Rules 1970

Made - - - *3rd June* 1970

* *To be laid before Parliament*

Coming into Operation *10th July* 1970

The Secretary of State for Education and Science, with the consent of the Minister for the Civil Service, in exercise of the powers conferred on him by sections 2 and 15 of the Superannuation (Miscellaneous Provisions) Act 1948(**a**), as amended by section 11 of the Superannuation (Miscellaneous Provisions) Act 1967(**b**) and the Minister for the Civil Service Order 1968(**c**), hereby makes the following Rules :—

PART I

GENERAL

Citation and Commencement

1. These Rules may be cited as the Superannuation (Teaching and Northern Ireland Civil Service) Interchange Rules 1970 and shall come into operation on 10th July 1970.

Revocation

2.—(1) The Superannuation (Teaching and Northern Ireland Civil Service) Interchange Rules 1962(**d**) are hereby revoked :

Provided that the Rules hereby revoked shall continue to apply in relation to any person who, before the beginning of April 1967, became employed in contributory service or as a civil servant within the meaning of those Rules in like manner as they would have applied if these Rules had not been made.

(2) Section 38(2) of the Interpretation Act 1889(**e**) (which relates to the effect of repeals) shall have effect in relation to the Rules revoked by this rule as if they were an enactment repealed by an Act.

Interpretation

3.—(1) In these Rules, unless the context otherwise requires—

"the Act" means the Superannuation (Miscellaneous Provisions) Act 1948 ;

"the Superannuation Acts" means the Superannuation Acts (Northern Ireland) 1967 and 1969(**f**) ;

* This instrument was laid before Parliament on 3rd July 1970.

(**a**) 1948 c. 33.
(**b**) 1967 c. 28.
(**c**) S.I. 1968/1656 (1968 III, p. 4485).
(**d**) S.I. 1962/538 (1962 I, p. 510).
(**e**) 1889 c. 63.
(**f**) 1967 c. 24 (N.I.); 1969 c. 7 (N.I.).

"civil servant" means a person serving in an established capacity in the permanent civil service of Northern Ireland ;

"contributing service" and "contributory employee" have the same respective meanings as in the Local Government Superannuation Acts 1937 to 1953(**a**) ;

"the Ministry of Finance" means the Ministry of Finance for Northern Ireland ;

"national service", in relation to any person, means service which is relevant service within the meaning of the Reserve and Auxiliary Forces (Protection of Civil Interests) Act 1951(**b**) ; and any similar service immediately following relevant service entered into with the consent of the body or person by whom he was last employed before undertaking the service ;

"pension" has the meaning assigned to it by the Act ;

"prescribed period" has the meaning assigned to it by rule 4 ;

"reckonable service" means reckonable service within the meaning of the Teachers' Superannuation Act 1967(**c**) ;

"the Secretary of State" means the Secretary of State for Education and Science ;

"the Teachers' Regulations" means the Teachers' Superannuation Regulations 1967 to 1970(**d**) ; and "the principal Teachers' Regulations" means the Teachers' Superannuation Regulations 1967(**e**) ;

"teaching service" means—

(*a*) reckonable service ; and

(*b*) service which for the purposes of the Teachers' Regulations is service as an organiser, a teacher in an admitted school, a services civilian teacher, a services education officer or a part-time teacher ;

"the Transfer Value Regulations" means the Local Government Superannuation (Transfer Value) Regulations 1954(**f**) ;

"voluntary contributions" means additional contributions being paid under section 19 of the Teachers (Superannuation) Act 1956(**g**) or regulation 32 of the principal Teachers' Regulations in respect of a period of previous employment and any contributions being paid as a condition of any other period (not being a period of war service or national service) being reckoned as teaching service.

(2) Any reference in these Rules to the provisions of any enactment, rules, regulations or other instrument shall, unless the context otherwise requires, be construed as a reference to those provisions as amended, modified, affected or re-enacted by any subsequent enactment, rules, regulations or instrument.

(3) References in these Rules to a rule or to a Part shall, unless the context otherwise requires, be construed as references to a rule or to a Part of these Rules, as the case may be.

(4) The Interpretation Act 1889 shall apply for the interpretation of these Rules as it applies for the interpretation of an Act of Parliament.

(**a**) 1937 c. 68; 1939 c. 18; 1953 c. 25. (**b**) 1951 c. 65.
(**c**) 1967 c. 12.
(**d**) S.I. 1967/489, 948, 1286, 1968/1353, 1969/80, 1970/10, 753 (1967 I, p. 1562; II, p. 2904; II, p. 3721, 1968 II, p. 3753; 1969 I, p. 241; 1970 I, p.11; II, p. 2394).
(**e**) S.I. 1967/489 (1967 I, p. 1562). (**f**) S.I. 1954/1212 (1954 II, p. 1723).
(**g**) 1956 c. 53.

Prescribed Period

4.—(1) For the purposes of these Rules, subject as hereafter in this rule provided, the expression "prescribed period" shall mean—

(*a*) in the case of a person who, immediately after ceasing to be employed in teaching service or to be a civil servant became engaged in national service, a period of six months after the date of termination of the national service ; and

(*b*) in the case of any other person, a period of twelve months after the date on which he ceased to be employed in teaching service or to be a civil servant.

(2) The Secretary of State in the case of a person entering teaching service and the Ministry of Finance in the case of a person becoming a civil servant may, with the agreement of the other, in any particular case extend any period specified in paragraph (1) above.

(3) In reckoning the periods of six months and twelve months specified in paragraph (1) above in the case of a person who in his new employment is in teaching service no account shall be taken of any period spent by him on a course of study or training after ceasing to be a civil servant if—

(*a*) his undertaking the said course was approved by the Ministry of Finance ; and

(*b*) the Secretary of State is satisfied that by reason of his having undertaken the said course he is better fitted for the duties of his new employment.

PART II

TRANSFER FROM TEACHING SERVICE TO CIVIL SERVICE

Application

5.—(1) Subject as in paragraph (3) below provided, this Part shall apply to a person who—

(*a*) within the prescribed period after ceasing to be employed in teaching service becomes, or since the beginning of April 1967 has become, a civil servant ; and

(*b*) within three months after becoming a civil servant or within such longer period as the Ministry of Finance with the agreement of the Secretary of State may in any particular case allow—

(i) notifies the Ministry of Finance in writing that he desires this Part to apply to him and furnishes that Ministry with particulars in writing of his teaching service ; and

(ii) pays to the Secretary of State an amount determined in accordance with paragraph (2) below.

(2) The amount to be paid by a person to the Secretary of State under paragraph (1)(*b*)(ii) above shall be the aggregate of—

(*a*) any sum paid to him after he last ceased to be employed in teaching service by way of return of contributions (other than voluntary contributions and contributions made or deemed to be made for the purpose of securing benefits for a widow, children or other dependants), together with any interest included therein ;

(*b*) any sum deducted from such payment as aforesaid in respect of liability to income tax arising by reason of its payment ; and

(*c*) compound interest on the sums specified in sub-paragraphs (*a*) and (*b*) above calculated at the rate of three and a half per cent. per annum with yearly rests from the date of the payment to him to the date of the payment by him to the Secretary of State.

(3) This Part shall not apply to a person who has received payment of any pension (other than repayment of contributions) under the Teachers (Superannuation) Acts 1918 to 1956 or the Teachers' Regulations.

Transfer Value

6.—(1) In respect of a person to whom this Part applies the Secretary of State shall, out of moneys provided by Parliament, pay to the Ministry of Finance a transfer value of an amount calculated in accordance with the following provisions of this rule.

(2) Subject as hereafter in this rule provided, the transfer value shall be an amount equal to the transfer value which would have been payable under the Transfer Value Regulations if the person, at the date when he ceased to be employed in teaching service, had ceased to be a contributory employee under one local authority and had become such an employee under another local authority and had been entitled to reckon as contributing service his reckonable service and his service reckonable for the purposes of Parts VII, IX and X of the principal Teachers' Regulations at the length at which it is so reckonable.

(3) For the purposes of paragraph (2) above service which is reckoned as contributing service shall be deemed to have been affected or modified in accordance with regulations applicable to contributing service made under Section 110 of the National Insurance Act 1965(**a**), or under any provision corresponding thereto contained in an enactment repealed by that Act, in like manner and to the like extent, as nearly as may be, as it was affected or modified by other such regulations.

(4) In calculating the amount of a transfer value there shall be excluded—

(*a*) any period of war service within the meaning of the Teachers' Superannuation (War Service) Act 1939(**b**) and of national service within the meaning of the Teachers Superannuation (National Service) Rules 1949(**c**) in respect of which, at the time the transfer value is paid, the contributions remain unpaid ; and

(*b*) any period of previous employment and any period additional to actual service in respect of which the person was immediately before ceasing to be employed in teaching service paying voluntary contributions and in respect of which, at the time the transfer value is paid, contributions are not payable to the Ministry of Finance under rules made by that Ministry ;

(5) The amount of the transfer value shall, in lieu of being reduced in accordance with the proviso to paragraph 2 of the First Schedule to the Transfer Value Regulations, be reduced by—

(*a*) an amount equal to any sum which remained to be paid by him on his ceasing to be employed in teaching service towards the discharge of a fixed sum as a condition of any period of service being reckoned for the purposes of the Teachers' Regulations ;

(**a**) 1965 c. 51. (**b**) 1939 c. 95. (**c**) S.I. 1949/468 (1949 I, p. 1533).

(b) an amount equal to the capital value of any voluntary contributions which on his ceasing to be employed in teaching service remained to be paid by him in respect of any period not excluded from the calculation of the amount of the transfer value by paragraph (4)(b) above; and

(c) an amount equal to any sum payable by the Secretary of State by way of income tax by reason of the payment.

(6) In respect of a person who became a civil servant more than twelve months after ceasing to be employed in teaching service or more than six months after ceasing to be engaged in national service, the transfer value shall be calculated by reference to his age on the date on which he became a civil servant.

Benefits under Teachers' Regulations

7. Subject to the provisions of Part III and any provisions similar thereto contained in other rules made under the Act, no payment of any pension shall be made under the Teachers' Regulations to or in respect of any person in respect of any service which is taken into account in calculating the amount of a transfer value under rule 6.

PART III

TRANSFER FROM CIVIL SERVICE TO TEACHING SERVICE

Application

8.—(1) Subject as in paragraph (2) below provided, this Part shall apply to a person who—

(a) within the prescribed period after ceasing to be a civil servant becomes, or since the beginning of April 1967 has become, employed in teaching service with the consent of the Department in which he was last employed as a civil servant;

(b) within three months after becoming employed in teaching service or within such longer period as the Secretary of State with the agreement of the Ministry of Finance may in any particular case allow, notifies the Secretary of State in writing that he desires this Part to apply to him and furnishes the Secretary of State with particulars in writing of his service as a civil servant; and

(c) is a person in respect of whom the Secretary of State receives from the Ministry of Finance a transfer value of an amount calculated in accordance with the provisions of rule 9.

(2) This Part shall not apply to a person who has received payment of any pension under the Superannuation Acts.

Transfer Value

9.—(1) Subject as hereafter in this rule provided, the transfer value receivable by the Secretary of State from the Ministry of Finance in respect of a person to whom this Part applies shall be an amount equal to the transfer value which would have been payable under the Transfer Value Regulations if the person, at the date when he ceased to be a civil servant or ceased to be engaged in national service, as the case may be, had ceased to be a contributory employee under one local authority and had become such an employee under another local authority and had been entitled to reckon his service reckonable for the purposes of the Superannuation Acts as contributing service.

(2) For the purposes of paragraph (1) above, service reckonable for the purposes of the Superannuation Acts which is to be reckoned as contributing service shall be deemed to have been affected or modified in accordance with regulations applicable to contributing service made under section 110 of the National Insurance Act 1965, or under any provision corresponding thereto contained in an enactment repealed by that Act, in like manner and to the like extent, as nearly as may be, as it was affected or modified in accordance with regulations made under section 103 of the National Insurance Act (Northern Ireland) 1966(**a**), or under any provision corresponding thereto contained in an enactment repealed by that Act.

(3) In respect of a person who became employed in teaching service more than twelve months after ceasing to be a civil servant or more than six months after ceasing to be engaged in national service, the transfer value shall be calculated by reference to his age on the date on which he became employed in teaching service.

(4) The transfer value shall be reduced by an amount equal to any sum which the Ministry of Finance is liable to pay by way of income tax by reason of its payment.

Reckoning of Service

10.—(1) In respect of a person to whom this Part applies there shall be reckoned as reckonable service—

(*a*) the period of service which under rule 9 is reckoned as contributing service for the purpose of calculating the amount of the transfer value payable in respect of him ; and

(*b*) any period in respect of which he was, at the time he ceased to be a civil servant, in course of making payments as a condition of his service reckonable for the purposes of the Superannuation Acts being increased by its addition thereto if—

(i) within three months of becoming employed in teaching service or within such longer period as the Secretary of State may in any particular case allow he elects to pay to the Secretary of State sums equal to the aforesaid payments and thereafter pays such sums at the times at which they would have been payable if he had continued to be a civil servant ; and

(ii) the transfer value paid in respect of him is calculated so as to include the liability of which the Ministry of Finance is relieved in respect of that period, reduced by the value of the payments he would have been liable to make if he had continued to be a civil servant.

(2) In relation to any period to which paragraph (1)(*b*) above applies:—

(*a*) the provisions of paragraphs (5)(*b*), (6), (7), (8) and (12) of regulation 32 and of regulation 38 of the principal Teachers' Regulations shall apply to the sums payable to the Secretary of State under that subparagraph as if those sums were additional contributions payable in respect of previous employment within the meaning of those Regulations ; and

(**a**) 1966 c. 6 (N.I.).

(*b*) if no election to pay those sums is made or if they are repaid under regulation 38 of the principal Teachers' Regulations, the period shall be reckoned for the purposes of those Regulations only to the extent, if any, to which it would have been so reckoned if no payments had been made in respect thereof.

(3) Any period of service of a person to whom this Part applies which under the Superannuation Acts was at the time he ceased to be a civil servant reckonable only for the purpose of calculating the amount of any pension payable to or in respect of him or only for the purpose of determining whether he was entitled to any pension shall be reckoned only for the corresponding like purpose under the Teachers' Regulations.

Return of Contributions

11.—(1) Where a person to whom this Part applies ceases to be employed in teaching service or dies, then, to any sum to which he or his personal representatives shall be entitled under the Teachers' Regulations by way of repayment of contributions there shall be added the following sums :—

(*a*) a sum equal to the amount of any contributions paid by him in respect of service which by virtue of this Part is reckoned as reckonable service ;

(*b*) a sum equal to the amount of any voluntary contributions paid by him before becoming employed in teaching service which have not been returned to him ; and

(*c*) compound interest on the foregoing sums calculated in accordance with paragraph (2) below.

(2) For the purposes of paragraph (1) above compound interest shall be calculated—

(*a*) as respects the period ending immediately before the date on which the person became employed in teaching service, in the manner in which such interest, if any, would have been calculated if the occasion for making the calculation had occurred immediately before that date ; and

(*b*) as respects the period beginning with that date, in accordance with the provisions of Part IV of the principal Teachers' Regulations.

Commencement of Employment

12. For the purposes of regulation 41(1)(*a*)(ii) of the principal Teachers' Regulations the date on which a person to whom this Part applies became a civil servant shall be deemed to be a date on which he became employed in teaching service.

Modification of Contributions and Benefits by reason of National Insurance

13.—(1) In relation to a person to whom this Part applies—

(*a*) the following paragraphs of Schedule 5 to the principal Teachers' Regulations, that is to say—

paragraph 2 (which provides for the reduction of contributions),

paragraph 4 (which provides for the reduction of pensions by fixed annual amounts specified therein) and

paragraph 5 (which provides for the reduction of pensions by annual amounts ascertained by reference to a table and age at a given date) shall not apply if, on the date on which he ceased to be a civil servant, the National Insurance (Modification of the Superannuation Acts) Regulations (Northern Ireland) 1948(a) did not apply to him ; and

(*b*) paragraphs 2 and 4 of the said Schedule 5 shall apply if, on the date on which he ceased to be a civil servant, the last mentioned Regulations applied to him.

Given under the Official Seal of the Secretary of State for Education and Science on 28th May 1970.

(L.S.)

Edward Short,
Secretary of State for Education and Science.

Consent of the Minister for the Civil Service given under his Official Seal on 3rd June 1970.

(L.S.)

K. H. McNeill,
Authorised by the Minister for the Civil Service.

EXPLANATORY NOTE

(*This Note is not part of the Rules.*)

These Rules continue, with minor alterations, the arrangements made by earlier Rules for the preservation of superannuation rights upon changes of employment between teaching in England and Wales and the Civil Service of Northern Ireland.

In accordance with Section 2(5) of the Superannuation (Miscellaneous Provisions) Act 1948 the Rules have effect retrospectively to 1st April 1967.

(a) S. R. & O. (N.I.) 1948, No. 91.

1970 No. 865

LAND REGISTRATION

The Land Registration (District Registries) Order 1970

Made - - -	1*st June* 1970
Coming into Operation	1*st October* 1970

The Lord Chancellor, in exercise of the powers conferred on him by sections 132 and 133 of the Land Registration Act 1925(**a**), and with the concurrence of the Treasury, hereby makes the following Order:—

Title, commencement and interpretation

1.—(1) This Order may be cited as the Land Registration (District Registries) Order 1970 and shall come into operation on 1st October 1970.

(2) The Interpretation Act 1889(**b**) shall apply to the interpretation of this Order as it applies to the interpretation of an Act of Parliament.

(3) In this Order, unless the context otherwise requires—

"the Act" means the Land Registration Act 1925 ;

"application" means an application made or delivered under the Land Registration Rules 1925(**c**) and the Land Registration (Official Searches) Rules 1969(**d**), and includes a notice or other instrument so made or delivered ;

"district registry" means a district registry of the Land Registry within the meaning of section 132 of the Act ;

"the Schedule" means the Schedule to this Order.

District Registries

2.—(1) There shall continue to be district registries bearing the names and at the places specified in column 1 of the Schedule.

(2) Each district registry shall be the proper office for the registration of titles to land and for the delivery of any application relating to land in its district, which shall comprise the administrative areas specified opposite its name in columns 2 and 3 of the Schedule :

Provided that the administrative county of Staffordshire and the county boroughs of Burton upon Trent, Dudley, Stoke-on-Trent, Walsall, West Bromwich and Wolverhampton shall not form part of the district of the Gloucester District Land Registry before 1st December 1970 and shall not form part of the district of the Nottingham District Land Registry on or after that date and the provisions of the Schedule shall be construed accordingly.

(**a**) 1925 c. 21. (**b**) 1889 c. 63.
(**c**) S.R. & O. 1925/1093 (Rev. XII, p. 81: 1925, p. 717).
(**d**) S.I. 1969/1179 (1969 II, p. 3474).

(3) The district registrar appointed for each district shall have the powers and indemnity conferred by section 133 of the Act :

Provided that—

(*a*) nothing in this paragraph shall be construed as giving a district registrar any powers or duties which are exercisable only by the Chief Land Registrar ; and

(*b*) all powers and duties of the district registrar shall be exercised under the general direction and authority of the Chief Land Registrar.

Delivery of instruments and applications at the proper office

3. No application shall be duly delivered until it is delivered at the proper office, namely :—

(*a*) where an application relates to land wholly within a district, the district registry for that district ;

(*b*) where an application relates to land in two or more districts, any one of the district registries for those districts.

Revocation

4. The Land Registration (District Registries) Order 1969(**a**) is hereby revoked.

Dated 27th May 1970.

Gardiner, C.

We concur,
Dated 1st June 1970.

Walter Harrison,
E. G. Perry,
Two of the Lords Commissioners
of Her Majesty's Treasury.

(**a**) S.I. 1969/115 (1969 I, p. 344).

SCHEDULE

Rules 2(1), 2(2)

DISTRICT REGISTRIES

1 District Registry	2 Administrative Counties	3 County Boroughs, London Boroughs, etc.
The Croydon District Land Registry at Croydon		Bexley Bromley Croydon Greenwich Kingston upon Thames Lambeth Lewisham Merton Richmond upon Thames Southwark Sutton Wandsworth
The Durham District Land Registry at Durham	Durham Northumberland Yorkshire, East Riding Yorkshire, North Riding	Darlington Gateshead Hartlepool Kingston upon Hull Newcastle upon Tyne South Shields Sunderland Teesside Tynemouth York
The Gloucester District Registry at Gloucester	Berkshire Gloucestershire Hampshire Isle of Wight Oxfordshire	Bournemouth Bristol Gloucester Oxford Portsmouth Reading Southampton
	Staffordshire (on and after 1st December 1970)	Burton upon Trent Dudley Stoke-on-Trent Walsall West Bromwich Wolverhampton (on and after 1st December 1970.)

1 District Registry	2 Administrative Counties	3 County Boroughs, London Boroughs, etc.
The Harrow District Land Registry at Harrow-on-the-Hill		The City of London The Inner Temple and the Middle Temple Barking Barnet Brent Camden City of Westminster Ealing Enfield Hackney Hammersmith Haringey Harrow Havering Hillingdon Hounslow Islington Kensington and Chelsea Newham Redbridge Tower Hamlets Waltham Forest
The Lytham District Land Registry at Lytham St. Annes	Cheshire Cumberland Herefordshire Lancashire Monmouthshire Shropshire Westmorland All the counties in Wales	Barrow-in-Furness Birkenhead Blackburn Blackpool Bolton Bootle Burnley Bury Carlisle Chester Liverpool Manchester Newport Oldham Preston Rochdale St. Helens Salford Southport Stockport Wallasey Warrington Wigan All the county boroughs in Wales

1 District Registry	2 Administrative Counties	3 County Boroughs, London Boroughs, etc.
The Nottingham District Land Registry at Nottingham	Derbyshire Leicestershire Nottinghamshire Warwickshire Worcestershire Yorkshire, West Riding	Barnsley Birmingham Bradford Coventry Derby Dewsbury Doncaster Halifax Huddersfield Leeds Leicester Nottingham Rotherham Sheffield Solihull Wakefield Warley Worcester
	—	—
	Staffordshire (only before 1st December 1970)	Burton upon Trent Dudley Stoke-on-Trent Walsall West Bromwich Wolverhampton (only before 1st December 1970.)
The Plymouth District Land Registry at Plymouth	Cornwall Devon Dorset Somerset Wiltshire	Bath Exeter Plymouth Torbay
The Stevenage District Land Registry at Stevenage	Bedfordshire Buckinghamshire Cambridgeshire and Isle of Ely Essex Hertfordshire Huntingdon and Peterborough Lincoln, parts of Holland Lincoln, parts of Kesteven Lincoln, parts of Lindsey Norfolk Northamptonshire Rutland Suffolk, East Suffolk, West	Great Yarmouth Grimsby Ipswich Lincoln Luton Northampton Norwich Southend-on-Sea
The Tunbridge Wells District Land Registry at Tunbridge Wells	Kent Surrey Sussex, East Sussex, West	Brighton Canterbury Eastbourne Hastings

EXPLANATORY NOTE

(This Note is not part of the Order.)

This Order, which replaces the Land Registration (District Registries) Order 1969, transfers responsibility for the registration of titles in the West Riding of Yorkshire, Barnsley, Bradford, Dewsbury, Doncaster, Halifax, Huddersfield, Leeds, Rotherham, Sheffield and Wakefield from the Durham to the Nottingham District Land Registry as from 1st October 1970 and in Staffordshire, Burton upon Trent, Dudley, Stoke-on-Trent, Walsall, West Bromwich and Wolverhampton from the Nottingham to the Gloucester District Land Registry as from 1st December 1970. The areas of the remaining district registries at Croydon, Harrow, Lytham St. Annes, Plymouth, Stevenage and Tunbridge Wells are unchanged.

The Order continues the requirement that applications for the registration of titles shall be delivered at the appropriate district registry as defined in the Order.

1970 No. 867

EDUCATION, ENGLAND AND WALES

The Awards (First Degree, etc. Courses) (Amendment) Regulations 1970

Made - - -	*8th June* 1970
* *To be laid before Parliament*	
Coming into Operation	*3rd July* 1970

The Secretary of State for Education and Science, in exercise of the powers conferred upon him by sections 1 and 4 of the Education Act 1962(**a**) as amended by the Secretary of State for Education and Science Order 1964(**b**), hereby makes the following regulations:—

Citation, commencement and interpretation

1.—(1) These regulations may be cited as the Awards (First Degree, etc. Courses) (Amendment) Regulations 1970 and shall come into operation on 3rd July 1970.

(2) The Interpretation Act 1889(**c**) shall apply for the interpretation of these Regulations as it applies for the interpretation of an Act of Parliament.

Amendment of Regulations

2.—(1) The Awards (First Degree, etc. Courses) Regulations 1970(**d**) shall have effect subject to the amendments specified in paragraph (2) below.

(2) (*a*) In regulation 6 (which prescribes the requisite educational qualifications), after paragraph (*a*)(iv) there shall be added—

> "(ivA) a pass in three subjects in the higher grade gained at not more than two sittings of the Scottish Universities Preliminary Examination, the Scottish Certificate of Education Examination or the examination for the Scottish Leaving Certificate."

(*b*) In regulation 7 (which prescribes designated courses), after paragraph (*c*) there shall be inserted as a new paragraph—

> "(*cc*) a sandwich course in preparation for any such degree, Certificate or Diploma as is mentioned in the three preceding paragraphs."

(*c*) In paragraph 3 of Schedule 1 (which prescribes the higher rates of ordinary maintenance), for the references to £395, £360 and £290 there shall be substituted references to £420, £380 and £305 respectively.

* This instrument was laid before Parliament on 2nd July 1970.

(**a**) 1962 c. 12.
(**b**) S.I. 1964/490 (1964 I, p. 800).
(**c**) 1889 c. 63.
(**d**) S.I. 1970/497 (1970 I, p. 1676).

(*d*) In paragraph 7 of Schedule 1 (which prescribes the amounts of supplementary maintenance for the purchase of equipment), after the word "incurred" there shall be inserted the words "by a medical student, a veterinary student or a dental student respectively".

(*e*) In paragraph 14 of Schedule 1 (which prescribes the requirements of older students), for the reference to £360 there shall be substituted a reference to £380.

(*f*) In paragraph 2 of Schedule 2 (which defines the expressions used in Part 2 of that Schedule), for the definition of "income" there shall be substituted—

> " "income of the student's parent" means the total income of the parent from all sources computed as for income tax purposes, except that no deduction shall be made which is of a kind for which provision is made by paragraph 6 below".

(*g*) In paragraph 5 of Schedule 2 (which defines gross income), for sub-paragraph (4) there shall be substituted—

> "(4) There shall be treated as part of the gross income all income arising from an office or employment which by virtue of any enactment is as such exempt from tax."

(*h*) In paragraph 2 of Schedule 4 (which modifies the provisions of Schedule 1 in its application to sandwich courses), for the references in paragraph 2(*a*) and (*b*) to £36 there shall be substituted references to £38.

Given under the Official Seal of the Secretary of State for Education and Science on 8th June 1970.

(L.S.)

Alice Bacon,
Minister of State for Education and Science.

EXPLANATORY NOTE

(*This Note is not part of the Regulations.*)

These Regulations increase the rates of ordinary maintenance prescribed by, and make minor amendments to, the Awards (First Degree, etc. Courses) Regulations 1970.

1970 No. 868

ANIMALS

The Animals (Restriction of Importation) Order 1970

Made - - - *8th June* 1970

* *To be laid before Parliament*

Coming into Operation *1st September* 1970

Whereas the Secretary of State, after consulting the Advisory Committee established under section 3 of the Animals (Restriction of Importation) Act 1964(**a**) (in this Order called "the Act"), is satisfied that the scope of section 1 of the Act should be extended so as to include Felidae (except Felis catus) and Tapiridae, being wild animals of kinds appearing to him to stand in need of conservation :

Now, therefore, the Secretary of State, in exercise of the powers conferred on him by section 2 of the Act, hereby makes the following Order :—

Citation and Commencement

1. This Order may be cited as the Animals (Restriction of Importation) Order 1970 and shall come into operation on 1st September 1970.

Modification of Schedule to Act

2. There shall be added to the Schedule to the Act (which specifies the kinds of animals the importation of individuals whereof is restricted)—

Felidae (except Felis catus).

Tapiridae.

Given under the Official Seal of the Secretary of State for Education and Science on 8th June 1970.

(L.S.)

Alice Bacon,
Minister of State for Education and Science.

* This instrument was laid before Parliament on 3rd July 1970.
(**a**) 1964 c. 61.

EXPLANATORY NOTE

(This Note is not part of the Order.)

This Order prohibits the importation of all live animals (other than domestic cats) of the cat and tapir families save under the authority, and in accordance with the terms, of a licence granted by the Board of Trade.

1970 No. 869

INFERIOR COURT, ENGLAND

The Salford Hundred Court of Record (Extension of Jurisdiction) Order 1970

Made - - - -	4*th June* 1970
Coming into Operation	1*st July* 1970

I, George Morgan Thomson Chancellor of the Duchy and County Palatine of Lancaster in exercise of the powers conferred on me by section 3(1) of the Salford Hundred Court of Record Act 1911(**a**) as amended by sub-section (2) of section 83 of the Manchester Corporation Act 1954(**b**) and all other powers enabling me in that behalf hereby order and direct that as from the first day of July One thousand nine hundred and seventy the jurisdiction of the Court of Record for the Hundred of Salford shall be extended so as to include personal actions within the meaning of sub-section (1) of section 6 of the Salford Hundred Court of Record Act 1868(**c**) in which the debt or damages sought to be recovered shall not exceed the sum of seven hundred and fifty pounds.

2. This Order may be cited as the Salford Hundred Court of Record (Extension of Jurisdiction) Order 1970 and shall come into operation on 1st July 1970.

G. M. Thomson.

Dated 4th June 1970.

EXPLANATORY NOTE

(*This Note is not part of the Order.*)

This Order increases the jurisdiction of the Salford Hundred Court of Record in personal actions from £500 to £750. (The jurisdiction was increased to £500 by the Salford Hundred Court of Record (Extension of Jurisdiction) Order 1966 (S.I. 1966/430)).

(**a**) 1 & 2 Geo. 5. c. clxxii. (**b**) 2 & 3 Eliz. 2. c. xlviii. (**c**) 31 & 32 Vict. c. cxxx.

STATUTORY INSTRUMENTS

1970 No. 877

AGRICULTURE

HILL LANDS

The Hill Cattle (Breeding Herds) (England and Wales) (Amendment) Scheme 1970

Made - - - - 8*th June* 1970

*To be laid before Parliament**

Coming into Operation 10*th June* 1970

The Minister of Agriculture, Fisheries and Food and the Secretary of State, acting jointly, in pursuance of sections 13, 14, 15 and 17 of the Hill Farming Act 1946(**a**), as extended by section 43 of the Agriculture Act 1967(**b**) and as read with the Transfer of Functions (Wales) Order 1969(**c**), and all their other enabling powers, with the approval of the Treasury, hereby make the following scheme:—

Citation and commencement

1. This scheme, which may be cited as the Hill Cattle (Breeding Herds) (England and Wales) (Amendment) Scheme 1970, shall come into operation on 10th June 1970.

Interpretation

2.—(1) This scheme shall be construed as one with the Hill Cattle (Breeding Herds) (England and Wales) Scheme 1968(**d**), as amended(**e**), in this scheme referred to as " the principal scheme ".

(2) In this scheme, unless the context otherwise requires—

" accredited herd " means a herd which, to the satisfaction of the Minister—

(*a*) has been found to be free from brucellosis by means of a series of blood tests carried out by him or on his behalf, and

(*b*) has been, since the date of commencement of such tests, the subject of adequate precautions against the introduction or re-introduction and consequent spreading of brucellosis ;

" brucellosis " means the disease caused by *brucella abortus* ;

" reactor " means an animal which, when tested for brucellosis by or on behalf of the Minister, gives rise to a reaction consistent with its being affected with that disease.

Reduction of subsidy where compensation for reactors is payable

3.—(1) This paragraph applies where an order under section 14(3) of the Act prescribes higher amounts of subsidy payments in relation to cattle comprised in accredited herds, or in certain herds which subsequently become accredited herds, than in relation to other cattle.

* This instrument was laid before Parliament on 29th June 1970.

(**a**) 1946 c. 73. For change of title of the Minister see S.I. 1955/554 (1965 I, p.1200).
(**b**) 1967 c. 22. (**c**) S.I. 1969/388 (1969 I, p. 1070). (**d**) S.I. 1968/875 (1968 II, p. 2310).
(**e**) S.I. 1969/695 (1969 II, p. 1909).

(2) Where on 31st December in the year 1970 or on the qualifying day in any subsequent year there is in force an arrangement between the Minister and the owner of a herd by which, if an animal in the herd is slaughtered as a reactor while the herd is an accredited herd, the owner is to be paid out of public funds, otherwise than under section 17 of the Diseases of Animals Act 1950(**a**), compensation equivalent to the value of the animal before slaughter (subject to any overriding limit which may be part of the arrangement), the amounts of any subsidy payments which may be made under the principal scheme in respect of any cattle in the herd in respect of that year shall be reduced to such amounts as would have been payable if the cattle were comprised in a herd which had never been, and never would become, an accredited herd.

In Witness whereof the Official Seal of the Minister of Agriculture, Fisheries and Food is hereunto affixed on 1st June 1970.

(L.S.) *Cledwyn Hughes,*
Minister of Agriculture, Fisheries and Food.

Given under my hand on 3rd June 1970.

George Thomas,
Secretary of State for Wales.

We approve,
8th June 1970.

Ernest Armstrong,
Joseph Harper,
Two of the Lord Commissioners of Her Majesty's Treasury.

EXPLANATORY NOTE

(*This Note is not part of the Scheme.*)

Under the Hill Cattle Subsidy (Breeding Herds) (England and Wales) Payment Order 1970 (S.I. 1970/878), made on the same date as this scheme, higher rates of subsidy are introduced for cattle in accredited herds, i.e. herds which have been found to be free from brucellosis by means of official tests and which have been the subject of adequate precautions against the re-introduction and consequent spreading of the disease.

The herd must have become an accredited herd by the qualifying day (usually 4th June) in the year to which the subsidy payment relates, or must subsequently become an accredited herd as a result of a final blood test commenced on or before that day.

This scheme reduces subsidy payments to the lower rate if on 31st December 1970 or on the qualifying day in any subsequent year there is an arrangement between the Minister and the owner of the herd by which compensation is to be paid for reactors at their value before slaughter (subject to any overriding limit), a characteristic of the informal voluntary eradication scheme introduced in 1967.

(**a**) 1950 c. 36.

STATUTORY INSTRUMENTS

1970 No. 878

AGRICULTURE

HILL LANDS

The Hill Cattle Subsidy (Breeding Herds) (England and Wales) Payment Order 1970

Made - - - - *8th June* 1970

**To be laid before Parliament*

Coming into Operation *10th June* 1970

The Minister of Agriculture, Fisheries and Food and the Secretary of State, acting jointly, in pursuance of sections 14(3) and 17 of the Hill Farming Act 1946(**a**), as amended by section 8 of the Livestock Rearing Act 1951(**b**) and as read with the Transfer of Functions (Wales) Order 1969(**c**), and all their other enabling powers, with the approval of the Treasury, hereby make the following order :—

Citation and Commencement

1. This order which may be cited as the Hill Cattle Subsidy (Breeding Herds) (England and Wales) Payment Order 1970, shall come into operation on 10th June 1970.

Interpretation

2.—(1) Unless the context otherwise requires, expressions used in this order shall have the same meaning as in the Hill Cattle (Breeding Herds) (England and Wales) Scheme 1968(**d**), as amended(**e**).

(2) The Interpretation Act 1889(**f**) shall apply to the interpretation of this order as it applies to the interpretation of an Act of Parliament.

Amounts of subsidy payments for 1970-72

3. Subject to the provisions of the Hill Cattle (Breeding Herds) (England and Wales) Scheme 1968, as amended, the amount which may be paid in respect of each of the years 1970, 1971 and 1972 by way of subsidy payments under that scheme in respect of any animal to which it applies shall be—

(*a*) in the case of an animal comprised in a herd which is an accredited herd on the qualifying day or which subsequently becomes such a herd as a result of a final blood test for brucellosis commenced on or before that day, £25 12s. 6d. ;

(*b*) in the case of any other animal, £23 15s. 0d.

* This instrument was laid before Parliament on 29th June 1970.

(**a**) 1946 c. 73. For change of title of the Minister, see S.I. 1955/554 (1955 I, p. 1200).
(**b**) 1951 c. 18. (**c**) S.I. 1969/388 (1969 I, p. 1070).
(**d**) S.I. 1968/875 (1968 II, p. 2310). (**e**) S.I. 1970/877 (1970 II, p. 2805). (**f**) 1889 c. 63.

Existing orders not to apply

4. The Hill Cattle Subsidy (Breeding Herds) (England and Wales) Payment Order 1968(**a**), as amended(**b**), shall cease to apply to subsidy payments in respect of the years 1970, 1971 and 1972.

In Witness whereof the Official Seal of the Minister of Agriculture, Fisheries and Food is hereunto affixed on 1st June 1970.

(L.S.) *Cledwyn Hughes,*

Minister of Agriculture, Fisheries and Food.

Given under my hand on 3rd June 1970.

George Thomas,

Secretary of State for Wales.

We approve,
8th June 1970.

Ernest Armstrong,
Joseph Harper,
Two of the Lords Commissioners of Her Majesty's Treasury.

EXPLANATORY NOTE

(*This Note is not part of the Order.*)

This order increases the amount of the Hill Cattle subsidy for the years 1970, 1971 and 1972. The old rate was a uniform sum of £22 5s. per cow; this order fixes two alternative rates. The higher rate, £25 12s. 6d., will be payable if the herd in which the cow is comprised is an accredited herd on the qualifying day (usually 4th June) or subsequently becomes such a herd as a result of a final blood test commenced on or before that day. For other animals the rate will be £23 15s.

In order to qualify as accredited, a herd must have been found by the Minister to be free from brucellosis by means of blood tests and must also have been the subject of adequate precautions against the re-introduction and consequent spreading of the disease.

(**a**) S.I. 1968/876 (1968 II, p. 2317). (**b**) S.I. 1969/696 (1969 II, p. 1911).

STATUTORY INSTRUMENTS

1970 No. 879

AGRICULTURE

The Price Stability of Imported Products (Rates of Levy) (Eggs) (No. 5) Order 1970

Made - - - - *8th June* 1970

Coming into Operation *9th June* 1970

The Minister of Agriculture, Fisheries and Food, in exercise of the powers conferred upon him by section 1(2), (4), (5), (6) and (7) of the Agriculture and Horticulture Act 1964(**a**) and of all other powers enabling him in that behalf, hereby makes the following order:—

1. This order may be cited as the Price Stability of Imported Products (Rates of Levy) (Eggs) (No. 5) Order 1970, and shall come into operation on 9th June 1970.

2.—(1) In this order—

" the Principal Order " means the Price Stability of Imported Products (Levy Arrangements) (Eggs) Order 1970(**b**) as amended by any subsequent order, and if any such order is replaced by any subsequent order the expression shall be construed as a reference to such subsequent order;

AND other expressions have the same meaning as in the Principal Order.

(2) The Interpretation Act 1889(**c**) shall apply to the interpretation of this order as it applies to the interpretation of an Act of Parliament and as if this order and the order hereby revoked were Acts of Parliament.

3. In accordance with and subject to the provisions of the Principal Order (which provides for the charging of levies on imports of those eggs and egg products which are specified commodities for the purposes of the Agriculture and Horticulture Act 1964) the rate of general levy for such imports into the United Kingdom of any specified commodity as are described in column 2 of the Schedule to this order in relation to a tariff heading indicated in column 1 of that Schedule shall be the rate set forth in relation thereto in column 3 of that Schedule.

4. The Price Stability of Imported Products (Rates of Levy) (Eggs) (No. 4) Order 1970(**d**) is hereby revoked.

In Witness whereof the Official Seal of the Minister of Agriculture, Fisheries and Food is hereunto affixed on 8th June 1970.

(L.S.)

J. A. Barrah,
Assistant Secretary.

(**a**) 1964 c. 28. (**b**) S.I. 1970/359 (1970 I, p. 1277). (**c**) 1889 c. 63.
(**d**) S.I. 1970/764 (1970 II, p. 2407).

SCHEDULE

1. Tariff Heading	2. Description of Imports	3. Rate of General Levy
	Imports of:—	(per 120 eggs)
04.05	*Birds' eggs in shell:—*	*s. d.*
	1. Not exceeding 11 lb. in weight per 120 ..	4 0
	2. Over 11 lb. but not exceeding 12½ lb. in weight per 120	4 0
	3. Over 12½ lb. but not exceeding 14 lb. in weight per 120	4 6
	4. Over 14 lb. but not exceeding 15½ lb. in weight per 120	4 6
	5. Over 15½ lb. but not exceeding 17 lb. in weight per 120	4 6
	6. Over 17 lb. in weight per 120	4 6

EXPLANATORY NOTE

(*This Note is not part of the Order.*)

This order, which comes into operation on 9th June 1970, supersedes the Price Stability of Imported Products (Rates of Levy) (Eggs) (No. 4) Order 1970. It—

(*a*) increases the rates of general levy on imports of eggs in shell in the weight grades which are numbered 1 to 4 in the Schedule to the order ;

(*b*) reimposes unchanged the rates of general levy for the other two weights of eggs which were in force immediately before the commencement of this order.

STATUTORY INSTRUMENTS

1970 No. 883

WAGES COUNCILS

The Wages Regulation (Hat, Cap and Millinery) Order 1970

Made - - - *10th June* 1970

Coming into Operation *8th July* 1970

Whereas the Secretary of State has received from the Hat, Cap and Millinery Wages Council (Great Britain) the wages regulation proposals set out in the Schedule hereto;

Now, therefore, the Secretary of State in exercise of her powers under section 11 of the Wages Councils Act 1959(**a**), and of all other powers enabling her in that behalf, hereby makes the following Order:—

1. This Order may be cited as the Wages Regulation (Hat, Cap and Millinery) Order 1970.

2.—(1) In this Order the expression "the specified date" means the 8th July 1970, provided that where, as respects any worker who is paid wages at intervals not exceeding seven days, that date does not correspond with the beginning of the period for which the wages are paid, the expression "the specified date" means, as respects that worker, the beginning of the next such period following that date.

(2) The Interpretation Act 1889(**b**) shall apply to the interpretation of this Order as it applies to the interpretation of an Act of Parliament and as if this Order and the Order hereby revoked were Acts of Parliament.

3. The wages regulation proposals set out in the Schedule hereto shall have effect as from the specified date and as from that date the Wages Regulation (Hat, Cap and Millinery) Order 1968(**c**) shall cease to have effect.

Signed by order of the Secretary of State.
10th June 1970.

A. A. Jarratt,
Deputy Under Secretary of State,
Department of Employment and Productivity.

SCHEDULE — Article 3

The following minimum remuneration shall be substituted for the statutory minimum remuneration fixed by the Wages Regulation (Hat, Cap and Millinery) Order 1968 (Order H.C.M. (13)).

(a) 1959 c. 69. **(b)** 1889 c. 63.
(c) S.I. 1968/1562 (1968 III, p. 4351).

PART I

GENERAL

1.—(1) The minimum remuneration payable to a worker to whom this Schedule applies for all work except work to which a minimum overtime rate applies under Part V of this Schedule is:—

(*a*) in the case of a time worker, the hourly general minimum time rate;

(*b*) in the case of a worker employed on piece work, piece rates each of which would yield, in the circumstances of the case, to an ordinary worker at least the same amount of money as the hourly piece work basis time rate.

(2) In this Schedule:—

"hourly general minimum time rate" means the general minimum time rate applicable to the worker under Part II or Part III of this Schedule divided by 40;

"hourly piece work basis time rate" means the piece work basis time rate applicable to the worker under Part II or Part III of this Schedule divided by 40;

"per week" means per week of 40 hours.

PART II

MALE WORKERS
GENERAL MINIMUM TIME RATES

2. The general minimum time rates applicable to male workers are as follows:—

	Per week s.	d.
(1) Cutters, blockers, body makers or finishers, stiffeners or shapers employed in a section of the trade other than the felt hat section ...	*246*	*8*
(2) Workers employed in the felt hat (wool) section of the trade on any of the operations of— hardening; planking processes of barrel twisting, hand planking or hand stretching; proofing (head man only); dyeing (head man only); blocking (other than coning when the operation is preparatory to blocking); pressing; finishing; curling; flanging; cutting; ironing and paring; velouring; if they have worked in any section of the trade on one or more of such operations for at least 3 years after the age of 18 years ...	*246*	*8*
(3) Workers employed in the felt hat (fur) section of the trade on any of the operations of— forming; hardening; planking; proofing (head man only); dyeing (head man only); blocking; pressing; finishing; brushing; curling and steaming; flanging; cutting; ironing and paring; trimming; velouring; if they have worked in any section of the trade on one or more of such operations for at least 3 years after the age of 18 years ...	*246*	*8*

(4) All other workers—

	Per week s.	d.
Aged 21 years or over	*228*	*4*
„ 20 and under 21 years	*202*	*6*
„ 19 „ „ 20 „	*183*	*4*
„ 18 „ „ 19 „	*165*	*10*
„ 17 „ „ 18 „	*147*	*6*
„ 16 „ „ 17 „	*127*	*6*
„ under 16 years	*105*	*10*

Provided that the general minimum time rate applicable during his first year's employment in the trade to a worker specified in this sub-paragraph, who enters, or has entered, the trade for the first time at or over the age of 19 years shall be:—

	s.	d.
During the first six months of such employment	*168*	*4*
" " second " " " "	*178*	*4*

PIECE WORK BASIS TIME RATES

3. The piece work basis time rates applicable to male workers of any age employed on piece work are—

	Per week s.	d.
(1) Workers specified in sub-paragraph (1), (2) or (3) of paragraph 2	*257*	*6*
(2) All other workers	*240*	*0*

PART III

FEMALE WORKERS

FEMALE WORKERS IN ALL BRANCHES OF THE TRADE OTHER THAN THE RETAIL BRANCH IN SCOTLAND

GENERAL MINIMUM TIME RATES

4. The general minimum time rates applicable to female workers other than those referred to in paragraph 6 are as follows:—

	Per week s.	d.
(1) Learners during the following periods of employment in the trade:—		
1st six months	*100*	*10*
2nd " "	*110*	*0*
2nd year	*136*	*8*
3rd "	*155*	*0*

Provided that a learner who enters, or has entered, the trade for the first time at or over the age of 18 years, shall be treated for the purpose of this sub-paragraph as though she had, at the date of her entry, completed 2 years of employment as a learner in the trade.

	s.	d.
(2) All other workers	*181*	*8*

PIECE WORK BASIS TIME RATE

	Per week s.	d.
5. The piece work basis time rate applicable to female workers other than those referred to in Paragraph 7 of any age employed on piece work is	*190*	*10*

FEMALE WORKERS IN THE RETAIL BRANCH OF THE TRADE IN SCOTLAND

GENERAL MINIMUM TIME RATES

6. The general minimum time rates payable to female workers employed in the retail branch of the trade, in Scotland, are as follows:—

	Per week s.	d.
(1) Learners during the following periods of employment in the trade:—		
1st six months	*100*	*10*
2nd " "	*110*	*0*
2nd year	*136*	*8*
3rd "	*155*	*0*
(2) All other workers	*181*	*8*

PIECE WORK BASIS TIME RATE

	Per week s. d.
7. The piece work basis time rate applicable to female workers of any age employed on piece work in the retail branch of the trade in Scotland is ...	*190 10*

PART IV

EXPERIENCE UNDER THE GOVERNMENT VOCATIONAL TRAINING SCHEME

8. Where any worker has completed a full course of training as a machinist in the cloth hat and cap section of the trade under the Government Vocational Training Scheme for resettlement training, such period of training shall, for the purpose of reckoning the period of the worker's employment in the trade, be treated as if it were—

(1) in the case of a female worker, a period of 3 years' employment as a learner in the trade, or

(2) in the case of a male worker, a period of at least one year's employment in the trade at or over the age of 21 years.

PART V

OVERTIME RATES AND WAITING TIME

ALL BRANCHES OF THE TRADE OTHER THAN THE RETAIL BRANCH

OVERTIME

9. Subject to the provisions of this Part of this Schedule, the minimum overtime rates set out in paragraph 10 are payable to a worker other than a worker employed in the retail branch of the trade in respect of any time worked:—

(1) in excess of the hours following, that is to say:

(*a*) in any week ... ... 40 hours

(*b*) on any day other than a Saturday, Sunday or customary holiday—
where the normal working hours exceed 8½ ... ... 9 hours
or
where the normal working hours are more than 8 but not more than 8½ ... ... 8½ hours
or
where the normal working hours are not more than 8... ... 8 hours

(2) on a Saturday, Sunday or customary holiday.

MINIMUM OVERTIME RATES

10.—(1) Minimum overtime rates are payable to any worker other than a worker employed in the retail branch of the trade as follows:—

(*a*) on any day other than a Sunday or customary holiday—

(i) for the first 2 hours of overtime worked ... ... time-and-a-quarter

(ii) for the next 2 hours ... ... time-and-a-half

(iii) thereafter ... ... double time

(*b*) on a Sunday or customary holiday—
for all time worked ... ... double time

Provided that where it is the practice in a Jewish undertaking for the employer to require attendance on Sunday instead of Saturday the provisions of this paragraph shall apply as if in such provisions the word "Saturday" were substituted for "Sunday", except where such substitution is unlawful.

(*c*) in any week, exclusive of any time in respect of which any minimum overtime rate is payable under the foregoing provisions of this sub-paragraph—

for all time worked in excess of 40 hours ... ... time-and-a-quarter

(2) The minimum overtime rates set out in sub-paragraph (1)(*a*) or (*b*) of this paragraph are payable in any week whether or not the minimum overtime rate set out in sub-paragraph (1)(*c*) is also payable.

RETAIL BRANCH
OVERTIME

11. Subject to the provisions of this Part of this Schedule, the minimum overtime rates set out in paragraph 12 are payable to workers in the retail branch of the trade as follows:—

(1) in any week, for all time worked in excess of ... ... 40 hours

(2) on any day other than a Saturday, Sunday or customary holiday, for all time worked in excess of ... ... 8 hours

Provided that where the worker normally attends on five days only in the week, minimum overtime rates shall apply to all time worked after ... ... 9 hours

(3) on a Saturday, not being a customary holiday,

(*a*) where the worker normally attends on six days in the week, for all time worked in excess of ... ... 4 hours

(*b*) where the worker normally attends on five days only in the week, for all time worked;

(4) on a Sunday or a customary holiday, for all time worked.

MINIMUM OVERTIME RATES

12.—(1) Subject to the provisions of this Part of this Schedule, minimum overtime rates are payable to a worker in the retail branch of the trade as follows:—

(*a*) on any day other than a Saturday, Sunday or customary holiday—

(i) for the first two hours worked in excess of 8 hours ...time-and-a-quarter

(ii) thereafter ... ... time-and-a-half

Provided that where the worker normally attends on five days only in the week, the said minimum overtime rates of time-and-a-quarter and time-and-a-half shall be payable after 9 and 11 hours' work respectively;

(*b*) on a Saturday, not being a customary holiday—

(i) where the worker normally attends on six days in the week—

for all time worked in excess of 4 hours ... ... time-and-a-half

(ii) where the worker normally attends on five days only in the week—

for the first 2 hours worked ... ... time-and-a-quarter
for the next 2 hours worked ... ... time-and-a-half
thereafter ... ... double time

(*c*) on a Sunday or a customary holiday—
for all time worked ... ... double time

(*d*) in any week, exclusive of any time in respect of which a minimum overtime rate is payable under the foregoing provisions of this sub-paragraph—

for all time worked in excess of 40 hours ... ... time-and-a-quarter

(2) The minimum overtime rates set out in sub-paragraph (1)(*a*), (*b*) or (*c*) of this paragraph are payable in any week, whether or not the minimum overtime rate set out in sub-paragraph (1)(*d*) of this paragraph is also payable.

(3) Where the worker normally attends on Sunday and not on Saturday, for the purposes of this Part of this Schedule (except where such attendance is unlawful), Saturday shall be treated as a Sunday and subject to the provisions of sub-paragraph (4) of this paragraph, Sunday as a Saturday.

(4) Where the worker normally attends on six days in the week and an ordinary weekday is substituted for Saturday or, in a case where the provisions of sub-paragraph (3) of this paragraph apply, for Sunday, as the worker's weekly short day, for the purposes of this Part of this Schedule (except where such substitution is unlawful) that ordinary weekday shall be treated as a Saturday and Saturday or Sunday, as the case may be, as an ordinary weekday.

(5) Where the worker normally attends on five days only in the week, including Saturday, a weekday on which he normally does not attend shall, for the purposes of this Part of this Schedule, be treated as a Saturday, and Saturday as another weekday.

13. In this Part of this Schedule—

(1) the expression "customary holiday" means:—

(*a*) In England and Wales—

(i) Christmas Day (or, if Christmas Day falls on a Sunday, such weekday as may be appointed by national proclamation, or, if none is so appointed, the next following Tuesday), Boxing Day, Good Friday, Easter Monday, Whit Monday, August Bank Holiday, and one other day to be agreed between the employer and the worker; or

(ii) in the case of each of the said days a day substituted by the employer therefor, being a day recognised by local custom as a day of holiday in substitution for the said day.

(*b*) In Scotland—

(i) New Year's Day (or the following day if New Year's Day falls on a Sunday);

the local Spring holiday;

the local Autumn holiday:

Provided that, where in any establishment it is not the custom or practice to observe all or any of such days as holidays, another day or other days, not fewer in number, may, by agreement between the employer and the worker, be substituted therefor; and

(ii) four other days to be agreed between the employer and the worker.

(2) the expressions "time-and-a-quarter", "time-and-a-half" and "double time" mean, respectively—

(*a*) in the case of a time worker, one and a quarter times, one and a half times and twice the hourly general minimum time rate otherwise payable to the worker;

(*b*) in the case of a piece worker—

(i) a time rate equal to one quarter, one half and the whole of the hourly piece work basis time rate otherwise applicable to the worker and, in addition thereto,

(ii) piece rates each of which would yield, in the circumstances of the case, to any ordinary worker, at least the same amount of money as the said hourly piece work basis time rate.

WAITING TIME

14.—(1) A worker is entitled to payment of the minimum remuneration specified in this Schedule for all time during which he is present on the premises of his employer unless he is present thereon in any of the following circumstances:—

(*a*) without the employer's consent, express or implied;

(*b*) for some purpose unconnected with his work and other than that of waiting for work to be given to him to perform;

(*c*) by reason only of the fact that he is resident thereon;

(*d*) during normal meal times in a room or place in which no work is being done and he is not waiting for work to be given to him to perform.

(2) The minimum remuneration payable under sub-paragraph (1) of this paragraph to a piece worker when not engaged on piece work is that which would be payable if he were a time worker.

PART VI
INTERPRETATION

15. In this Schedule, unless the context otherwise requires, the following expressions have the meanings hereby respectively assigned to them, that is to say:—

(1) "the trade" means the trade specified in paragraph 17.

(2) "the retail branch" means that branch of the trade in which the employer supplies the article direct to the individual wearer and employs the worker direct.

(3) A cutter is a male person who—

(*a*) is employed in a section of the trade, other than the silk hat section, on one or more of the operations of marking in or cutting any kind of material, laying up, hooking up or stripping and,

(*b*) for not less than 3 years after the age of 18 years has been employed in any section of the trade mainly on one or more of the last mentioned operations:

Provided that the work of a cutter shall not include the cutting of cloth or other textile materials for stitchers of hat leathers or for use as hat linings.

(4) A blocker, body maker, or finisher is a male person who is employed on one or more of the operations of—

(*a*) covering, pulling-on, or blocking hats or caps; or

(*b*) blocking straws, hoods or shapes, of any materials; or

(*c*) making shapes by means of a gas block;

and for not less than 3 years after the age of 18 years had been employed in any section of the trade mainly on one or more of the last mentioned operations.

(5) A stiffener is a male person who is employed in stiffening and has been employed in any section of the trade mainly in stiffening for not less than 3 years after the age of 18 years.

(6) A shaper is a male person who is employed in putting into shape by hand work the brim part of any hat or helmet which is made on a body or foundation of any material, and has been so employed in any section of the trade for not less than 3 years after the age of 18 years.

(7) A learner means a female worker who is employed by an employer who provides her with reasonable facilities for learning, practically and efficiently, any branch of the trade or the various processes involved in the making of any of the articles specified in the definition of the trade referred to in paragraph 17.

PART VII
WORKERS TO WHOM THIS SCHEDULE APPLIES

16. This Schedule shall not apply to workers employed as machinists in the cloth hat or cap section of the trade during any period in respect of which they are in receipt of allowances as provided under the Government Vocational Training Scheme for resettlement training if they are trainees who have been placed by the Department of Employment and Productivity with the employer for a period of approved training and if the requirements of the said scheme are duly complied with.

17. Subject to the provisions of paragraph 16, this Schedule applies to workers in relation to whom the Hat, Cap and Millinery Wages Council (Great Britain) operates, that is to say, workers employed in Great Britain in the trade specified in the Schedule to the Hat, Cap and Millinery Wages Councils (Abolition and Establishment) Order 1963(a), that is to say:—

"All workers employed in Great Britain in the making from any material of men's, women's or children's headgear, or the trimming thereof; including:—

Warehousing, packing or other operations incidental to or appertaining to the making or trimming of men's, women's or children's headgear; but excluding:—

(1) The casting and making of solid metal helmets;

(2) The making of rubberised or oilskin headgear where carried on in association with or in conjunction with the making of other rubberised or oilskin articles;

(3) The making of nurses' or servants' caps, chefs' caps, hospital ward caps, or similar articles;

(4) The making of field bonnets, sun bonnets, boudoir caps, or infants' millinery where carried on in association with or in conjunction with the making of dresses, non-tailored skirts, wraps, blouses, blouse-robes, jumpers, sports coats, neckwear, tea-gowns, dressing-gowns, dressing-jackets, pyjamas, underclothing, under-skirts, aprons, overalls, nurses' and servants' caps, juvenile clothing, baby linen or similar articles;

(5) The making of fur hats, where made in association with or in conjunction with the manufacture of furs or furriers' skins into garments, rugs or similar articles;

(6) The making of knitted headgear and the making of headgear from knitted fabrics where carried on in association with or in conjunction with the manufacture of the knitted fabrics;

(7) Warehousing and packing of men's, women's or children's headgear and other similar operations carried on in shops mainly engaged in the retail distribution of articles of any description that are not made or trimmed on the premises."

EXPLANATORY NOTE

(*This Note is not part of the Order.*)

This Order, which has effect from 8th July 1970, sets out the statutory minimum remuneration payable in substitution for that fixed by the Wages Regulation (Hat, Cap and Millinery) Order 1968 (Order H.C.M.(13)), which Order is revoked.

New provisions are printed in italics.

(a) S.I. 1963/122 (1963 I, p. 126).

1970 No. 886 (C. 21)

SUPREME COURT OF JUDICATURE, ENGLAND

CRIMINAL PROCEDURE, ENGLAND

JUDGMENTS

LANDLORD AND TENANT

The Administration of Justice Act 1970 (Commencement No. 1) Order 1970

Made - - - - 10*th June* 1970

The Lord Chancellor, in exercise of the power conferred on him by section 54(4) of the Administration of Justice Act 1970(a), hereby makes the following Order:—

1.—(1) This Order may be cited as the Administration of Justice Act 1970 (Commencement No. 1) Order 1970.

(2) In this Order " the Act " means the Administration of Justice Act 1970.

(3) The Interpretation Act 1889(b) shall apply to this order as it applies to an Act of Parliament.

2. The provisions of the Act specified in the schedule to this Order shall come into operation on 1st July 1970.

Dated 10th June 1970.

Gardiner, C.

SCHEDULE

Provisions of the Act	Subject matter of provisions
Section 5	The Vice-Chancellor.
Section 6	Divisional Courts.
Section 7	Extension of power to dispense with holding of assizes.
Section 8	Sittings of Central Criminal Court.
Section 9	Constitution of criminal division of the Court of Appeal and powers of single judge.

(a) 1970 c. 31. (b) 1889 c. 63.

Provisions of the Act	Subject matter of provisions
Section 10	Patents and Registered Designs Appeal Tribunals.
Section 40	Punishment for unlawful harassment of debtors.
Section 44	Interest on judgment debts.
Section 45	Removal of limit on number of county court judges assignable to a district and of certain registrars appointed jointly.
Section 46	Deputy county court registrar not to act as such in certain proceedings.
Section 47	Extension of power to make rules etc. for purposes of Rent Act 1968(**a**).
Section 49	Amendments relating to guardianship of minors.
Section 52	Financial provisions.
Section 54(1) and (2), (3) so far as it relates to the provisions of Schedule 11 mentioned in the last item of this Schedule, (4) and (5)	Citation, interpretation, repeals, commencement and extent.
Schedule 11 so far as it relates to sections 5 and 11 of the Guardianship of Infants Act 1886(**b**), section 63 of the Supreme Court of Judicature (Consolidation) Act 1925(**c**), the Patents Act 1949(**d**), the Registered Designs Act 1949(**e**), the Administration of Justice Act 1964(**f**), the Criminal Appeal Act 1966(**g**) and section 45(2) of the Criminal Appeal Act 1968(**h**)	Enactments repealed.

EXPLANATORY NOTE

(*This Note is not part of the Order.*)

This Order brings a number of provisions of the Administration of Justice Act 1970 into operation on 1st July 1970 together with the consequential repeals. The matters dealt with by the provisions to be brought into operation are indicated in the schedule to the Order.

(**a**) 1968 c. 23. (**b**) 1886 c. 27. (**c**) 1925 c. 49. (**d**) 1949 c. 87.
(**e**) 1949 c. 88. (**f**) 1964 c. 42. (**g**) 1966 c. 31. (**h**) 1968 c. 19.

1970 No. 887 (S. 67)

HIGH COURT OF JUSTICIARY, SCOTLAND

Act of Adjournal (Fees in the High Court of Justiciary) 1970

Made - - -	29*th May* 1970
Coming into Operation	1*st October* 1970

The Lord Justice-General, the Lord Justice-Clerk, and the Lords Commissioners of Justiciary, under and by virtue of the powers conferred upon them by section 2 of the Courts of Law Fees (Scotland) Act 1895**(a)** and of all other powers competent to them in that behalf, do hereby with the approval of the Treasury enact and declare as follows:—

1. The Act of Adjournal regulating the Fees of the High Court of Justiciary dated 18th December 1896**(b)** is hereby repealed.

2.—(1) The fees chargeable in the High Court of Justiciary shall be those specified in the Schedule hereto, and shall be paid when the writ is lodged, or when the step of procedure is taken, or when the act is done (as the case may be) in respect of which the fee is chargeable.

(2) Such fees shall be paid by means of stamps, or in such other manner as may be prescribed from time to time, by the Treasury by order made under section 2 of the Public Office Fees Act 1879**(c)**.

(3) Such fees shall be paid in the office of the Clerk of Justiciary to the Clerk of Justiciary or any officer acting for him, with the exception of fees for business performed on Circuit which shall be paid at the Circuit Town to the Circuit Clerk.

(4) The books of account to be kept in connection with such fees shall be in the form at present in use, or in such other form as the Clerk of Justiciary may consider expedient with a view to simplifying the form or to facilitate inspection of the books.

(5) In addition to the fees specified in the said Table there shall be payable to the Auditor of the Court of Session the like fees for taxing accounts of expenses as are prescribed from time to time by Act of Sederunt for the taxation of accounts of expenses in the Court of Session.

3. This Act of Adjournal may be cited as the Act of Adjournal (Fees in the High Court of Justiciary) 1970, and shall come into operation on 1st October 1970.

And the Lords appoint this Act of Adjournal to be recorded in the Books of Adjournal, and to be published in the *Edinburgh Gazette*.

J. L. Clyde,
I.P.D.

29th May 1970.

(a) 1895 c. 14. **(b)** S.R. & O. 1897/30 (Rev. XI, p. 566). **(c)** 1879 c. 58.

SCHEDULE

TABLE OF FEES

PAYABLE IN THE HIGH COURT OF JUSTICIARY

		£	s.	d.
1.	Bills of Suspension or Advocation, Appeals, Summary and other Applications, Answers, and other Papers not being Inventories or Notes	1	0	0
2.	Inventories, Productions, or Notes	0	10	0
3.	Bond of Caution	1	0	0
4.	Certificate of Caution	0	10	0
5.	Borrowing, each receipt	0	4	0
6.	Returnings, each	0	2	0
7.	Extract Decree	2	0	0
8.	Lodging Account of Expenses	0	10	0
9.	Criminal Letters—not exceeding 4 sheets	4	0	0
	each additional sheet	0	10	0
10.	Extract Conviction and sentence per sheet	0	15	0
11.	Certified Copy Interlocutor	0	7	0
12.	Copy Interlocutor	0	4	0
13.	Certified copy of any paper in print or manuscript, per sheet ...	0	5	0
14.	Lodging Caveats	0	5	0

EXPLANATORY NOTE

(This Note is not part of the Act of Adjournal.)

This Act of Adjournal prescribes a new Table of Fees payable in the High Court of Justiciary in substitution for the Table which has been continuously in force since 1897.

STATUTORY INSTRUMENTS

1970 No. 891

REPRESENTATION OF THE PEOPLE

The Elections (Welsh Forms) (No. 6) Regulations 1970

Made - - -	10*th June* 1970
Coming into Operation	11*th June* 1970

In pursuance of the powers conferred on me by section 1(1) of the Elections (Welsh Forms) Act 1964(**a**), I hereby make the following Regulations :—

1. These Regulations may be cited as the Elections (Welsh Forms) (No. 6) Regulations 1970 and shall come into operation on 11th June 1970.

2. The Elections (Welsh Forms) Regulations 1964(**b**), the Elections (Welsh Forms) Regulations 1965(**c**), and the form numbered 1 set out in the Schedule to the Elections (Welsh Forms) Regulations 1969(**d**) are hereby revoked.

James Callaghan,
One of Her Majesty's Principal
Secretaries of State.

Home Office,
Whitehall.

10th June 1970.

EXPLANATORY NOTE
(*This Note is not part of the Regulations.*)

These Regulations revoke the Regulations specified in Regulation 2 of these Regulations. The revoked Regulations prescribe translations into the Welsh language of certain electoral forms. These translations have been superseded by later translations prescribed by other statutory instruments under the Welsh Language Act 1967 (c.66).

(**a**) 1964 c. 31.
(**b**) S.I. 1964/1295 (1964 II, p. 2975).
(**c**) S.I. 1965/717 (1965 I, p. 2202).
(**d**) S.I. 1969/1407 (1969 III, p. 4144).

1970 No. 892

SOUTHERN RHODESIA

The Southern Rhodesia (Higher Authority for Power) Order 1970

Made - - - -	12*th June* 1970
Laid before Parliament	2*nd July* 1970
Coming into Operation	1*st October* 1970

At the Court at Buckingham Palace, the 12th day of June 1970

Present,

The Queen's Most Excellent Majesty in Council

Her Majesty, in exercise of the powers conferred on Her by section 3(1)(*c*) of the Southern Rhodesia Constitution Order 1965(**a**), is pleased, by and with the advice of Her Privy Council, to order, and it is hereby ordered, as follows :—

Citation, commencement and construction

1.—(1) This Order may be cited as the Southern Rhodesia (Higher Authority for Power) Order 1970 and shall come into operation on 1st October 1970.

(2) Save where the context otherwise requires, expressions used in this Order shall have the same meaning as in Part III of the Federation of Rhodesia and Nyasaland (Dissolution) Order in Council 1963(**b**) (hereinafter referrd to as " the principal Order ").

(3) Subject to the foregoing provisions of this Article, the Interpretation Act 1889(**c**) shall apply, with the necessary adaptations, for the purpose of interpreting this Order and otherwise in relation thereto as it applies for the purpose of interpreting and in relation to Acts of Parliament.

Membership of Higher Authority for Power

2. So long as this Order is in operation, and notwithstanding anything to the contrary contained in the principal Order, the Higher Authority for Power shall comprise, in addition to the two members who are Ministers of the Government of Zambia appointed by that Government, two members who shall be appointed under Article 3 of this Order and persons so appointed shall be members of the Higher Authority in place of Ministers of the Government of Southern Rhodesia.

Appointment of Members of Higher Authority by Secretary of State

3.—(1) So long as this Order is in operation and notwithstanding anything to the contrary contained in the principal Order, the Secretary of State may,

(**a**) S.I. 1965/1952 (1965 III, p. 5812). (**b**) S.I. 1963/2085 (1963 III, p. 4477).
(**c**) 52 & 53 Vict. c. 63.

by instrument in writing under his hand, appoint two members of the Higher Authority who may exercise the functions of their offices either in Southern Rhodesia or elsewhere.

(2) A person appointed as a member of the Higher Authority under this Article shall hold office until he resigns or until the Secretary of State otherwise directs by instrument under his hand, and shall then vacate office, but without prejudice to his eligibility for reappointment.

(3) Persons appointed members of the Higher Authority under this Article shall hold office upon such terms and conditions as may from time to time be determined by the Secretary of State.

(4) The Secretary of State may from time to time give to the members of the Higher Authority appointed under this Article such general or special directions relating to the exercise of their functions as members of the Higher Authority as he may think fit, and it shall be the duty of every person to whom any such directions are given to comply with them.

References to principal Order

4. Any reference in the Central African Power Act 1963(**a**) to the principal Order shall, in relation to any period during which this Order is in operation, be construed as a reference to the principal Order as modified by this Order.

W. G. Agnew.

EXPLANATORY NOTE

(*This Note is not part of the Order.*)

This Order makes temporary provision for the composition of the Higher Authority for Power established by the Federation of Rhodesia and Nyasaland (Dissolution) Order in Council 1963, substituting for two Ministers of the Government of Southern Rhodesia, two persons appointed by the Secretary of State.

(**a**) Act 62 of the Legislature of Southern Rhodesia.

1970 No. 897

JUVENILE COURTS AND OFFENDERS

The Juvenile Courts (London) Order 1970

Made - - -	11*th June* 1970
Coming into Operation	1*st July* 1970

In exercise of the powers conferred upon me by paragraphs 14 and 20 of Schedule 2 to the Children and Young Persons Act 1933**(a)**, as amended by section 17(1) of the Children and Young Persons Act 1963**(b)** read with section 12(1) of the Administration of Justice Act 1964**(c)**, I hereby make the following Order:—

1. This Order may be cited as the Juvenile Courts (London) Order 1970 and shall come into operation on 1st July 1970.

2. In the Schedule to the Juvenile Courts (London) Order 1965**(d)**, as amended**(e)** (which assigns divisions to juvenile courts in the metropolitan area and specifies the places of sitting of the courts), for the entry in column 2 relating to the place of sitting of a juvenile court for the South Central division of the metropolitan area there shall be substituted the following entry:—

"4 Kimpton Road,
Camberwell Green, S.E.5.".

James Callaghan,
One of Her Majesty's Principal
Secretaries of State.

Home Office,
Whitehall.
11th June 1970.

EXPLANATORY NOTE

(*This Note is not part of the Order*.)

This Order amends the Juvenile Courts (London) Order 1965 (which assigned divisions to juvenile courts in the inner London area and the City of London and specified the places of sitting of the courts) by substituting 4 Kimpton Road, Camberwell Green, S.E.5 as the place of sitting for a juvenile court for the South Central division for the place of sitting at present specified in the Order.

(a) 1933 c. 12.
(b) 1963 c. 37.
(c) 1964 c. 42.
(d) S.I. 1965/584 (1965 I, p. 1833).
(e) The amending instruments are not relevant to the subject matter of this Order.

STATUTORY INSTRUMENTS

1970 No. 898

AGRICULTURE

The Price Stability of Imported Products (Rates of Levy No. 8) Order 1970

Made - - - - 15*th June* 1970

Coming into Operation - 16*th June* 1970

The Minister of Agriculture, Fisheries and Food, in exercise of the powers conferred upon him by section 1(2), (4), (5), (6) and (7) of the Agriculture and Horticulture Act 1964(**a**) and of all other powers enabling him in that behalf, hereby makes the following order:—

1. This order may be cited as the Price Stability of Imported Products (Rates of Levy No. 8) Order 1970, and shall come into operation on 16th June 1970.

2.—(1) In this order—

" the Principal Order " means the Price Stability of Imported Products (Levy Arrangements) Order 1966(**b**) as amended(**c**) and as amended by any subsequent order, and if any such order is replaced by any subsequent order the expression shall be construed as a reference to such subsequent order;

AND other expressions have the same meaning as in the Principal Order.

(2) The Interpretation Act 1889(**d**) shall apply to the interpretation of this order as it applies to the interpretation of an Act of Parliament and as if this order and the orders hereby revoked were Acts of Parliament.

3. In accordance with and subject to the provisions of Part II of the Principal Order (which provides for the charging of levies on imports of certain specified commodities)—

(*a*) the rate of general levy for such imports into the United Kingdom of any specified commodity as are described in column 2 of Part I of the Schedule to this order in relation to a tariff heading indicated in column 1 of that Part shall be the rate set forth in relation thereto in column 3 of that Part;

(*b*) the rate of country levy for such imports into the United Kingdom of any specified commodity as are described in column 2 of Part II of the Schedule to this order in relation to a tariff heading indicated in column 1 of that Part shall be the rate set forth in relation thereto in column 3 of that Part.

(**a**) 1964 c. 28. (**b**) S.I. 1966/936 (1966 II, p. 2271).
(**c**) S.I. 1969/758, 1564 (1969 II, p. 2137; III, p. 5018). (**d**) 1889 c. 63.

4. The Price Stability of Imported Products (Rates of Levy No. 6) Order 1970(**a**) and the Price Stability of Imported Products (Rates of Levy No. 7) Order 1970(**b**) are hereby revoked.

In Witness whereof the Official Seal of the Minister of Agriculture, Fisheries and Food is hereunto affixed on 15th June 1970.

(L.S.)

R. J. E. Taylor,
Assistant Secretary.

(**a**) S.I. 1970/641 (1970 I, p. 2066). (**b**) S.I. 1970/765 (1970 II, p. 2409).

SCHEDULE

PART I

1. Tariff Heading	2. Description of Imports	3. Rate of General Levy
		per ton £ s. d.
	Imports of:—	
10.03	Barley	2 0 0
11.01	Wheat flours	15 0
11.02	Cereal groats— of barley	2 10 0
	Cereal meal— of barley	2 10 0
	Kibbled or cut cereals— barley	2 10 0
	Rolled, flaked, crushed or bruised cereals— barley	2 10 0
	Other processed cereals— barley	2 10 0

PART II

1. Tariff Heading	2. Description of Imports	3. Rate of Country Levy
		per ton £ s. d.
	Imports of:—	
10.03	Barley which has been grown in and consigned to the United Kingdom from—	
	the United States of America	2 0 0
	the Kingdom of the Netherlands	10 0
	the French Republic	10 0
	Canada	1 0 0
11.02	Barley groats, barley meal, kibbled or cut barley, rolled, flaked, crushed or bruised barley and other processed barley which, in each case, is the product of the Kingdom of the Netherlands and has been consigned to the United Kingdom from that country	2 10 0

EXPLANATORY NOTE

(*This Note is not part of the Order.*)

This order, which comes into operation on 16th June 1970, supersedes the Price Stability of Imported Products (Rates of Levy No. 6) Order 1970 and the Price Stability of Imported Products (Rates of Levy No. 7) Order 1970. It reduces the rates of all general and country levies in force immediately before the commencement of this order in relation to cereals and cereal products and by-products as follows:—

(*a*) the rate of general levy for each description of imports included in Part I of the Schedule to the order is reduced to the rate specified in relation thereto in column 3 of that Part; and

(*b*) the rate of country levy for each description of imports included in Part II of the Schedule is reduced to the rate specified in relation thereto in column 3 of that Part.

STATUTORY INSTRUMENTS

1970 No. 899

NATIONAL HEALTH SERVICE, ENGLAND AND WALES

The National Health Service (General Dental Services) Amendment Regulations 1970

Made - - - -	15*th June* 1970
Laid before Parliament	29*th June* 1970
Coming into Operation	1*st July* 1970

The Secretary of State for Social Services, in exercise of his powers under section 40 of the National Health Service Act 1946(**a**), as amended by section 11 of the National Health Service (Amendment) Act 1949(**b**), hereby makes the following regulations :—

1.—(1) These regulations may be cited as the National Health Service (General Dental Services) Amendment Regulations 1970 and shall come into operation on 1st July 1970.

(2) In these regulations—

" the principal regulations " means the National Health Service (General Dental Services) Regulations 1967(**c**) as amended(**d**) ; and

" regulation 28 " means regulation 28 of the principal regulations as amended by regulation 2(3) of the National Health Service (General Dental Services) Amendment (No. 2) Regulations 1969(**e**) (which provided for a new scale of fees for treatment).

(3) The Interpretation Act 1889(**f**) applies to the interpretation of these regulations as it applies to the interpretation of an Act of Parliament.

2. The principal regulations, as amended by regulation 2(3) of the said regulations of 1969, shall be further amended as follows:—

(1) Where an advice of payment from the Board to a Council is in respect of a contract or arrangement entered into or made on or after 1st July 1970 the Council shall pay to a practitioner in addition to the fees authorised under regulation 28 a sum equal to 10 per cent of the amount of these fees.

(2) (*a*) Subject to the following provisions of this regulation, these regulations shall not apply to general dental services provided under a contract or arrangement entered into or made before 1st July 1970 and such services shall continue to be subject to the provisions of the regulations in force immediately before that date.

(*b*) In respect of an advice of payment from the Board to a Council dated during the period beginning with 1st April 1970 and ending with 30th June 1970, the Council shall pay to a practitioner an additional sum equal to 7 per cent of the amounts authorised for payment.

(**a**) 1946 c. 81. (**b**) 1949 c. 93. (**c**) S.I. 1967/937 (1967 II, p. 2816).
(**d**) The relevant amending instrument is S.I. 1969/399 (1969 I, p. 1118).
(**e**) S.I. 1969/399 (1969 I, p. 1118). (**f**) 1889 c. 63.

(*c*) Where an advice of payment from the Board to a Council dated on or after 1st July 1970 is in respect of a contract or arrangement entered into or made on or after 1st April 1969 and before 1st July 1970 the Council shall pay to a practitioner in addition to the fees authorised under regulation 28 a sum equal to 10 per cent of the amount of these fees.

(*d*) Where an advice of payment from the Board to a Council dated on or after 1st July 1970 is in respect of a contract or arrangement entered into or made on or after 1st July 1966 and before 1st April 1969, the Council shall pay to a practitioner in addition to the fees authorised under regulation 28 a sum equal to 13 per cent of the amount of these fees.

(*e*) Where an advice of payment from the Board to a Council dated on or after 1st July 1970 is in respect of a contract or arrangement entered into or made before 1st July 1966 the Council shall pay to a practitioner in addition to the fees authorised under regulation 28 a sum equal to 25 per cent of the amount of these fees.

R. H. S. Crossman,

Secretary of State for Social Services.

15th June 1970.

EXPLANATORY NOTE

(*This Note is not part of the Regulations.*)

These Regulations further amend the National Health Service (General Dental Services) Regulations 1967 by providing for certain additional payments for practitioners, other than salaried practitioners, providing general dental services.

STATUTORY INSTRUMENTS

1970 No. 904 (L.18)

COUNTY COURTS

The County Court Districts (Miscellaneous) Order 1970

Made - - -	12*th June* 1970
Coming into Operation	1*st July* 1970

The Lord Chancellor, in exercise of the powers conferred on him by section 2 of the County Courts Act 1959(**a**) hereby makes the following Order:—

1.—(1) The County Court Districts Order 1970(**b**), as amended (**c**), (hereinafter called the principal Order) shall have effect as further amended by this Order.

(2) This Order may be cited as the County Court Districts (Miscellaneous) Order 1970 and shall come into operation on 1st July 1970.

(3) The Interpretation Act 1889(**d**) shall apply to the interpretation of this Order as it applies to the interpretation of an Act of Parliament.

2. A county court shall be held at Corby under the name of the Corby County Court, and the new entry set out in schedule 1 to this Order shall be inserted in schedule 1 to the principal Order immediately after the entry relating to the Conway, Llandudno and Colwyn Bay County Court.

3. The holding of the Bridport, Camelford, Cirencester, Dursley, Helston, Holsworthy, Honiton, Kington, Llanidloes, Market Harborough, Marlborough, Newcastle-under-Lyme, Newquay, Oakham, Richmond, Ripon, Ross, Swanage, Tavistock and Wincanton County Courts shall be discontinued, and the entries relating to these courts in schedule 1 to the principal Order shall be deleted.

4. The parts of the district of the Torquay County Court mentioned in column 3 of section 22A of schedule 2 to this Order shall be transferred to and form part of the districts of the county courts mentioned opposite thereto in column 1 :

Provided that nothing in this Article shall affect the jurisdiction of the Torquay County Court to deal with proceedings pending in that court on the coming into operation of this Order.

5. The amendments set out in columns 2 and 3 of schedule 2 to this Order shall be made in the corresponding columns of schedule 1 to the principal Order opposite the names of the courts mentioned in column 1.

6. The amendments set out in column 2 of schedule 3 to this Order shall be made in schedule 1 to the principal Order opposite the names of the courts mentioned in column 1.

(**a**) 1959 c. 22.
(**b**) S.I. 1970/16 (1970 I, p. 17).
(**c**) S.I. 1970/191.
(**d**) 1889 c. 63.

7. Where, in pursuance of Article 5 or 6 of this Order, the names of parts of county court districts are to be inserted into an entry in column 3 of schedule 1 to the principal Order, the names shall be inserted in their proper alphabetical order among the names in the existing entry.

8. The courts mentioned in column 2 of schedule 4 to this Order shall have jurisdiction in proceedings commenced before this Order comes into operation in the courts mentioned opposite thereto in column 1.

9. The Workington and Cockermouth County Court shall cease to be held at Cockermouth and shall be held at Workington under the name of the Workington County Court, and the words "and Cockermouth" shall accordingly be deleted from column 1 of schedule 1 to the principal Order.

10. For schedule 2 to the principal Order there shall be substituted the schedule set out in the appendix to this Order.

Dated 12th June 1970.

Gardiner, C.

SCHEDULE 1

CORBY COUNTY COURT

Column 1	*Column* 2	*Column* 3	
CORBY	Corby Urban District.	Corby.	
	Kettering Rural District (part). *Other part* in Kettering County Court District.	Ashley, Brampton Ash, Cottingham, East Carlton, Dingley, Gretton,	Middleton, Rockingham, Stanion, Stoke Albany, Sutton Bassett, Weldon, Weston by Welland, Wilbarston.
	Market Harborough Rural District (part). *Other parts* in Kettering, Leicester and Rugby County Court Districts.	Blaston, Hallaton,	Horninghold, Stockerston.
	Oundle Urban District.	Oundle.	
	Oundle and Thrapston Rural District (part). *Other parts* in Huntingdon, Kettering, Peterborough, Stamford and Wellingborough County Court Districts.	Benefield, Cotterstock, Deene, Deenethorpe, Glapthorn,	Harringworth, Lilford cum Wigsthorpe, Southwick, Stoke Doyle.
	Uppingham Rural District (part). *Other parts* in Leicester, Melton Mowbray and Stamford County Court Districts.	Ayston, Beaumont Chase, Bisbrooke, Caldecott, Liddington,	Seaton, Stoke Dry, Thorp by Water, Uppingham, Wardley.

SCHEDULE 2

SECTION 1

CORBY COUNTY COURT

AMENDMENTS CONSEQUENT ON ESTABLISHMENT

Column 1	*Column* 2	*Column* 3
HUNTINGDON	In the entry relating to the Oundle and Thrapston Rural District:—	
	Insert: "Corby" immediately before "Kettering".	
KETTERING	Delete "Corby Urban District".	Delete "Corby".
	In the entry relating to the Kettering Rural District:—	
	For "Market Harborough" substitute "Corby".	Delete "Cottingham, East Carlton, Gretton, Middleton, Stanion, Weldon".
	In the entry relating to the Oundle and Thrapston Rural District:—	
	Insert: "Corby" immediately before "Huntingdon".	Delete "Benefield, Deene, Deenethorpe, Lilford cum Wigsthorpe".
PETERBOROUGH	Delete "Oundle Urban District".	Delete "Oundle".
	In the entry relating to the Oundle and Thrapston Rural District:—	
	Insert: "Corby" immediately before Huntingdon.	Delete: "Cotterstock, Glapthorn, Southwick, Stoke Doyle".
WELLINGBOROUGH	In the entry relating to the Oundle and Thrapston Rural District:—	
	Insert: "Corby" immediately before "Huntingdon".	

SECTION 2

BRIDPORT COUNTY COURT

Amendments consequent on closure

Column 1	*Column* 2	*Column* 3
AXMINSTER AND CHARD	In the entry relating to the Beaminster Rural District:—	
	Delete "Bridport".	Insert "Bettiscombe, Marshwood, Pilsdon".
	In the entry relating to the Bridport Rural District:—	
	For "Bridport" substitute "Dorchester".	Insert "Chideock, Stanton, St. Gabriel, Whitchurch Canonicorum."
DORCHESTER	In the entry relating to the Beaminster Rural District:—	
	Delete "Bridport"	Insert "Hooke, Mapperton, Netherbury, North Poorton, Powerstock, Rampisham."
	After the entry relating to the Bridport Rural District insert the following two entries:—	
	"Bridport Municipal Borough.	Bridport".
	"Bridport Rural District (part). *Other part* in Axminster and Chard County Court District.	Allington, Askerswell, Bothenhampton, Bradpole, Burton Bradstock, Chilcombe, Litton Cheney, Loders, Puncknowle, Shipton, Gorge, Swyre, Symondsbury."
YEOVIL	In the entry relating to the Beaminster Rural District:—	
	Delete "Bridport".	Insert "Beaminster, Broadwindsor, Burstock, Stoke Abbott."

SECTION 3

CAMELFORD COUNTY COURT

AMENDMENTS CONSEQUENT ON CLOSURE

Column 1	*Column* 2	*Column* 3
BODMIN	After the entry relating to the Bodmin Municipal Borough insert the following entry:—	
	"Camelford Rural District (part). *Other part* in Launceston County Court District.	Advent, Camelford, Michaelstow, St. Breward, St. Teath, St. Endellion, St. Kew, St. Tudy."
	In the entry relating to the Wadebridge and Padstow Rural District:—	
	For the words "*Other parts* in Camelford and Newquay County Court Districts" substitute "*Other part* in Truro and Falmouth County Court District".	
LAUNCESTON	Before the entry relating to the Holsworthy Rural District insert the following entry:—	
	"Camelford Rural District (part). *Other part* in Bodmin County Court District.	Davidstow, Forrabury and Minster, Lesnewth, Otterham, St. Clether, St. Juliot, Tintagel, Travalga.
	In the entry relating to the Stratton Rural District:—	
	For "Holsworthy" substitute "Bideford"	Insert "Jacobstow, St. Genny's".

SECTION 4

CIRENCESTER COUNTY COURT

Amendments consequent on closure

Column 1	*Column* 2	*Column* 3
CHELTENHAM	Immediately after the entry relating to the Cheltenham Rural District insert the following entry:—	
	"Cirencester Rural District (part). *Other parts* in Malmesbury, Stroud and Swindon County Court Districts.	Bagendon, Barnsley, Baunton, Brimpsfield, Colesborne, Daglingworth, Duntisbourne Abbots, Duntisbourne Rouse, Elkstone, Hatherop, North Cerney, Quenington, Rendcombe, Syde, Winstone."
	In the entry relating to the Northleach Rural District:—	
	For "Cirencester" substitute "Swindon".	Insert "Bibury, Chedworth, Coln St. Aldwyn, Coln St. Dennis, Southrop, Winson".
MALMESBURY	Before the entry relating to the Malmesbury Municipal Borough insert the following entry:—	
	"Cirencester Rural District (part). *Other parts* in Cheltenham, Stroud and Swindon County Court Districts.	Kemble, Poole Keynes, Somerford Keynes, South Cerney."
STROUD	Before the entry relating to the Gloucester Rural District insert the following entry:—	
	"Cirencester Rural District (part). *Other parts* in Cheltenham, Malmesbury and Swindon County Court Districts.	Coates, Edgeworth, Rodmarton, Sapperton."
SWINDON	Immediately after the entry relating to the Calne and Chippenham Rural District insert the following two entries:—	
	"Cirencester Urban District.	Cirencester".
	"Cirencester Rural District (part). *Other parts* in Cheltenham, Malmesbury and Stroud County Court Districts.	Ampney Crucis, Ampney St. Mary, Ampney St. Peter, Down Ampney, Driffield, Fairford, Kempsford, Lechlade, Maiseyhampton, Poulton, Preston, Siddington."
	In the entry relating to the Cricklade and Wootton Bassett Rural District :—	
	Delete "(part)" and "*Other part* in Cirencester County Court District."	Insert "Ashton Keynes, Latton, Leigh, Marston Meysey".
	Immediately after the entry relating to the Marlborough and Ramsbury Rural District insert the following entry:—	
	"Northleach Rural District (part). *Other part* in Cheltenham County Court District.	Eastleach."

SECTION 5

DURSLEY COUNTY COURT

AMENDMENTS CONSEQUENT ON CLOSURE

Column 1	*Column* 2	*Column* 3
CHELTEN-HAM	In the entry relating to the Gloucester Rural District:—	
	Delete "Dursley".	
GLOUCES-TER	In the entry relating to the Gloucester Rural District:—	
	Delete "Dursley".	
MALMES-BURY	In the entry relating to the Tetbury Rural District:—	
	For "*Other parts* in Dursley and Stroud County Court Districts" substitute "*Other part* in Stroud County Court District".	
THORN-BURY	In the entry relating to the Thornbury Rural District:—	
	For "Dursley" substitute "Stroud".	Insert: "Charfield, Cromhall, Tortworth."
STROUD	Before the entry relating to the Gloucester Rural District insert the following entry:—	
	"Dursley Rural District.	Cam, Coaley, Dursley, Kingswood, North Nibley, Nympsfield, Slimbridge, Stinchcombe, Uley and Owlpen, Wotton under Edge."
	In the entry relating to the Gloucester Rural District:—	
	Delete "Dursley".	Insert "Frocester".
	In the entry relating to the Tetbury Rural District:—	
	For "*Other parts* in Dursley and Malmesbury County Court Districts" substitute "*Other part* in Malmesbury County Court District".	Insert "Kingscote, Ozleworth."
	After the entry relating to the Tetbury Rural District insert the following entry:—	
	"Thornbury Rural District (part). *Other part* in Thornbury County Court District.	Alkington, Berkeley, Ham and Stone, Hamfallow, Hinton."

SECTION 6

HELSTON COUNTY COURT

AMENDMENTS CONSEQUENT ON CLOSURE

Column 1	*Column* 2	*Column* 3
PENZANCE	Before the entry relating to the Penzance Municipal Borough insert the following two entries:—	
	"Helston Municipal Borough.	Helston."
	"Kerrier Rural District (part). *Other parts* in Redruth and Truro and Falmouth County Court Districts.	Breage, Cury, Germoe, Grade Ruan, Gunwalloe, Landewednack, Manaccan, Mawgan in Meneage, Mullion, St. Anthony in Meneage, St. Keverne, St. Martin in Meneage, Sithney, Wendron".
REDRUTH	In the entry relating to the Kerrier Rural District:—	
	For "Helston" substitute "Penzance".	Insert "Crowan".
TRURO AND FALMOUTH	In the entry relating to the Kerrier Rural District:—	
	For "Helston substitute "Penzance".	Insert "Constantine."

SECTION 7

HOLSWORTHY COUNTY COURT

AMENDMENTS CONSEQUENT ON CLOSURE

Column 1	*Column* 2	*Column* 3
BARN-STAPLE	In the entry relating to the Torrington Rural District:—	
	For "*Other parts* in Bideford and Holsworthy County Court Districts" substitute "*Other part* in Bideford County Court District".	
BIDEFORD	In the entry relating to the Bideford Rural District:—	
	Delete "(part) *Other part* in Holsworthy County Court District".	Insert "Welcombe".
	After the entry relating to the Bideford Rural District insert the following entry:—	
	"Bude-Stratton Urban District.	Bude-Stratton."
	In the entry relating to the Holsworthy Rural District:—	
	For "*Other parts* in Holsworthy and Launceston County Court Districts substitute "*Other part* in Launceston County Court District".	Insert "Abbots Bickington, Black Torrington, Bradford, Bradworthy, Cookbury, Holsworthy, Holsworthy Hamlets, Milton Damerel, Pancrasweek, Sutcombe, Thornbury."
	Immediately after the entry relating to the Northam Urban District insert the following entry:—	
	"Stratton Rural District (part). *Other part* in Launceston County Court District.	Kilkhamton, Launcells, Morwenstow."
	In the entry relating to the Torrington Rural District:—	
	For "*Other parts* in Barnstaple and Holsworthy County Court Districts" substitute "*Other part* in Barnstaple County Court District".	Insert "Buckland Filleigh, Shebbear, Sheepwash."
LAUNCES-TON	In the entry relating to the Holsworthy Rural District:—	
	For "*Other parts* in Bideford and Holsworthy County Court Districts" substitute "*Other part* in Bideford County Court District".	Insert "Ashwater, Bridgerule, Clawton, Halwill, Hollacombe, Luffincott, Pyworthy, Tetcott".
	Immediately after the entry relating to the Launceston Rural District insert the following entry:—	
	"Stratton Rural District (part). *Other part* in Bideford County Court District.	Marhamchurch, North Tamerton, Poundstock, Week St. Mary, Whitstone."

SECTION 8

HONITON COUNTY COURT

AMENDMENTS CONSEQUENT ON CLOSURE

Column 1	*Column* 2	*Column* 3	
AXMINSTER AND CHARD	Immediately after the entry relating to the Chard Rural District insert the following entry:—		
	"Honiton Rural District (part). *Other part* in Exeter County Court District.	Branscombe, Cotleigh, Northleigh, Offwell,	Southleigh, Widworthy, Yarcombe."
EXETER	Immediately after the entry relating to the Exmouth Urban District insert the following three entries:—		
	"Honiton Municipal Borough.	Honiton".	
	"Honiton Rural District (part). *Other part* in Axminster and Chard County Court District.	Awliscombe, Broadhembury, Buckerell, Combe Raleigh, Dunkeswell, Farway, Feniton,	Gittisham, Luppitt, Monkton, Payhembury, Plymtree, Sheldon, Talaton, Upottery."
	"Ottery St. Mary Urban District.	Ottery St. Mary."	
	After the entry relating to the St. Thomas Rural District insert the following entry:—		
	"Sidmouth Urban District.	Sidmouth."	

SECTION 9

KINGTON COUNTY COURT

Amendments consequent on closure

Column 1	*Column* 2	*Column* 3
BUILTH	In the entry relating to the New Radnor Rural District:—	
	For "Kington" substitute "Knighton".	Insert "Colva, Gladestry, Llanfihangel Nant Melan, Michaelchurch on Arrow, Newchurch, Trewern and Gwaithla".
HEREFORD	Immediately after the entry relating to the Hereford Rural District insert the following two entries:—	
	"Kington Rural District (part). *Other part* in Leominster County Court District.	Brilley, Eardisley, Huntington, Kington Rural, Lyonshall, Whitney, Winforton with Willersley."
	"Kington Urban District.	Kington."
	In the entry relating to the Weobley Rural District:—	
	For "*Other parts* in Kington and Leominster County Court Districts" substitute "*Other part* in Leominster County Court District."	Insert "Almeley, Kinnersley, Sarnesfield".
KNIGHTON	Immediately after the entry relating to the Leominster and Wigmore Rural District insert the following entry:—	
	"New Radnor Rural District (part). *Other parts* in Builth and Llandrindod Wells County Court Districts.	Ednol, Evenjobb, Newcastle, Burland and Burva, Harpton and Wolfpits, Kinnerton Salford and Badland, New Radnor, Old Radnor and Burlingjobb, Walton and Womaston."
LEOMINSTER	Immediately after the entry relating to the Bromyard Rural District insert the following entry:—	
	"Kington Rural District (part). *Other part* in Hereford County Court District.	Byton, Combe, Kinsham, Knill, Lower Harpton, Pembridge, Rodd, Nash and Little Brampton, Stapleton, Staunton on Arrow, Titley."
	In the entry relating to the Weobley Rural District:—	
	For "*Other parts* in Hereford and Kington County Court Districts" substitute "*Other part* in Hereford County Court District".	
LLANDRINDOD WELLS	In the entry relating to the New Radnor Rural District:—	
	For "Kington" substitute "Knighton".	

SECTION 10

LLANIDLOES COUNTY COURT

AMENDMENTS CONSEQUENT ON CLOSURE

Column 1	*Column* 2	*Column* 3
NEWTOWN	Immediately after the entry relating to the Knighton Rural District insert the following entry:—	
	"Llanidloes Municipal Borough.	Llanidloes".
	In the entry relating to the Newton and Llanidloes Rural District:—	
	Delete "(part). *Other part* in Llanidloes County Court District".	Insert "Llangurig, Llanidloes Without, Trefeglwys".

SECTION 11

MARKET HARBOROUGH COUNTY COURT

AMENDMENTS CONSEQUENT ON CLOSURE

Column 1	*Column* 2	*Column* 3
HINCKLEY	In the entry relating to the Lutterworth Rural District:— Delete "Market Harborough".	
KETTERING	Before the entry relating to the Burton Latimer Urban District insert the following entry:—	
	"Brixworth Rural District (part). *Other part* in Northampton County Court District.	East Farndon."
	In the entry relating to the Kettering Rural District:—	
	Delete "(part). *Other part* in Market Harborough County Court District".	Insert "Braybrooke".
	After the entry relating to the Kettering Rural District insert the following two entries:—	
	"Market Harborough Urban District.	Market Harborough".
	"Market Harborough Rural District (part). *Other parts* in Corby, Leicester and Rugby County Court Districts.	Bringhurst, Cranoe, Drayton, Great Easton, Medbourne, Nevill, Holt Slawston, Welham".
LEICESTER	In the entry relating to the Lutterworth Rural District:— Delete "Market Harborough".	
	Immediately after the entry relating to the Market Bosworth Rural District insert the following entry:—	
	"Market Harborough Rural District (part). *Other parts* in Corby, Kettering and Rugby County Court Districts.	East Langton, Fleckney, Foxton, Glooston, Gumley, Kibworth Beauchamp, Kibworth Harcourt, Laughton, Lubenham, Mowsley, Saddington, Shangton, Smeeton Westerby, Stonton Wyville, Thorpe Langton, Tur Langton, West Langton."
NORTHAMPTON	In the entry relating to the Brixworth Rural District:—	
	For "Market Harborough" substitute "Kettering".	Insert "Arthingworth, Clipston, Great Oxendon, Haselbech, Kelmarsh, Marston Trussell, Naseby, Sibbertoft, Sulby, Welford".
RUGBY	In the entry relating to the Lutterworth Rural District:—	
	For "*Other parts* in Hinckley, Leicester and Market Harborough County Court Districts" substitute "*Other parts* in Hinckley and Leicester County Court Districts".	Insert "Knaptoft, North Kilworth".
	Immediately after the entry relating to the Lutterworth Rural District insert the following entry:—	
	"Market Harborough Rural District (part). *Other parts* in Corby, Kettering and Leicester County Court Districts.	Husbands Bosworth, Theddingworth."

SECTION 12

MARLBOROUGH COUNTY COURT

Amendments consequent on closure

Column 1	*Column* 2	*Column* 3
ANDOVER	In the entry relating to the Marlborough and Ramsbury Rural District:—	
	Delete "Marlborough".	
	In entry relating to the Pewsey Rural District:—	
	For "*Other parts* in Devizes, Marlborough and Salisbury County Court Districts" substitute *Other parts* in Devizes, Salisbury and SwindonCounty Court Districts".	Insert "Collingbourne Ducis, Collingbourne Kingston, Everleigh".
DEVIZES	In the entry relating to the Pewsey Rural District:—	
	For "*Other parts* in Andover, Marlborough and Salisbury County Court Districts" substitute "*Other parts* in Andover, Salisbury and Swindon County Court Districts".	Insert "Alton".
NEWBURY	In the entry relating to the Marlborough and Ramsbury Rural District:—	
	Delete "Marlborough".	Insert "Shalbourne".
SALISBURY	In the entry relating to the Pewsey Rural District:—	
	For "Marlborough" substitute "Swindon".	
SWINDON	Immediately after the entry relating to the Highworth Rural District insert the following entry:—	
	"Marlborough Municipal Borough.	Marlborough".
	In the entry relating to the Marlborough and Ramsbury Rural District:—	
	Delete "Marlborough".	Insert "Avebury, Berwick Bassett, Broad Hinton, Chilton Foliat, East Kennett, Froxfield, Fyfield, Grafton, Great Bedwyn, Little Bedwyn, Mildenhall, Ogbourne St. Andrew, Ogbourne St. George, Preshute, Ramsbury, Savernake, West Overton, Winterbourne Bassett, Winterbourne Monkton".
	After the entry relating to the Marlborough and Ramsbury Rural District insert the following entry:—	
	"Pewsey Rural District (part). *Other parts* in Andover, Devizes and Salisbury County Court Districts.	Burbage, Easton Royal, Manningford, Milton, Lilbourne, Pewsey, Wilcot and Huish, Wootton Rivers."

SECTION 13

NEWCASTLE UNDER LYME COUNTY COURT

AMENDMENTS CONSEQUENT ON CLOSURE

Column 1	*Column* 2	*Column* 3
CREWE	In the entry relating to the Newcastle under Lyme Rural District:—	
	For "Newcastle under Lyme" substitute "Stoke on Trent".	
MARKET DRAYTON	In the entry relating to the Newcastle under Lyme Rural District:—	
	For "Newcastle under Lyme" substitute "Stoke on Trent".	
STAFFORD	In the entry relating to the Stone Rural District:—	
	For "*Other parts* in Stoke on Trent and Newcastle under Lyme County Court Districts" substitute "*Other part* in Stoke on Trent County Court District".	
STOKE ON TRENT	"After the entry relating to the Leek Rural District insert the following two entries:—	
	"Newcastle under Lyme Municipal Borough.	Newcastle under Lyme."
	"Newcastle under Lyme Rural District (part). *Other parts* in Crewe and Market Drayton County Court Districts.	Audley Rural, Chapel and Hill Chorlton, Keele, Madeley, Maer, Whitmore."
	In the entry relating to Stone Rural District:—	
	For "*Other parts* in Newcastle under Lyme and Stafford County Court Districts" substitute "*Other part* in Stafford County Court District".	Insert "Standon, Swynnerton".

SECTION 14

NEWQUAY COUNTY COURT

AMENDMENTS CONSEQUENT ON CLOSURE

Column 1	*Column* 2	*Column* 3	
BODMIN	In the entry relating to the St. Austell Rural District:—		
	For "*Other parts* in Newquay and St. Austell County Court Districts" substitute "*Other parts* in St. Austell and Truro and Falmouth County Court Districts".		
	In the entry relating to the Wadebridge and Padstow Rural District:—		
	For "*Other parts* in Camelford and Newquay County Court Districts" substitute "*Other part* in Truro and Falmouth County Court District".		
REDRUTH	In the entry relating to the Truro Rural District:—		
	For "*Other parts* in Newquay and Truro and Falmouth County Court Districts substitute "*Other part* in Truro and Falmouth County Court District".		
ST. AUSTELL	In the entry relating to the St. Austell Rural District:—		
	For "Newquay" substitute "Truro and Falmouth".		
TRURO AND FALMOUTH	Immediately after the entry relating to the Kerrier Rural District insert the following entry:—		
	"Newquay Urban District.	Newquay."	
	Immediately after the entry relating to the Penryn Municipal Borough insert the following entry:—		
	"St. Austell Rural District (part). *Other parts* in Bodmin and St. Austell County Court Districts.	Colan, Mawgan in Pydor,	St. Columb Major, St. Enoder."
	In the entry relating to the Truro Rural District:—		
	For "*Other parts* in Newquay and Redruth County Court Districts" substitute "*Other part* in Redruth County Court District".	Insert "Cubert, Newlyn".	
	After the entry relating to the Truro Rural District insert the following entry:—		
	"Wadebridge and Padstow Rural District (part). *Other part* in Bodmin County Court District.	St. Ervan,	St. Eval."

SECTION 15

OAKHAM COUNTY COURT

Amendments consequent on closure

Column 1	*Column* 2	*Column* 3	
GRANTHAM	In the entry relating to Melton and Belvoir Rural District:—		
	For "*Other parts* in Melton Mowbray and Oakham County Court Districts" substitute "*Other part* in Melton Mowbray County Court District".		
HUNTINGDON	In the entry relating to the Oundle and Thrapston Rural District:—		
	Delete "Oakham".		
KETTERING	In the entry relating to the Oundle and Thrapston Rural District:—		
	Delete "Oakham".		
LEICESTER	In the entry relating to the Billesdon Rural District:—		
	For "Oakham" substitute "Melton Mowbray".		
	Immediately after the entry relating to the Oadby Urban District insert the following entry:—		
	"Uppingham Rural District (part). *Other parts* in Corby, Melton Mowbray and Stamford County Court Districts.	Belton."	
MELTON MOWBRAY	Before the entry relating to the Bingham Rural District insert the following entry:—		
	"Billesdon Rural District (part). *Other part* in Leicester County Court District.	Owston, Whatborough,	Newbold, Withcote."
	In the entry relating to the Melton and Belvoir Rural District:—		
	For "*Other parts* in Grantham and Oakham County Court Districts" substitute "*Other part* in Grantham County Court District".	Insert "Knossington".	
	After the entry relating to the Melton Mowbray Urban District insert the following three entries:—		
	"Oakham Rural District (part). *Other part* in Stamford County Court District.	Ashwell, Barleythorpe, Barrow, Braunston, Brooke, Burley, Cottesmore, Egleton, Greetham, Gunthorpe, Hambleton,	Horn, Langham, Leighfield, Manton, Market Overton, Martinsthorpe, Streeton, Teigh, Thistleton, Wissendine."
	"Oakham Urban District.	Oakham."	
	"Uppingham Rural District (part). *Other parts* in Corby, Leicester and Stamford County Court Districts.	Preston, Ridlington,	Wing."

SECTION 15 (cont.).

Column 1	*Column* 2	*Column* 3
PETER-BOROUGH	In the entry relating to the Oundle and Thrapston Rural District:—	
	Delete "Oakham".	
STAMFORD	In the entry relating to Ketton Rural District:—	
	Delete "(part). *Other part* in Oakham County Court District".	Insert "Ketton".
	In the entry relating to the Oakham Rural District:—	
	For "Oakham" substitute "Melton Mowbray".	Insert "Edith Weston, Empingham, Exton, Lyndon, Normanton, Whitwell."
	In the entry relating to Oundle and Thrapston Rural District:—	
	Delete "Oakham" and insert "Corby" immediately before "Huntingdon".	Insert "Wakerley".
	After the entry relating to the Stamford Municipal Borough insert the following entry:—	
	"Uppingham Rural District (part). *Other parts* in Corby, Leicester and Melton Mowbray County Court Districts.	Barrowden, Glaston, Morcott, North Luffenham, Pilton, South Luffenham."
WELLING-BOROUGH	In the entry relating to the Oundle and Thrapston Rural District:—	
	Delete "Oakham".	

SECTION 16

RICHMOND COUNTY COURT

AMENDMENTS CONSEQUENT ON CLOSURE

Column 1	*Column* 2	*Column* 3	
DARLINGTON	Immediately after the entry relating to the Darlington Rural District insert the following three entries:—		
	"Reeth Rural District.	Arkengarthdale, Ellerton Abbey, Grinton, Marrick,	Melbecks, Muker, Reeth."
	"Richmond Municipal Borough.	Richmond."	
	"Richmond Rural District.	Aldbrough, Appleton, Aske Bolton upon Swale, Brompton upon Swale, Brough, Caldwell, Catterick, Colburn, Dalton, Downholme, Easby, East Layton, Ellerton upon Swale, Eppleby, Forcett with Carkin, Gayles, Gilling, Hipswell,	Hudswell, Kirby Hill, Marske, Melsonby, Middleton Tyas, Moulton, New Forest, Newsham, North Cowton, Ravensworth, St. Martin, Scorton, Scotton, Skeeby, Stainton, Stanwick St. John, Tunstall, Uckerby, Walburn, West Layton, Whashton."

SECTION 17

RIPON COUNTY COURT

Amendments consequent on closure

Column 1	*Column* 2	*Column* 3
HARRO-GATE	Before the entry relating to the Harrogate Municipal Borough insert the following entry:—	
	"Bedale Rural District (part). *Other part* in Northallerton County Court District.	Burnston, Carthorpe, East Tanfield, Howgrave, Kirklington cum Upsland, Snape with Thorpe, Sutton with Howgrave, Well, West Tanfield."
	After the entry relating to the Knaresborough Urban District insert the following entry:—	
	"Masham Rural District.	Burton upon Ure, Colsterdale, Ellingstring, Ellingtons, Fearby, Healey, Ilton cum Pott, Masham, Swinton with Wathermarske."
	In the entry relating to the Nidderdale Rural District:—	
	For "*Other parts* in Ripon and York County Court Districts" substitute "*Other part* in York County Court District".	Insert "Burton Leonard, South Stainley with Cayton, Westwick".
	Immediately after the entry relating to the Nidderdale Rural District insert the following entry:—	
	"Ripon Municipal Borough.	Ripon."
	In the entry relating to the Ripon and Pateley Bridge Rural District:—	
	Delete "(part). *Other part* in Ripon County Court District".	Insert "Aldfield, Azerley, Bishop Monkton, Bridge Hewick, Clotherholme, Copt Hewick, Eavestone, Givendale, Grantley, Grewelthorpe, Kirby Malzeard, Laverton, Lindrick with Studley Royal and Fountains, Littlethorpe, Markingfield Hall, Markington with Wallerthwaite, Newby with Mulwith, North Stainley with Scenningford, Nunwick with Howgrave, Sawley, Sharow, Skelding, Skelton, Studley Roger, Sutton Grange, Winksley".
	In the entry relating to the Thirsk Rural District:—	
	For "*Other parts* in Northallerton and Ripon County Court Districts" substitute "*Other part* in Northallerton County Court District".	Insert "Humberton, Kirby Hill, Lanthorpe, Milby, Norton le Clay, Thornton Bridge."
	After the entry relating to the Thirsk Rural District insert the following entry:—	
	"Wath Rural District.	Asenby, Baldersby, Cundall with Leckby, Dishforth, Hutton Conyers, Marton le Moor, Melmerby, Middleton Quernhow, Norton Conyers, Rainton with Newby, Wath."

SECTION 18

ROSS COUNTY COURT

AMENDMENTS CONSEQUENT ON CLOSURE

Column 1	*Column* 2	*Column* 3
GLOUCESTER	In the entry relating to the East Dean Rural District:—	
	Delete "(part). *Other part* in Ross County Court District".	Insert "Ruardean".
	Immediately after the entry relating to the Newent Rural District insert the following entry:—	
	"Ross and Whitchurch Rural District (part). *Other parts* in Hereford and Monmouth County Court Districts.	Aston Ingham, Hope Mansell, Lea, Linton, Upton Bishop, Weston under Penyard."
HEREFORD	Immediately after the entry relating to the Ledbury Rural District insert the following entry:—	
	"Ross and Whitchurch Rural District (part). *Other parts* in Gloucester and Monmouth County Court Districts.	Ballingham, Brockhampton, Harewood, Hentland, How Caple, King's Caple, Llandinabo, Llanwarne, Pencoyd, St. Weonards, Sollors Hope, Tretire with Michaelchurch, Yatton."
MONMOUTH	In the entry relating to the Ross and Whitchurch Rural District:—	
	For "*Other part* in Ross County Court District" substitute "*Other parts* in Gloucester and Hereford County Court Districts".	Insert "Brampton Abbots, Bridstow, Foy, Goodrich, Llangarron, Marstow, Peterstow, Ross Rural, Sellack, Walford".
	Immediately after the entry relating to the Ross and Whitchurch Rural District insert the following entry:—	
	"Ross on Wye Urban District.	Ross on Wye."

SECTION 19

SWANAGE COUNTY COURT

Amendments consequent on closure

Column 1	*Column* 2	*Column* 3
DORCHESTER	In the entry relating to the Beaminster Rural District:—	
	Delete "Bridport".	
	In the entry relating to the Wareham and Purbeck Rural District:—	
	Delete "Swanage".	Insert "Coombe Keynes, East Lulworth, West Lulworth, Wool".
POOLE	Immediately after the entry relating to the Poole Municipal Borough insert the following two entries:—	
	"Swanage Urban District.	Swanage."
	"Wareham Municipal Borough.	Wareham."
	In the entry relating to the Wareham and Purbeck Rural District:—	
	Delete "Swanage".	Insert "Arne, Bere Regis, Church Knowle, Corfe Castle, (part), viz. the entire Civil Parish except Furzey, Green, Long and Round Islands. East Holme, East Stoke, Kimmeridge, Langton Matravers, Morden, Steeple, Studland (part) viz. The entire Civil Parish except Brownsea Island, Tyneham, Wareham St. Martin, Worth Matravers."
WEYMOUTH	In the entry relating to the Wareham and Purbeck Rural District :—	
	For "*Other parts* in Dorchester, Poole and Swanage County Court Districts" substitute "*Other parts* in Dorchester and Poole County Court Districts".	

SECTION 20

TAVISTOCK COUNTY COURT

Amendments consequent on closure

Column 1	*Column* 2	*Column* 3
LAUNCESTON	In the entry relating to the Tavistock Rural District:—	
	For "Tavistock" substitute "Plymouth".	
LISKEARD	In the entry relating to the St. Germans Rural District:—	
	For "*Other parts* in Plymouth and Tavistock County Court Districts" substitute "*Other part* in Plymouth County Court District".	
PLYMOUTH	In the entry relating to the St. Germans Rural District:—	
	For "*Other parts* in Liskeard and Tavistock County Court Districts" substitute "*Other part* in Liskeard County Court District".	Insert "Calstock".
	Immediately after the entry relating to the Saltash Municipal Borough insert the following entry:—	
	"Tavistock Rural District (part). *Other part* in Launceston County Court District.	Bere Ferrers, Brentor, Buckland Monachorum, Coryton, Horrabridge, Lamerton, Lewtrenchard, Lydford, Marystowe, Mary Tavy, Meavy, Milton Abbott, Peter Tavy, Sampford Spiney, Sheepstor, Stowford, Sydenham Damerel, Tavistock, Tavistock Hamlets, Thrushelton, Walkhampton, Whitchurch."

SECTION 21

WINCANTON COUNTY COURT

Amendments consequent on closure

Column 1	*Column* 2	*Column* 3
SHAFTESBURY	In the entry relating to the Shaftesbury Rural District:—	
	For "Wincanton" substitute "Yeovil".	Insert "Bourton."
YEOVIL	Immediately after the entry relating to the Langport Rural District insert the following entry:—	
	"Shaftesbury Rural District (part). *Other part* in Shaftesbury County Court District.	Buckhorn Weston."
	After the entry relating to the Sturminster Rural District insert the following entry:—	
	"Wincanton Rural District.	Abbas and Templecombe, Alford, Ansford, Bratton Seymour, Brewham, Bruton, Castle Cary, Charlton Horethorne, Charlton Musgrove, Compton Pauncefoot, Corton Denham, Cucklington, Henstridge, Holton, Horsington, Lovington, Maperton, Milborne Port, North Barrow, North Cadbury, North Cheriton, Penselwood, Pitcombe, Queen Camel, Shepton Montague, South Barrow, South Cadbury, Sparkford, Stoke Trister, Wincanton, Yarlington."

SECTION 22

TORQUAY COUNTY COURT

A

BOUNDARY ALTERATION AND CONSEQUENT AMENDMENTS

Column 1	*Column* 2	*Column* 3
KINGS-BRIDGE	After the entry relating to the Salcombe Urban District insert the following entry:—	
	"Totnes Rural District (part). *Other parts* in Newton Abbot, Plymouth and Torquay County Court Districts.	Diptford, Halwell, Harberton, Moreleigh."
NEWTON ABBOT	Immediately after the entry relating to the Ashburton Urban District, insert the following entry:—	
	"Buckfastleigh Urban District.	Buckfastleigh."
	After the entry relating to the Teignmouth Urban District, insert the following entry:—	
	"Totnes Rural District (part). *Other parts* in Kingsbridge, Plymouth and Torquay County Court Districts.	Dean Prior, Holne, Littlehempston, Staverton, West Buckfastleigh."
PLY-MOUTH	After the entry relating to the Torpoint Urban District, insert the following entry:—	
	"Totnes Rural District (part). *Other parts* in Kingsbridge, Newton Abbot and Torquay County Court Districts.	North Huish, Ugborough."

B

FURTHER CONSEQUENTIAL AMENDMENTS

Column 1	*Column* 2	*Column* 3
TORQUAY	Delete "Buckfastleigh Urban District".	Delete "Buckfastleigh".
	In the entry relating to the Totnes Rural District:—	
	After the word "District", add "(part). *Other parts* in Kingsbridge, Newton Abbot and Plymouth County Court Districts."	Delete "Dean Prior, Diptford, Halwell, Harberton, Holne, Littlehempston, Moreleigh, North Huish, Staverton, Ugborough, West Buckfastleigh."

SCHEDULE 3

Column 1	*Column* 2
BANBURY	In the entry relating to the Banbury Rural District, delete "Alkerton" and, for the word "Shenington", substitute "Shenington with Alkerton".
BARNET	Immediately after the entry relating to the London Borough of Enfield, insert the following new entry:— *Column* 1: "Potters Bar Urban District. *Column* 2: Potters Bar ".
BIRMINGHAM	In the entry relating to the Meriden Rural District insert "Chelmsley Wood" and "Fordbridge" in column 3.
CREWE	In the entry relating to the Congleton Rural District, delete "Elton and Tetton" and, insert "Moston" in column 3.
NEWARK	In the entry relating to the Newark Rural District, delete "North Collingham" and "South Collingham" and insert "Collingham" in column 3.
READING	In the entry relating to the Wokingham Rural District, insert "Charvil" in column 3.
RUGBY	In the entry relating to the Rugby Rural District, delete "Binley".

SCHEDULE 4

COURTS HAVING JURISDICTION IN PROCEEDINGS PENDING IN CLOSED COURTS.

Column 1	*Column* 2
Bridport	Dorchester
Camelford	Bodmin
Cirencester	Swindon
Dursley	Stroud
Helston	Penzance
Holsworthy	Bideford
Honiton	Exeter
Kington	Hereford
Llanidloes	Newtown
Market Harborough	Kettering
Marlborough	Swindon
Newcastle under Lyme	Stoke on Trent
Newquay	Truro & Falmouth
Oakham	Melton Mowbray
Richmond	Darlington
Ripon	Harrogate
Ross	Monmouth
Swanage	Poole
Tavistock	Plymouth
Wincanton	Yeovil

APPENDIX

SCHEDULE 2

Column 1 Name of court	*Column* 2 Place of sitting
Aldershot and Farnham	Aldershot
Ashton under Lyne and Stalybridge	Stalybridge
Axminster and Chard	Axminster
Bideford	Bideford and Holsworthy
Bletchley and Leighton Buzzard	Leighton Buzzard
Bloomsbury and Marylebone	Bloomsbury
Chichester	Arundel, Chichester and Petworth
Darlington	Darlington and Richmond
Dorchester	Bridport and Dorchester
King's Lynn	Fakenham and Swaffham
Monmouth	Monmouth and Ross
Norwich	Cromer, Diss and Norwich
Penzance	Helston and Penzance
Plymouth	Plymouth and Tavistock
Poole	Poole and Swanage
Rhyl	Prestatyn
Stroud	Dursley and Stroud
Swindon	Cirencester and Swindon
Truro and Falmouth	Falmouth, Newquay and Truro"

EXPLANATORY NOTE

(This Note is not part of the Order.)

This Order establishes a new county court at Corby, and closes the county courts at Camelford, Honiton, Kington, Llanidloes, Market Harborough, Marlborough, Newcastle-under-Lyme, Oakham, Ripon and Wincanton. The courts are also closed, but provision made for occasional county court sittings, at Bridport, Cirencester, Dursley, Helston, Holsworthy, Newquay, Richmond (Yorkshire), Ross, Swanage and Tavistock, and the districts of all the closed courts are divided among those of neighbouring courts. The Order also closes the Cockermouth court of the Workington and Cockermouth County Court, and alters the boundary of the district of the Torquay County Court. Consequential and other amendments are made in the schedules to the County Court Districts Order 1970.

STATUTORY INSTRUMENTS

1970 No. 905 (L.19)

COUNTY COURTS

The County Courts (Bankruptcy and Companies Winding-up Jurisdiction) (Amendment) Order 1970

Made - - -	12*th June* 1970
Coming into Operation	1*st July* 1970

The Lord Chancellor, in exercise of the powers conferred on him by section 96 of the Bankruptcy Act 1914(**a**) and section 218(5) of the Companies Act 1948(**b**), hereby makes the following Order :—

1.—(1) This Order may be cited as the County Courts (Bankruptcy and Companies Winding-up Jurisdiction) (Amendment) Order 1970 and shall come into operation on 1st July 1970.

(2) The Interpretation Act 1889(**c**) shall apply to the interpretation of this Order as it applies to the interpretation of an Act of Parliament.

2. The County Courts (Bankruptcy and Companies Winding-up Jurisdiction) Order 1966(**d**), as amended (**e**), (which excludes certain county courts from having jurisdiction in bankruptcy and the winding-up of companies, and attaches their districts to other courts for these purposes) shall have effect subject to the further amendments set out in the schedule to this Order.

Dated 12th June 1970.

Gardiner, C.

SCHEDULE

1.—(1) In this Schedule, a schedule referred to by number means the schedule so numbered in the County Courts (Bankruptcy and Companies Winding-up Jurisdiction) Order 1966.

(2) For the purpose of this Schedule, an entry in Schedule 1 or 2 shall be treated as relating to the county court named in the first column of that schedule.

2. In Schedule 1, the entries relating to the following courts shall be deleted:—

Bridport
Camelford
Cirencester
Dursley
Helston
Holsworthy
Honiton
Kington
Llanidloes
Market Harborough
Marlborough
Newcastle under Lyme
Newquay
Oakham
Richmond
Ripon
Ross
Swanage
Tavistock
Wincanton

(**a**) 1914 c. 59. (**b**) 1948 c. 38. (**c**) 1889 c. 63.
(**d**) S.I. 1966/1548 (1966 III, p. 4386).
(**e**) S.I. 1968/939, 1969/1170 (1968 II, p. 2451; 1969 II, p. 3440).

3. Immediately after the entry in Schedule 1 relating to the Conway, Llandudno and Colwyn Bay County Court, there shall be inserted the following new entry:—

First Column	*Second Column*
Corby	Northampton

4. For Schedule 2, there shall be substituted the following:—

"SCHEDULE 2

COURTS HELD AT MORE THAN ONE PLACE

Name of Court	Place at which jurisdiction is exercisable
Ashton under Lyne and Stalybridge	Ashton under Lyne
Barrow in Furness and Ulverston	Barrow in Furness
Blackwood, Tredegar and Abertillery	Blackwood
Colchester and Clacton	Colchester
Darlington	Darlington
Dorchester	Dorchester
King's Lynn	King's Lynn
Neath and Port Talbot	Neath
Norwich	Norwich
Plymouth	Plymouth
Pontypridd and Ystradyfodwg	Pontypridd
Swindon	Swindon
Truro and Falmouth	Truro "

EXPLANATORY NOTE

(*This Note is not part of the Order.*)

This Order amends the County Courts (Bankruptcy and Companies Winding-up Jurisdiction) Order 1966 to take account of the closure of a number of small county courts and of the establishment of a new county court at Corby.

STATUTORY INSTRUMENTS

1970 No. 917

WAGES COUNCILS

The Wages Regulation (Retail Furnishing and Allied Trades) Order 1970

Made - - -	18*th June* 1970
Coming into Operation	3*rd August* 1970

Whereas the Secretary of State has received from the Retail Furnishing and Allied Trades Wages Council (Great Britain) the wages regulation proposals set out in the Schedule hereto ;

Now, therefore, the Secretary of State in exercise of her powers under section 11 of the Wages Councils Act 1959(**a**), and of all other powers enabling her in that behalf, hereby makes the following Order :—

1. This Order may be cited as the Wages Regulation (Retail Furnishing and Allied Trades) Order 1970.

2.—(1) In this Order the expression "the specified date" means the 3rd August 1970, provided that where, as respects any worker who is paid wages at intervals not exceeding seven days, that date does not correspond with the beginning of the period for which the wages are paid, the expression "the specified date" means, as respects that worker, the beginning of the next such period following that date.

(2) The Interpretation Act 1889(**b**) shall apply to the interpretation of this Order as it applies to the interpretation of an Act of Parliament and as if this Order and the Orders hereby revoked were Acts of Parliament.

3. The wages regulation proposals set out in the Schedule hereto shall have effect as from the specified date and as from that date the Wages Regulation (Retail Furnishing and Allied Trades) Order 1967(**c**) and the Wages Regulation (Retail Furnishing and Allied Trades) (Amendment) Order 1968(**d**) shall cease to have effect.

Signed by order of the Secretary of State.

18th June 1970.

A. A. Jarratt,
Deputy Under Secretary of State,
Department of Employment and Productivity.

(**a**) 1959 c. 69.
(**b**) 1889 c. 63.
(**c**) S.I. 1967/907 (1967 II, p. 2707).
(**d**) S.I. 1968/1890 (1968 III, p. 5035).

ARRANGEMENT OF SCHEDULE

PART I

STATUTORY MINIMUM REMUNERATION

PART II

ANNUAL HOLIDAY AND HOLIDAY REMUNERATION

PART III

GENERAL

Article 3

SCHEDULE

The following minimum remuneration and provisions as to holidays and holiday remuneration shall be substituted for the statutory minimum remuneration and the provisions as to holidays and holiday remuneration fixed by the Wages Regulation (Retail Furnishing and Allied Trades) Order 1967 (hereinafter referred to as "Order R.F.A. (48)"), as amended by the Wages Regulation (Retail Furnishing and Allied Trades) (Amendment) Order 1968 (Order R.F.A. (50)).

PART I

STATUTORY MINIMUM REMUNERATION

APPLICATION

1. Subject to the provisions of paragraphs 6, 9 and 10, the minimum remuneration payable to workers to whom this Schedule applies shall be the remuneration set out in paragraphs 2, 3, 4 and 5: Provided that any increase in remuneration payable under the provisions of paragraph 4 or 5 shall become effective on the first day of the first full pay week following the date upon which the increase would otherwise become payable under those provisions.

SHOP MANAGERS AND SHOP MANAGERESSES

2. Subject to the provisions of this paragraph, the minimum remuneration payable to Shop Managers and Shop Manageresses employed in the areas specified in Column 2 of the next following table shall be the amount appearing in the said Column 2 against the amount of weekly trade shown in Column 1.

Column 1	Column 2					
	LONDON AREA per week		PROVINCIAL A AREA per week		PROVINCIAL B AREA per week	
WEEKLY TRADE	Male	Female	Male	Female	Male	Female
	£ s.	£ s.	£ s.	£ s.	£ s.	£ s.
Under £175	*14 15*	*13 1*	*14 7*	*12 13*	*13 15*	*12 3*
£175 and under £200	*15 0*	*13 6*	*14 12*	*12 18*	*14 0*	*12 8*
£200 " " £240	*15 4*	*13 10*	*14 16*	*13 2*	*14 4*	*12 12*
£240 " " £280	*15 8*	*13 14*	*15 0*	*13 6*	*14 8*	*12 16*
£280 " " £320	*15 12*	*13 18*	*15 4*	*13 10*	*14 12*	*13 0*
£320 " " £360	*15 16*	*14 2*	*15 8*	*13 14*	*14 16*	*13 4*
£360 " " £400	*16 0*	*14 6*	*15 12*	*13 18*	*15 0*	*13 8*
£400 " " £440	*16 4*	*14 10*	*15 16*	*14 2*	*15 4*	*13 12*
£440 " " £480	*16 8*	*14 14*	*16 0*	*14 6*	*15 8*	*13 16*
£480 " " £520	*16 12*	*14 18*	*16 4*	*14 10*	*15 12*	*14 0*
£520 " " £560	*16 16*	*15 2*	*16 8*	*14 14*	*15 16*	*14 4*
£560 " " £600	*17 0*	*15 6*	*16 12*	*14 18*	*16 0*	*14 8*
£600 " " £640	*17 4*	*15 10*	*16 16*	*15 2*	*16 4*	*14 12*
£640 " " £680	*17 8*	*15 14*	*17 0*	*15 6*	*16 8*	*14 16*
£680 " " £720	*17 12*	*15 18*	*17 4*	*15 10*	*16 12*	*15 0*
£720 " " £760	*17 16*	*16 2*	*17 8*	*15 14*	*16 16*	*15 4*
£760 " " £800	*18 0*	*16 6*	*17 12*	*15 18*	*17 0*	*15 8*
£800 " " £840	*18 4*	*16 10*	*17 16*	*16 2*	*17 4*	*15 12*
£840 " " £880	*18 8*	*16 14*	*18 0*	*16 6*	*17 8*	*15 16*
£880 " " £920	*18 12*	*16 18*	*18 4*	*16 10*	*17 12*	*16 0*
£920 " " £960	*18 16*	*17 2*	*18 8*	*16 14*	*17 16*	*16 4*
£960 " " £1,000	*19 0*	*17 6*	*18 12*	*16 18*	*18 0*	*16 8*
£1,000 and over	*19 4*	*17 10*	*18 16*	*17 2*	*18 4*	*16 12*

For the purposes of this paragraph "weekly trade" shall be calculated half-yearly and based on the period of 12 months immediately preceding the commencement of each half-year in the following manner:—

For the period of 26 weeks beginning (1) with the fifth week or (2) with the 31st week following the accounting date in any year, the weekly trade of a shop shall be one fifty-second of the amount of the total receipts for goods sold at that shop during the 52 weeks immediately preceding the accounting date (in the case of (1) hereof) or the 26th week following the accounting date (in the case of (2) hereof).

Except as provided as aforesaid, the weekly trade in respect of any week shall be the amount of the total receipts for goods sold at the shop in the preceding week.

In this paragraph—

(*a*) "accounting date" means that date in each year on which the books of accounts of a shop are closed for the purpose of preparing the annual accounts in respect of that shop, or, in the absence of any such date, the 5th April in any year;

(*b*) the expression "receipts for goods sold" includes receipts in respect of hire purchase transactions;

(*c*) "shop" includes any part of the shop not engaged in the retail furnishing and allied trades.

TEMPORARY SHOP MANAGERS AND TEMPORARY SHOP MANAGERESSES

3.—(1) Subject to the provisions of this paragraph, the minimum remuneration payable to Temporary Shop Managers and Temporary Shop Manageresses, for each continuous period of employment as Temporary Shop Manager or Temporary Shop Manageress (reckoned in accordance with the provisions of sub-paragraph (2) of this paragraph), shall be the appropriate minimum remuneration for a Shop Manager or Shop Manageress, as the case may be, under the provisions of paragraph 2.

(2) In reckoning any continuous period of employment as Temporary Shop Manager or Temporary Shop Manageress for the purposes of sub-paragraph (1) of this paragraph, no account shall be taken of any period of employment:—

(*a*) not exceeding two consecutive working days; or

(*b*) not exceeding a total of two weeks in any year, being a period when the Shop Manager or Shop Manageress is absent on holiday:

Provided that for the purposes of this paragraph where in any year a worker is employed by the same employer as a Temporary Shop Manager or Temporary Shop Manageress at more than one shop during the absence on holiday of the Shop Manager or Shop Manageress, the first period of such employment and any subsequent periods of such employment in the same year shall be treated as a continuous period of employment.

(3) The minimum remuneration payable to Temporary Shop Managers and Temporary Shop Manageresses for any period of employment mentioned in (*a*) or (*b*) of sub-paragraph (2) of this paragraph, shall be not less than the appropriate minimum remuneration for a Shop Assistant under the provisions of this Schedule.

(4) For the purposes of this paragraph "year" means the 12 months commencing with 1st January and ending with 31st December.

WORKERS OTHER THAN SHOP MANAGERS, SHOP MANAGERESSES, TEMPORARY SHOP MANAGERS, TEMPORARY SHOP MANAGERESSES OR TRANSPORT WORKERS

4. Subject to the provisions of paragraph 1, the minimum remuneration payable to male or female workers of the classes specified in Column 1 of the next following table employed in the London Area, Provincial A Area or Provincial B Area, as the case may be, shall be the appropriate amount set out in Column 2.

Column 1	Column 2					
	LONDON AREA per week		PROVINCIAL A AREA per week		PROVINCIAL B AREA per week	
	Male	Female	Male	Female	Male	Female
	£ s.	£ s.	£ s.	£ s.	£ s.	£ s.
(1) CLERK GRADE I, AGED 23 YEARS OR OVER ...	*13 9*	*10 8*	*12 19*	*10 3*	*12 7*	*9 13*
(2) CLERK GRADE I, AGED UNDER 23 YEARS, CLERK GRADE II, SHOP ASSISTANT, CASHIER, CENTRAL WAREHOUSE WORKER, STOCKHAND OR VAN SALESMAN:—						
Aged 22 years or over	*12 19*	*10 0*	*12 9*	*9 15*	*11 17*	*9 5*
„ 21 and under 22 years ...	*11 19*	*9 5*	*11 9*	*9 0*	*10 17*	*8 10*
„ 20 „ „ 21 „ ...	*10 3*	*8 2*	*9 18*	*7 17*	*9 6*	*7 9*
„ 19 „ „ 20 „ ...	*9 8*	*7 12*	*9 3*	*7 7*	*8 11*	*6 19*
„ 18 „ „ 19 „ ...	*8 13*	*7 4*	*8 8*	*6 19*	*7 16*	*6 11*
„ 17 „ „ 18 „ ...	*7 8*	*6 2*	*7 3*	*5 17*	*6 11*	*5 9*
„ 16 „ „ 17 „ ...	*6 18*	*5 17*	*6 13*	*5 12*	*6 1*	*5 4*
„ under 16 years	*6 8*	*5 12*	*6 3*	*5 7*	*5 11*	*4 19*
(3) ALL OTHER WORKERS (OTHER THAN TRANSPORT WORKERS):—						
Aged 22 years or over	*12 9*	*9 12*	*11 19*	*9 7*	*11 7*	*8 17*
„ 21 and under 22 years ...	*11 9*	*8 17*	*10 19*	*8 12*	*10 7*	*8 2*
„ 20 „ „ 21 „ ...	*9 15*	*7 16*	*9 10*	*7 11*	*8 18*	*7 3*
„ 19 „ „ 20 „ ...	*9 0*	*7 6*	*8 15*	*7 1*	*8 3*	*6 13*
„ 18 „ „ 19 „ ...	*8 5*	*6 18*	*8 0*	*6 13*	*7 8*	*6 5*
„ 17 „ „ 18 „ ...	*7 3*	*5 18*	*6 18*	*5 13*	*6 6*	*5 5*
„ 16 „ „ 17 „ ...	*6 13*	*5 13*	*6 8*	*5 8*	*5 16*	*5 0*
„ under 16 years	*6 3*	*5 8*	*5 18*	*5 3*	*5 6*	*4 15*

TRANSPORT WORKERS

5. Subject to the provisions of paragraph 1, the minimum remuneration payable to Transport Workers employed in the London Area, Provincial A Area or Provincial B Area, as the case may be, shall be the appropriate amount set out in Column 3 of the next following table:—

Column 1	Column 2	Column 3		
Age of transport worker	Mechanically propelled vehicle with carrying capacity of	LONDON AREA per week	PROVINCIAL A AREA per week	PROVINCIAL B AREA per week
		£ s.	£ s.	£ s.
21 years or over ...	1 ton or less	12 *18*	*12 8*	*11 16*
20 and under 21 years	1 ton or less	10 13	*10 8*	*9 16*
19 „ „ 20 „	1 ton or less	*9 18*	*9 13*	*9 1*
18 „ „ 19 „	1 ton or less	*9 3*	*8 18*	*8 6*
under 18 years ...	1 ton or less	*7 18*	*7 13*	*7 1*
All ages	Over 1 ton and up to 2 tons	*13 3*	*12 13*	*12 1*
	Over 2 tons and up to 5 tons	*13 8*	*12 18*	*12 6*
	Over 5 tons	*13 13*	*13 3*	*12 11*

MINIMUM OVERTIME RATES

6. Overtime shall be payable at the following minimum rates:—

(1) To any worker, for work on a Sunday or customary holiday,

(*a*) where time worked does not exceed 4½ hours .. double time for 4½ hours

(*b*) where time worked exceeds 4½ hours but does not exceed 8 hours .. .. double time for 8 hours

(*c*) where time worked exceeds 8 hours .. .. .. double time for all time worked

Provided that—

(i) Overtime rates in accordance with the foregoing provisions of this paragraph shall be payable to a Shop Manager, Temporary Shop Manager, Shop Manageress or Temporary Shop Manageress only if the overtime worked is specifically authorised in writing by the employer or his representative;

(ii) Where it is or becomes the practice in a Jewish undertaking for the employer to require the worker's attendance on Sunday instead of Saturday, the provisions of this paragraph shall apply as if in such provisions the word "Saturday" were substituted for "Sunday", except where such attendance on Sunday is unlawful.

(2) To any worker, on the weekly short day in any week during which, under sub-section (3) of section 40 of the Shops Act 1950(**a**), the employer is relieved of his obligation to allow the worker a weekly half day,

for any time worked after 1.30 p.m. .. .. .. double time

(**a**) 1950 c. 28.

(3) To any worker, other than a Shop Manager, Temporary Shop Manager, Shop Manageress or Temporary Shop Manageress—

(*a*) on the weekly short day (not being a weekly short day to which sub-paragraph (2) of this paragraph applies)
for any time worked after 1.30 p.m. .. .. time-and-a-half

(*b*) in any week, exclusive of any time in respect of which a minimum overtime rate is payable under the foregoing provisions of this paragraph,
for all time worked in excess of 42 hours .. .. time-and-a-half

Provided that in any week which includes one customary holiday "35 hours" shall be substituted for "42 hours" and in any week which includes two customary holidays "28 hours" shall be substituted for the said "42 hours".

WAITING TIME

7. A worker shall be entitled to payment of the minimum remuneration specified in this Schedule for all the time during which he is present on the premises of the employer unless he is present thereon in any of the following circumstances, that is to say—

(1) without the employer's consent, express or implied;

(2) for some purpose unconnected with his work, and other than that of waiting for work to be given to him to perform;

(3) by reason only of the fact that he is resident thereon; or

(4) during normal meal times, and he is not waiting for work to be given to him to perform.

WORKERS WHO ARE NOT REQUIRED TO WORK ON A CUSTOMARY HOLIDAY

8.—(1) Subject to the provisions of sub-paragraph (2) of this paragraph, a worker who is not required to work on a customary holiday shall be paid for that holiday not less than the amount to which he would have been entitled under the foregoing provisions had the day not been a customary holiday and had he worked the number of hours ordinarily worked by him on that day of the week.

(2) A worker shall not be entitled to any payment under this paragraph unless he—

(*a*) worked for the employer throughout the last working day on which work was available for him preceding the holiday; and

(*b*) presents himself for employment at the usual starting time on the first working day after the holiday:

Provided that (*a*) or (*b*), as the case may be, of this sub-paragraph shall be deemed to be complied with where the worker is excused by his employer or is prevented by his proved illness or injury from working or presenting himself for employment as aforesaid.

GUARANTEED WEEKLY REMUNERATION PAYABLE TO A FULL-TIME WORKER

9.—(1) Notwithstanding the other provisions of this Schedule, where in respect of any week the total remuneration (including holiday remuneration but excluding remuneration in respect of overtime) payable to a full-time worker under those other provisions is less than the guaranteed weekly remuneration provided under this paragraph, the minimum remuneration payable to that worker for that week shall be that guaranteed weekly remuneration with the addition of any amount excluded as aforesaid.

(2) The guaranteed weekly remuneration payable in respect of any week to a full-time worker is the remuneration to which he would be entitled under paragraph 2, 4 or 5 for 42 hours' work in his normal occupation:

Provided that—

(*a*) where the worker normally works for the employer on work to which this Schedule applies for less than 42 hours in the week by reason only of the fact that he does not hold himself out as normally available for work for more than the number of hours he normally works in the week and the worker has informed the employer in writing that he does not so hold himself out, the guaranteed weekly remuneration shall be the remuneration to which the worker would be entitled (calculated as in paragraph 10) for the number of hours in the week normally worked by the worker for the employer on work to which this Schedule applies;

(*b*) where in any week a worker at his request and with the written consent of his employer is absent from work during any part of his normal working hours on any day (other than a holiday allowed under Part II of this Schedule or a customary holiday or a holiday allowed to all persons employed in the undertaking or branch of an undertaking in which the worker is employed), the guaranteed weekly remuneration payable in respect of that week shall be reduced in respect of each day on which he is absent as aforesaid by one-sixth where the worker's normal working week is six days or by one-fifth where his normal working week is five days.

(3) Guaranteed weekly remuneration is not payable in respect of any week unless the worker throughout his normal working hours in that week (excluding any time allowed to him as a holiday or during which he is absent from work in accordance with proviso (*b*) to sub-paragraph (2) of this paragraph) is

(*a*) capable of and available for work; and

(*b*) willing to perform such duties outside his normal occupation as the employer may reasonably require if his normal work is not available in the establishment in which he is employed.

(4) Guaranteed weekly remuneration is not payable in respect of any week if the worker's employment is terminated before the end of that week.

(5) If the employer is unable to provide the worker with work by reason of a strike or other circumstances beyond his control and gives the worker four clear days' notice to that effect, guaranteed weekly remuneration shall not be payable after the expiry of such notice in respect of any week during which or during part of which the employer continues to be unable to provide work as aforesaid:

Provided that in respect of the week in which the said notice expires there shall be paid to the worker, in addition to any remuneration payable in respect of time worked in that week, any remuneration that would have been payable if the worker had worked his normal hours of work on every day in the week prior to the expiry of the notice.

HOURS ON WHICH REMUNERATION IS BASED

10.—(1) The minimum remuneration specified in this Part of this Schedule relates to a week of 42 hours exclusive of overtime and, except in the case of guaranteed weekly remuneration under paragraph 9, is subject to a proportionate reduction according as the number of hours worked is less than 42.

(2) In calculating the remuneration for the purpose of this Schedule recognised breaks for meal times shall, subject to the provisions of paragraph 7, be excluded.

BENEFITS AND ADVANTAGES

11. The following benefits or advantages, being benefits or advantages provided, in pursuance of the terms and conditions of the employment of the worker, by the employer or some other person under arrangements with the employer and not being benefits or advantages the provision of which is illegal by virtue of the Truck Acts 1831 to 1940(a), or of any other enactment, are authorised to be reckoned as payment of wages by the employer in lieu of payment in cash in the following manner:—

(1) board and lodging for seven days a week, as the appropriate amount set out in the following table—

In the case of a worker aged	LONDON AREA per week	PROVINCIAL A AREA per week	PROVINCIAL B AREA per week
	s. d.	s. d.	s. d.
21 years or over	36 9	32 9	27 9
20 and under 21 years	34 9	30 9	25 9
19 „ „ 20 „	32 6	28 6	23 6
18 „ „ 19 „	30 0	26 0	21 0
17 „ „ 18 „	28 0	24 0	19 0
under 17 years	25 0	21 0	16 0

or, where board and lodging is not so provided,

(2) dinner of good and sufficient quality and quantity provided on each day on which the worker normally works in the week, other than the weekly short day, as an amount of 9s. 9d. per week;

(3) tea of good and sufficient quality and quantity provided as aforesaid, as an amount of 3s. 6d. per week.

PART II

ANNUAL HOLIDAY AND HOLIDAY REMUNERATION

ANNUAL HOLIDAY

12.—(1) Subject to the provisions of sub-paragraph (2) of this paragraph and of paragraph 13, an employer shall, between the date on which this Schedule becomes effective and 31st October 1970 and in each succeeding year between 1st April and 31st October allow a holiday (hereinafter referred to as an "annual holiday") to every worker in his employment to whom this Schedule applies who has been employed by him during the 12 months immediately preceding the commencement of the holiday season for any one of the periods of employment (calculated in accordance with the provisions of paragraph 19) set out in the first column of the table below and the duration of the annual holiday shall in the case of each such worker be related to that period as follows:—

Period of employment	Duration of annual holiday — Where the worker's normal working week is: Six days	Five days	Four days	Three days or less
12 months	12 days	10 days	8 days	6 days
Not less than 11 months but less than 12 months	11 „	9 „	7 „	5 „
„ „ 10 „ „ „ 11 „	10 „	8 „	7 „	5 „
„ „ 9 „ „ „ 10 „	9 „	7 „	6 „	4 „
„ „ 8 „ „ „ 9 „	8 „	7 „	5 „	4 „
„ „ 7 „ „ „ 8 „	7 „	6 „	5 „	3 „
„ „ 6 „ „ „ 7 „	6 „	5 „	4 „	3 „
„ „ 5 „ „ „ 6 „	5 „	4 „	3 „	2 „
„ „ 4 „ „ „ 5 „	4 „	3 „	3 „	2 „
„ „ 3 „ „ „ 4 „	3 „	2 „	2 „	1 day
„ „ 2 „ „ „ 3 „	2 „	2 „	1 day	1 „
„ „ 1 month „ „ 2 „	1 day	1 day	1 „	nil

(a) 1831 c. 37; 1887 c. 46; 1896 c. 44; 1940 c. 38.

(2) Notwithstanding the provisions of the last foregoing sub-paragraph—

(*a*) the number of days of annual holiday which an employer is required to allow to a worker in any holiday season shall not exceed in the aggregate twice the number of days constituting the worker's normal working week ;

(*b*) where the worker does not wish to take his annual holiday or part thereof during the holiday season in any year and, before the expiration of such holiday season, enters into an agreement in writing with his employer that the annual holiday or part thereof shall be allowed, at a date or dates to be specified in that agreement, after the expiration of the holiday season but before the first day of January in the following year, then any day or days of annual holiday so allowed shall be treated as having been allowed during the holiday season ;

(*c*) the duration of the worker's annual holiday during the holiday season ending on 31st October 1970 shall be reduced by any days of annual holiday duly allowed to him by the employer under the provisions of Order R.F.A. (48) as amended between 1st April 1970 and the date on which this Schedule becomes effective.

(3) In this Schedule the expression "holiday season" means in relation to the year 1970 the period commencing on 1st April 1970, and ending on 31st October 1970, and, in each succeeding year, the period commencing on 1st April and ending on 31st October of the same year.

13. Where at the written request of the worker at any time during the three months immediately preceding the commencement of the holiday season in any year, his employer allows him any day or days of annual holiday and pays him holiday remuneration in respect thereof calculated in accordance with the provisions of paragraphs 16 and 17, then

(1) the annual holiday to be allowed in accordance with paragraph 12 in the holiday season in that year shall be reduced by the day or days of annual holiday so allowed prior to the commencement of that holiday season ; and

(2) for the purpose of calculating accrued holiday remuneration under paragraph 18 any day or days of annual holiday deducted in accordance with sub-paragraph (1) hereof shall be treated as if they had been allowed in the holiday season.

14.—(1) An annual holiday shall be allowed on consecutive working days, being days on which the worker is normally called upon to work for the employer.

(2) Where the number of days of annual holiday for which a worker has qualified exceeds the number of days constituting his normal working week, the holiday may be allowed in two periods of consecutive working days ; so however that when a holiday is so allowed, one of the periods shall consist of a number of such days not less than the number of days constituting the worker's normal working week.

(3) For the purposes of this paragraph, days of annual holiday shall be treated as consecutive notwithstanding that a customary holiday on which the worker is not required to work for the employer or a day on which he does not normally work for the employer intervenes.

(4) Where a customary holiday on which the worker is not required to work for the employer immediately precedes a period of annual holiday or occurs during such a period and the total number of days of annual holiday required to be allowed in the period under the foregoing provisions of this paragraph, together with any customary holiday, exceeds the number of days constituting the worker's normal working week, then, notwithstanding the foregoing provisions of this paragraph, the duration of that period of annual holiday may be reduced by one day and in such a case one day of annual holiday may be allowed on a day on which the worker normally works for the employer (not being the worker's weekly short day) in the holiday season or after the holiday season in the circumstances specified in sub-paragraph (2)(*b*) of paragraph 12.

(5) No day of annual holiday shall be allowed on a customary holiday.

(6) A day of annual holiday under this Schedule may be allowed on a day on which the worker is entitled to a day of holiday (not being a customary holiday) or to a half-holiday under any enactment other than the Wages Councils Act 1959:

Provided that where the total number of days of annual holiday allowed to a worker under this Schedule is less than the number of days in his normal working week, the said annual holiday shall be in addition to the said day of holiday or the said half-holiday.

15. An employer shall give to a worker reasonable notice of the commencing date or dates and of the duration of his annual holiday. Such notice may be given individually to the worker or by the posting of a notice in the place where the worker is employed.

REMUNERATION FOR ANNUAL HOLIDAY

16.—(1) Subject to the provisions of paragraph 17, a worker qualified to be allowed an annual holiday under this Schedule shall be paid by his employer, on the last pay day preceding such holiday, one day's holiday pay in respect of each day thereof.

(2) Where an annual holiday is taken in more than one period the holiday remuneration shall be apportioned accordingly.

17. Where any accrued holiday remuneration has been paid by the employer to the worker (in accordance with paragraph 18 of this Schedule or with Order R.F.A. (48) as amended), in respect of employment during any of the periods referred to in that paragraph, the amount of holiday remuneration payable by the employer in respect of any annual holiday for which the worker has qualified by reason of employment during the said period shall be reduced by the amount of the said accrued holiday remuneration, unless that remuneration has been deducted from a previous payment of holiday remuneration made under the provisions of this Schedule or of Order R.F.A. (48) as amended.

ACCRUED HOLIDAY REMUNERATION PAYABLE ON TERMINATION OF EMPLOYMENT

18. Where a worker ceases to be employed by an employer after the provisions of this Schedule become effective, the employer shall, immediately on the termination of the employment (hereinafter referred to as the "termination date"), pay to the worker as accrued holiday remuneration:—

(1) in respect of employment occurring in the 12 months up to 1st April immediately preceding the termination date, a sum equal to the holiday remuneration for any days of annual holiday for which he has qualified except days of annual holiday which he has been allowed or has become entitled to be allowed before leaving the employment; and

(2) in respect of any employment since the said 1st April, a sum equal to the holiday remuneration which would have been payable to him if he could have been allowed an annual holiday in respect of that employment at the time of leaving it:

Provided that—

(*a*) no worker shall be entitled to the payment by his employer of accrued holiday remuneration if he is dismissed on the grounds of misconduct and is so informed by the employer at the time of dismissal;

(*b*) where a worker is employed under a contract of service under which he is required to give not less than one week's notice before terminating his employment and the worker, without the consent of his employer, terminates his employment without having given not less than one week's notice, or before one week has expired from the beginning of such notice, the amount of accrued holiday remuneration payable to the worker shall be the amount payable under the foregoing provisions of this paragraph less an amount equal to the statutory minimum remuneration which would be payable to him at the termination date for one week's work if working his normal working week and the normal number of daily hours worked by him ;

(*c*) where during the period or periods in respect of which the said accrued holiday remuneration is payable the worker has at his written request been allowed any day or days of holiday (other than days of holiday allowed by the employer under paragraph 13) for which he has not qualified under the provisions of this Schedule, any accrued holiday remuneration payable as aforesaid may be reduced by the amount of any sum paid by the employer to the worker in respect of such day or days of holiday.

CALCULATION OF EMPLOYMENT

19. For the purpose of calculating any period of employment qualifying a worker for an annual holiday or for any accrued holiday remuneration, the worker shall be treated as if he were employed for a month in respect of any month throughout which he has been in the employment of the employer.

PART III

GENERAL

DEFINITIONS

20. For the purposes of this Schedule—

"BOARD" means not less than three meals a day, of good and sufficient quality and quantity, one of which shall be dinner ; and "LODGING" means clean and adequate accommodation and clean and adequate facilities for eating, sleeping, washing and leisure.

"CARRYING CAPACITY" means the weight of the maximum load normally carried by the vehicle, and such carrying capacity when so established shall not be affected either by variations in the weight of the load resulting from collections or deliveries or emptying of containers during the course of the journey, or by the fact that on any particular journey a load greater or less than the established carrying capacity is carried.

"CASHIER" means a worker employed in a shop and engaged wholly or mainly in receiving cash or giving change.

"CENTRAL WAREHOUSE WORKER" means a worker wholly or mainly employed in a central warehouse, that is to say, a warehouse from which an undertaking in the retail furnishing and allied trades supplies its shops.

"CLERK GRADE I" means a worker engaged wholly or mainly on clerical work which includes responsibility for maintaining ledgers or wages books or for preparing financial accounts of the undertaking or of a branch or department thereof.

"CLERK GRADE II" means a worker, other than a Clerk Grade I, engaged wholly or mainly on clerical work.

"CUSTOMARY HOLIDAY" means

(1)(*a*) In England and Wales—

Christmas Day (or, if Christmas Day falls on a Sunday, such week-day as may be appointed by national proclamation, or, if none is so appointed, the next following Tuesday), Boxing Day, Good Friday, Easter Monday, Whit Monday (or where another day is substituted therefor by national proclamation, that day), August Bank Holiday and any day proclaimed as a public holiday throughout England and Wales ;

(*b*) in Scotland—

New Year's Day (or, if New Year's Day falls on a Sunday, the following Monday) ;

the local Spring holiday ;

the local Autumn holiday;

Christmas Day (when Christmas Day falls on any day other than a Sunday); two other days or, when Christmas Day falls on a Sunday, three other days (being days on which the worker would normally work) in the course of a calendar year, to be fixed by the employer and notified to the worker not less than three weeks before the holiday and any day proclaimed as a public holiday throughout Scotland;

or (2) where in any undertaking it is not the custom or practice to observe such days as are specified in (1)(*a*) or (1)(*b*) above as holidays, such other days, not fewer in number, as may by agreement between the employer or his representative and the worker or his representative be substituted for the specified days.

"FULL-TIME WORKER" means a worker who normally works for the employer for at least 36 hours in the week on work to which this Schedule applies.

"LONDON AREA", PROVINCIAL A AREA" and "PROVINCIAL B AREA" have the meanings respectively assigned to them in paragraph 21.

"MONTH" means the period commencing on a date of any number in one month and ending on the day before the date of the same number in the next month or, if the commencing date is the 29th, 30th or 31st day of a month and there is no date of the same number in the next month, then on the last day of that month.

"NORMAL WORKING WEEK" means the number of days on which it has been usual for the worker to work in a week while in the employment of the employer during the 12 months immediately preceding the commencement of the holiday season or, where under paragraph 18 accrued holiday remuneration is payable on the termination of the employment, during the 12 months immediately preceding the date of the termination of the employment:

Provided that—

(1) part of a day shall count as a day;

(2) no account shall be taken of any week in which the worker did not perform any work for which statutory minimum remuneration has been fixed.

"ONE DAY'S HOLIDAY PAY" means the appropriate proportion of the remuneration which the worker would be entitled to receive from his employer at the date of the annual holiday (or where the holiday is taken in more than one period at the date of the first period) or at the termination date, as the case may be, for one week's work—

(1) if working his normal working week, and the number of daily hours normally worked by him (exclusive of overtime),

(2) if the employer were not providing him with meals or board and lodging, and

(3) if he were paid at the appropriate rate of statutory minimum remuneration for work for which statutory minimum remuneration is payable and at the same rate for any work for the same employer for which such remuneration is not payable,

and in this definition "appropriate proportion" means—

where the worker's normal working week is	six days ..	one-sixth
" " " " "	five days ..	one-fifth
" " " " "	four days ..	one-quarter
" " " " "	three days ..	one-third
" " " " "	two days ..	one-half
" " " " "	one day ..	the whole.

"SHOP ASSISTANT" means a worker who is wholly or mainly engaged in the serving of customers.

"SHOP MANAGER", "SHOP MANAGERESS" means a worker who is employed at, and is normally immediately in charge of the operation of, an undertaking or branch (but not of a department of an undertaking or branch), including the custody of cash and stock, and, if employed in the London Area or in Provincial A Area, has immediate control of staff, if any, or, if employed in Provincial B Area, has immediate control of at least one full-time or two part-time staff; and for the purpose of this definition a worker shall not be deemed not to be immediately in charge of the operation of an undertaking or branch by reason only of being subject to the supervision of the employer or some person acting on his behalf, being in either case a person who is not normally, during the hours when the undertaking or branch is open to the public, wholly or mainly engaged in work at the undertaking or branch.

"STOCKHAND" means a worker employed in a shop or in a warehouse operated in connection with a shop, and wholly or mainly engaged in the reception, checking and re-issuing of goods together with the keeping of records in connection therewith.

"TEMPORARY SHOP MANAGER", "TEMPORARY SHOP MANAGERESS" means a worker who, in the absence of the Shop Manager or Shop Manageress as the case may be, is employed at and is temporarily immediately in charge of the operation of an undertaking or branch (but not of a department of an undertaking or branch) including the custody of cash and stock, whilst the worker is so in charge; and for the purpose of this definition a worker shall not be deemed not to be immediately in charge of the operation of an undertaking or branch by reason only of being subject to the supervision of the employer or some person acting on his behalf, being in either case a person who is not normally, during the hours when the undertaking or branch is open to the public, wholly or mainly engaged in work at the undertaking or branch.

"TIME-AND-A-HALF" and "DOUBLE TIME" mean, respectively, one and a half times and twice the hourly rate obtained by dividing by 42 the minimum weekly remuneration to which the worker is entitled under the provisions of paragraph 2, 3, 4 or 5.

"TRANSPORT WORKER" means a male worker (other than a van salesman) engaged wholly or mainly in driving a mechanically propelled road vehicle for the transport of goods and on work in connection with the vehicle and its load (if any) while on the road.

"VAN SALESMAN" means a worker wholly or mainly employed in the sale of goods to customers from a van or other vehicle.

"WATCHMAN" means a worker wholly or mainly engaged in guarding the employer's premises for the prevention of theft, fire, damage or trespass.

"WEEK" means pay week.

"WEEKLY SHORT DAY" means:—

(1) that day in any week on which the worker is, in accordance with the provisions of section 17 of the Shops Act 1950, required not to be employed about the business of a shop after half-past one o'clock in the afternoon, or,

(2) where there is no such day, or where the day falls on a customary holiday, a working day in the week not being a customary holiday, fixed by the employer and notified to the worker not later than the Saturday preceding the week during which it is to have effect; or, failing such notification, the last working day in the week which is not a customary holiday:

Provided that where the day specified in (1) of this definition falls on Christmas Day or Boxing Day in England and Wales or Christmas Day or New Year's Day in Scotland the employer may fix as the weekly short day for that week a working day in the following week not being either a customary holiday or the weekly short day for that following week.

AREAS

21. In this Schedule:—

(1) "LONDON AREA" means the Metropolitan Police District, as defined in the London Government Act 1963(**a**), the City of London, the Inner Temple and the Middle Temple.

(2) "PROVINCIAL A AREA" means

(*a*) in Scotland

(i) the following burghs:—

ABERDEEN COUNTY
Aberdeen (including part in Kincardine County)
Fraserburgh
Peterhead

ANGUS COUNTY
Arbroath
Brechin
Dundee
Forfar
Montrose

ARGYLL COUNTY
Dunoon

AYR COUNTY
Ardrossan
Ayr
Irvine
Kilmarnock
Largs
Prestwick
Saltcoats
Stevenston
Troon

BANFF COUNTY
Buckie

BUTE COUNTY
Rothesay

CLACKMANNAN COUNTY
Alloa

DUMFRIES COUNTY
Dumfries

DUNBARTON COUNTY
Bearsden
Clydebank
Dumbarton
Helensburgh
Kirkintilloch
Milngavie

EAST LOTHIAN COUNTY
North Berwick

FIFE COUNTY
Buckhaven and Methil
Burntisland
Cowdenbeath
Dunfermline
Kirkcaldy
Leven
Lochgelly
St. Andrews

INVERNESS COUNTY
Inverness

KINCARDINE COUNTY
Stonehaven

LANARK COUNTY
Airdrie
Coatbridge
Glasgow
Hamilton
Lanark
Motherwell and Wishaw
Rutherglen

MIDLOTHIAN COUNTY
Dalkeith
Edinburgh
Musselburgh

MORAY COUNTY
Elgin

ORKNEY COUNTY
Kirkwall

PERTH COUNTY
Perth

RENFREW COUNTY
Barrhead
Gourock
Greenock
Johnstone
Paisley
Port Glasgow
Renfrew

ROSS AND CROMARTY COUNTY
Stornaway

ROXBURGH COUNTY
Hawick

SELKIRK COUNTY
Galashiels

STIRLING COUNTY
Denny and Dunipace
Falkirk
Grangemouth
Kilsyth
Stirling

WEST LOTHIAN COUNTY
Armadale
Bathgate
Bo'ness

WIGTOWN COUNTY
Stranraer

ZETLAND COUNTY
Lerwick

(**a**) 1963 c. 33.

(ii) the following Special Lighting Districts, the boundaries of which have been defined, namely, Vale of Leven and Renton in the County of Dunbarton, and Larbert and Airth in the County of Stirling, and

(iii) the following areas the boundaries of which were defined as Special Lighting Districts prior to 10th March 1943, namely, Bellshill and Mossend, Blantyre, Cambuslang, Larkhall and Holytown, New Stevenston and Carfin, all in the County of Lanark.

(*b*) In England and Wales, the areas administered by County Borough, Municipal Borough or Urban District Councils, except where they are included in the London area or are listed in (3)(*b*) of this paragraph.

(3) "PROVINCIAL B AREA" means

(*a*) In Scotland, all areas other than those listed in (2)(*a*) of this paragraph ;

(*b*) In England and Wales, all areas not included in the London area administered by Rural District Councils, and the areas administered by the following Municipal Borough and Urban District Councils:—

ENGLAND (excluding Monmouthshire)

BEDFORDSHIRE
Ampthill
Sandy

BERKSHIRE
Wallingford
Wantage

BUCKINGHAMSHIRE
Buckingham
Linslade
Marlow
Newport Pagnell

CHESHIRE
Alsager
Longdendale

CORNWALL
Bodmin
Bude Stratton
Fowey
Helston
Launceston
Liskeard
Looe
Lostwithiel
Padstow
Penryn
St. Just
Torpoint

DERBYSHIRE
Bakewell
Whaley Bridge
Wirksworth

DEVON
Ashburton
Buckfastleigh
Budleigh Salterton
Crediton
Dartmouth
Great Torrington
Holsworthy
Honiton
Kingsbridge
Lynton
Northam
Okehampton
Ottery St. Mary
Salcombe
Seaton
South Molton
Tavistock
Totnes

DORSET
Blandford Forum
Lyme Regis
Shaftesbury
Sherborne
Wareham
Wimborne Minster

DURHAM
Barnard Castle
Tow Law

ELY, ISLE OF
Chatteris

ESSEX
Brightlingsea
Burnham-on-Crouch
Saffron Walden
West Mersea
Wivenhoe

GLOUCESTERSHIRE
Nailsworth
Tewkesbury

HEREFORDSHIRE
Bromyard
Kington
Ledbury

HERTFORDSHIRE
Baldock
Chorleywood
Royston
Sawbridgeworth

HUNTINGDONSHIRE
Huntingdon and Godmanchester
Ramsey
St. Ives
St. Neots

KENT
Lydd
New Romney
Queenborough
Sandwich
Tenterden

LANCASHIRE
Carnforth
Grange

LINCOLNSHIRE
Alford
Barton-upon-Humber
Bourne
Brigg
Horncastle
Mablethorpe and Sutton
Market Rasen
Woodhall Spa

NORFOLK
- Cromer
- Diss
- Downham Market
- Hunstanton
- North Walsham
- Sheringham
- Swaffham
- Thetford
- Wells-next-the-Sea
- Wymondham

NORTHAMPTON-SHIRE
- Brackley
- Burton Latimer
- Higham Ferrers
- Oundle

NORTHUMBERLAND
- Alnwick
- Amble

OXFORDSHIRE
- Bicester
- Chipping Norton
- Thame
- Woodstock

RUTLAND
- Oakham

SHROPSHIRE
- Bishop's Castle
- Church Stretton
- Ellesmere
- Market Drayton
- Newport
- Wem

SOMERSET
- Chard
- Crewkerne
- Glastonbury
- Ilminster
- Portishead
- Shepton Mallet
- Street
- Watchet
- Wellington

SUFFOLK
- Aldeburgh
- Beccles
- Bungay
- Eye
- Hadleigh
- Halesworth
- Haverhill
- Leiston-cum-Sizewell
- Saxmundham
- Southwold
- Sudbury
- Stowmarket
- Woodbridge

SUSSEX
- Arundel
- Rye

WESTMORLAND
- Appleby
- Lakes

WILTSHIRE
- Bradford-on-Avon
- Calne
- Malmesbury
- Marlborough
- Melksham
- Westbury
- Wilton

WORCESTERSHIRE
- Bewdley
- Droitwich

YORKSHIRE
- Hedon
- Hornsea
- Malton
- Norton
- Pickering
- Richmond
- Tickhill
- Withernsea

WALES AND MONMOUTHSHIRE

ANGLESEY
- Amlwch
- Beaumaris
- Llangefni
- Menai Bridge

BRECONSHIRE
- Builth Wells
- Hay
- Llanwrtyd Wells

CAERNARVONSHIRE
- Bethesda
- Betws-y-Coed
- Criccieth
- Llanfairfechan
- Penmaenmawr
- Portmadoc
- Pwllheli

CARDIGANSHIRE
- Aberayron
- Cardigan
- Lampeter
- New Quay

CARMARTHENSHIRE
- Cwmamman
- Kidwelly
- Llandeilo
- Llandovery
- Newcastle Emlyn

DENBIGHSHIRE
- Llangollen
- Llanrwst
- Ruthin

FLINTSHIRE
- Buckley
- Mold

GLAMORGAN
- Cowbridge

MERIONETHSHIRE
- Bala
- Barmouth
- Dolgellau
- Towyn

MONMOUTHSHIRE
- Caerleon
- Chepstow
- Usk

MONTGOMERYSHIRE
- Llanfyllin
- Llanidloes
- Machynlleth
- Montgomery
- Newtown and Llanllwchaiarn
- Welshpool

PEMBROKESHIRE
- Fishguard and Goodwick
- Narberth
- Neyland
- Tenby

RADNORSHIRE
- Knighton
- Llandrindod Wells
- Presteign

(4) Any reference to a local government area shall be construed as a reference to that area as it was on 23rd April 1961, unless otherwise stated.

WORKERS TO WHOM THIS SCHEDULE APPLIES

22.—(1) (i) Subject to the provisions of sub-paragraph (2) of this paragraph the workers to whom this Schedule applies are all workers employed in Great Britain in any undertaking or any branch or department of an undertaking, being an undertaking, branch or department engaged—

(*a*) wholly or mainly in the retail furnishing and allied trades; or

(*b*) wholly or mainly in those trades and one or more of the groups of retail distributive trades set out in the Appendix to this paragraph, and to a greater extent in the retail furnishing and allied trades than in any one of those groups:

Provided that if a branch or department of an undertaking is not so engaged this Schedule shall not apply to workers employed in that branch or department (notwithstanding that the undertaking as a whole is so engaged), except in the case of workers as respects their employment in a department of that branch if that department is so engaged.

(ii) For the purposes of this sub-paragraph

(*a*) in determining the extent to which an undertaking or branch or department of an undertaking is engaged in a group of trades, regard shall be had to the time spent in the undertaking, branch or department on work in that group of trades;

(*b*) an undertaking or branch or department of an undertaking which is engaged in any operation in a group of trades shall be treated as engaged in that group of trades.

(2) This Schedule does not apply to any of the following workers in respect of their employment in any of the following circumstances, that is to say:—

(i) workers in relation to whom the Road Haulage Wages Council operates in respect of any employment which is within the field of operation of that Council;

(ii) workers employed on post office business;

(iii) workers employed on the maintenance or repair of buildings, plant, equipment or vehicles (but not including workers employed as cleaners);

(iv) workers employed on the installation, maintenance or repair of radio or television sets;

(v) workers employed on the repair or renovation of furniture (including mattresses), the making up, planning or laying of carpets, linoleum or similar floor coverings, or the measuring, cutting, sewing, making up or fixing of blinds, curtains, pelmets or loose covers;

(vi) workers employed on the packing, storing or removal of furniture or other household effects in connection with a household removal;

(vii) workers employed in the assembling, installation, maintenance, alteration or repair of electrical or gas appliances and apparatus of all kinds;

(viii) workers employed by a Gas or Electricity Supply Undertaking;

(ix) workers employed as watchmen.

(3) For the purpose of this Schedule the retail furnishing and allied trades consist of:—

(i) the sale by retail of:—

(*a*) household and office furniture, including garden furniture, mattresses, floor coverings and mirrors, but excluding billiard tables, clocks, pianos, gramophones and pictures;

(*b*) ironmongery, turnery and hardware, of kinds commonly used for household purposes, including gardening implements;

(*c*) hand tools ;

(*d*) woodware, basketware, glassware, potteryware, chinaware, brassware, plasticware and ceramic goods, being articles or goods of kinds commonly used for household purposes or as household ornaments ;

(*e*) electrical and gas appliances and apparatus, of kinds commonly used for household purposes (excluding clocks), and accessories and component parts thereof ;

(*f*) heating, lighting and cooking appliances and apparatus, of kinds commonly used for household purposes, and accessories and component parts thereof ;

(*g*) radio and television sets and their accessories and component parts ;

(*h*) pedal cycles and their accessories and component parts ;

(*i*) perambulators, push chairs and invalid carriages ;

(*j*) toys, indoor games, requisites for outdoor games, gymnastics and athletics, but excluding billiard tables and sports clothing ;

(*k*) saddlery, leather goods (other than articles of wearing apparel), travel goods and ladies' handbags ;

(*l*) paint, distemper and wallpaper and oils of all kinds commonly used for household purposes (excluding petrol and lubricating oils) ;

(*m*) brushes, mops and brooms, used for household purposes, and similar articles ;

(*n*) disinfectants, chemicals, candles, soaps and polishes, of kinds commonly used for household purposes ;

(ii) operations in or about the shop or other place where any of the articles specified in (i) of this sub-paragraph are sold by retail, being operations carried on for the purpose of such sale or otherwise in connection with such sale ;

(iii) operations in connection with the warehousing or storing of any of the articles specified in (i) of this sub-paragraph for the purpose of the sale thereof by retail, or otherwise in connection with such sale, where the warehousing or storing takes place at a warehouse or store carried on in conjunction with one or more shops or other places where the said articles are sold by retail ;

(iv) operations in connection with the transport of any of the articles specified in (i) of this sub-paragraph when carried on in conjunction with their sale by retail or with the warehousing or storing operations specified in (iii) of this sub-paragraph ; and

(v) clerical or other office work carried on in conjunction with the sale by retail of any of the articles specified in (i) of this sub-paragraph and relating to such sale or to any of the operations specified in (ii) to (iv) of this sub-paragraph ;

and for the purpose of this definition the sale by retail of any of the articles specified in (i) of this sub-paragraph does not include sale by auction (except where the auctioneer sells articles by retail which are his property or the property of his master) but includes the sale of any of the articles therein specified to a person for use in connection with a trade or business carried on by him if such sale takes place at or in connection with a shop engaged in the retail sale to the general public of any of the said articles.

APPENDIX TO PARAGRAPH 22

GROUPS OF RETAIL DISTRIBUTIVE TRADES

Group 1.—The Retail Food Trades, that is to say, the sale by retail of food or drink for human consumption and operations connected therewith including:—

(i) operations in or about the shop or other place where the food or drink aforesaid is sold, being operations carried on for the purpose of such sale or otherwise in connection with such sale ;

(ii) operations in connection with the warehousing or storing of such food or drink for the purpose of sale by retail, or otherwise in connection with such sale, where the warehousing or storing takes place at a warehouse or store carried on in conjunction with one or more shops or other places where such food or drink is sold by retail ;

(iii) operations in connection with the transport of such food or drink when carried on in conjunction with its sale by retail or with the warehousing or storing operations specified in (ii) above ; and

(iv) clerical or other office work carried on in conjunction with the sale by retail aforesaid and relating to such sale or to any of the operations in (i) to (iii) above ;

but not including

the sale by retail of bread, pastry or flour confectionery (other than biscuits or meat pastries) or the sale by retail of meat (other than bacon, ham, pressed beef, sausages, or meat so treated as to be fit for human consumption without further preparation or cooking) or the sale by retail of milk (other than dried or condensed milk) or the sale by retail of ice-cream, aerated waters, chocolate confectionery or sugar confectionery, or the sale of food or drink for immediate consumption.

For the purpose of this definition "sale by retail" includes any sale of food or drink to a person for use in connection with a catering business carried on by him, when such sale takes place at or in connection with a shop engaged in the retail sale of food or drink to the general public.

Group 2.—The Retail Drapery, Outfitting and Footwear Trades, that is to say—

(1) the sale by retail of

(*a*) wearing apparel of all kinds (including footwear, headwear and handwear) and accessories, trimmings and adornments for wearing apparel (excluding jewellery and imitation jewellery) ;

(*b*) haberdashery ;

(*c*) textile fabrics in the piece, leather cloth, plastic cloth and oil cloth (but not including carpets, linoleum and other kinds of floor covering) ;

(*d*) knitting, rug, embroidery, crochet and similar wools or yarns ;

(*e*) made-up household textiles (but excluding mattresses and floor coverings) ;

(*f*) umbrellas, sunshades, walking sticks, canes and similar articles ;

(2) operations in or about the shop or other place where any of the articles included in (1) above are sold by retail, being operations carried on for the purpose of such sale or otherwise in connection with such sale ;

(3) operations in connection with the warehousing or storing of any of the articles included in (1) above for the purpose of the sale thereof by retail, or otherwise in connection with such sale, where the warehousing or storing takes place at a warehouse or store carried on in conjunction with one or more shops or other places where the said articles are sold by retail ;

(4) operations in connection with the transport of any of the articles included in (1) above when carried on in conjunction with their sale by retail or with the warehousing or storing operations specified in (3) above ; and

(5) clerical or other office work carried on in conjunction with the sale by retail of any of the articles included in (1) above and relating to such sale or to any of the operations specified in (2) to (4) above ;

and for the purpose of this definition the sale by retail of any of the articles in (1) above includes the sale of that article to a person for use in connection with a trade or business carried on by him if such sale takes place at or in connection with a shop engaged in the retail sale to the general public of any of the articles included in (1) above.

Group 3.—The Retail Bookselling and Stationery Trades, that is to say—

(1) the sale by retail of the following articles:—

(*a*) books (excluding printed music and periodicals);

(*b*) all kinds of stationery including printed forms, note books, diaries and similar articles, and books of kinds used in an office or business for the purpose of record;

(*c*) pens, pencils, ink, blotting paper and similar articles;

(*d*) maps and charts;

(*e*) wrapping and adhesive paper, string, paste and similar articles;

(2) operations in or about the shop or other place where any of the articles specified in (1) above are sold by retail, being operations carried on for the purpose of such sale or otherwise in connection with such sale;

(3) operations in connection with the warehousing or storing of any of the articles specified in (1) above for the purpose of the sale thereof by retail, or otherwise in connection with such sale, where the warehousing or storing takes place at a warehouse or store carried on in conjunction with one or more shops or other places where the said articles are sold by retail;

(4) operations in connection with the transport of any of the articles specified in (1) above when carried on in conjunction with their sale by retail or with the warehousing or storing operations specified in (3) above; and

(5) clerical or other office work carried on in conjunction with the sale by retail of any of the articles specified in (1) above and relating to such sale or to any of the operations specified in (2) to (4) above.

Group 4.—The Retail Newsagency, Tobacco and Confectionery Trades, that is to say—

(1) the sale by retail of the following articles:—

(*a*) newspapers, magazines and other periodicals;

(*b*) tobacco, cigars, cigarettes, snuff and smokers' requisites;

(*c*) articles of sugar confectionery and chocolate confectionery and ice-cream;

(2) operations in or about the shop or other place where any of the articles specified in (1) above are sold by retail, being operations carried on for the purpose of such sale or otherwise in connection with such sale;

(3) operations in connection with the warehousing or storing of any of the articles specified in (1) above for the purpose of the sale thereof by retail, or otherwise in connection with such sale, where the warehousing or storing takes place at a warehouse or store carried on in conjunction with one or more shops or other places where the said articles are sold by retail;

(4) operations in connection with the transport of any of the articles specified in (1) above when carried on in conjunction with their sale by retail or with the warehousing or storing operation specified in (3) above; and

(5) clerical or other office work carried on in conjunction with the sale by retail of any of the articles specified in (1) above and relating to such sale or to any of the operations specified in (2) to (4) above.

EXPLANATORY NOTE

(This Note is not part of the Order.)

This Order, which has effect from 3rd August 1970, sets out the statutory minimum remuneration payable and the holidays to be allowed to workers in substitution for the statutory minimum remuneration fixed, and holidays provided for, by the Wages Regulation (Retail Furnishing and Allied Trades) Order 1967 (Order R.F.A. (48)) as amended by the Wages Regulation (Retail Furnishing and Allied Trades) (Amendment) Order 1968 (Order R.F.A. (50)), which Orders are revoked.

New provisions are printed in italics.

STATUTORY INSTRUMENTS

1970 No. 920

CUSTOMS AND EXCISE

The Anti-Dumping (Provisional Charge to Duty) (No. 5) Order 1970

Made - - - -	19*th June* 1970
* *To be laid before the House of Commons*	
Coming into Operation	24*th June* 1970

The Board of Trade, in pursuance of the powers conferred upon them by sections 1, 2, 8 and 9(3) of the Customs Duties (Dumping and Subsidies) Act 1969(**a**), hereby make the following Order :—

1. This Order may be cited as the Anti-Dumping (Provisional Charge to Duty) (No. 5) Order 1970 and shall come into operation on 24th June 1970.

2. Goods of the description set out in the Schedule hereto (being goods classified in the Customs Tariff 1959(**b**) under the heading mentioned in the first column of that Schedule) shall be subject to a provisional charge to duty in respect of a duty of customs at the rate set out in the third column of that Schedule.

3. Section 2 of the Customs Duties (Dumping and Subsidies) Act 1969 (which allows relief to be given where goods are shown not to have been dumped or where the margin of dumping is less than the provisional charge) shall apply to the provisional charge imposed by this Order.

Antony Part,
Permanent Secretary to the
Board of Trade.

19th June 1970.

SCHEDULE

Relevant Tariff Heading	Description of Goods	Relevant Rate
ex 07·01 (IJ)	New potatoes originating in France	10s. 0d. per cwt.

*This instrument was laid before the House of Commons on 29th June 1970

(**a**) 1969 c. 16. (**b**) See S.I. 1969/1413 (1969 III, p. 4150).

EXPLANATORY NOTE

(This Note is not part of the Order.)

This Order makes imports of new potatoes originating in France subject to a provisional charge in respect of an anti-dumping duty.

The making of the Order enables the Commissioners of Customs and Excise to require security for the payment of any anti-dumping duty which may be imposed retrospectively on such imports under section 8(1) of the Customs Duties (Dumping and Subsidies) Act 1969. If any duty is imposed retrospectively, it may only be so imposed on goods imported while the Order is in force, and its rate may not exceed the rate mentioned in the Schedule to the Order.

The Order expires automatically after three months unless previously revoked or extended (for not more than three months) by a further Order.

The Order applies section 2 of the 1969 Act to the charge, which enables relief to be granted where particular goods have not been dumped or the margin of dumping is less than the amount of the provisional charge.

STATUTORY INSTRUMENTS

1970 No. 922 (C. 22)

LANDS TRIBUNAL

The Law of Property Act 1969 (Commencement) Order 1970

Made - - - - -	16*th June* 1970
* *To be laid before Parliament*	
Coming into Operation -	1*st July* 1970

The Lord Chancellor, in exercise of the powers conferred on him by section 28(11)(*b*) of the Law of Property Act 1969(**a**), hereby makes the following Order:—

1. This Order may be cited as the Law of Property Act 1969 (Commencement) Order 1970.

2. Section 28(6) of the Law of Property Act 1969 shall come into operation on 1st July 1970.

Dated 16th June 1970.

Gardiner, C.

EXPLANATORY NOTE

(*This Note is not part of the Order.*)

This Order brings into operation, on 1st July 1970, section 28(6) of the Law of Property Act 1969, which amends the procedure on applications to the Lands Tribunal under section 84 of the Law of Property Act 1925 (c. 20) for the discharge or modification of restrictive covenants.

*This instrument was laid before Parliament on 29th June 1970

(**a**) 1969 c. 59.

1970 No. 924 (S.71)

NATIONAL HEALTH SERVICE, SCOTLAND

The National Health Service (General Dental Services) (Scotland) Amendment Regulations 1970

Made - - -	17*th June* 1970
Laid before Parliament	29*th June* 1970
Coming into Operation	1*st July* 1970

In exercise of the powers conferred on me by section 39 of the National Health Service (Scotland) Act 1947**(a)**, as amended by section 11 of the National Health Service (Amendment) Act 1949**(b)**, and of all other powers enabling me in that behalf I hereby make the following regulations:—

1.—(1) These regulations may be cited as the National Health Service (General Dental Services) (Scotland) Amendment Regulations 1970 and shall come into operation on 1st July 1970.

(2) In these regulations:—

"the principal regulations" means the National Health Service (General Dental Services) (Scotland) Regulations 1966**(c)** as amended **(d)**; and

"regulation 27" means regulation 27 of the principal regulations as amended by regulation 2(2) of the National Health Service (General Dental Services) (Scotland) Amendment (No. 2) Regulations 1969**(e)** (which substituted provisions for a new scale of fees for treatment).

(3) The Interpretation Act 1889**(f)** applies for the interpretation of these regulations as it applies for the interpretation of an Act of Parliament.

2. The principal regulations, as amended by regulation 2(2) of the said regulations of 1969, shall be further amended as follows:—

(1) Where an advice of payment from the Board to a Council is in respect of a contract or arrangement entered into or made on or after 1st July 1970, the Council shall pay to a practitioner in addition to the fees authorised under regulation 27 a sum equal to 10 per cent of the amount of these fees.

(2) (*a*) Subject to the following provisions of this regulation, these regulations shall not apply to general dental services provided under a contract or arrangement entered into or made before 1st July 1970 and such services shall continue to be subject to the provisions of the regulations in force immediately before that date.

(a) 1947 c. 27.
(b) 1949 c. 93.
(c) S.I. 1966/1449 (1966 III, p. 3802).
(d) The relevant amending instrument is S.I. 1969/436 (1969 I, p. 1276).
(e) S.I. 1969/436 (1969 I, p. 1276).
(f) 1889 c. 63.

(*b*) In respect of an advice of payment from the Board to a Council dated during the period beginning with 1st April 1970 and ending with 30th June 1970, the Council shall pay to a practitioner an additional sum equal to 7 per cent of the amounts authorised for payment.

(*c*) Where an advice of payment from the Board to a Council dated on or after 1st July 1970 is in respect of a contract or arrangement entered into or made on or after 1st April 1969 and before 1st July 1970, the Council shall pay to a practitioner in addition to the fees authorised under regulation 27 a sum equal to 10 per cent of the amount of these fees.

(*d*) Where an advice of payment from the Board to a Council dated on or after 1st July 1970 is in respect of a contract or arrangement entered into or made on or after 1st July 1966 and before 1st April 1969, the Council shall pay to a practitioner in addition to the fees authorised under regulation 27 a sum equal to 13 per cent of the amount of these fees.

(*e*) Where an advice of payment from the Board to a Council dated on or after 1st July 1970 is in respect of a contract or arrangement entered into or made before 1st July 1966 the Council shall pay to a practitioner, in addition to the fees authorised under regulation 27 a sum equal to 25 per cent of the amount of these fees.

William Ross,
One of Her Majesty's Principal
Secretaries of State.

St. Andrew's House,
Edinburgh.
17th June 1970.

EXPLANATORY NOTE

(*This Note is not part of the Regulations.*)

These Regulations further amend the National Health Service (General Dental Services) (Scotland) Regulations 1966 by providing for certain additional payments for practitioners, other than salaried practitioners, providing general dental services.

1970 No. 926

NATIONAL HEALTH SERVICE, ENGLAND AND WALES

HOSPITAL AND SPECIALIST SERVICES

The National Health Service (Designation of London Teaching Hospitals) Amendment Order 1970

Made - - -	23*rd June* 1970
Coming into Operation	1*st July* 1970

The Secretary of State for Social Services in exercise of his powers under sections 11 and 75 of the National Health Service Act 1946(**a**), and of all other powers enabling him in that behalf and after consultation with the University of London, hereby orders as follows:—

1. This order may be cited as the National Health Service (Designation of London Teaching Hospitals) Amendment Order 1970, and shall come into operation on the 1st July 1970.

2.—(1) In this order—

"the Act" means the National Health Service Act 1946;

"the appointed day" means the 1st July 1970;

"the Board" means the Board of Governors of the London Hospital;

"the Committee" means the Brentwood Group Hospital Management Committee;

"the hospital" means the London Hospital Annexe, Brentwood, Essex.

(2) The Interpretation Act 1889(**b**), shall apply to the interpretation of this order as it applies to the interpretation of an Act of Parliament.

3. In column 2 of the First Schedule to the National Health Service (Designation of London Teaching Hospitals) Order 1957(**c**), as amended (**d**), the words "the London Hospital Annexe, Brentwood, Essex" shall be deleted.

4. Any property immediately before the appointed day belonging to the Board and held solely for the purposes of the hospital shall on that day be transferred to the Committee.

5. Subject as aforesaid all right and liabilities to which the Board were entitled or subject immediately before the appointed day, being rights or liabilities acquired or incurred solely in respect of the hospital premises shall on that day be transferred to and vest in the Committee.

(**a**) 1946 c. 81. (**b**) 1889 c. 63. (**c**) S.I. 1957/488 (1957 I, p. 1452).
(**d**) There is no amendment which relates to the subject matter of this order.

Signed by authority of the Secretary of State for Social Services.

J. Hauff,
Assistant Under Secretary of State,
Department of Health and Social Security.

23rd June 1970.

EXPLANATORY NOTE

(This Note is not part of the Order.)

This Order deletes the London Hospital Annexe, Brentwood, Essex from the list of hospitals designated by the Secretary of State for Social Services as a teaching hospital under the name of The London Hospital, and provides for consequential matters relating to property connected with the said Annexe.

1970 No. 931

INDUSTRIAL ASSURANCE

DECIMAL CURRENCY

The Industrial Assurance (Decimal Currency) Regulations 1970

Made - - -	23*rd June* 1970
Laid before Parliament	6*th July* 1970
Coming into Operation	1*st August* 1970

The Industrial Assurance Commissioner pursuant to the powers conferred upon him by subsections (2) to (5) of section 6 of the Decimal Currency Act 1969(**a**) and to all other powers enabling him in that behalf hereby makes the following Regulations :—

1.—(1) These Regulations may be cited as the Industrial Assurance (Decimal Currency) Regulations 1970, and shall come into operation on 1st August 1970.

(2) In these Regulations—

"industrial assurance company", "industrial assurance business" and "collecting society" have the meanings assigned by section 1 of the Industrial Assurance Act 1923(**b**) as amended by Schedule 6 to the Companies Act 1967(**c**) ;

"industrial assurance contract" means a contract of assurance made by an industrial assurance company in the course of its industrial assurance business in Great Britain or a contract made by a collecting society with a member of the society in the course of its industrial assurance business in Great Britain, whether contained in the rules of the society or not ;

"collecting society contract" means a contract, other than an industrial assurance contract, made by a collecting society with a member of the society in the course of its business in Great Britain, whether contained in the rules of the society or not ;

"the new currency" and "the old currency" have the meanings assigned by section 16(1) of the Decimal Currency Act 1969 ;

"the prescribed scheme" means the scheme prescribed in Schedule 4 to these Regulations ;

"approved scheme" means a special scheme approved by the Industrial Assurance Commissioner in the circumstances provided for in regulation 6 of these Regulations ;

"actuary" means an actuary having such qualifications as may be prescribed by Regulations made under section 16(1) of the Friendly and Industrial and Provident Societies Act 1968(**d**).

(3) The Interpretation Act 1889(**e**) shall apply to the interpretation of these Regulations as it applies to the interpretation of an Act of Parliament.

(**a**) 1969 c. 19.
(**b**) 1923 c. 8.
(**c**) 1967 c. 81.
(**d**) 1968 c. 55.
(**e**) 1889 c. 63.

2.—(1) Subject to regulation 3, this regulation applies to payments payable under any industrial assurance or collecting society contract made before 15th February 1971 that fall due on or after that date.

(2) The amount payable in respect of any payment to which this regulation applies and which is payable by an industrial assurance company or collecting society shall be the amount in the new currency provided for in Schedule 1 to these Regulations.

(3) The amount payable in respect of any payment to which this regulation applies and which is payable to an industrial assurance company or collecting society shall be—

(*a*) if the payment is payable under a collecting society contract as one of a series of payments payable at intervals greater than two weeks, the amount in the new currency provided for in Schedule 1 to these Regulations,

(*b*) if the payment is payable under an industrial assurance contract as one of a series of payments payable at intervals greater than two weeks, the amount in the new currency provided for in Schedule 2 to these Regulations,

(*c*) if the payment is payable under an industrial assurance or collecting society contract as one of a series of payments payable weekly or fortnightly, the amount in the new currency provided for in Schedule 3 to these Regulations.

3. Regulation 2 shall not apply to any payment payable under an industrial assurance or collecting society contract—

(*a*) which is contained in or by its terms subject to the rules of a collecting society and those rules provide for the amount in the new currency payable in respect of the payment, or

(*b*) to which the prescribed scheme or an approved scheme applies.

4.—(1) An industrial assurance company or a collecting society may by resolution of its board of directors or, as the case may be, of its committee of management, passed before 15th February 1971 adopt—

(*a*) the prescribed scheme, or

(*b*) an approved scheme, or

(*c*) both the prescribed scheme and an approved scheme

for the purpose of securing that under any industrial assurance or collecting society contract made before 15th February 1971 to which the prescribed scheme or an approved scheme applies no amount other than a new halfpenny or multiple thereof will be payable in respect of any payment that falls due on or after that date.

(2) Where an industrial assurance company or collecting society has so adopted any such scheme, the amount payable to or by the company or society in respect of a payment payable under any contract to which the scheme applies that falls due as aforesaid shall be the amount in the new currency provided for in the scheme.

(3) Written notice of a resolution adopting the prescribed or an approved scheme shall within fourteen days of the passing thereof be sent by the industrial assurance company or collecting society to the Industrial Assurance Commissioner.

5.—(1) Where payments payable to an industrial assurance company or collecting society which has adopted the prescribed scheme are increased by virtue of paragraph 3 of the scheme, the company or society shall on being requested so to do by the person by whom the increased payments are payable notify him in writing of the corresponding increase in the benefit payable by virtue of paragraph 8 of the scheme.

(2) Any person by whom payments so increased are payable may, within six months of first receiving written notification from the company or society of the increase in the benefit, appeal to the Industrial Assurance Commissioner on the ground that the increase in the benefit is not fair in relation to the increased payments payable by him.

(3) If on such appeal, and after giving the appellant and the company or society an opportunity of being heard, the Industrial Assurance Commissioner is satisfied that the increase in benefit is not fair, he may direct the company or society to make such increase as he may consider appropriate in the benefit to which the appeal relates and in like benefits payable under other like contracts.

6. The Industrial Assurance Commissioner may before 15th February 1971 approve a special scheme intended to be adopted by an industrial assurance company or collecting society for the purpose mentioned in regulation 4 if—

(*a*) in his opinion regulation 2 or the prescribed scheme cannot be made to apply to payments under the contracts to which the special scheme applies without difficulty or inconvenience having regard to the times or method of their payment or to any other relevant matter, and

(*b*) where by virtue of the scheme any payments payable to the company or society are increased, an actuary has certified that the scheme provides where actuarially appropriate for suitable adjustments to the benefits for which those payments are payable.

7. Notwithstanding anything contained in the rules of a collecting society which has adopted the prescribed scheme or an approved scheme, the committee of management of the society may by resolution passed before 15th February 1972 make amendments to the rules of the society in connection with the adoption by the society of any such scheme.

S. D. Musson,
Industrial Assurance Commissioner

Date 23rd June 1970.

SCHEDULE 1

AMOUNT IN THE NEW CURRENCY OF A PAYMENT REFERRED TO IN PARAGRAPHS (2) AND (3)(*a*) OF REGULATION 2

The amount in the new currency payable in respect of a payment referred to in paragraphs (2) and (3)(*a*) of regulation 2 shall be the amount corresponding to the amount in the old currency payable under the contract calculated as follows—

(*a*) for an amount or for so much of an amount as consists of one or more whole pounds the corresponding amount in the new currency is the same number of pounds; and (*b*) for any whole two shillings or multiple thereof of an amount or remaining amount of less than one pound the corresponding amount in the new currency is ten new pence or that multiple thereof ; and

(*c*) for an amount or remaining amount of less than two shillings shown in column 1 of the following table, the corresponding amount in the new currency is the amount (if any) in new pence shown opposite that amount in column 2 of that table and accordingly an amount or remaining amount of one penny shall be disregarded.

TABLE

Amount in old currency	*Corresponding amount in new pence*
1d	—
2d	1p
3d	1p
4d	2p
5d	2p
6d	3p
7d	3p
8d	3p
9d	4p
10d	4p
11d	5p
1s 0d	5p
1s 1d	5p
1s 2d	6p
1s 3d	6p
1s 4d	7p
1s 5d	7p
1s 6d	7p
1s 7d	8p
1s 8d	8p
1s 9d	9p
1s 10d	9p
1s 11d	10p

SCHEDULE 2

Amount in the New Currency of a Payment Referred to in Paragraph (3)(*b*) of Regulation 2

The amount in the new currency payable in respect of a payment referred to in paragraph (3)(*b*) of regulation 2 shall be the amount corresponding to the amount in the old currency payable under the contract or, if that amount would apart from the Industrial Assurance (Halfpenny) Regulations 1969(**a**) be or include a halfpenny, to the amount in the old currency payable under the contract apart from those Regulations, calculated as follows—

(*a*) for an amount or for so much of an amount as consists of one or more whole pounds the corresponding amount in the new currency is that number of pounds ; and

(*b*) for any whole shilling or multiple thereof of an amount or remaining amount of less than one pound the corresponding amount in the new currency is five new pence or that multiple thereof ; and

(a) S.I. 1969/887 (1969 II, p. 2525).

(*c*) for an amount or remaining amount of less than one shilling shown in column 1 of the following table, the corresponding amount in the new currency is the amount (if any) in new pence shown opposite that amount in column 2 of that table and accordingly an amount or remaining amount of one halfpenny shall be disregarded.

TABLE

Amount in old currency	*Corresponding amount in new pence*
½d	—
1d	½p
1½d	½p
2d	1p
2½d	1p
3d	1p
3½d	1½p
4d	1½p
4½d	2p
5d	2p
5½d	2½p
6d	2½p
6½d	2½p
7d	3p
7½d	3p
8d	3½p
8½d	3½p
9d	4p
9½d	4p
10d	4p
10½d	4½p
11d	4½p
11½d	5p

SCHEDULE 3

Amount in the New Currency of a Payment Referred to in Paragraph (3)(*c*) of Regulation 2

Payments payable weekly

1. The amount in the new currency payable in respect of a payment referred to in paragraph (3)(*c*) of regulation 2 which is payable weekly and which falls due on or after the relevant date shall be the amount corresponding to the amount in the old currency payable under the contract or, if that amount would apart from the Industrial Assurance (Halfpenny) Regulations 1969 be or include a halfpenny, to the amount in the old currency payable under the contract apart from those Regulations, calculated as follows—

(*a*) for any whole shilling or multiple thereof the corresponding amount in the new currency is five new pence or that multiple thereof; and

(*b*) for any amount or remaining amount of less than one shilling shown in column 1 of the following table the corresponding amount in the new currency is, in relation to any one of four successive weekly payments in a series beginning with the payment first falling due on or after the relevant date, the amount (if any) in new pence shown opposite that amount under the appropriate weekly payment in columns 2 to 5 of that table and an amount or remaining amount of one penny or a halfpenny shall be disregarded in relation to the weekly payment under which no amount in new pence is so shown.

TABLE

Amount in old currency	*Corresponding amount in new pence*			
	1st weekly payment	*2nd weekly payment*	*3rd weekly payment*	*4th weekly payment*
½d	—	½p	—	½p
1d	—	½p	½p	½p
1½d	½p	½p	½p	1p
2d	½p	1p	1p	1p
2½d	1p	1p	1p	1p
3d	1p	1½p	1p	1½p
3½d	1½p	1½p	1½p	1½p
4d	1½p	1½p	1½p	2p
4½d	1½p	2p	2p	2p
5d	2p	2p	2p	2½p
5½d	2p	2½p	2p	2½p
6d	2½p	2½p	2½p	2½p
6½d	2½p	3p	2½p	3p
7d	2½p	3p	3p	3p
7½d	3p	3p	3p	3½p
8d	3p	3½p	3½p	3½p
8½d	3½p	3½p	3½p	3½p
9d	3½p	4p	3½p	4p
9½d	4p	4p	4p	4p
10d	4p	4p	4p	4½p
10½d	4p	4½p	4½p	4½p
11d	4½p	4½p	4½p	5p
11½d	4½p	5p	4½p	5p

Payments payable fortnightly

2. The amount in the new currency payable in respect of a payment referred to in paragraph (3)(*c*) of regulation 2 which is payable fortnightly and which falls due on or after the relevant date shall be the amount corresponding to the amount in the old currency payable under the contract or, if that amount would apart from the Industrial Assurance (Halfpenny) Regulations 1969 be or include a halfpenny, to the amount in the old currency payable under the contract apart from those Regulations, calculated as follows—

(*a*) for any whole shilling or multiple thereof the corresponding amount in the new currency is five new pence or that multiple thereof ; and

(*b*) for any amount or remaining amount of less than one shilling shown in column 1 of the following table the corresponding amount in the new currency is, in relation to any one of two successive fortnightly payments in a series beginning with the payment first falling due on or after the relevant date, the amount (if any) in new pence shown opposite that amount under the appropriate fortnightly payment in columns 2 and 3 of that table and an amount or remaining amount of a halfpenny shall be disregarded in relation to the first of every two successive fortnightly payments.

TABLE

Amount in old currency		*Corresponding amount in new pence*	
		1st fortnightly payment	*2nd fortnightly payment*
½d	... ...	—	½p
1d	... ...	½p	½p
1½d	... ...	½p	½p
2d	... ...	½p	1p
2½d	... ...	1p	1p
3d	... ...	1p	1½p
3½d	... ...	1½p	1½p
4d	... ...	1½p	2p
4½d	... ...	2p	2p
5d	... ...	2p	2p
5½d	... ...	2p	2½p
6d	... ...	2½p	2½p
6½d	... ...	2½p	3p
7d	... ...	3p	3p
7½d	... ...	3p	3p
8d	... ...	3p	3½p
8½d	... ...	3½p	3½p
9d	... ...	3½p	4p
9½d	... ...	4p	4p
10d	... ...	4p	4½p
10½d	... ...	4½p	4½p
11d	... ...	4½p	4½p
11½d	... ...	4½p	5p

3. "Relevant date" in paragraphs 1 and 2 of this Schedule means—

(*a*) 15th February 1971, or

(*b*) 22nd February 1971 in relation to any payment payable to an industrial assurance company or collecting society which before 15th February 1971 has determined that 22nd February 1971 shall be the relevant date.

4. Where an industrial assurance company or collecting society has determined as mentioned in subparagraph (*b*) of the preceding paragraph, the amount in the new currency payable in respect of a payment referred to in paragraph (3)(*c*) of regulation 2 which is payable to the company or society and which falls due before 22nd February 1971 shall be the amount corresponding to the amount in the old currency (being in the case of an amount reduced or increased by one halfpenny by virtue of the Industrial Assurance (Halfpenny) Regulations 1969 the amount so reduced or increased) payable under the contract calculated as follows—

(*a*) for any whole shilling or multiple thereof the corresponding amount in the new currency is five new pence or that multiple thereof; and

(*b*) for any amount or remaining amount of less than one shilling shown in column 1 of the following table the corresponding amount in the new currency is the amount in new pence shown opposite that amount in column 2 of that table.

TABLE

Amount in old currency	*Corresponding amount in new pence*
1d	½p
2d	1p
3d	1p
4d	1½p
5d	2p
6d	2½p
7d	3p
8d	3½p
9d	4p
10d	4p
11d	4½p

SCHEDULE 4

PRESCRIBED SCHEME

1. The scheme applies to any industrial assurance or collecting society contract made before 15th February 1971 under which a series of weekly or fortnightly payments are payable to the industrial assurance company or collecting society which has adopted the scheme in accordance with regulation 4 of these Regulations.

2. The amount in the new currency of a payment payable under a contract to which the scheme applies and falling due on or after 15th February 1971 shall be the amount herein provided.

Weekly payment of not more than one shilling and fortnightly payment of not more than two shillings

3. In the case of a payment payable as one of a series to the company or society in respect of which the amount in the old currency payable does not exceed, if a weekly payment, one shilling or, if a fortnightly payment, two shillings, and which falls due on or after the relevant date, the amount in the new currency shall be the amount corresponding to the amount in the old currency payable under the contract or, if that amount would apart from the Industrial Assurance (Halfpenny) Regulations 1969 be or include a halfpenny, to the amount in the old currency payable under the contract apart from those Regulations, calculated as follows—

(*a*) for any whole shilling or two shillings the corresponding amount in the new currency is respectively five new pence and ten new pence, and

(*b*) for any amount or remaining amount of less than one shilling shown in column 1 of the following table the corresponding amount in the new currency is the amount in new pence shown opposite that amount in column 2 of that table.

TABLE

Amount in old currency	*Corresponding amount in new pence*
½d	½p
1d	½p
1½d	1p
2d	1p
2½d	1½p
3d	1½p
3½d	1½p
4d	2p
4½d	2p
5d	2½p
5½d	2½p
6d	2½p
6½d	3p
7d	3p
7½d	3½p
8d	3½p
8½d	4p
9d	4p
9½d	4p
10d	4½p
10½d	4½p
11d	5p
11½d	5p

4. "Relevant date" in paragraph 3 of the scheme means—

(*a*) 15th February 1971, or

(*b*) 22nd February 1971 if the company or society on adopting the scheme has determined that that date shall be the relevant date.

5. Where the company or society has determined as mentioned in subparagraph (*b*) of the preceding paragraph, the amount in the new currency of a payment falling due before 22nd February 1971 which would otherwise fall to be determined under paragraph 3 shall be the amount corresponding to the amount in the old currency (being in the case of an amount reduced or increased by one halfpenny by virtue of the Industrial Assurance (Halfpenny) Regulations 1969 the amount so reduced or increased) payable under the contract calculated as follows—

(*a*) for any whole shilling or two shillings the corresponding amount in the new currency is respectively five new pence and ten new pence ; and

(*b*) for any amount or remaining amount of less than one shilling shown in column 1 of the following table the corresponding amount in the new currency is the amount in new pence shown opposite that amount in column 2 of that table.

TABLE

Amount in old currency	*Corresponding amount in new pence*
1d	½p
2d	1p
3d	1p
4d	1½p
5d	2p
6d	2½p
7d	3p
8d	3½p
9d	4p
10d	4p
11d	4½p

Other weekly and fortnightly payments

6. In the case of a weekly or fortnightly payment payable as one of a series to the company or society in respect of which the amount in the old currency payable exceeds the amount referred to in paragraph 3, the amount in the new currency shall be the amount corresponding to the amount in the old currency payable under the contract or, if that amount would apart from the Industrial Assurance (Halfpenny) Regulations 1969 include a halfpenny, to the amount in the old currency payable under the contract apart from those Regulations, calculated in accordance with subparagraphs (*a*) to (*c*) of Schedule 2 to these Regulations.

Benefits

7. Subject to paragraph 8 the amount in the new currency payable by the company or society in respect of a benefit shall be the amount corresponding to the amount in the old currency payable under the contract calculated in accordance with subparagraphs (*a*) to (*c*) of Schedule 1 to these Regulations.

8. Where by virtue of paragraph 3 the payments payable under a contract are increased, the benefit payable by the company or society under the contract shall also be increased and shall be of such amount in the new currency as an actuary shall certify to be fair in relation to the increased payments payable.

EXPLANATORY NOTE

(*This Note is not part of the Regulations.*)

These Regulations prescribe the method of converting into decimal currency payments falling due on or after 15th February 1971 under industrial assurance contracts and friendly society contracts with collecting societies, made before that date. They also enable an industrial assurance company or collecting society to adopt any special scheme approved by the Industrial Assurance Commissioner for the purpose of converting such payments into decimal currency and provide for the circumstances in which a special scheme may be approved.

STATUTORY INSTRUMENTS

1970 No. 932

FRIENDLY SOCIETIES

DECIMAL CURRENCY

The Friendly Societies (Decimal Currency) Regulations 1970

Made - - -	*23rd June* 1970
Laid before Parliament	*6th July* 1970
Coming into Operation	*1st August* 1970

The Chief Registrar of Friendly Societies pursuant to the powers conferred upon him by sub-sections (2) to (5) of section 6 of the Decimal Currency Act 1969(**a**) and to all other powers enabling him in that behalf hereby makes the following Regulations :—

1.—(1) These Regulations may be cited as the Friendly Societies (Decimal Currency) Regulations 1970, and shall come into operation on 1st August 1970.

(2) In these Regulations—

"friendly society" means a friendly society, not being a collecting society, registered in any part of the United Kingdom under the Friendly Societies Act 1896(**b**) or a branch so registered under that Act of a friendly society so registered ;

"collecting society" has the meaning assigned by section 1 of the Industrial Assurance Act 1923(**c**) as amended by Schedule 6 to the Companies Act 1967(**d**) ;

"friendly society contract" means a contract made by a friendly society with a member of the society in the course of its business in Great Britain, whether contained in the rules of the society or not ;

"the new currency" and "the old currency" have the meanings assigned by section 16(1) of the Decimal Currency Act 1969 ;

"approved scheme" means a special scheme approved by the Chief Registrar of Friendly Societies in the circumstances provided for in regulation 5 of these Regulations ;

(**a**) 1969 c. 19. (**b**) 1896 c. 25.
(**c**) 1923 c. 8. (**d**) 1967 c. 81.

"actuary" means an actuary having such qualifications as may be prescribed by Regulations made under section 16(1) of the Friendly and Industrial and Provident Societies Act 1968(**a**).

(3) The Interpretation Act 1889(**b**) shall apply to the interpretation of these Regulations as it applies to the interpretation of an Act of Parliament.

2.—(1) Subject to regulation 3, this regulation applies to payments payable under any friendly society contract made before 15th February 1971 that fall due on or after that date.

(2) The amount payable in respect of any payment to which this regulation applies and which is payable by a friendly society shall be the amount in the new currency provided for in Schedule 1 to these Regulations.

(3) The amount payable in respect of any payment to which this regulation applies and which is payable to a friendly society shall be—

(*a*) if the payment is payable under a friendly society contract as one of a series of payments payable at intervals of two months or more, the amount in the new currency provided for in Schedule 1 to these Regulations,

(*b*) if the payment is payable under a friendly society contract as one of a series of payments payable at intervals of less than two months but more than two weeks, the amount in the new currency provided for in Schedule 2 to these Regulations,

(*c*) if the payment is payable under a friendly society contract as one of a series of payments payable at intervals of two weeks or less, the amount in the new currency provided for in Schedule 3 to these Regulations.

3. Regulation 2 shall not apply to any payment payable under a friendly society contract—

(*a*) which is contained in or is by its terms subject to the rules of a friendly society and those rules provide for the amount in the new currency payable in respect of the payment, or

(*b*) to which an approved scheme applies.

4.—(1) A friendly society may by resolution of its committee of management passed before 15th February 1971 adopt an approved scheme for the purpose of securing that under any friendly society contract made before that date to which the approved scheme applies no amount other than a new halfpenny or multiple thereof will be payable in respect of any payment that falls due on or after that date.

(2) Where a friendly society has so adopted an approved scheme the amount payable to or by the society in respect of a payment payable under any contract to which the scheme applies that falls due as aforesaid shall be the amount in the new currency provided for in the scheme.

(**a**) 1968 c. 55. (**b**) 1889 c. 63.

(3) Written notice of a resolution adopting an approved scheme shall within fourteen days of the passing thereof be sent by the friendly society to the Chief Registrar of Friendly Societies.

5. The Chief Registrar of Friendly Societies may before 15th February 1971 approve a special scheme intended to be adopted by a friendly society for the purpose mentioned in regulation 4 if—

(*a*) in his opinion regulation 2 cannot be made to apply to payments under the contracts to which the special scheme applies without difficulty or inconvenience having regard to the times or method of their payment or to any other relevant matter, and

(*b*) where by virtue of the scheme any payments payable to the friendly society are increased, an actuary has certified that the scheme provides where actuarially appropriate for suitable adjustments to the benefits for which those payments are payable.

6. Notwithstanding anything contained in the rules of a friendly society which has adopted an approved scheme, the committee of management of the society may by resolution passed before 15th February 1972 make amendments to the rules of the society in connection with the adoption by the society of the scheme.

7.—(1) A friendly society which has adopted an approved scheme shall before 15th February 1971 give to any person by whom a payment that falls due on or after that date is payable under a contract to which the scheme applies a written statement explaining the effect of that scheme.

(2) The statement aforesaid may be given by hand or by sending it by post to a person at his last known address or where the society has provided the person with a book for the recording of payments under the friendly society contract to which the scheme applies by inserting it in that book.

S. D. Musson,
Chief Registrar of Friendly Societies.

Date 23rd June 1970.

SCHEDULE 1

Amount in the New Currency of a Payment Referred to in Paragraphs (2) and (3)(*a*) of Regulation 2

The amount in the new currency payable in respect of a payment referred to in paragraphs (2) and (3)(*a*) of regulation 2 shall be the amount corresponding to the amount in the old currency payable under the contract calculated as follows—

(*a*) for an amount or for so much of an amount as consists of one or more whole pounds the corresponding amount in the new currency is the same number of pounds; and

(*b*) for any whole two shillings or multiple thereof of an amount or remaining amount of less than one pound the corresponding amount in the new currency is ten new pence or that multiple thereof; and

(*c*) for an amount or remaining amount of less than two shillings shown in column 1 of the following table, the corresponding amount in the new currency is the amount (if any) in new pence shown opposite that amount in column 2 of that table and accordingly an amount or remaining amount of one penny shall be disregarded.

TABLE

Amount in old currency	*Corresponding amount in new pence*
1d	—
2d	1p
3d	1p
4d	2p
5d	2p
6d	3p
7d	3p
8d	3p
9d	4p
10d	4p
11d	5p
1s 0d	5p
1s 1d	5p
1s 2d	6p
1s 3d	6p
1s 4d	7p
1s 5d	7p
1s 6d	7p
1s 7d	8p
1s 8d	8p
1s 9d	9p
1s 10d	9p
1s 11d	10p

SCHEDULE 2

AMOUNT IN THE NEW CURRENCY OF A PAYMENT REFERRED TO IN PARAGRAPH (3)(*b*) OF REGULATION 2

The amount in the new currency payable in respect of a payment referred to in paragraph (3)(*b*) of regulation 2 shall be the amount corresponding to the amount in the old currency payable under the contract or, if that amount would apart from the Friendly Societies (Halfpenny) Regulations 1969(**a**) be or include a halfpenny, to the amount in the old currency payable under the contract apart from those Regulations, calculated as follows—

(*a*) for an amount or for so much of an amount as consists of one or more whole pounds the corresponding amount in the new currency is that number of pounds; and

(*b*) for any whole shilling or multiple thereof of an amount or remaining amount of less than one pound the corresponding amount in the new currency is five new pence or that multiple thereof; and

(*c*) for an amount or remaining amount of less than one shilling shown in column 1 of the following table, the corresponding amount in the new currency is the amount (if any) in new pence shown opposite that amount in column 2 of that table and accordingly an amount or remaining amount of one halfpenny shall be disregarded.

TABLE

Amount in old currency	*Corresponding amount in new pence*
½d	—
1d	½p
1½d	½p
2d	1p
2½d	1p
3d	1p
3½d	1½p
4d	1½p
4½d	2p
5d	2p
5½d	2½p
6d	2½p
6½d	2½p
7d	3p
7½d	3p
8d	3½p
8½d	3½p
9d	4p
9½d	4p
10d	4p
10½d	4½p
11d	4½p
11½d	5p

(**a**) S.I. 1969/886 (1969 II, p. 2523).

SCHEDULE 3

Amount in the New Currency of a Payment Referred to in Paragraph (3)(c) of Regulation 2

Payments payable weekly

1. The amount in the new currency payable in respect of a payment referred to in paragraph (3)(*c*) of regulation 2 which is payable weekly and which falls due on or after the relevant date shall be the amount corresponding to the amount in the old currency payable under the contract or, if that amount would apart from the Friendly Societies (Halfpenny) Regulations 1969 be or include a halfpenny, to the amount in the old currency payable under the contract apart from those Regulations, calculated as follows—

(*a*) for any whole shilling or multiple thereof the corresponding amount in the new currency is five new pence or that multiple thereof ; and

(*b*) for any amount or remaining amount of less than one shilling shown in column 1 of the following table the corresponding amount in the new currency is, in relation to any one of four successive weekly payments in a series beginning with the payment first falling due on or after the relevant date, the amount (if any) in new pence shown opposite that amount under the appropriate weekly payment in columns 2 to 5 of that table and an amount or remaining amount of one penny or a halfpenny shall be disregarded in relation to the weekly payment under which no amount in new pence is so shown.

TABLE

Amount in old currency	*Corresponding amount in new pence*			
	1st weekly payment	*2nd weekly payment*	*3rd weekly payment*	*4th weekly payment*
½d	—	½p	—	½p
1d	—	½p	½p	½p
1½d	½p	½p	½p	1p
2d	½p	1p	1p	1p
2½d	1p	1p	1p	1p
3d	1p	1½p	1p	1½p
3½d	1½p	1½p	1½p	1½p
4d	1½p	1½p	1½p	2p
4½d	1½p	2p	2p	2p
5d	2p	2p	2p	2½p
5½d	2p	2½p	2p	2½p
6d	2½p	2½p	2½p	2½p
6½d	2½p	3p	2½p	3p
7d	2½p	3p	3p	3p
7½d	3p	3p	3p	3½p
8d	3p	3½p	3½p	3½p
8½d	3½p	3½p	3½p	3½p
9d	3½p	4p	3½p	4p
9½d	4p	4p	4p	4p
10d	4p	4p	4p	4½p
10½d	4p	4½p	4½p	4½p
11d	4½p	4½p	4½p	5p
11½d	4½p	5p	4½p	5p

Payments payable fortnightly

2. The amount in the new currency payable in respect of a payment referred to in paragraph (3)(*c*) of regulation 2 which is payable fortnightly and which falls due on or after the relevant date shall be the amount corresponding to the amount in the old currency payable under the contract or, if that amount would apart from the Friendly Societies (Halfpenny) Regulations 1969 be or include a halfpenny, to the amount in the old currency payable under the contract apart from those Regulations, calculated as follows—

(*a*) for any whole shilling or multiple thereof the corresponding amount in the new currency is five new pence or that multiple thereof ; and

(*b*) for any amount or remaining amount of less than one shilling shown in column 1 of the following table the corresponding amount in the new currency is, in relation to any one of two successive fortnightly payments in a series beginning with the payment first falling due on or after the relevant date, the amount (if any) in new pence shown opposite that amount under the appropriate fortnightly payment in columns 2 and 3 of that table and an amount or remaining amount of a halfpenny shall be disregarded in relation to the first of every two successive fortnightly payments.

TABLE

Amount in old currency	*Corresponding amount in new pence*	
	1st fortnightly payment	*2nd fortnightly payment*
½d	—	½p
1d	½p	½p
1½d	½p	½p
2d	½p	1p
2½d	1p	1p
3d	1p	1½p
3½d	1½p	1½p
4d	1½p	2p
4½d	2p	2p
5d	2p	2p
5½d	2p	2½p
6d	2½p	2½p
6½d	2½p	3p
7d	3p	3p
7½d	3p	3p
8d	3p	3½p
8½d	3½p	3½p
9d	3½p	4p
9½d	4p	4p
10d	4p	4½p
10½d	4½p	4½p
11d	4½p	4½p
11½d	4½p	5p

3. "Relevant date" in paragraphs 1 and 2 of this Schedule means—

(*a*) 15th February 1971, or

(*b*) 22nd February 1971 in relation to any payment payable to a friendly society which before 15th February 1971 has determined that 22nd February 1971 shall be the relevant date.

4. Where a friendly society has determined as mentioned in subparagraph (*b*) of the preceding paragraph, the amount in the new currency payable in respect of a payment referred to in paragraph (3)(*c*) of regulation 2 which is payable to the society and which falls due before 22nd February 1971 shall be the amount corresponding to the amount in the old currency (being in the case of an amount reduced or increased by one halfpenny by virtue of the Friendly Societies (Halfpenny) Regulations 1969 the amount so reduced or increased) payable under the contract calculated as follows—

(*a*) for any whole shilling or multiple thereof the corresponding amount in the new currency is five new pence or that multiple thereof ; and

(*b*) for any amount or remaining amount of less than one shilling shown in column 1 of the following table the corresponding amount in the new currency is the amount in new pence shown opposite that amount in column 2 of that table.

TABLE

Amount in old currency	*Corresponding amount in new pence*
1d	½p
2d	1p
3d	1p
4d	1½p
5d	2p
6d	2½p
7d	3p
8d	3½p
9d	4p
10d	4p
11d	4½p

EXPLANATORY NOTE

(*This Note is not part of the Regulations.*)

These Regulations prescribe the method of converting into decimal currency payments falling due on or after 15th February 1971 under contracts with friendly societies, not being collecting societies, made before that date. They also enable a friendly society to adopt any special scheme approved by the Chief Registrar of Friendly Societies for converting such payments into decimal currency and provide for the circumstances in which a special scheme may be approved.

1970 No. 933

CUSTOMS AND EXCISE

The Import Duties (General) (No. 4) Order 1970

Made - - - -	12*th June* 1970
Laid before the House of Commons	29*th June* 1970
Coming into Operation	2*nd July* 1970

The Lords Commissioners of Her Majesty's Treasury, by virtue of the powers conferred on them by sections 1, 2 and 13 of the Import Duties Act 1958(**a**), and of all other powers enabling them in that behalf, on the recommendation of the Board of Trade hereby make the following Order:—

1.—(1) This Order may be cited as the Import Duties (General) (No. 4) Order 1970.

(2) The Interpretation Act 1889(**b**) shall apply for the interpretation of this Order as it applies for the interpretation of an Act of Parliament.

(3) This Order shall come into operation on 2nd July 1970.

2. Schedule 1 to the Import Duties (General) (No. 3) Order 1969(**c**) (which Schedule by reference to the Customs Tariff 1959 sets out the import duties chargeable under the Import Duties Act 1958) shall be amended at heading 15.10 (fatty acids; acid oils from refining; fatty alcohols) by substituting for subheading (A) of that heading the subheading set out in the Schedule to this Order.

Neil McBride,
Walter Harrison,
Two of the Lords Commissioners of Her Majesty's Treasury.

12*th June* 1970.

(**a**) 1958 c. 6. (**b**) 1889 c. 63. (**c**) S.I. 1969/1413 (1969 III, p. 4150).

SCHEDULE

SUBSTITUTED SUBHEADING 15.10(A)

(A) Normal aliphatic alcohols containing eight or more carbon atoms in the molecule and having an iodine value not greater than 10:		
(1) Having a radioactivity of less than 3 disintegrations per minute per gramme of total carbon from β particles of energy between 18 kiloelectronvolts and 156 kiloelectronvolts and containing an even number of carbon atoms in each molecule, not less than 70 per cent. by weight of the alcohols having 12 and 14 carbon atoms per molecule and not more than 5 per cent. by weight of the alcohols having 8 carbon atoms per molecule.	10%	—
(2) Other	20%	—

EXPLANATORY NOTE

(*This Note is not part of the Order.*)

This Order reduces the full rate of duty on certain synthetic fatty alcohols from twenty per cent. to ten per cent. ad valorem.

1970 No. 934

CUSTOMS AND EXCISE

The Import Duties (Temporary Exemptions) (No. 7) Order 1970

Made - - - - -	*17th June* 1970
Laid before the House of Commons	*29th June* 1970
Coming into Operation	*2nd July* 1970

The Lords Commissioners of Her Majesty's Treasury, by virtue of the powers conferred on them by sections 3(6) and 13 of the Import Duties Act 1958(**a**), and of all other powers enabling them in that behalf, on the recommendation of the Board of Trade hereby make the following Order:—

1.—(1) This Order may be cited as the Import Duties (Temporary Exemptions) (No. 7) Order 1970.

(2) The Interpretation Act 1889(**b**) shall apply for the interpretation of this Order as it applies for the interpretation of an Act of Parliament.

(3) This Order shall come into operation on 2nd July 1970.

2.—(1) Until the beginning of 1st January 1971 or, in the case of goods in relation to which an earlier day is specified in Schedule 1 to this Order, until the beginning of that day, any import duty which is for the time being chargeable on goods of a heading of the Customs Tariff 1959 specified in that Schedule shall not be chargeable in respect of goods of any description there specified in relation to that heading.

(2) The period for which the goods of the headings of the Customs Tariff 1959 and descriptions specified in Schedule 2 to this Order are exempt from import duty shall be extended until the beginning of 1st January 1971 or, in the case of goods in relation to which an earlier day is specified in that Schedule, until the beginning of that day.

(3) Any entry in column 2 in Schedule 1 or 2 to this Order is to be taken to comprise all goods which would be classified under an entry in the same terms constituting a subheading (other than the final subheading) in the relevant heading in the Customs Tariff 1959.

(4) For the purposes of classification under the Customs Tariff 1959, in so far as that depends on the rate of duty, any goods to which paragraph (1) or (2) above applies shall be treated as chargeable with the same duty as if this Order had not been made.

(**a**) 1958 c. 6. (**b**) 1889 c. 63.

3. In Article 3 of the Import Duties (Temporary Exemptions) (No. 9) Order 1969(a) (which, until 2nd July 1970, limits import duty to 10 per cent. in the case of certain film base cellulose acetate), for " 2nd July 1970 " there shall be substituted " 1st January 1971 ".

Neil McBride,
E. G. Perry,
Two of the Lords Commissioners
of Her Majesty's Treasury.

17*th June* 1970

SCHEDULE 1

GOODS TEMPORARILY EXEMPT FROM IMPORT DUTY

Tariff Heading	*Description*
28.24	Cobaltous hydroxide (until 3rd September 1970)
29.04	2,2-Di(bromoethyl)propanediol
29.08	1,3-Dimethoxybenzene Guaiacol having a melting point of not less than 27° centigrade
29.12	Chloroacetaldehyde
29.13	α-*n*-Butoxybenzyl phenyl ketone
29.14	4-Chloro-17β-hydroxyandrost-4-en-3-one acetate *iso*Propyl chloroformate
29.15	Dimethyl isophthalate Itaconic acid
29.16	Sodium *cis*-3-bromo-3-(4-methoxybenzoyl)acrylate
29.22	αα′-Diaminoxylene, mixed isomers *NN*-Dimethyl-*n*-tetradecylamine
29.23	6-Amino-4-hydroxynaphthalene-2-sulphonic acid
29.25	*N*-Benzoyl-*N′N′*-di-*n*-propylisoglutamine *N*-[2,2,2-Trichloro-1-(3,4-dichloroanilino)ethyl]formamide
29.26	Guanidinium nitrate (until 3rd September 1970)
29.29	Bufexamac *O*-α-Cyanobenzylideneamino *OO*-diethyl phosphorothioate 1,3-Di-(4-chlorobenzylideneamino)guanidinium chloride
29.31	Di-(4-hydroxyphenyl) sulphone having a melting point not less than 236° centigrade (until 3rd September 1970) Diphenyl sulphone (until 3rd September 1970) 5-(1-Methylbutyl)-5-(2-methylthioethyl)-2-thiobarbituric acid, sodium derivative Toluenethiol, mixed isomers
29.35	Adenosine 5′-tosylate 6-Azauridine Dropropizine (±)-2,3,5,6-Tetrahydro-6-phenylimidazo[2,1-*b*]thiazole
29.38	Vitamin D_2 resin
29.39	Dexamethasone 21-(3-phenylpropionate)

(a) S.I. 1969/1751 (1969 III, p. 5484).

Tariff Heading	*Description*
29.42	(+)-9-*N′N′*-Diethylureido-4,6,6a,7,8,9-hexahydro-7-methylindolo[4,3-*f,g*]quinoline hydrogen maleate
29.44	Lucensomycin (until 3rd September 1970)
30.02	Foot-and-mouth disease vaccine (until 3rd September 1970)
39.02	Polystyrene, incorporating a volatile blowing agent capable of expanding the material to a rigid foam at a temperature of 90° centigrade or more, in the form of pieces having an overall length of not less than 8 millimetres and an overall width of not less than 4 millimetres
	Sticks of polystyrene, incorporating a volatile blowing agent capable of expanding the sticks to a rigid foam at a temperature of 90° centigrade or more
51.02	Monofil of polystyrene, incorporating a volatile blowing agent capable of expanding the filament to a rigid foam at a temperature of 90° centigrade or more
73.02	Ferro-vanadium
73.40	Circular can ends of tinplate, of a thickness of not less than 0·2 millimetre nor more than 0·26 millimetre, of an overall diameter of not less than 81 millimetres nor more than 94 millimetres, enamelled or lacquered on one side or on both sides and having a curled edge (until 3rd September 1970)
	Circular can ends of tinplate, of a thickness of not less than 0·3 millimetre nor more than 0·32 millimetre, of an overall diameter of not less than 163 millimetres nor more than 166 millimetres, enamelled or lacquered on one side or on both sides and having a curled edge (until 3rd September 1970)
76.02	Rod of aluminium, or of aluminium alloy containing not less than 95 per cent. by weight of aluminium, copper clad, the cladding comprising not less than 25 per cent. by weight nor more than 39 per cent. by weight of the whole, and of an overall diameter of not less than 6 millimetres and not more than 20 millimetres
81.04	Wrought titanium alloy containing not less than 3 per cent. nor more than 5 per cent. by weight of vanadium, not less than 5 per cent. nor more than 7 per cent. by weight of aluminium, balance titanium, in the form of billets of not less than 4 inches nor more than 7 inches in diameter or not less than 4 inches nor more than 7 inches square, in any lengths, and in the form of slab of a thickness of not less than 2¾ inches nor more than 3¼ inches, of a width of not less than 8¾ inches nor more than 12¼ inches in any lengths (until 3rd September 1970)
	Wrought titanium of a purity exceeding 99·6 per cent. titanium, in the form of slabs of a thickness of not less than 114 millimetres nor more than 153 millimetres, of a width of not less than 914 millimetres nor more than 1,220 millimetres, in any lengths, and in the form of square billets of a cross-sectional area of not less than 25·80 square centimetres nor more than 161·30 square centimetres in any lengths, and in the form of square or rectangular blooms of a cross-sectional area of not less than 929 square centimetres nor more than 2,091 square centimetres and of a thickness exceeding 153 millimetres in any lengths (until 3rd September 1970)

SCHEDULE 2

GOODS FOR WHICH EXEMPTION FROM IMPORT DUTY EXTENDED

Tariff Heading	*Description*
12.05	Dried chicory root (until 3rd September 1970)
25.19	Magnesite, dead-burned, containing (*a*) not less than 90 per cent. by weight of magnesium compounds expressed as MgO, (*b*) a total of not more than 1·0 per cent. by weight of aluminium compounds and iron compounds expressed as Al_2O_3 and Fe_2O_3, (*c*) a total of not less than 2·5 per cent. by weight and not more than 8·5 per cent. by weight of calcium compounds and silicon compounds expressed as CaO and SiO_2, and in which the weight of calcium compounds expressed as CaO is not less than 1·5 times the weight of silicon compounds expressed as SiO_2
27.07	Anthracene
28.17	Sodium peroxide
28.18	Magnesium oxide, dead-burned but not fused, of a purity not less than 96 per cent., containing (*a*) a total of not more than 1·0 per cent. by weight of aluminium compounds and iron compounds expressed as Al_2O_3 and Fe_2O_3, (*b*) a total of not more than 3·5 per cent. by weight of calcium compounds and silicon compounds expressed as CaO and SiO_2, the weight of silicon compounds being not less than 1·5 times and not more than 3·0 times the weight of calcium compounds; and (*c*) of which not less than 50 per cent. by weight is retained by a sieve having a nominal width of aperture of $\frac{3}{16}$ inch
	Magnesium oxide, dead-burned but not fused, of a purity not less than 96 per cent., which contains (*a*) not more than 0·05 per cent. by weight of boron compounds expressed as B_2O_3, (*b*) a total of not more than 0·5 per cent. by weight of aluminium compounds and iron compounds expressed as Al_2O_3 and Fe_2O_3, and (*c*) a total of not less than 1·0 per cent. by weight and not more than 3·5 per cent. by weight of calcium compounds and silicon compounds expressed as CaO and SiO_2, the weight of calcium compounds being not less than 1·5 times and not more than 2·5 times the weight of silicon compounds; and (*d*) of which not less than 35 per cent. by weight is retained by a sieve having a nominal width of aperture of $\frac{3}{16}$ inch
28.30	Nickel chloride (until 5th November 1970)
28.38	Aqueous barium sulphate paste containing not less than 70 per cent. and not more than 80 per cent. by weight of barium sulphate and containing in the dried material not more than four parts per million by weight of iron compounds calculated as Fe and not more than forty parts per hundred million by weight of ethanol soluble sulphur
	Nickel sulphate (until 5th November 1970)
28.39	Barium nitrate containing not more than 0·006 per cent. by weight of heavy metals calculated as Pb
28.43	Cuprous potassium cyanide
29.01	Anthracene
29.02	Chloropentafluoroethane (until 3rd September 1970)
	Vinyl chloride
29.04	2,3-Dibromopropan-1-ol containing not more than 0·1 per cent. by weight of 1,2,3-tribromopropane (until 3rd September 1970)
	Tridecyl alcohol, mixed isomers (until 3rd September 1970)

Tariff Heading	*Description*
29.06	2-Naphthol 3,5-Xylenol (until 3rd September 1970)
29.13	Cyclo-octanone Indanetrione hydrate (until 3rd September 1970)
29.14	*n*-Octanoic acid
29.19	Di-*n*-butyl phenyl phosphate Tri-(2,3-dibromopropyl) phosphate containing not more than 0·20 per cent. by weight of 2,3-dibromopropanol (until 3rd September 1970)
29.22	1,2-Diaminoethane (until 3rd September 1970) *NN*-Diethylaniline Diethylenetriamine (until 3rd September 1970) Tetraethylenepentamine Triethylenetetramine
29.27	Acrylonitrile (until 5th November 1970)
29.31	Dithiocyanatomethane having a melting point not less than 100° centigrade (until 3rd September 1970) 3-Mercaptopropane-1,2-diol 3-Mercaptopropionic acid
29.34	Nickel carbonyl (until 3rd September 1970)
29.35	Phenothiazine of a purity not less than 98 per cent., which contains not more than 0·0035 per cent. by weight of total iodine, and which yields not more than 0·05 per cent. by weight of sulphated ash Quinoline 5-Vinyl-2-picoline
29.36	Sulphanilamide Sulphaquinoxaline
29.39	Triamcinolone 16,21-diacetate
39.02	Acrylic sheet, transparent, colourless, of a thickness not less than 1·5 millimetres and not greater than 25·0 millimetres, which, when kept for 24 hours at a temperature of 110° centigrade, undergoes a linear shrinkage of not more than 10 per cent. and which, when kept for 24 hours at a temperature of 145° centigrade, undergoes a linear shrinkage of not less than 37·5 per cent. Polystyrene sheet, in rolls, colourless, of a thickness not less than 0·1 millimetre and not greater than 0·9 millimetre and having a light transmission not less than 85 per cent.
49.11	Identification kits, consisting essentially of a series of transparent slides or foils printed to depict individual characteristics of the human face or head; parts of such kits
68.13	Asbestos paper, rubber impregnated, in rolls, being not less than 0·55 millimetre and not more than 0·65 millimetre in thickness, weighing not less than 0·55 kilogramme and not more than 0·65 kilogramme per square metre, and which, when heated to a temperature of 1,000° centigrade, has a loss in weight of not less than 24 per cent. and not more than 28 per cent. (until 3rd September 1970) Asbestos paper, rubber impregnated, in rolls, being not less than 0·75 millimetre and not more than 0·85 millimetre in thickness, weighing not less than 0·71 kilogramme and not more than 0·78 kilogramme per square metre, and which, when heated to a temperature of 1,000° centigrade, has a loss in weight of not less than 28 per cent. and not more than 32 per cent. (until 3rd September 1970)

Tariff Heading	*Description*
70.18	Optical glass in the form of sheets, slabs or moulded lens blanks, having, with reference to the D line of sodium, a refractive index (n_D) not less than 1·5625 and not greater than 1·5650 and a dispersive power (ν_D) not less than 60·0 and not greater than 61·5 (until 3rd September 1970)
	Optical glass in the form of sheets, slabs or moulded lens blanks, having, with reference to the D line of sodium, a refractive index (n_D) not less than 1·612 and not greater than 1·615 and a dispersive power (ν_D) not less than 43·5 and not greater than 45·0; having also at a wavelength of 400 nanometres a light transmission for a 25 millimetres path of not less than 83 per cent.; and which acquires no visible stain when kept for 15 minutes at a temperature of 25° centigrade in contact with a buffered sodium acetate solution having a pH value of 4·6 (until 3rd September 1970)
73.06	Iron or steel ingots, blocks, lumps and similar forms, other than those manufactured entirely from pig iron smelted wholly with charcoal
73.07	Iron or steel blooms, billets, slabs and sheet bars
73.08	Iron or steel coils for re-rolling (until 5th November 1970)
73.12	Strip of iron or steel, coated with tin, of a width not less than 304 millimetres, and not more than 500 millimetres, of a thickness of not less than 0·12 millimetre and not more than 0·5 millimetre, and of a length of not more than 1,016 millimetres (until 3rd September 1970)
	Strip of iron or steel, in coil form, coated with tin, of a width of not less than 140 millimetres, and not more than 500 millimetres, and of a thickness of not less than 0·12 millimetre and not more than 0·5 millimetre (until 3rd September 1970)
73.13	Cold reduced sheets and plates of iron or steel, rectangular or in coils, of a width exceeding 500 millimetres, and of a thickness of less than 3 millimetres, not plated, coated, clad, drilled, punched or otherwise worked (until 3rd September 1970)
	Sheets of iron or steel, coated with tin, of a width exceeding 500 millimetres but not more than 966 millimetres, of a thickness of not less than 0·12 millimetre and not more than 0·5 millimetre, and of a length of not more than 1,016 millimetres (until 3rd September 1970)
	Sheets of iron or steel, in coil form, coated with tin, of a width exceeding 500 millimetres but not more than 966 millimetres, and of a thickness of not less than 0·12 millimetre and not more than 0·5 millimetre (until 3rd September 1970)
73.14	Iron or steel wire of a diameter not less than 0·019 inch nor more than 0·200 inch, and having a coating of nickel of not less than 0·0001 inch in thickness
73.15	Alloy steel coils for re-rolling, containing not more than 3·5 per cent. by weight of silicon as the major alloying element, and of a thickness of not more than 3 millimetres
73.19	Hot rolled seamless circular steel tubes of an outside diameter of not less than 19½ inches and not more than 24½ inches, and of a wall thickness of not less than $\frac{7}{16}$ inch and not more than $\frac{5}{8}$ inch
74.05	Tape consisting of a layer of niobium alloy containing tin, laminated between two layers of copper foil whether or not coated with tin, and being (*a*) not less than 0·25 inch nor more than 0·75 inch in width and (*b*) not more than 0·005 inch in thickness
76.03	Aluminium discs of a minimum value of 8s. per lb., not less than 6 inches nor more than 18 inches in diameter and not less than 0·033 inch nor more than 0·036 inch in thickness and which, when either face is placed on a flat surface, do not deviate from the flat by more than 0·010 inch at any point

Tariff Heading	*Description*
81.04	Chromium, electrolytic, in the form of cathode chips, which contains not more than 0·10 per cent. by weight of total oxygen, not more than 0·015 per cent. by weight of total aluminium, and not more than 0·001 per cent. by weight of aluminium compounds insoluble in boiling 5N hydrochloric acid and in boiling fuming perchloric acid, and estimated as Al
	Titanium sponge
	Vanadium, unwrought, of a purity not less than 99 per cent. and containing not more than 0·1 per cent. by weight of iron calculated as Fe
85.18	Tantalum capacitors greater than 10 microfarads in capacitance, of a kind for incorporation in deaf aids, with a maximum length not exceeding 7 millimetres exclusive of leads and with a transverse cross section having a circumference not exceeding 14 millimetres
	Tantalum capacitors, of a kind for incorporation in deaf aids, with a maximum length not exceeding 7 millimetres exclusive of leads and with a transverse cross section having a circumference not exceeding 10 millimetres
85.20	Glass neon discharge lamps, having a metal cap fitted to each end and not exceeding 1 inch in overall length and ½ inch in diameter over the caps
90.01	Lenses, Fresnel, converging, being composite sheets of artificial plastics, bearing a concentric system of grooves of a uniform density, not less than 18 grooves per centimetre; the lenses being not more than 1·0 centimetres in thickness, not less than 27 centimetres and not more than 29 centimetres square, with chamfered corners and having a focal length not greater than 16 centimetres (until 3rd September 1970)
	Material consisting of a polarising film supported on one or both sides by transparent material, and analysers and polarisers made therefrom
	Photographic process screens of the contact type, consisting of a base of cellulose acetate or of poly(ethylene terephthalate) on which is a regularly spaced pattern of grey-coloured or magenta-coloured dots
90.09	Blockwriters for step and repeat photo-reduction apparatus
90.19	Aortic heart valves
	Mitral heart valves
90.20	Beryllium metal windows of a thickness less than 0·004 inch for X-ray tubes (until 3rd September 1970)

EXPLANATORY NOTE

(*This Note is not part of the Order.*)

This Order provides that the goods listed in Schedule 1 shall be temporarily exempt from import duty, and those listed in Schedule 2 shall continue to be exempt from import duty, both until 1st January 1971, except for items for which an earlier day is specified.

The Order also continues until 1st January 1971 the partial exemption for photographic film base of cellulose acetate.

1970 No. 940

WAGES COUNCILS

The Wages Regulation (Corset) Order 1970

Made - - -	*24th June* 1970
Coming into Operation	*20th July* 1970

Whereas the Secretary of State has received from the Corset Wages Council the wages regulation proposals set out in the Schedule hereto;

Now, therefore, the Secretary of State in exercise of his powers under section 11 of the Wages Councils Act 1959(**a**), and of all other powers enabling him in that behalf, hereby makes the following Order:—

1. This Order may be cited as the Wages Regulation (Corset) Order 1970.

2.—(1) In this Order the expression "the specified date" means the 20th July 1970, provided that where, as respects any worker who is paid wages at intervals not exceeding seven days, that date does not correspond with the beginning of the period for which the wages are paid, the expression "the specified date" means, as respects that worker, the beginning of the next such period following that date.

(2) The Interpretation Act 1889(**b**) shall apply to the interpretation of this Order as it applies to the interpretation of an Act of Parliament and as if this Order and the Order hereby revoked were Acts of Parliament.

3. The wages regulation proposals set out in the Schedule hereto shall have effect as from the specified date and as from that date the Wages Regulation (Corset) Order 1968(**c**) shall cease to have effect.

Signed by order of the Secretary of State.

24th June 1970.

R. R. D. McIntosh,
Deputy Under Secretary of State,
Department of Employment and Productivity.

(**a**) 1959 c. 69. (**b**) 1889 c. 63.
(**c**) S.I. 1968/1420 (1968 III, p. 4137).

Article 3

SCHEDULE

The following minimum remuneration shall be substituted for the statutory minimum remuneration fixed by the Wages Regulation (Corset) Order 1968 (Order K. (66)).

STATUTORY MINIMUM REMUNERATION

PART I

GENERAL

1. The minimum remuneration payable to a worker to whom this Schedule applies for all work except work to which a minimum overtime rate applies under Part IV of this Schedule is:—

(1) in the case of a time worker, the general minimum time rate payable to the worker under Part II or Part III of this Schedule;

(2) *in the case of a worker employed on piece work, piece rates each of which would yield, in the circumstances of the case, to an ordinary worker at least the same amount of money as the general minimum time rate applicable to the worker under Part II or Part III of this Schedule.*

PART II

FEMALE WORKERS

GENERAL MINIMUM TIME RATES

2. Subject to the provisions of this Schedule, the general minimum time rates payable to female time workers are as follows:—

(*1*) *LEARNERS (as defined in paragraph 8) during the following periods of employment in the trade:—*

Entering the trade	*First 6 months of employment*	*Second 6 months of employment*	*Second year of employment*
	per hour *s. d.*	*per hour* *s. d.*	*per hour* *s. d.*
Aged 15 and under 16 years	*2 9*	*3 3*	*4 0*
" 16 " " 17 "	*3 0*	*3 6*	*4 3*
" 17 " " 18 "	*3 3*	*3 9*	*4 3*
" 18 years or over	*4 0*	*4 3*	*4 9*

(2) ALL OTHER WORKERS ... ... s. d. *4 9 per hour*

PART III

MALE WORKERS

GENERAL MINIMUM TIME RATES

3. Subject to the provisions of this Schedule, the general minimum time rates payable to male time workers are as follows:

	General Minimum Time Rates Per hour s. d.
(1) Workers employed in CUTTING, MARKING-OUT (other than process working), HAND PRESSING, MATCHING-UP or SHADING whose experience in any of the said occupations after the age of 18 years is:—	
(*a*) Not less than 5 years	*6 7*
(*b*) Less than 5 years but not less than 3 years	*6 5*

Provided that in reckoning such experience, there shall be included any experience of a worker after the age of 18 years in folding, hand-fitting, parting, separating or making-up, up to a maximum of 12 months.

(2) Workers employed in FOLDING, HAND-FITTING, PARTING, SEPARATING or MAKING-UP, with not less than three years' experience in any of the said occupations after the age of 18 years	*6 4*
(3) WAREHOUSEMEN OR PACKERS aged 21 years or over with not less than two years' experience as warehousemen or packers	*6 4*
(4) ALL OTHERS WORKERS (including process workers):—	
Aged 21 years or over	*6 2*
„ 20 and under 21 years	*5 6*
„ 19 „ „ 20 „	*5 3*
„ 18 „ „ 19 „	*4 9*
„ 17 „ „ 18 „	*4 0*
„ 16 „ „ 17 „	*3 6*
„ under 16 years	*3 0*

Provided that the minimum rates applicable during his first year's employment in the trade to a male worker who enters, or has entered, the trade for the first time at or over the age of 19 years shall be:—

	General Minimum Time Rates Per hour s. d.
Aged 21 years or over	*5 3*
Aged under 21 years	*4 9*

PART IV

OVERTIME AND WAITING TIME

NORMAL NUMBER OF HOURS

4. Subject to the provisions of this Part of this Schedule, the minimum overtime rates set out in paragraph 6 are payable to a worker in respect of any time worked—

(1) in excess of the hours following, that is to say,

(*a*) in any week .. .. 40 hours

(*b*) on any day other than a Saturday, Sunday or customary holiday—

where the normal working hours exceed 8½ .. .. 9 hours;

or

where the normal working hours are more than 8, but not more than 8½ .. .. 8½ hours;

or

where the normal working hours are not more than 8 — 8 hours;

(2) on a Saturday, Sunday or customary holiday.

MINIMUM OVERTIME RATES

5.—(1) Minimum overtime rates are payable to any worker as follows:—

(*a*) on any day other than a Sunday or customary holiday—

(i) for the first 2 hours of overtime worked ... time-and-a-quarter

(ii) for the next 2 hours ... ... time-and-a-half

(iii) thereafter ... ... double time

(*b*) on a Sunday or customary holiday—

for all time worked ... ... double time

(*c*) in any week, exclusive of any time in respect of which any minimum overtime rate is payable under the foregoing provisions of this sub-paragraph—

for all time worked in excess of 40 hours ... ... time-and-a-quarter

(2) The minimum overtime rates set out in sub-paragraph (1)(*a*) or (*b*) of this paragraph are payable in any week whether or not the minimum overtime rate set out in sub-paragraph (1)(*c*) is also payable.

6. In this Schedule—

(1) the expression "customary holiday" means:—

(*a*) (i) in England and Wales—

Christmas Day (or, if Christmas Day falls on a Sunday, such week-day as may be appointed by national proclamation, or, if none is so appointed, the next following Tuesday), Boxing Day, Good Friday, Easter Monday, Whit Monday (or where another day is substituted therefor by national proclamation, that day) and August Bank Holiday;

(ii) in Scotland—

New Year's Day (or, if New Year's Day falls on a Sunday, the following Monday);
the local Spring holiday;
the local Autumn holiday; and

three other days (being days of the week on which the worker normally works for the employer) in the course of each calendar year, to be fixed by the employer and notified to the worker not less than three weeks before the holiday ; or

(*b*) in the case of each of the said days, a day substituted by the employer therefor, being a day recognised by local custom as a day of holiday in substitution for the said day ;

(2) the expression "time-and-a-quarter", "time-and-a-half" and "double time" mean respectively—

(*a*) in the case of a time worker, one and a quarter times, one and a half times and twice the general minimum time rate otherwise payable to the worker ;

(b) in the case of a worker employed on piece work,

(i) a time rate equal respectively to one quarter, one half and the whole of the general minimum time rate which would be payable to the worker under Part II or Part III of this Schedule if the worker were a time worker and a minimum overtime rate did not apply, and, in addition thereto,

(ii) the piece rates otherwise payable to the worker under paragraph 1(2).

(*c*) in the case of a male worker aged less than 21 years who is employed on piece work or of a learner who is employed on piece work,

(i) a time rate equal respectively to one quarter, one half and the whole of the general minimum time rate which would be payable to the worker under Part II or Part III of this Schedule if the worker were a time worker and the minimum overtime rate did not apply, and, in addition thereto,

(ii) the piece rates otherwise payable to the worker under paragraph 1(2).

WAITING TIME

7.—(1) A worker is entitled to payment of the minimum remuneration specified in this Schedule for all time during which he is present on the premises of his employer, unless he is present thereon in any of the following circumstances:—

(*a*) without the employer's consent, express or implied ;

(*b*) for some purpose unconnected with his work and other than that of waiting for work to be given to him to perform ;

(*c*) by reason only of the fact that he is resident thereon ;

(*d*) during normal meal times in a room or place in which no work is being done, and he is not waiting for work to be given to him to perform.

(2) The minimum remuneration payable under sub-paragraph (1) of this paragraph to a piece worker when not engaged on piece work is that which would be payable if he were a time worker.

Part V

INTERPRETATION

8. In this Schedule—

(1) the expression "LEARNER" means a female worker who—

(*a*) is employed during the whole or a substantial part of her time in learning any branch of the trade by an employer who provides her with reasonable facilities for such learning, and (*b*) does not work in a room used for dwelling purposes except where she is in the employment of her parent or guardian.

(2) "THE TRADE" means the corset trade as specified in the next following paragraph.

APPLICABILITY OF STATUTORY MINIMUM REMUNERATION

9. Subject to the provisions of paragraph 10, this Schedule applies to workers in relation to whom the Corset Wages Council operates, that is to say, workers employed in Great Britain in the trade specified in the Schedule to the Trade Boards (Corset Trade, Great Britain) (Amendment) Regulations 1927(**a**), which is as follows:—

"1. All work in connection with—

(*a*) the manufacture of corsets, corselettes, stays, children's corset bodies, and infants' staybands.

(*b*) the manufacture of bust confiners.

(*c*) the manufacture of support or abdominal belts or similar articles.

(*d*) the manufacture (including assembling) of stocking suspenders, suspender belts and suspender pads, when carried on in conjunction with, or in association with the manufacture of any of the above articles.

2. Work in connection with the manufacture specified in paragraph 1 hereof shall include—

(*a*) the altering, repairing, renovating or remaking of any of the articles specified in paragraph 1 hereof, when carried on in conjunction with or in association with such manufacture.

(*b*) warehousing, packing, marking, letter-press stamping, when incidental to such manufacture.

3. Notwithstanding anything in this Schedule the following operations shall not be operations in the Corset Trade:—

(*a*) the manufacture of bust confiners, when carried on in a department mainly engaged on the making of articles specified in the Appendix to the Trade Boards (Women's Clothing) Order 1919(**b**);

(*b*) the manufacture of any of the articles specified in paragraph 1 hereof when made in association with or in conjunction with the manufacture of surgical instruments or appliances;

(*c*) the manufacture of corset steels and busks;

(*d*) printing, clerical work, cleaning, caretaking, and general maintenance work."

TRAINING UNDER THE GOVERNMENT VOCATIONAL TRAINING SCHEME

10. Notwithstanding anything hereinbefore contained, this Schedule shall not apply to—

(1) female workers employed on Machining, Pressing, Eyeletting and Boning,

(2) male workers employed on Cutting, Marking-out, Folding and Parting,

during any period in respect of which they are in receipt of allowances as provided under the Government Vocational Training Scheme for resettlement training if they are trainees who have been placed by the Department of Employment and Productivity with the employer for a period of approved training and if the requirements of the said Scheme are duly complied with.

(**a**) S.R. & O. 1927/534 (1927, p. 1814). (**b**) S.R. & O. 1919/1263 (1919 II, p. 531).

EXPLANATORY NOTE

(This Note is not part of the Order.)

This Order, which has effect from 20th July 1970, sets out the statutory minimum remuneration payable in substitution for that fixed by the Wages Regulation (Corset) Order 1968 (Order K. (66)), which Order is revoked.

New provisions are printed in italics.

1970 No. 941

INDUSTRIAL TRIBUNALS

The Industrial Tribunals (England and Wales) (Amendment) Regulations 1970

Made - - -	*24th June* 1970
Laid before Parliament	*2nd July* 1970
Coming into Operation	*3rd July* 1970

The Secretary of State in exercise of his powers under section 12 of the Industrial Training Act 1964**(a)** and after consultation with the Council on Tribunals hereby makes the following Regulations:—

Citation and commencement

1.—(1) These Regulations may be cited as the Industrial Tribunals (England and Wales) (Amendment) Regulations 1970, and the Industrial Tribunals (England and Wales) Regulations 1965**(b)** (hereinafter referred to as "the principal Regulations"), the Industrial Tribunals (England and Wales) (Amendment) Regulations 1967**(c)** and these Regulations may be cited together as the Industrial Tribunals (England and Wales) Regulations 1965 to 1970.

(2) These Regulations shall come into operation on 3rd July 1970.

Interpretation

2. The Interpretation Act 1889**(d)** shall apply to the interpretation of these Regulations as it applies to the interpretation of an Act of Parliament.

Amendment of the principal Regulations

3. For Regulation 3(2) of the principal Regulations there shall be substituted the following—

"(2) The President shall vacate his office at the end of the completed year of service in the course of which he attains the age of seventy-two years."

24th June 1970.

Robert Carr,
Secretary of State
for Employment and Productivity.

(a) 1964 c. 16.
(b) S.I. 1965/1101 (1965 II, p. 2805).
(c) S.I. 1967/301 (1967 I, p. 1040).
(d) 1889 c. 63.

EXPLANATORY NOTE

(*This Note is not part of the Regulations.*)

These Regulations amend the Industrial Tribunals (England and Wales) Regulations 1965, as previously amended, by providing that the President of the Industrial Tribunals (England and Wales) shall vacate his office at the end of the completed year of service in the course of which he attains the age of seventy-two years.

1970 No. 942

INDUSTRIAL TRAINING

The Industrial Training Levy (Water Supply) Order 1970

Made - - -	24*th June* 1970
Laid before Parliament	3*rd July* 1970
Coming into Operation	15*th July* 1970

The Secretary of State after approving proposals submitted by the Water Supply Industry Training Board for the imposition of a further levy on employers in the water supply industry and in exercise of his powers under section 4 of the Industrial Training Act 1964(**a**) and of all other powers enabling him in that behalf hereby makes the following Order:—

Title and commencement

1. This Order may be cited as the Industrial Training Levy (Water Supply) Order 1970 and shall come into operation on 15th July 1970.

Interpretation

2.—(1) In this Order unless the context otherwise requires :—

(*a*) "activities of the water supply industry" means any activities (not being agriculture) which, subject to the provisions of paragraph 2 of Schedule 1 to the industrial training order, are specified in paragraph 1 of that Schedule as activities of the water supply industry ;

(*b*) "agriculture" has the same meaning as in section 109(3) of the Agriculture Act 1947(**b**) or, in relation to Scotland, as in section 86(3) of the Agriculture (Scotland) Act 1948(**c**) ;

(*c*) "an appeal tribunal" means an industrial tribunal established under section 12 of the Industrial Training Act 1964 ;

(*d*) "assessment" means an assessment of an employer to the levy ;

(*e*) "emoluments" means all emoluments assessable to income tax under Schedule E (other than pensions), being emoluments from which tax under that Schedule is deductible, whether or not tax in fact falls to be deducted from any particular payment thereof ;

(*f*) "employer" means an employer in the water supply industry, being on the day upon which this Order comes into operation statutory water undertakers or a regional water board ;

(**a**) 1964 c. 16.
(**b**) 1947 c. 48.
(**c**) 1948 c. 45.

(*g*) "the fifth base period" means the period of twelve months that commenced on 6th April 1969 ;

(*h*) "the fifth levy period" means the period commencing with the day upon which this Order comes into operation and ending on 31st March 1971 ;

(*i*) "the Industrial Training Board" means the Water Supply Industry Training Board ;

(*j*) "the industrial training order" means the Industrial Training (Water Supply Board) Order 1965(**a**) ;

(*k*) "the levy" means the levy imposed by the Board in respect of the fifth levy period ;

(*l*) "local water authority" means a local water authority within the meaning of the Water (Scotland) Act 1946(**b**) ;

(*m*) "notice" means a notice in writing ;

(*n*) "regional water board" means a regional water board within the meaning of the Water (Scotland) Act 1967(**c**) ;

(*o*) "statutory water undertakers" means any statutory water undertakers within the meaning of the Water Act 1945(**d**).

(2) The Interpretation Act 1889(**e**) shall apply to the interpretation of this Order as it applies to the interpretation of an Act of Parliament.

Imposition of the Levy

3.—(1) The levy to be imposed by the Industrial Training Board on employers in respect of the fifth levy period shall be assessed in accordance with the provisions of this Article.

(2) The levy shall be assessed by the Industrial Training Board in respect of each employer.

(3) The amount of the levy imposed on an employer shall be a sum equal to 1·6 per cent. of the emoluments of the persons following—

(*a*) in the case of statutory water undertakers, all persons employed by the employer in the fifth base period in activities of the water supply industry and any other persons employed at any time in that period in a water undertaking or part of a water undertaking that on the day upon which this Order comes into operation forms part of the water undertaking of the employer ;

(*b*) in the case of a regional water board, all persons employed in activities of the water supply industry in the fifth base period by the regional water board or by a local water authority whose functions have been transferred in whole or in part to that regional water board under the Water (Scotland) Act 1967, being, in the case of a local water authority, persons who were solely employed in connection with the functions so transferred.

(4) For the purposes of this Article no regard shall be had to persons wholly engaged in agriculture or in the supply of food or drink for immediate consumption.

(**a**) S.I. 1965/1258 (1965 II, p. 3556).
(**b**) 1946 c. 42.
(**c**) 1967 c. 78.
(**d**) 1945 c. 42.
(**e**) 1889 c. 63.

Assessment Notice

4.—(1) The Industrial Training Board shall serve an assessment notice on every employer.

(2) An assessment notice shall state the address of the said Board for the service of a notice of appeal or of an application for an extension of time for appealing.

(3) An assessment notice may be served on an employer by sending it by post to the employer's registered or principal office.

Payment of the Levy

5.—(1) Subject to the provisions of this Article and of Articles 6 and 7, the amount of an assessment appearing in an assessment notice served by the Industrial Training Board shall be payable to the Board in two equal instalments, which shall be due respectively one month and five months after the date of the notice.

(2) An instalment of an assessment shall not be recoverable by the Industrial Training Board until there has expired the time allowed for appealing against the assessment by Article 7(1) of this Order and any further period or periods of time that the said Board or an appeal tribunal may have allowed for appealing under paragraph (2) or (3) of that Article or, where an appeal is brought, until the appeal is decided or withdrawn.

Withdrawal of Assessment

6.—(1) The Industrial Training Board may, by a notice served on the person assessed to the levy in the same manner as an assessment notice, withdraw an assessment if that person has appealed against that assessment under the provisions of Article 7 of this Order and the appeal has not been entered in the Register of Appeals kept under the appropriate Regulations specified in paragraph (4) of that Article.

(2) The withdrawal of an assessment shall be without prejudice to the power of the Industrial Training Board to serve a further assessment notice on the person assessed to the levy.

Appeals

7.—(1) A person assessed to the levy may appeal to an appeal tribunal against the assessment within one month from the date of the service of the assessment notice or within any further period or periods of time that may be allowed by the Industrial Training Board or an appeal tribunal under the following provisions of this Article.

(2) The Industrial Training Board by notice may for good cause allow a person assessed to the levy to appeal to an appeal tribunal against the assessment at any time within the period of four months from the date of the service of the assessment notice or within such further period or periods as the Board may allow before such time as may then be limited for appealing has expired.

(3) If the Industrial Training Board shall not allow an application for extension of time for appealing, an appeal tribunal shall upon application made to the tribunal by the person assessed to the levy have the like powers as the Board under the last foregoing paragraph.

(4) An appeal or an application to an appeal tribunal under this Article shall be made in accordance with the Industrial Tribunals (England and Wales)

Regulations 1965(**a**) as amended by the Industrial Tribunals (England and Wales) (Amendment) Regulations 1967(**b**) except in the case of a regional water board when the appeal or application shall be made in accordance with the Industrial Tribunals (Scotland) Regulations 1965(**c**) as amended by the Industrial Tribunals (Scotland) (Amendment) Regulations 1967(**d**).

(5) The powers of an appeal tribunal under paragraph (3) of this Article may be exercised by the President of the Industrial Tribunals (England and Wales) or by the President of the Industrial Tribunals (Scotland) as the case may be.

Evidence

8.—(1) Upon the discharge by a person assessed to the levy of his liability under an assessment the Industrial Training Board shall if so requested issue to him a certificate to that effect.

(2) The production in any proceedings of a document purporting to be certified by the Secretary of the Industrial Training Board to be a true copy of an assessment or other notice issued by the Board or purporting to be a certificate such as is mentioned in the foregoing paragraph of this Article shall, unless the contrary is proved, be sufficient evidence of the document and of the facts stated therein.

24th June 1970.

Robert Carr,
Secretary of State
for Employment and Productivity.

EXPLANATORY NOTE

(*This Note is not part of the Order.*)

This Order gives effect to proposals submitted by the Water Supply Industry Training Board to the Secretary of State for Employment and Productivity for the imposition of a further levy on employers in the water supply industry for the purpose of raising money towards the expenses of the Board.

The levy is to be imposed in respect of the fifth levy period commencing with the date on which this Order comes into operation and ending on 31st March 1971. The levy will be assessed by the Industrial Training Board and there will be a right of appeal against an assessment to an industrial tribunal.

(**a**) S.I. 1965/1101 (1965 II, p. 2805).
(**b**) S.I. 1967/301 (1967 I, p. 1040).
(**c**) S.I. 1965/1157 (1965 II, p. 3266).
(**d**) S.I. 1967/302 (1967 I, p. 1050).

1970 No. 944 (L.20)

SUPREME COURT OF JUDICATURE, ENGLAND

PROCEDURE

The Rules of the Supreme Court (Amendment No. 2) 1970

Made - - -	16*th June* 1970
Laid before Parliament	1*st July* 1970
Coming into Operation	20*th July* 1970

We, the Rule Committee of the Supreme Court, being the authority having for the time being power under section 99(4) of the Supreme Court of Judicature (Consolidation) Act 1925(**a**) to make, amend or revoke rules regulating the practice and procedure of the Supreme Court of Judicature, hereby exercise those powers and all other powers enabling us in that behalf as follows:—

1.—(1) These Rules may be cited as the Rules of the Supreme Court (Amendment No. 2) 1970 and shall come into operation on 20th July 1970.

(2) In these Rules an Order referred to by number means the Order so numbered in the Rules of the Supreme Court 1965(**b**), as amended (**c**).

(3) The Interpretation Act 1889(**d**) shall apply to the interpretation of these Rules as it applies to the interpretation of an Act of Parliament.

2. The Arrangement of Orders at the beginning of the Rules of the Supreme Court 1965 shall be amended as follows:—

(1) In the title of Order 29 after the word "property" there shall be inserted the words "interim payments".

(2) After Order 112 there shall be inserted the following entry:—

"113. Summary proceedings for possession of land".

3. The following paragraph shall be substituted for paragraph (6) of Order 4, rule 1:—

"(6) Where any cause or matter begun in the Chancery Division is so connected with a cause or matter already assigned to a group of judges in accordance with this rule that the later cause or matter ought to be assigned to the same group, it shall, if practicable, be assigned to that group.

A note indorsed on the document by which the later cause or matter is begun stating that it is to be assigned to a group in accordance with this paragraph shall, if made by a master of that group or by the district registrar of the registry in which the earlier cause or matter was begun, be sufficient authority for the later cause or matter to be so assigned."

(**a**) 1925 c. 49. (**b**) S.I. 1965/1776 (1965 III, p. 4995).
(**c**) The relevant amending instrument is S.I. 1968/1244 (1968 II, p. 3360).
(**d**) 1889 c. 63.

4. In Order 16, rule 10, for the words "before the trial of an action, a party to the action" there shall be substituted the words "at any time after he has entered an appearance, a party to an action".

5. Order 29 shall be amended as follows :—

(1) In the title after the word "PROPERTY" there shall be inserted the words "INTERIM PAYMENTS".

(2) Immediately before rule 1 there shall be inserted the words "I. INTERLOCUTORY INJUNCTIONS, INTERIM PRESERVATION OF PROPERTY, ETC.".

(3) At the end there shall be added the following Part :—

"II. INTERIM PAYMENTS

Interpretation of Part II

9. In this Part of this Order—

"an action for personal injuries" means an action in which there is a claim for damages in respect of personal injuries to the plaintiff or any other person or in respect of a person's death ;

"personal injuries" includes any disease and any impairment of a person's physical or mental condition ;

"interim payment", in relation to a defendant, means a payment on account of any such damages as aforesaid which that defendant may be held liable to pay to or for the benefit of the plaintiff ;

any reference to the plaintiff or defendant includes a reference to any person who, for the purpose of the proceedings, acts as next friend to the plaintiff or guardian of the defendant.

Application for interim payment

10. In an action for personal injuries the plaintiff may, at any time after the writ has been served on a defendant and the time limited for him to appear has expired, apply to the Court for an order requiring that defendant to make an interim payment.

Manner in which application under rule 10 *must be made*

11.—(1) An application under rule 10 must be made by summons, stating the grounds on which the application is made, and be supported by an affidavit, which must—

(*a*) verify the special damages, if any, claimed by the plaintiff up to the date of the application ;

(*b*) exhibit the hospital and medical reports, if any, relied upon by the plaintiff in support of the application ; and

(*c*) if the plaintiff's claim is made under the Fatal Accidents Acts 1846 to 1959, contain the particulars mentioned in section 4 of the Fatal Accidents Act 1846(**a**).

(2) The summons and a copy of the affidavit in support and any exhibit referred to therein must be served on the defendant against whom the order is sought not less than 10 clear days before the return day.

(**a**) 1846 c. 93.

(3) Notwithstanding the making or refusal of an order for an interim payment, a second or subsequent application may be made upon cause shown by reason of a change of circumstances.

Order for interim payment

12.—(1) If, on the hearing of an application under rule 10, the Court is satisfied—

(*a*) that the defendant against whom the order is sought (in this paragraph referred to as "the respondent") has admitted liability for the plaintiff's claim ; or

(*b*) that the plaintiff has obtained judgment against the respondent for damages to be assessed ; or

(*c*) that, if the action proceeded to trial, the plaintiff would succeed in the action on the question of liability without any substantial reduction of the damages for fault on his part or on the part of any person in respect of whose injury or death the plaintiff's claim arises and would obtain judgment for damages against the respondent or, where there are two or more defendants, against any of them,

the Court may, if it thinks fit and subject to paragraph (2), order the respondent to make an interim payment of such amount as it thinks just, not exceeding a reasonable proportion of the damages which in the opinion of the Court are likely to be recovered by the plaintiff.

(2) No order shall be made under paragraph (1) if it appears to the Court that the defendant, or, if there are two or more defendants, any of them, is not a person falling within one of the following categories, namely—

(*a*) a person who is insured in respect of the plaintiff's claim ;

(*b*) a public authority ;

(*c*) a person whose means and resources are such as to enable him to make the interim payment.

(3) Subject to Order 80, rule 12, the amount of any interim payment ordered to be made shall be paid to the plaintiff unless the order provides for it to be paid into court, and where the amount is paid into court, the Court may, on the ex parte application of the plaintiff, order the whole or any part of it to be paid out to him at such time or times as the Court thinks fit.

(4) An interim payment may be ordered to be made in one sum or by such instalments as the Court thinks fit.

Directions on application under rule 10

13.—(1) Where an application is made under rule 10, the Court may give directions as to the further conduct of the action.

(2) If, in a case to which sub-paragraph (*c*) of rule 12(1) applies, the Court thinks fit to give directions under this rule before the summons for directions, Order 25, rules 2 to 7, shall, with the omission of so much of rule 7(1) as requires parties to serve a notice specifying the orders and directions which they desire and with any other necessary modifications, apply as if the application were a summons for directions, and in particular the Court may order an early trial of the action.

Non-disclosure of order for interim payment

14. The fact that an order has been made under rule 12 shall not be pleaded and no communication of that fact shall be made to the Court at the trial or hearing of the action or of any question or issue as to liability or damages until all questions of liability and the amount of the damages have been decided.

Payment into court

15. Where, after making an interim payment pursuant to an order under rule 12, a defendant pays a sum of money into court under Order 22, rule 1, the notice of payment must state that the defendant has taken into account the interim payment.

Adjustment on final judgment or order

16. Where a defendant has made an interim payment pursuant to an order under rule 12, the Court may, on giving or making a final judgment or order determining that defendant's liability to the plaintiff in the action, make any such order with respect to the interim payment as may be necessary for giving effect to the determination and in particular—

(*a*) an order for the repayment by the plaintiff of any sum by which the interim payment exceeds the amount which that defendant is liable to pay the plaintiff, or

(*b*) an order for the payment by any other defendant of any part of the interim payment which the defendant who made it is entitled to recover from him by way of contribution or indemnity or in respect of any remedy or relief relating to or connected with the plaintiff's claim.

Interim order on counterclaim

17. A defendant who makes a counterclaim for damages in respect of personal injuries to himself or any other person or in respect of a person's death may apply for an order requiring the plaintiff to make an interim payment and this Part of this Order shall apply accordingly with the necessary modifications."

6. In Order 45, rule 12(3), for the words "in Appendix A" there shall be substituted the words "or 66A in Appendix A, whichever is appropriate".

7. Order 59 shall be amended as follows:—

(1) The following paragraph shall be added at the end of rule 4:—

"(3) In the case of an appeal from a decision in respect of which a certificate has been granted under section 12 of the Administration of Justice Act 1969(**a**) the period referred to in paragraph (1) shall be calculated from the end of the time during which, in accordance with section 13(5) of that Act, no appeal lies to the Court of Appeal".

(2) In rule 14(2) the words "if the appellant is acting in person" shall be omitted.

(3) In rule 18(2) for the words "14 days" there shall be substituted the words "6 weeks".

(**a**) 1969 c. 58.

8. Order 75, rule 24, shall be amended as follows :—

(1) In paragraph (2) for the words "paragraph (3)" there shall be substituted the words "paragraphs (3) and (4)".

(2) At the end there shall be added the following paragraph :—

"(4) Where in an Admiralty action money has been paid into court pursuant to an order made under Order 29, rule 12, the registrar or, in the case of an action which is proceeding in a district registry, the registrar of that registry, may make an order under paragraph (3) of that rule for the money to be paid out to the person entitled thereto".

9. The following Order shall be inserted after Order 112 :—

"ORDER 113

SUMMARY PROCEEDINGS FOR POSSESSION OF LAND

Proceedings to be brought by originating summons

1. Where a person claims possession of land which he alleges is occupied solely by a person or persons (not being a tenant or tenants holding over after the termination of the tenancy) who entered into or remained in occupation without his licence or consent or that of any predecessor in title of his, the proceedings may be brought by originating summons in accordance with the provisions of this Order.

Forms of originating summons

2.—(1) Subject to paragraph (2), the originating summons shall be in Form No. 10 in Appendix A.

(2) Where the person claiming possession is unable, after taking reasonable steps, to identify every person occupying the land for the purpose of making him a defendant, the originating summons shall be in Form No. 11A in Appendix A.

(3) No appearance need be entered to the originating summons.

Affidavit in support

3. The plaintiff shall file in support of the originating summons an affidavit stating—

(*a*) his interest in the land ;

(*b*) the circumstances in which the land has been occupied without licence or consent and in which his claim to possession arises ; and

(*c*) where the summons is in Form No. 11A, that he has taken all reasonable steps (describing them) to identify the persons occupying the land who are not named in the summons.

Service of originating summons

4.—(1) Where the plaintiff has identified any person in occupation of the land the originating summons together with a copy of the affidavit in support shall be served on him—

(*a*) in accordance with Order 10, rule 5, or

(*b*) by leaving a copy of the summons and of the affidavit, or sending them to him, at the premises, or

(*c*) in such other manner as the Court may direct.

(2) Where the plaintiff has not identified every person in occupation of the land, the originating summons shall, in addition to being served on the identified defendants (if any) in accordance with paragraph (1), be served by affixing a copy of it to the main door or other conspicuous part of the premises, unless the Court directs service in some other manner.

(3) Order 28, rule 3, shall not apply to proceedings under this Order.

Application by occupier to be made a party

5. Without prejudice to Order 15, rules 6 and 10, any person not named as a defendant who is in occupation of the land and wishes to be heard on the question whether an order for possession should be made may apply at any stage of the proceedings to be joined as a defendant.

Order for possession

6.—(1) A final order shall not be made on the originating summons except by a judge in person and shall, except in case of urgency and by leave of the Court, not be made less than 7 clear days after the date of service.

(2) An order for possession in proceedings under this Order shall be in Form No. 42A.

Writ of possession

7.—(1) Notwithstanding the provisions of Order 45, rule 3, a writ of possession to enforce an order for possession under this Order may be issued without the leave of the Court.

(2) The writ of possession shall be in Form No. 66A.

Setting aside order

8. The judge may, on such terms as he thinks just, set aside or vary any order made in proceedings under this Order."

10. Appendix A to the Rules of the Supreme Court 1965 shall be amended as follows :—

(1) The following form shall be inserted after Form No. 11 :—

"No. 11A

Originating summons for possession under Order 113

(O.113, r. 2)

In the High Court of Justice 19 , No.
Division
[Group]
In the matter of
[A.B. Plaintiff
C.D. Defendant (if any) whose name is known to the plaintiff]

Let all persons concerned attend before
Royal Courts of Justice, Strand, London, WC2A 2LL, on day, the day of 19 , at o'clock, on the hearing of an application by A.B. for an order that he do recover possession of on the ground that he is entitled to possession and

that the person(s) in occupation is(are) in occupation without licence or consent.

Dated the day of 19 .

This summons was taken out by of
solicitor for the said plaintiff whose address is
[*or* This summons was taken out by of agent
for of solicitor for the said plaintiff whose
address is] [*or when the plaintiff acts in person*

This summons was taken out by the said plaintiff who resides at
and is (*state occupation*) *and* (*if the plaintiff does not reside within the jurisdiction*) whose address for service is
]

Note. Any person occupying the premises who is not named as a defendant by this summons may apply to the Court personally or by counsel or solicitor to be joined as a defendant. If a person occupying the premises does not attend personally or by counsel or solicitor at the time and place above-mentioned, such order will be made as the Court may think just and expedient."

(2) The following form shall be inserted after Form No. 42 :—

"No. 42A

Order for possession under Order 113

(O.113, r. 6)

[*Heading as in summons*]

Upon hearing and upon reading the affidavit of
filed the day of 19 , it is ordered
that the plaintiff A.B. do recover possession of the land described in the originating summons as [and that the defendant do pay
the plaintiff £ costs [*or* costs to be taxed]]

The above costs, etc. [as in No. 39]].

Dated the day of 19 ."

(3) The following form shall be inserted after Form No. 66 :—

"No. 66A

Writ of possession under Order 113

(O.113, r. 7)

[*Heading as in summons*]

ELIZABETH THE SECOND [as in No. 53]

To the Sheriff of greeting:

Whereas it was on the day of 19
ordered that the plaintiff A.B. do recover possession of [*describe the land recovery of which has been ordered*] in your county [and that the defendant C.D. do pay
him £ costs [*or* costs to be taxed, which costs have been taxed and allowed
at £ as appears by the taxing officer's certificate dated the day
of 19]]:

We command you that you enter the said land and cause A.B. to have possession of it

[And we also command you that of the goods, chattels and other property [*remainder as in No.* 53]]."

Dated 16th June 1970.

Gardiner, C.
Parker of Waddington, C.J.
Denning, M.R.
J. E. S. Simon, P.
Denys B. Buckley, L.J.
Nigel Bridge, J.
E. S. Fay.
Oliver Lodge.
Arthur J. Driver.

EXPLANATORY NOTE

(*This Note is not part of the Rules.*)

These Rules introduce a rapid new procedure for the recovery of possession of land against trespassers (Rules 6, 9 and 10) and enable an order to be made for an interim payment on account of the damages which may be recovered in an action for personal injuries (Rules 5 and 8). They also make minor amendments in the Rules of the Supreme Court relating to the assignment of cases in the Chancery Division (Rule 3), offers of contribution by third parties and joint tortfeasors (Rule 4) and appeals to the Court of Appeal (Rule 7).

1970 No. 950

PACIFIC ISLANDS

The New Hebrides Order in Council 1970

Made - - - -	*26th June* 1970
Laid before Parliament	*2nd July* 1970
Coming into Operation	*3rd July* 1970

At the Court at Buckingham Palace, the 26th day of June 1970

Present,

The Queen's Most Excellent Majesty in Council

Her Majesty, by virtue and in exercise of the powers in that behalf by the Foreign Jurisdiction Act 1890(**a**) or otherwise in Her vested, is pleased, by and with the advice of Her Privy Council, to order, and it is hereby ordered, as follows:—

Citation and commencement.

1.—(1) This Order may be cited as the New Hebrides Order in Council 1970.

(2) This Order and the New Hebrides Orders in Council 1922 to 1963(**b**) may be cited together as the New Hebrides Orders in Council 1922 to 1970.

(3) This Order shall come into operation on the 3rd day of July 1970.

Interpretation.

2.—(1) This Order shall be construed as one with the New Hebrides Order in Council 1922(**c**) (hereinafter called " the principal Order ").

(2) In this Order, " the Protocol " means the Protocol made the 6th day of August 1914 between the Government of His late Majesty King George the Fifth and the Government of the French Republic in the terms set forth in the Schedule to the principal Order as interpreted in accordance with the agreement to that effect contained in the notes exchanged between the two Governments dated the 16th day of December 1922 and the 26th day of December 1922 respectively, and set out in the Schedule to the New Hebrides Order in Council 1923(**d**) and as modified, added to, or amended by any of the agreements set out in the Schedule to the New Hebrides Order in Council 1961(**e**) or in the Schedule to the New Hebrides Order in Council 1963(**f**).

(**a**) 53 & 54 Vict. c. 37.
(**b**) S.R. & O. 1922/717, 1923/356 (Rev. VIII, pp. 719, 757: 1922, p. 324; 1923, p. 337); S.I. 1955/553, 1961/1831, 1963/1324 (1955 II, p. 1700; 1961 III, p. 3456; 1963 II, p. 2297).
(**c**) S.R. & O. 1922/717 (Rev. VIII, p. 719: 1922, p. 324).
(**d**) S.R. & O. 1923/356 (Rev. VIII, p. 757: 1923, p. 337).
(**e**) S.I. 1961/1831 (1961 III, 3456).
(**f**) S.I. 1963/1324 (1963 II, p. 2297).

3. The principal Order shall be amended by the insertion, after section 10 thereof, of the following new section:—

Insertion of new section 10A in New Hebrides Order in Council 1922.

"10A. If, at any time after the coming into operation of the New Hebrides Order in Council 1970, the High Commissioner is informed by the Secretary of State for Foreign and Commonwealth Affairs that Her Majesty's Government and the Government of the French Republic have agreed by Exchange of Notes or otherwise to modify, add to or amend the Protocol, the High Commissioner shall cause the modification, addition or amendment to be published in the New Hebrides in the manner customarily adopted for the publication of regulations made under section 6 of this Order, and upon such publication the Protocol shall have the force of law and be binding within the New Hebrides subject to such modification, addition or amendment."

4.—(1) The Protocol shall have the force of law and shall be binding upon all such persons as are referred to in section 2 of the principal Order subject to the amendments set out in the Exchanges of Notes between the Government of the United Kingdom of Great Britain and Northern Ireland and the Government of the French Republic dated at London the 14th day of February 1967(**a**) and the 15th day of February 1967(**b**), that is to say:—

Agreements modifying the Protocol given the force of law, etc.

(*a*) Article 9 of the Protocol shall be abrogated and replaced by the following:—

"*Article* 9

The High Commissioners shall arrange, by Joint Regulation made after consultation with their Governments, for the registration wherever possible of births, marriages and deaths, and more generally of all civil status acts, of persons who are not nationals of the administering powers, or of persons who are not required to opt for the civil legislation of one or the other of those powers.

They may make this registration compulsory."

(*b*) Paragraph 3 of Article 12 of the Protocol shall be abrogated and replaced by the following:—

"3. Over all matters in respect of Joint Labour Regulations, under Article 31 of the present Convention."

(*c*) Articles 31 to 56 (inclusive) of the Protocol shall be abrogated and replaced by the following:—

"*Article* 31

1. Without prejudice to the generality of the powers conferred by Article 7, the High Commissioners may, after receipt of the authorisation of their respective Governments to that effect, issue Joint Labour Regulations, and may, as often as may be necessary, amend and revoke such Regulations after having, in each case, obtained such authorisation.

2. The procedure in relation to the prosecution and trial of offences against Joint Labour Regulations and the hearing of labour and trade disputes shall be prescribed by rules made in that behalf by the Joint Court based on British and French legislation on such matters."

(**a**) Cmnd. 3864. (**b**) Cmnd. 3276.

(2) The Protocol shall be deemed to have had the force of law and to have been binding in the manner prescribed in subsection (1) of this section with effect from the dates upon which the relevant agreements came into operation, that is to say :—

(*a*) in the case of the amendment set out in paragraph (*a*) of subsection (1), the 15th day of February 1967 ; and

(*b*) in the case of the amendments set out in paragraphs (*b*) and (*c*) of subsection (1), the 14th day of February 1967.

W. G. Agnew.

EXPLANATORY NOTE

(*This Note is not part of the Order.*)

This Order further amends the New Hebrides Order in Council 1922 by giving the force of law to further amendments to the Anglo-French Protocol respecting the New Hebrides of 6th August 1914. It also makes provision so that such amendments to the Protocol in future can be given the force of law without making further Orders in Council.

STATUTORY INSTRUMENTS

1970 No. 951

CIVIL AVIATION

The Civil Aviation (Isle of Man) Order 1970

Made - - -	26*th June* 1970
Laid before Parliament	2*nd July* 1970
Coming into Operation	6*th July* 1970

At the Court at Buckingham Palace, the 26th day of June 1970

Present,

The Queen's Most Excellent Majesty in Council

Her Majesty, in exercise of the powers conferred on Her by sections 61(1) and 67(1) of the Civil Aviation Act 1949(**a**), is pleased, by and with the advice of Her Privy Council, to order, and it is hereby ordered, as follows:—

1. This Order may be cited as the Civil Aviation (Isle of Man) Order 1970 and shall come into operation on 6th July 1970.

2. Section 40 of the Civil Aviation Act 1949, as extended to the Isle of Man by the Civil Aviation Act (Isle of Man) Order 1952(**b**), shall apply in the Isle of Man to aircraft belonging to or exclusively employed in the service of Her Majesty, not being military aircraft.

W. G. Agnew.

EXPLANATORY NOTE

(*This Note is not part of the Order.*)

This Order applies the provisions of section 40 of the Civil Aviation Act 1949 (which relates to liability in tort for civil aircraft belonging to or exclusively employed in the service of the Crown (which would include Concorde aircraft falling within those categories and the aircraft of the Board of Trade's Civil Aviation Flying Unit)) to the Isle of Man. The Order corresponds to the Civil Aviation (Crown Aircraft) Order 1970 (S.I. 1970/289), which made similar provision for the United Kingdom.

(**a**) 1949 c. 67.

(**b**) S.I. 1952/1032 (1952 I, p. 561).

1970 No. 952

INCOME TAX

The Double Taxation Relief (Taxes on Income) (Barbados) Order 1970

Laid before the House of Commons in draft

Made - - - *26th June* 1970

At the Court at Buckingham Palace, the 26th day of June 1970

Present,

The Queen's Most Excellent Majesty in Council

Whereas a draft of this Order was laid before the Commons House of Parliament in accordance with the provisions of section 497(8) of the Income and Corporation Taxes Act 1970(**a**), and an Address has been presented to Her Majesty by that House praying that an Order may be made in the terms of this Order:

Now, therefore, Her Majesty, in exercise of the powers conferred upon Her by section 497 of the said Income and Corporation Taxes Act 1970 and section 39 of the Finance Act 1965(**b**), as amended, and of all other powers enabling Her in that behalf, is pleased, by and with the advice of Her Privy Council, to order, and it is hereby ordered, as follows:—

1. This Order may be cited as the Double Taxation Relief (Taxes on Income) (Barbados) Order 1970.

2. It is hereby declared—

(*a*) that the arrangements specified in the Agreement set out in the Schedule to this Order have been made with the Government of Barbados with a view to affording relief from double taxation in relation to income tax, corporation tax or capital gains tax and taxes of a similar character imposed by the laws of Barbados; and

(*b*) that it is expedient that those arrangements should have effect.

W. G. Agnew.

(**a**) 1970 c. 10. (**b**) 1965 c. 25.

SCHEDULE

Agreement between the Government of the United Kingdom of Great Britain and Northern Ireland and the Government of Barbados for the Avoidance of Double Taxation and the Prevention of Fiscal Evasion with respect to Taxes on Income and Capital Gains

The Government of the United Kingdom of Great Britain and Northern Ireland and the Government of Barbados;

Desiring to conclude an agreement for the avoidance of double taxation and the prevention of fiscal evasion with respect to taxes on income and capital gains;

Have agreed as follows:

Article 1

Taxes covered

(1) The taxes which are the subject of this Agreement are:

(*a*) in the United Kingdom of Great Britain and Northern Ireland:

(i) the income tax (including surtax);

(ii) the corporation tax; and

(iii) the capital gains tax

(hereinafter referred to as "United Kingdom tax");

(*b*) in Barbados:

(i) the income tax;

(ii) the petroleum winning operations tax; and

(iii) the trade tax

(hereinafter referred to as "Barbados tax").

(2) This Agreement shall also apply to any identical or substantially similar taxes which are imposed by either Contracting State after the date of signature of this Agreement in addition to, or in place of, the existing taxes.

Article 2

General definitions

(1) In this Agreement, unless the context otherwise requires:

(*a*) "United Kingdom" means Great Britain and Northern Ireland, including any area outside the territorial sea of the United Kingdom which in accordance with international law has been or may hereafter be designated, under the laws of the United Kingdom concerning the Continental Shelf, as an area within which the rights of the United Kingdom with respect to the sea bed and sub-soil and their natural resources may be exercised;

(*b*) "Barbados" means the island of Barbados and the territorial waters thereof including any area outside such territorial waters which in accordance with international law and the laws of Barbados is an area within which the rights of Barbados with respect to the sea bed and sub-soil and their natural resources may be exercised;

(*c*) "company" means any body corporate or any entity which is treated as a body corporate for tax purposes;

(*d*) "a Contracting State" and "the other Contracting State" mean the United Kingdom or Barbados, as the context requires;

(*e*) "enterprise of a Contracting State" and "enterprise of the other Contracting State" mean respectively an enterprise carried on by a resident of a Contracting State and an enterprise carried on by a resident of the other Contracting State;

(*f*) "international traffic" includes traffic between places in one country in the course of a voyage which extends over more than one country;

(*g*) "national" means:

(i) in relation to the United Kingdom:

(*aa*) any citizen of the United Kingdom and Colonies who derives his status as such from connection with the United Kingdom;

(*bb*) any legal person, association or other entity deriving its status as such from the law of the United Kingdom;

(ii) in relation to Barbados:

(*aa*) any individual who is a citizen of Barbados;

(*bb*) any legal person, partnership or association deriving its status as such from the law of Barbados;

(*h*) "person" comprises an individual, a company and any other body of persons;

(*i*) "tax" means United Kingdom tax or Barbados tax, as the context requires;

(*j*) "taxation authorities" means, in the case of the United Kingdom, the Commissioners of Inland Revenue or their authorised representative; in the case of Barbados, the Commissioner of Inland Revenue or his authorised representative.

(2) In the application of the provisions of this Agreement by a Contracting State, any term not otherwise defined shall, unless the context otherwise requires, have the meaning which it has under the laws of that Contracting State relating to the taxes which are the subject of this Agreement.

ARTICLE 3

Fiscal domicile

(1) For the purposes of this Agreement, "resident of a Contracting State" means, subject to the provisions of paragraphs (2) and (3) of this Article, any person who, under the law of that State, is liable to taxation therein by reason of his domicile, residence, place of management or any other criterion of a similar nature; the term does not include any individual who is liable to tax in that Contracting State only if he derives income from sources therein. The terms "resident of the United Kingdom" and "resident of Barbados" shall be construed accordingly.

(2) Where by reason of the provisions of paragraph (1) of this Article an individual is a resident of both Contracting States, then his status shall be determined in accordance with the following rules:

(*a*) he shall be deemed to be a resident of the Contracting State in which he has a permanent home available to him. If he has a permanent home available to him in both Contracting States, he shall be deemed to be a resident of the Contracting State with which his personal and economic relations are closest (hereinafter referred to as his "centre of vital interests");

(*b*) if the Contracting State in which he has his centre of vital interests cannot be determined, or if he has not a permanent home available to him in either Contracting State, he shall be deemed to be a resident of the Contracting State in which he has an habitual abode;

(*c*) if he has an habitual abode in both Contracting States or in neither of them, he shall be deemed to be a resident of the Contracting State of which he is a national;

(*d*) if he is a national of both Contracting States or of neither of them, the taxation authorities of the Contracting States shall determine the question by mutual agreement.

(3) Where by reason of the provisions of paragraph (1) of this Article a person other than an individual is a resident of both Contracting States then it shall be deemed to be a resident of the Contracting State in which its place of effective management is situated.

Article 4

Permanent establishment

(1) For the purposes of this Agreement, "permanent establishment" means a fixed place of business in which the business of the enterprise is wholly or partly carried on.

(2) A permanent establishment shall include especially:

(*a*) a place of management;

(*b*) a branch;

(*c*) an office;

(*d*) a factory;

(*e*) a workshop;

(*f*) a mine, quarry or other place of extraction of natural resources;

(*g*) a building site or construction or assembly project which exists for more than six months;

(*h*) a farm or plantation.

(3) "Permanent establishment" shall not be deemed to include:

(*a*) the use of facilities solely for the purpose of storage, display or delivery of goods or merchandise belonging to the enterprise;

(*b*) the maintenance of a stock of goods or merchandise belonging to the enterprise solely for the purpose of storage, display or delivery;

(*c*) the maintenance of a stock of goods or merchandise belonging to the enterprise solely for the purpose of processing by another enterprise;

(*d*) the maintenance of a fixed place of business solely for the purpose of purchasing goods or merchandise, or for collecting information for the enterprise;

(*e*) the maintenance of a fixed place of business solely for the purpose of advertising, for the supply of information, for scientific research or for similar activities which have a preparatory or auxiliary character, for the enterprise.

(4) An enterprise of a Contracting State shall be deemed to have a permanent establishment in the other Contracting State if:

(*a*) it carries on supervisory activities in that other State for more than six months in connection with a construction, installation or assembly project which is being undertaken in that other State;

(*b*) it carries on a business which consists of providing the services within that other State of public entertainers or athletes referred to in Article 18.

(5) A person acting in a Contracting State on behalf of an enterprise of the other Contracting State (other than an agent of an independent status to whom the provisions of paragraph (6) of this Article apply) shall be deemed to be a permanent establishment in the former Contracting State if:

(*a*) he has, and habitually exercises in that former State, an authority to conclude contracts in the name of the enterprise, unless his activities are limited to the purchase of goods or merchandise for the enterprise; or

(*b*) he maintains in that former State a stock of goods or merchandise belonging to the enterprise from which he regularly fills orders on behalf of the enterprise.

(6) An enterprise of a Contracting State shall not be deemed to have a permanent establishment in the other Contracting State merely because it carries on business in that other State through a broker, a general commission agent or any other agent of an independent status, where such persons are acting in the ordinary course of their business.

(7) The fact that a company which is a resident of a Contracting State controls or is controlled by a company which is a resident of the other Contracting State, or which carries on business in that other State (whether through a permanent establishment or otherwise), shall not of itself constitute either company a permanent establishment of the other.

ARTICLE 5

Limitation of relief

Where under any provision of this Agreement any income is exempt from tax or is taxed at a reduced rate in a Contracting State if (with or without other conditions) it is subject to tax in the other Contracting State and that income is subject to tax in that other State by reference to the amount thereof which is remitted to or received in that other State, the exemption or reduction of tax to be allowed under this Agreement in the first-mentioned Contracting State shall apply only to the amounts so remitted or received.

ARTICLE 6

Business profits

(1) The industrial or commercial profits of an enterprise of a Contracting State shall be taxable only in that State unless the enterprise carries on a trade or business in the other Contracting State through a permanent establishment situated therein. If it carries on a trade or business as aforesaid, tax may be imposed on those profits by that other State, but only on so much of them as is attributable to that permanent establishment.

(2) Where an enterprise of a Contracting State carries on a trade or business in the other Contracting State through a permanent establishment situated therein, there shall in each Contracting State be attributed to that permanent establishment the industrial or commercial profits which it might be expected to make if it were an independent enterprise engaged in the same or similar activities under the same or similar conditions and dealing at arm's length with the enterprise of which it is a permanent establishment.

(3) In determining the industrial or commercial profits of a permanent establishment, there shall be allowed as deductions all expenses of the enterprise which are incurred for the purposes of the permanent establishment, including executive and general administration expenses so incurred, whether incurred in the Contracting State in which the permanent establishment is situated or elsewhere (other than expenses which would not be deductible if the permanent establishment were a separate enterprise).

(4) No profits shall be attributed to a permanent establishment by reason of the mere purchase by that permanent establishment of goods or merchandise for the enterprise.

(5) Nothing in this Article shall apply to either Contracting State to prevent the operation in the State of any provisions of its law relating specifically to the taxation of any person who carries on a business of any form of insurance. Provided that if the law in force in either Contracting State at the date of signature of this Agreement relating to the taxation of such persons is varied (otherwise than in minor respects so as not to affect its general character, or by this Agreement), the Contracting Government's shall consult with each other with a view to agreeing to such amendment of this paragraph as may be necessary.

ARTICLE 7

Associated enterprises

Where—

(*a*) an enterprise of a Contracting State participates directly or indirectly in the management, control or capital of an enterprise of the other Contracting State; or

(*b*) the same persons participate directly or indirectly in the management, control or capital of an enterprise of a Contracting State and an enterprise of the other Contracting State;

and, in either case, conditions are made or imposed between the two enterprises, in their commercial or financial relations, which differ from those which would be made between independent enterprises, then any profits which would, but for those conditions, have accrued to one of the enterprises, but, by reason of those conditions, have not so accrued, may be included in the profits of that enterprise and taxed accordingly.

ARTICLE 8

Shipping and air transport

A resident of a Contracting State shall be exempt from tax in the other Contracting State on profits from the operation of ships or aircraft other than profits from voyages of ships or aircraft confined solely to places in that other State.

ARTICLE 9

Dividends

(1) Dividends paid by a company which is a resident of a Contracting State to a resident of the other Contracting State who is subject to tax in that other State in respect thereof shall be exempt from any tax in that first-mentioned Contracting State which is chargeable on dividends in addition to the tax chargeable in respect of the profits or income of the company.

(2) The provisions of paragraph (1) of this Article shall not apply where a resident of a Contracting State has a permanent establishment in the other Contracting State and the holding giving rise to the dividends is effectively connected with that permanent establishment; in such event the dividends shall be treated as if they were industrial or commercial profits to which the provisions of Article 6 are applicable.

(3) Where a company which is a resident of a Contracting State derives profits or income from sources within the other Contracting State, that other State shall not impose any form of taxation on dividends paid by the company to persons not resident in that other State, or any tax in the nature of an undistributed profits tax on undistributed profits of the company, by reason of the fact that those dividends or undistributed profits represent, in whole or in part, profits or income so derived.

(4) Subject to the provisions of paragraph (5) of Article 10 and paragraph (5) of Article 11 the term "dividends" includes any item which, under the law of the Contracting State of which the company paying the dividend is a resident, is treated as a distribution of a company.

(5) If the recipient of a dividend is a company which owns 10 per cent or more of the class of shares in respect of which the dividend is paid then the provisions of paragraph (1) of this Article shall not apply to the dividend to the extent that it can have been paid only out of profits which the company paying the dividend earned or other income which it received in a period ending twelve months or more before the relevant date. For the purposes of this paragraph the term "relevant date" means the date on which the beneficial owner of the dividend became the

owner of 10 per cent or more of the class of shares in question. Provided that this paragraph shall not apply if the beneficial owner of the dividend shows that the shares were acquired for bona fide commercial reasons and not primarily for the purpose of securing the benefit of this Article.

Article 10

Interest

(1) Where interest is derived from sources within a Contracting State by a resident of the other Contracting State who is subject to tax in that other State in respect thereof, the rate of tax imposed thereon in the first-mentioned Contracting State shall not exceed 15 per cent.

(2) The provisions of paragraph (1) of this Article shall not apply where a resident of a Contracting State has a permanent establishment in the other Contracting State and such interest is attributable to that permanent establishment; in such event such interest as is attributable to that permanent establishment shall be treated as if it were industrial or commercial profits to which the provisions of Article 6 are applicable.

(3) In this Article, the term "interest" means income from Government securities, from bonds or debentures, whether or not secured by mortgage, or from any other form of indebtedness, as well as all other income assimilated to income from money lent by the taxation law of the Contracting State in which the income arises.

(4) Where, owing to a special relationship between the payer and the recipient or between both of them and some other person, the amount of the interest paid, having regard to the indebtedness in respect of which it is paid, exceeds the amount which would have been agreed upon by the payer and the recipient in the absence of such relationship, the provisions of this Article shall apply only to the last-mentioned amount. In that case, the excess part of the payments shall remain taxable according to the laws of each Contracting State, due regard being had to the other provisions of this Agreement.

(5) Any provision of the law of a Contracting State which relates only to interest paid to a non-resident company shall not operate so as to require such interest paid to a company which is a resident of the other Contracting State to be left out of account as a deduction in computing the taxable profits of the company paying the interest as being a dividend or distribution.

(6) The provisions of this Article shall not apply if the form of indebtedness in respect of which the interest is payable was created or assigned mainly for the purpose of taking advantage of this Article and not for bona fide commercial reasons.

Article 11

Royalties

(1) Any royalty derived from sources within a Contracting State by a resident of the other Contracting State who is subject to tax in that other State in respect thereof, shall be exempt from tax in that first-mentioned Contracting State. Provided that, where any such royalty is in respect of cinematograph or television films, tax may be imposed thereon in the Contracting State from which the royalty is derived, but the tax so imposed shall not exceed tax at the rate applicable to companies on 15 per cent of the gross amount of the royalty.

(2) In this Article, the term "royalty" means any royalty or other amount paid as consideration for the use of, or for the privilege of using, any copyright, patent, design, secret process or formula, trade-mark, or other like property, and includes any rental or like payment in respect of cinematograph or television films, but does not include any royalty or other amount paid in respect of the operation of a mine or quarry or of any other extraction of natural resources.

(3) The provisions of paragraph (1) of this Article shall not apply where a resident of a Contracting State has a permanent establishment in the other Contracting State and the royalty is attributable to that permanent establishment; in such event the royalty shall be treated as if it were industrial or commercial profits to which the provisions of Article 6 are applicable.

(4) Where, owing to a special relationship between the payer and the recipient or between both of them and some other person, the amount of the royalty, having regard to the use, right or property for which it is paid, exceeds the amount which would have been agreed upon by the payer and the recipient in the absence of such relationship, the provisions of the preceding paragraphs of this Article shall apply only to the last-mentioned amount. In that case, the excess part of the payments shall remain taxable according to the laws of each Contracting State, due regard being had to the other provisions of this Agreement.

(5) Royalties paid by a company which is a resident of a Contracting State to a resident of the other Contracting State shall not be treated as a distribution of that company. The preceding sentence shall not apply to royalties paid to a company where:

(*a*) the same persons participate directly or indirectly in the management or control of the company paying the royalties and the company deriving the royalties; and

(*b*) more than 50 per cent of the voting power in the company deriving the royalties is controlled, directly or indirectly, by a person or persons resident in the first-mentioned Contracting State.

Article 12

Immovable property

(1) Income from immovable property may be taxed in the Contracting State in which such property is situated.

(2) The term "immovable property" shall be defined in accordance with the laws of the Contracting State in which the property in question is situated. The term shall in any case include property accessory to immovable property, livestock and equipment of agricultural and forestry enterprises, rights to which the provisions of general law respecting landed property apply, usufruct of immovable property and rights to variable or fixed payments as consideration for the working of mineral deposits, sources and other natural resources; ships, boats and aircraft shall not be regarded as immovable property.

(3) The provisions of paragraph (1) of this Article shall apply to income derived from the direct use or from the letting of immovable property or the use in any other form of such property, including income from agricultural or forestry enterprises.

(4) The provisions of paragraphs (1) and (3) of this Article shall also apply to the income from immovable property of any enterprises other than agricultural or forestry enterprises and to income from immovable property used for the performance of professional services.

Article 13

Capital gains

(1) Capital gains from the alienation of immovable property, as defined in paragraph (2) of Article 12, may be taxed in the Contracting State in which such property is situated.

(2) Capital gains from the alienation of movable property forming part of the business property of a permanent establishment which an enterprise of a Contracting State has in the other Contracting State or of movable property pertaining to a fixed base available to a resident of a Contracting State in the other Contracting State for the purpose of performing professional services, including such gains from the alienation of such a permanent establishment (alone or together with the whole enterprise) or of such a fixed base, may be taxed in the other State.

(3) Notwithstanding the provisions of paragraph (1) of this Article, capital gains derived by a resident of a Contracting State from the alienation of ships and aircraft operated in international traffic and of movable property pertaining to the operation of such ships and aircraft shall be taxable only in that State.

(4) Capital gains from the alienation of any property other than those mentioned in paragraphs (1) and (2) of this Article which are subject to tax in the Contracting State of which the alienator is a resident shall be taxable only in that State.

(5) The provisions of paragraph (4) of this Article shall not affect the right of a Contracting State to levy according to its own law a tax on capital gains from the alienation of any property derived by an individual who is a resident of the other Contracting State and has been a resident of the first-mentioned Contracting State at any time during the five years immediately preceding the alienation of the property.

ARTICLE 14

Governmental functions

(1) Remuneration, including pensions, paid by a Contracting State to an individual for services rendered to that State in the discharge of governmental functions shall be exempt from tax in the other Contracting State if the individual is not ordinarily resident in that other State or (where the remuneration is not a pension) is ordinarily resident in that other State solely for the purpose of rendering those services.

(2) The provisions of this Article shall not apply to payments in respect of services rendered in connection with any trade or business carried on by either of the Contracting States for purposes of profit.

ARTICLE 15

Pensions

(1) Any pension (other than a pension of the kind referred to in paragraph (1) of Article 14) and any annuity, derived from sources within a Contracting State by an individual who is a resident of the other Contracting State and subject to tax in that other State in respect thereof, shall be exempt from tax in the first-mentioned Contracting State.

(2) The term "annuity" means a stated sum payable periodically at stated times, during life or during a specified or ascertainable period of time, under an obligation to make the payments in return for adequate and full consideration in money or money's worth.

ARTICLE 16

Independent personal services

(1) Income derived by a resident of a Contracting State in respect of professional services or other independent activities of a similar character shall be subjected to tax only in that State unless he has a fixed base regularly available to him in the other Contracting State for the purpose of performing his activities. If he has such a fixed base, such part of that income as is attributable to that base may be taxed in that other Contracting State.

(2) The term "professional services" includes especially independent scientific, literary, artistic, educational or teaching activities as well as the independent activities of physicians, lawyers, engineers, architects, dentists and accountants.

ARTICLE 17

Employments

(1) Subject to the provisions of Articles 14, 15 and 19, salaries, wages and other similar remuneration derived by a resident of a Contracting State in respect of an employment shall be subjected to tax only in that State unless the employment is exercised in the other Contracting State. If the employment is so exercised, such remuneration as is derived therefrom may be taxed in that other State.

(2) Notwithstanding the provisions of paragraph (1) of this Article, remuneration derived by a resident of a Contracting State in respect of an employment exercised in the other Contracting State shall be subjected to tax only in the first-mentioned State if:

(*a*) the recipient is present in the other State for a period or periods not exceeding in the aggregate 183 days in the fiscal year concerned ; and

(*b*) the remuneration is paid by or on behalf of an employer who is not a resident of the other State ; and

(*c*) the remuneration is not deducted from the profits of a permanent establishment or a fixed base which the employer has in the other State.

(3) In relation to remuneration of a director of a company derived from the company the preceding provisions of this Article shall apply as if the remuneration were remuneration of an employee in respect of an employment, and as if references to employers were references to the company.

(4) Notwithstanding the preceding provisions of this Article, remuneration for personal services performed aboard a ship or aircraft in international traffic may be taxed in the Contracting State of which the person deriving the profits from the operation of the ship or aircraft is a resident.

ARTICLE 18

Artistes and athletes

Notwithstanding anything contained in this Agreement, income derived by public entertainers, such as theatre, motion picture, radio or television artistes, and musicians, and by athletes, from their personal activities as such may be taxed in the Contracting State in which these activities are exercised.

ARTICLE 19

Teachers

A professor or teacher who visits a Contracting State for a period not exceeding two years for the purpose of teaching at a university, college, school or other educational institution and who immediately before that visit is a resident of the other Contracting State shall be exempt from tax in the first-mentioned Contracting State on any remuneration for such teaching in respect of which he is subject to tax in the other Contracting State.

ARTICLE 20

Students

Payments which a student or business apprentice, who is or was immediately before visiting a Contracting State a resident of the other Contracting State and who is present in the first-mentioned Contracting State solely for the purpose of his education or training, receives for the purpose of his maintenance, education or training, shall not be taxed in the first-mentioned State, provided that such payments are made to him from sources outside that State.

ARTICLE 21

Income not expressly mentioned

Items of income of a resident of a Contracting State being income of a class or from sources not expressly mentioned in the foregoing Articles of this Agreement in respect of which he is subject to tax in that State shall be taxable only in that State. Provided that this Article shall not be construed as affecting the taxation of income attributable to a permanent establishment which a resident of one Contracting State has in the other Contracting State.

ARTICLE 22

Elimination of double taxation

(1) Subject to the provisions of the law of the United Kingdom regarding the allowance as a credit against United Kingdom tax of tax payable in a territory outside the United Kingdom (which shall not affect the general principle hereof):

(*a*) Barbados tax payable under the laws of Barbados and in accordance with this Agreement, whether directly or by deduction, on profits or income from sources within Barbados shall be allowed as a credit against any United Kingdom tax computed by reference to the same profits or income by reference to which the Barbados tax is computed. Provided that in the case of a dividend the credit shall only take into account such tax in respect thereof as is additional to any tax payable by the company on the profits out of which the dividend is paid and is ultimately borne by the recipient without reference to any tax so payable.

(*b*) Where a company which is a resident of Barbados pays a dividend to a company resident in the United Kingdom which controls directly or indirectly at least 10 per cent of the voting power in the first-mentioned company, the credit shall take into account (in addition to any Barbados tax for which credit may be allowed under the provisions of sub-paragraph (*a*) of this paragraph) the Barbados tax payable by that first-mentioned company in respect of the profits out of which such dividend is paid.

(2) For the purposes of paragraph (1) of this Article, the term "Barbados tax payable" shall be deemed to include any amount which would have been payable as Barbados tax for any year but for an exemption or reduction of tax granted for that year or any part thereof under—

(*a*) any of the following provisions, that is to say:

(i) Sections 14(2), 15(2), 19(2) and 20 of the Pioneer Industries Act, 1958-54, as amended;

(ii) Sections 10, 15(2) and 16(1) of the Industrial Development (Export Industries) Act, 1969-43;

(iii) Sections 12, 14(2), 17(2) and 18(1) of the Industrial Incentives Act, 1963-31;

(iv) Sections 12, 14(2) and 15(1) of the Industrial Incentives (Factory Construction) Act, 1965-29;

(v) Sections 3 and 5 of the Hotel Aids Act, 1967-25;

(vi) Sections 21 and 46 of the Income Tax Act, 1968-51 ;
so far as they were in force on, and have not been modified since, the date when this Agreement was signed, or have been modified only in minor respects so as not to affect their general character ; or

(*b*) any other provision which may subsequently be made granting an exemption which is agreed by the taxation authorities of the United Kingdom and Barbados to be of a substantially similar character, if it has not been modified thereafter or has been modified only in minor respects so as not to affect its general character.

Provided:

(i) that relief from United Kingdom tax shall not be given by virtue of this paragraph in respect of income from any source if the income arises in a period starting more than ten years after the exemption from, or reduction of, Barbados tax was first granted in respect of that source ;

(ii) that where the relief is a relief accorded by the Industrial Development (Export Industries) Act, 1969-43, it shall be taken into account for the purposes of this Article if, and only if, the company qualifying for the relief could have been declared to be a company either:

(*aa*) which was engaging in a pioneer industry under the provisions of Section 3 of the Pioneer Industries Act, 1958-54, as amended ; or

(*bb*) which was an approved enterprise under the provisions of Section 4 of the Industrial Incentives Act, 1963-31.

(3) Subject to the provisions of the law of Barbados regarding the allowance as a credit against Barbados tax of tax payable in a territory outside Barbados (which shall not affect the general principle hereof):

(*a*) United Kingdom tax payable under the laws of the United Kingdom and in accordance with this Agreement, whether directly or by deduction, on profits or income from sources within the United Kingdom shall be allowed as a credit against any Barbados tax computed by reference to the same profits or income by reference to which the United Kingdom tax is computed. Provided that in the case of a dividend the credit shall only take into account such tax in respect thereof as is additional to any tax payable by the company on the profits out of which the dividend is paid and is ultimately borne by the recipient without reference to any tax so payable.

(*b*) Where a company which is a resident of the United Kingdom pays a dividend to a company resident in Barbados which controls directly or indirectly at least 10 per cent of the voting power in the first-mentioned company, the credit shall take into account (in addition to any United Kingdom tax for which credit may be allowed under the provisions of sub-paragraph (*a*) of this paragraph) the United Kingdom tax payable by that first-mentioned company in respect of the profits out of which such dividend is paid.

(4) For the purposes of this Article:

(*a*) profits or remuneration for personal (including professional) services performed in a Contracting State shall be deemed to be income from sources within that State ;

(*b*) the services of an individual whose services are wholly or mainly performed in ships or aircraft shall be deemed to be performed in the Contracting State of which the person deriving the profits from the operation of the ships or aircraft is a resident ;

(*c*) any amount which is included, for the purposes of tax in a Contracting State, in the chargeable profits or taxable income of a person who is a resident of the other Contracting State, and which is so included under any provision of the law of the first-mentioned Contracting State for the time being in force regarding taxation of income of a business of any form of insurance shall be treated as having a source in that first-mentioned Contracting State.

ARTICLE 23

Excluded companies

This Agreement shall not apply to companies entitled to any special tax benefit under the Barbados International Business Companies (Exemption from Income Tax) Act 1965-50 as in effect on 26th July 1965 or any substantially similar law enacted by Barbados after that date.

ARTICLE 24

Exchange of information

The taxation authorities of the Contracting States shall exchange such information (being information which is at their disposal under their respective taxation laws in the normal course of administration) as is necessary for carrying out the provisions of this Agreement or for the prevention of fraud or for the administration of statutory provisions against legal avoidance in relation to the taxes which are the subject of this Agreement. Any information so exchanged shall be treated as secret and shall not be disclosed to any persons other than those concerned with the assessment and collection of the taxes which are the subject of this Agreement. No information as aforesaid shall be exchanged which would disclose any trade, business, industrial or professional secret or trade process.

ARTICLE 25

Consultation

The taxation authorities of the Contracting States may communicate with each other directly for the purpose of giving effect to the provisions of this Agreement and for resolving any difficulty or doubt as to the application or interpretation of the Agreement.

ARTICLE 26

Non-discrimination

(1) The residents of a Contracting State shall not be subjected in the other Contracting State to any taxation or any requirement connected therewith which is other or more burdensome than the taxation and connected requirements to which the residents of that other State in the same circumstances are or may be subjected.

(2) Subject to the provisions of paragraph (5) of Article 6 of this Agreement, the taxation on a permanent establishment which an enterprise of a Contracting State has in the other Contracting State shall not be less favourably levied in that other State than the taxation levied on enterprises of that other State carrying on the same activities.

(3) Enterprises of a Contracting State, the capital of which is wholly or partly owned or controlled, directly or indirectly, by one or more residents of the other Contracting State, shall not be subjected in the first-mentioned Contracting State to any taxation or any requirement connected therewith which is other or more burdensome than the taxation and connected requirements to which other similar enterprises of that first-mentioned State are or may be subjected.

(4) In this Article the term "taxation" means taxes of every kind and description.

(5) Nothing contained in this Article shall be construed as obliging either of the Contracting States to grant to persons not resident in that State those personal allowances and reliefs for tax purposes which are by law available only to persons who are so resident, nor as restricting the taxation of dividends paid to a company which is a resident of the other Contracting State.

ARTICLE 27

Territorial extension

(1) This Agreement may be extended, either in its entirety or with modifications, to any territory for whose international relations the United Kingdom is responsible, and which imposes taxes substantially similar in character to those which are the subject of this Agreement, and any such extension shall take effect from such date and subject to such modifications and conditions (including conditions as to termination) as may be specified and agreed between the Contracting States in letters to be exchanged for this purpose.

(2) The termination in respect of the United Kingdom or Barbados of this Agreement under Article 29 shall, unless otherwise expressly agreed by both Contracting States, terminate the application of this Agreement to any territory to which the Agreement has been extended under this Article.

ARTICLE 28

Entry into force

(1) This Agreement shall come into force(**a**) on the date when the last of all such things shall have been done in the United Kingdom and Barbados as are necessary to give the Agreement the force of law in the United Kingdom and Barbados respectively, and shall thereupon have effect:

(*a*) in the United Kingdom:

(i) as respects income tax, surtax and capital gains tax, for any year of assessment beginning on or after 6th April, 1969;

(ii) as respects corporation tax, for any financial year beginning on or after 1st April, 1969;

(*b*) in Barbados:

(i) as respects income tax, for any year of assessment beginning on or after 1st January, 1969;

(ii) as respects petroleum winning operations tax, for any accounting period beginning on or after 1st January, 1969;

(iii) as respects trade tax, for any taxing period beginning on or after 1st April, 1969.

(2) Subject to the provisions of paragraph (3) of this Article, the Arrangement which was made in 1949 between the Government of the United Kingdom of Great Britain and Northern Ireland and the Government of Barbados(**b**), shall terminate and cease to be effective as respects taxes to which this Agreement in accordance with paragraph (1) of this Article applies.

(3) Where any provision of the Arrangement referred to in paragraph (2) of this Article would have afforded any greater relief from tax than is afforded by this Agreement any such provision as aforesaid shall continue to have effect for the first year of assessment or financial year for which this Agreement has effect in accordance with paragraph (1) of this Article.

ARTICLE 29

Termination

(1) This Agreement shall continue in effect indefinitely but either of the Contracting Governments may, on or before the thirtieth day of June in any calendar year after the year 1974, give notice of termination to the other Contracting

(a) The Agreement came into force on 26th June 1970. (b) S.I. 1949/358 (1949 I, p. 2236).

Government and, in such event, the Agreement shall cease to be effective:

(*a*) in the United Kingdom:

(i) as respects income tax, surtax and capital gains tax, for any year of assessment beginning on or after 6th April in the calendar year next following that in which the notice is given;

(ii) as respects corporation tax, for any financial year beginning on or after 1st April in the calendar year next following that in which the notice is given;

(*b*) in Barbados:

(i) as respects income tax, for any year of assessment beginning on or after 1st January in the calendar year next following that in which such notice is given;

(ii) as respects petroleum winning operations tax, for any accounting period beginning on or after 1st January in the calendar year next following that in which such notice is given;

(iii) as respects trade tax, for any taxing period beginning on or after 1st April in the calendar year next following that in which such notice is given.

(2) The termination of this Agreement shall not have the effect of reviving any agreement or arrangement abrogated by this Agreement.

In Witness Whereof the undersigned, duly authorised thereto, have signed this Agreement.

Done in duplicate at Bridgetown, this 26th day of March one thousand nine hundred and seventy.

For the Government of the United Kingdom of Great Britain and Northern Ireland:

JOHN S. BENNETT,
High Commissioner.

For the Government of Barbados:

ERROL W. BARROW,
Prime Minister and Minister of Finance.

EXPLANATORY NOTE

(*This Note is not part of the Order.*)

Under the Agreement with Barbados scheduled to this Order (which is to replace the Arrangement made in 1949), shipping and air transport profits, certain trading profits not arising through a permanent establishment, dividends, royalties (other than royalties in respect of cinematograph or television films), pensions (other than Government pensions) purchased annuities and the earnings of temporary business visitors are (subject to certain conditions) to be taxed only in the country of the taxpayer's residence. Government salaries and pensions are normally to be taxed by the paying Government. The remuneration of visiting professors and teachers and payments made for the maintenance of visiting students are (subject to certain conditions) to be exempt in the country visited. Capital gains arising from the disposal of movable property are normally to be taxed only in the country of the taxpayer's residence unless they arise from the disposal of assets of a permanent establishment which the taxpayer has in the other country.

The rate of tax in the source country on interest paid to residents of the other country is, in general, not to exceed 15 per cent.

Where income continues to be taxable in both countries, the country of the taxpayer's residence will relieve the double taxation by giving a credit for the other country's tax. In the case of dividends credit for the tax on the profits out of which the dividends are paid is to be given where the recipient of the dividends is a company which controls at least 10 per cent of the voting power in the paying company. The credit to be given by the United Kingdom includes credit for Barbados tax which would have been payable but for relief granted under certain provisions of Barbados law in order to encourage development there.

The Agreement is not to apply to companies entitled to certain special tax benefits under Barbados law.

There are provisions safeguarding residents and enterprises of one country against discriminatory taxation in the other country and for the exchange of information and consultation between the taxation authorities of the two countries.

The Agreement is in general to take effect in the United Kingdom for 1969-70 and subsequent years.

1970 No. 953

INCOME TAX

The Double Taxation Relief (Taxes on Income) (Botswana) Order 1970

Laid before the House of Commons in draft

Made - - - *26th June* 1970

At the Court at Buckingham Palace, the 26th day of June 1970

Present,

The Queen's Most Excellent Majesty in Council

Whereas a draft of this Order was laid before the Commons House of Parliament in accordance with the provisions of section 497(8) of the Income and Corporation Taxes Act 1970(**a**), and an Address has been presented to Her Majesty by that House praying that an Order may be made in the terms of this Order:

Now, therefore, Her Majesty, in exercise of the powers conferred upon Her by section 497 of the said Income and Corporation Taxes Act 1970 and of all other powers enabling Her in that behalf, is pleased, by and with the advice of Her Privy Council, to order, and it is hereby ordered, as follows:—

1. This Order may be cited as the Double Taxation Relief (Taxes on Income) (Botswana) Order 1970.

2. It is hereby declared—

(*a*) that the arrangements specified in the Agreement set out in the Schedule to this Order have been made with the Government of the Republic of Botswana with a view to affording relief from double taxation in relation to income tax or corporation tax and taxes of a similar character imposed by the laws of Botswana varying the arrangements set out in the Schedule to the Double Taxation Relief (Taxes on Income) (Bechuanaland Protectorate) Order 1949(**b**); and

(*b*) that it is expedient that those arrangements should have effect.

W. G. Agnew.

(**a**) 1970 c. 10. (**b**) S.I. 1949/2198 (1949 I, p. 2249).

SCHEDULE

Agreement amending the Arrangement between the Government of the United Kingdom of Great Britain and Northern Ireland and the Government of the Republic of Botswana for the Avoidance of Double Taxation and the Prevention of Fiscal Evasion with respect to Taxes on Income

The Government of the United Kingdom of Great Britain and Northern Ireland and the Government of the Republic of Botswana,

Desiring to amend the Arrangement for the avoidance of double taxation and the prevention of fiscal evasion with respect to taxes on income in force between Her Majesty's Government and the Government of the Bechuanaland Protectorate immediately before 30th September, 1966, when the Bechuanaland Protectorate was established as an independent republic under the name of Botswana, and continued in force since that date between the Government of the United Kingdom and the Government of the Republic of Botswana (hereinafter referred to as "the Arrangement"),

Have agreed as follows:

Article 1

The Arrangement shall be amended—

(*a*) by the substitution for paragraph 2(1)(*b*) of the following new paragraph—

"(*b*) The term "Botswana" means the Republic of Botswana.";

(*b*) by the substitution for the references therein to "Bechuanaland" or "Bechuanaland Protectorate", "Bechuanaland enterprise" and "Bechuanaland tax" of references to "Botswana", "Botswana enterprise" and "Botswana tax" respectively;

(*c*) by the addition at the end of paragraph 6 of the following new sub-paragraph—

"(3) If the recipient of a dividend is a company which owns 10 per cent or more of the class of shares in respect of which the dividend is paid then sub-paragraph (1) shall not apply to the dividend to the extent that it can have been paid only out of profits which the company paying the dividend earned or other income which it received in a period ending twelve months or more before the relevant date. For the purposes of this sub-paragraph the term "relevant date" means the date on which the beneficial owner of the dividend became the owner of 10 per cent or more of the class of shares in question. Provided that this sub-paragraph shall not apply if the beneficial owner of the dividend shows that the shares were acquired for bona fide commercial reasons and not primarily for the purpose of securing the benefit of this paragraph."; and

(*d*) by the substitution for sub-paragraphs (1) and (2) of paragraph 14 of the following two new sub-paragraphs—

"(1) Subject to the provisions of the law of the United Kingdom regarding the allowance as a credit against United Kingdom tax of tax payable in a territory outside the United Kingdom (which shall not affect the general principle hereof)—

(*a*) Botswana tax payable under the laws of Botswana and in accordance with this Arrangement, whether directly or by deduction, on profits or income from sources within Botswana shall be allowed as a credit against any United Kingdom tax computed by reference to the same profits or income by reference to which the Botswana tax is computed. Provided that in the case of a dividend the credit shall only take into account such tax in respect thereof as is additional to any tax payable by the company on the profits out of which the dividend is paid and is ultimately borne by the recipient without reference to any tax so payable.

(*b*) Where a company which is a resident of Botswana pays a dividend to a company resident in the United Kingdom which controls directly or indirectly at least 10 per cent of the voting power in the first-mentioned company, the credit shall take into account (in addition to any Botswana tax for which credit may be allowed under (*a*) of this sub-paragraph) the Botswana tax payable by that first-mentioned company in respect of the profits out of which such dividend is paid.

(2) If Botswana tax is payable, whether directly or by deduction, in respect of income derived from sources within the United Kingdom, then, subject to the provisions of the law of Botswana regarding the allowance as a credit against Botswana tax of tax payable in a territory outside Botswana (which shall not affect the general principle hereof)—

(*a*) United Kingdom tax payable under the laws of the United Kingdom and in accordance with this Arrangement, whether directly or by deduction, on profits or income from sources within the United Kingdom shall be allowed as a credit against any Botswana tax computed by reference to the same profits or income by reference to which the United Kingdom tax is computed. Provided that in the case of a dividend the credit shall only take into account such tax in respect thereof as is additional to any tax payable by the company on the profits out of which the dividend is paid and is ultimately borne by the recipient without reference to any tax so payable.

(*b*) Where a company which is a resident of the United Kingdom pays a dividend to a company resident in Botswana which controls directly or indirectly at least 10 per cent of the voting power in the first-mentioned company, the credit shall take into account (in addition to any United Kingdom tax for which credit may be allowed under (*a*) of this sub-paragraph) the United Kingdom tax payable by that first-mentioned company in respect of the profits out of which such dividend is paid."

ARTICLE 2

(1) This Agreement shall enter into force when the last of all such things shall have been done in the United Kingdom and Botswana as are necessary to give the Agreement the force of law in the United Kingdom and Botswana respectively.

(2) Upon the entry into force of this Agreement in accordance with paragraph (1) the new sub-paragraph (3) of paragraph 6 of the Arrangement and the new sub-paragraphs (1) and (2) of paragraph 14 thereof shall have effect immediately.

IN WITNESS WHEREOF the undersigned, duly authorised thereto, have signed this Agreement.

DONE in duplicate at Gaborone this Ninth day of April 1970.

For the Government of the United Kingdom of Great Britain and Northern Ireland:	For the Government of the Republic of Botswana:
DAVID ANDERSON	J. G. HASKINS

EXPLANATORY NOTE

(*This Note is not part of the Order.*)

This Agreement makes two amendments to the Arrangement between the United Kingdom and Botswana which is scheduled to the Double Taxation Relief (Taxes on Income) (Bechuanaland Protectorate) Order 1949.

First it provides that the exemption of dividends from any tax chargeable in addition to the tax on the paying company's profits is not to be allowed in certain cases where the shareholder is a company having a substantial holding in the paying company. The restriction does not apply to dividends on shares acquired for *bona fide* commercial reasons.

Secondly, it amends paragraph 14 of the 1949 Arrangement in its application to dividends by providing that credit for tax on the profits out of which dividends are paid, whether that tax is deducted from the dividends or not, is to be given only where the recipient is a company which holds not less than 10 per cent of the voting power in the paying company.

The Agreement applies to dividends paid after the date on which it enters into force.

1970 No. 954

CIVIL AVIATION

The Air Navigation Order 1970

Made - - -	26*th June* 1970
Laid before Parliament	13*th July* 1970
Coming into Operation—	
(*a*) *for making regulations*	15*th July* 1970
(*b*) *for all other purposes*	31*st July* 1970

ARRANGEMENT OF ORDER

CITATION, COMMENCEMENT AND REVOCATION

PART IV

AIRCRAFT CREW AND LICENSING

PART V

OPERATION OF AIRCRAFT

PART VI

FATIGUE OF CREW

At the Court at Buckingham Palace, the 26th day of June 1970

Present,

The Queen's Most Excellent Majesty in Council

Her Majesty in exercise of the powers conferred upon Her by sections 8, 41, 57, 58, 59 and 61 of the Civil Aviation Act 1949(**a**), and section 20 of the Civil Aviation Act 1968(**b**), and of all other powers enabling Her in that behalf, is pleased, by and with the advice of Her Privy Council, to order, and it is hereby ordered, as follows:

(**a**) 1949 c. 67. (**b**) 1968 c. 61.

CITATION, COMMENCEMENT AND REVOCATION

Citation and commencement

1.—(1) This Order may be cited as the Air Navigation Order 1970.

(2) This Order shall come into operation—

(*a*) on 15th July 1970, for the purpose of enabling the Board to make regulations thereunder and

(*b*) on 31st July 1970, for all other purposes.

Revocation

2.—(1) Subject to the following provisions of this Article, the following Orders are hereby revoked, that is to say—

The Air Navigation Order 1966(**a**).
The Air Navigation (Amendment) Order 1966(**b**).
The Air Navigation (Second Amendment) Order 1967(**c**).
The Air Navigation (Third Amendment) Order 1968(**d**).
The Air Navigation (Fourth Amendment) Order 1969(**e**).
The Air Navigation (Fifth Amendment) Order 1970(**f**).

(2) (*a*) Section 38(2) of the Interpretation Act 1889(**g**) (which relates to the effect of repeals) shall apply to this Order as if this Order were an Act of Parliament and as if the Orders revoked by paragraph (1) of this Article were Acts of Parliament thereby repealed.

(*b*) This Order shall apply to or in relation to any certificate, licence, approval, permission, exemption, authority, log book, record or other document issued, granted, made or having effect under any Order revoked by this Order, as it applies to a certificate, licence, approval, permission, exemption, authority, log book, record or other document issued, granted or made under this Order.

(*c*) Any certificate, licence, approval, permission, exemption, authority or other document issued, granted or having effect under any Order revoked by this Order in force at the date of the coming into operation of this Order shall, subject to the provisions of Article 58 of this Order, remain in force and shall have effect for the purposes of this Order as if it had been granted under the corresponding provisions thereof:

Provided that any such document which is expressed to remain in force for a definite period shall remain in force, unless renewed, only until the expiration of that period.

PART I

REGISTRATION AND MARKING OF AIRCRAFT

Aircraft to be registered

3.—(1) An aircraft shall not fly over the United Kingdom unless it is registered in:

(*a*) some part of the Commonwealth; or

(*b*) a Contracting State; or

(**a**) S.I. 1966/1184 (1966 III, p. 3073).
(**b**) S.I. 1966/1408 (1966 III, p. 3769).
(**c**) S.I. 1967/1678 (1967 III, p. 4592).
(**d**) S.I. 1968/1857 (1968 III, p. 4883).
(**e**) S.I. 1969/1082 (1969 II, p. 3153).
(**f**) S.I. 1970/156 (1970 I, p. 709).
(**g**) 1889 c. 63.

(c) some other country in relation to which there is in force an agreement between Her Majesty's Government in the United Kingdom and the Government of that country which makes provision for the flight over the United Kingdom of aircraft registered in that country:

Provided that:

(i) a glider may fly unregistered, and shall be deemed to be registered in the United Kingdom for the purposes of Articles 12, 13, 18 and 29 of this Order, on any flight which:

(a) begins and ends in the United Kingdom without passing over any other country, and

(b) is not for the purpose of public transport or aerial work;

(ii) any aircraft may fly unregistered on any flight which:

(a) begins and ends in the United Kingdom without passing over any other country, and

(b) is in accordance with the "B Conditions" set forth in Schedule 2 to this Order;

(iii) this paragraph shall not apply to any kite or captive balloon.

(2) If an aircraft flies over the United Kingdom in contravention of paragraph (1) of this Article in such manner or circumstances that if the aircraft had been registered in the United Kingdom an offence against this Order or any regulations made thereunder would have been committed, the like offence shall be deemed to have been committed in respect of that aircraft.

Registration of aircraft in the United Kingdom

4.—(1) The Board shall be the authority for the registration of aircraft in the United Kingdom.

(2) Subject to the provisions of this Article, an aircraft shall not be registered or continue to be registered in the United Kingdom if it appears to the Board that:

(a) the aircraft is registered anywhere outside the United Kingdom and that such registration does not cease by operation of law upon the aircraft being registered in the United Kingdom; or

(b) an unqualified person is entitled as owner to any legal or beneficial interest in the aircraft or any share therein; or

(c) the aircraft could more suitably be registered in some other part of the Commonwealth; or

(d) it would be inexpedient in the public interest for the aircraft to be or to continue to be registered in the United Kingdom.

(3) The following persons and no others shall be qualified to be the owner of a legal or beneficial interest in an aircraft registered in the United Kingdom or a share therein:

(a) the Crown in right of Her Majesty's Government in the United Kingdom;

(b) British subjects and citizens of the Republic of Ireland;

(c) British protected persons;

(d) bodies incorporated in some part of the Commonwealth, and having their principal place of business in any part of the Commonwealth;

(e) firms carrying on business in Scotland.

In this sub-paragraph "firm" has the same meaning as in the Partnership Act 1890**(a)**.

(a) 1890 c. 39.

(4) If an unqualified person residing or having a place of business in the United Kingdom is entitled as owner to a legal or beneficial interest in an aircraft, or a share therein, the Board, upon being satisfied that the aircraft may otherwise be properly so registered, may register the aircraft in the United Kingdom. The person aforesaid shall not cause or permit the aircraft, while it is registered in pursuance of this paragraph, to be used for the purpose of public transport or aerial work.

(5) If an aircraft is chartered by demise to a person qualified as aforesaid the Board may, whether or not an unqualified person is entitled as owner to a legal or beneficial interest therein, register the aircraft in the United Kingdom in the name of the charterer upon being satisfied that the aircraft may otherwise be properly so registered, and subject to the provisions of this Article the aircraft may remain so registered during the continuation of the charter.

(6) Application for the registration of an aircraft in the United Kingdom shall be made in writing to the Board, and shall include or be accompanied by such particulars and evidence relating to the aircraft and the ownership and chartering thereof as they may require to enable them to determine whether the aircraft may properly be registered in the United Kingdom and to issue the certificate referred to in paragraph (8) of this Article. In particular, the application shall include the proper description of the aircraft according to column 4 of the "General Classification of Aircraft" set forth in Part A of Schedule 1 to this Order.

(7) Upon receiving an application for the registration of an aircraft in the United Kingdom and being satisfied that the aircraft may properly be so registered, the Board shall register the aircraft, wherever it may be, and shall include in the register the following particulars:

(*a*) the number of the certificate;

(*b*) the nationality mark of the aircraft, and the registration mark assigned to it by the Board;

(*c*) the name of the constructor of the aircraft and its designation;

(*d*) the serial number of the aircraft;

(*e*) (i) the name and address of every person who is entitled as owner to a legal interest in the aircraft or a share therein, or, in the case of an aircraft which is the subject of a hire-purchase agreement, the name and address of the hirer; and

(ii) in the case of an aircraft registered in pursuance of paragraphs (4) or (5) of this Article, an indication that it is so registered.

(8) The Board shall furnish to the person in whose name the aircraft is registered (hereinafter in this Article referred to as "the registered owner") a certificate of registration, which shall include the foregoing particulars and the date on which the certificate was issued:

Provided that the Board shall not be required to furnish a certificate of registration if the registered owner is the holder of an aircraft dealer's certificate granted under this Order who has made to the Board and has not withdrawn a statement of his intention that the aircraft is to fly only in accordance with the "C Conditions" set forth in Schedule 2 to this Order, and in that case the aircraft shall fly only in accordance with those Conditions.

(9) The Board may grant to any person an aircraft dealer's certificate if they are satisfied that he has a place of business in the United Kingdom for buying and selling aircraft.

(10) Subject to paragraphs (4) and (5) of this Article, if at any time after an aircraft has been registered in the United Kingdom an unqualified person becomes entitled as owner to a legal or beneficial interest in the aircraft or a share therein, the registration of the aircraft shall thereupon become void and the certificate of registration shall forthwith be returned by the registered owner to the Board for cancellation.

(11) Any person who is the registered owner of an aircraft registered in the United Kingdom shall forthwith inform the Board in writing of:

(*a*) any change in the particulars which were furnished to the Board upon application being made for the registration of the aircraft;

(*b*) the destruction of the aircraft, or its permanent withdrawal from use;

(*c*) in the case of an aircraft registered in pursuance of paragraph (5) of this Article, the termination of the demise charter.

(12) Any person who becomes the owner of an aircraft registered in the United Kingdom shall forthwith inform the Board in writing to that effect.

(13) The Board may, whenever it appears to them necessary or appropriate to do so for giving effect to this Part of this Order or for bringing up to date or otherwise correcting the particulars entered on the register, amend the register or, if they think fit, may cancel the registration of the aircraft, and shall cancel that registration if they are satisfied that there has been a change in the ownership of the aircraft.

(14) The Board may, by regulations, adapt or modify the foregoing provisions of this Article as they deem necessary or expedient for the purpose of providing for the temporary transfer of aircraft to or from the United Kingdom register, either generally or in relation to a particular case or class of cases.

(15) In this Article references to an interest in an aircraft do not include references to an interest in an aircraft to which a person is entitled only by virtue of his membership of a flying club and the reference in paragraph (11) of this Article to the registered owner of an aircraft includes in the case of a deceased person, his legal personal representative, and in the case of a body corporate which has been dissolved, its successor.

(16) Nothing in this Article shall require the Board to cancel the registration of an aircraft if in their opinion it would be inexpedient in the public interest to do so.

Nationality and registration marks

5.—(1) An aircraft (other than an aircraft permitted by or under this Order to fly without being registered) shall not fly unless it bears painted thereon or affixed thereto, in the manner required by the law of the country in which it is registered, the nationality and registration marks required by that law.

(2) The marks to be borne by aircraft registered in the United Kingdom shall comply with Part B of Schedule 1 to this Order.

(3) An aircraft shall not bear any marks which purport to indicate:

(*a*) that the aircraft is registered in a country in which it is not in fact registered; or

(*b*) that the aircraft is a State aircraft of a particular country if it is not in fact such an aircraft, unless the appropriate authority of that country has sanctioned the bearing of such marks.

PART II

AIR OPERATORS' CERTIFICATES

Issue, revocation, etc., of air operators' certificates

6.—(1) The Board shall appoint an official of their Department to be the Director of Aviation Safety for civil aviation (hereafter in this Article referred to as "the Director"). The Board may also appoint officials of their Department to be deputies to the Director to perform the functions of the Director under this Article whenever the Board so instruct. The Board may at any time revoke the appointment of any person as Director or as his deputy.

(2) An aircraft registered in the United Kingdom, and having a maximum total weight authorised of more than 5,000 lb., shall not fly on any flight for the purpose of public transport, otherwise than under and in accordance with the terms of an air operator's certificate granted to the operator of the aircraft under paragraph (3) of this Article, certifying that the holder of the certificate is competent to secure that aircraft operated by him on such flights as that in question are operated safely.

(3) The Director shall grant to any person applying therefor an air operator's certificate if he is satisfied that that person is competent, having regard in particular to his previous conduct and experience, his equipment, organisation, staffing, maintenance and other arrangements, to secure the safe operation of aircraft of the types specified in the certificate on flights of the description and for the purposes so specified. The certificate may be granted subject to such conditions as the Director thinks fit, and, subject to the provisions of paragraph (4) of this Article, shall remain in force for the period specified in the certificate.

(4) Subject to the provisions of paragraph (5) of this Article the Director may, if he thinks fit, suspend or revoke any air operator's certificate, and may vary any such certificate whether or not application has been made for the variation.

(5) The Director shall not suspend, revoke or vary any air operator's certificate, except in accordance with an application made by the holder thereof, unless:

(*a*) the Director has previously given the holder of the certificate such written notice in such a manner and at such a time as may be prescribed, containing concise particulars of the Director's proposal and the reasons for it;

(*b*) the notice has expired; and

(*c*) the Director has considered any representations which the holder of the certificate may have made to him in writing before the expiration of the notice:

Provided that the foregoing requirements of this paragraph need not be complied with in any case in which the Director certifies that in the interests of the safety of air navigation it is essential for the revocation, suspension or variation of the certificate to take effect immediately.

(6) The Director shall serve the applicant for or holder of the certificate (as the case may be) with written notice of his decision as to that certificate and shall within such period as may be prescribed furnish the applicant for or holder of the certificate with reasons in writing for his decision:

(*a*) if he refuses to grant the certificate, or grants it subject to a condition to which the applicant has not agreed; or (*b*) if he suspends, revokes or varies the certificate otherwise than in accordance with an application by the holder.

(7) Any applicant for or holder of an air operator's certificate who is aggrieved by a decision of the Director as to that application or certificate may, within such period and in such manner as may be prescribed, appeal to a person to be appointed for the purpose:

(*a*) where the appellant has his principal place of business in Scotland, by the Lord President of the Court of Session,

(*b*) where the appellant has his principal place of business in Northern Ireland, by the Lord Chief Justice of Northern Ireland, and

(*c*) in any other case by the Lord Chancellor,

sitting with such technical assessors, if any, as may be so appointed. The Board may by regulations make provision as to the giving of notice of appeal, the liability of any of the parties in respect of costs or expenses incurred in connection therewith, and generally for the procedure relating to appeals.

(8) In this Article "holder", in relation to a certificate, includes the holder of a certificate which has been revoked or suspended.

PART III

AIRWORTHINESS AND EQUIPMENT OF AIRCRAFT

Certificate of airworthiness to be in force

7.—(1) An aircraft shall not fly unless there is in force in respect thereof a certificate of airworthiness duly issued or rendered valid under the law of the country in which the aircraft is registered, and any conditions subject to which the certificate was issued or rendered valid are complied with:

Provided that the foregoing prohibition shall not apply to flights, beginning and ending in the United Kingdom without passing over any other country, of:

(*a*) a glider, if it is not being used for the public transport of passengers or aerial work;

(*b*) a balloon, if it is not being used for the public transport of passengers;

(*c*) a kite;

(*d*) an aircraft flying in accordance with the "A Conditions" or the "B Conditions" set forth in Schedule 2 to this Order;

(*e*) an aircraft flying in accordance with the conditions of a permit to fly issued by the Board in respect of that aircraft.

(2) In the case of an aircraft registered in the United Kingdom the certificate of airworthiness referred to in paragraph (1) of this Article shall be a certificate issued or rendered valid in accordance with the provisions of Article 8 of this Order.

Issue and renewal of certificates of airworthiness

8.—(1) The Board may issue in respect of any aircraft a certificate of airworthiness if they are satisfied that the aircraft is fit to fly having regard to:

(*a*) the design, construction, workmanship and materials of the aircraft (including in particular any engines fitted therein), and of any equipment carried in the aircraft which they consider necessary for the airworthiness of the aircraft; and (*b*) the results of flying trials, and such other tests of the aircraft as they may require:

Provided that, if the Board have issued a certificate of airworthiness in respect of an aircraft which, in their opinion, is a prototype aircraft or a modification of a prototype aircraft, they may dispense with flying trials in the case of any other aircraft if they are satisfied that it conforms to such prototype or modification.

(2) Every certificate of airworthiness shall specify such categories as are, in the opinion of the Board, appropriate to the aircraft in accordance with Schedule 3 to this Order and the certificate shall be issued subject to the condition that the aircraft shall be flown only for the purposes indicated in the said Schedule in relation to those categories.

(3) The Board may issue the certificate of airworthiness subject to such other conditions relating to the airworthiness of the aircraft as they think fit.

(4) The certificate of airworthiness may designate the performance group to which the aircraft belongs for the purposes of the requirements referred to in Article 27(1) of this Order.

(5) The Board may, subject to such conditions as they think fit, issue a certificate of validation rendering valid for the purposes of this Order a certificate of airworthiness issued in respect of any aircraft under the law of any country other than the United Kingdom.

(6) Subject to the provisions of this Article and of Article 58 of this Order, a certificate of airworthiness or validation issued under this Article shall remain in force for such period as may be specified therein, and may be renewed from time to time by the Board for such further period as they think fit.

(7) A certificate of airworthiness or a certificate of validation issued in respect of an aircraft shall cease to be in force:

(*a*) if the aircraft, or such of its equipment as is necessary for the airworthiness of the aircraft is overhauled, repaired or modified, or if any part of the aircraft or of such equipment is removed or is replaced, otherwise than in a manner and with material of a type approved by the Board either generally or in relation to a class of aircraft or to the particular aircraft; or

(*b*) until the completion of any inspection of the aircraft or of any such equipment as aforesaid, being an inspection required by the Board to be made for the purpose of ascertaining whether the aircraft remains airworthy.

(8) Without prejudice to any other provision of this Order the Board may, for the purposes of this Article, accept reports furnished to them by a person whom they may approve, either absolutely or subject to such conditions as they think fit, as qualified to furnish such reports.

(9) The Board shall cause to be prepared and preserved in relation to each aircraft registered in the United Kingdom a record enabling the aircraft (including in particular its engines) and such of its equipment as they may have considered necessary for the airworthiness of the aircraft in issuing, varying or rendering valid a certificate of airworthiness, to be identified with the drawings and other documents on the basis of which the certificate was issued, varied or rendered valid as the case may be. All equipment so identified shall for the purposes of this Order be deemed to be equipment necessary for the airworthiness of the aircraft. The Board shall cause such record to be produced for examination upon request being made therefor at any reasonable time by any person having, in the opinion of the Board, reasonable grounds for requiring to examine it.

Certification of maintenance

9.—(1) An aircraft registered in the United Kingdom shall not fly for the purpose of public transport or dropping or projecting any material for agricultural, public health or similar purposes unless:

(*a*) the aircraft (including in particular its engines), together with its equipment and radio station, is maintained in accordance with maintenance schedules approved by the Board in relation to that aircraft;

(*b*) there are in force in respect of that aircraft certificates (in this Order referred to as "certificates of maintenance") issued in accordance with the provisions of this Article and certifying that maintenance has been carried out in accordance with such maintenance schedules:

Provided that an aircraft may, notwithstanding that sub-paragraphs (*a*) and (*b*) have not been complied with in relation to the radio station therein, fly for the sole purpose of enabling persons to be trained to perform duties in aircraft.

(2) Every certificate of maintenance shall come into force upon being issued and shall cease to be in force upon the expiration of the period of its validity in elapsed time or flying time, whichever may be the earlier, as specified in the relevant maintenance schedule, and the period of validity of the certificate shall be recorded in the certificate at the time when it is issued.

(3) A certificate of maintenance may be issued for the purposes of this Article only by:

(*a*) the holder of a licence granted under this Order as an aircraft maintenance engineer being a licence of a category appropriate in accordance with Article 11 of and Schedule 4 to this Order; or

(*b*) the holder of a licence as such an engineer granted under the law of a country other than the United Kingdom and rendered valid under this Order, in accordance with the privileges endorsed on the licence; or

(*c*) the holder of a licence as such an engineer granted under the law of any such country as may be prescribed, in accordance with the privileges endorsed on the licence and subject to any conditions which may be prescribed; or

(*d*) a person whom the Board have authorised to issue a certificate of maintenance in a particular case, and in accordance with that authority:

Provided that, upon approving a maintenance schedule, the Board may direct that certificates of maintenance relating to that schedule, or to any part thereof specified in their direction, may be issued only by the holder of such a licence as is so specified.

(4) Certificates of maintenance shall be issued in duplicate. One of the duplicates shall, during the period of validity of the certificate, be carried in the aircraft when Article 55 of this Order so requires, and the other shall be kept by the operator elsewhere than in the aircraft.

(5) On the termination of every flight by an aircraft registered in the United Kingdom for any of the purposes specified in paragraph (1) of this Article, the commander of the aircraft shall enter in a technical log:

(*a*) the times at which the flight began and ended; and

(*b*) particulars of any defect in any part of the aircraft or its equipment which is known to him, being a part to which a maintenance schedule relates, or, if no such defect is known to him, an entry to that effect;

and shall sign and date such entries:

Provided that in the case of a number of consecutive flights beginning and ending on the same day and with the same person as commander of the aircraft, the commander of an aircraft:

(i) flying for the purpose of public transport where each of the aforesaid consecutive flights begins at the same aerodrome and ends at that aerodrome, or

(ii) flying for the purpose of dropping or projecting any material for agricultural, public health or similar purposes,

may, except where he becomes aware of a defect during an earlier flight, make the entries as aforesaid in a technical log at the end of the last of such consecutive flights.

(6) Upon the rectification of any defect which has been entered in a technical log in accordance with paragraph (5) of this Article, a copy of the certificate of compliance required by Article 10 of this Order in respect of the work done for the rectification of the defect shall be entered in the technical log in such a position or manner as to be readily identifiable with the entry of the defect to which it relates.

(7) The technical log referred to in paragraphs (5) and (6) of this Article shall be carried in the aircraft when Article 55 of this Order so requires and copies of the entries referred to in those paragraphs shall be kept on the ground.

(8) Subject to the provisions of Article 57 of this Order every certificate of maintenance shall be preserved by the operator of the aircraft for a period of two years following the expiry of the period of validity of the certificate and for such further period as the Board may require in any particular case.

Inspection, overhaul, repair, replacement and modification

10.—(1) An aircraft registered in the United Kingdom, being an aircraft in respect of which a certificate of airworthiness issued or rendered valid under this Order is in force, shall not fly if any part of the aircraft or of such of its equipment as is necessary for the airworthiness of the aircraft, has been overhauled, repaired, replaced or modified, or has been inspected as provided in Article 8(7)(*b*) of this Order, unless there is in force a certificate of compliance issued in accordance with this Article and relating to the overhaul, repair, replacement, modification or inspection, as the case may be:

Provided that if a repair or replacement of a part of an aircraft or its equipment is carried out when the aircraft is at such place that it is not reasonably practicable:

(*a*) for the repair or replacement to be carried out in such a manner that a certificate of compliance can be issued under this Article in respect thereof, or

(*b*) for such a certificate to be issued while the aircraft is at that place,

the aircraft may fly to a place at which such a certificate can be issued, being the nearest place:

(i) to which the aircraft can, in the reasonable opinion of the commander thereof, safely fly by a route for which it is properly equipped, and

(ii) to which it is reasonable to fly having regard to any hazards to the liberty or health of any person on board;

and in such case the commander of the aircraft shall cause written particulars of the flight, and the reasons for making it, to be given to the Board within ten days thereafter.

(2) Neither:

(*a*) equipment provided in compliance with Schedule 5 to this Order (except paragraph (3) thereof), nor (*b*) in the case of a public transport aircraft, radio apparatus provided for use therein or in any survival craft carried therein, whether or not such apparatus is provided in compliance with this Order or any regulation made thereunder,

shall be installed, or placed on board for use, in an aircraft registered in the United Kingdom after being overhauled, repaired or modified, unless there is in force in respect thereof at the time when it is installed or placed on board a certificate of compliance issued in accordance with this Article and relating to the overhaul, repair or modification, as the case may be.

(3) For the purposes of this Order, "certificate of compliance" means a certificate that the part of the aircraft or its equipment has been overhauled, repaired, replaced or modified, as the case may be, in a manner and with material of a type approved by the Board either generally or in relation to a class of aircraft or the particular aircraft and which identifies the overhaul, repair, replacement or modification to which it relates and includes particulars of the work done; and in relation to an inspection required by the Board, that the inspection has been made in accordance with the requirement of the Board and that any consequential repair or replacement has been carried out as aforesaid.

(4) A certificate of compliance may be issued for the purposes of this Article only by—

(*a*) the holder of a licence granted under this Order as an aircraft maintenance engineer being a licence of a category appropriate in accordance with Article 11 of and Schedule 4 to this Order; or

(*b*) the holder of a licence as such an engineer granted under the law of a country other than the United Kingdom and rendered valid under this Order, in accordance with the privileges endorsed on the licence; or

(*c*) the holder of a licence as such an engineer granted under the law of any such country as may be prescribed, in accordance with the privileges endorsed on the licence and subject to any conditions which may be prescribed; or

(*d*) a person approved by the Board as being competent to issue such certificates; or

(*e*) a person whom the Board have authorised to issue the certificate in a particular case; or

(*f*) in relation only to the adjustment and compensation of direct reading magnetic compasses, the holder of an Airline Transport Pilot's Licence (Aeroplanes), a Senior Commercial Pilot's Licence (Aeroplanes) or a Flight Navigator's Licence.

(5) Subject to the provisions of Article 57 of this Order, if the aircraft to which a certificate of compliance relates is a public transport aircraft or an aerial work aircraft, the certificate of compliance shall be preserved by the operator of the aircraft for the period of time for which he is required to preserve the log book relating to the same part of the aircraft or to the same equipment or apparatus as the case may be. In the case of any other aircraft the certificate shall be preserved by the operator of the aircraft for a period of two years.

(6) In this Article, the expression "repair" includes in relation to a compass the adjustment and compensation thereof and the expression "repaired" shall be construed accordingly.

Licensing of maintenance engineers

11.—(1) The Board may grant to any person a licence to act for the purposes of this Order as an aircraft maintenance engineer, of one of the categories specified in Schedule 4 to this Order, upon their being satisfied that the applicant is a fit and proper person to hold the licence and is qualified by his knowledge and experience to do so, and for that purpose the applicant shall furnish such evidence and undergo such examinations and tests as the Board may require of him. The Board may include a rating in the licence limiting the licence to particular types of aircraft or equipment.

(2) A licence of any category shall, subject to any rating as aforesaid, entitle the holder to issue certificates of maintenance, certificates of compliance or certificates of fitness for flight in accordance with Schedule 4 to this Order.

(3) A licence and a rating shall, subject to the provisions of Article 58 of this Order, remain in force for the periods specified therein, not exceeding twelve months, but may be renewed by the Board from time to time upon their being satisfied that the applicant is a fit and proper person and is qualified as aforesaid.

(4) The Board may issue a certificate rendering valid for the purposes of this Order any licence as an aircraft maintenance engineer or aircraft radio maintenance engineer granted under the law of any country other than the United Kingdom. Such certificate may be issued subject to such conditions, and for such period, as the Board think fit.

(5) Upon receiving a licence granted under this Article, the holder shall forthwith sign his name thereon in ink with his ordinary signature.

Equipment of aircraft

12.—(1) An aircraft shall not fly unless it is so equipped as to comply with the law of the country in which it is registered, and to enable lights and markings to be displayed, and signals to be made, in accordance with this Order and any regulations made thereunder.

(2) In the case of aircraft registered in the United Kingdom the equipment required to be provided (in addition to any other equipment required by or under this Order) shall be that specified in such parts of Schedule 5 to this Order as are applicable in the circumstances and shall comply with the provisions of that Schedule. The equipment, except that specified in paragraph (3) of the said Schedule, shall be of a type approved by the Board either generally or in relation to a class of aircraft or in relation to that aircraft and shall be installed in a manner so approved.

(3) In any particular case the Board may direct that an aircraft registered in the United Kingdom shall carry such additional or special equipment or supplies as they may specify for the purpose of facilitating the navigation of the aircraft, the carrying out of search and rescue operations, or the survival of the persons carried in the aircraft.

(4) The equipment carried in compliance with this Article shall be so installed or stowed and kept stowed, and so maintained and adjusted, as to be readily accessible and capable of being used by the person for whose use it is intended.

(5) The position of equipment provided for emergency use shall be indicated by clear markings in or on the aircraft. In particular there shall be exhibited in a prominent position in every passenger compartment of every public transport aircraft registered in the United Kingdom a notice stating where the lifejackets (if any) are to be found, and containing instructions as to how they are to be used.

(6) All equipment installed or carried in an aircraft, whether or not in compliance with this Article, shall be so installed or stowed and kept stowed and so maintained and adjusted as not to be a source of danger in itself or to impair the airworthiness of the aircraft or the proper functioning of any equipment or services necessary for the safety of the aircraft.

(7) Without prejudice to paragraph (2) of this Article, all navigational equipment (other than radio apparatus) of any of the following types, namely:

(*a*) equipment capable of establishing the aircraft's position in relation to its position at some earlier time by computing and applying the resultant of the acceleration and gravitational forces acting upon it, and

(*b*) equipment capable of establishing automatically the altitude and relative bearing of selected celestial bodies,

when carried in an aircraft registered in the United Kingdom (whether or not in compliance with this Order or any regulations made thereunder) shall be of a type approved by the Board either generally or in relation to a class of aircraft or in relation to that aircraft and shall be installed in a manner so approved.

(8) This Article shall not apply in relation to radio apparatus except that specified in Schedule 5 to this Order.

Radio equipment of aircraft

13.—(1) An aircraft shall not fly unless it is so equipped with radio apparatus as to comply with the law of the country in which the aircraft is registered and to enable communications to be made, and the aircraft to be navigated, in accordance with the provisions of this Order and any regulations made thereunder.

(2) In the case of aircraft registered in the United Kingdom, the aircraft shall be equipped with radio apparatus in accordance with Schedule 6 to this Order.

(3) In any particular case the Board may direct that an aircraft registered in the United Kingdom shall carry such additional or special radio apparatus as they may specify for the purpose of facilitating the navigation of the aircraft, the carrying out of search and rescue operations or the survival of the persons carried in the aircraft.

(4) Subject to such exceptions as may be prescribed the radio apparatus provided in compliance with this Article in an aircraft registered in the United Kingdom shall always be maintained in serviceable condition.

(5) All radio apparatus installed in an aircraft registered in the United Kingdom (whether or not in compliance with this Order or any regulations made thereunder) shall be of a type approved by the Board in relation to the purpose for which it is to be used, and shall, except in the case of a glider which is permitted by Article 3(1) of this Order to fly unregistered, be installed in a manner approved by the Board. Neither the apparatus nor the manner in which it is installed shall be modified except with the approval of the Board.

Aircraft, engine and propeller log books

14.—(1) In addition to any other log books required by or under this Order, the following log books shall be kept in respect of every public transport aircraft and aerial work aircraft registered in the United Kingdom:

(*a*) an aircraft log book; and

(*b*) a separate log book in respect of each engine fitted in the aircraft; and (*c*) a separate log book in respect of each variable pitch propeller fitted to the aircraft.

The log books shall include the particulars respectively specified in Schedule 7 to this Order.

(2) Each entry in the log book shall be made as soon as is practicable after the occurrence to which it relates, but in no event more than seven days after the expiration of the certificate of maintenance (if any) in force in respect of the aircraft at the time of the occurrence.

(3) Entries in a log book may refer to other documents, which shall be clearly identified, and any other document so referred to shall be deemed, for the purposes of this Order, to be part of the log book.

(4) It shall be the duty of the operator of every aircraft in respect of which log books are required to be kept as aforesaid to keep them or cause them to be kept in accordance with the foregoing provisions of this Article.

(5) Subject to the provisions of Article 57 of this Order every log book shall be preserved by the operator of the aircraft until a date two years after the aircraft, the engine or the variable pitch propeller, as the case may be, has been destroyed or has been permanently withdrawn from use.

Aircraft weight schedule

15.—(1) Every flying machine and glider in respect of which a certificate of airworthiness issued or rendered valid under this Order is in force shall be weighed, and the position of its centre of gravity determined, at such times and in such manner as the Board may require in the case of that aircraft.

(2) Upon the aircraft being weighed as aforesaid the operator of the aircraft shall prepare a weight schedule showing the basic weight of the aircraft, that is to say, the weight of the aircraft empty together with the weight of unusable fuel and unusable oil in the aircraft and of such items of equipment as are indicated in the weight schedule; and showing the position of the centre of gravity of the aircraft when the aircraft contains only the items included in the basic weight.

(3) Subject to the provisions of Article 57 of this Order the weight schedule shall be preserved by the operator of the aircraft until the expiry of a period of six months following the next occasion on which the aircraft is weighed for the purposes of this Article.

Access and inspection for airworthiness purposes

16. The Board may cause such inspections, investigations, tests, experiments and flight trials to be made as they deem necessary for the purposes of this Part of this Order and any person authorised to do so in writing by the Board may at any reasonable time inspect any part of, or material intended to be incorporated in or used in the manufacture or any part of, an aircraft or its equipment or any documents relating thereto and may for that purpose go upon any aerodrome or aircraft factory.

PART IV

AIRCRAFT CREW AND LICENSING

Composition of crew of aircraft

17.—(1) An aircraft shall not fly unless it carries a flight crew of the number and description required by the law of the country in which it is registered.

(2) An aircraft registered in the United Kingdom shall carry a flight crew adequate in number and description to ensure the safety of the aircraft and of at least the number and description specified in the certificate of airworthiness issued or rendered valid under this Order or, if no certificate of airworthiness is required under this Order to be in force, the certificate of airworthiness, if any, last in force under this Order, in respect of that aircraft.

(3) A flying machine registered in the United Kingdom and flying for the purpose of public transport, having a maximum total weight authorised of 12,500 lb. or more, shall carry not less than two pilots as members of the flight crew thereof.

(4) An aircraft registered in the United Kingdom engaged on a flight for the purpose of public transport shall carry a flight navigator as a member of the flight crew if on the route or any diversion therefrom, being a route or diversion planned before take-off, the aircraft is intended to be more than 500 nautical miles from the point of take-off measured along the route to be flown, and to pass over part of an area specified in Schedule 8 to this Order. The flight navigator carried in compliance with this paragraph shall be carried in addition to any person who is carried in accordance with this Article to perform other duties.

(5) An aircraft registered in the United Kingdom which is required by the provisions of Article 13 of this Order to be equipped with radio communication apparatus shall carry a flight radio operator as a member of the flight crew, who, if he is required to operate radiotelegraph apparatus, shall be carried in addition to any other person who is carried in accordance with this Article to perform other duties.

(6) If it appears to them to be expedient to do so in the interests of safety, the Board may direct any particular operator that the aircraft operated by him or any such aircraft shall not fly in such circumstances as the Board may specify unless those aircraft carry in addition to the flight crew required to be carried therein by the foregoing provisions of this Article such additional persons as members of the flight crew as they may specify in the direction.

(7) (*a*) When an aircraft registered in the United Kingdom carries twenty or more passengers on a flight for the purpose of public transport, the crew of the aircraft shall include persons carried for the purpose of performing in the interest of the safety of passengers duties to be assigned by the operator or the person in command of the aircraft, but who shall not act as members of the flight crew. The number of such persons carried when the aircraft is carrying the number of passengers specified in column 1 of the table set out at the end of this sub-paragraph shall be not less than the number set opposite that number in column 2 of that table:

Column 1	*Column* 2
20–50 passengers	1 person
51–100 ,, ...	2 persons
101–150 ,, ...	3 persons
Over 150 ,, ...	4 persons

(*b*) The Board may give a direction to the operator of any aircraft registered in the United Kingdom requiring him to include among the crew thereof whenever the aircraft is flying for the purpose of public transport at least one such person as aforesaid, notwithstanding that the aircraft may be carrying fewer than 20 passengers.

Members of flight crew—licences

18.—(1) Subject to the provisions of this Article, a person shall not act as a member of the flight crew of an aircraft registered in the United Kingdom unless he is the holder of an appropriate licence granted or rendered valid under this Order:

Provided that a person may, within the United Kingdom, act as a flight radiotelephony operator without being the holder of such a licence if—

(*a*) he does so as the pilot of a glider not flying for the purpose of public transport or aerial work, or as a person being trained in an aircraft registered in the United Kingdom to perform duties as a member of the flight crew of an aircraft; and

(*b*) he is authorised to operate the radiotelephony station by the holder of the licence granted in respect of that station under any enactment; and

(*c*) messages are transmitted only for the purposes of instruction, or of the safety or navigation of the aircraft; and

(*d*) messages are transmitted only on a frequency exceeding 60 megacycles per second assigned by the Board for use on flights on which a flight radiotelephony operator acts in one of the capacities specified in paragraph (*a*) of this proviso; and

(*e*) the transmitter is pre-set to one or more of the frequencies so assigned and cannot be adjusted in flight to any other frequency; and

(*f*) the operation of the transmitter requires the use only of external switches; and

(*g*) the stability of the frequency radiated is maintained automatically by the transmitter.

(2) Subject as aforesaid, a person shall not act as a member of the flight crew required by or under this Order to be carried in an aircraft registered outside the United Kingdom unless—

(*a*) in the case of an aircraft flying for the purpose of public transport or aerial work he is the holder of an appropriate licence granted or rendered valid under the law of the country in which the aircraft is registered; and

(*b*) in the case of any other aircraft, he is the holder of an appropriate licence granted or rendered valid under the law of the country in which the aircraft is registered or under this Order, and the Board do not in the particular case give a direction to the contrary.

(3) For the purposes of this Article a licence granted under the law of a Contracting State purporting to authorise the holder thereof to act as a member of the flight crew of an aircraft, not being a licence purporting to authorise him to act as a student pilot only, shall unless the Board in the particular case give a direction to the contrary be deemed to be a licence rendered valid under this Order but shall not entitle the holder to act as member of the flight crew of any aircraft flying for the purpose of public transport or aerial work.

(4) Notwithstanding the provisions of paragraph (1) of this Article, a person may, unless the certificate of airworthiness in force in respect of the aircraft otherwise requires, act as pilot of an aircraft registered in the United Kingdom for the purpose of undergoing training or tests—

(*a*) for the grant or renewal of a pilot's licence or for the inclusion, renewal or extension of a rating thereon or

(*b*) for admission into any of Her Majesty's naval, military or air forces, without being the holder of an appropriate licence, if the following conditions are complied with:

(i) no other person shall be carried in the aircraft or in an aircraft being towed thereby except a person carried as a member of the flight crew in compliance with this Order, a person authorised by the Board to witness the aforesaid training or tests or to conduct the aforesaid tests, or, if the pilot in command of the aircraft is the holder of an appropriate licence, a person carried for the purpose of being trained or tested as a member of the flight crew of an aircraft; and

(ii) the person acting as the pilot of the aircraft without being the holder of an appropriate licence shall not be the pilot in command of the aircraft unless within the period of six months immediately preceding he was serving as a qualified pilot of aircraft in any of Her Majesty's naval, military or air forces, and his physical condition has not, so far as he is aware, so deteriorated during that period as to render him unfit for the licence for which he intends to qualify.

(5) Notwithstanding the provisions of paragraph (1) of this Article, a person may act as a member of the flight crew of an aircraft registered in the United Kingdom without being the holder of an appropriate licence if, in so doing, he is acting in the course of his duty as a member of any of Her Majesty's naval, military or air forces.

(6) An appropriate licence for the purposes of this Article means a licence which entitles the holder to perform the functions which he undertakes in relation to the aircraft concerned and the flight on which it is engaged.

(7) This Article shall not apply to a person (other than a flight radio operator) by reason of his acting as a member of the flight crew of a glider which is not flying for the purpose of public transport or aerial work.

(8) Notwithstanding anything in this Article—

(i) the holder of a licence granted or rendered valid under this Order, being a licence endorsed to the effect that the holder does not satisfy in full the relevant international standard, shall not act as a member of the flight crew of an aircraft registered in the United Kingdom in or over the territory of a Contracting State other than the United Kingdom, except in accordance with permission granted by the competent authorities of that State;

(ii) the holder of a licence granted or rendered valid under the law of a Contracting State other than the United Kingdom, being a licence endorsed as aforesaid, shall not act as a member of the flight crew of any aircraft in or over the United Kingdom except in accordance with permission granted by the Board, whether or not the licence is or is deemed to be rendered valid under this Order.

Grant and renewal of licences to members of flight crew

19.—(1) The Board may grant licences, subject to such conditions as they think fit, of any of the following classes:

Student pilot's licence,

Private pilot's licence (aeroplanes),

Commercial pilot's licence (aeroplanes),

Senior commercial pilot's licence (aeroplanes),

Airline transport pilot's licence (aeroplanes),

Private pilot's licence (helicopters and gyroplanes),
Commercial pilot's licence (helicopters and gyroplanes),
Airline transport pilot's licence (helicopters and gyroplanes),
Private pilot's licence (balloons and airships),
Commercial pilot's licence (balloons),
Commercial pilot's licence (airships),
Commercial pilot's licence (gliders),
Flight navigator's licence,
Flight engineer's licence,
Flight radiotelephony operator's general licence,
Flight radiotelephony operator's restricted licence,
Flight radiotelegraphy operator's licence,
Flight radiotelegraphy operator's temporary licence,

upon their being satisfied that the applicant is a fit and proper person to hold the licence and is qualified by reason of his knowledge, experience, competence, skill and physical fitness to act in the capacity to which the licence relates, and for that purpose the applicant shall furnish such evidence, and undergo such examinations and tests (including in particular medical examinations) as the Board may require of him. A licence of any class shall not be granted to any person who is under the minimum age specified for that class of licence in Part A of Schedule 9 to this Order.

(2) Subject to any conditions of the licence, a licence of any class shall entitle the holder to perform the functions specified in respect of that licence in Part A of the said Schedule 9 under the heading "privileges":

Provided that—

(*a*) subject to the provisions of paragraphs (11) and (12) of this Article, Article 18(4) and Article 22(1) of this Order a person shall not be entitled to perform any of the functions specified in Part B of the said Schedule in respect of a rating unless his licence includes that rating;

(*b*) a person shall not be entitled to perform any of the functions to which his licence relates if he knows or has reason to believe that his physical condition renders him temporarily or permanently unfit to perform such function;

(*c*) the holder of a licence, other than a flight radiotelephony operator's licence, shall not be entitled to perform any of the functions to which his licence relates unless it includes a medical certificate issued and in force under paragraph (7) of this Article;

(*d*) the holder of a pilot's licence shall not be entitled to perform functions on a flight unless the licence bears a valid certificate of test or a valid certificate of experience, which certificate shall in either case be appropriate to the functions he is to perform on that flight in accordance with Part C of the said Schedule and shall otherwise comply with that Part;

(*e*) a person shall not be entitled to perform the functions to which an instrument rating (aeroplanes), flying instructor's rating, assistant flying instructor's rating, or instrument meteorological conditions rating (aeroplanes) relate unless his licence bears a certificate signed by a person authorised by the Board to sign such certificates, indicating that the holder of the licence has, within the period of 13 months in the case of an instrument rating (aeroplanes) and an assistant flying instructor's rating, and 25 months in the case of a flying instructor's rating and an instrument meteorological conditions rating (aeroplanes) preceding the day on which he performs those functions, passed a test of his ability to perform the functions to which the rating relates, being a test carried out in flight in the case of the three last-named ratings, and in the case of the first-named rating, either in flight or by means of apparatus approved by the Board in which flight conditions are simulated on the ground;

(*f*) a person who, on the last occasion when he took a test for the purposes of sub-paragraphs (*d*) or (*e*) of this paragraph, failed that test shall not be entitled to fly in the capacity for which that test would have qualified him had he passed it.

(3) The Board may, if they are satisfied that the applicant is qualified as aforesaid to act in the capacity to which the rating relates, include in a licence a rating of any of the classes specified in Part B of the said Schedule 9, and such rating shall be deemed to form part of the licence and shall entitle the holder to perform such functions as are specified in Part B of the said Schedule in respect of that rating.

(4) A licence shall, subject to the provisions of Article 58 of this Order, remain in force for the periods indicated in the licence, not exceeding those respectively specified in Schedule 9 to this Order, and may be renewed by the Board from time to time upon their being satisfied that the applicant is a fit and proper person and is qualified as aforesaid.

(5) Upon receiving a licence granted under this Article, the holder shall forthwith sign his name thereon in ink with his ordinary signature.

(6) Every applicant for and holder of a licence granted under this Article other than a flight radiotelephony operator's licence shall upon such occasions as the Board may require submit himself to medical examination by a person approved by the Board either generally or in a particular case who shall make a report to the Board in such form as the Board may require.

(7) On the basis of the medical examination referred to in paragraph (6) of this Article, the Board or any person approved by them as competent to do so may issue a medical certificate subject to such conditions as they think fit to the effect that they have assessed the holder of the licence as fit to perform the functions to which the licence relates. The certificate shall, without prejudice to proviso (*b*) to paragraph (2) of this Article, be valid for such period as is therein specified, and shall be deemed to form part of the licence;

(8) Every holder of a licence, other than a flight radiotelephony operator's licence, granted under this Article or rendered valid under Article 20 of this Order who suffers—

(*a*) any personal injury involving incapacity to undertake the functions to which his licence relates; or

(*b*) any illness involving incapacity to undertake those functions throughout a period of twenty days or more,

shall inform the Board in writing of such injury or illness, as soon as possible in the case of an injury, and as soon as the period of twenty days has elapsed in the case of illness.

(9) A licence, other than a flight radiotelephony operator's licence, granted under this Part of this Order shall be deemed to be suspended upon the occurrence of such an injury, or the elapse of such period of illness as is referred to in paragraph (8) of this Article. The suspension of the licence shall cease:

(*a*) upon the holder being medically examined under arrangements made by the Board and pronounced fit to resume his functions under the licence; or

(*b*) upon the Board exempting the holder from the requirement of a medical examination, subject to such conditions as the Board may think fit.

(10) A licence granted under this Article shall be deemed to be suspended upon the pregnancy of the holder being diagnosed and shall remain suspended until the holder has been medically examined after the pregnancy has ended and pronounced fit to resume her duties under the licence.

(11) Nothing in this Order shall be taken to prohibit the holder of a commercial pilot's, senior commercial pilot's or airline transport pilot's licence from acting as pilot in command of an aircraft carrying passengers by night by reason of the lack of a night rating in his licence.

(12) Nothing in this Order shall prohibit the holder of a pilot's licence from acting as pilot of an aircraft not exceeding 12,500 lb. maximum total weight authorised when with the authority of the Board he is testing any person in pursuance of Article 19(1) or (3) of this Order, notwithstanding that the type of aircraft in which the test is conducted is not specified in the aircraft rating included in his licence.

Validation of licences

20. The Board may issue a certificate of validation rendering valid for the purposes of this Order any licence as a member of the flight crew of aircraft granted under the law of any country other than the United Kingdom. A certificate of validation may be issued subject to such conditions and for such period as the Board think fit.

Personal flying log book

21. Every member of the flight crew of an aircraft registered in the United Kingdom and every person who engages in flying for the purpose of qualifying for the grant or renewal of a licence under this Order or undergoing tests or receiving instruction in flying for admission into any of Her Majesty's naval, military or air forces shall keep a personal flying log book in which the following particulars shall be recorded:

The name and address of the holder of a log book.

Particulars of holder's licence (if any) to act as a member of the flight crew of an aircraft.

The name and address of his employer (if any).

Particulars of all flights made as a member of the flight crew of aircraft, including—

(*a*) the date, duration and places of arrival and departure of each flight;

(*b*) the type and registration marks of the aircraft;

(*c*) the capacity in which the holder acted in flight;

(*d*) particulars of any special conditions under which the flight was conducted, including night flying and instrument flying;

(*e*) particulars of any test or examination undertaken whilst in flight.

Instruction in flying

22.—(1) A person shall not give any instruction in flying to any person flying or about to fly a flying machine for the purpose of becoming qualified for—

(a) the grant of a pilot's licence; or

(b) the inclusion in a pilot's licence of an aircraft rating entitling the holder of the licence to act as pilot of—

(i) a multi-engined aircraft, or

(ii) an aircraft of any class appearing in column 4 of the Table in Part A of Schedule 1 to this Order,

if the person under instruction has not been previously entitled under the Act, or qualified in any of Her Majesty's naval, military or air forces, to act as pilot of a multi-engined aircraft, or of an aircraft of that class as the case may be; or

(c) the inclusion or variation of any rating, other than an aircraft rating, in a pilot's licence,

unless:

(i) the person giving the instruction holds a licence, granted or rendered valid under this Order, entitling him to act as pilot in command of the aircraft for the purpose and in the circumstances under which instruction is to be given; and

(ii) such licence includes a flying instructor's rating or an assistant flying instructor's rating entitling the holder, in accordance with the privileges specified in Schedule 9 to this Order in respect of that rating, to give the instructions; and

(iii) if consideration is given for the instruction, such licence entitles the holder to act as pilot in command of an aircraft flying for the purpose of public transport:

Provided that sub-paragraph (iii) of this paragraph shall not apply if the aircraft is owned, or is operated under arrangements entered into, by a flying club of which both the person giving and the person receiving the instruction are members.

(2) For the purpose of this Article payment shall be deemed to be made for instruction if any reward is given or promised by any person to any other person in consideration of the flight being made or of the instruction being given or if the instruction is given by a person employed for reward primarily for the purpose of giving such instruction.

Glider pilot—minimum age

23. A person under the age of sixteen years shall not act as pilot in command of a glider.

PART V

OPERATION OF AIRCRAFT

Operations Manual

24.—(1) This Article shall apply to public transport aircraft registered in the United Kingdom except aircraft used for the time being solely for flights not intended to exceed 60 minutes in duration, which are either—

(a) flights solely for training persons to perform duties in an aircraft, or

(b) flights intended to begin and end at the same aerodrome.

(2) (a) The operator of every aircraft to which this Article applies shall—

(i) make available to each member of his operating staff an operations manual, and

(ii) ensure that each copy of the operations manual is kept up to date, and

(iii) ensure that on each flight every member of the crew has access to a copy of every part of the operations manual which is relevant to his duties on the flight.

(*b*) Each operations manual shall contain all such information and instructions as may be necessary to enable the operating staff to perform their duties as such including in particular, information and instructions relating to the matters specified in Part A of Schedule 10 to this Order:

Provided that the operations manual shall not be required to contain any information or instructions available in a flight manual accessible to the persons by whom the information or instructions may be required.

(3) The operator of the aircraft shall, if the Board shall so require, furnish the Board with a copy of the whole of the operations manual for the time being in effect, or of such parts thereof as the Board may specify. The operator shall make such amendments of or additions to the operations manual as the Board may require for the purpose of ensuring the safety of the aircraft or of persons or property carried therein or the safety, efficiency or regularity of air navigation.

(4) For the purposes of this Article and Schedule 10 to this Order "operating staff" means the servants and agents employed by the operator, whether or not as members of the crew of the aircraft, to ensure that the flights of the aircraft are conducted in a safe manner, and includes an operator who himself performs those functions.

(5) If in the course of a flight on which the equipment specified in Scale O in paragraph 5 of Schedule 5 hereto is required to be provided the said equipment becomes unserviceable, the aircraft shall be operated on the remainder of that flight in accordance with any relevant instructions in the operations manual.

Public transport—operators' responsibilities

25.—(1) The operator of an aircraft registered in the United Kingdom shall not permit the aircraft to fly for the purpose of public transport without first—

(*a*) designating from among the flight crew a pilot to be the commander of the aircraft for the flight; and

(*b*) satisfying himself by every reasonable means that the aeronautical radio stations and navigational aids serving the intended route or any planned diversion therefrom are adequate for the safe navigation of the aircraft; and

(*c*) satisfying himself by every reasonable means that the aerodromes at which it is intended to take-off or land and any alternate aerodrome at which a landing may be made are suitable for the purpose and in particular are adequately manned and equipped (including such manning and equipment as may be prescribed) to ensure the safety of the aircraft and its passengers:

Provided that the operator of the aircraft shall not be required to satisfy himself as to the adequacy of fire-fighting, search, rescue or other services which are required only after the occurrence of an accident.

(2) The operator of an aircraft registered in the United Kingdom shall not permit any person to be a member of the crew thereof during any flight for the purpose of public transport (except a flight for the sole purpose of training persons to perform duties in aircraft) unless such person has had the training,

experience, practice and periodical tests specified in Part B of Schedule 10 to this Order in respect of the duties which he is to perform and unless the operator has satisfied himself that such person is competent to perform his duties, and in particular to use the equipment provided in the aircraft for that purpose. The operator shall maintain, preserve, produce and furnish information respecting records relating to the foregoing matters in accordance with Part B of the said Schedule 10.

Loading—public transport aircraft and suspended loads

26.—(1) The operator of an aircraft registered in the United Kingdom shall not cause or permit it to be loaded for a flight for the purpose of public transport or any load to be suspended therefrom except under the supervision of a person whom he has caused to be furnished with written instructions as to the distribution and securing of the load so as to ensure that—

(*a*) the load may safely be carried on the flight, and

(*b*) any conditions subject to which the certificate of airworthiness in force in respect of the aircraft was issued or rendered valid, being conditions relating to the loading of the aircraft, are complied with.

(2) The instructions shall indicate the weight of the aircraft prepared for service, that is to say the aggregate of the basic weight (shown in the weight schedule referred to in Article 15 of this Order) and the weight of such additional items in or on the aircraft as the operator thinks fit to include; and the instructions shall indicate the additional items included in the weight of the aircraft prepared for service, and shall show the position of the centre of gravity of the aircraft at that weight:

Provided that this paragraph shall not apply in relation to a flight if—

(*a*) the aircraft's maximum total weight authorised does not exceed 2,500 lb., or

(*b*) the aircraft's maximum total weight authorised does not exceed 6,000 lb. and the flight is intended not to exceed 60 minutes in duration and is either—

(i) a flight solely for training persons to perform duties in an aircraft, or

(ii) a flight intended to begin and end at the same aerodrome.

(3) The operator of an aircraft shall not cause or permit it to be loaded in contravention of the instructions referred to in paragraph (1) of this Article.

(4) The person supervising the loading of the aircraft shall, before the commencement of any such flight, prepare and sign a load sheet in duplicate conforming to the prescribed requirements, and shall (unless he is himself the commander of the aircraft) submit the load sheet for examination of the commander of the aircraft who shall sign his name thereon:

Provided that the foregoing requirements of this paragraph shall not apply if—

(*a*) the load and the distributing and securing thereof upon the next intended flight are to be unchanged from the previous flight and the commander of the aircraft makes and signs an endorsement to that effect upon the load sheet for the previous flight, indicating the date of the endorsement, the place of departure upon the next intended flight and the next intended place of destination; or

(*b*) paragraph (2) of this Article does not apply in relation to the flight.

(5) One copy of the load sheet shall be carried in the aircraft when Article 55 of this Order so requires until the flights to which it relates have been completed and one copy of that load sheet and of the instructions referred to in this Article

shall be preserved by the operator until the expiration of a period of 6 months thereafter and shall not be carried in the aircraft.

Public transport—operating conditions

27.—(1) An aircraft registered in the United Kingdom shall not fly for the purpose of public transport, except for the sole purpose of training persons to perform duties in aircraft, unless such requirements as may be prescribed in respect of its weight and related performance are complied with.

(2) The assessment of the ability of an aircraft to comply with paragraph (1) of this Article shall be based on the information as to its performance contained in the certificate of airworthiness relating to the aircraft. In the event of the information given therein being insufficient for that purpose such assessment shall be based on the best information available to the commander of the aircraft.

(3) Such requirements as may be prescribed in respect of the weather conditions required for take-off, approach to landing and landing shall be complied with in respect of every aircraft to which Article 24 of this Order applies.

(4) A flying machine registered in the United Kingdom when flying over water for the purpose of public transport shall fly, except as may be necessary for the purpose of take-off or landing, at such an altitude as would enable the aircraft—

(*a*) if it has one engine only, in the event of the failure of that engine,

(*b*) if it has more than one engine, in the event of the failure of one of those engines and with the remaining engine or engines operating within the maximum continuous power conditions specified in the certificate of airworthiness relating to the aircraft,

to reach a place at which it can safely land at a height sufficient to enable it to do so.

(5) Without prejudice to the provisions of paragraph (4) of this Article, an aeroplane in respect of which there is in force under this Order a certificate of airworthiness designating the aeroplane as being of performance group X shall not fly over water for the purpose of public transport so as to be more than 60 minutes flying time from the nearest shore, unless the aeroplane has more than two power units. For the purposes of this paragraph, flying time shall be calculated at normal cruising speed with one power unit inoperative.

Aircraft not registered in the United Kingdom—weather conditions

28.—(1) A public transport aircraft registered in a country other than the United Kingdom shall not fly unless the operator thereof shall have furnished to the Board such particulars as they may from time to time have required relating to the weather conditions specified by the operator in relation to aerodromes in the United Kingdom for the purpose of limiting their use by the aircraft for take-off or landing, including any instructions given by the operator in relation to such weather conditions. The aircraft shall not fly in or over the United Kingdom unless the operator shall have made such amendments of or additions to the weather conditions so specified and any instructions so given as the Board may require for the purpose of ensuring the safety of the aircraft or the safety, efficiency or regularity of air navigation.

(2) The aircraft shall not begin or end a flight at an aerodrome in the United Kingdom in weather conditions less favourable than those so specified in relation to that aerodrome, or in contravention of the instructions referred to in paragraph (1) of this Article.

(3) Without prejudice to the provisions of paragraph (2) of this Article a public transport aircraft registered in a country other than the United Kingdom shall not commence or continue an approach to landing at any aerodrome in the United Kingdom if the runway visual range at that aerodrome is at the time less than the relevant minimum for landing established in accordance with paragraph (1) of this Article.

(4) For the purpose of this Article "runway visual range" in relation to a runway or landing strip means the maximum distance in the direction of landing at which the runway or landing strip or the markers or lights delineating it can be seen from a point of 15 feet above its centre line; and if that distance has been communicated to the commander of the aircraft by or on behalf of the person in charge of the aerodrome as being the runway visual range, the distance so communicated shall be taken to be the runway visual range for the time being.

Pre-flight action by commander of aircraft

29. The commander of an aircraft registered in the United Kingdom shall satisfy himself before the aircraft takes off—

(*a*) that the flight can safely be made, taking into account the latest information available as to the route and aerodromes to be used, the weather reports and forecasts available, and any alternative course of action which can be adopted in case the flight cannot be completed as planned;

(*b*) that the equipment (including radio apparatus) required by or under this Order to be carried in the circumstances of the intended flight is carried and is in a fit condition for use;

(*c*) that the aircraft is in every way fit for the intended flight, and that where certificates of maintenance are required by Article 9(1) of this Order to be in force, they are in force and will not cease to be in force during the intended flight;

(*d*) that the load carried by the aircraft is of such weight, and is so distributed and secured, that it may safely be carried on the intended flight;

(*e*) in the case of a flying machine or airship, that sufficient fuel, oil and engine coolant (if required) are carried for the intended flight, and that a safe margin has been allowed for contingencies, and, in the case of a flight for the purpose of public transport, that the instructions in the operations manual relating to fuel, oil and engine coolant have been complied with;

(*f*) in the case of an airship or balloon that sufficient ballast is carried for the intended flight;

(*g*) in the case of a flying machine, that, having regard to the performance of the flying machine in the conditions to be expected on the intended flight, and to any obstructions at the places of departure and intended destination and on the intended route, it is capable of safely taking off, reaching and maintaining a safe height thereafter, and making a safe landing at the place of intended destination;

(*h*) that any pre-flight check system established by the operator and set forth in the operations manual or elsewhere has been complied with by each member of the crew of the aircraft.

Pilots to remain at controls

30. The commander of an aircraft registered in the United Kingdom, being a flying machine or glider, shall cause one pilot to remain at the controls at all times while the aircraft is in flight. If the aircraft is required by or under this Order to carry two pilots, the commander shall cause both pilots to remain at the controls during take-off and landing. Each pilot at the controls shall be secured in his seat by either a safety belt or a safety harness except that during take-off and landing a safety harness shall be used if it is required by Article 12 of this Order to be provided.

Public transport of passengers—duties of commander

31.—(1) This Article applies to flights for the purpose of the public transport of passengers by aircraft registered in the United Kingdom.

(2) In relation to every flight to which this Article applies the commander of the aircraft shall—

(*a*) before the aircraft takes off, take all reasonable steps to ensure that all passengers are made familiar with the position and method of use of emergency exits, safety belts, safety harnesses, oxygen equipment and lifejackets, and all other devices required by or under this Order and intended for use by passengers individually in case of an emergency occurring to the aircraft:

Provided that in relation to lifejackets this requirement may, except in the case of a seaplane, be complied with at any time before the aircraft reaches a point beyond gliding distance from land;

(*b*) if the aircraft is not a seaplane but is intended in the course of the flight to reach a point more than 30 minutes flying time (while flying in still air at the speed specified in the relevant certificate of airworthiness as the speed for compliance with regulations governing flights over water) from the nearest land, take all reasonable steps to ensure that before that point is reached, all passengers are given a practical demonstration of the method of use of the lifejackets required by or under this Order for the use of passengers;

(*c*) if the aircraft is a seaplane, take all reasonable steps to ensure that before the aircraft takes off all passengers are given a practical demonstration of the method of use of the equipment referred to in the preceding sub-paragraph;

(*d*) before the aircraft takes off, and before it lands, take all reasonable steps to ensure that the crew of the aircraft are properly secured in their seats and that any persons carried in compliance with Article 17(7) of this Order are properly secured in seats which shall be in a passenger compartment and which shall be so situated that they can readily assist passengers;

(*e*) before the aircraft takes off, and before it lands, and whenever by reason of turbulent air or any emergency occurring during flight he considers the precaution necessary, take all reasonable steps to ensure that all passengers are properly secured in their seats by safety belts or safety harnesses;

(*f*) in any emergency, take all reasonable steps to ensure that all passengers are instructed in the emergency action which they should take;

(*g*) except in a case where a pressure greater than 700 millibars is maintained in all passenger and crew compartments throughout the flight, take all reasonable steps to ensure that—

(i) before the aircraft reaches flight level 130 the method of use of the oxygen provided in the aircraft in compliance with the requirements of Article 12 of this Order is demonstrated to all passengers;

(ii) on reaching such altitude all passengers are recommended to use oxygen;

(iii) during any continuous period exceeding 30 minutes when the aircraft is flying above flight level 100 but not above flight level 130, and whenever the aircraft is flying above flight level 130, oxygen is used by all the crew of the aircraft.

Operation of radio in aircraft

32.—(1) The radio station in an aircraft shall not be operated, whether or not the aircraft is in flight, except in accordance with the conditions of the licence issued in respect of that station under the law of the country in which the aircraft is registered, and by a person duly licensed or otherwise permitted to operate the radio station under that law.

(2) Whenever an aircraft is in flight in such circumstances that it is required by or under this Order to be equipped with radio communication apparatus, a continuous radio watch shall be maintained by a member of the flight crew listening to the signals transmitted upon the frequency notified, or designated by a message received from an appropriate aeronautical radio station, for use by that aircraft:

Provided that—

(*a*) the radio watch may be discontinued or continued on another frequency to the extent that a message as aforesaid so permits; and

(*b*) the watch may be kept by a device installed in the aircraft if—

(i) the appropriate aeronautical radio station has been informed to that effect and has raised no objection; and

(ii) that station is notified, or in the case of a station situated in a country other than the United Kingdom, otherwise designated as transmitting a signal suitable for that purpose.

(3) The radio station in an aircraft shall not be operated so as to cause interference which impairs the efficiency of aeronautical telecommunications or navigational services, and in particular emissions shall not be made except as follows:

(*a*) emissions of the class and frequency for the time being in use, in accordance with general international aeronautical practice, in the air-space in which the aircraft is flying;

(*b*) distress, urgency and safety messages and signals, in accordance with general international aeronautical practice;

(*c*) messages and signals relating to the flight of the aircraft, in accordance with general international aeronautical practice;

(*d*) such public correspondence messages as may be permitted by or under the aircraft radio station licence referred to in paragraph (1) of this Article.

(4) In every aircraft registered in the United Kingdom which is equipped with radio communication apparatus a telecommunication log book shall be kept in which the following entries shall be made:

(*a*) the identification of the aircraft radio station;

(*b*) the date and time of the beginning and end of every radio watch maintained in the aircraft and of the frequency on which it was maintained;

(*c*) the date and time, and particulars of all messages and signals sent or received, including in particular details of any distress traffic sent or received;

(d) particulars of any action taken upon the receipt of a distress signal or message;

(e) particulars of any failure or interruption of radio communications and the cause thereof:

Provided that a telecommunication log book shall not be required to be kept in respect of communication by radiotelephony with a radio station on land or on a ship which provides a radio service for aircraft.

(5) The flight radio operator maintaining radio watch shall sign the entries in the telecommunication log book indicating the times at which he began and ended the maintenance of such watch.

(6) The telecommunication log book shall be preserved by the operator of the aircraft until a date six months after the date of the last entry therein.

(7) In any flying machine registered in the United Kingdom which is engaged on a flight for the purpose of public transport, the pilot and the flight engineer (if any) shall not make use of a hand-held microphone (whether for the purpose of radio communication or of intercommunication within the aircraft) whilst the aircraft is flying in controlled airspace at an altitude less than 15,000 feet above mean sea level or is taking off or landing.

Use of flight recorders and preservation of records

33.—(1) On any flight on which a flight recorder is required by or under this Order to be carried in an aeroplane, it shall always be in use from the beginning of the take-off run until the end of the landing run.

(2) The operator of the aircraft shall, subject to the provisions of Article 57 of this Order, preserve the record made by the flight recorder, together with means of identifying the record with the flight to which it relates, for a period of 30 days after the end of the flight or such longer period as the Board may in a particular case direct.

Towing of gliders

34.—(1) An aircraft in flight shall not tow a glider unless the certificate of airworthiness issued or rendered valid in respect of the towing aircraft under the law of the country in which that aircraft is registered includes an express provision that it may be used for that purpose.

(2) The length of the combination of towing aircraft, tow rope and glider in flight shall not exceed 500 feet.

(3) The commander of an aircraft which is about to tow a glider shall satisfy himself, before the towing aircraft takes off—

(a) that the tow rope is in good condition and is of adequate strength for the purpose, and that the combination of towing aircraft and glider is capable of flying in the manner referred to in Article 29(g) of this Order;

(b) that signals have been agreed and communication established with persons suitably stationed so as to enable the glider to take off safely;

(c) that emergency signals have been agreed between the commander of the towing aircraft and the commander of the glider, to be used, respectively, by the commander of the towing aircraft to indicate that the tow should immediately be released by the glider, and by the commander of the glider to indicate that the tow cannot be released.

(4) The glider shall be attached to the towing aircraft by means of the tow rope before the aircraft takes off.

Towing, picking up and raising of persons and articles

35.—(1) Subject to the provisions of this Article, an aircraft in flight shall not, by means external to the aircraft, tow any article, other than a glider, or pick up or raise any person, animal or article, unless the certificate of airworthiness issued or rendered valid in respect of that aircraft under the law of the country in which the aircraft is registered includes an express provision that it may be used for that purpose.

(2) An aircraft in flight shall not tow any article, other than a glider, at night or when flight visibility is less than one nautical mile.

(3) The length of the combination of towing aircraft, tow rope, and article in tow, shall not exceed 500 feet.

(4) A helicopter shall not fly at any height over a congested area of a city, town or settlement at any time when an article, person or animal is suspended from the helicopter.

(5) Nothing in this Article shall—

(*a*) prohibit the towing in a reasonable manner by an aircraft in flight of any radio aerial, any instrument which is being used for experimental purposes, or any signal, apparatus or article required or permitted by or under this Order to be towed or displayed by an aircraft in flight;

(*b*) prohibit the picking up or raising of any person, animal or article in an emergency or for the purpose of saving life;

(*c*) apply to any aircraft while it is flying in accordance with the "B Conditions" set forth in Schedule 2 to this Order.

(*d*) be taken to permit the towing or picking up of a glider otherwise than in accordance with Article 34 of this Order.

Dropping of persons and articles

36.—(1) Articles and animals (whether or not attached to a parachute) shall not be dropped, or permitted to drop, from an aircraft in flight so as to endanger persons or property.

(2) Articles, animals and persons (whether or not attached to a parachute) shall not be dropped, or permitted to drop, to the surface from an aircraft flying over the United Kingdom:

Provided that this paragraph shall not apply to the descent of persons by parachute from an aircraft in an emergency, or to the dropping of articles by, or with the authority of, the commander of the aircraft in the following circumstances:

(*a*) the dropping of articles for the purpose of saving life;

(*b*) the jettisoning, in case of emergency, of fuel or other articles in the aircraft;

(*c*) the dropping of ballast in the form of fine sand or water;

(*d*) the dropping of articles solely for the purpose of navigating the aircraft in accordance with ordinary practice or with the provisions of this Order;

(*e*) the dropping at an aerodrome in accordance with prescribed regulations of ropes, banners or similar articles towed by aircraft.

(3) For the purposes of this Article dropping includes projecting and lowering.

(4) Nothing in this Article shall prohibit the lowering of any person, animal or article from a helicopter to the surface, if the certificate of airworthiness

issued or rendered valid in respect of the helicopter under the law of the country in which it is registered includes an express provision that it may be used for that purpose.

Carriage of munitions of war

37.—(1) An aircraft shall not carry any munitions of war.

(2) It shall be unlawful for any person to take or cause to be taken on board an aircraft, or to deliver or cause to be delivered for carriage thereon, any goods which he knows or has reason to believe or suspect to be munitions of war.

(3) For the purposes of this Article "munitions of war" means such weapons and ammunition as are designed for use in warfare.

Carriage of dangerous goods

38.—(1) Dangerous goods shall not be carried in an aircraft except as follows:

(*a*) goods carried in accordance with any regulations which the Board may make to permit dangerous goods to be carried either in aircraft generally or in aircraft of any class specified in the regulations;

(*b*) goods, carried with the written permission of the Board, and in accordance with any conditions to which such permission may be subject;

(*c*) goods carried in aircraft with the consent of the operator thereof for the purpose of ensuring the proper navigation or safety of the aircraft or the well-being of any person on board;

(*d*) goods permitted to be carried under the laws of the country in which the aircraft is registered, if there is in force in relation to such country an agreement between Her Majesty's Government in the United Kingdom and the Government of that country permitting the carriage of dangerous goods within the United Kingdom in aircraft registered in that country.

(2) Dangerous goods permitted by or under this Order to be carried in an aircraft shall not be loaded as cargo therein unless:

(*a*) the consignor of the goods has furnished the operator of the aircraft with particulars in writing of the nature of the goods and the danger to which they give rise; and

(*b*) the goods or any container in which they are packed are clearly marked so as to indicate that danger to the person loading the goods in the aircraft.

The operator of the aircraft shall, before the flight begins, inform the commander of the aircraft of the identity of the goods, the danger to which they give rise and the weight or quantity of the goods.

(3) It shall be unlawful for any person to take or cause to be taken on board an aircraft, or to deliver or cause to be delivered for loading thereon, any goods which he knows or has reason to believe or suspect to be dangerous goods the carriage of which is prohibited by this Article.

(4) The provisions of this Article shall be additional to and not in derogation from the provisions of Article 37 of this Order.

Method of carriage of persons

39. A person shall not be in or on any part of an aircraft in flight which is not a part designed for the accommodation of persons and in particular a person shall not be on the wings or undercarriage of an aircraft. A person shall not be in or on any object, other than a glider or flying machine, towed by or attached to an aircraft in flight:

Provided that a person may have temporary access to—

(*a*) any part of an aircraft for the purpose of taking action necessary for the safety of the aircraft or of any person, animal or goods therein;

(*b*) any part of an aircraft in which cargo or stores are carried, being a part which is designed to enable a person to have access thereto while the aircraft is in flight.

Exits and break-in markings

40.—(1) This Article shall apply to every public transport aircraft registered in the United Kingdom.

(2) Whenever an aircraft to which this Article applies is carrying passengers, every exit therefrom and every internal door in the aircraft shall, during take-off and landing and during any emergency, be kept free of obstruction and shall not be fastened by locking or otherwise so as to prevent, hinder or delay its use by passengers:

Provided that an exit may be obstructed by cargo if it is an exit which, in accordance with arrangements approved by the Board, either generally or in relation to a class of aircraft or a particular aircraft, is not required for use by passengers and a door between the flight crew compartment and any adjacent compartment to which passengers have access may be locked or bolted if the commander of the aircraft so determines, for the purpose of preventing access by passengers to the flight crew compartment.

(3) Every exit from the aircraft, being an exit intended to be used by passengers in normal circumstances, shall be marked with the word "Exit" in capital letters and every exit, being an exit intended to be used by passengers in an emergency only, shall be marked with the words "Emergency Exit" in capital letters.

(4) (*a*) Every exit from the aircraft shall be marked with instructions in English and with diagrams, to indicate the correct method of opening the exit.

(*b*) The markings shall be placed on or near the inside surface of the door or other closure of the exit and, if it is openable from the outside of the aircraft, on or near the exterior surface.

(5) (*a*) Every aircraft to which this Article applies, being an aircraft of which the maximum total weight authorised exceeds 8,000 lb., shall be marked upon the exterior surface of its fuselage with markings to show the areas (in this paragraph referred to as "break-in areas") which can, for purposes of rescue in an emergency, be most readily and effectively broken into by persons outside the aircraft.

(*b*) The break-in areas shall be rectangular in shape and shall be marked by right-angled corner markings, each arm of which shall be 4 inches in length along its outer edge and 1 inch in width.

(*c*) The words "Cut Here in Emergency" shall be marked across the centre of each break-in area in capital letters.

(6) The markings required by this Article shall—

(*a*) be painted, or affixed by other equally permanent means;

(*b*) be red in colour and, in any case in which the colour of the adjacent background is such as to render red markings not readily visible, be outlined in white or some other contrasting colour in such a manner as to render them readily visible;

(*c*) be kept at all times clean and unobscured.

Imperilling safety of aircraft

41. A person shall not wilfully or negligently act in a manner likely to endanger an aircraft, or any person therein.

Imperilling safety of any person or property

42. A person shall not wilfully or negligently cause or permit an aircraft to endanger any person or property.

Drunkenness in aircraft

43.—(1) A person shall not enter any aircraft when drunk, or be drunk in any aircraft.

(2) A person shall not, when acting as a member of the crew of any aircraft or being carried in any aircraft for the purpose of so acting, be under the influence of drink or a drug to such an extent as to impair his capacity so to act.

Smoking in aircraft

44.—(1) Notices indicating when smoking is prohibited shall be exhibited in every aircraft registered in the United Kingdom so as to be visible from each passenger seat therein.

(2) A person shall not smoke in any compartment of an aircraft registered in the United Kingdom at a time when smoking is prohibited in that compartment by a notice to that effect exhibited by or on behalf of the commander of the aircraft.

Authority of commander of aircraft

45. Every person in an aircraft registered in the United Kingdom shall obey all lawful commands which the commander of that aircraft may give for the purpose of securing the safety of the aircraft and of persons or property carried therein, or the safety, efficiency or regularity of air navigation.

Stowaways

46. A person shall not secrete himself for the purpose of being carried in an aircraft without the consent of either the operator or the commander thereof or of any other person entitled to give consent to his being carried in the aircraft.

PART VI

FATIGUE OF CREW

Application and interpretation of Part VI

47.—(1) Articles 48 to 52, inclusive, of this Order apply in relation to an aircraft if, but only if, it is an aircraft registered in the United Kingdom which is either—

(*a*) engaged on a flight for the purpose of public transport, or

(*b*) operated by an air transport undertaking:

Provided that the said Articles shall not apply in relation to a flight made only for the purpose of instruction in flying given by or on behalf of a flying club or a flying school, or a person who is not an air transport undertaking.

(2) In this Part of this Order, the following expressions shall, except where the context otherwise requires, have the meanings hereby respectively assigned to them, that is to say—

(*a*) "flight time", in relation to any person, means all time spent by that person in an aircraft (other than an aircraft of which the maximum total weight authorised does not exceed 3,500 lb. and which is not flying for the purpose of public transport or aerial work) while it is in flight and he is carried therein as a member of the flight crew thereof;

(*b*) "duty period", in relation to any person who flies in an aircraft as a member of the crew thereof, means any continuous period throughout which he is, under the provisions of paragraphs (3) or (4) of this Article, to be treated as being on duty:

Provided that where two or more periods which would, but for this proviso, be separate duty periods are separated by an interval of less than 10 hours, the period starting when the first of those duty periods began and finishing when the last of them ended shall be treated as constituting a single continuous duty period;

(*c*) "rest period", in relation to any person, means any continuous period no part of which forms part of a duty period of that person;

(*d*) "day" means a continuous period of 24 hours beginning at midnight Greenwich mean time.

(3) For the purposes of this Part of this Order, a person who is employed under a contract of service to fly in an aircraft as a member of the crew thereof shall be treated as being on duty at any time when in the course of that employment he flies in any aircraft (whether as a member of its crew or as a passenger and whether or not the aircraft is such an aircraft as is referred to in paragraph (1) of this Article) or he is otherwise acting in the course of that employment:

Provided that when he is not flying in an aircraft—

(*a*) subject to paragraph (*c*) of this proviso, he shall not be treated as being on duty during any period which he is allowed for rest;

(*b*) subject to paragraph (*c*) of this proviso, he shall not be treated as being on duty at any time by reason only of his being required at that time to be available at a particular place to report for duty if required to do so;

(*c*) he shall be treated as being on duty at any time when he is required to be available at a particular place to report for duty if required to do so if—

(i) that place is at an aerodrome, or

(ii) that place, not being at an aerodrome, is a place at which his employer requires persons similarly employed to be available as aforesaid and adequate facilities for rest are not available for his use while he is required to be so available.

(4) For the purposes of this Part of this Order, a person who flies in an aircraft as a member of the crew thereof, otherwise than in the course of his employment under a contract of service to fly as aforesaid, shall be treated as being on duty at any time when, in connection with any business of operating aircraft, he flies in any aircraft (whether as a member of its crew or as a passenger and whether or not the aircraft is such an aircraft as is referred to in paragraph (1) of this Article) or does any work.

(5) For the purposes of this Part of this Order, references to a person flying in an aircraft as a member of the crew thereof include references to the operator of the aircraft who himself flies in the aircraft in any such capacity and references to the work and other duties which a person is required or permitted by an operator to carry out shall in any such case be construed as references to any work carried out by that operator in connection with the management of aircraft or with any business which includes the flying of aircraft.

Duties of operators to prevent excessive fatigue of crew

48. It shall be the duty of every operator of an aircraft to which this Article applies to ensure, as respects each person flying as a member of the crew of that aircraft, that the periods during which that person is required or permitted by that operator to carry out any work or other duties are so limited in length and frequency, and that that person is afforded such periods for rest, that his said work and duties are not likely to cause him such fatigue while he is flying in the aircraft as may endanger the safety thereof or of the persons therein.

Establishment of limits on flight times, flying duty periods and rest periods

49.—(1) Without prejudice to the provisions of Article 48 of this Order, and for the purposes of securing that the requirements of those provisions are complied with, every operator of an aircraft to which this Article applies shall establish—

(*a*) for every person flying in that aircraft as a member of the crew thereof:
(i) limits on his flying periods, and
(ii) minimum rest periods which he is to have immediately before any duty period in the course of which flies as aforesaid; and

(*b*) for every person flying in that aircraft as a member of the flight crew thereof, limits on the aggregate of all his flight times during every period of 28 consecutive days,

being limits and minimum rest periods which the operator is satisfied after taking into account the matters mentioned in paragraph (2) of this Article, are such that, if every member of the crew observes such of those limits as are applicable to him and has those minimum rest periods, the safety of neither the aircraft nor of the persons therein is likely to be endangered on the flight by reason of any fatigue which may be caused by the work or other duties which the members of the crew are required or permitted by the operator to carry out. Different limits and different minimum rest periods may be established either for different persons or for different classes of persons and for different circumstances.

(2) The matters which an operator shall take into account in establishing under paragraph (1) of this Article limits and minimum rest periods as therein mentioned for the persons therein mentioned are the nature of the work and other duties which those persons will carry out and all circumstances arising out of the carrying out of that work and those duties which may affect the degree of fatigue from which those persons may suffer while they are making a flight in an aircraft to which this Article applies in any such capacity as is mentioned in the said paragraph (1) including, without prejudice to the generality of the foregoing—

(*a*) the type of aircraft in which the flight will be made;

(*b*) the area in which the flight will be made;

(*c*) the number of landings which will be made during the course of each flying duty period;

(*d*) the amount of night flying during each flying duty period;

(*e*) for every person who is to fly in that aircraft as a member of the flight crew thereof, the number of consecutive occasions on which he will be required to fly for the maximum period permitted under this Part of the Order.

(3) No limits or minimum rest periods may be established under paragraph (1) of this Article which would require or permit any person to fly in any aircraft at a time when such flying would constitute a contravention of any of the provisions of Articles 50, 51 and 53 of this Order, or would require or permit any person to fly in any aircraft as a member of the flight crew thereof within the period of one hour immediately preceding the end of the specified time referred to in Article 50(2), or, when the specified time is 24 hours, within the period of two hours immediately preceding the end of the specified time.

(4) An operator of an aircraft to which this Article applies shall not permit that aircraft to make a flight unless limits and minimum rest periods have been established in accordance with the foregoing provisions of this Article so as to apply to every member of the crew thereof.

(5) Every operator of an aircraft to which this Article applies shall take all such steps as are reasonably practicable to secure that all limits for the time being established by that operator in accordance with the foregoing provisions of this Article are observed and that no person for whom minimum rest periods are for the time being so established makes any flight in an aircraft to which this Article applies as a member of the crew thereof unless, immediately before the duty period in the course of which he makes the flight, he has had the appropriate rest period so established.

(6) Notwithstanding anything contained in the foregoing provisions of this Article, an operator of an aircraft to which this Article applies may confer upon the commander of that aircraft a discretion to make, or authorise any person to make a flight in that aircraft in such circumstances that the commander or, as the case may be, that other person will not observe the limits or will not have had the minimum rest period established by that operator under the foregoing provisions of this Article and applicable to the commander or that other person:

Provided that the said discretion shall not be exercisable unless the following conditions are fulfilled, that is to say—

(*a*) that it appears to the commander—

(i) that arrangements had been made for the flight to be made with such a crew and so as to begin and end at such times that if the flight had been made in accordance with those arrangements each member of the crew would have observed the limits and have had the minimum rest periods established by the operator and applicable to them as aforesaid, and that since those arrangements were made the flight has been or will be prevented from being made in accordance with those arrangements by reason of exceptional circumstances or by reason of circumstances which were not foreseen as likely to prevent that flight from being so made, or

(ii) that the flight is one which ought to be carried out in the interests of the safety or health of any person, and

(*b*) that the commander is satisfied that the safety of neither the aircraft nor the persons therein will be endangered on that flight if he or that other person makes that flight.

(7) Every operator of an aircraft to which this Article applies shall include in every operations manual to be provided under Article 24 of this Order for the use and guidance of the members of the crew of that aircraft, or, in any case where no such manual is required to be provided by that Article, in a document which shall be provided for the use and guidance of those members, full particulars of all limits and minimum rest periods for the time being established under the foregoing provisions of this Article which may affect any of those members, and of any discretion conferred upon the commander of that aircraft under paragraph (6) of this Article and (without prejudice to the provisions of Article 24 of this Order) every such operator shall, whenever requested to do so by a person authorised in that behalf by the Board, furnish that person with a copy of all particulars from time to time included in any such operations manual or document in accordance with the requirements of this paragraph.

(8) In this Article the expression "flying duty period", in relation to any person, means the time, reckoned from the beginning of each duty period of that person, in the course of which he is permitted to make any flight to which this Article applies and after expiration of which he is not in the course of the same duty period, to make any such flight.

Maximum flying duty periods for flight crew

50.—(1) Without prejudice to the provisions of Article 48 of this Order, a person shall not fly in an aircraft to which this Article applies as a member of the flight crew thereof in the course of any duty period of that person after more than the specified time has elapsed since the beginning of that duty period.

(2) In paragraph (1) of this Article the expression "the specified time" means—

(*a*) in relation to a pilot whenever sub-paragraph (*b*) does not apply, 11 hours:

Provided that if, during the duty period, there has been a period of not less than five continuous hours throughout which that person has not flown in any aircraft to which this Article applies or performed any duties, the foregoing provisions of this sub-paragraph shall have effect as if 13 hours were substituted therein for 11 hours;

(*b*) in relation to a person who, at all times when he flies as a pilot in the course of his duty period, is one of two or more persons carried as pilots of the aircraft, 16 hours:

Provided that the foregoing provisions of this sub-paragraph shall have effect as if 24 hours were substituted therein for 16 hours if that person is one of three or more persons carried as pilots of the aircraft and the following conditions are fulfilled:

(i) at least two of the pilots are qualified to act as commander of the aircraft in the circumstances both by their respective licences and in accordance with the requirements of paragraph 1(5)(*a*) (i) and (ii) of Part B of Schedule 10 to this Order (except in respect of their knowledge of the aerodromes of take-off and landing and any alternate aerodromes);

(ii) at least one of the pilots is carried in addition to those members of the flight crew who are required to be carried in the circumstances by or under this Order;

(iii) one suitable bunk is always available for the use only of pilots; and

(iv) each of the pilots has, during the duty period, been afforded opportunities of resting for a reasonable time;

(*c*) in relation to a flight engineer, 16 hours:

Provided that the foregoing provisions of this sub-paragraph shall have effect as if 24 hours were substituted therein for 16 hours in relation to a person who, at all times when he flies as a flight engineer in the course of his duty period, is one of two or more persons carried as flight engineers of the aircraft, if the following conditions are fulfilled:

(i) at least one of the flight engineers is carried in addition to the members of the flight crew who are required to be carried in the circumstances by or under this Order;

(ii) one suitable bunk is always available for the use only of flight engineers;

(iii) each of the flight engineers has, during the duty period, been afforded opportunities of resting for a reasonable time;

(*d*) in relation to a flight navigator and a flight radio operator, 16 hours:

Provided that the foregoing provisions of this sub-paragraph shall have effect—

(i) as if 20 hours were substituted therein for 16 hours if one suitable bunk is always available for the use only of flight navigators or flight radio operators as the case may be; and

(ii) subject to the proviso to sub-paragraph (*c*), which shall apply to flight navigators and to flight radio operators as it applies to flight engineers.

Minimum rest periods for flight crew

51. Without prejudice to the provisions of Article 48 of this Order a person shall not fly in an aircraft to which this Article applies as a member of the flight crew thereof, unless immediately before the duty period in the course of which he makes that flight he had a sufficient rest period, that is to say, a rest period of a length not less than the minimum length specified in the first column of Table A in this Article and therein set opposite to the length specified in the second column of that Table which corresponds to the length of the duty period of that person which immediately precedes that rest period.

TABLE A

Minimum length of sufficient rest period	*Length of immediately preceding duty period*
10 hours	Not exceeding 10 hours
11 "	Exceeding 10 but not exceeding 11 hours
12 "	" 11 " " " 12 "
13 "	" 12 " " " 13 "
14 "	" 13 " " " 14 "
15 "	" 14 " " " 15 "
16 "	" 15 " " " 16 "
18 "	" 16 " " " 17 "
20 "	" 17 " " " 18 "
22 "	" 18 " " " 19 "
24 "	" 19 " " " 20 "
26 "	" 20 " " " 21 "
28 "	" 21 " " " 22 "
30 "	" 22 " " " 23 "
32 "	" 23 " " " 24 "
an additional 1½ hours	For every hour and every fraction of an hour in excess of 24 hours.

Provided that where a rest period is taken by a person at a place which is outside the United Kingdom and, if he ordinarily resides outside the United Kingdom, is not within 50 miles of his ordinary place of residence, it shall be deemed to be a sufficient rest period if it includes a period of eight hours falling between 2200 and 0800 hours local time and is of a length not less than the minimum length specified in the first column of Table B in this Article and therein set opposite to the length specified in the second column of that Table which corresponds to the length of the duty period of that person which immediately precedes that rest period.

TABLE B

Minimum length of sufficient rest period	*Length of immediately preceding duty period*
10 hours	Not exceeding 10 hours
11 "	Exceeding 10 but not exceeding 11 hours
12 "	" 11 " " " 12 "
13 "	" 12 " " " 14 "
14 "	" 14 " " " 17 "
15 "	" 17 " " " 19 "
16 "	" 19 " " " 21 "
17 "	" 21 " " " 23 "
18 "	" 23 " " " 24 "
an additional 1½ hours	For every hour and every fraction of an hour in excess of 24 hours.

Records of flight times and duty periods

52.—(1) The operator of an aircraft to which this Article applies shall not cause or permit any person to fly therein as a member of the crew thereof unless the operator has in his possession an accurate and up-to-date record maintained by him or by another operator of aircraft in respect of that person and in respect of the 28 days immediately preceding the flight showing—

(*a*) the times of the beginning and end of each flight in any aircraft made by that person as a member of its crew in the course of any of his duty periods, and

(*b*) the times of the beginning and end of each duty period of that person in the course of which he makes a flight in any aircraft as a member of its crew, and

(*c*) the times of the beginning and end of each duty period of that person ending within a period of 72 hours immediately preceding the beginning of any duty period of that person in the course of which he makes a flight in any aircraft as a member of its crew, and

(*d*) brief particulars of the nature of the work or other duties carried out by that person during each of his duty periods of which a record is required to be kept under this paragraph.

(2) The Board may prescribe the form and manner in which any records required to be kept under the last foregoing paragraph shall be kept and where they have so prescribed the said records shall be kept accordingly.

(3) Subject to the provisions of Article 57 of this Order the operator of the aircraft shall preserve the records referred to in paragraph (1) of this Article for a period of at least 12 months after the end of the flight, duty period or rest period to which they relate.

Maximum flight times for flight crews

53. A person shall not fly in any aircraft registered in the United Kingdom as a member of the flight crew thereof at any time on any day after the aggregate of all his flight times (whether arising from flight in an aircraft to which this Article applies or in any other aircraft) during the period of 28 consecutive days expiring at the end of that day amounts to 100 hours:

Provided that the foregoing prohibition shall not apply—

(*a*) to a flight made in an aircraft of which the maximum total weight authorised does not exceed 3,500 lb. and which is not flying for the purpose of public transport or aerial work; or

(*b*) to a flight made in an aircraft not flying for the purpose of public transport nor operated by an air transport undertaking, if at the time of the flight the aggregate of all the flight times of the person making the flight since he was last medically examined under this Order and found fit does not exceed 100 hours.

Provision for particular cases

54.—(1) Notwithstanding anything contained in Articles 50, 51 and 53 of this Order (hereinafter referred to as "the relevant Articles") a person shall be deemed not to have contravened any of the provisions of those Articles by reason of a flight made at any time by that person or by another person if the first mentioned person proves—

(*a*) that it was due to an unavoidable delay in the completion of the flight that the person so flying was flying at that time, and

(*b*) that the said first mentioned person could not reasonably be expected to have foreseen before the flight began that the delay was likely to occur.

(2) Without prejudice to the provisions of Article 80(2) of this Order and notwithstanding anything contained in the relevant Articles, the commander of an aircraft may make, or authorise any other person to make, and that other person if so authorised may make, a flight in that aircraft which he would, but for this paragraph, be prohibited from making by virtue of any provision contained in the relevant Articles if—

(*a*) it appears to the commander:

(i) that arrangements had been made for the flight to be made with such a crew and so as to begin and end at such times that no member of that crew would have been prohibited from making the flight in accordance with those arrangements by any provision contained in the relevant Articles, and that since those arrangements were made the flight has been or will be prevented from being made in accordance with those arrangements by reason of exceptional circumstances or by reason of circumstances which were not foreseen as likely to prevent that flight from being so made, or

(ii) that the flight is one which ought to be carried out in the interests of the safety or health of any person, and

(*b*) the commander is satisfied that the safety of the aircraft on that flight will not be endangered if he or that other person makes that flight.

(3) Where the commander or any other person makes a flight in an aircraft which he or that other person is permitted to make under the last foregoing paragraph, a report in writing that he or that other person has made that flight, giving full particulars of the circumstances in which it was made and the reasons why the commander made that flight or, as the case may be, authorised that other person to do so, shall be made as soon as is reasonably

practicable by the commander to the operator of the aircraft and in any event by the operator to the Board; and the operator and the commander shall furnish any authorised person with such further information in his possession relating to the flight and to the circumstances in which it was made as that person may require.

PART VII

DOCUMENTS AND RECORDS

Documents to be carried

55.—(1) An aircraft shall not fly unless it carries the documents which it is required to carry under the law of the country in which it is registered.

(2) An aircraft registered in the United Kingdom shall, when in flight, carry documents in accordance with Schedule 11 to this Order:

Provided that, if the flight is intended to begin and end at the same aerodrome and does not include passage over the territory of any country other than the United Kingdom, the documents may be kept at that aerodrome instead of being carried in the aircraft.

Production of documents and records

56.—(1) The commander of an aircraft, shall within a reasonable time after being requested to do so by an authorised person, cause to be produced to that person—

(*a*) the certificates of registration and airworthiness in force in respect of the aircraft;

(*b*) the licences of its flight crew;

(*c*) such other documents as the aircraft is required by Article 55 of this Order to carry when in flight.

(2) The operator of an aircraft registered in the United Kingdom shall, within a reasonable time after being requested to do so by an authorised person, cause to be produced to that person such of the following documents or records as may have been requested by that person being documents or records which are required, by or under this Order, to be in force or to be carried preserved or made available:

(*a*) the documents referred to in Schedule 11 to this Order as Documents A, B and G;

(*b*) the aircraft log book, engine log books and variable pitch propeller log books required under this Order to be kept;

(*c*) the weight schedule, if any, required to be preserved under Article 15 of this Order;

(*d*) in the case of a public transport aircraft or aerial work aircraft, the documents referred to in Schedule 11 to this Order as Documents D, E, F and H;

(*e*) any records of flight times, duty periods and rest periods which he is required by Article 52(3) of this Order to preserve, and such other documents and information in the possession or control of the operator, as the authorised person may require for the purpose of determining whether those records are complete and accurate.

(*f*) any such operations manuals as are required to be made available under Article 24(2)(*a*)(i) of this Order;

(*g*) the record made by any flight recorder required to be carried by or under this Order.

(3) The holder of a licence granted or rendered valid under this Order shall, within a reasonable time after being requested to do so by an authorised person, cause to be produced to that person his licence, including any certificate of validation. The requirements of this paragraph shall be deemed to have been complied with, except in relation to licences required by Article 55 of this Order to be carried in the aircraft or kept at an aerodrome, if the licence requested is produced within five days after the request has been made, at a police station in the United Kingdom specified, at the time of the request, by the person to whom the request is made.

(4) Every person required by Article 21 of this Order to keep a personal flying log book shall cause it to be produced within a reasonable time to an authorised person after being requested to do so by him within two years after the date of the last entry therein.

Preservation of documents, etc.

57. A person required by this Order to preserve any document or record by reason of his being the operator of an aircraft shall, if he ceases to be the operator of the aircraft, continue to preserve the document or record as if he had not ceased to be the operator, and in the event of his death the duty to preserve the document or record shall fall upon his personal representative:

Provided that if—

(*a*) another person becomes the operator of the aircraft and it remains registered in the United Kingdom he or his personal representative shall deliver to that other person upon demand the certificates of maintenance and compliance, the log books and the weight schedule and any record made by a flight recorder and preserved in accordance with Article 33(2) of this Order which are in force or required to be preserved in respect of that aircraft;

(*b*) an engine or variable pitch propeller is removed from the aircraft and installed in another aircraft operated by another person and registered in the United Kingdom he or his personal representative shall deliver to that other person upon demand the log book relating to that engine or propeller;

(*c*) any person in respect of whom a record has been kept by him in accordance with Article 52 of this Order becomes a member of the flight crew of a public transport aircraft registered in the United Kingdom and operated by another person he or his personal representative shall deliver those records to that other person upon demand,

and it shall be the duty of that other person to deal with the document or record delivered to him as if he were the first-mentioned operator.

Revocation, suspension and variation of certificates, licences and other documents

58.—(1) The Board may, if they think fit, provisionally suspend any certificate, licence, approval, permission, exemption or other document issued, granted or having effect under this Order, pending investigation of the case. The Board may, on sufficient ground being shown to their satisfaction after due inquiry, revoke, suspend or vary any such certificate, licence, approval, permission, exemption or other document.

(2) The holder or any person having the possession or custody of any certificate, licence, approval, permission, exemption or other document which has

been revoked, suspended or varied under this Order shall surrender it to the Board within a reasonable time after being required to do so by them.

(3) The breach of any condition subject to which any certificate, licence, approval, permission, exemption or other document, other than a licence issued in respect of an aerodrome, has been granted or issued, or which has effect under this Order shall render the document invalid during the continuance of the breach.

(4) Paragraphs (1) and (3) of this Article shall not apply to an air operator's certificate granted under Article 6 of this Order.

Offences in relation to documents and records

59.—(1) A person shall not with intent to deceive—

(*a*) use any certificate, licence, approval, permission, exemption or other document issued or having effect or required by or under this Order which has been forged, altered, revoked or suspended, or to which he is not entitled; or

(*b*) lend any certificate, licence, approval, permission, exemption or other document issued or having effect or required by or under this Order to, or allow it to be used by, any other person; or

(*c*) make any false representation for the purpose of procuring for himself or any other person the grant, issue, renewal or variation of any such certificate, licence, approval, permission or exemption or other document.

(2) A person shall not wilfully mutilate, alter or render illegible any log book or other record required by or under this Order to be maintained or any entry made therein, or knowingly make, or procure or assist in the making of, any false entry in or material omission from any such log book or record or destroy any such log book or record during the period for which it is required under this Order to be preserved.

(3) All entries made in writing in any log book or record referred to in paragraph (2) of this Article shall be made in ink or indelible pencil.

(4) A person shall not wifully or negligently make in a load sheet any entry which is incorrect in any material particular, or any material omission from such a load sheet.

(5) A person shall not purport to issue any certificate for the purposes of this Order or the Regulations made thereunder unless he is authorised to do so under this Order.

(6) A person shall not issue any such certificate as aforesaid unless he has satisfied himself that all statements in the certificate are correct.

PART VIII

CONTROL OF AIR TRAFFIC

Rules of the air and air traffic control

60.—(1) The Board may make regulations (hereinafter referred to in this Order as the Rules of the Air and Air Traffic Control) prescribing:

(*a*) the manner in which aircraft may move or fly including in particular provision for requiring aircraft to give way to military aircraft:

(*b*) the lights and other signals to be shown or made by aircraft or persons;

(*c*) the lighting and marking of aerodromes;

(*d*) the air traffic control services to be provided at aerodromes;

(*e*) the licensing of persons providing air traffic control services;

(*f*) any other provisions for securing the safety of aircraft in flight and in movement and the safety of persons and property on the surface.

(2) Subject to the provisions of paragraph (3) of this Article, it shall be an offence to contravene, to permit the contravention of, or to fail to comply with, the Rules of the Air and Air Traffic Control.

(3) It shall be lawful for the Rules of the Air and Air Traffic Control to be departed from to the extent necessary—

(*a*) for avoiding immediate danger; or

(*b*) for complying with the law of any country other than the United Kingdom within which the aircraft then is; or

(*c*) for complying with Ministry of Defence Flying Orders in relation to an aircraft of which the commander is acting as such in the course of his duty as a member of any of Her Majesty's naval, military or air forces.

(4) If any departure from the Rules of the Air and Air Traffic Control is made for the purpose of avoiding immediate danger, the commander of the aircraft shall cause written particulars of the departure, and of the circumstances giving rise to it, to be given within ten days thereafter to the competent authority of the country in whose territory the departure was made or if the departure was made over the high seas, to the Board.

(5) Nothing in the Rules of the Air and Air Traffic Control shall exonerate any person from the consequences of any neglect in the use of lights or signals or of the neglect of any precautions required by ordinary aviation practice or by the special circumstances of the case.

Power to prohibit or restrict flying

61.—(1) Where the Board deem it necessary in the public interest to restrict or prohibit flying over any area of the United Kingdom or along any route therein by reason of—

(*a*) the intended gathering or movement of a large number of persons,

(*b*) the intended holding of an aircraft race or contest or of an exhibition of flying, or

(*c*) national defence or any other reason affecting the public interest,

the Board may make regulations prohibiting, restricting or imposing conditions on flight, either generally or in relation to any class of aircraft, over any such area or along any such route, and an aircraft shall not fly in contravention of such regulations.

(2) If the commander of an aircraft becomes aware that the aircraft is flying in contravention of any such regulations which have been made for any of the reasons referred to in paragraph (1)(*c*) of this Article he shall forthwith cause a signal of distress to be made by radio or by one of the prescribed visual signals, and shall (unless otherwise instructed by the appropriate air traffic control unit or by a commissioned officer of Her Majesty's naval, military or air forces), cause the aircraft to land at the aerodrome, being an aerodrome suitable for that purpose, which it can reach by flying to the least possible extent over the area to which the regulations relate. The aircraft shall not begin to descend while over such area.

Balloons, kites and airships

62.—(1) Within the United Kingdom—

(*a*) a captive balloon or kite shall not be flown at a height of more than 200 feet above the ground level or within 200 feet of any vessel, vehicle or structure;

(*b*) a captive balloon shall not be flown within 3 miles of an aerodrome;

(*c*) a balloon exceeding 6 feet in any linear dimension at any stage of its flight, including any basket or other equipment attached to the balloon, shall not be flown in controlled airspace;

(*d*) a kite shall not be flown within 3 miles of an aerodrome;

(*e*) an airship shall not be moored,

without the permission in writing of the Board, and in accordance with any conditions subject to which that permission may be granted.

(2) A captive balloon when in flight shall be securely moored, and shall not be left unattended unless it is fitted with a device which ensures its automatic deflation if it breaks free of its moorings.

PART IX

AERODROMES, AERONAUTICAL LIGHTS AND DANGEROUS LIGHTS

Aerodromes: public transport of passengers and instruction in flying

63.—(1) An aircraft engaged on a flight for the purpose of the public transport of passengers or for the purpose of instruction in flying shall not take off or land at any place in the United Kingdom other than—

(*a*) a Government aerodrome notified as available for the take-off and landing of aircraft so engaged, or in respect of which the person in charge of the aerodrome has given his permission for the particular aircraft to take off or land, as the case may be;

(*b*) an aerodrome licensed under this Order for the take-off and landing of aircraft so engaged,

and in accordance with any condition subject to which the aerodrome may have been so licensed or notified, or subject to which such permission may have been given:

Provided that the foregoing prohibition shall not apply to any aircraft so engaged if it is—

(i) an aeroplane of which the maximum total weight authorised does not exceed 6,000 lb. unless it is so engaged on either (*a*) a scheduled journey, or (*b*) a flight intended to begin and end at the same aerodrome or (*c*) a flight for the purpose of instruction in flying;

(ii) a helicopter, unless it is so engaged on a journey or flight as aforesaid;

(iii) a glider being flown under arrangements made by a flying club and carrying no person other than a member of the club.

(2) An aircraft engaged on a flight for the public transport of passengers shall not take off or land by night at any place in the United Kingdom unless adequate lighting is in operation on the aerodrome.

Use of Government aerodromes

64. The Board may cause to be notified, subject to such conditions as they think fit, any Government aerodrome as an aerodrome available for take-off and landing by aircraft engaged on flights for the purpose of the public transport of passengers or for instruction in flying or by any classes of such aircraft.

Licensing of aerodromes

65.—(1) The Board may licence any aerodrome in the United Kingdom subject to such conditions as they think fit, for the take-off and landing of aircraft engaged in flights for the purpose of the public transport of passengers, or for the purpose of instruction in flying, or of any classes of such aircraft.

(2) Without prejudice to the generality of paragraph (1) of this Article, if the person applying for the licence so requests, the Board may grant a licence (in this Order referred to as "a licence for public use") which shall be subject to the condition that the aerodrome shall at all times when it is available for the take-off or landing of aircraft be so available to all persons on equal terms and conditions.

(3) The licensee of an aerodrome in respect of which a licence for public use is in force shall display in a prominent place at the aerodrome a copy of the licence and shall furnish to any person on request information concerning the terms of the licence.

(4) The licensee of an aerodrome licensed under this Order shall not cause or permit any condition of the licence to be contravened, in relation to an aircraft engaged on a flight for the public transport of passengers or for instruction in flying, but the licence shall not cease to be valid by reason only of such a contravention.

(5) A licence granted by the Board in respect of an aerodrome shall, subject to the provisions of Article 58 of this Order, remain in force as may be specified in the licence.

Records at aerodromes

66.—(1) The licensee of every aerodrome licensed under this Order which is provided with means of two-way radio communication with aircraft and either with radar equipment or with very high frequency direction finding apparatus for the purpose of providing holding aid, let-down aid or approach aid, shall provide at the aerodrome apparatus which is capable of recording the terms or content of any radio message or signal transmitted to any aircraft (either alone or in common with other aircraft) or received from any aircraft, by the air traffic control unit at the aerodrome.

(2) The apparatus provided in compliance with this Article shall—

(*a*) be of a type approved by the Board in relation to the aerodrome;

(*b*) be installed in a manner so approved;

(*c*) always be maintained in serviceable condition; and

(*d*) be in use at all times when any navigation services are being provided by the air traffic control unit at the aerodrome to any aircraft flying for the purpose of the public transport of passengers.

(3) The licensee of the aerodrome shall ensure that each record made by the apparatus provided in compliance with this Article includes—

(*a*) the date or dates on which the record was made;

(*b*) a means of identifying the person at the aerodrome by whom the message or signal was transmitted, the aircraft to or from which and the frequency on which the message or signal was transmitted or received, and the time at which each message or signal transmitted from the aerodrome was transmitted;

(*c*) the time (if any) at which the radio station at the aerodrome opened or closed as the case may be within the period covered by each such record.

(4) If at any time the apparatus provided in compliance with this Article ceases to be capable of recording the matters required by this Article to be included in the record, the licensee of the aerodrome shall ensure that those matters are recorded in writing.

(5) The licensee of the aerodrome shall preserve any record made in compliance with this Article for a period of 30 days from the date on which the message or signal was recorded or for such longer period as the Board may in a particular case direct, and shall, within a reasonable time after being requested to do so by an authorised person, cause it to be produced to that person.

(6) A person required by this Article to preserve any record by reason of his being the licensee of an aerodrome shall, if he ceases to be the licensee of the aerodrome, continue to preserve the record as if he had not ceased to be licensee, and in the event of his death the duty to preserve the record shall fall upon his personal representative:

Provided that if another person becomes the licensee of the aerodrome he or his personal representative shall deliver the record to that other person on demand, and it shall be the duty of that other person to deal with the record delivered to him as if he were the first mentioned licensee.

Charges at aerodromes licensed for public use

67.—(1) The Board may, in relation to any aerodrome in respect of which a licence for public use has been granted, or to such aerodromes generally or to any class thereof, prescribe the charges, or the maximum charges, which may be made for the use of the aerodrome and for any services performed at the aerodrome to or in connection with aircraft, and may further prescribe the conditions to be observed in relation to those charges and the performance of those services.

(2) The licensee of an aerodrome in relation to which the Board have made any regulations under paragraph (1) of this Article shall not cause or permit any charges to be made in contravention of those regulations and shall cause particulars of the prescribed charges to be kept exhibited at the aerodrome in such a place and manner as to be readily available for the information of any person affected thereby.

(3) The licensee of any aerodrome in respect of which a licence for public use has been granted shall, when required by the Board, furnish to the Board such particulars as they may require of the charges established by the licensee for the use of the aerodrome or of any facilities provided at the aerodrome for the safety, efficiency or regularity of air navigation.

Use of aerodromes by aircraft of Contracting States and of the Commonwealth

68. The person in charge of any aerodrome in the United Kingdom which is open to public use by aircraft registered in the United Kingdom (whether or not the aerodrome is a licensed aerodrome) shall cause the aerodrome, and all air navigation facilities provided thereat, to be available for use by aircraft registered in other Contracting States or in any part of the Commonwealth on the same terms and conditions as for use by aircraft registered in the United Kingdom.

Noise and vibration caused by aircraft on aerodromes

69. The Board may prescribe the conditions under which noise and vibration may be caused by aircraft (including military aircraft) on Government aerodromes, licensed aerodromes or on aerodromes at which the manufacture, repair or maintenance of aircraft is carried out by persons carrying on business as manufacturers or repairers of aircraft, and section 41(2) of the Act shall apply to any aerodrome in relation to which the Board have prescribed conditions as aforesaid.

Aeronautical lights

70.—(1) A person shall not establish or maintain an aeronautical light within the United Kingdom except with the permission of the Board and in accordance with any conditions which may be prescribed, or subject to which the permission may be granted.

(2) A person shall not alter the character of an aeronautical light within the United Kingdom except with the permission of the Board and in accordance with any conditions subject to which the permission may be granted.

(3) In the case of an aeronautical light, being a beacon, which is or may be visible from any waters within an area of a general lighthouse authority, the Board shall not give their permission for the purpose of this Article except with the consent of that authority.

(4) A person shall not wilfully or negligently injure or interfere with any aeronautical light established and maintained by, or with the permission of, the Board.

Dangerous lights

71.—(1) A person shall not exhibit in the United Kingdom any light which—

(*a*) by reason of its glare is liable to endanger aircraft taking off from or landing at an aerodrome; or

(*b*) by reason of its liability to be mistaken for an aeronautical light is liable to endanger aircraft.

(2) If any light which appears to the Board to be such a light as aforesaid is exhibited the Board may cause a notice to be served upon the person who is the occupier of the place where the light is exhibited or having charge of the light, directing that person, within a reasonable time to be specified in the notice, to take such steps as may be specified in the notice for extinguishing or screening the light and for preventing for the future the exhibition of any other light which may similarly endanger aircraft.

(3) The notice may be served either personally or by post, or by affixing it in some conspicuous place near to the light to which it relates.

(4) In the case of a light which is or may be visible from any waters within the area of a general lighthouse authority, the powers of the Board under this Article shall not be exercised except with the consent of that authority.

Customs airports

72.—(1) The Board may, with the concurrence of the Commissioners of Customs and Excise and subject to such conditions as they may think fit, by order designate any aerodrome to be a place for the landing or departure of aircraft for the purpose of the enactments for the time being in force relating to customs.

(2) The Board may, with the concurrence of the Commissioners of Customs and Excise, by order revoke any designation so made.

PART X

GENERAL

Restriction with respect to carriage for hire or reward in aircraft registered outside the United Kingdom

73. An aircraft registered in a Contracting State other than the United Kingdom, or in a foreign country, shall not take on board or discharge any passengers or cargo in the United Kingdom, being passengers or cargo carried or to be carried for hire or reward, except with the permission of the Board granted under this Article to the operator or the charterer of the aircraft or to the Government of the country in which the aircraft is registered, and in accordance with any conditions to which such permission may be subject.

Power to prevent aircraft flying

74.—(1) If it appears to the Board or an authorised person that any aircraft is intended or likely to be flown—

(*a*) in such circumstances that any provision of Articles 3, 5, 6, 7, 17, 18, 26, 33, 37, or 73 of this Order would be contravened in relation to the flight; or

(*b*) in such circumstances that the flight would be in contravention of any other provision of this Order or any regulations made thereunder and be a cause of danger to any person or property whether or not in the aircraft;

(*c*) while in a condition unfit for the flight, whether or not the flight would otherwise be in contravention of any provision of this Order or of any regulation made thereunder,

the Board or that authorised person may direct the operator or the commander of the aircraft that he is not to permit the aircraft to make the particular flight or any other flight of such description as may be specified in the direction, until the direction has been revoked by the Board or by an authorised person, and the Board or that authorised person may take such steps as are necessary to detain the aircraft.

(2) For the purposes of paragraph (1) of this Article the Board or any authorised person may enter upon and inspect any aircraft.

Right of access to aerodromes and other places

75. The Board and any authorised person shall have the right of access at all reasonable times—

(*a*) to any aerodrome, for the purpose of inspecting the aerodrome, or

(*b*) to any aerodrome for the purpose of inspecting any aircraft on the aerodrome or any document which he has power to demand under this Order, or for the purpose of detaining any aircraft under the provisions of this Order; and

(*c*) to any place where an aircraft has landed, for the purpose of inspecting the aircraft or any document which he has power to demand under this Order and for the purpose of detaining the aircraft under the provisions of this Order:

Provided that access to a Government aerodrome shall only be obtained with the permission of the person in charge of the aerodrome.

Obstruction of persons

76. A person shall not wilfully obstruct or impede any person acting in the exercise of his powers or the performance of his duties under this Order.

Enforcement of directions

77. Any person who fails to comply with any direction given to him by the Board or by any authorised person under any provision of this Order or any regulations made thereunder shall be deemed for the purposes of this Order to have contravened that provision.

Fees

78. The Board may, with the consent of the Treasury, prescribe the fees to be paid in respect of the issue, validation, renewal, extension or variation of any certificate, licence or other document (including an application for, or the issue of a copy of, any such document) or the undergoing of any examination, test, inspection or investigation or the grant of any permission or approval, required by, or for the purpose of, any Order made under section 8 of the Act or any regulations made thereunder.

Exercise of powers etc. of the Board outside the United Kingdom

79. In so far as the exercise of any power or the performance of any duty of the Board under this Order may be required outside the United Kingdom in any country where there is no representative of the Board competent to exercise such power or to perform such duty the Board may authorise in writing any person appearing to them to be qualified so to do or the holder for the time being of any office, to exercise such power or to perform such duty.

Penalties

80.—(1) If any provision of this Order or of any regulations made thereunder is contravened in relation to an aircraft, the operator of that aircraft and the commander thereof, if the operator or, as the case may be, the commander is not the person who contravened that provision shall (without prejudice to the liability of any other person under this Order for that contravention) be deemed for the purposes of the following provisions of this Article to have contravened that provision unless he proves that the contravention occurred without his consent or connivance and that he exercised all due diligence to prevent the contravention.

(2) If it is proved that an act or omission of any person which would otherwise have been a contravention by that person of a provision of this Order or of any regulations made thereunder was due to any cause not avoidable by the exercise of reasonable care by that person the act or omission shall be deemed not to be a contravention by that person of that provision.

(3) Where a person is charged with contravening a provision of this Order or of any regulations made thereunder by reason of his having been a member of the flight crew of an aircraft on a flight for the purpose of public transport or aerial work the flight shall be treated (without prejudice to the liability of any other person under this Order) as not having been for that purpose if he proves that he neither knew nor had reason to know that the flight was for that purpose.

(4) If any person contravenes any provision of this Order, or of any regulations made thereunder, not being a provision referred to in paragraph (5) or paragraph (6) of this Article, he shall be liable on summary conviction, to a fine not exceeding ten pounds; or in the case of a second or subsequent conviction for the like offence to a fine not exceeding twenty pounds.

(5) If any person contravenes any provision specified in Part A of Schedule 12 to this Order he shall be liable on summary conviction to a fine not exceeding fifty pounds; or in the case of a second or subsequent conviction for the like offence to a fine not exceeding one hundred pounds, or to imprisonment for a term not exceeding three months or to both such fine and imprisonment.

(6) If any person contravenes any provision specified in Part B of the said Schedule he shall be liable on summary conviction or indictment to a fine not exceeding two hundred pounds or to imprisonment for a term of six months or to both such fine and imprisonment.

Extra-territorial effect of the Order

81.—(1) Except where the context otherwise requires, the provisions of this Order,

(*a*) in so far as they apply (whether by express reference or otherwise) to aircraft registered in the United Kingdom, shall apply to such aircraft wherever they may be;

(*b*) in so far as they apply as aforesaid to other aircraft shall apply to such aircraft when they are within the United Kingdom;

(*c*) in so far as they prohibit, require or regulate (whether by express reference or otherwise) the doing of anything by persons in, or by any of the crew of, any aircraft registered in the United Kingdom, shall apply to such persons and crew, wherever they may be; and

(*d*) in so far as they prohibit, require or regulate as aforesaid the doing of anything in relation to any aircraft registered in the United Kingdom by other persons shall, where such persons are British subjects or citizens of the Republic of Ireland, apply to them wherever they may be.

(2) Nothing in this Article shall be construed as extending to make any person guilty of an offence in any case in which it is provided by section 3(1) of the British Nationality Act 1948**(a)** (which limits the criminal liability of certain persons who are not citizens of the United Kingdom and colonies) that that person shall not be guilty of an offence.

Application of Order to British-controlled aircraft not registered in the United Kingdom

82. The Board may direct that such of the provisions of this Order and of any Regulations made or having effect thereunder as may be specified in the direction shall have effect as if references in those provisions to British aircraft registered in the United Kingdom included references to the aircraft specified in the direction, being an aircraft not so registered but for the time being under the management of a person who, or of persons each of whom, is qualified to be the owner of a legal or beneficial interest in an aircraft registered in the United Kingdom.

Application of Order to the Crown and visiting forces etc.

83.—(1) Subject to the following provisions of this Article, the provisions of this Order shall apply to or in relation to aircraft belonging to or exclusively

(a) 1948 c. 56.

employed in the service of Her Majesty, as they apply to or in relation to other aircraft and for the purposes of such application the Department or other authority for the time being responsible on behalf of Her Majesty for the management of the aircraft shall be deemed to be the operator of the aircraft and in the case of an aircraft belonging to Her Majesty, to be the owner of the interest of Her Majesty in the aircraft:

Provided that nothing in this Article shall render liable to any penalty any Department or other authority responsible on behalf of Her Majesty for the management of any aircraft.

(2) Save as otherwise expressly provided the naval, military and air force authorities and members of any visiting force and any international headquarters and the members thereof and property held or used for the purpose of such a force or headquarters shall be exempt from the provisions of this Order and of any regulations made thereunder to the same extent as if that force or headquarters formed part of the forces of Her Majesty raised in the United Kingdom and for the time being serving there.

(3) Save as otherwise provided by paragraph (4) of this Article, Article 60(1)(*a*) and Article 69 of this Order, nothing in this Order shall apply to or in relation to any military aircraft.

(4) Where a military aircraft is flown by a civilian pilot and is not commanded by a person who is acting in the course of his duty as a member of any of Her Majesty's naval, military or air forces or as a member of a visiting force or international headquarters, the following provisions of this Order shall apply on the occasion of that flight, that is to say, Articles 41, 42, 43 and 61, and in addition Article 60 (so far as applicable) shall apply unless the aircraft is flown in compliance with Ministry of Defence Flying Orders or Ministry of Technology Flying Orders for Military Aircraft.

Exemption from Order

84. The Board may exempt from any of the provisions of this Order or any regulations made thereunder any aircraft or persons or classes of aircraft or persons, either absolutely or subject to such conditions as they think fit.

Interpretation

85.—(1) In this Order, unless the context otherwise requires—

"The Act" means the Civil Aviation Act 1949;

"Aerial work" means any purpose (other than public transport) for which an aircraft is flown if hire or reward is given or promised in respect of the flight or the purpose of the flight;

"Aerial work aircraft" means an aircraft (other than a public transport aircraft) flying, or intended by the operator to fly, for the purpose of aerial work;

"Aerial work undertaking" means an undertaking whose business includes the performance of aerial work;

"Aerobatic manoeuvres" includes loops, spins, rolls, bunts, stall turns, inverted flying and any other similar manoeuvre;

"Aerodrome" means any area of land or water designed, equipped, set apart or commonly used for affording facilities for the landing and departure of aircraft and includes any area or space, whether on the ground, on the roof of a building or elsewhere, which is designed, equipped or set apart for affording facilities for the landing and departure of aircraft capable of descending or climbing vertically, but shall not include any area the use of which for affording facilities for the landing and departure of aircraft has been abandoned and has not been resumed;

"Aerodrome traffic zone" in relation to any aerodrome means the airspace extending from the aerodrome to a height of 2,000 feet above the level of the aerodrome and within a distance of 3,000 yards of its boundaries except any part of that airspace which is within the aerodrome traffic zone of another aerodrome which is notified for the purposes of this Order as being the controlling aerodrome;

"Aeronautical light" means any light established for the purpose of aiding air navigation;

"Aeronautical radio station" means a radio station on the surface, which transmits or receives signals for the purpose of assisting aircraft;

"Air traffic control unit" means a person appointed by the Board or by any other person maintaining an aerodrome or place to give instructions or advice or both instructions and advice by means of radio signals to aircraft in the interests of safety and "Air traffic control service" shall be construed accordingly;

"Air transport undertaking" means an undertaking whose business includes the carriage by air of passengers or cargo for hire or reward;

"Appropriate aeronautical radio station" means in relation to an aircraft an aeronautical radio station serving the area in which the aircraft is for the time being;

"Appropriate air traffic control unit" means in relation to an aircraft the air traffic control unit serving the area in which the aircraft is for the time being;

"Authorised person" for the purposes of any provision of this Order means:

(*a*) any constable, and

(*b*) any person authorised by the Board either generally or in relation to a particular case or class of cases;

"Beneficial interest" has the same meaning as in section 57 of the Merchant Shipping Act 1894(**a**);

"The Board" means the Board of Trade;

"Cargo" includes mail and animals;

"Certificate of airworthiness" includes any validation thereof and any flight manual or performance schedule relating to the certificate of airworthiness;

"Certificate of maintenance" and "certificate of compliance" have the meanings respectively assigned to them by Article 9(1) and Article 10(3) of this Order;

"Commander" in relation to an aircraft means the member of the flight crew designated as commander of that aircraft by the operator thereof, or, failing such a person the person who is for the time being the pilot in command of the aircraft;

"The Commonwealth" means the United Kingdom, the Channel Islands, the Isle of Man, the countries mentioned in section 1(3) of the British Nationality Act 1948 and all other territories forming part of Her Majesty's dominions or in which Her Majesty has jurisdiction;

"Competent authority" means in relation to the United Kingdom, the Board, and in relation to any other country the authority responsible under the law of that country for promoting the safety of civil aviation;

(**a**) 1894 c. 60.

"Congested area" in relation to a city, town or settlement, means any area which is substantially used for residential, industrial, commercial or recreational purposes;

"Contracting State" means any State (including the United Kingdom) which is a party to the Convention on International Civil Aviation signed on behalf of the Government of the United Kingdom at Chicago on the 7th December 1944;

"Controlled airspace" means control areas and control zones;

"Control area" means airspace which has been notified as such and which extends upwards from a notified altitude;

"Control zone" means airspace which has been notified as such and which extends upwards from the surface;

"Co-pilot" in relation to an aircraft means a pilot who in performing his duties as such is subject to the direction of another pilot carried in the aircraft;

"Country" includes a territory;

"Crew" has the meaning assigned to it by paragraph (4) of this Article;

"Flight" and "to fly" have the meanings respectively assigned to them by paragraph (3) of this Article;

"Flight crew" in relation to an aircraft means those members of the crew of the aircraft who respectively undertake to act as pilot, flight navigator, flight engineer and flight radio operator of the aircraft;

"Flight level" means one of a series of levels of equal atmospheric pressure, separated by notified intervals and each expressed as the number of hundreds of feet which would be indicated at that level on a pressure altimeter calibrated in accordance with the International Standard Atmosphere and set to 1013·2 millibars;

"Flight visibility" means the visibility forward from the flight deck of an aircraft in flight;

"General lighthouse authority" has the same meaning as in section 634 of the Merchant Shipping Act 1894;

"Government aerodrome" means any aerodrome in the United Kingdom which is in the occupation of any Government Department or visiting force;

"Hire-purchase agreement" and "hirer" have the same meanings respectively as in sections 1(1) and 58(1) of the Hire-Purchase Act 1965**(a)**, and, in relation to Northern Ireland, as in section 1(1) of the Hire-Purchase Act (Northern Ireland) 1966**(b)**;

"Instrument Flight Rules" means Instrument Flight Rules prescribed under Article 60 of this Order;

"Instrument Meteorological Conditions" means weather precluding flight in compliance with the Visual Flight Rules;

"International Headquarters" means an international headquarters designated by Order in Council under section 1 of the International Headquarters and Defence Organisations Act 1964**(c)**;

"To land" in relation to aircraft includes alighting on the water;

"Legal personal representative" has the same meaning as in section 742 of the Merchant Shipping Act 1894;

(a) 1965 c. 66. **(b)** 1966 c. 42. (N.I.).
(c) 1964 c. 5.

"Licence" includes any certificate of competency or certificate of validity issued with the licence or required to be held in connection with the licence by the law of the country in which the licence is granted;

"Licence for public use" has the meaning assigned to it by Article 65(2) of this Order;

"Licensed aerodrome" means an aerodrome licensed under this Order;

"Lifejacket" includes any device designed to support a person individually in or on the water;

"Log Book" in the case of an aircraft log book, engine log book or variable pitch propeller log book, includes a record kept either in a book, or by any other means approved by the Board in the particular case;

"Maximum total weight authorised" in relation to an aircraft means the maximum total weight of the aircraft and its contents at which the aircraft may take off anywhere in the world, in the most favourable circumstances in accordance with the certificate of airworthiness in force in respect of the aircraft;

"Military aircraft" includes the naval, military or air force aircraft of any country and—

(*a*) any aircraft being constructed for the naval, military or air forces of any country under a contract entered into by the Minister;

(*b*) any aircraft belonging to Her Majesty in respect of which there is in force a certificate issued by the Secretary of State for Defence that the aircraft is to be treated for the purposes of this Order as a military aircraft; and

(*c*) any aircraft in respect of which there is in force a certificate as aforesaid issued by the Minister;

"The Minister" means the Minister of Technology;

"Nautical mile" means a distance of 6,080 feet;

"Navigation services" has the same meaning as in the Civil Aviation (Eurocontrol) Act 1962**(a)**;

"Night" means the time between half an hour after sunset and half an hour before sunrise, sunset and sunrise being determined at surface level;

"Notified" means set forth in a document issued by the Board and entitled "Notam—United Kingdom" or "United Kingdom Air Pilot";

"Operator" has the meaning assigned to it by paragraph (5) of this Article;

"Pilot in command" in relation to an aircraft means a person who for the time being is in charge of the piloting of the aircraft without being under the direction of any other pilot in the aircraft;

"Prescribed" means prescribed by regulations made by the Board under this Order, and the expression "prescribe" shall be construed accordingly;

"Pressurised aircraft" means an aircraft provided with means of maintaining in any compartment a pressure greater than that of the surrounding atmosphere;

"Public transport" has the meaning assigned to it by paragraph (6) of this Article;

"Public transport aircraft" means an aircraft flying, or intended by the operator of the aircraft to fly, for the purpose of public transport;

"Record" has the same meaning as in the Civil Aviation (Eurocontrol) Act 1962;

(a) 1962 c. 8.

"Replacement" in relation to any part of an aircraft or its equipment includes the removal and replacement of that part whether or not by the same part, and whether or not any work is done on it, but does not include the removal and replacement of a part which is designed to be removable solely for the purpose of enabling another part to be inspected, repaired, removed or replaced or cargo to be loaded;

"Rules of the Air and Air Traffic Control" has the meaning assigned to it by Article 60(1) of this Order;

"Scheduled journey" means one of a series of journeys which are undertaken between the same two places and which together amount to a systematic service;

"Seaplane" has the same meaning as for the purpose of section 52 of the Act;

"Special VFR flight" means a flight which is a special VFR flight for the purposes of rules prescribed under Article 60(1) of this Order;

"Visiting force" means any such body, contingent or detachment of the forces of any country as is a visiting force for the purpose of the provisions of the Visiting Forces Act 1952(**a**)—

(*a*) which apply to that country by virtue of section 1(1)(*a*) of that Act, or

(*b*) which from time to time apply to that country by virtue of the said section 1(1)(*b*) and of any Order in Council made or hereafter to be made under the said section 1 designating that country for the purpose of all the provisions of that Act following the said section 1(2);

"Visual Flight Rules" means Visual Flight Rules prescribed under Article 60(1) of this Order;

"Visual Meteorological Conditions" means weather permitting flight in accordance with the Visual Flight Rules.

(2) In this Order any reference (except in the last foregoing paragraph) to a hire-purchase agreement includes a reference to a hire-purchase or conditional sale agreement as defined by section 1 of the Hire-Purchase (Scotland) Act 1965(**b**); and in relation to any such agreement any reference to the hirer includes a reference to the hirer as defined in section 54(1) of that Act, or, as the case may require, the buyer as defined in the said section 54(1).

(3) An aircraft shall be deemed to be in flight—

(*a*) in the case of a piloted flying machine, from the moment when, after the embarkation of its crew for the purpose of taking off, it first moves under its own power, until the moment when it next comes to rest after landing;

(*b*) in the case of a pilotless flying machine, or a glider, from the moment when it first moves for the purpose of taking off until the moment when it next comes to rest after landing;

(*c*) in the case of an airship or free balloon, from the moment when it first becomes detached from the surface until the moment when it next becomes attached thereto or comes to rest thereon;

and the expressions "a flight" and "to fly" shall be construed accordingly.

(4) Every person employed or engaged in an aircraft in flight on the business of the aircraft shall be deemed to be a member of the crew thereof.

(5) References in this Order to the operator of an aircraft are, for the purpose of the application of any provision of this Order in relation to any particular

(**a**) 1952 c. 67. (**b**) 1965 c. 67.

aircraft, references to the person who at the relevant time has the management of that aircraft, and cognate expressions shall be construed accordingly:

Provided that for the purposes of the application of any provision in Part III of this Order, when by virtue of any charter or other agreement for the hire or loan of an aircraft a person other than an air transport undertaking or an aerial work undertaking has the management of that aircraft for a period not exceeding 14 days, the foregoing provisions of this paragraph shall have effect as if that agreement had not been entered into.

(6) (*a*) Subject to the provisions of this paragraph, an aircraft in flight shall for the purposes of this Order be deemed to fly for the purpose of public transport—

(i) if hire or reward is given or promised for the carriage of passenger or cargo in the aircraft on that flight; or

(ii) if any passengers or cargo are carried gratuitously in the aircraft on that flight by an air transport undertaking, not being persons in the employment of the undertaking (including, in the case of a body corporate, its directors and, in the case of a corporation established by the Air Corporations Act 1967(**a**), members of the Corporation), persons with the authority of the Board either making any inspection or witnessing any training, practice or test for the purposes of this Order, or cargo intended to be used by any such passengers as aforesaid, or by the undertaking; or

(iii) for the purposes of Part III of this Order, if hire or reward is given or promised for the right to fly the aircraft on that flight otherwise than under a hire-purchase agreement;

and the expression "public transport of passengers" shall be construed accordingly:

Provided that, notwithstanding that an aircraft may be flying for the purpose of public transport by reason of sub-paragraph (*a*)(iii) of this paragraph it shall not be deemed to be flying for the purpose of the public transport of passengers unless hire or reward is given for the carriage of those passengers.

(*b*) Where under a transaction effected by or on behalf of a member of an unincorporated association of persons on the one hand and the association of persons or any member thereof on the other hand, a person is carried in, or is given the right to fly, an aircraft in such circumstances that hire or reward would be deemed to be given or promised if the transaction were effected otherwise than as aforesaid, hire or reward shall, for the purposes of this Order, be deemed to be given.

(7) The expressions appearing in the "General Classification of Aircraft" set forth in Part A of Schedule 1 to this Order shall have the meanings thereby assigned to them.

(8) The Interpretation Act 1889 applies for the purpose of the interpretation of this Order as it applies for the purpose of the interpretation of an Act of Parliament.

(9) A power to make regulations under this Order shall include the power to make different provisions with respect to different classes of aircraft, aerodromes, persons or property and with respect to different circumstances and with respect to different parts of the United Kingdom and to make such incidental and supplementary provisions as are necessary or expedient for carrying out the purposes of the Order.

(**a**) 1967 c. 33.

(10) Unless the context otherwise requires any reference in the Order to any Act of Parliament shall be construed as a reference to that Act as amended, extended or applied by under any other Act.

Saving

86. Subject to the provisions of Articles 65 and 68 of this Order, nothing in this Order or the regulations made thereunder shall confer any right to land in any place as against the owner of the land or other persons interested therein.

Small aircraft

87. The provisions of this Order, other than Articles 42 and 62 thereof, shall not apply to or in relation to—

(*a*) any balloon which at any stage of its flight is not more than 6 feet in any linear dimension including any basket or other equipment attached to the balloon;

(*b*) any kite weighing not more than 4 lb.;

(*c*) any other aircraft weighing not more than 11 lb. without its fuel.

W. G. Agnew.

SCHEDULE 1

Articles 4 (6), 22 (1) and 85 (7)

PART A

TABLE OF GENERAL CLASSIFICATION OF AIRCRAFT

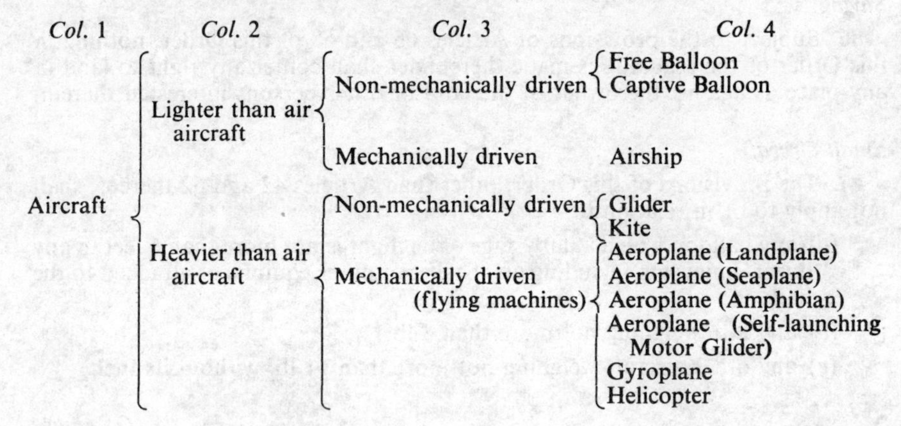

Col. 1	*Col.* 2	*Col.* 3	*Col.* 4
Aircraft	Lighter than air aircraft	Non-mechanically driven	Free Balloon Captive Balloon
		Mechanically driven	Airship
	Heavier than air aircraft	Non-mechanically driven	Glider Kite
		Mechanically driven (flying machines)	Aeroplane (Landplane) Aeroplane (Seaplane) Aeroplane (Amphibian) Aeroplane (Self-launching Motor Glider) Gyroplane Helicopter

Article 5 (2)

PART B

NATIONALITY AND REGISTRATION MARKS OF AIRCRAFT REGISTERED IN THE UNITED KINGDOM

1. The nationality mark of the aircraft shall be the capital letter "G" in Roman character and the registration mark shall be a group of four capital letters in Roman character assigned by the Board on the registration of the aircraft. The letters shall be without ornamentation and a hyphen shall be placed between the nationality mark and the registration mark.

2. The nationality and registration marks shall be painted on the aircraft or shall be affixed thereto by any other means ensuring a similar degree of permanence in the following manner:

I. *Position of marks*

(*a*) *Flying machines and Gliders*

(i) *Wings:* Except on aircraft having no fixed wing surface, the marks shall appear on the lower surface of the wing structure, and shall be on the left half of the lower surface of the wing structure unless they extend across the whole surface of both wings. So far as possible the marks shall be located equidistant from the leading and trailing edges of the wings. The tops of the letters shall be towards the leading edge of the wing.

(ii) *Fuselage* (*or equivalent structure*) *or Vertical Tail Surface:* The marks shall also be either on each side of the fuselage (or equivalent structure) between the wings and the tail surfaces, or on the upper halves of the vertical tail surfaces. When on a single vertical tail surface they shall be on both sides of the tail. When there is more than one vertical tail surface, the marks shall appear on the outboard sides of the outer tails.

(*b*) *Airships and Balloons*

(i) *Airships:* The marks shall be on each side of the airship and also on the upper surface on the line of symmetry. They shall be placed lengthwise near the maximum cross-section of the airship.

(ii) *Spherical Balloons:* The marks shall be in two places diametrically opposite. They shall be placed near the maximum horizontal circumference of the balloon.

(iii) *Non-Spherical Balloons:* The marks shall be on each side. They shall be placed near the maximum cross-section of the balloon immediately above either the rigging band or the points of attachment of the basket suspension cables.

(iv) In the case of all airships and balloons the side marks shall be so placed as to be visible both from the sides and from the ground.

II. *Size of Marks*

(*a*) *Flying Machines and Gliders*

(i) *Wings:* The letters constituting each group of marks shall be of equal height. The height of the letters shall be at least 20 inches.

(ii) *Fuselage (or equivalent structure) or Vertical Tail Surfaces:* The marks on the fuselage (or equivalent structure) shall not interfere with the visible outlines of the fuselage (or equivalent structure). The marks on the vertical tail surfaces shall be such as to leave a margin of at least two inches along each side of the vertical tail surface. The letters constituting each group of marks shall be of equal height. The height of the marks shall be at least 12 inches:

Provided that where owing to the structure of the aircraft a height of 12 inches is not reasonably practicable, the height shall be the greatest height reasonably practicable in the circumstances, but not less than 6 inches.

(*b*) *Airships and Balloons*

The letters constituting each group of marks shall be of equal height. The height of the letters shall be at least 30 inches.

III. *Width and Spacing of Marks*

(*a*) The width of each letter (except the letter I) and the length of the hyphen between the nationality mark and registration mark shall be two-thirds of the height of a letter.

(*b*) The letters and hyphens shall be formed by solid lines and shall be of a colour clearly contrasting with the background on which they appear. The thickness of the lines shall be one-sixth of the height of a letter.

(*c*) Each letter shall be separated from the letter which it immediately precedes or follows by a space equal to half the width of a letter. A hyphen shall be regarded as a letter for this purpose.

3. The nationality and registration marks shall be displayed to the best advantage, taking into consideration the constructional features of the aircraft and shall always be kept clean and visible.

4. In addition to the foregoing requirements of this Schedule the nationality and registration marks shall also be inscribed, together with the name and address of the registered owner of the aircraft, on a fireproof metal plate affixed in a prominent position to the fuselage or car or basket, as the case may be, and near the main entrance to the aircraft.

SCHEDULE 2

Articles 3 (1), 4 (8), 7 (1) and 35 (5)

A, B, AND C CONDITIONS

The A Conditions, B Conditions and C Conditions referred to in Articles 3(1), 4(8), 7(1) and 35(5) of this Order are as follows:

A Conditions

(1) The aircraft shall be either an aircraft in respect of which a certificate of airworthiness or validation has previously been in force under the provisions

of this Order, or an aircraft identical in design with an aircraft in respect of which such a certificate is or has been in force.

(2) The aircraft shall fly only for the purpose of enabling it to:

(*a*) qualify for the issue or renewal of a certificate of airworthiness or of the validation thereof or the approval of a modification of the aircraft, after an application has been made for such issue, renewal, validation or approval, as the case may be; or

(*b*) proceed to or from a place at which any inspection, test or weighing of the aircraft is to take place for a purpose referred to in sub-paragraph (*a*).

(3) The aircraft and its engines shall be certified as fit for flight by the holder of a licence as an aircraft maintenance engineer entitled in accordance with the provisions of Schedule 4 to this Order so to certify, or by a person approved by the Board for the purpose of issuing certificates under this condition.

(4) The aircraft shall carry the minimum flight crew specified in any certificate of airworthiness or validation which has previously been in force under this Order in respect of the aircraft, or is or has previously been in force in respect of any other aircraft of identical design.

(5) The aircraft shall not carry any passengers or cargo except passengers performing duties in the aircraft in connection with the flight.

(6) The aircraft shall not fly over any congested area of a city, town or settlement except to the extent that it is necessary to do so in order to take off from or land at a Government aerodrome or a licensed aerodrome in accordance with normal aviation practice.

(7) Without prejudice to the provisions of Article 17(2) of this Order, the aircraft shall carry such flight crew as may be necessary to ensure the safety of the aircraft.

B Conditions

(1) The flight shall be made under the supervision of a person approved by the Board for the purposes of these Conditions, and subject to any additional conditions which may be specified in such approval.

(2) If it is not registered in the United Kingdom or under the law of any country referred to in Article 3 of this Order, the aircraft shall be marked in a manner approved by the Board for the purposes of these Conditions, and the provisions of Articles 13, 14, 18, 29, 32, 55 and 56 of this Order shall be complied with in relation to the aircraft as if it was registered in the United Kingdom so far as such provisions are applicable to the aircraft in the circumstances.

(3) The aircraft shall fly only for the purpose of:

(*a*) experimenting with or testing the aircraft (including in particular its engines) and its equipment; or

(*b*) enabling the aircraft to qualify for the issue or validation of a certificate of airworthiness or the approval of a modification of the aircraft; or

(*c*) proceeding to or from a place at which any experiment, test, inspection or weighing of the aircraft is to take place for a purpose referred to in sub-paragraph (*a*) or (*b*).

(4) The aircraft shall carry such flight crew as may be necessary to ensure the safety of the aircraft.

(5) The aircraft shall not carry any cargo, or any persons other than the flight crew except the following:

(*a*) persons employed by the operator who carry out during the flight duties in connection with the purposes specified in paragraph (3) of these Conditions;

(*b*) persons employed by manufacturers of component parts of the aircraft (including the engine) who carry out during the flight duties in connection with the purposes so specified;

(*c*) persons approved by the Board under Article 8(8) of this Order as qualified to furnish reports for the purposes of that Article;

(*d*) persons, other than those carried under the preceding provisions of this paragraph, who are carried in the aircraft in order to carry out a technical evaluation of the aircraft or its operation.

(6) The aircraft shall not fly, except in accordance with procedures which have been approved by the Board in relation to that flight, over any congested area of a city, town or settlement.

C Conditions

(1) The operator of the aircraft shall be the registered owner of the aircraft, who shall be the holder of an aircraft dealer's certificate granted under this Order.

(2) The aircraft shall fly only for the purpose of—

(*a*) testing the aircraft; or

(*b*) demonstrating the aircraft with a view to the sale of that aircraft or of other similar aircraft; or

(*c*) proceeding to or from a place at which the aircraft is to be tested or demonstrated as aforesaid, or overhauled, repaired or modified; or

(*d*) delivering the aircraft to a person who has agreed to buy or lease it.

(3) The aircraft shall fly only within the United Kingdom.

SCHEDULE 3

Article 8

1. *Categories of Aircraft*

Transport Category (Passenger).

Transport Category (Cargo).

Aerial Work Category.

Private Category.

Special Category.

2. The purposes for which the aircraft may fly are as follows:

Transport Category (Passenger): Any purpose.

Transport Category (Cargo): Any purpose, other than the public transport of passengers.

Aerial Work Category: Aerial work only.

Private Category: Any purpose other than public transport or aerial work.

Special Category: Any other purpose specified in the certificate of airworthiness but not including the carriage of passengers unless expressly permitted.

SCHEDULE 4

Article 11(2)

Maintenance Engineers: Privileges of Licences

An aircraft maintenance engineer may, subject to the conditions of his licence issue certificates as follows:

Aircraft Maintenance Engineers—Category A (Aircraft)

In relation to aircraft (not including engines)—

(a) certificates of maintenance in accordance with the maintenance schedules approved under this Order;

(*b*) certificates of compliance in respect of inspections, repairs, replacements and modifications so approved;

(*c*) certificates of fitness of aircraft for flight under the "A Conditions".

Aircraft Maintenance Engineers—Category B (Aircraft)

In relation to aircraft (not including engines)—

Certificates of compliance in respect of inspections, overhauls, repairs, replacements and modifications approved under this Order.

Aircraft Maintenance Engineers—Category C (Engines)

In relation to engines—

(*a*) certificates of maintenance in accordance with the maintenance schedules approved under this Order;

(*b*) certificates of compliance in respect of inspections, repairs, replacements and modifications so approved;

(*c*) certificates of fitness of aircraft engines for flight under the "A Conditions".

Aircraft Maintenance Engineers—Category D (Engines)

In relation to engines—

Certificates of compliance in respect of inspections, overhauls, repairs, replacements and modifications approved under this Order.

Aircraft Maintenance Engineers—Category X

Compasses
Instruments
Electrical
Automatic Pilots.

In relation respectively to compasses, instruments, electrical or automatic pilots—

(*a*) certificates of maintenance in accordance with the maintenance schedules approved under this Order;

(*b*) certificates of compliance in respect of inspections, repairs, replacements and modifications so approved.

Aircraft Radio Maintenance Engineers—Category R (Radio)

In relation to aircraft radio stations—

(*a*) certificates of maintenance in accordance with the maintenance schedules approved under this Order;

(*b*) certificates of compliance in respect of inspections, repairs, replacements and modifications so approved.

The privileges of the licence shall also include the issue of certificates of compliance in respect of inspections, overhauls, repairs, replacements and modifications of any aircraft radio apparatus approved under this Order, if the licence bears an endorsement to that effect.

SCHEDULE 5

Articles 10(2) and 12(2)

AIRCRAFT EQUIPMENT

1. Every aircraft registered in the United Kingdom shall be provided, when flying in the circumstances specified in the first column of the Table set forth in paragraph (4) of this Schedule with adequate equipment, and for the purpose of this paragraph the expression "adequate equipment" shall mean the scales of equipment respectively indicated in that Table:

Provided that, if the aircraft is flying in a combination of such circumstances the scales of equipment shall not on that account be required to be duplicated.

2. The equipment carried in an aircraft as being necessary for the airworthiness of the aircraft shall be taken into account in determining whether this Schedule is complied with in respect of that aircraft.

3. The following items of equipment shall not be required to be of a type approved by the Board:

(i) The equipment referred to in Scale A (ii).

(ii) First Aid Equipment and Handbook, referred to in Scale B.

(iii) Time-pieces, referred to in Scale F.

(iv) Torches, referred to in Scales G, H and J.

(v) Whistles, referred to in Scale H.

(vi) Sea anchors, referred to in Scales I and J.

(vii) Rocket signals, referred to in Scale I.

(viii) Equipment for mooring, anchoring or manoeuvring aircraft on the water, referred to in Scale I.

(ix) Paddles, referred to in Scale J.

(x) Food and water, referred to in Scale J.

TABLE

Aircraft and Circumstances of Flight	Scale of Equipment Required																		
	A	B	C	D	E	F	G	H	I	J	K	L	M	N	O	P	Q	R	Extras
(1) *Flying machines flying for purposes other than public transport*																			
(*a*) when flying at night	A		C	D															
(*b*) when flying under Instrument Flight Rules (i) outside controlled airspace	A			D															
(ii) within controlled airspace	A				E	F													E (iv) duplicated
(*c*) when carrying out aerobatic manoeuvres ...	A												M						
(*d*) on all other flights	A																		
(2) *Flying machines flying for the purpose of public transport*																			
(*a*) when flying under Instrument Flight Rules (i) in the case of flying machines of which the maximum total weight authorised exceeds 2,500 lb.	A	B			E	F													E (iv) duplicated
(ii) in the case of flying machines of which the maximum total weight authorised does not exceed 2,500 lb. (*a*) outside controlled airspace	A	B		D		F (i) only													
(*b*) within controlled airspace	A	B			E	F													E (iv) duplicated

Aircraft and Circumstances of Flight	Scale of Equipment Required																		
	A	B	C	D	E	F	G	H	I	J	K	L	M	N	O	P	Q	R	Extras
(*b*) when flying at night (i) in the case of flying machines of which the maximum total weight authorised exceeds 2,500 lb.	A	B	C		E	F	G												E (iv) duplicated
(ii) in the case of flying machines of which the maximum total weight authorised does not exceed 2,500 lb.	A	B	C	D		F (i) only	G												
(*c*) when flying over water beyond gliding distance from land	A	B		D		F (i) only		H											
(*d*) when flying over water (i) in the case of an aeroplane (*a*) classified in its certificate of airworthiness as being of performance group A, C or X, or (*b*) having no performance group classification in its certificate of airworthiness and of such a weight and performance that with any one of its power units inoperative and the remaining power unit or units operating within the maximum continuous power conditions specified in the certificate of airworthiness, performance schedule or flight manual relating to the aeroplane issued or rendered valid by the Board, it is capable of a gradient																			

of climb of at least 1 in 200 at an altitude of 5,000 feet in the International Standard Atmosphere specified in or ascertainable by reference to the certificate of airworthiness in force in respect of that aircraft, when either more than 400 nautical miles or more than 90 minutes flying time* from the nearest aerodrome at which an emergency landing can be made;																		
(ii) in the case of all other flying machines, when more than 30 minutes flying time* from such an aerodrome	A	B		D		F (i) only		H		J								
(*e*) on all flights which involve manoeuvres on water	A	B		D		F (i) only		H	I	J								
(*f*) when flying at a height of 10,000 feet or more above mean sea level	A	B		D		F (i) only						K						
(*g*) on flights when the weather reports or forecasts available at the aerodrome at the time of departure indicate that conditions favouring ice formation are likely to be met	A	B		D		F (i) only						L						
(*h*) when carrying out aerobatic manoeuvres ...	A	B		D		F (i) only							M					
(*i*) on all flights on which the aircraft carries a flight crew of more than one person														N				

*For the purposes of this Table, flying time shall be calculated on the assumption that the aircraft is flying in still air at the speed specified in the relevant Certificate of Airworthiness as the speed for compliance with regulations governing flights over water.

Aircraft and Circumstances of Flight	Scale of Equipment Required																		
	A	B	C	D	E	F	G	H	I	J	K	L	M	N	O	P	Q	R	Extras
(*j*) (i) on all flights by flying machines first registered (whether in the United Kingdom or elsewhere) on or after 1st January 1967 being turbine-jet aircraft with a maximum total weight authorised over 12,500 lb. or pressurised aircraft with a maximum total weight authorised over 25,000 lb.; (ii) on all flights by such flying machines as aforesaid, being aircraft first registered (whether in the United Kingdom or elsewhere) before 1st January 1967; with the exception of any flight on which the radar set specified in Scale O in paragraph 5 of this Schedule is unserviceable on take-off but the weather report or forecasts available to the commander of the aircraft at that time indicate that cumulo-nimbus clouds or other potentially hazardous weather conditions which can be detected by the set when in working order are unlikely to be encountered on the intended route or any planned diversion therefrom, or the commander of the aircraft has satisfied himself that any such weather conditions will be encountered in daylight and can be seen and avoided, and the aircraft is in either case operated throughout the flight in accordance with any relevant instructions given in the operations manual															O				
(*k*) on all flights for the purpose of the public transport of passengers																	Q		

(*l*) on all flights by a pressurised aircraft ...																		R	
(*m*) on all other flights	A	B		D		F (i) only													
(3) *Gliders flying for purposes other than public transport or aerial work* when flying by night	A(ii) only		C																
(4) *Gliders flying for the purpose of public transport or aerial work* (*a*) when outside controlled airspace under Instrument Flight Rules...	A	B		D		F (i) only													
(*b*) when flying by night	A	B	C	D		F (i) only	G												
(*c*) when carrying out aerobatic manoeuvres ...	A	B		D		F (i) only							M						
(*d*) on all other flights	A	B		D		F (i) only													
(5) *Turbined-engined aeroplanes over 12,500 lb. maximum total weight authorised and piston-engined aeroplanes over 60,000 lb. maximum total weight authorised* (*a*) *which are operated by an air transport undertaking under a certificate of air-worthiness of the Transport Category (Passenger) or the Transport Category (Cargo); or* (*b*) *in respect of which application has been made and not withdrawn or refused for such a certificate, and which fly under the "A" Conditions or under a certificate of air-worthiness of the Special Category* when flying on any flight																P			

5. The scales of equipment indicated in the foregoing Table shall be as follows:

Scale A

(i) Spare fuses for all electrical circuits the fuses of which can be replaced in flight, consisting of 10 per cent. of the number of each rating or three of each rating whichever is the greater;

(ii) Maps, charts, codes and other documents and navigational equipment necessary, in addition to any other equipment required under this Order, for the intended flight of the aircraft, including any diversion which may reasonably be expected.

(iii) Subject to Scale B (iii), a safety belt or safety harness for every seat in use.

Scale B

(i) First-aid equipment of good quality, sufficient in quantity, having regard to the number of persons on board the aircraft, and including the following:

Roller bandages, triangular bandages, absorbent gauze, adhesive plaster, white absorbent lint, cotton wool (or wound dressings in place of the lint and cotton wool), burn dressings, safety pins;

Haemostatic bandages or tourniquet, scissors;

Antiseptic, analgesic and stimulant drugs;

A handbook on First Aid.

(ii) In the case of a flying machine used for the public transport of passengers in which, while the flying machine is at rest on the ground, the sill of any external door intended for the disembarkation of passengers, whether normally or in an emergency,

(*a*) is more than six feet from the ground when the undercarriage of the machine is in the normal position for taxying, or

(*b*) would be more than six feet from the ground if the undercarriage or any part thereof should collapse, break or fail to function,

apparatus readily available for use at each such door consisting of a device or devices which will enable passengers to reach the ground safely in an emergency while the flying machine is on the ground, and can be readily fixed in position for use.

(iii) If the maximum total weight authorised of the aircraft is more than 6,000 lb. a safety harness for every pilot's seat in use, in place of the safety belt referred to under Scale A:

Provided that the Board may permit a safety belt to be fitted if they are satisfied that it is not reasonably practicable to fit a safety harness.

(iv) If the commander cannot, from his own seat, see all the passengers' seats in the aircraft, a means of indicating to the passengers that seat belts should be fastened.

Scale C

(i) Equipment for displaying the lights required by the Rules of the Air and Air Traffic Control;

(ii) Electrical equipment, supplied from the main source of supply in the aircraft, to provide sufficient illumination to enable the flight crew properly to carry out their duties during flight;

(iii) Unless the aircraft is equipped with radio, devices for making the visual signal specified in the Rules of the Air and Air Traffic Control as indicating a request for permission to land.

Scale D

(i) Either (*a*) a turn and slip indicator; or

(*b*) a gyroscopic bank and pitch indicator and a gyroscopic direction indicator;

(ii) A sensitive pressure altimeter adjustable for changes in barometric pressure.

Scale E

(i) A turn and slip indicator;

(ii) A gyroscopic bank and pitch indicator;

(iii) A gyroscopic direction indicator;

(iv) A sensitive pressure altimeter adjustable for changes in barometric pressure.

Scale F

(i) A timepiece with a sweep second hand;

(ii) A means of indicating whether the power supply to the gyroscopic instruments is adequate;

(iii) A rate of climb and descent indicator;

(iv) If the maximum total weight authorised of the aircraft is more than 12,500 lb., a means of indicating the outside air temperature;

(v) If the maximum total weight authorised of the aircraft is more than 12,500 lb., two air speed indicators.

Scale G

(i) Landing lights consisting of two single filament lamps, or one dual filament lamp with separately energised filaments;

(ii) An electric lighting system to provide illumination in every passenger compartment;

(iii) (*a*) If the aircraft, in accordance with its certificate of airworthiness, may carry more than nineteen persons over three years of age; two electric torches and an emergency lighting system to provide illumination in the passenger compartments sufficient to facilitate the evacuation of the aircraft notwithstanding the failure of the lighting systems specified in sub-paragraph (ii);

(*b*) In the case of any other aircraft, one electric torch for each member of the crew of the aircraft;

(iv) In the case of an aircraft of which the maximum total weight authorised exceeds 12,500 lb., means of observing the existence and build up of ice on the aircraft.

Scale H

For each person on board, a lifejacket equipped with a whistle and waterproof torch:

Provided that lifejackets constructed and carried solely for use by children under three years of age need not be equipped with a whistle.

Scale I

(i) Additional flotation equipment, capable of supporting one-fifth of the number of persons on board, and provided in a place of stowage accessible from outside the flying machine;

(ii) Parachute distress rocket signals capable of making, from the surface of the water, the pyrotechnical signal of distress specified in the Rules of the Air and Air Traffic Control and complying with Part III of Schedule 14 to the Merchant Shipping (Life-Saving Appliances) Rules 1965(a);

(iii) A sea anchor and other equipment necessary to facilitate mooring, anchoring or manoeuvring the flying machine on water, appropriate to its size, weight, and handling characteristics.

Scale J

(i) Liferafts sufficient to accommodate all persons on board the flying machine with the following equipment:

(*a*) means for maintaining buoyancy;

(*b*) a sea anchor;

(a) S.I. 1965/1105 (1965 II, p. 2940).

(*c*) life lines, and means of attaching one liferaft to another;

(*d*) paddles or other means of propulsion;

(*e*) means of protecting the occupants from the elements;

(*f*) waterproof torch;

(*g*) marine type pyrotechnical distress signals;

(*h*) means of making sea water drinkable;

(*i*) for each person the liferaft is designed to carry:
8 ounces of glucose toffee tablets;
4 ounces of sweetened condensed milk in durable containers;
2 pints of fresh water in durable containers:

Provided that in any case in which it is not reasonably practicable owing to lack of stowage space in the liferaft to carry the quantities of condensed milk and water above prescribed, an equal quantity by weight of glucose toffee tablets may be substituted for the former and as large a quantity of fresh water as is reasonably practicable in the circumstances may be substituted for the latter. In no case however shall the quantity of water carried be less than is sufficient, when added to the amount of fresh water capable of being produced by means of the equipment specified in item (*h*) of this sub-paragraph, to provide 2 pints of water for each person the liferaft is designed to carry;

(*j*) first aid equipment.

Items (*f*) to (*j*), inclusive, shall be contained in a pack stowed with the liferaft.

(ii) For every four, or proportion of four liferafts, one liferaft radio transmitter.

Scale K

PART I

(i) In every flying machine which is provided with means for maintaining a pressure greater than 700 millibars throughout the flight in the flight crew compartment and in the compartments in which passengers are carried—

(*a*) a supply of oxygen sufficient, in the event of failure to maintain such pressure, occurring in the circumstances specified in columns 1 and 2 of the Table set out in Part II of this Scale, for continuous use, during the periods specified in column 3 of the said Table, by the persons for whom oxygen is to be provided in accordance with column 4 of that Table, and

(*b*) in addition, in every case where the flying machine flies above flight level 350, a supply of oxygen in a portable container sufficient for the simultaneous first aid treatment of two passengers,

together with suitable and sufficient apparatus to enable such persons to use the oxygen.

(ii) In any other flying machine—

(*a*) a supply of oxygen sufficient for continuous use by all the crew, and, if passengers are carried, by 10 per cent. of the number of passengers, for any period exceeding 30 minutes during which the flying machine flies above flight level 100 but not above flight level 130; and

(*b*) a supply of oxygen sufficient for continuous use by all persons on board for the whole time during which the flying machine flies above flight level 130,

together with suitable and sufficient apparatus to enable such person to use the oxygen.

(iii) The quantity of oxygen required for the purpose of complying with paragraphs (i) and (ii) of this Part of this Scale shall be computed in accordance with the information and instructions relating thereto specified in the operations manual relating to the aircraft pursuant to Item (vi) of Part A of Schedule 10 to this Order.

PART II

Column 1	Column 2	Column 3	Column 4
Vertical displacement of the flying machine in relation to flight levels	*Capability of flying machine to descend (where relevant)*	*Period of supply of oxygen*	*Persons for whom oxygen is to be provided*
Above flight level 100	—	30 minutes or the period specified at A hereunder whichever is the greater	In addition to any passengers for whom oxygen is provided as specified below, all the crew
Above flight level 100 but not above flight level 300	Flying machine is either flying at or below flight level 150 or is capable of descending and continuing to destination as specified at X hereunder	30 minutes or the period specified at A hereunder whichever is the greater	10 per cent of number of passengers
	Flying machine is flying above flight level 150 and is not so capable	10 minutes or the period specified at B hereunder whichever is the greater	All passengers
		and in addition	
		30 minutes or the period specified at C hereunder whichever is the greater	10 per cent of number of passengers
Above flight level 300 but not above flight level 350	Flying machine is capable of descending and continuing to destination as specified at Y hereunder	30 minutes or the period specified at A hereunder whichever is the greater	15 per cent of number of passengers

PART II (*cont.*)

	Flying machine is not so capable	10 minutes or the period specified at B hereunder whichever is the greater	All passengers
			and in addition
		30 minutes or the period specified at C hereunder whichever is the greater	15 per cent of number of passengers
Above flight level 350	—	10 minutes or the period specified at B hereunder whichever is the greater	All passengers
			and in addition
		30 minutes or the period specified at C hereunder whichever is the greater	15 per cent of number of passengers

A. The whole period during which, after a failure to maintain a pressure greater than 700 millibars in the control compartment and in the compartments in which passengers are carried has occurred, the flying machine flies above flight level 100.

B. The whole period during which, after failure to maintain such pressure had occurred, the flying machine flies above flight level 150.

C. The whole period during which, after a failure to maintain such pressure has occurred, the flying machine flies above flight level 100, but not above flight level 150.

X. The flying machine is capable, at the time when a failure to maintain such pressure occurs, of descending in accordance with the emergency descent procedure specified in the relevant flight manual and without flying below the minimum altitudes for safe flight specified in the operations manual relating to the aircraft, to flight level 150 within 6 minutes, and of continuing at or below that flight level to its place of intended destination or any other place at which a safe landing can be made.

Y. The flying machine is capable, at the time when a failure to maintain such pressure occurs of descending in accordance with the emergency descent procedure specified in the relevant flight manual and without flying below the minimum altitudes for safe flight specified in the operations manual relating to the aircraft, to flight level 150 within 4 minutes and of continuing at or below that flight level to its place of intended destination or any other place at which a safe landing can be made.

Scale L

Equipment to prevent the impairment through ice formation of the functioning of the controls, means of propulsion, lifting surfaces, windows or equipment of the aircraft so as to endanger the safety of the aircraft.

Scale M

Safety harness for every seat in use.

Scale N

An intercommunication system for use by all members of the flight crew and including microphones, not of a hand-held type, for use by the pilot and flight engineer (if any).

Scale O

A radar set capable of giving warning to the pilot in command of the aircraft and to the co-pilot of the presence of cumulo-nimbus clouds and other potentially hazardous weather conditions: provided that if the set becomes unserviceable so as to give the warning only to one pilot, it shall nevertheless be sufficient so long as the aircraft is flying only to the place at which it first becomes reasonably practicable for the set to be repaired.

Scale P

A flight recorder which is capable of recording, by reference to a time-scale, the following data—

(*a*) indicated air speed;

(*b*) indicated altitude;

(*c*) vertical accelaration:

(*d*) magnetic heading;

(*e*) pitch attitude, if the equipment provided in the aircraft is of such a nature as to enable this item to be recorded.

The recorder shall be so constructed that the record would likely to be preserved in the event of an accident to the aircraft.

Scale Q

If the maximum total weight authorised of the flying machine exceeds 12,500 lb. and it was first registered, whether in the United Kingdom or elsewhere, on or after 1st June 1965, a door between the flight crew compartment and any adjacent compartment to which passengers have access, which door shall be fitted with a lock or bolt capable of being worked from the flight crew compartment.

Scale R

(i) Equipment sufficient to protect the eyes, nose and mouth of the pilot in command of the aircraft from the effects of smoke and noxious gases for a period of not less than 15 minutes; and

(ii) Portable equipment sufficient to protect the eyes, nose and mouth of one other member of the crew of the aircraft from the effects of smoke and noxious gases for a period of not less than 8 minutes; and

(iii) Equipment sufficient to protect from the effects of smoke and noxious gases the eyes of all members of the flight crew of the aircraft whose eyes are not adequately protected by other equipment.

SCHEDULE 6

Article 13

Radio Apparatus to be carried in Aircraft

1. Every aircraft registered in the United Kingdom shall be provided, when flying in the circumstances specified in the first column of the Table set forth in paragraph (2) of this Schedule, with the scales of equipment respectively indicated in that Table:

Provided that, if the aircraft is flying in a combination of such circumstances the scales of equipment shall not on that account be required to be duplicated.

2. Table

Aircraft and Circumstances of Flight	Scale of Equipment Required			
	A	B	C	D
(1) *All aircraft*				
(a) when flying under Instrument Flight Rules within controlled airspace ..	A	B		
(b) where required by Regulations made under Article 60 of this Order to comply in whole or in part with instrument Flight Rules in Visual Meteorological Conditions	A*	B*		
(c) when flying within any airspace in respect of which special rules may be prescribed by the said Regulations in relation to a particular aerodrome, so as to require two-way radio communication with that aerodrome	A*			
(2) *All aircraft when flying for the purpose of public transport under Instrument Flight Rules:*				
(i) while making an approach to landing	A	B	C	D
(ii) on all other occasions	A	B	C	
(3) *All aircraft over 5,000 lb. maximum total weight authorised when flying for the purpose of public transport under visual Flight Rules*	A	B		
(4) *All aircraft not over 5,000 lb. maximum total weight authorised when flying for the purpose of public transport under Visual Flight Rules:*				
(i) over a route on which navigation is not effected solely by visual reference to landmarks	A	B		
(ii) over water, beyond gliding distance from any land	A			

*Unless the appropriate Air Traffic Control Unit otherwise permits in relation to the particular flight.

3. The scales of radio apparatus indicated in the foregoing Table shall be as follows:

Scale A

Radio apparatus capable of maintaining two-way communication with the appropriate aeronautical radio stations.

Scale B

Radio apparatus capable of enabling the aircraft to be navigated on the intended route including such apparatus as may be prescribed.

Scale C

Radio apparatus capable of receiving from the appropriate aeronautical radio stations meteorological broadcasts relevant to the intended flight.

Scale D

Radio apparatus capable of receiving signals from one or more aeronautical radio stations on the surface to enable the aircraft to be guided to a point from which a visual landing can be made at the aerodrome at which the aircraft is to land.

4. All aircraft when flying to, from, or over Berlin, Germany, shall be equipped with radio navigation apparatus appropriate to the route, including automatic direction finding apparatus and any one of the following:

(i) apparatus which will enable the aircraft to be navigated by means of signals received from radio navigation land stations forming part of the Decca radio navigation system, or

(ii) apparatus capable of giving visual indications of bearings of the aircraft by means of signals received from very high frequency omni-directional radio ranges.

In this sub-paragraph "automatic direction finding apparatus" means radio navigation apparatus which automatically indicates the bearing of any radio station transmitting the signals received by such apparatus.

SCHEDULE 7

Article 14

Aircraft, Engine and Propeller Log Books

1. *Aircraft Log Book*

The following entries shall be included in the aircraft log book:

(*a*) the name of the constructor, the type of the aircraft, the number assigned to it by the constructor and the date of the construction of the aircraft;

(*b*) the nationality and registration marks of the aircraft;

(*c*) the name and address of the operator of the aircraft;

(*d*) particulars of the date and duration of each flight, or, if more than one flight was made on one day, the number of flights and total duration of flights on that day;

(*e*) particulars of all maintenance work carried out on the aircraft or its equipment;

(*f*) particulars of any defects ocurring in the aircraft or in any equipment required to be carried therein by or under this Order, and of the action taken to rectify such defects including a reference to the relevant entries in the technical log required by Article 9(5) and (6) of this Order;

(*g*) particulars of any overhauls, repairs, replacements and modifications relating to the aircraft or any such equipment as aforesaid:

Provided that entries shall not be required to be made under sub-paragraphs (*e*), (*f*) and (*g*) in respect of any engine or variable pitch propeller.

2. *Engine Log Book*

The following entries shall be included in the engine log book:

(*a*) the name of the constructor, the type of the engine, the number assigned to it by the constructor and the date of the construction of the engine;

(*b*) the nationality and registration marks of each aircraft in which the engine is fitted;

(*c*) the name and address of the operator of each such aircraft;

(*d*) particulars of the date and duration of each occasion on which the engine is run in flight, or, if the engine is run on more than one occasion on one day the number of occasions and the total duration of the running of the engine on that day;

(*e*) particulars of all maintenance work done on the engine;

(*f*) particulars of any defects occuring in the engine, and of the rectification of such defects, including a reference to the relevant entries in the technical log required by Article 9(5) and (6) of this Order;

(*g*) particulars of all overhauls, repairs, replacements and modifications relating to the engine or any of its accessories.

3. *Variable Pitch Propeller Log Book*

The following entries shall be included in the variable pitch propeller log book:

(*a*) the name of the constructor, the type of the propeller, the number assigned to it by the constructor and the date of the construction of the propeller;

(*b*) the nationality and registration marks of each aircraft, and the type and number of each engine, to which the propeller is fitted;

(*c*) the name and address of the operator of each such aircraft;

(*d*) particulars of the date and duration of each occasion on which the propeller is run in flight, or, if the propeller is run on more than one occasion on one day, the number of occasions and the total duration of the running of the propeller on that day;

(*e*) particulars of all maintenance work done on the propeller;

(*f*) particulars of any defects occurring in the propeller, and of the rectification of such defects, including a reference to the relevant entries in the technical log required by Article 9(5) and (6) of this Order;

(*g*) particulars of any overhauls, repairs, replacements and modifications relating to the propeller.

SCHEDULE 8

Article 17(4)

Areas Specified in Connection with the Carriage of Flight Navigators as Members of the Flight Crews of Public Transport Aircraft

The following areas are hereby specified for the purposes of Article 17(4) of this Order.

Area A—Arctic

All that area north of latitude 66° 33′ north, excluding any part thereof lying within 300 nautical miles of Norway.

Area B—Antarctic

All that area south of latitude 50° south.

Area C—Sahara

All that area enclosed by rhumb lines joining successively the following points:

32°	north latitude	03° west	longitude
24°	,, ,,	14° ,,	,,
14°	,, ,,	14° ,,	,,
18°	,, ,,	28° east	,,
24°	,, ,,	28° ,,	,,
28°	,, ,,	23° ,,	,,
32°	,, ,,	03° west	,,

Area D—Arabian Desert

All that area enclosed by rhumb lines joining successively the following points:

30°	north	latitude	38°	east	longitude
16°	„	„	46°	„	„
20°	„	„	52°	„	„
29°	„	„	43°	„	„
30°	„	„	38°	„	„

Area E—South America (Central)

All that area enclosed by rhumb lines joining successively the following points:

05°	north	latitude	75°	west	longitude
04°	„	„	60°	„	„
10°	south	„	40°	„	„
30°	„	„	60°	„	„
30°	„	„	70°	„	„
18°	„	„	69°	„	„
14°	„	„	75°	„	„
05°	„	„	80°	„	„
05°	north	„	75°	„	„

Area F—South America (Patagonia)

All that area enclosed by rhumb lines joining successively the following points:

50°	south	latitude	75°	west	longitude
40°	„	„	75°	„	„
40°	„	„	62°	„	„
50°	„	„	65°	„	„
50°	„	„	75°	„	„

Area G—Pacific Ocean

All that area enclosed by rhumb lines joining successively the following points:

50°	south	latitude	75°	west	longitude
20°	„	„	73°	„	„
05°	„	„	85°	„	„
05°	north	latitude	80°	west	longitude
15°	„	„	105°	„	„
30°	„	„	125°	„	„
55°	„	„	140°	„	„
67°	„	„	180°	„	„
60°	„	„	180°	„	„
20°	„	„	128°	east	„
04°	„	„	128°	„	„
00°	„	„	160°	„	„
50°	south	„	160°	„	„
50°	„	„	75°	west	„

excluding any part thereof lying within 300 nautical miles of New Zealand.

Area H—Australia

All that area enclosed by rhumb lines joining successively the following points:

18°	south	latitude	123°	east	longitude
26°	„	„	118°	„	„
30°	„	„	118°	„	„
30°	„	„	145°	„	„
26°	„	„	145°	„	„
21°	„	„	140°	„	„
18°	„	„	123°	„	„

Area I—Indian Ocean

All that area enclosed by rhumb lines joining successively the following points:

50°	south	latitude	110°	east	longitude
20°	,,	,,	110°	,,	,,
13°	,,	,,	120°	,,	,,
10°	,,	,,	100°	,,	,,
18°	north	,,	89°	,,	,,
00°			80°	,,	,,
24°	north	,,	65°	,,	,,
05°	south	,,	43°	,,	,,
20°	,,	,,	60°	,,	,,
25°	,,	,,	60°	,,	,,
30°	,,	,,	35°	,,	,,
50°	,,	,,	35°	,,	,,
50°	,,	,,	110°	,,	,,

Area J—Atlantic Ocean

All that area enclosed by rhumb lines joining successively the following points:

50°	south	latitude	15°	east	longitude
05°	,,	,,	10°	,,	,,
02°	north	,,	05°	,,	,,
02°	,,	,,	10°	west	,,
15°	,,	,,	25°	,,	,,
55°	,,	,,	15°	,,	,,
67°	,,	,,	40°	,,	,,
67°	,,	,,	60°	,,	,,
45°	,,	,,	45°	,,	,,
40°	,,	,,	63°	,,	,,
19°	,,	,,	63°	,,	,,
05°	south	,,	30°	,,	,,
50°	,,	,,	55°	,,	,,
50°	,,	,,	15°	east	,,

SCHEDULE 9

Article 19

Flight Crew of Aircraft: Licences and Ratings

Part A—Licences

Minimum Age, Period of Validity, Privileges

1. *Student Pilots*

Student Pilots' Licence (Flying Machines, Balloons and Airships)

Minimum age—17 years

Maximum Period of Validity

(*a*) 24 months, if the holder is less than 40 years of age on the date on which the licence is granted or renewed; or

(*b*) 12 months, if the holder is 40 years of age or more on that date.

Privileges: The licence—

(*a*) shall entitle the holder to fly as pilot in command of an aircraft for the purpose of becoming qualified for the grant or renewal of a pilot's licence;

(*b*) shall be valid only for flights within the United Kingdom, the Channel Islands and the Isle of Man, and within any other territory specified in the licence;

(*c*) shall not entitle the holder to fly as pilot in command of an aircraft in which any other person is carried;

(*d*) shall be valid only for flights carried out in accordance with instructions given by a person holding a pilot's licence granted under this Order, being a licence which includes a flying instructor's rating or an assistant flying instructor's rating entitling him to give instruction in flying the type of aircraft to be flown.

2. *Aeroplane pilots*

Private Pilot's Licence (Aeroplanes)

Minimum age—17 years

Maximum Period of Validity—5 years

Privileges: The holder of the licence shall be entitled to fly as pilot in command or co-pilot of an aeroplane of any of the types specified in the aircraft rating included in the licence:

Provided that:

(*a*) he shall not fly such an aeroplane for the purpose of public transport or aerial work;

(*b*) he shall not receive any remuneration for his services as pilot on the flight, other than remuneration for the giving of instruction in an aeroplane owned, or operated under arrangements entered into, by a flying club of which the person giving and the person receiving the instruction are members;

(*c*) he shall not, unless his licence includes an instrument meteorological conditions rating, fly as pilot in command of such an aeroplane:

(i) on a flight outside controlled airspace:

(*aa*) when the flight visibility is less than one nautical mile; or

(*bb*) when any passenger is carried and the aeroplane is flying either above 3,000 feet above mean sea level in Instrument Meteorological Conditions or at or below 3,000 feet above mean sea level in a flight visibility of less than 3 nautical miles; or

(ii) on a special VFR flight in a control zone in a flight visibility of less than 5 nautical miles, except on a route or in an aerodrome traffic zone notified for the purposes of this sub-paragraph;

(*d*) he shall not fly as pilot in command of such an aeroplane at night on a flight on which any passenger is carried unless:

(i) his licence includes a night rating (aeroplanes); and

(ii) his licence includes an instrument rating (aeroplanes) or he has within the immediately preceding 6 months carried out as pilot in command not less than 5 take-offs and 5 landings at a time when the depression of the centre of the sun was not less than 12° below the horizon.

Commercial Pilot's Licence (Aeroplanes)

Minimum age—18 years

Maximum Period of Validity—5 years

Privileges: In addition to the privileges given above for the Private Pilot's Licence (Aeroplanes), which includes an instrument meteorological conditions rating, the holder of the licence shall be entitled to fly as—

(i) pilot in command of any aeroplane of a type specified in Part 1 of the aircraft rating included in the licence when the aeroplane is engaged in a flight for any purpose whatsoever:

Provided that—

(*a*) he shall not, unless his licence includes an instrument rating, fly such an aeroplane on any scheduled journey;

(*b*) he shall not fly such an aeroplane at night on a flight on which any passenger is carried unless his licence includes an instrument rating or he has within the immediately preceding 90 days carried out as pilot in command not less than 5 take-offs and 5 landings at a time when the depression of the centre of the sun was not less than 12 degrees below the horizon;

(*c*) he shall not, unless his licence includes an instrument rating, fly any such aeroplane of which the maximum total weight authorised exceeds 5,000 lb. on any flight for the purpose of public transport, except a flight beginning and ending at the same aerodrome and not extending beyond 25 nautical miles from that aerodrome;

(d) he shall not fly such an aeroplane on a flight for the purpose of public transport if its maximum total weight authorised exceeds 12,500 lb.;

(ii) co-pilot of any aeroplane of a type specified in Part 1 or Part 2 of such aircraft rating when the aeroplane is engaged in a flight for any purpose whatsoever.

Senior Commercial Pilot's Licence (Aeroplanes)

Minimum age—21 years

Maximum Period of Validity—5 years

Privileges: In addition to the privileges given above for the Private Pilot's Licence (Aeroplanes), which includes an instrument meteorological conditions rating, the holder of the licence shall be entitled to fly as—

(i) pilot in command of any aeroplane of a type specified in Part 1 of the aircraft rating included in the licence when the aeroplane is engaged in a flight for any purpose whatsoever:

Provided that—

(a) he shall not, unless his licence includes an instrument rating, fly such an aeroplane on any scheduled journey;

(b) he shall not fly such an aeroplane at night on a flight on which any passenger is carried unless his licence includes an instrument rating or he has within the immediately preceding 90 days carried out as pilot in command not less than 5 take-offs and 5 landings at a time when the depression of the centre of the sun was not less than 12 degrees below the horizon;

(c) he shall not, unless his licence includes an instrument rating, fly any such aeroplane of which the maximum total weight authorised exceeds 5,000 lb. on any flight for the purpose of public transport, except a flight beginning and ending at the same aerodrome and not extending beyond 25 nautical miles from that aerodrome;

(d) he shall not fly such an aeroplane on a flight for the purpose of public transport if its maximum total weight authorised exceeds 45,000 lb.;

(ii) co-pilot of any aeroplane of a type specified in Part 1 or Part 2 of such aircraft rating when the aeroplane is engaged in a flight for any purpose whatsoever.

Airline Transport Pilot's Licence (Aeroplanes)

Minimum age—21 years

Maximum Period of Validity—5 years

Privileges: In addition to the privileges given above for the Private Pilot's Licence (Aeroplanes), which includes an instrument meteorological conditions rating, the holder of the licence shall be entitled to fly as—

(i) pilot in command of any aeroplane of a type specified in Part 1 of the aircraft rating included in the licence when the aeroplane is engaged in a flight for any purpose whatsoever:

Provided that—

(a) he shall not, unless his licence includes an instrument rating, fly such an aeroplane on any scheduled journey;

(b) he shall not fly such an aeroplane at night on a flight on which any passenger is carried unless his licence includes an instrument rating or he has within the immediately preceding 90 days carried out as pilot in command not less than 5 take-offs and 5 landings at a time when the depression of the centre of the sun was not less than 12 degrees below the horizon;

(c) he shall not, unless his licence includes an instrument rating, fly any such aeroplane of which the maximum total weight authorised exceeds 5,000 lb. on any flight for the purpose of public transport, except a flight beginning and ending at the same aerodrome and not extending beyond 25 nautical miles from that aerodrome;

(*d*) he shall not at any time after he attains the age of 60 years, fly such an aeroplane on a flight for the purpose of public transport if its maximum total weight authorised exceeds 45,000 lb.;

(ii) co-pilot of any aeroplane of a type specified in Part I or Part 2 of such aircraft rating when the aeroplane is engaged in a flight for any purpose whatsoever.

3. *Helicopter and Gyroplane Pilots*

Private Pilot's Licence (*Helicopters and Gyroplanes*)

Minimum age—17 years

Maximum Period of Validity—5 years

Privileges: The licence—

(i) shall entitle the holder to fly as pilot in command or co-pilot of a helicopter or gyroplane of any of the types specified in the aircraft rating included in the licence, except when—

(*a*) the helicopter or gyroplane is flying for the purpose of public transport or aerial work; or

(*b*) the holder of the licence receives any remuneration in respect of the flight, not being remuneration for the giving of instruction in a helicopter or gyroplane owned, or operated under arrangements entered into, by a flying club of which the person giving and the person receiving the instruction are members;

(ii) shall not entitle the holder to act as pilot in command at night on a flight on which any passenger is carried unless his licence includes a night rating (helicopters and gyroplanes) and he has within the preceding 90 days carried out as pilot in command not less than 5 flights each consisting of a take-off, a transition from hover to forward flight, a climb to at least 500 ft., and a landing, at a time when the depression of the centre of the sun was not less than 12 degrees below the horizon.

Commercial Pilot's Licence (*Helicopters and Gyroplanes*)

Minimum age—18 years

Maximum Period of Validity—5 years

Privileges: In addition to the privileges given above for the Private Pilot's Licence (Helicopters and Gyroplanes), the holder of the licence shall be entitled to fly as—

(i) pilot in command of any helicopter or gyroplane of a type specified in Part 1 of the aircraft rating included in the licence when the helicopter or gyroplane is engaged on a flight for any purpose whatsoever:

Provided that—

(*a*) he shall not fly such a helicopter or gyroplane at night on a flight on which any passenger is carried unless he has within the preceding 90 days carried out as pilot in command not less than 5 flights, each consisting of a take-off, a transition from hover to forward flight, a climb to at least 500 ft., and a landing, at a time when the depression of the centre of the sun was not less than 12 degrees below the horizon;

(*b*) he shall not fly such a helicopter or gyroplane on a flight for the purpose of public transport if its maximum total weight authorised exceeds 12,500 lb.;

(ii) co-pilot of any helicopter or gyroplane to a type specified in Part 1 or Part 2 of such aircraft rating when the helicopter or gyroplane is engaged in a flight for any purpose whatsoever.

Airline Transport Pilot's Licence (*Helicopters and Gyroplanes*)

Minimum age—21 years

Maximum Period of Validity —5 years

Privileges: In addition to the privileges given above for the Private Pilot's Licence (Helicopters and Gyroplanes) the holder of the licence shall be entitled to fly as—

(i) pilot in command of any helicopter or gyroplane of a type specified in Part 1 of the aircraft rating included in the licence when the helicopter or gyroplane is engaged in a flight for any purpose whatsoever:

Provided that he shall not fly such a helicopter or gyroplane at night on a flight on which any passenger is carried unless he has within the immediately preceding 90 days carried out as pilot in command not less than 5 flights, each consisting of a take-off, a transition from hover to forward flight, a climb to at least 500 ft., and a landing, at a time when the depression of the centre of the sun was not less than 12 degrees below the horizon;

(ii) co-pilot of any helicopter or gyroplane of a type specified in Part 1 or Part 2 of such aircraft rating when the helicopter or gyroplane in engaged in a flight for any purpose whatsoever.

4. *Balloon and Airship Pilots*

Private Pilot's Licence (Balloon and Airships)

Minimum age—17 years

Maximum Period of Validity

(*a*) 24 months, if the holder is less than 40 years of age on the date on which the licence is granted or renewed; or

(*b*) 12 months, if the holder is 40 years of age or more on that date.

Privileges: The holder of the licence shall be entitled to fly, when the balloon or airship is flying for any purpose other than public transport or aerial work, as

(i) pilot in command of any type of balloon or airship specified in Part 1 of the aircraft type rating included in the licence;

(ii) co-pilot of any type of balloon or airship specified in Part 1 or Part 2 of such aircraft rating.

Commercial Pilot's Licence (Balloons)

Minimum age—18 years

Maximum Period of Validity—6 months*

Privileges: In addition to the privileges given above for the Private Pilot's Licence in respect of balloons, the holder of the licences shall be entitled to fly as pilot in command or co-pilot of any type of balloon specified in the aircraft rating included in the licence.

Commercial Pilot's Licence (Airships)

Minimum age—18 years

Maximum Period of Validity—6 months*

Privileges: In addition to the privileges given above for the Private Pilot's Licence in respect of airships, the holder of the licence shall be entitled to fly as—

(i) pilot in command of any airship of a type specified in Part 1 of the aircraft rating included in the licence;

(ii) co-pilot of any airship of a type specified in Part 2 of such aircraft rating.

5. *Glider Pilots*

Commercial Pilot's Licence (Gliders)

Minimum age—18 years

Maximum Period of Validity—6 months

Privileges: The holder of the licence shall be entitled to fly as pilot in command or co-pilot of—

(*a*) any glider of which the maximum total weight authorised does not exceed 1,500 lb.;

(*b*) any glider of which the maximum total weight authorised exceeds 1,500 lb. and which is of a type specified in the rating included in the licence.

*In respect of the privileges of a Private Pilot's Licence the maximum period of validity shall be as given for that licence.

6. *Other Flight Crew*

Flight Navigator's Licence

Minimum age—21 years

Maximum Period of Validity—12 months

Privileges: The holder of the licence shall be entitled to act as flight navigator in any aircraft.

Flight Engineer's Licence

Minimum age—21 years

Maximum Period of Validity—12 months

Privileges: The holder of the licence shall be entitled to act as flight engineer in any type of aircraft specified in the aircraft rating included in the licence.

Flight Radiotelephony Operator's General Licence

Minimum age—18 years

Maximum Period of Validity—5 years

Privileges: The holder of the licence shall be entitled to operate radiotelephony apparatus in any aircraft.

Flight Radiotelephony Operator's Restricted Licence

Minimum age—17 years

Maximum Period of Validity—5 years

Privileges: The holder of the licence shall be entitled to operate radiotelephony apparatus in any aircraft if the stability of the frequency radiated by the transmitter is maintained automatically but shall not be entitled to operate the transmitter, or to adjust its frequency, except by the use of external switching devices.

Flight Radiotelegraphy Operator's Licence

Minimum age—20 years

Maximum Period of Validity—12 months

Privileges: The holder of the licence shall be entitled to operate radiotelegraphy and radiotelephony apparatus in any aircraft.

Flight Radiotelegraphy Operator's Temporary Licence

Minimum age—18 years

Maximum Period of Validity—12 months

Privileges: The holder of the licence shall be entitled to operate radiotelegraphy and radiotelephony apparatus in any aircraft under the supervision of a person who is the holder of a flight radiotelegraphy operator's licence.

PART B—RATINGS

1. The following ratings may be included in a pilot's licence (other than a student pilot's licence) granted under Part IV of this Order, and, subject to the provisions of this Order and of the licence, the inclusion of a rating in a licence shall have the consequences respectively specified as follows:

Aircraft Rating. The licence shall entitle the holder to act as pilot only of aircraft of the types specified in the aircraft rating and different types of aircraft may be specified in respect of different privileges of a licence.

Instrument Meteorological Conditions Rating (*Aeroplanes*) shall entitle the holder of a private pilot's licence (aeroplanes) to fly as pilot in command of an aeroplane:

(*a*) on a flight outside controlled airspace with or without passengers, in either Visual Meteorological Conditions or Instrument Meteorological Conditions; or

(*b*) on a special VFR flight in a control zone in a flight visibility of not less than 1½ nautical miles.

Instrument Rating (Aeroplanes) shall entitle the holder of the licence to act as pilot of an aeroplane flying in controlled airspace in accordance with the instrument flight rules.

Night Rating (Aeroplanes) shall entitle the holder of a private pilot's licence (aeroplanes) to act as pilot in command at night of an aeroplane in which any passenger is carried.

Night Rating (Helicopters and Gyroplanes) shall entitle the holder of a private pilot's licence (helicopters and gyroplanes) to act as pilot in command at night of a helicopter or gyroplane in which any passenger is carried.

Towing Rating (Flying Machines) shall entitle the holder of the licence to act as pilot of a flying machine while towing a glider in flight for the purpose of public transport or aerial work.

Flying Instructor's Rating shall entitle the holder of the licence to give instruction in flying aircraft of such types as may be specified in the rating for that purpose.

Assistant Flying Instructor's Rating shall entitle the holder of the licence to give instruction in flying aircraft of such types as may be specified in the rating for that purpose:

Provided that—

(*a*) such instruction shall only be given under the supervision of a person present during the take-off and landing at the aerodrome at which the instruction is to begin and end and holding a pilot's licence endorsed with a flying instructor's rating; and

(*b*) an assistant flying instructor's rating shall not entitle the holder of the licence to give directions to the person undergoing instruction in respect of the performance by that person of:

(i) his first solo flight; or

(ii) his first solo flight by night; or

(iii) his first solo cross-country flight otherwise than by night; or

(iv) his first solo cross-country flight by night.

2. An aircraft rating may be included in every flight engineer's licence. The licence shall entitle the holder to act as flight engineer only of aircraft of a type specified in the aircraft rating.

3. For the purposes of this Schedule:

"Solo flight" means a flight on which the pilot of the aircraft is not accompanied by a person holding a pilot's licence granted or rendered valid under this Order.

"Cross-country flight" means any flight during the course of which the aircraft is more than 3 nautical miles from the aerodrome of departure.

PART C—CERTIFICATE OF TEST OR EXPERIENCE (AIRCRAFT RATING)

Person who may sign Certificate

1. A certificate of test or a certificate of experience required by proviso (*d*) to Article 19(2) of this Order shall be signed by a person authorised by the Board to sign certificates of that kind and shall comply with the following provisions of this Part of this Schedule.

Matters to be certified

2. The certificate shall certify the following particulars:

(*a*) the date on which it was signed;

(*b*) (i) in the case of a certificate of test, that the person signing the certificate is satisfied that on a date specified in the certificate the holder of the licence of which the certificate forms part passed a flying test;

(ii) in the case of a certificate of experience, that on the date on which the certificate was signed the holder of the licence of which it forms part produced his personal flying log book to the person signing the certificate and satisfied him that he had five hours' experience as a pilot of aircraft within the period of 6 months or 13 months preceding that date, whichever is the case;

(*c*) the type of aircraft or apparatus in or by means of which the test was conducted, or the type or types of aircraft in which the experience was gained;

(*d*) whether the test or experience was in the capacity of pilot in command or co-pilot.

Nature of flying test

3. The flying test referred to in paragraph 2 of this Part of this Schedule shall be a test of the pilot's competence to fly the aircraft as pilot in command or co-pilot and may, at the discretion of the Board, be conducted either in an aircraft in flight or by means of apparatus approved by the Board in which flight conditions are simulated on the ground.

Classification of flights into Groups

4. For the purposes of this Part of this Schedule, flights shall be divided into Groups according to the following Table.

Group	Circumstances of flight		
	Aircraft flown	Remuneration of licence-holder in respect of flight	Other circumstances
A	Single-engined aircraft below 12,500 lb.*	Unremunerated	Not public transport or aerial work
B	Multi-engined aircraft below 12,500 lb.*	Unremunerated	Not public transport or aerial work
C	Above 12,500 lb.*	Unremunerated	Not public transport or aerial work
D	Any aircraft	Remunerated	Not public transport, aerial work or carriage of passengers
E	Any aircraft	Remunerated	For the carriage of passengers but not for public transport or aerial work
F	Any aircraft	Remunerated or unremunerated	For aerial work
G	Any aircraft	Remunerated or unremunerated	For public transport

*Maximum total weight authorised

Requirement of test or experience

5. A certificate shall not be appropriate to the functions to be performed on flights in Group E or G unless it is a certificate of test, but in the case of Groups A,B,C, D and F it may be either a certificate of test or a certificate of experience.

Type or Class of Aircraft

6.—(1) A certificate of test shall not be appropriate to the functions to be performed unless it certifies that the test was conducted as follows—

For the purposes of Group A: in an aircraft of the same class as that in which the functions are to be performed;

For the purposes of Group B: in a multi-engined aircraft of the same class as that in which the functions are to be performed;

For the purposes of Groups C to G: in an aircraft of the same type as that in which the functions are to be performed or by means of apparatus approved by the Board in which flight conditions in such an aircraft are simulated on the ground.

(2) A certificate of experience shall not be appropriate to the functions to be performed unless it certifies that the experience was gained as follows:

For the purposes of Group A: 5 hours' experience in an aircraft of the same class as that in which the functions are to be performed;

For the purposes of Group B: 5 hours' experience in an aircraft of the same class as that in which the functions are to be performed, of which at least one flight shall have been in a multi-engined aircraft;

For the purposes of Groups C, D and F: 5 hours' experience in an aircraft of the same class as that in which the functions are to be performed of which at least one flight shall have been in an aircraft of the same type as that in which the functions are to be performed.

(3) For the purposes of this paragraph the class to which an aircraft belongs shall be determined according to column 4 of the Table in Part A of Schedule 1 to this Order.

Capacity in which functions are performed

7. A certificate of test or of experience in the capacity of pilot in command shall be appropriate to functions performed in the capacity of pilot in command or co-pilot. A certificate of test or of experience in the capacity of co-pilot shall be appropriate to functions performed in the capacity of co-pilot.

Period of experience

8. A certificate of experience shall have no effect unless the experience certified was gained within the period of 13 months preceding the signing of the certificate in the case of Groups A to D, and 6 months preceding the signing of the certificate in the case of Group F.

Period of validity of certificate

9.—(*a*) A certificate of test shall not be valid in relation to a flight made more than 13 months in the case of Groups A to E, or 6 months in the case of Groups F and G, after the date of the flying test which it certifies:

Provided that in the case of Groups F and G two certificates of test shall together be deemed to constitute a valid certificate if they certify flying tests conducted on two occasions within the period of 13 months preceding the flight on which the functions are to be performed, such occasions being separated by an interval of not less than 4 months, and if both certificates are appropriate to those functions.

(*b*) A certificate of experience shall not be valid in relation to a flight made more than 6 months after it was signed in the case of Group F or more than 13 months after it was signed in the case of any other Group.

SCHEDULE 10

Public Transport—Operational Requirements

Part A.—Operations Manual

Article 24

Information and instructions relating to the following matters shall be included in the operations manual referred to in Article 24(2) of this Order:

(i) the number of the crew to be carried in the aircraft, on each stage of any route to be flown, and the respective capacities in which they are to act, and instructions as to the order and circumstances in which command is to be assumed by members of the crew;

(ii) the respective duties of each member of the crew and the other members of the operating staff;

(iii) the particulars referred to in Article 49(7) of this Order;

(iv) such technical particulars concerning the aircraft, its engines and equipment and concerning the performance of the aircraft as may be necessary to enable the flight crew of the aircraft to perform their respective duties;

(v) the manner in which the quantities of fuel and oil to be carried by the aircraft are to be computed and records of fuel and oil carried and consumed on each stage of the route to be flown are to be maintained; the instructions shall take account of all circumstances likely to be encountered on the flight including the possibility of failure of one or more of the aircraft engines;

(vi) the manner in which the quantity, if any, of oxygen and oxygen equipment to be carried in the aircraft for the purpose of complying with Scale K in Schedule 5 to this Order is to be computed;

(vii) the check system to be followed by the crew of the aircraft prior to and on take-off, on landing and in an emergency, so as to ensure that the operating procedures contained in the operations manual and in the flight manual or performance schedule forming part of the relevant certificate of airworthiness are complied with;

(viii) the circumstances in which a radio watch is to be maintained;

(ix) the circumstances in which oxygen is to be used by the crew of the aircraft, and by passengers;

(x) communication, navigational aids, aerodromes, local regulations, in-flight procedures, approach and landing procedures and such other information as the operator may deem necessary for the proper conduct of flight operations; the information referred to in this paragraph shall be contained in a route guide, which may be in the form of a separate volume;

(xi) the reporting in flight to the notified authorities of meteorological observations;

(xii) the minimum altitudes for safe flight on each stage of the route to be flown and any planned diversion therefrom, such minimum altitudes being not lower than any which may be applicable under the law of the United Kingdom or of the countries whose territory is to be flown over;

(xiii) such matters as may be prescribed relating to weather conditions for take-off and landing;

(xiv) emergency flight procedures, including procedures for the instruction of passengers in the position and use of emergency equipment and procedures to be adopted when the commander of the aircraft becomes aware that another aircraft or a vessel is in distress and needs assistance:

Provided that in relation to any flight which is not one of a series of flights between the same two places it shall be sufficient if, to the extent that it is not practicable to comply with paragraphs (x) and (xii), the manual contains such information and instructions as will enable the equivalent data to be ascertained before take-off.

Part B.—Crew Training and Tests

Article 25

1. The training, experience, practice and periodical tests required under Article 25(2) of this Order in the case of members of the crew of an aircraft engaged on a flight for the purpose of public transport shall be as follows:

(1) *The Crew*

Every member of the crew shall—

(*a*) have been tested within the relevant period by or on behalf of the operator as to his knowledge of the use of the emergency and life saving equipment required to be carried in the aircraft on the flight; and

(*b*) have practised within the relevant period under the supervision of the operator or of a person appointed by him for the purpose the carrying out of the duties required of him in case of an emergency occurring to the aircraft, either in an aircraft of the type to be used on the flight or in apparatus approved by the Board for the purpose and controlled by persons so approved.

(2) *Pilots*

(*a*) Every pilot included in the flight crew who is intended by the operator to fly as pilot in circumstances requiring compliance with the Instrument Flight Rules shall within the relevant period have been tested by or on behalf of the operator—

(i) as to his competence to perform his duties while executing normal manoeuvres and procedures in flight, in an aircraft of the type to be used on the flight, including the use of the instruments and equipment provided in the aircraft;

(ii) as to his competence to perform his duties in instrument flight conditions while executing emergency manoeuvres and procedures in flight, in an aircraft of the type to be used on the flight, including the use of the instruments and equipment provided in the aircraft.

A pilot's ability to carry out normal manoeuvres and procedures shall be tested in the aircraft in flight.

The other tests required by this sub-paragraph may be conducted either in the aircraft in flight, or under the supervision of a person approved by the Board for the purpose by means of apparatus so approved in which flight conditions are simulated on the ground. The tests specified in sub-paragraph (2)(*a*)(ii) of this paragraph when conducted in the aircraft in flight shall be carried out either in actual instrument flight conditions or in instrument flight conditions simulated by means approved by the Board.

(*b*) Every pilot included in the flight crew whose licence does not include an instrument rating or who, notwithstanding the inclusion of such a rating in his licence, is not intended by the operator to fly in circumstances requiring compliance with the Instrument Flight Rules, shall within the relevant period have been tested, by or on behalf of the operator in flight in an aircraft of the type to be used on the flight

(i) as to his competence to act as pilot thereof, while executing normal manoeuvres and procedures, and

(ii) as to his competence to act as pilot thereof while executing emergency manoeuvres and procedures.

(3) *Flight Engineers*

Every flight engineer included in the flight crew shall within the relevant period have been tested by or on behalf of the operator, either in flight, or, under the supervision of a person approved by the Board for the purpose, by means of apparatus so approved in which flight conditions are simulated on the ground, as to his competence to perform the duties of flight engineer in aircraft of the type to be used on the flight, including his ability to execute emergency procedures in the course of such duties.

(4) *Flight Navigators and Flight Radio Operators*

Every flight navigator and flight radio operator whose inclusion in the flight crew is required under Article 17(4) and (5) respectively of this Order shall within the relevant period have been tested by or on behalf of the operator as to his competence to perform his duties in conditions corresponding to those likely to be encountered on the flight—

(*a*) in the case of a flight navigator, using equipment of the type to be used in the aircraft on the flight for purposes of navigation;

(*b*) in the case of a flight radio operator using radio equipment of the type installed in the aircraft to be used on the flight, and including a test of his ability to carry out emergency procedures.

(5) *Aircraft Commanders*

(*a*) The pilot designated as commander of the aircraft for the flight shall within the relevant period—

(i) have demonstrated to the satisfaction of the operator that he has adequate knowledge of the route to be taken, the aerodromes of take-off and landing, and any alternate aerodromes, including in particular his knowledge of—
the terrain,
the seasonal meteorological conditions,
the meteorological, communications, and air traffic facilities, services and procedures,
the search and rescue procedures, and
the navigational facilities,
relevant to the route;

(ii) have been tested as to his proficiency in using instrument approach-to-land systems of the type in use at the aerodrome of intended landing and any alternate aerodromes, such test being carried out either in flight in instrument flight conditions or in instrument flight conditions simulated by means approved by the Board or under the supervision of a person approved by the Board for the purpose by means of apparatus so approved in which flight conditions are simulated on the ground.

(iii) have carried out as pilot in command not less than three take-offs and three landings in aircraft of the type to be used on the flight.

(*b*) In determining whether a pilot's knowledge of the matters referred to in sub-paragraph (*a*)(i) is sufficient to render him competent to perform the duties of aircraft commander on the flight, the operator shall take into account the pilot's flying experience in conjunction with the following—

(i) the experience of other members of the intended flight crew;

(ii) the influence of terrain and obstructions on departure and approach procedures at the aerodromes of take-off and intended landing and at alternate aerodromes;

(iii) the similarity of the instrument approach procedures and let-down aids to those with which the pilot is familiar;

(iv) the dimensions of runways which may be used in the course of the flight in relation to the performance limits of aircraft of the type to be used on the flight;

(v) the reliability of meteorological forecasts and the probability of difficult meteorological conditions in the areas to be traversed;

(vi) the adequacy of the information available regarding the aerodrome of intended landing and any alternate aerodromes;

(vii) the nature of air traffic control procedures and familiarity of the pilot with such procedures;

(viii) the influence of terrain on route conditions and the extent of the assistance obtainable en route from navigational aids and air-to-ground communication facilities;

(ix) the extent to which it is possible for the pilot to become familiar with unusual aerodrome procedures and features of the route by means of ground instruction and training devices.

(6) For the purposes of this paragraph—

"instrument flight conditions" means weather conditions such that the pilot is unable to fly by visual reference to objects outside the aircraft;

"relevant period" means a period which immediately procedes the commencement of the flight, being a period—

(*a*) in the case of sub-paragraph (5)(*a*)(iii) of this paragraph, of three months;

(*b*) in the case of sub-paragraphs (2)(*a*)(ii), (2)(*b*)(ii), (3) and (5)(*a*)(ii) of this paragraph, of six months;

(*c*) in the case of sub-paragraphs (1), (2)(*a*)(i), (2)(*b*)(i), (4) and (5)(*a*)(i) of this paragraph, of thirteen months:

Provided that—

(i) any pilot of the aircraft to whom the provisions of sub-paragraphs (2)(*a*)(ii), (2)(*b*)(ii), or (5)(*a*)(ii) and any flight engineer of the aircraft to whom the provisions of sub-paragraph (3) of this paragraph apply shall for the purposes of the flight be deemed to have complied with such requirements respectively within the relevant period if he has qualified to perform his duties in accordance therewith on two occasions within the period of thirteen months immediately preceding the flight, such occasions being separated by an interval of not less than four months;

(ii) the requirements of sub-paragraph (5)(*a*)(i) shall be deemed to have been complied with within the relevant period by a pilot designated as commander of the aircraft for the flight if, having become qualified so to act on flights between the same places over the same route more than thirteen months before commencement of the flight, he has within the period of thirteen months immediately preceding the flight flown as pilot of an aircraft between those places over that route.

2.—(1) The records required to be maintained by an operator under Article 25(2) of this Order shall be accurate and up-to-date records so kept as to show, on any date, in relation to each person who has during the period of two years immediately preceding that date flown as a member of the crew of any public transport aircraft operated by that operator—

(*a*) the date and particulars of each test required by this Schedule undergone by that person during the said period including the name and qualifications of the examiner;

(*b*) the date upon which that person last practised the carrying out of duties referred to in paragraph 1(1)(*b*) of this Schedule;

(*c*) the operator's conclusions based on each such test and practice as to that person's competence to perform his duties;

(*d*) the date and particulars of any decision taken by the operator during the said period in pursuance of paragraph 1(5)(*a*)(i) of this Schedule including particulars of the evidence upon which that decision was based.

(2) The operator shall whenever called upon to do so by any authorised person produce for the inspection of any person so authorised all records referred to in the preceding sub-paragraph and furnish to any such person all such information as he may require in connection with any such records and produce for his inspection all log books, certificates, papers and other documents whatsoever which he may reasonably require to see for the purpose of determining whether such records are complete or of verifying the accuracy of their contents.

(3) The operator shall at the request of any person in respect of whom he is required to keep records as aforesaid furnish to that person, or to any operator of aircraft for the purpose of public transport by whom that person may subsequently be employed, particulars of any qualifications in accordance with this Schedule obtained by such person whilst in his service.

SCHEDULE 11

Articles 55 and 56

DOCUMENTS TO BE CARRIED BY AIRCRAFT REGISTERED IN THE UNITED KINGDOM

On a flight for the purpose of public transport:

Documents A, B, C, D, E, F, H and, if the flight is international air navigation, Document G.

On a flight for the purpose of aerial work:

Documents A, B, C, E, F, and, if the flight is international air navigation, Document G.

On a flight, being international air navigation, for a purpose other than public transport or aerial work:

Documents A, B, C and G.

For the purposes of this Schedule:

"A" means the licence in force under the Wireless Telegraphy Act 1949**(a)** in respect of the aircraft radio station installed in the aircraft, and the current telecommunication log book required by this Order;

"B" means the certificate of airworthiness in force in respect of the aircraft;

"C" means the licences of the members of the flight crew of the aircraft;

"D" means one copy of the load sheet, if any, required by Article 26 of this Order in respect of the flight;

"E" means one copy of each certificate of maintenance, if any, in force in respect of the aircraft;

"F" means the technical log, if any, in which entries are required to be made under Article 9(5) of this Order;

"G" means the certificate of registration in force in respect of the aircraft;

"H" means the operations manual, if any, required by Article 24(2)(*a*)(iii) of this Order to be carried on the flight.

For the purposes of this Schedule:

"International air navigation" means any flight which includes passage over the territory of any country other than the United Kingdom, except any of the Channel Islands, the Isle of Man, any country to which there is power to extend the Act under, section 66(1) thereof or any British Protected State.

(a) 1949 c. 54.

SCHEDULE 12

Article 80

PENALTIES

PART A—PROVISIONS REFERRED TO IN ARTICLE 80(5)

Article 3.
Article 5.
Article 10(5).
Article 14.
Article 15(3).
Article 21.
Article 23.
Article 24.
Article 26(5).
Article 32 (except paragraph (2)).
Article 33(2).
Article 43(1).
Article 44(1).
Article 52.
Article 57.
Article 61(2).
Article 66(5) and (6).
Article 68.
Article 71(1).
Article 73.
Article 76.

PART B—PROVISIONS REFERRED TO IN ARTICLE 80(6)

Article 7.
Article 9(1).
Article 10 (except paragraph (5)).
Article 12.
Article 13.
Article 15 (except paragraph (3)).
Article 17.
Article 18.
Article 22.
Article 25.
Article 26 (except paragraph (5)).
Articles 27 to 31, inclusive.
Article 32(2).
Article 33(1).
Articles 34 to 42, inclusive.
Article 43(2).
Article 44(2).
Article 45.
Article 46.
Articles 48 to 51, inclusive.
Article 53.
Article 59 (except paragraph (3)).
Article 60 (except paragraph (4)).
Article 61 (except paragraph (2)).
Article 62.
Article 63.
Article 65(4).
Article 66 (except paragraphs (5) and (6)).
Article 70.
Article 77.

EXPLANATORY NOTE

(*This Note is not part of the Order.*)

This Order consolidates the Air Navigation Order 1966 as amended. In addition to some minor and drafting amendments, a new Article (Article 82) is introduced which confers power on the Board of Trade to direct that, for the purposes of such provisions of the Order and regulations made thereunder as may be specified in the direction, the aircraft to which the direction relates is to be treated as if it was registered in the United Kingdom. Such a direction may be given only in respect of an aircraft managed by a person qualified to own an aircraft registered in the United Kingdom.

The following Table shows, in relation to each Article of the Air Navigation Order 1966, as amended, the Article of the 1970 Order in which it is reproduced:—

TABLE OF COMPARISON

1966 Order as amended	1970 Order	1966 Order as amended	1970 Order
87	1	42	44
86	2	43	45
1	3	44	46
2	4	45	47
3	5	46	48
4	6	47	49
5	7	48	50
6	8	49	51
7	9	50	52
8	10	51	53
9	11	52	54
10	12	53	55
11	13	54	56
12	14	55	57
13	15	56	58
14	16	57	59
15	17	59	60
16	18	60	61
17	19	61	62
18	20	62	63
19	21	63	64
20	22	64	65
21	23	65	66
22	24	66	67
23	25	67	68
24	26	68	69
25	27	69	70
26	28	70	71
27	29	71	72
28	30	72	73
29	31	73	74
30	32	74	75
31	33	75	76
32	34	76	77
33	35	77	78
34	36	78	79
35	37	79	80
36	38	80	81
37	39	— (New Article)	82
38	40	81	83
39	41	82	84
40	42	83	85
41	43	84	86
		85	87

1970 No. 955

PATENTS

The Patents (Amendment) Rules 1970

Made - - -	*26th June* 1970
Laid before Parliament	*3rd July* 1970
Coming into Operation	*4th July* 1970

The Board of Trade, in pursuance of the powers conferred upon them by section 94 of the Patents Act 1949(**a**), and of all other powers enabling them in that behalf, and after consultation with the Council on Tribunals, hereby make the following Rules:—

1. These Rules may be cited as the Patents (Amendment) Rules 1970 and shall come into operation on 4th July 1970.

2. The Interpretation Act 1889(**b**) shall apply to the interpretation of these Rules as it applies to the interpretation of an Act of Parliament and as if these Rules and the Rules hereby revoked were Acts of Parliament.

3. The Patents Rules 1968(**c**), as amended (**d**), shall have effect as if—

(*a*) for Rule 5(1) there were substituted the following:—

"**5.**—(1) All documents and copies of documents, except drawings, filed at the Office shall, unless the Comptroller otherwise directs, be written, typewritten, lithographed or printed in the English language—

(*a*) upon strong white paper of a size 330 mm by 200 to 210 mm (13 inches by 8 inches to 8¼ inches) or of A4 size (297 mm by 210 mm: 11¾ inches by 8¼ inches);

(*b*) in legible characters with a dark indelible ink;

(*c*) with the lines widely spaced;

(*d*) except in the case of statutory declarations and affidavits, on one side only;

(*e*) leaving a margin of at least 25 mm (1 inch) on the left-hand part thereof; and

(*f*) in the case of each of the forms set out in Schedule 2 hereto, leaving a space of about 80 mm (3 inches) blank at the top of the form.";

(*b*) for Rule 19 there were substituted the following:—

"**19.**—(1) Subject to the provisions of this Rule drawings shall be on sheets of a size 330 mm by 200 to 210 mm (13 inches by 8 to

(**a**) 1949 c. 87. (**b**) 1889 c. 63. (**c**) S.I. 1968/1389 (1968 II, p. 3958).
(**d**) The relevant amending instrument is S.I. 1968/1702 (1968 III, p. 4603).

8¼ inches) or of A4 size (297 mm by 210 mm : 11¾ inches by 8¼ inches) and a clear margin of 13 mm (½ an inch) shall be left at the edges of each sheet.

(2) If a figure or figures cannot be shown satisfactorily on one sheet of either of these dimensions it or they may be continued on subsequent sheets of the same dimensions.

(3) If it can be shown to the satisfaction of the Comptroller that a large figure cannot be shown satisfactorily, even on a reduced scale, on a sheet or sheets of the above mentioned dimensions, a sheet or sheets each of a size 330 mm by 400 to 420 mm (13 inches by 16 to 16½ inches) may be used and a clear margin of 13 mm (½ an inch) shall be left at the edges of each sheet.

(4) In a case falling within sub-rule (3) of this Rule one or more of the smaller sheets shall additionally be used only when it is not possible to show all the figures comprising the drawings on the sheet or sheets used by virtue of that sub-rule.

(5) No more sheets shall be employed than are necessary.

(6) The figures shall be numbered consecutively without regard to the number of sheets, and shall as far as possible be arranged in numerical order, separated by a sufficient space to keep them distinct.

(7) Where figures on a number of sheets form in effect a single complete figure, they shall be so arranged that the complete figure can be assembled without concealing any part of another figure." ;

(*c*) in Rule 20(*h*) after the word "inch" there were inserted the words "(3·2 mm)" ;

(*d*) for Rule 146 there were substituted the following:—

"**146.**—(1) In addition to the documents open to public inspection by virtue of section 13(2) and Rule 38(1), and subject to the provisions of this Rule, every Patents Form filed in pursuance of an application for a patent or in relation to a patent shall be open to public inspection after the date of publication of the complete specification and every document filed with or sent to the Office after the said date for the purposes of any proceedings relating to a patent or an application for a patent shall be open to public inspection after the expiry of the period of 14 days from its being filed or sent.

(2) Sub-rule (1) of this Rule shall not apply to—

(*a*) Patents Forms Nos. 1, 1 Con., 2, 3, 8, 37, 66 and 67 ;

(*b*) any document sent to the Office, at its request or otherwise, for inspection and subsequent return to the sender.

(3) (*a*) Where a document other than a Patents Form is filed or sent after the date of the publication of the complete specification and the person filing or sending it or any other party to the proceedings to which the document relates so requests, giving his reasons, within 14 days of the filing or sending of the document, the Comptroller may direct it to be treated as confidential ; and the document shall not be open to public inspection while the matter is being determined by the Comptroller.

(*b*) Where such a direction has been given and not withdrawn, nothing in this Rule shall be taken to authorise or require any person to be allowed to inspect the document to which the direction relates except by leave of the Comptroller.

(*c*) The Comptroller shall not withdraw any direction given under this sub-rule nor shall he give leave for any person to inspect any document to which a direction which has not been withdrawn relates without prior consultation with the person at whose request the direction was given, unless the Comptroller is satisfied that such prior consultation is not reasonably practicable.

(*d*) Where such a direction is given or withdrawn a record of the fact shall be filed with the document to which it relates.

(*e*) Where the time prescribed in paragraph (*a*) of this sub-rule is extended under Rule 154, the relevant document shall not be, or if the time is extended after the time has expired shall cease to be, open to public inspection until the expiry of the extended time, and if a request for a direction is made the document shall not be open to public inspection while the matter is being determined by the Comptroller.

(4) Nothing in this Rule shall be construed as imposing upon the Comptroller the duty of making available for public inspection any documents filed with or sent to the office before 1st November 1968.".

4. The Patents (Amendment) Rules 1968(**a**) are hereby revoked.

Anthony Grant,

Parliamentary Secretary
to the Board of Trade.

26th June 1970.

EXPLANATORY NOTE

(*This Note is not part of the Rules.*)

These Rules further amend the Patents Rules 1968. The principal amendments are as follows:—

(1) paper of A4 size may now be used for documents and drawings filed at the Office (Rules 5 and 19);

(2) the use of large sheets for drawings is permitted only in exceptional circumstances (Rule 19);

(3) additional documents are specifically excepted from the public inspection provided by Rule 146; and a request under that Rule that a document is to be treated as confidential may now be made within 14 days of the filing or sending of the document by any party to the proceedings and not, as hitherto, only at the time of filing by the person filing or sending the document.

(a) S.I. 1968/1702 (1968 III, p. 4603).

1970 No. 957

LOCAL GOVERNMENT, ENGLAND AND WALES

The Isles of Scilly (Land) Order 1970

Made - - - *26th June* 1970

The Minister of Housing and Local Government, after consultation with the Council of the Isles of Scilly, in exercise of his powers under section 11 of the Local Authorities (Land) Act 1963(**a**) and of all other powers enabling him in that behalf, hereby makes the following order:—

1. This order may be cited as the Isles of Scilly (Land) Order 1970.

2. The Interpretation Act 1889(**b**) applies to the interpretation of this order as it applies to the interpretation of an Act of Parliament.

3. The Local Authorities (Land) Act 1963 (except sections 6 to 8 thereof) shall apply to the Isles of Scilly with the modifications set out in the Schedule to this order.

SCHEDULE

For section 13 there shall be substituted—

"13. Section 159(1) of the Local Government Act 1933 (which as applied to the Isles of Scilly by the Isles of Scilly Order 1943 provides that the Council of the Isles of Scilly may be authorised to purchase land for the purposes of any of their functions under any public general Act) shall not apply in relation to any function conferred on the said Council by any provision of this Act which is applied to the Isles of Scilly by the Isles of Scilly (Land) Order 1970.".

In section 14(1), for the definition of "local authority" there shall be substituted

" "local authority" includes the Council of the Isles of Scilly;".

Given under the official seal of the Minister of Housing and Local Government on 26th June 1970.

(L.S.)

James W. Vernon,
Under Secretary,
Ministry of Housing and
Local Government.

(**a**) 1963 c. 29 (**b**) 1889 c. 63.

EXPLANATORY NOTE

(*This Note is not part of the Order.*)

This Note applies the Local Authorities (Land) Act 1963, other than sections 6 to 8 thereof, to the Isles of Scilly.

STATUTORY INSTRUMENTS

1970 No. 964

AGRICULTURE

The Price Stability of Imported Products (Rates of Levy) (Eggs) (No. 6) Order 1970

Made - - - - *29th June* 1970

Coming into Operation *30th June* 1970

The Minister of Agriculture, Fisheries and Food, in exercise of the powers conferred upon him by section 1(2), (4), (5), (6) and (7) of the Agriculture and Horticulture Act 1964(**a**) and of all other powers enabling him in that behalf, hereby makes the following order:—

1. This order may be cited as the Price Stability of Imported Products (Rates of Levy) (Eggs) (No. 6) Order 1970, and shall come into operation on 30th June 1970.

2.—(1) In this order—

" the Principal Order " means the Price Stability of Imported Products (Levy Arrangements) (Eggs) Order 1970(**b**) as amended by any subsequent order, and if any such order is replaced by any subsequent order the expression shall be construed as a reference to such subsequent order;

AND other expressions have the same meaning as in the Principal Order.

(2) The Interpretation Act 1889(**c**) shall apply to the interpretation of this order as it applies to the interpretation of an Act of Parliament and as if this order and the order hereby revoked were Acts of Parliament.

3. In accordance with and subject to the provisions of the Principal Order (which provides for the charging of levies on imports of those eggs and egg products which are specified commodities for the purposes of the Agriculture and Horticulture Act 1964) the rate of general levy for such imports into the United Kingdom of any specified commodity as are described in column 2 of the Schedule to this order in relation to a tariff heading indicated in column 1 of that Schedule shall be the rate set forth in relation thereto in column 3 of that Schedule.

4. The Price Stability of Imported Products (Rates of Levy) (Eggs) (No. 5) Order 1970(**d**) is hereby revoked.

In Witness whereof the Official Seal of the Minister of Agriculture, Fisheries and Food is hereunto affixed on 29th June 1970.

(L.S.)

J. A. Barrah,
Assistant Secretary.

(**a**) 1964 c. 28. (**b**) S.I. 1970/359 (1970 I, p. 1277). (**c**) 1889 c. 63.
(**d**) S.I. 1970/879 (1970 II, p.2809).

SCHEDULE

1. Tariff Heading	2. Description of Imports	3. Rate of General Levy
	Imports of:—	
		(per 120 eggs)
04.05	*Birds' eggs in shell:—*	*s. d.*
	1. Not exceeding 11 lb. in weight per 120 ..	4 0
	2. Over 11 lb. but not exceeding 12½ lb. in weight per 120	4 0
	3. Over 12½ lb. but not exceeding 14 lb. in weight per 120	5 6
	4. Over 14 lb. but not exceeding 15½ lb. in weight per 120	6 6
	5. Over 15½ lb. but not exceeding 17 lb. in weight per 120	6 6
	6. Over 17 lb. in weight per 120	4 6

EXPLANATORY NOTE

(This Note is not part of the Order.)

This order, which comes into operation on 30th June 1970, supersedes the Price Stability of Imported Products (Rates of Levy) (Eggs) (No. 5) Order 1970.

It—

(*a*) increases the rates of general levy on imports of eggs in shell for those eggs in the weight grades which are numbered 3 to 5 in the Schedule to the order ;

(*b*) reimposes unchanged the rates of general levy for the other three weights of eggs which were in force immediately before the commencement of this order.

STATUTORY INSTRUMENTS

1970 No. 965 (C.23)

ROAD TRAFFIC

The Road Traffic (Driving Instruction) Act 1967 (Commencement No. 2) Order 1970

Made - - - *24th June* 1970

The Minister of Transport, in exercise of his powers under section 22(2) of the Road Traffic (Driving Instruction) Act 1967(a) and of all other enabling powers, hereby makes the following Order :—

1. The provisions of the Road Traffic (Driving Instruction) Act 1967 specified in columns 1 and 2 of the Schedule to this Order (which relate to the subject matter specified in column 3 of that Schedule in relation to those provisions) shall, except in the case of the provisions specified in column 2 of that Schedule in so far as they have already come into operation, come into operation on the 1st October 1970.

2. This Order may be cited as the Road Traffic (Driving Instruction) Act 1967 (Commencement No. 2) Order 1970.

Given under the Official Seal of the Minister of Transport the 24th June 1970.

(L.S.)

L. E. Dale,
An Under Secretary of the Ministry of Transport.

(a) 1967 c. 79.

SCHEDULE

Column 1 Provisions coming into operation on 1st October 1970	Column 2 Provisions coming into operation on 1st October 1970, except in so far as they have already come into operation	Column 3 Subject matter
Section 1		Driving instruction for payment to be given only by registered or licensed persons.
Section 2		Exemption of police instructors from prohibition imposed by section 1 of this Act.
Section 6		Licences to give instruction.
	Section 7 and Schedule 1	Appeals against decisions of the Registrar in connection with licences.
	Section 9	Power to alter conditions for grant or revocation of licences.
	Section 11	Surrender of licences.
	Section 12	Production of licences to police constables and authorised persons.
	Section 13 and Schedule 2	Application of provisions of Road Traffic Act 1960 as to offences and fines and minor modifications thereof.
	Section 14	Evidence by certificate as to licences.

EXPLANATORY NOTE

(*This Note is not part of the Order.*)

This Order brings into operation all the provisions of the Road Traffic (Driving Instruction) Act 1967 which were not brought into force on 17th March 1969 by the Road Traffic (Driving Instruction) Act 1967 (Commencement No. 1) Order 1969 (S.I. 1969/84).

Section 1 now brought into operation makes it, in general, an offence for a person to give instruction, which is paid for by or in respect of the pupil, in driving a motor car, unless the instructor's name is in the Register of Approved Driving Instructors or he holds a current licence to give instruction granted under section 6 of the Act.

There is an exemption for serving police instructors, in certain circumstances, from the prohibition on giving driving instruction for which payment is made while unregistered or unlicensed—section 2.

Under section 6, for the purpose of acquiring practical experience of giving instruction with a view to undergoing the qualifying examination for entry in the Register, licences to give instruction may be issued by the Registrar to trainee instructors who possess the specified qualifications. Under that section, too, power is given to the Minister of Transport to prescribe by regulations the fee for a licence, its form, period of validity and conditions of issue.

The existing right of appeal to the Minister by a person aggrieved by a decision of the Registrar is extended to decisions refusing to issue a licence or revoking a licence. The existing procedure (specified in Schedule 1 to the 1967 Act) is to apply to appeals against such decisions—section 7.

1970 No. 966

ROAD TRAFFIC

The Motor Cars (Driving Instruction) (Amendment) Regulations 1970

Made - - -	*24th June* 1970
Laid before Parliament	*7th July* 1970
Coming into Operation	*1st October* 1970

The Minister of Transport, in exercise of his powers under sections 3(1) and (2), 6(1) and (4), 8(1), 9(*a*) and 18 of the Road Traffic (Driving Instruction) Act 1967(**a**) (hereinafter referred to as "the Act") and of all other enabling powers, hereby makes the following Regulations:—

1. These Regulations shall come into operation on the 1st October 1970 and may be cited as the Motor Cars (Driving Instruction) (Amendment) Regulations 1970.

2. The Interpretation Act 1889(**b**) shall apply for the interpretation of these Regulations as it applies for the interpretation of an Act of Parliament.

3. The conditions in the Act as to which the Registrar is required to be satisfied for the entry of a name in the register, the retention of a name therein and the grant of a licence shall be altered to the following extent, namely—

(*a*) by the substitution in section 3(1) of the Act—

(i) in paragraph (*b*), for the words from "and, at no time" to the end of that paragraph of the following words—

"and that, during the period of six years ending with the day on which the application is made, he has held for periods amounting in the aggregate to at least four years a current licence of one of the kinds aforesaid or a current foreign licence, that is to say a document issued under the law of a country outside the United Kingdom authorising the holder to drive a motor vehicle in that country;"; and

(ii) in paragraph (*c*), for the words "of the said period" of the words "of the period of four years ending with the day on which the application is made"; and

(*b*) by the omission in section 4(1) of the Act, in paragraph (*c*), of the words from "and at no time" to the end of that paragraph.

(**a**) 1967 c. 79. (**b**) 1889 c. 63.

4. The Motor Cars (Driving Instruction) Regulations 1969(**a**), as amended (**b**), shall have effect as though—

(1) at the end of Regulation 6 there were added the following paragraph— "and

(*h*) the book "Driving—The Ministry of Transport Manual", issued by the Ministry of Transport and published by H.M. Stationery Office." ;

(2) in Regulation 7(2) the word "white" and the words "on a black surface" were omitted, ;

(3) in Regulation 10—

(*a*) for paragraph (1), there were substituted the following paragraph—

"(1) The test shall consist of the attendance of the examiner while the candidate is giving instruction to a pupil or pupils, except that when required to do so by the examiner for the purpose of the test, the candidate shall give such instruction in a motor car on a road." ;

(*b*) at the beginning of paragraph (3), there were inserted the following words "Where the test is to be conducted in a motor car," ;

(4) after Part III there were inserted the following Part—

"PART IIIA

LICENCES UNDER SECTION 6 OF THE ACT

10A. In addition to the conditions referred to in section 6(1) of the Act as respects which the Registrar has to be satisfied are fulfilled in the case of an applicant for a licence, the following condition shall also apply in the case of such an applicant, that is to say, the Registrar shall be satisfied that the applicant at the time of his application for a licence—

(*a*) is eligible under Regulation 5(3) of these Regulations to submit himself for the practical part of the examination ; or

(*b*) has made an application to submit himself for the written part of the examination, the result of which has not been notified to him ; or

(*c*) is prevented from submitting himself for that written part only by virtue of Regulation 9(2) of these Regulations.

10B. Subject to section 6(5), (7) and (8) of the Act, a licence shall be in force for a period of six months from the date of issue.

10C. A licence shall be granted subject to the following conditions:—

(1) the holder thereof shall give instruction thereunder in the driving of a motor car only from an establishment of which the name and address is specified in the licence ;

(2) if any such establishment is a driving school or a branch thereof, the holder of the licence shall give such instruction only if the relevant condition as to the employment of instructors at that school or branch is complied with.

(**a**) S.I. 1969/85 (1969 I, p. 248).

(**b**) The relevant amending instrument is S.I. 1969/713 (1969 II, p. 1944).

In this sub-paragraph, "the relevant condition as to the employment of instructors" means that, for each holder of a licence in which the school or branch thereof is specified, there is employed thereat one or more persons whose names are in the Register at the rate of one such person for each holder of a licence ;

(3) that in the case of any licence other than the second of two licences issued in respect of consecutive periods, the holder thereof shall, while giving instruction in the driving of a motor car, receive direct personal supervision from a person whose name is in the Register for at least one fifth of the total time the holder spends giving such instruction during the first three months for which the licence is in force ;

(4) the holder shall maintain in respect of each working day during the first three months of a licence to which the last preceding paragraph applies a record of the time he spends giving such instruction containing the particulars specified in the next succeeding paragraph, shall preserve such record for three months from the date of expiry of that licence and shall produce such record on request to an officer authorised by the Minister to inspect such a record who shall be entitled to retain it, if he so desires ;

(5) the particulars referred to in the last preceding paragraph are:—

(*a*) the name of the holder of the licence ;

(*b*) its number ;

(*c*) the name of the establishment from which the holder of the licence has given instruction ;

(*d*) the name of the person under whose direct personal supervision the holder of the licence has given instruction ;

(*e*) in respect of each working day :—

(i) the date ;

(ii) the total number of hours spent giving instruction from the establishment ;

(iii) the periods spent under the direct personal supervision of the person referred to at (*d*) above ;

(iv) the signature of the holder of the licence ;

(v) the counter-signature of the person referred to at (*d*) above.

10D. A licence shall be in the form in, and contain the particulars required by, Schedule 2 to these Regulations." ;

(5) in Regulation 11, at the end thereof there were added the following paragraph—

"(4) A person applying for a licence shall pay a fee of one pound." ;

(6) the Schedule thereto were numbered "1", and after that Schedule there were added Schedule 2 set out in the Schedule to these Regulations.

Given under the Official Seal of the Minister of Transport the 24th June 1970.

John Peyton,
Minister of Transport.

SCHEDULE

Regulation 10D

SCHEDULE 2

FORM OF LICENCE UNDER S.6 OF THE ACT

Serial No.

REGISTER OF APPROVED DRIVING INSTRUCTORS
LICENCE TO GIVE INSTRUCTION IN DRIVING MOTOR CARS

Name of holder ....
Address ....
....
Name of training establishment ....
Address ....
....
Date of expiry of licence ....

Issued under the Road Traffic (Driving Instruction) Act 1967.

Signature ....
Registrar

Date of issue ....

EXPLANATORY NOTE

(*This Note is not part of the Regulations.*)

These Regulations alter the conditions in the Road Traffic (Driving Instruction) Act 1967 as to which the Registrar is required by the Act to be satisfied for the entry of a name in the Register of Approved Driving Instructors, the retention of a name therein and for the grant of a licence.

The Regulations also further amend the Motor Cars (Driving Instruction) Regulations 1969. The main changes are :—

1. The book "Driving—the Ministry of Transport Manual" is added to the list in Regulation 6 of the 1969 Regulations of subjects on which the written part of the examination of ability to give instruction is based (Regulation 4(1)) ;
2. The motor vehicle registration mark used in the test of eyesight referred to in Regulation 7(2) of the 1969 Regulations need no longer have white letters and figures on a black surface (Regulation 4(2)) ;
3. As respects the test of continued ability and fitness to give instruction, referred to in Regulation 10 of the 1969 Regulations, the person receiving the instruction is no longer required to be the holder of a provisional driving licence (Regulation 4(3)) ;
4. Provision is made in regard to licences under section 6 of the Road Traffic (Driving Instruction) Act 1967 dealing with their duration, the conditions on which they are granted, their form and the amount of the fee payable on applying therefor (Regulation 4(4), 4(5), 4(6) and the Schedule).

STATUTORY INSTRUMENTS

1970 No. 967

ROAD TRAFFIC

The Motor Cars (Driving Instruction) (Appeals) (Amendment) Rules 1970

Made - - - -	24*th June* 1970
Coming into Operation	1*st October* 1970

The Minister of Transport, in exercise of the powers conferred on him by paragraph 3 of Schedule 1 to the Road Traffic (Driving Instruction) Act 1967(**a**) and of all other enabling powers, hereby makes the following Rules:—

1.—(1) These Rules shall come into operation on the 1st October 1970 and may be cited as the Motor Cars (Driving Instruction) (Appeals) (Amendment) Rules 1970.

(2) The Interpretation Act 1889(**b**) shall apply for the interpretation of these Rules as it applies for the interpretation of an Act of Parliament.

2. The Motor Cars (Driving Instruction) (Appeals) Rules 1969(**c**) shall have effect as though:—

(1) in Rule 1, at the end of paragraph (2) there were added the following sub-paragraph—

" or,

(*d*) refusing an application for the grant of a licence under section 6 of the Act or revoking such a licence." ;

(2) in Rule 2, in the definition of " appeal ", the words " except in so far as that section relates to licences granted under section 6 of the Act " were omitted.

Given under the Official Seal of the Minister of Transport the 24th June 1970.

(L.S.)

L. E. Dale,
An Under Secretary of
the Ministry of Transport.

(**a**) 1967 c. 79. (**b**) 1889 c. 63. (**c**) 1969/86 (1969 I, p. 255).

EXPLANATORY NOTE

(*This Note is not part of the Rules.*)

These Rules extend the Motor Cars (Driving Instruction) (Appeals) Rules 1969 so that the latter apply to appeals under section 7 of the Road Traffic (Driving Instruction) Act 1967 against decisions of the Registrar refusing an application for the grant of a licence under section 6 of the Act, or revoking such a licence.

STATUTORY INSTRUMENTS

1970 No. 968

NATIONAL HEALTH SERVICE, ENGLAND AND WALES
NATIONAL HEALTH SERVICE, SCOTLAND

The National Health Service (Employers of Mariners Contributions) (Amendment) Regulations 1970

Made - - -	30*th June* 1970
Laid before Parliament	3*rd July* 1970
Coming into Operation	6*th July* 1970

The Treasury, in exercise of the powers conferred on them by section 2(7) of the National Health Service Contributions Act 1965**(a)**, and of all other powers enabling them in that behalf, hereby make the following Regulations:—

1. These Regulations may be cited as the National Health Service (Employers of Mariners Contributions) (Amendment) Regulations 1970, and shall come into operation on 6th July 1970.

2. The Interpretation Act 1889**(b)** shall apply for the interpretation of these Regulations as it applies for the interpretation of an Act of Parliament, and as if these Regulations and the Regulations hereby revoked were Acts of Parliament.

3. The National Health Service (Employers of Mariners Contributions) Regulations 1957**(c)**, as amended **(d)**, shall be further amended by substituting, in Regulation 4 thereof, for the words "by fourpence", the words "in respect of any period before 15th February 1971 by elevenpence, and in respect of any period beginning on or after that day by £0.047".

4.—(1) Where a mariner is employed for a voyage (including any period of leave on pay immediately following the voyage) which begins after the coming into operation of these Regulations and ends during the transitional period, the reduction falling to be made under Regulation 4 of the said Regulations of 1957 may, for the purpose of calculating the employer's national health service contributions payable in respect of that voyage, be taken to be either elevenpence or £0.047.

(2) In this Regulation "the transitional period" has the meaning assigned to it by section 16(1) of the Decimal Currency Act 1969**(e)**.

5. The National Health Service (Employers of Mariners Contributions) Amendment Regulations 1961**(d)** are hereby revoked.

Hector Munro,
Walter Clegg,
Two of the Lords Commissioners
of Her Majesty's Treasury.

30th June 1970.

(a) 1965 c. 54. **(b)** 1889 c. 63.
(c) S.I. 1957/1327 (1957 I, p. 1484). **(d)** S.I. 1961/751 (1961 I, p. 1559).
(e) 1969 c. 19.

EXPLANATORY NOTE

(*This Note is not part of the Regulations.*)

These Regulations further amend Regulation 4 of the National Health Service (Employers of Mariners Contributions) Regulations 1957, which provides for a reduction of 4d. in the N.H.S. contribution payable by the employers of mariners who are domiciled or resident in the United Kingdom and are employed in foreign-going ships. In consequence of the increase of 1s. 0d. in the employer's N.H.S. contribution provided for by the National Health Service Contributions Act 1970 (c.16), these Regulations increase the above mentioned reduction from 4d. to 11d. The Regulations also provide for the corresponding amount of the reduction in decimal currency to be £0.047.

STATUTORY INSTRUMENTS

1970 No. 969

LOCAL GOVERNMENT, ENGLAND AND WALES

The Police (Compensation) (Amendment) Regulations 1970

Made - - -	29*th June* 1970
Laid before Parliament	8*th July* 1970
Coming into Operation	1*st August* 1970

Whereas the Minister for the Civil Service has determined under section 60(2) of the Local Government Act 1958(**a**) (read with Article 2(1) of the Minister for the Civil Service Order 1968(**b**)) that the Secretary of State is the appropriate Minister in relation to members of police forces :

Now, therefore, in exercise of the powers conferred on me by the said section 60(2) (as extended by Schedule 9 to, and read with section 58(4) of, the Police Act 1964(**c**)), I hereby make the following Regulations :—

1. These Regulations may be cited as the Police (Compensation) (Amendment) Regulations 1970 and shall come into operation on 1st August 1970.

2. In these Regulations any reference to the principal Regulations is a reference to the Police (Compensation) Regulations 1965(**d**), as amended (**e**).

3.—(1) Notwithstanding anything contained in the principal Regulations, Regulations 4, 5 and 6 of these Regulations shall apply with effect from the date of the coming into operation of these Regulations in relation to any compensation under the principal Regulations awarded before that date.

(2) Nothing in Regulation 7 of these Regulations shall affect the entitlement of any person to compensation under the principal Regulations where that entitlement has been determined before the date of the coming into operation of these Regulations.

4. For Regulation 6(1)(*a*) of the principal Regulations (deductions to be made in calculating resettlement compensation) there shall be substituted the following provision :—

"(*a*) unemployment, sickness or injury benefit under any Act relating to national insurance claimable by him in respect of such week (excluding any amount claimable by him in respect of any dependant) ;".

5. After Regulation 26 of the principal Regulations (adjustment of compensation) there shall be inserted the following Regulation :—

"*Deduction in respect of national insurance benefit*

26A.—(1) Where in any week a person is entitled to long-term compensation for loss or diminution of emoluments and is also entitled to unemploy-

(**a**) 1958 c. 55. (**b**) S.I. 1968/1656 (1968 III, p. 4485). (**c**) 1964 c. 48.
(**d**) S.I. 1965/564 (1965 I, p. 1751). (**e**) S.I. 1966/730 (1966 II, p. 1692).

ment, sickness or injury benefit under any Act relating to national insurance, other than a benefit claimable by him in respect of a dependant, there shall be deducted from the long-term compensation payable for that week a sum equal to the amount by which the aggregate of such national insurance benefits claimable in respect of that week, the weekly rate at which the long-term compensation would be payable but for this Regulation, and the weekly rate of any superannuation benefit taken into account for the purpose of Regulation 13(4) of these Regulations, exceeds two-thirds of the weekly rate of the net emoluments of the employment which he has lost or in which the emoluments have been diminished :

Provided that this paragraph shall not apply in relation to any such sickness or injury benefit in so far as an equivalent sum is deducted from the emoluments of his current employment and such deduction from those emoluments has not occasioned an increase in his long-term compensation.

(2) For the purposes of paragraph (1) of this Regulation the expression "weekly rate" means seven three hundred and sixty-fifths of the relevant annual rate.".

6. In Regulation 27 of the principal Regulations (certain changes in circumstances to be notified to the compensating authority) there shall be inserted after sub-paragraph (*c*) the following provision :—

"or,

(*d*) a person entitled to long-term compensation is receiving or starts to receive any benefit, any increase in benefit or any further benefit under any Act relating to national insurance,".

7. After Regulation 38(2) of the principal Regulations (which relates to interpretation) there shall be inserted the following provision :—

"(2A) Except as provided in Regulations 4(2) and 10(2) of these Regulations, the expression "relevant employment" shall not include service in the armed forces of the Crown.".

R. Maudling,
One of Her Majesty's Principal
Secretaries of State.

Home Office,
Whitehall.
29th June 1970.

EXPLANATORY NOTE

(This Note is not part of the Regulations.)

These Regulations amend the Police (Compensation) Regulations 1965 (the principal Regulations) as follows:—

(i) all national insurance benefits (other than benefits payable in respect of dependants) are to be taken into account in assessing resettlement compensation and not only, as at present, benefits at the flat rate applicable to a single person (Regulation 4);

(ii) national insurance benefits (other than benefits payable in respect of dependants) are to be deducted from long-term compensation to such extent as is necessary to ensure that the total of benefits and compensation received in any week does not exceed two-thirds of the emoluments for the loss or reduction of which compensation is payable. This was until recently secured by Regulations under the National Insurance Acts (Regulation 5);

(iii) a person entitled to long-term compensation is required to inform the compensating authority about national insurance benefits received by him (Regulation 6);

(iv) the expression "relevant employment" (which is defined in Regulation 38(1) of the principal Regulations and which affects qualification for compensation and calculation of the amount) is not to include service in the armed forces of the Crown other than certain national service which is expressly made relevant employment for determining whether a person is qualified to claim compensation (Regulation 7).

The provisions mentioned in (i) to (iii) above apply to compensation in payment at the date of commencement of these Regulations as well as compensation awarded after that date (Regulation 3).

1970 No. 975

SUGAR

The Sugar (Rates of Surcharge and Surcharge Repayments) (No. 8) Order 1970

Made - - - -	*1st July* 1970
Laid before Parliament	*2nd July* 1970
Coming into Operation	*3rd July* 1970

The Minister of Agriculture, Fisheries and Food, in exercise of the powers conferred on him by sections 7(4), 8(6) and 33(4) of the Sugar Act 1956(**a**) having effect subject to the provisions of section 3 of, and Part II of Schedule 5 to, the Finance Act 1962(**b**), and section 58 of the Finance Act 1968(**c**) and of all other powers enabling him in that behalf, with the concurrence of the Treasury, on the advice of the Sugar Board, hereby makes the following order:—

1.—(1) This order may be cited as the Sugar (Rates of Surcharge and Surcharge Repayments) (No. 8) Order 1970; and shall come into operation on 3rd July 1970.

(2) The Interpretation Act 1889(**d**) shall apply for the interpretation of this order as it applies for the interpretation of an Act of Parliament.

2. Notwithstanding the provisions of Article 2 of the Sugar (Rates of Surcharge and Surcharge Repayments) (No. 7) Order 1970(**e**), the rates of surcharge payable under and in accordance with the provisions of section 7 of the Sugar Act 1956, having effect as aforesaid, in respect of sugar and invert sugar imported or home produced or used in the manufacture of imported composite sugar products shall on and after 3rd July 1970 be those rates specified in Schedule 1 to this order.

3. For the purpose of section 8(3)(*b*) of the Sugar Act 1956, having effect as aforesaid, the rates of surcharge repayments in respect of invert sugar produced in the United Kingdom from materials on which on or after 3rd July 1970 sugar duty has been paid or, by virtue of paragraph 1 of Part II of Schedule 5 to the Finance Act 1962, is treated as having been paid shall, notwithstanding the provisions of Article 3 of the Sugar (Rates of Surcharge and Surcharge Repayments) (No. 7) Order 1970 be those specified in Schedule 2 to this order.

(**a**) 1956 c. 48. (**b**) 1962 c. 44.
(**c**) 1968 c. 44. (**d**) 1889 c. 63.
(**e**) S.I. 1970/766 (1970 II, p. 2411).

In Witness whereof the Official Seal of the Minister of Agriculture, Fisheries and Food is hereunto affixed on 24th June 1970.

(L.S.)

R. P. Fraser,
Authorised by the Minister.

We concur.

1st July 1970.

Reginald Eyre,

H. F. P. Monro,

Two of the Lords Commissioners of Her Majesty's Treasury.

SCHEDULE 1

PART I

SURCHARGE RATES FOR SUGAR

Polarisation	Rate of Surcharge per cwt.
	s. d.
Exceeding—	
99°	9 4·0
98° but not exceeding 99°	8 9·6
97° „ „ „ 98°	8 7·0
96° „ „ „ 97°	8 4·3
95° „ „ „ 96°	8 1·6
94° „ „ „ 95°	7 10·9
93° „ „ „ 94°	7 8·2
92° „ „ „ 93°	7 5·6
91° „ „ „ 92°	7 2·9
90° „ „ „ 91°	7 0·2
89° „ „ „ 90°	6 9·5
88° „ „ „ 89°	6 6·8
87° „ „ „ 88°	6 4·6
86° „ „ „ 87°	6 2·3
85° „ „ „ 86°	6 0·3
84° „ „ „ 85°	5 10·3
83° „ „ „ 84°	5 8·3
82° „ „ „ 83°	5 6·3
81° „ „ „ 82°	5 4·5
80° „ „ „ 81°	5 2·7
79° „ „ „ 80°	5 0·9
78° „ „ „ 79°	4 11·1
77° „ „ „ 78°	4 9·3
76° „ „ „ 77°	4 7·5
Not exceeding 76°	4 6·0

Part II

Surcharge Rates for Invert Sugar

Sweetening matter content by weight	Rate of Surcharge per cwt.
	s. d.
70 per cent. or more	5 11
Less than 70 per cent. and more than 50 per cent.	4 3
Not more than 50 per cent.	2 1

SCHEDULE 2

Surcharge Repayment Rates for Invert Sugar

Sweetening matter content by weight	Rate of Surcharge Repayment per cwt.
	s. d.
More than 80 per cent.	7 0
More than 70 per cent. but not more than 80 per cent.	5 11
More than 60 per cent. but not more than 70 per cent.	4 3
More than 50 per cent. but not more than 60 per cent.	3 4
Not more than 50 per cent. and the invert sugar not being less in weight than 14 lb. per gallon	2 1

EXPLANATORY NOTE

(*This Note is not part of the Order.*)

This order prescribes—

(*a*) reductions equivalent to 2s. 4d. per cwt. of refined sugar in the rates of surcharge payable on sugar and invert sugar which become chargeable with surcharge on or after 3rd July 1970;

(*b*) correspondingly reduced rates of surcharge repayment in respect of invert sugar produced in the United Kingdom from materials on which surcharge has been paid.

STATUTORY INSTRUMENTS

1970 No. 976

SUGAR

The Composite Sugar Products (Surcharge and Surcharge Repayments—Average Rates) (No. 9) Order 1970

Made - - - -	*1st July* 1970
Laid before Parliament	*2nd July* 1970
Coming into Operation	*3rd July* 1970

Whereas the Minister of Agriculture, Fisheries and Food (hereinafter called " the Minister ") has on the recommendation of the Commissioners of Customs and Excise (hereinafter called " the Commissioners ") made an order(**a**) pursuant to the powers conferred upon him by sections 9(1) and 9(4) of the Sugar Act 1956(**b**), having effect subject to the provisions of section 3 of, and Part II of Schedule 5 to, the Finance Act 1962(**c**), to the provisions of section 52(2) of the Finance Act 1966(**d**), and to the provisions of section 58 of the Finance Act 1968(**e**), providing that in the case of certain descriptions of composite sugar products surcharge shall be calculated on the basis of an average quantity of sugar or invert sugar taken to have been used in the manufacture of the products, and that certain other descriptions of composite sugar products shall be treated as not containing any sugar or invert sugar, and that in the case of certain descriptions of goods in the manufacture of which sugar or invert sugar is used, surcharge repayments shall be calculated on the basis of an average quantity of sugar or invert sugar taken to have been so used:

Now, therefore, the Minister, on the recommendation of the Commissioners and in exercise of the powers conferred upon him by sections 9(1), 9(4) and 33(4) of the Sugar Act 1956, having effect as aforesaid, and of all other powers enabling him in that behalf, hereby makes the following order:—

1.—(1) This order may be cited as the Composite Sugar Products (Surcharge and Surcharge Repayments—Average Rates) (No. 9) Order 1970, and shall come into operation on 3rd July 1970.

(2) The Interpretation Act 1889(**f**) shall apply for the interpretation of this order as it applies for the interpretation of an Act of Parliament.

2. Surcharge payable on or after 3rd July 1970 under and in accordance with the Sugar Act 1956, having effect as aforesaid, in respect of sugar and invert sugar used in the manufacture of the descriptions of imported composite sugar products specified in column 2 of Schedule 1 to this order shall, notwithstanding the provisions of the Sugar (Rates of Surcharge and Surcharge Repayments) (No. 8) Order 1970(**g**) and the Composite Sugar Products (Surcharge and Surcharge Repayments—Average Rates) (No. 8) Order 1970(**a**), be calculated by reference to the weight of the products at the rates specified in relation thereto in column 3 of the said Schedule.

(**a**) S.I. 1970/767 (1970 II, p. 2414). (**b**) 1956 c. 48. (**c**) 1962 c. 44.
(**d**) 1966 c. 18. (**e**) 1968 c. 44. (**f**) 1889 c. 63.
(**g**) S.I. 1970/975 (1970 II, p.3082).

3. Imported composite sugar products other than those of a description specified in Schedules 1 and 2 to this order shall be treated as not containing any sugar or invert sugar for the purposes of surcharge payable on or after 3rd July 1970.

4. Surcharge repayments payable on and after 3rd July 1970 under and in accordance with the provisions of section 8 of the Sugar Act 1956, having effect as aforesaid, in respect of sugar and invert sugar used in the manufacture of the descriptions of goods specified in column 1 of Schedule 3 to this order shall, notwithstanding the provisions of the Sugar (Rates of Surcharge and Surcharge Repayments) (No. 8) Order 1970(**a**) and the Composite Sugar Products (Surcharge and Surcharge Repayments—Average Rates) (No. 8) Order 1970(**b**), be calculated by reference to the quantity of the goods at the rates specified in relation thereto in column 2 of the said Schedule.

In Witness whereof the Official Seal of the Minister of Agriculture, Fisheries and Food is hereunto affixed on 1st July 1970.

(L.S.) *R. P. Fraser*,
Authorised by the Minister.

SCHEDULE 1

In this Schedule:—

" Tariff heading " means a heading or, where the context so requires, a subheading of the Customs Tariff 1959 (see paragraph (1) of Article 2 of the Import Duties (General) (No. 3) Order 1969(**c**)).

Tariff heading	Description of Imported Composite Sugar Products	Rate of Surcharge
		Per cwt. s. d.
04.02	Milk and cream, preserved, concentrated or sweetened, containing more than 10 per cent. by weight of added sugar	4 2
17.02 (B) (2) and 17.05 (B)	Syrups containing sucrose sugar, whether or not flavoured or coloured, but not including fruit juices containing added sugar in any proportion:—	
	containing 70 per cent. or more by weight of sweetening matter	5 11
	containing less than 70 per cent., and more than 50 per cent., by weight of sweetening matter ..	4 3
	containing not more than 50 per cent. by weight of sweetening matter	2 1

(a) S.I. 1970/975 (1970 II, p. 3082). (b) S.I. 1970/767 (1970 II, p. 2414).
(c) S.I. 1969/1413 (1969 III, p. 4150).

Tariff heading	Description of Imported Composite Sugar Products	Rate of Surcharge
		Per cwt. s. d.
17.02 (F) ..	Caramel:—	
	Solid	9 4
	Liquid	6 6
17.04	Sugar confectionery, not containing cocoa ..	7 7
18.06	Chocolate and other food preparations containing cocoa and added sugar:—	
	Chocolate couverture not prepared for retail sale; chocolate milk crumb, liquid ..	4 2
	Chocolate milk crumb, solid	5 1
	Solid chocolate bars or blocks, milk or plain, with or without fruit or nuts; other chocolate confectionery consisting wholly of chocolate or of chocolate and other ingredients not containing added sugar, but not including such goods when packed together in retail packages with goods liable to surcharge at a higher rate	4 2
	Other	5 5
19.08	Pastry, biscuits, cakes and other fine bakers' wares containing added sugar:—	
	Biscuits, wafers and rusks containing more than 12½ per cent. by weight of added sugar, and other biscuits, wafers and rusks included in retail packages with such goods.. ..	2 4
	Cakes with covering or filling containing added sugar; meringues	3 1
	Other	1 2
20.01	Vegetables and fruit, prepared or preserved by vinegar or acetic acid, containing added sugar:—	
	Containing 10 per cent. or more by weight of added sugar	3 3
	Other	8
20.03	Fruit preserved by freezing, containing added sugar	1 2
20.04	Fruit, fruit-peel and parts of plants, preserved by sugar (drained, glacé or crystallised)	6 2
20.05	Jams, fruit jellies, marmalades, fruit purée and fruit pastes, being cooked preparations, containing added sugar	5 10
20.06	Fruit otherwise prepared or preserved, containing added sugar:—	
	Ginger	4 8
	Other	1 2

SCHEDULE 2

Tariff heading	Description of Imported Composite Sugar Products
17.05 (A) and (B)	Sugar and invert sugar, flavoured or coloured.

SCHEDULE 3

Description of goods	Rate of surcharge repayment per bulk barrel of 36 gallons
Lager	4·6d.
All beer other than lager	4·1d.

EXPLANATORY NOTE

(*This Note is not part of the Order.*)

This order provides for reductions on and after 3rd July 1970 in the average rates of surcharge payable on imported composite sugar products of the descriptions specified in Schedule 1 and in the average rates of surcharge repayment in respect of exported goods of the descriptions specified in Schedule 3. These correspond to the reductions in surcharge rates effected by the Sugar (Rates of Surcharge and Surcharge Repayments) (No. 8) Order 1970 (S.I.1970/975). Provision is also made for certain imported composite sugar products to be treated as not containing any sugar or invert sugar.

STATUTORY INSTRUMENTS

1970 No. 977

SOCIAL SECURITY

The Family Allowances, National Insurance, Industrial Injuries and Miscellaneous Provisions (Decimalisation of the Currency) Amendment (No. 2) Regulations 1970

Made - - - - -	1*st July* 1970
Laid before Parliament	3*rd July* 1970
Coming into Operation	6*th July* 1970

The Secretary of State for Social Services, in conjunction with the Treasury, in exercise of his powers under section 8 of the National Insurance Act 1969(**a**), hereby makes the following regulations which, by virtue of the provisions of section 10(1)(*b*) of the said Act of 1969, are exempt from the requirements of section 108 of the National Insurance Act 1965(**b**) (preliminary draft of regulations under that Act to be submitted to the National Insurance Advisory Committee) and section 62(2) of the National Insurance (Industrial Injuries) Act 1965(**c**) (proposal to make regulations under that Act to be submitted to the Industrial Injuries Advisory Council):—

Citation, interpretation and commencement

1. These regulations, which may be cited as the Family Allowances, National Insurance, Industrial Injuries and Miscellaneous Provisions (Decimalisation of the Currency) Amendment (No. 2) Regulations 1970, shall be read as one with the Family Allowances, National Insurance, Industrial Injuries and Miscellaneous Provisions (Decimalisation of the Currency) Regulations 1970(**d**) as amended(**e**) (hereinafter referred to as "the principal regulations") and shall come into operation on 6th July 1970.

Amendment to regulation 1 *of the principal regulations*

2. In regulation 1 of the principal regulations (citation, commencement and interpretation), in paragraph (3) thereof, after the words "any enactment", there shall be inserted the words "scheme, order or regulation"; after the words "that enactment" the words "scheme, order or regulation"; and after the words "other enactment" the word "scheme".

Amendment to the National Insurance Classification Regulations

3.—(1) After regulation 5 of the principal regulations there shall be inserted the following regulation:—

"*Amendment to the National Insurance Classification Regulations*

5A. In the First Schedule to the National Insurance (Classification) Regulations 1948(**f**) as amended(**g**) (classification of insured persons), in paragraph 17 of column (A) thereof, for the reference to forty shillings there shall, from and including the appointed day, be substituted a reference to £2·00."

(**a**) 1969 c. 44. (**b**) 1965 c. 51. (**c**) 1965 c. 52. (**d**) S.I. 1970/46 (1970 I, p. 243).
(**e**) S.I. 1970/507 (1970 I, p. 1713). (**f**) S.I. 1948/1425 (Rev. XVI, p. 95: 1948 I, p. 2738).
(**g**) The relevant amending instrument is S.I. 1957/2175 (1957 I, p. 1623).

(2) In the Arrangement of Regulations, after the entry relating to regulation 5 of the principal regulations, there shall be inserted the following entry:—

"5A. Amendment to the First Schedule to the National Insurance (Classification) Regulations."

Amendment to regulation 13 *of the principal regulations*

4. In regulation 13 of the principal regulations (amendments to the National Insurance Mariners Regulations), for paragraph (1) thereof, there shall be substituted the following paragraph:—

"(1) In regulation 2(2) of the National Insurance (Mariners) Regulations 1967(**a**) as amended(**b**) (insurance of mariners who are neither domiciled nor have a place of residence in the United Kingdom), the words 'subject to the qualification that where any such contribution would, apart from this provision, include a fraction of a penny, that fraction shall be disregarded if it is less than a halfpenny and shall be treated as a penny if it is a halfpenny or more' shall be omitted; and after proviso (*c*) to the said regulation 2(2) there shall be added the following proviso:—

'(*d*) where the amount of any contribution payable under this paragraph, or, in a case where any contribution payable under this paragraph is payable with an employer's contribution under the National Insurance (Industrial Injuries) Act 1965(**c**), the National Health Service Contributions Act 1965(**d**) or the Redundancy Payments Act 1965(**e**), the total amount payable by way of any such contributions, would, apart from this provision, include a fraction of a new penny, that fraction shall be disregarded if it is less than a new halfpenny and shall be treated as a new penny if it is a new halfpenny or more'".

Amendments to Schedules 1, 10 *and* 28 *to the principal regulations*

5.—(1) In Schedule 1 to the principal regulations, for the provisions therein substituted for Parts I and II of Schedule 1 to the National Insurance Act, there shall be substituted the provisions set out in the Schedule to these regulations.

(2) In Schedule 10 to the principal regulations, the provisions therein substituted for Schedule 3 to the National Insurance (Members of the Forces) Regulations shall be amended by substituting in column 2 0·094 for 0·104 and in column 3 0·107 for 0·117 and 0·053 for 0·043.

(3) In Schedule 28 to the principal regulations, the provisions therein substituted for the Schedule to the National Health Service Contributions Act 1965 shall be amended by substituting for 0·033 (weekly rate of contribution by employers) 0·083.

Signed by authority of the Secretary of State for Social Services

Paul Dean,

Parliamentary Under-Secretary of State, Department of Health and Social Security.

29th June 1970.

Reginald Eyre,
H. S. P. Monro,

Two of the Lords Commissioners of Her Majesty's Treasury.

1st July 1970.

(**a**) S.I. 1967/386 (1967 I, p. 1294). (**b**) The relevant amending instruments are S.I. 1967/1573, 1969/1277 (1967 III, p. 4382; 1969 III, p. 3811). (**c**) 1965 c. 52. (**d**) 1965 c. 54. (**e**) 1965 c. 62.

SCHEDULE Regulation 5(1)

Provisions substituted for Parts I and II of Schedule 1 to the National Insurance Act 1965

Rates of Flat-Rate Contributions

Part I

Employed persons except for periods during which employment outside Great Britain is treated as employed contributor's employment by virtue of the provisions of regulation 3 *of the National Insurance (Residence and Persons Abroad) Regulations* 1948(**a**) *as amended*(**b**).

Description of employed person 1	Weekly Rate of Contribution Unless by virtue of a non-participating employment 2	Weekly Rate of Contribution If by virtue of a non-participating employment 3
	£	£
Men between the ages of 18 and 70 (other than men over the age of 65 who have retired from regular employment)—		
Earning remuneration at a weekly rate exceeding £6	0·676	0·796
Earning remuneration at a weekly rate of £6 or less	0·406	0·466
Women between the ages of 18 and 65 (other than women over the age of 60 who have retired from regular employment)—		
Earning remuneration at a weekly rate exceeding £6	0·592	0·672
Earning remuneration at a weekly rate of £6 or less	0·342	0·392
Boys under the age of 18	0·470	—
Girls under the age of 18	0·389	—

(**a**) S.I. 1948/1275 (Rev. XVI, p. 88: 1948 I, p. 2864).

(**b**) The relevant amending instruments are S.I. 1958/1084, 1960/1210 (1958 II, p. 1581; 1960 II, p. 2234).

Employed persons for periods during which employment outside Great Britain is treated as employed contributor's employment by virtue of the provisions of regulation 3 *of the National Insurance (Residence and Persons Abroad) Regulations* 1948 *as amended.*

Description of employed person 1	Weekly Rate of Contribution	
	Unless by virtue of a non-participating employment 2	If by virtue of a non-participating employment 3
	£	£
Men between the ages of 18 and 70 (other than men over the age of 65 who have retired from regular employment)—		
Earning remuneration at a weekly rate exceeding £6	0·682	0·802
Earning remuneration at a weekly rate of £6 or less	0·412	0·472
Women between the ages of 18 and 65 (other than women over the age of 60 who have retired from regular employment)—		
Earning remuneration at a weekly rate exceeding £6	0·595	0·665
Earning remuneration at a weekly rate of £6 or less	0·355	0·385
Boys under the age of 18	0·471	—
Girls under the age of 18	0·391	—

For the purposes of this Part and Part II of this Schedule a person shall be deemed to be earning remuneration at a weekly rate of £6 or less if, but only if, his remuneration does not include the provision of board and lodging by the employer and the rate of the remuneration neither exceeds, nor is deemed in accordance with regulations made under section 114(5) of this Act to exceed, £6 a week, and to be earning remuneration at a weekly rate exceeding £6 in any other case.

PART II

Employers except for periods during which employment outside Great Britain is treated as employed contributor's employment by virtue of the provisions of regulation 3 of the National Insurance (Residence and Persons Abroad) Regulations 1948 as amended.

Description of employed person	Weekly Rate of Contribution	
	Unless by virtue of a non-participating employment	If by virtue of a non-participating employment
1	2	3
	£	£
Men over the age of 18—		
Earning remuneration at a weekly rate exceeding £6 or not being liable to pay a contribution as an employed person ...	0·754	0·874
Earning remuneration at a weekly rate of £6 or less and being liable to pay a contribution as an employed person	1·024	1·204
Women over the age of 18—		
Earning remuneration at a weekly rate exceeding £6 or not being liable to pay a contribution as an employed person ...	0·650	0·730
Earning remuneration at a weekly rate of £6 or less and being liable to pay a contribution as an employed person	0·900	1·010
Boys under the age of 18	0·516	—
Girls under the age of 18	0·430	—

Employers for periods during which employment outside Great Britain is treated as employed contributor's employment by virtue of the provisions of regulation 3 *of the National Insurance (Residence and Persons Abroad) Regulations* 1948 *as amended.*

Description of employed person 1	Weekly Rate of Contribution Unless by virtue of a non-participating employment 2	If by virtue of a non-participating employment 3
	£	£
Men over the age of 18—		
Earning remuneration at a weekly rate exceeding £6 or not being liable to pay a contribution as an employed person ...	0·754	0·874
Earning remuneration at a weekly rate of £6 or less and being liable to pay a contribution as an employed person	1·024	1·204
Women over the age of 18—		
Earning remuneration at a weekly rate exceeding £6 or not being liable to pay a contribution as an employed person ...	0·658	0·728
Earning remuneration at a weekly rate of £6 or less and being liable to pay a contribution as an employed person	0·898	1·008
Boys under the age of 18	0·517	—
Girls under the age of 18	0·427	—

For the purposes of this Part of this Schedule a person over pensionable age, not being an insured person, shall be treated as an employed person if he would be an insured person were he under pensionable age and would be an employed person were he an insured person.

EXPLANATORY NOTE

(*This Note is not part of the Regulations.*)

These Regulations, which further amend the Family Allowances, National Insurance, Industrial Injuries and Miscellaneous Provisions (Decimalisation of the Currency) Regulations 1970 (hereafter called "the Principal Regulations") are made under powers conferred by section 8 of the National Insurance Act 1969 and, accordingly, by virtue of section 10(1)(*b*) of that Act, they have not been referred to the National Insurance Advisory Committee or the Industrial Injuries Advisory Council.

Regulation 2 remedies an omission in Regulation 1(3) of the Principal Regulations; Regulation 3 converts into decimal currency terms a reference to forty shillings in the First Schedule to the National Insurance (Classification) Regulations 1948, which Regulations are now unlikely to be consolidated before 15th February 1971 (date of introduction of decimal currency); Regulation 4 amends Regulation 13 of the Principal Regulations so as to secure that in all cases a contribution, or the total of any contributions, payable in respect of certain mariners who are neither domiciled nor have a place of residence in the United Kingdom which would not be of a whole new penny amount will be rounded to a whole new penny amount; Regulation 5(1) and the Schedule amend Schedule 1 to the Principal Regulations, altering, as a consequence of the increase in the rate of national health service contributions payable by employers by virtue of the National Health Service Contributions Act 1970 (c. 16), the rate of national insurance contributions payable by employers in respect of girls under the age of 18 who are employed in employed contributor's employment in Great Britain from £0·420 to £0·430 and securing that the total contributions payable in respect of certain persons whose employment outside Great Britain is treated as employed contributor's employment will be of a whole new penny amount; and Regulation 5(3) amends Schedule 28 to the Principal Regulations to reflect the increase in the rate of national health service contributions payable by employers by virtue of the said Act of 1970. With the exception of the substitution of £0·094 for £0·104 contained in Schedule 10 to the Principal Regulations, which corrects an anomaly which has come to light since the making of those Regulations, the remaining amendments to the Principal Regulations are consequential upon the increase in the rate of national health service contributions payable by employers.

1970 No. 978

WAGES COUNCILS

The Wages Regulation (Rope, Twine and Net) Order 1970

Made - - - *1st July* 1970
Coming into Operation *24th July* 1970

Whereas the Secretary of State has received from the Rope, Twine and Net Wages Council (Great Britain) the wages regulation proposals set out in the Schedule hereto;

Now, therefore, the Secretary of State in exercise of his powers under section 11 of the Wages Councils Act 1959(**a**), and of all other powers enabling him in that behalf, hereby makes the following Order:—

1. This Order may be cited as the Wages Regulation (Rope, Twine and Net) Order 1970.

2.—(1) In this Order the expression "the specified date" means the 24th July 1970, provided that where, as respects any worker who is paid wages at intervals not exceeding seven days, that date does not correspond with the beginning of the period for which the wages are paid, the expression "the specified date" means, as respects that worker, the beginning of the next such period following that date.

(2) The Interpretation Act 1889(**b**) shall apply to the interpretation of this Order as it applies to the interpretation of an Act of Parliament and as if this Order and the Order hereby revoked were Acts of Parliament.

3. The wages regulation proposals set out in the Schedule hereto shall have effect as from the specified date and as from that date the Wages Regulation (Rope, Twine and Net) Order 1969(**c**) shall cease to have effect.

Signed by order of the Secretary of State.
1st July 1970.

R. R. D. McIntosh,
Deputy Under Secretary of State,
Department of Employment and Productivity.

SCHEDULE — Article 3

The following minimum remuneration shall be substituted for the statutory minimum remuneration fixed by the Wages Regulation (Rope, Twine and Net) Order 1969 (Order R. (153)).

(**a**) 1959 c. 69. (**b**) 1889 c. 63.
(**c**) S.I. 1969/654 (1969 II, p. 1789).

STATUTORY MINIMUM REMUNERATION

PART I

GENERAL

1. The minimum remuneration payable to a worker to whom this Schedule applies for all work except work to which a minimum overtime rate applies under Part III of this Schedule is:—

(1) in the case of a time worker, the general minimum time rate, or, where appropriate, the minimum weekly remuneration payable to the worker under Part II of this Schedule;

(2) in the case of a worker employed on piece work—

(*a*) where a general minimum piece rate applies under Part II of this Schedule, that piece rate increased by *50 per cent.*, or

(*b*) where no general minimum piece rate applies, piece rates each of which would yield, in the circumstances of the case, to an ordinary worker at least the same amount of money as the piece work basis time rate applicable to the worker under paragraph 3(5) of this Schedule.

DEFINITIONS

2. In this Schedule, unless the context otherwise requires,

(1) SHIFT WORKER means a worker employed on a shift system in accordance with which—

(*a*) a 24-hour period is divided into two or more shifts, one of which is a night shift; or

(*b*) there is no night shift and the remainder of the day is divided into two or more shifts;

and for the purposes of this definition NIGHT SHIFT means a turn of duty which includes some period of employment between 10 p.m. on one day and 6 a.m. on the next following day.

(2) HARD FIBRES mean manilla, sisal, maguey fibre, New Zealand hemp or coir or a mixture thereof;

SHRINK NETTING means that the netting is made by shrinking or gaining, that is to say, the process of putting two meshes into one mesh or vice versa in order to obtain the required taper, shrink or gain;

PLAIN NETTING is ordinary braiding, single selvedge, the net mesh when straight hanging diamond;

A RAN SHORT REEL is the amount of twine wound on a reel 69 inches in circumference in 400 revolutions or 766⅔ yards;

SIZE OF MESH means in the case of all nets, other than the stack nets referred to in paragraph 9, the total length of two adjacent sides of the mesh, measured from the inside of one knot to the outside of the other.

PART II

ALL SECTIONS OF THE TRADE

GENERAL MINIMUM TIME RATES, MINIMUM WEEKLY REMUNERATION AND PIECE WORK BASIS TIME RATES

3.—(1) Subject to the provisions of sub-paragraphs (2) to (4) of this paragraph, the general minimum time rates payable to male and female workers specified in Column 1 of the next following Table are the rates set out in Column 2 of that Table.

(2) Where, in any week, the remuneration payable to a worker for the hours worked (excluding overtime) in that week, calculated at the appropriate general minimum time rate, together with any bonus payments or holiday remuneration payable to the worker in that week amounts to less than the minimum weekly remuneration specified for that worker in Column 3 of the next following Table, the minimum remuneration (exclusive of any amount payable in respect of overtime) payable to that worker in that week shall be the minimum weekly remuneration so specified.

(3) *For the purposes of the preceding sub-paragraph the minimum weekly remuneration shall be reduced proportionately according as the number of hours worked (excluding overtime) is less than 40 where—*

(*a*) *The worker is a part-time worker who normally works for the employer for less than 40 hours a week by reason only of the fact that*

(*i*) *he does not hold himself out as normally available for work for more than the number of hours he normally works in the week ;*

or

(*ii*) *he was engaged to work under a system of part-time working in operation in the factory or workshop where he is employed.*

(*b*) *The worker works for less than 40 hours in any week by reason of absence at any time during that week with the consent of the employer or because of proved incapacity due to illness or injury ;*

or

(*c*) *The employer is unable to provide the worker with work by reason of a strike or shortage of work or circumstances beyond his control and gives the worker notice to that effect two clear weeks before the week or weeks in question in the case of a shortage of work and four clear days in any other case ;*

or

(*d*) *The worker's employment is terminated before the end of the week.*

(4) Except as provided by sub-paragraph (3)(*b*) of this paragraph, the minimum weekly remuneration specified in Column 3 of the next following Table shall not be payable to a worker in any week in which that worker at any time in that week is absent from work without the consent of the employer.

TABLE OF GENERAL MINIMUM TIME RATES AND MINIMUM WEEKLY REMUNERATION

TIME WORKERS	General Minimum Time Rate		Minimum Weekly Remuneration	
Column 1	Column 2		Column 3	
	Up to and including 14th Feb., 1971	On and after 15th Feb., 1971	Up to and including 14th Feb., 1971	On and after 15th Feb., 1971
MALE WORKERS OTHER THAN SHIFT WORKERS (including home-workers) being aged—	Per hour s. d.	Per hour p	s. d.	£
18 years or over	*6 0*	*30*	*265 0*	*13·25*
17 and under 18 years	*3 11½*	*20*	*158 4*	*8·00*
16 " " 17 "	*3 4½*	*17*	*135 0*	*6·80*
under 16 years	*2 10½*	*14½*	*115 0*	*5·80*
FEMALE WORKERS OTHER THAN SHIFT WORKERS (including home-workers) being aged—				
18 years or over	*4 9*	*23¾*	*205 0*	*10·25*
17½ and under 18 years	*4 0½*	*20*	*161 8*	*8·00*
17 " " 17½ "	*3 7*	*18*	*143 4*	*7·20*

TIME WORKERS	General Minimum Time Rate		Minimum Weekly Remuneration	
Column 1	Column 2		Column 3	
	Up to and including 14th Feb., 1971	On and after 15th Feb., 1971	Up to and including 14th Feb., 1971	On and after 15th Feb., 1971
FEMALE WORKERS OTHER THAN SHIFT WORKERS (*continued*) (including home-workers) being aged—	Per hour s. d.	Per hour p	s. d.	£
16½ " " 17 "	*3 4*	*16½*	*133 4*	*6·60*
16 " " 16½	*3 0*	*15*	*120 0*	*6·00*
under 16 years	*2 10½*	*14½*	*115 0*	*5·80*
MALE SHIFT WORKERS, WHEN EMPLOYED ON DAY SHIFTS, being aged—				
18 years or over	*6 9*	*33¾*	*299 0*	*14·95*
17 and under 18 years	*4 5½*	*22½*	*178 4*	*9·00*
16 " " 17 "	*3 9½*	*19*	*151 8*	*7·60*
FEMALE SHIFT WORKERS, WHEN EMPLOYED ON DAY SHIFTS, being aged—				
18 years or over	*5 4*	*26¾*	*231 0*	*11·55*
17½ and under 18 years	*4 6½*	*22¾*	*181 8*	*9·10*
17 " " 17½ "	*4 0½*	*20*	*161 8*	*8·00*
16½ " " 17 "	*3 9*	*18¾*	*150 0*	*7·50*
16 " " 16½	*3 4½*	*17*	*135 0*	*6·80*
MALE SHIFT WORKERS, WHEN EMPLOYED ON NIGHT SHIFTS, being aged—				
18 years or over	*7 2½*	*36*	*318 0*	*15·90*
PROVIDED THAT the following rates shall apply to new entrants who enter or have entered the trade for the first time at or over the age of 18 years:—				
Male Workers—for the first eight weeks of employment	*6 0*	*30*	*240 0*	*12·00*
Female Workers—for the first eight weeks of employment	*4 9*	*23¾*	*190 0*	*9·50*

(5) The piece work basis time rates applicable to the male or female workers specified in Column 1 of the next following Table, when employed on piece work with the materials specified in Column 2 or 3 as the case may be, are the rates set out in Column 2 or 3 respectively.

TABLE OF PIECE WORK BASIS TIME RATES

WORKERS EMPLOYED ON PIECE WORK	Fibres other than man-made fibres of continuous filament		Man-made fibres of continuous filament	
Column 1	Column 2		Column 3	
	Up to and including 14th Feb., 1971	On and after 15th Feb., 1971	Up to and including 14th Feb., 1971	On and after 15th Feb., 1971
	s. d.	p	s. d.	p
Male workers other than shift workers ...	*6 1½*	*30¾*	—	—
Female " " " " " " ...	*4 10½*	*24½*	*5 3½*	*26½*
Male shift workers on day shift	*6 11*	*34¾*	—	—
Female " " " " " ...	*5 6*	*27½*	*5 11½*	*30*
Male workers on night shift	*7 4½*	*37*	—	—

(6) In this paragraph—

"bonus payments" means any production, merit, incentive or similar bonus payments payable at intervals of not more than one month;

"the Trade" means the Rope, Twine and Net Trade as specified in paragraph 14.

GENERAL MINIMUM PIECE RATES

MAKING COTTON NORSELLS

4. The general minimum piece rates payable per pound to female home-workers for making cotton norsells are as follows:—

11 inches and upwards:—

	s. d.		s. d.
32s/18 ply norsells ...	11 2	32s/36 ply norsells ...	4 9
32s/21 " " ...	9 3	32s/42 " " ...	3 9⅜
32s/24 " " ...	7 4⅞	32s/48 " " ...	3 5½
32s/27 " " ...	6 6½	32s/54 " " ...	3 1½
32s/30 " " ...	5 7	32s/60 " " ...	2 8¼

MAKING HEMP NORSELLS

5. The general minimum piece rates payable per 1,000 to female home-workers for making hemp norsells are as follows:—

	Natural Colour	Tanned		Natural Colour	Tanned
	s. d.	s. d.		s. d.	s. d.
18 inch ...	5 7	6 7½	36 inch ...	9 6	11 2
20 " ...	5 8	6 9⅜	42 " ...	10 9¼	12 4¾
22 " ...	5 11	7 1	48 " ...	12 4¾	13 10⅛
24 " ...	6 8⅝	7 6¼			

HANDBRAIDING, HANDKNOTTING OR HANDBAITING NETS FROM FIBRES NOT BEING HARD FIBRES OR MAN-MADE FIBRES OF CONTINUOUS FILAMENT

NETS MADE FROM SINGLE TWINE

6.—(1) The general minimum piece rates set out in the next following Table are per dozen rans short reel or per 9,200 yards and are payable, subject to the provisions of this paragraph, to female home-workers employed on handbraiding, handknotting or handbaiting nets made from single twine (of sizes up to and including 36 lbs. per dozen rans short reel or per 9,200 yards) from fibres not being hard fibres or man-made fibres of continuous filament.

(2) The length of the nets referred to in Columns 3 to 8 inclusive of the said Table is the length measured by stretched mesh or through the hand.

TABLE OF PIECE RATES

Twines of sizes up to and including 36 lbs. per dozen rans short reel or per 9,200 yards

Size of mesh	Plain netting Column 1	Shrink or square mesh work irrespective of numbers of meshes begun or ended (single or double selvedge) and plain netting with double selvedge Column 2	Netting braided in the form of a hose or bag, including shrimp and landing nets, billiard table pockets and other fancy nets: Length 30 inches and over Column 3	Length 20 inches and over but under 30 inches Column 4	Length 15 inches and over but under 20 inches Column 5	Length 10 inches and over but under 15 inches Column 6	Length 5 inches and over but under 10 inches Column 7	Length under 5 inches Column 8
	s. d.	s. d.	s. d.	s. d.	s. d.	s. d.	s. d.	s. d.
Over 7 inch	88 5½	93 0½	97 7	111 10½	123 5	132 8	139 3½	146 3
5 inch and over up to and including 7 inch ...	92 7½	97 6	101 11½	117 3	128 11	138 7	145 6½	152 10
4 inch and over up to but not including 5 inch ...	99 8½	105 0½	109 10	126 3½	138 11	149 4	156 9½	164 7
Rows per yard:—								
Over 18 and up to and including 21	106 3	111 2½	116 10	134 5	147 10	158 11	166 10½	175 2½
" 21 " " 24	111 9½	117 4½	123 3	141 9	155 11	167 7½	175 11½	184 9
" 24 " " 27	117 4½	123 3	129 2½	148 7	163 5½	175 8½	184 5½	193 8
" 27 " " 30	123 3	129 6	135 7½	155 11½	171 6½	184 5½	193 7½	203 4
" 30 " " 33	128 7½	135 3½	141 9½	163 0½	179 4½	192 9½	202 5½	212 7
" 33 " " 36	134 6	141 6	147 11½	171 1½	187 2½	201 2½	211 3	221 10
" 36 " " 39	140 1½	146 10½	154 1	177 2½	194 11	209 6	220 0	231 0
" 39 " " 42	145 11½	152 11	160 6	184 7	203 0½	218 3	229 1½	240 8
" 42 " " 45	151 3½	158 10	166 5	191 5	210 6½	226 4	237 8	249 6
" 45 " " 48	157 2½	164 11½	172 11	198 10	218 9	235 1½	246 10½	259 2½
" 48 " " 54	168 4	176 11½	185 6	213 4	234 8	252 3	264 10½	278 1½
" 54 " " 60	179 10	188 10½	197 9½	227 5½	250 2½	268 11½	282 5	296 5½
" 60 " " 66	191 1	200 11	210 5	241 11	266 2½	286 1½	300 5	315 5
" 66 " " 72	202 6	212 3½	222 8½	256 0½	281 8½	302 10	317 11½	333 10½
" 72 " " 78	213 9	224 4	235 1	270 4	297 4½	319 8	335 8	352 5½
" 78 " " 84	225 3	236 4½	247 7½	284 9	313 3	336 9	353 7	371 3
" 84 " " 90	236 4½	248 3	260 3	299 3	329 2	353 10½	371 7	390 2
" 90 " " 96	247 7	260 2½	272 7½	313 6	344 10	370 8½	389 3	408 8½
" 96 " " 108	270 5	283 10	297 5	342 0½	376 1½	404 5	424 8	445 11
" 108 " " 120	292 11½	307 10	322 1½	370 5	407 6	438 1	459 11½	482 11½
" 120 " " 132	315 9	331 5½	347 5½	399 7	439 6½	472 6	496 1½	520 11
" 132 " " 144	338 6	355 2	372 5	428 3	471 1	506 5	531 9	558 4
" 144 " " 162	372 5	390 9	409 10	471 4	518 5½	557 4	585 2½	614 4½

(3) Where the twine is of a size larger than 36 lbs. per dozen rans short reel or per 9,200 yards the general minimum piece rates payable to the said workers are the rates set out in the said Table increased as follows:—

Size of Twine	Additions s. d.
Over 36 lbs. and up to and including 48 lbs.	10 1
" 48 " " " " " " 60 "	20 4
" 60 " " " " " " 84 "	31 4
" 84 " " " " " " 96 "	32 0
" 96 " " " " " " 108 "	36 0
" 108 " " " " " " 120 "	42 0
" 120 " " " " " " 132 "	48 0
" 132 " " " " " " 144 "	54 0
" 144 " " " " " " 156 "	60 0
" 156 "	66 0

(4) Where the work is double knotted work, the general minimum piece rates payable to the said workers shall be one and two-thirds times the rates payable for single knotted work.

NETS MADE FROM DOUBLE OR TREBLE TWINE

7. The general minimum piece rates payable to female home-workers employed on handbraiding, handknotting or handbaiting nets made from double or treble twine from fibres not being hard fibres or man-made fibres of continuous filament are respectively three-quarters and two-thirds of the general minimum piece rates which would be payable under paragraph 6 if the nets were made from single twine.

HANDBRAIDING OF TRAWL, SEINE OR OTHER NETS FROM HARD FIBRES

8.—(1) The general minimum piece rates set out in the next following Table are per lb. of twine and are payable, subject to the provisions of this paragraph, to female workers (including home-workers) employed in the handbraiding of trawl, seine or other nets (other than stack nets to which paragraph 9 applies) from hard fibres.

(2) The general minimum piece rates set out in the said Table are payable where the needles are filled at the expense of the worker. Where the needles are filled at the expense of the employer, the said rates shall be reduced by ten per cent.

(3) Where a net section contains meshes of more than one size, the general minimum piece rate payable for the whole section is that for a mesh size ascertained by a weighted average arrived at as follows: Multiply the number of rows of each separate mesh size by the size of the mesh, add the product, and divide the result by the total number of rows in the net section.

For example: The belly of a new trawl net consisting of 75 rows of 3-inch mesh, 50 rows of 4-inch mesh, 25 rows of 5-inch mesh: Calculation of weighted average mesh—

$75 \times 3 = 225$
$50 \times 4 = 200$
$25 \times 5 = 125$

150 550

Weighted average mesh size $= \frac{550}{150} = 3\frac{2}{3}$ inches.

The whole net section must be paid for as though the mesh was $3\frac{2}{3}$ inches throughout, viz., under Col. 8 of the said Table.

TABLE OF PIECE RATES

	Col. 1		Col. 2		Col. 3		Col. 4		Col. 5		Col. 6	
Size of mesh { less than	2 in.		2¼ in.		2½ in.		2¾ in.		3 in.		3¼ in.	
and not less than...	—		2 in.		2¼ in.		2½ in.		2¾ in.		3 in.	
Twine used as { S.=Single D.=Double }	S.	D.	S.	D.	S.	D.	S.	D.	S.	D.	S.	D.
Twine sizes:—	s. d.	s. d.	s. d.	s. d.	s. d.	s. d.	s. d.	s. d.	s. d.	s. d.	s. d.	s. d.
Up to and including 60 yds. per lb.	4 11⅝	3 4⅜	3 2¾	2 3	2 9⅝	1 11¼	2 5½	1 8⅜	2 1¼	1 6	1 9¼	1 3⅛
Over 60 up to and including 75 yds. per lb.	5 3½	3 6⅝	3 5⅛	2 4⅜	2 11½	2 0½	2 6¾	1 9¼	2 2½	1 6⅝	1 10⅞	1 3⅞
" 75 " " 90 " "	5 8⅛	3 9⅜	3 8	2 5⅞	3 2⅛	2 2⅛	2 8⅝	1 10⅞	2 4½	1 8⅛	2 0¼	1 5¼
" 90 " " 105 " "	6 1¾	4 1	3 11½	2 7¾	3 4¾	2 3⅛	2 11¼	2 0⅛	2 6⅝	1 8⅞	2 2½	1 6¼
" 105 " " 120 " "	6 7½	4 5	4 3⅝	2 10	3 7¾	2 4⅞	3 2⅛	2 1¾	2 8⅝	1 10½	2 4⅝	1 7¼
" 120 " " 135 " "	7 2⅝	4 9½	4 8¼	3 1¼	3 11¾	2 6½	3 5¼	2 3⅝	2 11⅝	1 11⅞	2 7⅛	1 9
" 135 " " 150 " "	7 11⅛	5 2⅜	5 1⅞	3 4¾	4 4⅞	2 10⅞	3 8¾	2 5⅞	3 2¾	2 1⅞	2 9¾	1 11
" 150 " " 165 " "	8 9¼	5 8	5 8⅜	3 9	4 10¾	3 3	4 1⅛	2 8⅞	3 6⅝	2 4⅜	3 1⅜	2 1
" 165 " " 180 " "	9 8⅜	6 3⅛	6 3⅝	4 1⅜	5 5⅝	3 6⅞	4 6½	3 0⅛	3 11½	2 7½	3 5⅜	2 3¾
" 180 " " 195 " "	10 11	6 11½	7 0¾	4 6½	6 1⅝	3 11¼	5 1⅜	3 4¼	4 5⅞	2 10⅞	3 10⅞	2 6⅝
" 195 " " 210 " "	12 3½	7 8⅜	7 10¾	5 0⅛	6 10⅜	4 4⅜	5 9⅜	3 9⅛	5 1⅜	3 3¼	4 5⅜	2 10¼
" 210 " " 255 " "	15 3⅞	9 6⅞	9 9¾	6 2⅞	8 5½	5 4⅝	7 2⅞	4 8⅛	6 3¼	4 0	5 7	3 7

	Col. 7		Col. 8		Col. 9		Col. 10		Col. 11		Col. 12	
Size of mesh { less than	3½ in.		3¾ in.		4 in.		4¼ in.		4½ in.		4¾ in.	
and not less than	3¼ in.		3½ in.		3¾ in.		4 in.		4¼ in.		4½ in.	
Twine used as { S. = Single, D. = Double }	S.	D.	S.	D.	S.	D.	S.	D.	S.	D.	S.	D.
Twine sizes:—	s. d.	s. d.	s. d.	s. d.	s. d.	s. d.	s. d.	s. d.	s. d.	s. d.	s. d.	s. d.
Up to and including 60 yds. per lb.	1 6¼	1 0¾	1 4⅝	11½	1 3¼	10¾	1 2¼	10	1 1⅜	9½	1 0¾	8⅞
Over 60 up to and including 75 yds. per lb.	1 7⅜	1 1½	1 6	1 0½	1 4⅜	11½	1 3⅜	10¾	1 2¾	10¼	1 2⅛	9⅝
„ 75 „ „ 90 „ „	1 9	1 2⅞	1 7	1 1¼	1 5⅝	1 0½	1 4⅝	11⅝	1 4⅛	11⅛	1 3¼	10¾
„ 90 „ „ 105 „ „	1 11	1 3⅝	1 9	1 2¼	1 7¼	1 1¼	1 6¼	1 0⅝	1 5⅜	1 0⅜	1 4⅞	11⅝
„ 105 „ „ 120 „ „	2 0¾	1 5¼	1 11	1 3⅝	1 9⅛	1 2¾	1 8¼	1 1¾	1 7¼	1 1¼	1 6⅝	1 0¾
„ 120 „ „ 135 „ „	2 2⅞	1 6⅝	2 1⅛	1 5⅜	1 11⅜	1 4¼	1 10½	1 3⅜	1 9¼	1 2¾	1 8¾	1 2¼
„ 135 „ „ 150 „ „ „	2 5¾	1 8½	2 3⅞	1 7⅛	2 2¼	1 6⅛	2 1	1 5¼	2 0⅛	1 4⅜	1 11¼	1 3⅝
„ 150 „ „ 165 „ „	2 9½	1 10½	2 6⅞	1 9	2 4¾	1 7⅞	2 3⅛	1 7⅛	2 2⅝	1 6½	2 1¾	1 6
„ 165 „ „ 180 „ „	3 0⅜	2 0¾	2 10	1 11	2 7⅞	1 10	2 6½	1 9	2 5⅝	1 8⅜	2 4⅜	1 8⅛
„ 180 „ „ 195 „ „	3 5⅛	2 3¾	3 2½	2 1⅞	3 0⅛	2 0½	2 10⅜	1 11⅜	2 9½	1 10¾	2 7⅞	1 9⅞
„ 195 „ „ 210 „ „	3 10½	2 6½	3 7½	2 4½	3 4¾	2 3⅛	3 3¼	2 2¼	3 1⅜	2 1¼	3 0⅛	2 0½
„ 210 „ „ 255 „ „	4 11⅜	3 2½	4 6	2 11¾	4 2⅞	2 10¼	4 1	2 8⅝	3 10¾	2 7⅝	3 9	2 6¾

	Col. 13		Col. 14		Col. 15		Col. 16		Col. 17		Col. 18	
Size of mesh { less than	5 in.		5¼ in.		5½ in.		5¾ in.		6 in.		—	
and not less than	4¾ in.		5 in.		5¼ in.		5½ in.		5¾ in.		6 in.	
Twine used as { S.=Single D.=Double }	S.	D.	S.	D.	S.	D.	S.	D.	S.	D.	S.	D.
Twine sizes:—	s. d.	s. d.	s. d.	s. d.	s. d.	s. d.	s. d.	s. d.	s. d.	s. d.	s. d.	s. d.
Up to and including 60 yds. per lb.	1 0½	8¾	11⅞	8⅝	11⅝	8½	11⅛	8	11⅛	7⅞	10¾	7¾
Over 60 up to and including 75 yds. per lb.	1 1⅜	9½	1 1⅛	9⅜	1 0⅝	8⅞	1 0½	8¾	11⅞	8⅝	11⅝	8½
„ 75 „ „ 90 „ „	1 2¾	10¼	1 2¼	10	1 1¾	9⅝	1 1⅜	9½	1 1⅛	9⅜	1 0¾	8⅞
„ 90 „ „ 105 „ „	1 4⅜	11⅛	1 3⅝	10⅞	1 3⅜	10¾	1 3⅛	10½	1 2¾	10¼	1 2½	10
„ 105 „ „ 120 „ „ „	1 6¼	1 0½	1 5⅜	1 0⅜	1 5⅛	11⅝	1 4½	11½	1 4¼	11⅛	1 3⅞	10⅞
„ 120 „ „ 135 „ „	1 8⅜	1 1¾	1 7⅜	1 1¼	1 7	1 0¾	1 6½	1 0⅝	1 6¼	1 0½	1 6	1 0½
„ 135 „ „ 150 „ „	1 10⅞	1 3⅜	1 10⅜	1 2⅞	1 9¼	1 2½	1 8⅞	1 2¼	1 8⅜	1 2⅛	1 8¼	1 1⅝
„ 150 „ „ 165 „ „	2 1	1 5¼	2 0¼	1 4½	1 11⅜	1 4¼	1 11⅛	1 3⅞	1 10¾	1 3⅝	1 10½	1 3½
„ 165 „ „ 180 „ „	2 3⅞	1 7⅛	2 2⅞	1 6⅝	2 2½	1 6¼	2 2	1 6	2 1⅛	1 5⅝	2 1	1 5⅜
„ 180 „ „ 195 „ „	2 7⅛	1 9	2 6	1 8¾	2 4⅞	1 8⅛	2 4½	1 7⅞	2 4⅛	1 7¼	2 3⅞	1 7⅛
„ 195 „ „ 210 „ „	2 10⅜	1 11⅜	2 9½	1 11	2 8	1 10½	2 7⅝	1 9⅞	2 7⅛	1 9¾	2 6¾	1 9¼
„ 210 „ „ 255 „ „	3 6⅞	2 5¾	3 5⅝	2 4½	3 3½	2 3⅛	3 2⅜	2 2⅝	3 1¼	2 1⅞	2 11¾	2 1

HANDBRAIDING OF STACK NETS

9.—(1) The general minimum piece rates set out in the next following Table are payable to female workers (including home-workers) employed in the hand-braiding of stack nets and shall apply to the making by hand of all such nets irrespective of the method of manufacture and the type of material used.

(2) The general minimum piece rates set out in the said Table are payable where the needles are filled at the expense of the worker. Where the needles are filled at the expense of the employer, the said rates shall be reduced by ten per cent.

TABLE OF PIECE RATES

Diamond mesh throughout		Square mesh throughout	
Size of mesh	Per dozen meshes	Size of mesh	Per square yard
	d.		d.
		Less than 6 ins.	1 3/8
		Not less than 6 ins. but less than 7ins.	1 5/16
Less than 16 ins.	1	Not less than 7 ins. but less than 8 ins.	1 1/4
Not less than 16 ins. but less than 18 ins.	1 3/16	Not less than 8 ins. but less than 9 ins.	1 3/16
Not less than 18 ins. but less than 20 ins.	1 5/16	Not less than 9 ins. but less than 10 ins.	1 1/8
Not less than 20 ins. but less than 22 ins.	1 9/16	Not less than 10 ins. but less than 11 ins.	1 1/16
Not less than 22 ins. but less than 24 ins.	1 3/4	Not less than 11 ins. but less than 12 ins.	15/16
Not less than 24 ins. but less than 26 ins.	2	Not less than 12 ins. but less than 13 ins.	7/8
Not less than 26 ins. but less than 28 ins.	2 1/8	Not less than 13 ins. but less than 14 ins.	13/16
28 ins. and over	2 5/16	14 ins. and over	3/4

(3) For the purposes of this paragraph—

(*a*) Square yardage shall be calculated by multiplying in feet the length by the breadth of the net and dividing the result by nine.

(*b*) SIZE OF MESH is—

(i) in the case of diamond mesh, the total length of two adjacent sides of the mesh measured from the inside of one knot to the outside of the other;

(ii) in the case of square mesh, the length of one side of the mesh measured from the inside of one knot to the outside of the other.

PART III

OVERTIME AND WAITING TIME

10. This Part of this Schedule applies to a worker in any section of the Trade, not being—

(1) a home-worker employed in the net section on piece work or

(2) a female home-worker employed in a section other than the net section.

MINIMUM OVERTIME RATES

11.—(1) Subject to the provisions of sub-paragraph (2) of this paragraph, minimum overtime rates are payable to any worker to whom this Part of this Schedule applies as follows:—

(*a*) on any day other than a Saturday, Sunday or a customary holiday—

(i) for the first two hours worked in excess of 8 hours ... time-and-a-quarter

(ii) thereafter ... ... time-and-a-half

(*b*) on a Saturday, not being a customary holiday—

(i) for the first two hours worked ... ... time-and-a-quarter

(ii) thereafter ... ... time-and-a-half

(c) on a Sunday or a customary holiday—
for all time worked ... ... double time

(2) Where the employer and the worker by agreement in writing fix in respect of each weekday the number of hours after which a minimum overtime rate shall be payable and the total number of such hours amounts to 40 weekly, the following minimum overtime rates shall be payable in substitution for those set out in sub-paragraph (1) of this paragraph:—

(*a*) on any day other than a Saturday, Sunday or a customary holiday—

(i) for the first two hours worked in excess of the agreed number of hours ... ... time-and-a-quarter

(ii) thereafter ... ... time-and-a-half

(*b*) on a Saturday, not being a customary holiday—
for all time worked in excess of the agreed number of hours ... ... time-and-a-half

Provided that where the said agreement provides that Saturday shall not normally be a working day, the following minimum overtime rates shall apply—

(i) for the first two hours worked ... ... time-and-a-quarter

(ii) thereafter ... ... time-and-a-half

(*c*) on a Sunday or a customary holiday—
for all time worked ... ... double time

12. In this Part of this Schedule—

(1) The expression "customary holiday" means:—

(*a*) (i) In England and Wales:—

Good Friday, Easter Monday, Whit Monday (or where another day is substituted therefor by national proclamation, that day), August Bank Holiday (or, in the case of August Bank Holiday, such day, other than a weekly short day, as may be substituted therefor by the employer, being a day which is by local custom recognised as a day of holiday and which falls within three months of the day for which it is substituted), Christmas Day (or, if Christmas Day falls on a Sunday, such weekday as may be appointed by national proclamation, or, if none is so appointed, the next following Tuesday) and Boxing Day;

(ii) In Scotland:—

The New Year's holidays (2 days),
The local Spring holiday (1 day),
The local Autumn holiday (1 day) and
two other weekdays(being days upon which the worker normally attends for work) in the course of a calendar year, to be fixed by the employer and notified to the workers not less than three weeks before the holiday;

or (*b*) in the case of each of the said days, such weekday falling between 1st April and 30th September as may be substituted therefor by agreement between the employer and the workers.

(2) The expressions "time-and-a-quarter", "time-and-a-half" and "double time" mean respectively:—

(*a*) in the case of a time worker, one and a quarter times, one and a half times and twice the general minimum time rate otherwise payable to the worker;

(*b*) in the case where a piece work basis time rate is otherwise applicable to a piece worker,

(i) a time rate equal respectively to one quarter, one half and the whole of the said piece work basis time rate, and, in addition thereto,

(ii) the piece rates otherwise applicable under paragraph 1(2);

(*c*) in the case where a general minimum piece rate is otherwise payable to a piece worker employed in the net section of the trade on hand net braiding, knotting or baiting,

(i) a time rate equal respectively to one quarter, one half and the whole of the piece work basis time rate which would be applicable to a female worker under the provisions of paragraph 3 if a minimum overtime rate did not apply and, in addition thereto,

(ii) the said general minimum piece rate.

WAITING TIME

13.—(1) A worker is entitled to payment of the minimum remuneration specified in this Schedule for all time during which he is present on the premises of the employer, unless he is present thereon in any of the following circumstances:—

(*a*) without the employer's consent, express or implied;

(*b*) for some purpose unconnected with his work and other than that of waiting for work to be given to him to perform;

(*c*) by reason only of the fact that he is resident thereon;

(*d*) during normal meal times in a room or place in which no work is being done and he is not waiting for work to be given to him to perform.

(2) The minimum remuneration payable under sub-paragraph (1) of this paragraph to a piece worker when not engaged on piece work is that which would be payable if he were a time worker.

PART IV

APPLICABILITY OF STATUTORY MINIMUM REMUNERATION

14. This Schedule applies to workers in relation to whom the Rope, Twine and Net Wages Council (Great Britain) operates, that is to say, workers employed in Great Britain in the branches of work specified in the Schedule to the Trade Boards (Rope, Twine and Net Trade, Great Britain) (Constitution and Proceedings) Regulations 1933(**a**), but excluding therefrom the splicing or braiding of rope, cord or twine performed by hand or machine when incidental to, or carried on in association with or in conjunction with, the operations specified in paragraphs 1 and 2 of the Appendix to the Trade Boards (Made-up Textiles) Order 1920(**b**), or any other processes or operations which are specifically mentioned in the said Appendix.

(**a**) S.R. & O. 1933/1023 (1933, p. 2049). (**b**) S.R. & O. 1920/1901 (1920 II, p. 782).

The Schedule to the said Regulations reads as follows:—

"The Rope, Twine and Net Trade, that is to say—

(1) The making or re-making of (*a*) rope (including driving rope and banding), (*b*) cord (including blind and window cord, but excluding silk, worsted and other fancy cords), (*c*) core for wire-ropes, (*d*) lines, (*e*) twine (including binder and trawl twine), (*f*) lanyards, (*g*) net and similar articles.

(2) The bleaching, teazing, hackling, carding, preparing and spinning of the materials required for the making or re-making of any of the articles (*a*) to (*g*) above when carried on in the same factory or workshop as such making or re-making.

(3) The manufacture of packings, gaskins and spun yarns, when carried on in the same factory or workshop as the making or re-making of any of the articles (*a*) to (*g*) above.

(4) The braiding or splicing of articles made from rope, cord, twine or net.

(5) The mending of nets and the winding, twisting, doubling, laying, polishing, dressing, tarring, tanning, dyeing, balling, reeling, finishing, packing, despatching, warehousing and storing of any of the above articles, where these operations or any of them are carried on in a factory or workshop in which any of the articles (*a*) to (*g*) above are made or re-made;

but excluding the making of wire rope (unless made in the same factory or workshop as hemp or similar rope or core for wire rope), and also excluding the making of net in connection with the lace-curtain trade and the weaving of cloth."

EXPLANATORY NOTE

(*This Note is not part of the Order.*)

This Order which has effect from 24th July 1970, sets out the statutory minimum remuneration payable in substitution for that fixed by the Wages Regulation (Rope, Twine and Net) Order 1969 (Order R. (153)), which Order is revoked.

New provisions are printed in italics.

1970 No. 979

WAGES COUNCILS

The Wages Regulation (Rope, Twine and Net) (Holidays) Order 1970

Made - - -	1*st July* 1970
Coming into Operation	24*th July* 1970

Whereas the Secretary of State has received from the Rope, Twine and Net Wages Council (Great Britain) the wages regulation proposals set out in the Schedule hereto;

Now, therefore, the Secretary of State in exercise of his powers under section 11 of the Wages Councils Act 1959(**a**), and of all other powers enabling him in that behalf, hereby makes the following Order:—

1. This Order may be cited as the Wages Regulation (Rope, Twine and Net) (Holidays) Order 1970.

2.—(1) In this Order the expression "the specified date" means the 24th July 1970, provided that where, as respects any worker who is paid wages at intervals not exceeding seven days, that date does not correspond with the beginning of the period for which the wages are paid, the expression "the specified date" means, as respects that worker, the beginning of the next such period following that date.

(2) The Interpretation Act 1889(**b**) shall apply to the interpretation of this Order as it applies to the interpretation of an Act of Parliament and as if this Order and the Order hereby revoked were Acts of Parliament.

3. The wages regulation proposals set out in the Schedule hereto shall have effect as from the specified date and as from that date the Wages Regulation (Rope, Twine and Net) (Holidays) Order 1968(**c**), as amended by Schedule 2 to the Wages Regulation (Rope, Twine and Net) Order 1969(**d**), shall cease to have effect.

Signed by order of the Secretary of State.

1st July 1970.

R. R. D. McIntosh,
Deputy Under Secretary of State,
Department of Employment and Productivity.

SCHEDULE Article 3

The following provisions as to holidays and holiday remuneration shall be substituted for the provisions as to holidays and holiday remuneration set out in the Wages Regulation (Rope, Twine and Net) (Holidays) Order 1968 (hereafter in this Order referred to as "Order R. (151)") as amended by Schedule 2 to the Wages Regulation (Rope, Twine and Net) Order 1969 (Order R. (153)).

(**a**) 1959 c. 69.
(**b**) 1889 c. 63.
(**c**) S.I. 1968/1051 (1968 II, p. 2761).
(**d**) S.I. 1969/654 (1969 II, p. 1789).

PART I

APPLICATION

1. This Schedule applies to every worker (other than a home-worker) for whom statutory minimum remuneration has been fixed.

PART II

CUSTOMARY HOLIDAYS

2.—(1) An employer shall allow to every worker in his employment to whom this Schedule applies a holiday (hereinafter referred to as a "customary holiday") in each year on the days specified in the following sub-paragraph, provided that the worker was in his employment for a period of not less than four weeks during the six months immediately preceding the customary holiday and (unless excused by the employer or absent by reason of the proved illness of the worker) worked for the employer throughout the last working day on which work was available to him immediately prior to the customary holiday.

(2) The said customary holidays are:—

(*a*) (i) in England and Wales:—

Good Friday, Easter Monday, Whit Monday (or where another day is substituted therefor by national proclamation, that day), August Bank Holiday (or in the case of August Bank Holiday such day, other than a weekly short day, as may be substituted therefor by the employer, being a day which is by local custom recognised as a day of holiday and which falls within three months of the day for which it is substituted), Christmas Day (or, if Christmas Day falls on a Sunday, such weekday as may be appointed by national proclamation, or, if none is so appointed, the next following Tuesday) and Boxing Day;

(ii) in Scotland:—

the New Year's holidays (2 days);

the local Spring holiday (1 day);

the local Autumn holiday (1 day); and

two other weekdays (being days upon which the worker normally attends for work) in the course of a calendar year, to be fixed by the employer and notified to the workers not less than three weeks before the holiday;

or (*b*) in the case of each of the said days, such weekday falling within the holiday season as may be substituted therefor by agreement between the employer and the workers.

(3) Notwithstanding the preceding provisions of this paragraph, an employer may (except where in the case of a woman or young person such a requirement would be unlawful) require a worker who is otherwise entitled to any customary holiday under the foregoing provisions of this Schedule to work thereon, and, in lieu of any customary holiday on which he so works, the employer shall allow to the worker a day's holiday (hereinafter referred to as a "holiday in lieu of a customary holiday") on a weekday on which he would normally work for the employer within the period of four weeks next ensuing.

(4) A worker who is required to work on a customary holiday shall be paid:—

(*a*) for all time worked thereon at the minimum rate then appropriate to the worker for work on a customary holiday; and

(*b*) in respect of the holiday in lieu of the customary holiday, holiday remuneration in accordance with paragraph 6.

PART III

ANNUAL HOLIDAY

3.—(1) Subject to the provisions of paragraph 4, in addition to the holidays specified in Part II of this Schedule an employer shall, between the date on which this Schedule becomes effective and 30th September 1970, and in each succeeding year between 1st April and 30th September allow a holiday (hereinafter referred to as an "annual holiday") to every worker in his employment to whom this Schedule applies who has been employed by him during the 12 months immediately preceding the commencement of the holiday season for any of the periods of employment set out in the appropriate column in the table below and the duration of the annual holiday shall, in the case of each such worker, be related to that period as follows:—

Period of employment	Workers with a normal working week of six days	Workers with a normal working week of five days	Workers with a normal working week of four days	Workers with a normal working week of three days or less
	Duration of annual holiday			
	Days	Days	Days	Days
At least 48 weeks	18	15	12	9
" " 47 "	17	14	11	8
" " 46 "	17	14	11	8
" " 45 "	16	14	11	8
" " 44 "	16	13	10	8
" " 43 "	15	13	10	8
" " 42 "	15	13	10	7
" " 41 "	14	12	10	7
" " 40 "	14	12	9	7
" " 39 "	13	12	9	7
" " 38 "	13	11	9	7
" " 37 "	12	11	9	6
" " 36 "	12	11	8	6
" " 35 "	11	10	8	6
" " 34 "	11	10	8	6
" " 33 "	11	10	8	6
" " 32 "	10	9	7	5
" " 31 "	10	9	7	5
" " 30 "	10	9	7	5
" " 29 "	9	8	7	5
" " 28 "	9	8	6	5
" " 27 "	9	8	6	4
" " 26 "	8	7	6	4
" " 25 "	8	7	6	4
" " 24 "	8	7	5	4
" " 23 "	7	6	5	4
" " 22 "	7	6	5	3
" " 21 "	7	6	5	3
" " 20 "	6	5	4	3
" " 19 "	6	5	4	3
" " 18 "	6	5	4	3
" " 17 "	5	4	4	2
" " 16 "	5	4	3	2
" " 15 "	5	4	3	2
" " 14 "	4	3	3	2
" " 13 "	4	3	3	2
" " 12 "	4	3	2	1
" " 11 "	3	2	2	1
" " 10 "	3	2	2	1
" " 9 "	3	2	2	1
" " 8 "	2	2	1	1
" " 7 "	2	1	1	1
" " 6 "	2	1	1	—
" " 5 "	1	1	1	—
" " 4 "	1	1	—	—

(2) Notwithstanding the provisions of the last foregoing sub-paragraph:—

(*a*) the number of days of annual holiday which an employer is required to allow to a worker in any holiday season shall not exceed in the aggregate three times the number of days constituting the worker's normal working week ;

(*b*) the duration of the worker's annual holiday during the holiday season ending on 30th September 1970 shall be reduced by any days of annual holiday duly allowed to him by the employer under the provisions of Order R. (151) as amended by Schedule 2 to Order R. (153) between 1st April 1970 and the date on which the provisions of this Schedule become effective.

(3) Where before 17th September in any holiday season a worker (or his representative) and his employer (or his representative) enter into an agreement in writing that the worker shall be allowed after the end of the holiday season and before 1st November next following, the annual holiday, or any part thereof, for which he has qualified under this paragraph, any such days of annual holiday may, subject to the provisions of paragraph 4, be allowed in accordance with the agreement, and if so allowed shall be treated for the purposes of this Schedule as having been allowed during the holiday season.

(4) In this Schedule the expression "holiday season" means in relation to the year 1970 the period commencing on 1st April 1970 and ending on 30th September 1970 and, in each succeeding year, the period commencing on 1st April and ending on 30th September of the same year.

4.—(1) Except as hereinafter in this paragraph otherwise provided, an annual holiday shall be allowed on consecutive working days, being days on which the worker is normally called upon to work for the employer.

(2) (*a*) Where the number of days of annual holiday for which a worker has qualified exceeds the number of days constituting his normal working week, but does not exceed twice that number, the holiday may be allowed in two periods of consecutive working days ; so, however, that when a holiday is so allowed, one of the periods shall consist of a number of such days not less than the number of days constituting the worker's normal working week.

(*b*) Where the number of days of annual holiday for which a worker has qualified exceeds twice the number of days constituting his normal working week the holiday may be allowed as follows:—

(i) as to two periods of consecutive working days, each such period not being less than the period constituting the worker's normal working week, during the holiday season ; and

(ii) as to any additional days, on working days which need not be consecutive, to be fixed by the employer either during the holiday season or on any working day before the beginning of the next following holiday season.

(3) For the purposes of this paragraph, days of annual holidays shall be treated as consecutive notwithstanding that a day of holiday allowed to a worker under Part II of this Schedule or a day upon which he does not normally work for the employer intervenes.

(4) Where a day of holiday allowed to a worker under Part II of this Schedule immediately precedes or follows a period of annual holiday or occurs during such a period and the total number of days of annual holiday required to be allowed in the period under the foregoing provisions of this paragraph, together with any such day of holiday allowed under Part II of this Schedule, exceeds the number of days constituting the worker's normal working week then, notwithstanding the foregoing provisions of this paragraph, the duration of that period of annual holiday may be reduced by one day and in such a case one day of annual holiday may be allowed on any working day (not being the worker's weekly short day) in the holiday season or before the commencement of the next holiday season.

(5) Subject to the provisions of sub-paragraph (1) of this paragraph, any day of annual holiday under this Schedule may be allowed on a day on which the worker is entitled to a day of holiday or to a half-holiday under any enactment other than the Wages Councils Act 1959.

5. An employer shall give to a worker notice of the commencing date or dates and duration of the period or periods of his annual holiday. Such notice shall be given at least 21 days before the first day of the holiday or, where, under the provisions of paragraph 4, an annual holiday is allowed in more than one period, before each period, and may be given individually to the worker or by the posting of a notice in the place where the worker is employed.

PART IV

HOLIDAY REMUNERATION

A—CUSTOMARY HOLIDAYS AND HOLIDAYS IN LIEU OF CUSTOMARY HOLIDAYS

6.—(1) Subject to the provisions of this paragraph, for each day of holiday to which a worker is entitled under Part II of this Schedule he shall be paid by the employer holiday remuneration equal to the amount, calculated at the appropriate rate of statutory minimum remuneration, to which he would have been entitled as a time worker if the day had not been a day of holiday and he had worked on that day on work for which statutory minimum remuneration is payable for the time (excluding overtime) usually worked by him on that day of the week:

Provided that—

(*a*) where the customary holiday falls on a Saturday—

(i) in the case of a worker who normally works on six days of the week, in addition to any amount to which he is entitled under the other provisions of this Schedule, he shall be paid an amount equal to the statutory minimum remuneration (excluding overtime) to which he would be entitled if he were employed as a time worker for four and a half hours on work for which statutory minimum remuneration is payable;

(ii) in the case of a worker who normally attends on five days only in the week, he shall be paid an amount equal to the appropriate statutory minimum remuneration (excluding overtime) to which he would have been entitled as a time worker if the day had not been a day of customary holiday and he had worked on that day for one-fifth of the number of hours he normally works in a week on work for which statutory minimum remuneration is payable.

(*b*) (i) Payment of the said holiday remuneration is subject to the condition that the worker presents himself for employment at the usual starting hour on and works throughout the first working day following the holiday or, if he fails to do so, such failure is by reason of the proved incapacity of the worker due to illness or injury or with the consent of the employer;

(ii) when two customary holidays occur on successive days (or so that no working day intervenes) the said condition shall apply only to the second customary holiday.

(2) The holiday remuneration in respect of any customary holiday shall be paid by the employer to the worker not later than the pay day on which the wages for the pay week including the first working day following the customary holiday are paid.

(3) The holiday remuneration in respect of any holiday in lieu of a customary holiday shall be paid not later than the pay day on which the wages for the pay week including the first working day following the holiday in lieu of a customary holiday are paid:

Provided that the said payment shall be made immediately upon the termination of the worker's employment in the case where he ceases to be employed before being allowed a holiday in lieu of a customary holiday to which he is entitled, and in that case the proviso (*b*) to sub-paragraph (1) of this paragraph shall not apply.

B—ANNUAL HOLIDAY

7.—(1) Subject to the provisions of paragraph 8, a worker qualified to be allowed an annual holiday under this Schedule shall be paid by his employer in respect thereof, on the last pay day preceding such annual holiday, one day's holiday pay (as defined in paragraph 11) in respect of each day of annual holiday.

(2) Where under the provisions of paragraph 4 an annual holiday is allowed in more than one period, the holiday remuneration shall be apportioned accordingly.

8. Where any accrued holiday remuneration has been paid by the employer to the worker in accordance with paragraph 9 or in accordance with the provisions of Order R. (151) as amended by Schedule 2 to Order R. (153), in respect of employment during any of the periods referred to in that paragraph or that Order respectively, the amount of holiday remuneration payable by the employer in respect of any annual holiday for which the worker has qualified by reason of employment during the said period shall be reduced by the amount of the said accrued holiday remuneration unless that remuneration has been deducted from previous payment of holiday remuneration made under the provisions of this Schedule or of Order R. (151) as amended.

ACCRUED HOLIDAY REMUNERATION PAYABLE ON TERMINATION OF EMPLOYMENT

9. Where a worker ceases to be employed by an employer after the provisions of this Schedule become effective the employer shall, immediately on the termination of the employment, pay to the worker as accrued holiday remuneration:—

(1) in respect of employment in the 12 months up to the 31st day of the preceding March, a sum equal to the holiday remuneration which would be payable for any days of annual holiday for which he has qualified (except days of annual holiday which he has been allowed or has become entitled to be allowed before leaving the employment) if they were allowed at the time of leaving the employment ; and

(2) in respect of any employment since the 31st day of the preceding March, a sum equal to the holiday remuneration which would have been payable to him if he could have been allowed an annual holiday in respect of that employment at the time of leaving it.

PART V
GENERAL

10. For the purpose of calculating any period of employment qualifying a worker for an annual holiday or for any accrued holiday remuneration under this Schedule, the worker shall be treated—

(1) as if he were employed for a week in respect of any week in which—

(*a*) in the case of a worker other than a part-time worker, he has worked for the employer for not less than 34 hours and has performed some work for which statutory minimum remuneration is payable ;

(*b*) in the case of a part-time worker, he has worked for the employer and has performed some work for which statutory minimum remuneration is payable ; or

(*c*) in the case of any worker, he has worked for the employer for less than 34 hours by reason of proved incapacity due to sickness or injury or for a like reason he has been absent throughout the week or has been suspended throughout the week owing to shortage of work: Provided that the number of weeks which may be so treated as weeks of employment shall not exceed:—

(i) 26 weeks in the case of proved incapacity in respect of which the worker is entitled to injury benefit under the National Insurance (Industrial Injuries) Acts 1965 to 1967 ; and

(ii) six weeks in the case of any other proved incapacity or of suspension owing to shortage of work;

(2) as if he were employed on any day of holiday allowed under the provisions of this Schedule or of Order R. (151) as amended by Schedule 2 to Order R. (153), and, for the purposes of the provisions of sub-paragraph (1) of this paragraph, a worker who is absent on such a holiday shall be treated as having worked thereon for the employer on work for which statutory minimum remuneration is payable for the number of hours (excluding overtime) ordinarily worked by him on that day of the week.

11. In this Schedule, unless the context otherwise requires, the following expressions have the meanings hereby respectively assigned to them, that is to say:—

"home-worker" means a worker who works in his or her own home or in any other place not under the control or management of the employer.

"normal working week" means the number of days on which it has been usual for the worker to work in a week in the employment of the employer during the 12 months immediately preceding the commencement of the holiday season or, where under paragraph 9 accrued holiday remuneration is payable on the termination of the employment, during the 12 months immediately preceding the date of the termination of the employment:

Provided that—

(1) part of a day shall count as a day;

(2) no account shall be taken of any week in which the worker did not perform any work for which statutory minimum remuneration has been fixed.

"one day's holiday pay" means—

the appropriate proportion of the amount which the worker would be entitled to receive from his employer, at the beginning of the holiday or the first period of the holiday, as the case may be, for a week's work, if working his normal working week and the number of daily hours usually worked by him (exclusive of overtime), and if paid—

(*a*) in the case of a time worker, at the appropriate *General Minimum Time Rate* for work to which that rate applies *plus 12½%* and at the same rate for work (if any) to which that rate does not apply;

(*b*) in the case of a piece worker, the appropriate *General Minimum Time Rate* that would have been applicable to him if he had been employed as a time worker, *plus 12½%*.

In this definition "appropriate proportion" means—

where the worker's normal working week is six days ... one-sixth

" " " " " " five days ... one-fifth

" " " " " " four days ... one-quarter

" " " " " " three days or less one-third

"part-time worker" means a worker who normally works for the employer for less than 40 hours a week by reason only of the fact that he does not hold himself out as normally available for work for more than the number of hours he normally works in the week.

"statutory minimum remuneration" means remuneration (other than holiday remuneration) fixed by a wages regulation order made by the Secretary of State to give effect to proposals submitted to him by the Rope, Twine and Net Wages Council (Great Britain).

"week" in paragraphs 3 and 10 means "pay week".

"weekly short day" means Saturday or any other day (not being Sunday) which may be substituted therefor by agreement between an employer and a worker.

12. The provisions of this Schedule are without prejudice to any agreement for the allowance of any further holidays with pay or for the payment of additional holiday remuneration.

EXPLANATORY NOTE

(*This Note is not part of the Order.*)

This Order, which has effect from 24th July 1970, sets out the holidays which an employer is required to allow to workers and the remuneration payable for those holidays, in substitution for the holidays and holiday remuneration set out in the Wages Regulation (Rope, Twine and Net) (Holidays) Order 1968 (Order R. (151)) as amended by Schedule 2 to the Wages Regulation (Rope, Twine and Net) Order 1969 (Order R. (153)). Order R. (151) is revoked.

New provisions are printed in italics.

1970 No. 984

PUBLIC OFFICE

The Courts of Law, Scotland (Fees) Order 1970

Made - - - *30th June* 1970
Coming into Operation *1st October* 1970

The Treasury, in exercise of the powers conferred on them by section 2 of the Public Offices Fees Act 1879(**a**) and of all other powers enabling them in that behalf, hereby make the following Order:—

1. This Order may be cited as the Courts of Law, Scotland (Fees) Order 1970, and shall come into operation on 1st October 1970.

2. The Interpretation Act 1889(**b**) shall apply for the interpretation of this Order as it applies for the interpretation of an Act of Parliament.

3. All fees payable in the Office of the Accountant of Court, of the Court of Teinds, of the Court of Justiciary and of the Scottish Land Court or to the officers thereof shall be collected in money.

4. The Treasury Minute dated 25th March 1873 and the Treasury Order (**c**) dated 29th October 1912 regulating the collection of fees by the Offices of the said Courts and their officers by means of stamps is hereby revoked.

30th June 1970.

Hector Monro,
Walter Clegg,
Two of the Lords Commissioners of
Her Majesty's Treasury.

EXPLANATORY NOTE
(*This Note is not part of the Order.*)

This Order directs that fees payable in the Office of the Accountant of Court, Court of Teinds, Court of Justiciary, Scottish Land Court, and to the Officers thereof shall be collected in money, and not, as previously, in stamps. It revokes the Treasury Minute and Treasury Order which directed collection in stamps.

(**a**) 42 & 43 Vict. c. 58. (**b**) 52 & 53 Vict. c. 63.
(**c**) S.R. & O. 1912/1752 (Rev. XII p. 369).

1970 No. 985

CINEMATOGRAPHS AND CINEMATOGRAPH FILMS

EXHIBITION OF FILMS

The Films (Exhibitors) (Amendment) Regulations 1970

Made - - -	*2nd July* 1970
Coming into Operation	*1st August* 1970

The Board of Trade, in pursuance of the powers conferred upon them by section 44 of the Films Act 1960(**a**), as amended and extended by the Films Act 1970(**b**), and, so far as they prescribe fees, with the consent of the Treasury, hereby makes the following Regulations :—

1. These Regulations may be cited as the Films (Exhibitors) (Amendment) Regulations 1970 and shall come into operation on 1st August 1970.

2. The Interpretation Act 1889(**c**) shall apply to the interpretation of these Regulations as it applies to the interpretation of an Act of Parliament.

3. The Films (Exhibitors) Regulations 1961(**d**) shall have effect as if :—

(1) for Regulation 1(4) there were substituted the following :—

"(4) The fee referred to in paragraph (3) of this Regulation shall be in the case of a licence to be issued

(*a*) for a calendar year	£10.
(*b*) for a quarterly period	£3.
(*c*) for 2 quarterly periods	£5 15s. 0d.
(*d*) for 3 quarterly periods	£8 10s. 0d." ;

(2) for Schedule 1 thereto there were substituted the Schedule to these Regulations ;

(3) in Schedule 2, the words "except British films which do not count for quota" at the head of column (1) were omitted.

H. Bailey,
An Under Secretary of the
Board of Trade.

2nd July 1970.

The Treasury hereby consent,
so far as prescribing fees.

Reginald Eyre,
H. S. P. Monro,
Two of the Lord's Commissioners
of Her Majesty's Treasury.

2nd July 1970.

(**a**) 1960 c. 57. (**b**) 1970 c. 26. (**c**) 1889 c. 63.
(**d**) S.I. 1961/1824 (1961 III, p. 3436).

SCHEDULE

APPLICATION FOR EXHIBITOR'S LICENCE

Name of Applicant(s) ....

(i.e. the person or partnership or company being the proprietor of the business of exhibiting films at the cinema in respect of which the licence is desired, whether the owner of the cinema or not).

Address of place of business within Great Britain..........................

(In the case of a company, the address of the registered office.)

....

Name of Cinema ....

Address of Cinema ....

(If the applicant desires a licence to authorise the exhibition of registered films at more than one cinema but on not more than six days in the year at any cinema and at not more than one cinema at the same time the words "Section 26 (2) Licence" should be inserted here.)

Number of licence now held in respect of above cinema E.L..................

If the applicant(s) has/have not previously held a licence for this cinema, state the date on which the exhibition of registered films to the public was commenced by him/them there 197

I/We, the above named applicant(s) hereby apply for the issue of an exhibitor's licence authorising me/us to carry on the business of exhibiting registered films to the public at the cinema above described during the

(*a*) year commencing..................and ending........................

(*b*) period commencing...............and ending { 31st March, 197 / 30th June, 197 / 30th September, 197 / 31st December, 197

Delete (a) or (b) whichever does not apply. If (b) applies strike out dates not applicable.

I/We enclose the licence fee.

Date.................... Signature of applicant.......................

(In the case of partnership, of a partner; or, in the case of a company, of the secretary or a director.)

EXPLANATORY NOTE

(This Note is not part of the Regulations.)

These Regulations amend the Films (Exhibitors) Regulations 1961. The principal amendments are as follows:—

(1) the fees payable in respect of applications for exhibitors' licences are increased; and

(2) the form of application for an exhibitor's licence is amended to take account of the repeal by the Films Act 1970 of section 27 of the Films Act 1960 which related to circuit cinemas.

1970 No. 986

CINEMATOGRAPHS AND CINEMATOGRAPH FILMS

EXHIBITION OF FILMS

The Films (Renters' Licences) (Amendment) Regulations 1970

Made - - -	*2nd July* 1970
Coming into Operation	*16th July* 1970

The Board of Trade, in pursuance of the powers conferred upon them by section 44 of the Films Act 1960(**a**), as amended and extended by the Films Act 1970(**b**), and with the consent of the Treasury, hereby make the following Regulations :—

1. These Regulations may be cited as the Films (Renters' Licences) (Amendment) Regulations 1970 and shall come into operation on 16th July 1970.

2. The Interpretation Act 1889(**c**) shall apply to the interpretation of these Regulations as it applies to the interpretation of an Act of Parliament.

3. The Films (Renters' Licences) Regulations 1961(**d**) shall have effect as if in Regulation 2, for "£15 15s. 0d." there were substituted "£25".

H. Bailey,
An Under Secretary of the
Board of Trade.

2nd July 1970.

The Treasury hereby consent to the making of these Regulations.

Reginald Eyre,
H. S. P. Monro,
Two of the Lords Commissioners
of Her Majesty's Treasury.

2nd July 1970.

EXPLANATORY NOTE

(*This Note is not part of the Regulations.*)

These Regulations amend the Films (Renters' Licences) Regulations 1961 by increasing from £15 15s. 0d. to £25 the fee payable for a renter's licence.

(**a**) 1960 c. 57. (**b**) 1970 c. 26. (**c**) 1889 c. 63.
(**d**) S.I. 1961/1827 (1961 III, p. 3449).

1970 No. 987

CINEMATOGRAPHS AND CINEMATOGRAPH FILMS

REGISTRATION OF FILMS

The Films (Registration of Newsreels) (Amendment) Regulations 1970

Made - - -	*2nd July* 1970
Coming into Operation	16*th July* 1970

The Board of Trade, in pursuance of the powers conferred upon them by section 44 of the Films Act 1960(**a**), as amended and extended by the Films Act 1970(**b**), and with the consent of the Treasury, hereby make the following Regulations:—

1. These Regulations may be cited as the Films (Registration of Newsreels) (Amendment) Regulations 1970 and shall come into operation on 16th July 1970.

2. The Interpretation Act 1889(**c**) shall apply to the interpretation of these Regulations as it applies to the interpretation of an Act of Parliament.

3. The Films (Registration of Newsreels) Regulations 1961(**d**), as amended (**e**), shall have effect as if:—

(1) in Regulation 2, for "£6 6s. 0d." there were substituted "£10";

(2) in Regulation 7, for "1s. 6d." there were substituted "3s. 0d.";

(3) in Regulation 8, for "7s. 6d." there were substituted "12s. 0d.".

H. Bailey,
An Under Secretary of the Board of Trade.

2nd July 1970.

The Treasury hereby consent to the making of these Regulations.

Reginald Eyre,
H. S. P. Monro,
Two of the Lords Commissioners of Her Majesty's Treasury.

2nd July 1970.

EXPLANATORY NOTE

(*This Note is not part of the Regulations.*)

These Regulations further amend the Films (Registration of Newsreels) Regulations 1961 by increasing the fees payable in respect of applications for the registration of newsreels, inspections of the register and applications for certified copies of entries in the register.

(**a**) 1960 c. 57.
(**b**) 1970 c. 26.
(**c**) 1889 c. 63.
(**d**) S.I. 1961/1825 (1961 III, p. 3442).
(**e**) The amendment does not relate expressly to the subject matter of these Regulations.

STATUTORY INSTRUMENTS

1970 No. 988

CINEMATOGRAPHS AND CINEMATOGRAPH FILMS

REGISTRATION OF FILMS

The Films (Registration) (Amendment) Regulations 1970

Made - - -	2nd *July* 1970
Coming into Operation	16*th July* 1970

The Board of Trade, in pursuance of the powers conferred upon them by section 44 of the Films Act 1960**(a)**, as amended and extended by the Films Act 1970**(b)**, and with the consent of the Treasury, hereby make the following Regulations:—

1. These Regulations may be cited as the Films (Registration) (Amendment) Regulations 1970 and shall come into operation on 16th July 1970.

2. The Interpretation Act 1889**(c)** shall apply to the interpretation of these Regulations as it applies to the interpretation of an Act of Parliament.

3. The Films (Registration) Regulations 1960**(d)**, as amended **(e)**, shall have effect as if:—

(1) in Regulation 2(1), for "£300" there were substituted "£350" and for "£6 6s. 0d." there were substituted "£10";

(2) in Regulation 2(2), for "£3 3s. 0d." there were substituted "£4 15s. 0d.";

(3) in Regulation 10, for "1s. 6d." there were substituted "3s. 0d.";

(4) in Regulation 11, for "7s. 6d." there were substituted "12s. 0d.".

H. Bailey,
An Under Secretary of the
Board of Trade.

2nd July 1970.

The Treasury hereby consent to the making of these Regulations.

Reginald Eyre,
H.S.P. Monro,
Two of the Lords Commissioners of
Her Majesty's Treasury.

2nd July 1970.

(a) 1960 c. 57.
(b) 1970 c. 26.
(c) 1889 c. 63.
(d) S.I. 1960/2291 (1960 I, p. 532).
(e) The relevant amending instruments are S.I. 1961/1826, 1967/400 (1961 III, p. 3447; 1967 I, p. 1337).

EXPLANATORY NOTE

(*This Note is not part of the Regulations.*)

These Regulations further amend the Films (Registration) Regulations 1960 by increasing the fees payable in respect of applications for the registration of all films, applications to amend the register, inspections of the register and applications for certified copies of entries in the register.

1970 No. 989 (S. 72)

SHERIFF COURT, SCOTLAND

Act of Sederunt (Alteration of Fees collected by Sheriff Clerks) 1970

Made - - -	30*th June* 1970
Laid before Parliament	9*th July* 1970
Coming into Operation	1*st August* 1970

The Lords of Council and Session, under and by virtue of the powers conferred upon them by section 2 of the Courts of Law Fees (Scotland) Act 1895**(a)** and by section 40 of the Sheriff Courts (Scotland) Act 1907**(b)** as amended by section 39 of and the Schedule to the Administration of Justice (Scotland) Act 1933**(c)**, and of all other powers competent to them in that behalf, and with the approval and concurrence of the Treasury, do hereby enact and declare as follows:—

1. The Act of Sederunt (Alteration of Sheriff Court Fees) 1963**(d)** and the Table of Fees annexed thereto shall be amended as follows:—

(1) In paragraph 1 of the Act of Sederunt there shall be deleted the interpretation of the word "Decree", and there shall be substituted therefor a new interpretation as follows:

" 'Decree' in section 17 of A, Part II, shall include licence, appointment, discharge, certificate of registration of a club, or other written statement of the Sheriff's decision in any proceeding under sections 15 or 23 of A, Part II."

(2) Paragraph 4 of the Act of Sederunt shall be deleted and there shall be substituted therefor a new paragraph 4 as follows:

"4. The fee in section 1 of A, Part I, shall cover extract. The *ad valorem* fees in section 3 of A, Part I, shall cover all proceedings, including correspondence, but not including petitions for appointment of executor, for restriction of caution, or for special warrants. The fee in section 5 of A, Part II, shall cover all proceedings, including extract, but not including appeal. The fees in sections 6 to 13 inclusive, and 18 to 22 inclusive, of A, Part II, shall cover all proceedings, including, in bankruptcy cases, the necessary extracts and abbreviates for the Accountant of Court and other Government departments. The fee in section 14 of A, Part II, shall cover all proceedings, including extract, but not including stated case. In criminal cases at the instance of a private prosecutor, when more persons than one are proceeded against in one complaint, the fee shall cover one extract conviction or order in respect of each person. The fees in sections 15 to 17 inclusive of A, Part II, shall cover all proceedings (except appeal or stated case) in any action or proceeding for which special fees are not provided elsewhere.

(a) 1895 c. 14. **(b)** 1907 c. 51. **(c)** 1933 c.41. **(d)** S.I. 1963/133 (1963 I, p. 128).

Any subsequent extracts or copies required shall be charged under section 4 of A, Part I, or section 1 of A, Part II. The extracting or copying fees, sections 4(b) of A, Part I and 1(c) of A, Part II, shall be alternative fees to those in sub-section (a) of each of the said sections, in the option of the applicant. In litigated commissary, service of heirs, and bankruptcy cases, the same fees shall be charged as for similar business in the ordinary Sheriff Court.

When a small debt case is remitted to the ordinary roll, the parties shall pay fees as for an ordinary action, under deduction of any fees already paid."

(3) Paragraph 6 of the Act of Sederunt shall be deleted.

(4) Part II of Section A of the Table of Fees shall be deleted, and there shall be substituted therefor a new Part II of Section A in the terms set forth in the Schedule annexed hereto.

2. This Act of Sederunt may be cited as the Act of Sederunt (Alteration of Fees collected by Sheriff Clerks) 1970 and shall come into operation on 1st August 1970.

And the Lords appoint this Act of Sederunt to be inserted in the Books of Sederunt.

J. L. Clyde,
I.P.D.

Edinburgh,
30th June 1970.

SCHEDULE

PART II—SHERIFF COURT PROCEEDINGS

General (applicable to all business under Part II)

	£	s.	d.
1. (a) Recording, extracting, or copying, per sheet	0	4	0
(b) Preservation of deeds, each	0	4	0
(c) Extracting or copying when three or more printed copies are supplied by the applicant—For each print	0	10	0
2. Single search, to include inspection, per hour	0	2	0
3. Inspection by a trade protection society or trade publication of protests, Act Books and Court Rolls—			
Weekly for three months (payable in advance)	1	0	0
Twice weekly for three months (payable in advance)	2	0	0
4. Application for stated case...	3	0	0
(Note:—*If the application is withdrawn, £2 of this fee shall be repayable on the certificate of the Sheriff that the stated case has not been drafted.*)			

Small debt, and Summary Removings under Section 38 *of the Sheriff Courts (Scotland) Act* 1907, *and proceedings under the Tenancy of Shops (Scotland) Act* 1949, *and the Housing (Repairs and Rents) (Scotland) Act* 1954.

	£	s.	d.
5. Summons, petition or sist for rehearing	0	10	0

Bankruptcy Proceedings	£	s.	d.
6. Petition for sequestration of estates	2	0	0
7. Act and warrant of trustee	1	10	0
8. Writing examination of bankrupt or minute of meeting, per sheet ...	0	4	0
9. Application (written or oral) for discharge of trustee	1	0	0
10. Petition for discharge of bankrupt or application for approval of composition or deed of arrangement	1	10	0
11. Request to act in aid of English Court of Bankruptcy	0	10	0
Service of Heirs			
12. Petition for general or special service or completion of title, or note for a Crown or Prince's charter, writ or precept	4	0	0
Inferior Courts Judgment Extension Act			
13. Any proceeding	0	10	0
Summary Jurisdiction Acts			
14. Complaint	1	0	0
Ordinary and Miscellaneous			
15. Initial writ in any proceeding for which no special fee is provided elsewhere	2	0	0
16. First paper, reponing, or attendance to state a defence, each defender or compearer	2	0	0
17. Extract of Decree	0	10	0
18. Caveat, to be in operation for one month	0	4	0
19. Sealing up repositories, or the like, per hour	0	10	0
20. Summary warrant for recovery of rates	2	0	0
21. Recording protest of a bill or promissory note	0	10	0
22. Lodging each set of plans or other Parliamentary deposit	2	0	0
23. Application for registration of a club	2	0	0

EXPLANATORY NOTE

(*This Note is not part of the Act of Sederunt.*)

This Act of Sederunt prescribes a new Table of Fees for Sheriff Court Proceedings, other than Commissary Proceedings in the Sheriff Court, and also makes certain consequential amendments to the Act of Sederunt (Alteration of Sheriff Court Fees) 1963 which prescribed the Table of Fees at present in force.

1970 No. 990

NATIONAL HEALTH SERVICE, ENGLAND AND WALES

The National Health Service (Southampton University Hospital Designation) Order 1970

Made - - -	2nd *July* 1970
Laid before Parliament	10*th July* 1970
Coming into Operation	1*st April* 1971

The Secretary of State for Social Services, being satisfied that the group of hospitals specified in Schedule 1 to this order and vested in him provides for the University of Southampton facilities for undergraduate and post-graduate clinical teaching and after consultation with that University, in exercise of his powers under section 5 of the Health Services and Public Health Act 1968(**a**) and of all other powers enabling him in that behalf, hereby makes the following order :—

1.—(1) This order may be cited as the National Health Service (Southampton University Hospital Designation) Order 1970 and shall come into operation on 1st April 1971.

(2) The Interpretation Act 1889(**b**) applies to the interpretation of this order as it applies to the interpretation of an Act of Parliament.

2. The group of hospitals specified in Schedule 1 to this order (hereinafter in this order referred to as "the group") is hereby designated as a university hospital.

3. Part II of Schedule 3 to the National Health Service Act 1946(**c**) (constitution of Hospital Management Committees) shall have effect in relation to the Committee appointed to exercise functions with respect to the management and control of the group, as modified and set out in Schedule 2 to this order.

SCHEDULE 1

LIST OF HOSPITALS

1. Southampton General Hospital.
2. Royal South Hants Hospital, Southampton (including Fred Woolley House, Chilworth and Widger House, Southampton).
3. Hythe Hospital.
4. Ashurst Hospital.
5. Moorgreen Hospital, Southampton.
6. Southampton Chest Hospital.
7. Southampton Children's Hospital (including Bursledon Annexe).
8. Southampton Eye Hospital.

(**a**) 1968 c. 46. (**b**) 1889 c. 63. (**c**) 1946 c. 81.

9. Rookwood Maternity Hospital, Eastleigh.
10. Fenwick Hospital, Lyndhurst.
11. Hill Rise Maternity Hospital, Lyndhurst.
12. Romsey Hospital.
13. Netley Castle Convalescent Home, Netley Abbey.
14. Lymington Infirmary.
15. Lymington Hospital.

SCHEDULE 2

CONSTITUTION OF THE SOUTHAMPTON UNIVERSITY HOSPITAL MANAGEMENT COMMITTEE

The provisions of Part II of Schedule 3 to the National Health Service Act 1946 shall have effect as modified and set out below:—

(1) subject to the following provisions of this Schedule, the Hospital Management Committee shall consist of a Chairman, appointed by the Wessex Regional Hospital Board after consultation with the University of Southampton, and 15 other members appointed by the Board;

(2) of the 15 other members 3 shall be nominated by the University of Southampton but of these 3 not more than 2 shall be medical practitioners or dental practitioners, and 3 shall be nominated by the medical and dental staff of the group after consultation with the Wessex Regional Hospital Board and the University of Southampton;

(3) other members shall include persons appointed after consultation with:—
   (i) any local health authority whose area comprises the area or any part of the area served by the group; and
   (ii) any Executive Council whose area comprises the area or any part of the area served by the group; and
   (iii) the senior medical and dental staff of the group; and
   (iv) such other organisations as appear to the Board to be concerned;

(4) not more than 6 members shall be medical practitioners or dental practitioners;

(5) before making appointments to fill vacancies, the Board shall consult the Committee.

Keith Joseph,
Secretary of State for Social Services.

2nd July 1970.

EXPLANATORY NOTE

(*This Note is not part of the Order.*)

This Order designates the group of hospitals set out in Schedule 1 as a university hospital, associated with the University of Southampton, and provides for a modified form of Hospital Management Committee (as set out in Schedule 2) to manage and control it.

1970 No. 991

EXCHANGE CONTROL

The Exchange Control (Authorised Dealers and Depositaries) (Amendment) (No. 3) Order 1970

Made - - -	2nd *July* 1970
Coming into Operation	13*th July* 1970

The Treasury, in exercise of the powers conferred upon them by sections 36(5) and 42(1) of the Exchange Control Act 1947(**a**), hereby make the following Order :—

1.—(1) This Order may be cited as the Exchange Control (Authorised Dealers and Depositaries) (Amendment) (No. 3) Order 1970, and shall come into operation on 13th July 1970.

(2) The Interpretation Act 1889(**b**) shall apply for the interpretation of this Order as it applies for the interpretation of an Act of Parliament.

2. Schedule 2 to the Exchange Control (Authorised Dealers and Depositaries) Order 1970(**c**) shall be amended as follows :—

(*a*) by deleting the words "District Bank Ltd." ;

(*b*) by inserting the words "Harris Trust and Savings Bank." after the words "Hambros (Jersey) Ltd." ;

(*c*) by inserting the words "Manufacturers Hanover Ltd." after the words "Lloyds Bank Ltd." ;

(*d*) by deleting the words "National Provincial Bank Ltd." ;

(*e*) by deleting the words "Société Centrale de Banque." ; and

(*f*) by deleting the words "Westminster Bank Ltd.".

3. This Order shall extend to the Channel Islands, and any reference in this Order to the Exchange Control Act 1947 includes a reference to that Act as extended by the Exchange Control (Channel Islands) Order 1947(**d**).

Hector Monro,
Bernard Weatherill,
Two of the Lords Commissioners of Her Majesty's Treasury.

2nd July 1970.

(**a**) 1947 c. 14. (**b**) 1889 c. 63. (**c**) S.I. 1970/691 (1970 II, p. 2207).
(**d**) S.R. & O. 1947/2034 (Rev. VI, p. 1001: 1947 I, p. 660).

EXPLANATORY NOTE

(This Note is not part of the Order.)

This Order amends the list of persons authorised by the Treasury under the Exchange Control Act 1947 to act as dealers in gold and foreign currencies and as depositaries for the purpose of the deposit of securities.

1970 No. 992

PARTNERSHIP

The Partnerships (Unrestricted Size) No. 3 Regulations 1970

Made - - - 1*st July* 1970

The Board of Trade in pursuance of the powers conferred upon them by section 120(2) of the Companies Act 1967(**a**) hereby make the following Regulations:—

1. These Regulations may be cited as the Partnerships (Unrestricted Size) No. 3 Regulations 1970.

2. Section 434 of the Companies Act 1948(**b**) shall not apply to the formation for the purpose of carrying on practice as consulting engineers of a partnership consisting of persons the majority of whom are recognised by the Council of Engineering Institutions as Chartered Engineers.

C. W. Jardine,
An Under-Secretary of the Board of Trade.

1st July 1970.

EXPLANATORY NOTE

(*This Note is not part of the Regulations.*)

Section 434 of the Companies Act 1948 prohibits the formation of partnerships consisting of more than 20 members. These Regulations exempt from that prohibition partnerships of the description, and formed for the purpose, specified in the Regulations.

(**a**) 1967 c. 81. (**b**) 1948 c. 38.

STATUTORY INSTRUMENTS

1970 No. 993 (S. 73)

EDUCATION, SCOTLAND

The Remuneration of Teachers (Scotland) Order 1970

Made - - -	*3rd July* 1970
Coming into Operation	*6th July* 1970

Whereas—

(1) under section 2(2) of the Remuneration of Teachers (Scotland) Act 1967**(a)** (hereinafter referred to as "the Act") the Scottish Teachers Salaries Committee (hereinafter referred to as "the Committee") constituted under section 1 of the Act for the purpose of considering the remuneration of (a) teachers employed whole-time by education authorities in the provision of school education under the Education (Scotland) Acts 1939 to 1969 and duly qualified for appointment other than temporary appointment in terms of regulations for the time being in force under the said Acts; and (b) teachers employed whole-time by education authorities in the provision of further education under the said Acts, transmitted to the Secretary of State recommendations agreed on by them with respect to the remuneration of teachers of the said descriptions;

(2) under section 2(3) of the Act the Secretary of State has prepared a draft memorandum setting out the scales and other provisions required for determining the remuneration of teachers of the said descriptions in the form in which, in his opinion, those scales and provisions should be so as to give effect to the recommendations of the Committee;

(3) the Secretary of State, as required by section 2(4) of the Act, has consulted the Committee with respect to the draft memorandum and the Committee have made no representations with respect thereto; and

(4) the Secretary of State has arranged for a memorandum setting out the requisite scales and other provisions in the form of the draft to be published on 2nd July 1970 by Her Majesty's Stationery Office under the title "SCOTTISH TEACHERS' SALARIES MEMORANDUM 1970";

Now therefore, the Secretary of State, in exercise of the powers conferred on him by section 2(4)(*b*) and section 8(2) and (3) of the Act and of all other powers enabling him in that behalf, hereby orders as follows—

Citation and commencement

1. This order may be cited as the Remuneration of Teachers (Scotland) Order 1970 and shall come into operation on 6th July 1970.

Interpretation

2.—(1) In this order—

"education authority" has the meaning assigned to it by section 145(16) of the Education (Scotland) Act 1962**(b)**;

"registered" has the meaning assigned to it by section 17(1) of the Teaching Council (Scotland) Act 1965**(c)**; and

"regulations of 1966" means the Teachers' Salaries (Scotland) Regulations 1966**(d)**.

(a) 1967 c. 36.
(b) 1962 c. 47. **(c)** 1965 c. 19. **(d)** S.I. 1966/831 (1966 II, p. 1919).

(2) The Interpretation Act 1889(**a**) shall apply for the interpretation of this order as it applies for the interpretation of an Act of Parliament.

(3) Section 38 of the Interpretation Act 1889 shall apply as if this order were an Act of Parliament and as if the orders revoked by this order were an Act of Parliament repealed by an Act of Parliament.

Remuneration of teachers

3. The remuneration payable to teachers employed whole-time by education authorities solely or mainly in or in connection with (a) school education under the Education (Scotland) Acts 1939 to 1969 and who are registered teachers, or (b) further education under the said Acts shall with effect from 1st April 1970 be determined in accordance with the scales and other provisions set out in the memorandum published by Her Majesty's Stationery Office as aforesaid.

Revocation

4.—(1) The Remuneration of Teachers (Scotland) Order 1968(**b**), the Remuneration of Teachers (Scotland) Amendment Order 1969(**c**) and the Remuneration of Teachers (Scotland) Amendment Order 1970(**d**) are hereby revoked; provided that such revocation shall not prevent the Secretary of State or the education authority from exercising any of their functions under the said orders in respect of employment of any teachers to which the said orders apply in the period during which the said orders were in operation.

(2) Notwithstanding the provisions of the last foregoing paragraph any power, whether under the said orders or under the regulations of 1966 or under regulations made before the regulations of 1966, to reassess the length of service of a teacher for the purpose of the calculation of his salary in respect of employment in the period during which the said orders, or the regulations of 1966 or the regulations made before the regulations of 1966 were in operation shall not be exercised save in exceptional circumstances.

Given under the seal of the Secretary of State for Scotland.

(L.S.) *Norman W. Graham,*
Secretary.

Scottish Education Department,
St Andrew's House,
Edinburgh.

3rd July 1970.

(**a**) 1889 c. 63. (**b**) S.I. 1968/420 (1968 I, p. 1098). (**c**) S.I. 1969/1090 (1969 II, p. 3164).
(**d**) S.I. 1970/473 (1970 I, p. 1577).

EXPLANATORY NOTE

(*This Note is not part of the Order.*)

This Order brings into operation with effect from 1st April 1970 the scales and other provisions contained in a memorandum published by Her Majesty's Stationery Office relating to the remuneration of registered teachers employed whole-time by education authorities in schools and of teachers employed whole-time by education authorities in further education centres. The memorandum gives effect to agreed recommendations made to the Secretary of State by the Scottish Teachers Salaries Committee.

The scales and other provisions have been given retrospective effect by virtue of the power in section 8(3) of the Remuneration of Teachers (Scotland) Act 1967.

Article 4 of the Order revokes the Remuneration of Teachers (Scotland) Order 1968 but provides for the continued exercise by the Secretary of State and education authorities of functions under the 1968 Order in relation to employment during the currency of that Order.

1970 No. 998

WAGES COUNCILS

The Wages Regulation (Shirtmaking) Order 1970

Made - - - *6th July* 1970
Coming into Operation *3rd August* 1970

Whereas the Secretary of State has received from the Shirtmaking Wages Council (Great Britain) the wages regulation proposals set out in the Schedule hereto ;

Now, therefore, the Secretary of State in exercise of his powers under section 11 of the Wages Councils Act 1959(**a**), and of all other powers enabling him in that behalf, hereby makes the following Order :—

1. This Order may be cited as the Wages Regulation (Shirtmaking) Order 1970.

2.—(1) In this Order the expression "the specified date" means the 3rd August 1970, provided that where, as respects any worker who is paid wages at intervals not exceeding seven days, that date does not correspond with the beginning of the period for which the wages are paid, the expression "the specified date" means, as respects that worker, the beginning of the next such period following that date.

(2) The Interpretation Act 1889(**b**) shall apply to the interpretation of this Order as it applies to the interpretation of an Act of Parliament and as if this Order and the Orders hereby revoked were Acts of Parliament.

3. The wages regulation proposals set out in the Schedule hereto shall have effect as from the specified date and as from that date the Wages Regulation (Shirtmaking) Order 1966(**c**) and the Wages Regulation (Shirtmaking) (Amendment) Order 1968(**d**) shall cease to have effect and the Wages Regulation (Shirtmaking) (Holidays) Order 1967(**e**) shall have effect as if Schedule 2 were omitted.

Signed by order of the Secretary of State.
6th July 1970.

R. R. D. McIntosh,
Deputy Under Secretary of State,
Department of Employment and Productivity.

Article 3

SCHEDULE

The following minimum remuneration shall be substituted for the statutory minimum remuneration fixed by the Wages Regulation (Shirtmaking) Order 1966 (Order S. (66)) as amended by the Wages Regulation (Shirtmaking) (Amendment) Order 1968 (Order S. (71)) and Schedule 2 to the Wages Regulation (Shirtmaking) (Holidays) Order 1967 (Order S. (69)).

(**a**) 1959 c. 69.
(**b**) 1889 c. 63.
(**c**) S.I. 1966/786 (1966 II, p. 1806).
(**d**) S.I. 1968/1319 (1968 II, p. 3649).
(**e**) S.I. 1967/1361 (1967 III, p. 4002).

STATUTORY MINIMUM REMUNERATION

PART I

GENERAL

1. The minimum remuneration payable to a worker to whom this Schedule applies for all work except work to which a minimum overtime rate applies under Part IV of this Schedule is:—

(1) in the case of a time worker, the general minimum time rate payable to the worker under Part II or Part III of this Schedule;

(2) *in the case of a worker employed on piece work, piece rates each of which would yield in the circumstances of the case, to an ordinary worker at least the same amount of money as the general minimum time rate which would be payable if the worker were a time worker.*

PART II

MALE WORKERS

GENERAL MINIMUM TIME RATES

	General minimum time rates
2. Subject to the provisions of this Schedule, the general minimum time rates payable to male time workers are as follows:—	Per hour s. d.
(1) SPECIAL OR MEASURE CUTTERS, PATTERN CUTTERS OR PATTERN TAKERS, who are employed as such during the whole or a substantial part of their time and have had after the age of 18 years not less than three years' employment as a cutter of any class specified in this or the next following sub-paragraph including not less than two years as a measure cutter	*6 7*
(2) CUTTERS, aged 21 years or over, who are employed as such during the whole or a substantial part of their time and have had not less than four years' employment as a cutter of any class specified in this or the last preceding sub-paragraph	*6 5*
(3) TIE CUTTERS, aged 22 years or over, who are employed during the whole or a substantial part of their time in tie cutting and have had at least five years' experience therein	*6 7*
(4) TIE CUTTERS (not being workers to whom sub-paragraph (3) applies) aged 21 years or over, who are employed during the whole or a substantial part of their time in tie cutting and have had at least four years' experience therein	*6 5*
(5) ALL OTHER MALE WORKERS being aged—	
21 years or over	*6 1*
20 and under 21 years	*5 6*
19 „ „ 20 „	*5 3*
18 „ „ 19 „	*4 9*
17 „ „ 18 „	*4 0*
16 „ „ 17 „	*3 6*
under 16 years	*3 0*

PART III

FEMALE WORKERS

GENERAL MINIMUM TIME RATES

3.—(1) Subject to the provisions of this Schedule, the general minimum time rates payable to female time workers are as follows:—

(*a*) *LEARNERS during the following periods of employment in the trade:—*

	1st 6 months per hour	*2nd 6 months per hour*	*2nd year per hour*
Entering the trade—	s. d.	s. d.	s. d.
Aged 15 and under 16 years	*2 9*	*3 3*	*4 0*
" 16 " " 17 "	*3 0*	*3 6*	*4 3*
" 17 " " 18 "	*3 3*	*3 9*	*4 3*
" 18 years or over	*4 0*	*4 3*	*4 9*

(*b*) ALL OTHER WORKERS (including home-workers) ... ... s. d. *4 9* per hour

(2) For the purpose of determining the period of a learner's employment in the trade and the date on which she ceases to be a learner, there shall be reckoned as employment in the trade any employment in any branch of the trade or in the making, wherever carried on, of overalls for male or female persons.

PART IV

OVERTIME AND WAITING TIME

NORMAL NUMBER OF HOURS

4. Subject to the provisions of this Part of this Schedule, the minimum overtime rates set out in paragraph 5 are payable to a worker in respect of any time worked—

(1) in excess of the hours following, that is to say,

(*a*) in any week .. .. 40 hours

(*b*) on any day other than a Saturday, Sunday or customary holiday—

where the normal working hours exceed $8\frac{1}{2}$ .. .. 9 hours

or

where the normal working hours are more than 8 but not more than $8\frac{1}{2}$ .. .. $8\frac{1}{2}$ hours

or

where the normal working hours are not more than 8 8 hours

(2) on a Saturday, Sunday or customary holiday.

MINIMUM OVERTIME RATES

5.—(1) Minimum overtime rates are payable to any worker as follows:—

(*a*) on any day other than a Sunday or customary holiday—

(i) for the first 2 hours of overtime worked ... ... time-and-a-quarter

(ii) for the next 2 hours ... ... time-and-a-half

(iii) thereafter ... ... double time

(*b*) on a Sunday or customary holiday—
for all time worked ... ... double time

(*c*) in any week, exclusive of any time in respect of which any minimum overtime rate is payable under the foregoing provisions of this sub-paragraph—

for all time worked in excess of 40 hours... ... time-and-a-quarter

(2) The minimum overtime rates set out in sub-paragraph (1)(*a*) or (*b*) of this paragraph are payable in any week whether or not the minimum overtime rate set out in sub-paragraph (1)(*c*) is also payable.

6. In this Part of the Schedule—

(1) the expression "CUSTOMARY HOLIDAY" means:—

(*a*) (i) in England and Wales—

Christmas Day (or, if Christmas Day falls on a Sunday, such week-day as may be appointed by national proclamation, or, if none is so appointed, the next following Tuesday), Boxing Day, Good Friday, Easter Monday, Whit Monday (or where another day is substituted therefore by national proclamation, that day), and August Bank Holiday;

(ii) in Scotland—

New Year's Day (or, if New Year's Day falls on a Sunday, the following Monday);

the local Spring holiday;

the local Autumn holiday; and

three other days (being days of the week on which the worker normally works for the employer), in the course of a calendar year, to be fixed by the employer and notified to the worker not less than three weeks before the holiday;

or (*b*) in the case of each of the said days a day substituted by the employer therefor, being a day recognised by local custom as a day of holiday in substitution for the said day.

(2) the expressions "TIME-AND-A-QUARTER", "TIME-AND-A-HALF" and "DOUBLE TIME" mean respectively—

(*a*) in the case of a time worker, one and a quarter times, one and a half times and twice the general minimum time rate otherwise payable to the worker;

(*b*) *in the case of a worker employed on piece work*—

(*i*) *a time rate equal respectively to one quarter, one half and the whole of the general minimum time rate which would be payable to him if he were a time worker and a minimum overtime rate did not apply and, in addition thereto,*

(*ii*) *the piece rates otherwise payable to him under paragraph* 1(2).

WAITING TIME

7.—(1) A worker is entitled to payment of the minimum remuneration specified in this Schedule for all time during which he is present on the premises of his employer unless he is present thereon in any of the following circumstances:—

(*a*) without the employer's consent, express or implied;

(*b*) for some purpose unconnected with his work and other than that of waiting for work to be given to him to perform;

(*c*) by reason only of the fact that he is resident thereon;

(*d*) during normal meal times in a room or place in which no work is being done, and he is not waiting for work to be given to him to perform.

(2) The minimum remuneration payable under sub-paragraph (1) of this paragraph to a piece worker when not engaged on piece work is that which would be payable if he were a time worker.

PART V

INTERPRETATION

8. In this Schedule, unless the context otherwise requires, the following expressions have the meanings hereby expressly assigned to them:—

(1) A CUTTER is a worker (other than a special or measure cutter, a pattern cutter or a pattern taker) substantially employed in one or more of the following processes:—

(*a*) marking-in or marking-out or marking-up materials;

(*b*) laying-up or hooking-up or folding materials;

(*c*) cutting materials; and

(*d*) dividing, that is to say, the process ordinarily carried on by cutters or their assistants of dividing, parting or separating parts of garments which are being cut and of assembling them into suitable bundles for making-up;

(2) A LEARNER is a female worker who—

(*a*) is employed during the whole or a substantial part of her time in learning any branch or process of the trade by an employer who provides her with reasonable facilities for such learning; and

(*b*) does not work in a room used for dwelling purposes, except where she is in the employment of her parent or guardian;

(3) A SPECIAL OR MEASURE CUTTER is a worker who—

(*a*) is able to take a complete set of measures and cut from model patterns; and

(*b*) has sufficient technical knowledge to alter patterns (excluding stock patterns);

(4) "THE TRADE" means the shirtmaking trade as specified in paragraph 10.

STATUTORY INSTRUMENTS

1970 No. 1003

MERCHANT SHIPPING

SAFETY

The Merchant Shipping (Load Line) (Amendment) Rules 1970

Made - - -	7*th July* 1970
Laid before Parliament	14*th July* 1970
Coming into Operation	21*st July* 1970

The Board of Trade in exercise of the powers conferred upon them by section 2 of the Merchant Shipping (Load Lines) Act 1967(**a**) and of all other powers enabling them in that behalf hereby make the following Rules:—

1. These Rules may be cited as the Merchant Shipping (Load Line) (Amendment) Rules 1970 and shall come into operation on 21st July 1970.

2. The Merchant Shipping (Load Line) Rules 1968(**b**) shall have effect subject to the amendment that for paragraph (6) of Rule 30 there shall be substituted the following paragraph:—

"(6)(*a*) This paragraph shall apply to any ship in respect of which a load line certificate issued under the Merchant Shipping (Safety and Load Line Conventions) Act 1932(**c**) was in force on 21st July 1968 (the date on which these Rules came into operation) not being a ship in respect of which information as to stability including particulars appropriate to the ship in respect of the matters specified in Schedule 7 has been approved by the Board under paragraph (5) of this Rule.

(*b*) The owner of a ship to which this paragraph applies shall provide for the information of the master such information relating to the stability of the ship as was required to be provided under the law in force immediately prior to 21st July 1968(**d**).

(*c*) The preceding sub-paragraph shall have effect in relation to any ship until either—

(i) the expiration of the period of 12 months next following the date of issue of the first load line certificate to be issued in respect of the ship after 20th July 1970; or

(ii) 20th July 1975

whichever shall first occur".

F. V. Corfield,
Minister of State,
Board of Trade.

7th July 1970.

1967 c. 27. (**b**) S.I. 1968/1053 (1968 II, p. 2774). (**c**) 1932 c. 9.
ee section 18 of the Merchant Shipping (Safety Convention) Act 1949 (12, 13
14 Geo. 6 c. 43) and section 14 of the Merchant Shipping Act 1964 (1964 c. 47).

EXPLANATORY NOTE

(This Note is not part of the Rules.)

These Rules amend the Merchant Shipping (Load Line) Rules 1968 in relation to the provision of stability information for ships which held valid load line certificates when those Rules came into force on 21st July 1968. They extend the period during which in the case of such ships the stability information to be provided is that prescribed under the law applicable immediately prior to that date. This extension will not apply in any case in which the fuller information set out in Schedule 7 to the 1968 Rules has been approved by the Board of Trade.

1970 No. 1004 (L.21)

MAGISTRATES' COURTS

PROCEDURE

The Magistrates' Courts (Amendment) Rules 1970

Made - - -	*2nd July* 1970
Laid before Parliament	*14th July* 1970
Coming into Operation	*15th July* 1970

The Lord Chancellor, in exercise of the power conferred on him by section 15 of the Justices of the Peace Act 1949**(a)**, as extended by section 122 of the Magistrates' Courts Act 1952**(b)**, after consultation with the Rule Committee appointed under the said section 15, hereby makes the following Rules:—

1. These Rules may be cited as the Magistrates' Courts (Amendment) Rules 1970 and shall come into operation on 15th July 1970.

2. Rule 84 of the Magistrates' Courts Rules 1968**(c)**, as amended **(d)**, shall be amended as follows:—

(*a*) for paragraph (1) there shall be substituted the following paragraph:—

"(1) An application under section 106 of the Road Traffic Act 1960**(e)** or section 2 of the Road Traffic (Disqualification) Act 1970**(f)** for an order removing a disqualification or disqualifications for holding or obtaining a licence shall be by complaint.";

(*b*) in paragraph (3) for the words "under the said section 106" there shall be substituted the words "under either of the aforesaid sections".

Dated 2nd July 1970.

Hailsham of St. Marylebone, C.

EXPLANATORY NOTE

(*This Note is not part of the Rules.*)

Section 2 of the Road Traffic (Disqualification) Act 1970 enables a person who is disqualified for driving by an order made before the commencement of the Act to apply for the disqualification to be removed if the disqualification resulted from a conviction for driving whilst disqualified and was additional to a previous disqualification. These Rules amend Rule 84 of the Magistrates' Courts Rules 1968 so as to provide that the procedure for the removal of such a disqualification shall be the same as that in respect of disqualification on other grounds.

(a) 1949 c. 101. **(b)** 1952 c. 55. **(c)** S.I. 1968/1920 (1968 III, p. 5175).
(d) The amending Rules are not relevant to the subject matter of these Rules.
(e) 1960 c. 16. **(f)** 1970 c. 23.

1970 No. 1008

RATING AND VALUATION

The Natural Gas Terminals (Rating) Order 1970

Made - - -	*8th July* 1970
Laid before Parliament	*15th July* 1970
Coming into Operation	*21st November* 1970

The Minister of Housing and Local Government, after consultation with the Gas Council, with the associations of local authorities appearing to him to be concerned and with the local authorities with whom consultation appeared to him to be desirable, in exercise of his powers under section 33(5) of, and paragraph 14 of Schedule 6 to, the General Rate Act 1967(**a**) and of all other powers enabling him in that behalf, hereby makes the following order :—

1. This order may be cited as the Natural Gas Terminals (Rating) Order 1970 and shall come into operation on 21st November 1970.

2. This order shall apply, in respect of the rate periods beginning on 1st April 1971 and subsequent rate periods, to the premises specified in column (1) of the Schedule, being premises occupied and used by the Gas Council for the reception of gas purchased by such Council, or in the case of the premises specified in item 1 for such reception and the evaporation of gas in a liquid state.

3.—(1) The Interpretation Act 1889(**b**) applies to the interpretation of this order as it applies to the interpretation of an Act of Parliament.

(2) In this order—

"Gas Board" means an Area Board within the meaning of the Gas Act 1948(**c**) other than the Scottish Gas Board ;

"the Schedule" means the Schedule to this order ;

"valuation officer", in relation to a valuation list, a rating area or any premises, means any officer of the Commissioners of Inland Revenue who is for the time being appointed to be the valuation officer or one of the valuation officers, or to be the deputy valuation officer or one of the deputy valuation officers, in relation to that list, the valuation list for that rating area or the valuation list for the rating area in which those premises are situated, as the case may be ;

"year" means a period of twelve months beginning with 1st April.

(**a**) 1967 c. 9. (**b**) 1889 c. 63. (**c**) 1948 c. 67.

4. The premises specified in column (1) of the Schedule are hereby designated for the purposes of section 33(5) of the General Rate Act 1967.

5. For any year, the value of the premises specified in any item in column (1) of the Schedule shall be—

$$\frac{x}{1000} \times \frac{y}{100} \text{ pounds,}$$

x being the number estimated as provided in article 6(2)(*a*) as being the total number of therms of natural gas supplied from the premises in the penultimate year; and

y being the number specified in respect of such premises in column (2).

6.—(1) Paragraphs (2) to (4) shall have effect in respect of any year, and in those paragraphs "penultimate year" means the year beginning 24 months before such year.

(2) The Gas Council shall, before the end of the month of October (or in relation to the year 1971-72 the month of November) preceding the year, transmit

(*a*) to the rating authority for the area in which the premises specified in any item in column (1) of the Schedule are situated and to the valuation officer for such area, an estimate of the total number of therms of natural gas supplied from the premises in the penultimate year; and

(*b*) to the rating authorities for the areas in which the premises specified in column (1) of the Schedule are situated and to the valuation officers for such areas, for the purposes of the direction to be given under section 33(5), an estimate of the total number of therms of natural gas supplied by them in the penultimate year to, or direct for consumption in the area of, any Gas Board.

(3) On receipt of the estimates under paragraph (2) the valuation officer shall calculate the value of the premises specified in any item in column (1) of the Schedule for the purposes of section 33(5) of the General Rate Act 1967 for the year and apportion such value among the Gas Boards in the proportions included in the estimates under paragraph (2)(*b*) and shall notify the amounts of such value and apportionments to the rating authority for the area in which the premises are situated and to the Gas Boards before the end of the month of December preceding the year.

(4) The duty imposed on the Gas Council by paragraph (2) shall be enforceable by mandamus at the instance of the rating authority or of the valuation officer; and the duty imposed on the valuation officer by paragraph (3) shall be enforceable by mandamus at the instance of the rating authority.

7. Where the valuation officer notifies the amount apportioned to a rating authority in respect of any Gas Board in accordance with article 6(3)—

(*a*) the rating authority, in making and levying any rate for a rate period in the year to which the notification relates, shall include the Gas Board as the occupier of a hereditament of a rateable value equal to such amount; and

(*b*) the valuation officer, at or as soon as may be after the beginning of such year, shall cause such alterations (if any) to be made in the valuation list as may be requisite for showing the Gas Board in the list as the occupier of a hereditament of that rateable value ; and if any such alteration is made after the beginning of such year it shall be treated as having been made at the beginning of such year:

Provided that if such year is a year beginning with the date on which a new valuation list comes into force, this sub-paragraph shall not apply, but the valuation officer shall include the Gas Board in the list as the occupier of a hereditament of the said rateable value.

SCHEDULE

(1) Premises to which the order applies	(2) Number constituting *y* in article 5
1. Premises in the urban district of Canvey Island	37·5
2. Premises in the parishes of Bacton and Paston in the rural district of Smallburgh	2·5
3. Premises in the parish of Easington in the rural district of Holderness	2·5

Given under the official seal of the Minister of Housing and Local Government on 8th July 1970.

(L.S.) *Peter Walker,*

Minister of Housing and Local Government.

EXPLANATORY NOTE

(*This Note is not part of the Order.*)

Under section 33 of the General Rate Act 1967 premises occupied by gas authorities are in general not rated ; the authorities are treated as occupying notional hereditaments. Section 33(5), however, empowers the Minister of Housing and Local Government to make an order designating certain premises occupied and used by, inter alia. the Gas Council as premises in respect of which rate payments should be made and providing for the determination by such method as may be specified in the order of a value for the premises for such purposes. Where such an order is in force the Minister may direct that such value shall be apportioned among Gas Boards, that such Boards shall be treated as occupying hereditaments of such values, and that the Board's basic totals of rateable values, from which the rateable values of the Boards' notional hereditaments are calculated, shall be adjusted. Paragraph 14 of Schedule 6 to the Act of 1967 empowers the order to contain incidental, supplemental and consequential provisions. This Order designates the premises specified in the Schedule for the purposes indicated, provides for the determination of a value for them and makes the necessary incidental, supplemental and consequential provision. The Natural Gas Terminals (Rating) Direction 1970 was made concurrently with this Order.

STATUTORY INSTRUMENTS

1970 No. 1009

ECCLESIASTICAL LAW

The Compensation of Clergy Rules 1970

Made (Approved by the Church Assembly)	*8th July* 1970
Laid before Parliament	*15th July* 1970
Coming into Operation	*1st August* 1970

We, the Church Commissioners for England, in exercise of the powers conferred on us by paragraph 15(1) of Schedule 4 of the Pastoral Measure 1968(**a**) do hereby order as follows:—

1.—(1) These Rules may be cited as the Compensation of Clergy Rules 1970 and shall come into operation on the 1st day of August 1970.

(2) The Interpretation Measure 1925(**b**) shall apply to the interpretation of these Rules as it applies to the interpretation of a Measure of the Church Assembly.

2. In these Rules unless the context otherwise requires, the following expressions have the meanings hereby respectively assigned to them, that is to say:—

"the Committee" means, in relation to a claim and other proceedings, the Pastoral Committee for the diocese in which the incumbent, vicar in a team ministry or archdeacon concerned in the proceedings, was serving before the date of the coming into operation of the relevant provision of the pastoral scheme or order affecting his benefice or office or, in the case of a claim made before that date, the diocese in which the claimant is serving;

"the registrar of the diocese" and "chancellor of the diocese" mean the registrar and chancellor of the aforesaid diocese;

"the Measure" means the Pastoral Measure 1968;

"the secretary" means the secretary of the Committee.

3.—(1) A claim for compensation under Schedule 4 to the Measure by any incumbent, vicar in a team ministry or archdeacon, shall be in writing and shall be sent or delivered to the secretary.

(2) A claim for such compensation may be made before the date on which the relevant provision of the pastoral scheme or order comes into operation and shall be made not later than thirteen weeks after that date; but the Committee may extend the time for making a claim, and the making of a claim shall not preclude the giving of supplementary information in writing or the making of any addition to or amendment of the claim.

(**a**) 1968 No. 1.
(**b**) 15 & 16 Geo. 5 No. 1.

(2) The Appeal Tribunal :—

(*a*) may, if they think fit, receive oral or written evidence, and shall not be bound to observe strict rules as to the admissibility of evidence ;

(*b*) may require evidence to be given on oath, but need not do so ;

(*c*) may confirm the decision of the Committee or substitute such other decision as they think just, or send the case back to the Committee for reconsideration, with such directions as they think fit.

(3) At any hearing before the Appeal Tribunal the appellant may be represented by a barrister or solicitor or may be assisted by a friend.

12.—(1) An application for the refunding in accordance with paragraph 16 of Schedule 4 to the Measure of costs reasonably incurred in proceedings under that Schedule shall—

(*a*) be made in writing to the registrar of the diocese and sent or delivered to him at his office ; and

(*b*) give particulars of the costs incurred and be accompanied by vouchers and other documents relating thereto ;

and the registrar shall determine whether any such costs have been reasonably so incurred and, if so, the amount thereof.

(2) The registrar may by notice in writing request the applicant to give such further information and supply such further documents as he may reasonably require and shall, if the applicant so wishes, arrange for a hearing.

(3) The registrar shall give his decision in writing and send it to the applicant and, unless he grants the application in full, shall state the reasons therefor ; and the applicant may, by notice sent or delivered to the registrar within fourteen days after the decision was sent to the applicant, appeal from it to the chancellor of the diocese.

(4) On receipt of the notice of appeal, the registrar shall—

(*a*) send to the chancellor the application and all other documents relating thereto and a note of what took place at any hearing before him, and send a copy of any such note to the applicant ;

(*b*) if the applicant so wishes, arrange for a hearing before the chancellor, and give to the applicant not less than seven days' notice of the time and place thereof.

(5) At any hearing before the registrar or chancellor under this rule the applicant may be represented by a barrister or solicitor or may be assisted by a friend ; and the costs of proceedings under this rule shall be dealt with in those proceedings.

(6) The registrar shall certify to the Central Board of Finance the amount of any costs determined under this rule to have been reasonably incurred as aforesaid.

13. The Committee shall take steps to inform all persons who have or may have a right to compensation under Schedule 4 to the Measure of the name of the secretary and the address to which documents shall be sent or delivered to him, and it shall be the duty of the secretary to give assistance to such persons in connection with claims or other proceedings under these rules, and, if the Committee make a determination or decision from which an appeal lies to the Appeal Tribunal, to inform the person concerned of the name and address of the secretary of the Appeal Tribunal.

The Common Seal of the Church Commissioners was hereunto affixed this 19th day of May 1970.

L. N. King,
Assistant Secretary.

Approved by the Church Assembly the 8th July 1970.

John Guillum Scott.
Secretary.

APPENDIX

FORM OF UNDERTAKING UNDER RULE 7(1)

Diocese

I , of ,
having been awarded compensation under Schedule 4 to the Pastoral Measure 1968, hereby undertake to give to the secretary of the Pastoral Committee of the above diocese, the information specified below:—

(*a*) If at any time I am appointed to any ecclesiastical office or engage in any other remunerated employment, I will forthwith inform the secretary and give him full particulars of the office or employment.

(*b*) If at any time I am offered an ecclesiastical office which I intend to refuse or have refused, I will forthwith inform the secretary and give him full particulars of the office and my reasons for refusing.

(*c*) If at any time:—

(i) I execute a deed of relinquishment under the Clerical Disabilities Act 1870(a); or

(ii) I become a member of a religious body which is not in communion with the Church of England; or

(iii) I become disqualified under the Ecclesiastical Jurisdiction Measure 1963(b) from holding preferment in the Church of England;

I will inform the secretary and give him full particulars of the circumstances.

Signed...

DATED the day of , 19 .

EXPLANATORY NOTE

(*This Note is not part of the Rules.*)

These Rules provide a uniform code of procedure to be followed in claiming and determining rights to and amounts of compensation under Schedule 4 (Compensation of Clergy) of the Pastoral Measure 1968, and in altering terminating or suspending payments of compensation, and in proceedings before the Appeal Tribunal and in any other proceedings under the Schedule.

(a) 1870 c.91. (b) 1963 No. 1.

1970 No. 1010

LOCAL GOVERNMENT, ENGLAND AND WALES

The Rate Support Grant (Amendment) Regulations 1970

Made - - -	*9th July* 1970
Laid before Parliament	*16th July* 1970
Coming into Operation	*1st August* 1970

The Minister of Housing and Local Government, in exercise of his powers under section 5(1)(*a*) of the Local Government Act 1966**(a)**, and of all other powers enabling him in that behalf, hereby makes the following regulations:—

Title and commencement

1. These regulations may be cited as the Rate Support Grant (Amendment) Regulations 1970 and shall come into operation on 1st August 1970.

Interpretation

2.—(1) The Interpretation Act 1889**(b)** shall apply for the interpretation of these regulations as it applies for the interpretation of an Act of Parliament.

(2) In these regulations "the principal regulations" means the Rate Support Grant Regulations 1967**(c)** as amended **(d)**.

Amendment of the schedule to the principal regulations

3. For sub-paragraph (3) of paragraph 2 of the schedule to the principal regulations (which provides for calculating the number of education units for an area, and *inter alia* describes the method of estimating the number of pupils) there shall be substituted the following:—

"(3) Pupils who fall within sub-paragraph (2)(*a*) above shall be treated as secondary school pupils where—

(*a*) proposals with respect to the school have been approved by the Secretary of State under section 1 of the Education Act 1964**(e)** (which relates to new schools with special age limits) and

(*b*) they were 11 years of age on the 1st September preceding the time as at which, pursuant to paragraph 7 of this schedule, numbers are required to be estimated,

and otherwise shall be treated as primary school pupils.

(3A) Pupils or children who fall within sub-paragraph (2)(*b*) or (*c*) above shall be treated as primary school pupils if under 12 years of age and as secondary school pupils if 12 years of age or over."

Given under the official seal of the Minister of Housing and Local Government on 9th July 1970.

(L.S.)

Peter Walker,
Minister of Housing and
Local Government.

(a) 1966 c. 42.
(b) 1889 c. 63.
(c) S.I. 1967/363 (1967 I, p. 1235).
(d) S.I. 1969/105 (1969 I, p. 339).
(e) 1964 c. 82.

EXPLANATORY NOTE

(This Note is not part of the Regulations.)

The Rate Support Grant Regulations 1967 provide for the carrying into effect of sections 1 to 4 of the Local Government Act 1966 (under which rate support grants are paid to local authorities). They determine *inter alia* the method of calculating the number of education units for any area for the purpose of assessing the amounts payable to individual authorities in respect of the needs element of rate support grants. As amended by the Rate Support Grant (Amendment) Regulations 1969, they divide by age pupils at schools approved by the Secretary of State for Education and Science under section 1 of the Education Act 1964 (middle schools) and at independent schools: middle school pupils are treated as secondary school pupils if they are 12 years of age at the time of the count (which is made as at January in each financial year). These Regulations provide that they shall instead be treated as secondary school pupils if they are 11 years of age on the 1st September preceding the count.

1970 No. 1012

INDUSTRIAL ASSURANCE

DECIMAL CURRENCY

The Industrial Assurance (Premium Receipt Books) (Decimal Currency) Regulations 1970

Made - - -	7*th July* 1970
Laid before Parliament	17*th July* 1970
Coming into Operation	1*st September* 1970

The Industrial Assurance Commissioner, with the approval of the Treasury, pursuant to section 8(2) of the Industrial Assurance and Friendly Societies Act 1948**(a)**, section 7(5) of the Decimal Currency Act 1969**(b)** and of all other powers enabling him in that behalf, hereby makes the following Regulations:—

1.—(1) These Regulations may be cited as the Industrial Assurance (Premium Receipt Books) (Decimal Currency) Regulations 1970, and shall come into operation on 1st September 1970.

(2) In these Regulations—

"principal Regulations" means the Industrial Assurance (Premium Receipt Books) Regulations 1948**(c)** as amended by the Industrial Assurance (Premium Receipt Books) (Amendment) Regulations 1961**(d)**;

"policy" and "premium receipt book" have the meanings assigned by regulation 6 of the principal Regulations;

"new currency" and "old currency" have the meanings assigned by section 16(1) of the Decimal Currency Act 1969;

"prescribed scheme" means the scheme prescribed in Schedule 4 to the Industrial Assurance (Decimal Currency) Regulations 1970**(e)**;

"approved scheme" means a special scheme approved in pursuance of section 6(3) of the Decimal Currency Act 1969;

"collector" has the meaning assigned by section 45(1) of the Industrial Assurance Act 1923**(f)**;

"industrial assurance company" and "collecting society" have the meanings assigned by section 1 of the Industrial Assurance Act 1923 as amended by Schedule 6 to the Companies Act 1967**(g)**.

(3) The Interpretation Act 1889**(h)** shall apply to the interpretation of these Regulations as it applies to the interpretation of an Act of Parliament.

2.—(1) A premium receipt book provided for use in respect of a policy effected before 15th February 1971 under which premiums are payable weekly or fortnightly may on and after that date, if the condition specified in paragraph (2) of this regulation is fulfilled, contain particulars of the total amount in the new currency of four successive weekly or, as the case may be, of two successive fortnightly premiums payable under the policy instead of the particulars of the

(a) 1948 c. 39.
(b) 1969 c. 19.
(c) S.I. 1948/2770 (Rev. VIII, p. 915: 1948 I, p. 1619).
(d) S.I. 1961/597 (1961 I, p. 1312).
(e) S.I. 1970/931 (1970 II, p. 2892).
(f) 1923 c. 8.
(g) 1967 c. 81.
(h) 1889 c. 63.

premiums as required by subparagraph (*d*) of regulation 1 of the principal Regulations.

(2) The condition referred to in paragraph (1) of this regulation is that the amounts in the new currency payable in respect of premiums payable under the policy are determined under—

(*a*) paragraphs 1 or 2 of Schedule 3 to the Industrial Assurance (Decimal Currency) Regulations 1970, or

(*b*) the provisions of an approved scheme under which the amount in the new currency payable in respect of all or any part of each of four successive weekly or each of two successive fortnightly premiums is separately provided for.

3.—A collector who on or after 15th February 1971 receives in respect of a policy a payment in the old currency which is not a whole number of pounds may instead of entering so much of that amount as is in shillings and pence in the appropriate premium receipt book in accordance with regulation 3 of the principal Regulations enter therein the corresponding amount in the new currency calculated in accordance with the provisions of the Schedule to these Regulations.

4.—A premium receipt book provided for use in respect of a policy effected before 15th February 1971 shall on and after that date contain—

(*a*) a statement approved by the Industrial Assurance Commissioner explaining the effect of the provisions of the Industrial Assurance (Decimal Currency) Regulations 1970, being Regulations made under section 6 of the Decimal Currency Act 1969, relating to the determination of the amounts in the new currency payable in respect of premiums payable under the policy that fall due on or after that date, or,

(*b*) if the policy is one to which the prescribed or an approved scheme applies, information explaining the effect of the scheme on that policy including:—

(i) how the amounts in the new currency payable in respect of premiums payable under the policy that fall due on or after 15th February 1971 are determined,

(ii) if increased benefit is payable under the policy by virtue of the scheme, that the owner of the policy will be notified at his request of its amount, and

(iii) in the case of a policy to which the prescribed scheme applies, the conditions under which the owner of the policy may appeal to the Industrial Assurance Commissioner if he considers that the increased benefit payable under the policy by virtue of the scheme is unfair in relation to any increased payments payable by him.

S. D. Musson,
Industrial Assurance Commissioner.

Date 3rd July 1970.

We approve these Regulations.

Reginald Eyre,
Bernard Weatherill,
Two of the Lords Commissioners of Her Majesty's Treasury.

Date 7th July 1970.

SCHEDULE

METHOD OF CALCULATING THE AMOUNT IN NEW PENCE CORRESPONDING TO AN AMOUNT IN SHILLINGS AND PENCE FOR THE PURPOSE OF REGULATION 3.

The amount in the new currency corresponding to an amount in shillings and pence or pence which may be entered in a premium receipt book under regulation 3 of these Regulations shall be calculated as follows:—

(*a*) for any whole shilling or multiple thereof the corresponding amount in the new currency shall be taken to be five new pence, or that multiple thereof, and

(*b*) for any amount or remaining amount of less than one shilling shown in column 1 of the following table the corresponding amount in the new currency shall be taken to be the amount in new pence shown opposite that amount in column 2 of that table.

TABLE

Amount in old currency	*Amount in new pence*
1d.	½p
2d.	1p
3d.	1p
4d.	1½p
5d.	2p
6d.	2½p
7d.	3p
8d.	3½p
9d.	4p
10d.	4p
11d.	4½p

EXPLANATORY NOTE

(*This Note is not part of the Regulations.*)

These Regulations supplement the Industrial Assurance (Premium Receipt Books) Regulations 1948 under which the premium, the interval at which it is payable and the payment received by a collector are required to be entered in a premium receipt book relating to an industrial assurance policy. They provide that in the case of weekly or fortnightly premiums payable under a policy effected before 15th February 1971 (the date of the introduction of decimal currency) the premium receipt book may show the total amount in decimal currency payable in respect of four premiums, if payable weekly, or two premiums, if payable fortnightly. The Regulations also permit the amount of a payment made in the old currency to be entered in a premium receipt book as a payment of the corresponding amount in the new currency and provide for information to be contained in premium receipt books about decimal currency payments under policies effected before 15th February 1971.